THEORIZING FEMINISMS

THEORIZING FEMINISMS

A Reader

Elizabeth Hackett and
Sally Haslanger

New York   Oxford
OXFORD UNIVERSITY PRESS
2006

Oxford University Press, Inc., publishes works that further Oxford University's
objective of excellence in research, scholarship, and education.

Oxford   New York
Auckland   Cape Town   Dar es Salaam   Hong Kong   Karachi
Kuala Lumpur   Madrid   Melbourne   Mexico City   Nairobi
New Delhi   Shanghai   Taipei   Toronto

With offices in
Argentina   Austria   Brazil   Chile   Czech Republic   France   Greece
Guatemala   Hungary   Italy   Japan   Poland   Portugal   Singapore
South Korea   Switzerland   Thailand   Turkey   Ukraine   Vietnam

Published by Oxford University Press, Inc.
198 Madison Avenue, New York, New York 10016
http://www.oup.com

Oxford is a registered trademark of Oxford University Press

Library of Congress Cataloging-in-Publication Data

Theorizing feminisms : a reader / [edited] by Elizabeth Hackett
and Sally Haslanger.
     p. cm.
   Includes bibliographical references.
   ISBN-13: 978-0-19-515009-4 (pbk.)
  1. Feminist theory. 2. Feminism. I. Hackett, Elizabeth. II.
Haslanger, Sally Anne.
   HQ1190.T475 2005
   305.4201–dc22

2005026364

Printing number: 9 8 7 6 5 4 3

Printed in the United States of America
on acid-free paper

To the students of Agnes Scott College, Eastern Michigan University, Massachusetts Institute of Technology, the University of Michigan, and the University of Pennsylvania, with whom we had the pleasure of exploring this material, and to all future students of feminist theory. May this anthology serve as inspiration to your work.

CONTENTS

SECTION III   LOCALIZING APPROACHES TO SEX OPPRESSION

SECTION IV   FEMINIST ALLIES?

ACKNOWLEDGMENTS

We thank Clare Batty, Roxanne Fay, Elizabeth Harman, Ishani Maitra, and Ásta Sveinsdóttir for their research assistance in preparing this text. Tracy Edwards offered valuable advice while working as Sally's teaching assistant. Thank you to Sue Delonis for the matching socks. Heartfelt thanks to Stephen Yablo for his constancy. Finally, we are grateful for financial support provided by Agnes Scott College and the dean of the School of Humanities, Arts, and Social Sciences, Massachusetts Institute of Technology.

CONTRIBUTORS

Addams, Jane (1860–1935): founder of Hull House, a social settlement house in Chicago.

Alcoff, Linda: Associate Professor of Philosophy and Women's Studies and the Meredith Professor for Teaching Excellence at Syracuse University.

Allen, Paula Gunn: Professor of English/Creative Writing/American Indian Studies at the University of California at Los Angeles (retired).

Anzaldúa, Gloria (1942–2004): Chicana lesbian-feminist, poet, writer, and cultural critic.

Bartky, Sandra Lee: Professor of Philosophy at the University of Illinois at Chicago.

Beauvoir, Simone de (1908–1986): French existentialist, writer, and cultural critic.

Bordo, Susan: Professor of English and Women's Studies and holder of the Otis A. Singletary Chair in the Humanities at the University of Kentucky.

Bornstein, Kate: author and performance artist, currently living in Spanish Harlem, New York.

Butler, Judith: Maxine Elliot Professor in the departments of Rhetoric and Comparative Literature at the University of California, Berkeley.

Christ, Carol P.: taught at Columbia University, Pomona College, and Harvard Divinity School, and is currently director of the Ariadne Institute.

Christian, Barbara (1943–2000): Professor of African American Studies at the University of California, Berkeley.

Collins, Patricia Hill: Chair of and Charles Phelps Taft Professor of Sociology within the Department of African American Studies at the University of Cincinnati.

Combahee River Collective: Formed in 1974 in Boston, the Combahee River Collective took its name from the South Carolina river that was the site of a military action led by Harriet Tubman that freed hundreds of slaves.

Crenshaw, Kimberlé: Professor of Law, Columbia University and University of California, Los Angeles, law schools.

Davis, Angela: Professor of History of Consciousness, University of California, Santa Cruz, University of California Presidential Chair.

Duggan, Lisa: Associate Professor, History and American Studies, New York University.

Feinberg, Leslie: novelist, historian, and transgender activist.

Fraser, Nancy: Henry A. and Louise Loeb Professor of Political and Social Science, New School University.

Frye, Marilyn: Professor of Philosophy, Michigan State University.

Gandhi, Leela: Senior Lecturer, English, LaTrobe University, Australia.

Gilligan, Carol: Patricia Albjerg Graham Professor of Gender Studies, Harvard Graduate School of Education.

Goldman, Emma (1869–1940): famous anarchist, dubbed "one of the most dangerous women in America" by J. Edgar Hoover.

Grillo, Trina (1948–1996): University of San Francisco School of Law.

Hackett, Elizabeth: Associate Professor of Women's Studies and Philosophy, Agnes Scott College.

Hammonds, Evelynn: Professor of the History of Science and of Afro-American Studies, Harvard University.

Haslanger, Sally: Professor of Philosophy, Massachusetts Institute of Technology.

hooks, bell: Distinguished Professor of English at City College in New York.

Hunter, Nan D.: Professor of Law, Brooklyn Law School.

Kadi, Joanna: writer, musician, poet, teacher, and cultural critic living in Florida.

Kirk, Gwyn: scholar and activist; academic interests include feminism, militarism, and ecology.

Lorde, Audre (1934–1992): theorist and self-described "Black lesbian, mother, warrior, poet."

MacKinnon, Catharine: Elizabeth A. Long Professor of Law, University of Michigan.

Marcus, Sharon: Associate Professor of English, University of California, Berkeley.

Matsuda, Mari: Professor of Law, Georgetown University.

Mill, John Stuart (1806–1873): influential political philosopher.

Narayan, Uma: Associate Professor of Philosophy, Vassar College.

Nicholson, Linda J.: Susan E. and William P. Stiritz Distinguished Professor in Women's Studies and History, Washington University in St. Louis.

Nussbaum, Martha C.: Ernst Freund Distinguished Service Professor of Law and Ethics, University of Chicago Law School.

Roberts, Dorothy E.: Kirkland & Ellis Professor of Law, Northwestern University.

Rubin, Gayle S.: Assistant Professor, Ethnology, Department of Anthropology, University of Michigan.

Ruddick, Sara: New School for Social Research, New York City.

Schechter, Susan (1946–2004): leader in the domestic violence prevention movement; Clinical Professor, University of Iowa School of Social Work.

Sen, Amartya: Lament University Professor, Harvard University, and Professor of Economics and Philosophy, Harvard University.

Shiva, Vandana: Director, Research Foundation for Science, Technology, and Ecology, New Delhi.

Stoler, Ann Laura: Professor, Anthropology and History, University of Michigan.

Stoltenberg, John: pro-feminist activist and author.

Truth, Sojourner (1797?–1883): famous abolitionist and women's rights activist.

Vance, Carole S.: Program for the Study of Sexuality, Gender, Health, and Human Rights, Columbia University.

Walker, Alice: womanist novelist, poet, and essayist.

Wendell, Susan: Professor Emerita, Women's Studies, Simon Fraser University, British Columbia.

Young, Iris M.: Professor, Department of Political Science, University of Chicago.

INTRODUCTION

GENERAL OVERVIEW

Although most women's studies programs (and many philosophy, literature, and political science departments) include an upper-level course entitled Feminist Theory, little consensus exists about the appropriate content of such courses. Some of these courses simply expose students to feminists doing theory in different disciplines; others serve as "methods" courses, teaching students how to criticize traditional research methods and to design and carry out feminist research; and still others cover a narrower selection of feminist theoretical work in the instructor's home discipline. While undeniably these courses are valuable, we believe that another important model for an interdisciplinary feminist theory course is one that surveys approaches to the theoretical issues raised by the quest for gender justice. Such a course takes two questions as its central topic: What is sexist oppression? What ought to be done about it? The goal of the course is to provide an overview of feminist responses to—including a critique of—these questions. This book collects and organizes a set of essays that are ideally suited to a course framed in this way.

The book is divided into four main sections. In the first section we include essays that introduce students to some of the basic concepts used in thinking about sexism, e.g., oppression, social construction, essentialism, intersectionality, gender, race, and class, and to issues that problematize the position of theorist, e.g., what is the task of feminist theory? What biases should we be alert to? Can we speak only from/about our own experience, or can we legitimately analyze the experience of others?

The second main section covers three approaches to sex oppression that attempt to characterize in a general way the source of injustice toward women. Humanist feminism, also sometimes referred to as "the sameness approach," and counted as a form of liberal feminism, maintains that a social system is unjust toward women insofar as women are viewed and treated as different from men. The humanist approach often favors a "gender-blind" strategy in assuring the fair treatment of men and women. Gynocentric feminists criticize humanists for failing to acknowledge that women are different from men and, more importantly, for failing to value women's distinctive capacities, contributions, and virtues. Gynocentric feminism, also known as "the difference approach," favors a more substantial integration of womanly values into the structure of society. Dominance feminists reject the sameness/ difference dichotomy as not adequately identifying the crux of the problem. Regardless of the similarities or dissimilarities between women and men, in order to achieve justice the distribution of power between the sexes must be equal. According to the dominance feminists, to a large extent women's "difference," their "femininity," is intimately tied to their lack of power; but this is not to say that if powerful they would be like men, or should be like men. If women and men had equal power, gender as we know it would no longer exist.

The third section of the book rejects the project of offering a general analysis of sex oppression that supposedly targets the problem and provides the solution. "Localizing" approaches, as we have termed them, are wary of theories that attempt to analyze social phenomena across history and culture. They charge that such theories typically do no more than project the perspective of those in a particular social position (historically, the white middle-class feminist) onto everyone else. We consider two versions of this critique, one grounded in postmodernism, the other in the politics of identity, or what is also called "identity politics." As we understand the localizing critique, the point is not that we should throw out everything offered by the universalizing approaches, for there may be contexts in which the tools and strategies they developed are useful. But the very task of feminist theory must be rethought.

The fourth and final section considers the relationship of feminist theory to three other liberatory projects that do not characterize themselves as feminist, yet take gender as a significant category of analysis. Specifically, this section contains articles that raise questions about the relationship between feminist theory and postcolonialism, neo-materialism, and queer theory.

Based on our experience teaching courses in feminist theory over a number of years, we are convinced that a course of this kind is accessible and helpful to all women's studies students, regardless of their disciplinary focus. Feminist work depends on assumptions about how the current sex/gender system is problematic; the task in a given course is typically to expose what "the problem" is, to construct possible remedies, or to critique others' proposed remedies. But across disciplines and authors within disciplines, there are varying interpretations of "the problem" posed by the sex/gender system, e.g., feminist political theory, literary theory, and psychology frame the central issues of feminism in quite different ways. Although this variation can lead to important insights in interdisciplinary dialogue, it is not always clear to students (or to their professors) what the presuppositions of their inquiry are or how their inquiry is related to other feminist work. A course of the kind we propose explicitly refuses to privilege one framing of "the problem" of sex oppression and is instead designed to give students a structure for thinking about a variety of different and interconnected problems under this broad rubric. As a result, it helps students see both connections and tensions between the far-ranging material they have studied in other women's studies classes and provides an opportunity to clarify and organize their thinking. Once students are alert to a broad constellation of problems concerning sex/gender, they are in a good position to problematize the original guiding questions to ask whether there is a unified phenomenon of "sex oppression." If there is, how might it be differently reflected in different social and historical contexts? And how can it be addressed it in its full complexity? If not, what should the task of feminism and feminist theory be?

We acknowledge that some may charge that our choice to organize the course around the concept of "sex oppression" biases the discussion. First, one might object that the focus on "oppression" reveals a social-scientific emphasis that neglects the important work by humanists on issues of representation and "culture." Although it is true that our text does not include some works that might be seen as central to, e.g., feminist literary theory, it is not our goal to provide an introduction to any particular disciplinary approach to feminist theory. That said, however, we also want to emphasize that the politics of representation is an important theme throughout the text, from consideration of metatheoretical issues of standpoint and epistemic position to political and legal debates over pornography. Moreover, it is our belief that the more abstract questions of representation taken up in literary theory (and related fields) are well motivated by considering, e.g., the challenges of doing cross-cultural comparisons, the symbols of patriarchal religion and pornography, and the political repercussions of cultural scripts.

A second concern might be that the focus on "oppression" leaves untouched many methodological questions about feminist research that students need to encounter in a theory course. Again, we agree that there is a place in a women's studies curriculum for a methods course; but ours is not attempting to be that course. Nonetheless, our text raises central methodological questions both explicitly and implicitly through the controversies generated between different approaches and different authors. For example, the question of essentialism and the problem of intersectionality is an underlying thread throughout the essays, as is the related question of who can legitimately speak for (and about) whom. More importantly to our minds, however, the course does not shy away from discussion of values and the normative dimension of feminist theorizing. The authors we have selected take a stand (actually, a variety of different stands) on what gender justice consists in, and how different forms of theorizing do or do not further the cause of justice. Because the course is explicitly political in its guiding questions, it engages different forms of academic feminism by revealing their political roots and normative implications.

Further, one might complain that this text does not provide an adequate representation of the history of feminism, and so suggests that feminist theory can pose and answer once and for all the organizing questions "What is sex oppression and what should we do about it?" In order to understand feminism, the objection continues, one must be attentive to the social and historical contexts of women's discontent. And when attempting to understand contemporary forms of feminism, we gain valuable insight by reflecting on past feminist movements.

We acknowledge the importance of historical perspective in understanding feminism, and agree that a study of historical texts and the work of feminist historians is essential to feminist theorizing. We have included a small number of historical texts in this volume, and urge instructors and students to pursue additional sources. Many historical texts are available on the Internet and can be easily accessed without charge; as a result, we felt it was more important to include material here that was less easily available. In addition, we believe that some of the advantages of historical perspective can also be gained by cross-cultural, cross-race, and cross-class comparisons, and we urge readers to attend to the ways in which time, culture, and social position can affect how one frames feminist issues and what one finds satisfying in a solution.

ORGANIZATIONAL HIGHLIGHTS

In addition to structuring the text around the central thematic questions, the following are further organizational features we'd like to emphasize:

• Given that the text is framed by questions concerning the nature of sex oppression, our text is organized by theoretical approach (e.g., humanist feminism, gynocentric feminism) rather than topic (e.g., work, families). We have also chosen not to organize approaches according to their non-feminist intellectual roots (e.g., Marxist feminism, socialist feminism, ecofeminism). We find our rubrics organize the material more effectively in response to the framing questions, presuppose less background knowledge about nonfeminist intellectual traditions, and also reveal that there are disagreements internal to feminism that cannot be traced to nonfeminist sources.

• In an effort to highlight the tight connection between feminist theory and practice, our text includes for each theoretical approach several essays illustrating some important political inspirations or applications. We have found this approach extremely useful in making highly theoretical pieces more accessible, and in engaging students who are wary of "high" theory. Our intention is not to reinforce a theory/practice divide; rather, we seek to demonstrate how theory is inspired by, emerges out of, returns to inform, and then is corrected by political work.

• Although early versions of many of the approaches we consider may be justifiably criticized for not taking women's diversity into account, we believe that in some cases the core commitments of the theory are compatible with a more complex understanding of gender and the phenomenon of intersectionality; moreover, in some cases defenders of an approach have responded to charges of exclusion. As a result, we have made an effort to include under each approach not only a "classical" statement of it, but further developments or extensions of it. This is important, we believe, in order to demonstrate that theories are not static entities, but grow and change as we engage and critique them. We have also incorporated writings by women of color within the "Theoretical Frames" section of each approach, making clear that women of color are contributing authors to the approaches, not only sources of critique.

• One of the current controversies in women's studies is how to incorporate a "global" perspective in our teaching and research. In choosing strategies for thinking globally we want to avoid tokenism, or casting those outside the United States as "exotic" or "Other"; we also want to avoid making the United States the "superior site of feminisms." However, a course that incorporated international issues as a centrally organizing theme along with the others we have identified would stretch an already overloaded course (and text) too thin. Our compromise is to provide a text that focuses on the United States, but that also includes several articles that invite students to broaden their perspective to consider international issues. Clearly, those who are concerned to place global issues more centrally in their course will find our compromise unsatisfying; though we also hope that this text could provide a springboard for further discussion of and readings on global feminism.

• One of the central themes of our text is the challenge of doing theory that takes the full diversity of women into account. We have chosen, in particular, to highlight at different points in the text the effects of race, ethnicity, nationality, class, sexuality, and religion. We have not represented all sources of difference, e.g., we do not include essays specifically addressing age; and some dimensions of women's experience, e.g., disability, nationality, and appearance, are represented to a very limited extent. Our goal in this text cannot be to cover everything. Instead our hope is to have provided an assortment of tools and strategies for thinking about the issue of sexist oppression and intersectionality that students can then be encouraged to extend more broadly to cases and complexities that are not explicitly covered.

PEDAGOGICAL ISSUES

Feminist theory provides a number of pedagogical challenges that we have considered in organizing the text:

• One objective of a feminist theory course such as ours is to position students as theorists themselves, rather than only as witnesses to or passive receivers of theory. We have found that one way to achieve this is to present students with different and opposing viewpoints on a particular question, and to invite them into the broader conversation occurring between the authors. Our text provides several different sorts of opportunity to participate in the theoretical conversation.

First, the text as a whole is structured so that each section responds to the one before it: in particular, essays beginning a section offer a critique of the strategies proposed in the previous one. And yet, the organizing ideas of each approach are not treated as "refuted," but emerge at later points, sometimes transformed and recontextualized. For example, although the dominance approach begins with a critique of gynocentrism, gynocentric themes reemerge later (transformed) in later essays.

Second, the essays selected as "contextual studies" provide more than one example of how the approach in question might be worked out in practice. In some cases clear tensions between the different agendas develop. This provides an opportunity for students to think through for themselves how theories might be differently interpreted and implemented, and to make judgments about their successes and failures.

Finally, rather than simply providing a selection of canonical works and ending at the boundaries of the well-established positions, our text introduces cutting-edge material in the last section that points in many possible directions. As the debates represented in the text demonstrate, it is not clear that a single unified phenomenon of "sex oppression" exists, and at the very least "sex oppression" must be analyzed together with other forms of injustice. So, in particular, we are concerned in the last section to provide examples of ways in which women's studies can be linked with other academic programs and political movements, encouraging students to participate in even broader conversations. Because the subsections under "Feminist Allies?" are areas of ongoing research, we are hoping to modify the text for further editions to keep it current.

• A disadvantage of broad survey courses is that they do not enable students to study particular authors in depth. Out of this concern, we provide full versions of almost all of the essays or book chapters, and excerpt only a few exceptionally long pieces. We also believe that there are benefits to including in several cases more than one essay by a single author, e.g., Butler, hooks, Young. Having available (even if not assigned) more than one essay by an author enables students to see how an idea might evolve in response to different concerns.

• Much of the work in recent feminist theory is written for an academic audience and is inaccessible to undergraduates; yet, more accessible single-authored surveys of the field provide only one person's interpretation of the rich, multidisciplinary terrain. Although students usually come to the course without a background in (and often a resistance to) theory, they often have some background in thinking politically about sex oppression. We have discovered that as a result, an effective technique for giving the students the entrée they need to the complex domain of theory is to have them engage different theoretical accounts of what sex oppression consists of that have emerged out of and inform feminist politics. By reaching out to students on topics that they already know something about (and also care about) and using these as a springboard for introducing more abstract theoretical issues and debates, we have found that students develop the ability and patience to read even very difficult material.

• A related problem is motivation: students do not want to work through the details of a difficult text if they think the ideas do not matter, but if they can be shown how they matter, they will make the effort. For example, students often think that "humanism" is an abstract, obsolete theory that characterized a previous era of thinking about sex equality, and so are impatient with the suggestion that they should study it. To counter this, we include historical selections such as a chapter from J. S. Mill's *Subjection of Women* in combination with contemporary representatives of liberal feminism such as Martha Nussbaum; we include Susan Schechter's account of the battered women's movement in the United States, together with humanist critiques from the perspective of women of color, immigrant women, and global politics. By showing the potentially radical implications and current usefulness of humanist (or certain forms of liberal) theory, students are motivated to take the material seriously.

• Normally, the students taking an upper-division feminist theory course are a broadly interdisciplinary group. They may have had some exposure to gender issues in previous coursework, but do not have a shared background in thinking about feminism or feminist approaches. Coming from different disciplines, they also lack a shared background in theories or debates internal to particular fields.

Topically arranged courses provide one solution to this problem, and yet have two major drawbacks in this context: first, because feminist work on broad topics such as "work" or "families" is usually framed as responding to ongoing mainstream debates, students who are not familiar with the mainstream disciplinary research often find it difficult to appreciate the force of the arguments presented; but attempting to provide the disciplinary background to the debates is usually too big a task to take on in a course devoted to feminist theory. Second, topical anthologies usually represent several different feminist responses to a particular topic; but without some way to frame these responses as part of a broader approach, students tend to see feminism as highly fragmented and divisive.

We find that a course organized around feminist approaches is much more self-contained and more effective for an interdisciplinary audience. By including with the approaches essays that focus on particular topics, such as marriage, religion, sexuality, and pornography, we also achieve some of the benefits of a topical approach.

• All courses that strive to provide students with an overview of a broad body of work struggle with balancing breadth and depth. Our goal is to introduce students to a representative array of writing, while providing enough rigor that the students do not leave with only a caricature of the views considered. We believe that anthologies comprising extensively edited excerpts tend to encourage cartoonish understandings of feminist debates; however, collections that include only full-length, highly abstract—though complete—works make for insufficiently broad courses because so much time must be invested in each article. By providing introductions to each section, study questions, and a broad conception of what counts as "theory," our text hopes to strike a good balance between breadth and depth.

One of the most difficult tasks in putting together this text was to limit ourselves to a reasonable number of essays. The range of excellent material available is remarkable, and there are many different strategies for entering into the lively and important debates. (A helpful and substantial bibliography of work in feminist theory is "The Core Reading Lists in Women's Studies" compiled by the Association of College and Research Libraries, Women's Studies Section: http://www.library.wisc.edu/libraries/WomensStudies/core/coremain.htm.) We offer here a selection of essays framed in one of many ways; we hope and expect that classes using this text will undertake to challenge and improve upon this framing. Our highest hope, however, is that this text will provide a valuable resource for the next generations of feminist theorists.

THEORIZING FEMINISMS

Section I

BACKGROUND CONCEPTS

Elizabeth Hackett and Sally Haslanger, *"Introduction"*

OPPRESSION

Iris M. Young, *"Five Faces of Oppression"*

SOCIAL CONSTRUCTION

Sally Haslanger, *"Gender and Social Construction: Who? What? When? Where? How?"*
Susan Wendell, *"The Social Construction of Disability"*
Trina Grillo, *"Anti-Essentialism and Intersectionality Tools to Dismantle the Master's House"*

EPISTEMIC POSITION

Joanna Kadi, *"Stupidity 'Deconstructed'"*
Patricia Hill Collins, *"The Politics of Black Feminist Thought"*
Uma Narayan, *"Cross-Cultural Connections, Border-Crossings, and 'Death by Culture'"*
Linda Alcoff, *"The Problem of Speaking for Others"*

INTRODUCTION

Feminist theory is interdisciplinary in two ways. It is a body of work by scholars in many different disciplines, and it includes individual writings that incorporate methods and ideas from more than one discipline, sometimes transforming those methods and ideas into something new and original. One challenge when reading feminist scholarship is that the same term might not be used in the same way by different authors, possibly because of the disciplinary backgrounds of the authors, perhaps because the authors are extending its meaning in novel but different ways. A consequence of this variation is that although two authors may seem to be addressing the same question, they might have quite different understandings of what issue the question raises and what methods should be used to answer it.

Articles in this section introduce a small selection of central, though contested, concepts that are useful to understanding the readings throughout the rest of the book. Our goal is to provide enough background about the concepts in question that they will be familiar when encountered in later readings; however, we also aim to provide enough critical perspective on the concepts that differences in their use will not be surprising. We also attempt to provide some tools to enable and encourage active contestation of the concepts' meanings.

As explained in the introduction, to this text, two questions organize this survey of feminist theory: What is sex oppression? and What should be done about it? Although many important concepts occur frequently in feminist work, our guiding questions call for special attention to the concepts of *oppression*, *social construction*, and *epistemic position*.

Iris Young's article asks: what is *oppression*? She argues that oppression is a structural phenomenon that positions groups in relations of subordination and privilege. Her view is distinctive insofar as it neither reduces oppression to a single form of subordination, nor fragments it to suggest there are separate systems subordinating different targeted groups (e.g., sexism, racism, heterosexism). Rather, she catalogues the variety of ways groups can be oppressed, in particular, by exploitation, marginalization, powerlessness, cultural imperialism, and violence.

Sally Haslanger, Susan Wendell, and Trina Grillo introduce the idea of *social construction*. It is by now virtually a platitude of feminist work that gender is socially constructed. But what exactly does that mean? Do feminists all mean the same thing when they say that something is socially constructed? Haslanger argues that there are at least two importantly different uses of the notion, one concerned with the construction of concepts or classification schemes, the other with things. Wendell provides examples of both of these uses of the notion of social construction in her description of the social construction of disability.

Grillo's discussion of oppression and social construction focuses on the intersectionality of oppressive systems. She points out that race, like gender, is socially constructed; it is a classification system that is imposed upon and lived by us. However, gender and race do not function independently; they are coupled in our experience and in their oppressive impact on our lives. (Grillo's article also provides a useful introduction to the notion of essentialism.)

The third group of essays focuses on the idea of *epistemic position*. *Episteme* is a Greek word for knowledge; epistemology is the theory of knowledge. Feminists have argued that all knowers are situated, i.e., they stand in a variety of relationships to other knowers and to the objects of knowledge. The specific features of our bodies, our cognitive styles, our emotions and values, our cultural backgrounds, and our social status all affect what we know and how we know. Joanna Kadi, Patricia Collins, Uma Narayan, and Linda Alcoff discuss how social position plays a role in the production of knowledge, and consider how feminists should take this into account. Kadi's essay illuminates both sources and consequences of the assumption that members of the working class are stupid, and challenges the lack of attention to class as an epistemic position. Collins explores the "distinctive standpoint" of Black women and urges a reconsideration of the domain within which knowledge can be generated and the forms it can take. Narayan considers the challenges of speaking "across cultures" and understanding the position of women in other national settings. She argues for a contextualized understanding of feminist issues, but one that resists the temptation to attribute the oppression of women in "Third World" countries to their "culture." Alcoff explicitly raises the issue that threads through these essays: to what extent and in what contexts is it legitimate to speak for/speak about others? Alcoff argues that although "[t]he effect of the practice of speaking for others is often, though not always, erasure and a reinscription of sexual, national, and other kinds of hierarchies," speaking for others is sometimes important and valuable, particularly if one is appropriately attentive to "the probable or actual effects of the words on the discursive and material context."

In the analyses of sexual oppression that will be considered in later parts of the book, the concepts of oppression, social construction, and epistemic position play a crucial role, even if they are not explicitly employed. Ongoing attention to the complexity of the issues as demonstrated by the articles in this section will be tremendously valuable.

OPPRESSION

Iris M. Young

Five Faces of Oppression

In this chapter I offer some explication of the concept of oppression as I understand its use by new social movements in the United States since the 1960s. My starting point is reflection on the conditions of the groups said by these movements to be oppressed: among others women, Blacks, Chicanos, Puerto Ricans and other Spanish-speaking Americans, American Indians, Jews, lesbians, gay men, Arabs, Asians, old people, working-class people, and the physically and mentally disabled. I aim to systematize the meaning of the concept of oppression as used by these diverse political movements, and to provide normative argument to clarify the wrongs the term names.

Obviously the above-named groups are not oppressed to the same extent or in the same ways. In the most general sense, all oppressed people suffer some inhibition of their ability to develop and exercise their capacities and express their needs, thoughts, and feelings. In that abstract sense all oppressed people face a common condition. Beyond that, in any more specific sense, it is not possible to define a single set of criteria that describe the condition of oppression of the above groups. Consequently, attempts by theorists and activists to discover a common description or the essential causes of the oppression of all these groups have frequently led to fruitless disputes about whose oppression is more fundamental or more grave. The contexts in which members of these groups use the term oppression to describe the injustices of their situation suggest that oppression names in fact a family of concepts and conditions, which I divide into five categories: exploitation, marginalization, powerlessness, cultural imperialism, and violence. [. . .]

OPPRESSION AS A STRUCTURAL CONCEPT

One reason that many people would not use the term oppression to describe injustice in our society is that they do not understand the term in the same way as do new social movements. In its traditional usage, oppression means the exercise of tyranny by a ruling group. Thus many Americans would agree with radicals in applying the term oppression to the situation of Black South Africans under apartheid. Oppression also traditionally carries a strong connotation of conquest and colonial domination. The Hebrews were oppressed in Egypt, and many uses of the term oppression in the West invoke this paradigm.

Dominant political discourse may use the term oppression to describe societies other than our own, usually Communist or purportedly Communist

societies. Within this anti-Communist rhetoric both tyrannical and colonialist implications of the term appear. For the anti-Communist, Communism denotes precisely the exercise of brutal tyranny over a whole people by a few rulers, and the will to conquer the world, bringing hitherto independent peoples under that tyranny. In dominant political discourse it is not legitimate to use the term oppression to describe our society, because oppression is the evil perpetrated by the Others.

New left social movements of the 1960s and 1970s, however, shifted the meaning of the concept of oppression. In its new usage, oppression designates the disadvantage and injustice some people suffer not because a tyrannical power coerces them, but because of the everyday practices of a well-intentioned liberal society. In this new left usage, the tyranny of a ruling group over another, as in South Africa, must certainly be called oppressive. But oppression also refers to systemic constraints on groups that are not necessarily the result of the intentions of a tyrant. Oppression in this sense is structural, rather than the result of a few people's choices or policies. Its causes are embedded in unquestioned norms, habits, and symbols, in the assumptions underlying institutional rules and the collective consequences of following those rules. It names, as Marilyn Frye puts it, "an enclosing structure of forces and barriers which tends to the immobilization and reduction of a group or category of people" (Frye, 1983, p. 11). In this extended structural sense oppression refers to the vast and deep injustices some groups suffer as a consequence of often unconscious assumptions and reactions of well-meaning people in ordinary interactions, media and cultural stereotypes, and structural features of bureaucratic hierarchies and market mechanisms—in short, the normal processes of everyday life. We cannot eliminate this structural oppression by getting rid of the rulers or making some new laws, because oppressions are systematically reproduced in major economic, political, and cultural institutions.

The systemic character of oppression implies that an oppressed group need not have a correlate oppressing group. While structural oppression involves relations among groups, these relations do not always fit the paradigm of conscious and intentional oppression of one group by another. Foucault (1977) suggests that to understand the meaning and operation of power in modern society we must look beyond the model of power as "sovereignty," a dyadic relation of ruler and subject, and instead analyze the exercise of power as the effect of often liberal and "humane" practices of education, bureaucratic administration, production and distribution of consumer goods, medicine, and so on. The conscious actions of many individuals daily contribute to maintaining and reproducing oppression, but those people are usually simply doing their jobs or living their lives, and do not understand themselves as agents of oppression.

I do not mean to suggest that within a system of oppression individual persons do not intentionally harm others in oppressed groups. The raped woman, the beaten Black youth, the locked-out worker, the gay man harrassed on the street, are victims of intentional actions by identifiable agents. I also do not mean to deny that specific groups are beneficiaries of the oppression of other groups, and thus have an interest in their continued oppression. Indeed, for every oppressed group there is a group that is *privileged* in relation to that group.

The concept of oppression has been current among radicals since the 1960s partly in reaction to Marxist attempts to reduce the injustices of racism and sexism, for example, to the effects of class domination or bourgeois ideology. Racism, sexism, ageism, homophobia, some social movements asserted, are distinct forms of oppression with their own dynamics apart from the dynamics of class, even though they may interact with class oppression. From often heated discussions among socialists, feminists, and antiracism activists in the last ten years a consensus is emerging that many different groups must be said to be oppressed in our society, and that no single form of oppression can be assigned causal or moral primacy. The same discussion has also led to the recognition that group differences cut across individual lives in a multiplicity of ways that can entail privilege and oppression for the same person

in different respects. Only a plural explication of the concept of oppression can adequately capture these insights.

Accordingly, I offer below an explication of five faces of oppression as a useful set of categories and distinctions which I believe is comprehensive, in the sense that it covers all the groups said by new left social movements to be oppressed and all the ways they are oppressed. I derive the five faces of oppression from reflection on the condition of these groups. Because different factors, or combinations of factors, constitute the oppression of different groups, making their oppression irreducible, I believe it is not possible to give one essential definition of oppression. The five categories articulated in this chapter, however, are adequate to describe the oppression of any group, as well as its similarities with and differences from the oppression of other groups. But first we must ask what a group is. [. . .]

THE FACES OF OPPRESSION

Exploitation

The central function of Marx's theory of exploitation is to explain how class structure can exist in the absence of legally and normatively sanctioned class distinctions. In precapitalist societies domination is overt and accomplished through directly political means. In both slave society and feudal society the right to appropriate the product of the labor of others partly defines class privilege, and these societies legitimate class distinctions with ideologies of natural superiority and inferiority.

Capitalist society, on the other hand, removes traditional juridically enforced class distinctions and promotes a belief in the legal freedom of persons. Workers freely contract with employers and receive a wage; no formal mechanisms of law or custom force them to work for that employer or any employer. Thus the mystery of capitalism arises: when everyone is formally free, how can there be class domination? Why do class distinctions persist between the wealthy, who own the means of production, and the mass of people, who work for them? The theory of exploitation answers this question.

Profit, the basis of capitalist power and wealth, is a mystery if we assume that in the market goods exchange at their values. The labor theory of value dispels this mystery. Every commodity's value is a function of the labor time necessary for its production. Labor power is the one commodity which in the process of being consumed produces new value. Profit comes from the difference between the value of the labor performed and the value of the capacity to labor which the capitalist purchases. Profit is possible only because the owner of capital appropriates any realized surplus value.

In recent years Marxist scholars have engaged in considerable controversy about the viability of the labor theory of value this account of exploitation relies on. John Roemer (1982), for example, develops a theory of exploitation which claims to preserve the theoretical and practical purposes of Marx's theory, but without assuming a distinction between values and prices and without being restricted to a concept of abstract, homogeneous labor. My purpose here is not to engage in technical economic disputes, but to indicate the place of a concept of exploitation in a conception of oppression.

Marx's theory of exploitation lacks an explicitly normative meaning, even though the judgment that workers are exploited clearly has normative as well as descriptive power in that theory. C. B. Macpherson (1973, chap. 3) reconstructs this theory of exploitation in a more explicitly normative form. The injustice of capitalist society consists in the fact that some people exercise their capacities under the control, according to the purposes, and for the benefit of other people. Through private ownership of the means of production, and through markets that allocate labor and the ability to buy goods, capitalism systematically transfers the powers of some persons to others, thereby augmenting the power of the latter. In this process of the transfer of powers, according to Macpherson, the capitalist class acquires and maintains an ability to extract benefits from workers. Not only are powers transferred from workers to capitalists, but also the powers of workers diminish by more

than the amount of transfer, because workers suffer material deprivation and a loss of control, and hence are deprived of important elements of self-respect. Justice, then, requires eliminating the institutional forms that enable and enforce this process of transference and replacing them with institutional forms that enable all to develop and use their capacities in a way that does not inhibit, but rather can enhance, similar development and use in others.

The central insight expressed in the concept of exploitation, then, is that this oppression occurs through a steady process of the transfer of the results of the labor of one social group to benefit another. The injustice of class division does not consist only in the distributive fact that some people have great wealth while most people have little. Exploitation enacts a structural relation between social groups. Social rules about what work is, who does what for whom, how work is compensated, and the social process by which the results of work are appropriated operate to enact relations of power and inequality. These relations are produced and reproduced through a systematic process in which the energies of the have-nots are continuously expended to maintain and augment the power, status, and wealth of the haves.

Many writers have cogently argued that the Marxist concept of exploitation is too narrow to encompass all forms of domination and oppression. In particular, the Marxist concept of class leaves important phenomena of sexual and racial oppression unexplained. Does this mean that sexual and racial oppression are nonexploitative, and that we should reserve wholly distinct categories for these oppressions? Or can the concept of exploitation be broadened to include other ways in which the labor and energy expenditure of one group benefits another, and reproduces a relation of domination between them?

Feminists have had little difficulty showing that women's oppression consists partly in a systematic and unreciprocated transfer of powers from women to men. Women's oppression consists not merely in an inequality of status, power, and wealth resulting from men's excluding them from privileged activities. The freedom, power, status, and self-realization of men is possible precisely because women work for them. Gender exploitation has two aspects, transfer of the fruits of material labor to men and transfer of nurturing and sexual energies to men.

Christine Delphy (1984), for example, describes marriage as a class relation in which women's labor benefits men without comparable remuneration. She makes it clear that the exploitation consists not in the sort of work that women do in the home, for this might include various kinds of tasks, but in the fact that they perform tasks for someone on whom they are dependent. Thus, for example, in most systems of agricultural production in the world, men take to market the goods women have produced, and more often than not men receive the status and often the entire income from this labor.

With the concept of sex-affective production, Ann Ferguson (1989, chap. 4) identifies another form of the transference of women's energies to men. Women provide men and children with emotional care and provide men with sexual satisfaction, and as a group receive relatively little of either from men. The gender socialization of women makes us tend to be more attentive to interactive dynamics than men, and makes women good at providing empathy and support for people's feelings and at smoothing over interactive tensions. Both men and women look to women as nurturers of their personal lives, and women frequently complain that when they look to men for emotional support they do not receive it. The norms of heterosexuality, moreover, are oriented around male pleasure, and consequently many women receive little satisfaction from their sexual interaction with men.

Most feminist theories of gender exploitation have concentrated on the institutional structure of the patriarchal family. Recently, however, feminists have begun to explore relations of gender exploitation enacted in the contemporary workplace and through the state. Carol Brown argues that as men have removed themselves from responsibility for children, many women have become dependent on the state for subsistence as they continue to bear nearly total responsibility for childrearing (Brown, 1981). This creates a new system of the exploitation of women's domestic labor mediated by state institutions, which she calls public patriarchy.

In twentieth-century capitalist economies the workplaces that women have been entering in increasing numbers serve as another important site of gender exploitation. David Alexander (1987) argues that typically feminine jobs involve gender-based tasks requiring sexual labor, nurturing, caring for others' bodies, or smoothing over workplace tensions. In these ways women's energies are expended in jobs that enhance the status of, please, or comfort others, usually men; and these gender-based labors of waitresses, clerical workers, nurses, and other caretakers often go unnoticed and undercompensated.

To summarize, women are exploited in the Marxist sense to the degree that they are wage workers. Some have argued that women's domestic labor also represents a form of capitalist class exploitation insofar as it is labor covered by the wages a family receives. As a group, however, women undergo specific forms of gender exploitation in which their energies and power are expended, often unnoticed and unacknowledged, usually to benefit men by releasing them for more important and creative work, enhancing their status or the environment around them, or providing them with sexual or emotional service.

Race is a structure of oppression at least as basic as class or gender. Are there, then, racially specific forms of exploitation? There is no doubt that racialized groups in the United States, especially Blacks and Latinos, are oppressed through capitalist superexploitation resulting from a segmented labor market that tends to reserve skilled, high-paying, unionized jobs for whites. There is wide disagreement about whether such superexploitation benefits whites as a group or only benefits the capitalist class, and I do not intend to enter into that dispute here.

However one answers the question about capitalist superexploitation of racialized groups, is it possible to conceptualize a form of exploitation that is racially specific on analogy with the gender-specific forms just discussed? I suggest that the category of *menial* labor might supply a means for such conceptualization. In its derivation "menial" designates the labor of servants. Wherever there is racism, there is the assumption, more or less enforced, that members of

the oppressed racial groups are or ought to be servants of those, or some of those, in the privileged
group. In most white racist societies this means that
many white people have dark- or yellow-skinned
domestic servants, and in the United States today
there remains significant racial structuring of private
household service. But in the United States today
much service labor has gone public: anyone who
goes to a good hotel or a good restaurant can have
servants. Servants often attend the daily—and
nightly—activities of business executives, government officials, and other high-status professionals.
In our society there remains strong cultural pressure
to fill servant jobs—bellhop, porter, chambermaid,
busboy, and so on—with Black and Latino workers.
These jobs entail a transfer of energies whereby the
servers enhance the status of the served.

Menial labor usually refers not only to service,
however, but also to any servile, unskilled, low-
paying work lacking in autonomy, in which a person
is subject to taking orders from many people. Menial
work tends to be auxiliary work, instrumental to the
work of others, where those others receive primary
recognition for doing the job. Laborers on a construction site, for example, are at the beck and call of
welders, electricians, carpenters, and other skilled
workers, who receive recognition for the job done.
In the United States explicit racial discrimination
once reserved menial work for Blacks, Chicanos,
American Indians, and Chinese, and menial work still
tends to be linked to Black and Latino workers. I offer
this category of menial labor as a form of racially
specific exploitation, as a provisional category in
need of exploration.

The injustice of exploitation is most frequently
understood on a distributive model. For example,
though he does not offer an explicit definition of the
concept, by "exploitation" Bruce Ackerman seems
to mean a seriously unequal distribution of wealth,
income, and other resources that is group based and
structurally persistent (Ackerman, 1980, chap. 8).
John Roemer's definition of exploitation is narrower
and more rigorous: "An agent is exploited when the
amount of labor embodied in *any* bundle of goods he
could receive, in a feasible distribution of society's
net product, is less than the labor he expended"
(Roemer, 1982, p. 122). This definition too turns the
conceptual focus from institutional relations and
processes to distributive outcomes.

Jeffrey Reiman argues that such a distributive
understanding of exploitation reduces the injustice of
class processes to a function of the inequality of the
productive assets classes own. This misses, according
to Reiman, the relationship of force between capitalists and workers, the fact that the unequal exchange in
question occurs within coercive structures that give
workers few options (Reiman, 1987). The injustice
of exploitation consists in social processes that bring
about a transfer of energies from one group to another
to produce unequal distributions, and in the way in
which social institutions enable a few to accumulate
while they constrain many more. The injustices of
exploitation cannot be eliminated by redistribution
of goods, for as long as institutionalized practices
and structural relations remain unaltered, the process
of transfer will re-create an unequal distribution
of benefits. Bringing about justice where there is
exploitation requires reorganization of institutions
and practices of decisionmaking, alteration of the
division of labor, and similar measures of institutional, structural, and cultural change.

Marginalization

Increasingly in the United States racial oppression
occurs in the form of marginalization rather than
exploitation. Marginals are people the system of
labor cannot or will not use. Not only in Third World
capitalist countries, but also in most Western capitalist societies, there is a growing underclass of people
permanently confined to lives of social marginality,
most of whom are racially marked—Blacks or
Indians in Latin America, and Blacks, East Indians,
Eastern Europeans, or North Africans in Europe.

Marginalization is by no means the fate only of
racially marked groups, however. In the United States
a shamefully large proportion of the population is
marginal: old people, and increasingly people who are
not very old but get laid off from their jobs and cannot
find new work; young people, especially Black or

Latino, who cannot find first or second jobs; many single mothers and their children; other people involuntarily unemployed; many mentally and physically disabled people; American Indians, especially those on reservations.

Marginalization is perhaps the most dangerous form of oppression. A whole category of people is expelled from useful participation in social life and thus potentially subjected to severe material deprivation and even extermination. The material deprivation marginalization often causes is certainly unjust, especially in a society where others have plenty. Contemporary advanced capitalist societies have in principle acknowledged the injustice of material deprivation caused by marginalization, and have taken some steps to address it by providing welfare payments and services. The continuance of this welfare state is by no means assured, and in most welfare state societies, especially the United States, welfare redistributions do not eliminate large-scale suffering and deprivation.

Material deprivation, which can be addressed by redistributive social policies, is not, however, the extent of the harm caused by marginalization. Two categories of injustice beyond distribution are associated with marginality in advanced capitalist societies. First, the provision of welfare itself produces new injustice by depriving those dependent on it of rights and freedoms that others have. Second, even when material deprivation is somewhat mitigated by the welfare state, marginalization is unjust because it blocks the opportunity to exercise capacities in socially defined and recognized ways. I shall explicate each of these in turn.

Liberalism has traditionally asserted the right of all rational autonomous agents to equal citizenship. Early bourgeois liberalism explicitly excluded from citizenship all those whose reason was questionable or not fully developed, and all those not independent. Thus poor people, women, the mad and the feebleminded, and children were explicitly excluded from citizenship, and many of these were housed in institutions modeled on the modern prison: poorhouses, insane asylums, schools.

Today the exclusion of dependent persons from equal citizenship rights is only barely hidden beneath the surface. Because they depend on bureaucratic institutions for support or services, the old, the poor, and the mentally or physically disabled are subject to patronizing, punitive, demeaning, and arbitrary treatment by the policies and people associated with welfare bureaucracies. Being a dependent in our society implies being legitimately subject to the often arbitrary and invasive authority of social service providers and other public and private administrators, who enforce rules with which the marginal must comply, and otherwise exercise power over the conditions of their lives. In meeting needs of the marginalized, often with the aid of social scientific disciplines, welfare agencies also construct the needs themselves. Medical and social service professionals know what is good for those they serve, and the marginals and dependents themselves do not have the right to claim to know what is good for them. Dependency in our society thus implies, as it has in all liberal societies, a sufficient warrant to suspend basic rights to privacy, respect, and individual choice.

Although dependency produces conditions of injustice in our society, dependency in itself need not be oppressive. One cannot imagine a society in which some people would not need to be dependent on others at least some of the time: children, sick people, women recovering from childbirth, old people who have become frail, depressed or otherwise emotionally needy persons, have the moral right to depend on others for subsistence and support.

An important contribution of feminist moral theory has been to question the deeply held assumption that moral agency and full citizenship require that a person be autonomous and independent. Feminists have exposed this assumption as inappropriately individualistic and derived from a specifically male experience of social relations, which values competition and solitary achievement. Female experience of social relations, arising both from women's typical domestic care responsibilities and from the kinds of paid work that many women do, tends to recognize dependence as a basic human condition. Whereas on the autonomy model a just society would as much as possible give people the opportunity to be independent, the feminist model envisions justice as according respect and participation in decisionmaking to those who are dependent as well as to those who are independent. Dependency should not be a reason to be deprived of choice and respect, and much of the oppression many marginals experience would be lessened if a less individualistic model of rights prevailed.

Marginalization does not cease to be oppressive when one has shelter and food. Many old people, for example, have sufficient means to live comfortably but remain oppressed in their marginal status. Even if marginals were provided a comfortable material life within institutions that respected their freedom and dignity, injustices of marginality would remain in the form of uselessness, boredom, and lack of self-respect. Most of our society's productive and recognized activities take place in contexts of organized social cooperation, and social structures and processes that close persons out of participation in such social cooperation are unjust. Thus while marginalization definitely entails serious issues of distributive justice, it also involves the deprivation of cultural, practical, and institutionalized conditions for exercising capacities in a context of recognition and interaction.

The fact of marginalization raises basic structural issues of justice, in particular concerning the appropriateness of a connection between participation in productive activities of social cooperation, on the one hand, and access to the means of consumption, on the other. As marginalization is increasing, with no sign of abatement, some social policy analysts have introduced the idea of a "social wage" as a guaranteed socially provided income not tied to the wage system. Restructuring of productive activity to address a right of participation, however, implies organizing some socially productive activity outside of the wage system, through public works or self-employed collectives.

Powerlessness

As I have indicated, the Marxist idea of class is important because it helps reveal the structure of exploitation: that some people have their power and wealth because they profit from the labor of others. For this reason I reject the claim some make that a traditional class exploitation model fails to capture the structure of contemporary society. It remains the case that the labor of most people in the society augments the power of relatively few. [. . .]

While it is false to claim that a division between capitalist and working classes no longer describes our society, it is also false to say that class relations have remained unaltered since the nineteenth century. An adequate conception of oppression cannot ignore the experience of social division reflected in the colloquial distinction between the "middle class" and the "working class," a division structured by the social division of labor between professionals and nonprofessionals. Professionals are privileged in relation to nonprofessionals, by virtue of their position in the division of labor and the status it carries. Nonprofessionals suffer a form of oppression in addition to exploitation, which I call powerlessness.

In the United States, as in other advanced capitalist countries, most workplaces are not organized democratically, direct participation in public policy decisions is rare, and policy implementation is for the most part hierarchical, imposing rules on bureaucrats and citizens. Thus most people in these societies do not regularly participate in making decisions that affect the conditions of their lives and actions, and in this sense most people lack signficant power. At the same time, . . . domination in modern society is enacted through the widely dispersed powers of many agents mediating the decisions of others. To that extent many people have some power in relation to others, even though they lack the power to decide policies or results. The powerless are those who lack authority or power even in this mediated sense, those over whom power is exercised without their exercising it; the powerless are situated so that they must take orders and rarely have the right to give them. Powerlessness also designates a position in the division of labor and the concomitant social position that allows persons little opportunity to develop and exercise skills. The powerless have little or no work autonomy, exercise little creativity or judgment in their work, have no technical expertise or authority, express themselves awkwardly, especially in public or bureaucratic settings, and do not command respect.

Powerlessness names the oppressive situations Sennett and Cobb (1972) describe in their famous study of working-class men.

This powerless status is perhaps best described negatively: the powerless lack the authority, status, and sense of self that professionals tend to have. The status privilege of professionals has three aspects, the lack of which produces oppression for nonprofessionals.

First, acquiring and practicing a profession has an expansive, progressive character. Being professional usually requires a college education and the acquisition of a specialized knowledge that entails working with symbols and concepts. Professionals experience progress first in acquiring the expertise, and then in the course of professional advancement and rise in status. The life of the nonprofessional by comparison is powerless in the sense that it lacks this orientation toward the progressive development of capacities and avenues for recognition.

Second, while many professionals have supervisors and cannot directly influence many decisions or the actions of many people, most nevertheless have considerable day-to-day work autonomy. Professionals usually have some authority over others, moreover— either over workers they supervise, or over auxiliaries, or over clients. Nonprofessionals, on the other hand, lack autonomy, and in both their working and their consumer-client lives often stand under the authority of professionals.

Though based on a division of labor between "mental" and "manual" work, the distinction between "middle class" and "working class" designates a division not only in working life, but also in nearly all aspects of social life. Professionals and nonprofessionals belong to different cultures in the United States. The two groups tend to live in segregated neighborhoods or even different towns, a process itself mediated by planners, zoning officials, and real estate people. The groups tend to have different tastes in food, decor, clothes, music, and vacations, and often different health and educational needs. Members of each group socialize for the most part with others in the same status group. While there is some intergroup mobility between generations, for the most part the children of professionals become professionals and the children of nonprofessionals do not.

Thus, third, the privileges of the professional extend beyond the workplace to a whole way of life. I call this way of life "respectability." To treat people with respect is to be prepared to listen to what they have to say or to do what they request because they have some authority, expertise, or influence. The norms of respectability in our society are associated specifically with professional culture. Professional dress, speech, tastes, demeanor, all connote respectability. Generally professionals expect and receive respect from others. In restaurants, banks, hotels, real estate offices, and many other such public places, as well as in the media, professionals typically receive more respectful treatment than nonprofessionals. For this reason nonprofessionals seeking a loan or a job, or to buy a house or a car, will often try to look "professional" and "respectable" in those settings.

The privilege of this professional respectability appears starkly in the dynamics of racism and sexism. In daily interchange women and men of color must prove their respectability. At first they are often not treated by strangers with respectful distance or deference. Once people discover that this woman or that Puerto Rican man is a college teacher or a business executive, however, they often behave more respectfully toward her or him. Working-class white men, on the other hand, are often treated with respect until their working-class status is revealed. [. . .]

Cultural Imperialism

Exploitation, marginalization, and powerlessness all refer to relations of power and oppression that occur by virtue of the social division of labor—who works for whom, who does not work, and how the content of work defines one institutional position relative to others. These three categories refer to structural and institutional relations that delimit people's material lives, including but not restricted to the resources they have access to and the concrete opportunities they have or do not have to develop and exercise their capacities. These kinds of oppression are a matter of concrete power in relation to others—of who benefits from whom, and who is dispensable.

Recent theorists of movements of group liberation, notably feminist and Black liberation theorists, have also given prominence to a rather different form of oppression, which following Lugones and Spelman (1983) I shall call cultural imperialism. To experience cultural imperialism means to experience how the dominant meanings of a society render the particular perspective of one's own group invisible at the same time as they stereotype one's group and mark it out as the Other.

Cultural imperialism involves the universalization of a dominant group's experience and culture, and its establishment as the norm. Some groups have exclusive or primary access to what Nancy Fraser (1987) calls the means of interpretation and communication in a society. As a consequence, the dominant cultural products of the society, that is, those most widely disseminated, express the experience, values, goals, and achievements of these groups. Often without noticing they do so, the dominant groups project their own experience as representative of humanity as such. Cultural products also express the dominant group's perspective on and interpretation of events and elements in the society, including other groups in the society, insofar as they attain cultural status at all.

An encounter with other groups, however, can challenge the dominant group's claim to universality. The dominant group reinforces its position by bringing the other groups under the measure of its dominant norms. Consequently, the difference of women from men, American Indians or Africans from Europeans, Jews from Christians, homosexuals from heterosexuals, workers from professionals, becomes reconstructed largely as deviance and inferiority. Since only the dominant group's cultural expressions receive wide dissemination, their cultural expressions become the normal, or the universal, and thereby the unremarkable. Given the normality of its own cultural expressions and identity, the dominant group constructs the differences which some groups exhibit as lack and negation. These groups become marked as Other.

The culturally dominated undergo a paradoxical oppression, in that they are both marked out by stereotypes and at the same time rendered invisible. As remarkable, deviant beings, the culturally imperialized are stamped with an essence. The stereotypes confine them to a nature which is often attached in some way to their bodies, and which thus cannot easily be denied. These stereotypes so permeate the society that they are not noticed as contestable. Just as everyone knows that the earth goes around the sun, so everyone knows that gay people are promiscuous, that Indians are alcoholics, and that women are good with children. White males, on the other hand, insofar as they escape group marking, can be individuals.

Those living under cultural imperialism find themselves defined from the outside, positioned, placed, by a network of dominant meanings they experience as arising from elsewhere, from those with whom they do not identify and who do not identify with them. Consequently, the dominant culture's stereotyped and inferiorized images of the group must be internalized by group members at least to the extent that they are forced to react to behavior of others influenced by those images. This creates for the culturally oppressed the experience that W. E. B. Du Bois called "double consciousness"—"this sense of always looking at one's self through the eyes of others, of measuring one's soul by the tape of a world that looks on in amused contempt and pity" (Du Bois, 1969 [1903], p. 45). Double consciousness arises when the oppressed subject refuses to coincide with these devalued, objectified, stereotyped visions of herself or himself. While the subject desires recognition as human, capable of activity, full of hope and possibility, she receives from the dominant culture only the judgment that she is different, marked, or inferior.

The group defined by the dominant culture as deviant, as a stereotyped Other, *is* culturally different from the dominant group, because the status of Otherness creates specific experiences not shared by the dominant group, and because culturally oppressed groups also are often socially segregated and occupy specific positions in the social division of labor. Members of such groups express their specific group experiences and interpretations of the world to one another, developing and perpetuating their own culture. Double consciousness, then, occurs because one finds one's being defined by two cultures: a dominant and a subordinate culture. Because they can affirm and recognize one another as sharing similar experiences and perspectives on social life, people in culturally imperialized groups can often maintain a sense of positive subjectivity.

Cultural imperialism involves the paradox of experiencing oneself as invisible at the same time that one is marked out as different. The invisibility comes about when dominant groups fail to recognize the perspective embodied in their cultural expressions as a perspective. These dominant cultural expressions often simply have little place for the experience of other groups, at most only mentioning or referring to them in stereotyped or marginalized ways. This, then, is the injustice of cultural imperialism: that the oppressed group's own experience and interpretation of social life finds little expression that touches the dominant culture, while that same culture imposes on the oppressed group its experience and interpretation of social life. [. . .]

Violence

Finally, many groups suffer the oppression of systematic violence. Members of some groups live with the knowledge that they must fear random, unprovoked attacks on their persons or property, which have no motive but to damage, humiliate, or destroy the person. In American society women, Blacks, Asians, Arabs, gay men, and lesbians live under such threats of violence, and in at least some regions Jews, Puerto Ricans, Chicanos, and other Spanish-speaking Americans must fear such violence as well. Physical violence against these groups is shockingly frequent. Rape Crisis Center networks estimate that more than one-third of all American women experience an attempted or successful sexual assault in their lifetimes. Manning Marable (1984, pp. 238–41) catalogues a large number of incidents of racist violence and terror against blacks in the United States between 1980 and 1982. He cites dozens of incidents of the

severe beating, killing, or rape of Blacks by police officers on duty, in which the police involved were acquitted of any wrongdoing. In 1981, moreover, there were at least five hundred documented cases of random white teenage violence against Blacks. Violence against gay men and lesbians is not only common, but has been increasing in the last five years. While the frequency of physical attack on members of these and other racially or sexually marked groups is very disturbing, I also include in this category less severe incidents of harrassment, intimidation, or ridicule simply for the purpose of degrading, humiliating, or stigmatizing group members.

Given the frequency of such violence in our society, why are theories of justice usually silent about it? I think the reason is that theorists do not typically take such incidents of violence and harrassment as matters of social injustice. No moral theorist would deny that such acts are very wrong. But unless all immoralities are injustices, they might wonder, why should such acts be interpreted as symptoms of social injustice? Acts of violence or petty harrassment are committed by particular individuals, often extremists, deviants, or the mentally unsound. How then can they be said to involve the sorts of institutional issues I have said are properly the subject of justice?

What makes violence a face of oppression is less the particular acts themselves, though these are often utterly horrible, than the social context surrounding them, which makes them possible and even acceptable. What makes violence a phenomenon of social injustice, and not merely an individual moral wrong, is its systemic character, its existence as a social practice.

Violence is systemic because it is directed at members of a group simply because they are members of that group. Any woman, for example, has a reason to fear rape. Regardless of what a Black man has done to escape the oppressions of marginality or powerlessness, he lives knowing he is subject to attack or harassment. The oppression of violence consists not only in direct victimization, but in the daily knowledge shared by all members of oppressed groups that they are *liable* to violation, solely on account of their group identity. Just living under such a threat of attack on oneself or family or friends deprives the oppressed of freedom and dignity, and needlessly expends their energy.

Violence is a social practice. It is a social given that everyone knows happens and will happen again. It is always at the horizon of social imagination, even for those who do not perpetrate it. According to the prevailing social logic, some circumstances make such violence more "called for" than others. The idea of rape will occur to many men who pick up a hitch-hiking woman; the idea of hounding or teasing a gay man on their dorm floor will occur to many straight male college students. Often several persons inflict the violence together, especially in all-male group-ings. Sometimes violators set out looking for people to beat up, rape, or taunt. This rule-bound, social, and often premeditated character makes violence against groups a social practice.

Group violence approaches legitimacy, moreover, in the sense that it is tolerated. Often third parties find it unsurprising because it happens frequently and lies as a constant possibility at the horizon of the social imagination. Even when they are caught, those who perpetrate acts of group-directed violence or harrass-ment often receive light or no punishment. To that extent society renders their acts acceptable.

An important aspect of random, systemic violence is its irrationality. Xenophobic violence differs from the violence of states or ruling-class repression. Re-pressive violence has a rational, albeit evil, motive: rulers use it as a coercive tool to maintain their power. Many accounts of racist, sexist, or homophobic viol-ence attempt to explain its motivation as a desire to maintain group privilege or domination. I do not doubt that fear of violence often functions to keep oppressed groups subordinate, but I do not think xenophobic violence is rationally motivated in the way that, for example, violence against strikers is.

On the contrary, the violation of rape, beating, killing, and harrassment of women, people of color, gays, and other marked groups is motivated by fear or hatred of those groups. Sometimes the motive may be a simple will to power, to victimize those marked as vulnerable by the very social fact that they are subject to violence. If so, this motive is secondary in the sense that it depends on a social practice of group viol-ence. Violence-causing fear or hatred of the other at least partly involves insecurities on the part of the violators; its irrationality suggests that unconscious processes are at work. . . . I offer a psychoanalytic account of the fear and hatred of some groups as bound up with fears of identity loss. I think such unconscious fears account at least partly for the oppression I have here called violence. It may also partly account for cultural imperialism.

Cultural imperialism, moreover, itself intersects with violence. The culturally imperialized may reject the dominant meanings and attempt to assert their own subjectivity, or the fact of their cultural difference may put the lie to the dominant culture's implicit claim to universality. The dissonance generated by such a challenge to the hegemonic cultural meanings can also be a source of irrational violence. [. . .]

APPLYING THE CRITERIA

Social theories that construct oppression as a unified phenomenon usually either leave out groups that even the theorists think are oppressed, or leave out important ways in which groups are oppressed. Black liberation theorists and feminist theorists have argued persuasively, for example, that Marxism's reduction of all oppressions to class oppression leaves out much about the specific oppression of Blacks and women. By pluralizing the category of oppression in the way explained in this chapter, social theory can avoid the exclusive and oversimplifying effects of such reductionism.

I have avoided pluralizing the category in the way some others have done, by constructing an account of separate systems of oppression for each oppres-sed group: racism, sexism, classism, heterosexism, ageism, and so on. There is a double problem with considering each group's oppression a unified and distinct structure or system. On the one hand, this way of conceiving oppression fails to accommodate the similarities and overlaps in the oppressions of dif-ferent groups. On the other hand, it falsely represents the situation of all group members as the same.

I have arrived at the five faces of oppression—exploitation, marginalization, powerlessness, cultural imperialism, and violence—as the best way to avoid such exclusions and reductions. They function as criteria for determining whether individuals and groups are oppressed, rather than as a full theory of oppression. I believe that these criteria are objective. They provide a means of refuting some people's belief that their group is oppressed when it is not, as well as a means of persuading others that a group is oppressed when they doubt it. Each criterion can be operationalized; each can be applied through the assessment of observable behavior, status relationships, distributions, texts and other cultural artifacts. I have no illusions that such assessments can be value-neutral. But these criteria can nevertheless serve as means of evaluating claims that a group is oppressed, or adjudicating disputes about whether or how a group is oppressed.

The presence of any of these five conditions is sufficient for calling a group oppressed. But different group oppressions exhibit different combinations of these forms, as do different individuals in the groups. Nearly all, if not all, groups said by contemporary social movements to be oppressed suffer cultural imperialism. The other oppressions they experience vary. Working-class people are exploited and powerless, for example, but if employed and white do not experience marginalization and violence. Gay men, on the other hand, are not qua gay exploited or powerless, but they experience severe cultural imperialism and violence. Similarly, Jews and Arabs as groups are victims of cultural imperialism and violence, though many members of these groups also suffer exploitation or powerlessness. Old people are oppressed by marginalization and cultural imperialism, and this is also true of physically and mentally disabled people. As a group women are subject to gender-based exploitation, powerlessness, cultural imperialism, and violence. Racism in the United States condemns many Blacks and Latinos to marginalization, and puts many more at risk, even though many members of these groups escape that condition; members of these groups often suffer all five forms of oppression.

Applying these five criteria to the situation of groups makes it possible to compare oppressions without reducing them to a common essence or claiming that one is more fundamental than another. One can compare the ways in which a particular form of oppression appears in different groups. For example, while the operations of cultural imperialism are often experienced in similar fashion by different groups, there are also important differences. One can compare the combinations of oppressions groups experience, or the intensity of those oppressions. Thus with these criteria one can plausibly claim that one group is more oppressed than another without reducing all oppressions to a single scale.

REFERENCES

Ackerman, Bruce. 1980. *Social Justice and the Liberal State*. New Haven: Yale University Press.

Alexander, David. 1987. "Gendered Job Traits and Women's Occupations." PhD. dissertation, Economics, University of Massachusetts.

Brown, Carol. 1981. "Mothers, Fathers and Children: From Private to Public Patriarchy." In Lydia Sargent, ed., *Women and Revolution*. Boston: South End.

Delphy, Christine. 1984. *Close to Home: A Materialist Analysis of Women's Oppression*. Amherst: University of Massachusetts Press.

Du Bois, W. E. B. 1969 [1903]. *The Souls of Black Folks*. New York: New American Library.

Fergeson, Ann. 1989. *Blood at the Root*. London: Pandora.

Foucault, Michel. 1977. *Discipline and Punish*. New York: Pantheon.

Fraser, Nancy. 1987. "Social Movements vs. Disciplinary Democracy." CHS Occasional Papers No. 8, Center for Humanistic Studies, University of Minnesota.

Frye, Marilyn. 1983. "Oppression." In *The Politics of Reality*. Trumansburg, NY: Crossing.

Lugones, Maria and Elizabeth V. Spelman. 1983. "Have We Got a Theory for You!" *Women's Studies International Forum* 6: 573–81.

Macherson, C. B. 1973. *Democratic Theory: Essays in Retrieval*. Oxford: Oxford University Press.

Marable, Manning. 1984. *Race, Reform and Rebellion*. Jackson: University of Mississippi Press.

Reiman, Jeffrey. 1987. "Exploitation, Force, and the Moral Assessment of Capitalism." *Philosophy and Public Affairs* 16 (Winter): 3–41.

Roemer, John. 1982. *A General Theory of Exploitation and Class*. Cambridge: Harvard University Press.

Sennett, Richard and Jonathan Cobb. 1972. *The Hidden Injuries of Class*. New York: Vintage.

Study Questions

1. Explain the shift from "oppression" as defined in dominant political discourse to its use by the new left social movements described at the beginning of Young's article.

2. What does Young mean by a "face" of oppression?

3. Explain the five faces of oppression discussed by Young.

4. Young claims that her list is comprehensive. Is she right about this? Think about each of the groups that new left social movements typically take to be oppressed in light of each of Young's five "faces"; e.g., does cultural imperialism adequately capture the "Othering" experienced by women?

SOCIAL CONSTRUCTION

Sally Haslanger

Gender and Social Construction: Who? What? When? Where? How?

I. INTRODUCTION[1]

The idea of social construction is a crucial tool of contemporary feminist theory. No longer willing to regard the differences between women and men as "natural", feminists have studied the variety of cultural processes by which one "becomes" a woman (or a man), ultimately with the hope of subverting them. Along with this has come a critique of those patterns of thought by which gender, as well as other hierarchical social relations, has been sustained.

Although there is consensus that we need the notion of social construction to theorize adequately about women, there is a broad diversity in how the term "social construction" is used and where it should be applied. As just indicated, beyond the thesis that *gender* and other social categories such as *race* and *nationality* are socially constructed, one also finds the claims that the "subject", "knowledge" and "truth" are each socially constructed. On occasion it is possible to find the claim that "everything" is socially constructed, or that "reality" is socially constructed. But once we come to the claim that everything is socially constructed, it appears a short step to the conclusion that there is no reality independent of our practices or of our language, and that "truth" and "reality" are only fictions employed by the dominant to mask their power.

Dramatic claims rejecting the legitimacy of such notions as "truth" and "reality" do appear in the work of feminist theorists, yet one also finds there a deep resistance to slipping into any form of idealism or relativism. For example, to quote Catharine MacKinnon's typically vivid words:

> Epistemologically speaking, women know the male world is out there because it hits them in the face. No matter how they think about it, try to think it out of existence or into a different shape, it remains independently real, keeps forcing them into certain molds. No matter what they think or do, they cannot get out of it. It has all the indeterminacy of a bridge abutment hit at sixty miles per hour. (MacKinnon 1989: 123)

To start, it will be useful to consider carefully different things one might mean in saying that something is socially constructed. Although I won't address the full range of cases mentioned above, I hope that the distinctions I discuss will be useful in exploring options for interpreting, criticizing or defending such claims. My focus here will be to consider how the different senses of construction might apply in the case of gender.

II. KINDS OF SOCIAL CONSTRUCTION

In the very broadest sense, something is a social construction if it is an intended or unintended product of a social practice. Artifacts such as washing machines and power drills might on some views count as social constructions, but more interesting cases include: the Supreme Court of the US, chess games, languages, literature, and scientific inquiry.[2] Because each of these depend for their existence on a complex social context, they are in the broad sense in question social constructions. Note, however, that there is also a sense in which professors and wives are only possible within a social context: you can't be a *wife* unless you stand in a marriage relationship to a man that is sanctioned by the state. Insofar as the features which qualify one as a member of a particular type or kind include *social* (properties and) relations, things of that kind could count as social constructions too. Although these various items, be they objects, events, sets of individuals, etc., are very different sorts of things and are "constructed" in different ways, at this point there is no reason whatsoever to think they are anything less than fully *real*; and their reality is perfectly concrete, i.e., they don't just exist "in our heads".

A. The Construction of Ideas and Concepts

However, things get more complicated quite quickly. It is important to distinguish first the construction of *ideas* and the construction of *objects*. (Hacking 1999: 9–16). Let's start with ideas.[3] On one reading, the claim that an idea or a concept is only possible within and due to a social context is utterly obvious. It would

seem to be a matter of common sense that concepts are taught to us by our parents through our language; different cultures have different concepts (that go along with their different languages); and concepts evolve over time as a result of historical changes, science, technological advances, etc. Let's (albeit contentiously) call this the "ordinary view" of concepts and ideas. Even someone who believes that our scientific concepts perfectly map "nature's joints" can allow that scientists come to have the ideas and concepts they do through social-historical processes. After all, social and cultural forces (including, possibly, the practices and methods of science) may help us develop concepts that are apt or accurate, and beliefs that are true.

We may sometimes forget that what and how we think is affected by social forces because our experiences seem to be caused simply and directly by world itself. However, it does not take much prompting to recall that our culture is largely responsible for the interpretive tools we bring to the world in order to understand it. Once we've noted that our experience of the world is already an interpretation of it, we can begin to raise questions about the adequacy of our conceptual framework. Concepts help us organize phenomena; different concepts organize it in different ways. It is important, then, to ask: what phenomena are highlighted and what are eclipsed by a particular framework of concepts? What assumptions provide structure for the framework?

For example, our everyday framework for thinking about human beings is structured by the assumptions that there are two (and only two) sexes, and that every human is either a male or a female. But in fact a significant percentage of humans have a mix of male and female anatomical features. Intersexed bodies are eclipsed in our everyday framework. (Fausto-Sterling 1993). This should invite us to ask: why? Whose interests are served, if anyone's, by the intersexed being ignored in the dominant conceptual framework? (It can't be plausibly argued that sex isn't important enough to us to make fine-grained distinctions between bodies!) Further, once we recognize the intersexed, how should we revise our conceptual framework? Should we group bodies into more than two sexes, or are there reasons instead to complicate the definitions of male and female to include everyone in just two sex categories? More generally, on what basis should we decide what categories to use? (Fausto-Sterling 1993; Butler 1990, Ch. 1). In asking these questions it is important to remember that an idea or conceptual framework may be inadequate without being false, e.g., a claim might be true and yet incomplete, misleading, unjustified, biased, etc. (Anderson 1995).

The point of saying that a concept or idea is socially constructed will vary depending on context; sometimes it may have little or no point, if everyone is fully aware of the social history of the idea in question or if the social history isn't relevant to the issue at hand. On other occasions, saying that this or that idea is socially constructed is a reminder of the ordinary view of concepts and, more importantly, an invitation to notice the motivations behind and limitations of our current framework. Every framework will have some limits; the issue is whether the limits eclipse something that, given the (legitimate) goals of our inquiry, matters. However, sometimes a social constructionist is making a more controversial claim. The suggestion would be that something or other is "merely" a social construction, in other words, that what we are taking to be real is only a fiction, an idea that fails to capture reality. Feminists have argued, for example, that certain mental "disorders" that have been used to diagnose battered women are *merely* social constructions. Andrea Westlund points out how

> [b]attered women's "abnormalities" have been described and redescribed within the psychiatric literature of the twentieth century, characterized as everything from hysteria to masochistic or self-defeating personality disorders (SDPD) to co-dependency . . . Moreover, such pathologies measure, classify, and define battered women's deviance not just from "normal" female behavior but also from universalized male norms of independence and self-interest. (Westlund 1999)

Such diagnoses invite us to explain domestic violence by reference to the woman's psychological state rather than the batterer's need for power and control; they also "deflect attention from the social and political aspects of domestic violence to the private neuroses to which women as a group are thought to be prone." (Westlund 1999, 1051). Westlund and others have argued that although victims of domestic violence often do suffer from psychological conditions, e.g., major depression, there is a range of gender coded mental disorders included in the *Diagnostic and Statistical Manual of Mental Disorder* (DSM) for which there is little, if any, good evidence. These diagnoses, it could be claimed, are *merely* social constructions in the sense that they are ideas used to interpret and regulate social phenomena, but do not describe anything real. Applying this to the case at hand would entail that "Self-Defeating Personality Disorder" doesn't really exist. The description of SDPD, if it captures anything at all, isn't a mental disorder of the sort alleged.

So in considering the claim that something is socially constructed, we should ask first: Is it an object or an idea? If it is an idea, it is important to determine how that idea functions within a broader framework of ideas and concepts and to consider how the framework structures our experience: does it illegitimately or inappropriately privilege one set of phenomena over another? Of course in some contexts privileging certain phenomena is useful and even necessary: medical sciences are not "neutral" with respect to what phenomena count as significant and how they are categorized; medicine has a legitimate concern with human health and the organisms that affect human health. However, other things being equal, medicine that privileges phenomena related to men's health, or the health of the wealthy, would not be epistemically or politically legitimate. (Anderson 1995). Considering what is left out of a framework of categories and what assumptions structure it can reveal biases of many sorts. In extreme cases we may find that the idea in question does not describe anything real at all, and instead is just a fiction being treated as real. In such cases work must be done to demonstrate that what's at issue is only a fiction. But that's not all, for we should also ask: How are such fictions established and maintained? Whose interests do they serve?

B. The Construction of Objects

Now consider objects (understanding "objects" in the broadest sense as virtually anything that's not an idea). There is a sense in which any artifact is a construction; but claiming that scissors or cars are social constructions would not have much point, given how obvious it is. Social constructionists, on the whole, are arguing for a surprising thesis that they believe challenges our everyday view of things. It is much more surprising to say that women or Asian-Americans, homosexuals, child abusers, or refugees, are social constructions. What could this mean?

In considering the construction of objects the first point to note is that our classificatory schemes, at least in social contexts, may do more than just map pre-existing groups of individuals; rather our attributions have the power to both establish and reinforce groupings which may eventually come to "fit" the classifications. This works in several ways. Forms of description or classification provide for kinds of intention; e.g., given the classification "cool", I can set about to become cool, or avoid being cool, etc. But also, such classifications can function in justifying behavior; e.g., "we didn't invite him because he's not cool", and such justifications, in turn, can reinforce the distinction between those who are cool and those who are uncool. In an earlier essay, drawing on Ian Hacking's work, I referred to this as "discursive" construction:

> discursive construction: something is discursively constructed just in case it is (to a significant extent) the way it is because of what is attributed to it or how it is classified. (Haslanger 1995, 99)

Admittedly, the idea here is quite vague (e.g., how much is "a significant extent"?). However, social construction in this sense is ubiquitous. Each of us is socially constructed in this sense because we are (to a significant extent) the individuals we are today as a result of what has been attributed (and self-attributed) to us. For example, being classified as an able-bodied female from birth has profoundly affected the paths available to me in life and the sort of person I have become.

Note, however, that to say that an entity is "discursively constructed", is not to say that language or discourse brings a material object into existence de novo. Rather something in existence comes to have—partly as a result of having been categorized in a certain way—a set of features that qualify it as a member of a certain kind or sort.[4] My having been categorized as a female at birth (and consistently since then) has been a factor in how I've been viewed and treated; these views and treatments have, in turn, played an important causal role in my becoming gendered a woman. (See also Haslanger 1993). But discourse didn't bring me into existence.

It would appear that gender (in different senses) is both an idea-construction and an object-construction. Gender is an idea-construction because the *classification* men/women is the contingent result of historical events and forces. As we saw above, the everyday distinction between males and females leaves out the intersexed population that might have been given its own sex/gender category. Arguably, in fact, some cultures have divided bodies into three sexual/reproductive groups (Herdt 1993). At the same time the classifications "woman" and "man" are what Hacking calls "interactive kinds": gender classifications occur within a complex matrix of institutions and practices, and being classified as a woman (or not), or a man (or not), or third, fourth, fifth . . . sex/gender or not, has a profound effect on an individual. Such classification will have a material affect on her social position as well as effect her experience and self-understanding. In this sense, women and men—concrete individuals—are constructed *as gendered kinds of people*, i.e., we are each object constructions.

There is yet a further sense, I'd like to argue, in which something might be a social construction. (Haslanger 2003). So far we've been focusing on social *causation*: to say that something is socially constructed is to say that it is caused to be a certain way, and the causal process involves social factors, e.g., social forces were largely responsible for my coming to have the idea of a husband, and social forces were largely responsible for there being husbands. But often when theorists argue that something is a social construction their point is not about causation. Rather, the point is to distinguish social kinds from physical kinds. In the case of gender, the idea would be that gender is not a classification scheme based simply on anatomical or biological differences, but marks social differences between individuals. Gender, as opposed to sex, is not about testicles and ovaries, the penis and the uterus, but about the location of groups within a system of social relations.

Consider, for example, the category of landlords. To be a landlord one must be located within a broad system of social and economic relations which includes tenants, private property, and the like. It might be that all and only landlords have a mole behind their left ear. But even if this were the case, having this physical mark is not what it is to be a landlord. Similarly, one might want to draw a distinction between sex and gender, *sex* being an anatomical distinction based on locally salient sexual/reproductive differences, and *gender* being a distinction between the social/political positions of those with bodies marked as of different sexes. One could allow that the categories of sex and gender interact (so concerns with distinctions between bodies will influence social divisions and vice versa); but even to be clear how they interact, we should differentiate them. Using the terms "male"/"female" to mark the current familiar sex distinction and "man"/"woman" the gender distinction, one should allow that on this account of gender, it is plausible that some males are women and some females are men. Because one is a female by virtue of some (variable) set of anatomical features, and one is a woman by virtue of one's position within a social and economic system, the sex/gender distinction gives us some (at least preliminary) resources for including transgendered as well as transsexual persons within our conceptual framework.

I shall return to the question of what social positions might constitute gender below. Before that, however, it is important to note that social kinds cannot be equated with things that have social causes. Sociobiologists claim that some social phenomena have biological causes; some feminists claim that some anatomical phenomena have social causes, e.g., that height and strength differences between the sexes are caused by a long history of gender norms

concerning food and exercise.[5] It is also significant that not all social kinds are *obviously* social. Sometimes it is assumed that the conditions for membership in a kind concern only or primarily biological or physical facts. Pointing out that this is wrong can have important consequences. For example, the idea that whether or not a person is White is not simply a matter of their physical features but concerns their position in a social matrix, has been politically significant, and to many surprising. How should we construe the constructionist project of arguing that a particular kind is a social kind? What could be interesting or radical about such a project?

I am a White woman. What does this mean? Suppose we pose these questions to someone who is not a philosopher, someone not familiar with the academic social constructionist literature. A likely response will involve mention of my physical features: reproductive organs, skin color, etc. The gender and race constructionists will reject this response and will argue that what makes the claim apt concerns the social relations in which I stand. On this construal, the important social constructionist import in Beauvoir's claim that "one is not born but rather becomes a woman" (de Beauvoir 1989/1949) is not that one is caused to be feminine by social forces (even if this is true); rather, the important insight was that being a woman is not an anatomical matter concerning, e.g., one's reproductive organs, but a social matter.[6]

Because being a woman is a function of one's role in a social framework broadly speaking, if we allow that social phenomena are highly variable across time, cultures, groups, then this also allows us to recognize that the specific details of what it is to be a woman will differ depending on one's race, ethnicity, class, etc. My being a woman occurs in a context in which I am also White and privileged; my actual social position will therefore be affected by multiple factors simultaneously. I learned the norms of WASP womanhood, not Black womanhood. And even if I reject many of those norms, I benefit from the fact that they are broadly accepted.

The social constructionist's goal is often to challenge the appearance of inevitability of the category in question; as things are arranged now, there are men and women, and people of different races. But if social conditions changed substantially, there would be no men and women, and no people of different races. It would be possible, then, to do away with the conceptual frameworks that we currently use. But an important first step is to make the category visible as a *social* as opposed to *physical* category. This sometimes requires a rather radical change in our thinking. For example, elsewhere, following in Beauvoir's now long tradition, I have argued for the following definitions of man and woman (Haslanger 2000)[7]:

S *is a woman* if and only if

i. S is regularly and for the most part observed or imagined to have certain bodily features presumed to be evidence of a female's biological role in reproduction;

ii. that S has these features marks S within the dominant ideology of S's society as someone who ought to occupy certain kinds of social position that are in fact subordinate (and so motivates and justifies S's occupying such a position); and

iii. the fact that S satisfies (i) and (ii) plays a role in S's systematic subordination, i.e., *along some dimension*, S's social position is oppressive, and S's satisfying (i) and (ii) plays a role in that dimension of subordination.

S *is a man* if and only if

i. S is regularly and for the most part observed or imagined to have certain bodily features presumed to be evidence of a male's biological role in reproduction;

ii. that S has these features marks S within the dominant ideology of S's society as someone who ought to occupy certain kinds of social position that are in fact privileged (and so motivates and justifies S's occupying such a position); and

iii. the fact that S satisfies (i) and (ii) plays a role in S's systematic privilege, i.e., *along some dimension*, S's social position is privileged, and S's satisfying (i) and (ii) plays a role in that dimension of privilege.

Allowing for the possibility of new and non-hierarchical genders, I also suggest:

A group G *is a gender* relative to context C if and only if members of G are (all and only) those:

i. who are regularly observed or imagined to have certain bodily features presumed in C to be evidence of their reproductive capacities[8];

ii. whose having (or being imagined to have) these features marks them within the context of the ideology in C as motivating and justifying some aspect(s) of their social position; and

iii. whose satisfying (i) and (ii) plays (or would play) a role in C in their social position's having one or another of these designated aspects.

These definitions are proposed, not as reconstructions of our common sense understanding of the terms "man" and "woman", but as providing a better explanation of how gender works.

What is involved in explaining "how gender works"? There are two clusters of questions that should be distinguished:

1. Is the classification C (e.g., a distinction between the two groups as defined above) theoretically or politically useful?

2. Does the proposed theoretical understanding of C capture an ordinary social category? Is it legitimate or warranted to claim that the proposed definitions reveal the commitments of our ordinary discourse?

I offer the definitions above as a "debunking" of our ordinary understanding of the distinction between men and women as primarily anatomical/biological. The best way of understanding the groups of individuals so familiar to us, men and women, is to understand them in social and hierarchical terms. The anatomical understandings we take for granted, in effect, mask the social reality. So in response to question (1) I claim that the definitions proposed are theoretically and politically useful; but in response to question (2) I allow that I have not captured our ordinary understanding of the terms. But this is intentional.

III. CONCLUSION

On the account of social construction I've sketched, there are several different senses in which gender, race, and the like are socially constructed. First, the conceptual framework of gender that we take as just "common sense" is only one way of dividing up people according to the shape and functioning of their bodies. There are (and have been) other ways; there are (I believe) better ways.

Moreover, there are ideas associated with gender that are "merely" constructions, e.g., fictions about biological essences and genetic determination are used to reinforce belief in the rightness and inevitability of the classifications. This is not to say, however, that gender is not "real". Although some ideas about gender are fictions, these fictional ideas have functioned to create and reinforce gender reality, i.e., hierarchical social groups based on beliefs about reproductive differences, that are all too real. These categories of people are, I would argue, not just ideas, but are social entities. Such entities are socially constructed in the sense that they are caused by social forces, but also because the conditions for membership in a gender group are social (as opposed to, say, merely physical or anatomical) conditions.

Finally, individual members of such groups are, in a rather extended sense socially constructed, insofar as they are affected by the social processes that constitute the groups. Human beings are social beings in the sense that we are deeply responsive to our social context and become the physical and psychological beings we become through interaction with others. One feminist hope is that we can become, through the construction of new and different practices, no longer men and women, but new sorts of beings.

NOTES

1. Note that this essay draws significantly from my previous work, in particular (Haslanger 1995, Haslanger 2000, Haslanger 2003).

2. Some (e.g., Hacking 1999, Ch. 1) have argued that in cases of something obviously social, it is incorrect, or at least inapt, to say that it is socially constructed, suggesting that it is part of the meaning of the claim that the item in question is typically "taken for granted," "inevitable". (Hacking 1999, 12). I prefer to say that the unmasking element of social contruction claims are not part of the meaning, though it may be inapt to make such claims in the case of obviously social phenomena. The inaptness of the assertion can be explained by saying that in general, there is a linguistic maxim against stating the obvious. (Grice 1975).

3. Like Hacking, I will use the terms "idea" and "concept" without making precise distinctions between them for the purposes of our discussion. In contrast to concepts, ideas are often propositional, and plausibly more specific to the individual.

4. Note that the notion of *kind* in philosophy has several different uses. On one use it is meant to capture a classification of things by essence: things fall into kinds based on their essence, and each thing falls only into one kind. On this view, horses constitute a kind because they share an equine essence, but red things don't constitute a kind because apples, t-shirts, and sunsets don't share an essence. However, on a more common use, the term "kind" is used as equivalent to "type" or "sort" or "grouping". So far I've been using the term "kind" in the latter sense, and will continue to do so.

5. More generally, it is an error to treat the conditions by virtue of which a social entity exists as causing the entity. Consider, for example, what must be the case in order for someone to be a husband in the contemporary US: A husband is a man legally married to a woman. Being a man legally married to a woman does not *cause* one to be a husband; it is just what being a husband consists in.

6. For Beauvoir, roughly, women are positioned as "Absolute Other", i.e., as "Other" in relation to a group counting as "Subject" where the relation between these two groups never reverses so the "Other" becomes "Subject". (Beauvoir 1989, xxii; also Beauvoir 1989, xv–xxxiv)

7. Note that in the fuller account I suggest a "focal analysis" of gender that distinguishes gender as a social category from gender norms, gender identity, gender symbolism, and other gendered phenomena. For example, on my account one may be in the social category of woman if one is socially positioned in the way described, but still not have a woman's *gender identity*, understanding gender identity to be a psychological or subjective matter.

8. It is important here that the "observations" or "imaginings" in question not be idiosyncratic but part of a broader pattern of social perception; however, they need not occur, as in the case of *man* and *woman*, "for the most part". They may even be both regular and rare.

REFERENCES

Anderson, Elizabeth. (1995) "Knowledge, Human Interests, and Objectivity in Feminist Epistemology," *Philosophical Topics* 23:2: 27–58.

Butler, Judith. (1990) *Gender Trouble*. New York: Routledge.

de Beauvoir, Simone. (1989/1949) *The Second Sex*. Trans. H. M. Parshley. New York: Vintage.

Fausto-Sterling, Anne. (1993) "The Five Sexes: Why Male and Female Are Not Enough," *The Sciences* 33:2: 20–24.

Grice, H. Paul. (1975) "Logic and Conversation." In *Syntax and Semantics*, vol. 3, ed., P. Cole and J. L. Morgan. New York: Academic Press, pp. 41–58.

Hacking, Ian. (1999) *The Social Construction of What?* Cambridge, MA: Harvard University Press.

Haslanger, Sally. (1993) "On Being Objective and Being Objectified," *A Mind of One's Own*, ed., L. Antony and C. Witt. Boulder: Westview, 85–125.

———. (1995) "Ontology and Social Construction," *Philosophical Topics* 23:2: 95–125.

———. (2000) "Gender and Race: (What) Are They? (What) Do We Want Them To Be?" *Nous* 34(1): 31–55.

———. (2003) "Social Construction: The 'Debunking' Project," in *Socializing Metaphysics*, ed., F. Schmitt. (Lanham, MD: Rowman and Littlefield).

Herdt, Gilbert. (1993) *Third Sex, Third Gender: Beyond Sexual Dimorphism in Culture and History*. New York: Zone Books.

MacKinnon, Catharine. (1989) *Towards a Feminist Theory of the State*. Cambridge, MA: Harvard University Press.

Westlund, Andrea. (1999) "Pre-Modern and Modern Power: Foucault and the Case of Domestic Violence." *Signs* 24(4): 1045–1066.

Study Questions

1. How does Haslanger characterize the "ordinary" view of concepts and ideas? In her view, are all concepts and ideas "socially constructed"? What is interesting or important about claiming that a particular idea or concept is socially constructed?

2. What is "discursive construction" in Haslanger's view? Is everything discursively constructed? If not, give an example of something that is not.

3. Haslanger proposes definitions of "woman," "man," and "gender" that make explicit that these are positions in a social framework and so are social kinds. Explain Haslanger's definition of "woman" in your own words.

4. Haslanger states that her definitions do not capture people's ordinary understandings of "woman," "man," and "gender." Given this, in what way does she believe that her definitions are useful?

Susan Wendell

The Social Construction of Disability

I [have] argued that neither impairment nor disability can be defined purely in biomedical terms, because social arrangements and expectations make essential contributions to impairment and disability, and to their absence. In this chapter, I develop that argument further. I maintain that the distinction between the biological reality of a disability and the social construction of a disability cannot be made sharply, because the biological and the social are interactive in creating disability. They are interactive not only in that complex interactions of social factors and our bodies affect health and functioning, but also in that social arrangements can make a biological condition more or less relevant to almost any situation. I call the interaction of the biological and the social to create (or prevent) disability "the social construction of disability."

Disability activists and some scholars of disability have been asserting for at least two decades that disability is socially constructed. Moreover, feminist scholars have already applied feminist analyses of the social construction of the experience of being female to their analyses of disability as socially constructed. Thus I am saying nothing new when I claim that disability, like gender, is socially constructed. Nevertheless, I understand that such an assertion may be new and even puzzling to many readers, and that not everyone who says that disability is socially constructed means the same thing by it. Therefore, I will explain what I mean in some detail.

I see disability as socially constructed in ways ranging from social conditions that straightforwardly create illnesses, injuries, and poor physical functioning, to subtle cultural factors that determine standards of normality and exclude those who do not meet them from full participation in their societies. I could not possibly discuss all the factors that enter into the social construction of disability here, and I feel sure that I am not aware of them all, but I will try to explain and illustrate the social construction of disability by discussing what I hope is a representative sample from a range of factors.

SOCIAL FACTORS THAT CONSTRUCT DISABILITY

First, it is easy to recognize that social conditions affect people's bodies by creating or failing to prevent sickness and injury. Although, since disability is relative to a person's physical, social, and cultural environment, none of the resulting physical conditions is necessarily disabling, many do in fact cause disability given the demands and lack of support in the environments of the people affected. In this direct sense of damaging people's bodies in ways that are disabling in their environments, much disability is created by the violence of invasions, wars, civil wars, and terrorism, which cause disabilities not only through direct injuries to combatants and noncombatants, but also through the spread of disease and the deprivations of basic needs that result from the chaos they create. In addition, although we more often hear about them when they cause death, violent crimes such as shootings, knifings, beatings, and rape all cause disabilities, so that a society's success or failure in protecting its citizens from injurious crimes has a significant effect on its rates of disability.

The availability and distribution of basic resources such as water, food, clothing, and shelter have major effects on disability, since much disabling physical damage results directly from malnutrition and indirectly from diseases that attack and do more lasting harm to the malnourished and those weakened by exposure. Disabling diseases are also contracted from contaminated water when clean water is not available. Here too, we usually learn more about the deaths caused by lack of basic resources than the (often lifelong) disabilities of survivors.

Many other social factors can damage people's bodies in ways that are disabling in their environments, including (to mention just a few) tolerance of high-risk working conditions, abuse and neglect of children, low public safety standards, the degradation of the environment by contamination of air, water, and food, and the overwork, stress, and daily grinding deprivations of poverty. The social factors that can damage people's bodies almost always affect some groups in a society more than others because of racism, sexism, heterosexism, ageism, and advantages of class background, wealth, and education.

Medical care and practices, traditional and Western-scientific, play an important role in both preventing and creating disabling physical damage. (They also play a role in defining disability. [. . .]) Lack of good prenatal care and dangerous or inadequate obstetrical practices cause disabilities in babies and in the women giving birth to them. Inoculations against diseases such as polio and measles prevent quite a lot of disability. Inadequate medical care of those who are already ill or injured results in unnecessary disablement. On the other hand, the rate of disability in a society increases with improved medical capacity to save the lives of people who are dangerously ill or injured in the absence of the capacity to prevent or cure all the physical damage they have incurred. Moreover, public health and sanitation measures that increase the average lifespan also increase the number of old people with disabilities in a society, since more people live long enough to become disabled.

The *pace of life* is a factor in the social construction of disability that particularly interests me, because it is usually taken for granted by non-disabled people, while many people with disabilities are acutely aware of how it marginalizes or threatens to marginalize us. I suspect that increases in the pace of life are important social causes of damage to people's bodies through rates of accident, drug and alcohol abuse, and illnesses that result from people's neglecting their needs for rest and good nutrition. But the pace of life also affects disability as a second form of social construction, the social construction of disability through expectations of performance.

When the pace of life in a society increases, there is a tendency for more people to become disabled, not only because of physically damaging consequences of efforts to go faster, but also because fewer people can meet expectations of "normal" performance; the physical (and mental) limitations of those who cannot meet the new pace become conspicuous and disabling, even though the same limitations were inconspicuous and irrelevant to full participation in the slower-paced society. Increases in the pace of life can be counterbalanced for some people by improvements in accessibility, such as better transportation and easier communication, but for those who must move or think slowly, and for those whose energy is severely limited, expectations of pace can make work, recreational, community, and social activities inaccessible.

Let me give a straightforward, personal illustration of the relationship between pace and disability. I am currently just able (by doing very little else) to work as a professor three-quarter time, on one-quarter disability leave. There has been much talk recently about possible increases in the teaching duties of professors at my university, which would not be accompanied by any reduction in expectations for the other two components of our jobs, research and administration. If there were to be such an increase in the pace of professors' work, say by one additional course per term, I would be unable to work more than half-time (by the new standards) and would have to request half-time disability leave, even though there had been no change in my physical condition. Compared to my colleagues, I would be more work-disabled than I am now. Some professors with less physical limitation than I have, who now work full-time, might be unable to work at the new full-time pace and be forced to go on part-time disability leave. This sort of change could contribute to disabling anyone in any job.

Furthermore, even if a person is able to keep up with an increased pace of work, any increase in the pace of work will decrease the energy available for other life activities, which may upset the delicate balance of energy by which a person manages to participate in them and eventually exclude her/him from those activities. The pace of those other activities may also render them inaccessible. For example, the more the life of a society is conducted on the assumption of quick travel, the more disabling are those physical conditions that affect movement and travel, such as needing to use a wheelchair or having a kind of epilepsy that prevents one from driving a car, unless compensating help is provided. These disabling effects extend into people's family, social, and sexual lives and into their participation in recreation, religious life, and politics.

Pace is a major aspect of expectations of performance; non-disabled people often take pace so much for granted that they feel and express impatience with the slower pace at which some people with disabilities need to operate, and accommodations of pace are often crucial to making an activity accessible to people with a wide range of physical and mental abilities. Nevertheless, expectations of pace are not the only expectations of performance that contribute to disability. For example, expectations of individual productivity can eclipse the actual contributions of people who cannot meet them, making people unemployable when they can in fact do valuable work. There are often very definite expectations about *how* tasks will be performed (not the standards of performance, but the methods). For example, many women with disabilities are discouraged from having children because other people can only imagine caring for children in ways that are impossible for women with their disabilities, yet everything necessary could be done in other ways, often with minor accommodations.

Furthermore, the expectation that many tasks will be performed by individuals on their own can create or expand the disability of those who can perform the tasks only in cooperative groups or by instructing a helper.

Expectations of performance are reflected, because they are assumed, in the social organization and physical structure of a society, both of which create disability. Societies that are physically constructed and socially organized with the unacknowledged assumption that everyone is healthy, non-disabled, young but adult, shaped according to cultural ideals, and, often, male, create a great deal of disability through sheer neglect of what most people need in order to participate fully in them.

Feminists talk about how the world has been designed for the bodies and activities of men. In many industrialized countries, including Canada and the United States, life and work have been structured as though no one of any importance in the public world, and certainly no one who works outside the home for wages, has to breast-feed a baby or look after a sick child. Common colds can be acknowledged publicly, and allowances are made for them, but menstruation cannot be acknowledged and allowances are not made for it. Much of the public world is also structured as though everyone were physically strong, as though all bodies were shaped the same, as though everyone could walk, hear, and see well, as though everyone could work and play at a pace that is not compatible with any kind of illness or pain, as though no one were ever dizzy or incontinent or simply needed to sit or lie down. (For instance, where could you rest for a few minutes in a supermarket if you needed to?) Not only the architecture, but the entire physical and social organization of life tends to assume that we are either strong and healthy and able to do what the average young, non-disabled man can do or that we are completely unable to participate in public life.

A great deal of disability is caused by this physical structure and social organization of society. For instance, poor architectural planning creates physical obstacles for people who use wheelchairs, but also for people who can walk but cannot walk far or cannot climb stairs, for people who cannot open doors, and for people who can do all of these things but only at the cost of pain or an expenditure of energy they can ill afford. Some of the same architectural flaws cause problems for pregnant women, parents with strollers, and young children. This is no coincidence. Much architecture has been planned with a young adult, non-disabled male paradigm of humanity in mind. In addition, aspects of social organization that take for granted the social expectations of performance and productivity, such as inadequate public transportation (which I believe assumes that no one who is needed in the public world needs public transportation), communications systems that are inaccessible to people with visual or hearing impairments, and inflexible work arrangements that exclude part-time work or rest periods, create much disability.

When public and private worlds are split, women (and children) have often been relegated to the private, and so have the disabled, the sick, and the old. The public world is the world of strength, the positive (valued) body, performance and production, the non-disabled, and young adults. Weakness, illness, rest and recovery, pain, death, and the negative (devalued) body are private, generally hidden, and often neglected. Coming into the public world with illness, pain, or a devalued body, people encounter resistance to mixing the two worlds; the split is vividly revealed. Much of the experience of disability and illness goes underground, because there is no socially acceptable way of expressing it and having the physical and psychological experience acknowledged. Yet acknowledgement of this experience is exactly what is required for creating accessibility in the public world. The more a society regards disability as a private matter, and people with disabilities as belonging in the private sphere, the more disability it creates by failing to make the public sphere accessible to a wide range of people.

Disability is also socially constructed by the failure to give people the amount and kind of help they need to participate fully in all major aspects of life in the society, including making a significant contribution in the form of work. Two things are important to remember about the help that people with disabilities may need. One is that most industrialized societies give non-disabled people (in different degrees and kinds, depending on class, race, gender, and other factors) a lot of help in the form of education, training, social support, public communication and transportation facilities, public recreation, and other services. The help that non-disabled people receive tends to be taken for granted and not considered help but entitlement, because it is offered to citizens who fit the social paradigms, who by definition are not considered dependent on social help. It is only when people need a different kind or amount of help than that given to "paradigm" citizens that it is considered help at all, and they are considered socially dependent. Second, much, though not all, of the help that people with disabilities need is required because their bodies were damaged by social conditions, or because they cannot meet social expectations of performance, or because the narrowly-conceived physical structure and social organization of society have placed them at a disadvantage; in other words, it is needed to overcome problems that were created socially.

Thus disability is socially constructed through the failure or unwillingness to create ability among people who do not fit the physical and mental profile of "paradigm" citizens. Failures of social support for people with disabilities result in inadequate rehabilitation, unemployment, poverty, inadequate personal and medical care, poor communication services, inadequate training and education, poor protection from physical, sexual, and emotional abuse, minimal opportunities for social learning and interaction, and many other disabling situations that hurt people with disabilities and exclude them from participation in major aspects of life in their societies.

For example, Jongbloed and Crichton (1990, 35) point out that, in Canada and the United States, the belief that social assistance benefits should be less than can be earned in the work force, in order to provide an incentive for people to find and keep employment, has contributed to poverty among people with disabilities. Although it was recognized in the 1950s

that they should receive disability pensions, these were set, as were other forms of direct economic help, at socially minimal levels. Thus, even though unemployed people with disabilities have been viewed by both governments as surplus labour since at least the 1970s (because of persistently high general rates of unemployment), and efforts to increase their employment opportunities have been minimal, they are kept at poverty level incomes[1] based on the "incentive" principle. Poverty is the single most disabling social circumstance for people with disabilities, since it means that they can barely afford the things that are necessities for non-disabled people, much less the personal care, medicines, and technological aids they may need to live decent lives outside institutions, or the training or education or transportation or clothing that might enable them to work or to participate more fully in public life.

Failure or unwillingness to provide help often takes the form of irrational rules governing insurance benefits and social assistance, long bureaucratic delays, and a pervasive attitude among those administering programs for people with disabilities that their "clients" are trying to get more than they deserve. In her semiautobiographical novel, *The Body's Memory*, Jean Stewart describes the cluster of assumptions a woman discovers behind the questions of her social worker when she first applies for some "vocational rehabilitation," that is, the money to buy a basic wheelchair:

> (1) The client-applicant is ineligible for services until proven eligible. (2) The client-applicant's Vocational Goals are outlandish, greedy, arrogant, must be trimmed down to appropriately humble scale. (3) The client-applicant's motive in seeking services is, until proven otherwise, to rip off the system. (4) The function of the Agency is to facilitate (favorite word) adaptation (second favorite) of client to job (client to world), not the reverse. (5) The client is a fraud. (6) The client is helpless. (Stewart 1989, 190)

I do not want to claim or imply that social factors alone cause all disability. I do want to claim that the social response to and treatment of biological difference constructs disability from biological reality, determining both the nature and the severity of disability. I recognize that many disabled people's relationships to their bodies involve elements of struggle that perhaps cannot be eliminated, perhaps not even mitigated, by social arrangements. But many of the struggles of people with disabilities and much of what is disabling, are the consequences of having those physical conditions under social arrangements that could, but do not, either compensate for their physical conditions, or accommodate them so that they can participate fully, or support their struggles and integrate those struggles into the cultural concept of life as it is ordinarily lived.

CULTURAL CONSTRUCTION OF DISABILITY

Culture makes major contributions to disability. These contributions include not only the omission of experiences of disability from cultural representations of life in a society, but also the cultural stereotyping of people with disabilities, the selective stigmatization of physical and mental limitations and other differences (selective because not all limitations and differences are stigmatized, and different limitations and differences are stigmatized in different societies), the numerous cultural meanings attached to various kinds of disability and illness, and the exclusion of people with disabilities from the cultural meanings of activities they cannot perform or are expected not to perform.

The lack of realistic cultural representations of experiences of disability not only contributes to the "Otherness" of people with disabilities by encouraging the assumption that their lives are inconceivable to non-disabled people but also increases non-disabled people's fear of disability by suppressing knowledge of how people live with disabilities. Stereotypes of disabled people as dependent, morally depraved, superhumanly heroic, asexual, and/or pitiful are still the most common cultural portrayals of people with disabilities. Stereotypes repeatedly get in the way of full participation in work and social life. For example, Francine Arsenault, whose leg was damaged by childhood polio and later by gangrene, describes the following incident at her wedding:

> When I got married, one of my best friends came to the wedding with her parents. I had known her parents all the time I was growing up; we visited in each other's homes and I thought that they knew my situation quite well.
> But as the father went down the reception line and shook hands with my husband, he said, "You know, I used to think that Francine was intelligent, but to put herself on you as a burden like this shows that I was wrong all along." (Arsenault 1994, 6)

Here the stereotype of a woman with a disability as a helpless, dependent burden blots out, in the friend's father's consciousness, both the reality that Francine simply has one damaged leg and the probability that her new husband wants her for her other qualities. Moreover, the man seems to take for granted that the new husband sees Francine in the same stereotyped way (or else he risks incomprehension or rejection), perhaps because he counts on the cultural assumptions about people with disabilities. I think both the stigma of physical "imperfection" (and possibly the additional stigma of having been damaged by disease) and the cultural meanings attached to the disability contribute to the power of the stereotype in situations like this. Physical "imperfection" is more likely to be thought to "spoil" a woman than a man by rendering her unattractive in a culture where her physical appearance is a large component of a woman's value; having a damaged leg probably evokes the metaphorical meanings of being "crippled," which include helplessness, dependency, and pitifulness. Stigma, stereotypes, and cultural meanings are all related and interactive in the cultural construction of disability. [. . .]

The power of culture alone to construct a disability is revealed when we consider bodily differences— deviations from a society's conception of a "normal" or acceptable body—that, although they cause little or no functional or physical difficulty for the person who has them, constitute major social disabilities. An important example is facial scarring, which is a disability of appearance only, a disability constructed totally by stigma and cultural meanings. Stigma, stereotypes, and cultural meanings are also the primary components of other disabilities, such as mild epilepsy and not having a "normal" or acceptable body size.

I believe that culture plays a central role in constructing (or not constructing) disability. However, I want to distinguish this view from approaches to cultural construction of "the body" that seem to confuse the lived reality of bodies with cultural discourse about and representations of bodies, or that deny or ignore bodily experience in favour of fascination with bodily representations. For example, this approach troubles me in Donna Haraway's "The Biopolitics of Postmodern Bodies: Constitutions of Self in Immune System Discourse" (Haraway 1991), where Haraway discusses the biomedical construction of "immune system discourse" as though discourse and its political context are all there is, without acknowledging either the reality of physical suffering (for example, by people with AIDS, ME, MS, Amyotrophic Lateral Sclerosis (ALS), rheumatoid arthritis), which surely has *some* relationship to the development of immune system discourse, or the effects of this discourse on the lives of people who are thought to be suffering from immune disorders.

I do not think my body *is* a cultural representation, although I recognize that my experience of it is both highly interpreted and very influenced by cultural (including medical) representations. Moreover, I think it would be cruel, as well as a distortion of people's lives, to erase or ignore the everyday, practical, experienced limitations of people's disabilities simply because we recognize that human bodies and their varied conditions are both changeable and highly interpreted. That I can imagine having an energetic, pain-free body or living in a society where my body is considered acceptable or normal and its limitations are compensated by social and physical arrangements does not make it any easier to get out of bed or to function as an academic in my present circumstances.

In most postmodern cultural theorizing about the body, there is no recognition of—and, as far as I can see, no room for recognizing—the hard physical realities that are faced by people with disabilities. (Or would postmodernists deny that there are such "realities," suggestive as they are of something that is not constructed or constituted by discourse? I cannot tell, because nothing like it is discussed.) The experiences of people with disabilities are as invisible in the discourses of postmodernism, which has the virtue of being critical of idealized, normalized, and universalized representations of bodies, as they are in discourses which employ concepts of bodily "normality" uncritically.

I believe that in thinking about the social construction of disability we need to strike a balance between, on the one hand, thinking of a body's abilities and limitations as given by nature and/or accident, as immutable and uncontrollable, and, on the other hand, thinking of them as so constructed by society and culture as to be controllable by human thought, will, and action. We need to acknowledge that social justice and cultural change can eliminate a great deal of disability while recognizing that there may be much suffering and limitation that they cannot fix.

NOTE

1. Here I am speaking about people who do not receive private disability insurance benefits, settlements from accident claims, veterans' disability benefits, or workers' compensation benefits, any of which *may* be high enough to keep them out of poverty. In Canada, the majority of people with disabilities are not eligible for these more adequate forms of support.

REFERENCES

Arsenault, Francine. 1994. "Stakeholder Speech—Chairperson of the Council of Canadians with Disabilities." *Transition* April/May: 6.
Haraway, Donna J. 1991. *Simians, Cyborgs, and Women: The Reinvention of Nature*. New York: Routledge.

Jongbloed, Lyn and Anne Crichton. 1990. "A New Definition of Disability: Implications for Rehabilitation Practice and Social Policy." *Canadian Journal of Occupational Therapy* 57 (1): 32–38.

Stewart, Jean. 1993. *The Body's Memory*. St. Martin's Press.

Study Questions

1. Wendell distinguishes between social and cultural factors that contribute to the construction of disability. Explain this distinction.

2. Compare and contrast Wendell's description of the social construction of disability with your own understanding of the social construction of gender.

3. What relationship, if any, do you see between the "faces of oppression" described in Young's article in this section of the text and the social construction of disability and/or gender?

4. Does thinking about ableism suggest shortcomings in Young's list of the faces of oppression?

Trina Grillo

Anti-Essentialism and Intersectionality: Tools to Dismantle the Master's House

I am pleased to be here today to celebrate the tenth anniversary of the *Berkeley Women's Law Journal* ("BWLJ"). From its inception, the BWLJ has devoted itself to giving voice to underrepresented women and has continued this mission even through difficult times. In preparing for this talk I reviewed a number of past volumes of this journal. I was impressed with how often articles published in the BWLJ foreshadowed controversies that were later discussed in more traditional journals.

I want to begin my talk with a quote from the late poet Audre Lorde: "The master's tools will never dismantle the master's house."[1] I was asked to speak today about anti-essentialism and intersectionality. I am glad to do so, for I believe both concepts are indispensable tools for dismantling the master's house. I will begin by briefly describing these concepts to you. I will suggest that it is time to turn inward, to use the tools of intersectionality and anti-essentialism to guide our own academic, political, and spiritual work, and I will give you a few examples of how we might do so.

My thesis today is that sometimes the governing paradigms which have structured all of our lives are so powerful that we can think we are doing progressive work, dismantling the structures of racism and other oppressions, when in fact we are reinforcing the paradigms. These paradigms are so powerful that sometimes we find ourselves unable to talk at all, even or especially about those things closest to our hearts. When I am faced with such uncertainty and find myself unable to speak, anti-essentialism and intersectionality are to me like life preservers. They give me a chance to catch my breath as the waves come crashing over me and they help me sort through my own confusion about what work I should be doing and how I should be doing it.

The basis of intersectionality and anti-essentialism is this:

> Each of us in the world sits at the intersection of many categories: She is Latina, woman, short, mother, lesbian, daughter, brown-eyed, long-haired, quick-witted, short-tempered, worker, stubborn. At

Trina Grillo, "Anti-Essentialism and Intersectionality: Tools to Dismantle the Master's House." © 1995 by The Regents of the University of California. Reprinted from the *Berkeley Women's Law Journal* Vol. 10, Pp: 16–30 by permission of the Regents of the University of California. Notes have been edited.

any one moment in time and in space, some of these categories are central to her being and her ability to act in the world. Others matter not at all. Some categories, such as race, gender, class, and sexual orientation, are important most of the time. Others are rarely important. When something or someone highlights one of her categories and brings it to the fore, she may be a dominant person, an oppressor of others. Other times, even most of the time, she may be oppressed herself. She may take lessons she has learned while in a subordinated status and apply them for good or ill when her dominant categories are highlighted. For example, having been mistreated as a child, she may be either a carefully respectful or an abusive parent.[2]

I am going to talk now about intersectionality and anti-essentialism and will begin by talking about them separately. I believe these two concepts embody what is essentially the same critique, but made from two different starting points. For simplicity's sake, as I continue I am often going to talk about them together.

INTERSECTIONALITY

Above, I described a single, whole woman. Yet if we turn the traditional tools of legal analysis upon this woman, we find she is someone entirely different. She is fragmented, capable of being only one thing at a time. For example, under a traditional legal approach, when her situation is analyzed as a woman, it is not analyzed as a Latina. She is a mother or a worker, but never both at the same time. Her characteristics are not connected one to the other; instead, they exist separately, suspended in time and space. This fragmenting of identity by legal analysis, a fragmenting entirely at odds with the concrete life of this woman, is the subject of the intersectionality critique.

The intersectionality critique is described succinctly in the title of a book on Black women's studies: *All the Women Are White, All the Blacks Are Men, But Some of Us Are Brave*.[3] Kimberlé Crenshaw explodes the discussion of race and gender discrimination in her work on intersectionality.[4] She notes that women of color stand at the intersection of the categories of race and gender, and that their

experiences are not simply that of racial oppression plus gender oppression. One case she uses for her analysis says it all: When a group of Black women faced discrimination, they were held to have no legal cause of action because neither white women nor Black men were discriminated against in the same way.[5] Therefore, they were recognized as victims of neither race nor gender discrimination.[6] Makes perfect sense. And, of course, you have all seen the many newspaper articles talking about the progress of "women and Blacks"; Black women are completely lost in this description.[7]

An example of why the situation of Black women is not a composite of the situations of white women and Black men appears in a wonderful article by Paulette Caldwell in which she discusses restrictions on the rights of Black women to wear braided hairstyles.[8] She writes of the mixed shame and pride that many Black women feel about their hair, shame and pride shared neither by white women *nor* Black men.[9]

The intersectionality critique has been extended by both Stephanie Wildman and Elvia Arriola.[10] Both note that while Professor Crenshaw discusses a woman standing at the single intersection of race and gender,[11] in fact we all stand at multiple intersections of our fragmented legal selves. Professor Arriola notes that a single discriminatory act can be based on many characteristics of the victim and calls for a radical dismantling of the traditional analytical framework.[12] Professor Wildman supplies the necessary element for this dismantling. She explains why the "woman" experience of, for example, a woman of color is different from that of a white woman. In every set of categories there is not only subordination, but also its counterpart, privilege.[13]

The most vivid description of this interrelationship has been given by Adrienne Davis. Professor Davis has described privilege and subordination as a "double-headed hydra": you cannot get rid of the subordination without eliminating the privilege as well.[14]

To look at white, middle-class women as subordinated *as women* is accurate as far as it goes, but their experience of oppression is not interchangeable with the oppression of non-white, non-middle-class women.

The whiteness and middle-class status supply privilege even as the femaleness conveys oppression.

ANTI-ESSENTIALISM

Essentialism is the notion that there is a single woman's, or Black person's, or any other group's, experience that can be described independently from other aspects of the person—that there is an "essence" to that experience. An essentialist outlook assumes that the experience of being a member of the group under discussion is a stable one, one with a clear meaning, a meaning constant through time, space, and different historical, social, political, and personal contexts.

The perceived need to define what "women's" experience is and what oppression "as women" means has prompted some feminists to analyze the situation of woman by stripping away race and class. To be able to separate out the oppressions of race and class (as well as sexual orientation and other bases of oppressions), the theory goes, we must look at someone who is not experiencing those oppressions and then we will see what oppression on the basis of gender alone looks like.[15] This approach, however, assumes that the strands of identity are separable, that the experience of a white woman dealing with a white man, or raising a white child, is the same experience that a Black woman has dealing with a Black man, or raising a Black child. But as the intersectionality critique has taught us, they are different and not just additively.

Race and class can never be just "subtracted" because they are in ways inextricable from gender. The attempt to subtract race and class elevates white, middle-class experience into the norm, making it the prototypical experience. As Elizabeth Spelman says in her thoughtful and far-ranging book, such essentialism "makes the participation of other women inessential to the production of the story. How lovely: the many turn out to be one, and the one that they are is me."[16]

For a Black woman, race and gender are not separate, but neither are they for white women. White women often think of themselves as "without a race" rather than as white.[17] Thus, exploring white women's experiences, although a worthy task, does not produce a picture of a raceless "essential woman." Spelman urges us to think of white slaveowners and their wives: "the meaning of the sexual difference between them was constructed in part by the alleged contrast between them as whites and other men and women who were Black; what was supposed to characterize their relationship was not supposed to characterize the relationship between white men and Black women or white women and Black men."[18]

john powell—a former colleague of mine and also the legal affairs director of the ACLU—tells a story of going to a Thanksgiving dinner with his son, Fon. john and Fon are vegetarians. The host said to Fon, "This is the regular dressing and the other is the vegetarian dressing." john said to his host, "No, there is vegetarian dressing and there is meat-eater's dressing, but neither one of them is regular dressing."[19] In the world of feminism, the white, middle-class experience is considered the "regular" dressing; the lesson john taught his host was that of anti-essentialism.

In a thoughtful and at times devastating critique, Angela Harris has shown how essentialism in feminist legal theory has betrayed feminism's promise to listen to the experiences of real women.[20] Her suggestion is that we focus on the notion of multiple consciousness as an appropriate way "to describe a world in which people are not oppressed only or primarily on the basis of gender, but also on the bases of race, class, sexual orientation and other categories in inextricable webs."[21] Those of us who are outsiders or who do not fit neatly within standard categories have various voices within ourselves. We speak partly with one voice and partly with another, going back and forth, a process that Mari Matsuda has said can lead to genius or madness or both.[22]

But remember, we speak with multiple voices only because we have categories that describe these voices as separate from one another. Let's think for a minute about something that is in truth impossible to imagine—that the Latina mother I first described was the definer of categories. She would not have to speak with multiple voices, because once she said she was, for example, Latina (or lesbian, or a woman), we would automatically know she was these other things. In fact, a whole different set of categories would exist. We cannot even begin to speculate what these categories might be because we are all still ordering our world by the categories given us by the dominant culture. We have no words and perhaps no circuits in our brains for thinking about these other categories.[23] But suppose my Latina mother (by this shorthand, I identify what are for me her most salient qualities) was the definer. We could then leave it to those whose wholeness was not included in her described categories to say, "Wait, I need to add my voice to this. When you talk about women, why are you automatically assuming they are Latinas, lesbian, and working class? Why does woman, unmodified, have to mean that? Don't make me fragment parts of my identity by talking about women and whites as if they were mutually exclusive categories; after all, it *is* possible to be a woman and be white at the same time." And then the Latina mother could say, "Well, I appreciate what you're saying and I think we need to take into account your differences. Perhaps we can give you ten minutes at the end of the program. And next time we'll make sure we have a white face on the panel. But, we're all in this together, and by putting forth your separate identity you're making it hard for us to fight the patriarchy."[24]

Some have described the anti-essentialism and intersectionality critiques as dangerous in that, if carried to their furthest conclusions, they make it impossible to talk of any oppression. If each woman, if each Black, has a different experience, how can one say that women as women, or Blacks as Blacks, are oppressed? How can we use the feminist method of paying attention to our experience, without being essentialist ourselves? Elizabeth Spelman asks whether it is "possible to give the things women have in common their full significance without thereby implying that the differences among us are less important."[25] If we emphasize our differences, then do we not risk losing all credence *as women*? We have seen something similar happen in academic circles with respect to scholars of color. The argument goes: If these voices are very diverse, and if conservatives of color differ with critical race theorists, then why should

we, the hiring committee or the bestower of other goodies, listen to any of you? Why shouldn't we just anoint those who are most comfortable for us to listen to? Of course, if the "insiders" were listening to the lessons of anti-essentialism, they would know that the voices they need to listen to are precisely those that make them most uncomfortable.

I think it is important to emphasize that essentialism is not always a bad thing; however, unconscious, self-protective, self-advancing essentialism is. The question is whether the essentialism, which is sometimes unavoidable, is explicit, is considered temporary, and is contingent.[26]

In the end, the anti-essentialism and intersectionality critiques ask only this: that we define complex experiences as closely to their full complexity as possible and that we not ignore voices at the margin. The fact is, the choice with which we seem to be presented is either to accept a white, middle-class woman's view of the world or to talk explicitly about different types of women. No one is trying to make it appear as though our Latina mother's experience can represent that of all women. Spelman describes a group of pebbles on the beach; they are all pebbles, but they are all shaped and colored in different ways.[27] Essentialist feminist theory has picked one pebble and asked it to represent all.

LESSONS TO BE LEARNED FROM THE ANTI-ESSENTIALISM AND INTERSECTIONALITY CRITIQUES

Now that I have summarized the anti-essentialism and intersectionality critiques of feminist legal theory, I want to talk about at least three lessons they bring to our own work.

Lesson One

The anti-essentialism and intersectionality critiques teach us to look carefully at what is in front of our faces. When things are being described in ways contrary to our sensory experiences, we must pay particular attention. We must look at the evidence of our bodies, and we must believe what our bodies tell us. They teach us to check for the deep, internal discomfort we feel when something is being stated as gospel but does not match our truth. Then they teach us how to spin that feeling out, to analyze it, to accept that it is true but to be able to show why that is so. They also teach us to be brave.

My father was born in Tampa, Florida of Cuban Black parents. Much of his life was spent firmly claiming his place among American Blacks. My mother was the daughter of Italian immigrants. I was born in 1948 and soon thereafter moved to the San Francisco Bay Area. There were four children in my family. At times it seemed to me that we were half the biracial population of the Bay Area. We were stared at wherever we went, although it took me awhile, probably until I was five, to realize that the stares were not always ones of admiration. Of course, we did not define ourselves as biracial then. Instead, we were considered, and considered ourselves, Black, or Negro as we then said. Still, our skin color and our parents' interracial marriage were always causes for comment. My race and my skin color have been issues that have preoccupied me for a good part of my life, and I see little prospect of this changing anytime soon.

When I began teaching at Hastings Law School in 1977, I knew that I wanted to write about multiraciality. I did a little research, and proceeded to write— nothing. At that time there was little interest in the popular culture in that subject, and virtually nothing in the legal literature, so it is easy to see why I gave up on my project. Multiraciality did not seem to matter to anyone but me.

But now I cannot turn on "Oprah" without seeing a segment on multiraciality, right in between the shows on incest and the shows on weight loss. There is a movement (I think a misguided one in the particular form it takes) on the part of some people of mixed race to have a separate census category.[28] We are everywhere, in numbers hard to ignore. But one thing has not changed. No one knows how to talk about us.

I looked at two newspapers yesterday, and saw the racial descriptions of the jurors in the O.J. Simpson trial. One paper said there were "eight Blacks, one Anglo, one Hispanic and two persons of mixed race."[29] The other paper said there were eight Blacks, two Hispanics, one Anglo, and one person who identified himself as half white and half American Indian.[30] There were four items about each juror described in the paper: gender, age, occupation, and racial background.[31] From a more complete description of the racial backgrounds of the jurors, I found out that one of the Hispanics was a Hispanic/Black, classified as mixed race by one paper and as Hispanic by another.[32] Interestingly, neither paper classified this juror as Black, although that would be my "first" classification of myself.

So we have no stable conventions for describing multiracial persons, at least none that match what we perceive to be reality. However, that someone is of mixed race is a fact now being noted and thought to be of enough importance to be mentioned separately in a news story.

There have also been hundreds of articles and a number of books on multiraciality written in the past five years.[33] This is an important topic to me, one that affects my life, and the lives of my children every single day. Still, seventeen years after I first decided to write in this area, I am silent. My one, feeble attempt to write about issues of multiraciality was abandoned the first time my tentative musings (which, now that I think of it, were actually put to paper by one of my co-authors, such was my state of paralysis) were criticized. And I am not alone; I have talked to two multiracial colleagues who have described to me similar experiences.

I explained yesterday to my friend Catharine Wells that I had abandoned my original plan to talk a little bit today about multiraciality. "It is too much," I said, "to describe anti-essentialism and intersectionality and also get into this other complicated terrain. I feel so unsure about what I think anyway. Besides, there really just isn't time. They only gave me an hour." She saw right through my excuses, and convinced me that I would be lacking in courage if I spoke about intersectionality and anti-essentialism and yet was unwilling to speak about the place in my life where these concepts have the most meaning. She also convinced me that my example is a good one for showing the silencing effect of essentialism and the role that an intersectional, anti-essentialist analysis can have in permitting us to talk. She told me that it would be enough to just tell you about the problems I am having figuring this out and that I didn't have to provide you with any conclusions.

To begin with, we must fully understand that race is not a biological concept, but a social and historical construct.[34] The reason that I grew up considering myself, as we then said, Negro, is that a racist system described me in that way. Most Blacks in the United States are persons of "mixed blood," if such a thing can be said to exist, and have both white and Black ancestors. If there were such as thing as a biological white, I would be at least half that, and so would many other Blacks. However, the fact that race is an historical and social construct certainly does not mean that it does not exist. Experiences, histories, and communities have all developed around this concept; so if we abandon race, we abandon communities that may have been initially formed as a result of racism but have become something else entirely.

All the scientific literature says that biological races do not exist. Instead, races were created as a mechanism for the oppression of certain groups of people. But once created, they remain. We are then left with these questions: How should we regard people of mixed race? How is it possible to take our experiences seriously without having them turned into a means of separating ourselves from other Blacks or into a means of ranking people of color, with those of mixed race given more power than other Blacks? (I should say that my focus is on mixtures which include Black because that is the experience with which I am familiar; because the history is different, the issues are surely different for persons of mixed race who are, for example, Asian and white).

If we accept the definition of Black which we have been given—a definition which historically defined anyone with "one drop of Black blood" as Black—we ignore the existence of multiracial people. We ignore people whose experiences may be different from those experiences which have been defined as constituting the Black experience—that is, the "essentialized" Black experience. By so essentializing, we assume that the taxonomy of race proposed by nineteenth-century white supremacists—that human beings can be classified into four races and everyone fits neatly into one slot—is a valid one. On the other hand, if we do classify multiracial people as Black, the potential for group solidarity is much greater. "We are all Black," we say. "You cannot divide us."

The move for a "multiracial" category, both on census and other forms, and in terms of how we talk in daily life, is in part an attempt to recognize what is in fact the case—that some people have parents of two races, that even people who have parents of the same race may have other ancestors of a different race.[35] A multiracial category would permit children to claim a racial relationship to both, or all, their parents, rather than being forced to choose. Moreover, even though over the years many Black leaders have been biracial,[36] today some multiracial people, especially those with very light skin or who have been raised only by a white parent, may not feel completely comfortable or accepted in Black groups.

But the move to define people as multiracial has serious risks. How would we distinguish between those who are multiracial because they have one white parent, such as myself, and the general Black population of the United States, many of whom in one way or another have a similar amount of white ancestry?[37] Why would we *want* to make such a distinction? Echoes of the way people in "colored" categories have been used in other countries—as mediators, enforcers, the secret police—make many Blacks fear that the multiracial movement has to do with establishing a higher category in the social hierarchy for multiracial people than for Blacks. There is a fear that multiracial people want to "get out of" being Black, that it is a new form of passing. The history in this country of colorism—the discrimination even within communities of color against those with darker skins—makes the attempt by multiracial persons to leave the Black category more stinging still.[38]

The multiracial movement is not helped by the fact that some of those pressing most vigorously for a multiracial category are the white mothers of children whose fathers are Black. I went to a conference on multiraciality a few years ago that included time for discussion in small groups. There were a number of white mothers of biracial children in my group. The refrain I heard from these mothers was this: "My child is not Black. My child is *golden*." So it is not simply because of paranoia that some members of the multiracial movement are perceived as wanting to dissociate from Blacks. (Other members of the movement, of course, have a completely different set of motivations.) We have to acknowledge that if we count people as mixed race rather than Black when the census is taken, it is going to mean that social services to Black communities will be decreased even further than they have been already.

What does anti-essentialism teach about this situation? Does it help me struggle with my dilemma? Perhaps. The confusion that a biracial child feels does not derive from being classified as Black, but from essentialist notions that being Black is one particular experience, and that this experience is not hers or his. Take for example a family, my family in fact, where one child appears so essentially "Black" that he sees no reason to look further for an identification, and the other is so fair, and so blond, that identity issues for her are a constant struggle. Some of her Black friends are bothered if she presumes to call herself Black and suspicious if she does not. Given the history, this is a perfectly coherent reaction on their part, but it is a hard one for her to deal with. Of course, multiracial people will try to find a place to call home if they cannot be at home being Black.

At the conference I previously mentioned, a Black man chastised those in the group pressing for a multiracial designation. "Black," he said in a booming voice, opening his arms wide, "is the ocean into which all rivers flow."

I wonder if it is possible for that to be true. Is it possible to create a Black-identified biracial identity? Can one be biracial or multiracial and also be Black? Or is the historical freight still too great for that to be possible? One thing I am sure of: The fact that a person is biracial is an important piece of who she is. It is something I would find of interest if I were reading her work or listening to her speak. We need a way to say that, a way which does not compromise the community of Black people.

Lesson Two

Another way that anti-essentialism and intersectionality critiques help us is by keeping us from being diverted by what Regina Austin calls "the running of the oppression sweepstakes."[39]

Oppression based on my race has always seemed closer to my rage and has reached a place more central to my being than oppression based on my gender or on other aspects of my self. For years I would have said without a doubt, without a moment's hesitation, that for me, race came first; gender, though important, came second. In the oppression sweepstakes, I had my money on the "race" horse. If pressed, I would still say today that there is a way in which, in my heart, race trumps gender. But now I understand a little better the anti-essentialist lesson which says I should not permit myself to be pressed, to be made to choose which part of myself is most important to me. The lessons of anti-essentialism and intersectionality are that the oppressions cannot be dismantled separately because they mutually reinforce each other. Racism uses sexism as its enforcer. Homophobia enforces sexism by making people pay a heavy price for departing from socialized gender roles. And those of us who are middle-class, or members of otherwise privileged elites, can be used as unwitting perpetuators of the subordination of others.[40]

We have spent a lot of time arguing over whose pain is greater. That time would be better used trying to understand the complex ways that race, gender, sexual orientation, and class (among other things) are related.

A note: To say that the oppressions are related does not mean that they are the same. It is dangerous at the least to expect that experiencing one oppression means that one understands the others.[41] In fact, to expect so is disrespectful in that it wipes out the true, lived experience of that group in exchange for one's own, self-serving fantasy.

Lesson Three

We all have the impulse to essentialize. It is built into our brains. This means it is important to remember who we are. Even though we may be "underrepresented" persons in many ways, many of us are living in this very master's house that we are hoping to help dismantle. We may be living in the basement, and the others in the house are not always particularly nice to us, but our view is still shaped by where we are situated.

Think of the vast body of literature about the problem of women "being placed on pedestals." Don't you wonder what the authors could have been thinking when in front of their very eyes and, in fact, sometimes waiting on them, were women who not only were on no one's pedestal, but whose lot in life was to scour those pedestals?[42] It's scary to think that we could be, and no doubt are, doing the same thing in other contexts.

What this means in terms of process is that we should not deny this distance, but, as Regina Austin has advised, acknowledge it and attempt to bridge it.[43] What this means is that although our own experience is our touchstone, we must be careful about generalizing from that experience. In other words, we must be careful about essentializing the experiences of persons in the group to which we belong. I certainly cannot speak for all Black persons, Latinas, or women. What I can do is to pay careful attention to the lives and material conditions of women who are underrepresented in the law and to believe that their struggles have meaning and have much to teach me and the world. What I can also do is help their voices be heard, not by presuming to speak for them, but rather by doing what I can to put a microphone in front of them. What I can do is to work where I am today to make these changes.

What this means is that if I work in legal education, which I do, I can spend some of my time working in academic support programs, making it possible for students who otherwise would not be in law school to attend school, graduate, and get into positions in which their voices can be more easily heard. If I work in legal education, my scholarship, or some of it, can be a political act, bringing the lives of poor women, minority women, and other underrepresented women to the fore.[44] I can focus on how the law and the dominant culture structurally produce subordi-

nation. I know that laws and rules ignore the real lives of these women; I can do what I can to make ignoring them more difficult to do.

For example, wherever I work, I can begin to struggle against the tyranny we have permitted the Educational Testing Service, the Bar Examiners, and other such organizations—for the most part private, power-mad, and secret—over decisions about who gets into school, who gets a job, who is thought of as smart, and who thinks well of herself once having arrived.

Leslie Espinoza, in an article on the LSAT, shows that test questions are often a form of what she calls, kindly, "subtle, unconscious" psychological warfare.[45] Let me give you one of the questions she uses by way of example.

> In Evalsland, where it is legal to hold slaves, the guests at a dinner party get into a debate. One of the guests contends that slavery is a cruel institution. But the host contends that the slaves themselves like it. To prove his point, the host called in the household slaves, all of whom affirm that they do indeed find their condition not simply tolerable, but extremely pleasant. Which of the following would seriously weaken the host's argument in the passage above?[46]

The question goes on to list four statements and then asks which combination of statements best answers the question.

Professor Espinoza comments, "As one African American student expressed, first the question reminds you that you are Black, then it forces you to try to divorce yourself from yourself, to pretend that you can look at the question without *you* looking at the question."[47] Those of us in positions to do so must actively oppose these tests every single day.

I had lunch last week with Laura Nader who teaches at U.C. Berkeley. She said to me, "What can we do about these standardized tests?" I said to myself, "Do? I can't do anything else about anything. I'm doing well to get up in the morning, take care of my kids and get to work." And then I thought, well, there's this little piece I can do, and that is to talk about what an outrage these tests are every chance I get. So I decided that if I give a talk, I'm going to talk about what an outrage they are. If I go to lunch, I'm going to talk about what an outrage they are. And if I meet someone on the street, I'm going to say, "Hello, and isn't it terrible about the LSAT?" I urge you all to do the same so that we can challenge our own passive acceptance, our own assumption that this is how things must be.

Then we have the problem of determining which voices we need to help bring forward. When I told you about the Latina mother, I told you that in some situations she was dominant, privileged; in others, perhaps most, she was subordinated. The dangerous thing for her would be to go through life as if she were always subordinated, because she then might not notice situations in which she was ignoring someone else's voice. We need to notice the areas in which we are privileged, and in those areas we need to be careful to listen to the concrete, lived experiences of those who are less privileged. Although I am always willing to talk to the very privileged, I generally assume, I think rightly, that I have heard their story.

Anti-essentialism and intersectionality are checks on us; they help us make sure that we do not speak for those we cannot speak for or ask others to share our agenda while they patiently wait for their own. Pat Cain asks those of us who are heterosexual to *notice* that we are heterosexual and therefore privileged.[48] One of our privileges is to not notice that we are heterosexual, to assume that laws, customs, and habits should be, while non-discriminatory, based on the norm of our heterosexual lives. Cain asks us to think of our sexual identities as coming from choice, and to ask ourselves why we have chosen to be privileged in this way.[49] I think that the issue of choice obscures the true issue, which is one of privilege. Whether or not a person has chosen to be heterosexual, she has privilege based on that status; what she does about that fact is to my mind some measure of her moral worth.

Those of us who are part-time residents in the master's house have much to gain by taking this approach, which recognizes privilege. For our view may be in some ways more obstructed than the view of people who are comparatively less privileged. As Dorothy Roberts, who has done in a very short time a prodigious amount of work on Black mothers, in particular Black, single, teenage mothers, states: "Studying exclusively how the oppressed are defined by others is debilitating. It too often neglects how people resist these definitions and create their own concepts of justice, morality, and legality. It also ignores how imposed definitions and self-definitions shape each other."[50] Roberts asks "whether it is precisely in the lives of those most deviant that we will be able to discern a vision of liberation."[51] Of course, it is easy to romanticize the vision of the outsiders. Some acts labelled resistant actually reproduce and support the status quo. Still, I think it is important to accept what I view as fact: That each of us has a limited view of the world, that we have a better chance of forming a vision of a post-patriarchal, post-racist society both by trusting in our own experiences and by seeking out voices that are drowned out by essentialism in all its forms.

NOTES

Professor of Law, University of San Francisco School of Law; J.D., University of Minnesota Law School, 1974; A.B., University of California at Berkeley, 1969. My thanks to Stephanie Wildman, Catharine Wells, Adrienne Davis, and Marian Shostrom.

1. Audre Lorde, Sister Outsider 110, 111 (1984).

2. In 1992 Adrienne Davis, Stephanie Wildman, and I co-authored Categories and Koosh Balls: Rendering Privilege Visible and Other Subversive Practices (unpublished manuscript, on file with author). Much of the first section of this talk is based on ideas we developed in that paper. In particular, the discussion of categories, id. at 3–10, was inspired by the thoughts and writing of Adrienne Davis.

3. All the Women Are White, All the Blacks Are Men, But Some of Us Are Brave (Gloria Hull et al. eds., 1982).

4. Kimberlé Crenshaw, *Demarginalizing the Intersection of Race and Sex: A Black Feminist Critique of Antidiscrimination Doctrine, Feminist Theory and Antiracist Politics*, 1989 U. Chi. Legal F. 139.

5. Id. at 141–43 (discussing DeGraffenreid v. General Motors, 413 F. Supp. 142 (E.D. Mo. 1976)).

6. Id. at 142.

7. Elizabeth Spelman, Inessential Woman 114 (1988).

8. Paulette Caldwell, *A Hair Piece: Perspectives on the Intersection of Race and Gender*, 1991 Duke L.J. 365.

9. See generally id.

10. Stephanie Wildman, *Language and Silence: Making Systems of Privilege and Subordination Visible*, in Critical Race Theory: The Cutting Edge (Richard Delgado ed., forthcoming 1995); Elvia Arriola, *Gendered Inequality: Lesbians, Gays and Feminist Legal Theory*, 9 Berkeley Women's L.J. 103 (1994).

11. Crenshaw, supra note 4, at 140.

12. *See* Arriola, supra note 10.

13. Wildman, supra note 10, at 52.

14. Adrienne D. Davis, Toward a Post-Essentialist Methodology or a Call to Countercategorical Practices 35 (Sept. 1994) (unpublished manuscript, on file with author).

15. Spelman, supra note 7, at 75, 166.

16. Id. at 159.

17. Wildman, supra note 10, at 54. *See also* Martha Mahoney, *Whiteness and Women. In Practice and Theory: A Reply to Catharine MacKinnon*, 5 Yale J.L. & Feminism 217 (1993).

18. Spelman, supra note 7, at 104–05.

19. This story also appears in Charles Lawrence III, *If He Hollers Let Him Go: Regulating Racist Speech on Campus*, 1990 Duke L.J. 431, 473.

20. Angela P. Harris, *Race and Essentialism in Feminist Legal Theory*, 42 Stan. L. Rev. 581, 587 (1990).

21. Id.

22. Mari Matsuda, *When the First Quail Calls: Multiple Consciousness as Jurisprudential Method*, 11 Women's Rts. L. Rep. 7, 8 (1989).

23. See generally Davis, supra note 14. See also Harris, supra note 20, at 589.

24. Cf. Lorde, supra note 1, at 110–13 (setting forth the irony of such a hypothetical situation).

25. Spelman, supra note 7, at 3.

26. See Diane Fuss, Essentially Speaking 20 (1989) (saying the question is not whether the text is essentialist but, if it is essentialist, how, where, and by whom it is being deployed). Adrienne Davis has urged that this concept of strategic essentialism be imported into feminist legal theory. Davis, supra note 14, at 38. See also Harris, supra note 20, at 586 ("Even a jurisprudence based on multiple consciousness must categorize.... My suggestion is only that we make our categories tentative, relational and unstable.").

27. Spelman, supra note 7, at 1–5.

28. See Lawrence Wright, *One Drop of Blood*, The New Yorker, July 25, 1994, at 46.

29. Thomas D. Elias, *12 Jurors Sworn in For O.J.'s Trial; 8 Women and 4 Men to Hear Murder Case*, Ariz. Republic, Nov. 4, 1994, at A1.

30. Kenneth B. Noble, *A Jury is Chosen to Hear The Simpson Murder Case*, N.Y. Times, Nov. 4, 1994, at A18.

31. Elias, supra note 29.

32. Compare Elias, supra note 29, with Noble, supra note 30.

33. See, e.g., F. James Davis, Who Is Black? (1991); Racially Mixed People In America (Maria P.P. Root ed., 1992); Paul R. Spickard, Mixed Blood (1989). There are also several magazines devoted specifically to issues of multiraciality, interracial relationships, or both. See, e.g., Interrace Magazine, and Biracial Child.

34. This proposition has been discussed at length in both legal and scientific literature. See, e.g., Neil Gotanda, *A Critique of "Our Constitution is Color-Blind"*, 44 Stan. L. Rev. 1 (1991); Jayne C. S. Lee, *Navigating the Topology of Race*, 46 Stan. L. Rev. 747 (1994); Ian F. Haney López, *The Social Construction of Race: Some Observations on Illusion, Fabrication, and Choice*, 29 Harv. C.R.-C.L. L. Rev. 1 (1994).

35. Much of the formal racial classification in the United States has been in recent years shaped by a 1977 Office of Management and Budget directive, controlling the racial and ethnic designations on all federal forms. This directive acknowledges four racial groups: American Indian or Alaskan Native, Asian or Pacific Islander, Black, and White. Ethnicity is divided into "Hispanic Origin" and "Not of Hispanic Origin." These categories now appear not just on census forms, but on school enrollment forms and applications for jobs, schools, and scholarships. Each person is expected to choose one category. The categorizations are used to enforce civil rights legislation and entitlement and set-aside programs. See Wright, supra note 28, at 46. These categories have also begun to have a life of their own, shaping the self-definitions of individuals and groups. Id. at 52–53. At present there is no multiracial category. The Office of Management and Budget is considering whether it needs to create new categories that take into account "respect for individual dignity," including a new "multiracial" category. Cindy Skrzycki, *The Regulators: Classifying Race and Ethnicity*, Wash. Post, June 17, 1994, at F1. Such a category is supported by a number of organizations in the "mixed race" movement. Opponents of the multiracial category argue that such a category will devastate programs designed to enforce civil rights and lead to the political abandonment of dark-skinned Blacks by light-skinned Blacks. Wright, supra note 28, at 54. With respect

to the problem of colorism in the African-American community, see Kathy Russell et al., The Color Complex (1992).

36. Indeed, many of the most famous African-American leaders have been persons with substantial amounts of white ancestry, including Booker T. Washington, Frederick Douglass, and W.E.B. DuBois. Wright, supra note 28, at 48. A recently published book by the Delaney sisters, members of an exceptionally prominent African-American family, includes a family tree which shows mostly white ancestry. Sarah Delaney et al., Having Our Say (1993).

37. Kwame Anthony Appiah, whose mother is English and father Ghanaian, states that the multiracial category is not aimed at people of mixed ancestry (because most Americans are products of mixed ancestry), but rather at "people who have parents who are socially recognized as belonging to different races." Wright, supra note 28, at 47. He describes multiraciality as "an interesting social category" but wonders how the children of multiracial people might be categorized. Id. He adds that the multiracial category, "which is meant to solve anomalies, simply creates more anomalies of its own, and that's because the fundamental concept—that you should be able to assign every American to one of three or four races reliably—is crazy." Id. at 49.

38. See Russell, supra note 35.

39. Regina Austin, Sapphire Bound! 1989 Wis. L. Rev. 539, 546.

40. Id. at 554.

41. See Trina Grillo & Stephanie Wildman, Obscuring the Importance of Race: The Implications of Making Comparisons Between Racism and Sexism (Or Other Isms), 1991 Duke L.J. 397.

42. Spelman, supra note 7, at 9.

43. Austin, supra note 39, at 545.

44. Id. at 543.

45. Leslie Espinoza, The LSAT: Narratives and Bias, 1 J. Gender & L. 121 (1993).

46. Id. at 134.

47. Id. at 135.

48. Patricia A. Cain, Feminist Jurisprudence: Grounding the Theories, 4 Berkeley Women's L.J. 191, 209 (1989–90).

49. Id. at 209 (quoting Marilyn Frye).

50. Dorothy E. Roberts, Deviance, Resistance, and Love, 1994 Utah L. Rev. 179, 180.

51. Id.

Study Questions

1. What does Grillo mean by "intersectionality"?

2. What does Grillo mean by "essentialism," and what does she identify as a potential danger of essentialism?

3. Grillo discusses three "lessons" to be learned from the anti-essentialist and intersectionality critiques. According to Grillo, what lessons do these critiques teach about the proposed "multiracial" category, the "oppression sweepstakes," and "remembering who we are"?

4. Does thinking about intersectionality reveal weaknesses in Haslanger's discussion of the social construction of gender, Wendell's discussion of the social construction of disability, or Young's discussion of oppression?

EPISTEMIC POSITION

Joanna Kadi

Stupidity "Deconstructed"

Dozens of workers move deliberately around the building site at the University of Minnesota, driving huge machines, handling dangerous equipment, carrying heavy loads. They can barely talk over the noise, but they are communicating and working together well. A wrongly-interpreted nod, a misunderstood word, a petty quarrel could mean the loss of a hand or a life. Although that's not the only reason for cooperative efforts; they're a common working-class practice.

I connect with these workers. I've lived with people like them, worked with people like them—I'm one of them. The worst jobs I've had were made bearable thanks to our jokes, camaraderie, easy flow of conversation. The familiar sweat, dirty hands, missing teeth, and lined faces reassure me. Workers.

Workers at the university. We've built every university that has ever existed, yet we're shunned and despised within academia's hallowed halls. Explicitly and implicitly, we've been taught our place—and it's not in a student's desk or the professors' lounge. We're needed to construct the university, maintain, clean, and repair it.

Oh, we're welcome here, as long as we stay where we're supposed to. We know the monster that presents itself if we dare step out of place. *Stupid. We are too stupid to study, learn, think, analyze, critique. Because working-class people are stupid.* So much energy goes into the social lie that poor people are stupid; capitalism needs a basic rationalization to explain why things happen the way they do. So we hear, over and over, that our lousy jobs and living situations result from our lack of smarts. I internalized this lie. Rationally, I knew money and brains didn't go hand in hand. But on deep unconscious levels, I believed in my own stupidity and in the stupidity of working-class people.

I want to examine these dynamics in this essay which I titled "Stupidity 'Deconstructed'" in order to connect with construction workers *and* to express my irritation toward postmodernists who consistently use the term. This piece goes hand in hand with the writing of working-class people committed to theorizing about our experiences in universities and factories. It's past time for such a movement; *we* must create theory about our lives. No one else. If middle- and upper-middle-class people want to write about indoctrination into class privilege and unlearning it, great. But leave the rest to us.

A sordid history lurks here. Middle- and upper-middle class academics have traditionally sought out the experiences and stories of working-class/working-

poor people for use in shaping theory. That is, we provide the raw material of bare facts and touching stories; they transform these rough elements into theory. Sound familiar? Gosh, it sounds like an exact replication of factory activity. Academics have approached me after I've given presentations on class, and said, "The stories about your family are so *interesting*." (*Oh, thank you so much.*) "Don't you think they'd be stronger if you let them stand on their own?" Unedited translation: give me your stories, I'll write the theory. Leave it to the experts. *It's time to forget that shit.*

YES, I'M A WORTHY PERSON, I HAVE TWO UNIVERSITY DEGREES

I understand the workings of universities. I paid attention when I studied at the University of Toronto and the Episcopal Divinity School in Massachusetts. I've hung out on other campuses, and heard more than enough university stories. Levels of elitism and arrogance vary with regional difference, size, prestige, and how many misfits end up on the campus, but the core system remains: privileged people belong here.

If only I'd known this years ago! Then anger, instead of feeling crazy, alienated, and stupid, would have been uppermost. *Don't get me started. Even hearing that word makes my blood boil. Even hearing the word "smart" makes my blood boil. I want to wring your neck.*

From a young age, I loved to read and write and learn. But my future in that general motors city had been mapped out, and books didn't appear anywhere. I didn't like the map; nor did I like being surrounded by people who treated me like a handy repository for muddy boots and unmitigated rage. University offered a good solution (or so I thought). I started working paid jobs at age ten and saved every penny for the endeavor.

In Mr. Smythe's math class, the third floor of that ancient high school, sun streams through windows onto old wooden desks. Test results are read out loud—no surprises. Top marks for me, the Johnson twins, Brian Kingsley, Jonathon Woodley, Amanda

Britian. Their label: brain. Mine: jock and party-er. Their parents: doctor, lawyer, psychiatrist, executive. Mine: line worker. Mr. Smythe advised the Johnson twins to apply to Waterloo or Toronto but not McMaster, and the intricacies of differences between these universities went way over my head; our guidance counselor poured over pamphlets and reference books with Brian once a week; Mr. and Mrs. Woodley and Jonathon drove to a different campus each weekend. I got wrecked every Friday and Saturday night and cruised around in cars driven by boys as stoned and drunk as me.

Despite my party-er status, despite the lack of help in selecting the "right" school, despite my total cluelessness, I applied to three universities. Only my grades appeared on transcripts; no entries for parents' work history or weekend activities. Fresh out of high school, naive but steadfast, I carried my cheap vinyl suitcase up those marble steps of Queen's University. Four months. I had cash for two years, but not enough class privilege. My throat locked, my tongue twisted, I sat in back rows with arms wrapped around chest and stomach. To say I felt like a fish out of water hardly describes my overwhelming feelings of confusion, depression, inadequacy, and shame. People actually asked me the year my grandparents graduated! Not just my parents, my *grandparents*. I thought everyone's grandparents were poor. I knew everyone's parents weren't poor, but I assumed everyone in the previous generation experienced poverty. Now rich white girls with straight teeth asked, "When did your grandparents graduate?" Four months. I'm surprised I lasted that long.

Years later I returned to those hallowed halls. Not through any formal, reasonable plan—more because I was pissed off. Today the whole thing strikes me as a big joke. During a bitter separation, a lawyer told me I could get more money from my ex-husband if I enrolled in university. During our marriage, I worked and supported him while he earned a degree, and I deserved an equivalent education. "Sounds good," I told her. We got the money and I went back to school.

Women's studies, University of Toronto. Middle-class and upper-middle-class women. *I'm so stupid.* I sat surrounded by women years younger than me,

women exuding poise and confidence as they discussed graduate school options and Karl Marx. (Marx. Oh, yeah, that guy those other rich[1] people I worked with at CBC Radio used to spout off about.) *What am I doing here?* I talked to janitors and I talked to Kim, the last hold-out for cigarettes in the whole department. We scrunched in corners of the smoking lounge so she could indulge and the smoke gave me a headache, but I didn't care. Better a headache than crazy. Kim anchored me. A white girl, working-class, smart as a whip, skinny and tough. We sat close together in back rows and whispered comments to each other because we couldn't say them out loud. I couldn't have made it without her.

Another bizarre turn of events dropped me in graduate school. A professor at U of T actually took an interest in me. My brain flip-flopped. "You should go on to graduate school," she told me earnestly. "You're very smart. And you have such good study habits. You would do so well." Smart? No, stupid. Graduate school? No, janitor. What *is* graduate school? What happens there? What's an M.A.? A Ph.D.? They must be the same things with different names. I said nothing out loud; that would reveal my stupidity. A friend told me about a university with a master's program in feminist ethics. I didn't know any other graduate programs. I didn't know how to find them. *I can't believe I'm writing this down. Now people will know just how stupid I really am.* I didn't know jackshit.

I applied for the feminist ethics program and laid out stringent conditions to make it as unlikely as possible I would ever get there. *If* the school offered me acceptance, a scholarship covering tuition, a job on campus, housing for my lover and me. Then, and only then, would I take the leap. My divorce money had dried up, and I would never, never in a million years, take out a loan. I knew all about loans and debts. Every working-class person I grew up with laid down the law: never take out a loan for anything except a mortgage on a house. Loans are bad. Debts are bad. You'll never get rid of these horrible burdens. I'd fly to the moon before borrowing money for graduate school. *Graduate school. What is it?*

The school met my stringent conditions. Uh-oh. But once there, I found Joann and Sheri and Meck, and we laughed until we cried and cried until we laughed about academia and how stupid we felt. We didn't have Aristotle and Socrates as reference points, couldn't even spell the names. We didn't know how to use the library system. We hadn't grown up with parents and family friends waxing nostalgic about university days and cutesy pranks, thus easing our entry into this strange world.

Then, something truly amazing. A working-class professor. I studied with one of the most brilliant minds in this country, Dr. Katie Geneva Cannon, a working-class, African-American woman from the South, who pushed me and pushed me and pushed me to think critically about class. Take it apart, figure it out, analyze it, *it's just like my brother used to do when he started building stereo equipment at age ten*, pull and pull and pull, you are smart, she said, you need to write. I sat in class, sweating, tongue-tied, scared shitless, and looked at her, teaching, questioning, inspiring, her brilliance shining like a star. *She was destined to cook and clean for white people, that is, if she didn't get something worse—if she can do it, maybe I can too.*

Buildings cut from fine stone and beautiful wood. My hands ache with the remembering. The maintenance men I worked with: Tony, shy and sweet with a faint Portuguese accent; Al, tough hide covering a heart like worn flannel; Eddy, drifting from job to job, booze on his breath, twisted grin, broken front tooth. I worked with them through the summer and felt so comfortable in our little lounge, drinking coffee and smoking, smoking, always smoking—rich people have given it up but we're still puffing away.

I spent hours wrestling with voices in my head telling me "You're stupid," and listening to trusted friends telling me "You're not stupid. This system makes you feel stupid." We figured out our own analysis: the university system is intricately linked with the capitalist system. People with power at the university will do their part to reinforce and promote the capitalist explanation for class difference—smart rich people, stupid poor people—in return for continued benefits and privileges from the current structure. They don't want a motley bunch of upstart working-class urchins figuring any of this out and refusing to sit in quiet shame.

They don't want graduates of their system to end up like me: class identity and loyalties stronger than ever, angry about the others who never had a chance, who still believe they're stupid, who always will, some already in their graves. Yes, I'm angry.

CONSTRUCTING/DECONSTRUCTING: BUILDING/HIRING

For the capitalist system to continue ruthlessly grinding on (or for the capitalist system to "succeed," as you would say) those of us bred for stupid and/or dangerous work must believe we're not as smart as the people who boss us around. It's critical. Capitalism needs simple explanations about why poor people with lousy jobs take orders from men in suits. Lack of brains fits the bill. (So does the lie that rich people work harder. I'll tackle that in another essay.) Any noticeable class divisions stem from difference in intellectual capacity. Connected to this is the touting of "American ingenuity" as the doorway to upward mobility. It's as untrue as the existence of a whole class of stupid people, but if enough people believe it—even partially believe it—this idea will reinforce and strengthen capitalism. After all, if we believe brains lead to success, we'll blame ourselves for not getting ahead. Personal failure, not systemic oppression, explains why we're going nowhere so very fast.

I grew up learning the bulk of the population in our small general motors city—that is, workers—was stupid. Dumb, brutish, boring, close to animals. Did I believe it? In some ways, I knew people in my family had brains and the bosses didn't. My extended family joked about it frequently. But just as frequently, they indicated they believed it. And at deep levels, I internalized the lie and lived with it for years. It impacted my thoughts, decisions, and actions, and surfaced resoundingly when I entered university. The smugness and certainty with which upper-middle-class people paraded their brain cells jarred me; for a time I was taken in by this, and it contrasted so sharply with my inability to speak, let alone parade, that I felt

I really must be stupid. Thankfully, that didn't last long. *Who knows what will happen if we realize that we're not so stupid and you're not so smart? Maybe you'll lose privileges and status. Maybe you'll have to clean up your own messes. Maybe we'll find fulfilling work and the drudge work will be shared equally. Maybe we'll remove your feet from our necks.*

Of course, I didn't feel stupid at university only because of constructions concerning stupid workers. That coupled with an unfamiliar upper-middle-class world made me feel stupid. I didn't know any of the middle-class/upper-middle-class reference points and contexts, ranging from GRE's and LSAT's to Ph.D.'s and post-doc fellowships. I couldn't swish around with the entitlement of privileged students; I crept. I liked janitors more than professors; more to the point, I identified with janitors, not professors.

Language proved crucially important in opening a door into clarity, awareness, and class pride. It happened this way: I grew up around people who built things—houses, additions on houses, large buildings. They talked about it by saying, "I built that." This meant they planned and designed something, then picked up a hammer, nails, and saw, and began constructing.

University professors used this same phrase, often when discussing summer homes. They said authoritatively, "I built that." I knew what it meant to build something and I thought they meant they must have built their summer home. But they didn't look like they knew anything about construction work. I felt confused. I was astounded when I stumbled across the translation. "I built this" really meant "I hired some of you to build this for me."

So. Privileged people misuse language in ways that distort meanings of commonplace, easy-to-understand words like "build." This told me something. Then I read articles focusing on class, usually written by university professors. I looked forward to these, because I needed to develop my class analysis and thought these articles would help. But again disappointment and shame resulted. I didn't understand most of what I read. Abstract and impersonal, these essays stood three times removed from concrete reality of working-class life.

After confusion and shame, another door opened. If they misused a simple word like build, how could I trust them? If their articles used weird words like "proletariat" and showed they didn't know the first thing about us, maybe they weren't quite so smart. *Maybe we weren't quite so stupid.*

My hunch solidified after examining academic attraction to and use of postmodern theory and language. This horrible mix of distorted language and casual appropriation of our ideas allowed me once and for all to dismiss the ideology about stupid workers. As far as I can tell, postmodern theoreticians say nothing new, but their inaccessible language makes it appear as though they do. For example, they're fascinated with the notion that multiple realities exist in society, and they've written and theorized extensively about this.

Puh-lease. Everybody in my neighborhood, including the mechanics who had to sniff carbon monoxide in tiny, enclosed garages all day long, grasped that idea with no problem. We lived it. We had our reality, the bosses had theirs, and we understood them both. Theorists like W. E. B. Du Bois wrote about double consciousness—whereby African Americans understand their reality and white people's—at the turn of this century. But I've never seen postmodernists attribute these ideas to the people of color and/or working-class people who've lived and understood them for centuries. Instead, postmodernists steal these ideas and dress them up in language so inaccessible only a tiny, elite group can discuss them.

We need to ask, and begin answering, hard, practical questions. Who defines smart and stupid, and why? Who misuses language, and for whose benefit? Who writes theory, and why? Who goes to university, and why? Who does the academy serve? Can universities be transformed into places where everyone is welcomed and respected?

In this country, the first institutions of higher learning were trade or agricultural schools and theological centers, with liberal arts colleges and medical schools following. Around the turn of this century, with the establishment of standardization and class-biased guidelines, universities took on the task of serving middle- and upper-class white men. That group enjoyed peace and quiet for several decades, until the rest of us began banging on the door. Grudgingly, after years and years of hard work, little chinks appeared in those thick, stone doors. *The doors we built, with our hands. The doors we couldn't walk through.* The misfits demanded entrance: Africans, Asians, Natives, Arabs, Latinos, women, queers, even welfare mothers. Even the sons and daughters of factory workers and miners and janitors. What's a rich white man to do? The stress must be unbelievable. Poor guys.

Capitalism exists as a human construct, not a natural or innate system. We've been steeped in lies about its inevitability, and it seems to take on its own life as its institutions reinforce each other and the system. But it *is* a human construct, carefully set up to keep a small number of people stretched out comfortably along the backs of the rest of us. Remember: human constructs can be destroyed.

RICH EQUALS SMART, POOR EQUALS STUPID

I think of the university and a swift hot anger rushes from the pit of my stomach, sweeps through my throat, bursts out of my mouth. Stone buildings beautifully carved, wooden rooms beautifully balanced. Underpaid exploited workers. Our hands next to the hands of a professor "deconstructing" ideas with strings of six-syllable words. *Stupid.* Underpaid exploited workers keeping these buildings clean. *Stupid.* I think of myself and working-class friends sitting in back rows, saying nothing, sweating, fearful that one word from these stubborn, hurt mouths will betray us, will expose our selves/our class.

Many mechanisms have been created in this rigidly defined, class-structured society to keep poor people in our place. Our place. We crouch over and the rest of you keep your feet on our necks. You sit complacently, feet resting comfortably—"Could you move just a little bit to the left?"—crossing ankles, smiling in our direction—"Very nice." One such mechanism is the constant, cross-racial image of the

worker as stupid. Growing up, I attached "stupid" to workers and "smart" to executives. This didn't happen because of a weird personal quirk. It resulted from force-fed images and words of TV shows, newspapers, magazines, and movies. Any TV show with working-class characters, first "The Honeymooners" and "I Love Lucy," then "All In the Family," covertly and overtly highlighted the stupidity of bus drivers, factory workers, and plumbers. Movies, books, and comics followed suit. At school, middle-class kids called us stupid; we hurled back "stuck up," but never "stupid." Working-class/working-poor kids failed and dropped out, but not middle-class kids. Our town newspaper consistently portrayed general motors executives as calm, rational types, while union members appeared unthinking, wild, and chaotic.

Oh, you're exaggerating. You've gone too far. Stupid merely refers to someone not terribly intelligent. You've attached all these cultural, class-based meanings. You're way out on a limb. Chill out. People are gonna think you're nuts.

I look up "stupid" in the dictionary and find: 1. slow of mind, obtuse, brutish; 2. dulled in feeling or sensation, torpid; 3. marked by or resulting from dullness, senseless; 4. lacking interest or point, vexatious, exasperating.[2] I look up stupid in the dictionary and feel: 1. recognition; 2. affirmation of what I have felt my whole life and what I am saying in this essay; 3. fury; 4. disgust.

This dictionary definition fits precisely with what I learned in my bones before I could talk. A very particular set of cultural baggage goes along with stupid. Not a mere description of how well someone thinks, stupid has become a cultural concept with a particular code and set of signifiers that describe working-class people as the middle and upper classes perceive and construct us. It doesn't truthfully describe working-class people; rather, it speaks clearly to the particular understanding rich people created and maintain with a vengeance.

Brutish, dull, senseless. *I grew up believing we're thick-skinned, slow-witted, impervious to pain, boring.* The dominant culture drove this point home relentlessly. Someone called me sensitive and I couldn't grasp her meaning. *Working-class people can't be sensitive.* Rich people construct us as stupid and brainwash us Day One to make us believe it. We read their newspapers, watch their TV shows, take in their movies, and work jobs that reinforce what we see and hear. A vicious cycle.

What's the reality? I do know working-class people who fit the stereotype. Of course, their brains have been fried from decades of drudge work. Like Howie, my partner on the assembly line. Slow, barely able to get a complete sentence out of his mouth, unable to believe I learned his job in two hours. Vacant look, hollow eyes. Couldn't read. *You try working on an assembly line, at the same station, for thirty-eight years. How interesting will you be? How much will you know about world affairs? How creative will you feel?*

It's painful to acknowledge the fact that some of our brains have been fried. Not stupid from birth, as rich people insist, but fried from decades of the most boring, idiotic, repetitive work imaginable. I've done it. I fought every minute to keep my mind away from the hovering void. The boredom, lethargy, apathy, and meaninglessness surrounding that factory, surrounding every factory, constitutes a horrible and violating reality of daily life.

Stupid. They marked my family as stupid, and this confused me. I didn't think we were, but had no tools for arguing against such an intense social construct. I grew more confused and internalized the belief in my own stupidity, as all around me, my family proceeded with their lives and used their brains. My aunt went from grade school education to neighborhood CPA; she knew all the deductions, could add numbers ridiculously quickly, and did everyone's taxes for free. My grandfather, literate in three languages, poor, steered new Lebanese immigrants through the morass of landlords, bosses, lawyers. My father and uncles, with their tenth-grade educations, filled out daily crossword puzzles with pens and painstakingly planned, calculated, measured, added rooms on small houses, with wiring, plumbing, support beams, ceilings, floor tiles, never a sixteenth of an inch out. I once helped a friend build a porch, holding boards in place as she hammered, blinking in disbelief because half-inch gaps appeared. My mother and

aunts balanced budgets, paying bills with nonexistent funds, borrowing some from here, begging some from there, adding and subtracting large numbers in their heads.

Class socialization begins early. Material possessions, home environment, and neighborhood provide information about our present situation and our future. Family members' sense of/lack of entitlement and expectation provides more. Social constructions of class, put out by institutions such as media and school, are a third factor. Whether family members resist or unquestioningly take in these social constructions impacts class socialization.

For a continuous supply of expendable workers, capitalism must offer ideas and experiences that reinforce each other. If people who look, act, talk, and live like you are constantly portrayed as working particular jobs because they're too stupid to get anything better, chances are you'll believe the lie when you end up in the same factory.

Ideas help reinforce and explain different class locations. Capitalism relies on various institutions, such as the university, to pass on relevant knowledge about the system. Universities need to replicate and reinforce central ideologies. Such as poor people stupid, rich people smart—a perfect example of the kind of polarized thinking that has hindered and weakened Western thought for centuries. These categorizations feed into an either/or mentality and ignore complications and complexities. They also shore up oppressive systems of racism, sexism, and classism because of the positive meaning attached to one half of the equation and the negative meaning attached to the other—male/female, white/black, heterosexual/homosexual, virgin/whore, thinking/feeling. I always include rich/poor and smart/stupid in this list of important categories; lately I've begun to perceive the ways they map on to each other to become richsmart/poorstupid.

In the years I spent in Women's Studies, we spent hours and hours analyzing the superficial nature of dualistic thinking around men/women, white/black, and thinking/feeling, and reflected on more complicated and realistic understandings. But we never touched on the smart/stupid, rich/poor breakdown.

(Of course, we were in a university classroom.) This particular ideological split goes a long way to support the dangerous, classist myth I've discussed in this essay. It's time to pay attention.

In thinking about rich smart/poor stupid, we need to analyze stupidity and intelligence. Writing this essay might play into the belief that only one kind of intelligence exists, the kind defined and revered by the ruling class in conjunction with academics, because I focus on the university, the stupid/smart dichotomy, and class oppression. That's not my intention. In the same ways I understand the category of "race" as a myth while acknowledging the reality of racism and different physical/cultural traits, I want to put "intelligence" as defined in a limited and narrow way by the ruling class into the myth category, while acknowledging a variety of mental capacities and different types of intelligence.[3]

Many different kinds of intelligence exist, and these cross class lines. Universities revere the type of intelligence that can synthesize information rapidly and understand abstract concepts. Equally valid types of intelligence enable a child to design and build a bird house, a mother to balance a budget with no money, an "uneducated" man to enthrall listeners with stories, a young woman who hasn't had music lessons to compose a piano tune, a girl to write a poem, a homeless person to comprehend the poem, a neighborhood to devise a plan to stop a company from dumping toxic waste, three young women to invent scathing responses to catcalls and whistles. These types of intelligence require creativity, humor, ability to ask questions, care, a good memory, compassion, belief in solidarity, ability to project an image of something that doesn't physically exist.

Some manual-labor jobs require intelligent, creative thinking, such as carpentry, video technology, and grounds keeping/designing. Most manual-labor jobs require little thinking of any sort, and are marked by monotony and danger. Some executive jobs require intelligence and creative thinking, and most don't. (None, however, are likely to be dangerous.) On the whole, capitalism has offered little in the way of stimulating, educational, growth-enhancing work experiences.

CAN I REALLY BE WORKING-CLASS *AND* SMART?

The sarcasm in this heading is an attempt to get at underlying and often unconscious beliefs about stupidity which popped up constantly after I got my master's degree. People freaked out. Working-class people with university degrees freak out ourselves and our middle-class "brothers and sisters" (more sarcasm). We ask: "Am I still working-class?" Middle-class people inform us, delicately and sensitively: "You're not working-class anymore."

Where do these reactions come from? Let me first examine what working-class people mean when we say: *am I working-class now?* I have a university degree. A secret subtext, a critical message lurks here.

One day I figured out my translation. When I asked: "Am I working-class now that I have a university degree," I meant: "Am I working-class now that I'm smart?" Back to my theory about dualistic thinking. If the stupid/smart dichotomy is a cornerstone of the academy, and if this division rests clearly along class lines (rich people smart/poor people stupid) then conferring university degrees onto middle- and upper-class people isn't only about knowledge, courses passed, GPAs, degrees, and job security. University degrees constitute a symbol, a marker, so the world understands the bearer comes from the middle/upper-class. Degrees separate this group from lowly, unprivileged, stupid workers.

Then working-class people traverse the minefield of academia and end up with initials after our names. We get confused. Very confused, because those initials symbolize the separation between rich and poor. Rich people need these degrees to feel smart, to remind themselves they are not a lowly janitor sweeping halls, a lowly cook slopping out lousy cafeteria food. They need them, but somehow we end up with them. We get confused. Are we announcing we're smart? But working-class people can't be smart. *If we are working-class, we can't be smart. Therefore, since we've earned a university degree, we are no longer working-class.*

Now, that's not true, for at least three reasons. First, whatever is going on subconsciously, consciously I know rich people aren't necessarily smart. Having cleaned their houses, read their garbled manuscripts, and "typed" (code word for "re-wrote") their incoherent essays, I'm well aware of this.

Second, whatever silly initials my friends and I carry after our names, we're still working-class.[4] We still talk the same and feel the same and work shit jobs. We don't float around thinking we're entitled to everything; we don't grab whatever we want. We don't acquire privilege, entitlement, and arrogance after slogging it out in the academy.

Third, all of this begs the question: does class location change if one factor governing class location alters? Some people say yes. For them, once working-class people make a good salary they cease being working-class. By the same standard, if working-class people earn university degrees, they leave their class of origin.

I disagree with this, since I believe class identity comes from many places: education, values, culture, income, dwelling, lifestyle, manners, friends, ancestry, language, expectations, desires, sense of entitlement, religion, neighborhood, amount of privacy.[5] If one of these, such as education, shifts dramatically, class identity doesn't change.

Let me return to the statement of "fact" made by middle-class people: "You can't be working class. You have a university degree." I want to address this because I've heard it frequently, usually after I've asserted my working-class identity.

The remark contains arrogance that goes unnoticed by the speaker (*surprise, surprise*) but not by me (*surprise, surprise*). When a person with class privilege takes on the task of defining and articulating class location of someone from a lower class, it's arrogant and offensive.

Does this happen because working-class people claiming our identity threaten class-privileged people? In the United States, class is a taboo subject for everyone, let alone some upstart housecleaner or garbage man. Rich people need an automatic response, and seem to prefer a verbal attack that immediately silences the speaker. Discounting someone's identity usually does the trick.

This action is similar to the way white people try to shut me up when I critique racism: they question my identity as a person of color because of my light skin. Middle-class people attempt to shut me up by discrediting me, calling my identity into question, anything to stop me from claiming a working-class identity from which I might offer some criticism of their class privilege.

Implicit in middle-class people's assertion that I have indeed "moved up" is the ever popular belief that upward mobility is easily achieved and highly desirous. Neither of these is true, as far as I can tell. Some small percentage of working-class families have moved into the middle class in one or two generations, but they are the exception rather than the rule. As for upward mobility being highly desirable? Not for me. The values, ethics, simple lifestyles, and cultures of working-class people from any racial/ethnic group appeal to me more than the constrained emotional life, isolation, and gross materialism of rich people. The only aspect of class privilege I find desirable is rich people's innate belief/knowledge that options about life—from job choice to education to creative activities—really do exist. Not to mention the freedom from despair over whether the rent will be paid or whether food will appear on the table.

HOW DO YOU SPELL "CLASS"?

Universities have changed in the last twenty years. Critiques of the system, hard questions, cross-disciplinary dialogues, new programs and departments springing up—Women's Studies, Ethnic Studies, Queer Studies. This is great, but what about class? I know the kind of rampant sexism, racism, and heterosexism progressive professors and administrators deal with as they struggle to change curricula, but it's hard to deal with the classism of this crowd because I expect more. I'm dismayed to read the advanced theories these people offer when discussing race, gender, or sexuality, and contrast that to blank looks about the c-l-a-s-s word.[6]

I've heard progressive professors present information about social change movements, and been excited to study common people's history and struggles. But I'm angry when pertinent information about participants' class location doesn't enter the discussion. In a lecture about the 1960s' Black civil rights movement, a professor carefully delineated racial issues but somehow forgot to mention that most people putting their asses on the line were poor. Another professor discussed "gay men" and "lesbians" fighting back at the Stonewall riots. I didn't learn until later that Black and Puerto Rican drag queens and white butches and femmes really carried off the honors; none of them held executive day jobs.[7] I want to call progressive professors on their failure to integrate class into the curriculum, on their failure to notice they are as out-to-lunch about class as the straight white men they criticize.

Hand in hand with changes to existing institutions, I propose the establishment of new institutions. I want Working Class Studies set up. I want working-class and working-poor histories, cultures, ideologies, theories, languages studied. I want the many worthy individuals who spent their lives working for social justice studied and examined. I want us teaching each other, want the labor halls and community centers filled with janitors, secretaries, housecleaners, garbage men, lineworkers, want us in charge of curriculum and reading lists and teaching. I envision us at the center; I don't want "experts" explaining our lives to us, standing behind a lectern and pontificating for two hours on proletarians.

Maybe I'm paranoid, but I anticipate this reaction to my idea: *You've got to be kidding.* Eyes focused on the front of the room, looking anywhere else but toward me, silence, shifting bodies, unease, a bright smile from the professor: "Thank you for that interesting suggestion. Shall we move on?" *It's happened to me before. Once I actually told a group of rich, white students I thought we should have Class Speak-Outs where only poor people could speak. No one looked at me. My words rolled into a hole in the middle of the floor and disappeared from the face of the earth.* I know what the reaction to this will be: what

on earth are you suggesting? *Study a bunch of stupid rednecks?*[8] Chuckle, chuckle.

CONCLUSION

At 3:00 P.M., construction workers on the University of Minnesota campus finish up. Privileged university students grumble about what an easy job these guys have and how early they're leaving. They have no idea these workers arrived at 6:00 or 7:00 in the morning. They don't know how a body feels after eight hours of physical labor. They don't care.

As for me, I just watch the workers go by and feel many things. I feel at home, because these men look so familiar, from their flannel shirts, jeans, and workboots down to lunch pails and thermoses, cigarettes, and hard hats. I feel comfortable, because I like being around them. *These are my people. And we're not stupid.* I feel angry, because I know how students and professors perceive these workers. Because I know some of these workers believe the lies about who's stupid and who's smart, who has the right to think and study here and who has the right to build and clean here.

But I am clear. *I'm working-class. I'm smart. Just like the people I grew up with.* We know how to screw the system, we know how to take care of ourselves and survive when the odds are against us. We cook tasty meals with one onion, build our own stereo speakers, cut precisely-fitting pieces of wood for porches, know how to wire our houses and sew clothes, we like to read and think and talk to each other. We make music and art and tell stories. We know how to work cooperatively and we know how to give, generously, both hands open.

I've figured out I belong in the university. Not just when they need a janitor, or a cook, or a construction worker. But when I want to go. If I choose to study there, I won't let anyone make me feel stupid; I'll remember why it's so important they try. I won't let them turn me into an assimilationist, a fraud, a middle-class-identified polite girl who's grateful for all the help these nice rich people offer. I'll stay true to my roots. I'll use my brains, and my hands, to take this system apart. I'll use my brains, and my hands, to get your feet off my neck.

NOTES

Thanks to Jan Binder, Elizabeth Clare, Cynthia Lane, Jeff Nygaard, and Susan Raffo for their help with this piece.

1. In this essay, when I use the word "rich," I mean anyone middle-class and up. Poor means anyone working-class and down. That is the way the working-class and working-poor people I grew up with use the terms. I find these categories problematic on one hand because they miss a lot of the subtleties of class. For example, they ignore my privilege of being working-class instead of working-poor. On the other hand, I still find them powerful and appropriate categories. Middle-class people, who could choose to realize they are also being duped by rich people and decide they would be better off aligning themselves with working-class and working-poor people, continually align themselves with the rich. This is another reason to include middle-class people in the "rich" group.

2. From *Webster's New Collegiate Dictionary*, 1979.

3. Thanks to Jeff Nygaard for helping me articulate this point.

4. I also know other working-class people who have earned a university degree and are no longer working-class identified. These people are intent on passing and assimilating. I'm not sure if they are really middle-class, but they are certainly middle-class identified.

5. Thanks to Dr. Katie Cannon, for articulating all of this so clearly.

6. A notable exception to the lack of discussion/curriculum around this issue are the courses I took from Dr. Katie Cannon, which consistently dealt with critical questions relating to race, class, sex, ability, and sexuality. Dr. Cannon is continuing this groundbreaking work at Temple University in Philadelphia.

7. I want to mention here the regular inclusion, in Women's Studies, of the women's campaign to get the vote. I believe it is an important struggle to study, but I've also come to believe that part of its popularity in women's studies is that the social location of those activists reflects the social location of the women teaching in those programs in a way that other struggles usually do not.

8. For the best discussion I have ever read on the offensiveness of rich people using the term "redneck," read Elliott, "Whenever I Tell You the Language We Use is a Class Issue, You Nod Your Head in Agreement—and Then You Open Your Mouth," *Out of the Class Closet: Lesbians Speak*, Julia Penelope, editor (Freedom, CA: The Crossing Press, 1994). Elliott's article first appeared in *Lesbian Ethics*, vol. 4, no. 2 (Spring 1991).

Study Questions

1. Kadi argues that the identification of working-class people as stupid and "rich" people as smart serves a particular political purpose. What is that purpose?

2. Compare and contrast class and gender as social constructions.

3. Kadi holds that only working-class people should write about the working class. What considerations does she raise to support this claim? Do you agree?

4. Kadi asserts that simply changing one among the many elements that constitute one's class (e.g., one's educational level) does not move one out of one's class. Do you agree?

Patricia Hill Collins

The Politics of Black Feminist Thought

In 1831 Maria W. Stewart asked, "How long shall the fair daughters of Africa be compelled to bury their minds and talents beneath a load of iron pots and kettles?" Orphaned at age five, bound out to a clergyman's family as a domestic servant, Stewart struggled to gather isolated fragments of an education when and where she could. As the first American woman to lecture in public on political issues and to leave copies of her texts, this early Black woman intellectual foreshadowed a variety of themes taken up by her Black feminist successors (Richardson 1987).

Maria Stewart challenged African-American women to reject the negative images of Black womanhood so prominent in her times, pointing out that racial and sexual oppression were the fundamental causes of Black women's poverty. In an 1833 speech she proclaimed, "like King Solomon, who put neither nail nor hammer to the temple, yet received the praise; so also have the white Americans gained themselves a name . . . while in reality we have been their principal foundation and support." Stewart objected to the injustice of this situation: "We have pursued the shadow, they have obtained the substance: we have performed the labor, they have received the profits; we have planted the vines, they have eaten the fruits of them" (Richardson 1987, 59).

Maria Stewart was not content to point out the source of Black women's oppression. She urged Black women to forge self-definitions of self-reliance and independence. "It is useless for us any longer to sit with our hands folded, reproaching the whites; for that will never elevate us," she exhorted. "Possess the spirit of independence. . . . Possess the spirit of men, bold and enterprising, fearless and undaunted" (p. 53). To Stewart, the power of self-definition was essential, for Black women's survival was at stake. "Sue for your rights and privileges. Know the reason you cannot attain them. Weary them with your importunities. You can but die if you make the attempt; and we shall certainly die if you do not" (p. 38).

Stewart also challenged Black women to use their special roles as mothers to forge powerful mechanisms of political action. "O, ye mothers, what a responsibility rests on you!" Stewart preached. "You have souls committed to your charge. . . . It is you that must create in the minds of your little girls and boys a thirst for knowledge, the love of virtue, . . . and the cultivation of a pure heart." Stewart recognized the magnitude of the task at hand. "Do not say you cannot make any thing of your children; but say . . . we will try" (p. 35).

Maria Stewart was one of the first Black feminists to champion the utility of Black women's relationships with one another in providing a community for Black women's activism and self-determination. "Shall it any longer be said of the daughters of Africa, they have no ambition, they have no force?" she questioned. "By no means. Let every female heart become united, and let us raise a fund ourselves; and at the end of one year and a half, we might be able to lay the corner stone for the building of a High School, that the higher branches of knowledge might be enjoyed by us" (p. 37). Stewart saw the potential for Black women's activism as educators. She advised, "turn your attention to knowledge and improvement; for knowledge is power" (p. 41).

Though she said little in her speeches about the sexual politics of her time, her advice to African-American women suggests that she was painfully aware of the sexual abuse visited upon Black women. She continued to "plead the cause of virtue and the pure principles of morality" (p. 31) for Black women. And to those whites who thought that Black women were inherently inferior, Stewart offered a biting response: "Our souls are fired with the same love of liberty and independence with which your souls are fired . . . too much of your blood flows in our veins, too much of your color in our skins, for us not to possess your spirits" (p. 40).

Despite Maria Stewart's intellectual prowess, the ideas of this extraordinary woman come to us only in scattered fragments that not only suggest her brilliance but speak tellingly of the fate of countless Black women intellectuals. Recent scholarship has uncovered many Maria Stewarts, African-American women whose minds and talents have been suppressed by the pots and kettles symbolic of Black women's subordination. Far too many African-American women intellectuals have labored in isolation and obscurity and, like Zora Neale Hurston, lie buried in unmarked graves.

Some have been more fortunate, for they have become known to us, largely through the efforts of contemporary Black women scholars. Like Alice Walker, these scholars sense that "a people do not throw their geniuses away" and that, "if they are thrown away, it is our duty as artists, scholars, and witnesses for the future to collect them again for the sake of our children, . . . if necessary, bone by bone" (Walker 1983, 92).

This painstaking process of collecting the ideas and actions of "thrown away" Black women like Maria Stewart has revealed one important discovery.

Black women intellectuals have laid a vital analytical foundation for a distinctive standpoint on self, community, and society and, in doing so, created a Black women's intellectual tradition. While clear discontinuities in this tradition exist—times when Black women's voices were strong and others when assuming a more muted tone was essential—one striking dimension of the ideas of Maria W. Stewart and her successors is the thematic consistency of their work.

If such a rich intellectual tradition exists, why has it remained virtually invisible until now? In 1905 Fannie Barrier Williams lamented, "the colored girl . . . is not known and hence not believed in; she belongs to a race that is best designated by the term 'problem,' and she lives beneath the shadow of that problem which envelops and obscures her" (Williams 1987, 150). Why are African-American women and our ideas not known and not believed in?

The shadow obscuring the Black women's intellectual tradition is neither accidental nor benign. Suppressing the knowledge produced by any oppressed group makes it easier for dominant groups to rule because the seeming absence of an independent consciousness in the oppressed can be taken to mean that subordinate groups willingly collaborate in their own victimization. Maintaining the invisibility of Black women and our ideas is critical in structuring patterned relations of race, gender, and class inequality that pervade the entire social structure.

In spite of this suppression, African-American women have managed to do intellectual work, to have our ideas matter. Anna Julia Cooper, Sojourner Truth, Mary McLeod Behune, Toni Morrison, Barbara Smith, Ida B. Wells, and countless others have consistently struggled to make themselves heard and have used their voices to raise essential issues affecting Black women. Like the work of Maria W. Stewart, Black women's intellectual work has fostered Black women's resistance and activism.

This dialectic of oppression and activism, the tension between the suppression of Black women's ideas and our intellectual activism in the face of that suppression, comprises the politics of Black feminist thought. More important, understanding this dialectical relationship is critical in assessing how Black feminist thought—its definitions, core themes, and epistemological significance—is fundamentally embedded in a political context that has challenged its very right to exist.

THE SUPPRESSION OF BLACK FEMINIST THOUGHT

The vast majority of African-American women were brought to the United States to work as slaves. This initial condition shaped all subsequent relationships that Black women had within African-American families and communities, with employers, and among each other, and created the political context for Black women's intellectual work.

Black women's oppression has been structured along three interdependent dimensions. First, the exploitation of Black women's labor—the "iron pots and kettles" symbolizing Black women's longstanding ghettoization in service occupations—represents the economic dimension of oppression. Survival for most African-American women has been such an all-consuming activity that most have had few opportunities to do intellectual work as it has been traditionally defined. The drudgery of enslaved African-American women's work and the grinding poverty of "free" wage labor in the rural South tellingly illustrate the high costs Black women have paid for survival. The millions of impoverished African-American women currently ghettoized in inner cities demonstrate the continuation of these earlier forms of Black women's economic exploitation.

Second, the political dimension of oppression has denied African-American women the rights and privileges routinely extended to white male citizens. Forbidding Black women to vote, excluding African-Americans and women from public office, and withholding equitable treatment in the criminal justice system all substantiate the political subordination of Black women. Educational institutions have also fostered this pattern of disenfranchisement. Past practices such as denying literacy to slaves and rel-

egating Black women to underfunded, segregated Southern schools worked to ensure that a quality education for Black women remained the exception rather than the rule. The large numbers of young Black women in inner cities and impoverished rural areas who continue to leave school before attaining full literacy represent the continued efficacy of the political dimension of Black women's oppression.

Finally, the controlling images of Black women that originated during the slave era attest to the ideological dimension of Black women's oppression. Ideology represents the process by which certain assumed qualities are attached to Black women and how those qualities are used to justify oppression. From the mammies, Jezebels, and breeder women of slavery to the smiling Aunt Jemimas on pancake mix boxes, ubiquitous Black prostitutes, and ever-present welfare mothers of contemporary popular culture, the nexus of negative stereotypical images applied to African-American women has been fundamental to Black women's oppression.

Taken together, the seamless web of economy, polity, and ideology function as a highly effective system of social control designed to keep African-American women in an assigned, subordinate place. This larger system of oppression works to suppress the ideas of Black women intellectuals and to protect elite white male interests and worldviews. Denying African-American women the credentials to become literate certainly excluded most African-American women from positions as scholars, teachers, authors, poets, and critics. Moreover, while Black women historians, writers, and social scientists have long existed, until recently these women have not held leadership positions in universities, professional associations, publishing concerns, broadcast media, and other social institutions of knowledge validation. Black women's exclusion from positions of power within mainstream institutions has led to the elevation of elite white male ideas and interests and the corresponding suppression of Black women's ideas and interests in traditional scholarship and popular culture.

Women's studies has offered one major challenge to the allegedly hegemonic ideas of elite white men.

Ironically, feminist theory has also suppressed Black women's ideas. Even though Black women intellectuals have long expressed a unique feminist consciousness about the intersection of race and class in structuring gender, historically we have not been full participants in white feminist organizations. Even today African-American, Hispanic, Native American, and Asian-American women criticize the feminist movement and its scholarship for being racist and overly concerned with white, middle-class women's issues.

This historical suppression of Black women's ideas has had a pronounced influence on feminist theory. Theories advanced as being universally applicable to women as a group on closer examination appear greatly limited by the white, middle-class origins of their proponents. For example, Nancy Chodorow's work on sex role socialization and Carol Gilligan's study of the moral development of women both rely heavily on white, middle-class samples. While these two classics make key contributions to feminist theory, they simultaneously promote the notion of a generic woman who is white and middle class. The absence of Black feminist ideas from these and other studies places them in a much more tenuous position to challenge the hegemony of mainstream scholarship on behalf of all women.

Black social and political thought has also challenged mainstream scholarship. In this case the patterns of suppressing Black women's ideas have been quite different. Unlike the history of excluding Black women from both dominant academic discourse and white feminist arenas, African-American women have long been included in Black social and political organizations. But with the exception of Black women's organizations, male-run organizations have not stressed Black women's issues. Even though Black women intellectuals have asserted their right to speak both as African-Americans and as women, historically these women have not held top leadership positions in Black organizations.

Civil rights activist Ella Baker's experiences in the Southern Christian Leadership Conference illustrate one form that suppressing Black women's ideas and talents can take. Ms. Baker virtually ran the entire organization, yet had to defer to the decision-making authority of the exclusively male leadership group. Civil rights activist Septima Clark describes similar experiences: "I found all over the South that whatever the man said had to be right. They had the whole say. The woman couldn't say a thing" (C. Brown 1986, 79).

Black social and political thought has been limited by both the reformist postures toward change assumed by many Black intellectuals and the secondary status afforded the ideas and experiences of African-American women. Adhering to a male-defined ethos that far too often equates racial progress with the acquisition of an ill-defined manhood has left Black thought with a prominent masculinist bias. Calvin Hernton points out that the "masculine perspective itself, concerning the manhood of the black race, has always occupied center stage in the drama of Afro-American literature" (1985, 7). Black feminist activist Pauli Murray (1970) found that from its founding in 1916 to 1970, the *Journal of Negro History* published only five articles devoted exclusively to Black women.

Much of contemporary Black feminist thought stems from Black women's increasing willingness to strive for gender equality within African-American organizations. Septima Clark describes this transformation:

> I used to feel that women couldn't speak up, because when district meetings were being held at my home . . . I didn't feel as if I could tell them what I had in mind. . . . But later on, I found out that women had a lot to say, and what they had to say was really worthwhile. . . . So we started talking, and have been talking quite a bit since that time. (C. Brown 1986, 82)

African-American women intellectuals have been "talking quite a bit" since 1970 and have insisted that both the masculinist bias in Black social and political thought and the racist bias in feminist theory be corrected. Recent works in both African-American and feminist scholarship indicate that Black women's voices are being heard. For example, Manning Marable devotes an entire chapter in *How Capitalism*

Underdeveloped Black America to how sexism has been a primary deterrent to Black community development. Similarly, works by prominent white feminist theorists reflect similar efforts to incorporate Black women's ideas.

While these signs are promising, the recent resurgence of Black women's ideas has not gone unopposed. The virulent reaction to earlier Black women's writings by some Black men, such as Robert Staples's (1979) analysis of Ntozake Shange's choreopoem, *For Colored Girls Who Have Considered Suicide*, and Michele Wallace's admittedly flawed volume, *Black Macho and the Myth of the Superwoman*, illustrates the difficulty of challenging the masculinist bias in Black social and political thought. In describing the response of Black men to the outpouring of publications by Black women writers in the 1970s and 1980s, Calvin Hernton offers an incisive criticism of the seeming tenacity of a masculinist bias:

> The telling thing about the hostile attitude of black men toward black women writers is that they interpret the new thrust of the women as being "counter-productive" to the historical goal of the Black struggle. Revealingly, while black men have achieved outstanding recognition throughout the history of black writing, black women have not accused the men of collaborating with the enemy and setting back the progress of the race. (1985, 5)

Though less overtly hostile, the resistance to Black women's ideas in the white feminist scholarly community has been similarly entrenched. Alice Walker (1983) writes of her stint sharing an office with a prominent white feminist who expressed superficial interest in Black women's ideas yet compiled an anthology of women writers from which women of color were noticeably absent. Similarly, white women who possess great competence in researching a range of issues omit women of color from their work claiming that they are unqualified to understand the "Black woman's experience." Both examples reflect a basic unwillingness by many white feminists to alter the paradigms that guide their work.

THE SHAPE OF ACTIVISM

Even if they appear to be otherwise, oppressive situations such as the suppression of Black women's ideas within traditional scholarship and the struggles within the critiques of that established knowledge are inherently unstable. Conditions in the wider political economy simultaneously shape Black women's subordination and foster activism. People who are oppressed usually know it. For African-American women, the knowledge gained at the intersection of race, gender, and class oppression provides the stimulus for crafting and passing on the subjugated knowledge[1] of a Black women's culture of resistance.[2]

Prior to World War II, self-contained Black communities created under slavery and maintained by de jure and de facto segregation served as one contradictory location stimulating an African-American women's culture of resistance. Even though the overriding purpose of Black ghettoization was political control and economic exploitation, all-Black communities simultaneously provided a separate space where African-Americans could articulate an independent Afrocentric worldview.

Every culture has a worldview that it uses to order and evaluate its own experiences. For African-Americans this worldview originates in the Afrocentric ideas of classical African civilizations, ideas sustained by the cultures and institutions of diverse West African ethnic groups. By retaining significant elements of West African culture, communities of enslaved Africans offered their members alternative explanations for slavery than those advanced by slaveowners. Confining African-Americans to all-Black areas in the rural South and northern urban ghettos fostered the continuation of certain dimensions of this Afrocentric worldview. While essential to the survival of African-Americans, the knowledge produced in Black communities was hidden from and suppressed by the dominant group and thus remained extant but subjugated.

As mothers, othermothers, teachers and sisters, Black women were central to the retention and transformation of this Afrocentric worldview. Within African-American extended families and communities,

Black women fashioned an independent standpoint about the meaning of Black womanhood. These self-definitions enabled Black women to use African-derived conceptions of self and community to resist negative evaluations of Black womanhood advanced by dominant groups. In all, Black women's grounding in traditional African-American culture fostered the development of a distinctive Afrocentric women's culture.

Black women's position in the political economy, particularly ghettoization in domestic work, comprised another contradictory location where economic and political subordination created the conditions for Black women's resistance. Domestic work allowed African-American women to see white elites, both actual and aspiring, from perspectives largely obscured from Black men and from these groups themselves. In their white "families," Black women not only performed domestic duties but frequently formed strong ties with the children they nurtured, and with the employers themselves. On one level this insider relationship was satisfying to all concerned. Accounts of Black domestic workers stress the sense of self-affirmation the women experienced at seeing white power demystified. But on another level these Black women knew that they could never belong to their white "families," that they were economically exploited workers and thus would remain outsiders. The result was a curious outsider-within stance, a peculiar marginality that stimulated a special Black women's perspective.

Taken together, the outsider-within perspective generated by Black women's location in the labor market and this grounding in traditional African-American culture provide the material backdrop for a unique Black women's standpoint on self and society. As outsiders within, Black women have a distinct view of the contradictions between the dominant group's actions and ideologies. Nancy White, a Black inner-city resident, explores the connection between experience and beliefs:

> Now, I understand all these things from living. But you can't lay up on these flowery beds of ease and think that you are running your life, too. Some women, white women, can run their husband's lives

for a while, but most of them have to . . . see what he tells them there is to see. If he tells them that they ain't seeing what they know they *are* seeing, then they have to just go on like it wasn't there! (in Gwaltney 1980, 148)

Not only does this passage speak to the power of the dominant group to suppress the knowledge produced by subordinate groups, but it illustrates how an outsider-within stance functions to create a new angle of vision on the process of suppression. Ms. White's Blackness makes her a perpetual outsider. She can never be a white middle-class woman lying on a "flowery bed of ease." But her work of caring for white women allows her an insider's view of some of the contradictions between white women thinking that they are running their lives and the actual source of power and authority in white patriarchal households.

African-American women question the contradictions between ideologies of womanhood and Black women's devalued status. If women are allegedly passive and fragile, then why are Black women treated as "mules" and assigned heavy cleaning chores? With no compelling explanations offered by a viable culture of resistance, the angle of vision created by being a devalued worker could easily be turned inward, leading to internalized oppression. But the presence of a legacy of struggle suggests that African-American culture generally and Black women's culture in particular provide potent alternative interpretations.

African-American women intellectuals are nurtured in this larger Black women's community. While the economic, political, and ideological dimensions of Black women's oppression lead directly to the suppression of the Black feminist intellectual tradition, these same conditions simultaneously foster the continuation of Afrocentric culture and the creation of an outsider-within stance essential to Black women's activism. Black women intellectuals' critical posture toward mainstream, feminist, and Black scholarly inquiry has been similarly shaped by Afrocentric culture and the outsider-within stance characterizing a more generalized Black women's culture of resistance. Out of the dialectic of oppression and activism come the experiences of African-

American women generally that stimulate the ideas of Black women intellectuals.

The exclusion of Black women's ideas from mainstream academic discourse and the curious placement of African-American women intellectuals in both feminist and Black social and political thought has meant that Black women intellectuals have remained outsiders within in all three communities. The assumptions on which full group membership are based—whiteness for feminist thought, maleness for Black social and political thought, and the combination for mainstream scholarship—all negate a Black female reality. Prevented from becoming full insiders in any of these areas of inquiry, Black women remain outsiders within, individuals whose marginality provides a distinctive angle of vision on the theories put forth by such intellectual communities.

Alice Walker's work exemplifies both of these fundamental influences on the Black women's intellectual tradition. Walker describes the impact that an outsider-within stance had on her own thinking: "I believe . . . that it was from this period—from my solitary, lonely position, the position of an outcast—that I began really to see people and things, really to notice relationships" (Walker 1983, 244). Walker realizes that "the gift of loneliness is sometimes a radical vision of society or one's people that has not previously been taken into account" (p. 264). And yet marginality is not the only influence on her work. By reclaiming the works of Zora Neale Hurston and in other ways placing Black women's experiences and culture at the center of her work, she draws on the alternative Afrocentric feminist worldview extant in Black women's culture.

RECLAIMING THE BLACK FEMINIST INTELLECTUAL TRADITION

Starting from the assumption that African-American women have created an independent, viable, yet subjugated knowledge concerning our own subordination, contemporary Black women intellectuals are engaged in the struggle to reconceptualize all dimensions of the dialectic of oppression and activism as it applies to African-American women. Central to this enterprise is reclaiming the Black feminist intellectual tradition.

Black women academicians' positions as outsiders within fosters this reclamation process. Stimulated by the knowledge that the minds and talents of our grandmothers, mothers, and sisters have been suppressed, the task of reclaiming Black women's subjugated knowledge takes on special meaning for Black women intellectuals. Alice Walker describes how this sense of purpose affects her work: "In my own work I write not only what I want to read—understanding fully and indelibly that if I don't do it no one else is so vitally interested, or capable of doing it to my satisfaction—I write all the things *I should have been able to read*" (Walker 1983, 13).

Reclaiming this tradition involves discovering, reinterpreting, and, in many cases, analyzing for the first time the works of Black women intellectuals who were so extraordinary that they did manage to have their ideas preserved through the mechanisms of mainstream scholarly discourse. In some cases this process involves locating unrecognized and unheralded works, scattered and long out of print. Marilyn Richardson's (1987) painstaking editing of the writings and speeches of Maria Stewart, Gloria Hull's (1984) careful compilation of the journals of Black feminist intellectual Alice Dunbar-Nelson, and Mary Helen Washington's (1975, 1980, 1987) collections of Black women's writings typify this process. Similarly, Alice Walker's (1979) efforts to have Zora Neale Hurston's unmarked grave recognized parallel her intellectual quest to honor Hurston's important contributions to the Black feminist literary tradition.

Reinterpreting existing works through new theoretical frameworks is another component of this process of reclaiming the Black feminist intellectual tradition. Mary Helen Washington's (1987) reassessment of anger and voice in *Maud Martha*, a much-neglected work by novelist and poet Gwendolyn Brooks, Hazel Carby's (1987) use of the lens of race, class, and gender to reinterpret the works of nineteenth-century Black women novelists, and Evelyn Brooks Higginbotham's (1989) analysis of the emerging concepts and paradigms in Black women's history all exemplify this process of reinterpreting the works of African-American women intellectuals through new theoretical frameworks.

Reclaiming the Black feminist intellectual tradition also involves searching for its expression in alternative institutional locations and among women who are not commonly perceived as intellectuals. Denied formal education, nineteenth-century Black feminist activist Sojourner Truth is not typically seen as an intellectual.[3] Yet her 1851 speech at an Akron, Ohio, women's rights convention provides an incisive analysis of the definitions of the term *woman* forwarded in the mid-1800s:

> That man over there says women need to be helped into carriages, and lifted over ditches, and to have the best place everywhere. Nobody ever helps me into carriages, or over mud-puddles, or gives me any best place! And ain't I a woman? Look at me! Look at my arm! I have ploughed, and planted, and gathered into barns, and no man could head me! And ain't I a woman? I could work as much and eat as much as a man—when I could get it—and bear the lash as well! And ain't I a woman? I have borne thirteen children, and seen them most all sold off to slavery, and when I cried out with my mother's grief, none but Jesus heard me! And ain't I a woman? (Loewenberg and Bogin 1976, 235)

Sojourner Truth exposes the concept of woman as being culturally constructed by using the contradictions between her life as an African-American woman and the qualities ascribed to women. Her life as a second-class citizen has been filled with hard physical labor, with no assistance from men. Her question, "and ain't I a woman?" points to the contradictions inherent in blanket use of the term *woman*. For those who question Truth's femininity, she invokes her status as a mother of thirteen children, all sold off into slavery, and asks again, "and ain't I a woman?" Rather than accepting the existing assumptions about what a woman was and then trying to prove that she fit the standards, Truth challenged the very standards themselves. Her actions demonstrate the process of deconstruction—namely, exposing a concept as ideological or culturally constructed rather than as natural or a simple reflection of reality.

By deconstructing the concept *woman*, Truth proved herself to be a formidable intellectual. And yet Truth was a former slave who never learned to read or write.

Examining the contributions of women like Sojourner Truth suggests that a similar process of deconstruction must be applied to the concept of *intellectual*. Just as theories, epistemologies, and facts produced by any group of individuals represent the standpoints and interests of their creators, the very definition of who is legitimated to do intellectual work is also politically contested. Reclaiming the Black feminist intellectual tradition involves much more than developing Black feminist analyses using standard epistemological criteria. It also involves challenging the very definitions of intellectual discourse.

Assuming new angles of vision on the definitions of who can be a Black woman intellectual and on what constitutes Black feminist thought suggests that much of the Black women's intellectual tradition has been embedded in institutional locations other than the academy. At the core of Black feminist thought lie theories created by African-American women which clarify a Black women's standpoint—in essence, an interpretation of Black women's experiences and ideas by those who participate in them. African-American women not commonly certified as intellectuals by academic institutions have long functioned as intellectuals by representing the interests of Black women as a group and fostering Black feminist thought. Without tapping these so-called nontraditional sources, much of the Black women's intellectual tradition would remain "not known and hence not believed in" (Williams 1987, 150).

Reclaiming the Black women's intellectual tradition involves examining the everyday ideas of Black women not previously considered intellectuals. The ideas we share with one another as mothers in extended families, as othermothers in Black communities, as members of Black churches, and as teachers to the Black community's children have formed one pivotal area where African-American women have hammered out a Black women's standpoint. Musicians, vocalists, poets, writers, and other artists constitute another group of Black women intellectuals who have aimed to interpret Black women's experiences. Building on the Afrocentric oral tradition, musicians in particular have enjoyed close association with the larger community of African-American women comprising their audience. Through their words and actions, political activists have also contributed to the Black women's intellectual tradition. Producing intellectual work is generally not attributed to Black women artists and political activists. Such women are typically thought of as nonintellectual and nonscholarly, classifications that create a false dichotomy between scholarship and activism, between thinking and doing. Examining the ideas and actions of these excluded groups reveals a world in which behavior is a statement of philosophy and in which a vibrant, both/and, scholar/activist tradition remains intact.

OBJECTIVES OF THE VOLUME

Africa-American women's position in the economic, political, and ideological terrain bounding intellectual discourse has fostered a distinctive Black feminist intellectual tradition. Two basic components of Black feminist thought—its thematic content and its epistemological approach—have been shaped by Black women's outsider-within stance and by our embeddedness in traditional African-American culture.

My overall goal in this book is to describe, analyze, explain the significance of, and generally further the development of Black feminist thought. In addressing this general goal, I have several specific objectives. First, I summarize some of the essential themes in Black feminist thought by surveying their historical and contemporary expression. Drawing primarily on the works of African-American women scholars, and on the thought produced by Black women intellectuals in everyday and alternative locations for knowledge production, I explore several core themes that comprise a Black women's standpoint. The vast majority of thinkers discussed in the text are, to the best of my knowledge, Black women.

I cite a range of Black women thinkers not because I think Black women have a monopoly on the ideas presented; instead I aim to demonstrate the range and depth of thinkers who exist in my community. Placing the ideas of ordinary African-American women as well as those of better-known Black women intellectuals at the center of analysis produces a new angle of vision on feminist and African-American concerns, one infused with an Afrocentric feminist sensibility.

While Black women intellectuals have consistently investigated a series of core questions, namely the simultaneity of race, class, and gender oppression, the importance of self-definition in resisting oppression, and analyses of specific topics such as motherhood and political activism, not all issues have received equal theoretical attention. My second objective is to explore selected neglected themes currently lacking a comprehensive Black feminist analysis. For example, even though Black women have written about topics such as rape, sterilization abuse, and sexual harassment, comprehensive Black feminist analyses of sexual politics that incorporate the interlocking nature of race, gender, and class oppression remain scarce. While the ideas of African-American women intellectuals lie at the core of all arguments forwarded in this volume, I use Black women's ideas as a point of departure in exploring neglected topics. By synthesizing the ideas of thinkers from diverse race and gender groups, I develop my own independent analyses of themes important to Black women.

My third objective is to develop an epistemological framework that can be used both to assess existing Black feminist thought and to clarify some of the underlying assumptions that impede the development of Black feminist thought. This issue of epistemology raises some difficult questions. I see the need to define the boundaries that delineate Black feminist thought from other arenas of intellectual inquiry. What criteria can be applied to ideas to determine whether they are in fact Black and feminist? What essential features does Black feminist thought share with other bodies of intellectual criticism, particularly feminist theory, Afrocentric theory, Marxist analyses, and postmodernism? Do African-American women implicitly rely on alternative standards for determining whether ideas are true? Traditional epistemological assumptions concerning how we arrive at "truth" simply are not sufficient to the task of furthering Black feminist thought. In the same way that concepts such as woman and intellectual must be deconstructed, the process by which we arrive at truth merits comparable scrutiny.

Finally, I aim to use this same epistemological framework in preparing the book itself. Alice Walker describes this process as one whereby "to write the books one wants to read is both to point the direction of vision and, at the same time, to follow it" (1983, 8). This was a very difficult process for me, one requiring that I not only develop standards and guidelines for assessing Black feminist thought but that I then apply those same standards and guidelines to my own work while I was creating it. For example, one dimension of Black feminist thought . . . is that Black women intellectuals create Black feminist thought by using their own concrete experiences as situated knowers in order to express a Black women's standpoint. To adhere to this epistemological tenet required that I reject the pronouns "they" and "their" when describing Black women and our ideas and replace these terms with the terms "we," "us," and "our." Using the distancing terms "they" and "their" when describing my own group and our experiences might enhance both my credentials as a scholar and the credibility of my arguments in some academic settings. But by taking this epistemological stance that reflects my disciplinary training as a sociologist, I invoke standards of certifying truth about which I remain ambivalent.

In contrast, by identifying my position as a participant in and observer of my own community, I run the risk of being discredited as being too subjective and hence less scholarly. But by being an advocate for my material, I validate the epistemological stance that I claim is fundamental for Black feminist thought. To me, the suppression of the Black women's intellectual tradition has made this process of feeling one's way an unavoidable epistemological stance for Black women intellectuals. As Walker points out,

"she must be her own model as well as the artist attending, creating, learning from, realizing the model, which is to say, herself" (1983, 8).

NOTES

1. My use of the term *subjugated knowledge* differs somewhat from Michel Foucault's (1980) definition. According to Foucault, subjugated knowledges are "those blocs of historical knowledge which were present but disguised," namely, "a whole set of knowledges that have been disqualified as inadequate to their task or insufficiently elaborated: naive knowledges, located low down on the hierarchy, beneath the required level of cognition or scientificity" (p. 82). I suggest that Black feminist thought is not a "naive knowledge" but has been made to appear so by those controlling knowledge validation procedures. Moreover, Foucault argues that subjugated knowledge is "a particular, local, regional knowledge, a differential knowledge incapable of unanimity and which owes its force only to the harshness with which it is opposed by everything surrounding it" (p. 82). The component of Black feminist thought that analyzes Black women's oppression certainly fits this definition, but the long-standing, independent Afrocentric foundation of Black women's thought is omitted from Foucault's analysis.

2. My use of the term *culture of resistance* should not imply that a monolithic culture of resistance exists. Instead I suggest that such cultures contain contradictory elements that foster both compliance with and resistance to oppression. [. . .]

3. Sojourner Truth's actions exemplify Antonio Gramsci's (1971) contention that every social group creates one or more "strata of intellectuals which give it homogeneity and an awareness of its own function not only in the economic but also in the social and political fields" (p. 5). Academicians are the intellectuals trained to represent the interests of groups in power. In contrast, "organic" intellectuals depend on common sense and represent the interests of their own group. Sojourner Truth typifies an "organic" or everyday intellectual, but she may not be certified as such by the dominant group because her intellectual activity threatens the prevailing social order. The outsider-within position of Black women academicians encourages us to draw on the traditions of both our discipline of training and our experiences as Black women but to participate fully in neither.

REFERENCES

Brown, Cynthia Stokes, ed. 1986. *Ready From Within: Septima Clark and the Civil Rights Movement.* Navarro, CA: Wild Tree Press.

Carby, Hazel. 1987. *Reconstructing Womanhood: The Emergence of the Afro-American Woman Novelist.* New York: Oxford.

Foucault, Michel. 1980. *Power/Knowledge*, edited by Colin Gordon. New York: Pantheon.

Gramsci, Antonio. 1971. *Selections From the Prison Notebooks.* London: Lawrence and Wishart.

Gwaltney, John Langston. 1980. *Drylongso, A Self-Portrait of Black America.* New York: Vintage.

Hernton, Calvin. 1985. "The Sexual Mountain and Black Women Writers." *Black Scholar* 16(4): 2–11.

Higginbotham, Evelyn Brooks. 1989. "Beyond the Sound of Silence: Afro-American Women in History." *Gender and History* 1(1): 50–67.

Hull, Gloria. 1984. *Give Us Each Day: the Diary of Alice Dunbar-Nelson.* New York: W.W. Norton.

Loewenberg, Bert J., and Ruth Bogin, eds. 1976. *Black Women in Nineteenth-Century American Life.* University Park, Pennsylvania: Pennsylvania State University Press.

Murray, Pauli. 1970. "The Liberation of Black Women." In *Voices of the New Feminism*, ed. Mary Lou Thompson. 87–102. Boston: Beacon.

Richardson, Marilyn, ed. 1987. *Maria W. Stewart, America's First Black Woman Political Writer.* Bloomington: Indiana University Press.

Staples, Robert. 1979. "The Myth of Black Macho: A Response to Angry Black Feminists." *Black Scholar* 10(6): 24–33.

Walker, Alice, ed. 1979. *I Love Myself When I am Laughing, And Then Again When I am Looking Mean and Impressive: a Zora Neale Hurston Reader.* Old Westbury, NY: Feminist Press.

———. 1983. *In Search of Our Mothers' Gardens.* New York: Harcourt Brace Jovanovich.

Washington, Mary Helen, ed. 1975. *Black-Eyed Susans: An Approach to the Study of Black Women.* Garden City, NY: Anchor.

———, ed. 1980. *Midnight Birds.* Garden City, NY: Anchor.

———, ed. 1987. *Invented Lives: Narratives of Black Women 1860–1960.* Garden City, NY: Anchor.

Williams, Fannie Barrier. 1987. "The Colored Girl." In *Invented Lives: Narratives of Black Women 1860–1960*, edited by Mary Helen Washington, 150–59. Garden City, NY: Anchor.

Study Questions

1. Collins argues that while "Black women intellectuals have laid a vital analytical foundation for a distinctive standpoint on self, community, and society and, in doing so, created a Black women's intellectual tradition," this rich tradition "has remained virtually invisible until now." Why has the "distinctive standpoint" of Black women not been more visible? Where should we look to find the intellectual tradition(s) she is speaking of?

2. How has the suppression of Black women's intellectual contributions affected feminist theory?

3. What does Collins mean by the "outsider-within perspective"? (See the section entitled "The Shape of Activism," paragraph 6.) How have Black women, in particular, come to occupy this perspective? Do members of other groups also occupy this perspective?

4. In Collins's view, "Reclaiming the Black feminist intellectual tradition involves much more than developing Black feminist analyses using standard epistemological criteria. It also involves challenging the very definitions of intellectual discourse." (See the section entitled "Reclaiming the Black Feminist Intellectual Tradition," paragraph 7.) Give two examples of what Collins has in mind by "challenging the very definitions of intellectual discourse."

Uma Narayan

Cross-Cultural Connections, Border-Crossings, and "Death by Culture"

*Thinking About Dowry-Murders in India and Domestic-Violence
Murders in the United States*

INTRODUCTION

. . . While this essay calls attention to problems I have with the ways in which the issue of dowry-murder is framed and understood in my encounters with the topic in the United States, this essay is not primarily about the issue of dowry-murder. Rather, the central objective of this essay is to call attention to two sorts of problems that often beset the general project of "learning about Other cultures." I am specifically interested in how these problems affect the *feminist* commitment to attend to the problems of women in a variety of cultural contexts, and to "learning about the problems of women in Other cultures." The first cluster of problems has to do with the "effects" that national contexts have on the "construction" of feminist issues and the ways in which understandings of issues are then affected by their "border-crossings" across national boundaries. This first set of problems has to do with features of context that "bring" particular issues onto feminist agendas, mold the information that is available on the issue, and shape as well as distort the ways in which they are understood when the issue "crosses borders." The

second problem I am concerned with has to do with the ways in which "culture" is invoked in explanations of forms of violence against Third-World women, while it is not similarly invoked in explanations of forms of violence that affect mainstream Western women. I intend to argue that when such "cultural explanations" are given for *fatal* forms of violence against Third-World women, the effect is to suggest that Third-World women suffer "death by culture." I shall try to show that fatal forms of violence against mainstream Western women seem interestingly resistant to such "cultural explanations," leaving Western women seemingly more immune to "death by culture." I believe that such asymmetries in "cultural explanation" result in pictures of Third-World women as "victims of their culture" in ways that are interestingly different from the way in which victimization of mainstream Western women is understood. [. . .]

The first two sections of this essay both explore the ways in which "national contexts" shape feminist issues, and the implications of such shaping for "cross-cultural understanding." The first section of this essay attempts to show how national contexts shape feminist agendas by exploring the differences between the U.S. and Indian feminist agendas around issues of domestic violence. [. . .]

The second section of the essay attempts to call attention to another, perhaps less obvious, way in which "cross-cultural understanding" of issues is complicated. I wish to argue that the ways in which "issues" emerge in various national contexts, and the contextual factors that shape the specific issues that are named and addressed, *affect the information that is readily available for such connection-making* and hence our abilities to make connections across these contexts. [. . .]

The third section of the essay explores the effects that traveling across national borders has on the understanding of specific issues. It raises questions about the *sorts* of issues pertaining to Third-World women that predominantly cross national borders, and points to the adverse effects that "decontextualized information" has on the understanding of these issues in Western contexts. [. . .]

The last two sections explore "death by culture" and attempt to think critically about *how* "culture" is invoked in accounts of violence against women in Third-World contexts. [. . . while] domestic-violence murders in the United States seem resistant to problematic "cultural explanations" of the "death by culture" variety. [. . .]

FEMINIST MOVEMENTS, NATIONAL CONTEXTS, AND THE "MAKING" OF FEMINIST ISSUES

[. . .] Most Americans that I have talked to about dowry-murder know that many U.S. women are killed by their partners as a result of domestic violence. Given that many members of the U.S. public know that domestic violence has fatal forms, why is it that they make no connection between the "foreign" phenomenon of dowry-murder and the "familiar" phenomenon of domestic violence? What are the difficulties that stand in the way of this connection being made? I believe that part of the answer to this question lies in the ways in which domestic violence agendas have developed in the United States, and their effects on the ways in which the term "domestic violence" is widely understood. Let me explain what I mean.

When I began looking through the articles in my files, and through several books that either wholly or partly address issues of domestic violence in the U.S., I did not come across any book or article that *centrally focused* on U.S. women *murdered* as a result of domestic violence (even though I found a fair amount of writing on legal issues pertaining to women who killed their batterers). In all of the American "domestic-violence" readings I initially went through as I began writing this piece, I found no data about the number of women who are annually *killed* as a result of domestic violence, though I found plenty of other kinds of data on facets of domestic violence such as injuries and homelessness. None of several American feminist friends I called knew off-hand roughly how many women were killed by their partners each year in the United States. Nor could they find this figure easily when they went through their collections of books and articles on the subject. We were all struck by the fact that it was quite difficult for any one of us to find this particular piece of data, and also struck by the degree to which deaths resulting from domestic violence have *not* been much focused upon in U.S. literature on domestic violence. A friend who participated in my search for the numbers of U.S. women annually killed by their partners commented that she was surprised at the difference between the "disappearing dead women" in U.S. accounts of domestic violence and the "spectacular visibility" of women murdered over dowry in India.

Discussions of domestic violence in the U.S. contexts are not lacking in mention of grievous injury to women. Although fatalities are often mentioned along with injuries, most discussions do not centrally focus on the most "extreme cases" where the woman dies as a result of domestic violence. There is a striking contrast between the lack of focus on fatal cases that enters into the construction of the category "domestic violence" in the United States context, and the focus on deadly cases of domestic violence in the Indian context that has given visibility to the category "dowry-murder." I believe that this "asymmetry in focus" contributes to the lack of perceived connection between dowry-murders and domestic violence in the minds of many Americans.

How is this "asymmetry in focus" to be explained? I think these differences in focus are connected to the different ways in which issues of violence against women emerged within, and were taken up by, feminist movements in India and in the United States. In many areas of U.S. feminist effort around domestic violence, such as challenging police nonresponsiveness to domestic-violence complaints, and countering various laws and legal attitudes that trivialized domestic violence or dismissed it as a "private quarrel," there was little reason to single out cases of domestic violence that resulted in death. Rather, the focus was on generating legal and institutional responses that addressed a *wide spectrum* of domestic violence cases, ranging from the fairly minor to the potentially lethal. As a result of U.S. feminist efforts around issues of domestic violence, public attention was certainly drawn to the various ways in which women were often brutally and repeatedly injured in domestic violence attacks, terrorized and stalked, and often additionally endangered if they tried to leave violent relationships. But the bulk of the U.S. feminist responses to domestic violence, quite understandably, seem to have focused on victims who were still alive, who needed either shelters, counseling and assistance, or various forms of legal redress.

While the much publicized trial of O.J. Simpson for his wife's murder has put more of a spotlight on the fact that U.S. women are *killed* as a result of relationships plagued by domestic violence, such deaths have not necessarily been portrayed as the "typical" or "paradigmatic" outcomes of domestic-violence situations. The fact that domestic-violence situations *can* end in death seems to be used as an indicia of its potential seriousness and danger, rather than as an emblem. Let me reiterate that I believe this makes sense, given that there seem few reasons, in the U.S. context, to focus specifically on women *killed* in acts of domestic violence with respect to legal and

institutional attempts to address the problem. If anything, feminist efforts on the issue may have had good reason to move in the other direction, away from a focus on domestic-violence-related homicides, since homicides are likely, by dint of their seriousness, to receive police and legal attention where less drastic forms of domestic violence do not. Feminist efforts in the U.S. seem to have moved in the direction of *widening* the scope of what is understood to constitute "domestic violence," pointing out that verbal, emotional, and psychological abuse often constitute components of domestic violence.

If we are to understand the "asymmetry" between feminist engagement with domestic violence in the U.S. and Indian contexts, we also need to understand why the Indian feminist movement focused on domestic violence in the extreme form of "dowry-murder" and did not focus on general issues of domestic violence to the same degree as in the United States. In what follows, I will attempt to provide an answer by giving a brief sketch of the history of contemporary Indian feminist engagement with issues of violence against women. In an article on the Indian women's movement, Mary Fainsod Katzenstein points out that a report on Indian women, commissioned by the government of India in 1974 in anticipation of the International Women's Year declared by the United Nations in 1975, played a "catalytic role in the emergence of the contemporary women's movement in India."[1] Katzenstein adds:

> The report dramatically called attention to existing gender inequality with its documentation of a declining sex ratio (read as an indicator of differential female mortality) and its presentation of evidence of inequalities in education, income, access to health care and political representation. The report galvanized both academics and activists. Not only did it cite patterns of inequality that had not been widely recognized but no less important, the process of preparing the report caused several women members of the commission to redirect their scholarly and activist energies entirely.[2]

Although the report sparked an interest in organizing around gender issues, issues of sexual violence were given little attention at the start, as the movement initially focused largely on economic and demographic issues. Members of committee that wrote the 1974 report have, in retrospect, acknowledged their inattention to issues of violence against women. As one member puts it:

> I realise now that there were other things which we should have investigated. We did not include rape in our inquiry. We took some note of suicides when they were brought to our notice, but no one mentioned a single case of dowry-murder. Harassment, even torture was reported but never a murder. Today I realize that the issue of violence of crimes against women did not feature in our report as we had not investigated it. Even the practice of dowry was not in our initial questionnaire—it was forced on us by the women we met.[3]

However, by the late 1970s issues of violence against women began to move to the forefront of the feminist agenda. Katzenstein remarks that "it was the focus on violence against women, beginning in the late 1970s, that propelled the movement forward and endowed it with much of its strength."[4] The two most "visible" issues initially addressed by women's groups were the issue of dowry-murder and that of rape, especially police rape of poor women held in custody.[5] Many women's groups that addressed the issue of dowry-murders did not address the issue in isolation from the general issue of domestic violence, which was also addressed quite apart from dowry-related contexts. For instance, a number of women's groups addressed wife-beating in the context of male drinking and alcoholism.[6]

Although the issue of dowry-murder was hardly the only issue pertaining to violence against women that was addressed by the Indian women's movement, it has probably had the most widespread impact on public attention in India and received the most sustained media coverage, resulting in dowry-murders being reported in a more ongoing way than many other issues affecting Indian women. I believe that there are a number of reasons for the public attention that dowry-murders have received. While issues such as that of police rape of women in custody primarily affected poorer women, dowry-murders were predominantly a middle-class phenomenon. And

although the political energies of the women's movement were crucial in calling a number of issues of violence against women to public attention and to underlining their prevalence, I suspect that issues such as police rape, or domestic violence as a general problem, were not "surprising" to many Indians, while dowry-murders were. [. . .]

There also seem to be contextual reasons as to why some other aspects of domestic violence received less organizational attention and effort from women's groups in India than they did in the United States. A significant proportion of feminist efforts around domestic violence in the United States seems to have focused on publicizing the need for shelters for battered women and in setting up and organizing such shelters. While there have been some attempts by women's groups in India to organize shelters for battered women, there are considerably *fewer* efforts in this direction than has been the case in the United States. Understanding the reasons for this difference is, I think, interesting in its capacity to illuminate the degree to which specific feminist policies and solutions are dependent on the background social, economic, and institutional features of the national landscapes within which feminist groups operate.

Why did organizing battered women's shelters not have a central place in Indian feminist agendas? The answer is not, as some Western feminists seem to have assumed, that the Indian women's movement is "less developed." Madhu Kishwar alludes to these assumptions when she says:

> Over the last decade, innumerable western feminists have asked us: "Do you have battered women's homes in India?" The assumption is that not to have such homes is to be at a lower stage of development in the struggle against violence on women, and that such homes will be one inevitable outcome of the movement's development.[7]

Kishwar goes on to provide a very different kind of account for this difference, pointing to a number of factors that help make battered women's shelters a feasible strategy for affording assistance to battered women in countries like the United States, factors that play out differently in India. Kishwar says:

Battered women's homes in the west . . . seemed to act as a useful type of short term intervention because of (a) the existence of a welfare system which includes some, even though inadequate, provisions for public assistance, unemployment, benefits, subsidized housing, and free schooling for children; (b) the overall employment situation being very different from that in India; (c) the lower stigma on women living on their own and moving around on their own; and (d) the existence of certain avenues of employment that are not considered permissible for middle class women here.[8]

Although the situation is far from rosy in countries like the United States, and might conceivably get much worse if current attacks on state provisions such as welfare are successful, it is still feasible for U.S. battered women's shelters to help at least some women leave abusive domestic relationships. Enabling some battered women to secure welfare for themselves or their children, assisting others in securing paid employment, state-funded medical care, and legal aid around custody issues, are all ways in which U.S. battered women's shelters can offer more than temporary refuge. The provision of such services enables at least some women to leave relationships they would not otherwise be in a position to leave. The virtual absence in India of state-provided welfare, education, and medical care, the unavailability of state-provided legal services to deal with custody, and far greater levels of unemployment, render it very difficult for feminists to help generate structures that would enable Indian women to leave the family contexts where they are victims of violence. With the exception of the relatively small group of women who earn enough on their own to support themselves and their children, few women are materially in a position to leave abusive relationships. In addition, as Kishwar suggests, there is much greater stigma in India around issues such as divorce, separation from one's husband, and "women living on their own," factors that might well deter even women who could economically support themselves. Kishwar points out that groups attempting to help battered women often have no resources but to try and persuade the women's marital families to take them back on "slightly improved terms."[9]

In the Indian context, organizing around issues such as shelters for battered women, which require a variety of state and institutional structures that are not readily available, is not highly feasible.[10] In contrast, dowry-murder was an issue around which Indian women's groups *could* effectively organize in a number of ways. Women's groups in India had the resources to publicize cases of dowry-murders and hold public demonstrations and protests, often in the neighborhood where "suspicious burnings" had occurred. Such public efforts to call the phenomenon of dowry-murder to national attention had the important function of alerting Indian families to the potentially lethal situations in which marriage placed some of their daughters. Such efforts also provoked a considerable amount of public "consciousness raising" on the institution of dowry, led to calls-for people to pledge not to give or take dowries, and for people to boycott marriages where dowry was involved. Women's groups in India also engaged in pushing for a variety of legal changes that would enable more efficient prosecution of the family members responsible for these murders, and generated debates on possible changes in property and inheritance laws that might ameliorate the problem of dowry-murders. [. . .]

The preceding analysis helps call attention to some of the complexities inherent in the project of "learning about issues of women in Other cultures." It challenges the unreflective and naively optimistic view that sees this project primarily in terms of "information retrieval"—as a simple matter of acquiring information and learning "the facts" that illuminate these "problems of women in Other cultures," and then perhaps going on to understand our "commonalities and differences." It suggests that we need to understand the ways in which feminist agendas are shaped by the different conditions that obtain within different national contexts if we are to understand the connections between the "visibility" of dowry-murders in India and the relative "invisibility" of the issue of domestic-violence murder in the United States.

In the absence of such an understanding, it is not surprising that many Americans fail to connect the unfamiliar phenomenon of dowry-murder to the more familiar category of "domestic violence." [. . .]

THE EFFECTS OF "ABSENCES" ON PROJECTS OF CROSS-CULTURAL UNDERSTANDING

The preceding analysis suggests that the project of "understanding Other cultures" is made difficult by the problems one often has in "seeing" features of one's "own context" that might be relevant to this project, features that might make a difference to the sense of "similarities and differences" one develops. I think it is quite difficult to "notice" that a term like "domestic-violence murders" is "absent" in the U.S. context, and to perceive how this "lack" contributes to the phenomenon lacking specificity of a sort it might have had if a term had "picked it out" and made the underlying issue the focused subject of public and political concern. The absence in the U.S. context of a term such as "domestic-violence murders," and the lack of focus on this issue in U.S. feminist agendas on domestic violence, only forcibly struck me when I began working on this essay. I believe that the effects of this "absence" go beyond its functioning as an impediment to many Americans making connections between dowry-murders and domestic violence. I would like, in this section, to go on to explore some of the less obvious ways in which this absence works to complicate "cross-cultural understanding" of "similarities and differences" between forms of violence that affect women in Third-World nations and violence against women in Western national contexts.

One of the things I hoped to do when I began this essay was to work on making a stronger connection between Indian dowry-deaths and domestic violence in the United States by comparing the number of women annually killed in dowry-murders in India to the numbers of U.S. women annually killed by their partners. I wanted to make this comparison to see if data would support my suspicion that the incidence of "domestic-violence murders" in the United States was "numerically similar" to the incidence of dowry-murders in India. If I found the incidence of the two phenomena to be "numerically similar," I hoped to argue that, given their relatively equal seriousness as "social problems," it was even more interesting that one phenomenon had a specific name and activist

focus and that the other did not. What I completely failed to realize was the degree to which the absence of a term that conferred "specificity" on the phenomenon of "domestic-violence murders" in the United States would affect my very attempt to make this comparison. [. . .]

I am arguing that the complicated factors that have shaped different national agendas on issues of domestic violence seem to exert a considerable amount of influence on the kinds of "official data" that are generated on various aspects of the phenomenon. Given that very different kinds of domestic-violence data seem to be available in the Indian and U.S. contexts, any attempts to "compare" the figures on "domestic-violence murders in the U.S." and "dowry-murders in India" more than hint at comparing apples and oranges. However, working on the principle that there may be a point to comparing apples and oranges if one is interested in understanding some aspects of fruit, I will press on with the "comparison."

The population of India is roughly four times that of the United States. Given that roughly 1,400 U.S. women annually are (known to be) victims of "domestic-violence murder" and that roughly 5,000 Indian women annually are (suspected to be) victims of dowry-murders, it seems as if one could at least safely say that the proportion of the women in the U.S. population who are victims of "domestic-violence murder" seems *roughly similar* to the proportion of women in the Indian population murdered over dowry. These figures at least make plausible the claim that "death by domestic violence" in the U.S. seems to be numerically as significant a social problem as "dowry-murders" are in India. Given that roughly the same proportion of women in the U.S. population are possible victims of "domestic-violence murder" as women in the Indian population are possible victims of "dowry-murder," it is interesting that one of these phenomena is named, noted, and made into a "specific social issue" while the other is not.

I have already given an account of the reasons that may have shaped the U.S. domestic-violence agenda away from a focus on fatalities, and of the factors that led to the Indian feminist focus on dowry-murders. What I have pointed out in this section is how different kinds of "focus" and "lacks of focus" on various aspects of domestic violence in India and the United States also shape the kinds of data that are readily available in the two contexts. Such differences of data as well as "absences of data" are, by their nature, difficult to see and to make sense of. However, the ability to see them and make sense of them seems to me to be crucial to attempts to better understand "similarities and differences" between problems women confront in different national contexts.

BORDER-CROSSINGS, LACKS OF CONTEXT, AND THE CONSTRUCTION OF "DEATH BY CULTURE"

My previous analysis pointed to how some of the ways in which issues are "shaped" within different national contexts might affect the project of "cross-cultural understanding." In this section, I will attempt to explore the effects of "border-crossings" on issues affecting Third-World women, and the distortions that accompany such issues in their travels across national borders. I believe that Western feminists interested in the "problems of women in Other cultures" need to think about: (1) the kinds of Third-World women's issues that cross Western borders more frequently than others; and about (2) the effects of the "editing" and "re-framing" such issues undergo when they do cross borders. I will try to address these issues by focusing on dowry-murder.

In thinking about issues of "violence against Third-World women" that "cross borders" into Western national contexts, it strikes me that phenomena that seem "Different," "Alien," and "Other" cross these borders with considerably more frequency than problems that seem "similar" to those that affect mainstream Western women. Thus, clitorodectomy and infibulation have become virtually an "icon" of "African women's problems" in Western contexts, while a host of other "more familiar" problems that different groups of African women face are held up at the border. In a similar vein, the abandonment and

infanticide of female infants appears to be the one gender issue pertaining to China that receives coverage. These issues then become "common topics" for academics and feminists, and also cross over to a larger public audience that becomes "familiar" with these issues. It is difficult not to conclude that there is a premium on "Third-World difference" that results in greater interest being accorded those issues that seem strikingly "different" from those affecting mainstream Western women. The issues that "cross borders" then become the "Third-World gender issues" that are taught about and studied "across the border," reinforcing their "iconic" and "representative" status as issues.

My analysis in the first section of this essay suggested that the issue of dowry-murder has "crossed Western borders" in part because this issue occupied an early and visible place on the agendas of Indian women's groups and remains an ongoing Indian feminist issue today. While that *is* part of the explanation, I believe it can only be a very *partial explanation*, since many other issues that have received sustained attention from Indian women's groups have not acquired the same sort of "familiarity" to many Westerners. Thus, I believe that features of dowry-murder that mark it as "Other" also partly account for its "border-crossing." These features of "Otherness" simultaneously operate to cause the phenomenon to receive "notice" and to distort understandings of the phenomenon.

One factor that I believe helps dowry-murders receive Western attention is the history of Western fascination with "the Indian tradition" of *sati* or widow-immolation. This historic association of *sati* and "Indian culture" and "Indian women" results today in a metonymic blurring of *sati* with dowry-murder, generating a confused composite of "burnt Indian women" variously going up in flames as a result of "their Culture." "Women being burnt" thus becomes constituted as a "paradigmatic," "iconic," and "familiar" form of "violence suffered by Indian women." The terms "*sati*" and "dowry-murder" come to have a vaguely familiar ring, even though their exact referents are often not well understood. What is "understood," however, is their "Indianness," their status as "things that happen elsewhere," which in turn suggests that they are unlike "things that happen here."

This effect is only compounded by the fact that there is little "coverage" or information in the United States about the general issue of domestic violence as it affects women in India, and by the fact that reports about dowry-deaths are seldom framed in terms of the general issue of domestic violence.[11] Given that dowry-related domestic *harassment* is far more widespread in India than dowry-*murder*, and that non-dowry-related forms of domestic violence are likely the most widespread of all, this focus on dowry-murders as a paradigmatic case of "violence suffered by Indian women" is one that centers on the most "extreme" and "spectacular" forms of domestic violence suffered by Indian women. Domestic violence against Indian women thus becomes most widely known in Western contexts in its most *extreme incarnation*, underlining its " Otherness."

The "alien" features of "burning" and "dowry" help to further code the phenomenon as "Indian" and "Other" and intersect to expunge any trace of the phenomenon's connection to the more "familiar" domestic category of "domestic violence." Consider the possible effects on Western understandings of dowry-murder of the "lurid exoticism" of fire and of women being burnt to death. Given the lack of contextual information, Indian women's murder-by-fire seems mysterious, possibly ritualistic, and one of those factors that is assumed to have something to do with "Indian culture." While the use of fire as the pre-ferred instrument of dowry-murder does have much to do with details of the Indian context, these details are less "cultural" and "exotic," and more mundane and material, than they are often assumed to be.

Pointing out that fire is chiefly chosen for "the forensic advantage" it has over other methods of killing a wife, Veena Talwar Oldenburg goes on to say:

> It virtually destroys the evidence of murder along with the victim and can easily be made to look like an accident. It is also relatively simple to commit. It occurs in the kitchen, where the middle-class housewife spends a large amount of time each day. Pressurized kerosene stoves are in common use in such homes; a tin of fuel is always kept in reserve.

This can be quickly poured over the intended victim and a lighted match will do the rest. It is easy to pass off the event as an accident because these stoves are prone to explode (consumer reports confirm this), and the now ubiquitous but highly inflammable nylon sari easily catches fire and engulfs the wearer in flames. Signs of a struggle simply do not show up on bodies with 90 or more percent third-degree burns.[12]

Oldenburg's account underlines the fact that the use of fire as a murder weapon is far more a matter of expedience than it is a matter of exoticism. Burning a woman to death in the Indian context is no more "exotic" than shooting her to death is in the U.S. context. Conversely, death by shooting in a middle-class domestic context would be rather "exotic" in India, where firearms are not freely available and widely owned, and where widespread ownership of firearms and the prevalence of gun-related violence is often perceived of as "typically American."

I believe that the "exoticizing" features I have mentioned above have both contributed to dowry-murder's popularity as a border-crossing issue and have contributed to popular misunderstandings of the issue. In addition, I also believe that such misunderstandings are facilitated by the fact that certain kinds of "contextual information" are often left behind when issues cross national borders. For example, many Indians have sufficient "contextual information" to know that dowry-murders are just one extreme and specific form of domestic violence directed against Indian women. They are likely to know that mistreatment and harassment of Indian daughters-in-law by their marital families is widespread, that many women are harassed over dowry-related reasons even when they are not murdered, and that Indian women are also abused and mistreated for a range of reasons that have nothing to do with dowry. They are also likely to know that dowry-murders seem to be a fairly *recent* phenomenon that seem to have come into "systematic" existence in the last three decades, and that seem to be on the increase.

When the issue of dowry-murders "crosses national borders" and becomes "known" in Western national contexts as an "issue affecting Indian women," it becomes known "out of context" because many Westerners lack these forms of "contextual information." In traveling across national borders unaccompanied by such contextual information, "dowry-murder" loses its links to the category of "domestic violence" and becomes transmuted into some sort of bizarre "Indian ritual," a form of violence against women that surely must be "caused by Indian culture." The category "Indian culture" then becomes the diffuse culprit responsible for "women being burned to death everyday in India," producing the effect that I call "death by culture." [. . .]

While the factual weight of the information testifies to the "reality of the problem," the references to "culture" commonplace in these reports serves to "render intelligible" everything that might otherwise remain "puzzling" to the audience. Thus, while many Western readers might not know exactly what dowry is, or the factors that lead to dowry-murders, or the exact nature of the relationship of either dowry or dowry-murder to "Indian culture," the presence of references to "Indian culture" can provide a swift and convenient "explanation" for what they do not understand. The references to "culture" in these reports can then combine with more "free-floating" ideas of "Third-World backwardness" and the tendency to think of Third-World contexts as realms of "Very Other Cultures" to make "foreign phenomenon" seem comfortingly intelligible while preserving their "foreignness." Members of the Western audience are often left "feeling solidly informed," with nothing "in the picture" that suggests any need to re-examine the picture.

I am suggesting that the "distortions" that occur when "Third-World issues" cross over into Western national contexts are not reducible to "ethnocentrism" or "racism." While forms of ethnocentric and stereotypic thinking about "the Third World" do play a part in the perpetuation of such "distortions," there are also other different factors at work. One has to attend to the "multiple mediations" that occur between: (1) the ways in which "related" issues have been shaped in Western national contexts; (2) the "life" these issues have in Third-World national contexts, where their coverage and reception occur in a

space where members of the national public have a variety of contextual information that puts such issues "in perspective"; and (3) the decontextualization and recontextualization that accompanies these issues on their travels across national borders.

Critical attention to the complexities of the "multiple mediations" that work to "shape" issues in different national contexts, and to "filter" the information that crosses national borders, is vital to all of us who are participants in the project of making both academic curricula and feminist agendas more responsive to "Third-World issues" or problems affecting "Other women." Multicultural education cannot be seen as a simple task of replacing "ignorance about Other cultures" with "knowledge," since problems of the sort I am talking about are precisely not problems of "ignorance" per se, but problems related to understanding the "effects" of contexts on issues, and of decontextualized, refracted, and reframed "knowledge." These features of "context" as well as of decontextualization and refraction are, by their very nature, difficult to see and to call attention to, as are their "effects."

Such difficulties complicate the project of "understanding Other cultures." I would like to insist that they cannot be "solved" by simply "deploying" Third-World subjects familiar with the articulation of these issues in specific Third-World contexts to "point out" the distortions and problems that occur as a result of these border-crossing "mediations." While Third-World subjects who are familiar with the representations of an issue in both a Third-World and a Western national context might well have a sense of some of the distortions and misrepresentations that occur as a result of "border-crossing," it is hardly *easy* for them to develop a fine-grained sense of the ways in which various "mediations" on particular issues collaborate and cohere to create the widely shared misunderstandings that shape the understanding of the issue in a Western national context.

It has not been a simple task for me to figure out exactly what many Americans "don't seem to get" about dowry-murders, or the structures that might facilitate such "not getting." And this sort of task of "figuring out" what isn't "getting across" seems inevitably a messy, provisional, and uncertain business. One relies on particular encounters and conversations, the impressions and hunches one develops as a result, and a strange assortment of information, impression, and speculation. And, as I mentioned earlier, there is a variety of difficulties in trying to figure out how to "get across" what particular individuals may not "be getting." In short, I am fairly pessimistic about any "quick fixes" for these sorts of problems of informational "border-crossings."

DOWRY-MURDERS AND THE LIMITS AND LIMITATIONS OF "CULTURAL" EXPLANATIONS

In this section, I would like to move on to exploring the ways in which "culture" is deployed in explanations of dowry-murders in India and to point out the problems with some of these attempts at "cultural explanation." In doing so, I wish to lead up to thinking about why "Indian culture" is invoked in explanations for dowry-murders in ways in which "American culture" is not usually invoked in explanations for either U.S. domestic violence, in general, or for "domestic-violence murders" in the United States.

What I am calling "cultural explanations" of dowry-murders all too frequently invoke "Hindu religious views on women." I shall begin with an example that helps vividly underline what is problematic about such religious "cultural explanations" of dowry-murder. The example I shall use is a chapter from Elizabeth Bumiller's book, *May You Be the Mother of a Hundred Sons: A Journey Among the Women of India*. I choose this example not because this text is uniquely problematic, but because this is a book whose covers carry glowing review blurbs from *Newsweek, The New York Times Book Review*, and the *Philadelphia Inquirer*, all indicating that the book was a "national bestseller." It is a book I have seen in several bookstores, including the bookstore of the college where I teach, and it is a book that a friend of Indian background reports having several copies of, presented to her by friends. In short, I pick it only because it seems to have had a more significant

public presence and influence than most "academic" writing, and not because there are no "scholarly" examples of these same problems.

The third chapter in Bumiller's book is (alas all too predictably) entitled "Flames: A Bride Burning and a *Sati*." Opening with the line, "When Hindus look at fire, they see many things beyond flames," Bumiller's first paragraph goes on to describe the use of fire in several Hindu ceremonies and rites of passage.[13] The second paragraph opens with the line, "Fire is also a special presence in the lives of Hindu women" and launches into a narration of the mythological story of Sita throwing herself into a fire to prove her chastity to her husband Rama, in the Hindu epic the *Ramayana*, a story that is continued and concluded in the third paragraph.[14]

The fourth paragraph goes on to say:

> Sita's ordeal has left an indelible mark on the relationship of women to fire, which remains a major feature of their spiritual lives, a cause of their death and a symbol, in the end, of one of the most shocking forms of oppression. What follows is the story of two Indian women, Surinder Kaur and Roop Kanwar, both of them victims of fire and Hindu tradition.[15]

Let me briefly point to several problems with this "framing" of Bumiller's chapter. The mythological story of Sita, which has occupied two paragraphs, is a story about Sita *proving her chastity through an ordeal by fire*, and its deployment in this chapter is completely gratuitous, given that the Sita story is an instance of neither *sati* nor dowry-murder. Further, given that one of the two Indian women mentioned in the quote above, Roop Kanwar, was a victim of *sati*, and that the other, Surinder Kaur, is a survivor of an attempted *dowry-murder*, they are hardly victims of "one" form of oppression, as Bumiller claims. Bumiller's failure to make a clear distinction between *sati* and dowry-murder operates as yet one more example of the tedious "metonymic blurring" of completely unrelated phenomena having to do with "burning Indian women" I have previously discussed, a blurring whose ubiquitousness accounts for the headache that sets in when I read essays that start with sentences like "Women are being burnt to death everyday in India."

Bumiller also characterizes both women as "victims of Hindu tradition," a characterization that creates different kinds of problems with respect to *sati* and to dowry-murder. *Sati*, the immolation of a widow on her husband's funeral pyre, used to be a "traditional practice" in *some* Indian communities, and was the "exceptional" rather than the "routine" fate of widows even in these communities. Its endorsement by "Hinduism" has been a matter of debate for centuries, and incidents of *sati* have occurred only very rarely in the last half-century. Bumiller terms *sati* a "Hindu tradition" without specifying its contested and tenuous status qua "Hindu tradition," and her subsequent discussion of feminist protests triggered by the Roop Kanwar incident fails to emphasize the degree to which *sati*'s alleged status as a "Hindu tradition" was itself an important site of feminist contestation. Dowry-murder is, in contrast, neither Hindu nor a tradition, even in the "qualified" sense in which *sati* might be so characterized. Even in cases where it is Hindu women who are murdered for dowry, Hinduism neither endorses or condones such murders, allusions to Sita notwithstanding. Dowry-murder can hardly amount to the victimization of Indian women by "Hindu tradition" when there is no such tradition of burning women to death for dowry. In addition, the institution of dowry is not a Hindu institution in at least two important ways. Dowry is not a pan-Hindu practice, given that there are Hindu communities, such as the matrilineal Nair community of Kerala, where dowry was traditionally unknown. It is also a practice that exists within some non-Hindu Indian communities, as Surinder Kaur's case reveals.

Surinder Kaur, who is first invoked by Bumiller as a woman who survived an alleged attempted burning by her husband and sister-in-law, is a Sikh, and not a Hindu. While Bumiller mentions that Surinder Kaur is a Sikh, in the very next paragraph and several times later in the chapter, she seems not to notice its implications. None of the fire-related Hindu ceremonies and rituals that Bumiller thinks testify to the "special relationship" that Hindus and Hindu women have to fire, nor the Hindu mythological story of Sita that Bumiller uses to frame her discussion, are related to Surinder Kaur's own religious background. While Surinder Kaur may have been the victim of fire, she could hardly have been the victim of a Hindu tradition as Bumiller insists, given that she is a Sikh! Few Western readers are likely to unravel themselves from the trail of confusion whereby, in two pages, references to Hindu ceremonies, Sita, and *sati* collaborate to construct dowry-murder as "Indian women's victimization by Hindu tradition" to register the oddity of a Sikh woman being victimized by Hindu tradition, or to register the fact that dowry-murder is neither Hindu nor a tradition!

Quite apart from Bumiller's chapter, I would argue that references to Hindu religion, mythology, and "tradition" make very poor explanations for dowry-murders, since dowry-murders have not been a widespread social phenomenon before the late 1970s. Hindu myths and traditions have been around considerably longer. It is therefore hard to see that they have serious explanatory value with respect to the contemporary phenomenon of dowry-murders. Notwithstanding the contemporary nature of dowry-murders, many discussions on the subject besides Bumiller's tend to be replete with references to Hindu mythology and to texts such as the *Vedas* and the Laws of Manu, which are separated by centuries from the problem they are used to "explain."[16] The tendency to explain contemporary Indian women's problems by reference to religious views is by no means a tendency exclusive to Western writers, but crops up quite frequently in writings by contemporary Indians. In a context where she is talking about both dowry and dowry-murders, Sushila Mehta asserts, "If the scriptures propound that a woman is a man's property, it is axiomatic that a woman has less value than a man. To compensate she must, therefore, bring something of value along with herself for her husband and his people taking the trouble of marrying her!"[17]

Mehta's discussion exemplifies a common tendency to muddle together discussions of dowry (a traditional practice in some Indian communities) with discussions of dowry-murders (neither a traditional practice nor a historical phenomenon of long standing.) Such muddling frequently results in a failure to register that what the scriptures propound may have little explanatory power with respect to the more contemporary of the two phenomenon, dowry-murders, even where they have some connection to the traditional practice of dowry. (I also believe that Mehta misrepresents the institution of dowry, a point I will return to.) I wish to argue that Mehta's discussion is only a very mild example of a "problematic genre" of work on India and Indian culture, written by Indians. Such work frequently equates Indian culture to Hindu culture, Hindu culture to Hindu religious views, and Hindu religious views to views propounded in various Hindu scriptures, without any registering of how extremely problematic every step in this equation is.[18] [. . .]

Given that dowry-murders are a *contemporary* phenomenon, . . . I believe that a plausible explanation for dowry-murders must refer to the significant changes that the institution of dowry has undergone in recent decades, changes that have rendered it murderous. [. . .]

In the "explanations" that generate "death by culture," religious views or "traditional values" often become virtually synonymous with "culture." While the institution of dowry can certainly be meaningfully connected to "Indian culture" it is not, I think, given a satisfactory "explanation" by references to "religion." The fact that, for instance, the Laws of Manu (dating to the turn of the Christian era) endorse marriage involving dowry over other forms of marriage, such as marriage by capture or marriage involving bride-price, does little to illuminate the varying considerations about property and inheritance that have undoubtedly contributed to the continuous historical life of this institution.

I do think there are interesting questions (which I am not in the least equipped to answer) about why the institution of dowry has existed in some Indian communities and not in others, and as to why it has persisted in Indian communities when it has disappeared from those Western contexts where it historically existed. While I believe answers to these questions would make reference to many material, social, and cultural aspects of the Indian context, "religious views" alone would hardly suffice as explanation. In addition, while explanations for Indian women's vulnerability to dowry-murder might meaningfully refer to some aspects of "culture," such as underlying marriage and family arrangements that contribute to women's powerlessness, neither dowry-murders nor women's vulnerability to dowry-murder seem explainable as simply the outcome of adherence to a specific set of "religious" views.[19] [. . .]

DIFFERENCES OF "CULTURE" AND DIFFERENCES IN "CULTURE AS EXPLANATION"

I would like to end by considering an interesting asymmetry that exists between explanations of violence against women in "mainstream Western culture" and such "death by culture" explanations of violence against women specific to "Third-World cultural contexts." The best way I can think of to point to this asymmetry is the following kind of "thought experiment," which is also a kind of wicked fantasy whose "fantastical" elements are actually more interesting than its wickedness. Imagine yourself meeting a young Indian woman journalist who, after reading Bumiller's book, has decided to retaliate by working on a book entitled, *May You Be the Loser of A Hundred Pounds: A Journey Among the Women of the United States.* The young journalist plans to travel throughout the United States talking to an assortment of American women, trying to learn about "American women and American culture." The chapters she hopes to include in her book include vignettes on American women suffering from eating disorders; American women in weight-loss programs; American women who have undergone liposuctions, breast implants, and other types of cosmetic surgery; American women victims of domestic violence; American women in politics, and American women media stars.[20]

Ask yourself, "What are the structures of knowledge-production and information-circulation that make this book as difficult to imagine as it is impossible to find?" What are the factors that make it unlikely for a young Indian woman to conceive of such a project?[21] What is the likelihood of such a project being taken seriously enough to warrant the various forms of interest that are necessary to enable such a book to be written and published (in the United States *or* in India)? How likely is this book to be considered a serious source of information on "American culture" by the general public, or to appear on the reading list of any course on American culture? How likely is the book to receive reviews that credit the author with having "made the United States new and immediate again" and with being an "Eastern writer who has actually discovered the United States?"[22] What are the factors that make this imaginary book implausible and allow us to feel quite certain that there is no such book?

Pursuing my point about "cultural explanation," I shall continue with my fantasy, and go on to imagine how some of the contours of this Indian journalist's book on "women in American culture" would differ from Bumiller's Indian counterpart. I shall concentrate on her attempts to write the chapter linking domestic violence to American culture. Our intrepid Indian journalist would find it difficult, if not impossible, to account for many "American cultural phenomena" by references to Christian doctrines, myths, and practices. While "Christian values" have probably coexisted with domestic violence, fatal and nonfatal, in the United States much longer than "Hinduism" has coexisted with dowry-murder, one doubts that our journalist would be inclined, either on her own or as a result of her conversations with most Americans, to explain contemporary domestic violence in terms of Christian views about women's sinful nature, Eve's role in the Fall, the sanctity of marriage and the family, or the like.

Permit me to imagine the interesting difficulties that would confront our imaginary journalist as she attempted to write this chapter on "domestic violence and American culture." It just doesn't seem plausible, she has realized, to attempt an explanatory link between the two terms "domestic violence" and "American culture" through references to Christianity. How else, she wonders, is she to link the two terms,

enabling her discussion of domestic violence in the United States to illuminate "American culture?" Much of the U.S. literature on domestic violence turns out not very helpful for her particular project, since most of the accounts they give explain the phenomenon in terms of a "non-nation-specific, secularized, general patriarchy," that seems no more distinctively "American" than it is "Christian."

She will find criticisms, most notably by U.S. feminists of color, that the underlying picture of "patriarchy" at work in many U.S. accounts of domestic-violence is often overly generalized. She may find the article where Kimberle Crenshaw argues that strands in U.S. domestic violence discourse have "transformed the message that battering is not *exclusively* a problem of poor or minority communities into a claim that it *equally* affects all classes and races,"[23] and that such views impede attention to the specific needs of battered women of color.[24] She will find that Crenshaw argues that women of color suffer disproportionately higher unemployment, lack of job skills, and discriminatory employment and housing practices, that make it harder for them to leave abusive relationships.[25] She will learn that factors such as being non-English speaking and having an immigration status that is dependent on marriage to the abuser further work to disempower a number of battered women of color in the United States.[26] Through such work, the journalist may develop a better understanding of how American class and race structures, and the outcomes of U.S. immigration policies, affect victims of domestic violence in the United States. She will recognize, however, that such references to features of the American context seem quite different from the sorts of "religious" references to "Indian culture" Bumiller's chapter introduction uses to explain *sati* and dowry-murders.

Among the things she will learn in her readings and conversations are that American men batter their partners for "reasons" that range from sexual jealousy, alcoholism, stress, and pure unmitigated rage, to the desire to control the woman or to "prevent her leaving." She will learn that economic dependency, worries about the custody and welfare of children, low self-esteem due to abuse, and the threats and violence that have followed upon previous attempts at leaving are often given as reasons for American women staying in abusive relationships. With the possible exception of "low self-esteem,"[27] these sorts of reasons will seem similar to those that work to keep Indian women in abusive marriages, though they are often eclipsed in explanations that rely on elements such as Hindu mythology or the status of women in the Laws of Manu. She will notice that in U.S. accounts of domestic violence the sorts of reasons mentioned above appear to provide explanation enough, and that there is no felt need to explain why domestic violence in America is "American." None of this, she realizes, is helping her write a chapter that easily links U.S. domestic violence to "American culture."

Suddenly, she has a flash of inspiration! "Guns," she exclaims to herself, "gun-related domestic violence against women is what my chapter should be about. That will provide the tie into 'American culture' I have been looking for, since guns are so quintessentially 'American.' I need to find out how many women are injured annually by guns and how seriously, and how many of these injuries are inflicted by domestic partners. I need to find out how many domestic shooting incidents are claimed to be 'accidents' and how often there is good reason to doubt that they are. I need to find out how many American women are murdered annually by guns, and how many of them by their partners. Finding this information might help me depict guns as an 'icon' of violence against U.S. women, just as 'fire' seems to have become an icon of violence against Indian women."

What our imaginary Indian journalist might run up against as she tries to write this improbable chapter is revealing. Guns and lack of gun control, she will find in her conversations with Americans, are often acknowledged to be fairly distinctively "American" problems. However, in her attempts to relate gun-related violence to women and domestic violence, she will find that gun control and gun-related violence have not widely emerged specifically as "women's issues" or "domestic-violence issues." The journalist will run into difficulties as she tries to find "official data" on the "numbers of U.S. women killed and/or injured by guns in acts of domestic violence." If she starts with sources that have data on domestic violence, she will find figures for the numbers of U.S. women killed and for women injured in acts of domestic violence, but she will find that the sources do not specify how many of these deaths or injuries were gun-related. She will discover that it is not easy to figure out how many of the roughly 1,400 American women known to be killed annually by their partners were killed by guns. When she turns to data on gun-related violence, she will find similar problems. While it is fairly easy to find out that seven out of every ten American murders involved guns, it is less easy to find out whether seven out of ten murders *of women* involved guns. Figures for gun-related murders, she will find, do not often specify how many of these murders were domestic-violence related. While the data on the "handgun victimization rate" (which excludes murder and manslaughter) are broken down by sex, race, and age, they do not often specify how much of the "handgun victimization" suffered by U.S. women is domestic-violence related.[28]

In short, she will predominantly find that figures pertaining to U.S. domestic violence do not specifically focus on guns, and that data on gun-related violence in the U.S. lacks specific attention to domestic violence. The intersection between "domestic violence suffered by U.S. women" and "American gun-related violence"—which would be the space of "domestic violence against American women mediated by the use of guns"—seems not to be well marked either as an "American" or as a "women's" issue. If she eventually finds the data, she will be struck by the fact that although the majority of women murdered by partners are in fact murdered with firearms, gun control has not emerged strongly as a U.S. feminist issue or even as a "visible" issue in much of the literature on domestic violence.[29] The journalist will discover that her idea about linking "domestic violence" to "American culture" by focusing on gun-related violence against women is not a project easy to carry out, since the two issues seem not to be frequently connected by those engaged with gun-control issues or domestic-violence agendas.

She might, however, acquire some interesting "cross-cultural insights" as a result of her frustrations. She might come to see that while Indian women repeatedly suffer "death by culture" in a range of scholarly and popular works, even as the elements of "culture" proffered do little to explain their deaths, American women seem relatively immune to such analyses of "death or injury by culture" even as they are victimized by the fairly distinctively American phenomenon of wide-spread gun-related violence.

Given these difficulties, it is perhaps for the best that this is an imaginary chapter in an improbable book. I would like to end with the suggestion that books that cannot be written and chapters that are oddly difficult to write might have more to teach us about particular cultures and their relationships to "Other cultures" than many books and chapters that face few difficulties in being either imagined or written.

NOTES

1. Mary Fainsod Katzenstein, "Organizing Against Violence: Strategies of the Indian Women's Movement," *Pacific Affairs* 62, 1 (Spring 1989), p. 61.

2. Ibid.

3. From "Discussion Forum: From the Commission on the Status of Women in India to the End of the Women's Decade: Some Personal Reflections," *Samya Shakti* 2, 1 (1985), p. 80.

4. Katzenstein, "Organizing Against Violence: Strategies of the Indian Women's Movement," p. 54.

5. Katzenstein points out that the Delhi-based group, Saheli, "concerned itself particularly with issues of dowry and domestic violence" and that the Bombay-based Forum against Oppression of Women took up issues of police rape and dowry-murders. See "Organizing Against Violence," *Pacific Affairs* (1989), pp. 56–57.

6. For details, see Mary Fainsod Katzenstein, "Organizing Against Violence," pp. 57–58.

7. Madhu Kishwar, "Why I Do Not Call Myself a Feminist," *Manushi* 61 (Nov./Dec. 1990).

8. Madhu Kishwar, "Why I Do Not Call Myself a Feminist," p. 5.

9. Ibid., p. 6.

10. It is interesting to note that feminist groups in many diasporic South Asian communities in Western national contexts have organized shelters for battered women in their communities. For instance, there are shelters organized and operated by South Asian women in New Jersey and in Chicago.

11. While the Indian journal *Manushi* does cover general issues of domestic violence in India, I do not think it makes much difference at the level of popular U.S. public understanding.

12. Veena Talwar Oldenburg, "Dowry Murders in India: A Preliminary Examination of the Historical Evidence," in *Women's Lives and Public Policy: The International Experience*, Meredeth Turshen and Briavel Holcomb, eds. (Westport, Conn.: Greenwood Press, 1993), p. 146.

13. Elizabeth Bumiller, *May You Be the Mother of a Hundred Sons: A Journey Among the Women of India* (New York: Fawcett Columbine, 1990), p. 44.

14. Bumiller, *May You Be the Mother of a Hundred Sons*, p. 45.

15. Ibid.

16. Some of these works are "general discussions of women in Indian culture" that situate "Hindu religious doctrines" at the center of their "analysis of Indian culture" and mention dowry and dowry-murders "in passing," more or less as "examples of the effects of Hindu religious views on women's well-being." Others center their discussions on dowry and dowry-murder, and then deploy very many of the same elements of "Hindu religious doctrine" in ways that suggest they are "explanations" for dowry-murders.

17. Sushila Mehta, *Revolution and the Status of Women in India* (New Delhi: Metropolitan Book Co., 1982), p. 208.

18. Arguing that "there has been an overemphasis on the mystical and religious aspects of Indian society," Martha Nussbaum and Amartya Sen go on to add: "The image of the 'mystical East,' and specifically India, is not a matter only of popular conception but has a good deal of following in the typical Indologist's summary view of Indian intellectual history. In this respect there is also no real gulf between the things that the Western scholars have typically tended to emphasize in Indian culture and what Indian Indologists have themselves most often highlighted. This close correspondence may not, however, be particularly remarkable, since approaches to 'cultural summarizing' are generally quite 'infectious,' and, no less importantly, modern Indian scholarship is greatly derivative from the West." Martha C. Nussbaum and Amartya Sen, "Internal Criticism and Indian Rationalist Traditions," in *Relativism: Interpretation and Confrontation*, Michael Krauz, ed. (Notre Dame, Ind.: University of Notre Dame Press, 1989),

pp. 301–303. I argue that the "general picture" of "Indian culture" they point to seems to have problematic effects on social science explanations of Indian phenomena. I would also add that writings by Indians on "Indian culture" tend, in turn, to be assimilated into "Western scholarship" on India—whereby, for instance, Sushila Mehta's views on dowry and dowry-murder "reappear" in works by Western feminists on "Indian women's issues."

19. I also have problems with a different kind of "cultural explanation," quite common in Indian discussions of these issues, that sees the institution of dowry as the "central culprit" in dowry-murders. Let me try to explain my problem. Dowry has been illegal since the Dowry Prohibition Act of 1961. The Act outlaws dowry, defined as "the property a woman brings to her husband at marriage," and coercive demands for dowry. It does not prohibit either "gifts to the groom's family" that are of a "customary nature," or the giving of property to the daughter herself, thereby providing two clear loopholes that make the Act virtually impossible to apply. I am increasingly unsure whether the inefficacy of this law in prohibiting dowry is entirely a bad thing. If successful, it might prevent a great many women from receiving their "traditional" share of parental property, without necessarily ensuring that they get any share at all. Even if dowry prohibition was combined with a law that gave women rights to a full post-mortem share of parental property, there is little guarantee that many women might not be cheated out of it by brothers and male kin. Besides, while a successful prohibition of dowry would certainly prevent some women being killed, it may also leave many others without the margin of economic security dowry provides during their marriage. Dowryless women may be safe from dowry-murder but may be less empowered in having no assets of their own until their parents' death, leaving them more vulnerable when they confront other forms of harassment during those years.

20. Yes, this roughly approximates the range of topics on "Indian women" found in Bumiller's book.

21. I leave these questions unanswered in part because I think the answers are complicated and would require a great deal more thought and reflection than I can give them at this time.

22. Yes, Bumiller's book *did* receive reviews corresponding to these quotes!

23. Kimberle Crenshaw, "Intersectionality and Identity Politics: Learning from Violence Against Women of Color," in *Reconstructing Political Theory: Feminist Perspectives*, Mary L. Shanley and Uma Narayan, eds., forthcoming from Polity Press.

24. She may also find mention of a different problem, whereby greater incidence of wife assault among blue-collar workers, the unemployed, and the partially employed, as well as among African Americans and Hispanic Americans, results in "the popular explanation that these subcultures have proviolence norms." Daniel G. Saunders, "Husbands Who Assault: Multiple Profiles Requiring Multiple Responses," in *Legal Responses to Wife Assault: Current Trends and Evaluation*, edited by N. Zoe Hilton (Newbury Park, Cal.: Sage Publications, 1993), p. 12. Saunders goes on to argue against this view. However, it does point out the degree to which problems within minority racial or ethnic communities in the United States are more likely to receive explanations in terms of specific "*cultural* pathologies" that differ from the kinds of "general explanations" given for domestic violence.

25. Crenshaw, "Intersectionality and Identity Politics."

26. See both Crenshaw and Nancy Hirschman's "The Theory and Practice of Freedom: The Case of Battered Women," in *Reconstructing Political Theory: Feminist Perspectives*.

27. Initially, discourses about "self-esteem" and "low self-esteem" struck me as quite American and less likely to be deployed in the Indian context. But considering how rapidly ideas from Western contexts are "exported" to Third-World countries, I now do not feel sure about this.

28. I am not claiming that these statistics are *unavailable*—just that they have proved very *difficult* for myself, and even for others more skilled at locating empirical data, to find.

29. Thanks to my colleague Marque Miringoff, I eventually did find data that indicates that 69 percent of wives and ex-wives and 60 percent of girlfriends killed by intimates were killed by firearms in "Violence between Intimates," *Bureau of Justice Statistics, Selected Findings*, U.S. Department of Justice, November 1994. I also found data that indicated that 42 percent of all family murder victims were killed by firearms, and that 53 percent of spousal murder victims died from gun shots in "Murder in Families," *Bureau of Justice Statistics, Special Report*, Washington, D.C., July 1994.

Study Questions

1. Narayan argues that two central problems beset Western feminists' attempts to learn about other cultures. One involves "national context" and the other, imputations of "death by culture." Explain each of these problems.

2. Provide another example (other than dowry murder) of Westerners' (mis)interpretation of happenings in a non-Western country that evidences failure to take into account adequately national context and/or exhibits imputations of death by culture.

3. How does Narayan think that Western feminists can avoid such problems?

Linda Alcoff

The Problem of Speaking for Others

Consider the following true stories:

1. Anne Cameron, a very gifted white Canadian author, writes several first person accounts of the lives of Native Canadian women. At the 1988 International Feminist Book Fair in Montreal, a group of Native Canadian writers asks Cameron to, in their words, "move over" on the grounds that her writings are disempowering for indigenous authors. She agrees (Maracle 1989).

2. After Manuel Noriega overturns the 1989 elections in Panama U.S. President George Bush declares in a public address that Noriega's actions constitute an "outrageous fraud" and that "the voice of the Panamanian people have spoken. . . . The Panamanian people want democracy and not tyranny, and want Noriega out." He proceeds to plan the invasion of Panama.

3. At a recent symposium at my university, a prestigious theorist was invited to lecture on the political problems of postmodernism. The audience, which includes many white women and people of oppressed nationalities and races, waits in eager anticipation for his contribution to this important discussion. To the audience's disappointment, he introduces his lecture by explaining that he cannot cover the assigned topic because as a white male he does not feel that he can speak for the feminist and postcolonial perspectives that have launched the critical interrogation of postmodernism's politics. Instead he lectures on architecture.

These examples demonstrate the range of current practices of speaking for others in our society. While the prerogative of speaking for others remains unquestioned in the citadels of colonial administration, among activists and in the academy it elicits a growing unease and, in some communities of discourse, it is being rejected. There is a strong, albeit contested, current within feminism which holds that speaking for others—even for other women—is arrogant, vain, unethical, and politically illegitimate. Feminist scholarship has a liberatory agenda that almost requires that women scholars speak on behalf of other women; yet the dangers of speaking across differences of race, culture, sexuality, and power are becoming increasingly clear. Articles and letters in which the author states that she can only speak for herself are commonly found in feminist magazines such as *Sojourner*. In her important essay, "Dyke Methods," Joyce Trebilcot offers a philosophical articulation of this view. She renounces for herself the practice of speaking for others within a lesbian feminist community, arguing that she "will not try to get other wimmin to accept my beliefs in place of their own" on the grounds that to do so would be to practice a kind of discursive coercion and even a violence" (1).[1]

Linda M. Alcoff, "The Problem of Speaking for Others," *Cultural Critique* (Winter 1991–92): 5–32. Copyright 1991–2 by the University of Minnesota Press. Reprinted by permission of the publisher.

Feminist discourse is not the only site in which the problem of speaking for others has been acknowledged and addressed. In anthropology there is similar discussion about whether it is possible to speak for others either adequately or justifiably. Trinh T. Minh-hà explains the grounds for skepticism when she says that anthropology is "mainly a conversation of 'us' with 'us' about 'them,' of the white man with the white man about the primitive-nature man . . . in which 'them' is silenced. 'Them' always stands on the other side of the hill, naked and speechless . . . 'them' is only admitted among 'us,' the discussing subjects, when accompanied or introduced by an 'us'" (65, 67).[2] Given this analysis, even ethnographies written by progressive anthropologists are a priori regressive because of the structural features of anthropological discursive practice.

The recognition that there is a problem in speaking for others has followed from the widespread acceptance of two claims. First, there has been a growing awareness that where an individual speaks from affects both the meaning and truth of what she says and thus she cannot assume an ability to transcend her location. In other words, a speaker's location (which I take here to refer to her *social* location or social identity) has an epistemically significant impact on that speaker's claims and can serve either to authorize or de-authorize her speech. Women's studies and African American studies departments were founded on this very belief: that both the study of and the advocacy for the oppressed must be done principally by the oppressed themselves and that we must finally acknowledge that systematic divergences in social location between speakers and those spoken for will have a significant effect on the content of what is said. The unspoken premise is simply that a speaker's location is epistemically salient. I shall explore this issue further in the next section.

The second claim holds that not only is location epistemically salient but certain privileged locations are discursively dangerous.[3] In particular, the practice of privileged persons speaking for or on behalf of less privileged persons has actually resulted (in many cases) in increasing or reinforcing the oppression of the group spoken for. This was part of the argument made against Anne Cameron's speaking for indigenous women: Cameron's intentions were never in question, but the effects of her writing were argued to be harmful to the needs of indigenous authors because it is Cameron rather than they who will be listened to and whose books will be bought by readers interested in indigenous women. Persons from dominant groups who speak for others are often treated as authenticating presences that confer legitimacy and credibility on the demands of subjugated speakers; such speaking for others does nothing to disrupt the discursive hierarchies that operate in public spaces. For this reason, the work of privileged authors who speak on behalf of the oppressed is becoming increasingly criticized by members of those oppressed groups.[4]

As social theorists, we are authorized by virtue of our academic positions to develop theories that express and encompass the ideas, needs, and goals of others. We must begin to ask ourselves whether this is ever a legitimate authority, and if so, what are the criteria for legitimacy? In particular, is it ever valid to speak for others who are unlike us or who are less privileged than us?

We might try to delimit this problem as only arising when a more privileged person speaks for a less privileged one. In this case, we might say that I should only speak for groups of which I am a member. But this does not tell us how groups themselves should be delimited. For example, can a white woman speak for all women simply by virtue of being a woman? If not, how narrowly should we draw the categories? The complexity and multiplicity of group identifications could result in "communities" composed of single individuals. Moreover, the concept of groups assumes specious notions about clear-cut boundaries and "pure" identities. I am a Panamanian American and a person of mixed ethnicity and race: half white/Angla and half Panamanian mestiza. The criterion of group identity leaves many unanswered questions for a person such as myself, since I have membership in many conflicting groups but my membership in all of them is problematic. Group identities and boundaries are ambiguous and permeable, and decisions about demarcating identity are always partly arbitrary. Another problem concerns how specific an identity needs to be to confer epistemic authority. Reflection on such problems quickly reveals that no easy solution to the problem of speaking for others can be found by simply restricting the practice to speaking for groups of which one is a member.

Adopting the position that an individual should only speak for herself raises similarly difficult questions. If I don't speak for those less privileged than myself, am I abandoning my political responsibility to speak out against oppression, a responsibility incurred by the very fact of my privilege? If I should not speak for others, should I restrict myself to following their lead uncritically? Is my greatest contribution to *move over and get out of the way?* If so, what is the best way to do this—to keep silent or to deconstruct my own discourse?

The answers to these questions will certainly depend on who is asking them. While some of us may want to undermine, for example, the U.S. government's practice of speaking for the "third world," we may *not* want to undermine someone such as Rigoberta Menchu's ability to speak for Guatemalan Indians.[5] So the question arises about whether all instances of speaking for should be condemned and, if not, how we can justify a position that would repudiate some speakers while accepting others.

In order to answer these questions we need to become clearer on the epistemological and metaphysical issues involved in the articulation of the problem of speaking for others, issues that most often remain implicit. I will attempt to clarify these issues before discussing some of the possible responses to the problem and advancing a provisional, procedural solution of my own. But first I need to explain further my framing of the problem.

In the examples above, there may appear to be a conflation between the issue of speaking for others and the issue of speaking about others. This conflation was intentional on my part, because it is often difficult to distinguish speaking about from speaking for. There is an ambiguity in the two phrases: when A is speaking for B, A may be describing B's situation and thus also speaking about B. In fact, it may be impossible to speak for another without simultane-

ously conferring information about them. Similarly, when A is speaking about B, or simply trying to describe B's situation or some aspect of it, A may also be speaking in place of B, in other words, speaking for B. Thus, I would maintain that if the practice of speaking for others is problematic, so too must be the practice of speaking about others.[6] This is partly the case because of what has been called the "crisis of representation." For in both the practice of speaking for and the practice of speaking about others, I am engaging in the act of representing the other's needs, goals, situation, and in fact, *who they are*, based on my own situated interpretation. In poststructuralist terms, I am participating in the construction of their subject positions rather than simply discovering their true selves.

Once we pose it as a problem of representation, we see that, not only are speaking for and speaking about analytically close, so too are the practices of speaking for others and speaking for myself. For, in speaking for myself, I am also representing my self in a certain way, as occupying a specific subject position, having certain characteristics and not others, and so on. In speaking for myself, I (momentarily) create myself—just as much as when I speak for others I create them as a public, discursive self, a self that is more unified than any subjective experience can support. And this public self will in most cases have an effect on the self experienced as interiority.

The point here is that the problem of representation underlies all cases of speaking for, whether I am speaking for myself or for others. This is not to suggest that all representations are fictions: they have very real material effects, as well as material origins, but they are always mediated in complex ways by discourse, power, and location. However, the problem of speaking for others is more specific than the problem of representation generally and requires its own particular analysis.

There is one final point I want to make before we can pursue this analysis. The way I have articulated this problem may imply that individuals make conscious choices about their discursive practices free of ideology and the constraints of material reality. This is not what I wish to imply. The problem of speaking for others is a social one, the options available to us are socially constructed, and the practices we engage in cannot be understood as simply the results of autonomous individual choice. Yet to replace both "I" and "we" with a passive voice that erases agency results in an erasure of responsibility and accountability for one's speech, an erasure I would strenuously argue against (there is too little responsibility-taking already in Western practice!). When we sit down to write or stand up to speak, we experience ourselves as making choices. We may experience hesitation from fear of being criticized or from fear of exacerbating a problem we would like to remedy, or we may experience a resolve to speak despite existing obstacles, but in many cases we experience having the possibility to speak or not to speak. On the one hand, a theory that explains this experience as involving autonomous choices free of material structures would be false and ideological, but, on the other hand, if we do not acknowledge the activity of choice and the experience of individual doubt, we are denying a reality of our experiential lives.[7] So I see the argument of this chapter as addressing that small space of discursive agency we all experience, however multilayered, fictional, and constrained it in fact is.

Ultimately, the question of speaking for others bears crucially on the possibility of political effectivity. Both collective action and coalitions would seem to require the possibility of speaking for. Yet influential postmodernists such as Gilles Deleuze have characterized as "absolutely fundamental: the indignity of speaking for others" (209), and important feminist theorists have renounced the practice as irretrievably harmful. What is at stake in rejecting or validating speaking for others as a discursive practice? To answer this, we must come to understand more clearly the epistemological and metaphysical claims that are implicit in the articulation of the problem.

* * *

In this century, a plethora of sources have argued that the neutrality of the theorizer can no longer, can never again, be sustained, even for a moment. Critical theory, discourses of empowerment, psychoanalytic theory, poststructuralism, feminism, and anticolonialist theories have all concurred on this point. Who is speaking to whom turns out to be as important for meaning and truth as what is said; in fact what is said turns out to change according to who is speaking and who is listening. Following Michel Foucault, I will call these "rituals of speaking" to identify discursive practices of speaking or writing that involve not only the text or utterance but also their position within a social space that includes the persons involved in, acting upon, and/or affected by the words. Two elements within these rituals deserve our attention: the positionality or location of the speaker and the discursive context. The notion of a discursive context refers to the connections and relations of involvement between the utterance/text and other utterances and texts, as well as the material practices in the relevant environment, which should not be confused with an environment spatially adjacent to the particular discursive event.

Rituals of speaking are constitutive of the meaning of the words spoken as well as the meaning of the event. This claim requires us to shift the ontology of meaning from its location in a text or utterance to a larger space that includes the text or utterance as well as the discursive context. An important implication of this claim is that meaning must be understood as plural and shifting, since a single text can engender diverse meanings within diverse contexts. Not only what is emphasized, noticed, and how it is understood will be affected by the location of both speaker and hearer, but the truth-value or epistemic status will also be affected.

In many situations, for example, when a woman speaks the presumption is against her; when a man speaks he is usually taken seriously (unless his speech patterns mark him as socially inferior by dominant standards). When writers from oppressed races and nationalities have insisted that all writing is political, the claim has been dismissed as foolish or grounded in ressentiment or simply ignored; when prestigious European philosophers say that all writing is political, that statement is praised as a new and original "truth" (Judith Wilson calls this "the intellectual equivalent of the 'cover record' ").[8] The rituals of speaking, which involve the locations of speaker and listeners, affect whether a claim is taken as a true, well-reasoned, compelling argument or significant idea. Thus, how what is said gets heard depends on who says it and who says it will affect the style and language in which it is stated. The discursive style in which some European poststructuralists have claimed that all writing is political marks the claim as important and likely to be true for a certain (powerful) milieu, whereas the style in which African American writers made the same claim marked their speech as dismissable in the eyes of the same milieu.

This point might be conceded by those who admit to the political mutability of *interpretation*, but they might continue to maintain that *truth* is a different matter altogether. Moreover, they would be right that acknowledging the effect of location on meaning and even on whether something is *taken* as true within a particular discursive context does not entail that the "actual" truth of the claim is contingent upon its context. However, this objection presupposes a particular conception of truth, one in which the truth of a statement can be distinguished from its interpretation and acceptance. Such a concept would require truth to be independent of the speakers' or listeners' embodied and perspectival location. Thus, the question of whether location bears simply on what is taken to be true or what is really true, and whether such a distinction can be upheld, involves the very difficult problem of the meaning of truth. In the history of Western philosophy, there have existed multiple, competing definitions and ontologies of truth: correspondence, idealist, pragmatist, coherentist, and consensual notions. The dominant modernist view has been that truth represents a relationship of correspondence between a proposition and an extra-discursive reality. In this view, truth is about a realm completely independent of human action and expresses things "as they are in themselves," that is, free of human interpretation.

Arguably since Kant, more obviously since Hegel, it has been widely accepted that an understanding of truth that requires it to be free of human interpretation leads inexorably to skepticism, since it makes truth inaccessible by definition. This created an impetus to reconfigure the ontology of truth from a locus outside human interpretation to one within it. Hegel, for example, understood truth as an "identity in difference" between subjective and objective elements. Thus, in the Hegelian aftermath, so-called subjective elements, or the historically specific conditions in which human knowledge occurs, are no longer rendered irrelevant or even obstacles to truth.

In a coherentist account of truth, which is held by such philosophers as Richard Rorty, Donald Davidson, W. V. O. Quine, and (I would argue) Hans-Georg Gadamer and Michel Foucault, truth is defined as an emergent property of converging discursive and nondiscursive elements, when there exists a specific form of integration among these elements in a particular event. Such a view has no necessary relationship to idealism, but it allows us to understand how the social location of the speaker can be said to bear on truth. The speaker's location is one of the elements that converge to produce meaning and thus to determine epistemic validity.[9]

Let me return now to the formulation of the problem of speaking for others. There are two premises implied by the articulation of the problem, and unpacking these should advance our understanding of the issues involved.

> *Premise 1:* The "ritual of speaking" (as defined above) in which an utterance is located always bears on meaning and truth such that there is no possibility of rendering positionality, location, or context irrelevant to content.

The phrase "bears on" here should indicate some variable amount of influence short of determination or fixing.

One important implication of this first premise is that we can no longer determine the validity of a given instance of speaking for others simply by asking whether or not the speaker has done sufficient research to justify her claims. Adequate research will be a necessary but insufficient criterion of evaluation.

> *Premise 2:* All contexts and locations are differentially related in complex ways to structures of oppression. Given that truth is connected to politics, these political differences between locations will produce epistemic differences as well.

The claim in premise 2 that "truth is connected to politics" follows necessarily from premise 1. Rituals of speaking are politically constituted by power relations of domination, exploitation, and subordination. Who is speaking, who is spoken of, and who listens is a result, as well as an act, of political struggle. Simply put, the discursive context is a political arena. To the extent that this context bears on meaning, and meaning is in some sense the object of truth, we cannot make an epistemic evaluation of the claim without simultaneously assessing the politics of the situation.

Although we cannot maintain a neutral voice, according to the first premise we may at least all claim the right and legitimacy to speak. But the second premise suggests that some voices may be de-authorized on grounds that are simultaneously political and epistemic. Any statement will invoke the structures of power allied with the social location of the speaker, aside from the speaker's intentions or attempts to avoid such invocations.

The conjunction of premises 1 and 2 suggests that the speaker loses some portion of control over the meaning and truth of her utterance. Given that the context of listeners is partially determinant, the speaker is not the master or mistress of the situation. Speakers may seek to regain control by taking into account the context of their speech, but they can never know everything about this context. Moreover, with written and electronic communication it is becoming increasingly difficult to know anything at all about the context of reception.

This loss of control may be taken by some speakers to mean that no speaker can be held accountable for her discursive actions. The meaning of any discursive event will be shifting and plural, fragmented and even inconsistent. As it ranges over diverse spaces and transforms in the minds of its recipients according to their different horizons of interpretation, the effective control of the speaker over the meanings that she puts in motion may seem negligible. However, a *partial* loss of control does not entail a *complete* loss of accountability. Moreover, the better we understand the trajectories by which meanings proliferate, the more likely we can increase, though always only partially, our ability to direct the interpretations and transformations our speech undergoes. When I acknowledge that the listener's social location will affect the meaning of my words, I can more effectively generate the meaning I intend. Paradoxically, the view that holds the speaker or author of a speech act as solely responsible for its meanings ensures the speaker's least effective determinacy over the meanings that are produced.

We do not need to posit the existence of fully conscious acts or containable, fixed meanings in order to hold that speakers can alter their discursive practices and be held accountable for at least some of the effects of these practices. It is a false dilemma to pose the choice as one between no accountability or complete causal power.

*   *   *

In this section I shall consider some of the principal responses offered to the problem of speaking for others. First, I want to consider the argument that the very formulation of the problem with speaking for others involves a retrograde, metaphysically insupportable essentialism that assumes we can read off the truth and meaning of *what* we say straight from the discursive context. Let's call this response the "charge of reductionism," because it argues that a sort of reductionist theory of justification (or evaluation) is entailed by premises 1 and 2. Such a reductionist theory might, for example, reduce evaluation to a political assessment of the speaker's location where that location is seen as an insurmountable essence that fixes an individual, as if her feet are superglued to a spot on the sidewalk.

For instance, after I vehemently defended Barbara Christian's "The Race for Theory," a male friend who had a different evaluation of the piece couldn't help raising the possibility of whether a sort of apologetics structured my response, that I was motivated by a desire to valorize African American writing against all odds. In effect his question raised the issue of the reductionist/essentialist theory of justification that I have just described.

I, too, would reject reductionist theories of justification and essentialist accounts of what it means to have a location. To say that location *bears* on meaning and truth is not the same as saying that location *determines* meaning and truth. Location is not a fixed essence absolutely authorizing an individual's speech in the way that God's favor absolutely authorized the speech of Moses. Location and positionality should not be conceived as one-dimensional or static but as multiple and with varying degrees of mobility.[10] What it means, then, to speak from or within a group and/or a location is immensely complex. To the extent that location is not a fixed essence, and to the extent that there is an uneasy, underdetermined, and contested relationship between location on the one hand and meaning and truth on the other, we cannot reduce evaluation of meaning and truth to a simple identification of the speaker's location. Neither premise 1 nor premise 2 entail reductionism or essentialism. They argue for the relevance of location, not its singular power of determination, and they are noncommittal on how to construe the metaphysics of location.

While the "charge of reductionism" response has been popular among academic theorists, what I call the "retreat" response has been popular among some sections of the U.S. feminist movement. This response is simply to retreat from all practices of speaking for; it asserts that an individual can only know her own narrow individual experience and her "own truth" and thus that she can never make claims beyond this. This response is motivated in part by the desire to recognize difference and different priorities without organizing these differences into hierarchies.

Sometimes I think this is the proper response to the problem of speaking for others, depending on who is making it. We certainly want to encourage a more receptive listening on the part of the discursively privileged and to discourage presumptuous and oppressive practices of speaking for. The desire to retreat sometimes results from the desire to engage in political work but without practicing what might be called discursive imperialism. But a retreat from speaking for will not result in an increase in receptive listening in all cases; it may result merely in a retreat into a narcissistic yuppie lifestyle in which a privileged person takes no responsibility whatsoever for her society. She may even feel justified in exploiting

her privileged capacity for personal happiness at the expense of others on the grounds that she has no alternative.

The major problem with such a retreat is that it significantly undercuts the possibility of political effectivity. There are numerous examples of the practice of speaking for others that have been politically efficacious in advancing the needs of those spoken for, from Rigoberta Menchu to Edward Said and Steven Biko. Menchu's efforts to speak for the thirty-three Indian communities facing genocide in Guatemala have helped to raise money for the revolution and bring pressure against the Guatemalan and U.S. governments who have committed the massacres in collusion. The point is not that for some speakers the danger of speaking for others does not arise, but that in some cases certain political effects can be garnered in no other way.

Joyce Trebilcot's version of the retreat response acknowledges these political realities. She agrees that an absolute prohibition of speaking for would undermine political effectiveness and therefore says that she will avoid speaking for others only within her lesbian feminist community. So it might be argued that the retreat from speaking for others can be maintained without sacrificing political effectivity if it is restricted to particular discursive spaces. Why might we advocate such a partial retreat? Given that interpretations and meanings are discursive constructions made by embodied speakers, Trebilcot worries that attempting to persuade or speak for another will cut off that person's ability or willingness to engage in the constructive act of developing meaning. Since no embodied speaker can produce more than a partial account, and since the process of producing meaning is necessarily collective, everyone's account within a specified community needs to be encouraged.

I agree with a great deal of Trebilcot's argument. I certainly agree that in some instances speaking for others constitutes a violence and should be stopped. But Trebilcot's position, as well as a more general retreat position, presumes an ontological configuration of the discursive context that simply does not obtain. In particular, it assumes that an individual *can* retreat into her discrete location and make claims entirely and singularly within that location that do not range over others and, therefore, that an individual can disentangle herself from the implicating networks between her discursive practices and others' locations, situations, and practices. In other words, the claim that I can speak only for myself assumes the autonomous conception of the self in classical liberal theory—that I am unconnected to others in my authentic self or that I can achieve an autonomy from others given certain conditions. But there is no neutral place to stand free and clear in which my words do not prescriptively affect or mediate the experience of others, nor is there a way to demarcate decisively a boundary between my location and all others. Even a complete retreat from speech is of course not neutral since it allows the continued dominance of current discourses and acts by omission to reinforce their dominance.

As my practices are made possible by events spatially far away from my body, so too my own practices make possible or impossible others' practices. The declaration that I "speak only for myself" has the sole effect of allowing me to avoid responsibility and accountability for my effects on others; it cannot literally erase those effects.

Let me offer an illustration of this. The feminist movement in the United States has spawned many kinds of support groups for women with various needs: rape victims, incest survivors, battered wives, and so forth; some of these groups have been structured around the view that each survivor must come to her own "truth" which ranges only over herself and has no bearing on others. Thus, one woman's experience of sexual assault, its effect on her and her interpretation of it, should not be taken as a universal generalization to which others must subsume or conform their experience. This view works only up to a point. To the extent it recognizes irreducible differences in the way people respond to various traumas and is sensitive to the genuinely variable way in which women can heal themselves, it represents real progress beyond the homogeneous, universalizing approach that maps one road for all to follow.

However, it is an illusion to think that, even in the safe space of a support group, a member of the group can, for example, trivialize brother-sister incest as "sex play" without profoundly harming someone else in the group who is trying to maintain her realistic assessment of her brother's sexual activities with her as a harmful assault against his adult rationalization that "well, for me it was just harmless fun." Even if the speaker offers a dozen caveats about her views as restricted to her location, she will still affect the other woman's ability to conceptualize and interpret her experience and her response to it. This is true simply because we cannot neatly separate our mediating praxis, which interprets and constructs our experiences, from the praxis of others. We are collectively caught in an intricate, delicate web in which each action I take, discursive or otherwise, pulls on, breaks off, or maintains the tension in many strands of the web in which others also find themselves moving. When I speak for myself, I am constructing a possible self, a way to be in the world, and am offering that, whether I intend to or not, to others, as one possible form of existence.

Thus, the attempt to avoid the problematic of speaking for by retreating into an individualist realm is based on an illusion, well supported in the individualist ideology of the West, that a self is not constituted by multiple intersecting discourses but consists in a unified whole capable of autonomy from others. It is an illusion that I can separate from others to such an extent that I can avoid affecting them. This may be the intention of my speech, and even its meaning if we take that to be the formal entailments of the sentences, but it will not be the effect of the speech and therefore cannot capture the speech in its reality as a discursive practice. When I "speak for myself," I am participating in the creation and reproduction of discourses through which my own and other selves are constituted.

A further problem with the retreat response is that it may be motivated by a desire to find a method or practice immune from criticism. If I speak only for myself it may appear that I am immune from criticism because I am not making any claims that describe others or prescribe actions for them. If I am only speaking for myself I have no responsibility for being true to your experience or needs.

Surely it is both morally and politically objectionable to structure our actions around the desire to avoid criticism, especially if this outweighs other questions of effectivity. In some cases, the motivation is perhaps not so much to avoid criticism as to avoid errors, and we may believe that the only way to avoid errors is to avoid all speaking for others. Yet errors are unavoidable in theoretical inquiry as well as political struggle, and they usually make contributions. The pursuit of an absolute means to avoid making errors comes perhaps not from a desire to advance collective goals but from a desire for personal mastery, to establish a privileged discursive position wherein we cannot be undermined or challenged and thus become master of the situation. From such a position our own location and positionality would not require constant interrogation and critical reflection; we would not have to constantly engage in this emotionally troublesome endeavor and would be immune from the interrogation of others. Such a desire for mastery and immunity must be resisted.

The final response to the problem of speaking for others that I will consider occurs in Gayatri Chakravorty Spivak's rich essay "Can the Subaltern Speak?" Spivak rejects a total retreat from speaking for others, and she criticizes the "self-abnegating intellectual" pose that Foucault and Deleuze adopt when they reject speaking for others on the grounds that their position assumes the oppressed can transparently represent their own true interests. According to Spivak, Foucault's and Deleuze's self-abnegation serves only to conceal the actual authorizing power of the retreating intellectuals, who in their very retreat help to consolidate a particular conception of experience (as transparent and self-knowing). Thus, to promote "listening to" as opposed to speaking for essentializes the oppressed as nonideologically constructed subjects. But Spivak is also critical of speaking for that engages in dangerous representations. In the end Spivak prefers a "speaking to" in which the intellectual neither abnegates his or her discursive role nor presumes an authenticity of the oppressed, but still allows for the possibility that the oppressed will produce a "countersentence" that can then suggest a new historical narrative.

Spivak's arguments suggest that the speech of the oppressed will not necessarily be either liberatory or reflective of their "true interests," if such exist. At the same time, however, ignoring the subaltern's or oppressed person's speech is, as she notes, "to continue the imperialist project" (298). I would add that, even if the oppressed person's speech is not liberatory in its content, it remains the case that the very act of speaking constitutes a subject that challenges and subverts the opposition between the knowing agent and the object of knowledge, an opposition that has served as a key player in the reproduction of imperialist modes of discourse. Thus, the problem with speaking for others exists in the very structure of discursive practice, irrespective of its content, and subverting the hierarchical rituals of speaking will always have some liberatory effects.

I agree, then, that we should strive to create wherever possible the conditions for dialogue and the practice of speaking with and to rather than speaking for others. Often the possibility of dialogue is left unexplored or inadequately pursued by more privileged persons. Spaces in which it may seem impossible to engage in dialogic encounters (e.g., classrooms, hospitals, workplaces, welfare agencies, universities, institutions for international development and aid, and governments) need to be transformed in order to do so. It has long been noted that existing communication technologies have the potential to produce these kinds of interaction even though research and development teams have not found it advantageous under capitalism to do so.

While there is much theoretical and practical work to be done to develop such alternatives, the practice of speaking for others remains the best option in some existing situations. An absolute retreat weakens political effectivity, is based on a metaphysical illusion, and often produces only an obscuring of the intellectual's power. There can be no complete or definitive solution to the problem of speaking for others, but there is a possibility that its dangers can be decreased. The remainder of this chapter will try to contribute toward the development of that possibility.

*   *   *

In rejecting a general retreat from speaking for, I am not advocating a return to an unselfconscious appropriation of the other but rather that anyone who speaks for others should only do so out of a concrete analysis of the particular power relations and discursive effects involved. I want to develop this point by elucidating four sets of interrogatory practices that are meant to help evaluate possible and actual instances of speaking for. In list form they may appear to resemble an algorithm, as if we could plug in an instance of speaking for and factor out an analysis and evaluation. Yet they are meant only to suggest the questions that should be asked concerning any such discursive practice. These are by no means original: they have been learned and practiced by many activists and theorists.

1. The *impetus to speak* must be carefully analyzed and, in many cases (certainly for academics), fought against. This may seem an odd way to begin discussing how to speak for, but the point is that the impetus to *always* be the speaker and to speak in all situations must be seen for what it is: a desire for mastery and domination. If our immediate impulse is to teach rather than to listen to a less-privileged speaker, we should resist that impulse long enough to interrogate it carefully. Some of us have been taught that by right of having the dominant gender, class, race, letters after our name, or some other criterion, we are more likely to have the truth. Others have been taught the opposite and will speak haltingly, with apologies, if they speak at all.[11]

At the same time, we must acknowledge that the very decision to "move over" or retreat can occur only from a position of privilege. Those who are not in a position of speaking at all cannot retreat from an action they do not employ. Moreover, an individual's decision of whether or not to retreat is an extension or application of privilege, not an abdication of it. Still, it is sometimes called for.

2. We must also interrogate the *bearing of our location and context* on what we are saying, and this should be an explicit part of every serious discursive practice in which we engage. Constructing hypotheses about the possible connections between our location and our words is one way to begin. This procedure would be most successful if engaged in collectively with others, by which aspects of our location less obvious to us might be revealed.[12]

One deformed way in which this is too often carried out is when speakers offer up in the spirit of "honesty" autobiographical information about themselves as a kind of disclaimer, usually at the beginning of their discourse. This is meant to acknowledge their own understanding that they are speaking from a specified, embodied location without pretense to a transcendental truth. But as Maria Lugones and others have forcefully argued, such an act serves no good end when it is used as a disclaimer against the speaker's ignorance or errors and is made without critical interrogation of the bearing of such an autobiography on what is about to be said. All the real work is left for the listeners to do. For example, if a middle-class white man started a speech by sharing such autobiographical information and then used it as a kind of apologetics for any limitations of his speech, this would leave to the audience who do not share his social location all the work of translating his terms into their own, apprising the applicability of his analysis to their diverse situation, and determining the substantive relevance of his location on his claims. This is simply what less-privileged persons have always had to do for themselves when reading the history of philosophy, literature, and so on, which makes the task of appropriating these discourses more difficult and time-consuming (and more likely to result in alienation). Simple unanalyzed disclaimers do not improve on this familiar situation and may even make it worse to the extent that by offering such information the speaker may feel even more authorized to speak and be accorded more authority by his peers.

3. Speaking should always carry with it an *accountability and responsibility* for what an individual says. To whom we are accountable is a political/epistemological choice contestable, contingent, and as Donna Haraway says, constructed through the process of discursive action. What this entails in practice is a serious commitment to remain open to criticism and to attempt actively, attentively, and sensitively to

"hear" the criticism (i.e., understand it). A quick impulse to reject criticism must make us wary.

4. Here is my central point. In order to evaluate attempts to speak for others in particular instances, we need to analyze the *probable or actual effects of the words on the discursive and material context*. We cannot simply look at the location of the speaker or her credentials to speak; nor can we look merely at the propositional content of the speech; we must also look at where the speech goes and what it does there.

Looking merely at the content of a set of claims without looking at their effects cannot produce an adequate or even meaningful evaluation of it; this is partly because the notion of a content separate from effects does not hold up. The content of the claim, or its meaning, emerges in interaction between words and hearers within a very specific historical situation. Given this, we have to pay careful attention to the discursive arrangement in order to understand the full meaning of any given discursive event. For example, in a situation where a well-meaning first world person is speaking for a person or group in the third world, the very discursive arrangement may reinscribe the "hierarchy of civilizations" view where the United States lands squarely at the top. This effect occurs because the speaker is positioned as authoritative and empowered, as the knowledgeable subject, while the third world group is reduced, merely because of the structure of the speaking practice, to an object and victim that must be championed from afar. Though the speaker may he trying to materially improve the situation of some lesser-privileged group, one of the effects of her discourse is to reinforce racist, imperialist conceptions and perhaps also to further silence the lesser-privileged group's own ability to speak and be heard.[13] This illustrates why it is so important to reconceptualize discourse, as Foucault recommends, as an *event* that includes speaker, words, hearers, location, language, and so on.

All such evaluations produced in this way will be of necessity *indexed*. That is, they will obtain for a very specific location and cannot be taken as universal. This simply follows from the fact that the evaluations will be based on the specific elements of historical discursive context, location of speakers and hearers, and so forth. When any of these elements is changed, a new evaluation is called for.

Our ability to assess the effects of a given discursive event is limited; our ability to predict these effects is even more circumscribed. When meaning is plural and deferred, we can never hope to know the totality of effects. Still, we can know some of the effects our speech generates: I can find out, for example, whether the people I spoke for are angry or appreciative that I did so. By learning as much as possible about the context of reception I can increase my ability to discern at least some of the possible effects. This mandates incorporating a more dialogic approach to speaking that would include learning from and about the domains of discourse my words will affect.

I want to illustrate the implications of this fourth point by applying it to the examples at the beginning of this chapter. In the case of Anne Cameron, if the effects of her books are truly disempowering for indigenous women, then they are counterproductive to Cameron's own stated intentions, and she should indeed "move over." In the case of the white male theorist who discussed architecture instead of the politics of postmodernism, the effect of his refusal was that he offered no contribution to an important issue and his audience lost an opportunity to discuss and explore it.

Now let me turn to the example of George Bush. When Bush claimed that Noriega is a corrupt dictator who stands in the way of democracy in Panama, he repeated a claim that has been made almost word for word by the Opposition movement in Panama. Yet the effects of the two statements are vastly different because the meaning of the claim changes radically depending on who states it. When the president of the United States stands before the world passing judgment on a third world government and criticizes it on the basis of corruption and a lack of democracy, the immediate effect of *this* statement, as opposed to the Opposition's, is to reinforce the prominent Anglo view that Latin American corruption is the primary cause of the region's poverty and lack of democracy, that the United States is on the side of democracy in

the region, and that the United States opposes corruption and tyranny. Thus, the effect of a U.S. president's speaking for Latin America in this way is to
reconsolidate U.S. imperialism by obscuring its true
role in torturing and murdering hundreds of thousands of people who have tried to bring democratic
and progressive governments into existence in Latin
America. Moreover, this effect will continue until the
U.S. government admits its history of international
mass murder and radically alters it foreign policy.

CONCLUSION

Any discussion of discursive responsibility is complicated by the variable way in which the importance of the source, or location of the author, can be
understood, a topic alluded to earlier. In one view,
the author of a text is its "owner" and "originator,"
credited with creating its ideas and with being their
authoritative interpreter. In another view, the original
speaker or writer is no more privileged than any other
person who articulates these views and, in fact, the
"author" cannot be identified in a strict sense because
the concept of author is an ideological construction
many abstractions removed from the way in which
ideas emerge and become material forces.[14] Does this
latter position mean that the source or location of the
author is irrelevant?

It need not entail this conclusion, though it might
in some formulations. We can de-privilege the "original" author and reconceptualize ideas as traversing
(almost) freely in a discursive space, available from
many locations and without a clearly identifiable
originary track, and yet retain our sense that source
remains relevant to effect. Our metatheory of author-
ship does not preclude the material reality that in discursive spaces there is a speaker or writer credited as
the author of her utterances, or that, for example, the
feminist appropriation of the concept "patriarchy"
gets tied to Kate Millett, a white Anglo feminist, or
that the term feminism itself has been and is associated with a Western origin. These associations have
an effect of producing distrust on the part of some
third world nationalists and of reinscribing semicon-

scious imperialist attitudes on the part of some first
world feminists. These are not the only possible
effects. Some of the effects may not be pernicious but
all must be considered when evaluating the discourse
of "patriarchy."

The emphasis on effects should not imply, therefore, that an examination of the speaker's location
is any less crucial. Such an examination might be
called a kind of genealogy. In this sense, a genealogy
involves asking how a position or view is mediated
and constituted through and within the conjunction
and conflict of historical, cultural, economic, psychological, and sexual practices. But it seems to me that
the importance of the source of a view, and the importance of doing a genealogy, should be subsumed
within an overall analysis of effects, making the
central question what the effects are of the view on
material and discursive practices through which it
traverses and the particular configuration of power
relations emergent from these. Source is relevant
only to the extent that it has an impact on effect. As
Gayatri Chakravorty Spivak has repeatedly pointed
out, the invention of the telephone by a European
upper-class male in no way preempts its being put to
the use of an anti-imperialist revolution.

In conclusion, I would stress that the practice of
speaking for others is often born of a desire for mastery,
to privilege oneself as the one who more correctly
understands the truth about another's situation or as
the one who can champion a just cause and thus
achieve glory and praise. The effect of the practice of
speaking for others is often, though not always, erasure and a reinscription of sexual, national, and other
kinds of hierarchies. I hope that this analysis will
contribute toward rather than diminish the important
ongoing discussion about how to develop strategies
for a more equitable, just distribution of the ability
to speak and be heard. But this development should
not be taken as an absolute de-authorization of all
practices of speaking for. It is not *always* the case that
when others unlike me speak for me I have ended
up worse off or that when we speak for others they
end up worse off. Sometimes, as Loyce Stewart has
argued, we need a "messenger" to advocate for
our needs.

The source of a claim or discursive practice in suspect motives or maneuvers or in privileged social locations, I have argued, cannot be sufficient to repudiate it, though it is always relevant. We must ask further questions about its effects, questions that address the following: Will it enable the empowerment of oppressed peoples?

NOTES

For their generous help with this chapter, I am grateful to the Eastern Society for Women in Philosophy, the Central New York Women Philosophers' Group, Loyce Stewart, Richard Schmitt, Sandra Bartky, Laurence Thomas, Leslie Bender, Robyn Wiegman, Anita Canizares Molina, and Felicity Nussbaum. An earlier version of this essay appeared in *Cultural Critique* 20 (Winter 1991–92): 5–32.

1. Trebilcot is explaining here her own reasoning for rejecting these practices, but she is not advocating that other women join her. Thus, her argument does not fall into a self-referential incoherence.

2. For examples of anthropologists' concern with this issue, see James Clifford and George E. Marcus, eds., *Writing Culture*; James Clifford, "On Ethnographic Authority"; George Marcus and Michael Fischer, eds., *Anthropology as Cultural Critique*; and Paul Rabinow, "Discourse and Power."

3. To be privileged here means to be in a more favorable, mobile, and dominant position vis-à-vis the structures of power and knowledge in a society. This privilege carries with it, for example, presumption in one's favor when one speaks. Certain races, nationalities, genders, sexualities, and classes confer privilege, but a single individual (perhaps most individuals) may enjoy privilege in respect to some parts of their identity and a lack of privilege in respect to other parts. Therefore, privilege must always be indexed to specific relationships as well as to specific locations.

The term privilege is not meant to include positions of discursive power achieved through merit, but in any case these are rarely pure. In other words, some persons are accorded discursive authority because they are respected leaders or because they are teachers in a classroom and know more about the material at hand. Often, of course, the authority they may enjoy by virtue of their merit combines with the authority they may enjoy by virtue of their having the dominant gender, race, class, or sexuality. It is gender, race, class, and sexuality as sources of authority that I refer to by the term "privilege."

4. See also, Maria Lugones and Elizabeth Spelman, "Have We Got a Theory For You!" In their article, Lugones and Spelman explore the way in which the "demand for the women's voice" disempowered women of color by not attending to the difference in privilege within the category of women, resulting in a privileging of only white women's voices. They explore the effects this has had on the making of theory within feminism, and they attempt to find "ways of talking or being talked about that are helpful, illuminating, empowering, respectful" (25). My chapter takes inspiration from their essay and is meant to continue their discussion.

5. See Menchu's *I . . . Rigoberta Menchu*. The use of the term "Indian" here follows Menchu's use.

6. For example, if it is the case that no "descriptive" discourse is normative- or value-free, then no discourse is free of some kind of advocacy, and all speaking about will involve speaking for someone(s) or something.

7. Another distinction that might be made is between different material practices of speaking for: giving a speech, writing an essay or book, making a movie or TV program, as well as hearing, reading, watching, and so on. I will not address the possible differences that arise from these multifarious practices and will address myself to the (fictional) "generic" practice of speaking for.

8. See Wilson's "Down to the Crossroads: The Art of Alison Saar," for a discussion of this phenomenon in the art world (especially p. 36). See also Barbara Christian, "The Race for Theory," and Henry Louis Gates, Jr., "Authority, (White) Power and the (Black) Critic."

9. I know that my insistence on using the word "truth" swims upstream of current postmodernist orthodoxies. My insistence is not based on a commitment to transparent accounts of representation or a correspondence theory of truth but on my belief that the demarcation between epistemically better and worse claims continues to operate (indeed is inevitable) and that what happens when we eschew all epistemological issues of truth is that the terms upon which those demarcations are made go unseen and uncontested. A very radical revision of what we mean by truth is in order, but if we ignore the ways in which our discourses appeal to some version of truth for their persuasiveness, we are in danger of remaining blind to the operations of legitimation that function within our own texts. The task is therefore to explicate the relations between politics and knowledge rather than pronounce the death of truth. See my *Real Knowing* (forthcoming).

10. See also my "Cultural Feminism versus Post-Structuralism." For more discussions on the multidimensionality of social identity, see Maria Lugones, "Playfulness, 'World'-Travelling, and Loving Perception," and Gloria Anzaldúa, *Borderlands/La Frontera*.

11. See Edward Said, "Representing the Colonized" on this point. He shows how the "dialogue' between Western anthropology and colonized people has been nonreciprocal and supports the need for Westerners to begin to *stop talking*.

12. See Said, "Representing the Colonized" (212), where he encourages in particular the self-interrogation of privileged speakers. This seems to be a running theme in what are sometimes called "minority discourses": asserting the need for whites to study whiteness. The need for an interrogation of one's location exists with every discursive event by any speaker, but given the lopsidedness of current "dialogues" it seems especially important to push for this among the privileged, who sometimes seem to want to study everybody's social and cultural constructions but their own.

13. To argue for the relevance of effects for evaluation does not mean that there is only one way to do such an accounting nor does it dictate what kind of effects will be deemed desirable. How we evaluate a particular effect is left open; point number four argues simply that effects must always be taken into account.

14. I like the way Susan Bordo makes this point. In speaking about theories or ideas that gain prominence, she says: "All cultural formations . . . [are] complexly constructed out of diverse elements—intellectual, psychological, institutional, and sociological. Arising not from monolithic design but from all interplay of factors and forces, it is best understood not as a discrete, definable position which can be adopted or rejected, but as an emerging coherence which is being fed by a variety of currents, sometimes overlapping, sometimes quite distinct" (135). If these ideas arise in such a configuration of forces, does it make sense to ask for an author?

WORKS CITED

Alcoff, Linda. "Cultural Feminism versus Post-Structuralism: The Identity Crisis in Feminist Theory." *Signs: Journal of Women in Culture and Society* 13 (1988): 405–36.

———. *Real Knowing*. Ithaca, N.Y.: Cornell University Press, forthcoming.

Anzaldúa, Gloria. *Borderlands/La Frontera: The New Mestiza*. San Francisco: Spinsters/Aunt Lute, 1987.

Bordo, Susan. "Feminism, Postmodernism, and Gender-Skepticism." Pp. 133–56 in *Feminism/Postmodernism*, ed. Linda Nicholson. New York: Routledge, 1989.

Christian, Barbara. "The Race for Theory." *Feminist Studies* 14 (1988): 67–79.

Clifford, James. "On Ethnographic Authority." *Representations* 1 (1983): 118–46.

Clifford, James, and George Marcus, eds. *Writing Culture: The Poetics and Politics of Ethnography*. Berkeley: University of California Press, 1986.

Deleuze, Gilles, and Michel Foucault. "Intellectuals and Power." Pp. 205–17 in *Language, Counter-Memory, Practice*, ed. Donald Bouchard. Trans. Donald Bouchard and Sherry Simon. Ithaca, N.Y.: Cornell University Press, 1977.

Gates, Henry Louis, Jr. "Authority, (White) Power and the (Black) Critic: It's All Greek to Me." *Cultural Critique* 7 (fall 1987): 19–46.

Lugones, Maria. "Playfulness, 'World'-Travelling, and Loving Perception." *Hypatia* 2, no. 2 (1987): 3–19.

Lugones, Maria, and Elizabeth Spelman. "Have We Got a Theory For You! Feminist Theory, Cultural Imperialism, and the Demand for the 'Women's Voice.'" *Women's Studies International Forum* 6, no. 6 (1983): 573–81.

Maracle, Lee. "Moving Over." *Trivia* 14 (spring 1989): 9–10.

Marcus, George, and Michael Fisher, eds. *Anthropology as Cultural Critique*. Chicago: University of Chicago Press, 1986.

Menchu, Rigoberta. *I . . . Rigoberta Menchu*. Edited by Elisabeth Burgos-Debray. Trans. Ann Wright. London: Verso, 1984.

Nelson, Cary, and Lawrence Grossberg. *Marxism and the Interpretation of Culture*. Urbana: University of Illinois Press, 1988.

Rabinow, Paul. "Discourse and Power: On the Limits of Ethnographic Texts." *Dialectical Anthropology* 10, nos. 1–2 (1985): 1–14.

Said, Edward. "Representing the Colonized: Anthropology's Interlocutors." *Critical Inquiry* 15 (1989): 205–25.

Spivak, Gayatri Chakravorty. "Can the Subaltern Speak?" Pp. 271–313 in *Marxism and the Interpretation of Culture*, ed. Nelson and Grossberg.

Trebilcot, Joyce. "Dyke Methods." *Hypatia* 3, no. 2 (1988): 1–13.

Trinh T. Minh-hà. *Woman, Native, Other: Writing Postcoloniality and Feminism*. Bloomington: Indiana University Press, 1989.

Wilson, Judith. "Down to the Crossroads: The Art of Alison Saar." *Third Text* 10 (Spring 1990): 25–44.

Study Questions

1. According to Alcoff, what *is* the problem of speaking for others?

2. Before explaining her recommended response to this problem, Alcoff describes and criticizes a range of responses including

   a) silence
   b) speaking only for oneself
   c) speaking only for groups of which one is a member
   d) speaking "to or with" rather than "for" others.

   What is her estimation of each of these responses? Do you agree with her criticisms?

3. Does Alcoff think it is ever appropriate to speak for others? If not, why not? If so, under what circumstances?

4. What do you think? When—if ever—is it appropriate to speak for others?

5. What relationship do you see between this article and Narayan's "Cross-Cultural Connections, Border-Crossings, and 'Death by Culture'"?

 Section II

General Approaches to Sex Oppression

Elizabeth Hackett and Sally Haslanger, *"Introduction"*

THE SAMENESS APPROACH ("HUMANIST FEMINISM")

Theoretical Frames

John Stuart Mill, *The Subjection of Women*, Chapter 1
Sojourner Truth, *"Ar'n't I a Woman?"*
Simone de Beauvoir, *The Second Sex*, Introduction
Martha C. Nussbaum, *"Human Capabilities, Female Human Beings"*

Contextual Studies

Susan Schechter, *"Social Change on Behalf of Battered Women: Reforming the Criminal Justice System"*
Amartya Sen, *"More than 100 Million Women Are Missing"*
Kimberlé Crenshaw, *"Mapping the Margins: Intersectionality, Identity Politics, and Violence Against Women of Color"*

THE DIFFERENCE APPROACH ("GYNOCENTRIC FEMINISM")

Theoretical Frames

Iris M. Young, *"Humanism, Gynocentrism, and Feminist Politics"*
Jane Addams, *"Women and Public Housekeeping"*
Audre Lorde, *"Uses of the Erotic: The Erotic as Power"*
Paula Gunn Allen, *"Who Is Your Mother? Red Roots of White Feminism"*
Carol Gilligan, *"Moral Orientation and Moral Development"*

Contextual Studies

Carol P. Christ, *"Why Women Need the Goddess: Phenomenological, Psychological, and Political Reflections"*
Alice Walker, *"The Only Reason You Want to Go to Heaven Is That You Have Been Driven Out of Your Mind (Off Your Land and Out of Your Lover's Arms)"*
Sara Ruddick, *"Notes Toward a Feminist Maternal Peace Politics"*
Vandana Shiva, *"Women's Indigenous Knowledge and Biodiversity Conservation"*

THE DOMINANCE APPROACH

Theoretical Frames

Catharine MacKinnon, *"Difference and Dominance: On Sex Discrimination"*
Catharine MacKinnon, *"Desire and Power"* and *"Sex and Violence: A Perspective"*
Emma Goldman, *"Woman Suffrage"*
Sandra Lee Bartky, *"Foucault, Femininity, and the Modernization of Patriarchal Power"*
Audre Lorde, *"Age, Race, Class, and Sex: Women Redefining Difference"*

Contextual Studies

John Stoltenberg, *"Confronting Pornography as a Civil-Rights Issue"*
Lisa Duggan, Nan D. Hunter, and Carole S. Vance, *"False Promises: Feminist Antipornography Legislation"*
Marilyn Frye, *"Willful Virgin or Do You Have to Be a Lesbian to Be a Feminist?"*
bell hooks, *"Seduced by Violence No More"*

INTRODUCTION

As explained in the introduction to this text, the organizing questions used to group articles in this and the following section are, What is sex oppression? and What should be done about it? Articles contained in this section hold that these questions can be given a "general" or "universal" answer. That is, they maintain or assume that there is a single, generally applicable answer to each of these questions, as opposed to holding, as do postmodernists, for example, that answers to such questions are useful only if they take into account specific facts about social and historical context. Postmodernists, and others who take what we refer to in this text as "localizing approaches," focus on sexism in particular times and places, and propose solutions tailored to those particulars. Those who embrace *general approaches* are more at home with "grand" theory, proposing analyses and solutions that (at least purport to) have very broad application.

Although the three approaches covered in this section provide or presume general answers to our organizing questions, the content of their answers differs markedly. The first approach treated is the *sameness approach*, or what is sometimes referred to as *humanist feminism*. When taking a sameness approach to sex oppression, feminists stress similarities between women and men; they focus on sameness, often on underlying, shared humanity. In this approach, sex oppression results from women not being treated as men are treated, so the solution—not surprisingly—*is* to treat women as men are treated.

The argumentative strategy of the sameness approach is a familiar one: if two people or groups of people are similar in all relevant ways, most people's intuitions about fairness dictate that the two should be treated identically. The sameness approach employs this kind of strategy to argue for better treatment for women. The following pieces from John Stuart Mill, Sojourner Truth, Simone de Beauvoir, and Martha Nussbaum argue for improved treatment of women by appealing to features that both women and men possess, and that the author deems relevant to a certain kind of treatment that (in the context in question) only men enjoy, or that men enjoy to a greater extent than do women. While these theorists' arguments reflect their differing philosophical commitments,[1] the argumentative strategies the authors employ are strikingly similar. The remaining articles in the section implicitly or explicitly employ the same kind of argumentative strategy to address: the treatment of battered women by the U.S. legal system (Susan Schechter), the startlingly low ratio of women to men in the population of the world (Amartya Sen), and why women of color who are victims of violence do not get what they need (Kimberlé Crenshaw).[2]

It is interesting to note that the argumentative strategy identified here as characteristic of the sameness approach (or of humanist feminism) encompasses two very different kinds of projects. Schechter's piece, for example, focuses on women battered in domestic violence situations, and argues that they should be treated by the legal system as are any other victims of assault. The "sameness" upon which her argument turns is that battered women are the same as any other victims of assault, *in virtue of being victims of assault*. The treatment battered women are said to deserve is *identical* to the treatment received by like victims. Nussbaum's argument, in contrast, appeals to the sameness of *underlying humanity* (in this case, the potential to exercise certain human capabilities), and the treatment argued for is not identical treatment per se, but "the same" treatment in the sense that people deserve whatever it is that they need in order to be able to actualize their human capabilities. In other words, the sameness to which one appeals in grounding a sameness argument can be very specific or quite general, and the sameness of treatment that one calls for can be "the same" in the sense of being identical, or in the sense of all people being treated "the same" in virtue of getting what they need as individuals.

But what about when women and men are *not* the same? Consider again the case of battered women. Schechter argues, in "Social Change on Behalf of Battered Women," that "it is more effective to declare battered women equal to others rather than make them a more protected class." When trying to convince society that assaulting an intimate is equivalent to assaulting a stranger, rather than a lesser offense due to its "private" nature, arguing for battered women's similarity to other victims has been quite effective. But think, for example, of women who kill their batterers while the batterer is asleep. Should such women be treated in the same way as a person who kills a stranger while he sleeps? Perhaps not. Some worry that the sameness approach leaves one ill-equipped to address effectively situations in which women and men are different.[3]

For this and other reasons, some turn to the *difference approach*, also known as *gynocentric feminism*. Rather than stressing women's similarities to men in order to obtain for women what men have, the difference approach stresses the differences between women and men. On the difference approach, sex oppression results from societies' failure to recognize and value appropriately that which is distinctively feminine or womanly. Accordingly, on this approach, the solution to sex oppression is to revalue the feminine. Perhaps the most dramatic example of such revaluing is goddess worship. For, how can one value something more highly than by declaring it divine? (See Carol Christ's "Why Women Need the Goddess" for a discussion along these lines.)

This section opens with the article "Humanism, Gynocentrism, and Feminist Politics," in which Iris Young discusses the relative strengths and weaknesses of what she labels "gynocentric" and "humanist" feminism.[4] Essays that follow argue for revaluing the feminine in the context of running cities (Jane Addams), unlearning oppressive modes of being (Audre Lorde), moral reasoning (Carol Gilligan), religion (Carol Christ and Alice Walker), pacifism (Sara Ruddick), and biodiversity (Vandana Shiva). Paula Gunn Allen's essay, "Who Is Your Mother? Red Roots of White Feminism," raises interesting questions about the relationship between gynocentric feminism and Native American cultures.

A concern that some have about the difference approach, however, is that it seems to accept the definitions of "femininity" and "woman" dictated by patriarchy (albeit while calling for a revaluation of what is so defined), rather than challenging those sexist definitions themselves. This is one of the criticisms that Catharine MacKinnon raises in her essay, "Difference and Dominance: On Sex Discrimination." MacKinnon is equally unsatisfied with what she calls the "sameness path," however, and argues instead for the "*dominance approach*."[5] The dominance approach holds that whether women are the same as or different from men is beside the point. In this approach, sex oppression is about females being made into beings who are subordinate to men, and eliminating sex oppression means eliminating that subordination. Sexuality is an arena that many feminists identify as central to the subordination of women, and the subsequent articles by Catharine MacKinnon, John Stoltenberg, Lisa Duggan et al., Marilyn Frye, and bell hooks tackle this issue from various angles. The selection from Sandra Lee Bartky indicts femininity more generally, while Emma Goldman's "Woman Suffrage" makes a perhaps surprising argument against women's pursuit of suffrage. Audre Lorde's piece, "Age, Race, Class and Sex: Women Redefining Difference," identifies sexism as one among a range of forces that teaches us to use difference as a justification for dominance.[6]

NOTES

1. The excerpt from Mill's *The Subjection of Women* reflects the author's utilitarianism. At its most basic, utilitarianism is an ethical theory that holds that moral choices should be decided in favor of the option that will bring about the greatest good for the greatest number. (Mill understands our ultimate good to be happiness.) Similarly, anti-racism clearly informs the included speech by Sojourner Truth. Beauvoir's commitment to existentialism is evident in the excerpt from *The Second Sex*. Considered as an ethical theory, existentialism values, above all, people's capacity to author their own freely chosen projects. Finally, Nussbaum's focus on human capabilities in the selected essay is heavily influenced by the work of the ancient philosopher, Aristotle.

2. Some readers may note that a number of the theorists presented here as putting forth humanist/sameness feminist arguments are liberal feminists. The term "Liberal feminism" is used differently in different disciplines. For example, in philosophy, "liberalism" is the name for a broad group of political theories that emphasize individual liberty and equality of rights. In this context, a liberal feminist is one who applies her favored version of liberal theory to women and criticizes societies for not extending to women the full complement of rights and liberties to which they are entitled. In other contexts, e.g., in popular discourse, the term "liberal feminism" is used to refer to a cluster of ideas and policies promoted by the U.S. women's liberation movement of the 1970s, including, e.g., equal access to education and jobs, breakdown of the gendered division of labor, equal pay for equal work, and access to child care and abortion. While humanist feminism and liberal feminism share some features, they are distinct views; the characterization and criticisms presented in this volume of humanist feminist arguments cannot be assumed to apply to liberal feminism. For information about liberal feminism, see, for example, Susan Moller Okin's *Gender, Justice and the Family* (New York: Basic Books, 1989).

3. Although some have this concern, others believe that the sameness approach has resources perfectly adequate to such situations. It is interesting to think about this issue as you work your way through this section of the text.

4. As you read the essays that follow, consider whether Iris Young's definitions of humanist and gynocentric feminism—and her evaluation of them—correspond to your own developing understanding of the sameness and difference approaches presented in this text.

5. As with the Young piece that introduces the section on the difference approach, it is important to consider whether MacKinnon's understandings and criticisms map meaningfully onto the articles in this text.

6. It is interesting to consider the relationship between projects such as Mill's, Nussbaum's and Beauvior's and what is here called the dominance approach. Given how these three authors harshly criticize the subordination of women to men, does it make sense to characterize them as taking a sameness approach rather than a dominance approach to sex equality? As you read the following selections, consider whether you agree with how they have been grouped.

THE SAMENESS APPROACH

John Stuart Mill

The Subjection of Women

CHAPTER 1

The object of this Essay is to explain as clearly as I am able, the grounds of an opinion which I have held from the very earliest period when I had formed any opinions at all on social or political matters, and which, instead of being weakened or modified, has been constantly growing stronger by the progress of reflection and the experience of life: That the principle which regulates the existing social relations between the two sexes—the legal subordination of one sex to the other—is wrong in itself, and now one of the chief hindrances to human improvement; and that it ought to be replaced by a principle of perfect equality, admitting no power or privilege on the one side, nor disability on the other.

The very words necessary to express the task I have undertaken, show how arduous it is. But it would be a mistake to suppose that the difficulty of the case must lie in the insufficiency or obscurity of the grounds of reason on which my conviction rests. The difficulty is that which exists in all cases in which there is a mass of feeling to be contended against. So long as an opinion is strongly rooted in the feelings, it gains rather than loses in stability by having a preponderating weight of argument against it. For if it were accepted as a result of argument, the refutation of the argument might shake the solidity of the conviction; but when it rests solely on feeling, the worse it fares in argumentative contest, the more persuaded

its adherents are that their feeling must have some deeper ground, which the arguments do not reach; and while the feeling remains, it is always throwing up fresh intrenchments of argument to repair any breach made in the old. And there are so many causes tending to make the feelings connected with this subject the most intense and most deeply-rooted of all those which gather round and protect old institutions and customs, that we need not wonder to find them as yet less undermined and loosened than any of the rest by the progress of the great modern spiritual and social transition; nor suppose that the barbarisms to which men cling longest must be less barbarisms than those which they earlier shake off.

In every respect the burthen is hard on those who attack an almost universal opinion. They must be very fortunate as well as unusually capable if they obtain a hearing at all. They have more difficulty in obtaining a trial, than any other litigants have in getting a verdict. If they do extort a hearing, they are subjected to a set of logical requirements totally different from those exacted from other people. In all other cases, the burthen of proof is supposed to lie with the affirmative. If a person is charged with a murder, it rests with those who accuse him to give proof of his guilt, not with himself to prove his innocence. If there is a difference of opinion about the reality of any alleged historical event, in which the feelings of men in general are not much interested, as the Siege of Troy for example, those who maintain

From John Stuart Mill, *The Subjection of Women*, 1869.

that the event took place are expected to produce their proofs, before those who take the other side can be required to say anything; and at no time are these required to do more than show that the evidence produced by the others is of no value. Again, in practical matters, the burthen of proof is supposed to be with those who are against liberty; who contend for any restriction or prohibition; either any limitation of the general freedom of human action, or any disqualification or disparity of privilege affecting one person or kind of persons, as compared with others. The à priori presumption is in favour of freedom and impartiality. It is held that there should be no restraint not required by the general good, and that the law should be no respecter of persons, but should treat all alike, save where dissimilarity of treatment is required by positive reasons, either of justice or of policy. But of none of these rules of evidence will the benefit be allowed to those who maintain the opinion I profess. It is useless for me to say that those who maintain the doctrine that men have a right to command and women are under an obligation to obey, or that men are fit for government and women unfit, are on the affirmative side of the question, and that they are bound to show positive evidence for the assertions, or submit to their rejection. It is equally unavailing for me to say that those who deny to women any freedom or privilege rightly allowed to men, having the double presumption against them that they are opposing freedom and recommending partiality, must be held to the strictest proof of their case, and unless their success be such as to exclude all doubt, the judgment ought to go against them. These would be thought good pleas in any common case; but they will not be thought so in this instance. Before I could hope to make any impression, I should be expected not only to answer all that has ever been said by those who take the other side of the question, but to imagine all that could be said by them—to find them in reasons, as well as answer all I find: and besides refuting all arguments for the affirmative, I shall be called upon for invincible positive arguments to prove a negative. And even if I could do all this, and leave the opposite party with a host of unanswered arguments against them, and not a single unrefuted one on their side, I should be thought to

have done little; for a cause supported on the one hand by universal usage, and on the other by so great a preponderance of popular sentiment, is supposed to have a presumption in its favour, superior to any conviction which an appeal to reason has power to produce in any intellects but those of a high class.

I do not mention these difficulties to complain of them; first, because it would be useless; they are inseparable from having to contend through people's understandings against the hostility of their feelings and practical tendencies: and truly the understandings of the majority of mankind would need to be much better cultivated than has ever yet been the case, before they can be asked to place such reliance in their own power of estimating arguments, as to give up practical principles in which they have been born and bred and which are the basis of much of the existing order of the world, at the first argumentative attack which they are not capable of logically resisting. I do not therefore quarrel with them for having too little faith in argument, but for having too much faith in custom and the general feeling. It is one of the characteristic prejudices of the reaction of the nineteenth century against the eighteenth, to accord to the unreasoning elements in human nature the infallibility which the eighteenth century is supposed to have ascribed to the reasoning elements. For the apotheosis of Reason we have substituted that of Instinct; and we call everything instinct which we find in ourselves and for which we cannot trace any rational foundation. This idolatry, infinitely more degrading than the other, and the most pernicious of the false worships of the present day, of all of which it is now the main support, will probably hold its ground until it gives way before a sound psychology, laying bare the real root of much that is bowed down to as the intention of Nature and the ordinance of God. As regards the present question, I am willing to accept the unfavourable conditions which the prejudice assigns to me. I consent that established custom, and the general feeling, should be deemed conclusive against me, unless that custom and feeling from age to age can be shown to have owed their existence to other causes than their soundness, and to have derived their power from the worse rather than the better parts of human nature. I am willing that judgment should go against me, unless I can show that my judge has been tampered with. The concession is not so great as it might appear; for to prove this, is by far the easiest portion of my task.

The generality of a practice is in some cases a strong presumption that it is, or at all events once was, conducive to laudable ends. This is the case, when the practice was first adopted, or afterwards kept up, as a means to such ends, and was grounded on experience of the mode in which they could be most effectually attained. If the authority of men over women, when first established, had been the result of a conscientious comparison between different modes of constituting the government of society; if, after trying various other modes of social organization— the government of women over men, equality between the two, and such mixed and divided modes of government as might be invented—it had been decided, on the testimony of experience, that the mode in which women are wholly under the rule of men, having no share at all in public concerns, and each in private being under the legal obligation of obedience to the man with whom she has associated her destiny, was the arrangement most conducive to the happiness and well being of both; its general adoption might then be fairly thought to be some evidence that, at the time when it was adopted, it was the best: though even then the considerations which recommended it may, like so many other primeval social facts of the greatest importance, have subsequently, in the course of ages, ceased to exist. But the state of the case is in every respect the reverse of this. In the first place, the opinion in favour of the present system, which entirely subordinates the weaker sex to the stronger, rests upon theory only; for there never has been trial made of any other: so that experience, in the sense in which it is vulgarly opposed to theory, cannot be pretended to have pronounced any verdict. And in the second place, the adoption of this system of inequality never was the result of deliberation, or forethought, or any social ideas, or any notion whatever of what conduced to the benefit of humanity or the good order of society. It arose simply from the fact that from the very earliest twilight of human society, every woman (owing to the value attached to her by men, combined with her inferiority in muscular strength) was found in a state of bondage to some man. Laws and systems of polity always begin by recognising the relations they find already existing between individuals. They convert what was a mere physical fact into a legal right, give it the sanction of society, and principally aim at the substitution of public and organized means of asserting and protecting these rights, instead of the irregular and lawless conflict of physical strength. Those who had already been compelled to obedience became in this manner legally bound to it. Slavery, from being a mere affair of force between the master and the slave, became regularized and a matter of compact among the masters, who, binding themselves to one another for common protection, guaranteed by their collective strength the private possessions of each, including his slaves. In early times, the great majority of the male sex were slaves, as well as the whole of the female. And many ages elapsed, some of them ages of high cultivation, before any thinker was bold enough to question the rightfulness, and the absolute social necessity, either of the one slavery or of the other. By degrees such thinkers did arise: and (the general progress of society assisting) the slavery of the male sex has, in all the countries of Christian Europe at least (though, in one of them, only within the last few years) been at length abolished, and that of the female sex has been gradually changed into a milder form of dependence. But this dependence, as it exists at present, is not an original insitution, taking a fresh start from considerations of justice and social expediency— it is the primitive state of slavery lasting on, through successive mitigations and modifications occasioned by the same causes which have softened the general manners, and brought all human relations more under the control of justice and the influence of humanity. It has not lost the taint of its brutal origin. No presumption in its favour, therefore, can be drawn from the fact of its existence. The only such presumption which it could be supposed to have, must be grounded on its having lasted till now, when so many other things which came down from the same odious source have been done away with. And this, indeed, is what makes it strange to ordinary ears, to hear it asserted that the inequality of rights between men and women has no other source than the law of the strongest.

That this statement should have the effect of a paradox, is in some respects creditable to the progress of civilization, and the improvement of the moral sentiments of mankind. We now live—that is to say, one or two of the most advanced nations of the world now live—in a state in which the law of the strongest seems to be entirely abandoned as the regulating principle of the world's affairs: nobody professes it, and, as regards most of the relations between human beings, nobody is permitted to practise it. When any one succeeds in doing so, it is under cover of some pretext which gives him the semblance of having some general social interest on his side. This being the ostensible state of things, people flatter themselves that the rule of mere force is ended; that the law of the strongest cannot be the reason of existence of anything which has remained in full operation down to the present time. However any of our present institutions may have begun, it can only, they think, have been preserved to this period of advanced civilization by a well-grounded feeling of its adaptation to human nature, and conduciveness to the general good. They do not understand the great vitality and durability of institutions which place right on the side of might; how intensely they are clung to; how the good as well as the bad propensities and sentiments of those who have power in their hands, become identified with retaining it; how slowly these bad institutions give way, one at a time, the weakest first, beginning with those which are least interwoven with the daily habits of life; and how very rarely those who have obtained legal power because they first had physical, have ever lost their hold of it until the physical power had passed over to the other side. Such shifting of the physical force not having taken place in the case of women; this fact, combined with all the peculiar and characteristic features of the particular case, made it certain from the first that this branch of the system of right founded on might, though softened in its most atrocious features at an earlier period than several of the others, would be the very last to disappear. It was inevitable that this one case of a social relation grounded on force, would survive through generations of institutions grounded on equal justice, an almost solitary exception to the general

character of their laws and customs; but which, so long as it does not proclaim its own origin, and as discussion has not brought out its true character, is not felt to jar with modern civilization, any more than domestic slavery among the Greeks jarred with their notion of themselves as a free people.

The truth is, that people of the present and the last two or three generations have lost all practical sense of the primitive condition of humanity; and only the few who have studied history accurately, or have much frequented the parts of the world occupied by the living representatives of ages long past, are able to form any mental picture of what society then was. People are not aware how entirely, in former ages, the law of superior strength was the rule of life; how publicly and openly it was avowed, I do not say cynically or shamelessly—for these words imply a feeling that there was something in it to be ashamed of, and no such notion could find a place in the faculties of any person in those ages, except a philosopher or a saint. History gives a cruel experience of human nature, in shewing how exactly the regard due to the life, possessions, and entire earthly happiness of any class of persons, was measured by what they had the power of enforcing; how all who made any resistance to authorities that had arms in their hands, however dreadful might be the provocation, had not only the law of force but all other laws, and all the notions of social obligation against them; and in the eyes of those whom they resisted, were not only guilty of crime, but of the worst of all crimes, deserving the most cruel chastisement which human beings could inflict. The first small vestige of a feeling of obligation in a superior to acknowledge any right in inferiors, began when he had been induced, for convenience, to make some promise to them. Though these promises, even when sanctioned by the most solemn oaths, were for many ages revoked or violated on the most trifling provocation or temptation, it is probable that this, except by persons of still worse than the average morality, was seldom done without some twinges of conscience. The ancient republics, being mostly grounded from the first upon some kind of mutual compact, or at any rate formed by an union of persons not very unequal in strength, afforded, in consequence, the first instance of a portion of human relations fenced round, and placed under the dominion of another law than that of force. And though the original law of force remained in full operation between them and their slaves, and also (except so far as limited by express compact) between a commonwealth and its subjects, or other independent commonwealths; the banishment of that primitive law even from so narrow a field, commenced the regeneration of human nature, by giving birth to sentiments of which experience soon demonstrated the immense value even for material interests, and which thenceforward only required to be enlarged, not created. Though slaves were no part of the commonwealth, it was in the free states that slaves were first felt to have rights as human beings. The Stoics were, I believe, the first (except so far as the Jewish law constitutes an exception) who taught as a part of morality that men were bound by moral obligations to their slaves. No one, after Christianity became ascendant, could ever again have been a stranger to this belief, in theory; nor, after the rise of the Catholic Church, was it ever without persons to stand up for it. Yet to enforce it was the most arduous task which Christianity ever had to perform. For more than a thousand years the Church kept up the contest, with hardly any perceptible success. It was not for want of power over men's minds. Its power was prodigious. It could make kings and nobles resign their most valued possessions to enrich the Church. It could make thousands, in the prime of life and the height of worldly advantages, shut themselves up in convents to work out their salvation by poverty, fasting, and prayer. It could send hundreds of thousands across land and sea, Europe and Asia, to give their lives for the deliverance of the Holy Sepulchre. It could make kings relinquish wives who were the object of their passionate attachment, because the Church declared that they were within the seventh (by our calculation the fourteenth) degree of relationship. All this it did; but it could not make men fight less with one another, nor tyrannize less cruelly over the serfs, and when they were able, over burgesses. It could not make them renounce either of the applications of force; force militant, or force triumphant. This they could never be induced to do until they

were themselves in their turn compelled by superior force. Only by the growing power of kings was an end put to fighting except between kings, or competitors for kingship; only by the growth of a wealthy and warlike bourgeoisie in the fortified towns, and of a plebeian infantry which proved more powerful in the field than the undisciplined chivalry, was the insolent tyranny of the nobles over the bourgeoisie and peasantry brought within some bounds. It was persisted in not only until, but long after, the oppressed had obtained a power enabling them often to take conspicuous vengeance; and on the Continent much of it continued to the time of the French Revolution, though in England the earlier and better organization of the democratic classes put an end to it sooner by establishing equal laws and free national institutions.

If people are mostly so little aware how completely, during the greater part of the duration of our species, the law of force was the avowed rule of general conduct, any other being only a special and exceptional consequence of peculiar ties—and from how very recent a date it is that the affairs of society in general have been even pretended to be regulated according to any moral law; as little do people remember or consider, how institutions and customs which never had any ground but the law of force, last on into ages and states of general opinion which never would have permitted their first establishment. Less than forty years ago, Englishmen might still by law hold human beings in bondage as saleable property: within the present century they might kidnap them and carry them off, and work them literally to death. This absolutely extreme case of the law of force, condemned by those who can tolerate almost every other form of arbitrary power, and which, of all others, presents features the most revolting to the feelings of all who look at it from an impartial position, was the law of civilized and Christian England within the memory of persons now living: and in one half of Anglo-Saxon America three or four years ago, not only did slavery exist, but the slave trade, and the breeding of slaves expressly for it, was a general practice between slave states. Yet not only was there a greater strength of sentiment against it, but, in England at least, a less amount either of feeling or of interest in favour of it, than of any other of the customary abuses of force: for its motive was the love of gain, unmixed and undisguised; and those who profited by it were a very small numerical fraction of the country, while the natural feeling of all who were not personally interested in it, was unmitigated abhorrence. So extreme an instance makes it almost superfluous to refer to any other: but consider the long duration of absolute monarchy. In England at present it is the almost universal conviction that military despotism is a case of the law of force, having no other origin or justification. Yet in all the great nations of Europe except England it either still exists, or has only just ceased to exist, and has even now a strong party favourable to it in all ranks of the people, especially among persons of station and consequence. Such is the power of an established system, even when far from universal; when not only in almost every period of history there have been great and well-known examples of the contrary system, but these have almost invariably been afforded by the most illustrious and most prosperous communities. In this case, too, the possessor of the undue power, the person directly interested in it, is only one person, while those who are subject to it and suffer from it are literally all the rest. The yoke is naturally and necessarily humiliating to all persons, except the one who is on the throne, together with, at most, the one who expects to succeed to it. How different are these cases from that of the power of men over women! I am not now prejudging the question of its justifiableness. I am showing how vastly more permanent it could not but be, even if not justifiable, than these other dominations which have nevertheless lasted down to our own time. Whatever gratification of pride there is in the possession of power, and whatever personal interest in its exercise, is in this case not confined to a limited class, but common to the whole male sex. Instead of being, to most of its supporters, a thing desirable chiefly in the abstract, or, like the political ends usually contended for by factions, of little private importance to any but the leaders; it comes home to the person and hearth of every male head of a family, and of every one who looks forward to being so. The clodhopper exercises, or is to exercise,

his share of the power equally with the highest nobleman. And the case is that in which the desire of power is the strongest: for every one who desires power, desires it most over those who are nearest to him, with whom his life is passed, with whom he has most concerns in common, and in whom any independence of his authority is oftenest likely to interfere with his individual preferences. If, in the other cases specified, powers manifestly grounded only on force, and having so much less to support them, are so slowly and with so much difficulty got rid of, much more must it be so with this, even if it rests on no better foundation than those. We must consider, too, that the possessors of the power have facilities in this case, greater than in any other, to prevent any uprising against it. Every one of the subjects lives under the very eye, and almost, it may be said, in the hands, of one of the masters—in closer intimacy with him than with any of her fellow-subjects; with no means of combining against him, no power of even locally overmastering him, and, on the other hand, with the strongest motives for seeking his favour and avoiding to give him offence. In struggles for political emancipation, everybody knows how often its champions are bought off by bribes, or daunted by terrors. In the case of women, each individual of the subject-class is in a chronic state of bribery and intimidation combined. In setting up the standard of resistance, a large number of the leaders, and still more of the followers, must make an almost complete sacrifice of the pleasures or the alleviations of their own individual lot. If ever any system of privilege and enforced subjection had its yoke tightly riveted on the necks of those who are kept down by it, this has. I have not yet shown that it is a wrong system: but every one who is capable of thinking on the subject must see that even if it is, it was certain to outlast all other forms of unjust authority. And when some of the grossest of the other forms still exist in many civilized countries, and have only recently been got rid of in others, it would be strange if that which is so much the deepest-rooted had yet been perceptibly shaken anywhere. There is more reason to wonder that the protests and testimonies against it should have been so numerous and so weighty as they are.

Some will object, that a comparison cannot fairly be made between the government of the male sex and the forms of unjust power which I have adduced in illustration of it, since these are arbitrary, and the effect of mere usurpation, while it on the contrary is natural. But was there ever any domination which did not appear natural to those who possessed it? There was a time when the division of mankind into two classes, a small one of masters and a numerous one of slaves, appeared, even to the most cultivated minds, to be a natural, and the only natural, condition of the human race. No less an intellect, and one which contributed no less to the progress of human thought, than Aristotle, held this opinion without doubt or misgiving; and rested it on the same premises on which the same assertion in regard to the dominion of men over women is usually based, namely that there are different natures among mankind, free natures, and slave natures; that the Greeks were of a free nature, the barbarian races of Thracians and Asiatics of a slave nature. But why need I go back to Aristotle? Did not the slaveowners of the Southern United States maintain the same doctrine, with all the fanaticism with which men cling to the theories that justify their passions and legitimate their personal interests? Did they not call heaven and earth to witness that the dominion of white man over the black is natural, that the black race is by nature incapable of freedom, and marked out for slavery? some even going so far as to say that the freedom of manual labourers is an unnatural order of things anywhere. Again, the theorists of absolute monarchy have always affirmed it to be the only natural form of government; issuing from the patriarchal, which was the primitive and spontaneous form of society, framed on the model of the paternal, which is anterior to society itself, and, as they contend, the most natural authority of all. Nay, for that matter, the law of force itself, to those who could not plead any other, has always seemed the most natural of all grounds for the exercise of authority. Conquering races hold it to be Nature's own dictate that the conquered should obey the conquerors, or, as they euphoniously paraphrase it, that the feebler and more unwarlike races should submit to the braver and manlier. The smallest

acquaintance with human life in the middle ages, shows how supremely natural the dominion of the feudal nobility over men of low condition appeared to the nobility themselves, and how unnatural the conception seemed, of a person of the inferior class claiming equality with them, or exercising authority over them. It hardly seemed less so to the class held in subjection. The emancipated serfs and burgesses, even in their most vigorous struggles, never made any pretension to a share of authority; they only demanded more or less of limitation to the power of tyrannizing over them. So true is it that unnatural generally means only uncustomary, and that everything which is usual appears natural. The subjection of women to men being a universal custom, any departure from it quite naturally appears unnatural. But how entirely, even in this case, the feeling is dependent on custom, appears by ample experience. Nothing so much astonishes the people of distant parts of the world, when they first learn anything about England, as to be told that it is under a queen: the thing seems to them so unnatural as to be almost incredible. To Englishmen this does not seem in the least degree unnatural, because they are used to it; but they do feel it unnatural that women should be soldiers or members of Parliament. In the feudal ages, on the contrary, war and politics were not thought unnatural to women, because not unusual; it seemed natural that women of the privileged classes should be of manly character, inferior in nothing but bodily strength to their husbands and fathers. The independence of women seemed rather less unnatural to the Greeks than to other ancients, on account of the fabulous Amazons (whom they believed to be historical), and the partial example afforded by the Spartan women; who, though no less subordinate by law than in other Greek states, were more free in fact, and being trained to bodily exercises in the same manner with men, gave ample proof that they were not naturally disqualified for them. There can be little doubt that Spartan experience suggested to Plato, among many other of his doctrines, that of the social and political equality of the two sexes.

But, it will be said, the rule of men over women differs from all these others in not being a rule of force: it is accepted voluntarily; women make no complaint, and are consenting parties to it. In the first place, a great number of women do not accept it. Ever since there have been women able to make their sentiments known by their writings (the only mode of publicity which society permits to them), an increasing number of them have recorded protests against their present social condition: and recently many thousands of them, headed by the most eminent women known to the public, have petitioned Parliament for their admission to the Parliamentary Suffrage. The claim of women to be educated as solidly, and in the same branches of knowledge, as men, is urged with growing intensity, and with a great prospect of success; while the demand for their admission into professions and occupations hitherto closed against them, becomes every year more urgent. Though there are not in this country, as there are in the United States, periodical Conventions and an organized party to agitate for the Rights of Women, there is a numerous and active Society organized and managed by women, for the more limited object of obtaining the political franchise. Nor is it only in our own country and in America that women are beginning to protest, more or less collectively, against the disabilities under which they labour. France, and Italy, and Switzerland, and Russia now afford examples of the same thing. How many more women there are who silently cherish similar aspirations, no one can possibly know; but there are abundant tokens how many *would* cherish them, were they not so strenuously taught to repress them as contrary to the proprieties of their sex. It must be remembered, also, that no enslaved class ever asked for complete liberty at once. When Simon de Montfort called the deputies of the commons to sit for the first time in Parliament, did any of them dream of demanding that an assembly, elected by their constituents, should make and destroy ministries, and dictate to the king in affairs of state? No such thought entered into the imagination of the most ambitious of them. The nobility had already these pretensions; the commons pretended to nothing but to be exempt from arbitrary taxation, and from the gross individual oppression of the king's officers. It is a political law of nature that those who are under any power of ancient origin,

never begin by complaining of the power itself, but only of its oppressive exercise. There is never any want of women who complain of ill usage by their husbands. There would be infinitely more, if complaint were not the greatest of all provocatives to a repetition and increase of the ill usage. It is this which frustrates all attempts to maintain the power but protect the woman against its abuses. In no other case (except that of a child) is the person who has been proved judicially to have suffered an injury, replaced under the physical power of the culprit who inflicted it. Accordingly wives, even in the most extreme and protracted cases of bodily ill usage, hardly ever dare avail themselves of the laws made for their protection: and if, in a moment of irrepressible indignation, or by the interference of neighbours, they are induced to do so, their whole effort afterwards is to disclose as little as they can, and to beg off their tyrant from his merited chastisement.

All causes, social and natural, combine to make it unlikely that women should be collectively rebellious to the power of men. They are so far in a position different from all other subject classes, that their masters require something more from them than actual service. Men do not want solely the obedience of women, they want their sentiments. All men, except the most brutish, desire to have, in the woman most nearly connected with them, not a forced slave but a willing one, not a slave merely, but a favourite. They have therefore put everything in practice to enslave their minds. The masters of all other slaves rely, for maintaining obedience, on fear; either fear of themselves, or religious fears. The masters of women wanted more than simple obedience, and they turned the whole force of education to effect their purpose. All women are brought up from the very earliest years in the belief that their ideal of character is the very opposite to that of men; not self-will, and government by self-control, but submission, and yielding to the control of others. All the moralities tell them that it is the duty of women, and all the current sentimentalities that it is their nature, to live for others; to make complete abnegation of themselves, and to have no life but in their affections. And by their affections are meant the only ones they are allowed to have—those to the men with whom they are connected, or to the children who constitute an additional and indefeasible tie between them and a man. When we put together three things—first, the natural attraction between opposite sexes; secondly, the wife's entire dependence on the husband, every privilege or pleasure she has being either his gift, or depending entirely on his will; and lastly, that the principal object of human pursuit, consideration, and all objects of social ambition, can in general be sought or obtained by her only through him, it would be a miracle if the object of being attractive to men had not become the polar star of feminine education and formation of character. And, this great means of influence over the minds of women having been acquired, an instinct of selfishness made men avail themselves of it to the utmost as a means of holding women in subjection, by representing to them meekness, submissiveness, and resignation of all individual will into the hands of a man, as an essential part of sexual attractiveness. Can it be doubted that any of the other yokes which mankind have succeeded in breaking, would have subsisted till now if the same means had existed, and had been as sedulously used, to bow down their minds to it? If it had been made the object of the life of every young plebeian to find personal favour in the eyes of some patrician, of every young serf with some seigneur; if domestication with him, and a share of his personal affections, had been held out as the prize which they all should look out for, the most gifted and aspiring being able to reckon on the most desirable prizes; and if, when this prize had been obtained, they had been shut out by a wall of brass from all interests not centering in him, all feelings and desires but those which he shared or inculcated; would not serfs and seigneurs, plebeians and patricians, have been as broadly distinguished at this day as men and women are? and would not all but a thinker here and there, have believed the distinction to be a fundamental and unalterable fact in human nature?

The preceding considerations are amply sufficient to show that custom, however universal it may be, affords in this case no presumption, and ought not to create any prejudice, in favour of the arrangements which place women in social and political subjection to men. But I may go farther, and maintain that the course of history, and the tendencies of progressive human society, afford not only no presumption in favour of this system of inequality of rights, but a strong one against it; and that, so far as the whole course of human improvement up to this time, the whole stream of modern tendencies, warrants any inference on the subject, it is, that this relic of the past is discordant with the future, and must necessarily disappear.

For, what is the peculiar character of the modern world—the difference which chiefly distinguishes modern institutions, modern social ideas, modern life itself, from those of times long past? It is, that human beings are no longer born to their place in life, and chained down by an inexorable bond to the place they are born to, but are free to employ their faculties, and such favourable chances as offer, to achieve the lot which may appear to them most desirable. Human society of old was constituted on a very different principle. All were born to a fixed social position, and were mostly kept in it by law, or interdicted from any means by which they could emerge from it. As some men are born white and others black, so some were born slaves and others freemen and citizens; some were born patricians, other plebeians; some were born feudal nobles, others commoners and *roturiers*. A slave or serf could never make himself free, nor, except by the will of his master, become so. In most European countries it was not till towards the close of the middle ages, and as a consequence of the growth of regal power, that commoners could be ennobled. Even among nobles, the eldest son was born the exclusive heir to the paternal possessions, and a long time elapsed before it was fully established that the father could disinherit him. Among the industrious classes, only those who were born members of a guild, or were admitted into it by its members, could lawfully practise their calling within its local limits; and nobody could practise any calling deemed important, in any but the legal manner—by processes authoritatively prescribed. Manufacturers have stood in the pillory for presuming to carry on their business by new and improved methods. In modern Europe, and most in those parts of it which have participated

most largely in all other modern improvements, diametrically opposite doctrines now prevail. Law and
government do not undertake to prescribe by whom
any social or industrial operation shall or shall not be
conducted, or what modes of conducting them shall
be lawful. These things are left to the unfettered
choice of individuals. Even the laws which required
that workmen should serve an apprenticeship, have in
this country been repealed: there being ample assur-
ance that in all cases in which an apprenticeship is
necessary, its necessity will suffice to enforce it. The
old theory was, that the least possible should be left
to the choice of the individual agent; that all he had to
do should, as far as practicable, be laid down for him
by superior wisdom. Left to himself he was sure to go
wrong. The modern conviction, the fruit of a thous-
and years of experience, is, that things in which the
individual is the person directly interested, never go
right but as they are left to his own discretion; and
that any regulation of them by authority, except to
protect the rights of others, is sure to be mischievous.
This conclusion, slowly arrived at, and not adopted
until almost every possible application of the contrary
theory had been made with disastrous result, now (in
the industrial department) prevails universally in the
most advanced countries, almost universally in all
that have pretensions to any sort of advancement. It is
not that all processes are supposed to be equally
good, or all persons to be equally qualified for everything; but that freedom of individual choice is now
known to be the only thing which procures the adoption of the best processes, and throws each operation
into the hands of those who are best qualified for it.
Nobody thinks it necessary to make a law that only a
strong-armed man shall be a blacksmith. Freedom
and competition suffice to make blacksmiths strong-
armed men, because the weak-armed can earn more
by engaging in occupations for which they are more
fit. In consonance with this doctrine, it is felt to be an
overstepping of the proper bounds of authority to fix
beforehand, on some general presumption, that certain persons are not fit to do certain things. It is now
thoroughly known and admitted that if some such
presumptions exist, no such presumption is infallible.
Even if it be well grounded in a majority of cases,

which it is very likely not to be, there will be a minority of exceptional cases in which it does not hold: and
in those it is both an injustice to the individuals, and
a detriment to society, to place barriers in the way of
their using their faculties for their own benefit and for
that of others. In the cases, on the other hand, in
which the unfitness is real, the ordinary motives of
human conduct will on the whole suffice to prevent
the incompetent person from making, or from persisting in, the attempt.

If this general principle of social and economical
science is not true; if individuals, with such help as
they can derive from the opinion of those who know
them, are not better judges than the law and the
government, of their own capacities and vocation; the
world cannot too soon abandon this principle, and
return to the old system of regulations and disabilities. But if the principle is true, we ought to act as if
we believed it, and not to ordain that to be born a girl
instead of a boy, any more than to be born black
instead of white, or a commoner instead of a nobleman, shall decide the person's position through all
life—shall interdict people from all the more elevated
social positions, and from all, except a few, respectable occupations. Even were we to admit the utmost
that is ever pretended as to the superior fitness of men
for all the functions now reserved to them, the same
argument applies which forbids a legal qualification
for members of Parliament. If only once in a dozen
years the conditions of eligibility exclude a fit person,
there is a real loss, while the exclusion of thousands
of unfit persons is no gain; for if the constitution
of the electoral body disposes them to choose unfit
persons, there are always plenty of such persons to
choose from. In all things of any difficulty and importance, those who can do them well are fewer than the
need, even with the most unrestricted latitude of choice:
and any limitation of the field of selection deprives
society of some chances of being served by the competent, without ever saving it from the incompetent.

At present, in the more improved countries, the
disabilities of women are the only case, save one, in
which laws and institutions take persons at their birth,
and ordain that they shall never in all their lives be
allowed to compete for certain things. The one

exception is that of royalty. Persons still are born to the throne; no one, not of the reigning family, can ever occupy it, and no one even of that family can, by any means but the course of hereditary succession, attain it. All other dignities and social advantages are open to the whole male sex: many indeed are only attainable by wealth, but wealth may be striven for by any one, and is actually obtained by many men of the very humblest origin. The difficulties, to the majority, are indeed insuperable without the aid of fortunate accidents; but no male human being is under any legal ban: neither law nor opinion superadd artificial obstacles to the natural ones. Royalty, as I have said, is excepted: but in this case every one feels it to be an exception—an anomaly in the modern world, in marked opposition to its customs and principles, and to be justified only by extraordinary special expediencics, which, though individuals and nations differ in estimating their weight, unquestionably do in fact exist. But in this exceptional case, in which a high social function is, for important reasons, bestowed on birth instead of being put up to competition, all free nations contrive to adhere in substance to the principle from which they nominally derogate; for they circumscribe this high function by conditions avowedly intended to prevent the person to whom it ostensibly belongs from really performing it; while the person by whom it is performed, the responsible minister, does obtain the post by a competition from which no full-grown citizen of the male sex is legally excluded. The disabilities, therefore, to which women are subject from the mere fact of their birth, are the solitary examples of the kind in modern legislation. In no instance except this, which comprehends half the human race, are the higher social functions closed against any one by a fatality of birth which no exertions, and no change of circumstances, can overcome; for even religious disabilities (besides that in England and in Europe they have practically almost ceased to exist) do not close any career to the disqualified person in case of conversion.

The social subordination of women thus stands out an isolated fact in modern social institutions; a solitary breach of what has become their fundamental law; a single relic of an old world of thought and practice exploded in everything else, but retained in the one thing of most universal interest; as if a gigantic dolmen, or a vast temple of Jupiter Olympius, occupied the site of St. Paul's and received daily worship, while the surrounding Christian churches were only resorted to on fasts and festivals. This entire discrepancy between one social fact and all those which accompany it, and the radical opposition between its nature and the progressive movement which is the boast of the modern world, and which has successively swept away everything else of an analogous character, surely affords, to a conscientious observer of human tendencies, serious matter for reflection. It raises a primâ facie presumption on the unfavourable side, far outweighing any which custom and usage could in such circumstances create on the favourable; and should at least suffice to make this, like the choice between republicanism and royalty, a balanced question.

The least that can be demanded is, that the question should not be considered as prejudged by existing fact and existing opinion, but open to discussion on its merits, as a question of justice and expediency: the decision on this, as on any of the other social arrangements of mankind, depending on what an enlightened estimate of tendencies and consequences may show to be most advantageous to humanity in general, without distinction of sex. And the discussion must be a real discussion, descending to foundations, and not resting satisfied with vague and general assertions. It will not do, for instance, to assert in general terms, that the experience of mankind has pronounced in favour of the existing system. Experience cannot possibly have decided between two courses, so long as there has only been experience of one. If it be said that the doctrine of the equality of the sexes rests only on theory, it must be remembered that the contrary doctrine also has only theory to rest upon. All that is proved in its favour by direct experience, is that mankind have been able to exist under it, and to attain the degree of improvement and prosperity which we now see; but whether that prosperity has been attained sooner, or is now greater, than it would have been under the other system, experience does not say. On the other hand, experience does say, that every step in improvement has been so invariably accompanied by a step made in raising the social position of women, that historians and philosophers have been led to adopt their elevation or debasement as on the whole the surest test and most correct measure of the civilization of a people or an age. Through all the progressive period of human history, the condition of women has been approaching nearer to equality with men. This does not of itself prove that the assimilation must go on to complete equality; but it assuredly affords some presumption that such is the case.

Neither does it avail anything to say that the *nature* of the two sexes adapts them to their present functions and position, and renders these appropriate to them. Standing on the ground of common sense and the constitution of the human mind, I deny that any one knows, or can know, the nature of the two sexes, as long as they have only been seen in their present relation to one another. If men had ever been found in society without women, or women without men, or if there had been a society of men and women in which the women were not under the control of the men, something might have been positively known about the mental and moral differences which may be inherent in the nature of each. What is now called the nature of women is an eminently artificial thing—the result of forced repression in some directions, unnatural stimulation in others. It may be asserted without scruple, that no other class of dependents have had their character so entirely distorted from its natural proportions by their relation with their masters; for, if conquered and slave races have been, in some respects, more forcibly repressed, whatever in them has not been crushed down by an iron heel has generally been let alone, and if left with any liberty of development, it has developed itself according to its own laws; but in the case of women, a hot-house and stove cultivation has always been carried on of some of the capabilities of their nature, for the benefit and pleasure of their masters. Then, because certain products of the general vital force sprout luxuriantly and reach a great development in this heated atmosphere and under this active nurture and watering, while other shoots from the same root, which are left outside in the wintry air, with ice purposely heaped all round

them, have a stunted growth, and some are burnt off with fire and disappear; men, with that inability to recognise their own work which distinguishes the unanalytic mind, indolently believe that the tree grows of itself in the way they have made it grow, and that it would die if one half of it were not kept in a vapour bath and the other half in the snow.

Of all difficulties which impede the progress of thought, and the formation of well-grounded opinions on life and social arrangements, the greatest is now the unspeakable ignorance and inattention of mankind in respect to the influences which form human character. Whatever any portion of the human species now are, or seem to be, such, it is supposed, they have a natural tendency to be: even when the most elementary knowledge of the circumstances in which they have been placed, clearly points out the causes that made them what they are. Because a cottier deeply in arrears to his landlord is not industrious, there are people who think that the Irish are naturally idle. Because constitutions can be overthrown when the authorities appointed to execute them turn their arms against them, there are people who think the French incapable of free government. Because the Greeks cheated the Turks, and the Turks only plundered the Greeks, there are persons who think that the Turks are naturally more sincere: and because women, as is often said, care nothing about politics except their personalities, it is supposed that the general good is naturally less interesting to women than to men. History, which is now so much better understood than formerly, teaches another lesson: if only by showing the extraordinary susceptibility of human nature to external influences, and the extreme variableness of those of its manifestations which are supposed to be most universal and uniform. But in history, as in travelling, men usually see only what they already had in their own minds; and few learn much from history, who do not bring much with them to its study.

Hence, in regard to that most difficult question, what are the natural differences between the two sexes—a subject on which it is impossible in the present state of society to obtain complete and correct knowledge—while almost everybody dogmatizes upon it, almost all neglect and make light of the only means by which any partial insight can be obtained into it. This is, an analytic study of the most important department of psychology, the laws of the influence of circumstances on character. For, however great and apparently ineradicable the moral and intellectual differences between men and women might be, the evidence of their being natural differences could only be negative. Those only could be inferred to be natural which could not possibly be artificial—the residuum, after deducting every characteristic of either sex which can admit of being explained from education or external circumstances. The profoundest knowledge of the laws of the formation of character is indispensable to entitle any one to affirm even that there is any difference, much more what the difference is, between the two sexes considered as moral and rational beings; and since no one, as yet, has that knowledge, (for there is hardly any subject which, in proportion to its importance, has been so little studied), no one is thus far entitled to any positive opinion on the subject. Conjectures are all that can at present be made; conjectures more or less probable, according as more or less authorized by such knowledge as we yet have of the laws of psychology, as applied to the formation of character.

Even the preliminary knowledge, what the differences between the sexes now are, apart from all question as to how they are made what they are, is still in the crudest and most incomplete state. Medical practitioners and physiologists have ascertained, to some extent, the differences in bodily constitution; and this is an important element to the psychologist: but hardly any medical practitioner is a psychologist. Respecting the mental characteristics of women; their observations are of no more worth than those of common men. It is a subject on which nothing final can be known, so long as those who alone can really know it, women themselves, have given but little testimony, and that little, mostly suborned. It is easy to know stupid women. Stupidity is much the same all the world over. A stupid person's notions and feelings may confidently be inferred from those which prevail in the circle by which the person is surrounded. Not so with those whose opinions and feelings are an emanation from their own nature and

faculties. It is only a man here and there who has any tolerable knowledge of the character even of the women of his own family. I do not mean, of their capabilities; these nobody knows, not even themselves, because most of them have never been called out. I mean their actually existing thoughts and feelings. Many a man thinks he perfectly understands women, because he has had amatory relations with several, perhaps with many of them. If he is a good observer, and his experience extends to quality as well as quantity, he may have learnt something of one narrow department of their nature—an important department, no doubt. But of all the rest of it, few persons are generally more ignorant, because there are few from whom it is so carefully hidden. The most favourable case which a man can generally have for studying the character of a woman, is that of his own wife: for the opportunities are greater, and the cases of complete sympathy not so unspeakably rare. And in fact, this is the source from which any knowledge worth having on the subject has, I believe, generally come. But most men have not had the opportunity of studying in this way more than a single case: accordingly one can, to an almost laughable degree, infer what a man's wife is like, from his opinions about women in general, To make even this one case yield any result, the woman must be worth knowing, and the man not only a competent judge, but of a character so sympathetic in itself, and so well adapted to hers, that he can either read her mind by sympathetic intuition, or has nothing in himself which makes her shy of disclosing it. Hardly anything, I believe, can be more rare than this conjunction. It often happens that there is the most complete unity of feeling and community of interests as to all external things, yet the one has as little admission into the internal life of the other as if they were common acquaintance. Even with true affection, authority on the one side and subordination on the other prevent perfect confidence. Though nothing may be intentionally withheld, much is not shown. In the analogous relation of parent and child, the corresponding phenomenon must have been in the observation of every one. As between father and son, how many are the cases in which the father, in spite of real affection on both sides, obviously to all the world does not know, nor suspect, parts of the son's character familiar to his companions and equals. The truth is, that the position of looking up to another is extremely unpropitious to complete sincerity and openness with him. The fear of losing ground in his opinion or in his feelings is so strong, that even in an upright character, there is an unconscious tendency to show only the best side, or the side which, though not the best, is that which he most likes to see: and it may be confidently said that thorough knowledge of one another hardly ever exists, but between persons who, besides being intimates, are equals. How much more true, then, must all this be, when the one is not only under the authority of the other, but has it inculcated on her as a duty to reckon everything else subordinate to his comfort and pleasure, and to let him neither see nor feel anything coming from her, except what is agreeable to him. All these difficulties stand in the way of a man's obtaining any thorough knowledge even of the one woman whom alone, in general, he has sufficient opportunity of studying. When we further consider that to understand one woman is not necessarily to understand any other woman; that even if he could study many women of one rank, or of one country, he would not thereby understand women of other ranks or countries; and even if he did, they are still only the women of a single period of history; we may safely assert that the knowledge which men can acquire of women, even as they have been and are, without reference to what they might be, is wretchedly imperfect and superficial, and always will be so, until women themselves have told all that they have to tell.

And this time has not come; nor will it come otherwise than gradually. It is but of yesterday that women have either been qualified by literary accomplishments, or permitted by society, to tell anything to the general public. As yet very few of them dare tell anything, which men, on whom their literary success depends, are unwilling to hear. Let us remember in what manner, up to a very recent time, the expression, even by a male author, of uncustomary opinions, or what are deemed eccentric feelings, usually was, and in some degree still is, received; and we may form some faint conception under what impediments a

woman, who is brought up to think custom and opinion her sovereign rule, attempts to express in books anything drawn from the depths of her own nature. The greatest woman who has left writings behind her sufficient to give her an eminent rank in the literature of her country, thought it necessary to prefix as a motto to her boldest work, "Un homme peut braver l'opinion; une femme doit s'y soumettre." The greater part of what women write about women is mere sycophancy to men, In the case of unmarried women, much of it seems only intended to increase their chance of a husband. Many, both married and unmarried, overstep the mark, and inculcate a servility beyond what is desired or relished by any man, except the very vulgarest. But this is not so often the case as, even at a quite late period, it still was. Literary women are becoming more freespoken, and more willing to express their real sentiments. Unfortunately, in this country especially, they are themselves such artificial products, that their sentiments are compounded of a small element of individual observation and consciousness, and a very large one of acquired associations. This will be less and less the case, but it will remain true to a great extent, as long as social institutions do not admit the same free development of originality in women which is possible to men. When that time comes, and not before, we shall see, and not merely hear, as much as it is necessary to know of the nature of women, and the adaptation of other things to it.

I have dwelt so much on the difficulties which at present obstruct any real knowledge by men of the true nature of women, because in this as in so many other things "opinio copiae inter maximas causas inopiae est;" and there is little chance of reasonable thinking on the matter, while people flatter themselves that they perfectly understand a subject of which most men know absolutely nothing, and of which it is at present impossible that any man, or all men taken together, should have knowledge which can qualify them to lay down the law to women as to what is, or is not, their vocation. Happily, no such knowledge is necessary for any practical purpose connected with the position of women in relation to society and life. For, according to all the principles involved in modern society, the question rests with women themselves—to be decided by their own experience, and by the use of their own faculties. There are no means of finding what either one person or many can do, but by trying—and no means by which any one else can discover for them what it is for their happiness to do or leave undone.

One thing we may be certain of—that what is contrary to women's nature to do, they never will be made to do by simply giving their nature free play. The anxiety of mankind to interfere in behalf of nature, for fear lest nature should not succeed in effecting its purpose, is an altogether unnecessary solicitude. What women by nature cannot do, it is quite superfluous to forbid them from doing. What they can do, but not so well as the men who are their competitors, competition suffices to exclude them from; since nobody asks for protective duties and bounties in favour of women; it is only asked that the present bounties and protective duties in favour of men should be recalled. If women have a greater natural inclination for some things than for others, there is no need of laws or social inculcation to make the majority of them do the former in preference to the latter. Whatever women's services are most wanted for, the free play of competition will hold out the strongest inducements to them to undertake. And, as the words imply, they are most wanted for the things for which they are most fit; by the apportionment of which to them, the collective faculties of the two sexes can be applied on the whole with the greatest sum of valuable result.

The general opinion of men is supposed to be, that the natural vocation of a woman is that of a wife and mother. I say, is supposed to be, because, judging from acts—from the whole of the present constitution of society—one might infer that their opinion was the direct contrary. They might be supposed to think that the alleged natural vocation of women was of all things the most repugnant to their nature; insomuch that if they are free to do anything else—if any other means of living, or occupation of their time and faculties, is open, which has any chance of appearing desirable to them—there will not be enough of them who will be willing to accept the condition said to be

natural to them. If this is the real opinion of men in general, it would be well that it should be spoken out. I should like to hear somebody openly enunciating the doctrine (it is already implied in much that is written on the subject)—"It is necessary to society that women should marry and produce children. They will not do so unless they are compelled. Therefore it is necessary to compel them." The merits of the case would then be clearly defined. It would be exactly that of the slaveholders of South Carolina and Louisiana. "It is necessary that cotton and sugar should be grown. White men cannot produce them. Negroes will not, for any wages which we choose to give. Ergo they must be compelled." An illustration still closer to the point is that of impressment. Sailors must absolutely be had to defend the country. It often happens that they will not voluntarily enlist. Therefore there must be the power of forcing them. How often has this logic been used! and, but for one flaw in it, without doubt it would have been successful up to this day. But it is open to the retort—First pay the sailors the honest value of their labour. When you have made it as well worth their while to serve you, as to work for other employers, you will have no more difficulty than others have in obtaining their services. To this there is no logical answer except "I will not:" and as people are now not only ashamed, but are not desirous, to rob the labourer of his hire, impressment is no longer advocated. Those who attempt to force women into marriage by closing all other doors against them, lay themselves open to a similar retort. If they mean what they say, their opinion must evidently be, that men do not render the married condition so desirable to women, as to induce them to accept it for its own recommendations. It is not a sign of one's thinking the boon one offers very attractive, when one allows only Hobson's choice, "that or none." And here, I believe, is the clue to the feelings of those men, who have a real antipathy to the equal freedom of women. I believe they are afraid, not lest women should be unwilling to marry, for I do not think that any one in reality has that apprehension; but lest they should insist that marriage should be on equal conditions; lest all women of spirit and capacity should prefer doing almost anything else, not in their own eyes degrading, rather than marry, when marrying is giving themselves a master, and a master too of all their earthly possessions. And truly, if this consequence were necessarily incident to marriage, I think that the apprehension would be very well founded. I agree in thinking it probable that few women, capable of anything else, would, unless under an irresistible *entrainement*, rendering them for the time insensible to anything but itself, choose such a lot, when any other means were open to them of filling a conventionally honourable place in life: and if men are determined that the law of marriage shall be a law of despotism, they are quite right, in point of mere policy, in leaving to women only Hobson's choice. But, in that case, all that has been done in the modern world to relax the chain on the minds of women, has been a mistake. They never should have been allowed to receive a literary education. Women who read, much more women who write, are, in the existing constitution of things, a contradiction and a disturbing element: and it was wrong to bring women up with any acquirements but those of an odalisque, or of a domestic servant.

Study Questions

1. In the first paragraph of his essay, Mill proposes that there are two things wrong with the "legal subordination of one sex to the other." What are they?

2. Mill points out that when discussing political matters, typically the burden of proof lies with those who seek to restrict liberty and the presumption is in favor of freedom and equal treatment. But when considering the situation of women, the burden of proof is reversed. Why? Because it is commonly maintained that

   • What is customary is presumed correct, and it is customary that women should be subordinate.
   • What is natural is presumed correct, and it is natural that women should be subordinate.

   He then argues against each of these claims.

   a) Explain two reasons Mill gives for thinking that even though our custom is to subordinate women, we should not presume that this policy is sound.
   b) Explain two reasons he gives for thinking that we cannot presume that it is natural for women to be subordinate.

3. Mill proposes a principle that he thinks distinguishes modern life from life in times past: human beings should not be born to their place in life; they should be "free to employ their faculties, and such favourable chances as offer, to achieve the lot which may appear to them most desirable" (paragraph 13). What reasons does he offer to support the principle?

4. Summarize Mill's argument in this chapter supporting his two-pronged analysis of what is wrong with the legal subordination of women (see your answer to question 1). Is the argument convincing?

Sojourner Truth

"Ar'n't I a Woman?"

Jeffrey Stewart provides useful information about the following excerpt in his introduction to *Narrative of Sojourner Truth* (New York: Oxford University Press, 1991, p. xxxiv). "This is the text of Sojourner Truth's famous 'Ar'n't I a Woman?' speech as it was transcribed and printed by the *Anti-Slavery Bugle* in Salem, Ohio, on June 21, 1851, less than thirty days after she delivered it at the Women's Rights Convention in Akron, Ohio." It differs markedly from the more familiar version "transcribed by Frances Gage, the organizer of the convention," most significantly in that this version does not "render [the] speech in a rather crude Southern dialect." It is extremely unlikely that Truth spoke in such a dialect, given that she was "a New York-born, former slave [. . .] bilingual in English and Dutch."

"May I say a few words?" Receiving an affirmative answer, she proceeded; "I want to say a few words about this matter. I am a woman's rights. I have as much muscle as any man, and can do as much work as any man. I have plowed and reaped and husked and chopped and mowed, and can any man do more than that? I have heard much about the sexes being equal; I can carry as much as any man, and can eat as much too, if I can get it. I am as strong as any man that is now. As for intellect, all I can say is, if woman have a pint and man a quart—why can't she have her little pint full? You need not be afraid to give us our rights for fear we will take too much, for we can't take more than our pint'll hold. The poor men seem to be all in confusion, and don't know what to do. Why children, if you have woman's rights give it to her and you will feel better. You will have your own rights, and they won't be so much trouble. I can't read, but I can hear. I have heard the bible and have learned that Eve caused man to sin. Well if woman upset the world, do give her a chance to set it right side up again. The Lady has spoken about Jesus, how he never spurned woman from him, and she was right. When Lazarus died, Mary and Martha came to him with faith and love and besought him to raise their brother. And Jesus wept—and Lazarus came forth. And how came Jesus into the world? Through God who created him and woman who bore him. Man, where is your part? But the women are coming up, blessed be God, and a few of the men are coming with them. But man is in a tight place, the poor slave is on him, woman is coming on him, and he is surely between a hawk and a buzzard."

STUDY QUESTIONS

1. What kind of argument might have prompted Truth to begin her speech with the assertion, "I have as much muscle as any man"?

2. In what ways do Truth's remarks criticize both sexist and racist stereotypes about women?

3. In what sense is Truth making a sameness/humanist argument?

Simone de Beauvoir

The Second Sex

INTRODUCTION

For a long time I have hesitated to write a book on woman. The subject is irritating, especially to women; and it is not new. Enough ink has been spilled in the quarreling over feminism, now practically over, and perhaps we should say no more about it. It is still talked about, however, for the voluminous nonsense uttered during the last century seems to have done little to illuminate the problem. After all, is there a problem? And if so, what is it? Are there women, really? Most assuredly the theory of the eternal feminine still has its adherents who will whisper in your ear: "Even in Russia women still are *women*"; and other erudite persons—sometimes the very same—say with a sigh: "Woman is losing her way, woman is lost." One wonders if women still exist, if they will always exist, whether or not it is desirable that they should, what place they occupy in this world, what their place should be. "What has become of women?" was asked recently in an ephemeral magazine.[1]

But first we must ask: what is a woman? "*Tota mulier in utero*," says one, "woman is a womb." But in speaking of certain women, connoisseurs declare that they are not women, although they are equipped with a uterus like the rest. All agree in recognizing the fact that females exist in the human species; today as always they make up about one half of humanity. And yet we are told that femininity is in danger; we are exhorted to be women, remain women, become women. It would appear, then, that every female human being is not necessarily a woman; to be so considered she must share in that mysterious and threatened reality known as femininity. Is this attribute something secreted by the ovaries? Or is it a Platonic essence, a product of the philosophic imagination? Is a rustling petticoat enough to bring it down to earth? Although some women try zealously to incarnate this essence, it is hardly patentable. It is frequently described in vague and dazzling terms that seem to have been borrowed from the vocabulary of the seers, and indeed in the times of St. Thomas it was considered an essence as certainly defined as the somniferous virtue of the poppy.

But conceptualism has lost ground. The biological and social sciences no longer admit the existence of unchangeably fixed entities that determine given characteristics, such as those ascribed to woman, the Jew, or the Negro. Science regards any characteristic as a reaction dependent in part upon a *situation*. If today femininity no longer exists, then it never existed. But does the word *woman*, then, have no specific content? This is stoutly affirmed by those who hold to the philosophy of the enlightenment, of rationalism, of nominalism; women, to them, are merely the human beings arbitrarily designated by the word *woman*. Many American women particularly are prepared to think that there is no longer any place for woman as such; if a backward individual still takes herself for a woman, her friends advise her to be psychoanalyzed and thus get rid of this obsession. In regard to a work, *Modern Woman: The Lost Sex*, which in other respects has its irritating features, Dorothy Parker has written: "I cannot be just to books which treat of woman as woman. . . . My idea is that all of us, men as well as women, should be regarded as human beings." But nominalism is a rather inadequate doctrine, and the antifemininists have had no trouble in showing that women simply *are not* men. Surely woman is, like man, a human being; but such a declaration is abstract. The fact is that every concrete human being is always a singular, separate individual. To decline to accept such notions as the eternal feminine, the black soul, the Jewish character, is not to deny that Jews, Negroes, women exist today—this denial does not represent a liberation for those concerned, but rather a flight from reality. Some years ago a well-known woman writer refused to permit her portrait to appear in a series of photographs especially devoted to women writers; she wished to be counted among the men. But in order to gain this privilege she made use of her husband's influence! Women who assert that they are men lay claim none the less to masculine consideration and respect. I recall also a young Trotskyite standing on a platform at a boisterous meeting and getting ready to use her fists, in spite of her evident fragility. She was denying her feminine weakness; but it was for love of a militant male whose equal she wished to be. The attitude of defiance of many American women proves that they are haunted by a sense of their femininity. In truth, to go for a walk with one's eyes open is enough to demonstrate that humanity is divided into two classes of individuals whose clothes, faces, bodies, smiles, gaits, interests, and occupations are manifestly different. Perhaps these differences are superficial, perhaps they are destined to disappear. What is certain is that right now they do most obviously exist.

If her functioning as a female is not enough to define woman, if we decline also to explain her through "the eternal feminine," and if nevertheless we admit, provisionally, that women do exist, then we must face the question: what is a woman?

To state the question is, to me, to suggest, at once, a preliminary answer. The fact that I ask it is in itself significant. A man would never get the notion of writing a book on the peculiar situation of the human male.[2] But if I wish to define myself, I must first of all say: "I am a woman"; on this truth must be based all further discussion. A man never begins by presenting himself as an individual of a certain sex; it goes without saying that he is a man. The terms *masculine* and *feminine* are used symmetrically only as a matter of form, as on legal papers. In actuality the relation of the two sexes is not quite like that of two electrical poles, for man represents both the positive and the neutral, as is indicated by the common use of *man* to designate human beings in general; whereas woman represents only the negative, defined by limiting criteria, without reciprocity. In the midst of an abstract discussion it is vexing to hear a man say: "You think thus and so because you are a woman"; but I know that my only defense is to reply: "I think thus and so because it is true," thereby removing my subjective self from the argument. It would be out of the question to reply: "And you think the contrary because you are a man," for it is understood that the fact of being a man is no peculiarity. A man is in the right in being a man; it is the woman who is in the wrong. It amounts to this: just as for the ancients there was an absolute vertical with reference to which the oblique was defined, so there is an absolute human type, the masculine. Woman has ovaries, a uterus; these peculiarities imprison her in her subjectivity, circumscribe her within the limits of her own nature. It is often said that she thinks with her glands. Man superbly ignores the fact that his anatomy also includes glands, such as the testicles, and that they secrete hormones. He thinks of his body as a direct and normal connection with the world, which he believes he apprehends objectively, whereas he regards the body of woman as a hindrance, a prison, weighed down by everything peculiar to it. "The female is a female by virtue of a certain *lack* of qualities," said Aristotle; "we should regard the female nature as afflicted with a natural defectiveness." And St. Thomas for his part pronounced woman to be an "imperfect man," an "incidental" being. This is symbolized in Genesis where Eve is depicted as made from what Bossuet called "a supernumerary bone" of Adam.

Thus humanity is male and man defines woman not in herself but as relative to him; she is not regarded as an autonomous being. Michelet writes: "Woman, the relative being. . . ." And Benda is most positive in his *Rapport d'Uriel*: "The body of man makes sense in itself quite apart from that of woman, whereas the latter seems wanting in significance by itself. . . . Man can think of himself without woman. She cannot think of herself without man." And she is simply what man decrees; thus she is called "the sex," by which is meant that she appears essentially to the male as a sexual being. For him she is sex—absolute sex, no less. She is defined and differentiated with reference to man and not he with reference to her; she is the incidental, the inessential as opposed to the essential. He is the Subject, he is the Absolute—she is the Other.[3]

The category of the *Other* is as primordial as consciousness itself. In the most primitive societies, in the most ancient mythologies, one finds the expression of a duality—that of the Self and the Other. This duality was not originally attached to the division of the sexes; it was not dependent upon any empirical facts. It is revealed in such works as that of Granet on Chinese thought and those of Dumézil on the East Indies and Rome. The feminine element was at first no more involved in such pairs as Varuna-Mitra, Uranus-Zeus, Sun-Moon, and Day-Night than it was in the contrasts between Good and Evil, lucky and unlucky auspices, right and left, God and Lucifer. Otherness is a fundamental category of human thought.

Thus it is that no group ever sets itself up as the One without at once setting up the Other over against itself. If three travelers chance to occupy the same compartment, that is enough to make vaguely hostile "others" out of all the rest of the passengers on the train. In small-town eyes all persons not belonging to the village are "strangers" and suspect; to the native of a country all who inhabit other countries are "foreigners"; Jews are "different" for the anti-Semite, Negroes are "inferior" for American racists, aborigines are "natives" for colonists, proletarians are the "lower class" for the privileged.

Lévi-Strauss, at the end of a profound work on the various forms of primitive societies, reaches the following conclusion: "Passage from the state of Nature to the state of Culture is marked by man's ability to view biological relations as a series of contrasts; duality, alternation, opposition, and symmetry, whether under definite or vague forms, constitute not so much phenomena to be explained as fundamental and immediately given data of social reality."[4] These phenomena would be incomprehensible if in fact human society were simply a *Mitsein* or fellowship based on solidarity and friendliness. Things become clear, on the contrary, if, following Hegel, we find in consciousness itself a fundamental hostility toward every other consciousness; the subject can be posed only in being opposed—he sets himself up as the essential, as opposed to the other, the inessential, the object.

But the other consciousness, the other ego, sets up a reciprocal claim. The native traveling abroad is shocked to find himself in turn regarded as a "stranger" by the natives of neighboring countries. As a matter of fact, wars, festivals, trading, treaties, and contests among tribes, nations, and classes tend to deprive the concept *Other* of its absolute sense and to make manifest its relativity; willy-nilly, individuals and groups are forced to realize the reciprocity of their relations. How is it, then, that this reciprocity has not been recognized between the sexes, that one of the contrasting terms is set up as the sole essential, denying any relativity in regard to its correlative and defining the latter as pure otherness? Why is it that women do not dispute male sovereignty? No subject will readily volunteer to become the object, the inessential; it is not the Other who, in defining himself as the Other, establishes the One. The Other is posed as such by the One in defining himself as the One. But if the Other is not to regain the status of being the One, he must be submissive enough to accept this alien point of view. Whence comes this submission in the case of woman?

There are, to be sure, other cases in which a certain category has been able to dominate another completely for a time. Very often this privilege depends upon inequality of numbers—the majority imposes its rule upon the minority or persecutes it. But women are not a minority, like the American Negroes or the

Jews; there are as many women as men on earth. Again, the two groups concerned have often been originally independent; they may have been formerly unaware of each other's existence, or perhaps they recognized each other's autonomy. But a historical event has resulted in the subjugation of the weaker by the stronger. The scattering of the Jews, the introduction of slavery into America, the conquests of imperialism are examples in point. In these cases the oppressed retained at least the memory of former days; they possessed in common a past, a tradition, sometimes a religion or a culture.

The parallel drawn by Bebel between women and the proletariat is valid in that neither ever formed a minority or a separate collective unit of mankind. And instead of a single historical event it is in both cases a historical development that explains their status as a class and accounts for the membership of *particular individuals* in that class. But proletarians have not always existed, whereas there have always been women. They are women in virtue of their anatomy and physiology. Throughout history they have always been subordinated to men, and hence their dependency is not the result of a historical event or a social change—it was not something that *occurred*. The reason why otherness in this case seems to be an absolute is in part that it lacks the contingent or incidental nature of historical facts. A condition brought about at a certain time can be abolished at some other time, as the Negroes of Haiti and others have proved; but it might seem that a natural condition is beyond the possibility of change. In truth, however, the nature of things is no more immutably given, once for all, than is historical reality. If woman seems to be the inessential which never becomes the essential, it is because she herself fails to bring about this change. Proletarians say "We"; Negroes also. Regarding themselves as subjects, they transform the bourgeois, the whites, into "others." But women do not say "We," except at some congress of feminists or similar formal demonstration; men say "women," and women use the same word in referring to themselves. They do not authentically assume a subjective attitude. The proletarians have accomplished the revolution in Russia, the Negroes in Haiti, the Indo-Chinese are battling

for it in Indo-China; but the women's effort has never been anything more than a symbolic agitation. They have gained only what men have been willing to grant; they have taken nothing, they have only received.

The reason for this is that women lack concrete means for organizing themselves into a unit which can stand face to face with the correlative unit. They have no past, no history, no religion of their own; and they have no such solidarity of work and interest as that of the proletariat. They are not even promiscuously herded together in the way that creates community feeling among the American Negroes, the ghetto Jews, the workers of Saint-Denis, or the factory hands of Renault. They live dispersed among the males, attached through residence, housework, economic condition, and social standing to certain men—fathers or husbands—more firmly than they are to other women. If they belong to the bourgeoisie, they feel solidarity with men of that class, not with proletarian women; if they are white, their allegiance is to white men, not to Negro women. The proletariat can propose to massacre the ruling class, and a sufficiently fanatical Jew or Negro might dream of getting sole possession of the atomic bomb and making humanity wholly Jewish or black; but woman cannot even dream of exterminating the males. The bond that unites her to her oppressors is not comparable to any other. The division of the sexes is a biological fact, not an event in human history. Male and female stand opposed within a primordial *Mitsein*, and woman has not broken it. The couple is a fundamental unity with its two halves riveted together, and the cleavage of society along the line of sex is impossible. Here is to be found the basic trait of woman: she is the Other in a totality of which the two components are necessary to one another.

One could suppose that this reciprocity might have facilitated the liberation of woman. When Hercules sat at the feet of Omphale and helped with her spinning, his desire for her held him captive; but why did she fail to gain a lasting power? To revenge herself on Jason, Medea killed their children; and this grim legend would seem to suggest that she might have obtained a formidable influence over him through his love for his offspring. In *Lysistrata* Aristophanes gaily depicts a band of women who joined forces to gain social ends through the sexual needs of their men; but this is only a play. In the legend of the Sabine women, the latter soon abandoned their plan of remaining sterile to punish their ravishers. In truth woman has not been socially emancipated through man's need—sexual desire and the desire for off-spring—which makes the male dependent for satis-faction upon the female.

Master and slave, also, are united by a reciprocal need, in this case economic, which does not liberate the slave. In the relation of master to slave the master does not make a point of the need that he has for the other; he has in his grasp the power of satisfying this need through his own action; whereas the slave, in his dependent condition, his hope and fear, is quite con-scious of the need he has for his master. Even if the need is at bottom equally urgent for both, it always works in favor of the oppressor and against the oppressed. That is why the liberation of the working class, for example, has been slow.

Now, woman has always been man's dependent, if not his slave; the two sexes have never shared the world in equality. And even today woman is heavily handicapped, though her situation is beginning to change. Almost nowhere is her legal status the same as man's, and frequently it is much to her disadvan-tage. Even when her rights are legally recognized in the abstract, long-standing custom prevents their full expression in the mores. In the economic sphere men and women can almost be said to make up two castes; other things being equal, the former hold the better jobs, get higher wages, and have more opportunity for success than their new competitors. In industry and politics men have a great many more positions and they monopolize the most important posts. In addition to all this, they enjoy a traditional prestige that the education of children tends in every way to support, for the present enshrines the past—and in the past all history has been made by men. At the present time, when women are beginning to take part in the affairs of the world, it is still a world that belongs to men—they have no doubt of it at all and women have scarcely any. To decline to be the Other, to refuse to

be a party to the deal—this would be for women to renounce all the advantages conferred upon them by their alliance with the superior caste. Man-the-sovereign will provide woman-the-liege with material protection and will undertake the moral justification of her existence; thus she can evade at once both economic risk and the metaphysical risk of a liberty in which ends and aims must be contrived without assistance. Indeed, along with the ethical urge of each individual to affirm his subjective existence, there is also the temptation to forgo liberty and become a thing. This is an inauspicious road, for he who takes it—passive, lost, ruined—becomes henceforth the creature of another's will, frustrated in his transcen-dence and deprived of every value. But it is an easy road; on it one avoids the strain involved in under-taking an authentic existence. When man makes of woman the *Other*, he may, then, expect her to mani-fest deep-seated tendencies toward complicity. Thus, woman may fail to lay claim to the status of subject because she lacks definite resources, because she feels the necessary bond that ties her to man regard-less of reciprocity, and because she is often very well pleased with her role as the *Other*.

But it will be asked at once: how did all this begin? It is easy to see that the duality of the sexes, like any duality, gives rise to conflict. And doubtless the winner will assume the status of absolute. But why should man have won from the start? It seems possible that women could have won the victory; or that the outcome of the conflict might never have been decided. How is it that this world has always belonged to the men and that things have begun to change only recently? Is this change a good thing? Will it bring about an equal sharing of the world between men and women?

These questions are not new, and they have often been answered. But the very fact that woman *is the Other* tends to cast suspicion upon all the justifica-tions that men have ever been able to provide for it. These have all too evidently been dictated by men's interest. A little-known feminist of the seventeenth century, Poulain de la Barre, put it this way: "All that has been written about women by men should be suspect, for the men are at once judge and party to the lawsuit." Everywhere, at all times, the males have displayed their satisfaction in feeling that they are the lords of creation. "Blessed be God . . . that He did not make me a woman," say the Jews in their morning prayers, while their wives pray on a note of resignation: "Blessed be the Lord, who created me according to His will." The first among the blessings for which Plato thanked the gods was that he had been created free, not enslaved; the second, a man, not a woman. But the males could not enjoy this privilege fully unless they believed it to be founded on the absolute and the eternal; they sought to make the fact of their supremacy into a right. "Being men, those who have made and compiled the laws have favored their own sex, and jurists have elevated these laws into principles," to quote Poulain de la Barre once more.

Legislators, priests, philosophers, writers, and scientists have striven to show that the subordinate position of woman is willed in heaven and advantageous on earth. The religions invented by men reflect this wish for domination. In the legends of Eve and Pandora men have taken up arms against women. They have made use of philosophy and theology, as the quotations from Aristotle and St. Thomas have shown. Since ancient times satirists and moralists have delighted in showing up the weaknesses of women. We are familiar with the savage indictments hurled against women throughout French literature. Montherlant, for example, follows the tradition of Jean de Meung, though with less gusto. This hostility may at times be well founded, often it is gratuitous; but in truth it more or less successfully conceals a desire for self-justification. As Montaigne says, "It is easier to accuse one sex than to excuse the other." Sometimes what is going on is clear enough. For instance, the Roman law limiting the rights of woman cited "the imbecility, the instability of the sex" just when the weakening of family ties seemed to threaten the interests of male heirs. And in the effort to keep the married woman under guardianship, appeal was made in the sixteenth century to the authority of St. Augustine, who declared that "woman is a creature neither decisive nor constant," at a time when the

single woman was thought capable of managing her property. Montaigne understood clearly how arbitrary and unjust was woman's appointed lot: "Women are not in the wrong when they decline to accept the rules laid down for them, since the men make these rules without consulting them. No wonder intrigue and strife abound." But he did not go so far as to champion their cause.

It was only later, in the eighteenth century, that genuinely democratic men began to view the matter objectively. Diderot, among others, strove to show that woman is, like man, a human being. Later John Stuart Mill came fervently to her defense. But these philosophers displayed unusual impartiality. In the nineteenth century the feminist quarrel became again a quarrel of partisans. One of the consequences of the industrial revolution was the entrance of women into productive labor, and it was just here that the claims of the feminists emerged from the realm of theory and acquired an economic basis, while their opponents became the more aggressive. Although landed property lost power to some extent, the bourgeoisie clung to the old morality that found the guarantee of private property in the solidity of the family. Woman was ordered back into the home the more harshly as her emancipation became a real menace. Even within the working class the men endeavored to restrain woman's liberation, because they began to see the women as dangerous competitors—the more so because they were accustomed to work for lower wages.

In proving woman's inferiority, the antifeminists then began to draw not only upon religion, philosophy, and theology, as before, but also upon science—biology, experimental psychology, etc. At most they were willing to grant "equality in difference" to the *other* sex. That profitable formula is most significant; it is precisely like the "equal but separate" formula of the Jim Crow laws aimed at the North American Negroes. As is well known, this so-called equalitarian segregation has resulted only in the most extreme discrimination. The similarity just noted is in no way due to chance, for whether it is a race, a caste, a class, or a sex that is reduced to a position of inferiority, the methods of justification are the same. "The eternal feminine" corresponds to "the black soul" and to "the Jewish character." True, the Jewish problem is on the whole very different from the other two—to the anti-Semite the Jew is not so much an inferior as he is an enemy for whom there is to be granted no place on earth, for whom annihilation is the fate desired. But there are deep similarities between the situation of woman and that of the Negro. Both are being emancipated today from a like paternalism, and the former master class wishes to "keep them in their place"—that is, the place chosen for them. In both cases the former masters lavish more or less sincere eulogies, either on the virtues of "the good Negro" with his dormant, childish, merry soul—the submissive Negro—or on the merits of the woman who is "truly feminine"—that is, frivolous, infantile, irresponsible—the submissive woman. In both cases the dominant class bases its argument on a state of affairs that it has itself created. As George Bernard Shaw puts it, in substance, "The American white relegates the black to the rank of shoeshine boy; and he concludes from this that the black is good for nothing but shining shoes." This vicious circle is met with in all analogous circumstances; when an individual (or a group of individuals) is kept in a situation of inferiority, the fact is that he *is* inferior. But the significance of the verb *to be* must be rightly understood here; it is in bad faith to give it a static value when it really has the dynamic Hegelian sense of "to have become." Yes, women on the whole *are* today inferior to men; that is, their situation affords them fewer possibilities. The question is: should that state of affairs continue?

Many men hope that it will continue; not all have given up the battle. The conservative bourgeoisie still see in the emancipation of women a menace to their morality and their interests. Some men dread feminine competition. Recently a male student wrote in the *Hebdo-Latin*: "Every woman student who goes into medicine or law robs us of a job." He never questioned his rights in this world. And economic interests are not the only ones concerned. One of the benefits that oppression confers upon the oppressors is that the most humble among them is made to *feel* superior; thus, a "poor white" in the South can con-

sole himself with the thought that he is not a "dirty nigger"—and the more prosperous whites cleverly exploit this pride.

Similarly, the most mediocre of males feels himself a demigod as compared with women. It was much easier for M. de Montherlant to think himself a hero when he faced women (and women chosen for his purpose) than when he was obliged to act the man among men—something many women have done better than he, for that matter. And in September 1948, in one of his articles in the *Figaro littéraire*, Claude Mauriac—whose great originality is admired by all—could[5] write regarding woman: "*We* listen on a tone [*sic*!] of polite indifference . . . to the most brilliant among them, well knowing that her wit reflects more or less luminously ideas that come from *us*." Evidently the speaker referred to is not reflecting the ideas of Mauriac himself, for no one knows of his having any. It may be that she reflects ideas originating with men, but then, even among men there are those who have been known to appropriate ideas not their own; and one can well ask whether Claude Mauriac might not find more interesting a conversation reflecting Descartes, Marx, or Gide rather than himself. What is really remarkable is that by using the questionable *we* he identifies himself with St. Paul, Hegel, Lenin, and Nietzsche, and from the lofty eminence of their grandeur looks down disdainfully upon the bevy of women who make bold to converse with him on a footing of equality. In truth, I know of more than one woman who would refuse to suffer with patience Mauriac's "tone of polite indifference."

I have lingered on this example because the masculine attitude is here displayed with disarming ingenuousness. But men profit in many more subtle ways from the otherness, the alterity of woman. Here is miraculous balm for those afflicted with an inferiority complex, and indeed no one is more arrogant toward women, more aggressive or scornful, than the man who is anxious about his virility. Those who are not fear-ridden in the presence of their fellow men are much more disposed to recognize a fellow creature in woman; but even to these the myth of Woman, the Other, is precious for many reasons.[6] They cannot be blamed for not cheerfully relinquishing all the benefits they derive from the myth, for they realize what they would lose in relinquishing woman as they fancy her to be, while they fail to realize what they have to gain from the woman of tomorrow. Refusal to pose oneself as the Subject, unique and absolute, requires great self-denial. Furthermore, the vast majority of men make no such claim explicitly. They do not *postulate* woman as inferior, for today they are too thoroughly imbued with the ideal of democracy not to recognize all human beings as equals.

In the bosom of the family, woman seems in the eyes of childhood and youth to be clothed in the same social dignity as the adult males. Later on, the young man, desiring and loving, experiences the resistance, the independence of the woman desired and loved; in marriage, he respects woman as wife and mother, and in the concrete events of conjugal life she stands there before him as a free being. He can therefore feel that social subordination as between the sexes no longer exists and that on the whole, in spite of differences, woman is an equal. As, however, he observes some points of inferiority—the most important being unfitness for the professions—he attributes these to natural causes. When he is in a co-operative and benevolent relation with woman, his theme is the principle of abstract equality, and he does not base his attitude upon such inequality as may exist. But when he is in conflict with her, the situation is reversed: his theme will be the existing inequality, and he will even take it as justification for denying abstract equality.[7]

So it is that many men will affirm as if in good faith that women *are* the equals of man and that they have nothing to clamor for, while *at the same time* they will say that women can never be the equals of man and that their demands are in vain. It is, in point of fact, a difficult matter for man to realize the extreme importance of social discriminations which seem outwardly insignificant but which produce in woman moral and intellectual effects so profound that they appear to spring from her original nature. The most sympathetic of men never fully comprehend woman's concrete situation. And there is no

reason to put much trust in the men when they rush to the defense of privileges whose full extent they can hardly measure. We shall not, then, permit ourselves to be intimidated by the number and violence of the attacks launched against women, nor to be entrapped by the self-seeking eulogies bestowed on the "true woman," nor to profit by the enthusiasm for woman's destiny manifested by men who would not for the world have any part of it.

We should consider the arguments of the feminists with no less suspicion, however, for very often their controversial aim deprives them of all real value. If the "woman question" seems trivial, it is because masculine arrogance has made of it a "quarrel"; and when quarreling one no longer reasons well. People have tirelessly sought to prove that woman is superior, inferior, or equal to man. Some say that, having been created after Adam, she is evidently a secondary being; others say on the contrary that Adam was only a rough draft and that God succeeded in producing the human being in perfection when He created Eve. Woman's brain is smaller; yes, but it is relatively larger. Christ was made a man; yes, but perhaps for his greater humility. Each argument at once suggests its opposite, and both are often fallacious. If we are to gain understanding, we must get out of these ruts; we must discard the vague notions of superiority, inferiority, equality which have hitherto corrupted every discussion of the subject and start afresh.

Very well, but just how shall we pose the question? And, to begin with, who are we to propound it at all? Man is at once judge and party to the case; but so is woman. What we need is an angel—neither man nor woman—but where shall we find one? Still, the angel would be poorly qualified to speak, for an angel is ignorant of all the basic facts involved in the problem. With a hermaphrodite we should be no better off, for here the situation is most peculiar; the hermaphrodite is not really the combination of a whole man and a whole woman, but consists of parts of each and thus is neither. It looks to me as if there are, after all, certain women who are best qualified to elucidate the situation of woman. Let us not be misled by the sophism that because Epimenides was a Cretan he was necessarily a liar; it is not a mysterious essence that compels men and women to act in good or in bad faith, it is their situation that inclines them more or less toward the search for truth. Many of today's women, fortunate in the restoration of all the privileges pertaining to the estate of the human being, can afford the luxury of impartiality—we even recognize its necessity. We are no longer like our partisan elders; by and large we have won the game. In recent debates on the status of women the United Nations has persistently maintained that the equality of the sexes is now becoming a reality, and already some of us have never had to sense in our femininity an inconvenience or an obstacle. Many problems appear to us to be more pressing than those which concern us in particular, and this detachment even allows us to hope that our attitude will be objective. Still, we know the feminine world more intimately than do the men because we have our roots in it, we grasp more immediately than do men what it means to a human being to be feminine; and we are more concerned with such knowledge. I have said that there are more pressing problems, but this does not prevent us from seeing some importance in asking how the fact of being women will affect our lives. What opportunities precisely have been given us and what withheld? What fate awaits our younger sisters, and what directions should they take? It is significant that books by women on women are in general animated in our day less by a wish to demand our rights than by an effort toward clarity and understanding. As we emerge from an era of excessive controversy, this book is offered as one attempt among others to confirm that statement.

But it is doubtless impossible to approach any human problem with a mind free from bias. The way in which questions are put, the points of view assumed, presuppose a relativity of interest; all characteristics imply values, and every objective description, so called, implies an ethical background. Rather than attempt to conceal principles more or less definitely implied, it is better to state them openly at the beginning. This will make it unnecessary to specify on every page in just what sense one uses such words as *superior, inferior, better, worse, progress, reaction*, and the like. If

we survey some of the works on woman, we note that one of the points of view most frequently adopted is that of the public good, the general interest; and one always means by this the benefit of society as one wishes it to be maintained or established. For our part, we hold that the only public good is that which assures the private good of the citizens; we shall pass judgment on institutions according to their effectiveness in giving concrete opportunities to individuals. But we do not confuse the idea of private interest with that of happiness, although that is another common point of view. Are not women of the harem more happy than women voters? Is not the housekeeper happier than the working-woman? It is not too clear just what the word *happy* really means and still less what true values it may mask. There is no possibility of measuring the happiness of others, and it is always easy to describe as happy the situation in which one wishes to place them.

In particular those who are condemned to stagnation are often pronounced happy on the pretext that happiness consists in being at rest. This notion we reject, for our perspective is that of existentialist ethics. Every subject plays his part as such specifically through exploits or projects that serve as a mode of transcendence; he achieves liberty only through a continual reaching out toward other liberties. There is no justification for present existence other than its expansion into an indefinitely open future. Every time transcendence falls back into immanence, stagnation, there is a degradation of existence into the "*en-soi*"—the brutish life of subjection to given conditions—and of liberty into constraint and contingence. This downfall represents a moral fault if the subject consents to it; if it is inflicted upon him, it spells frustration and oppression. In both cases it is an absolute evil. Every individual concerned to justify his existence feels that his existence involves an undefined need to transcend himself, to engage in freely chosen projects.

Now, what peculiarly signalizes the situation of woman is that she—a free and autonomous being like all human creatures—nevertheless finds herself living in a world where men compel her to assume the status of the Other. They propose to stabilize her as object and to doom her to immanence since her transcendence is to be overshadowed and forever transcended by another ego (*conscience*) which is essential and sovereign. The drama of woman lies in this conflict between the fundamental aspirations of every subject (ego)—who always regards the self as the essential—and the compulsions of a situation in which she is the inessential. How can a human being in woman's situation attain fulfillment? What roads are open to her? Which are blocked? How can independence be recovered in a state of dependency? What circumstances limit woman's liberty and how can they be overcome? These are the fundamental questions on which I would fain throw some light. This means that I am interested in the fortunes of the individual as defined not in terms of happiness but in terms of liberty.

Quite evidently this problem would be without significance if we were to believe that woman's destiny is inevitably determined by physiological, psychological, or economic forces. Hence I shall discuss first of all the light in which woman is viewed by biology, psychoanalysis, and historical materialism. Next I shall try to show exactly how the concept of the "truly feminine" has been fashioned—why woman has been defined as the Other—and what have been the consequences from man's point of view. Then from woman's point of view I shall describe the world in which women must live; and thus we shall be able to envisage the difficulties in their way as, endeavoring to make their escape from the sphere hitherto assigned them, they aspire to full membership in the human race.

NOTES

1. *Franchise*, dead today.

2. The Kinsey Report [Alfred C. Kinsey and others: *Sexual Behavior in the Human Male* (W. B. Saunders Co., 1948)] is no exception, for it is limited to describing the sexual characteristics of American men, which is quite a different matter.

3. E. Lévinas expresses this idea most explicitly in his essay *Temps et l'Autre*. "Is there not a case in which otherness, alterity [*altérité*], unquestionably marks the nature of a being, as its essence, an instance of otherness not consisting purely and simply in the opposition of two species of the same genus? I think that the feminine represents the contrary in its absolute sense, this contrariness being in no wise affected by any relation between it and its correlative and thus remaining absolutely other. Sex is not a certain specific difference . . . no more is the sexual difference a mere contradiction. . . . Nor does this difference lie in the duality of two complementary terms, for two complementary terms imply a pre-existing whole. . . . Otherness reaches its full flowering in the feminine, a term of the same rank as consciousness but of opposite meaning."

I suppose that Lévinas does not forget that woman, too, is aware of her own consciousness, or ego. But it is striking that he deliberately takes a man's point of view, disregarding the reciprocity of subject and object. When he writes that woman is mystery, he implies that she is mystery for man. Thus his description, which is intended to be objective, is in fact an assertion of masculine privilege.

4. See C. Lévi-Strauss: *Les Structures élémentaires de la parenté*. My thanks are due to C. Lévi-Strauss for his kindness in furnishing me with the proofs of his work, ...

5. Or at least he thought he could.

6. A significant article on this theme by Michel Carrouges appeared in No. 292 of the *Cahiers du Sud*. He writes indignantly: "Would that there were no woman-myth at all but only a cohort of cooks, matrons, prostitutes, and bluestockings serving functions of pleasure or usefulness!" That is to say, in his view woman has no existence in and for herself; he thinks only of her *function* in the male world. Her reason for existence lies in man. But then, in fact, her poetic "function" as a myth might be more valued than any other. The real problem is precisely to find out why woman should be defined with relation to man.

7. For example, a man will say that he considers his wife in no wise degraded because she has no gainful occupation. The profession of housewife is just as lofty, and so on. But when the first quarrel comes, he will exclaim: "Why, you couldn't make your living without me!"

Study Questions

1. Beauvoir asserts that woman has been defined as "the Other." What does this mean?

2. What are some reasons Beauvoir gives for women's failure to rebel against this definition?

3. As an existentialist, what is Beauvoir's estimation of woman's status as "the Other"?

4. According to Beauvoir, who is best positioned to shed light on women's true condition?

5. In what sense can this excerpt by Beauvoir be read as an example of sameness/humanist feminist thinking?

Martha C. Nussbaum

Human Capabilities, Female Human Beings

Human beings are not by nature kings, or nobles, or courtiers, or rich. All are born naked and poor. All are subject to the miseries of life, to frustrations, to ills, to needs, to pains of every kind. Finally, all are condemned to death. That is what is really the human being; that is what no mortal can avoid. Begin, then, by studying what is the most inseparable from human nature, that which most constitutes humanness.

Jean-Jacques Rousseau, *Emile*, Book IV

Women, a majority of the world's population, receive only a small share of developmental opportunities. They are often excluded from education or from the better jobs, from political systems or from adequate health care . . . In the countries for which relevant data are available, the female human development index is only 60% that of males.

Human Development Report 1993, United Nations Development Program

Were our state a pure democracy there would still be excluded from our deliberations women, who, to prevent depravation of morals and ambiguity of issue, should not mix promiscuously in gatherings of men.

Thomas Jefferson

Being a woman is not yet a way of being a human being.

Catharine MacKinnon

1 FEMINISM AND COMMON HUMANITY

Begin with the human being: with the capacities and needs that join all humans, across barriers of gender and class and race and nation. To a person concerned with the equality and dignity of women, this advice should appear in one way promising. For it instructs us to focus on what all human beings share, rather than on the privileges and achievements of a dominant group, and on needs and basic functions, rather than power or status. Women have rarely been kings, or nobles, or courtiers, or rich. They have, on the other hand, frequently been poor and sick and dead.

But this starting point will be regarded with scepticism by many contemporary feminists. For it is all too obvious that throughout the history of political thought, both Western and non-Western, such allegedly-unbiased general concepts have served in various ways to bolster male privilege and to marginalize women. Human beings are not born kings, or nobles, or courtiers. They are, or so it seems,[1] born male and female. The nakedness on which Rousseau places such emphasis reveals a difference that is taken by Rousseau himself to imply profound differences in capability and social role. His remarks about human nature are the prelude to his account of Emile's education. Sophie, Emile's female companion, will be said to have a different "nature" and a different education. Whether, as here, women are held to be bearers of a different "nature" from unmarked "human nature", or whether they are simply said to be degenerate and substandard exemplars of the same "nature", the result is usually the same: a judgement of female inferiority, which can then be used to justify and stabilize oppression.

I shall argue nonetheless that we should in fact begin with a conception of the human being and human functioning in thinking about women's equality in developing countries. This notion can be abused. It can be developed in a gender-biased way. It can be unjustly and prejudicially applied. It can be developed in ways that neglect relevant differences among women of different nationalities, classes, and races. But I shall argue that, articulated in a certain way (and I shall be emphatically distinguishing my approach from others that use an idea of "human nature") it is our best starting point for reflection. It is . . . the best basis for claims of justice . . . on behalf of the huge numbers of women in the world who are currently being deprived of their full "human development". [. . .]

My proposal is frankly universalist and "essentialist". That is, it asks us to focus on what is common to all, rather than on differences (although, as we

shall see, it does not neglect these), and to see some capabilities and functions as more central, more at the core of human life, than others. Its primary opponents on the contemporary scene will be "anti-essentialists" of various types, thinkers who urge us to begin not with sameness but with difference—both between women and men and across groups of women—and to seek norms defined relatively to a local context and locally held beliefs. This opposition takes many forms, and I shall be responding to several distinct objections that opponents may bring against my universalist proposal. But I can begin to motivate my enterprise by telling several true stories of conversations that have taken place at WIDER, in which the relativist position[2] seemed to have alarming implications for women's lives. I have in some cases conflated two separate conversations into one; otherwise things happened as I describe them.

1. At a conference on "Value and Technology", an American economist who has long been a left-wing critic of neoclassical economics delivers a paper urging the preservation of traditional ways of life in a rural area of India, now under threat of contamination from Western development projects. As evidence of the excellence of this rural way of life, he points to the fact that, whereas we Westerners experience a sharp split between the values that prevail in the workplace and the values that prevail in the home, here, by contrast, there exists what the economist calls "the embedded way of life"; the same values obtaining in both places. His example: just as in the home a menstruating woman is thought to pollute the kitchen and therefore may not enter it, so too in the workplace a menstruating woman is taken to pollute the loom and may not enter the room where looms are kept. Amartya Sen objects that this example is repellant, rather than admirable: surely such practices both degrade the women in question and inhibit their freedom. The first economist's collaborator, an elegant French anthropologist (who would, I suspect, object violently to a purity check at the seminar room door), replies to Sen. Doesn't he realize that there is, in these matters, no privileged place to stand? This, after all, has been shown by both Derrida and Foucault.

Doesn't he know that he is neglecting the otherness of Indian ideas by bringing his Western essentialist values into the picture?

2. The same French anthropologist now delivers her paper. She expresses regret that the introduction of smallpox vaccination to India by the British eradicated the cult of Sittala Devi, the goddess to whom one used to pray in order to avert smallpox. Here, she says, is another example of Western neglect of difference. Someone (it might have been me) objects that it is surely better to be healthy rather than ill, to live rather than to die. The answer comes back: Western essentialist medicine conceives of things in terms of binary oppositions: life is opposed to death, health to disease. But if we cast away this binary way of thinking, we will begin to comprehend the otherness of Indian traditions.

At this point Eric Hobsbawm, who has been listening to the proceedings in increasingly uneasy silence, rises to deliver a blistering indictment of the traditionalism and relativism that prevail in this group. He lists historical examples of ways in which appeals to tradition have been used to support oppression and violence. His final example is that of National Socialism in Germany. In the confusion that ensues, most of the relativist social scientists—above all those from far away, who do not know who Hobsbawm is—demand that he be asked to leave the room. The radical American economist, disconcerted by this apparent tension between his relativism and his affiliation with the left, convinces them, with difficulty, to let Hobsbawm remain.

3. We shift now to another conference two years later, a philosophical conference organized by Amartya Sen and me. Sen makes it clear that he holds the perhaps unsophisticated view that life is opposed to death in a very binary way, and that such binary oppositions can and should be used in development analysis. His paper contains much universalist talk of human functioning and capability; he begins to speak of freedom of choice as a basic human good. At this point he is interrupted by the radical economist of my first story, who insists that contemporary anthropology has shown that non-Western people are not especially attached to freedom of choice. His example: a new book on Japan

has shown that Japanese males, when they get home from work, do not wish to choose what to eat for dinner, what to wear, etc. They wish all these choices to be taken out of their hands by their wives. A heated exchange follows about what this example really shows. I leave it to your imaginations to reconstruct it. In the end, the confidence of the radical economist is unshaken: Sen and I are both victims of bad universalist thinking, who fail to respect "difference".

Here we see the relativist position whose influence in development studies motivated the work that has led to the present volume. The phenomenon is an odd one. For we see here highly-intelligent people, people deeply committed to the good of women and men in developing countries, people who think of themselves as progressive and feminist and anti-racist, people who correctly argue that the concept of development is an evaluative concept requiring normative argument—effectively eschewing normative argument and taking up positions that converge, as Hobsbawn correctly saw, with the positions of reaction, oppression, and sexism. Under the banner of their fashionable opposition to "essentialism" march ancient religious taboos, the luxury of the pampered husband, educational deprivation, unequal health care, and premature death. (And in my own universalist Aristotelian way, I say it at the outset, I do hold that death is opposed to life in the most binary way imaginable, and freedom to slavery, and hunger to adequate nutrition, and ignorance to knowledge. Nor do I believe that it is only, or even primarily, in Western thinking that such oppositions are, and should be, important.) [. . .]

2 THE ASSAULT ON UNIVERSALISM

Many critics of universalism in ethics are really critics of metaphysical realism who assume that realism is a necessary basis for universalism. I shall argue that this assumption is false. By metaphysical realism I mean the view (commonly held in both Western and non-Western philosophical traditions) that there is some determinate way the world is, apart from the interpretive workings of the cognitive faculties of living beings. Far from requiring technical metaphysics for its articulation, this is a very natural way to view things, and is in fact a very common daily-life view, in both Western and non-Western traditions. We did not make the stars, the earth, the trees they are what they are there outside of us, waiting to be known. And our activities of knowing do not change what they are. [. . .]

But universalism does not require such support. For universal ideas of the human do arise within history and from human experience, and they can ground themselves in experience. Indeed, if, as the critics of realism allege, we are always dealing with our own interpretations anyhow, they must acknowledge that universal conceptions of the human are prominent and pervasive among such interpretations, hardly to be relegated to the dustbin of metaphysical history along with rare and recondite philosophical entities such as the Platonic forms. [. . .]

But such an experiential and historical universalism is still vulnerable to some, if not all, of the objections standardly brought against universalism. I therefore need to introduce those objections, and later to test my account against them.

2.1. Neglect of Historical and Cultural Differences

The opposition charges that any attempt to pick out some elements of human life as more fundamental than others, even without appeal to a transhistorical reality, is bound to be insufficiently respectful of actual historical and cultural differences. People, it is claimed, understand human life and humanness in widely different ways: and any attempt to produce a list of the most fundamental properties and functions of human beings is bound to enshrine certain understandings of the human and to demote others. Usually, the objector continues, this takes the form of enshrining the understanding of a dominant group at the expense of minority understandings. This type of objection is frequently made by feminists, and can claim support from many historical examples, in which the human has indeed been defined by focusing on the characteristics of males, as manifested in the definer's culture.

It is far from clear what this objection shows. In particular it is far from clear that it supports the idea that we ought to base our ethical norms, instead, on the current preferences and the self-conceptions of people who are living what the objector herself claims to be lives of deprivation and oppression. But it does show at least that the project of choosing one picture of the human over another is fraught with difficulty, political as well as philosophical.

2.2. Neglect of Autonomy

A different objection is presented by liberal opponents of universalism; my relativist opponents, [. . .] endorse it as well. (Many such objectors, [. . .], are themselves willing to give a universal account of the human in at least some ways, holding freedom of choice to be everywhere of central importance.) The objection is that by determining in advance what elements of human life have most importance, the universalist project fails to respect the right of people to choose a plan of life according to their own lights, determining what is central and what is not. This way of proceeding is "imperialistic". Such evaluative choices must be left to each citizen. For this reason, politics must refuse itself a determinate theory of the human being and the human good.

2.3. Prejudicial Application

If we operate with a determinate conception of the human being that is meant to have some normative moral and political force, we must also, in applying it, ask which beings we shall take to fall under the concept. And here the objector notes that, all too easily—even if the conception itself is equitably and comprehensively designed—the powerless can be excluded. Aristotle himself, it is pointed out, held that women and slaves were not full-fledged human beings; and since his politics were based on his view of human functioning, the failure of these beings (in his view) to exhibit the desired mode of functioning contributed to their political exclusion and oppression.

It is, once again, hard to know what this objection is supposed to show. In particular, it is hard to know how, if at all, it is supposed to show that we would be better off without such determinate universal concepts. For it could be plausibly argued that it would have been even easier to exclude women and slaves on a whim if one did not have such a concept to contend with. Indeed, this is what I shall be arguing. On the other hand, it does show that we need to think not only about getting the concept right but also about getting the right beings admitted under the concept.

Each of these objections has some merit. Many universal conceptions of the human being have been insular in an arrogant way, and neglectful of differences among cultures and ways of life. Some have been neglectful of choice and autonomy. And many have been prejudicially applied. But none of this shows that all such conceptions must fail in one or more of these ways. But at this point I need to advance a definite example of such a conception, in order both to display its merits and to argue that it can in fact answer these charges.

3 A CONCEPTION OF THE HUMAN BEING: THE CENTRAL HUMAN CAPABILITIES

Here, then, is a sketch for an account of the most important functions and capabilities of the human being, in terms of which human life is defined. The basic idea is that we ask ourselves, "What are the characteristic activities of the human being? What does the human being do, characteristically, as such— and not, say, as a member of a particular group, or a particular local community?" To put it another way, what are the forms of activity, of doing and being, that constitute the human form of life and distinguish it from other actual or imaginable forms of life, such as the lives of animals and plants, or, on the other hand, of immortal gods as imagined in myths and legends (which frequently have precisely the function of delimiting the human)?

We can get at this question better if we approach it via two somewhat more concrete questions that we often really ask ourselves. First is a question about personal continuity. We ask ourselves what changes or transitions are compatible with the continued existence of that being as a member of the human kind, and what are not. (Since continued species identity seems to be at least necessary for continued personal identity, this is also a question about the necessary conditions for continuing as one and the same individual.) Some functions can fail to be present without threatening our sense that we still have a human being on our hands; the absence of others seems to signal the end of a human life. This question is asked regularly, when we attempt to make medical definitions of death in a situation in which some of the functions of life persist, or to decide, for others or (thinking ahead) for ourselves, whether a certain level of illness or impairment means the end of the life of the being in question.

The other question is a question about kind inclusion. We recognize other humans as human across many differences of time and place, of custom and appearance. Kwame Anthony Appiah writes about the experience of seeing his heterogenous nieces and nephews playing together, and the term "the human future" naturally occurs to him.[3] Much though we may love our dogs and cats, we recognize such scenes as crucially different from scenes of a child playing with a dog or cat. On what do we base these recognitions? We often tell ourselves stories, on the other hand, about anthropomorphic creatures who do not get classified as human, on account of some feature of their form of life and functioning. On what do we base these exclusions? In short, what do we believe must be there, if we are going to acknowledge that a given life is human?

This inquiry proceeds by examining a wide variety of self-interpretations of human beings in many times and places. Especially valuable are myths and stories that situate the human being in some way in the universe, between the "beasts" on the one hand and the "gods" on the other; stories that ask what it is to live as a being with certain abilities that set it apart from the rest of the world of nature and with, on the other hand, certain limits that derive from membership in the world of nature. The idea is that people in many different societies share a general outline of such a conception. This is not surprising, since they do recognize one another as members of the same species,[4] marry one another, have children together, and so forth—and indeed do tell one another such stories, without much difficulty of translation. This convergence gives us some reason for optimism, that if we proceed in this way, using our imaginations, we will have in the end a theory that is not the mere projection of local preferences, but is fully international and a basis for cross-cultural attunement.

Several important methodological points must now be emphasized:

1. The procedure through which this account of the human is derived is neither ahistorical nor a priori. It is an attempt to set down a very general record of broadly shared experiences of human beings within history. A related point can be made about the results of the inquiry: they do not claim to be ahistorical or a priori truth, but, rather, an especially deep and continuous sort of experiential and historical truth.

2. On the other hand, the guiding questions of the inquiry direct it to cross national and temporal boundaries, looking for features that ground recognitions of humanness across these boundaries. Thus we can expect that its results will embody what is continuous rather than rapidly changing, international rather than local.

3. The account is neither a biological account nor a metaphysical account. (For these reasons I have avoided using the term "human nature", which is usually associated with attempts to describe the human being either from the point of view of an allegedly value-free science or from the point of view of normative, often theological, metaphysics.) The inquiry pays attention to biology, but as it figures in and shapes human experience. It is an evaluative and, in a broad sense, ethical inquiry. It asks us to evaluate components of lives, asking which ones are so important that we would not call a life human without them. The result of this inquiry is, then, not a list of value-neutral facts, but a normative conception.

4. The account is meant to be both tentative and open-ended. We allow explicitly for the possibility that we will learn from our encounters with other human societies to recognize things about ourselves that we had not seen before, or even to change in certain ways, according more importance to something we had thought more peripheral. (We may also shift to reach a political consensus.)

5. The account is not intended to deny that the items it enumerates are to some extent differently constructed by different societies. It claims only that in these areas there is considerable continuity and overlap, sufficient to ground a working political consensus.

6. Although the account appeals to consensus in this way, it should be understood that the consensus is acceptable only if it is reached by reasonable procedures, where the notion of reasonableness has normative content. In this way it is different from consensus as mere overlap.

7. The list is heterogeneous: for it contains both limits against which we press and capabilities through which we aspire. This is not surprising, since we began from the intuitive idea of a creature who is both capable and needy.

8. The concept "human being", as this view understands it, is in one way like the concept "person" as used elsewhere in moral philosophy: that is, it is a normative ethical concept. On the other hand, because of its link with an empirical study of a species-specific form of life, and with what is most central in such a form of life, it may prove more difficult to withhold from certain beings in an arbitrary way (see Section 7 below). This may commend it to feminists: for the label "person" has frequently been withheld from women, without substantial argument.

Here then, as a first approximation, is a story about what seems to be part of any life we will count as a human life:

3.1. Level One of the Conception of the Human Being: The Shape of the Human Form of Life

3.1.1. Mortality All human beings face death and, after a certain age, know that they face it. This fact shapes more or less every other element of human life. Moreover, all human beings have an aversion to death. Although in many circumstances death will be preferred to the available alternatives, the death of a loved one, or the prospect of one's own death, is an occasion for grief and/or fear. If we encountered an immortal anthropomorphic being, or a mortal being who showed no aversion to death and no tendency at all to avoid death, we would judge, in both of these cases, that the form of life was so different from our own that the being could not be acknowledged as human.

3.1.2. The Human Body We live all our lives in bodies of a certain sort, whose possibilities and vulnerabilities do not as such belong to one human society rather than another. These bodies, similar far more than dissimilar (given the enormous range of possibilities) are our homes, so to speak, opening certain options and denying others, giving us certain needs and also certain possibilities for excellence. The fact that any given human being might have lived anywhere and belonged to any culture is a great part of what grounds our mutual recognitions; this fact, in turn, has a great deal to do with the general humanness of the body, its great distinctness from other bodies. The experience of the body is culturally shaped, to be sure; the importance we ascribe to its various functions is also culturally shaped. But the body itself, not culturally variant in its nutritional and other related requirements, sets limits on what can be experienced and valued, ensuring a great deal of overlap.

There is much disagreement, of course, about how much of human experience is rooted in the body. Here religion and metaphysics enter the picture in a non-trivial way. Therefore, in keeping with the non-metaphysical character of the list, I shall include at this point only those features that would be agreed to be bodily even by determined dualists. The more controversial features, such as thinking, perceiving, and emotion, I shall discuss separately, taking no stand on the question of dualism.

1. *Hunger and thirst: the need for food and drink.* All human beings need food and drink in order to live; all have comparable, though varying, nutritional requirements. Being in one culture rather than another does not make one metabolize food differently. Furthermore, all human beings have appetites that are indices of need. Appetitive experience is to some extent culturally shaped; but we are not surprised to discover much similarity and overlap. Moreover, human beings in general do not wish to be hungry or thirsty (though of course they might choose to fast for some reason). If we discovered someone who really did not experience hunger and thirst at all, or, experiencing them, really did not care about eating and drinking, we would judge that this creature was (in Aristotle's words) "far from being a human being".

2. *Need for shelter.* A recurrent theme in myths of humanness is the nakedness of the human being, its relative unprotectedness in the animal world, its susceptibility to heat, cold, and the ravages of the elements. Stories that explore the difference between our needs and those of furry or scaly or otherwise protected creatures remind us how far our life is constituted by the need to find protection through clothing and housing.

3. *Sexual Desire.* Though less urgent as a need than the needs for food, drink, and shelter (in the sense that one can live without its satisfaction) sexual need and desire are features of more or less every human life, at least beyond a certain age. It is, and has all along been, a most important basis for the recognition of others different from ourselves as human beings.

4. *Mobility.* Human beings are, as the old definition goes, featherless bipeds—that is, creatures whose form of life is in part constituted by the ability to move from place to place in a certain characteristic way, not only through the aid of tools that they have made, but with their very own bodies. Human beings like moving about, and dislike being deprived of mobility. An anthropomorphic being who, without disability, chose never to move from birth to death would be hard to view as human.

3.1.3. Capacity for Pleasure and Pain Experiences of pain and pleasure are common to all human life (though, once again, both their expression and, to some extent, the experience itself may be culturally shaped). Moreover, the aversion to pain as a fundamental evil is a primitive and, it appears, unlearned part of being a human animal. A society whose members altogether lacked that aversion would surely be judged to be beyond the bounds of humanness.

3.1.4. Cognitive Capability: Perceiving, Imagining, Thinking   All human beings have sense-perception, the ability to imagine, and the ability to think, making distinctions and "reaching out for understanding".[5] And these abilities are regarded as of central importance. It is an open question what sorts of accidents or impediments to individuals in these areas will be sufficient for us to judge that the life in question is not really human any longer. But it is safe to say that if we imagine a group of beings whose members totally lack sense-perception, or totally lack imagination, or totally lack reasoning and thinking, we are not in any of these cases imagining a group of human beings, no matter what they look like.

3.1.5. Early Infant Development   All human beings begin as hungry babies, aware of their own helplessness, experiencing their alternating closeness to and distance from that, and those, on whom they depend. This common structure to early life—which is clearly shaped in many different ways by different social arrangements—gives rise to a great deal of overlapping experience that is central in the formation of desires, and of complex emotions such as grief, love, and anger. This, in turn, is a major source of our ability to recognize ourselves in the emotional experiences of those whose lives are very different in other respects from our own. If we encountered a group of apparent humans and then discovered that they never had been babies and had never, in consequence, had those experiences of extreme dependency, need, and affection, we would, I think, have to conclude that their form of life was sufficiently different from our own that they could not be considered part of the same kind.

3.1.6. Practical Reason   All human beings participate (or try to) in the planning and managing of their own lives, asking and answering questions about what is good and how one should live. Moreover, they wish to enact their thought in their lives—to be able to choose and evaluate, and to function accordingly. This general capability has many concrete forms, and is related in complex ways to the other capabilities, emotional, imaginative, and intellectual. But a being who altogether lacks this would not be likely to be regarded as fully human, in any society.

3.1.7. Affiliation With Other Human Beings   All human beings recognize and feel some sense of affiliation and concern for other human beings. Moreover, we value the form of life that is constituted by these recognitions and affiliations. We live with and in relation to others, and regard a life not lived in affiliation with others to be a life not worth the living. (Here I would really wish, with Aristotle, to spell things out further. We define ourselves in terms of at least two types of affiliation: intimate family and/or personal relations, and social or civic relations.)

3.1.8. Relatedness to Other Species and to Nature Human beings recognize that they are not the only living things in their world: that they are animals living alongside other animals, and also alongside plants, in a universe that, as a complex interlocking order, both supports and limits them. We are dependent upon that order in countless ways; and we also sense that we owe that order some respect and concern, however much we may differ about exactly what we owe, to whom, and on what basis. Again, a creature who treated animals exactly like stones and could not be brought to see any difference would probably be regarded as too strange to be human. So too would a creature who did not in any way respond to the natural world.

3.1.9. Humour and Play   Human life, wherever it is lived, makes room for recreation and laughter. The forms play takes are enormously varied—and yet we recognize other humans, across cultural barriers, as the animals who laugh. Laughter and play are frequently among the deepest and also the first modes of our mutual recognition. Inability to play or laugh is taken, correctly, as a sign of deep disturbance in a child; if it proves permanent we will doubt whether the child is capable of leading a fully human life. An entire society that lacked this ability would seem to us both terribly strange and terribly frightening.

3.1.10. Separateness

However much we live with and for others, we are, each of us, "one in number",[7] proceeding on a separate path through the world from birth to death. Each person feels only his or her own pain and not anyone else's. Each person dies without entailing logically the death of anyone else. When one person walks across the room, no other person follows automatically. When we count the number of human beings in a room, we have no difficulty figuring out where one begins and the other ends. These obvious facts need stating, since they might have been otherwise. We should bear them in mind when we hear talk about the absence of individualism in certain societies. Even the most intense forms of human interaction, for example sexual experience, are experiences of responsiveness, not of fusion. If fusion is made the goal, the result is bound to be disappointment.

3.1.11. Strong Separateness

Because of separateness, each human life has, so to speak, its own peculiar context and surroundings—objects, places, a history, particular friendships, locations, sexual ties—that are not exactly the same as those of anyone else, and in terms of which the person to some extent identifies herself. Though societies vary a great deal in the degree and type of strong separateness that they permit and foster, there is no life yet known that really does (as Plato wished) fail to use the words "mine" and "not mine" in some personal and non-shared way. What I use, live in, respond to, I use, live in, respond to from my own separate existence. And on the whole, human beings recognize one another as beings who wish to have at least some separateness of context, a little space to move around in, some special items to use or love.

This is a working list. It is put out to generate debate. It has done so and will continue to do so, and it will be revised accordingly.

As I have said, the list is composed of two different sorts of items; limits and capabilities. As far as capabilities go, to call them parts of humanness is to make a very basic sort of evaluation. It is to say that a life without this item would be too lacking, too impoverished, to be human at all. Obviously, then, it could not be a good human life. So this list of capabilities is a ground-floor or minimal conception of the good. (In the sense that it does not fully determine the choice of a way of life, but simply regulates the parameters of what can be chosen, it plays, however, the role traditionally played in liberal political theory by a conception of the right.)

With the limits, things are more complicated. In selecting the limits for attention, we have, once again, made a basic sort of evaluation, saying that these things are so important that life would not be human without them. But what we have said is that human life, in its general form, consists of the awareness of these limits plus a struggle against them. Humans do not wish to be hungry, to feel pain, to die. (Separateness is highly complex, both a limit and a capability. Much the same is true of many of the limits implied by the shape and the capacities of the body.) On the other hand, we cannot assume that the correct evaluative conclusion to draw is that we should try as hard as possible to get rid of the limit altogether. It is characteristic of human life to prefer recurrent hunger plus eating to a life with neither hunger nor eating; to prefer sexual desire and its satisfaction to a life with neither desire nor satisfaction. Even where death is concerned, the desire for immortality, which many human beings certainly have, is a peculiar desire: for it is not clear that the wish to lose one's finitude completely is a desire that one can coherently entertain for oneself or for someone one loves. It seems to be a wish for a transition to a way of life so wholly different, with such different values and ends, that it seems that the identity of the individual will not be preserved. So the evaluative conclusion, in mapping out a ground-floor conception of the good (saying what functioning is necessary for a life to be human) will have to be expressed with much caution, clearly, in terms of what would be a humanly good way of countering the limitation.

4 THE TWO THRESHOLDS

Things now get very complicated. For we want to describe two distinct thresholds: a threshold of capability to function beneath which a life will be so impoverished that it will not be human at all; and a somewhat higher threshold, beneath which those characteristic functions are available in such a reduced way that, though we may judge the form of life a human one, we will not think it a *good* human life. The latter threshold is the one that will eventually concern us when we turn to public policy: for we don't want societies to make their citizens capable of the bare minimum. My view holds, with Aristotle, that a good political arrangement is one "in accordance with which anyone whatsoever might do well and live a flourishing life".[7]

These are clearly, in many areas, two distinct thresholds, requiring distinct levels of resource and opportunity. One may be alive without being well nourished. As Marx observed, one may be able to use one's senses without being able to use them in a fully human way. And yet there is need for caution here. For in many cases the move from human life to good human life is supplied by the citizen's own powers of choice and self-definition, in such a way that once society places them above the first threshold, moving above the second is more or less up to them. This is especially likely to be so, I think, in areas such as affiliation and practical reasoning, where in many cases once social institutions permit a child to cross the first threshold its own choices will be central in raising it above the second. (This is not always so, however: for certain social conditions, for example certain mindless forms of labour or, we may add, traditional hierarchical gender relations, may impede the flourishing of affiliation and practical reason, while not stamping it out entirely.) On the other hand, it is clear that where bodily health and nutrition, for example, are concerned, there is a considerable difference between the two thresholds, and a difference that is standardly made by resources over which individuals do not have full control. It would then be the concern of quality-of-life assessment to ask whether all citizens are capable, not just of the bare minimum,

but of *good life* in these areas. Clearly there is a continuum here. Nor will it in practise be at all easy to say where the upper threshold, especially, should be located.

I shall not say much about the first threshold, but shall illustrate it by a few examples. What is an existence that is so impoverished that it cannot properly be called a human life? Here we should count, I believe, many forms of existence that take place at the end of a human life—all those in which the being that survives has irretrievably lost sensation and consciousness (in what is called a "permanent vegetative condition"); and also, I would hold, some that fall short of this, but in which the capacity to recognize loved ones, to think and to reason, has irreversibly decayed beyond a certain point. I would include the extreme absence of ability to engage in practical reasoning that is often the outcome of the notorious frontal lobotomy. I would also include an absence of mobility so severe that it makes speech, as well as movement from place to place, impossible.

It follows from this that certain severely damaged infants are not human ever, even if born from two human parents: again, those with global and total sensory incapacity and/or no consciousness or thought; also, I think, those with no ability at all to recognize or relate to others. (This of course tells us nothing about what we owe them morally, it just separates that question from moral questions about human beings.)

Again, we notice the evaluative character of these threshold judgements. The fact that a person who has lost her arms cannot play a piano does not make us judge that she no longer lives a human life; had she lost the capacity to think and remember, or to form affectionate relationships, it would have been a different matter.

Many such disasters are not to be blamed on social arrangements, and in those cases the first threshold has no political implications. But many are, where bad nutrition and health care enter in. The role of society is even more evident if we think of a more controversial group of first-threshold cases, in which the non-human outcome was environmentally caused: the rare cases of children who have grown up outside a human community, or in a severely dysfunctional home, and utterly lack language and reason, or lack social abilities in an extreme and irreversible way. We can focus the political question more productively, however, if we now turn from the question of mere human life to the question of good life, the level we would really like to see a human being attain.

Here, as the next level of the conception of the human being, I shall now specify certain basic functional capabilities at which societies should aim for their citizens, and which quality of life measurements should measure. In other words, this will be an account of the second threshold—although in some areas it may coincide, for the reasons I have given, with the first: once one is capable of human functioning in this area one is also capable, with some further effort and care, of good functioning. I introduce this list as a list of capabilities to function, rather than of actual functionings, since I shall argue that capability, not actual functioning, should be the goal of public policy.

4.1. Level 2 of the Conception of the Human Being: Basic Human Functional Capabilities

1. Being able to live to the end of a human life of normal length,[8] not dying prematurely, or before one's life is so reduced as to be not worth living.

2. Being able to have good health; to be adequately nourished,[9] to have adequate shelter; having opportunities for sexual satisfaction, and for choice in matters of reproduction; being able to move from place to place.

3. Being able to avoid unnecessary and non-beneficial pain, so far as possible, and to have pleasurable experiences.

4. Being able to use the senses; being able to imagine, to think, and to reason—and to do these things in a way informed and cultivated by an adequate education, including, but by no means limited to, literacy and basic mathematical and scientific training. Being able to use imagination and thought in connection with experiencing and producing spiritually enriching materials and events of one's own choice; religious, literary, musical, and so forth. I believe that the protection of this capability requires not only the provision of

education, but also legal guarantees of freedom of expression with respect to both political and artistic speech, and of freedom of religious exercise.

5. Being able to have attachments to things and persons outside ourselves; to love those who love and care for us, to grieve at their absence; in general, to love, to grieve, to experience longing and gratitude. Supporting this capability means supporting forms of human association that can be shown to be crucial in their development.

6. Being able to form a conception of the good and to engage in critical reflection about the planning of one's own life. This includes, today, being able to seek employment outside the home and to participate in political life.

7. Being able to live for and to others, to recognize and show concern for other human beings, to engage in various forms of social interaction; to be able to imagine the situation of another and to have compassion for that situation; to have the capability for both justice and friendship. Protecting this capability means, once again, protecting institutions that constitute such forms of affiliation, and also protecting the freedoms of assembly and political speech.

8. Being able to live with concern for and in relation to animals, plants, and the world of nature.

9. Being able to laugh, to play, to enjoy recreational activities.

10. Being able to live one's own life and nobody else's. This means having certain guarantees of non-interference with certain choices that are especially personal and definitive of selfhood, such as choices regarding marriage, childbearing, sexual expression, speech, and employment.

10a. Being able to live one's own life in one's own surroundings and context. This means guarantees of freedom of association and of freedom from unwarranted search and seizure; it also means a certain sort of guarantee of the integrity of personal property, though this guarantee may be limited in various ways by the demands of social equality, and is always up for negotiation in connection with the interpretation of the other capabilities, since personal property, unlike personal liberty, is a tool of human functioning rather than an end in itself.

My claim is that a life that lacks any one of these capabilities, no matter what else it has, will fall short of being a good human life. So it would be reasonable to take these things as a focus for concern, in assessing the quality of life in a country and asking about the role of public policy in meeting human needs. The list is certainly general—and this is deliberate, in order to leave room for plural specification and also for further negotiation. But I claim that it does, rather like a set of constitutional guarantees, offer real guidance in the ongoing historical process of further refinement and specification, and far more accurate guidance than that offered by the focus on utility, or even on resources. . . .

The list is, emphatically, a list of separate components. We cannot satisfy the need for one of them by giving a larger amount of another. All are of central importance and all are distinct in quality. This limits the trade-offs that it will be reasonable to make, and thus limits the applicability of quantitative cost-benefit analysis. At the same time, the items on the list are related to one another in many complex ways. For example our characteristic mode of nutrition, unlike that of sponges, requires moving from here to there. And we do whatever we do as separate beings, tracing distinct paths through space and time. Notice that reproductive choices involve both sexual capability and issues of separateness, and bind the two together in a deep and complex way.

A further comment is in order, concerning the relationship of this threshold list to an account of human equality. A commitment to bringing all human beings across a certain threshold of capability to choose represents a certain sort of commitment to equality: for the view treats all persons as equal bearers of human claims, no matter where they are starting from in terms of circumstances, special talents, wealth, gender, or race. On the other hand, I have said nothing so far about how one should regard inequalities that persist once the threshold level has been attained for all persons. To some extent I feel this would be premature, since the threshold level has so rarely been attained for the complete capability set. On the other hand, one can imagine a situation—perhaps it could be that of the USA or Japan, given certain large changes in health support here, or educational distribution there, that would meet threshold conditions and still exhibit inequalities of attainment between the genders or the races. We have two choices here: either to argue that this situation actually contains capability failure after all; or to grant that the capability view needs to be supplemented by an independent theory of equality. I am not yet certain what I want to say about this, but I am inclined to the first alternative, since I think that gender inequality of the sort one sees in a prosperous nation does none the less push the subordinated racial or gender group beneath an acceptable threshold of autonomy, dignity, and emotional well being. Indeed, subordination is itself a kind of capability failure, a failure to attain complete personhood. So I am inclined to say that, properly fleshed out, the second threshold would be incompatible with systematic subordination of one group to another. . . .

6 ANSWERING THE OBJECTIONS: HUMAN FUNCTIONING AND PLURALISM

I have commended the human-function view by contrast to its rivals on the development scene. But I must now try to show how it can answer the objections I described earlier.

Concerning *neglect of historical and cultural difference*, I can begin by insisting that this normative conception of human capability and functioning is general, and in a sense vague, for precisely this reason. The list claims to have identified in a very general way components that are fundamental to any human life. But it allows in its very design for the possibility of multiple specifications of each of the components. This is so in several different ways. First, the constitutive circumstances of human life, while broadly shared, are themselves realized in different forms in different societies. The fear of death, the love of play, relationships of friendship and affiliation with others, even the experience of the bodily appetites never turn up in simply the vague and general form in which we have introduced them here, but always in some specific and historically rich cultural realization, which can profoundly shape not only the conceptions used by the citizens in these areas, but also their experiences themselves. Nonetheless, we do have in these areas of our common humanity sufficient overlap to sustain a general conversation, focusing on our common problems and prospects. And sometimes the common conversation will permit us to criticize some conceptions of the grounding experiences themselves, as at odds with other things human beings want to do and to be.

When we are choosing a conception of good functioning with respect to these circumstances, we can expect an even greater degree of plurality to become evident. Here the approach wants to retain plurality in two significantly different ways: what I may call the way of *plural specification*, and what I may call the way of *local specification*.

Plural specification means what its name implies. Public policy, while using a determinate conception of the good at a high level of generality, leaves a great deal of latitude for citizens to specify each of the components more concretely, and with much variety, in accordance with local traditions, or individual tastes. Many concrete forms of life, in many different places and circumstances, display functioning in accordance with all the major capabilities.

As for local specification: good public reasoning, I believe and have argued, is always done, when well done, with a rich sensitivity to the concrete context, to the characters of the agents and their social situation. This means that in addition to the pluralism I have just described, the Aristotelian needs to consider a different sort of plural specification of the good. For sometimes what is a good way of promoting education in one part of the world will be completely ineffectual in another. Forms of affiliation that flourish in one community may prove impossible to sustain in another. In such cases, the Aristotelian must aim at some concrete specification of the general list that suits, and develops out of, the local conditions. This will always most reasonably be done in a participatory dialogue with those who are most deeply immersed in those conditions. For though Aristotelianism does not hesitate to criticize tradition

where tradition perpetrates injustice or oppression, it also does not believe in saying anything at all without rich and full information, gathered not so much from detached study as from the voices of those who live the ways of life in question. [. . .]

The liberal charges the capability approach with *neglect of autonomy*, arguing that any such determinate conception removes from the citizens the chance to make their own choices about the good life. This is a complicated issue: three points can be stressed. First, the list is a list of capabilities, not a list of actual functions, precisely because the conception is designed to leave room for choice. Government is not directed to push citizens into acting in certain valued ways; instead, it is directed to make sure that all human beings have the necessary resources and conditions for acting in those ways. It leaves the choice up to them. A person with plenty of food can always choose to fast. A person who has been given the capability for sexual expression can always choose celibacy. The person who has access to subsidized education can always decide to do something else instead. By making opportunities available, government enhances, and does not remove, choice. It will not always be easy to say at what point someone is really capable of making a choice, especially in areas where there are severe traditional obstacles to functioning. Sometimes our best strategy may well be to look at actual functioning and infer negative capability (tentatively) from its absence. But the conceptual distinction remains very important.

Secondly, this respect for choice is built deeply into the list itself, in the architectonic role it gives to practical reasoning. One of the most central capabilities promoted by the conception will be the capability of choice itself. [. . .]

Finally, the capability view insists that choice is not pure spontaneity, flourishing independent of material and social conditions. If one cares about autonomy, then one must care about the rest of the form of life that supports it, and the material conditions that enable one to live that form of life. Thus the approach claims that its own comprehensive concern with flourishing across all areas of life is a better way of promoting choice than is the liberal's narrower concern with spontaneity alone, which sometimes tolerates situations in which individuals are in other ways cut off from the fully human use of their faculties.

I turn now to the objection about application; it raises especially delicate questions where women are concerned.

7 WHO GETS INCLUDED? WOMEN AS HUMAN BEINGS

In a now well-known remark, which I cite here as an epigraph, the feminist lawyer Catharine MacKinnon claimed that "being a woman is not yet a way of being a human being."[10] This means, I think, that most traditional ways of categorizing and valuing women have not accorded them full membership in the human species, as that species is generally defined. MacKinnon is no doubt thinking in particular of the frequent denials to women of the rational nature that is taken to be a central part of what it is to be human. It is sobering to remind oneself that quite a few leading philosophers, including Aristotle and Rousseau, the "fathers" (certainly not mothers) of my idea, did deny women full membership in human functioning as they understood that notion. If this is so, one might well ask, of what use is it really to identify a set of central human capabilities? For the basic (lower-level) capacity to develop these can always be denied to women, even by those who grant their centrality. Does this problem show that the human function idea is either hopelessly in league with patriarchy or, at best, impotent as a tool for justice?

I believe that it does not. For if we examine the history of these denials we see, I believe, the great power of the conception of the human as a source of moral claims. Acknowledging the other person as a member of the very same kind would have generated a sense of affiliation and a set of moral and educational duties. That is why, to those bent on shoring up their own power, the stratagem of splitting the other off from one's own species seems so urgent and so seductive. But to deny humanness to beings with

whom one lives in conversation and interaction is a fragile sort of self-deceptive stratagem, vulnerable to sustained and consistent reflection, and also to experiences that cut through self-deceptive rationalization. Any moral conception can be withheld, out of ambition or hatred or shame. But the conception of the human being, spelled out, as here, in a roughly determinate way, in terms of circumstances of life and functions in these circumstances, seems much harder to withhold than other conceptions that have been made the basis for ethics—"rational being", for example, or (as I have suggested) "person".

To illustrate this point, I now turn to the earliest argument known to me in the Western philosophical tradition that uses a conception of the human being for feminist ends. It is not the first feminist argument in the Western tradition: for Plato's *Republic* precedes (and influences) it. But Plato's argument in favour of equal education for women is heavily qualified by his élitism with respect to all functions for all human beings; thus it is able to generate only élitist conclusions for males and females alike. Platonic justice is not the "humanist justice" of Susan Okin's powerful phrase. The argument I have in mind is, instead, the first argument of the Roman Stoic thinker Musonius Rufus in his brief treatise, "That Women Too Should Do Philosophy", written in the first century A.D. This argument is all the more interesting in that it, in effect, uses Aristotelian concepts to correct Aristotle's mistake about women—showing, I think, that an Aristotelian who is both internally consistent and honest about the evidence cannot avoid the egalitarian normative conclusion that women, as much as men, should receive a higher education (for that is in effect what is meant by doing philosophy).

The argument has a tacit premise. It is that—at least with respect to certain central functions of the human being—the presence in a creature of a basic (untrained, lower-level) capability to perform the functions in question, given suitable support and education, exerts a claim on society that those capabilities should be developed to the point at which the person is fully capable of choosing the functions in question. This premise needed no argument in the

philosophical culture of Greco-Roman antiquity, since
that moral claim is more or less taken to be implicit in
the notion of capability itself. I have tried to give it
intuitive support in the argument of this paper.

The argument itself now follows with a truly
radical simplicity. Its second premise consists of an
appeal to the experience of the imaginary recalcitrant
male interlocutor. Women, he is asked to concede
on the basis of experience, do in fact have the basic
capabilities to perform a wide variety of the most
important human functions. They have the five senses.
They have the same number of bodily parts, implying
similar functional possibilities in that sphere. They
have the ability to think and reason, just as males do.
And, finally, they have responsiveness to ethical
distinctions, making (whether well or badly) distinctions between the good and the bad. Some time is
then spent establishing a third premise: that "higher
education" of the sort offered by the Stoic ideal of
liberal education, is necessary for the full development of the perceptual, intellectual, and moral capabilities. Conclusion: women, like men, should have
this education.

The puzzle, for us, is the second premise. Why
does the interlocutor accept it? We see from the surrounding material that the interlocutor is a husband
who interacts with his wife in a number of areas of
life that are explicitly enumerated: planning and
managing a household (where she is the one who
manages most of the daily business); having and raising children (where he observes, or imagines, her in
labour, enduring risk and pain for the sake of the
family and, later, caring for and educating the child);
having sexual relations with him, and refusing to
have sex with others; having a real friendship with
him, based on common contemporary ideas of "sharing life together"; deciding how to treat the people
around her; being fair, for example, to the household
staff; and, finally, confronting all the dangers and the
moral ambiguities of the politics of first century A.D.
Rome—refusing to capitulate, he says, to the unjust
demands of a tyrant. In all of these operations of life,
the argument seems to be, he tacitly acknowledges, in
fact strongly relies upon, his wife's capability to
engage in practical reasoning and ethical distinction

making. Indeed, he is depicted as someone who
would like these things done *well*—for he wants his
wife not to reason badly when political life gets
tough, or to treat the servants with cruelty, or to botch
the education of the children. So in his daily life he
acknowledges her humanity, her possession of the
basic (lower-level) capabilities for fully human functioning. How, then, Musonius reasonably asks him,
can he consistently deny her what would be necessary in order to develop and fulfil that humanity?

This, I believe, is an impressively radical argument. And it led to (or reflected) a social situation that
marked a high point for women in the Western tradition for thousands of years since and to come. We
do not need to show that the views of Musonius on
women were perfect in all respects; in many ways
they were not. But his argument shows, I believe, the
power of a universal conception of the human being
in claims of justice for women. For the interlocutor
might have refused to acknowledge that his wife was
a "person": it was to some extent up to him to define
that rather refined and elusive concept. He could
not fail to acknowledge that she was a human being,
with the basic capability for the functions in question.
For he had acknowledged that already, in his daily
life. . . .

Being a woman is indeed not yet a way of being a
human being. Women in much of the world lack support for the most central human functions, and this
denial of support is frequently caused by their being
women. But women, unlike rocks and plants and
even dogs and horses, are human beings, have the
potential to become capable of these human functions, given sufficient nutrition, education, and other
support. That is why their unequal failure in capability is a problem of justice. It is up to us to solve this
problem. I claim that a conception of human functioning gives us valuable assistance as we undertake
this task.

NOTES

1. By this I mean that the difference in external genitalia
figures in social life as it is interpreted by human cultures;

thus we are never dealing simply with facts given at birth, but always with what has been made of them [. . .] . Thus, even the common distinction between "gender", a cultural concept, and "sex", the allegedly pure biological concept, is inadequate to capture the depth of cultural interpretation in presenting even the biological "facts" to human beings, from the very start of a child's life. See Anne Fausto-Sterling, *Myths of Gender* (2nd edn., New York: Basic Books, 1992). I have discussed these issues further in "Constructing Love, Desire, and Care", forthcoming in D. Estlund and M. Nussbaum (eds.), *Laws and Nature: Shaping Sex, Preference, and Family* (Oxford University Press).

2. By relativism, I mean the view that the only available criterion of adjudication is some local group or individual. Thus relativism, as I understand it, is a genus of which the brand of reliance on individuals' subjective preferences frequently endorsed in neoclassical economics is one species. (Economists, of course, are relativist only about value, not about what they construe as the domain of scientific "fact".) [. . .] My opponents also frequently employ the term "postmodernist" to characterize their position: this is a vaguer term, associated in a very general way with the repudiation of both metaphysical realism (to be defined below) and universalism.

3. Kwame Anthony Appiah, *In My Father's House: Africa in the Philosophy of Culture* (New York and Oxford: Oxford University Press, 1992), p. viii.

4. This of course is not incompatible with calling certain groups non-human or subhuman for political purposes. But such denials are usually either transparent propaganda or forms of self-deception, which can be unmasked by critical argument. . . .

5. Aristotle, *Metaphysics* I.I.

6. Aristotle, ubiquitously in the accounts of substance.

7. Aristotle, *Politics* VII.I: see "Nature, Function, and Capability".

8. Although "normal length" is clearly relative to current human possibilities, and may need, for practical purposes, to be to some extent relativized to local conditions, it seems important to think of it—at least at a given time in history—in universal and comparative terms, as the *Human Development Report* does, to give rise to complaint in a country that has done well with some indicators of life quality, but badly on life expectancy. And although some degree of relativity may be put down to the differential genetic possibilities of different groups (the "missing women" statistics, for example, allow that on the average women live somewhat longer than men), it is also import-

ant not to conclude prematurely that inequalities between groups—for example, the growing inequalities in life expectancy between blacks and whites in the USA—are simply genetic variation, not connected with social injustice.

9. The precise specification of these health rights is not easy, but the work currently being done on them in drafting new constitutions in South Africa and Eastern Europe gives reason for hope that the combination of a general specification of such a right with a tradition of judicial interpretation will yield something practicable. It should be noticed that I speak of health, not just health care: and health itself interacts in complex ways with housing, with education, with dignity. Both health and nutrition are controversial as to whether the relevant level should be specified universally, or relatively to the local community and its traditions: for example, is low height associated with nutritional practices to be thought of as "stunting", or as felicitous adaptation to circumstances of scarcity? . . .

10. The remark was cited by Richard Rorty in "Feminist and Pragmatism", *Michigan Quarterly Review*, 30 (1989), 231; it has since been confirmed and repeated by MacKinnon herself.

Study Questions

1. Nussbaum describes her project as "frankly universalist and 'essentialist.'" What does she mean by this?

2. Nussbaum discusses four common criticisms of universalizing projects:

   a) that they entail metaphysical realism
   b) that they neglect historical and cultural differences
   c) that they negate human autonomy
   d) that they result in prejudicial applications

   Explain these criticisms and Nussbaum's responses to them.

3. Why does Nussbaum wish to answer the question, "What are the characteristic activities of the human being?" What method does she recommend that one employ when seeking the answer?

4. What do you think of Nussbaum's list of "Basic Human Functional Capabilities"? Does Wendell's discussion of disability suggest problems for Nussbaum's list?

5. In what sense can this piece by Nussbaum be read as an example of sameness/humanist feminist thinking?

Susan Schechter

Social Change on Behalf of Battered Women: Reforming the Criminal Justice System

CHANGING POLICE PRACTICES

One survey reports that in almost half the violence cases, women turn to no one,[1] a shocking reminder of the depth of their isolation. Thousands of battered women, however, do ask for assistance. Many turn in desperation to the police, the only "helping" agency open twenty-four hours a day. Before the movement began, the typical attitude toward intervention on behalf of battered women was recorded unashamedly in the Michigan Police Training Academy procedures.

   a. Avoid arrest if possible. Appeal to their vanity.
   b. Explain the procedure of obtaining a warrant.
      1. Complainant must sign complaint.
      2. Must appear in court.
      3. Consider loss of time.
      4. Cost of court.
   c. State that your only interest is to prevent a breach of the peace.
   d. Explain that attitudes usually change by court time.
   e. Recommend a postponement.
      1. Court not in session.
      2. No judge available.
   f. *Don't* be too harsh or critical.[2]

The failure to weigh the seriousness of assault and its potential for escalating into homicide had grave consequences. In a Kansas City study of domestic assault, the Police Department found that "they had responded to disturbance calls at the address of homicide victims or suspects at least once in the 2 years before the homicide in 90 percent of the cases, and five or more times in the 2 years before the homicide in 50 percent of the cases."[3]

At the beginning of the movement, battered women complained frequently that the police simply would not come when called. If they did come, they would refuse to arrest, saying: "There's nothing we can do. It's a family matter; go to Family Court tomorrow." Or they would side with the husband, walking him around the block or joking with him about the violence. Police refused to escort women to hospitals or to wait and protect them as they gathered their children and clothing. Continually looking through sexist blinders, the police failed to acknowledge that this victim was often frightened and intimidated because she lived with her assailant.

James Bannon, Commander of the Detroit Police Department, corroborates battered women's stories as he explains the procedures police used.

The second example of a not atypical strategy is what has become known as "call screening." Some years back, calls for police service exceeded the department's ability to respond. The decision was made not to respond to certain types of calls. Wouldn't you know that the first calls screened out were family troubles.[4]

Bannon describes how battered women's cases "disappeared" as they proceeded through the criminal justice system in Detroit.

In 1972 for instance, there were 4900 assaults of this kind which had survived the screening process long enough to at least have a request for warrant prepared and the complainant referred to the assault and battery squad. Through the process of conciliation, complainant harassment and prosecutor discretion, fewer than 300 of these cases were ultimately tried by a court of law.[5]

Calling this treatment malfeasance, Bannon offered his explanation for why only 300 out of 4900 assaults were tried.

It is my view that police, and later prosecutors and courts, contribute to domestic violence by their laissez-faire attitudes toward what they view as essentially a "personal problem." This is made even more problematic because police are socialized to regard females in general as subordinate.[6]

Laws against assault and battery existed in every state before the battered women's movement began. Assault and battery is always a crime, either a misdemeanor or felony, depending on the seriousness of the attack. But, as Del Martin notes:

Usually, in misdemeanor cases a police officer can only make an arrest on the spot if the act is committed in his presence or if a warrant has been issued. . . .

When a felony has been committed, an officer is authorized to make an arrest on "reasonable belief" or "probable cause," that is, if he has sufficient reason to believe that a felony has been committed and that the person identified by the victim or witnesses committed the crime. But this provision, being the most subjective and also the easiest to ignore, is rarely invoked in wife-abuse cases.[7]

Although laws vary significantly from state to state, the battered women's movement worked legislatively to see that wife beating was treated as a crime—a social, not a private matter. The movement argued that battered women deserved the same rights as any other crime victims, and worked with the police, legislators, and courts to enforce already existing laws or to create new ones. Additionally, parts of the movement asserted that because this victim lives with her victimizer and faces recurrent intimidation and danger, police arrest powers should be expanded. As one lawyer noted, "in battered women's cases, the police tend to view serious attacks as misdemeanors rather than felonies so you must specify in legislation that the police may arrest without a warrant for a misdemeanor offense."[8] As a result of the movement:

Twenty-seven of the recent state laws on domestic violence expand police power to arrest in domestic abuse cases. In twenty-one states, arrest without a warrant is permitted where a police officer has probable cause to believe that an abuser has committed a misdemeanor. In fourteen states, police may arrest without a warrant if they have probable cause to believe that an abuser has violated a protection order. (Eight states allow probable cause arrest in both cases.) . . .

Almost half the statutes impose some duties on police responding to domestic disturbance calls, including transporting the victim to a hospital or shelter, informing her of her legal options, staying until she is no longer in danger. . . .[9]

In much new legislation, the emphasis is on enforcing the victim's rights, increasing her legal options, and protecting her from further assaults.

In Oakland and New York, the battered women's movement decided that the best way to deal with recalcitrant police was through legal confrontation rather than legislative change or bureaucratic negotiation. In October 1976, battered women filed a class action suit, Scott v. Hart, against the Oakland Police Department, and in December 1976, battered wives leveled a suit, Bruno v. Codd, against the New York

City Police Department, the New York City Department of Probation, and the clerks of the Family Court.[10] In New York City, the Litigation Coalition for Battered Women charged the police and courts with gross failure to comply with the law. One plaintiff's deposition stated that the police refused to arrest her husband even though he was still hitting her when they arrived and they had to pry his hands from around her neck. Another woman, beaten many times, was told by Family Court personnel that she would have to bring her husband with her to the court's family counseling program before she could get an order of protection.[11] In an unstated admission of their guilt, the police settled the NY suit before it went to trial. The agreement stipulated that the police must: 1. arrest men who commit felonious assaults; 2. send out officers for every call from a battered woman; 3. arrest in misdemeanor cases unless there is justification not to arrest; 4. arrest where the husband has violated a Family Court protection order; 5. assist the woman in receiving medical help; and 6. search for a husband who has fled the scene of the crime as the police do in other cases.[12]

Lawsuits were one tactic that dramatically focused national attention on the institutional complicity that kept women battered. The examples provided by activists in New York and Oakland encouraged women in New Haven, Chicago, and Atlanta to threaten their police departments with lawsuits and inspired Los Angeles women to sue in 1979. Although only a few lawsuits were filed, their impact reached far beyond the departments sued. As one activist noted, "some of us . . . have been able to use the leverage of other cities' suits to get our police departments to review their policies, procedures and training . . ."[13]

Time is needed to fully assess the impact of these suits. They helped activists find one another across the country, share information, strategize, and build a movement. Locally, the early lawsuits brought together lawyers, grassroots groups, and battered women in a joint effort to reclaim women's rights. Where these coalitions have remained organized to monitor the police, abuses, while still frequent, have decreased. In one New York City neighborhood with an active grassroots service program, police compliance with the law is significantly better than in neighborhoods with no watchdog agency. In general, change is described as small, based on individual officer's attitudes. In evaluating the lawsuits, a veteran feminist lawyer cautions, "don't do lawsuits unless you are in this for life. Police attitudes are embedded in centuries of sexism, and if you don't have an organized movement behind you, lawsuits won't help."[14] Another activist lawyer notes, "litigation can be used for social change. It is not a change agent in itself but rather a public relations tactic that gives the movement power to negotiate."[15]

A final focus of statutory or regulatory change was police training procedures. One Michigan study revealed that although almost half of all police calls for assistance are about domestic violence, only 3 to 5 out of 240 hours of police recruit training are spent learning to handle domestic violence complaints.[16] While hailed by many, police training legislation can be problematic unless carefully written and monitored. Because so many police officers are killed answering "domestic disturbance" calls, it is in the interest of the police to protect officers, mediate the conflict, and leave as soon as possible. Training can easily fall into teaching the police crisis intervention and mediation techniques. These skills, while helpful to officers, leave battered women in a vulnerable position. In a context where one person unpredictably resorts to force to get his way, "mediation" offers no safety for the victim. It holds no legal sanction. The victim learns nothing about her rights. Because of these problems, the battered women's movement has often opposed mediation and pushed for very specific training legislation that encourages officers to arrest the batterer and to assist the victim. One example from Washington is cited as a model.

All training relating to the handling of domestic violence complaints by law enforcement officers shall stress enforcement of criminal laws in domestic situations, availability of community resources, and protection of the victim. Law enforcement agencies and community organizations with expertise in the issue of domestic violence shall cooperate in all aspects of the training.[17]

Even model legislation, however, can be ineffective without monitoring by women's programs. Police training mandates can be easily ignored and subverted, and behavior can stay remarkably fixed in sexist patterns.

COURT REFORM

Courts, like the police, reflect sexist values and often provide little aid to victims of battering. Court orders are supposed to protect battered women.

> A protection order (also called a restraining order or temporary injunction) is an order issued to an abuser by a court requiring him to change his conduct. The court may, depending on state law, order an abuser to move out of a residence shared with the victim, to refrain from abuse or contact with the victim, to attend a counseling program, or to pay support, restitution, or attorney's fees. The court may award child custody and visitation rights or may restrict use or disposition of personal property . . .[18]

At the beginning of the battered women's movement, in many states such protective orders were available only to women filing for divorce; as of 1981, twelve states still granted such injunctions pending only divorce, separation, or custody proceedings.[19] For religious, economic, moral, or emotional reasons, many battered women will not file for divorces; such women were, and in some cases still are, without civil court protection.

My observations as a battered women's advocate in 1978–79 in Manhattan Family Court, a civil court, suggest typical problems battered women's groups have sought to remedy. This Family Court offers women Orders of Protection, pieces of paper that order the abuser to refrain from harassing, menacing, or assaulting the petitioner for one year. Failure to comply with such orders can result in six months in jail, although in my twelve month experience, only one husband, violating a court order for the eighth time by throwing his wife from a second story window, went to jail. His sentence was thirty days.

The law states that the purpose of Family Court is to keep the family together. Twisting the law to their own ends, probation officers used this mandate to keep women out of court. As noted in the New York City lawsuit, Family Court probation employees— those who interview each court petitioner before she sees a judge—denied women access to court by illegally coercing them into family counseling. Unlike the potential inherent in a court order of protection, family counseling offers neither protection nor any enforcement mechanism to punish men if further abuse occurs. As a result, battered women felt the seriousness of their cases denied. Heaping one abuse on top of another, hostile attitudes toward victims were commonly expressed; one probation officer carefully explained to me that battered women are generally, "shrewish, unfeminine, and crushing."

Even when granting orders of protection, judges urged counseling. Only rarely did they exercise their authority to remove an abusive man from the home; women and their children, therefore, bore the burden of leaving. Three or four week delays were common between the date of a woman's first court appearance in which she was granted a Temporary Order of Protection and a second hearing in which her husband was entitled to legal counsel. Long delays and adjournments often resulted. In the meantime, she might be beaten again and advised by the police to go back to court and file a violation of an Order of Protection; no arrest would occur. If her husband appeared for this hearing, he was usually verbally reprimanded. Many men learned that the court would do nothing to stop their abuse. Sometimes they even watched judges grant mutual orders of protection in which non-violent women were ordered to stop "harassing" their husbands. The humiliation was often unbearable for women.

Family Court can also grant visitation, support, and custody rights. Men who batter often use visitation as a form of tormenting their wives by failing to return children on time. Since most order of protection hearings, especially those without attorneys, last no more than minutes, few women ever have the chance to explain to judges their unique fears about further violence or their concerns about child snatching. In addition, if violations of visitation rights occurred on a weekend, women had no immediate access to the courts.

Legal remedies for unmarried women were even more problematic. In New York City, for example, Family Court serves married women only. Unmarried women are sent to a totally ineffective summons court or to criminal court if their cases are serious. Fearful of retaliation or protective of their men, many women do not want to use criminal court and find themselves with no civil court remedies.

In some states, where battered women's advocates were well organized, activists wrote, lobbied for, and helped implement state legislation that offers women more substantial remedies. A member of the Battered Women's Action Committee describes the provisions of the Abuse Prevention Act passed in Massachusetts in 1978 which is modeled on the Pennsylvania legislation enacted in 1976.

1. *Broad definition of abuse.* "Abuse" is defined as attempting to cause or actually causing physical harm, putting another in fear of imminent physical harm, or making another engage involuntarily in sexual relations by fear, fear of force, or duress.

2. *Greater availability of emergency protective orders.* Unmarried people living together, as well as women married to their abusers, may request emergency orders. Married women are eligible for emergency orders whether or not they choose to file for divorce or separation. These emergency orders include protective orders as well as those for custody and support. The request is made on a simple complaint form which is free and can be filled out without the assistance of an attorney. Orders are issued the same day; a hearing will be held within 5 days to give the abuser the opportunity to respond. Local police stations can advise women of judges available on a rotating basis during hours when the court is closed.[20]

The Massachusetts law mandates that victims can request compensation for injuries, moving expenses, and loss of income; that violation of the order is a criminal offense; that police must take whatever steps necessary to prevent further abuse. Police must arrest the attacker if a felony has occurred, if a misdemeanor has been committed in their presence, or if a

protective order has been violated. And finally, "recognizing that jail is not a solution to violence, . . ." the law suggests referrals to counseling, a residential treatment facility, or probation officer in sentencing while contact with the victim of abuse remains restricted.[21]

Although courts have had the judicial right to evict a violent man based on legal precedents of just and fair treatment, they never offered this option to battered women. This inequity was partially corrected as state legislatures passed laws specifying that the abuser, not the victim, bears the burden of leaving. In some states where these laws are in effect, women hail them as significant reforms. For example, rural service projects, without local shelters, often successfully use court vacate orders and then support women in their efforts to stand firm against their husbands' recurring threats. Thirty-two of the new protection order laws have eviction clauses which give victims a right to their homes.[22] From surveys done around the country, however, it is clear that courts are not consistently granting protection and vacate orders.

In assessing any criminal justice system changes, it is important to distinguish large urban areas from small towns. It is also crucial to recognize differences between coalitions and local programs that have allocated significant resources to police and court training and monitoring from those that have not. Reports from small towns, while very varied, generally are more optimistic than those from large urban areas. In small towns, police and judges have been confronted about their sexist behavior by advocates who are often their neighbors. Personal contact frequently allows ongoing discussion and has sometimes brought noticeable improvements in law enforcement. In some areas, judges and police have felt the weight of social criticism as women mobilize others in the community to condemn sloppy law enforcement. Even more marked changes are sometimes recounted by those coalitions, like Pennsylvania, that received grants to train police and district justices throughout the state. In one year, staff trained all 580 of Pennsylvania's district justices and 400 police officers, noting attitudinal and behavioral changes in many.[23]

Divorce, support, and child custody laws were also amended as a result of the activity of the battered women's movement. In states that maintain "fault" divorces, desertion is defined as one ground for divorce. Battered women who left their husbands to avoid abuse were sometimes found to have abandoned their families and thus could be divorced by their husbands. Facing the maddening logic of sexist double-binds, women then discovered that desertion charges were used against them in child custody battles. New Jersey, therefore, adopted specific legislation stating that abuse is a defense to any action alleging desertion.[24] In Illinois, a sixth factor was added to the five existing ones for determining the best interests of the child in custody cases.

> The physical violence or threat of physical violence by the child's potential custodian, whether directed against the child or directed against another person but witnessed by the child.[25]

Another Illinois statutory provision allowed victims, often harassed by their abusers even after they leave them, to avoid divulging their addresses on court orders if such disclosures might endanger them or their children.[26]

In their search for legal support in civil cases, most battered women, with access to few, if any, financial resources, found that courts were not the only cause for complaint. With some notable exceptions, like the Family Law Unit at South Brooklyn Legal Services, advocates bemoan the lack of help available through Legal Services, the agency mandated and funded to offer legal assistance to the poor. As several activist attorneys have remarked, "most lawyers see family law as the boring junk, or worse, the sphere that forces them to serve hysterical women." Although Legal Services is mandated to help anyone who fits into its eligibility criteria, each office chooses its priorities. Some offices subvert their mandate by including husbands' income in eligibility determinations and declaring battered women "over-income" and thus ineligible for services. In others, only routine divorce cases are handled, while emergency protective orders are not. Complicated cases—in which rights to protection, custody, and support are contested—

may be passed on to the youngest, least experienced attorneys.

Poor legal treatment is not just the result of local decisions. The National Center on Women and Family Law, a Legal Services back-up center mandated to scrutinize the needs of women and disseminate information nationally, receives the lowest allocation of any Legal Services back-up center. It will be hardest hit by cutbacks, and probably will be the first center phased out by President Reagan. Women attorneys organized and pressured Legal Services to establish this Center, yet from the beginning, these attorneys were told that battered women were an inappropriate priority.

Like Civil courts, Criminal courts demeaned battered women and trivialized their experiences. Badly beaten women, desperate for protection, often saw charges reduced or dismissed by prosecutors and heard attorneys and judges alike recommend counseling or mediation. The constant taunts: "You don't want to lock him up; he'll lose his job; your kids need a father," greeted battered women who tried to prosecute. Prosecutors considered these cases a bother, demanding proof of severe injury, promises to follow through, and "character" checks to verify battered women's credibility as witnesses. Like rape victims, battered women often felt like the criminal.

Ten states have passed legislation making spouse abuse a separate criminal offense; this legislation creates no new substantive law but rather emphasizes the need for enforcement of criminal law and makes data collection easier.[27] Some states have passed legislation setting conditions for pre-trial release and deferred prosecution. These include orders of protection specifying that the abuser is to stay away from the victim. Michigan and California legislation has created diversionary counseling programs, ordering defendants to participate in counseling. If the defendant completes the program successfully, charges are dismissed; if he fails to comply with program criteria, criminal proceedings can be resumed.[28]

Some women have opposed mandatory therapy on the grounds that it deprives people of their civil rights; that mandated, rather than chosen treatment never works; and that men who batter should face serious consequences that only criminal sanctions bring. Moreover, some courts use counseling diversion as a way of throwing cases out. Many worry that court-appointed therapists hold sexist views about treatment. Focusing on keeping the family unit together, they fail to understand the seriousness of violence and have few skills to stop it. Men will not only be released unchanged but also might have their sexist views reinforced.

Other feminists, however, argue that mandated counseling should be tried because it is one of the only tools available to help men to change their behavior. For them, the important issue becomes the ideology and therapeutic practice of the counselors as well as the conditions for counseling that the court imposes. As a result of court demonstration projects that have tested mandated therapy, feminists have drawn several tentative conclusions about the nature of such counseling. These include that: 1. the victim retain the right to express her wishes about court diversion decisions; 2. men who have histories of repeated arrests and severe violent attacks should not be diverted to counseling; 3. abusers must participate regularly in a program in which stopping their violence is the treatment focus and alternative methods of handling anger are provided; the counselor's goal is to stop the violence, not to keep the family together. 4. if further violence or threats occur or the counseling contract is violated, prosecution will resume; 5. contact between the victim and abuser is restricted or if the couple is still living together, the counseling program must maintain a relationship with the woman to determine if further abuse is occurring; 6. the woman also is entitled to advocacy and support; 7. battered women should be informed that counseling is a long process that often fails with violent men. No woman should be falsely assured about the efficacy of counseling. Because men who batter minimize or deny the seriousness of their threats and assaults, counselor involvement with the battered woman is essential. Diversionary programs which do not meet regularly with the abuser or those that use traditional psychotherapeutic methods, like couple counseling, and refrain from focusing on changing violent behavior are ineffective and dangerous.

The battered women's movement has tried a variety of solutions to deal with the many problems victims face within the criminal court system. Women's groups have organized court watching projects, gathering evidence about battered women's experiences to use as leverage in negotiations for institutional change. Reminding judges that they are publicly accountable for their actions, some groups send large contingents to court, especially for trials involving women who were badly brutalized. And in some cases, attorneys advocate using criminal and civil remedies jointly, especially against those men who would rather see a woman dead than free.

At the same time that they serve as individual women's advocates, feminist attorneys and shelter workers attempt to educate court personnel about the seriousness of violence. These educational efforts have included formal training sessions for judges and police as well as informal meetings and discussions about the meaning and impact of violence. Many advocates report that frequently criminal justice personnel, including judges, have little awareness of and inaccurate information about family law. If the legislature has recently enacted new laws, ignorance tends to multiply. Heightening the problem, many judges hold stereotypic attitudes toward battered women, either seeing them as nags or as women who drop their cases. Education and training, therefore, are essential. Although reports from advocates in states like Pennsylvania are optimistic about the effectiveness of training, it is too early to assess long-term change, even where the movement has allocated significant resources to this work.

Sometimes advocates working to reform court procedures must spend time on petty matters. In Pennsylvania, for example, advocates not only had to oversee the development of new legal forms but also push each county court to buy them. Activists encounter infuriating resistance at literally every step in the process through which law is translated into practice. They are often forced to take their complaints back to the legislature and lobby over minor matters like who is mandated to distribute legal forms.

As in the anti-rape movement, a debate flares up repeatedly over whether to raise or lower the severity of criminal court punishments for violent men. The argument for increased severity suggests that to be taken seriously, violence against women must be labeled the crime it is and punished. Felony charges are a logical and necessary protection because of the unequal power context in which battered women operate. The reality is, however, that an overworked criminal justice system still largely sees women's problems, including violence, as inconsequential and a waste of police and court time. As a result, if the police are aware that abusers will be charged with felonies and punished more severely, they may simply stop arresting; similarly, judges might find fewer men guilty. The law's intention could be easily subverted. A more practical counter suggestion is to force the courts to treat family violence like other forms of assault with a range of penalties, higher for felonies and lower for misdemeanors. This argument recognizes that although education and monitoring are a continual necessity to insure that battered women's cases are even treated as assaults, it is more effective to declare battered women equal to others rather than make them a more protected class.[29] It also counters the alternative suggestion of lower penalties for all wife beating, including felonies, and suggests that such lowering feeds into the sexism that views battering as insignificant.

The battered women's movement currently faces major challenges about civil and criminal court legislation and proceedings. Because several potentially dangerous bills have been introduced within state legislatures, the movement must remain vigilant and mobilized to insure that seemingly "helpful" legislation fails to pass. For example, the New Hampshire legislature introduced a bill that required medical personnel to report all cases of adult abuse. In Kentucky, following the precedent of child abuse statutes, the legislature mandated not only reporting but also investigation of all adult abuse and neglect cases, turning battered women into children. An *Aegis* writer offered a critique of the New Hampshire bill.

> If legislation is to be passed, it should assist women in taking direct control over their lives: it should not sanction unsolicited intermeddling by doctors, social workers and judges. There are more than abstract issues of personal control, confidentiality and privacy involved here: battered women will probably be deterred from seeking necessary medical attention if the bill is passed.[30]

As one activist noted, "the movement has put out hundreds of such small fires. If successful, some of these proposed changes would have further robbed battered women or shelters of their autonomy. No one ever hears about these time-consuming, draining efforts but we have had to mobilize frequently to prevent disasters."[31]

Although advocates predicted long battles to see legislation implemented correctly, they never expected the numerous appeals and constitutional challenges that men have initiated. Fending off a backlash against women, activists have fought court battles successfully in Minnesota, Pennsylvania, California, and Ohio. In Pennsylvania, an abusive husband challenged the right of the court to grant a temporary order of protection, excluding him from his home; in Ohio, a defendant argued that issuing a temporary order of protection as a condition of bail was a violation of state constitutional rights and that ordering a man from his home denied him federal constitutional rights to travel. California law was challenged because it was limited to female victims.[32] Although new laws have been upheld as constitutional in these test cases, activists are forced to mobilize repeatedly, depleting movement resources, yet reminding us of the importance of an organized feminist community. Only a movement, advocating for women and monitoring legal change, insures that the altered power dynamics that are symbolized by new legislation will become a reality.

COMPLICATED CHOICES AHEAD

[. . .] The battered women's movement must continue its advocacy and social change efforts within the criminal justice system. At the same time, however, a fine tension needs to be maintained so that advocacy and reform are balanced with building a broad-based, well organized feminist movement and continuing community education efforts. Only in this way will battered women's organizations retain the power base and community support from which to demand institutional change. Although criminal sanctions to stop abuse are a vital part of a solution to battered women's immediate problems, in the long run, the community, not just the criminal justice system, must understand that violence against women is rooted in male domination. Only by developing a philosophy of and struggle for gender equality will a movement change public consciousness which in turn will force individuals and institutions to treat violence against women as a serious offense.

In evaluating reform efforts, criteria are needed which assess how much control women gain over the decisions affecting their lives. An additional assessment must weigh whether these options are actually available or are presently legal fictions.

One advocate suggests a position for the movement to adopt about reform work.

> We have to assert that battered women deserve the same protection from the system as anybody else. They are not an exempt category. On the other hand, the system is not a solution for them and they know it. Reforms aren't a solution to their problem.
>
> The movement must acknowledge winning reforms and the difference they make and say where they come from. This is the only way of dealing with the problem of just helping the system look good. We can't cloud over the motivations of institutions.[33]

If the movement allows institutions to claim reforms as a result of benevolence, then the movement loses the opportunity to acknowledge its strength and impact. This tension suggests another important criteria by which to assess reforms—are women brought together to participate democratically and struggle? If women gain new skills and a sense of power by working together on behalf of all women, then new strength and energy is brought to the movement. Reforms introduced to take control away from autonomous women's programs or from individual battered women must be defined as unacceptable.

Weighing reforms in terms of their impact on collective and individual self-determination is essential

but not sufficient. Reforms that can be turned against women or other groups without power also need to be carefully discussed and possibly opposed. For example, preventive detention for batterers would give power to the police and courts that can easily be abused.

A series of questions might help guide an analysis of reforms.

1. How are social relationships of domination by sex, class, and race challenged or reinforced by each proposed reform?
2. How does this reform effect the male right to beat?
3. Does the suggested change further empower women or make them more dependent?
4. Which women of which class or race benefit or are harmed by this activity?
5. If there are racist consequences to specific work, can they be minimized, avoided or fought against?
6. Do women gain control by proposed changes? If not, who gains control or legitimacy, and in what way might this harm the movement?
7. How do specific institutions reinforce the subordination of women—through policies, practices, structures, lack of community control? Can the movement effect these different areas and is it worth the energy?
8. Does the fight help build the movement and organize women?

Feminist theoretician and activist Charlotte Bunch proposes five similar criteria to evaluate reforms so that women can gain the power to eliminate patriarchy and create a more humane society.

1. Does this reform materially improve the lives of women, and if so, which women, and how many?
2. Does it build an individual woman's self-respect, strength, and confidence?
3. Does it give women a sense of power, strength, and imagination as a group and help build structures for further change?

4. Does it educate women politically, enhancing our ability to criticize and challenge the system in the future?

5. Does it weaken patriarchal control of society's institutions and help women gain power over them?[34]

Because so many practices affecting battered women need changing, choices are difficult. Each must be defined in its complexity, facing the limitations and tensions within it. Equally important to measure is the fact that just as reform efforts build the movement by recruiting more women to work on problems, reforms can also unnecessarily deplete energy needed for other tasks, like community education and outreach to battered women.

In its assessment of reforms, the movement must ultimately face other layers of contradictions. Many women want to use neither shelters nor courts. They do not want police to arrest; they just want the violence to stop. For another group of women, leaving their husbands or communities is unthinkable, and going to court feels like cutting themselves off from their only base of support. In this case, the movement's necessary push to enforce battered women's rights collides with endemic problems within a male-dominated, capitalist society. The lack of community and social mechanisms to stop male violence or to support women staying within their neighborhoods meets a society that fails to provide many women with the decent incomes and housing that would free them from violent men. These failings cannot be solved within our current criminal justice system. To transform this reality, reforms must go far beyond the parameters currently defined by the police or courts; the need for a broad-based, progressive political movement, fighting to democratically redistribute resources, power, and control is clear and pressing if battered women are to be protected and violence ended. If we fail to win far reaching change, criminal justice and other institutions will continue to reflect the racism, sexism, and class bias of the larger society. Without a larger feminist community, supported by anti-racist and working class movements committed to ending oppression, the impact of the courageous

and important efforts to secure battered women justice and autonomy will be limited.

NOTES

1. Mark A. Schulman, *A Survey of Spousal Violence Against Women in Kentucky*, U.S. Department of Justice, Law Enforcement Assistance Administration, Study No. 792701, July 1979, p. 48.

2. Eisenberg and Micklow, cited in Del Martin, *Battered Wives* (San Francisco: Glide Publications, 1976), p. 93.

3. Breedlove et al., cited in Marjory D. Fields, "Wife Beating: Government Intervention Policies and Practices," U.S. Commission on Civil Rights, *Battered Women: Issues of Public Policy*, a consultation, Washington, D.C., 30–13 January 1978, p. 247.

4. James Bannon, "Law Enforcement Problems with Intra-Family Violence," paper presented to the American Bar Association Convention, 12 August 1975, p. 6.

5. Ibid., p. 5.

6. James Bannon, "Law Enforcement Problems with Intra-Family Violence," Reprinted by American Friends Service Committee, Women's Issues Program, Cambridge, Massachusetts, undated, p. 1.

7. Del Martin, *Battered Wives*, p. 90.

8. Author's interview with Lisa Lerman.

9. Lisa Lerman with the assistance of Leslie Landis and Sharon Goldzweig, "State Legislation on Domestic Violence," *Response to Violence in the Family* 4, No. 7 (September/October 1981): 3.

10. See Summary of Developments in Bruno v. Codd sub nom Bruno v. McGuire and Scott v. Hart, National Center on Women and Family Law,

11. Holly Ladd and Esther Mosak, "Bruno v. McGuire: Battered Women Sue Police and Courts," American Friends Service Committee, Women's Issues Program, Cambridge, Massachusetts, unpaged.

12. Ibid.

13. Candace Wayne, "Working on Woman Abuse, Confronting the Present-Future Goals," speech presented at Woman Abuse: A Working Conference for the Midwest, 23–24 April 1979, Chicago, p. 4.

14. Author's interview with Laurie Woods.

15. Author's interview with Barbara Hart.

16. Eisenberg and Micklow cited in Marjory Fields, "Wife Beating: Government Intervention Policies and Practices," p. 233.

17. Julie E. Hamos, National Coalition Against Domestic Violence, *State Domestic Violence Laws and How to Pass Them: A Manual for Lobbyists*, National Clearinghouse on Domestic Violence, No. 2, June 1980, p. 45.

18. Lisa Lerman with the assistance of Mary Bottum and Susan Wiviott, "State Legislation on Domestic Violence," *Response to Violence in the Family* 3, No. 12 (August/September 1980): 1.

19. Lisa Lerman, "State Legislation on Domestic Violence," *Response* 4, No. 7 (September–October 1981): 2.

20. Esther Mosak, "Massachusetts Abuse Prevention Act," American Friends Service Committee, Women's Issues Program, unpaged.

21. Ibid.

22. Lisa Lerman, "State Legislation on Domestic Violence," *Response* 4, No. 7, p. 2.

23. Susan Kelly-Dreiss, personal communication.

24. Julie E. Hamos, *State Domestic Violence Laws and How to Pass Them*, p. 34.

25. Ibid., pp. 34–35.

26. Ibid., p. 35.

27. Lisa Lerman, "State Legislation on Domestic Violence," *Response* 3, No. 12, p. 2.

28. Julie E. Hamos, *State Domestic Violence Laws and How to Pass Them*, p. 41.

29. Author's interview with Barbara Hart.

30. Sue Herz, "Update on State Legislation," *Aegis*, May/June 1979, p. 20.

31. Author's interview with Barbara Hart.

32. Author's interview with Laurie Woods.

33. Author's interview with Esther Mosak.

34. Charlotte Bunch, "The Reform Tool Kit," *Aegis*, July/August 1979, p. 31.

Study Questions

1. Why does Schechter hold that battered women should be treated like other victims of assault rather than as "a more protected class"?

2. In what sense can this article be read as an example of sameness/humanist feminist thinking?

3. What is Schechter's overarching strategy for eradicating domestic violence?

Amartya Sen

More than 100 Million Women Are Missing

It is often said that women make up a majority of the world's population. They do not. This mistaken belief is based on generalizing from the contemporary situation in Europe and North America, where the ratio of women to men is typically around 1.05 or 1.06, or higher. In South Asia, West Asia, and China, the ratio of women to men can be as low as 0.94, or even lower, and it varies widely elsewhere in Asia, in Africa, and in Latin America. How can we understand and explain these differences, and react to them?

1.

At birth, boys outnumber girls everywhere in the world, by much the same proportion—there are around 105 or 106 male children for every 100 female children. Just why the biology of reproduction leads to this result remains a subject of debate. But after conception, biology seems on the whole to favor women. Considerable research has shown that if men and women receive similar nutritional and medical attention and general health care, women tend to live

Amartya Sen, "More than 100 Million Women Are Missing," *The New York Review of Books*, December 20, 1990, pp. 61–66. Reprinted with permission from *The New York Review of Books*. Copyright © 1990 NYREV, Inc.

noticeably longer than men. Women seem to be, on the whole, more resistant to disease and in general hardier than men, an advantage they enjoy not only after they are forty years old but also at the beginning of life, especially during the months immediately following birth, and even in the womb. When given the same care as males, females tend to have better survival rates than males.[1]

Women outnumber men substantially in Europe, the US, and Japan, where, despite the persistence of various types of bias against women (men having distinct advantages in higher education, job specialization, and promotion to senior executive positions, for example), women suffer little discrimination in basic nutrition and health care. The greater number of women in these countries is partly the result of social and environmental differences that increase mortality among men, such as a higher likelihood that men will die from violence, for example, and from diseases related to smoking. But even after these are taken into account, the longer lifetimes enjoyed by women given similar care appear to relate to the biological advantages that women have over men in resisting disease. Whether the higher frequency of male births over female births has evolutionary links to this potentially greater survival rate among women is a question of some interest in itself. Women seem to have lower death rates than men at most ages whenever they get roughly similar treatment in matters of life and death.

The fate of women is quite different in most of Asia and North Africa. In these places the failure to give women medical care similar to what men get and to provide them with comparable food and social services results in fewer women surviving than would be the case if they had equal care. In India, for example, except in the period immediately following birth, the death rate is higher for women than for men fairly consistently in all age groups until the late thirties. This relates to higher rates of disease from which women suffer, and ultimately to the relative neglect of females, especially in health care and medical attention.[2] Similar neglect of women vis-à-vis men can be seen also in many other parts of the world. The result is a lower proportion of women than would be the case if they had equal care—in most of Asia and North Africa, and to a lesser extent Latin America.

This pattern is not uniform in all parts of the third world, however. Sub-Saharan Africa, for example, ravaged as it is by extreme poverty, hunger, and famine, has a substantial excess rather than deficit of women, the ratio of women to men being around 1.02. The "third world" in this matter is not a useful category, because it is so diverse. Even within Asia, which has the lowest proportion of women in the world, Southeast Asia and East Asia (apart from China) have a ratio of women to men that is slightly higher than one to one (around 1.01). Indeed, sharp diversities also exist within particular regions—sometimes even within a particular country. For example, the ratio of women to men in the Indian states of Punjab and Haryana, which happen to be among the country's richest, is a remarkably low 0.86, while the state of Kerala in southwestern India has a ratio higher than 1.03, similar to that in Europe, North America, and Japan.

To get an idea of the numbers of people involved in the different ratios of women to men, we can estimate the number of "missing women" in a country, say, China or India, by calculating the number of extra women who would have been in China or India if these countries had the same ratio of women to men as obtain in areas of the world in which they receive similar care. If we could expect equal populations of the two sexes, the low ratio of 0.94 women to men in South Asia, West Asia, and China would indicate a 6 percent deficit of women; but since, in countries where men and women receive similar care, the ratio is about 1.05, the real shortfall is about 11 percent. In China alone this amounts to 50 million "missing women," taking 1.05 as the benchmark ratio. When that number is added to those in South Asia, West Asia, and North Africa, a great many more than 100 million women are "missing." These numbers tell us, quietly, a terrible story of inequality and neglect leading to the excess mortality of women.

2.

To account for the neglect of women, two simplistic explanations have often been presented or, more often, implicitly assumed. One view emphasizes the cultural contrasts between East and West (or between the Occident and the Orient), claiming that Western civilization is less sexist than Eastern. That women outnumber men in Western countries may appear to lend support to this Kipling-like generalization. (Kipling himself was not, of course, much bothered by concerns about sexism, and even made "the twain" meet in romantically masculine circumstances: "But there is neither East nor West, Border, nor Breed, nor Birth,/When two strong men stand face to face, tho' they come from the ends of the earth!") The other simple argument looks instead at stages of economic development, seeing the unequal nutrition and health care provided for women as a feature of underdevelopment, a characteristic of poor economies awaiting economic advancement.

There may be elements of truth in each of these explanations, but neither is very convincing as a general thesis. To some extent, the two simple explanations, in terms of "economic development" and "East-West" divisions, also tend to undermine each other. A combined cultural and economic analysis would seem to be necessary, and, I will argue, it would have to take note of many other social conditions in addition to the features identified in the simple aggregative theses.

To take the cultural view first, the East-West explanation is obviously flawed because experiences within the East and West diverge so sharply. Japan, for example, unlike most of Asia, has a ratio of women to men that is not very different from that in Europe or North America. This might suggest, at least superficially, that real income and economic development do more to explain the bias against providing women with the conditions for survival than whether the society is Western or Oriental. In the censuses of 1899 and 1908 Japan had a clear and substantial deficit of women, but by 1940 the numbers of men and women were nearly equal, and in the postwar decades, as Japan became a rich and highly industrialized country, it moved firmly in the direction of a large surplus, rather than a deficit, of women. Some countries in East Asia and Southeast Asia also provide exceptions to the deficit of women; in Thailand and Indonesia, for example, women substantially outnumber men.

In its rudimentary, undiscriminating form, the East-West explanation also fails to take into account other characteristics of these societies. For example, the ratios of women to men in South Asia are among the lowest in the world (around 0.94 in India and Bangladesh, and 0.90 in Pakistan—the lowest ratio for any large country), but that region has been among the pioneers in electing women as top political leaders. Indeed, each of the four large South Asian countries—India, Pakistan, Bangladesh, and Sri Lanka—either has had a woman as the elected head of government (Sri Lanka, India, and Pakistan), or has had women leading the main opposition parties (as in Bangladesh).

It is, of course, true that these successes in South Asia have been achieved only by upper-class women, and that having a woman head of government has not, by itself, done much for women in general in these countries. However, the point here is only to question the tendency to see the contrast between East and West as simply based on more sexism or less. The large electoral successes of women in achieving high positions in government in South Asia indicate that the analysis has to be more complex.

It is, of course, also true that these women leaders reached their powerful positions with the help of dynastic connections—Indira Gandhi was the daughter of Jawaharlal Nehru, Benazir Bhutto the daughter of Zulfikar Bhutto, and so on. But it would be absurd to overlook—just on that ground—the significance of their rise to power through popular mandate. Dynastic connections are not new in politics and are pervasive features of political succession in many countries. That Indira Gandhi derived her political strength partly from her father's position is not in itself more significant than the fact that Rajiv Gandhi's political credibility derived largely from his mother's political eminence, or the fact (perhaps less well known) that Indira Gandhi's father—the great Jawaharlal Nehru—initially rose to prominence as the son of Motilal Nehru, who had been president of the Congress party. The dynastic aspects of South Asian politics have certainly helped women to come to power through electoral support, but it is still true that so far as winning elections is concerned, South Asia would seem to be some distance ahead of the United States and most European countries when it comes to discrimination according to gender.

In this context it is useful also to compare the ratios of women in American and Indian legislatures. In the US House of Representatives the proportion of women is 6.4 percent, while in the present and the last lower houses of the Indian Parliament, women's proportions have been respectively 5.3 and 7.9 percent. Only two of the 100 US Senators are women, and this 2 percent ratio contrasts with more than 9 and 10 percent women respectively in the last and present "upper house," Rajya Sabha, in India. (In a different, but not altogether unrelated, sphere, I had a much higher proportion of tenured women colleagues when I was teaching at Delhi University than I now have at Harvard.) The cultural climate in different societies must have a clear relevance to differences between men and women—both in survival and in other ways as well—but it would be hopeless to see the divergences simply as a contrast between the sexist East and the unbiased West.

How good is the other (i.e., the purely economic) explanation for women's inequality? Certainly all the countries with large deficits of women are more or less poor, if we measure poverty by real incomes, and no sizable country with a high gross national product per head has such a deficit. There are reasons to expect a reduction of differential female mortality with economic progress. For example, the rate of maternal mortality at childbirth can be expected to decrease both with better hospital facilities and the reduction in birth rate that usually accompanies economic development.

However, in this simple form, an economic analysis does not explain very much, since many poor countries do not, in fact, have deficits of women. As was noted earlier, sub-Saharan Africa, poor and underdeveloped as it is, has a substantial excess of women. Southeast and East Asia (but not China) also differ from many other relatively poor countries in this respect, although to a lesser degree. Within India, as was noted earlier, Punjab and Haryana—among the richest and most economically advanced Indian states—have very low ratios of women to men (around 0.86), in contrast to the much poorer state of Kerala, where the ratio is greater than 1.03.

Indeed, economic development is quite often accompanied by a relative worsening in the rate of survival of women (even as life expectancy improves in absolute terms for both men and women). For example, in India the gap between the life expectancy of men and women has narrowed recently, but only after many decades when women's relative position deteriorated. There has been a steady decline in the ratio of women to men in the population, from more than 97 women to 100 men at the turn of the century (in 1901), to 93 women in 1971, and the ratio is only a little higher now. The deterioration in women's position results largely from their unequal sharing in the advantages of medical and social progress. Economic development does not invariably reduce women's disadvantages in mortality.

A significant proportional decline in the population of women occurred in China after the economic and social reforms introduced there in 1979. The Chinese Statistical Yearbooks show a steady decline in the already very low ratio of women to men in the population, from 94.32 in 1979 to 93.42 in 1985 and 1986. (It has risen since then, to 93.98 in 1989—still lower than what it was in 1979). Life expectancy was significantly higher for females than for males until the economic reforms, but seems to have fallen behind since then.[3] Of course, the years following the reforms were also years of great economic growth and, in many ways, of social progress, yet women's relative prospects for survival deteriorated. These and other cases show that rapid economic development may go hand in hand with worsening relative mortality of women.

3.

Despite their superficial plausibility, neither the alleged contrast between "East" and "West," nor the simple hypothesis of female deprivation as a characteristic of economic "underdevelopment" gives us anything like an adequate understanding of the geography of female deprivation in social well-being and survival. We have to examine the complex ways in which economic, social, and cultural factors can influence the regional differences.

It is certainly true that, for example, the status and power of women in the family differ greatly from one region to another, and there are good reasons to expect that these social features would be related to the economic role and independence of women. For example, employment outside the home and owning assets can both be important for women's economic independence and power; and these factors may have far-reaching effects on the divisions of benefits and chores within the family and can greatly influence what are implicitly accepted as women's "entitlements."

Indeed, men and women have both interests in common and conflicting interests that affect family decisions; and it is possible to see decision making in the family taking the form of the pursuit of cooperation in which solutions for the conflicting aspects of family life are implicitly agreed on. Such "cooperative conflicts" are a general feature of many group relations, and an analysis of cooperative conflicts can provide a useful way of understanding the influences that affect the "deal" that women get in the division of benefits within the family. There are gains to be made by men and women through following implicitly agreed-on patterns of behavior; but there are many possible agreements—some more favorable to one party than others. The choice of one such cooperative arrangement from among the range of possibilities leads to a particular distribution of joint benefits. (Elsewhere, I have tried to analyze the general nature of "cooperative conflicts" and the application of the analysis of such conflicts to family economics.[4])

Conflicts in family life are typically resolved through implicitly agreed-on patterns of behavior that may or may not be particularly egalitarian. The very nature of family living—sharing a home and experiences—requires that the elements of conflict must not be explicitly emphasized (giving persistent attention to conflicts will usually be seen as aberrant behavior); and sometimes the deprived woman would not even have a clear idea of the extent of her relative deprivation. Similarly, the perception of who is doing "productive" work, who is "contributing" how much to the family's prosperity, can be very influential, even though the underlying principles regarding how "contributions" or "productivity" are to be assessed may be rarely discussed explicitly. These issues of social perception are, I believe, of pervasive importance in gender inequality, even in the richer countries, but they can have a particularly powerful influence in sustaining female deprivation in many of the poorer countries.[5]

The division of a family's joint benefits is likely to be less unfavorable to women if (1) they can earn an outside income; (2) their work is recognized as productive (this is easier to achieve with work done outside the home); (3) they own some economic resources and have some rights to fall back on; and (4) there is a clear-headed understanding of the ways in which women are deprived and a recognition of the possibilities of changing this situation. This last category can be much influenced by education for women and by participatory political action.

Considerable empirical evidence, mostly studies of particular localities, suggests that what is usually defined as "gainful" employment (i.e., working outside the home for a wage, or in such "productive" occupations as farming), as opposed to unpaid and unhonored housework—no matter how demanding—can substantially enhance the deal that women get.[6] Indeed, "gainful" employment of women can make the solution of "cooperative conflicts" less unfavorable to women in many ways. First, outside employment for wages can provide women with an income to which they have easier access, and it can also serve as a means of making a living on which women can rely, making them less vulnerable. Second, the social respect that is associated with being a "bread winner" (and a "productive" contributor to the family's joint prosperity) can improve women's status and standing in the family, and may influence the prevailing cultural traditions regarding who gets what in the division of joint benefits. Third, when outside employment takes the form of jobs with some security and legal protection, the corresponding rights that women get can make their economic position much less vulnerable and precarious. Fourth, working outside the home also provides experience of the outside world, and this can be socially important in improving women's position within the family. In this respect outside work may be "educational" as well.

These factors may not only improve the "deal" women get in the family, they can also counter the relative neglect of girls as they grow up. Boys are preferred in many countries because they are expected to provide more economic security for their parents in old age; but the force of this bias can be weakened if women as well as men can regularly work at paid jobs. Moreover, if the status of women does in general rise and women's contributions become more recognized, female children may receive more attention. Similarly, the exposure of women to the world through work outside the home can weaken, through its educational effect, the hold of traditional beliefs and behavior.

In comparing different regions of Asia and Africa, if we try to relate the relative survival prospects of women to the "gainful employment" of both sexes—i.e., work outside the home, possibly for a wage—we do find a strong association. If the different regions of Asia and Africa (with the exception of China) are ranked according to the proportion of women in so-called gainful employment relative to the proportion of men in such employment, we get the following ranking, in descending order:[7]

1. Sub-Saharan Africa
2. Southeast and Eastern Asia
3. Western Asia
4. Southern Asia
5. Northern Africa

Ranking the ratios of life expectancy of females to those of males produces a remarkably similar ordering:

1. Sub-Saharan Africa
2. Southeast and Eastern Asia
3. Western Asia
4. Northern Africa
5. Southern Asia

That the two rankings are much the same, except for a switch between the two lowest-ranking regions (lowest in terms of both indicators), suggests a link between employment and survival prospects. In addition to the overall correspondence between the two rankings, the particular contrasts between sub-Saharan Africa and North Africa, and that between Southern (and Western) Asia and Southeast (and Eastern) Asia are suggestive distinctions within Africa and Asia respectively, linking women's gainful employment and survival prospects.

It is, of course, possible that what we are seeing here is not a demonstration that gainful employment causes better survival prospects but the influence of some other factor correlated with each. In fact, on the basis of such broad relations, it is very hard to draw any firm conclusion; but evidence of similar relations can be found also in other comparisons.[8] For example, Punjab, the richest Indian state, has the lowest ratio of women to men (0.86) in India; it also has the lowest ratio of women in "gainful" employment compared to men. The influence of outside employment on women's well-being has also been documented in a number of studies of specific communities in different parts of the world.[9]

4.

The case of China deserves particular attention. It is a country with a traditional bias against women, but after the revolution the Chinese leaders did pay considerable attention to reducing inequality between men and women.[10] This was helped both by a general expansion of basic health and medical services accessible to all and by the increase in women's gainful employment, along with greater social recognition of the importance of women in the economy and the society.

There has been a remarkable general expansion of longevity, and despite the temporary setback during the terrible famines of 1958–1961 (following the disastrous failure of the so-called Great Leap Forward), the Chinese life expectancy at birth increased from the low forties around 1950 to the high sixties by the time the economic reforms were introduced in 1979. The sharp reduction in general mortality (including female mortality) is all the more remarkable in view of the fact that it took place despite deep economic problems in the form of widespread industrial inefficiency, a rather stagnant agriculture, and relatively little increase in output per head. Female death rates declined sharply—both as a part of a general mortality reduction and also relatively, vis-à-vis male mortality. Women's life expectancy at birth overtook that of men—itself much enhanced—and was significantly ahead at the time the economic and social reforms were introduced in 1979.

Those reforms immediately increased the rate of economic growth and broke the agricultural stagnation. The official figures suggest a doubling of agricultural output between 1979 and 1986—a remarkable achievement even if some elements of exaggeration are eliminated from these figures. But at the same time, the official figures also record an increase in the general mortality rates after the reforms, with a consistently higher death rate than what China had achieved by 1979. There seems to be also a worsening of the relative survival of women, including a decline, discussed earlier, of the ratio of women to men in the population, which went down from 94.3 in 1979 to 93.4 in 1985 and 1986. There are problems in interpreting the available data and difficulties in arriving at firm conclusions, but the view that women's life expectancy has again become lower than that of men has gained support. For example, the World Bank's most recent World Development Report suggests a life expectancy of sixty-nine years for men and sixty-six years for women (even though the confounded nature of the subject is well reflected by the fact that the same Report also suggests an average life expectancy of seventy years for men and women put together).[11]

Why have women's survival prospects in China deteriorated, especially in relative terms, since 1979?

Several experts have noted that recently Chinese leaders have tended, on the whole, to reduce the emphasis on equality for women; it is no longer much discussed, and indeed, as the sociologist Margery Wolf puts it, it is a case of a "revolution postponed."[12] But this fact, while important, does not explain why the relative survival prospects of women would have so deteriorated during the early years of the reforms, just at the time when there was a rapid expansion of overall economic prosperity.

The compulsory measures to control the size of families which were introduced in 1979 may have been an important factor. In some parts of the country the authorities insisted on the "one-child family." This restriction, given the strong preference for boys in China, led to a neglect of girls that was often severe. Some evidence exists of female infanticide. In the early years after the reforms, infant mortality for girls appeared to increase considerably. Some estimates had suggested that the rate of female infant mortality rose from 37.7 per thousand in 1978 to 67.2 per thousand in 1984.[13] Even if this seems exaggerated in the light of later data, the survival prospects of female children clearly have been unfavorably affected by restrictions on the size of the family. Later legal concessions (including the permission to have a second child if the first one is a girl) reflect some official recognition of these problems.

A second factor relevant to the survival problems of Chinese women is the general crisis in health services since the economic reforms. As the agricultural production brigades and collectives, which had traditionally provided much of the funding for China's extensive rural health programs, were dismantled, they were replaced by the so-called "responsibility system," in which agriculture was centered in the family. Agricultural production improved, but cutbacks in communal facilities placed severe financial restrictions on China's extensive rural medical services. Communal agriculture may not have done much for agricultural production as such, but it had been a main source of support for China's innovative and extensive rural medical services. So far as gender is concerned, the effects of the reduced scope of these services are officially neutral, but in view of the pro-male bias in Chinese rural society, the cutback in medical services would have had a particularly severe impact on women and female children. (It is also the pro-male bias in the general culture that made the one-child policy, which too is neutral in form, unfavorable to female children in terms of its actual impact.)

Third, the "responsibility system" arguably has reduced women's involvement in recognized gainful employment in agriculture. In the new system's more traditional arrangement of work responsibilities, women's work in the household economy may again suffer from the lack of recognition that typically affects household work throughout the world.[14] The impact of this change on the status of women within the household may be negative, for the reasons previously described. Expanded employment opportunities for women outside agriculture in some regions may at least partially balance this effect. But the weakening of social security arrangements since the reforms would also have made old age more precarious, and since such insecurity is one of the persistent motives for families' preferring boys over girls, this change too can be contributing to the worsening of care for female children.[15]

5.

Analyses based on simple conflicts between East and West or on "under-development" clearly do not take us very far. The variables that appear important—for example, female employment or female literacy—combine both economic and cultural effects. To ascribe importance to the influence of gainful employment on women's prospects for survival may superficially look like another attempt at a simple economic explanation, but it would be a mistake to see it this way. The deeper question is why such outside employment is more prevalent in, say, sub-Saharan Africa than in North Africa, or in Southeast and Eastern Asia than in Western and Southern Asia. Here the cultural, including religious, backgrounds of the respective regions are surely important. Economic causes for women's deprivation have to be integrated with other—social and cultural—factors to give depth to the explanation.

Of course, gainful employment is not the only factor affecting women's chances of survival. Women's education and their economic rights—including property rights—may be crucial variables as well.[16] Consider the state of Kerala in India, which I mentioned earlier. It does not have a deficit of women—its ratio of women to men of more than 1.03 is closer to that of Europe (1.05) than those of China, West Asia, and India as a whole (0.94). The life expectancy of women at birth in Kerala, which had already reached sixty-eight years by the time of the last census in 1981 (and is estimated to be seventy-two years now), is considerably higher than men's sixty-four years at that time (and sixty-seven now). While women are generally able to find "gainful employment" in Kerala—certainly much more so than in Punjab—the state is not exceptional in this regard. What is exceptional is Kerala's remarkably high literacy rate; not only is it much higher than elsewhere in India, it is also substantially higher than in China, especially for women.

Kerala's experience of state-funded expansion of basic education, which has been consolidated by left-wing state governments in recent decades, began, in fact, nearly two centuries ago, led by the rulers of the kingdoms of Travancore and Cochin. (These two native states were not part of British India; they were joined together with a small part of the old Madras presidency to form the new state of Kerala after independence.) Indeed, as early as 1817, Rani Gouri Parvathi Bai, the young queen of Travancore, issued clear instructions for public support of education: The state should defray the entire cost of education of its people in order that there might be no backwardness in the spread of enlightenment among them, that by diffusion of education they might be better subjects and public servants and that the reputation of the State might be advanced thereby.[17]

Moreover, in parts of Kerala, property is usually inherited through the family's female line. These factors, as well as the generally high level of communal medicine, help to explain why women in Kerala do not suffer disadvantages in obtaining the means for survival. While it would be difficult to "split up" the respective contributions made by each of these different influences, it would be a mistake not to include all these factors among the potentially interesting variables that deserve examination.

In view of the enormity of the problems of women's survival in large parts of Asia and Africa, it is surprising that these disadvantages have received such inadequate attention. The numbers of "missing women" in relation to the numbers that could be expected if men and women received similar care in health, medicine, and nutrition, are remarkably large. A great many more than a hundred million women are simply not there because women are neglected compared with men. If this situation is to be corrected by political action and public policy, the reasons why there are so many "missing" women must first be better understood. We confront here what is clearly one of the more momentous, and neglected, problems facing the world today.

NOTES

1. An assessment of the available evidence can be found in Ingrid Waldron's "The Role of Genetic and Biological Factors in Sex Differences in Mortality," in A. D. Lopez and L. T. Ruzicka, eds., *Sex Differences in Mortality* (Canberra: Department of Demography, Australian National University, 1983). On the pervasive cultural influences on mortality and the difficulties in forming a biological view of survival advantages, see Sheila Ryan Johansson, "Mortality, Welfare and Gender: Continuity and Change in Explanations for Male/Female Mortality Differences over Three Centuries," in *Continuity and Change*, forthcoming.

2. These and related data are presented and assessed in my joint paper with Jocelyn Kynch, "Indian Women: Wellbeing and Survival," *Cambridge Journal of Economics*, Vol. 7 (1983), and in my *Commodities and Capabilities* (Amsterdam: North-Holland, 1985), Appendix B. See also Lincoln Chen et al., "Sex Bias in the Family Allocation of Food and Health Care in Rural Bangladesh," in *Population and Development Review*, Vol. 7 (1981); Barbara Miller, *The Endangered Sex: Neglect of Female Children in Rural North India* (Cornell University Press, 1981); Pranab Bardhan, *Land, Labor, and Rural Poverty* (Columbia

University Press, 1984); Devaki Jain and Nirmala Banerji, eds., *Tyranny of the Household* (New Delhi: Vikas, 1985); Barbara Harriss and Elizabeth Watson, "The Sex Ratio in South Asia," in J. H. Momsen and J. G. Townsend, eds., *Geography of Gender in the Third World* (State University of New York Press, 1987); Monica Das Gupta, "Selective Discrimination against Female Children in Rural Punjab, India," in *Population and Development Review*, Vol. 13 (1987).

3. See the World Bank's *World Development Report 1990* (Oxford University Press, 1990), Table 32. See also Judith Banister, *China's Changing Population* (Stanford University Press, 1987), Chapter 4, though the change in life expectancy may not have been as large as these early estimates had suggested, as Banister herself has later noted.

4. "Gender and Cooperative Conflicts," Working Paper of the World Institute of Development Economics Research (1986), in Irene Tinker, ed., *Persistent Inequalities: Women and World Development* (Oxford University Press, 1990). In the same volume see also the papers of Ester Boserup, Hanna Papanek, and Irene Tinker on closely related subjects.

5. The recent literature on the modeling of family relations as "bargaining problems," despite being usefully suggestive and insightful, has suffered a little from giving an inadequate role to the importance of perceptions (as opposed to objectively identified interests) of the parties involved. On the relevance of perception, including perceptual distortions (a variant of what Marx had called "false perception"), in family relations, see my "Gender and Cooperative Conflicts." See also my *Resources, Values and Development* (Harvard University Press, 1984), Chapters 15 and 16; Gail Wilson, *Money in the Family* (Avebury/Gower, 1987).

6. See the case studies and the literature cited in my "Gender and Cooperative Conflicts." A pioneering study of some of these issues was provided by Ester Boserup, *Women's Role in Economic Development* (St. Martin's, 1970). See also Bina Agarwal, "Social Security and the Family," in E. Ahmad, et al., *Social Security in Developing Countries*, to be published by Oxford University Press in 1991.

7. Details can be found in my "Gender and Cooperative Conflicts."

8. For example, see Pranab Bardhan, *Land, Labor, and Rural Poverty* on different states in India and the literature cited there.

9. See the literature cited in my "Gender and Cooperative Conflicts."

10. See Elisabeth Croll, *Chinese Women Since Mao* (M. E. Sharpe, 1984).

11. See *World Development Report 1990*, Tables 1 and 32. See also Banister, *China's Changing Population*, Chapter 4, and Athar Hussain and Nicholas Stern, *On the recent increase in death rate in China*, China Paper #8 (London: STICERD/London School of Economics, 1990).

12. See Margery Wolf, *Revolution Postponed: Women in Contemporary China* (Stanford University Press, 1984).

13. See Banister, *China's Changing Population*, Table 4.12.

14. On this and related matters, see Nahid Aslanbeigui and Gale Summerfield, "The Impact of the Responsibility System on Women in Rural China: A Theoretical Application of Sen's Theory of Entitlement," in *World Development*, Vol. 17 (1989).

15. These and other aspects of the problem are discussed more extensively in my joint book with Jean Drèze, *Hunger and Public Action* (Oxford University Press, 1989).

16. For interesting investigations of the role of education, broadly defined, in influencing women's well-being in Bangladesh and India, see Martha Chen, *A Quiet Revolution: Women in Transition in Rural Bangladesh* (Schenkman Books, 1983); and Alaka Basu, *Culture, the Status of Women and Demographic Behavior* (New Delhi: National Council of Applied Economic Research, 1988).

17. Kerala has also had considerable missionary activity in schooling (a fifth of the population is, in fact, Christian), has had international trading and political contacts (both with east and west Asia) for a very long time, and it was from Kerala that the great Hindu philosopher and educator Sankaracarya, who lived during A.D. 788–820, had launched his big movement of setting up centers of study and worship across India.

Study Questions

1. Sen argues that "100 million women are missing." What does he mean by this?

2. Sen rejects two common explanations for this situation on his way to suggesting what he believes accounts for it. What explanations does he reject, and what explanation does he endorse?

3. In what sense can this article be read as an example of sameness/humanist feminist thinking?

Kimberlé Crenshaw

Mapping the Margins

Intersectionality, Identity Politics, and Violence Against Women of Color

Over the last two decades, women have organized against the almost routine violence that shapes their lives.[1] Drawing from the strength of shared experience, women have recognized that the political demands of millions speak more powerfully than the pleas of a few isolated voices. This politicization in turn has transformed the way we understand violence against women. For example, battering and rape, once seen as private (family matters) and aberrational (errant sexual aggression), are now largely recognized as part of a broad-scale system of domination that affects women as a class.[2] This process of recognizing as social and systemic what was formerly perceived as isolated and individual has also characterized the identity politics of African-Americans, other people of color, and gays and lesbians, among others. For all these groups, identity-based politics has been a source of strength, community, and intellectual development.

The embrace of identity politics, however, has been in tension with dominant conceptions of social justice. Race, gender, and other identity categories are most often treated in mainstream liberal discourse as vestiges of bias or domination—that is, as intrinsically negative frameworks in which social power works to exclude or marginalize those who are different. According to this understanding, our liberatory objective should be to empty such categories of any social significance. Yet implicit in certain strands of feminist and racial liberation movements, for example, is the view that the social power, in delineating difference, need not be the power of domination; it can instead be the source of social empowerment and reconstruction.

The problem with identity politics is not that it fails to transcend difference, as some critics charge, but rather the opposite—that it frequently conflates or ignores intragroup differences. In the context of violence against women, this elision of difference in identity politics is problematic, fundamentally because the violence that many women experience is often shaped by other dimensions of their identities, such as race and class. Moreover, ignoring difference *within* groups contributes to tension *among* groups, another problem of identity politics that bears on efforts to politicize violence against women. Feminist efforts to politicize experiences of women and antiracist efforts to politicize experiences of people of color have frequently proceeded as though the issues and experiences they each detail occur on mutually exclusive terrains. Although racism and sexism readily intersect in the lives of real people, they seldom do in feminist and antiracist practices. And so, when the practices expound identity as woman or person of color as an either/or proposition, they relegate the identity of women of color to a location that resists telling.

My objective in this essay is to advance the telling of that location by exploring the race and gender dimensions of violence against women of color.[3] Contemporary feminist and antiracist discourses have failed to consider intersectional identities such as women of color. Focusing on male violence against women through battering, I consider how the experi-

ences of women of color are frequently the product of intersecting patterns of racism and sexism,[4] and how these experiences tend not to be represented within the discourses of either feminism or antiracism. Because of their intersectional identity as both women *and* of color within discourses that are shaped to respond to one *or* the other, women of color are marginalized within both.

In an earlier article, I used the concept of intersectionality to denote the various ways in which race and gender interact to shape the multiple dimensions of black women's employment experiences.[5] My objective there was to illustrate that many of the experiences black women face are not subsumed within the traditional boundaries of race or gender discrimination as these boundaries are currently understood, and that the intersection of racism and sexism factors into black women's lives in ways that cannot be captured wholly by looking at the race or gender dimensions of those experiences separately. I build on those observations here by exploring the various ways in which race and gender intersect in shaping structural, political, and representational aspects of violence against women of color.

I should say at the outset that intersectionality is not being offered here as some new, totalizing theory of identity. Nor do I mean to suggest that violence against women of color can be explained only through the specific frameworks of race and gender considered here. Indeed, factors I address only in part or not at all, such as class or sexuality, are often as critical in shaping the experiences of women of color. My focus on the intersections of race and gender only highlights the need to account for multiple grounds of identity when considering how the social world is constructed.[6]

I have divided the issues presented in this article into two categories. In the first section, I discuss structural intersectionality, the ways in which the location of women of color at the intersection of race and gender makes our actual experience of domestic violence and remedial reform qualitatively different than that of white women. I shift the focus in the next section to political intersectionality, where I analyze how both feminist and antiracist politics have, paradoxically, often helped to marginalize the issue of violence against women of color.

STRUCTURAL INTERSECTIONALITY

I observed the dynamics of structural intersectionality during a brief field study of battered women's shelters located in minority communities in Los Angeles.[7] In most cases, the physical assault that leads women to these shelters is merely the most immediate manifestation of the subordination they experience. Many women who seek protection are unemployed or underemployed, and a good number of them are poor. Shelters serving these women cannot afford to address only the violence inflicted by the batterer; they must also confront the other multilayered and routinized forms of domination that often converge in these women's lives, hindering their ability to create alternatives to the abusive relationships that brought them to shelters in the first place. Many women of color, for example, are burdened by poverty, child care responsibilities, and the lack of job skills. These burdens, largely the consequence of gender and class oppression, are then compounded by the racially discriminatory employment and housing practices women of color often face,[8] as well as by the disproportionately high unemployment among people of color that makes battered women of color less able to depend on the support of friends and relatives for temporary shelter.

Where systems of race, gender, and class domination converge, as they do in the experiences of battered women of color, intervention strategies based solely on the experiences of women who do not share the same class or race backgrounds will be of limited help to women who because of race and class face different obstacles. Such was the case in 1990 when Congress amended the marriage fraud provisions of the Immigration and Nationality Act to protect immigrant women who were battered or exposed to extreme cruelty by the United States citizens or permanent residents these women immigrated to the United States to marry. Under the marriage fraud provisions of the Act, a person who immigrated to the

United States to marry a United States citizen or permanent resident had to remain "properly" married for two years before even applying for permanent resident status,[9] at which time applications for the immigrant's permanent status were required of both spouses.[10] Predictably, under these circumstances, many immigrant women were reluctant to leave even the most abusive of partners for fear of being deported.[11] When faced with the choice between protection from their batterers and protection against deportation, many immigrant women chose the latter. Reports of the tragic consequences of this double subordination put pressure on Congress to include in the Immigration Act of 1990 a provision amending the marriage fraud rules to allow for an explicit waiver for hardship caused by domestic violence.[12] Yet many immigrant women, particularly immigrant women of color, have remained vulnerable to battering because they are unable to meet the conditions established for a waiver. The evidence required to support a waiver "can include, but is not limited to, reports and affidavits from police, medical personnel, psychologists, school officials, and social service agencies."[13] For many immigrant women, limited access to these resources can make it difficult to obtain the evidence needed for a waiver. And cultural barriers often further discourage immigrant women from reporting or escaping battering situations. Tina Shum, a family counselor at a social service agency, points out that "[t]his law sounds so easy to apply, but there are cultural complications in the Asian community that make even these requirements difficult. . . . Just to find the opportunity and courage to call us is an accomplishment for many."[14] The typical immigrant spouse, she suggests, may live "[i]n an extended family where several generations live together, there may be no privacy on the telephone, no opportunity to leave the house and no understanding of public phones."[15] As a consequence, many immigrant women are wholly dependent on their husbands as their link to the world outside their homes.[16]

Immigrant women are also vulnerable to spousal violence because so many of them depend on their husbands for information regarding their legal status. Many women who are now permanent residents continue to suffer abuse under threats of deportation by their husbands. Even if the threats are unfounded, women who have no independent access to information will still be intimidated by such threats. And even though the domestic violence waiver focuses on immigrant women whose husbands are United States citizens or permanent residents, there are countless women married to undocumented workers (or who are themselves undocumented) who suffer in silence for fear that the security of their entire families will be jeopardized should they seek help or otherwise call attention to themselves.[17]

Language barriers present another structural problem that often limits opportunities of non-English-speaking women to take advantage of existing support services. Such barriers not only limit access to information about shelters, but also limit access to the security shelters provide. Some shelters turn non-English-speaking women away for lack of bilingual personnel and resources.[18]

These examples illustrate how patterns of subordination intersect in women's experience of domestic violence. Intersectional subordination need not be intentionally produced; in fact, it is frequently the consequence of the imposition of one burden that interacts with preexisting vulnerabilities to create yet another dimension of disempowerment. In the case of the marriage fraud provisions of the Immigration and Nationality Act, the imposition of a policy specifically designed to burden one class—immigrant spouses seeking permanent resident status—exacerbated the disempowerment of those already subordinated by other structures of domination. By failing to take into account the vulnerability of immigrant spouses to domestic violence, Congress positioned these women to absorb the simultaneous impact of its anti-immigration policy and their spouses' abuse.

The enactment of the domestic violence waiver of the marriage fraud provisions similarly illustrates how modest attempts to respond to certain problems can be ineffective when the intersectional location of women of color is not considered in fashioning the remedy. Cultural identity and class affect the likelihood that a battered spouse could take advantage of the waiver. Although the waiver is formally available

to all women, the terms of the waiver make it inaccessible to some. Immigrant women who are socially, culturally, or economically privileged are more likely to be able to marshall the resources needed to satisfy the waiver requirements. Those immigrant women least able to take advantage of the waiver—women who are socially or economically the most marginal—are most likely to be women of color.

POLITICAL INTERSECTIONALITY

The concept of political intersectionality highlights the fact that women of color are situated within at least two subordinated groups that frequently pursue conflicting political agendas. The need to split one's political energies between two sometimes opposing groups is a dimension of intersectional disempowerment that men of color and white women seldom confront. Indeed, their specific raced *and* gendered experiences, although intersectional, often define as well as confine the interests of the entire group. For example, racism as experienced by people of color who are of a particular gender—male—tends to determine the parameters of antiracist strategies, just as sexism as experienced by women who are of a particular race—white—tends to ground the women's movement. The problem is not simply that both discourses fail women of color by not acknowledging the "additional" issue of race or of patriarchy but that the discourses are often inadequate even to the discrete tasks of articulating the full dimensions of racism and sexism. Because women of color experience racism in ways not always the same as those experienced by men of color and sexism in ways not always parallel to experiences of white women, antiracism and feminism are limited, even on their own terms.

Among the most troubling political consequences of the failure of antiracist and feminist discourses to address the intersections of race and gender is the fact that, to the extent they can forward the interests of "people of color" and "women," respectively, one analysis often implicitly denies the validity of the other. The failure of feminism to interrogate race means that the resistance strategies of feminism will often replicate and reinforce the subordination of people of color, and the failure of antiracism to interrogate patriarchy means that antiracism will frequently reproduce the subordination of women. These mutual elisions present a particularly difficult political dilemma for women of color. Adopting either analysis constitutes a denial of a fundamental dimension of our subordination and precludes the development of a political discourse that more fully empowers women of color.

That the political interests of women of color are obscured and sometimes jeopardized by political strategies that ignore or suppress intersectional issues is illustrated by my experiences in gathering information for this essay. I attempted to review Los Angeles Police Department statistics reflecting the rate of domestic violence interventions by precinct because such statistics can provide a rough picture of arrests by racial group, given the degree of racial segregation in Los Angeles.[19] L.A.P.D., however, would not release the statistics. A representative explained that one reason the statistics were not released was that domestic violence activists both within and outside the Department feared that statistics reflecting the extent of domestic violence in minority communities might be selectively interpreted and publicized so as to undermine long-term efforts to force the Department to address domestic violence as a serious problem. I was told that activists were worried that the statistics might permit opponents to dismiss domestic violence as a minority problem and, therefore, not deserving of aggressive action.

The informant also claimed that representatives from various minority communities opposed the release of these statistics. They were concerned, apparently, that the data would unfairly represent Black and Brown communities as unusually violent, potentially reinforcing stereotypes that might be used in attempts to justify oppressive police tactics and other discriminatory practices. These misgivings are based on the familiar and not unfounded premise that certain minority groups—especially Black men—have already been stereotyped as uncontrollably violent. Some worry that attempts to make domestic violence an object of political action may only serve to confirm such stereotypes and undermine efforts to combat negative beliefs about the Black community.

This account sharply illustrates how women of color can be erased by the strategic silences of antiracism and feminism. The political priorities of both were defined in ways that suppressed information that could have facilitated attempts to confront the problem of domestic violence in communities of color.

DOMESTIC VIOLENCE AND ANTIRACIST POLITICS

Within communities of color, efforts to stem the politicization of domestic violence are often grounded in attempts to maintain the integrity of the community. The articulation of this perspective takes different forms. Some critics allege that feminism has no place within communities of color, that the issues are internally divisive, and that they represent the migration of white women's concerns into a context in which they are not only irrelevant but also harmful. At its most extreme, this rhetoric denies that gender violence is a problem in the community and characterizes any effort to politicize gender subordination as itself a community problem. This is the position taken by Shahrazad Ali in her controversial book, *The Blackman's Guide to Understanding the Blackwoman*.[20] In this stridently antifeminist tract, Ali draws a positive correlation between domestic violence and the liberation of African-Americans. Ali blames the deteriorating conditions within the Black community on the insubordination of Black women and on the failure of Black men to control them.[21] Ali goes so far as to advise Black men to physically chastise Black women when they are "disrespectful."[22] While she cautions that Black men must use moderation in disciplining "their" women, she argues that they must sometimes resort to physical force to reestablish the authority over Black women that racism has disrupted.

Ali's premise is that patriarchy is beneficial for the Black community, and that it must be strengthened through coercive means if necessary.[23] Yet the violence that accompanies this will to control is devastating, not only for the Black women who are victimized, but also for the entire Black community. The recourse to violence to resolve conflicts establishes a dangerous pattern for children raised in such environments and contributes to many other pressing problems.[24] It has been estimated that nearly forty percent of all homeless women and children have fled violence in the home,[25] and an estimated sixty-three percent of young men between the ages of eleven and twenty who are imprisoned for homicide have killed their mothers' batterers.[26] And yet, while gang violence, homicide, and other forms of Black-on-Black crime have increasingly been discussed within African-American politics, patriarchal ideas about gender and power preclude the recognition of domestic violence as yet another compelling incidence of Black-on-Black crime.

Efforts such as Ali's to justify violence against women in the name of Black liberation are indeed extreme.[27] The more common problem is that the political or cultural interests of the community are interpreted in a way that precludes full public recognition of the problem of domestic violence. While it would be misleading to suggest that white Americans have come to terms with the degree of violence in their own homes, it is nonetheless the case that race adds yet another dimension to why the problem of domestic violence is suppressed within nonwhite communities. People of color often must weigh their interests in avoiding issues that might reinforce distorted public perceptions against the need to acknowledge and address intracommunity problems. Yet the cost of suppression is seldom recognized, in part because the failure to discuss the issue shapes perceptions of how serious the problem is in the first place.

The controversy over Alice Walker's novel *The Color Purple* can be understood as an intracommunity debate about the political costs of exposing gender violence within the Black community.[28] Some critics chastised Walker for portraying Black men as violent brutes.[29] One critic lambasted Walker's portrayal of Celie, the emotionally and physically abused protagonist who finally triumphs in the end. Walker, the critic contended, had created in Celie a Black woman whom she couldn't imagine existing in any Black community she knew or could conceive of.[30]

The claim that Celie was somehow an unauthentic character might be read as a consequence of silencing discussion of intracommunity violence. Celie may be unlike any Black woman we know because the real terror experienced daily by minority women is routinely concealed in a misguided (though perhaps understandable) attempt to forestall racial stereotyping. Of course, it is true that representations of Black violence—whether statistical or fictional—are often written into a larger script that consistently portrays Black and other minority communities as pathologically violent. The problem, however, is not so much the portrayal of violence itself as it is the absence of other narratives and images portraying a fuller range of Black experience. Suppression of some of these issues in the name of antiracism imposes real costs. Where information about violence in minority communities is not available, domestic violence is unlikely to be addressed as a serious issue.

The political imperatives of a narrowly focused antiracist strategy support other practices that isolate women of color. For example, activists who have attempted to provide support services to Asian and African-American women report intense resistance from those communities.[31] At other times, cultural and social factors contribute to suppression. Nilda Rimonte, director of Everywoman's Shelter in Los Angeles, points out that in the Asian community, saving the honor of the family from shame is a priority.[32] Unfortunately, this priority tends to be interpreted as obliging women not to scream rather than obliging men not to hit.

Race and culture contribute to the suppression of domestic violence in other ways as well. Women of color are often reluctant to call the police, a hesitancy likely due to a general unwillingness among people of color to subject their private lives to the scrutiny and control of a police force that is frequently hostile. There is also a more generalized community ethic against public intervention, the product of a desire to create a private world free from the diverse assaults on the public lives of racially subordinated people. The home is not simply a man's castle in the patriarchal sense, but may also function as a safe haven from the indignities of life in a racist society.

However, but for this "safe haven" in many cases, women of color victimized by violence might otherwise seek help.

There is also a general tendency within antiracist discourse to regard the problem of violence against women of color as just another manifestation of racism. In this sense, the relevance of gender domination within the community is reconfigured as a consequence of discrimination against men. Of course, it is probably true that racism contributes to the cycle of violence, given the stress that men of color experience in dominant society. It is therefore more than reasonable to explore the links between racism and domestic violence. But the chain of violence is more complex and extends beyond this single link. Racism is linked to patriarchy to the extent that racism denies men of color the power and privilege that dominant men enjoy. When violence is understood as an acting-out of being denied male power in other spheres, it seems counterproductive to embrace constructs that implicitly link the solution to domestic violence to the acquisition of greater male power. The more promising political imperative is to challenge the legitimacy of such power expectations by exposing their dysfunctional and debilitating effect on families and communities of color. Moreover, while understanding links between racism and domestic violence is an important component of any effective intervention strategy, it is also clear that women of color need not await the ultimate triumph over racism before they can expect to live violence-free lives.

RACE AND THE DOMESTIC VIOLENCE LOBBY

Not only do race-based priorities function to obscure the problem of violence suffered by women of color; feminist concerns often suppress minority experiences as well. Strategies for increasing awareness of domestic violence within the white community tend to begin by citing the commonly shared assumption that battering is a minority problem. The strategy then focuses on demolishing this strawman, stressing that spousal abuse also occurs in the white commu-

nity. Countless first-person stories begin with a statement like, "I was not supposed to be a battered wife." That battering occurs in families of all races and all classes seems to be an ever-present theme of anti-abuse campaigns.[33] First-person anecdotes and studies, for example, consistently assert that battering cuts across racial, ethnic, economic, educational, and religious lines.[34] Such disclaimers seem relevant only in the presence of an initial, widely held belief that domestic violence occurs primarily in minority or poor families. Indeed some authorities explicitly renounce the "stereotypical myths" about battered women.[35] A few commentators have even transformed the message that battering is not *exclusively* a problem of the poor or minority communities into a claim that it *equally* affects all races and classes.[36] Yet these comments seem less concerned with exploring domestic abuse within "stereotyped" communities than with removing the stereotype as an obstacle to exposing battering within white middle and upper-class communities.

Efforts to politicize the issue of violence against women challenge beliefs that violence occurs only in homes of "others." While it is unlikely that advocates and others who adopt this rhetorical strategy intend to exclude or ignore the needs of poor and colored women, the underlying premise of this seemingly univeralistic appeal is to keep the sensibilities of dominant social groups focused on the experiences of those groups. Indeed, as subtly suggested by the opening comments of Senator David Boren (D-Okla.) in support of the Violence Against Women Act of 1991, the displacement of the "other" as the presumed victim of domestic violence works primarily as a political appeal to rally white elites. Boren said,

Violent crimes against women are not limited to the streets of the inner cities, but also occur in homes in the urban and rural areas across the country.

Violence against women affects not only those who are actually beaten and brutalized, but indirectly affects all women. Today, our wives, mothers, daughters, sisters, and colleagues are held captive by fear generated from these violent crimes—held captive not for what they do or who they are, but solely because of gender.[37]

Rather than focusing on and illuminating how violence is disregarded when the home is "othered," the strategy implicit in Senator Boren's remarks functions instead to politicize the problem only in the dominant community. This strategy permits white women victims to come into focus, but does little to disrupt the patterns of neglect that permitted the problem to continue as long as it was imagined to be a minority problem. The experience of violence by minority women is ignored, except to the extent it gains white support for domestic violence programs in the white community.

Senator Boren and his colleagues no doubt believe that they have provided legislation and resources that will address the problems of all women victimized by domestic violence. Yet despite their universalizing rhetoric of "all" women, they were able to empathize with female victims of domestic violence only by looking past the plight of "other" women and by recognizing the familiar faces of their own. The strength of the appeal to "protect our women" must be its race and class specificity. After all, it has always been someone's wife, mother, sister, or daughter that has been abused, even when the violence was stereotypically Black, Brown, and poor. The point here is not that the Violence Against Women Act is particularistic on its own terms, but that unless the Senators and other policymakers ask why violence remained insignificant as long as it was understood as a minority problem, it is unlikely that women of color will share equally in the distribution of resources and concern. It is even more unlikely, however, that those in power will be forced to confront this issue. As long as attempts to politicize domestic violence focus on convincing whites that this is not a "minority" problem but *their* problem, any authentic and sensitive attention to the experiences of Black and other minority women probably will continue to be regarded as jeopardizing the movement.

While Senator Boren's statement reflects a self-consciously political presentation of domestic violence, an episode of the CBS news program *48 Hours*[38] shows how similar patterns of "othering" nonwhite women are apparent in journalistic accounts of domestic violence as well. The program presented seven women who were victims of abuse. Six were interviewed at some length along with their family members, friends, supporters, and even detractors. The viewer got to know something about each of these women. These victims were humanized. Yet the seventh woman, the only non-white one, never came into focus. She was literally unrecognizable throughout the segment, first introduced by photographs showing her face badly beaten and later shown with her face electronically altered in the videotape of a hearing at which she was forced to testify. Other images associated with this woman included shots of a bloodstained room and blood-soaked pillows. Her boyfriend was pictured handcuffed while the camera zoomed in for a close-up of his bloodied sneakers. Of all the presentations in the episode, hers was the most graphic and impersonal. The overall point of the segment "featuring" this woman was that battering might not escalate into homicide if battered women would only cooperate with prosecutors. In focusing on its own agenda and failing to explore why this woman refused to cooperate, the program diminished this woman, communicating, however subtly, that she was responsible for her own victimization.

Unlike the other women, all of whom, again, were white, this Black woman had no name, no family, no context. The viewer sees her only as victimized and uncooperative. She cries when shown pictures. She pleads not to be forced to view the bloodstained room and her disfigured face. The program does not help the viewer to understand her predicament. The possible reasons she did not want to testify—fear, love, or possibly both—are never suggested.[39] Most unfortunately, she, unlike the other six, is given no epilogue. While the fates of the other women are revealed at the end of the episode, we discover nothing about the Black woman. She, like the "others" she represents, is simply left to herself and soon forgotten.

I offer this description to suggest that "other" women are silenced as much by being relegated to the margin of experience as by total exclusion. Tokenistic, objectifying, voyeuristic inclusion is at least as disempowering as complete exclusion. The effort to politicize violence against women will do little to address Black and other minority women if their images are retained simply to magnify the problem rather than to humanize their experiences. Similarly, the antiracist agenda will not be advanced significantly by forcibly suppressing the reality of battering in minority communities. As the *48 Hours* episode makes clear, the images and stereotypes we fear are readily available and are frequently deployed in ways that do not generate sensitive understanding of the nature of domestic violence in minority communities.

RACE AND DOMESTIC VIOLENCE SUPPORT SERVICES

Women working in the field of domestic violence have sometimes reproduced the subordination and marginalization of women of color by adopting policies, priorities, or strategies of empowerment that either elide or wholly disregard the particular intersectional needs of women of color. While gender, race, and class intersect to create the particular context in which women of color experience violence, certain choices made by "allies" can reproduce intersectional subordination within the very resistance strategies designed to respond to the problem.

This problem is starkly illustrated by the inaccessibility of domestic violence support services to many non-English-speaking women. In a letter written to the deputy commissioner of the New York State Department of Social Services, Diana Campos, Director of Human Services for Programas de Ocupaciones y Desarrollo Económico Real, Inc. (PODER), detailed the case of a Latina in crisis who was repeatedly denied accommodation at a shelter because she could not prove that she was English-proficient. The woman had fled her home with her teenaged son, believing her husband's threats to kill them both. She called the domestic violence hotline administered by PODER seeking shelter for herself and her son. Because most shelters would not accommodate the woman with her son, they were forced to live on the streets for two days. The hotline counselor was finally able to find an agency that would take both the mother and the son, but when the counselor told the intake coordinator at the shelter that the woman spoke limited English, the coordinator told her that they could not take anyone who was not English-proficient. When the woman in crisis called back and was told of the shelter's "rule," she replied that she could understand English if spoken to her slowly. As Campos explains, Mildred, the hotline counselor, told Wendy, the intake coordinator

that the woman said that she could communicate a little in English. Wendy told Mildred that they could not provide services to this woman because they have house rules that the woman must agree to follow. Mildred asked her, "What if the woman agrees to follow your rules? Will you still not take her?" Wendy responded that all of the women at the shelter are required to attend [a] support group and they would not be able to have her in the group if she could not communicate. Mildred mentioned the severity of this woman's case. She told Wendy that the woman had been wandering the streets at night while her husband is home, and she had been mugged twice. She also reiterated the fact that this woman was in danger of being killed by either her husband or a mugger. Mildred expressed that the woman's safety was a priority at this point, and that once in a safe place, receiving counseling in a support group could be dealt with.[40]

The intake coordinator restated the shelter's policy of taking only English-speaking women, and stated further that the woman would have to call the shelter herself for screening. If the woman could communicate with them in English, she might be accepted. When the woman called the PODER hotline later that day, she was in such a state of fear that the hotline counselor who had been working with her had difficulty understanding her in Spanish.[41] Campos directly intervened at this point, calling the executive director of the shelter. A counselor called back from the shelter. As Campos reports,

Marie [the counselor] told me that they did not want to take the woman in the shelter because they felt that the woman would feel isolated. I explained that the son agreed to translate for his mother during the intake process. Furthermore, that we would assist them in locating a Spanish-speaking battered women's advocate to assist in counseling her. Marie stated that utilizing the son was not an acceptable means of communication for them, *since it further victimized the victim*. In addition, she stated that they had similar experiences with women who were non-English-speaking, and that the women eventually just left because they were not able to communicate with anyone. I expressed my extreme concern for her safety and reiterated that we would assist them in providing her with the necessary services until we could get her placed someplace where they had bilingual staff.[42]

After several more calls, the shelter finally agreed to take the woman. The woman called once more during the negotiation; however, after a plan was in place, the woman never called back. Said Campos, "After so many calls, we are now left to wonder if she is alive and well, and if she will ever have enough faith in our ability to help her to call us again the next time she is in crisis."[43]

Despite this woman's desperate need, she was unable to receive the protection afforded English-speaking women, due to the shelter's rigid commitment to exclusionary policies. Perhaps even more troubling than the shelter's lack of bilingual resources was its refusal to allow a friend or relative to translate for the woman. This story illustrates the absurdity of a feminist approach that would make the ability to attend a support group without a translator a more significant consideration in the distribution of resources than the risk of physical harm on the street. The point is not that the shelter's image of empowerment is empty, but rather that it was imposed without regard to the disempowering consequences for women who didn't match the kind of client the shelter's administrators imagined. And thus they failed to accomplish the basic priority of the shelter movement—to get the woman out of danger.

Here the woman in crisis was made to bear the burden of the shelter's refusal to anticipate and provide for the needs of non-English-speaking women. Said Campos, "It is unfair to impose more stress on victims by placing them in the position of having to demonstrate their proficiency in English in order to

receive services that are readily available to other battered women."[44] The problem is not easily dismissed as one of well-intentioned ignorance. The specific issue of monolingualism and the monistic view of women's experience that set the stage for this tragedy were not new issues in New York. Indeed, several women of color reported that they had repeatedly struggled with the New York State Coalition Against Domestic Violence over language exclusion and other practices that marginalized the interests of women of color.[45] Yet despite repeated lobbying, the Coalition did not act to incorporate the specific needs of non-white women into their central organizing vision.

Some critics have linked the Coalition's failure to address these issues to the narrow vision of coalition that animated its interaction with women of color in the first place. The very location of the Coalition's headquarters in Woodstock, New York—an area where few people of color live—seemed to guarantee that women of color would play a limited role in formulating policy. Moreover, efforts to include women of color came, it seems, as something of an afterthought. Many were invited to participate only after the Coalition was awarded a grant by the state to recruit women of color. However, as one "recruit" said, "they were not really prepared to deal with us or our issues. They thought that they could simply incorporate us into their organization without rethinking any of their beliefs or priorities and that we would be happy."[46] Even the most formal gestures of inclusion were not to be taken for granted. On one occasion when several women of color attended a meeting to discuss a special task force on women of color, the group debated all day over including the issue on the agenda.[47]

The relationship between the white women and the women of color on the Board was a rocky one from beginning to end. Other conflicts developed over differing definitions of feminism. For example, the Board decided to hire a Latina staffperson to manage outreach programs to the Latino community, but the white members of the hiring committee rejected candidates favored by Latina committee members who did not have recognized feminist credentials. As Campos pointed out, by measuring Latinas against their own biographies, the white members of the Board failed to recognize the different circumstances under which feminist consciousness develops and manifests itself within minority communities. Many of the women who interviewed for the position were established activists and leaders within their own community, a fact in itself suggesting that these women were probably familiar with the specific gender dynamics in their communities and were accordingly better qualified to handle outreach than other candidates with more conventional feminist credentials.[48]

The Coalition ended a few months later when the women of color walked out.[49] Many of these women returned to community-based organizations, preferring to struggle over women's issues within their communities rather than struggle over race and class issues with white middle-class women. Yet as illustrated by the case of the Latina who could find no shelter, the dominance of a particular perspective and set of priorities within the shelter community continues to marginalize the needs of women of color.

The struggle over which differences matter and which do not is neither an abstract nor an insignificant debate among women. Indeed, these conflicts are about more than difference as such; they raise critical issues of power. The problem is not simply that women who dominate the anti-violence movement are different from women of color but that they frequently have power to determine, either through material or rhetorical resources, whether the intersectional differences of women of color will be incorporated at all into the basic formulation of policy. Thus, the struggle over incorporating these differences is not a petty or superficial conflict about who gets to sit at the head of the table. In the context of violence, it is sometimes a deadly serious matter of who will survive—and who will not.[50]

NOTES

1. Feminist academics and activists have played a central role in forwarding an ideological and institutional challenge to the practices that condone and perpetuate violence against women. See generally Susan Brownmiller, Against Our Will: Men, Women and Rape (1975); Lorenne M. G. Clark & Debra J. Lewis, Rape: The Price of Coercive Sexuality (1977); R. Emerson Dobash & Russell Dobash, Violence Against Wives: A Case Against the Patriarchy (1979); Nancy Gager & Cathleen Schurr, Sexual, Assault: Confronting Rape in America (1976); Diana E. H. Russell, The Politics of Rape: The Victim's Perspective (1974); Elizabeth Anne Stanko, Intimate Intrusions: Women's Experience of Male Violence (1985); Lenore E. Walker, Terrifying Love: Why Battered Women Kill and How Society Responds (1989); Lenore E. Walker, The Battered Woman Syndrome (1984); Lenore E. Walker, The Battered Woman (1979).

2. See, e.g., Susan Schechter, Women and Male Violence: The Visions and Struggles of the Battered Women's Movement (1982) (arguing that battering is a means of maintaining women's subordinate position); Brownmiller, supra note 1 (arguing that rape is a patriarchal practice that subordinates women to men); Elizabeth Schneider, *The Violence of Privacy*, 23 Conn. L. Rev. 973, 974 (1991) (discussing how "concepts of privacy permit, encourage and reinforce violence against women"); Susan Estrich, *Rape*, 95 Yale L.J. 1087 (1986) (analyzing rape law as one illustration of sexism in criminal law); *see also* Catharine A. MacKinnon, Sexual Harassment of Working Women: A Case of Sex Discrimination 143–213 (1979) (arguing that sexual harassment should be redefined as sexual discrimination actionable under Title VII, rather than viewed as misplaced sexuality in the workplace).

3. This article arises out of and is inspired by two emerging scholarly discourses. The first is critical race theory. For a cross-section of what is now a substantial body of literature, see Patricia J. Williams, The Alchemy of Race and Rights (1991); Robin D. Barnes, *Race Consciousness: The Thematic Content of Racial Distinctiveness in Critical Race Scholarship*, 103 Harv. L. Rev. 1864 (1990); John O. Calmore, *Critical Race Theory, Archie Shepp, and Fire Music: Securing an Authentic Intellectual Life in a Multicultural World*, 65 S. Cal. L. Rev. 2129 (1992); Anthony E. Cook, *Beyond Critical Legal Studies: The Reconstructive Theology of Dr. Martin Luther King*, 103 Harv. L. Rev. 985 (1990); Kimberlé Williams Crenshaw, *Race, Reform and Retrenchment: Transformation and Legitimation in Antidiscrimination Law*, 101 Harv. L. Rev. 1331 (1988); Richard Delgado, *When a Story is Just a Story: Does Voice Really Matter?*, 76 Va. L. Rev. 95 (1990); Neil Gotanda, *A Critique of "Our Constitution is Colorblind,"* 44 Stan. L. Rev. 1 (1991); Mari J. Matsuda, *Public Response to Racist Speech: Considering the Victim's*

Story, 87 Mich. L. Rev. 2320 (1989); Charles R. Lawrence III, *The Id, the Ego, and Equal Protection: Reckoning with Unconscious Racism*, 39 Stan. L. Rev. 317 (1987); Gerald Torres, *Critical Race Theory: The Decline of the Universalist Ideal and the Hope of Plural Justice—Some Observations and Questions of an Emerging Phenomenon*, 75 Minn. L. Rev. 993 (1991). For a useful overview of critical race theory, see Calmore, supra, at 2160–2168.

A second, less formally linked body of legal scholarship investigates the connections between race and gender. See, e.g., Regina Austin, *Sapphire Bound!*, 1989 Wisc. L. Rev. 539; Crenshaw, supra; Angela P. Harris, *Race and Essentialism in Feminist Legal Theory*, 42 Stan. L. Rev. 581 (1990); Marlee Kline, *Race, Racism and Feminist Legal Theory*, 12 Harv. Women's L.J. 115 (1989); Dorothy E. Roberts, *Punishing Drug Addicts Who Have Babies: Women of Color, Equality and the Right of Privacy*, 104 Harv. L. Rev. 1419 (1991); Cathy Scarborough, *Conceptualizing Black Women's Employment Experiences*, 98 Yale L.J. 1457 (1989); Peggie R. Smith, *Separate Identities: Black Women, Work and Title VII*, 14 Harv. Women's L.J. 21 (1991); Judy Scales-Trent, *Black Women and the Constitution: Finding Our Place, Asserting Our Rights*, 24 Harv. C.R.-C.L. L. Rev. 9 (1989); Judith A. Winston, *Mirror, Mirror on the Wall: Title VII, Section 1981, and the Intersection of Race and Gender in the Civil Rights Act of 1990*, 79 Cal. L. Rev. 775 (1991).

4. Although this article deals with violent assault perpetrated by men against women, women are also subject to violent assault by women. Violence among lesbians is a hidden but significant problem. One expert reported that in a study of ninety lesbian couples, roughly 46% of lesbians have been physically abused by their partners. Jane Garcia, *The Cost of Escaping Domestic Violence: Fear of Treatment in a Largely Homophobic Society May Keep Lesbian Abuse Victims from Calling for Help*, L.A. Times, May 6, 1991, at 2; see also Naming the Violence: Speaking Out About Lesbian Battering (Kerry Lobel ed., 1986); Ruthann Robson, *Lavender Bruises: Intralesbian Violence, Law and Lesbian Legal Theory*, 20 Golden Gate U. L. Rev. 567 (1990). There are clear parallels between violence against women in the lesbian community and violence against women in communities of color. Lesbian violence is often shrouded in secrecy for similar reasons that have suppressed the exposure of heterosexual violence in communities of color—fear of embarrassing other members of the community, which is already stereotyped as deviant, and fear of being ostracized from the community. Despite these similarities, there are nonetheless distinctions between

male abuse of women and female abuse of women that in the context of patriarchy, racism and homophobia, warrants more focused analysis than is possible here.

5. Kimberlé Crenshaw, *Demarginalizing the Intersection of Race and Sex*, 1989 U. Chi. Legal F. 139.

6. Professor Mari Matsuda calls this inquiry "asking the other question." Mari J. Matsuda, *Beside My Sister, Facing the Enemy: Legal Theory Out of Coalition*, 43 Stan. L. Rev. 1183 (1991). For example, we should look at an issue or condition traditionally regarded as a gender issue and ask, "Where's the racism in this?"

7. During my research in Los Angeles, California, I visited Jenessee Battered Women's Shelter, the only shelter in the Western states primarily serving Black women, and Everywoman's Shelter, which primarily serves Asian women. I also visited Estelle Chueng at the Asian Pacific Law Foundation and I spoke with a representative of La Casa, a shelter in the predominantly Latino community of East L.A.

8. Together they make securing even the most basic necessities beyond the reach of many. Indeed one shelter provider reported that nearly eighty-five percent of her clients returned to the battering relationships, largely because of difficulties in finding employment and housing.

9. 8 U.S.C. § 1186a (1988). The Marriage Fraud Amendments provide that an alien spouse "shall be considered, at the time of obtaining the status of an alien lawfully admitted for permanent residence, to have obtained such status on a conditional basis subject to the provisions of this section." § 1186a(a)(1). An alien spouse with permanent resident status under this conditional basis may have her status terminated if the Attorney General finds that the marriage was "improper," § 1186a(b)(1), or if she fails to file a petition or fails to appear at the personal interview. § 1186a(c)(2)(A).

10. The Marriage Fraud Amendments provided that for the conditional resident status to be removed, "the alien spouse and the petitioning spouse (if not deceased) *jointly* must submit to the Attorney General . . . a petition which requests the removal of such conditional basis and which states, under penalty of perjury, the facts and information." § 1186a(b)(1)(A) (emphasis added). The Amendments provided for a waiver, at the Attorney General's discretion, if the alien spouse was able to demonstrate that deportation would result in extreme hardship, or that the qualifying marriage was terminated for good cause. § 1186a(c)(4). However, the terms of this hardship waiver have not adequately protected battered spouses. For example, the requirement that the marriage be terminated for good cause

may be difficult to satisfy in states with no-fault divorces. Eileen P. Lynsky, *Immigration Marriage Fraud Amendments of 1986: Till Congress Do Us Part*, 41 U. Miami L. Rev. 1087, 1095 n.47 (1987) (citing Jerome B. Ingber & R. Leo Prischet, *The Marriage Fraud Amendments, in* The New Simpson-Rodino Immigration Law of 1986, 564–65 (Stanley Mailman ed., 1986)).

11. Immigration activists have pointed out that "[t]he 1986 Immigration Reform Act and the Immigration Marriage Fraud Amendment have combined to give the spouse applying for permanent residence a powerful tool to control his partner." Jorge Banales, *Abuse Among Immigrants; As Their Numbers Grow So Does the Need for Services*, Wash. Post, Oct. 16, 1990, at E5. Dean Ito Taylor, executive director of Nihonmachi Legal Outreach in San Francisco, explained that the Marriage Fraud Amendments "bound these immigrant women to their abusers." Deanna Hodgin, *"Mail-Order" Brides Marry Pain to Get Green Cards*, Wash. Times, Apr. 16, 1991, at E1. In one egregious instance described by Beckie Masaki, executive director of the Asian Women's Shelter in San Francisco, the closer the Chinese bride came to getting her permanent residency in the United States, the more harshly her Asian-American husband beat her. Her husband, kicking her in the neck and face, warned her that she needed him, and if she did not do as he told her, he would call immigration officials. Id.

12. Immigration Act of 1990, Pub. L. No. 101–649, 104 Stat. 4978. The Act, introduced by Representative Louise Slaughter (D-N.Y.), provides that a battered spouse who has conditional permanent resident status can be granted a waiver for failure to meet the requirements if she can show that "the marriage was entered into in good faith and that after the marriage the alien spouse was battered by or was subjected to extreme mental cruelty by the U.S. citizen or permanent resident spouse". H.R. Rep. No. 723(1), 101st Cong., 2d Sess. 78 (1990), reprinted in 1990 U.S.C.C.A.N. 6710, 6758; see also 8 C.F.R. § 216.5(3) (1992) (regulations for application for waiver based on claim of having been battered or subjected to extreme mental cruelty).

13. H.R. Rep. No. 723(1), supra note 12, at 79, reprinted in 1990 U.S.C.C.A.N. 6710, 6759.

14. Hodgin, supra note 11.

15. Id.

16. Mildred Daley Pagelow, Woman-Battering: Victims and Their Experiences 96 (1981). The seventy minority women in the study "had a double disadvantage in this society that serves to tie them more strongly to their spouses." Id.

17. Incidents of sexual abuse of undocumented women abound. Marta Rivera, director of the Hostos College Center for Women's and Immigrant's Rights, tells of how a 19-year-old Dominican woman had "arrived shaken . . . after her boss raped her in the women's restroom at work." The woman told Rivera that "70 to 80 percent of the workers [in a Brooklyn garment factory] were undocumented, and they all accepted sex as part of the job. . . . She said a 13-year-old girl had been raped there a short while before her, and the family sent her back to the Dominican Republic." Vivienne Walt, *Immigrant Abuse: Nowhere to Hide; Women Fear Deportation, Experts Say*, Newsday, Dec. 2, 1990, at 8.

18. Pagelow, supra note 16, at 96–97.

19. Most crime statistics are classified by sex or race but none are classified by sex *and* race. Because we know that most rape victims are women, the racial breakdown reveals, at best, rape rates for Black women. Yet, even given this head start, rates for other non-white women are difficult to collect. While there are some statistics for Latinas, statistics for Asian and Native American women are virtually non-existent. Cf. G. Chezia Carraway, *Violence Against Women of Color*, 43 Stan. L. Rev. 1301 (1991).

20. Shahrazad Ali, The Blackman's Guide to Understanding the Blackwoman (1989).

21. Shahrazad Ali suggests that the "[Blackwoman] certainly does not believe that her disrepect for the Blackman is destructive, *nor* that her opposition to him has deteriorated the Black nation." Ali, supra note 20, at viii. Blaming the problems of the community on the failure of the Black woman to accept her "real definition," Ali explains that "[n]o nation can rise when the natural order of the behavior of the male and the female have been altered against their wishes by force. No species can survive if the female of the genus disturbs the balance of her nature by acting other than herself." Id. at 76.

22. Ali advises the Blackman to hit the Blackwoman in the mouth, "[b]ecause it is from that hole, in the lower part of her face, that all her rebellion culminates into words. Her unbridled tongue is a main reason she cannot get along with the Blackman. She often needs a reminder." Id. at 169. Ali warns that "if [the Blackwoman] ignores the authority and superiority of the Blackman, there is a penalty. When she crosses this line and becomes viciously insulting it is time for the Blackman to soundly slap her in the mouth." Id.

23. In this regard, Ali's arguments bear much in common with those of neoconservatives who attribute many of the social ills plaguing Black America to the breakdown of patriarchal family values. See, e.g., William Raspberry, *If*

We Are to Rescue American Families, We Have to Save the Boys, Chi. Trib., July 19, 1989, at C15; George F. Will, *Voting Rights Won't Fix It*, Wash. Post, Jan. 23, 1986, at A23; George F. Will, *"White Racism" Doesn't Make Blacks Mere Victims of Fate*, Milwaukee J., Feb. 21, 1986, at 9. Ali's argument shares remarkable similarities to the controversial "Moynihan Report" on the Black family, so called because its principal author was now-Senator Daniel P. Moynihan (D-N.Y.). In the infamous chapter entitled "The Tangle of Pathology," Moynihan argued that

> the Negro community has been forced into a matriarchal structure which, because it is so out of line with the rest of American society, seriously retards the progress of the group as a whole, and imposes a crushing burden on the Negro male and, in consequence, on a great many Negro women as well.

Office of Policy Planning and Research, U.S. Department of Labor, The Negro Family: The Case for National Action 29 (1965), reprinted in Lee Rainwater & William L. Yancey, The Moynihan Report and the Politics of Controversy 75 (1967).

24. A pressing problem is the way domestic violence reproduces itself in subsequent generations. It is estimated that boys who witness violence against women are ten times more likely to batter female partners as adults. *Women and Violence: Hearings Before the Senate Comm. on the Judiciary on Legislation to Reduce the Growing Problem of Violent Crime Against Women*, 101st Cong., 2d Sess., pt. 2, at 89 (1991) [hereinafter *Hearings on Violent Crime Against Women*] (testimony of Charlotte Fedders). Other associated problems for boys who witness violence against women include higher rates of suicide, violent assault, sexual assault, and alcohol and drug use. Id., pt. 2, at 131 (statement of Sarah M. Buel, Assistant District Attorney, Massachusetts, and Supervisor, Harvard Law School Battered Women's Advocacy Project).

25. Id. at 142 (statement of Susan Kelly-Dreiss) (discussing several studies in Pennsylvania linking homelessness to domestic violence).

26. Id. at 143 (statement of Susan Kelly-Dreiss).

27. Another historical example includes Eldridge Cleaver, who argued that he raped white women as an assault upon the white community. Cleaver "practiced" on black women first. Eldridge Cleaver, Soul. on Ice 14–15 (1968).

28. Alice Walker, The Color Purple (1982).

29. See, e.g., Gerald Early, *Her Picture in the Papers: Remembering Some Black Women*, Antaeus, Spring 1988,

at 9; Daryl Pinckney, *Black Victims, Black Villains*, N.Y. Review of Books, Jan. 29, 1987, at 17; Jacqueline Trescott, *Passions Over Purple; Anger and Unease Over Film's Depiction of Black Men*, Wash. Post, Feb. 5, 1986, at C1.

30. Trudier Harris, *On the Color Purple, Stereotypes, and Silence*, 18 Black Am. Lit. F. 155, 155 (1984).

31. The source of the resistance reveals an interesting difference between the Asian-American and African-American communities. In the African-American community, the resistance is usually grounded in efforts to avoid confirming negative stereotypes of African-Americans as violent; the concern of members in some Asian-American communities is to avoid tarnishing the model minority myth. Interview with Nilda Rimonte, Director of the Everywoman Shelter, in Los Angeles, California (Apr. 19, 1991).

32. Nilda Rimonte, *Cultural Sanction of Violence Against Women in the Pacific-Asian Community*, 43 Stan. L. Rev. 1183 (1991); see also Nilda Rimonte, *Domestic Violence Against Pacific Asians, in* Making Waves: An Anthology of Writings By and About Asian American Women 327, 328 (Asian Women United of California ed., 1989).

33. See, e.g., *Hearings on Violent Crime Against Women*, supra note 24, pt. 1, at 101 (testimony of Roni Young, Director of Domestic Violence Unit, Office of the State's Attorney for Baltimore City, Baltimore, Maryland) ("The victims do not fit a mold by any means."); Id., pt. 2, at 89 (testimony of Charlotte Fedders) ("Domestic violence occurs in all economic, cultural, racial, and religious groups. There is not a typical woman to be abused."); Id. at 139 (statement of Susan Kelly-Dreiss, Executive Director, Pennsylvania Coalition Against Domestic Violence) ("Victims come from a wide spectrum of life experiences and backgrounds. Women can be beaten in any neighborhood and in any town.").

34. See, e.g., Lenore F. Walker, Terrifying Love: Why Battered Women Kill and How Society Responds 101–02 (1989) ("Battered women come from all types of economic, cultural, religious, and racial backgrounds. . . . They are women like you. Like me. Like those whom you know and love."); Murray A. Straus, Richard J. Gelles & Suzanne K. Steinmetz, Behind Closed Doors: Violence in the American Family 31 (1980) ("Wife-beating is found in every class, at every income level."); Natalie Loder Clark, *Crime Begins At Home: Let's Stop Punishing Victims and Perpetuating Violence*, 28 Wm. & Mary L. Rev. 263, 282 n.74 (1987) ("The problem of domestic violence cuts across all social lines and affects 'families regardless of

their economic class, race, national origin, or educational background.' Commentators have indicated that domestic violence is prevalent among upper middle-class families.") (citations omitted).

35. For example, Susan Kelly-Dreiss states:

The public holds many myths about battered women—they are poor, they are women of color, they are uneducated, they are on welfare, they deserve to be beaten and they even like it. However, contrary to common misperceptions, domestic violence is not confined to any one socioeconomic, ethnic, religious, racial or age group.

Hearings on Violent Crime Against Women, supra note 24, pt. 2, at 139 (testimony of Susan Kelly-Dreiss, Executive Director, Pa. Coalition Against Domestic Violence).

36. However, no reliable statistics support such a claim. In fact, some statistics suggest that there is a greater frequency of violence among the working classes and the poor. See Straus, Gelles & Steinmetz, supra note 34, at 31. Yet these statistics are also unreliable because, to follow Waits's observation, violence in middle and upper-class homes remains hidden from the view of statisticians and governmental officials alike. See note 35, supra. I would suggest that assertions that the problem is the same across race and class are driven less by actual knowledge about the prevalence of domestic violence in different communities than by advocates' recognition that the image of domestic violence as an issue involving primarily the poor and minorities complicates efforts to mobilize against it.

37. 137 Cong. Rec. S611 (daily ed. Jan. 14, 1991) (statement of Sen. Boren).

38. *48 Hours: Till Death Do Us Part* (CBS television broadcast, Feb. 6, 1991).

39. See Christine A. Littleton, *Women's Experience and the Problem of Transition: Perspectives on Male Battering of Women*, 1989 U. Chi. Legal F. 23.

40. Letter of Diana M. Campos, Director of Human Services, PODER, to Joseph Semidei, Deputy Commissioner, New York State Department of Social Services (Mar. 26, 1992) [hereinafter *PODER Letter*].

41. The woman had been slipping back into her home during the day when her husband was at work. She remained in a heightened state of anxiety because he was returning shortly and she would be forced to go back out into the streets for yet another night.

42. *PODER Letter*, Supra note 40 (emphasis added).

43. Id.

44. Id.

45. Roundtable Discussion on Racism and the Domestic Violence Movement (April 2, 1992).

46. Id.

47. Id.

48. Id.

49. Ironically, the specific dispute that led to the walkout concerned the housing of the Spanish-language domestic violence hotline. The hotline was initially housed at the Coalition's headquarters, but languished after a succession of coordinators left the organization. Latinas on the Coalition board argued that the hotline should be housed at one of the community service agencies, while the board insisted on maintaining control of it. The hotline is now housed at PODER. Id.

50. Said Campos, "It would be a shame that in New York state a battered woman's life or death were dependent upon her English language skills." *PODER Letter*, supra note 40.

Study Questions

1. Crenshaw argues that failure to attend to the intersectional location of women of color results in women of color who are victims of domestic violence not getting what they need. Provide two examples from the article to illustrate her point.

2. On the face of it, this article focuses on differences between women (i.e., racial differences in particular) rather than on sameness. In what sense, then, can Crenshaw's piece be read as an example of sameness/humanist feminist thinking?

3. Does thinking about Crenshaw's article reveal any weaknesses in Schechter's discussion of domestic violence policy?

THE DIFFERENCE APPROACH

Iris M. Young

Humanism, Gynocentrism, and Feminist Politics

December 1978. At a mostly male conference I hug, chat, eat, drink, listen with my sisters in philosophy. My body avalanches from its recent maternal swellings to the plateaus of a folded uterus, milkless breasts. I left my baby daughter in Chicago, who used to suckle for ninety minutes at a time while I read *The Women's Room*. For the first time in fifteen months that warm red flow moves through my clitoral canals. No quiet transition, but a body revolution throbbing my back and neck. Clouded in this private woman-state, I glide around the chandeliered ballroom finding one woman's face and another and another. Fervently we converse about the day's papers and one another's questions. We catch up on the news about one another's lovers or children or jobs.

That night in my restless sleep, I dream. A ball-room filled with women, hundreds under the chand-eliers, a reception after business at the Society for Women in Philosophy. I flit from one group of women to another in smiling comfort. As I turn to find another friend I see her tall figure across the room, as though overlooking the sisterly crowd: Simone de Beauvoir. Then, just before I wake, a single object, shimmering: a glass of milk.

No other woman can so occupy our dreams as the mother of feminist philosophy (who in her time, in her view, could be a writing mother only by leaving her body out of mothering, and I think she was right).

Yet most feminists in the United States today find irredeemable flaws in Beauvoir's story of women's oppression and her hope for liberation. What has happened between the childhood and puberty of our feminist revolution?

In this essay I explore the shift in feminist thinking from a Beauvoirian sort of position, which I define as humanist feminism, to an analysis that I call gynocentric feminism. Humanist feminism defines women's oppression as the inhibition and distortion of women's potential by a society that allows the self-development of men. Most feminists of the nineteenth and twentieth centuries, including feminists of the early second wave, have been humanist feminists. In recent years a different account of women's oppression has gained influence, however, partly growing from a critique of humanist feminism. Gynocentric feminism defines women's oppression as the devaluation and repression of women's experience by a masculinist culture that exalts violence and individualism. It argues for the superiority of the values embodied in traditionally female experience and rejects the values it finds in traditionally male dominated institutions. Gynocentric feminism, I suggest, contains a more radical critique of male dominated society than does humanist feminism. But at the same time, especially within the social context of antifeminist backlash, however, its effect can be quieting and accommodating to official powers.

Iris M. Young, "Humanism, Gynocentrism, and Feminist Politics," *Women's Studies International Forum* 8:3 (1985): 173–85.

I

Humanist feminism consists of a revolt against femininity. Patriarchal culture has ascribed to women a distinct feminine nature by which it has justified the exclusion of women from most of the important and creative activity of society—science, politics, invention, industry, commerce, the arts. By defining women as sexual objects, decorative charmers, and mothers, the patriarchal culture enforces behavior in women that benefits men by providing them with domestic and sexual servants. Women's confinement to femininity stunts the development of their full potential and makes women passive, dependent, and weak. Humanist feminism defines femininity as the primary vehicle of women's oppression and calls upon male dominated institutions to allow women the opportunity to participate fully in the public world-making activities of industry, politics, art, and science.

Women's liberation, in this view, consists of freeing women from the confines of traditional femininity and making it possible for women to pursue the projects that have hitherto been dominated by men. Any assumptions that women are not capable of achieving the excellence that men have attained must be suspended until women are allowed to develop their full potential. When gender differences are transcended in this manner, people will be able to choose whatever activities they wish to pursue, will be able to develop their full potential as individuals. Women's liberation consists of eliminating a separate women's sphere and giving women the opportunity to do what men have done. This implies that men will have to do more of the work traditionally assigned to women.

I call this position humanist feminist because it defines gender difference as accidental to humanity. The goal of liberation is for all persons to pursue self-development in those creative and intellectual activities that distinguish human beings from the rest of nature. Women's liberation means sexual equality. Sexual equality means bringing women and men under a common measure, judged by the same standards. We should judge all by the standards according to which men have judged one another: courage, rationality, strength, cunning, quick-wittedness.

Humanist feminism, in one version or another, has dominated feminist accounts for most of the nineteenth and twentieth centuries. The feminist classics of Wollstonecraft, Mill, and Taylor, as well as the views of many of the suffragettes in nineteenth-century England and the United States, exhibit the main outlines of humanist feminism. Until recently humanist feminism was also the dominant strain in contemporary feminism. Simone de Beauvoir's description of the oppression of women and her vision of liberation in *The Second Sex* stands as one of the most theoretically grounded and thorough articulations of humanist feminism.[1]

Beauvoir's account of women's oppression depends on the distinction between transcendence and immanence. Transcendence designates the free subjectivity that defines its own nature and makes projects that bring new entities into the world. The free subject moves out into the world, takes initiative, faces the world boldly, creates his own individualized life. According to Beauvoir, patriarchal society allows only men such transcendence. Masculinity entails no particular attributes but in patriarchal society is identified with transcendence, free activity that fashions artifacts and history. A man is confined to no particular nature but has all manner of projects open to him—he can be a soldier or an artist, a politician or a chef, a scientist or a gambler. To be sure, Beauvoir understands the class and race oppression that puts more limits on the possibilities of some men than on those of others. Gender does not restrict oppressed men, however. The possibility of action is still open to oppressed men, in the form of wily sabotage or open rebellion. Masculinity entails individual existence, where the person defines his own individual projects and creates his own nature.

Patriarchal culture confines women, on the other hand, to immanence. Immanence designates being an object, a thing with an already defined nature lined up within a general category of things with the same nature. Femininity is an essence, a set of general attributes that define a class, that restricts women to immanence and to being defined as the Other. Whereas a man exists as a transcending subject who defines his own individual projects, patriarchal institutions require a woman to be the object for the gaze and touch of a subject, to be the pliant responder to his commands.

Beauvoir discusses several respects in which femininity confines women's existence to immanence and the repetition of the species rather than individual existence. She finds female biology itself in part responsible for rooting women in immanence; women's reproductive processes limit their individual capacities for the sake of the needs of the species. But gender determines women's oppression more significantly than does biology. Whatever might be her position in the world and whatever her individual accomplishments, a women is appraised first *as a woman*, and only afterward for her position or accomplishments. Others will evaluate her beauty or lack of it; ascertain whether her clothes are tasteful and becoming; determine whether her smiles, gestures, and manner of speech exhibit charm. Whether a woman conforms to the requirements of feminine attractiveness, is indifferent to them, or rebels against them, both her and other people's attitudes toward her will be determined by this definition. Women have been barred from the important business of government and commerce, or from fashioning products that achieve recognition, and instead have been expected to expend most of their energy keeping a home for husband and children. From early childhood women learn that the world of individual achievement is closed to them and that their primary vocation is to please and serve men. Thus women learn to be deferential, accommodating, and attentive to the desires of others.

The expectations of femininity that circumscribe the lives of women inhibit the development of their possibilities. Beauvoir describes how in their childhood, girls learn early that the world of action and daring is closed to them, learn not to move freely and openly and do not develop an ability to fight.[2] Women's sexual being is clouded with masochism, a desire to love the strong actor but not to be actors themselves.[3] Women often become timid and lacking in confidence, or fear that success will conflict with their femininity.

More than merely inhibiting possibilities, in Beauvoir's account femininity often produces muti-

lated or deformed persons. In my view this is the most ingenious aspect of Beauvoir's account. She explains characteristics that many have found undesirable about women as the effects of imprisonment in femininity. Despite the culture's denial, women are subjects, full of creative energy, intelligence, and the desire to make their mark on the world. Patriarchal institutions, however, restrict their recognized activity to caring for their appearance, for a household, and for children. Women thus channel their creativity into these activities. They try to make a project out of turning themselves into mannequins; keeping a house clean, orderly, and pleasing; and rearing children. These activities, however, belong to immanence, to objectification and mere life maintenance. Trying to make them the freely chosen projects of a transcending subject only produces a monstrous caricature of expressiveness and individuality: the haughty vanity of a woman preoccupied with her image in the mirror; the shrewish woman who will not allow living action to occur in her house, for fear that it will soil the rug or knock over a plant; the clutching mother who tries to mold her child's life according to her own plan.

To summarize, Beauvoir defines women's oppression as the confinement and mutilation of women's potentialities by patriarchal requirements that she be a pleasing and deferential object for men. Unlike femininity, masculinity does not entail confinement to an essence or nature, but the freedom to make oneself and assert oneself in the world. Women's liberation consists of freeing women from the confines of traditional femininity and making it possible for women to pursue the projects that have hitherto been dominated by men.

While Beauvoir's book remains one of the most sensitive, thorough, and theoretically grounded descriptions of women's oppression under patriarchy, most feminists today find it deeply marred by at least two related factors: Beauvoir does not call into question the definition of being human that traditional Western society holds, and she devalues traditionally female activity in the same way as does patriarchal culture.

Beauvoir fiercely rails at the male privilege that restricts such transcendence to men, but she does not question the value of the activities through which men compete with one another and achieve recognition. Power, achievement, individual expression, rationality, mastery of natural processes are for her, as for the patriarchal culture she criticizes, the most human values. She is a socialist, of course, and therefore asserts that the achievement of full humanity by both men and women requires the elimination of capitalist domination. She calls for participation of women in these public world-making achievements but does not question the prominence that male-dominated society gives to achievement itself and to public activities of politics, competition, and individual creativity.

Beauvoir's humanism identifies the human with men. She points out in several places that whereas women experience a contradiction between being human and being feminine, men do not experience such a contradiction. The other side of her impressive and often sympathetic account of how patriarchy has victimized women is her description of the free subjectivity that she claims it gives to men. Boys roam, climb, play rough, and, very important for Beauvoir, learn to fight.

> Violence is the authentic proof of each one's loyalty to himself, to his passions, to his own will; radically to deny this will is to deny oneself any objective truth, it is to wall oneself up in an abstract subjectivity; anger or revolt that does not get into the muscles remains a figment of the imagination. It is a profound frustration not to be able to register one's feelings upon the face of the world. (p. 371)

Men are allowed, encouraged to be daring, to reach out and accomplish a project. Men are supposed to be rational, inventive, and creative. Thus, the great achievements of humanity have been accomplished almost entirely by men: exploring the world, charting and mapping it, formulating theories of the universe, writing great plays, developing constitutions and ruling cities and states. Even less-renowned or -accomplished men have a privilege not accorded to women, the privilege of being in public; they can achieve some public recognition in the workplace, among comrades or cronies at the bar. Men's situation allows or encourages them to be free subjects, transcending the given to bold new futures, confronting other subjects as equals.

The distinction between transcendence and immanence ensnares Beauvoir in the very definition of woman as a nonhuman Other, which her brilliant analysis reveals as patriarchal. Defining humanity as transcendence requires setting a human being in opposition to nonhuman objects and in particular nature. Fully human, free subjectivity transcends mere life, the processes of nature that repeat in an eternal cycle without individuality or history. Thus, risking life and being willing to kill are cardinal marks of humanity for Beauvoir as for Hegel. Taking control of one's needs and fashioning objects to satisfy them, confronting and mastering the forces of nature that threaten one's life or comfort—these are the aims of human projects.[4] Humanity achieves its greatest freedom, however, in the creation of moral ideals and works of art, for these express a wholly new and unnatural way of being in the world. Beauvoir's ontology reproduces the Western tradition's oppositions of nature and culture, freedom and mere life, spirit and body.

With those distinctions Beauvoir brilliantly shows that patriarchal culture has projected onto women all those aspects of human existence that participate in mere life. She does not, however (as Dinnerstein, rereading her later, does), call upon a transformation of culture in the direction of a greater acceptance of life, the body, and mortality.[5] Instead, she herself devalues women's lives insofar as she finds them closer to nature and the body than men's.

Beauvoir mirrors patriarchal culture in her exposition of the experiences of the female body. The young girl finds her puny clitoris less glorious than the boy's more apparent penis. At puberty girls react to menstruation with shame and disgust, though Beauvoir asserts this is due to the social status of femininity rather than to any natural reaction. Female sexuality is passive and masochistic:

> Feminine sex desire is the soft throbbing of a mollusk. Whereas a man is impetuous, woman is only impatient; her expectation can become ardent without ceasing to be passive; man dives upon his prey

like the eagle and the hawk; woman lies in wait like the carnivorous plant, the bog, in which insects and children are swallowed up. She is absorption, suction, humus, pitch and glue, a passive influx vaguely feels herself to be. (p. 431)[6]

Pregnancy is an "ordeal" (p. 559) in which the woman submits to the species and must suffer limitations on her capacity to individualize herself. Beauvoir expresses with understanding and sympathy how many women take pleasure in pregnancy and nursing. But clearly she regards such pleasures as examples of women's resignation to their condition of immanence, one among many ways women agree to relinquish their freedom.[7] That pregnancy itself can be a human project is impossible in her ontological framework.[8]

Beauvoir also devalues traditionally feminine activity, such as housework and mothering. The woman is imprisoned in her home, and since she is deprived there of activity, she loses herself in things and becomes dependent on them. Though she recognizes that housework and mothering are arduous and important tasks, in her account they have no truly human value. Housework has a negative basis: one gets rid of dirt, eliminates disorder, and in performing it the woman is condemned to endless repetition that results in no product, no work. Beauvoir finds cooking to be something of an exception here and explains that women thus rightly take pride in culinary achievements; but even these are only to be consumed, not to stand as lasting artifacts.

As a wife, the woman is abjectly dependent, not in control of her life. This makes her dangerous for rearing children, since she tends to be smotheringly possessive or brutally resentful. Even the best of mothers, in Beauvoir's account, do not attain transcendence—that is, full humanity—by caring for and loving their children; they only make it possible for their children to do so. Beauvoir thus devalues women's reproductive labor.[9]

Beauvoir's concrete descriptions of women's lives are full of insights, sympathy, and an understanding of the variations in each individual existence. (She does not, however, systematically examine variations in women's situation due to structural considerations such as class and race.) The overall picture she offers,

however, portrays woman only as victim—maimed, mutilated, dependent, confined to a life of immanence, and forced to be an object. She rarely describes the strength that women have had and the earthly value of their work: ways women have formed networks and societies among themselves, the lasting beauty of the caring social values women often exhibit. While she expresses outrage at the selfishness, blindness, and ruthlessness of the men who benefit from the mutilation of the personhood of half the human race, she finds little to criticize in the modern humanist conception of individuality and freedom.

II

Gynocentric feminism defines the oppression of women very differently from humanist feminism. Women's oppression consists not of being prevented from participating in full humanity, but of the denial and devaluation of specifically feminine virtues and activities by an overly instrumentalized and authoritarian masculinist culture. Unlike humanist feminism, gynocentric feminism does not focus its analysis on the impediments to women's self-development and the exclusion of women from spheres of power, prestige, and creativity. Instead, gynocentric feminism focuses its critique on the values expressed in the dominant social spheres themselves. The male-dominated activities with the greatest prestige in our society—politics, science, technology, warfare, business—threaten the survival of the planet and the human race. That our society accords these activities the highest value only indicates the deep perversity of patriarchal culture. Masculine values exalt death, violence, competition, selfishness, a repression of the body, sexuality, and affectivity.

Gynocentric feminism finds in women's bodies and traditionally feminine activity the source of more positive values. Women's reproductive processes keep us linked with nature and the promotion of life to a greater degree than men's. Female eroticism is more fluid, diffuse, and loving than violence-prone male sexuality. Our feminine socialization and traditional roles as mothers give to us a capacity to nurture and a sense of social cooperation that may be the only salvation of the planet. Gynocentric feminism thus defines the oppression of women quite differently from the way humanistic feminism defines it. Femininity is not the problem, not the source of women's oppression, but indeed within traditional femininity lie the values that we should promote for a better society. Women's oppression consists of the devaluation and repression of women's nature and female activity by the patriarchal culture.

In distinguishing between humanist feminism and gynocentric feminism I intend to mark out two tendencies or poles of feminism, which are held in various forms and degrees by different feminists. Feminism of the nineteenth century in the United States was marked by an oscillation between humanist and gynocentric feminism. For most of the period of the suffrage movement the humanist position prevailed, but the movements of moral motherhood and social housekeeping had a more gynocentric cast. In contemporary feminism both tendencies have been present, often in uneasy union. Nevertheless I think it is appropriate to distinguish periods of contemporary feminism when one of these tendencies has been stronger. Until the late 1970s feminism in the United States was predominantly humanist feminism, but in the mid- and late 1970s feminism has shifted more in the direction of gynocentrism.

The distinction between humanist feminism and gynocentric feminism cannot be mapped onto the more commonly held way of classifying feminism as liberal, radical, or socialist. The set of positions often referred to as liberal feminism is indeed a species of humanist feminism, and to the degree that these positions are still held by many feminists, humanist feminism is still a strong tendency among feminists. Many of those who called themselves radical feminists in the early and mid-'70s, however, asserted something similar to the humanist feminist position I have identified as Beauvoir's. They found women's oppression located primarily in confinement to femininity, which they claimed made women dependent on men and inhibited women's self-development, and they often called upon women to develop skills and attributes traditionally associated with men—

physical strength, mechanical ability, assertiveness, etc. Similarly, until recently most feminists who called themselves socialist feminists held humanist-feminist positions like that of Beauvoir. They took socialism as a necessary but not sufficient condition of the self-development of all human beings, and took the goal of feminism to be the elimination of gender differences and the requirements of femininity that inhibit the full development of women's capacities.

Starting about the mid- to late '70s, many of those called radical feminists and those called socialist feminists increasingly moved toward a more gynocentric feminism, and several of the writers treated in this section are self-identified socialist feminists. Those calling themselves radical feminists moved toward gynocentric analysis first, but by the late '70s this mode of feminism had become increasingly influential even among those who might in other ways be called liberal feminists. In the herstory of the contemporary women's movement I find at least three factors that have produced this shift from humanistic to gynocentric feminism: antifeminist reaction to feminism, the emergence of black feminism, and the development of women's history and feminist anthropology.

Antifeminists have identified feminism solely with humanist feminism. In their perception feminists eschew femininity, devalue traditional womanhood, and want to be equal to—that is, like, in identity with—men. Antifeminist women have sneered at such a naïve claim to eliminate difference and have argued without difficulty that treating men and women equally will often lead to injustice for women.[10] Early during the second wave of the women's movement, moreover, antifeminists protested what they regarded as feminist denigration of women. Many women take pride in the homes they decorate and bring warmth to and regard their caring for children as a noble vocation, they claimed. They dress well and do their hair to please themselves, not because men require it of them. How dare you feminists claim that these activities lack value, entail imprisonment?, they exclaimed. Furthermore, they asserted, we don't want to be like men—competitive, unfeeling, getting high blood pressure and ulcers at the office or cancer in the factory. Antifeminists still screech this line, even though contemporary feminism has changed considerably in response to such protests of antifeminist women.

One of the first jobs of black feminists was to attack the victim/dependent image of women's situation that held sway in the women's movement in the early '70s. Our women, they said, have rarely had the luxury to be housewives, kept relatively comfortably by men, having their capacity to act smothered by diapers, corsets, and girdles. On the contrary, to survive black women typically learned to be tough, physically strong, clever, but usually also warm, sexy, and nurturant. Black women have suffered endless injustice and humiliation, but it has not maimed their spirits, for they have acted with brilliance, courage, and righteousness.[11] Through such discussion the women's movement learned that the typical account of femininity as entailing weakness and dependence had a class and race bias.

The work of feminist historians also promoted awareness of the differences in women's situations and the historical specificity of bourgeois femininity, as well as a sense of women as active participants in history. We discovered the mother rulers of Mycenae and the wisdom of the witches. We found that in most cultures women's work contributes as much as or more than men's work does to the subsistence of the family and village, and we recovered the contributions women have made to agricultural development, diplomacy, healing, art, literature, music, philosophy. We reconstructed the lives of peasant and proletariat women and saw them as providing crucial strength and foci of resistance for dominated classes. From the protests of some feminists against the humanist image of women as forced to be inactive and less than human, and from these concrete studies of women's lives and action, a new focus on the positivity of women's culture was born.

Gynocentric feminism has received a number of expressions in the United States women's movement in recent years. Artists and poets have been among the leaders in developing images of celebration of this more positive understanding of women's history and contemporary self-understanding. Judy Chicago's *The Dinner Party*, for example, laboriously and beautifully recovers whole aspects of women's history and locates them within images of female genitalia and objects that rely on traditionally female arts.

Within the sphere of political activism, gynocentric feminism perhaps is best represented in the feminist antimilitarist and ecology movements of the past five years. In the Women's Pentagon Action or the action at the Seneca Army Depot, for example, a major aspect of the political protest has been the use of symbols and actions that invoke traditional labor, such as weaving, spinning, birthing, mothering. Feminist antimilitarist and ecological analysis has argued that the dangers to the planet that have been produced by the nuclear arms race and industrial technology are essentially tied to masculinist values.[12] The burgeoning movement of feminist spirituality entails a similar analysis and promotes values associated with traditional femininity.

A number of prominent recent theories of contemporary feminism express a gynocentric feminism. I see Susan Griffin's *Woman and Nature*[13] as one of the first written statements of gynocentric feminism in the second wave. It shows that one of the first steps of gynocentrism is to deny the nature/culture dichotomy held by humanists such as Beauvoir and to affirmatively assert the connection of women and nature. Daly's *Gyn/Ecology*[14] I see as a transition work. In it Daly asserts an analysis of the victimization of women by femininity that outdoes Beauvoir, but she also proposes a new gynocentric language.

Carol Gilligan's critique of male theories of moral development has had a strong influence on the formation of gynocentric analysis.[15] She questions dominant assumptions about moral valuation and affirms forms of moral reasoning associated with traditional femininity. Following Chodorow, she argues that gender socialization creates in women a relational communal orientation toward others, while it creates in men a more oppositional and competitive mode of relating to others. These gender differences produce two different forms of moral rationality: a masculine ethic of rights and justice, and a feminine ethic of responsibility and care. Traditional moral theory has ignored and repressed the particularistic ethic of care as being pre-moral. Women's moral oppression consists of being measured against male standards, according to Gilligan, in the silencing of women's different voice. The dominance of those male centered values of abstract reasoning, instrumentality, and individualism, moreover, produce a cold, uncaring, competitive world. Both the liberation of women and the restructuring of social relations require tempering these values with the communally oriented values derived from women's ethic of care.[16] While Gilligan herself would reject the label of gynocentric feminist, her work has exerted an enormous influence on feminists in fields as diverse as mathematics and philosophy, providing the foundation for a revaluation of attributes associated with femininity.

Mary O'Brien[17] articulates a gynocentric critique of traditional political theory starting from the biological fact that the reproductive process gives women a living continuity with their offspring that it does not give men. Women thus have a temporal consciousness that is continuous, whereas male temporal consciousness is discontinuous. Arising from the alienation from the child they experience in the reproductive process, masculine thought emphasizes dualism and separation. Men establish a public realm in which they give spiritual birth to a second nature, transcending the private realm of mere physicality and reproduction to which they confine women. Patriarchy develops an ideology of the male potency principle, which installs the father as ruler of the family and men as rulers of society, and substitutes an intellectual notion of creativity for the female principle of life generation. The contemporary women's movement has the potential to overturn such a conception of politics that is separated from life continuity because out of female reproductive consciousness can come a politics based on women's experience of life processes and species continuity.

Nancy Hartsock's theory of the feminist standpoint from which she analyzes patriarchal culture is a more sweeping version of gynocentric feminism. She argues that the sexual division of labor provides men and women with differing experiences that structure different standpoints upon nature and social relations.

Based on Chodorow's theory of the development of gender personalities, Hartsock argues that men experience the relation of self and other as one of hostility and struggle. The sexual division of labor also removes men from the needs of the body, from the vulnerability and basic demands of children and the aged, and provides men with an instrumentally calculative relation to nature. This division of labor, she argues, produces a way of thinking about the world that Hartsock calls abstract masculinity, which organizes experience and social relations into binary oppositions in which one term carries greater value than the other. This standpoint of abstract masculinity has determined the primary structure of Western social relations and culture. This male dominated culture's values are both partial and perverse. It embodies sexuality where desire for fusion with the other takes the form of domination of the other. Masculine consciousness denies and fears the body and associates birth with death. The only sense of community generated by abstract masculinity, moreover, is the community of warriors in preparation for combat.

From women's experience, Hartsock claims, we can both criticize masculinist values and conceptualization and develop a better vision of social relations. The gender personalities women develop in relation to their mothers give them a propensity to feel more connected with others than men do. The experiences of menstruation, coitus, pregnancy, and lactation, which challenge body boundaries, give women a greater experience of continuity with nature. Women's labor in caring for men and children and producing basic values in the home, finally, gives them a greater rootedness in nature than men's work gives them, a more basic understanding of life processes. These attributes of women's experience can ground, Hartsock argues, a form of conceptualization that does not depend on dichotomous thinking and that values connections among persons more than their separation, as does abstract masculinity.[18]

While Sara Ruddick is careful to claim that any recovery and revaluation of traditionally feminine attributes must be infused with a feminist politics, her notion of maternal thinking provides another example of a gynocentric feminist analysis. She argues that the specific daily practices of mothering generate specific modes of thinking motivated by the interests in preservation, growth, and the acceptability of the child to the society. Maternal practice is not restricted to mothers, but exists wherever such nurturing and preservation interests prevail. She suggests that maternal thinking provides antimilitarist values that feminists can use in promoting a politics of peace.[19]

Writing within a very different intellectual current from American feminists, using rather different assumptions and style, several women in France in recent years have developed distinctive versions of gynocentric feminism. I shall mention only Luce Irigaray and Julia Kristeva. Like a number of other contemporary French thinkers, Irigaray describes phallocentric culture as preoccupied by a metaphysics of identity dominated by visual metaphors. Male thinking begins by positing the One, the same, the essence, that generates binary oppositions in which the second term is defined by the first as what it is not, thus reducing it to its identity. Phallogocentric discourse defines the opposition male/female in just this way—woman is only not a man, a lack, a deficiency. Preoccupied with the straight, the true, the proper, men establish relations of property and exchange in which accounts are balanced. Women in the phallocentric system have been silenced and separated, exchanged as goods among men. Irigaray proposes that women must find and speak the specificity of female desire, which has completely different values from those of phallic thinking. Women's eroticism is neither one nor two but plural, as women's bodies themselves experience arousal and pleasure in a multiplicity of places that cannot all be identified. Touch, not sight, predominates, the autoeroticism of vaginal lips touching clitoris, of intimate bodies touching. A genuinely feminine language moves and twists, starts over again from different perspectives, does not go straight to the point. Such a language can displace the sterility and oppressiveness of phallogocentric categorization.[20]

Kristeva also focuses on language and the repression of specifically female experience. Language has two moments: the symbolic, the capacity of language to represent and define, to be literal; and the semiotic,

those elements of language that slip and play in ambiguities and nuance. Certain linguistic practices, such as poetry, make most explicit use of the semiotic, but for the most part the playful, the musical in language is repressed in Western culture and the symbolic, rational, legalistic discourse rules. For Kristeva this repression concerns the repression of the body and the installation of order, hierarchy, and authority. Repression of the body and the semiotic entails repression of the pre-oedipal experience of the maternal body before the subject emerges with a self-identical ego, as well as denial by the culture of the specificity and difference that the female body exhibits. Challenge to the dominant oppressions, to capitalism, racism, sexism, must come not only from specific demands within the political arena, but also from changing the speaking subject.

Kristeva finds in the repressed feminine the potential for such change, where feminine means at least two things: first, women's specific experience as female bodies, the daughters of mothers, and often mothers themselves, an experience of a decentered subject; second, the aspects of language and behavior Western culture has devalued and repressed: the poetic, rhythmic, musical, nurturant, and soothing, but also contradictory and shifting ways of being, that fickleness that women have been accused of. This revolution of the feminine Kristeva finds in a number of male avant-garde writers. The women's movement, however, also carries the possibility of displacing the rigidity of a subject that loves authority, provided that women do not fall into that humanist feminism by which they simply demand to get in on the masculinist power game.[21]

To summarize, humanist feminism defines femininity as the source of women's oppression and calls upon male-dominated institutions to allow women the opportunity to participate fully in public world-making activities of industry, politics, art, and science. In contrast, gynocentric feminism questions the values of these traditional public activities that have been dominated by men. Women's oppression consists not of being prevented from participating in full humanity, but of the denial and devaluation of specifically feminine virtues and activities by an overly instrumentalized and authoritarian masculinist culture. Femininity is not the problem for gynocentric feminism, and indeed is the source of a conception of society and the subject that can not only liberate women, but also all persons.

III

The polarity between humanist and gynocentric feminism might be considered part of the logic of feminism itself. Feminism consists of calling attention to and eradicating gender-based oppression. Humanism and gynocentrism are the two most obvious positions to take in that struggle. Either feminism means that we seek for women the same opportunities and privileges the society gives to men, or feminism means that we assert the distinctive value of womanhood against patriarchal denigration. While these positions need not be mutually exclusive, there is a strong tendency for both feminists and nonfeminists to make them so: Either we want to be like men or we don't.

I think that contemporary gynocentric feminism has a number of aspects that make it a better analysis than humanist feminism. At the same time, I think the swing toward gynocentrism has left behind some important elements of feminist politics that humanist feminism has emphasized. We need to rethink our analysis, not to form a synthesis of the two, but to cook up a better mixture out of some of the old ingredients.

Since it was first uttered in the eighteenth century, humanist feminism has assumed the liberation of women as an extension of the values of liberalism. The ideal of universal humanity—that all persons have equal rights whatever their station or class—should be extended to women. To be sure, many humanist feminists, such as Beauvoir, have been socialists and have called for radical transformation of economic and political institutions. The argument for such socialism, however, is that only publicly controlled and democratic economic and political institutions will make it possible to realize the ideal of equality and self-development promised by liber-

alism. Even socialist versions of humanist feminism, then, stand in continuity with the modern humanist tradition insofar as it seeks to realize the values articulated by that tradition for all persons, including and especially women.[22]

Gynocentric feminism confronts humanist feminism on one of its core assumptions, namely, that the ideal for feminists is a universal humanity in which all persons equally realize their potential for self-development. Nearly every term in this sentence can be put to gynocentric feminist critique, but I will restrict myself to the notion of universal humanity. In the humanist feminist view uttered by Beauvoir, differences between men and women are socially enforced oppressions. In their humanity there is no essential difference between men and women, and we look forward to a society in which sex difference will make no difference.

Gynocentric feminism can reveal this ideal of universal humanity as both unrealistic and oppressive. This ideal proposes to measure all persons according to the formal standards of rationality and rights. But the material differences among persons determined by history, region, or bodies continue to operate, so some will measure differently. Only an explicit affirmation of difference and social plurality, gynocentric feminism suggests, offers the hope of overcoming sexism, racism, ethnic oppression. Such affirmation of difference is difficult and threatening, however, because it challenges modes of individual and community self-identification.

As I already pointed out in discussing Beauvoir, humanist feminism focuses its investigation primarily on women's situation and criticizes patriarchy because of its specifically destructive effect on women's lives, without questioning the dominant culture's basic assumptions about the good human life. Gynocentric feminism, on the other hand, takes a much broader look at our society. It seeks to uncover and throw into question some of the most basic assumptions of the Western tradition of thought of which modern humanism is a part—the distinction between nature and culture, spirit and body, the universal and particular. Gynocentric feminism links masuclinist culture's equation of humanity with rationality, on the one hand, and to the repression of life spontaneity and the development of an oppressive web of social controls and organizational hierarchy, on the other. In these ways it is similar to and stands in the same category with critiques of Western culture uttered by Nietzsche, Adorno and Horkheimer, Foucault and Derrida.

As a result of its greater comprehensiveness, gynocentric feminism broadens its critique of our society beyond focus on specifically sexist institutions and practices and specific damage to women. Because it brings feminist critique to basic assumptions of the society as a whole, gynocentric feminism offers for the first time distinctively feminist analyses of social structures and forms of symbolization not tied to women in particular—such as racism, classism, the military, or the state. This has produced a broadened politics in which feminists participate as feminists in ecological, antimilitarist, antiracist struggles. Unlike humanist feminism, that is, gynocentric feminism has developed a perspective from which to criticize any institution or practice in our society, even if it does not distinguish women's specific oppression.

While gynocentric feminism is deeply radical in these ways, it also harbors some dangers to radical politics. Turning to femininity as the source of values by which to criticize patriarchal culture and form the image of a better society seems to lead to a disturbing essentialism. By "essentialism" I mean an account that theorizes women as a category with a set of essential attributes. O'Brien states that she describes the structure of womanhood in her articulation of the female mode of reproductive consciousness. Hartsock acknowledges historical and situational differences among women, but claims that feminist theory requires identifying common attributes of women's experience. Gynocentric feminists find these attributes in the same place as has patriarchy—in women's reproductive biology and the activity of mothering. Feminist antimilitarist and ecological analysis finds women more in touch with nature than men are because of the cycles and changes of our bodies, and more peace-loving because our nurturing impulses foster in us a love of life.

French theorists explicitly criticize feminist tendencies toward essentialism. On this account many of them reject the label "feminist." They fear replacing humanism, where universal humanity is projected as an ideal, with universal womanhood. "Woman" is a fiction, a metaphysical attempt to bring multiplicity into unity. The French theorists I have referred to nevertheless share some of the essentialist tendencies of gynocentric feminism in the United States. They rely on an opposition between the masculine and the feminine, even where, as in Kristeva, they do not necessarily associate these with men and women. Though these theories explicitly question Western dichotomous thinking, their use of the opposition of masculinity and femininity retains its traditional dichotomous terms, in revaluated form: the masucline is power, discursive rationality, calculation, abstraction, while the feminine is desire, sensuality, poetic language, immediacy of contact with nature. Like their counterparts across the ocean, these French theorists tend to reduce women's specificity to reproductive biology and the function of mothering,[23] though in some of her writing Irigaray reaches toward a woman-to-woman relation beyond the mother-daughter cycle.

Gynocentrism's most important contribution is its affirmation of difference against humanism's claim of a universal humanity. Gynocentric feminism, however, still tends to see gender difference as a relation of inside and outside. We need a conception of difference that is less like the icing bordering the layers of cake, however, and more like a marble cake, in which the flavors remain recognizably different but thoroughly insinuated in one another.

Gynocentric feminism has rightly restored dignity to the character of women, shown how within our confined roles and despite often severe domination by men, we have made new things, contributed to historical events, struggled actively against our oppression, and formed networks of solidarity. It has been especially necessary to topple the stance of women as victims, weak, passive, and only partial human beings.

In its effort to recover self-respect, agency, and authentic subjectivity of women by finding greater value in traditional women's culture than in the dominant masculinist culture, however, gynocentric feminism tends to swing too far away from understanding women as confined or enslaved. It rejects too completely the Beauvorian claim that femininity inhibits, distorts, and mutilates women's lives. Gilligan's accent on women's traditional sovereignty in the private realm, where she cares for each person in her particularity, for example, fails to note how this ethic of care often leads women to a sacrificing stance that can make us easily hurt.

The gynocentric revaluation of traditional femininity can weaken the claim that women are oppressed. If women's labor has been as creative or more so than men's labor is, if women's networks and relations with children have been the source of values more life-giving than the public activities of men are, if female desire is more playful, less rigid than male desire is, what warrants the claim that women need liberating? To be sure, all gynocentric feminists find that men rule society and in so doing devalue and repress this feminine sphere. Such a way of conceptualizing male domination, however, mutes the outrage against injustice that humanist feminism exhibits because it claims that women are not simply devalued, but also damaged, by male domination.

Gynocentric feminism, moreover, tends to reject too categorically the value of the activities and ambitions traditionally associated with masculinity. Men have traditionally reserved for themselves the public activities of political position, recognized artist, inventor, or scientist, and have recognized only other men worthy to compete for the accolades that reward excellence. If the activities that men have dominated really are less valuable than those in which women have traditionally engaged, as gynocentric feminism suggests, of what does male privilege consist? The other side of gynocentrism's denial of the damaging consequences of femininity is its denial of the growth-promoting aspects of traditional masculinity. If we claim that masculinity distorts men more than it contributes to their self-development and capacities, again, the claim that women are the victims of injustice loses considerable force.

Within the context of antifeminist backlash, the effect of gynocentric feminism may be accommodating to the existing structure. Gynocentric feminism relies on and reinforces gender stereotypes at just the time when the dominant culture has put new emphasis on marks of gender difference. It does so, moreover, by relying on many of those aspects of women's traditional sphere that traditional patriarchal ideology has most exploited and that humanist feminists such as Beauvoir found most oppressive—reproductive biology, motherhood, domestic concerns. Even though its intentions are subversive, such renewed attention to traditional femininity can have a reactionary effect on both ourselves and our listeners because it may echo the dominant claim that women belong in a separate sphere.

Humanist feminism calls upon patriarchal society to open places for women within those spheres of human activity that have been considered the most creative, powerful, and prestigious. Gynocentric feminism replies that wanting such things for women implies a recognition that such activities are the most humanly valuable. It argues that in fact, militarism, bureaucratic hierarchy, competition for recognition, and the instrumentalization of nature and people entailed by these activities are basic disvalues.[24]

Yet in contemporary society, men still have most institutionalized power, and gynocentric feminism shows why they do not use it well. If feminism turns its back on the centers of power, privilege, and individual achievement that men have monopolized, those men will continue to monopolize them, and nothing significant will change. Feminists cannot undermine masculinist values without entering some of the centers of power that foster them, but the attainment of such power itself requires at least appearing to foster those values. Still, without being willing to risk such co-optation, feminism can be only a moral position of critique rather than a force for institutional change.

Despite its intention, I fear that gynocentric feminism may have the same consequence as the stance of moral motherhood that grew out of nineteenth century feminism: a resegregation of women to a specifically women's sphere, outside the sites of power, privilege, and recognition. For me the symptom here is what the dominant culture finds more threatening. Within the dominant culture a middle-aged assertive woman's claim to co-anchor the news alongside a man appears considerably more threatening than women's claim to have a different voice that exposes masculinist values as body-denying and selfish. The claim of women to have a right to the positions and benefits that have hitherto been reserved for men, and that male dominated institutions should serve women's needs, is a direct threat to male privilege. While the claim that these positions of power themselves should be eliminated and the institutions eliminated or restructured is indeed more radical, when asserted from the gynocentric feminist position it can be an objective retreat.

Gynocentrism's focus on values and language as the primary target of its critique contributes to this blunting of its political force. Without doubt, social change requires changing the subject, which in turn means developing new ways of speaking, writing, and imagining. Equally indubitable is the gynocentric feminist claim that masculinist values in Western culture deny the body, sensuality, and rootedness in nature and that such denial nurtures fascism, pollution, and nuclear games. Given these facts, however, what shall we do? To this gynocentrism has little concrete answer. Because its criticism of existing society is so global and abstract, gynocentric critique of the values, language, and culture of masculinism can remove feminist theory from analysis of specific institutions and practices, and how they might be concretely structurally changed in directions more consonant with our visions.

NOTES

1. Simone de Beauvoir, *The Second Sex*, H. M. Parshley, trans. (New York: Random House, 1952); page citations from the 1974 Vintage paperback edition appear in the text.

2. See my paper "Throwing Like a Girl," in Young, *Throwing Like a Girl and Other Essays in Feminist Philosophy and Social Theory* (Bloomington, In: Indiana Univ. Press, 1990). On the issue of assertiveness of the female body.

3. On femininity and masochism, compare Sandra Bartky, "Feminine Masochism and the Politics of Personal Transformation," *Women's Studies International Forum*, vol. 7, no. 5 (1984), pp. 323–34.

4. Nancy Hartsock, *Money, Sex and Power: Toward a Feminist Historical Materialism* (New York: Longman, 1983), appendix 2.

5. Dorothy Dinnerstein, *The Mermaid and the Minotaur* (New York: Harper and Row, 1976).

6. On Beauvoir's views of female sexuality, see Jo-Ann Pilardi, "Female Eroticism in the Works of Simone de Beauvoir," in Allen and Young, ed., *The Thinking Muse: Feminism and Modern French Philosophy* (Bloomington: Indiana University Press, 1989), pp. 18–34.

7. See Mary O'Brien, *The Politics of Reproduction* (Boston: Routledge and Kegan Paul, 1981), pp. 67–76.

8. For an understanding of pregnancy as a woman's project, see my paper "Pregnant Embodiment," in Young, op. cit.

9. Alison Jaggar and William McBride argue for this claim in their essay "'Reproduction' As Male Ideology," *Women's Studies International Forum*, vol. 8, no. 3 (1985), pp. 185–96.

10. See, for example, Elizabeth G. Wolgast, *Equality and the Rights of Women* (Ithaca, N.Y.: Cornell University Press, 1978).

11. For two excellent examples of accounts of the strength of black women, see Carol B. Stack, *All Our Kin: Strategies for Survival in a Black Community* (New York: Harper and Row, 1975); and Angela Davis, *Women, Race and Class* (New York: Random House, 1981).

12. Lyn Blumenthal, et al., ed., *Heresies: A Feminist Publication of Art and Politics*, vol. 4, no. 1 (1981); this entire issue is devoted to articles and art works about feminism, environmentalism, and militarism; see also I. M. Young, "Review Essay: Feminism and Ecology," *Environmental Ethics*, vol. 5, no. 2 (1983), pp. 174–79.

13. Susan Griffin, *Woman and Nature: The Roaring Inside Her* (New York: Harper and Row, 1978).

14. Mary Daly, *Gyn/Ecology* (Boston: Beacon Press, 1978).

15. Carol Gilligan, *In a Different Voice* (Cambridge, Mass.: Harvard University Press, 1981).

16. See Carol Gould, "Private Rights and Public Virtues: Women, the Family and Democracy," in Carol Gould, ed., *Beyond Domination: New Perspectives on Women and Philosophy* (Totowa, N.J.: Rowman and Allenheld, 1983).

17. O'Brien, op. cit.

18. Hartsock, op. cit., especially chapter 10.

19. Sara Ruddick, "Maternal Thinking," *Feminist Studies*, vol. 6, no. 2 (1980), pp. 342–67; and "Preservative Love and Military Destruction," in Joyce Trebilcot, ed.,

Mothering: Essays in Feminist Theory (Totowa, N.J.: Rowman and Allenheld, 1984). pp. 231–62.

20. Irigaray's best text, in my opinion, is *Speculum of the Other Woman* (Ithaca, N.Y.: Cornell University Press, 1985), but the above remarks are also based on the important essays in *This Sex Which Is Not One* (Ithaca, N.Y.: Cornell University Press, 1985). For useful responses to Irigaray, see Jane Gallop, *The Daughter's Seduction* (Ithaca, N.Y.: Cornell University Press, 1981); Elizabeth L. Berg, "The Third Woman," *Diacritics*, vol. 12, no. 2 (1982), pp. 11–20; and Eleanor Kuykendall, "Toward an Ethic of Nurturance: Luce Irigaray on Mothering and Power," in Trebilcot, op. cit., pp. 263–74.

21. For this account of Kristeva I am relying on the following texts primarily: "The Ethics of Linguistics," "From One Identity to an Other," "The Novel as Polylogue," and "Motherhood According to Giovanni Bellini," all in *Desire in Language*, Leon S. Roudiez, ed. (New York: Columbia University Press, 1980); "Woman Can Never Be Defined," in Marks and de Courtivron, ed., *New French Feminism* (New York: Schocken Books, 1981); and "Women's Time," *Signs*, vol. 7, no. 1 (1981), pp. 5–12.

22. See Zillah Eisenstein, *The Radical Future of Liberal Feminism* (New York: Longman, 1980).

23. For a critical look at the use of mother as metaphor by French theorists, see Donma Stanton, "Difference on Trial: A Critique of the Maternal Metaphor in Cixous, Irigaray, and Kristeva," in Allen and Young, ed., op. cit, pp. 156–79.

24. Kathy E. Ferguson, "Feminism and Bureaucratic Discourse," *New Political Science*, vol. 11 (1983), pp. 53–73.

Study Questions

1. According to Young, how does "humanist feminism" define women's oppression?

2. Summarize briefly two of Young's criticisms of humanist feminism.

3. According to Young, how does "gynocentric feminism" define women's oppression?

4. Give one example of a gynocentric approach to a feminist issue.

5. Summarize briefly two strengths Young claims for gynocentric feminism, relative to humanist feminism.

6. Young writes that gynocentric feminism can be "quieting and accommodating to official powers." To what concerns about gynocentric feminism is she alluding in this phrase?

Jane Addams

Women and Public Housekeeping, 1913

A city is in many respects a great business corporation, but in other respects it is enlarged housekeeping. If American cities have failed in the first, partly because officeholders have carried with them the predatory instinct learned in competitive business, and cannot help "working a good thing" when they have an opportunity, may we not say that city housekeeping has failed partly because women, the traditional housekeepers, have not been consulted as to its multiform activities? The men of the city have been carelessly indifferent to much of its civic housekeeping, as they have always been indifferent to the details of the household. They have totally disregarded a candidate's capacity to keep the streets clean, preferring to consider him in relation to the national tariff or to the necessity for increasing the national navy, in a pure spirit of reversion to the traditional type of government, which had to do only with enemies and outsiders.

It is difficult to see what military prowess has to do with the multiform duties which, in a modern city, include the care of parks and libraries, superintendence of markets, sewers and bridges, the inspection of provisions and boilers, and the proper disposal of garbage. It has nothing to do with the building department, which the city maintains that it may see to it that the basements are dry, that the bedrooms are large enough to afford the required cubic feet of air, that the plumbing is sanitary, that the gas pipes do not leak, that the tenement house court is large enough to afford light and ventilation, that the stairways are fireproof. The ability to carry arms has nothing to do with the health department maintained by the city, which provides that children are vaccinated, that contagious diseases are isolated and placarded, that the spread of tuberculosis is curbed, that the water is free from typhoid infection. Certainly the military conception of society is remote from the functions of the school boards, whose concern it is that children are educated, that they are supplied with kindergartens, and are given a decent place in which to play. The very multifariousness and complexity of a city government demand the help of minds accustomed to detail and variety of work, to a sense of obligation for the health and welfare of young children, and to responsibility for the cleanliness and comfort of other people.

Because all these things have traditionally been in the hands of women, if they take no part in them now they are not only missing the education which the natural participation in civic life would bring to them, but they are losing what they have always had. From the beginning of tribal life, they have been held responsible for the health of the community, a function which is now represented by the health department. From the days of the cave dwellers, so far as the home was clean and wholesome, it was due to their efforts, which are now represented by the Bureau of Tenement House Inspection. From the period of the primitive village, the only public sweeping which was performed was what they undertook in their divers dooryards, that which is now represented by the Bureau of Street Cleaning. Most of the departments in a modern city can be traced to woman's traditional activity; but, in spite of this, so soon as these old affairs were turned over to the city they slipped from woman's hands, apparently because they then became matters for collective action and implied the use of the franchise—because the franchise had in the first instance been given to the man who could fight, because in the beginning he alone could vote who could carry a weapon, it was considered an improper thing for a woman to possess it.

Is it quite public spirited for woman to say, "We will take care of these affairs so long as they stay in our own houses, but if they go outside and concern so many people that they cannot be carried on without the mechanism of the vote, we will drop them; it is true that these activities which women have always had are not at present being carried on very well by the men in most of the great American cities, but, because we do not consider it 'lady-like' to vote, we will let them alone?"

Study Questions

1. What is Addams's argument in support of women's involvement in running cities?

2. Does Addams's argument rely on essentializing beliefs about women?

3. In what sense can Addams be read as utilizing a difference/gynocentric approach?

Audre Lorde

Uses of the Erotic: The Erotic as Power

There are many kinds of power, used and unused, acknowledged or otherwise. The erotic is a resource within each of us that lies in a deeply female and spiritual plane, firmly rooted in the power of our unexpressed or unrecognized feeling. In order to perpetuate itself, every oppression must corrupt or distort those various sources of power within the culture of the oppressed that can provide energy for change. For women, this has meant a suppression of the erotic as a considered source of power and information within our lives.

We have been taught to suspect this resource, vilified, abused, and devalued within western society. On the one hand, the superficially erotic has been encouraged as a sign of female inferiority; on the other hand, women have been made to suffer and to feel both contemptible and suspect by virtue of its existence.

It is a short step from there to the false belief that only by the suppression of the erotic within our lives and consciousness can women be truly strong. But that strength is illusory, for it is fashioned within the context of male models of power.

As women, we have come to distrust that power which rises from our deepest and nonrational knowledge. We have been warned against it all our lives by the male world, which values this depth of feeling enough to keep women around in order to exercise it in the service of men, but which fears this same depth too much to examine the possibilities of it within themselves. So women are maintained at a distant/inferior position to be psychically milked, much the same way ants maintain colonies of aphids to provide a life-giving substance for their masters.

But the erotic offers a well of replenishing and provocative force to the woman who does not fear its revelation, nor succumb to the belief that sensation is enough.

The erotic has often been misnamed by men and used against women. It has been made into the confused, the trivial, the psychotic, the plasticized sensation. For this reason, we have often turned away from the exploration and consideration of the erotic as a source of power and information, confusing it with its opposite, the pornographic. But pornography is a direct denial of the power of the erotic, for it represents the suppression of true feeling. Pornography emphasizes sensation without feeling.

The erotic is a measure between the beginnings of our sense of self and the chaos of our strongest feelings. It is an internal sense of satisfaction to which, once we have experienced it, we know we can aspire. For having experienced the fullness of this depth of feeling and recognizing its power, in honor and self-respect we can require no less of ourselves.

It is never easy to demand the most from ourselves, from our lives, from our work. To encourage excellence is to go beyond the encouraged mediocrity of our society. But giving in to the fear of feeling and working to capacity is a luxury only the unintentional can afford, and the unintentional are those who do not wish to guide their own destinies.

This internal requirement toward excellence which we learn from the erotic must not be misconstrued as demanding the impossible from ourselves nor from others. Such a demand incapacitates everyone in the process. For the erotic is not a question only of what we do; it is a question of how acutely and fully we can feel in the doing. Once we know the extent to which we are capable of feeling that sense of satisfaction and completion, we can then observe which of our various life endeavors bring us closest to that fullness.

The aim of each thing which we do is to make our lives and the lives of our children richer and more possible. Within the celebration of the erotic in all our endeavors, my work becomes a conscious decision—a longed-for bed which I enter gratefully and from which I rise up empowered.

Of course, women so empowered are dangerous. So we are taught to separate the erotic demand from most vital areas of our lives other than sex. And the lack of concern for the erotic root and satisfactions of our work is felt in our disaffection from so much of what we do. For instance, how often do we truly love our work even at its most difficult?

The principal horror of any system which defines the good in terms of profit rather than in terms of human need, or which defines human need to the exclusion of the psychic and emotional components of that need—the principal horror of such a system is that it robs our work of its erotic value, its erotic power and life appeal and fulfillment. Such a system reduces work to a travesty of necessities, a duty by which we earn bread or oblivion for ourselves and those we love. But this is tantamount to blinding a painter and then telling her to improve her work, and to enjoy the act of painting. It is not only next to impossible, it is also profoundly cruel.

As women, we need to examine the ways in which our world can be truly different. I am speaking here of the necessity for reassessing the quality of all the aspects of our lives and of our work, and of how we move toward and through them.

The very word *erotic* comes from the Greek word *eros*, the personification of love in all its aspects— born of Chaos, and personifying creative power and harmony. When I speak of the erotic, then, I speak of it as an assertion of the lifeforce of women; of that creative energy empowered, the knowledge and use of which we are now reclaiming in our language, our history, our dancing, our loving, our work, our lives.

There are frequent attempts to equate pornography and eroticism, two diametrically opposed uses of the sexual. Because of these attempts, it has become fashionable to separate the spiritual (psychic and emotional) from the political, to see them as contradictory or antithetical. "What do you mean, a poetic revolutionary, a meditating gunrunner?" In the same way, we have attempted to separate the spiritual and the erotic, thereby reducing the spiritual to a world of flattened affect, a world of the ascetic who aspires to feel nothing. But nothing is farther from the truth. For the ascetic position is one of the highest fear, the gravest immobility. The severe abstinence of the ascetic becomes the ruling obsession. And it is one not of self-discipline but of self-abnegation.

The dichotomy between the spiritual and the political is also false, resulting from an incomplete attention to our erotic knowledge. For the bridge which connects them is formed by the erotic—the sensual— those physical, emotional, and psychic expressions of what is deepest and strongest and richest within each of us, being shared: the passions of love, in its deepest meanings.

Beyond the superficial, the considered phrase, "It feels right to me," acknowledges the strength of the erotic into a true knowledge, for what that means is the first and most powerful guiding light toward any understanding. And understanding is a handmaiden which can only wait upon, or clarify, that knowledge,

deeply born. The erotic is the nurturer or nursemaid of all our deepest knowledge.

The erotic functions for me in several ways, and the first is in providing the power which comes from sharing deeply any pursuit with another person. The sharing of joy, whether physical, emotional, psychic, or intellectual, forms a bridge between the sharers which can be the basis for understanding much of what is not shared between them, and lessens the threat of their difference.

Another important way in which the erotic connection functions is the open and fearless underlining of my capacity for joy. In the way my body stretches to music and opens into response, hearkening to its deepest rhythms, so every level upon which I sense also opens to the erotically satisfying experience, whether it is dancing, building a bookcase, writing a poem, examining an idea.

That self-connection shared is a measure of the joy which I know myself to be capable of feeling, a reminder of my capacity for feeling. And that deep and irreplaceable knowledge of my capacity for joy comes to demand from all of my life that it be lived within the knowledge that such satisfaction is possible, and does not have to be called *marriage*, nor *god*, nor *an afterlife*.

This is one reason why the erotic is so feared, and so often relegated to the bedroom alone, when it is recognized at all. For once we begin to feel deeply all the aspects of our lives, we begin to demand from ourselves and from our life-pursuits that they feel in accordance with that joy which we know ourselves to be capable of. Our erotic knowledge empowers us, becomes a lens through which we scrutinize all aspects of our existence, forcing us to evaluate those aspects honestly in terms of their relative meaning within our lives. And this is a grave responsibility, projected from within each of us, not to settle for the convenient, the shoddy, the conventionally expected, nor the merely safe.

During World War II, we bought sealed plastic packets of white, uncolored margarine, with a tiny, intense pellet of yellow coloring perched like a topaz just inside the clear skin of the bag. We would leave the margarine out for a while to soften, and then we would pinch the little pellet to break it inside the bag, releasing the rich yellowness into the soft pale mass of margarine. Then taking it carefully between our fingers, we would knead it gently back and forth, over and over, until the color had spread throughout the whole pound bag of margarine, thoroughly coloring it.

I find the erotic such a kernel within myself. When released from its intense and constrained pellet, it flows through and colors my life with a kind of energy that heightens and sensitizes and strengthens all my experience.

We have been raised to fear the *yes* within ourselves, our deepest cravings. But, once recognized, those which do not enhance our future lose their power and can be altered. The fear of our desires keeps them suspect and indiscriminately powerful, for to suppress any truth is to give it strength beyond endurance. The fear that we cannot grow beyond whatever distortions we may find within ourselves keeps us docile and loyal and obedient, externally defined, and leads us to accept many facets of our oppression as women.

When we live outside ourselves, and by that I mean on external directives only rather than from our internal knowledge and needs, when we live away from those erotic guides from within ourselves, then our lives are limited by external and alien forms, and we conform to the needs of a structure that is not based on human need, let alone an individual's. But when we begin to live from within outward, in touch with the power of the erotic within ourselves, and allowing that power to inform and illuminate our actions upon the world around us, then we begin to be responsible to ourselves in the deepest sense. For as we begin to recognize our deepest feelings, we begin to give up, of necessity, being satisfied with suffering and self-negation, and with the numbness which so often seems like their only alternative in our society. Our acts against oppression become integral with self, motivated and empowered from within.

In touch with the erotic, I become less willing to accept powerlessness, or those other supplied states of being which are not native to me, such as resignation, despair, self-effacement, depression, self-denial.

And yes, there is a hierarchy. There is a difference between painting a back fence and writing a poem, but only one of quantity. And there is, for me, no difference between writing a good poem and moving into sunlight against the body of a woman I love.

This brings me to the last consideration of the erotic. To share the power of each other's feelings is different from using another's feelings as we would use a kleenex. When we look the other way from our experience, erotic or otherwise, we use rather than share the feelings of those others who participate in the experience with us. And use without consent of the used is abuse.

In order to be utilized, our erotic feelings must be recognized. The need for sharing deep feeling is a human need. But within the european-american tradition, this need is satisfied by certain proscribed erotic comings-together. These occasions are almost always characterized by a simultaneous looking away, a pretense of calling them something else, whether a religion, a fit, mob violence, or even playing doctor. And this misnaming of the need and the deed give rise to that distortion which results in pornography and obscenity—the abuse of feeling.

When we look away from the importance of the erotic in the development and sustenance of our power, or when we look away from ourselves as we satisfy our erotic needs in concert with others, we use each other as objects of satisfaction rather than share our joy in the satisfying, rather than make connection with our similarities and our differences. To refuse to be conscious of what we are feeling at any time, however comfortable that might seem, is to deny a large part of the experience, and to allow ourselves to be reduced to the pornographic, the abused, and the absurd.

The erotic cannot be felt secondhand. As a Black lesbian feminist, I have a particular feeling, knowledge, and understanding for those sisters with whom I have danced hard, played, or even fought. This deep participation has often been the forerunner for joint concerted actions not possible before.

But this erotic charge is not easily shared by women who continue to operate under an exclusively european-american male tradition. I know it was not available to me when I was trying to adapt my consciousness to this mode of living and sensation.

Only now, I find more and more women-identified women brave enough to risk sharing the erotic's electrical charge without having to look away, and without distorting the enormously powerful and creative nature of that exchange. Recognizing the power of the erotic within our lives can give us the energy to pursue genuine change within our world, rather than merely settling for a shift of characters in the same weary drama.

For not only do we touch our most profoundly creative source, but we do that which is female and self-affirming in the face of a racist, patriarchal, and anti-erotic society.

NOTE

Paper delivered at the Fourth Berkshire Conference on the History of Women, Mount Holyoke College, August 25, 1978. Published as a pamphlet by Out & Out Books (available from The Crossing Press).

Study Questions

1. According to Lorde, what is "the erotic"? Why is it threatening to patriarchy?

2. What does Lorde mean when she writes, "The erotic is a resource within each of us that lies in a deeply female . . . plane"? According to Lorde, can nonlesbian women access the erotic? Can males?

3. Does labeling the resource/force Lorde discusses in this piece "the erotic" seem appropriate/useful to you? Why or why not?

4. In what sense can Lorde be read as taking a difference/gynocentric approach?

Paula Gunn Allen

Who Is Your Mother? Red Roots of White Feminism

At Laguna Pueblo in New Mexico, "Who is your mother?" is an important question. At Laguna, one of several of the ancient Keres gynocratic societies of the region, your mother's identity is the key to your own identity. Among the Keres, every individual has a place within the universe—human and nonhuman—and that place is defined by clan membership. In turn, clan membership is dependent on matrilineal descent. Of course, your mother is not only that woman whose womb formed and released you—the term refers in every individual case to an entire generation of women whose psychic, and consequently physical, "shape" made the psychic existence of the following generation possible. But naming your own mother (or her equivalent) enables people to place you precisely within the universal web of your life, in each of its dimensions: cultural, spiritual, personal, and historical.

Among the Keres, "context" and "matrix" are equivalent terms, and both refer to approximately the same thing as knowing your derivation and place. Failure to know your mother, that is, your position and its attendant traditions, history, and place in the scheme of things, is failure to remember your significance, your reality, your right relationship to earth and society. It is the same as being lost—isolated, abandoned, self-estranged, and alienated from your own life. This importance of tradition in the life of every member of the community is not confined to Keres Indians; all American Indian Nations place great value on traditionalism.

The Native American sense of the importance of continuity with one's cultural origins runs counter to contemporary American ideas: in many instances, the immigrants to America have been eager to cast off cultural ties, often seeing their antecedents as backward, restrictive, even shameful. Rejection of tradition constitutes one of the major features of American life, an attitude that reaches far back into American colonial history and that now is validated by virtually every cultural institution in the country. Feminist practice, at least in the cultural artifacts the community values most, follows this cultural trend as well.

The American idea that the best and the brightest should willingly reject and repudiate their origins leads to an allied idea—that history, like everything in the past, is of little value and should be forgotten as quickly as possible. This all too often causes us to reinvent the wheel continually. We find ourselves discovering our collective pasts over and over, having to retake ground already covered by women in the preceding decades and centuries. The Native American view, which highly values maintenance of traditional customs, values, and perspectives, might result in slower societal change and in quite a bit less social upheaval, but it has the advantage of providing a solid sense of identity and lowered levels of psychological and interpersonal conflict.

Contemporary Indian communities value individual members who are deeply connected to the traditional ways of their people, even after centuries of concerted and brutal effort on the part of the American government, the churches, and the corporate system to break the connections between individuals and their tribal world. In fact, in the view of the traditionals, rejection of one's culture—one's traditions, language, people—is the result of colonial oppression and is hardly to be applauded. They believe that the roots of oppression are to be found in the loss of tradition and memory because that loss is always accompanied by a loss of a positive sense of self. In short, Indians think it is important to remember, while Americans believe it is important to forget.

The traditional Indians' view can have a significant impact if it is expanded to mean that the sources of social, political, and philosophical thought in the Americas not only should be recognized and honored by Native Americans but should be embraced by American society. If American society judiciously modeled the traditions of the various Native Nations, the place of women in society would become central, the distribution of goods and power would be egalitarian, the elderly would be respected, honored, and protected as a primary social and cultural resource, the ideals of physical beauty would be considerably enlarged (to include "fat," strong-featured women, gray-haired, and wrinkled individuals, and others who in contemporary American culture are viewed as "ugly"). Additionally, the destruction of the biota, the life sphere, and the natural resources of the planet would be curtailed, and the spiritual nature of human and nonhuman life would become a primary organizing principle of human society. And if the traditional tribal systems that are emulated included pacifist ones, war would cease to be a major method of human problem solving.

RE-MEMBERING CONNECTIONS AND HISTORIES

The belief that rejection of tradition and of history is a useful response to life is reflected in America's amazing loss of memory concerning its origins in the matrix and context of Native America. America does not seem to remember that it derived its wealth, its values, its food, much of its medicine, and a large part of its "dream" from Native America. It is ignorant of the genesis of its culture in this Native American land, and that ignorance helps to perpetuate the longstanding European and Middle Eastern monotheistic, hierarchical, patriarchal cultures' oppression of women, gays, and lesbians, people of color, working class, unemployed people, and the elderly. Hardly anyone in America speculates that the constitutional system of government might be as much a product of American Indian ideas and practices as of colonial American and Anglo-European revolutionary fervor.

Even though Indians are officially and informally ignored as intellectual movers and shapers in the

United States, Britain, and Europe, they are peoples with ancient tenure on this soil. During the ages when tribal societies existed in the Americas largely untouched by patriarchal oppression, they developed elaborate systems of thought that included science, philosophy, and government based on a belief in the central importance of female energies, autonomy of individuals, cooperation, human dignity, human freedom, and egalitarian distribution of status, goods, and services. Respect for others, reverence for life, and, as a by-product, pacifism as a way of life; importance of kinship ties in the customary ordering of social interaction; a sense of the sacredness and mystery of existence; balance and harmony in relationships both sacred and secular were all features of life among the tribal confederacies and nations. And in those that lived by the largest number of these principles, gynarchy was the norm rather than the exception. Those systems are as yet unmatched in any contemporary industrial, agrarian, or postindustrial society on earth.

As we have seen in previous essays, there are many female gods recognized and honored by the tribes and Nations. Femaleness was highly valued, both respected and feared, and all social institutions reflected this attitude. Even modern sayings, such as the Cheyenne statement that a people is not conquered until the hearts of the women are on the ground, express the Indians' understanding that without the power of woman the people will not live, but with it, they will endure and prosper.

Indians did not confine this belief in the central importance of female energy to matters of worship. Among many of the tribes (perhaps as many as 70 percent of them in North America alone), this belief was reflected in all of their social institutions. The Iroquois Constitution or White Roots of Peace, also called the Great Law of the Iroquois, codified the Matrons' decision-making and economic power:

> The lineal descent of the people of the Five Fires [the Iroquois Nations] shall run in the female line. Women shall be considered the progenitors of the Nation. They shall own the land and the soil. Men and women shall follow the status of their mothers. (Article 44)

> The women heirs of the chieftainship titles of the League shall be called Oiner or Otinner [Noble] for all time to come. (Article 45)

> If a disobedient chief persists in his disobedience after three warnings [by his female relatives, by his male relatives, and by one of his fellow council members, in that order], the matter shall go to the council of War Chiefs. The Chiefs shall then take away the title of the erring chief *by order of the women in whom the title is vested.* When the chief is deposed, the women shall notify the chiefs of the League . . . and the chiefs of the League shall sanction the act. The women will then select another of their sons as a candidate and the chiefs shall elect him. (Article 19) (Emphasis mine)[1]

The Matrons held so much policy-making power traditionally that once, when their position was threatened they demanded its return, and consequently the power of women was fundamental in shaping the Iroquois Confederation sometime in the sixteenth or early seventeenth century. It was women who fought what may have been the first successful feminist rebellion in the New World. The year was 1600, or thereabouts, when these tribal feminists decided that they had had enough of unregulated warfare by their men. Lysistratas among the Indian women proclaimed a boycott on lovemaking and childbearing. Until the men conceded to them the power to decide upon war and peace, there would be no more warriors. Since the men believed that the women alone knew the secret of childbirth, the rebellion was instantly successful.

In the Constitution of Deganawidah the founder of the Iroquois Confederation of Nations had said: "He caused the body of our mother, the woman, to be of great worth and honor. He purposed that she shall be endowed and entrusted with the birth and upbringing of men, and that she shall have the care of all that is planted by which life is sustained and supported and the power to breathe is fortified: *and moreover that the warriors shall be her assistants.*"

The footnote of history was curiously supplied when Susan B. Anthony began her "Votes for Women" movement two and a half centuries later. Unknowingly the feminists chose to hold their founding convention of latter-day suffragettes in the town of Seneca [Falls], New York. The site was just a stone's throw from the old council house where the Iroquois women had plotted their feminist rebellion. (Emphasis mine)[2]

Beliefs, attitudes, and laws such as these became part of the vision of American feminists and of other human liberation movements around the world. Yet feminists too often believe that no one has ever experienced the kind of society that empowered women and made that empowerment the basis of its rules of civilization. The price the feminist community must pay because it is not aware of the recent presence of gynarchical societies on this continent is unnecessary confusion, division, and much lost time.

THE ROOT OF OPPRESSION IS LOSS OF MEMORY

An odd thing occurs in the minds of Americans when Indian civilization is mentioned: little or nothing. As I write this, I am aware of how far removed my version of the roots of American feminism must seem to those steeped in either mainstream or radical versions of feminism's history. I am keenly aware of the lack of image Americans have about our continent's recent past. I am intensely conscious of popular notions of Indian women as beasts of burden, squaws, traitors, or, at best, vanished denizens of a long-lost wilderness. How odd, then, must my contention seem that the gynocratic tribes of the American continent provided the basis for all the dreams of liberation that characterize the modern world.

We as feminists must be aware of our history on this continent. We need to recognize that the same forces that devastated the gynarchies of Britain and the Continent also devastated the ancient African civilizations, and we must know that those same materialistic, antispiritual forces are presently engaged in wiping out the same gynarchical values, along with the peoples who adhere to them, in Latin America. I am convinced that those wars were and continue to be about the imposition of patriarchal civilization over the holistic, pacifist, and spirit-based gynarchies they supplant. To that end the wars of imperial con-

quest have not been solely or even mostly waged over the land and its resources, but they have been fought within the bodies, minds, and hearts of the people of the earth for dominion over them. I think this is the reason traditionals say we must remember our origins, our cultures, our histories, our mothers and grandmothers, for without that memory, which implies continuance rather than nostalgia, we are doomed to engulfment by a paradigm that is fundamentally inimical to the vitality, autonomy, and self-empowerment essential for satisfying, high-quality life.

The vision that impels feminists to action was the vision of the Grandmothers' society, the society that was captured in the words of the sixteenth-century explorer Peter Martyr nearly five hundred years ago. It is the same vision repeated over and over by radical thinkers of Europe and America, from François Villon to John Locke, from William Shakespeare to Thomas Jefferson, from Karl Marx to Friedrich Engels, from Benito Juarez to Martin Luther King, from Elizabeth Cady Stanton to Judy Grahn, from Harriet Tubman to Audre Lorde, from Emma Goldman to Bella Abzug, from Malinalli to Cherrie Moraga, and from Iyatiku to me. That vision as Martyr told it is of a country where there are "no soldiers, no gendarmes or police, no nobles, kings, regents, prefects, or judges, no prisons, no lawsuits . . . All are equal and free," or so Friedrich Engels recounts Martyr's words.[3]

Columbus wrote:

Nor have I been able to learn whether they [the inhabitants of the islands he visited on his first journey to the New World] held personal property, for it seemed to me that whatever one had, they all took shares of . . . They are so ingenuous and free with all they have, that no one would believe it who has not seen it; of anything that they possess, if it be asked of them, they never say no; on the contrary, they invite you to share it and show as much love as if their hearts went with it.[4]

At least that's how the Native Caribbean people acted when the whites first came among them; American Indians are the despair of social workers, bosses, and missionaries even now because of their deeply ingrained tendency to spend all they have, mostly on others. In any case, as the historian William Brandon notes,

> the Indian *seemed* free, to European eyes, gloriously free, to the European soul shaped by centuries of toil and tyranny, and this impression operated profoundly on the process of history and the development of America. Something in the peculiar character of the Indian world gave an impression of classlessness, of propertylessness, and that in turn led to an impression, as H. H. Bancroft put it, of "humanity unrestrained . . . in the exercise of liberty absolute."[5]

A FEMINIST HEROINE

Early in the women's suffrage movement, Eva Emery Dye, an Oregon suffragette, went looking for a heroine to embody her vision of feminism. She wanted a historical figure whose life would symbolize the strengthened power of women. She found Sacagawea (or Sacajawea) buried in the journals of Lewis and Clark. The Shoshoni teenager had traveled with the Lewis and Clark expedition, carrying her infant son, and on a small number of occasions acted as translator.[6]

Dye declared that Sacagawea, whose name is thought to mean Bird Woman, had been the guide to the historic expedition, and through Dye's work Sacagawea became enshrined in American memory as a moving force and friend of the whites, leading them in the settlement of western North America.[7]

But Native American roots of white feminism reach back beyond Sacagawea. The earliest white women on this continent were well acquainted with tribal women. They were neighbors to a number of tribes and often shared food, information, child care, and health care. Of course little is made of these encounters in official histories of colonial America, the period from the Revolution to the Civil War, or on the ever-moving frontier. Nor, to my knowledge, has either the significance or incidence of intermarriage between Indian and white or between Indian and Black been explored. By and large, the study of Indian-white relations has been focused on government and treaty relations, warfare, missionization, and education. It has been almost entirely documented in terms of formal white Christian patriarchal impacts and assaults on Native Americans, though they are not often characterized as assaults but as "civilizing the savages." Particularly in organs of popular culture and miseducation, the focus has been on what whites imagine to be degradation of Indian women ("squaws"), their equally imagined love of white government and white conquest ("princesses"), and the horrifyingly misleading, fanciful tales of "bloodthirsty, backward primitives" assaulting white Christian settlers who were looking for life, liberty, and happiness in their chosen land.

But, regardless of official versions of relations between Indians and whites or other segments of the American population, the fact remains that great numbers of apparently "white" or "Black" Americans carry notable degrees of Indian blood. With that blood has come the culture of the Indian, informing the lifestyles, attitudes, and values of their descendents. Somewhere along the line—and often quite recently—an Indian woman was giving birth to and raising the children of a family both officially and informally designated as white or Black—not Indian. In view of this, it should be evident that one of the major enterprises of Indian women in America has been the transfer of Indian values and culture to as large and influential a segment of American immigrant populations as possible. Their success in this endeavor is amply demonstrated in the Indian values and social styles that increasingly characterize American life. Among these must be included "permissive" childrearing practices, for as noted in an earlier chapter ("When Women Throw Down Bundles"), imprisoning, torturing, caning, strapping, starving, or verbally abusing children was considered outrageous behavior. Native Americans did not believe that physical or psychological abuse of children would result in their edification. They did not believe that children are born in sin, are congenitally predisposed to evil, or that a good parent who wishes the child to gain salvation, achieve success, or earn the respect of her or his fellows can be helped to those ends by physical or emotional torture.

The early Americans saw the strongly protective attitude of the Indian people as a mark of their "savagery"—as they saw the Indian's habit of bathing frequently, their sexual openness, their liking for scant clothing, their raucous laughter at most things, their suspicion and derision of authoritarian structures, their quick pride, their genuine courtesy, their willingness to share what they had with others less fortunate than they, their egalitarianism, their ability to act as if various lifestyles were a normal part of living, and their granting that women were of equal or, in individual cases, of greater value than men.

Yet the very qualities that marked Indian life in the sixteenth century have, over the centuries since contact between the two worlds occurred, come to mark much of contemporary American life. And those qualities, which I believe have passed into white culture from Indian culture, are the very ones that fundamentalists, immigrants from Europe, the Middle East, and Asia often find the most reprehensible. Third- and fourth-generation Americans indulge in growing nudity, informality in social relations, egalitarianism, and the rearing of women who value autonomy, strength, freedom, and personal dignity— and who are often derided by European, Asian, and Middle Eastern men for those qualities. Contemporary Americans value leisure almost as much as tribal people do. They find themselves increasingly unable to accept child abuse as a reasonable way to nurture. They bathe more than any other industrial people on earth—much to the scorn of their white cousins across the Atlantic, and they sometimes enjoy a good laugh even at their own expense (though they still have a less developed sense of the ridiculous than one might wish).

Contemporary Americans find themselves more and more likely to adopt a "live and let live" attitude in matters of personal sexual and social styles. Two-thirds of their diet and a large share of their medications and medical treatments mirror or are directly derived from Native American sources. Indianization is not a simple concept, to be sure, and it is one that Americans often find themselves resisting; but it is a process that has taken place, regardless of American resistance to recognizing the source of many if not most of American's vaunted freedoms in our personal, family, social, and political arenas.

This is not to say that Americans have become Indian in every attitude, value, or social institution. Unfortunately, Americans have a way to go in learning how to live in the world in ways that improve the quality of life for each individual while doing minimal damage to the biota, but they have adapted certain basic qualities of perception and certain attitudes that are moving them in that direction.

AN INDIAN-FOCUSED VERSION OF AMERICAN HISTORY

American colonial ideas of self-government came as much from the colonists' observations of tribal governments as from their Protestant or Greco-Roman heritage. Neither Greece nor Rome had the kind of pluralistic democracy as that concept has been understood in the United States since Andrew Jackson, but the tribes, particularly the gynarchical tribal confederacies, did. It is true that the *oligarchic* form of government that colonial Americans established was originally based on Greco-Roman systems in a number of important ways, such as its restriction of citizenship to propertied white males over twenty-one years of age, but it was never a form that Americans as a whole have been entirely comfortable with. Politics and government in the United States during the Federalist period also reflected the English common law system as it had evolved under patriarchal feudalism and monarchy—hence the United States' retention of slavery and restriction of citizenship to propertied white males.

The Federalists did make one notable change in the feudal system from which their political system derived on its Anglo side. They rejected blooded aristocracy and monarchy. This idea came from the Protestant Revolt to be sure, but it was at least reinforced by colonial America's proximity to American Indian nonfeudal confederacies and their concourse with those confederacies over the two hundred years of the colonial era. It was this proximity and concourse that enabled the revolutionary theorists to "dream up" a system in which all local polities would contribute to and be protected by a central governing body responsible for implementing policies that bore on the common interest of all. It should also be noted that the Reformation followed Columbus's contact with the Americas and that his and Martyr's reports concerning Native Americans' free and easy egalitarianism were in circulation by the time the Reformation took hold.

The Iroquois federal system, like that of several in the vicinity of the American colonies, is remarkably similar to the organization of the federal system of the United States. It was made up of local, "state," and federal bodies composed of executive, legislative, and judicial branches. The Council of Matrons was the executive: it instituted and determined general policy. The village, tribal (several villages), and Confederate councils determined and implemented policies when they did not conflict with the broader Council's decisions or with theological precepts that ultimately determined policy at all levels. The judicial was composed of the men's councils and the Matron's council, who sat together to make decisions. Because the matrons were the ceremonial center of the system, they were also the prime policymakers.

Obviously, there are major differences between the structure of the contemporary American government and that of the Iroquois. Two of those differences were and are crucial to the process of just government. The Iroquois system is spirit-based, while that of the United States is secular, and the Iroquois Clan Matrons formed the executive. The female executive function was directly tied to the ritual nature of the Iroquois politic, for the executive was lodged in the hands of the Matrons of particular clans across village, tribe, and national lines. The executive office was hereditary, and only sons of eligible clans could serve, at the behest of the Matrons of their clans, on the councils at the three levels. Certain daughters inherited the office of Clan Matron through their clan affiliations. No one could impeach or disempower a Matron, though her violation of certain laws could result in her ineligibility for the Matron's council. For example, a woman who married *and took her husband's name* could not hold the title Matron.

American ideas of social justice came into sharp focus through the commentaries of Iroquois observers who traveled in France in the colonial period. These observers expressed horror at the great gap between the lifestyles of the wealthy and the poor, remarking to the French philosopher Montaigne, who would heavily influence the radical communities of Europe, England, and America, that "they had noticed that in Europe there seemed to be two moities, consisting of the rich 'full gorged' with wealth, and the poor, starving 'and bare with need and povertie.' The Indian tourists not only marveled at the division, but marveled that the poor endured 'such an injustice, and that they took not the others by the throte, or set fire on their house.' "[8] It must be noted that the urban poor eventually did just that in the French Revolution. The writings of Montaigne and of those he influenced provided the theoretical framework and the vision that propelled the struggle for liberty, justice, and equality on the Continent and later throughout the British empire.

The feminist idea of power as it ideally accrues to women stems from tribal sources. The central importance of the clan Matrons in the formulation and determination of domestic and foreign policy as well as in their primary role in the ritual and ceremonial life of their respective Nations was the single most important attribute of the Iroquois, as of the Cherokee and Muskogee, who traditionally inhabited the southern Atlantic region. The latter peoples were removed to what is now Oklahoma during the Jackson administration, but prior to the American Revolution they had regular and frequent communication with and impact on both the British colonizers and later the American people, including the African peoples brought here as slaves.

Ethnographer Lewis Henry Morgan wrote an account of Iroquoian matriarchal culture, published in 1877,[9] that heavily influenced Marx and the development of communism, particularly lending it the idea of the liberation of women from patriarchal dominance. The early socialists in Europe, especially in Russia, saw women's liberation as a central aspect of the socialist revolution. Indeed, the basic ideas of socialism, the egalitarian distribution of goods and power, the peaceful ordering of society, and the right of every member of society to participate in the work and benefits of that society, are ideas that pervade

American Indian political thought and action. And it is through various channels—the informal but deeply effective Indianization of Europeans, and christianizing Africans, the social and political theory of the confederacies feuding and then intertwining with European dreams of liberty and justice, and, more recently, the work of Morgan and the writings of Marx and Engels—that the age-old gynarchical systems of egalitarian government found their way into contemporary feminist theory.

When Eva Emery Dye discovered Sacagawea and honored her as the guiding spirit of American womanhood, she may have been wrong in bare historical fact, but she was quite accurate in terms of deeper truth. The statues that have been erected depicting Sacagawea as a Matron in her prime signify an understanding in the American mind, however unconscious, that the source of just government, of right ordering of social relationships, the dream of "liberty and justice for all" can be gained only by following the Indian Matrons' guidance. For, as Dr. Anna Howard Shaw said of Sacagawea at the National American Woman's Suffrage Association in 1905:

Forerunner of civilization, great leader of men, patient and motherly woman, we bow our hearts to do you honor! . . . May we the daughters of an alien race . . . learn the lessons of calm endurance, of patient persistence and unfaltering courage exemplified in your life, in our efforts to lead men through the Pass of justice, which goes over the mountains of prejudice and conservatism to the broad land of the perfect freedom of a true republic; one in which men and women together shall in perfect equality solve the problems of a nation that knows no caste, no race, no sex in opportunity, in responsibility or in justice! May "the eternal womanly" ever lead us on![10]

NOTES

1. The White Roots of Peace, cited in *The Third Woman: Minority Women Writers of the United States*, ed. Dexter Fisher (Boston: Houghton Mifflin, 1980), p. 577. Cf. Thomas Sanders and William Peek, eds., *Literature of the American Indian* (New York: Glencoe Press, 1973),

pp. 208–239. Sanders and Peek refer to the document as "The Law of the Great Peace."

2. Stan Steiner, *The New Indians* (New York: Dell, 1968), pp. 219–220.

3. William Brandon, *The Last Americans: The Indian in American Culture* (New York: McGraw-Hill, 1974), p. 294.

4. Brandon, *Last Americans*, p. 6.

5. Brandon, *Last Americans*, pp. 7–8. The entire chapter "American Indians and American History" (pp. 1–23) is pertinent to the discussion.

6. Ella E. Clark and Margot Evans, *Sacagawea of the Lewis and Clark Expedition* (Berkeley: University of California Press, 1979), pp. 93–98. Clark details the fascinating, infuriating, and very funny scholarly escapade of how our suffragette foremothers created a feminist hero from the scant references to the teenage Shoshoni wife of the expedition's official translator, Pierre Charbonneau.

7. The implications of this maneuver did not go unnoticed by either whites or Indians, for the statues of the idealized Shoshoni woman, the Native American matron Sacagawea, suggest that American tenure on American land, indeed, the right to be on this land, is given to whites by her. While that implication is not overt, it certainly is suggested in the image of her that the sculptor chose: a tall, heavy woman, standing erect, nobly pointing the way westward with upraised hand. The impression is furthered by the habit of media and scholar of referring to her as "the guide." Largely because of the popularization of the circumstances of Sacagawea's participation in the famed Lewis and Clark expedition, Indian people have viewed her as a traitor to her people, likening her to Malinalli (La Malinche, who acted as interpreter for Cortés and bore him a son) and Pocahontas, that unhappy girl who married John Rolfe (not John Smith) and died in England after bearing him a son. Actually none of these women engaged in traitorous behavior. Sacagawea led a long life, was called Porivo (Chief Woman) by the Commanches, among whom she lived for more than twenty years, and in her old age engaged her considerable skill at speaking and manipulating white bureaucracy to help in assuring her Shoshoni people decent reservation holdings.

A full discussion is impossible here but an examination of American child-rearing practices, societal attitudes toward women and exhibited by women (when compared to the same in Old World cultures) as well as the foodstuffs, medicinal materials, countercultural and alternative cultural systems, and the deeply Indian values these reflect should demonstrate the truth about informal acculturation and cross-cultural connections in the Americas.

8. Brandon, *Last Americans*, p. 6.

9. Lewis Henry Morgan, *Ancient Society or Researches in the Lines of Human Progress from Savagery Through Barbarism to Civilization* (New York, 1877).

10. Clark and Evans, *Sacagawea*, p. 96.

Study Questions

1. What does Allen believe would occur "[i]f American society judiciously modeled the traditions of the various Native Nations"?

2. What does Allen mean by "gynarchical values"?

3. Is Allen's work an example of difference feminism, or does it instead pose a *challenge to* difference feminism by arguing that gynarchical values are rooted in Native American culture rather than in women or women's culture?

4. Does Allen's article make essentializing claims about women? About Native Americans?

Carol Gilligan

Moral Orientation and Moral Development

When one looks at an ambiguous figure like the drawing that can be seen as a young or old woman, or the image of the vase and the faces, one initially sees it in only one way. Yet even after seeing it in both ways, one way often seems more compelling. This phenomenon reflects the laws of perceptual organization that favor certain modes of visual grouping. But it also suggests a tendency to view reality as unequivocal and thus to argue that there is one right or better way of seeing.

The experiments of the Gestalt psychologists on perceptual organization provide a series of demonstrations that the same proximal pattern can be organized in different ways so that, for example, the same figure can be seen as a square or a diamond, depending on its orientation in relation to a surrounding frame. Subsequent studies show that the context influencing which of two possible organizations will be chosen may depend not only on the features of the array presented but also on the perceiver's past experience or expectation. Thus, a bird-watcher and a rabbit-keeper are likely to see the duck-rabbit figure in different ways; yet this difference does not imply that one way is better or a higher form of perceptual organization. It does, however, call attention to the fact that the rabbit-keeper, perceiving the rabbit, may not see the ambiguity of the figure until someone points out that it can also be seen as a duck.

This paper presents a similar phenomenon with respect to moral judgment, describing two moral perspectives that organize thinking in different ways. The analogy to ambiguous figure perception arises from the observation that although people are aware of both perspectives, they tend to adopt one or the other in defining and resolving moral conflict. Since moral judgments organize thinking about choice in difficult situations, the adoption of a single perspective may facilitate clarity of decision. But the wish for clarity may also imply a compelling human need for resolution or closure, especially in the face of decisions that give rise to discomfort or unease. Thus, the search for clarity in seeing may blend with a search for justification, encouraging the position that there is one right or better way to think about moral problems. This question, which has been the subject of intense theological and philosophical debate, becomes of interest to the psychologist not only because of its psychological dimensions—the tendency to focus on one perspective and the wish for justification—but also because one moral perspective currently dominates psychological thinking and is embedded in the most widely used measure for assessing the maturity of moral reasoning.

In describing an alternative standpoint, I will reconstruct the account of moral development around two moral perspectives, grounded in different dimensions of relationship that give rise to moral concern. The justice perspective, often equated with moral reasoning, is recast as one way of seeing moral problems and a care perspective is brought forward as an alternate vision or frame. The distinction between justice and care as alternative perspectives or moral orientations is based empirically on the observation that a shift in the focus of attention from concerns about justice to concerns about care changes the definition of what constitutes a moral problem, and leads the same situation to be seen in different ways. Theoretically, the distinction between justice and care cuts across the familiar divisions between thinking and feeling, egoism and altruism, theoretical and practical reasoning. It calls attention to the fact that all human relationships, public and private, can be characterized *both* in terms of equality and in terms of attachment, and that both inequality and detachment constitute grounds for moral concern. Since everyone is vulnerable both to oppression and to abandonment, two moral visions—one of justice and one of care—recur in human experience. The moral injunctions, not to act unfairly toward others, and not to turn away from someone in need, capture these different concerns.

The conception of the moral domain as comprised of at least two moral orientations raises new questions about observed differences in moral judgment and the disagreements to which they give rise. Key to this revision is the distinction between differences in developmental stage (more or less adequate positions within a single orientation) and differences in orientation (alternative perspectives or frameworks). The findings reported in this paper of an association between moral orientation and gender speak directly to the continuing controversy over sex differences in moral reasoning. In doing so, however, they also offer an empirical explanation for why previous thinking about moral development has been organized largely within the justice framework.

My research on moral orientation derives from an observation made in the course of studying the relationship between moral judgment and action. Two studies, one of college students describing their experiences of moral conflict and choice, and one of pregnant women who were considering abortion, shifted the focus of attention from the ways people reason about hypothetical dilemmas to the ways people construct moral conflicts and choices in their lives. This change in approach made it possible to see what experiences people define in moral terms, and to explore the relationship between the understanding of moral problems and the reasoning strategies used and the actions taken in attempting to resolve them. In this context, I observed that women, especially when speaking about their own experiences of moral conflict and choice, often define moral problems in a way that eludes the categories of moral theory and is at odds with the assumptions that shape psychological thinking about morality and about the self.[1] This discovery, that a different voice often guides the moral judgments and the actions of women, called attention to a major design problem in previous moral judgment research: namely, the use of all-male samples as the empirical basis for theory construction.

The selection of an all-male sample as the basis for generalizations that are applied to both males and females is logically inconsistent. As a research strategy, the decision to begin with a single-sex sample is inherently problematic, since the categories of analysis will tend to be defined on the basis of the initial data gathered and subsequent studies will tend to be restricted to these categories. Piaget's work on the moral judgment of the child illustrates these problems since he defined the evolution of children's consciousness and practice of rules on the basis of his study of boys playing marbles, and then undertook a study of girls to assess the generality of his findings. Observing a series of differences both in the structure of girls' games and "in the actual mentality of little girls," he deemed these differences not of interest because "it was not this contrast which we proposed to study." Girls, Piaget found, "rather complicated our interrogatory in relation to what we know about boys," since the changes in their conception of rules, although following the same sequence observed in boys, did not stand in the same relation to social experience. Nevertheless, he concluded that "in spite of these differences in the structure of the game and apparently in the players' mentality, we find the same process at work as in the evolution of the game of marbles."[2]

Thus, girls were of interest insofar as they were similar to boys and confirmed the generality of Piaget's findings. The differences noted, which included a greater tolerance, a greater tendency toward innovation in solving conflicts, a greater willingness to make exceptions to rules, and a lesser concern with legal elaboration, were not seen as germane to "the psychology of rules," and therefore were regarded as insignificant for the study of children's moral judgment. Given the confusion that currently surrounds the discussion of sex differences in moral judgment, it is important to emphasize that the differences observed by Piaget did not pertain to girls' understanding of rules per se or to the development of the idea of justice in their thinking, but rather to the way girls structured their games and their approach to conflict resolution—that is, to their use rather than their understanding of the logic of rules and justice.

Kohlberg, in his research on moral development, did not encounter these problems since he equated moral development with the development of justice reasoning and initially used an all-male sample as the basis for theory and test construction. In response to his critics, Kohlberg has recently modified his claims, renaming his test a measure of "justice reasoning" rather than of "moral maturity" and acknowledging the presence of a care perspective in people's moral thinking.[3] But the widespread use of Kohlberg's measure as a measure of moral development together with his own continuing tendency to equate justice reasoning with moral judgment leaves the problem of orientation differences unsolved. More specifically, Kohlberg's efforts to assimilate thinking about care

to the six-stage developmental sequence he derived and refined by analyzing changes in justice reasoning (relying centrally on his all-male longitudinal sample), underscores the continuing importance of the points raised in this paper concerning (1) the distinction between differences in developmental stage within a single orientation and differences in orientation, and (2) the fact that the moral thinking of girls and women was not examined in establishing either the meaning or the measurement of moral judgment within contemporary psychology.

An analysis of the language and logic of men's and women's moral reasoning about a range of hypothetical and real dilemmas underlies the distinction elaborated in this paper between a justice and a care perspective. The empirical association of care reasoning with women suggests that discrepancies observed between moral theory and the moral judgments of girls and women may reflect a shift in perspective, a change in moral orientation. Like the figure-ground shift in ambiguous figure perception, justice and care as moral perspectives are not opposites or mirror-images of one another, with justice uncaring and care unjust. Instead, these perspectives denote different ways of organizing the basic elements of moral judgment: self, others, and the relationship between them. With the shift in perspective from justice to care, the organizing dimension of relationship changes from inequality/equality to attachment/ detachment, reorganizing thoughts, feelings, and language so that words connoting relationship like "dependence" or "responsibility" or even moral terms such as "fairness" and "care" take on different meanings. To organize relationships in terms of attachment rather than in terms of equality changes the way human connection is imagined, so that the images or metaphors of relationship shift from hierarchy or balance to network or web. In addition, each organizing framework leads to a different way of imagining the self as a moral agent.

From a justice perspective, the self as moral agent stands as the figure against a ground of social relationships, judging the conflicting claims of self and others against a standard of equality or equal respect (the Categorical Imperative, the Golden Rule). From a care perspective, the relationship becomes the figure, defining self and others. Within the context of relationship, the self as a moral agent perceives and responds to the perception of need. The shift in moral perspective is manifest by a change in the moral question from "What is just?" to "How to respond?"

For example, adolescents asked to describe a moral dilemma often speak about peer or family pressure in which case the moral question becomes how to maintain moral principles or standards and resist the influence of one's parents or friends. "I have a right to my religious opinions," one teenager explains, referring to a religious difference with his parents. Yet, he adds, "I respect their views." The same dilemma, however, is also construed by adolescents as a problem of attachment, in which case the moral question becomes: how to respond both to oneself and to one's friends or one's parents, how to maintain or strengthen connection in the face of differences in belief. "I understand their fear of my new religious ideas," one teenager explains, referring to her religious disagreement with her parents, "but they really ought to listen to me and try to understand my beliefs."

One can see these two statements as two versions of essentially the same thing. Both teenagers present self-justifying arguments about religious disagreement; both address the claims of self and of others in a way that honors both. Yet each frames the problem in different terms, and the use of moral language points to different concerns. The first speaker casts the problem in terms of individual rights that must he respected within the relationship. In other words, the figure of the considering is the self looking on the disagreeing selves in relationship, and the aim is to get the other selves to acknowledge the right to disagree. In the case of the second speaker, figure and ground shift. The relationship becomes the figure of the considering, and relationships are seen to require listening and efforts at understanding differences in belief. Rather than the right to disagree, the speaker focuses on caring to hear and to be heard. Attention shifts from the grounds for agreement (rights and respect) to the grounds for understanding (listening and speaking, hearing and being heard). This shift is marked by a

change in moral language from the stating of separate claims to rights and respect ("I have a right . . . I respect their views.") to the activities of relationship—the injunction to listen and try to understand ("I understand . . . they ought to listen . . . and try to understand."). The metaphor of moral voice itself carries the terms of the care perspective and reveals how the language chosen for moral theory is not orientation neutral.

The language of the public abortion debate, for example, reveals a justice perspective. Whether the abortion dilemma is cast as a conflict of rights or in terms of respect for human life, the claims of the fetus and of the pregnant woman are balanced or placed in opposition. The morality of abortion decisions thus construed hinges on the scholastic or metaphysical question as to whether the fetus is a life or a person, and whether its claims take precedence over those of the pregnant woman. Framed as a problem of care, the dilemma posed by abortion shifts. The connection between the fetus and the pregnant woman becomes the focus of attention and the question becomes whether it is responsible or irresponsible, caring or careless, to extend or to end this connection. In this construction, the abortion dilemma arises because there is no way not to act, and no way of acting that does not alter the connection between self and others. To ask what actions constitute care or are more caring directs attention to the parameters of connection and the costs of detachment, which become subjects of moral concern.

Finally, two medical students, each reporting a decision not to turn in someone who has violated the school rules against drinking, cast their decision in different terms. One student constructs the decision as an act of mercy, a decision to override justice in light of the fact that the violator has shown "the proper degrees of contrition." In addition, this student raises the question as to whether or not the alcohol policy is just, i.e., whether the school has the right to prohibit drinking. The other student explains the decision not to turn in a proctor who was drinking on the basis that turning him in is not a good way to respond to this problem, since it would dissolve the relationship between them and thus cut off an avenue for help. In addition, this student raises the question as to whether the proctor sees his drinking as a problem.

This example points to an important distinction, between care as understood or construed within a justice framework and care as a framework or a perspective on moral decision. Within a justice construction, care becomes the mercy that tempers justice; or connotes the special obligations or supererogatory duties that arise in personal relationships; or signifies altruism freely chosen—a decision to modulate the strict demands of justice by considering equity or showing forgiveness; or characterizes a choice to sacrifice the claims of the self. All of these interpretations of care leave the basic assumptions of a justice framework intact: the division between the self and others, the logic of reciprocity or equal respect.

As a moral perspective, care is less well elaborated, and there is no ready vocabulary in moral theory to describe its terms. As a framework for moral decision, care is grounded in the assumption that self and other are interdependent, an assumption reflected in a view of action as responsive and, therefore, as arising in relationship rather than the view of action as emanating from within the self and, therefore, "self governed." Seen as responsive, the self is by definition connected to others, responding to perceptions, interpreting events, and governed by the organizing tendencies of human interaction and human language. Within this framework, detachment, whether from self or from others, is morally problematic, since it breeds moral blindness or indifference—a failure to discern or respond to need. The question of what responses constitute care and what responses lead to hurt draws attention to the fact that one's own terms may differ from those of others. Justice in this context becomes understood as respect for people in their own terms.

The medical student's decision not to turn in the proctor for drinking reflects a judgment that turning him in is not the best way to respond to the drinking problem, itself seen as a sign of detachment or lack of concern. Caring for the proctor thus raises the question of what actions are most likely to ameliorate this problem, a decision that leads to the question of what are the proctor's terms.

The shift in organizing perspective here is marked by the fact that the first student does not consider the terms of the other as potentially different but instead assumes one set of terms. Thus the student alone becomes the arbiter of what is *the* proper degree of contrition. The second student, in turn, does not attend to the question of whether the alcohol policy itself is just or fair. Thus each student discusses an aspect of the problem that the other does not mention.

These examples are intended to illustrate two cross-cutting perspectives that do not negate one another but focus attention on different dimensions of the situation, creating a sense of ambiguity around the question of what is the problem to be solved. Systematic research on moral orientation as a dimension of moral judgment and action initially addressed three questions: (1) Do people articulate concerns about justice and concerns about care in discussing a moral dilemma? (2) Do people tend to focus their attention on one set of concerns and minimally represent the other? and (3) Is there an association between moral orientation and gender? Evidence from studies that included a common set of questions about actual experiences of moral conflict and matched samples of males and females provides affirmative answers to all three questions.

When asked to describe a moral conflict they had faced, 55 out of 80 (69 percent) educationally advantaged North American adolescents and adults raised considerations of both justice and care. Two-thirds (54 out of 80) however, focused their attention on one set of concerns, with focus defined as 75 percent or more of the considerations raised pertaining either to justice or to care. Thus the person who presented, say, two care considerations in discussing a moral conflict was more likely to give a third, fourth, and fifth than to balance care and justice concerns—a finding consonant with the assumption that justice and care constitute organizing frameworks for moral decision. The men and the women involved in this study (high school students, college students, medical students, and adult professionals) were equally likely to demonstrate the focus phenomenon (two-thirds of both sexes fell into the outlying focus categories). There were, however, sex differences in the direction of focus.

With one exception, all of the men who focused, focused on justice. The women divided, with roughly one third focusing on justice and one third on care.[4]

These findings clarify the different voice phenomenon and its implications for moral theory and for women. First, it is notable that if women were eliminated from the research sample, care focus in moral reasoning would virtually disappear. Although care focus was by no means characteristic of all women, it was almost exclusively a female phenomenon in this sample of educationally advantaged North Americans. Second, the fact that the women were advantaged means that the focus on care cannot readily be attributed to educational deficit or occupational disadvantage—the explanation Kohlberg and others have given for findings of lower levels of justice reasoning in women.[5] Instead, the focus on care in women's moral reasoning draws attention to the limitations of a justice-focused moral theory and highlights the presence of care concerns in the moral thinking of both women and men. In this light, the Care/Justice group composed of one third of the women and one third of the men becomes of particular interest, pointing to the need for further research that attends to the way people organize justice and care in relation to one another—whether, for example, people alternate perspectives, like seeing the rabbit and the duck in the rabbit-duck figure, or integrate the two perspectives in a way that resolves or sustains ambiguity.

Third, if the moral domain is comprised of at least two moral orientations, the focus phenomenon suggests that people have a tendency to lose sight of one moral perspective in arriving at moral decision—a liability equally shared by both sexes. The present findings further suggest that men and women tend to lose sight of different perspectives. The most striking result is the virtual absence of care-focus reasoning among the men. Since the men raised concerns about care in discussing moral conflicts and thus presented care concerns as morally relevant, a question is why they did not elaborate these concerns to a greater extent.

In summary, it becomes clear why attention to women's moral thinking led to the identification of a different voice and raised questions about the place of justice and care within a comprehensive moral theory. It also is clear how the selection of an all-male sample for research on moral judgment fosters an equation of morality with justice, providing little data discrepant with this view. In the present study, data discrepant with a justice-focused moral theory comes from a third of the women. Previously, such women were seen as having a problem understanding "morality." Yet these women may also be seen as exposing the problem in a justice-focused moral theory. This may explain the decision of researchers to exclude girls and women at the initial stage of moral judgment research. If one begins with the premise that "all morality consists in respect for rules,"[6] or "virtue is one and its name is justice,"[7] then women are likely to appear problematic within moral theory. If one begins with women's moral judgments, the problem becomes how to construct a theory that encompasses care as a focus of moral attention rather than as a subsidiary moral concern.

The implications of moral orientation for moral theory and for research on moral development are extended by a study designed and conducted by Kay Johnston.[8] Johnston set out to explore the relationship between moral orientation and problem-solving strategies, creating a standard method using fables for assessing spontaneous moral orientation and orientation preference. She asked 60 eleven- and fifteen-year-olds to state and to solve the moral problem posed by the fable. Then she asked: "Is there another way to solve this problem?" Most of the children initially constructed the fable problems either in terms of justice or in terms of care; either they stood back from the situation and appealed to a rule or principle for adjudicating the conflicting claims or they entered the situation in an effort to discover or create a way of responding to all of the needs. About half of the children, slightly more fifteen- than eleven-year-olds, spontaneously switched moral orientation when asked whether there was another way to solve the problem. Others did so following an interviewer's cue as to the form such a switch might take. Finally, the children were asked which of the solutions they described was the best solution. Most of the children answered the question and explained why one way was preferable.

Johnston found gender differences parallel to those previously reported, with boys more often spontaneously using and preferring justice solutions and girls more often spontaneously using and preferring care solutions. In addition, she found differences between the two fables she used, confirming Langdale's finding that moral orientation is associated both with the gender of the reasoner and with the dilemma considered.[9] Finally, the fact that children, at least by the age of eleven, are able to shift moral orientation and can explain the logic of two moral perspectives, each associated with a different problem-solving strategy, heightens the analogy to ambiguous figure perception and further supports the conception of justice and care as organizing frameworks for moral decision.

The demonstration that children know both orientations and can frame and solve moral problems in at least two different ways means that the choice of moral standpoint is an element of moral decision. The role of the self in moral judgment thus includes the choice of moral standpoint, and this decision, whether implicit or explicit, may become linked with self-respect and self-definition. Especially in adolescence when choice becomes more self-conscious and self-reflective, moral standpoint may become entwined with identity and self-esteem. Johnston's finding that spontaneous moral orientation and preferred orientation are not always the same raises a number of questions as to why and under what conditions a person may adopt a problem-solving strategy that he or she sees as not the best way to solve the problem.

The way people chose to frame or solve a moral problem is clearly not the only way in which they can think about the problem, and is not necessarily the way they deem preferable. Moral judgments thus do not reveal *the* structure of moral thinking, since there are at least two ways in which people can structure moral problems. Johnston's demonstration of orientation-switch poses a serious challenge to the methods that have been used in moral judgment and moral development research, introducing a major interpretive caution. The fact that boys and girls at eleven and fifteen understand and distinguish the logics of

justice and care reasoning directs attention to the origins and the development of both ways of thinking. In addition, the tendency for boys and girls to use and prefer different orientations when solving the same problem raises a number of questions about the relationship between these orientations and the factors influencing their representation. The different patterns of orientation use and preference, as well as the different conceptions of justice and of care implied or elaborated in the fable judgments, suggest that moral development cannot be mapped along a single linear stage sequence.

One way of explaining these findings, suggested by Johnston, joins Vygotsky's theory of cognitive development with Chodorow's analysis of sex differences in early childhood experiences of relationship.[10] Vygotsky posits that all of the higher cognitive functions originate as actual relations between individuals. Justice and care as moral ideas and as reasoning strategies thus would originate as relationships with others—an idea consonant with the derivation of justice and care reasoning from experiences of inequality and attachment in early childhood. All children are born into a situation of inequality in that they are less capable than the adults and older children around them and, in this sense, more helpless and less powerful. In addition, no child survives in the absence of some kind of adult attachment—or care, and through this experience of relationship children discover the responsiveness of human connection including their ability to move and affect one another.

Through the experience of inequality, of being in the less powerful position, children learn what it means to depend on the authority and the good will of others. As a result, they tend to strive for equality of greater power, and for freedom. Through the experience of attachment, children discover the ways in which people are able to care for and to hurt one another. The child's vulnerability to oppression and to abandonment thus can be seen to lay the groundwork for the moral visions of justice and care, conceived as ideals of human relationship and defining the ways in which people "should" act toward one another.

Chodorow's work then provides a way of explaining why care concerns tend to be minimally represented by men and why such concerns are less frequently elaborated in moral theory. Chodorow joins the dynamics of gender identity formation (the identification of oneself as male or female) to an analysis of early childhood relationships and examines the effects of maternal child care on the inner structuring of self in relation to others. Further, she differentiates a positional sense of self from a personal sense of self, contrasting a self defined in terms of role or position from a self known through the experience of connection. Her point is that maternal child care fosters the continuation of a relational sense of self in girls, since female gender identity is consonant with feeling connected with one's mother. For boys, gender identity is in tension with mother-child connection, unless that connection is structured in terms of sexual opposition (e.g., as an Oedipal drama). Thus, although boys experience responsiveness or care in relationships, knowledge of care or the need for care, when associated with mothers, poses a threat to masculine identity.[11]

Chodorow's work is limited by her reliance on object relations theory and problematic on that count. Object relations theory ties the formation of the self to the experience of separation, joining separation with individuation and thus counterposing the experience of self to the experience of connection with others. This is the line that Chodorow traces in explicating male development. Within this framework, girls' connections with their mothers can only be seen as problematic. Connection with others or the capacity to feel and think *with* others is, by definition, in tension with self-development when self-development or individuation is linked to separation. Thus, object-relations theory sustains a series of oppositions that have been central in Western thought and moral theory, including the opposition between thought and feelings, self and relationship, reason and compassion, justice and love. Object relations theory also continues the conventional division of psychological labor between women and men. Since the idea of a self, experienced in the context of attachment with others, is theoretically impossible, mothers, described as objects, are viewed as selfless, without a self. This view is essentially problematic for women, divorcing the activity of mothering from desire, knowledge, and agency, and implying that insofar as a mother experiences herself as a subject rather than as an object (a mirror reflecting her child), she is "selfish" and not a good mother. Winnicott's phrase "good-enough mother" represents an effort to temper this judgment.

Thus, psychologists and philosophers, aligning the self and morality with separation and autonomy—the ability to be self-governing—have associated care with self-sacrifice, or with feelings—a view at odds with the current position that care represents a way of knowing and a coherent moral perspective. This position, however, is well represented in literature written by women. For example the short story "A Jury of Her Peers," written by Susan Glaspell in 1917, a time when women ordinarily did not serve on juries, contrasts two ways of knowing that underlie two ways of interpreting and solving a crime.[12] The story centers on a murder; Minnie Foster is suspected of killing her husband.

A neighbor woman and the sheriff's wife accompany the sheriff and the prosecutor to the house of the accused woman. The men, representing the law, seek evidence that will convince a jury to convict the suspect. The women, collecting things to bring Minnie Foster in jail, enter in this way into the lives lived in the house. Taking in rather than taking apart, they begin to assemble observations and impressions, connecting them to past experience and observations until suddenly they compose a familiar pattern, like the log-cabin pattern they recognize in the quilt Minnie Foster was making. "Why do we *know*—what we know this minute?" one woman asks the other, but she also offers the following explanation:

> We live close together, and we live far apart. We all go through the same things—it's all just a different kind of the same thing! If it weren't—why do you and I *understand*.[13]

The activity of quilt-making—collecting odd scraps and piecing them together until they form a pattern—becomes the metaphor for this way of knowing. Discovering a strangled canary buried under pieces of quilting, the women make a series of connections that lead them to understand what happened.

The logic that says you don't kill a man because he has killed a bird, the judgment that finds these acts wildly incommensurate, is counterposed to the logic that sees both events as part of a larger pattern—a pattern of detachment and abandonment that led finally to the strangling. "I *wish* I'd come over here once in a while," Mrs. Hale, the neighbor, exclaims. "That was a crime! Who's going to punish that?" Mrs. Peters, the sheriff's wife, recalls that when she was a girl and a boy killed her cat, "If they hadn't held me back I would have—" and realizes that there had been no one to restrain Minnie Foster. John Foster was known as "a good man . . . He didn't drink, and he kept his word as well as most, I guess, and paid his debts." But he also was "a hard man," Mrs. Hale explains, "like a raw wind that gets to the bone."

Seeing detachment as the crime with murder as its ultimate extension, implicating themselves and also seeing the connection between their own and Minnie Foster's actions, the women solve the crime by attachment—by joining together, like the "knotting" that joins pieces of a quilt. In the decision to remove rather than to reveal the evidence, they separate themselves from a legal system in which they have no voice but also no way of voicing what they have come to understand. In choosing to connect themselves with one another and with Minnie, they separate themselves from the law that would use their understanding and their knowledge as grounds for further separation and killing.

In a law school class where a film-version of this story was shown, the students were divided in their assessment of the moral problem and in their evaluation of the various characters and actions. Some focused on the murder, the strangling of the husband. Some focused on the evidence of abandonment or indifference to others. Responses to a questionnaire showed a bi-modal distribution, indicating two ways of viewing the film. These different perspectives led to different ways of evaluating both the act of murder and the women's decision to remove the evidence. Responses to the film were not aligned with the sex of the viewer in an absolute way, thus dispelling any implication of biological determinism or of a stark division between the way women and men know or judge events. The knowledge gained inductively by the women in the film, however, was also gained more readily by women watching the film, who came in this way to see a logic in the women's actions and to articulate a rationale for their silence.

The analogy to ambiguous figure perception is useful here in several ways. First, it suggests that people can see a situation in more than one way, and even alternate ways of seeing, combining them without reducing them—like designating the rabbit-duck figure both duck and rabbit. Second, the analogy argues against the tendency to construe justice and care as opposites or mirror-images and also against the implication that these two perspectives are readily integrated or fused. The ambiguous figure directs attention to the way in which a change in perspective can reorganize perception and change understanding, without implying an underlying reality or pure form. What makes seeing both moral perspectives so difficult is precisely that the orientations are not opposites nor mirror images or better and worse representations of a single moral truth. The terms of one perspective do not contain the terms of the other. Instead, a shift in orientation denotes a restructuring of moral perception, changing the meaning of moral language and thus the definition of moral conflict and moral action. For example, detachment is considered the hallmark of mature moral thinking within a justice perspective, signifying the ability to judge dispassionately, to weigh evidence in an even-handed manner, balancing the claims of others and self. From a care perspective, detachment is *the* moral problem.

> "I could've come," retorted Mrs. Hale . . . "I wish I had come over to see Minnie Foster sometimes. I can see now . . . If there had been years and years of— nothing, then a bird to sing to you, it would be awful—still—after the bird was still. . . . I know what stillness is."

The difference between agreement and understanding captures the different logics of justice and care reasoning, one seeking grounds for agreement, one seeking grounds for understanding, one assuming separation and thus the need for some external structure of connection, one assuming connection and thus the potential for understanding. These assumptions run deep, generating and reflecting different views of human nature and the human condition. They also point to different vulnerabilities and different sources of error. The potential error in justice reasoning lies in its latent egocentrism, the tendency to confuse one's perspective with an objective standpoint or truth, the temptation to define others in one's own terms by putting oneself in their place. The potential error in care reasoning lies in the tendency to forget that one has terms, creating a tendency to enter into another's perspective and to see oneself as "selfless" by defining oneself in other's terms. These two types of error underlie two common equations that signify distortions or deformations of justice and care: the equation of human with male, unjust in its omission of women; and the equation of care with self-sacrifice, uncaring in its failure to represent the activity and the agency of care.

The equation of human with male was assumed in the Platonic and in the Enlightenment tradition as well as by psychologists who saw all-male samples as "representative" of human experience. The equation of care with self-sacrifice is in some ways more complex. The premise of self-interest assumes a conflict of interest between self and other manifest in the opposition of egoism and altruism. Together, the equations of male with human and of care with self-sacrifice form a circle that has had a powerful hold on moral philosophy and psychology. The conjunction of women and moral theory thus challenges the traditional definition of human and calls for a reconsideration of what is meant by both justice and care.

To trace moral development along two distinct although intersecting dimensions of relationship suggests the possibility of different permutations of justice and care reasoning, different ways these two moral perspectives can be understood and represented in relation to one another. For example, one perspective may overshadow or eclipse the other, so that one is brightly illuminated while the other is dimly remembered, familiar but for the most part forgotten. The way in which one story about relationship obscures another was evident in high-school girls' definitions of dependence. These definitions

highlighted two meanings—one arising from the opposition between dependence and independence, and one from the opposition of dependence to isolation ("No woman," one student observed, "is an island.") As the word "dependence" connotes the experience of relationship, this shift in the implied opposite of dependence indicates how the valence of relationship changes, when connection with others is experienced as an impediment to autonomy or independence, and when it is experienced as a source of comfort and pleasure, and a protection against isolation. This essential ambivalence of human connection provides a powerful emotional grounding for two moral perspectives, and also may indicate what is at stake in the effort to reduce morality to a single perspective.

It is easy to understand the ascendance of justice reasoning and of justice-focused moral theories in a society where care is associated with personal vulnerability in the form of economic disadvantage. But another way of thinking about the ascendance of justice reasoning and also about sex differences in moral development is suggested in the novel *Masks*, written by Fumiko Enchi, a Japanese woman.[14] The subject is spirit possession, and the novel dramatizes what it means to be possessed by the spirits of others. Writing about the Rokujo lady in the *Tales of Genji*, Enchi's central character notes that:

> Her soul alternates uncertainly between lyricism and spirit possession, making no philosophical distinction between the self alone and in relation to others, and is unable to achieve the solace of a religious indifference.[15]

The option of transcendence, of a religious indifference or a philosophical detachment, may be less available to women because women are more likely to be possessed by the spirits and the stories of others. The strength of women's moral perceptions lies in the refusal of detachment and depersonalization, and insistence on making connections that can lead to seeing the person killed in war or living in poverty as someone's son or father or brother or sister, or mother, or daughter, or friend. But the liability of women's development is also underscored by Enchi's novel in that women, possessed by the spirits of others, also are more likely to be caught in a chain of false attachments. If women are at the present time the custodians of a story about human attachment and interdependence, not only within the family but also in the world at large, then questions arise as to how this story can be kept alive and how moral theory can sustain this story. In this sense, the relationship between women and moral theory itself becomes one of interdependence.

By rendering a care perspective more coherent and making its terms explicit, moral theory may facilitate women's ability to speak about their experiences and perceptions and may foster the ability of others to listen and to understand. At the same time, the evidence of care focus in women's moral thinking suggests that the study of women's development may provide a natural history of moral development in which care is ascendant, revealing the ways in which creating and sustaining responsive connection with others becomes or remains a central moral concern. The promise in joining women and moral theory lies in the fact that human survival, in the late twentieth century, may depend less on formal agreement than on human connection.

NOTES

1. Gilligan, C. (1977). "In a Different Voice: Women's Conceptions of Self and of Morality." *Harvard Educational Review* 47 (1982):481–517; *In a Different Voice: Psychological Theory and Women's Development*. Cambridge, Mass.: Harvard University Press.

2. Piaget, J. (1965). *The Moral Judgment of the Child*. New York, N.Y.: The Free Press Paperback Edition, pp. 76–84.

3. Kohlberg, L. (1984). *The Psychology of Moral Development*. San Francisco, Calif.: Harper & Row, Publishers, Inc.

4. Gilligan, C. and J. Attanucci. (1986). *Two Moral Orientations*. Harvard University, unpublished manuscript.

5. See Kohlberg, L. op. cit., also Walker, L. (1984). "Sex Differences in the Development of Moral Reasoning: A Critical Review of the Literature." *Child Development* 55 (3):677–91.

6. Piaget, R., op. cit.

7. Kohlberg, L., op. cit.

8. Johnston, K. (1985). *Two Moral Orientations—Two Problem-solving Strategies: Adolescents Solutions to Dilemmas in Fables*. Harvard University, unpublished doctoral dissertation.

9. Langdale, C. (1983). *Moral Orientation and Moral Development: The Analysis of Care and Justice Reasoning Across Different Dilemmas in Females and Males from Childhood through Adulthood*. Harvard University, unpublished doctoral dissertation.

10. Johnston, K., op. cit.; Vygotsky, L. (1978). *Mind in Society*. Cambridge, Mass.: Harvard University Press; Chodorow, N. (1974). "Family Structure and Feminine Personality" in *Women, Culture and Society*, L. M. Rosaldo and L. Lamphere, eds., Stanford, Calif.: Stanford University Press; see also Chodorow, N. (1978). *The Reproduction of Mothering: Psychoanalysis and the Sociology of Gender*, Berkeley, Calif.: University of California Press.

11. Chodorow, N., op. cit.

12. Glaspell, S. (1927). *A Jury of Her Peers*. London: E. Benn.

13. Ibid.

14. Fumiko, E. (1983). *Masks*. New York: Random House.

15. Ibid. p. 54.

Study Questions

1. How does the experience of viewing an ambiguous picture (such as the famous duck-rabbit drawing) help us understand the relationship between the justice perspective and the care perspective? Explain what *particular* features of perceiving an ambiguous picture are analogous to what *particular* features of moral thinking.

2. What is Gilligan's criticism of Piaget's work? Of Kohlberg's?

3. What are the differences between a justice perspective and a care perspective? Describe a moral problem (other than those Gilligan discusses) from a justice perspective and from a care perspective, demonstrating their differences.

4. Does Gilligan provide evidence that men and women systematically differ in their moral responses to situations? Describe the differences.

5. What implications does Gilligan take her research to have for moral theory? For psychology?

Carol P. Christ

Why Women Need the Goddess: Phenomenological, Psychological, and Political Reflections

At the close of Ntozake Shange's stupendously successful Broadway play *for colored girls who have considered suicide / when the rainbow is enuf*, a tall beautiful Black woman rises from despair to cry out, "I found God in myself and I loved her fiercely."[1] Her discovery is echoed by women around the country who meet spontaneously in small groups on full moons, solstices, and equinoxes to celebrate the Goddess as symbol of life and death powers and waxing and waning energies in the universe and in themselves.[2]

> It is the night of the full moon. Nine women stand in a circle, on a rocky hill above the city. The western sky is rosy with the setting sun; in the east the moon's face begins to peer above the horizon. . . . The woman pours out a cup of wine onto the earth, refills it and raises it high. "Hail, Tana, Mother of mothers!" she cries. "Awaken from your long sleep, and return to your children again!"[3]

What are the political and psychological effects of this fierce new love of the divine in themselves for women whose spiritual experience has been focused by the male God of Judaism and Christianity? Is the spiritual dimension of feminism a passing diversion, an escape from difficult but necessary political work? Or does the emergence of the symbol of Goddess among women have significant political

and psychological ramifications for the feminist movement?

To answer this question, we must first understand the importance of religious symbols and rituals in human life and consider the effect of male symbolism of God on women. According to anthropologist Clifford Geertz, religious symbols shape a cultural ethos, defining the deepest values of a society and the persons in it. "Religion," Geertz writes, "is a system of symbols which act to produce powerful, pervasive, and long-lasting moods and motivations"[4] in the people of a given culture. A "mood" for Geertz is a psychological attitude, such as awe, trust, and respect, while a "motivation" is the *social* and *political* trajectory created by a mood that transforms mythos into ethos, symbol system into social and political reality. Symbols have both psychological and political effects, because they create the inner conditions (deep-seated attitudes and feelings) that lead people to feel comfortable with or to accept social and political arrangements that correspond to the symbol system.

Because religion has such a compelling hold on the deep psyches of so many people, feminists cannot afford to leave it in the hands of the fathers. Even people who no longer "believe in God" or participate in the institutional structure of patriarchal religion still may not be free of the power of the symbolism of God the Father. A symbol's effect does not depend on rational assent, for a symbol also functions on levels of the psyche other than the rational. Religion fulfills deep psychic needs by providing symbols and rituals that enable people to cope with limit situations[5] in human life (death, evil, suffering) and to pass through life's important transitions (birth, sexuality, death). Even people who consider themselves completely secularized will often find themselves sitting in a church or synagogue when a friend or relative gets married, or when a parent or friend has died. The symbols associated with these important rituals cannot fail to affect the deep or unconscious structures of the mind of even a person who has rejected these symbolisms on a conscious level—especially if the person is under stress. The reason for the continuing effect of religious symbols is that the mind abhors a vacuum. Symbol systems cannot simply be rejected, they must be replaced. Where there is not any replacement, the mind will revert to familiar structures at times of crisis, bafflement, or defeat.

Religions centered on the worship of a male God create "moods" and "motivations" that keep women in a state of psychological dependence on men and male authority, while at the same time legitimating the *political* and *social* authority of fathers and sons in the institutions of society.

Religious symbol systems focused around exclusively male images of divinity create the impression that female power can never be fully legitimate or wholly beneficent. This message need never be explicitly stated (as, for example, it is in the story of Eve) for its effect to be felt. A woman completely ignorant of the myths of female evil in biblical religion nonetheless acknowledges the anomaly of female power when she prays exclusively to a male God. She may see herself as like God (created in the image of God) only by denying her own sexual identity and affirming God's transcendence of sexual identity. But she can never have the experience that is freely available to every man and boy in her culture, of having her full sexual identity affirmed as being in the image and likeness of God. In Geertz' terms, her "mood" is one of trust in male power as salvific and distrust of female power in herself and other women as inferior

or dangerous. Such a powerful, pervasive, and long-lasting "mood" cannot fail to become a "motivation" that translates into social and political reality.

In *Beyond God the Father*, feminist theologian Mary Daly detailed the psychological and political ramifications of father religion for women. "If God in 'his' heaven is a father ruling his people," she wrote, "then it is the 'nature' of things and according to divine plan and the order of the universe that society be male-dominated. Within this context, a *mystification of roles* takes place: The husband dominating his wife represents God 'himself.' The images and values of a given society have been projected into the realm of dogmas and 'Articles of Faith,' and these, in turn, justify the social structures which have given rise to them and which sustain their plausibility."[6]

Philosopher Simone de Beauvoir was well aware of the function of patriarchal religion as legitimater of male power; she wrote, "Man enjoys the great advantage of having a god endorse the code he writes; and since man exercises a sovereign authority over women it is especially fortunate that this authority has been vested in him by the Supreme Being. For the Jew, Mohammedans, and Christians, among others, man is Master by divine right; the fear of God will, therefore, repress any impulse to revolt in the downtrodden female."[7]

This brief discussion of the psychological and political effects of God religion puts us in an excellent position to begin to understand the significance of the symbol of Goddess for women. In discussing the meaning of the Goddess, my method will first be phenomenological. I will isolate a meaning of the symbol of the Goddess as it has emerged in the lives of contemporary women. I will then discuss its psychological and political significance by contrasting the "moods" and "motivations" engendered by Goddess symbols with those engendered by Christian symbolism. I will also correlate Goddess symbolism with themes that have emerged in the women's movement, in order to show how Goddess symbolism undergirds and legitimates the concerns of the women's movement, much as God symbolism in Christianity undergirded the interests of men in patriarchy. I will discuss four aspects of Goddess symbolism here: the Goddess as affirmation of female power, the female body, the female will, and women's bonds and heritage. There are, of course, many other meanings of the Goddess that I will not discuss here.

The sources for the symbol of the Goddess in contemporary spirituality are traditions of Goddess worship and modern women's experience. The ancient Mediterranean, pre-Christian European, Native American, Mesoamerican, Hindu, African, and other traditions are rich sources for Goddess symbolism. But these traditions are filtered through modern women's experiences. Traditions of goddesses, subordination to gods, for example, are ignored. Ancient traditions are tapped selectively and eclectically, but they are not considered authoritative for modern consciousness. The Goddess symbol has emerged spontaneously in the dreams, fantasies, and thoughts of many women around the country in the past several years. Kirsten Grimstad and Susan Rennie reported that they were surprised to discover widespread interest in spirituality, including the Goddess, among feminists around the country in the summer of 1974.[8] *WomanSpirit* magazine, which published its first issue in 1974 and has contributors from across the United States, has expressed the grass roots nature of the women's spirituality movement. In 1976, a journal, *Lady Unique*, devoted to the Goddess emerged. In 1975, the first women's spirituality conference was held in Boston and attended by 1,800 women. In 1978, a course on the Goddess at the University of California at Santa Cruz, drew over 500 people. Sources for this essay are these manifestations of the Goddess in modern women's experiences as reported in *WomanSpirit, Lady Unique*, and elsewhere, and as expressed in conversations I have had with women who have been thinking about the Goddess and women's spirituality.

The simplest and most basic meaning of the symbol of Goddess is the acknowledgment of the legitimacy of female power as a beneficent and independent power. A woman who echoes Ntozake Shange's dramatic statement, "I found God in myself and I loved her fiercely," is saying "Female power is strong and creative." She is saying that the divine principle, the saving and sustaining power, is in herself, that she will no longer look to men or male figures as saviors. The strength and independence of female power can be intuited by contemplating ancient and modern images of the Goddess. This meaning of the symbol of Goddess is simple and obvious, and yet it is difficult for many to comprehend. It stands in sharp contrast to the paradigms of female dependence on males that have been predominant in Western religion and culture. The internationally acclaimed novelist Monique Wittig captured the novelty and flavor of the affirmation of female power in her mythic work *Les Guérillères*:

> There was a time when you were not a slave, remember that. You walked alone, full of laughter, you bathed bare-bellied. You say you have lost all recollection of it, remember . . . you say there are no words to describe it, you say it does not exist. But remember. Make an effort to remember. Or, failing that, invent.[9]

While Wittig does not speak directly of the Goddess here, she captures the "mood" of joyous celebration of female freedom and independence that is created in women who define their identities through the symbol of Goddess. Artist Mary Beth Edelson expressed the political "motivations" inspired by the Goddess when she wrote,

> The ascending archetypal symbols of the feminine unfold today in the psyche of modern Everywoman. They encompass the multiple forms of the Great Goddess. Reaching across the centuries we take the hands of our Ancient Sisters. The Great Goddess, alive and well, is rising to announce to the patriarchs that their 5,000 years are up—Hallelujah! Here we come.[10]

The affirmation of female power contained in the Goddess symbol has both psychological and political consequences. Psychologically, it means the defeat of the view engendered by patriarchy that women's power is inferior and dangerous. This new "mood" of affirmation of female power also leads to new "motivations"; it supports and undergirds women's trust in their own power and the power of other women in family and society.

If the simplest meaning of the Goddess symbol is an affirmation of the legitimacy and beneficence of female power, then a question immediately arises, "Is the Goddess simply female power writ large, and, if so, why bother with the symbol of Goddess at all? Or does the symbol refer to a Goddess 'out there' who is not reducible to a human potential?" The many women who have rediscovered the power of Goddess would give three answers to this question: (1) The Goddess is divine female, a personification who can be invoked in prayer and ritual; (2) the Goddess is symbol of the life, death, and rebirth energy in nature and culture, in personal and communal life; and (3) the Goddess is symbol of the affirmation of the legitimacy and beauty of female power (made possible by the new becoming of women in the women's liberation movement). If one were to ask these women which answer is the "correct" one, different responses would be given. Some would assert that the Goddess definitely is *not* "out there," that the symbol of a divinity "out there" is part of the legacy of patriarchal oppression, which brings with it the authoritarianism, hierarchicalism, and dogmatic rigidity associated with biblical monotheistic religions. They might assert that the Goddess symbol reflects the sacred power within women and nature, suggesting the connectedness between women's cycles of menstruation, birth, and menopause, and the life and death cycles of the universe. Others seem quite comfortable with the notion of Goddess as a divine female protector and creator and would find their experience of Goddess limited by the assertion that she is not *also* out there as well as within themselves and in all natural processes. When asked what the symbol of Goddess means, Starhawk, a feminist priestess, replied, "It all depends on how I feel. When I feel weak, She is someone who can help and protect me. When I feel strong, She is the symbol of my own power. At other times I feel Her as the natural energy in my body and the world."[11] How are we to evaluate such a statement? Theologians might call these the words of a sloppy thinker. But my deepest intuition tells me they contain a wisdom that Western theological thought has lost.

To theologians, these differing views of the "meaning" of the symbol of Goddess might seem to threaten a replay of the trinitarian controversies. Is there, perhaps, a way of doing theology which would not lead immediately into dogmatic controversy, which would not require theologians to say definitively that one understanding is true and the others are false? Could people's relation to a common symbol be made primary and varying interpretations be acknowledged? The diversity of explications of the meaning of the Goddess symbol suggests that symbols have a richer significance than any explications of their meaning can express, a point literary critics have long insisted on. This phenomenological fact suggests that theologians may need to give more than lip service to a theory of symbol in which the symbol is viewed as the primary fact and the meanings are viewed as secondary. It also suggests that a *thea*logy[12] of the Goddess would be very different from the *theo*logy we have known in the West. But to spell out this notion of the primacy of *symbol* in thealogy in contrast to the primacy of the *explanation* in theology would be the topic of another paper. Let me simply state that women, who have been deprived of a female religious symbol system for centuries, are, therefore, in an excellent position to recognize the power and primacy of symbols. I believe women must develop a theory of symbol and thealogy congruent with their experience at the same time as they "remember and invent" new symbol systems.

A second important implication of the Goddess symbol for women is the affirmation of the female body and the life cycle expressed in it. Because of women's unique position as menstruants, birthgivers, and those who have traditionally cared for the young and the dying, women's connection to the body, nature, and this world has been obvious. Women were denigrated because they seemed more carnal, fleshy, and earthy than the culture-creating males.[13] The misogynist anti*body* tradition in Western thought is symbolized in the myth of Eve who is traditionally viewed as a sexual temptress, the epitome of women's carnal nature. This tradition reaches its nadir in the *Malleus Maleficarum* (*The Hammer of Evil-Doing Women*), which states, "All witchcraft stems from carnal lust, which in women is insatiable."[14] The Virgin Mary, the positive female image in Christianity does not contradict Christian denigration of the female body and its powers. The Virgin Mary is revered because she, in her perpetual virginity, transcends the carnal sexuality attributed to most women.

The denigration of the female body is expressed in cultural and religious taboos surrounding menstruation, childbirth, and menopause in women. While menstruation taboos may have originated in a perception of the awesome powers of the female body,[15] they degenerated into a simple perception that there is something "wrong" with female bodily functions. Menstruating women were forbidden to enter the sanctuary in ancient Hebrew and premodern Christian communities. Although only Orthodox Jews still enforce religious taboos against menstruant women, few women in our culture grow up affirming their menstruation as a connection to sacred power. Most women learn that menstruation is a curse and grow up believing that the bloody facts of menstruation are best hidden away. Feminists challenge this attitude to the female body. Judy Chicago's art piece "Menstruation Bathroom" broke these menstrual taboos. In a sterile white bathroom, she exhibited boxes of Tampax and Kotex on an open shelf, and the wastepaper basket was overflowing with bloody tampons and sanitary napkins.[16] Many women who viewed the piece felt relieved to have their "dirty secret" out in the open.

The denigration of the female body and its powers is further expressed in Western culture's attitudes toward childbirth.[17] Religious iconography does not celebrate the birthgiver, and there is no theology or ritual that enables a woman to celebrate the process of birth as a spiritual experience. Indeed, Jewish and Christian traditions also had blood taboos concerning the woman who had recently given birth. While these religious taboos are rarely enforced today (again, only by Orthodox Jews), they have secular equivalents. Giving birth is treated as a disease requiring hospitalization, and the woman is viewed as a passive object, anesthetized to ensure her acquiescence to the will of the doctor. The women's liberation movement has challenged these cultural attitudes, and many feminists have joined with advocates of natural childbirth and home birth in emphasizing the need for women to

control and take pride in their bodies, including the birth process.

Western culture also gives little dignity to the postmenopausal or aging woman. It is no secret that our culture is based on a denial of aging and death, and that women suffer more severely from this denial than men. Women are placed on a pedestal and considered powerful when they are young and beautiful, but they are said to lose this power as they age. As feminists have pointed out, the "power" of the young woman is illusory, since beauty standards are defined by men, and since few women are considered (or consider themselves) beautiful for more than a few years of their lives. Some men are viewed as wise and authoritative in age, but old women are pitied and shunned. Religious iconography supports this cultural attitude toward aging women. The purity and virginity of Mary and the female saints is often expressed in the iconographic convention of perpetual youth. Moreover, religious mythology associates aging women with evil in the symbol of the wicked old Witch. Feminists have challenged cultural myths of aging women and have urged women to reject patriarchal beauty standards and to celebrate the distinctive beauty of women of all ages.

The symbol of Goddess aids the process of naming and reclaiming the female body and its cycles and processes. In the ancient world and among modern women, the Goddess symbol represents the birth, death, and rebirth processes of the natural and human worlds. The female body is viewed as the direct incarnation of the waxing and waning, life and death cycles in the universe. This is sometimes expressed through the symbolic connection between the twenty-eight-day cycles of menstruation and the twenty-eight-day cycles of the moon. Moreover, the Goddess is celebrated in the triple aspect of youth, maturity, and age, or maiden, mother, and crone. The potentiality of the young girl is celebrated in the nymph or maiden aspect of the Goddess. The Goddess as mother is sometimes depicted giving birth, and giving birth is viewed as a symbol for all the creative, life-giving powers of the universe.[18] The life-giving powers of the Goddess in Her creative aspect are not limited to physical birth, for the Goddess is also seen as the creator of all the arts of civilization, including healing, writing, and the giving of just law. Women in the middle of life who are not physical mothers may give birth to poems, songs, and books, or nurture other women, men, and children. They, too, are incarnations of the Goddess in Her creative, life-giving aspect. At the end of life, women incarnate the crone aspect of the Goddess. The wise old woman, the woman who knows from experience what life is about, the woman whose closeness to her own death gives her a distance and perspective on the problems of life, is celebrated as the third aspect of the Goddess. Thus, women learn to value youth, creativity, and wisdom in themselves and other women.

The possibilities of reclaiming the female body and its cycles have been expressed in a number of Goddess-centered rituals. Hallie Iglehart and Barbry My Own created a summer solstice ritual to celebrate menstruation and birth. The women simulated a birth canal and birthed each other into their circle. They raised power by placing their hands on each other's bellies and chanting together. Finally they marked each other's faces with rich, dark menstrual blood saying, "This is the blood that promises renewal. This is the blood that promises sustenance. This is the blood that promises life."[19] From hidden dirty secret to symbol of the life power of the Goddess, women's blood has come full circle. Other women have created rituals that celebrate the crone aspect of the Goddess. Z. Budapest believes that the crone aspect of the Goddess is predominant in the fall, especially at Halloween, an ancient holiday. On this day, the wisdom of the old woman is celebrated, and it is also recognized that the old must die so that the new can he born.

The "mood" created by the symbol of the Goddess in triple aspect is one of positive, joyful affirmation of the female body and its cycles and acceptance of aging and death as well as life. The "motivations" are to overcome menstrual taboos, to return the birth process to the hands of women, and to change cultural attitudes about age and death. Changing cultural attitudes toward the female body could go a long way toward overcoming the spirit-flesh, mind-body dualisms of Western culture, since, as Rosemary

Ruether has pointed out, the denigration of the female body is at the heart of these dualisms. The Goddess as symbol of the revaluation of the body and nature, thus, also undergirds the human potential and ecology movements. The "mood" is one of affirmation, awe, and respect for the body and nature, and the "motivation" is to respect the teachings of the body and the rights of all living beings.

A third important implication of the Goddess symbol for women is the positive valuation of will in a Goddess-centered ritual, especially in Goddess-centered ritual magic and spellcasting in womanspirit and feminist Witchcraft circles. The basic notion behind ritual magic and spellcasting is energy as power. Here the Goddess is a center or focus of power and energy; She is the personification of the energy that flows between beings in the natural and human worlds. In Goddess circles, energy is raised by chanting or dancing. According to Starhawk, "Witches conceive of psychic energy as having form and substance that can be perceived and directed by those with a trained awareness. The power generated within the circle is built into a cone form and, at its peak, is released—to the Goddess, to reenergize the members of the coven, or to do a specific work such as healing."[20] In ritual magic, the energy raised is directed by willpower. Women who celebrate in Goddess circles believe they can achieve their wills in the world.

The emphasis on the will is important for women, because women traditionally have been taught to devalue their wills, to believe that they cannot achieve their will through their own power, and even to suspect that the assertion of will is evil. Faith Wilding's poem "Waiting," from which I will quote only a short segment, sums up women's sense that their lives are defined not by their own will, but by waiting for others to take the initiative:

Waiting for my breasts to develop
Waiting to wear a bra
Waiting to menstruate
. . .
Waiting for life to begin, Waiting—
Waiting to be somebody
. . .

Waiting to get married
Waiting for my wedding day
Waiting for my wedding night
. . .
Waiting for the end of the day
Waiting for sleep. Waiting . . .[21]

Patriarchal religion has enforced the view that female initiative and will are evil through the juxtaposition of Eve and Mary. Eve caused the fall by asserting her will against the command of God, while Mary began the new age with her response to God's initiative, "Let it be done to me according to Thy word" (Luke 1:38). Even for men, patriarchal religion values the passive will subordinate to divine initiative. The classical doctrines of sin and grace view sin as the prideful assertion of will and grace as the obedient subordination of the human will to the divine initiative or order. While this view of will might be questioned from a human perspective, Valerie Saiving has argued that it has particularly deleterious consequences for women in Western culture. According to Saiving, Western culture encourages males in the assertion of will, and, thus, it may make some sense to view the male form of sin as an excess of will. But since our culture discourages females in the assertion of will, the traditional doctrines of sin and grace encourage women to remain in their form of sin, which is self-negation or insufficient assertion of will.[22] One possible reason the will is denigrated in a patriarchal religious framework is that both human and divine will are often pictured as arbitrary, self-initiated, and exercised without regard for other wills.

In a Goddess-centered context, in contrast, the will is valued. *A woman is encouraged to know her will, to believe that her will is valid, and to believe that her will can be achieved in the world*, three powers traditionally denied to her in patriarchy. In a Goddess-centered framework, a woman's will is not subordinated to the Lord God as king and ruler, nor to men as his representatives. Thus, a woman is not reduced to waiting and acquiescing in the wills of others as she is in patriarchy. But neither does she adopt the egocentric form of will that pursues self-interest without regard for the interests of others.

The Goddess-centered context provides a different understanding of the will than that available in the traditional patriarchal religious framework. In the Goddess framework, will can be achieved only when it is exercised in harmony with the energies and wills of other beings. Wise women, for example, raise a cone of healing energy at the full moon or solstice when the lunar or solar energies are at their high points with respect to the earth. This discipline encourages them to recognize that not all times are propitious for the achieving of every will. Similarly, they know that spring is a time for new beginnings in work and love, summer a time for producing external manifestations of inner potentialities, and fall or winter a time for stripping down to the inner core and extending roots. Such awareness of waxing and waning processes in the universe discourages arbitrary ego-centered assertion of will, while at the same time encouraging the assertion of individual will in cooperation with natural energies and the energies created by the wills of others. Wise women also have a tradition that whatever is sent out will be returned, and this reminds them to assert their wills in cooperative and healing rather than egocentric and destructive ways. This view of will allows women to begin to recognize, claim, and assert their wills without adopting the worst characteristics of the patriarchal understanding and use of will. In the Goddess-centered framework, the "mood" is one of positive affirmation of personal will in the context of the energies of other wills or beings. The "motivation" is for women to know and assert their wills in cooperation with other wills and energies. This of course does not mean that women always assert their wills in positive and life-affirming ways. Women's capacity for evil is, of course, as great as men's. My purpose is simply to contrast the differing attitudes toward the exercise of will per se, and the female will in particular, in Goddess-centered religion and in the Christian God-centered religion.

The fourth and final aspect of Goddess symbolism that I will discuss here is the significance of the Goddess for a revaluation of woman's bonds and heritage. As Virginia Woolf has said, "Chloe liked Olivia," a statement about a woman's relation to another woman, is a sentence that rarely occurs in fiction. Men have written the stories, and they have written about women almost exclusively in their relations to men.[23] The celebrations of women's bonds to each other, as mothers and daughters, as colleagues and co-workers, as sisters, friends, and lovers, is beginning to occur in the new literature and culture created by women in the women's movement. While I believe that the revaluing of each of these bonds is important, I will focus on the mother-daughter bond, in part because I believe it may be the key to the others.

Adrienne Rich has pointed out that the mother-daughter bond, perhaps the most important of woman's bonds, "resonant with charges . . . the flow of energy between two biologically alike bodies, one of which has lain in amniotic bliss inside the other, one of which has labored to give birth to the other,"[24] is rarely celebrated in patriarchal religion and culture. Christianity celebrates the father's relation to the son and the mother's relation to the son, but the story of mother and daughter is missing. So, too, in patriarchal literature and psychology the mothers and the daughters rarely exist. Volumes have been written about the Oedipus complex, but little has been written about the girl's relation to her mother. Moreover, as de Beauvoir has noted, the mother-daughter relation is distorted in patriarchy because the mother must give her daughter over to men in a male-defined culture in which women are viewed as inferior. The mother must socialize her daughter to become subordinate to men, and if her daughter challenges patriarchal norms, the mother is likely to defend the patriarchal structures against her own daughter.[25]

These patterns are changing in the new culture created by women in which the bonds of women to women are beginning to be celebrated. Holly Near has written several songs that celebrate women's bonds and women's heritage. In one of her finest songs she writes of an "old-time woman" who is "waiting to die." A young woman feels for the life that has passed the old woman by and begins to cry, but the old woman looks her in the eye and says, "If I had not suffered, you wouldn't be wearing those jeans/Being an old-time woman ain't as bad as it seems."[26] This song, which Near has said was inspired by her grandmother, expresses and celebrates a bond and a heritage passed down from one woman to another. In another of Near's songs, she sings of "a hiking-boot mother who's seeing the world/For the first time with her own little girl." In this song, the mother tells the drifter who has been traveling with her to pack up and travel alone if he thinks "traveling three is a drag" because "I've got a little one who loves me as much as you need me/And darling, that's loving enough."[27] This song is significant because the mother places her relationship to her daughter above her relationship to a man, something women rarely do in patriarchy.[28]

Almost the only story of mothers and daughters that has been transmitted in Western culture is the myth of Demeter and Persephone that was the basis of religious rites celebrated by women only, the Thesmophoria, and later formed the basis of the Eleusinian mysteries, which were open to all who spoke Greek. In this story, the daughter, Persephone, is abducted away from her mother, Demeter, and raped by the God of the Underworld. Unwilling to accept this state of affairs, Demeter rages and withholds fertility from the Earth until Her daughter is returned to Her. What is important for women in this story is that a mother fights for her daughter and for her relation to her daughter. This is completely different from the mother's relation to her daughter in patriarchy. The "mood" created by the story of Demeter and Persephone is one of celebration of the mother-daughter bond, and the "motivation" is for mothers and daughters to affirm the heritage passed on from mother to daughter and to reject the patriarchal pattern where the primary loyalties of mother and daughter must be to men.

The symbol of Goddess has much to offer women who are struggling to be rid of the "powerful, pervasive, and long-lasting moods and motivations" of devaluation of female power, denigration of the female body, distrust of female will, and denial of the women's bonds and heritage that have been engendered by patriarchal religion. As women struggle to create a new culture in which women's power, bodies, will, and bonds are celebrated, it seems natural that the Goddess would re-emerge as symbol of the new-found beauty, strength, and power of women.

NOTES

1. From the original cast album, Buddah Records, 1976.

2. See Susan Rennie and Kirsten Grimstad, "Spiritual Explorations Cross-Country," *Quest*, 1975, vol. 1, no. 4, 1975, pp. 49–51; and *WomanSpirit* magazine.

3. See Starhawk, "Witchcraft and Women's Culture," in *Womanspirit Rising*.

4. Clifford Geertz, "Religion as a Cultural System," in William L. Lessa and Evon V. Vogt, eds., *Reader in Comparative Religion*, 2nd ed. (New York: Harper & Row, 1972), p. 206.

5. Geertz, p. 210.

6. Boston: Beacon Press, 1973, p. 13, italics added.

7. Simone de Beauvoir, *The Second Sex*, trans. H. M. Parshleys (New York: Alfred A. Knopf, 1953).

8. Grimstad and Rennie, loc. cit.

9. *Les Guérillères*, trans. David LeVay (New York: Avon Books, 1971), P. 89. Also quoted in Morgan MacFarland, "Witchcraft: The Art of Remembering," *Quest*, 1975, vol. 1, no. 4, p. 41.

10. "Speaking for Myself," *Lady Unique*, 1976, Cycle 1, p. 56.

11. Personal communication.

12. A term coined by Naomi Goldenberg to refer to reflection on the meaning of the symbol of Goddess.

13. This theory of the origins of the Western dualism is stated by Rosemary Ruether in *New Woman: New Earth* (New York: Seabury Press, 1975), and elsewhere.

14. Heinrich Kramer and Jacob Sprenger (New York: Dover, 1971), p. 47.

15. See Rita M. Gross, "Menstruation and Childbirth as Ritual and Religious Experience in the Religion of the Australian Aborigines," in *The Journal of the American Academy of Religion*, 1977, vol. 45, no. 41, Supplement, pp. 1147–1181.

16. Judy Chicago, *Through the Flower* (New York: Doubleday & Company, 1975), plate 4, pp. 106–107.

17. See Adrienne Rich, *Of Woman Born* (New York: Bantam Books, 1977), chaps. 6 and 7.

18. See James Mellaart, *Earliest Civilizations of the Near East* (New York: McGraw-Hill, 1965), p. 92.

19. Barbry My Own, "Ursa Maior: Menstrual Moon Celebration," *Moon, Moon*, Anne Kent Rush, ed. (Berkeley, Calif., and New York: Moon Books and Random House, 1976), pp. 374–387.

20. Starhawk, in *Womanspirit Rising*.

21. Judy Chicago, op. cit., pp. 213–217.

22. "The Human Situation: A Feminine View," *Journal of Religion*, 1960, vol. 40, pp. 100–112.

23. *A Room of One's Own* (New York: Harcourt Brace Jovanovich, 1928), p. 86.

24. Rich, op. cit., p. 226.

25. De Beauvoir, op. cit., pp. 448–449.

26. "Old Time Woman," lyrics by Jeffrey Langley and Holly Near, from *Holly Near: A Live Album*, Redwood Records, 1974.

27. "Started Out Fine," by Holly Near from *Holly Near: A Live Album*.

28. Rich, op. cit., p. 223.

Study Questions

1. According to Christ, why do symbols have both psychological and political effects?

2. Christ borrows the notions of "mood" and "motivation" from the work of Clifford Geertz. What are moods and motivations, as Christ uses the terms?

3. Christ writes, "[A woman] may see herself as like God (created in the image of God) only by denying her own sexual identity and affirming God's transcendence of sexual identity. But she can never have the experience that is freely available to every man and boy in her culture, of having her full sexual identity affirmed as being in the image and likeness of God." According to Christ, what are the implications of this for women?

4. According to Christ, what are the four libratory (for women) "moods" and corresponding "motivations" that accompany the change in symbol system from God to Goddess? In other words, according to Christ, why *do* women need the Goddess?

5. In what sense can Christ be read as making a sameness/gynocentric argument?

Alice Walker

The Only Reason You Want to Go to Heaven Is That You Have Been Driven Out of Your Mind (Off Your Land and Out of Your Lover's Arms)

Clear Seeing Inherited Religion and Reclaiming the Pagan Self

> Unto the woman God said: I will greatly multiply thy sorrow and thy conception; in sorrow thou shalt bring forth children; and thy desire shall be to thy husband, and he shall rule over thee.
>
> —Genesis

In my novel *The Color Purple* Celie and Shug discuss, as all thoughtful humans must, the meaning of God. Shug says, "I believe God is everything that is, ever was or ever will be." Celie, raised to worship a God that resembles "the little fat white man who works in the bank," only bigger and bearded, learns to agree. I agree also. It was years after writing these words for Shug that I discovered they were also spoken, millennia ago, by Isis, ancient Goddess of Africa, who, as an African, can be said to be a spiritual mother of us all.

There is a special grief felt by the children and grandchildren of those who were forbidden to read, forbidden to explore, forbidden to question or to know. Looking back on my parents' and grandparents' lives, I have often felt overwhelmed, helpless, as I've examined history and society, and especially religion, with them in mind, and have seen how they were manipulated away from a belief in their own judgment and faith in themselves.

It is painful to realize they were forever trying to correct a "flaw"—that of being black, female, human—that did not exist, except as "men of God," but really men of greed, misogyny, and violence, defined it. What a burden to think one is conceived in sin rather than in pleasure; that one is born into evil rather than into joy. In my work, I speak to my parents and to my most distant ancestors about what I myself have found as an Earthling growing naturally out of the Universe. I create characters who sometimes speak in the language of immediate ancestors, characters who are not passive but active in the discovery of what is vital and real in this world. Characters who explore what it would feel like not to be imprisoned by the hatred of women, the love of violence, and the destructiveness of greed taught to human beings as the "religion" by which they must guide their lives.

What is happening in the world more and more is that people are attempting to decolonize their spirits.

A crucial act of empowerment, one that might return reverence to the Earth, thereby saving it, in this fearful-of-Nature, spiritually colonized age. [. . .]

In day-to-day life, I worship the Earth as God— representing everything—and Nature as its spirit. But for a long time I was confused. After all, when someone you trust shows you a picture of a blond, blue-eyed Jesus Christ and tells you he's the son of God, you get an instant image of his father: an older version of him. When you're taught God loves you, but only if you're good, obedient, trusting, and so forth, and you know you're that way only some of the time, there's a tendency to deny your shadow side. Hence the hypocrisy I noted early on in our church.

The church I attended as a child still stands. It is small, almost tiny, and made of very old, silver-gray lumber, painted white a couple of decades ago, when an indoor toilet was also added. It is simple, serene, sweet. It used to nestle amid vivid green foliage at a curve in a sandy dirt road; inside, its rough-hewn benches smelled warmly of pine. Its yard was shaded by a huge red oak tree, from which people took bits of bark to brew a tonic for their chickens. I remember my mother boiling the bark she'd cut from the tree and feeding the reddish brown "tea" to her pullets, who, without it, were likely to cannibalize each other. The county, years later, and without warning, cut down the tree and straightened and paved the road. In an attempt to create a tourist industry where none had existed before, they flooded the surrounding countryside. The fisherpeople from far away who whiz by in their pickup trucks today know nothing about what they see. To us, they are so unconnected to the land they appear to hover above it, like ghosts. [. . .]

My mother, in addition to her other duties as worker, wife, and mother of eight children, was also mother of the church. I realize now that I was kind of a little church mother in training, as I set out for the church with her on Saturday mornings. We would mop the bare pine floors, run dust rags over the benches, and wash the windows. Take out the ashes, dump them behind the outhouse, clean the outhouse, and be sure there was adequate paper. We would sweep the carpeting around the pulpit and I would reverently dust off the Bible. Each Saturday my mother slipped a starched and ironed snowy-white doily underneath it.

One season she resolved to completely redo the pulpit area. With a hammer and tacks and rich, wine-dark cloth she'd managed to purchase from meager savings, she upholstered the chairs, including the thronelike one in which the preacher sat. She also laid new carpeting. On Sunday morning she would bring flowers from her garden.

There has never been anyone who amazed and delighted me as consistently as my mother did when I was a child. Part of her magic was her calm, no-nonsense manner. If it could be done, she could probably do it, was her attitude. She enjoyed being strong and capable. Anything she didn't know how to do, she could learn. I was thrilled to be her apprentice.

My father and brothers cleared the cemetery of brush and cut the grass around the church while we were inside. By the time we were finished, everything sparkled. We stood back and admired our work.

Sister Walker, my mother, was thanked for making the church so beautiful, but this wise woman, who knew so many things about life and the mysteries of the heart, the spirit, and the soul, was never asked to speak to the congregation. If she and other "mothers" and "sisters" of the church had been asked to speak, if it had been taken for granted that they had vision and insight to match their labor and their love, would the church be alive today?

And what would the women have said? Would they have protested that the Eve of the Bible did not represent them? That they had never been that curious? But of course they had been just as curious. If a tree had appeared in their midst with an attractive fruit on it, and furthermore one that they were informed would make them wise, they would have nibbled it. And what could be so wrong about that? Anyway, God had told Adam about the forbidden fruit; He hadn't said a word directly to Eve. And what kind of God would be so cruel as to curse women and men forever for eating a piece of fruit, no matter how forbidden? Would they have said that Adam was a weak man who evaded personal responsibility for his actions? Would they have pointed out how quickly and obsequiously he turned in his wife to God, as if she had forced him to eat the fruit rather than simply offered him a bite? Would they have said Adam's behavior reminded them of a man who got a woman pregnant and then blamed the woman for tempting him to have intercourse, thereby placing all the blame on her? Would they have said that God was unfair? Well, He was white, His son was white, and it truly was a white man's world, as far as they could see.

Would they have spoken of the God they had found, not in the Bible, but in life, as they wrestled death while delivering babies, or as they worked almost beyond, and sometimes beyond, capacity in the white man's fields? I remember my mother telling me of a time when she was hugely pregnant and had an enormous field of cotton, twenty-five or thirty acres, to chop, that is, to thin and weed. Her older children were in school, from which she refused to take them, her youngest trailed behind her and fell asleep in the furrows. My father, who was laborer, dairyman, and chauffeur, had driven the bosslady to town. As my mother looked out over the immense acreage still to be covered, she felt so ill she could barely lift the hoe. Never had she felt so alone. Coming to the end of a row, she lay down under a tree and asked to die. Instead, she fell into a deep sleep, and when she awakened, she was fully restored. In fact, she felt wonderful, as if a healing breeze had touched her soul. She picked up the hoe and continued her work.

What God rescued my mother? Was it the God who said women deserved to suffer and were evil anyway, or was it the God of nonjudgmental Nature, calming and soothing her with the green coolness of the tree she slept under and the warm earth she lay upon? I try to imagine my mother and the other women calling on God as they gave birth, and I shudder at the image of Him they must have conjured. He was someone, after all, they had been taught, who said black people were cursed to be drawers of water and hewers of wood. That some people enslaved and abused others was taken for granted by Him. He ordered the killing of women and children, by the hundreds of thousands, if they were not of his chosen tribe. The women would have had to know how little they and their newborns really mattered, because

they were female, poor, and black, like the accursed children of Hagar and of Ham, and they would have had to promise to be extra good, obedient, trusting, and so forth, to make up for it.

Life was so hard for my parents' generation that the subject of heaven was never distant from their thoughts. The preacher would gleefully, or so it seemed to me, run down all the trials and tribulations of an existence that ground us into dust, only to pull heaven out of the biblical hat at the last minute. I was intrigued. Where is heaven? I asked my parents. Who is going to be there? What about accommodations, and food? I was told what they sincerely believed: that heaven was in the sky, in space, as we would later describe it; that only the best people on earth would go there when they died. We'd all have couches to lounge on, great food to eat. Wonderful music, because all the angels played harp. It would be grand. Would there be any white people? Probably. Oh.

There was not one white person in the county that any black person felt comfortable with. And though there was a rumor that a good white woman, or man, had been observed sometime, somewhere, no one seemed to know this for a fact.

Now that there's been so much space travel and men have been on the moon, I wonder if preachers still preach about going to heaven, and whether it's the same place.

The truth was, we already lived in paradise but were worked too hard by the land-grabbers to enjoy it. This is what my mother, and perhaps the other women, knew, and this was one reason why they were not permitted to speak. They might have demanded that the men of the church notice Earth. Which always leads to revolution. In fact, everyone has known this for a very long time. For the other, more immediate and basic, reason my mother and the other women were not permitted to speak in church was that the Bible forbade it. And it is forbidden in the Bible because, in the Bible, men alone are sanctioned to own property, in this case, Earth itself. And woman herself *is* property, along with the asses, the oxen, and the sheep. [. . .]

"Pagan" means "of the land, country dweller, peasant," all of which my family was. It also means a person whose primary spiritual relationship is with Nature and the Earth. And this, I could see, day to day, was true not only of me but of my parents; but there was no way to ritually express the magical intimacy we felt with Creation without being accused of, and ridiculed for, indulging in "heathenism," that other word for paganism. And Christianity, we were informed, had fought long and hard to deliver us from *that*. In fact, millions of people were broken, physically and spiritually, literally destroyed, for nearly two millennia, as the orthodox Christian Church "saved" them from their traditional worship of the Great Mystery they perceived in Nature.

In the Sixties many of us scared our parents profoundly when we showed up dressed in our "African" or "Native American" or "Celtic" clothes. We shocked them by wearing our hair in its ancient naturalness. They saw us turning back to something that they'd been taught to despise and that, by now, they actively feared. Many of our parents had been taught that the world was only two or three thousand years old, and that spiritually, civilized life began with the birth of Jesus Christ. Their only hope of enjoying a better existence, after a lifetime of crushing toil and persistent abuse, was to be as much like the long-haired rabbi from a small Jewish sect in a far-off desert as possible; then, by the Grace of His father, who owned heaven, they might be admitted there, after death. It would be segregated, of course, who could imagine anything different? But perhaps Jesus Christ himself would be present, and would speak up on their behalf. After all, these were black people who were raised never to look a white person directly in the face.

I think now, and it hurts me to think it, of how tormented the true believers in our church must have been, wondering if, in heaven, Jesus Christ, a white man, the only good one besides Santa Claus and Abraham Lincoln they'd ever heard of, would deign to sit near them. [. . .]

[. . .] but only a very small number of us would get into heaven. There was hell, a pit of eternally burning fire, for the vast majority.

Where was hell? I wanted to know. Under the ground, I was informed. It was assumed most of the white people would be there, and therefore it would be more or less like here. Only fiery hot, hotter than the sun in the cotton field at midday. Nobody wanted to go there.

I had a problem with this doctrine at a very early age: I could not see how my parents had sinned. Each month my mother had what I would later recognize, because I unfortunately inherited it, as bad PMS. At those times her temper was terrible; the only safe thing was to stay out of her way. My father, slower to anger, was nonetheless a victim of sexist ideology learned from his father, the society, and the church, which meant I battled with him throughout childhood, until I left home for good at seventeen. But I did not see that they were evil, that they should be cursed because they were black, because my mother was a woman. They were as innocent as trees, I felt. And, at heart, generous and sweet. I resented the minister and the book he read from that implied they could be "saved" only by confessing their sin and accepting suffering and degradation as their due, just because a very long time ago, a snake had given a white woman an apple and she had eaten it and generously given a bite to her craven-hearted husband. This was insulting to the most drowsy intelligence, I thought. Noting that my exhausted father often napped while in church. But what could I do? I was three years old. [. . .]

It is ironic, to say the least, that the very woman out of whose body I came, whose pillowy arms still held me, willingly indoctrinated me away from herself and the earth from which both of us received sustenance, and toward a frightful, jealous, cruel, murderous "God" of another race and tribe of people, and expected me to forget the very breasts that had fed me and that I still leaned against. But such is the power of centuries-old indoctrination. [. . .]

In the black church we have loved and leaned on Moses, because he brought the enslaved Israelites out of Egypt. As enslaved and oppressed people, we have identified with him so completely that we have adopted his God. [. . .]

It is fatal to love a God who does not love you. A God specifically created to comfort, lead, advise, strengthen, and enlarge the tribal borders of someone else. We have been beggars at the table of a religion that sanctioned our destruction. Our own religions denied, forgotten; our own ancestral connections to All Creation something of which we are ashamed. I maintain that we are empty, lonely, without our pagan-heathen ancestors; that we must lively them up within ourselves, and begin to see them as whole and necessary and correct: their Earth-centered, female-reverencing religions, like their architecture, agriculture, and music, suited perfectly to the lives they led. And lead, those who are left, today. I further maintain that the Jesus most of us have been brought up to adore must be expanded to include the "wizard" and the dancer, and that when this is done, it becomes clear that he coexists quite easily with pagan indigenous peoples. Indeed, it was because the teachings of Jesus were already familiar to many of our ancestors, especially in the New World—they already practiced the love and sharing that he preached—that the Christian Church was able to make as many genuine converts to the Christian religion as it did.

All people deserve to worship a God who also worships them. A God that made them, and likes them. That is why Nature, Mother Earth, is such a good choice. Never will Nature require that you cut off some part of your body to please It; never will Mother Earth find anything wrong with your natural way. She made it, and She made it however it is so that you will be more comfortable as part of Her Creation, rather than less. Everyone deserves a God who adores our freedom: Nature would never advise us to do anything but be ourselves. Mother Earth will do all that She can to support our choices. Whatever they are. For they are of Her, and inherent in our creation is Her trust.

We are born knowing how to worship, just as we are born knowing how to laugh.

And what is the result of decolonizing the spirit? It is as if one truly does possess a third eye, and this eye opens. One begins to see the world from one's own point of view; to interact with it out of one's own conscience and heart. One's own "pagan" Earth spirit. We begin to flow, again, with and into the Universe. And out of this flowing comes the natural activism of wanting to survive, to be happy, to enjoy one another and Life, and to laugh. We begin to distinguish between the need, singly, to throw rocks at whatever is oppressing us, and the creative joy that arises when we bring our collective stones of resistance against injustice together. We begin to see that we must be loved very much by whatever Creation is, to find ourselves on this wonderful Earth. We begin to recognize our sweet, generously appointed place in the makeup of the Cosmos. We begin to feel glad, and grateful to be *here*.

NOTE

This exploration of my own spiritual quest was presented at Auburn Theological Seminary, New York City, in April of 1995.

Study Questions

1. Walker writes, "It is painful to realize that they [i.e., her parents and grandparents] were forever trying to correct a 'flaw'—that of being black, female, human." Explain this quotation. According to Walker, how is Christianity implicated by this statement?

2. Walker suggests that she and her parents were pagan but were unable to embrace that identity. What does she mean by this?

3. Compare and contrast Walker's argument here with Christ's in "Why Women Need the Goddess."

4. In what sense can Walker be read as making a sameness/gynocentric argument?

Sara Ruddick

Notes Toward a Feminist Maternal Peace Politics

Maternal Practice

Maternal practice begins in a response to the reality of a biological child in a particular social world. To be a "mother" is to take upon oneself the responsibility of child care, making its work a regular and substantial part of one's working life.

Mothers, as individuals, engage in all sorts of other activities, from farming to deep sea diving, from astrophysics to elephant training. Mothers as individuals are not defined by their work; they are lovers and friends; they watch baseball, ballet, or the soaps; they run marathons, play chess, organize church bazaars and rent strikes. Mothers are as diverse as any other humans and are equally shaped by the social milieu in which they work. In my terminology they are "mothers" just because and to the degree that they are committed to meeting demands that define maternal work.

Both her child and the social world in which a mother works make these demands. "Demands" is an artificial term. Children demand all sorts of things— to eat ice cream before dinner, stay up all night, take the subway alone, watch the latest horror show on TV. A mother's social group demands of her all sorts of behavior—that she learn to sew or get a high school degree, hold her tongue or speak wittily in public, pay her taxes or go to jail for refusing to do so,

sit ladylike in a restaurant or sit in at a lunch counter. A mother will decide in her own way which of these demands she will meet.

But in my discussion of maternal practice, I mean by "demands" those requirements that are imposed on anyone doing maternal work, in the way respect for experiment is imposed on scientists and racing past the finish line is imposed on jockeys. In this sense of demand, children "demand" that their lives be preserved and their growth fostered. In addition, the primary social groups with which a mother is identified, whether by force, kinship, or choice, demand that she raise her children in a manner acceptable to them. These three demands—for *preservation*, *growth*, and *social acceptability*—constitute maternal work; to be a mother is to be committed to meeting these demands by works of preservative love, nurturance, and training.

Conceptually and historically, the preeminent of these demands is that of preservation. As a species, human children share prolonged physical fragility and therefore prolonged dependence on adults for their safety and well-being. In all societies, children need protective care, though the causes and types of fragility and the means of protection vary widely. This universal need of human children creates and defines a category of human work. A mother who callously endangers her child's well-being is simply not doing maternal work. (This does not mean that she is a bad person. She may sacrifice maternal work out of desperation or in a noble cause.)

The demand for protection is both epistemological and practical. Meeting the demand presupposes a minimal attentiveness to children and an awareness that their survival depends upon protective care. Imaginatively grasping the significance of children's biological vulnerability is necessary but not sufficient for responding to them. The perception that someone is in need of care may lead to caring; but then again it may lead to running away. In the settings where I first encountered polliwogs and goldfish (usually in jars and bowls where I'd managed to put them), they were exceedingly vulnerable. When I was young, I saw that these little creatures were vulnerable and I cared for them. Much later, when I was dealing with my children's attachment to them, I found the vulnerability and total unpredictability of goldfish merely an annoyance. I cared for them because I cared for my children but, given the total inadequacy of our caring, I would have been delighted if my children had forgotten them altogether. Now I almost never think about goldfish and never want to care for one the rest of my life.

Given the passions that we have for children, comparing them to goldfish may seem frivolous. When you *see* children as demanding care, the reality of their vulnerability and the necessity of a caring response seem unshakable. But I deliberately stress the optional character first of perceiving "vulnerability" and then of responding with care. Maternal responses are complicated acts that social beings make to biological beings whose existence is inseparable from social interpretations. Maternal practice begins with a double vision—seeing the fact of biological vulnerability as socially significant and as demanding care. Neither birth nor the actual presence of a vulnerable infant guarantees care. In the most desperate circumstances mothers are more apt to feed their babies than to let them sicken and starve. Yet when infants were dependent solely on mothers' milk, biological mothers could refuse the food their children needed, for example, sending them away to wet-nurses, although this was known to have a high

risk of illness and even death.[1] To be committed to meeting children's demand for preservation does not require enthusiasm or even love; it simply means to see vulnerability and to respond to it with care rather than abuse, indifference, or flight. Preserving the lives of children is the central constitutive, invariant aim of maternal practice; the commitment to achieving that aim is the constitutive maternal act.

The demand to preserve a child's life is quickly supplemented by the second demand, to nurture its emotional and intellectual growth. Children grow in complex ways, undergoing radical qualitative as well as quantitative change from childhood to adulthood. They experience intense emotions and varieties of changing, complex sexual desire. As they grow they develop more or less useful ways of coping with other people and their own feelings—adaptive strategies and defenses against anxiety, fear, shame, and guilt. Children's minds also develop gradually, their cognitive capacities and uses of memory becoming different in kind as they move from early childhood through adolescence. In one sense, children grow "naturally," provided favorable conditions for growing. On the other hand, each child grows in her or his distinctive, often peculiar way. Children's desires, defenses, and goals can be hurtful to others and to themselves; their cognitive and emotional development is easily distorted or inhibited. They "demand" nurturance.

This demand to foster children's growth appears to be historically and culturally specific to a degree that the demand for preservation is not. To be aware of children's need for nurturance depends on a belief, prevalent in my social milieu, that children have complicated lives, that their minds and psyches need attending. But even in social groups I know firsthand, some people—in my experience more often men— claim that if children are protected and trained, growth takes care of itself. On the other hand, it is difficult to judge what mothers themselves really believe about the conditions of growth. Some mothers who say that children simply grow and need little nurturance nonetheless act in ways that indicate they believe their children are complex and needy beings.

To say that the demand to foster growth is culturally and historically specific does not mean that the complexity of children's lives is primarily a cultural creation. In cultures dramatically different from middle-class North American culture—where, for example, there are no notions of "adolescence" or "cognitive development"—children's growth is still complex. Only some cultures, and some people within a culture, may believe, as I do, that children's spiritual and intellectual growth requires nurturance. But what I believe, I believe about all children. When others claim that children are simple, naturally growing beings whose growth does not require attentive nurturance, we disagree in our beliefs about *all* children's needs. To believe that only the children of one's own or similar cultures are complex—that their complexity is essentially a cultural creation—is a familiar form of racism. Certainly, some children exist in conditions in which they can do no better than "simply" survive. It seems grotesque to speak of the complex psychological needs of children who are dying of famine. Yet those children, in my view, are as complicated and demanding of nurturance as any others. Where terror or deprivation reduces children to the most basic need for simple survival, they are nonetheless fragile, complicated human creatures who have been so reduced.

In the urban middle-class cultures I know best, mothers who believe that children's development is sufficiently complex to require nurturance shoulder a considerable burden. Many people other than mothers are interested in children's growth—fathers, lovers, teachers, doctors, therapists, coaches. But typically a mother assumes the primary task of maintaining conditions of growth: it is a mother who considers herself and is considered by others to be primarily responsible for arrested or defective growth. The demand to nurture children's growth is not as ineluctable as the demand to ensure their survival. Mothers often find themselves unable to deal with the complexities of their children's experience because they are overwhelmed simply tending to their children's survival or are preoccupied by their own projects or are simply exhausted and confused. Children survive nonetheless.

The third demand on which maternal practice is based is made not by children's needs but by the social groups of which a mother is a member. Social groups require that mothers shape their children's growth in "acceptable" ways. What counts as acceptable varies enormously within and among groups and cultures. The demand for acceptability, however, does not vary, nor does there seem to be much dissent from the belief that children cannot "naturally" develop in socially correct ways but must be "trained." I use the neutral, though somewhat harsh, term "training" to underline a mother's active aims to make her children "acceptable." Her training strategies may be persuasive, manipulative, educative, abusive, seductive, or respectful and are typically a mix of most of these.

A mother's group is that set of people with whom she identifies to the degree that she would count failure to meet their criteria of acceptability as her failure. The criteria of acceptability consist of the group values that a mother has internalized as well as the values of group members whom she feels she must please. Acceptability is not merely a demand imposed on a mother by her group. Indeed, mothers themselves as part of the larger social group formulate its ideals and are usually governed by an especially stringent form of acceptability that nonmothers in the group may not necessarily adhere to. Mothers want their children to grow into people whom they themselves and those closest to them can delightedly appreciate. This demand gives an urgency—sometimes exhilarating, sometimes painful—to mothers' daily lives.

In training their children, mature and socially powerful mothers find opportunities to express their own values as well as to challenge and invigorate dominant creeds. Often, however, a mother is ambivalent about her group's values and feels alienated or harassed by the group's demands on her and her children. Mothers are usually women, and women typically, though to varying degrees, have less power than men of their group. Many mothers are, at least at the beginning of their work, young women. Although they consider failing the group as their own failure, this assessment may be less motivated by moral self-definition than by fear or a need for social survival. If a group demands acceptable behavior that, in a mother's eyes, contradicts her children's need for protection and nurturance, then the mother will be caught in painful and self-fragmenting conflict. Nonetheless, however alienated they feel, mothers seem to recognize the demand to train their children as an ineluctable demand made on them as mothers.

In addition to preservation, growth, and social acceptability there may well be other demands that constitute maternal practices. Certainly there are other ways to categorize maternal commitment. But without any claim to exhaustiveness, I take the goals of preservation, growth, and social acceptability as constitutive of maternal practice.

Although in my view all social groups demand training, all mothers recognize their children's demand to be protected, and all children require some kind of nurturance, it may well be that some cultures do not recognize "children" or "mothers" in my sense of the terms. The concept of "mother" depends on that of "child," a creature considered to be of value and in need of protection. Only in societies that recognize children as creatures who demand protection, nurturance, and training is there a maternal practice that meets those demands. Social historians tell us that in many cultures, it was a normal practice to exploit, neglect, or abuse children.[2] What I call "maternal practice" is probably not ubiquitous, even though what I call "children" exist everywhere.

In any culture, maternal commitment is far more voluntary than people like to believe. Women as well as men may refuse to be aware of or to respond to the demands of children; some women abuse or abandon creatures who are, in all cultures, dependent and vulnerable. All mothers sometimes turn away, refuse to listen, stop caring. Both maternal work and the thinking that is provoked by it are decisively shaped by the possibility that any mother may refuse to see creatures as children or to respond to them as complicated, fragile, and needy.

Among those cultures who do recognize children, perceptions of their fragility and adult responses to it vary enormously and may be difficult for outsiders to understand. As anyone knows who listens to mothers, commonality of childhood demands does not preclude sharp disagreement about children's "nature" and appropriate maternal responses to it. Comparing and contrasting differing strategies of maternal work goes on among mothers all the time. When it is generous and thoughtful, this collective, self-reflective activity is a source of critical and creative maternal thinking.

To protect, nurture, and train—however abstract the schema, the story is simple. A child leans out of a high-rise window to drop a balloon full of water on a passerby. She must be hauled in from the window (preservation) and taught not to endanger innocent people (training), and the method used must not endanger her self-respect or confidence (nurturance). In any mother's day, the demands of preservation, growth, and acceptability are intertwined. Yet a reflective mother can separately identify each demand, partly because they are often in conflict. If a child wants to walk to the store alone, do you worry about her safety or applaud her developing capacity to take care of herself? If you overhear your son hurling insults at a neighbor's child, do you rush to instill decency and compassion in him, or do you let him act on his own impulses in his need to overcome shyness? If your older child, in her competitive zeal, pushes ahead of your younger, smaller child while climbing a high slide, do you inhibit her competitive pleasure or allow an aggressiveness you cannot appreciate? Should her younger brother learn to fight back? And if he doesn't, is he bowing too easily to greater strength? Most urgently, whatever you do, is somebody going to get hurt? Love may make these questions painful; it does not provide the answers. Mothers must *think*. [. . .]

NOTES TOWARD A FEMINIST MATERNAL PEACE POLITICS

Whenever a poet employs a figure or story previously accepted and defined by a culture, the poet is using a myth, and the potential is always there that the myth will be revisionist: that is, the figure or tale will be altered for appropriate ends, the old vessel filled with new wine, initially satisfying the thirst of the individual poet but ultimately making cultural change possible.

—*Alicia Ostriker*[3]

Maternal peace politics begins in a myth: mothers are peacemakers without power. War is men's business; mothers are outsiders or victims; their business is life. The myth is shattered by history. Everywhere that men fight, mothers support them. When powerful men have not discouraged them, women, and sometimes mothers, have fought as fiercely as their brothers. As feminists insist that women and men share fairly the burdens and pleasures of battle, many young women expect their lives to include, without contradiction, both fighting and mothering.

Yet the myth remains intoxicating. The contradiction between violence and maternal work is evident. Wherever there are wars, children are hurt, hungry, and frightened; homes are burned, crops destroyed, families scattered. The daily practice and long-term aims of women's caring labor are all threatened. Though mothers may be warlike, war is their enemy. Where there is peace, mothers engage in work that requires nonviolent battle, fighting while resisting the temptation to assault or abandon opponents. The connectedness of maternal nonviolence is symbolized in the relationship of a birthing woman to her infant and of the infant to her adoptive mother. Although mothers may not be peaceful, "peace" is their business. Despite clear historical evidence, the myth of maternal peacefulness survives.

Like revisionary poets, peacemakers set themselves to alter the myth so that it can survive contemporary realism about women and still serve the ends of peace. The contemporary mythmaker can point to the usefulness of mothers and maternal thinking to peace politics. Although a group of mothers, like any other group, includes ordinary militarists and peacemakers as well as fierce fighters and saintly pacifists, the practice of mothering taken as a whole gives rise to ways of thinking and acting that are useful to peace politics. Mothers might bring to *any* politics capaci-

ties honed in their work—for example, attentiveness, realism, and a welcoming attitude toward change. Some maternal characteristics, thought useful to any organized endeavor, seem specifically appropriate to nonviolent action. Nonviolent action, like maternal practice at its best, requires resilient cheerfulness, a grasping of truth that is caring, and a tolerance of ambiguity and ambivalence. For mothers, issues of proper trust, permissible force, and the possibility and value of control are alive and complex in daily work as they are in any nonviolent action. Peace itself can be conceived for both activists and mothers as depending on a connective "love" that still struggles "toward definition, grow[s] out of confusion, knowledge, misery and necessity."[4] None of this makes most mothers peaceful. Rather, those mothers who are already committed to public peacefulness—to fomenting suspicion of violence and inventing nonviolent action—can contribute distinctively to a collective peacemaking effort.

It is all to the good, from a peacemaker's perspective, that individual mothering women and men bring distinctly maternal abilities to peace work. But this is less than the revisionist myth needs. The promise of maternal peacefulness lies in the work and love to which mothers are committed. The mythical peacemaking mother does more than bring distinctive gifts to peace projects. By virtue of her mothering she is meant to be an initiator of peace and a witness against war. She represents a practice whose aims and strategies contradict those of war, which, like mothering, is also an organized human activity with moral pretensions. It is this potentially painful and lively contradiction between war and mothering as human activities that might motivate individual mothers to resist. Similarly, the principles of nonviolence by which ordinary mothers judge themselves govern a practice; it is the nonviolent aspirations of the practice, persisting through continuous and sometimes catastrophic individual failure, that suggest a wider, more public peace. Women and men whose maternal identity is central to their self-respect should, as mothers, be uneasy militarists and self-possessed peacemakers, whatever their individual proclivities.

It is here, at its deepest promise, that the myth of maternal peacefulness is most seriously challenged. It is no great surprise that many mothers love war and many more play their parts in military scripts. But it is troubling that the very demands of maternal practice often inspire a militarist politics. Maternal nonviolence is rooted in particular tribal, often racial, loyalties; the defensive and defended state celebrated by just-war theory is often the most likely object of an extended maternal love; maternal inclinations to dominate whatever is unruly threaten a vision of the body as a testament of hope. The many kinds of parochialism, denial, and inauthenticity to which maternal thinkers are prey often prevent them from seeing, let alone resisting, militarist violence.

How then can the myth of maternal peacefulness be revised? What actions or understanding can transform mothering itself? If there is no way to make the leap from mothers to peace, is it possible to build a conceptual-political bridge between them? Individual women such as Käthe Kollwitz are exemplary in their courage to change. Are there also ways to transform the *practices* of mothering, and hence the public conception of mothers? Is it possible to create a new, real and symbolic, publicly acknowledged maternal identity? Are there collective enterprises or political movements that transform the practice of those mothers who engage in them? How does participation in these movements undercut specifically militarist elements typical of maternal practices?

Among the many political movements that might serve as agents of political change, I have been struck by two that strengthen the peacefulness of mothers who participate in them and crystallize for witnesses and sympathizers new possibilities of maternal power and peacefulness. The first I call a women's politics of resistance, the second feminist politics. Although neither a women's politics of resistance nor a feminist politics is inherently a peace politics, each instructs and strengthens peacemaking. Both politics are intricately connected to mothering, yet each also challenges just those aspects of maternal practice that limit its public, effective peacefulness. Hence separately and, even more, in combination, they transform maternal practice into a work of peace.

A Women's Politics of Resistance

A women's politics of resistance is identified by three characteristics: its participants are women, they explicitly invoke their culture's symbols of femininity, and their purpose is to resist certain practices or policies of their governors.

Women, like men, typically act out of social locations and political allegiances unconnected to their sex; women are socialists or capitalists, patriots or dissidents, colonialists or nationalists. Unlike other politics, a women's politics is organized and acted out by women. Women "riot" for bread, picket against alcohol, form peace camps outside missile bases, protect their schools from government interference, or sit in against nuclear testing. A women's politics often includes men: women call on men's physical strength or welcome the protection that powerful male allies offer. Nonetheless it is women who organize themselves self-consciously as women. The reasons women give for organizing range from an appreciation of the protection afforded by "womanliness" to men's unwillingness to participate in "sentimental" politics to the difficulty in speaking, much less being taken seriously, with men around. Typically, the point of women's politics is not to claim independence from men but, positively, to organize as women. Whatever the reasons for their separatism, the fact that women organize, direct, and enact a politics enables them to exploit their culture's symbols of femininity.

Women can also organize together without evoking common understandings of femininity. Feminist actions, for example, are often organized by women who explicitly repudiate the roles, behavior, and attitudes expected of "women." What I am calling a women's politics of resistance affirms obligations traditionally assigned to women and calls on the community to respect them. Women are responsible for their children's health; in the name of their maternal duty they call on the government to halt nuclear testing, which, epitomizing a general unhealthiness, leaves strontium-90 in nursing mothers' milk. If women are to be able to feed their families, then the community must produce sufficient food and sell it at prices homemakers can afford. If women are responsible for educating young children, then they resist government efforts to interfere with local schools.

Not all women's politics are politics of resistance. There are politics organized by women that celebrate women's roles and attitudes but that serve rather than resist the state. In almost every war, mothers of heroes and martyrs join together in support of military sons, knitting, writing, and then mourning, in the service of the military state. The best-known instance of women's politics is the organization of Nazi women in praise of *Kinder, Küche, Kirche*.[5] Today in Chile, a women's organization under the direction of the dictator Pinochet's wife celebrates "feminine power" (*el poder femenino*), which expresses itself through loyalty to family and fatherland.

A women's politics of *resistance* is composed of women who take responsibility for the tasks of caring labor and then find themselves confronted with policies or actions that interfere with their right or capacity to do their work. In the name of womanly duties that they have assumed and that their communities expect of them, they resist. This feminine resistance has made some philosophers and feminists uneasy. Much like organized violence, women's resistance is difficult to predict or control. Women in South Boston resist racial integration; mothers resist the conscription of their children in just wars.

Even where women aim to resist tyranny, their "feminine" protest seems too acceptable to be effective. As Dorothy Dinnerstein eloquently laments, women are *meant* to weep while men rule and fight:

> Women's resigned, implicitly collusive, ventilation of everybody's intuition that the world men rule is murderously crazy is a central theme in folklore, literature, drama [and women's politics of resistance].
>
> Think, for instance, of the proverb that groups woman with wine and song as a necessary counterpoint to battle, a counterpoint that makes it possible for men to draw back from their will to kill just long and far enough so that they can then take it up again with new vigor. Or think of the saying "Men must work and women must weep." Woman's tears over what is lethal in man's work, this saying implies, are part of the world's eternal, unalterable way....

> [Her] tears serve not to deter man but to help him go on, for she is doing his weeping for him and he is doing what she weeps about for her.[6]

Christa Wolf expresses a related fear that women's resistance is as fragile as their dependence on individual men, loyalty to kin, and privileges of class:

> I was slow on the uptake. My privileges intruded between me and the most necessary insights; so did my attachment to my own family, which did not depend upon the privileges I enjoyed.[7]

For whatever reasons, feminists are apt to be disappointed in the sturdiness and extent of women's resistance. Dorothy Dinnerstein expresses this feminist disappointment:

> The absurd self-importance of his striving has been matched by the abject servility of her derision, which has on the whole been expressed only with his consent and within boundaries set by him, and which has on the whole worked to support the stability of the realm he rules.[8]

While some people fear that "feminine" resistance is inevitably limited—and their fears seem to me not groundless—I place my hope in its unique potential effectiveness, namely, women's social position makes them inherently "disloyal to the civilization"[9] that depends on them. Thus Hegel worries, and I hope, that ostensibly compliant women are on the edge of dissidence. The state, whose most powerful governors depend on women's work and whose stability rests on the authority of the Fathers, "creates for itself in what it suppresses and what it depends upon an internal enemy—womankind in general."[10] Underlining as Hegel does women's exclusion from power, Julia Kristeva celebrates a woman who is "an eternal dissident in relation to social and political consensus, in exile from power, and therefore always singular, fragmentary, demonic, a witch."[11] Yet like Kristeva, I find that the dissident mother, perhaps unlike other witches, is not only a potential critic of the order that excludes her but also and equally a conserver and legitimator of the order it is her duty to instill in her children. Kristeva expects from this dissident mother an "attentiveness to ethics" rooted in a collective

experience and tradition of mothering. And I would
expect from her the ambivalence that Jane Lazarre
believes keeps the heart alive, even as it slows the
trigger finger. This attentiveness to ethics can become
effectively militant in a women's politics of resistance. Its ambivalence, while a spur to compassion,
does not slow action if women are governed by principles of nonviolence that allow them to hate and
frustrate oppressors they neither mutilate nor murder.

Women's politics of resistance are as various as
the cultures from which they arise. Of the many
examples I could choose, I select one, the resistance
of Argentinian and Chilean women to military dictatorship, specifically to the policy of kidnapping,
imprisonment, torture, and murder of the "disappeared." The resistance of the Madres (mothers) of
Argentina to its military regime and the similar,
ongoing resistance of Chilean women to the Pinochet
dictatorship politically exemplify central maternal
concepts such as the primacy of bodily life and the
connectedness of self and other. At the same time,
these movements politically transform certain tendencies of maternal militarism such as cheery denial
and parochialism.

Although women's work is always threatened by
violence and although women in war always suffer
the hunger, illness, mutilation, and loss of their loved
ones, the crime of "disappearance" is especially
haunting. Kidnapping and rumors of torture and murder destroy lives and families. Yet because the fate
of the disappeared person is unclear, because no one
in power acknowledges her or his existence, let alone
disappearance, even mourning is impossible:

> To disappear means to be snatched off a street cor-
> ner, or dragged from one's bed, or taken from a
> movie theater or cafe, either by police, or soldiers, or
> men in civilian clothes, and from that moment on to
> disappear from the face of the earth leaving not a sin-
> gle trace. It means that all knowledge of the disap-
> peared is totally lost. Absolutely nothing is known
> about them. What was their fate? If they are alive,
> where are they? What are they enduring? If they are
> dead, where are their bones?[12]

Nathan Laks describes the Argentinian protest that
began in Buenos Aires in 1976:

Once in power [in Argentina in 1976], the military
systematized and accelerated the campaign of terror,
quickly annihilating the armed organizations of the
Left and the unarmed ones, as well as many individuals with little or no connection to either. The in-
discriminate nature of the kidnapping campaign and
the impunity with which it was carried out spread
terror—as intended. Relationships among friends
and relatives were shattered by unprecedented fear.
Perfectly decent individuals suddenly became afraid
even to visit the parents of a kidnap victim, for any
such gesture of compassion might condemn the visi-
tor to a terrible fate. In this terrorized society, a small
organization of women, mothers and other relatives
of kidnapped Argentines staged a stunning act of
defiance. One Thursday afternoon they gathered in
the Plaza de Mayo, the main square in Buenos Aires
and the site of countless historic incidents beginning
in 1810 with the events that led to Argentina's separation from the Spanish Empire. In the center of the
Plaza de Mayo, within clear sight of the presidential
palace, the national cathedral, and several headquarters of ministries and corporations, the Mothers
paraded in a closed circle.[13]

The Madres met each other outside hospitals or
prisons, where they took food and other provisions
and looked for traces of the disappeared, or outside
government offices, where they tried, almost invariably without success, to get some accounting of their
loved ones' whereabouts. When they marched, the
Madres wore white kerchiefs with the names of the
disappeared embroidered on them. Often they carried
lighted candles and almost always they wore or carried photographs of the disappeared. In Chile, women
chained themselves to the steps of the capitol, formed
a human chain to a mine, Lonquen, where a mass
grave was discovered, and took over a stadium where
disappeared people had been rounded up, later to be
tortured and killed.

The Latin American women's movements are
clearly politics of resistance. The women who engage
in them court imprisonment and torture and in some
cases have become "disappeared" themselves. Knowing what fearful things could happen to them, women
in Chile trained themselves to name and deal with
what they feared:

If they were afraid of facing police, they were told simply to find a policeman and stare at him until they could see him as a man and not as a representative of the state. [They] circled police vans on foot, until these symbols of the regime appeared as just another kind of motor vehicle. . . . The women also instructed one another how to deal with the tear gas . . . to stop eating two hours before demonstrations, to dress in casual clothing, to take off makeup but to put salt on their cheekbones to keep teargas powder from entering their eyes, . . . to carry lemon to avoid teargas sting and to get a jar with homemade smelling salts made up of salt and ammonia.[14]

The women talked among themselves about their terrors, found others who shared their fears, and marched with them in affinity groups. And thus they brought their bodies to bear against the state.

As in many women's politics of resistance, the Argentinian and Chilean women emphasize mothering among women's many relations. They are Madres, whether or not they are biological or adoptive mothers of individual disappeared; a later group is made up of Abuelas (grandmothers). Their presence and the character of their action, as well as the interviews they have given, invariably evoke an experience of mothering that is central to their lives, whatever other home work or wage labor they engage in. Repeatedly they remember and allude to ordinary tasks—clothing, feeding, sheltering, and most of all tending to extensive kin work. All these works, ordinarily taken for granted, are dramatically present just because they are interrupted; they are made starkly visible through the eerie "disappearance," the shattering mockery of a maternal and childlike "unchanging expectation of good in the heart."[15]

As these women honor mothering, they honor themselves. The destruction of the lives of their children, often just on the verge of adulthood, destroys years of their work; their loss and the impossibility of mourning it constitute a violent outrage against them. Yet there is something misleading about this way of talking. The women do not speak of their work but of their children; they carry children's photographs, not their own. The distinctive structuring of the relation between self and other, symbolized in birth and enacted in mothering, is now politicized. The children, the absent ones, are *not* their mothers, who have decidedly *not* disappeared but are bodily present. The singular, irreplaceable children are lost. Yet as the pictures the Madres carry suggest, the children are not, even in disappearance, apart from their mothers but, in their absence, are still inseparable from them.

For these Argentinian and Chilean women, as for women in most cultures, mothering is intuitively or "naturally" connected to giving birth. The Abuelas, especially, have made a political point of the emotional significance of genetic continuity. Since the fall of the military regime, one of their projects has been to form a genetic bank to trace the biological parentage of children adopted by people close to the ruling class at the time the military was in power. The insistence on genetic connection is one aspect of a general affirmation of the body. Indeed, the vulnerability, promise, and power of human bodies is central to this women's politics of resistance, as it is to maternal practice:

> Together with the affirmation of life, the human body is a very important reference for these women. They often speak of physical pain, the wounds caused by the disappearances. It seems that wearing a photograph of the missing one attached to the clothing or in a locket around the neck is a way of feeling closer to them.[16]

Because they have suffered military violence—have been stripped naked, sexually humiliated, and tortured—children's bodies have become a locus of pain. Because the violation of bodies is meant to terrify the body itself becomes a place where terror is wrought. In resistance to this violation mothers' bodies become instruments of nonviolent power. Adorned with representations of bodies loved and violated, they express the necessity of love even amid terror, "in the teeth of all experience of crimes committed, suffered and witnessed."[17]

In their protests, these women fulfill traditional expectations of femininity and at the same time violate them. These are women who may well have expected to live out an ideology of "separate spheres" in which men and women had distinct but complementary tasks. Whatever ideology of the sexual division of labor they may have espoused, their political circumstances, as well as the apparently greater vulnerability and the apparently greater timidity and conventionality of the men they lived among, required that they act publicly as women. Women who bring to the public plazas of a police state pictures of their loved ones, like women who put pillowcases, toys, and other artifacts of attachment against the barbed wire fences of missile bases, translate the symbols of mothering into political speech. Preservative love, singularity in connection, the promise of birth and the resilience of hope, the irreplaceable treasure of vulnerable bodily being—these clichés of maternal work are enacted in public, by women insisting that their governors name and take responsibility for their crimes. They speak a "women's language" of loyalty, love, and outrage; but they speak with a public anger in a public place in ways they were never meant to do.

Although not a "peace politics" in a conventional sense, the Latin American protest undermines tendencies of maternal practice and thinking that are identifiably militarist. To some extent, this is a matter of shifting a balance between tendencies in mothering that support militarism toward tendencies that subvert it. In this case, the balance shifts from denial to truthfulness, from parochialism to solidarity, and from inauthenticity to active responsibility. Writing about André Trocme and his parishioners in the French village of Le Chambon during World War II, Phillip Hallie identified three characteristics that enabled them to penetrate the confusion and misinformation with which Nazis covered their policy and then to act on their knowledge. "*Lucid knowledge, awareness of the pain of others*, and *stubborn decision* dissipated for the Chambonnais the Night and Fog that inhabited the minds of so many people in Europe, and the world at large, in 1942."[18] In the transformed maternal practice of the Argentinian and Chilean women, these same virtues of nonviolent resistance are at work.

Cheery denial is an endemic maternal temptation. A similar "willingness to be self-deceived," as the resistance leader André Trocme called it, also sustains many decent citizens' support of war policy. It is notorious that few people can bear, except very briefly, to acknowledge the dangers of nuclear weapons and the damage they have done and could still do. Similarly, few citizens really look at the political aims and material-emotional lives of people affected by their own country's interventionist war policies. By contrast, the Argentinian and Chilean women insist on, and then disseminate, "lucid knowledge" of military crimes. "What is so profoundly moving about them is their determination to find out the truth."[19] They insist that others, too, hear the truth. They are "ready to talk immediately; they need to talk, to make sure their story, so tragic and so common, . . . be told, be known."[20] In addition to talking, they make tapestries, "arpilleras," that tell stories of daily life including workers' organizing, police brutality, kidnapping, and resistance. The protests, tales, and arpilleras extend the maternal task of storytelling, maintaining ordinary maternal values of realism in the face of temptation to deny or distort. In this context, their ordinary extraordinary work becomes a politics of remembering.

After fighting in World War II the philosopher J. Glenn Gray wrote:

> The great god Mars tries to blind us when we enter his realm, and when we leave he gives us a generous cup of the waters of Lethe to drink. . . . When I consider how easily we forget the millions who suffered unbearably, either permanently maimed in body or mind, or who gave up their lives before they realized their purpose, I rebel at the whole insane spectacle of human existence.[21]

After the junta fell, Argentinian women insisted that violated bodies be *remembered*, which required that crimes be named, the men who committed them be brought to trial, and the bodies themselves, alive or dead, be accounted for and, where possible, returned.

"*Awareness of the pain of others*." The Argentinian and Chilean Madres spoke first of their own pain and the pain of relatives and friends of other disappeared. Similarly, maternal nonviolence is rooted, and typically limited by, a commitment to one's "own" children and the people they live among. [. . .]

I spoke of this limitation as a principal source of maternal militarism; the parochialism of maternal practice can become the racialism that fuels organized violence. This tribal parochialism was also broken down in the Argentinian and Chilean protests.

As in mothering generally, women found it easiest to extend their concern for their own children to other mothers "like them"; only in this political context likeness had to do not with race or ethnicity but with common suffering. In Argentina, where protests are marked by the "singularity" of photographs, the women came to wear identical masks to mark their commonality. In Chile one woman said:

> Because of all this suffering we are united. I do not ask for justice for my child alone, or the other women just for their children. We are asking for justice for all. All of us are equal. If we find one disappeared one I will rejoice as much as if they had found mine.[22]

Concern for all victims then sometimes extended to collective concern for all the people of the nation:

> We are the women and mothers of this land, of the workers, of the professionals, of the students, and of future generations.[23]

This is still "nationalism," though of a noble sort. Many of the women went further as they explicitly identified with all victims of military or economic violence:

> In the beginning we only wanted to rescue our children. But as time passed we acquired a different comprehension. We understood better what is going on in the world. We know that when babies do not have enough to eat that, too, is a violation of human rights.[24]
>
> We should commit ourselves to make Lonquen [the mine where a mass grave was discovered] a blessed spot. May it be a revered spot, so that never again will a hostile hand be raised against any other person that lives on the earth.[25]

It would be foolish to believe that every woman in the Argentinian and Chilean protest movements extended concern from her own children to all the disappeared then to all of the nation, and finally to all victims everywhere. Why should women whose children and loved ones have been singularly persecuted extend sympathetic protection to all victims, an extension that is extraordinary even among women and men who do not suffer singular assault? Yet many of these women did so extend themselves—intellectually, politically, emotionally. They did not "transcend" their particular loss and love; particularity was the emotional root and source of their protest. It is through acting on that particularity that they extended mothering to include sustaining and protecting any people whose lives are blighted by violence.

"Stubborn decision." As children remind us, stubborn decision is a hallmark of maternity. And mothers reply: what looks like stubborn decision may well be a compound of timidity, vacillation, and desperation. Women in resistance are (almost certainly) not free from ordinary mothers' temptations to inauthenticity, to letting others—teachers, employers, generals, Fathers, grandparents—establish standards of acceptability and delegating to them responsibility for children's lives. And like ordinary mothers, women in resistance probably include in their ranks *individuals* who in ordinary times could speak back to the teacher or organize opposition to the local corporate polluter. But "stubborn decision" takes on a new and collective political meaning when women acting together walk out of their homes to appropriate spaces they never were meant to occupy.

Like their counterparts in resistance elsewhere, these stubbornly decisive Argentinian and Chilean women, whatever their personal timidities, publicly announce that they take responsibility for protecting the world in which they and their children must live. These women are the daughters, the heirs, of Kollwitz's *mater dolorosa*. As in Kollwitz's representations, a mother is victimized through the victimization of her children. These women are themselves victims; moreover, they bear witness to victimization first of loved ones, then of strangers; they stand against those in power, in solidarity with those who are hurt. Yet there is also a sense in which, by their active courage, they refuse victimization. More accurately, they mock dichotomies that still riddle political thought. There is no contradiction between "playing the role of victim" and taking responsibility for public policies. It is possible to act powerfully while standing with those who are hurt. It is neither weak nor passive to reveal one's own suffering while refusing to damage or mutilate in return. The Latin American *mater dolorosa* has learned how to fight as a victim for victims, not by joining the strong, but by resisting them.

A women's politics of resistance is not inherently a peace politics. Women can organize to sabotage peace treaties or to celebrate the heroes and martyrs of organized violence. During the Malvinas-Falklands war, Argentinian and English women sought each other out at a women's meeting in New York to denounce together their countries' militarism and imperialism. Yet during that same war, the Argentinian Madres were reported to use patriotic rhetoric to reinforce their own aims: "The Malvinas belong to us and so do our sons."

Nonetheless, in their own contexts, the Argentinian protest had and the Chilean protest still has antimilitarist implications. The regimes against which the women protest were and are militarist; the omnipresence of the soldier as oppressor and the general as the torturers' commander was—and in Chile still is— sufficient to symbolize a contrast between women and war. Moreover, the generals' actions have not been accidentally related to militarism. As Plato saw, when he rejected militarist rule in his totalitarian state, torture, kidnapping and other physical terrorism infect the rule of fearful tyrants, just as atrocities infect the best organized war. In their deliberately and increasingly brutal strategies to ensure absolute control, the generals exemplify the excesses inherent in militarized tyranny. Hence in the women's protests, not only a particular government but military rule is brought to trial.

Whatever their militarist sentiments or rhetoric, the Argentinian and Chilean protests express to the world the ideals of nonviolence. Although effective protest inevitably hurts its opponents and those associated with them, the protesters did not set out to injure but to end injuring. None of their actions even risked serious, lasting physical damage. Their aim was steadfastly one of reconnection and restoration of a just community, even though and because those responsible for violence were held accountable and were punished. By providing an example of persistent, stubborn action, the Argentinian and Chilean women have offered a model of nonviolent resistance to other Latin American countries and to the world. They have therefore contributed to collective efforts to invent peace, whatever their degree of effectiveness within their own countries. Like the maternal practice from which it grows, a women's politics of resistance may remain racial, tribal, or chauvinist; we cannot expect of women in resistance the rare human ability to stand in solidarity with all victims of violence. Yet if these Latin American protests are at all emblematic, they suggest that the peacefulness latent in maternal practice tends to be realized as participants act against, and therefore reflect on, violence itself.

NOTES

1. The example is from Elisabeth Badinter, *Mother Love: Myth and Reality* (New York: Macmillan, 1980).

2. There is considerable controversy about parental attitudes toward children in different historical periods or in different subcultures of North America, particularly over the extent and degree to which children have been exploited and abused. What no one seems to dispute is that there is wide social as well as individual variation in the basic understanding of the needs and rights of children. Elisabeth Badinter, *Mother Love* is a good place to start reading about this issue. Lloyd De Mause has written extensively about the "nightmare" of childhood. See "The Evolution of Childhood," *The History of Childhood Quarterly*, Spring 1974, pp. 503–575. For a different perspective see John Demos, *Past, Present, and Personal* (New York: Oxford University Press, 1986).

3. Alicia Ostriker, *Stealing the Language* (Boston: Beacon Press, 1986), p. 212.

4. Jane Lazarre, *The Mother Knot* (Boston: Beacon Press, 1986), p. 156.

5. For a discussion of women's participation in (and occasional resistance to) the Nazi German government, see Claudia Koonz, *Mothers in the Fatherland: Women, the Family, and Nazi Politics* (New York: St. Martin's, 1987). Among the many virtues of this fascinating book is its tracing of the complex interconnections between women's

separate spheres, the Nazi and feminist use of women's difference, and women's participation in but also disappointment in the Nazi state.

6. Dorothy Dinnerstein, *The Mermaid and the Minotaur* (New York: Harper & Row, 1976), p. 226.

7. Christa Wolf, *Cassandra* (New York: Farrar Straus & Giroux, 1984), p. 53.

8. Dorothy Dinnerstein, "The Mobilization of Eros," in *Face to Face* (Greenwood Press, 1982). Manuscript courtesy of the author. For an intellectually sophisticated and high-spirited account of an American women's politics of resistance, see Amy Swerdlow's work on Women's Strike for Peace, forthcoming from the University of Chicago Press. For an example of her work, see "Pure Milk, Not Poison: Women's Strike for Peace and the Test Ban Treaty of 1963," in *Rocking the Ship of State: Toward a Feminist Peace Politics*, ed. Adrienne Harris and Ynestra King (Westview Press, 1989).

9. The title of a well-known essay by Adrienne Rich in *Lies, Secrets and Silence* (New York: Norton, 1979), pp. 275–310.

10. Hegel, *The Phenomenology of Mind*, part VI, A, b, "Ethical Action: Knowledge Human and Divine: Guilt and Destiny" (New York: Harper, 1967), p. 496.

11. Julia Kristeva, "Talking about *Polygoue*" (an interview with Françoise van Rossum-Guyon), in *French Feminist Thought*, ed. Toril Moi (Oxford: Basil Blackwell, 1987), p. 113.

12. Marjorie Agosin, "Emerging from the Shadows: Women of Chile," *Barnard Occasional Papers On Women's Issues*, vol. 2, no. 3, Fall 1987, p. 12. I am very grateful to Temma Kaplan, historian and director of the Barnard College Women's Center, whose interest in "motherist" and grass-roots women's resistance movements inspired this section. Temma Kaplan provided me with material on the Madres and discussed an earlier draft of the chapter.

13. Nathan Laks, cited in Nora Amalia Femenia, "Argentina's Mothers of Plaza de Mayo: The Mourning Process from Junta to Democracy," *Feminist Studies*, vol. 13, no. 1, p. 10. The Argentinian Madres protested until the fall of the military regime and still exist today, though they are now divided in their political aims.

14. Marjorie Agosin, Temma Kaplan, Teresa Valduz, "The Politics of Spectacle in Chile," *Barnard Occasional Papers on Women's Issues*, vol. 2, no. 3, Fall 1987, p. 6.

15. Simone Weil, "Human Personality," in *Simone Weil Reader*, p. 315.

16. Agosin, "Emerging," p. 18

17. Simone Weil, "Human Personality," in *Simone Weil Reader*, p. 315.

18. Phillip Hallie, *Lest Innocent Blood Be Shed* (New York: Harper & Row, 1979), p. 104. (Italics added.)

19. Agosin, "Emerging," p. 16.

20. Agosin, "Emerging," p. 14.

21. J. Glenn Gray, *The Warriors* (New York: Harper & Row, 1970), pp. 21, 23.

22. Agosin, "Emerging," p. 21.

23. Patricia M. Chuchryk, "Subversive Mothers: The Women's Opposition to the Military Regime in Chile," paper presented at the International Congress of the Latin American Studies Association, Boston, 1986, p. 9.

24. Rene Epelbaum, member of the Argentinian protest, in an interview with Jean Bethke Elshtain, personal communication.

25. Agosin, "Emerging," p. 18.

Study Questions

1. In Ruddick's view, what is a mother? Can a male be a mother?

2. Ruddick speaks of the "contradiction between violence and maternal work" (see the section entitled "Notes Toward a Feminist Maternal Peace Politics," paragraph 2). What is the contradiction? Does Ruddick take this contradiction to entail that mothers cannot be violent or support violence? Why or why not?

3. What stance does Ruddick take to the "myth" that "mothers are peacemakers without power"? Does she accept it? Reject it? Revise it? If she revises it, explain her revision.

4. What is "a woman's politics of resistance"? In what ways, according to Ruddick, does the Latin American movement she discusses challenge militarist tendencies in material practice?

5. In what sense can Ruddick be read as taking a difference/gynocentric approach?

Vandana Shiva

Women's Indigenous Knowledge and Biodiversity Conservation

Gender and diversity are linked in many ways. The construction of women as the "second sex" is linked to the same inability to cope with difference as is the development paradigm that leads to the displacement and extinction of diversity in the biological world. The patriarchal world view sees man as the measure of all value, with no space for diversity, only for hierarchy. Woman, being different, is treated as unequal and inferior. Nature's diversity is seen as not intrinsically valuable in itself, its value is conferred only through economic exploitation for commercial gain. This criterion of commercial value thus reduces diversity to a problem, a deficiency. Destruction of diversity and the creation of monocultures becomes an imperative for capitalist patriarchy.

The marginalization of women and the destruction of biodiversity go hand in hand. Loss of diversity is the price paid in the patriarchal model of progress which pushes inexorably towards monocultures, uniformity and homogeneity. In this perverted logic of progress, even conservation suffers. Agricultural "development" continues to work towards erasing diversity, while the same global interests that destroy biodiversity urge the Third World to conserve it. This separation of production and consumption, with "production" based on uniformity and "conservation" desperately attempting to preserve diversity militates against protecting biodiversity. It can be

protected only by making diversity the basis, foundation and logic of the technology and economics of production.

The logic of diversity is best derived from biodiversity and from women's links to it. It helps look at dominant structures from below, from the ground of diversity, which reveal monocultures to be unproductive and the knowledge that produces them as primitive rather than sophisticated.

Diversity is, in many ways, the basis of women's politics and the politics of ecology; gender politics is largely a politics of difference. Eco-politics, too, is based on nature's variety and difference, as opposed to industrial commodities and processes which are uniform and homogeneous.

These two politics of diversity converge when women and biodiversity meet in fields and forest, in arid regions and wetlands.

DIVERSITY AS WOMEN'S EXPERTISE

Diversity is the principle of women's work and knowledge. This is why they have been discounted in the patriarchal calculus. Yet it is also the matrix from which an alternative calculus of "productivity" and "skills" can be built that respects, not destroys, diversity.

The economies of many Third World communities depend on biological resources for their sustenance and well-being. In these societies, biodiversity is simultaneously a means of production, and an object of consumption. The survival and sustainability of livelihoods is ultimately connected to the conservation and sustainable use of biological resources in all their diversity. Tribal and peasant societies' biodiversity-based technologies, however, are seen as backward and primitive and are, therefore, displaced by "progressive" technologies that destroy both diversity and people's livelihoods.

There is a general misconception that diversity-based production systems are low-productivity systems. However, the high productivity of uniform and homogenous systems is a contextual and theoretically constructed category, based on taking into account only one-dimensional yields and outputs. The alleged low productivity of the one against the alleged high productivity of the other is, therefore, not a neutral, scientific measure but biased towards commercial interests for whom maximizing the one-dimensional output is an economic imperative.

Crop uniformity, however, undermines the diversity of biological systems which form the production system as well as the livelihoods of people whose work is associated with diverse and multiple-use systems of forestry, agriculture and animal husbandry. For example, in the state of Kerala in India (its name derives from the coconut palm), coconut is cultivated in a multi-layered, high-intensity cropping system, along with betel and pepper vines, bananas, tapioca, drumstick, papaya, jackfruit, mango and vegetables. The annual labour requirement in a monoculture of coconut palm is 157 man-days per ha, while in a mixed cropping system, it is 960 man-days per ha. In the dry-land farming systems of the Deccan, the shift from mixed cropping millets, pulses and oilseeds to eucalyptus monocultures led to an annual loss of employment of 250 man-days per ha.

When labour is scarce and costly, labour displacing technologies are productive and efficient, but when labour is abundant, labour displacement is unproductive because it leads to poverty, dispossession and destruction of livelihoods. In Third World situations, sustainability has therefore to be achieved at two levels simultaneously: sustainability of natural resources and sustainability of livelihoods. Consequently, biodiversity conservation must be linked to conservation of livelihoods derived from biodiversity.

Women's work and knowledge is central to biodiversity conservation and utilization both because they work between "sectors" and because they perform multiple tasks. Women, as farmers, have remained invisible despite their contribution. Economists tend to discount women's work as "production" because it falls outside the so-called "production boundary". These omissions arise not because too few women work, but too many women do too much work of too many different kinds.

Statisticians and researchers suffer a conceptual inability to define women's work inside and outside the house—and farming is usually part of both. This recognition of what is and is not labour is exacerbated by the great volume and variety of work that women do. It is also related to the fact that although women work to sustain their families and communities, most of what they do is not measured in wages. Their work is also invisible because they are concentrated outside market-related or remunerated work, and they are normally engaged in multiple tasks.

Time allocation studies, which do not depend on an a priori definition of work, reflect more closely the multiplicity of tasks undertaken, and the seasonal, even daily movement in and out of the conventional labour force which characterize most rural women's livelihood strategy. Gender studies now being published, confirm that women in India are major producers of food in terms of value, volume and hours worked.

In the production and preparation of plant foods, women need skills and knowledge. To prepare seeds they need to know about seed preparation, germination requirements and soil choice. Seed preparation requires visual discrimination, fine motor co-ordination, sensitivity to humidity levels and weather conditions. To sow and strike seeds demands knowledge of seasons, climate, plant requirements, weather conditions, microclimatic factors and soil-enrichment; sowing seeds requires physical dexterity and strength. To properly nurture plants calls for information about the nature of plant diseases, pruning, staking, water supplies, companion planting, predators, sequences, growing seasons and soil maintenance. Persistence and patience, physical strength and attention to plant needs are essential. Harvesting requires judgements in relation to weather, labour and grading; and knowledge of preserving, immediate use and propagation.

Women's knowledge has been the mainstay of the indigenous dairy industry. Dairying, as managed by women in rural India, embodies practices and logic rather different from those taught in dairy science at institutions of formal education in India, since the latter is essentially an import from Europe and North America. Women have been experts in the breeding and feeding of farm animals, including not only cows and buffaloes but also pigs, chickens, ducks and goats.

In forestry too, women's knowledge is crucial to the use of biomass for feed and fertilizer. Knowledge of the feed value of different fodder species, the fuel value of firewood types, and of food products and species is essential to agriculture-related forestry in which women are predominately active. In low input agriculture, fertility is transferred from forest and farm trees to the field by women's work either directly or via animals.

Women's work and knowledge in agriculture is uniquely found in the spaces "in between" the interstices of "sectors", the invisible ecological flows between sectors, and it is through these linkages that ecological stability, sustainability and productivity under resource-scarce conditions are maintained. The invisibility of women's work and knowledge arises from the gender bias which has a blind spot for realistic assessment of women's contributions. It is also rooted in the sectoral, fragmented and reductionist approach to development which treats forests, livestock and crops as independent of each other.

The focus of the "green revolution" has been increasing grain yields of rice and wheat by techniques such as dwarfing, monocultures and multicropping. For an Indian woman farmer, rice is not only food, but also a source of cattle fodder and straw for thatch. High yield varieties (HYVs) can increase women's work; the shift from local varieties and indigenous

crop-improvement strategies can also take away women's control over seeds and genetic resources. Women have been seed custodians since time immemorial, and their knowledge and skills should be the basis of all crop-improvement strategies.

WOMEN: CUSTODIANS OF BIODIVERSITY

In most cultures women have been the custodians of biodiversity. They produce, reproduce, consume and conserve biodiversity in agriculture. However, in common with all other aspects of women's work and knowledge, their role in the development and conservation of biodiversity has been rendered as non-work and non-knowledge. Their labour and expertise has been defined into nature, even though it is based on sophisticated cultural and scientific practises. But women's biodiversity conservation differs from the dominant patriarchal notion of biodiversity conservation.

Recent concern with biodiversity at the global level has grown as a result of the erosion of diversity due to the expansion of large-scale monoculture-based agricultural production and its associated vulnerability. Nevertheless, the fragmentation of farming systems linked to the spread of monocultures continues to be the guiding paradigm for biodiversity conservation. Each element of the farm eco-system is viewed in isolation, and conservation of diversity is seen as an arithmetical exercise of collecting varieties.

In contrast, in the traditional Indian setting, biodiversity is a relational category in which each element acquires its characteristics and value through its relationships with other elements. Biodiversity is ecologically and culturally embedded. Diversity is reproduced and conserved through the reproduction and conservation of culture, in festivals and rituals which not only celebrate the renewal of life, but also provide a platform for subtle tests for seed selection and propagation. The dominant world view does not regard these tests as scientific because they do not emerge from the laboratory and the experimental plot, but are integral to the total world-view and lifestyle of people and are carried out, not by men in white coats, but by village woman. But because it is thus that the rich biological diversity in agriculture has been preserved they are systematically reliable.

When women conserve seed, they conserve diversity and therefore conserve balance and harmony. *Navdanya* or nine seeds are the symbol of this renewal of diversity and balance, not only of the plant world, but of the planet and of the social world. This complex relationship web gives meaning to biodiversity in Indian culture and has been the basis of its conservation over millennia.

"SACREDNESS": A CONSERVATION CATEGORY

In the indigenous setting, sacredness is a large part of conservation. Sacredness encompasses the intrinsic value of diversity; sacredness denotes a relationship of the part to the whole—a relationship that recognizes and preserves integrity. Profane seed violates the integrity of ecological cycles and linkages and fragments agricultural ecosystems and the relationships responsible for sustainable production at all the following levels:

1. Sacred seed is perceived as a microcosm of the macrocosm with *navdanya* symbolizing the Navagraha. The influences of planets and climate are seen as essential to plant productivity. In contrast, HYVs break links with all seasonal climatic and cosmic cycles. Multiple-cropping and photo-insensitivity are two important ways in which the HYV seeds are separated from planetary and climatic influences. But, "freedom" from seasonal cycles is based on dependence on large dams and intensive irrigation.

2. Seed diversity and nutritional balance go hand in hand. Monocultures of HYV also cause nutritional deficiency and imbalance: pulses and oilseeds are sacrificed to increase the commodity-production of cereal crops.

3. Crop-diversity is essential for maintaining soil fertility. Monocultures fed on chemical fertilizers destroy the basis of soil fertility; biodiversity enhances

it. Dwarf varieties yield no straw for recycling organic matter to the soil; chemicals kill soil fauna and flora.

4. Biodiversity is also essential to maintain the sustainability of self-provisioning farm units, where producers are also consumers. HYV monocultures mean that more farmers will become consumers of purchased seed, thereby creating dependency, increasing production costs and decreasing food entitlements at the local level.

5. Finally, purchased seeds displace women from decision-making and custodianship of seeds and transform them into unskilled labour. Main cereal crop associates are called *akadi* in Karnataka and women make all decisions relating to the *akadi* crop. In the words of a Lambani woman, "What do (men) know about the *akadi*, they only know how to *besaya* (plough)." Due to women's involvement in the *akadi* crop traditional seeds are preserved over generations. One woman said, "they are the seeds grown by me, and my mother in my native family, and it is the seeds grown by the daughter."

What insights can be derived from the everyday practice of women in agricultural communities in the conservation and renewal of biodiversity?

Firstly, the meaning of biodiversity, as epitomized in *navdanya* indicates that biodiversity is a relational not reductionist category—a contextual not atomized concept. Conserving biodiversity therefore implies conserving the relationship from which derive balance and harmony. Biodiversity cannot be conserved in fragments, except to serve raw materials requirements, as such it cannot serve as the basis of the vitality of living ecosystems and living cultures.

Secondly, the conservation of relatedness involves a notion of sacredness and inviolability. The concept of sacredness and diversity of seed is located in an entirely different world view from that in which seed is only a commodity, with profit as its only value.

Thirdly, the self-provisioning nature of most sustainable agricultural systems implies a closed cycle of production and consumption. Dominant economics is unable to take such provision into account because it counts as production only that in which the producer and consumer are different, that means that only commodity production is production, and self-provisioning is non-productive work. This is the viewpoint that counts women's heavy work-load as non-work. Unfortunately, it also provides the framework that informs dominant strategies for the conservation of biodiversity.

Thus, while biological resources have social, ethical, cultural and economic values, it is the economic values that must be demonstrated to compete for the attention of government decision-makers. Three categories of the economic values of biological resources are named, as:

- "consumptive value": value of products consumed directly without passing through a market, such as firewood, fodder and game meat;
- "productive value": value of products commercially exploited; and
- "non-consumptive use value": indirect value of ecosystem functions, such as watershed protection, photosynthesis, regulation of climate and production of soil.

An interesting value framework has thus been constructed which predetermines analysis and opinions. If the Third World's poor, who derive their livelihoods directly from nature, only "consume", while trading and commercial interests are the "only" producers, it follows quite naturally that the Third World is responsible for the destruction of its biological wealth, and the North alone has the capacity to preserve it. The ideologically constructed divisions between consumption, production and conservation conceal the political economy of the processes which underlie the destruction of biological diversity.

In particular, it transforms women, the producers and conservers of biodiversity's value, into mere consumers. Instead of building conservation programmes based on their culture, values, skills, knowledge and wisdom, dominant conservation strategies erode them, and thereby create conditions for the erosion of biodiversity as the basis of sustainable livelihoods and production systems.

Diversity in the dominant world-view is seen as a numerical and arithmetical factor, not an ecological one. It relates to arithmetical variety not to relational symbiosis and complexity. Biodiversity is usually defined as the "degree of nature's variety, including both the number and frequency of ecosystems, species and genes in a given assemblage". In contrast, for cultures and economies which have practised diversity, biodiversity is a web of relationships which ensures balance and sustainability. On the grand scale this involves a relationship between planets and plants, between cosmic harmony and agricultural harmony captured in *navdanya*.

On the more earthly level, diversity and interrelationships are characteristic of all sustainable agricultural systems. Biodiversity in this context implies co-existence and interdependence of trees, crops and livestock, which maintains cycles of fertility through biomass flows. Women's work and knowledge is concentrated in these invisible "spaces between". In addition, there are ecological relationships between the diversity of crops in mixed and rotational cropping, relationships that maintain the ecological balance through multiple functions. Mixtures of cereals and pulses create nutrient balance in the nitrogen cycle; crop mixtures maintain pest-predator balance, controlling pests without chemical or genetic engineering. Diverse mixtures also maintain the water-cycle, and conserve the soil's moisture and fertility. This ecologically-rich meaning and practice of biodiversity has been conserved over millennia on India's small farms, and has provided food and nutrition on the basis of sustainability and justice.

BIOTECHNOLOGY AND THE DESTRUCTION OF BIODIVERSITY

There are a number of crucial ways in which the Third World women's relationship to biodiversity differs from corporate men's relationship to biodiversity. Women produce through biodiversity, whereas corporate scientists produce through uniformity.

For women farmers, biodiversity has intrinsic value—for global seed and agribusiness corporations, biodiversity derives its value only as "raw material" for the biotechnology industry. For women farmers the essence of the seed is the continuity of life. For multinational corporations, the value of the seed lies in the discontinuity of its life. Seed corporations deliberately breed seeds that cannot give rise to future generations so that farmers are transformed from seed custodians into seed consumers. Hybrid seeds are "biologically patented" in that the offspring cannot be used as seeds as farmers must go back to corporations to buy seed every year. Where hybrids do not force the farmers back to the market, legal patents and "intellectual property rights" are used to prevent farmers from saving seed. Seed patents basically imply that corporations treat seed as their "creation." Patents prevent others from "making" the patented product, hence patented seed cannot be used for making seed. Royalties have to be paid to the company that gets the patent.

The claim of "creation" of life by corporate scientists is totally unjustified, it is in fact an interruption in the life flow of creation. It is also unjustified because nature and Third World farmers have made the seed that corporations are attempting to own as their innovation and their private property. Patents on seeds are thus a twenty-first century form of piracy, through which the shared heritage and custody of Third World women peasants is robbed and depleted by multinational corporations, helped by global institutions like GATT.

Patents and biotechnology contribute to a two-way theft. From Third World producers they steal biodiversity. From consumers everywhere they steal safe and healthy food.

Genetic engineering is being offered as a "green" technology worldwide. President Bush ruled in May 1992 that genetically engineered foods should be treated as "natural" and hence safe. However, genetic engineering is neither natural nor safe.

A number of risks associated with genetically engineered foods have been listed recently by the Food and Drug Administration of the US:

- New toxicants may be added to genetically engineered food.
- Nutritional quality of engineered food may be diminished.
- New substances may significantly alter the composition of food.
- New proteins that cause allergic reactions may enter the food supply.
- Antibiotic resistant genes may diminish the effectiveness of some antibiotics to human and domestic animal diseases.
- The deletion of genes may have harmful side effects.
- Genetic engineering may produce "counterfeit freshness".
- Engineered food may pose risks to domestic animals.
- Genetically engineered food crops may harm wildlife and change habitats.

When we are being asked to trust genetically engineered foods, we are being asked to trust the same companies that gave us pesticides in our food. Monsanto, which is now selling itself as Green was telling us that "without chemicals, millions more would go hungry". Today, when Bhopal has changed the image of these poisons, we are being told by the Monsantos, Ciba-Geigys, Duponts, ICIs and Dows that they will now give us Green products. However, as Jack Kloppenberg has recently said, "Having been recognized as wolves, the industrial semioticians want to redefine themselves as sheep, and green sheep at that."

Study Questions

1. According to Shiva, why are women central to the preservation of biodiversity?

2. Is the connection between women and biodiversity that Shiva proffers essentializing? If so, is that a problem for her view?

3. Shiva calls for the creation of "an alternative calculus of 'productivity' and 'skills' . . . that respects, not destroys, diversity." According to Shiva, what are the central features of the dominant "calculus"? Of the alternative?

4. In what sense can Shiva be read as taking a difference/gynocentric approach?

THE DOMINANCE APPROACH

Catharine MacKinnon

Difference and Dominance: On Sex Discrimination

What is a gender question a question of? What is an inequality question a question of? These two questions underlie applications of the equality principle to issues of gender, but they are seldom explicitly asked. I think it speaks to the way gender has structured thought and perception that mainstream legal and moral theory tacitly gives the same answer to them both: these are questions of sameness and difference. The mainstream doctrine of the law of sex discrimination that results is, in my view, largely responsible for the fact that sex equality law has been so utterly ineffective at getting women what we need and are socially prevented from having on the basis of a condition of birth: a chance at productive lives of reasonable physical security, self-expression, individuation, and minimal respect and dignity. Here I expose the sameness/difference theory of sex equality, briefly show how it dominates sex discrimination law and policy and underlies its discontents, and propose an alternative that might do something.

.   .   .

According to the approach to sex equality that has dominated politics, law, and social perception, equality is an equivalence, not a distinction, and sex is a distinction. The legal mandate of equal treatment—which is both a systemic norm and a specific legal

doctrine—becomes a matter of treating likes alike and unlikes unlike; and the sexes are defined as such by their mutual unlikeness. Put another way, gender is socially constructed as difference epistemologically; sex discrimination law bounds gender equality by difference doctrinally. A built-in tension exists between this concept of equality, which presupposes sameness, and this concept of sex, which presupposes difference. Sex equality thus becomes a contradiction in terms, something of an oxymoron, which may suggest why we are having such a difficult time getting it.

Upon further scrutiny, two alternate paths to equality for women emerge within this dominant approach, paths that roughly follow the lines of this tension. The leading one is: be the same as men. This path is termed gender neutrality doctrinally and the single standard philosophically. It is testimony to how substance gets itself up as form in law that this rule is considered formal equality. Because this approach mirrors the ideology of the social world, it is considered abstract, meaning transparent of substance; also for this reason it is considered not only to be *the* standard, but *a* standard at all. It is so far the leading rule that the words "equal to" are code for, equivalent to, the words "the same as"—referent for both unspecified.

To women who want equality yet find that you are different, the doctrine provides an alternate route: be different from men. This equal recognition of difference is termed the special benefit rule or special protection rule legally, the double standard philosophically. It is in rather bad odor. Like pregnancy, which always calls it up, it is something of a doctrinal embarrassment. Considered an exception to true equality and not really a rule of law at all, this is the one place where the law of sex discrimination admits it is recognizing something substantive. Together with the Bona Fide Occupational Qualification (BFOQ), the unique physical characteristic exception under ERA policy, compensatory legislation, and sex-conscious relief in particular litigation, affirmative action is thought to live here.[1]

The philosophy underlying the difference approach is that sex *is* a difference, a division, a distinction, beneath which lies a stratum of human commonality, sameness. The moral thrust of the sameness branch of the doctrine is to make normative rules conform to this empirical reality by granting women access to what men have access to: to the extent that women are no different from men, we deserve what they have. The differences branch, which is generally seen as patronizing but necessary to avoid absurdity, exists to value or compensate women for what we are or have become distinctively as women (by which is meant, unlike men) under existing conditions.

My concern is not with which of these paths to sex equality is preferable in the long run or more appropriate to any particular issue, although most discourse on sex discrimination revolves about these questions as if that were all there is. My point is logically prior: to treat issues of sex equality as issues of sameness and difference *is to take a particular approach*. I call this the difference approach because it is obsessed with the sex difference. The main theme in the fugue is "we're the same, we're the same, we're the same." The counterpoint theme (in a higher register) is "but we're different, but we're different, but we're different." Its underlying story is: on the first day, difference was; on the second day, a division was created upon it; on the third day, irrational instances of dominance arose. Division may be rational or irrational. Dominance either seems or is justified. Difference *is*.

There is a politics to this. Concealed is the substantive way in which man has become the measure of all things. Under the sameness standard, women are measured according to our correspondence with man, our equality judged by our proximity to his measure. Under the difference standard, we are measured according to our lack of correspondence with him, our womanhood judged by our distance from his measure. Gender neutrality is thus simply the male standard, and the special protection rule is simply the female standard, but do not be deceived: masculinity, or maleness, is the referent for both. Think about it like those anatomy models in medical school. A male body is the human body; all those extra things women have are studied in ob/gyn. It truly is a situation in which more is less. Approaching sex discrimination in this way—as if sex questions are difference questions and equality questions are sameness questions—provides two ways for the law to hold women to a male standard and call that sex equality.

.   .   .

Having been very hard on the difference answer to sex equality questions, I should say that it takes up a very important problem: how to get women access to everything we have been excluded from, while also valuing everything that women are or have been allowed to become or have developed as a consequence of our struggle either not to be excluded from most of life's pursuits or to be taken seriously under the terms that have been permitted to be our terms. It negotiates what we have managed in relation to men. Legally articulated as the need to conform normative standards to existing reality, the strongest doctrinal expression of its sameness idea would prohibit taking gender into account in any way.

Its guiding impulse is: we're as good as you. Anything you can do, we can do. Just get out of the way. I have to confess a sincere affection for this approach. It has gotten women some access to employment[2] and education,[3] the public pursuits, including academic,[4] professional,[5] and blue-collar work;[6] the military;[7] and more than nominal access to athletics.[8] It has moved to change the dead ends that were all we were seen as good for and has altered what passed for women's lack of physical training, which was really serious training in passivity and enforced weakness. It makes you want to cry sometimes to know that it has had to be a mission for many women just to be permitted to do the work of this society, to have the dignity of doing jobs a lot of other people don't even want to do.

The issue of including women in the military draft[9] has presented the sameness answer to the sex equality question in all its simple dignity and complex equivocality. As a citizen, I should have to risk being killed just like you. The consequences of my resistance to this risk should count like yours. The undercurrent is: what's the matter, don't you want me to learn to kill . . . just like you? Sometimes I see this as a dialogue between women in the afterlife. The feminist says to the soldier, "we fought for your equality." The soldier says to the feminist, "oh, no, *we* fought for *your* equality."

Feminists have this nasty habit of counting bodies and refusing not to notice their gender. As applied, the sameness standard has mostly gotten men the benefit of those few things women have historically had—for all the good they did us. Almost every sex discrimination case that has been won at the Supreme Court level has been brought by a man.[10] Under the rule of gender neutrality, the law of custody and divorce has been transformed, giving men an equal chance at custody of children and at alimony.[11] Men often look like better "parents" under gender-neutral rules like level of income and presence of nuclear family, because men make more money and (as they say) initiate the building of family units.[12] In effect, they get preferred because society advantages them before they get into court, and law is prohibited from taking that preference into account because that would mean taking gender into account. The group realities that make women more in need of alimony are not permitted to matter, because only individual factors, gender-neutrally considered, may matter. So the fact that women will live their lives, as individuals, as members of the group women, with women's chances in a sex-discriminatory society, may not count, or else it is sex discrimination. The equality principle in this guise mobilizes the idea that the way

to get things for women is to get them for men. Men have gotten them. Have women? We still have not got equal pay,[13] or equal work,[14] far less equal pay for equal work,[15] and we are close to losing separate enclaves like women's schools through this approach.[16]

Here is why. In reality, which this approach is not long on because it is liberal idealism talking to itself, virtually every quality that distinguishes men from women is already affirmatively compensated in this society. Men's physiology defines most sports,[17] their needs define auto and health insurance coverage, their socially designed biographies define workplace expectations and successful career patterns, their perspectives and concerns define quality in scholarship, their experiences and obsessions define merit, their objectification of life defines art, their military service defines citizenship, their presence defines family, their inability to get along with each other— their wars and rulerships—defines history, their image defines god, and their genitals define sex. For each of their differences from women, what amounts to an affirmative action plan is in effect, otherwise known as the structure and values of American society. But whenever women are, by this standard, "different" from men and insist on not having it held against us, whenever a difference is used to keep us second class and we refuse to smile about it, equality law has a paradigm trauma and it's crisis time for the doctrine.

What this doctrine has apparently meant by sex inequality is not what happens to us. The law of sex discrimination that has resulted seems to be looking only for those ways women are kept down that have *not* wrapped themselves up as a difference—whether original, imposed, or imagined. Start with original: what to do about the fact that women actually have an ability men still lack, gestating children in utero. Pregnancy therefore is a difference. Difference doctrine says it is sex discrimination to give women what we need, because only women need it. It is not sex discrimination not to give women what we need because then only women will not get what we need.[18] Move into imposed: what to do about the fact that most women are segregated into low-paying jobs where there are no men. Suspecting that the structure of the marketplace will be entirely subverted if comparable worth is put into effect, difference doctrine says that because there is no man to set a standard from which women's treatment is a deviation, there is no sex discrimination here, only sex difference. Never mind that there is no man to compare with because no man would do that job if he had a choice, and of course he has because he is a man, so he won't.[19]

Now move into the so-called subtle reaches of the imposed category, the de facto area. Most jobs in fact require that the person, gender neutral, who is qualified for them will be someone who is not the primary caretaker of a preschool child.[20] Pointing out that this raises a concern of sex in a society in which women are expected to care for the children is taken as day one of taking gender into account in the structuring of jobs. To do that would violate the rule against not noticing situated differences based on gender, so it never emerges that day one of taking gender into account was the day the job was structured with the expectation that its occupant would have no child care responsibilities. Imaginary sex differences—such as between male and female applicants to administer estates or between males aging and dying and females aging and dying[21]—I will concede, the doctrine can handle.

I will also concede that there are many differences between women and men. I mean, can you imagine elevating one half of a population and denigrating the other half and producing a population in which everyone is the same? What the sameness standard fails to notice is that men's differences from women are equal to women's differences from men. There is an *equality* there. Yet the sexes are not socially equal. The difference approach misses the fact that hierarchy of power produces real as well as fantasied differences, differences that are also inequalities. What is missing in the difference approach is what Aristotle missed in his empiricist notion that equality means treating likes alike and unlikes unlike, and nobody has questioned it since. Why should you have to be the same as a man to get what a man gets simply because he is one? Why does maleness provide an original entitlement, not questioned on the basis of *its* gender, so that it is women—women who want to

make a case of unequal treatment in a world men have made in their image (this is really the part Aristotle missed)—who have to show in effect that they are men in every relevant respect, unfortunately mistaken for women on the basis of an accident of birth?

The women that gender neutrality benefits, and there are some, show the suppositions of this approach in highest relief. They are mostly women who have been able to construct a biography that somewhat approximates the male norm, at least on paper. They are the qualified, the least of sex discrimination's victims. When they are denied a man's chance, it looks the most like sex bias. The more unequal society gets, the fewer such women are permitted to exist. Therefore, the more unequal society gets, the *less* likely the difference doctrine is to be able to do anything about it, because unequal power creates both the appearance and the reality of sex differences along the same lines as it creates its sex inequalities.

The special benefits side of the difference approach has not compensated for the differential of being second class. The special benefits rule is the only place in mainstream equality doctrine where you get to identify as a woman and not have that mean giving up all claim to equal treatment—but it comes close. Under its double standard, women who stand to inherit something when their husbands die have gotten the exclusion of a small percentage of the inheritance tax, to the tune of Justice Douglas waxing eloquent about the difficulties of all women's economic situation.[22] If we're going to be stigmatized as different, it would be nice if the compensation would fit the disparity. Women have also gotten three more years than men get before we have to be advanced or kicked out of the military hierarchy, as compensation for being precluded from combat, the usual way to advance.[23] Women have also gotten excluded from contact jobs in male-only prisons because we might get raped, the Court taking the viewpoint of the reasonable rapist on women's employment opportunities.[24] We also get protected out of jobs because of our fertility. The reason is that the job has health hazards, and somebody who might be a real person some day and therefore could sue—that is, a fetus—might be hurt if women, who apparently are not real persons and therefore can't sue either for the hazard to our health or for the lost employment opportunity, are given jobs that subject our bodies to possible harm.[25] Excluding women is always an option if equality feels in tension with the pursuit itself. They never seem to think of excluding men. Take combat.[26] Somehow it takes the glory out of the foxhole, the buddiness out of the trenches, to imagine us out there. You get the feeling they might rather end the draft, they might even rather not fight wars at all than have to do it with us.

The double standard of these rules doesn't give women the dignity of the single standard; it also does not (as the differences standard does) suppress the gender of its referent, which is, of course, the female gender. I must also confess some affection for this standard. The work of Carol Gilligan on gender differences in moral reasoning[27] gives it a lot of dignity, more than it has ever had, more, frankly, than I thought it ever could have. But she achieves for moral reasoning what the special protection rule achieves in law: the affirmative rather than the negative valuation of that which has accurately distinguished women from men, by making it seem as though those attributes, with their consequences, really are somehow ours, rather than what male supremacy has attributed to us for its own use. For women to affirm difference, when difference means dominance, as it does with gender, means to affirm the qualities and characteristics of powerlessness.

Women have done good things, and it is a good thing to affirm them. I think quilts are art. I think women have a history. I think we create culture. I also know that we have not only been excluded from making what has been considered art; our artifacts have been excluded from setting the standards by which art is art. Women have a history all right, but it is a history both of what was and of what was not allowed to be. So I am critical of affirming what we have been, which necessarily is what we have been permitted, as if it is women's, ours, possessive. As if equality, in spite of everything, already ineluctably exists.

I am getting hard on this and am about to get harder on it. I do not think that the way women reason morally is morality "in a different voice."[28] I think it is morality in a higher register, in the feminine voice.

Women value care because men have valued us according to the care we give them, and we could probably use some. Women think in relational terms because our existence is defined in relation to men. Further, when you are powerless, you don't just speak differently. A lot, you don't speak. Your speech is not just differently articulated, it is silenced. Eliminated, gone. You aren't just deprived of a language with which to articulate your distinctiveness, although you are; you are deprived of a life out of which articulation might come. Not being heard is not just a function of lack of recognition, not just that no one knows how to listen to you, although it is that; it is also silence of the deep kind, the silence of being prevented from having anything to say. Sometimes it is permanent. All I am saying is that the damage of sexism is real, and reifying that into differences is an insult to our possibilities.

So long as these issues are framed this way, demands for equality will always appear to be asking to have it both ways: the same when we are the same, different when we are different. But this is the way men have it: equal and different too. They have it the same as women when they are the same and want it, and different from women when they are different and want to be, which usually they do. Equal and different too would only be parity.[29] But under male supremacy, while being told we get it both ways, both the specialness of the pedestal and an even chance at the race, the ability to be a woman and a person, too, few women get much benefit of either.

      ·   ·   ·

There is an alternative approach, one that threads its way through existing law and expresses, I think, the reason equality law exists in the first place. It provides a second answer, a dissident answer in law and philosophy, to both the equality question and the gender question. In this approach, an equality question is a question of the distribution of power. Gender is also a question of power, specifically of male supremacy and female subordination. The question of equality, from the standpoint of what it is going to take to get it, is at root a question of hierarchy, which—as power succeeds in constructing social perception and social reality—derivatively becomes a categorical distinction, a difference. Here, on the first day that matters, dominance was achieved, probably by force. By the second day, division along the same lines had to be relatively firmly in place. On the third day, if not sooner, differences were demarcated, together with social systems to exaggerate them in perception and in fact, *because* the systematically differential delivery of benefits and deprivations required making no mistake about who was who. Comparatively speaking, man has been resting ever since. Gender might not even code as difference, might not mean distinction epistemologically, were it not for its consequences for social power.

I call this the dominance approach, and it is the ground I have been standing on in criticizing mainstream law. The goal of this dissident approach is not to make legal categories trace and trap the way things are. It is not to make rules that fit reality. It is critical of reality. Its task is not to formulate abstract standards that will produce determinate outcomes in particular cases. Its project is more substantive, more jurisprudential than formulaic, which is why it is difficult for the mainstream discourse to dignify it as an approach to doctrine or to imagine it as a rule of law at all. It proposes to expose that which women have had little choice but to be confined to, in order to change it.

The dominance approach centers on the most sex-differential abuses of women as a gender, abuses that sex equality law in its difference garb could not confront. It is based on a reality about which little of a systematic nature was known before 1970, a reality that calls for a new conception of the problem of sex inequality. This new information includes not only the extent and intractability of sex segregation into poverty, which has been known before, but the range of issues termed violence against women, which has not been. It combines women's material desperation, through being relegated to categories of jobs that pay nil, with the massive amount of rape and attempted rape—44 percent of all women—about which virtually nothing is done;[30] the sexual assault of children— 38 percent of girls and 10 percent of boys—which is apparently endemic to the patriarchal family;[31] the

battery of women that is systematic in one quarter to one third of our homes;[32] prostitution, women's fundamental economic condition, what we do when all else fails, and for many women in this country, all else fails often;[33] and pornography, an industry that traffics in female flesh, making sex inequality into sex to the tune of eight billion dollars a year in profits largely to organized crime.[34]

These experiences have been silenced out of the difference definition of sex equality largely because they happen almost exclusively to women. Understand: for this reason, they are considered *not* to raise sex equality issues. Because this treatment is done almost uniquely to women, it is implicitly treated as a difference, the sex difference, when in fact it is the socially situated subjection of women. The whole point of women's social relegation to inferiority as a gender is that for the most part these things aren't done to men. Men are not paid half of what women are paid for doing the same work on the basis of their equal difference. Everything they touch does not turn valueless because they touched it. When they are hit, a person has been assaulted. When they are sexually violated, it is not simply tolerated or found entertaining or defended as the necessary structure of the family, the price of civilization, or a constitutional right.

Does this differential describe the sex difference? Maybe so. It does describe the systematic relegation of an entire group of people to a condition of inferiority and attribute it to their nature. If this differential were biological, maybe biological intervention would have to be considered. If it were evolutionary, perhaps men would have to evolve differently. Because I think it is political, I think its politics construct the deep structure of society. Men who do not rape women have nothing wrong with their hormones. Men who are made sick by pornography and do not eroticize their revulsion are not under-evolved. This social status in which we can be used and abused and trivialized and humiliated and bought and sold and passed around and patted on the head and put in place and told to smile so that we look as though we're enjoying it all is not what some of us have in mind as sex equality.

This second approach—which is not abstract, which is at odds with socially imposed reality and therefore does not look like a standard according to the standard for standards—became the implicit model for racial justice applied by the courts during the sixties. It has since eroded with the erosion of judicial commitment to racial equality. It was based on the realization that the condition of Blacks in particular was not fundamentally a matter of rational or irrational differentiation on the basis of race but was fundamentally a matter of white supremacy, under which racial differences became invidious as a consequence.[35] To consider gender in this way, observe again that men are as different from women as women are from men, but socially the sexes are not equally powerful. To be on the top of a hierarchy is certainly different from being on the bottom, but that is an obfuscatingly neutralized way of putting it, as a hierarchy is a great deal more than that. If gender were merely a question of difference, sex inequality would be a problem of mere sexism, of mistaken differentiation, of inaccurate categorization of individuals. This is what the difference approach thinks it is and is therefore sensitive to. But if gender is an inequality first, constructed as a socially relevant differentiation in order to keep that inequality in place, then sex inequality questions are questions of systematic dominance, of male supremacy, which is not at all abstract and is anything but a mistake.

If differentiation into classifications, in itself, is discrimination, as it is in difference doctrine, the use of law to change group-based social inequalities becomes problematic, even contradictory. This is because the group whose situation is to be changed must necessarily be legally identified and delineated, yet to do so is considered in fundamental tension with the guarantee against legally sanctioned inequality. If differentiation is discrimination, affirmative action, and any legal change in social inequality, is discrimination—but the existing social differentiations which constitute the inequality are not? This is only to say that, in the view that equates differentiation with discrimination, changing an unequal status quo is discrimination, but allowing it to exist is not.

Looking at the difference approach and the dominance approach from each other's point of view clarifies some otherwise confusing tensions in sex equality debates. From the point of view of the dominance approach, it becomes clear that the difference approach adopts the point of view of male supremacy on the status of the sexes. Simply by treating the status quo as "the standard," it invisibly and uncritically accepts the arrangements under male supremacy. In this sense, the difference approach is masculinist, although it can be expressed in a female voice. The dominance approach, in that it sees the inequalities of the social world from the standpoint of the subordination of women to men, is feminist.

If you look through the lens of the difference approach at the world as the dominance approach imagines it—that is, if you try to see real inequality through a lens that has difficulty seeing an inequality as an inequality if it also appears as a difference—you see demands for change in the distribution of power as demands for special protection. This is because the only tools that the difference paradigm offers to comprehend disparity equate the recognition of a gender line with an admission of lack of entitlement to equality under law. Since equality questions are primarily confronted in this approach as matters of empirical fit[36]—that is, as matters of accurately shaping legal rules (implicitly modeled on the standard men set) to the way the world is (also implicitly modeled on the standard men set)—any existing differences must be negated to merit equal treatment. For ethnicity as well as for gender, it is basic to mainstream discrimination doctrine to preclude any true diversity among equals or true equality within diversity.

To the difference approach, it further follows that any attempt to change the way the world actually is looks like a moral question requiring a separate judgment of how things ought to be. This approach imagines asking the following disinterested question that can be answered neutrally as to groups: against the weight of empirical difference, should we treat some as the equals of others, even when they may not be entitled to it because they are not up to standard? Because this construction of the problem is part of what the dominance approach unmasks, it does not arise with the dominance approach, which therefore does not see its own foundations as moral. If sex inequalities are approached as matters of imposed status, which are in need of change if a legal mandate of equality means anything at all, the question whether women should be treated unequally means simply whether women should be treated as less. When it is exposed as a naked power question, there is no separable question of what ought to be. The only real question is what is and is not a gender question. Once no amount of difference justifies treating women as subhuman, eliminating that is what equality law is for. In this shift of paradigms, equality propositions become no longer propositions of good and evil, but of power and powerlessness, no more disinterested in their origins or neutral in their arrival at conclusions than are the problems they address.

There came a time in Black people's movement for equality in this country when slavery stopped being a question of how it could be justified and became a question of how it could be ended. Racial disparities surely existed, or racism would have been harmless, but at that point—a point not yet reached for issues of sex—no amount of group difference mattered anymore. This is the same point at which a group's characteristics, including empirical attributes, become constitutive of the fully human, rather than being defined as exceptions to or as distinct from the fully human. To one-sidedly measure one group's differences against a standard set by the other incarnates partial standards. The moment when one's particular qualities become part of the standard by which humanity is measured is a millenial moment.

To summarize the argument: seeing sex equality questions as matters of reasonable or unreasonable classification is part of the way male dominance is expressed in law. If you follow my shift in perspective from gender as difference to gender as dominance, gender changes from a distinction that is presumptively valid to a detriment that is presumptively suspect. The difference approach tries to map reality; the dominance approach tries to challenge and change it. In the dominance approach, sex discrimination stops being a question of morality and starts being a question of politics.

You can tell if sameness is your standard for equality if my critique of hierarchy looks like a request for special protection in disguise. It's not. It envisions a change that would make possible a simple equal chance for the first time. To define the reality of sex as difference and the warrant of equality as sameness is wrong on both counts. Sex, in nature, is not a bipolarity; it is a continuum. In society it is made into a bipolarity. Once this is done, to require that one be the same as those who set the standard—those which one is already socially defined as different from—simply means that sex equality is conceptually designed never to be achieved. Those who most need equal treatment will be the least similar, socially, to those whose situation sets the standard as against which one's entitlement to be equally treated is measured. Doctrinally speaking, the deepest problems of sex inequality will not find women "similarly situated"[37] to men. Far less will practices of sex inequality require that acts be intentionally discriminatory.[38] All that is required is that the status quo be maintained. As a strategy for maintaining social power first structure reality unequally, then require that entitlement to alter it be grounded on a lack of distinction in situation; first structure perception so that different equals inferior, then require that discrimination be activated by evil minds who *know* they are treating equals as less.

I say, give women equal power in social life. Let what we say matter, then we will discourse on questions of morality. Take your foot off our necks, then we will hear in what tongue women speak. So long as sex equality is limited by sex difference, whether you like it or don't like it, whether you value it or seek to negate it, whether you stake it out as a grounds for feminism or occupy it as the terrain of misogyny, women will be born, degraded, and die. We would settle for that equal protection of the laws under which one would be born, live, and die, in a country where protection is not a dirty word and equality is not a special privilege.

NOTES

The most memorable occasions on which I delivered a version of this speech were: Harvard Law School, Cambridge, Massachusetts, Oct. 24, 1984; Conference on the Moral Foundations of Civil Rights Policy, Center for Philosophy and Public Policy, University of Maryland, College Park, Maryland, Oct. 19, 1984; and the James McCormick Mitchell Lecture, State University of Buffalo Law School, Buffalo, New York, Oct. 19, 1984. I thank the students of Harvard Law School for their response to so many of my initial thoughts.

1. The Bona Fide Occupational Qualification (BFOQ) exception to Title VII of the Civil Rights Act of 1964, 42 U.S.C. § 2000 e-(2)(e), permits sex to be a job qualification when it is a valid one. The leading interpretation of the proposed federal Equal Rights Amendment would, pursuing a similar analytic structure, permit a "unique physical characteristic" exception to its otherwise absolute embargo on taking sex into account. Barbara Brown, Thomas I. Emerson, Gail Falk, and Ann E. Freedman, "The Equal Rights Amendment: A Constitutional Basis for Equal Rights for Women," 80 *Yale Law Journal* 893 (1971).

2. Title VII of the Civil Rights Act of 1964, 42 U.S.C. § 2000 e; Phillips v. Martin-Marietta, 400 U.S. 542 (1971). Frontiero v. Richardson, 411 U.S. 484 (1974) is the high-water mark of this approach. See also City of Los Angeles v. Manhart, 435 U.S. 702 (1978); Newport News Shipbuilding and Dry Dock Co. v. EEOC, 462 U.S. 669 (1983).

3. Title IX of the Education Amendments of 1972, 20 U.S.C. § 1681; Cannon v. University of Chicago, 441 U.S. 677 (1981); Mississippi University for Women v. Hogan, 458 U.S. 718 (1982); see also De La Cruz v. Tormey, 582 F.2d 45 (9th Cir. 1978).

4. My impression is that women appear to lose most academic sex discrimination cases that go to trial, although I know of no systematic or statistical study on the subject. One case that won eventually, elevating the standard of proof in the process, is Sweeney v. Board of Trustees of Keene State College, 439 U.S. 29 (1979). The ruling for the plaintiff was affirmed on remand, 604 F.2d 106 (1st Cir. 1979).

5. Hishon v. King & Spalding, 467 U.S. 69 (1984).

6. See, e.g., Vanguard Justice v. Hughes, 471 F. Supp. 670 (D. Md. 1979); Meyer v. Missouri State Highway Commission, 567 F.2d 804, 891 (8th Cir. 1977). Payne v. Travenol Laboratories Inc., 416 F. Supp. 248 (N.D. Mass. 1976). See also Dothard v. Rawlinson, 433 U.S. 321 (1977) (height and weight requirements invalidated for prison guard contact positions because of disparate impact on sex).

7. Frontiero v. Richardson, 411 U.S. 484 (1974); Schlesinger v. Ballard, 419 U.S. 498 (1975).

8. This situation is relatively complex. See Gomes v. R.I. Interscholastic League, 469 F. Supp. 659 (D. R.I.

1979); Brenden v. Independent School District, 477 F.2d 1292 (8th Cir. 1973); O'Connor v. Board of Education of School District No. 23, 645 F.2d 578 (7th Cir. 1981); Cape v. Tennessee Secondary School Athletic Association, 424 F. Supp. 732 (E.D. Tenn. 1976), rev'd, 563 F.2d 793 (6th Cir. 1977); Yellow Springs Exempted Village School District Board of Education v. Ohio High School Athletic Association, 443 F. Supp. 753 (S.D. Ohio 1978); Aiken v. Lieuallen, 593 P.2d 1243 (Or. App. 1979).

9. Rostker v. Goldberg, 453 U.S. 57 (1981). See also Lori S. Kornblum, "Women Warriors in a Men's World: The Combat Exclusion," 2 *Law and Inequality: A Journal of Theory and Practice* 353 (1984).

10. David Cole, "Strategies of Difference: Litigating for Women's Rights in a Man's World," 2 *Law & Inequality: A Journal of Theory and Practice* 34 n.4 (1984) (collecting cases).

11. Devine v. Devine, 398 So. 2d 686 (Ala. Sup. Ct. 1981); Danielson v. Board of Higher Education, 358 F. Supp. 22 (S.D.N.Y. 1972); Weinberger v. Wiesenfeld, 420 U.S. 636 (1975); Stanley v. Illinois, 405 U.S. 645 (1971); Caban v. Mohammed, 441 U.S. 380 (1979); Orr v. Orr, 440 U.S. 268 (1979).

12. Lenore Weitzman, "The Economics of Divorce: Social and Economic Consequences of Property, Alimony and Child Support Awards," 28 *U.C.L.A. Law Review* 1118, 1251 (1982), documents a decline in women's standard of living of 73 percent and an increase in men's of 42 percent within a year after divorce.

13. Equal Pay Act, 29 U.S.C. § 206(d)(1) (1976) guarantees pay equality, as does case law, *but cf.* data on pay gaps, "Introduction," note 2. MacKinnon, *Feminism Unmodified*. Cambridge, Mass: Harvard University Press, 1987.

14. Examples include Christenson v. State of Iowa, 563 F.2d 353 (8th Cir. 1977); Gerlach v. Michigan Bell Tel. Co., 501 F. Supp. 1300 (E.D. Mich. 1980); Odomes v. Nucare, Inc., 653 F.2d 246 (6th Cir. 1981) (female nurse's aide denied Title VII remedy because her job duties were not substantially similar to those of better-paid male orderly); Power v. Barry County, Michigan, 539 F. Supp. 721 (W.D. Mich. 1982); Spaulding v. University of Washington, 740 F.2d 686 (9th Cir. 1984).

15. County of Washington v. Gunther, 452 U.S. 161 (1981) permits a comparable worth–type challenge where pay inequality can be proven to be a correlate of intentional job segregation. See also Lemons v. City and County of Denver, 17 FEP Cases 910 (D. Colo. 1978), aff'd, 620 F.2d 228 (10th Cir. 1977), cert. denied, 449 U.S. 888 (1980);

AFSCME v. State of Washington, 770 F.2d 1401 (9th Cir. 1985). See generally Carol Jean Pint, "Value, Work and Women," 1 *Law & Inequality: A Journal of Theory and Practice* 159 (1983).

16. Combine the result in Bob Jones University v. United States, 461 U.S. 547 (1983) with Mississippi University for Women v. Hogan, 458 U.S. 718 (1982), and the tax-exempt status of women-only schools is clearly threatened.

17. A particularly pungent example comes from a case in which the plaintiff sought to compete in boxing matches with men, since there were no matches sponsored by the defendant among women. A major reason that preventing the woman from competing was found not to violate her equality rights was that the "safety rules and precautions [were] developed, designed, and tested in the context of all-male competition." Lafler v. Athletic Board of Control, 536 F. Supp. 104, 107 (W.D. Mich. 1982). As the court put it: "In this case, the real differences between the male and female anatomy are relevant in considering whether men and women may be treated differently with regard to their participating in boxing. The plaintiff *admits* that she wears a protective covering for her breasts while boxing. Such a protective covering . . . would violate Rule Six, Article 9 of the Amateur Boxing Federation rules currently in effect. The same rule *requires* contestants to wear a protective cup, a rule obviously designed for the unique anatomical characteristics of men." Id. at 106 (emphasis added). The rule is based on the male anatomy, therefore not a justification for the discrimination but an example of it. This is not considered in the opinion, nor does the judge discuss whether women might benefit from genital protection, and men from chest guards, as in some other sports.

18. This is a reference to the issues raised by several recent cases which consider whether states' attempts to compensate pregnancy leaves and to secure jobs on return constitute sex discrimination. California Federal Savings and Loan Assn. v. Guerra, 758 F.2d 390 (9th Cir. 1985), cert. granted 54 U.S.L.W. 3460 (U.S. Jan. 13, 1986); see also Miller-Wohl v. Commissioner of Labor, 515 F. Supp. 1264 (D. Montana 1981), vacated and dismissed, 685 F.2d 1088 (9th Cir. 1982). The position argued in "Difference and Dominance" here suggests that if these benefits are prohibited under Title VII, Title VII is unconstitutional under the equal protection clause.

This argument was not made directly in either case. The American Civil Liberties Union argued that the provisions requiring pregnancy to be compensated in employment, without comparable coverage for men, violated Title VII's prohibition on pregnancy-based classifications and on sex. Montana had made it illegal for an employer to "terminate a woman's employment because of her pregnancy" or to "refuse to grant to the employee a reasonable leave of absence for such pregnancy." Montana Maternity Leave Act § 49-2-310(1) and (2). According to the ACLU this provision "grants pregnant workers certain employment rights not enjoyed by other workers . . . Legislation designed to benefit women has . . . perpetuated destructive stereotypes about their proper roles and operated to deny them rights and benefits enjoyed by men. The [Montana provision] deters employers from hiring women who are or may become pregnant, causes resentment and hostility in the workplace, and penalizes men." Brief of American Civil Liberties Union, et al. *amicus curiae*, Montana Supreme Court No. 84–172, at 7. The National Organization for Women argued that the California provision, which requires employers to give pregnant workers unpaid disability leave with job security for up to four months, would violate Title VII should Title VII be interpreted to permit it. Brief of National Organization for Women, et al., United States Court of Appeals for the Ninth Circuit, 685 F.2d 1088 (9th Cir. 1982).

When Congress passed the Pregnancy Discrimination Act, amending Title VII, 42 U.S.C. § 2000 e(k), it defined "because of sex" or "on the basis of sex" to include "because of or on the basis of pregnancy, childbirth, or related medical conditions; and women affected by pregnancy, childbirth, or related medical conditions shall be treated the same for all employment-related purposes." In so doing, Congress arguably decided that one did not have to be the same as a man to be treated without discrimination, since it guaranteed freedom from discriminatory treatment on the basis of a condition that is not the same for men as it is for women. It even used the word "women" in the statute.

Further, Congress made this decision expressly to overrule the Supreme Court decision in General Electric v. Gilbert, 429 U.S. 125 (1976), which had held that failure to cover pregnancy as a disability was not sex discrimination because the line between pregnant and nonpregnant was not the line between women and men. In rejecting this logic, as the Court found it did expressly in Newport News Shipbuilding and Dry Dock Co. v. EEOC, 462 U.S. 669, 678 (1983), Congress rejected the implicit measuring of women's entitlement to equality by a male standard. Nor need all women be the same, that is, pregnant or potentially so, to have pregnancy-based discrimination be sex-based discrimination.

Upholding the California pregnancy leave and job security law, the Ninth Circuit opinion did not require sameness for equality to be delivered: "The PDA does not require states to ignore pregnancy. It requires that women be treated equally . . . [E]quality under the PDA must be measured in employment opportunity, not necessarily in amounts of money expended—or in amounts of days of disability leave expended. Equality . . . compares coverage to actual need, not coverage to hypothetical identical needs." California Federal v. Guerra, 758 F.2d 390 (9th Cir. 1985) (Ferguson, J.). "We are not the first court to announce the goal of Title VII is equality of employment opportunity, not necessarily sameness of treatment." Id. at 396 n.7.

19. Most women work at jobs mostly women do, and most of those jobs are paid less than jobs that mostly men do. See, e.g., Pint, note 15 above, at 162–63 nn.19, 20 (collecting studies). To the point that men may not meet the male standard themselves, one court found that a union did not fairly represent its women in the following terms: "As to the yard and driver jobs, defendants suggest not only enormous intellectual requirements, but that the physical demands of those jobs are so great as to be beyond the capacity of any female. Again, it is noted that plaintiffs' capacity to perform those jobs was never tested, despite innumerable requests therefor. It is also noted that defendants have never suggested *which* of the innumerable qualifications they list for these jobs (for the first time) the plaintiffs might fail to meet. The court, however, will accept without listing here the extraordinary catalogue of feats which defendants argue must be performed in the yard, and as a driver. That well may be. However, one learns from this record that one cannot be too weak, too sick, too old and infirm, or too ignorant to perform these jobs, *so long as one is a man.* The plaintiffs appear to the layperson's eye to be far more physically fit than many of the drivers who moved into the yard, over the years, according to the testimony of defense witnesses . . . In short, they were all at least as fit as the men with serious physical deficits and disabilities who held yard jobs." Jones v. Cassens Transport, 617 F. Supp. 869, 892 (1985) (emphasis in original).

20. Phillips v. Martin-Marietta, 400 U.S. 542 (1971).

21. Reed v. Reed, 404 U.S. 71 (1971) held that a statute barring women from administering estates is sex discrimination. If few women were taught to read and write, as used to be the case, the gender difference would not be imaginary in this case, yet the social situation would be even more sex discriminatory than it is now. Compare City of Los Angeles v. Manhart, 434 U.S. 815 (1978), which held

that requiring women to make larger contributions to their retirement plan was sex discrimination, in spite of the allegedly proven sex difference that women on the average outlive men.

22. Kahn v. Shevin, 416 U.S. 351, 353 (1974).

23. Schlesinger v. Ballard, 419 U.S. 498 (1975).

24. Dothard v. Rawlinson, 433 U.S. 321 (1977); see also Michael M. v. Sonoma County Superior Court, 450 U.S. 464 (1981).

25. Doerr v. B.F. Goodrich, 484 F. Supp. 320 (N.D. Ohio 1979). Wendy Webster Williams, "Firing the Woman to Protect the Fetus: The Reconciliation of Fetal Protection with Employment Opportunity Goals Under Title VII," 69 *Georgetown Law Journal* 641 (1981). See also Hayes v. Shelby Memorial Hospital, 546 F. Supp. 259 (N.D. Ala. 1982); Wright v. Olin Corp., 697 F.2d 1172 (4th Cir. 1982).

26. Congress requires the Air Force (10 U.S.C. § 8549 [1983]) and the Navy (10 U.S.C. § 6015 [1983]) to exclude women from combat, with some exceptions. Owens v. Brown, 455 F. Supp. 291 (D.D.C. 1978), had previously invalidated the prior Navy combat exclusion because it prohibited women from filling jobs they could perform and inhibited Navy's discretion to assign women on combat ships. The Army excludes women from combat based upon its own policies under congressional authorization to determine assignment (10 U.S.C. § 3012 [e] [1983]).

27. Carol Gilligan, *In a Different Voice* (1982).

28. Id.

29. I argued this in Appendix A of my *Sexual Harassment of Working Women: A Case of Sex Discrimination* (1979). That book ends with "Women want to be equal and different, too." I could have added "Men are." As a standard, this would have reduced women's aspirations for equality to some corresponding version of men's actualities. But as an observation, it would have been true.

30. Diana Russell and Nancy Howell, "The Prevalence of Rape in the United States Revisited," 8 *Signs: Journal of Women in Culture and Society* 689 (1983) (44 percent of women in 930 households were victims of rape or attempted rape at some time in their lives).

31. Diana Russell, "The Incidence and Prevalence of Intrafamilial and Extrafamilial Sexual Abuse of Female Children," 7 *Child Abuse & Neglect: The International Journal* 133 (1983).

32. R. Emerson Dobash and Russell Dobash, *Violence against Wives: A Case against the Patriarchy* (1979); Bruno v. Codd, 90 Misc. 2d 1047, 396 N.Y.S. 2d 974 (Sup. Ct. 1977), rev'd, 64 A.D. 2d 582, 407 N.Y.S. 2d 165

(1st Dep't 1978), aff'd 47 N.Y. 2d 582, 393 N.E. 2d 976, 419 N.Y.S. 2d 901 (1979).

33. Kathleen Barry, *Female Sexual Slavery* (1979); Moira K. Griffin, "Wives, Hookers and the Law: The Case for Decriminalizing Prostitution," 10 *Student Lawyer* 18 (1982); Report of Jean Fernand-Laurent, Special Rapporteur on the Suppression of the Traffic in Persons and the Exploitation of the Prostitution of Others (a United Nations report), in *International Feminism: Networking against Female Sexual Slavery* 130 (Kathleen Barry, Charlotte Bunch, and Shirley Castley eds.) (Report of the Global Feminist Workshop to Organize against Traffic in Women, Rotterdam, Netherlands, Apr. 6–15, 1983 [1984]).

34. Galloway and Thornton, "Crackdown on Pornography—A No-Win Battle," *U.S. News and World Report*, June 4, 1984, at 84. See also "The Place of Pornography," *Harper's*, November 1984, at 31 (citing $7 billion per year).

35. Loving v. Virginia, 388 U.S. 1 (1967), first used the term "white supremacy" in invalidating an antimiscegenation law as a violation of equal protection. The law equally forbade whites and Blacks to intermarry. Although going nowhere near as far, courts in the athletics area have sometimes seen that "same" does not necessarily mean "equal" nor does "equal" require "same." In a context of sex inequality like that which has prevailed in athletic opportunity, allowing boys to compete on girls' teams may diminish overall sex equality. "Each position occupied by a male reduces the female participation and increases the overall disparity of athletic opportunity which generally exists." Petrie v. Illinois High School Association, 394 N.E. 2d 855, 865 (Ill. 1979). "We conclude that to furnish exactly the same athletic opportunities to boys as to girls would be most difficult and would be detrimental to the compelling governmental interest of equalizing general athletic opportunities between the sexes." Id.

36. The scholars Tussman and tenBroek first used the term "fit" to characterize the necessary relation between a valid equality rule and the world to which it refers. J. Tussman and J. tenBroek, "The Equal Protection of the Laws," 37 *California Law Review* 341 (1949).

37. Royster Guano Co. v. Virginia, 253 U.S. 412, 415 (1920): "[A classification] must be reasonable, not arbitrary, and must rest upon some ground of difference having a fair and substantial relation to the object of the legislation, so that all persons similarly circumstanced shall be treated alike." Reed v. Reed, 404 U.S. 71, 76 (1971): "Regardless of their sex, persons within any one of the enumerated classes . . . are similarly situated . . . By providing dissimilar treatment for men and women who are thus similarly situated, the challenged section violates the Equal Protection Clause."

38. Washington v. Davis, 426 U.S. 229 (1976) and Personnel Administrator of Massachusetts v. Feeney, 442 U.S. 256 (1979) require that intentional discrimination be shown for discrimination to be shown.

Study Questions

MacKinnon sketches two approaches to sex equality, viz., the *difference* approach and the *dominance* approach. Note that she also speaks of a "differences" (or "special benefits") path and a "sameness" path, both under the rubric of the *difference* approach. This can be confusing, so beware.

1. According to MacKinnon, how are sex and equality understood within the difference approach to sex equality? What does MacKinnon mean when she asserts that, given these definitions, "sex equality" is an oxymoron?

2. On the "sameness path" of the difference approach, how does one argue for equal treatment of women? And on the "differences path"?

3. State one criticism made by MacKinnon of the difference approach as a whole and one criticism of each of its paths.

4. According to MacKinnon, how are sex and equality understood within the dominance approach to sex equality? Why, according to MacKinnon, is this approach superior to the difference approach?

5. Do the "sameness path" and "difference path" map meaningfully onto the sameness and difference approaches outlined in this text? Do MacKinnon's criticisms of those paths apply to the works grouped under those headings in this text?

Catharine MacKinnon

Desire and Power

This conference, however broad its inspiration, sophisticated its conception, competent its organization, and elaborate in what is called here articulation, is not, I've noticed, principally set up to maximize conferring. Conferring happens interstitially. Those of us up here do what are called talks; however, we read them. They are called works in progress; although many of them are quite "done." You then respond with what are called questions, many of which are in the form of statements. This event presents itself as a dialogue but operates through a linear series of speeches. We are presented as being engaged in a process, when in actuality we are here to produce a product. We are in a production-consumption cycle, the product being the book that will come out of all of this. The silence that constitutes your half of the dialogue makes our half sound like the sound of one hand clapping. An ominous sound, I should think, for anyone trained on the left.

In partial, if entirely inadequate, response to these thoughts, I am going to speak rather than read what I have to say. I gather that it will still qualify as a text. At the beginning I will draw on parts of my published work. This will help me be concise in laying out what, I gather from people's responses to that work, is a fairly dense grounding. Things will become a little more open-textured after that, more raw than cooked. I am also now requesting that you interject. I will take your "interruptions" as participation. I've

been told that you can, in fact, be heard without those phallic microphones. I say this now because I think that once I get going, it's not going to seem all that clear that there are spaces for you to come in. What I want you to do is wave or say "Give an example" or "Say that again another way" or "Come on, what difference does that make?" I mean this.

Audience: It's not all that easy to do.

C.M.: I know. Thank you. Manners are often taken more seriously than politics. There's a politics to that. I wanted to break into small groups after Ellen Willis finished her critique, but I was talked out of it. I will respond to heat on this if you want to do it. I was told that part of the importance of this conference is to make it accessible to people who are not able to be here. I was moved by that. Another way of putting that is that the organizers want our conversations on tape. If we disperse into small places, that won't happen.

Audience: But it won't be the same conversation.

C.M.: That's true; it won't at all. To help in that direction, I am going to attempt, rather than referring to scholarship that has gone on elsewhere, much of which has been adequately covered by people speaking before me, to refer instead to remarks people have made here, as examples for my theoretical points. This conference is an experience I think I can rely on most of us having had. I will include conversations I've had with some of you here, questions you've asked from the floor, and things that have been said from this stage. I will be particularly interested to refer to those anonymous among you who have referred to my work without knowing it was me sitting at the next table or in the row in front of you. These expository choices are an attempt to make this more dialogic and open-textured, even if only marginally so.

One more thing about the politics of this situation and my place in it. We purport to want to change things, but we talk in ways that no one understands. We know that discourses have fashions, that we're in the midst of a certain fashion now, that a few years from now it will be another, that ten years ago it was different. We know better than to think that this is the pure onward progress of knowledge. We participate in these fashions, are swept along in them, but we don't set them. I'm particularly concerned that in talking fashionably about complicated realities—and what we have said here is central to real concerns— we often have highly coded conversations. Not only one-sided, but coded. What conditions create access to the latest code book?

Sometimes I think to myself, MacKinnon, you write. Do you remember that the majority of the world's illiterates are women? *What are you doing?* I feel that powerfully when I think about what brings us all here, which is to make the changes we are talking about. When someone condemns someone else for the use of jargon, they tend to suppose that they themselves speak plain plate glass. I'm not exempting myself from this criticism, I'm saying that I see it as fundamental to developing a politics of language that will be constructive as well as deconstructive.

This talk is in three parts. The first is in the form of an argument: I will state what I take to be feminism. I will take from and converse around my articles that appeared in *Signs*. I do take it upon myself to define feminism. I challenge everyone to do the same. I would like to open a discourse on what feminism means, rather than on who we think we are to think that we can define what it means. In other words, I'd rather talk substance than relative postures of authority. I undertake this in critical awareness that each of our biographies limits the experience from which we will

make such a substantive definition, knowing that none of us individually has the direct experience of all women, but that together we do, so that this theory must be collectively created. We are here to engage that process. Here and now. This is why the hierarchical structure of this conference is such a problem. What kind of theory does one create this way?

In the second part I will attempt to unpack and extend some of the implications from the initial, compressed declarative argument. It will get more discursive. The implications of the initial argument for some central concerns in marxist theory, including the aspiration toward a unified theory of social inequality, will be extended and directed principally to questions of method.

I will end with what I take to be some urgent questions on our agenda. Not that there aren't urgent questions unanswered throughout, but I want to end with some problems I have not yet adequately addressed. The posture of authority I take to speak to you comes because I agree with what I'm saying. Not to shove it down your throats, but to take responsibility for my position.

The first part. In my view, sexuality is to feminism what work is to marxism. (Those of you who know my work will recognize this from the first *Signs* article.)[1] By saying that sexuality is to feminism what work is to marxism, I mean that both sexuality and work focus on that which is most one's own, that which most makes one the being the theory addresses, as that which is most taken away by what the theory criticizes. In each theory you are made who you are by that which is taken away from you by the social relations the theory criticizes. In marxist theory, we see society fundamentally constructed of the relations people form as they do and make those things that are needed to survive humanly. Work is the social process of shaping and transforming the material and social worlds, the process that creates people as social beings, as their interactions create value. Work is that activity by which the theory comprehends people become who they socially are. Class is the social structure of their work, production is its process, capital is one congealed form. Control is its principal issue, that which is contested, that which we care about, the relations of which Marx wrote to attempt to alter.

A parallel argument is implicit in feminism. In my view—you will notice that I equate "in my view" with "feminism"—this argument is that the molding, direction, and expression of sexuality organize society into two sexes, women and men. This division underlies the totality of social relations; it is as structural and pervasive as class is in marxist theory, although of course its structure and quality of pervasion are different. Sexuality is the social process that creates, organizes, expresses, and directs desire. Desire here is parallel to value in marxist theory, not the same, though it occupies an analogous theoretical location. It is taken for a natural essence or presocial impetus but is actually *created by* the social relations, the hierarchical relations, in question. This process creates the social beings we know as women and men, as their relations create society. Sexuality to feminism is, like work to marxism, socially constructed and at the same time constructing. It is universal as activity, yet always historically specific, and jointly comprised of matter and mind. As the organized expropriation of the work of some for the use of others defines the class, workers, the organized expropriation of the sexuality of some for the use of others defines the sex, woman. Heterosexuality is its predominant structure, gender is its social process, the family is a congealed form, sex roles are its qualities generalized to two social personas, and reproduction is a consequence. (Theorists sometimes forget that in order to reproduce one must first, usually, have had sex.) Control is also the issue of gender.

In this analysis, both marxism and feminism are theories of power and of its unequal distribution. They each provide an account of how a systematically unequal social arrangement (by arrangement I don't mean to suggest it's equally chosen by all) is internally coherent and internally rational and pervasive yet unjust. Both theories are total theories. That is, they are both theories of the totality, of the whole thing, theories of a fundamental and critical underpinning of the whole they envision. The problem of the relation between marxism and feminism then becomes how both can be true at the same time. As the focus of my attempt to address this issue, I have taken the relationship between questions of power and questions of knowledge, that is, the relation between the political and the epistemological, as each theory conceives it. I will talk about the feminist theory of power and the feminist theory of knowledge and then move into their implications for an array of marxist methodological issues. I will then say what I think the relationship between marxism and feminism is.

By political, I mean here questions of power. The feminist theory of power is that sexuality is gendered as gender is sexualized. (This comes from the second *Signs* article.)[2] In other words, feminism is a theory of how the erotization of dominance and submission creates gender, creates woman and man in the social form in which we know them. Thus the sex difference and the dominance-submission dynamic define each other. The erotic is what defines sex as an inequality, hence as a meaningful difference. This is, in my view, the social meaning of sexuality and the distinctly feminist account of gender inequality. The feminist theory of knowledge begins with the theory of the point of view of all women on social life. It takes as its point of departure the criticism that the male point of view on social life has constructed both social life and knowledge about it. In other words, the feminist theory of knowledge is inextricable from the feminist critique of male power because the male point of view has forced itself upon the world, and does force itself upon the world, as its way of knowing.

An epistemology is an answer to the question, how do you know? What makes you think you know? Not exactly why should I believe you, but your account of why your account of reality is a true account. The content of the feminist theory of knowledge begins with its criticism of the male point of view by criticizing the posture that has been taken as the stance of "the knower" in Western political thought. That is the stance Stanley Aronowitz previously referred to, the neutral posture, which I will be calling objectivity—that is, the nonsituated, distanced standpoint. I'm claiming that this is the male standpoint socially, and I'm going to try to say why. I will argue that the relationship between objectivity as the stance from which the world is known and the world that is apprehended in this way is the relationship of objectification. Objectivity is the epistemological stance of which objectification is the social process, of which male dominance is the politics, the acted-out social practice. That is, to look at the world objectively is to objectify it. The act of control, of which what I have described is the epistemological level, is itself eroticized under male supremacy. To say women are sex objects is in this way redundant. Sexualized objectification is what defines women as sexual and as women under male supremacy.

I now want to develop some of the implications of this thesis. First, what is gender; then, what is sexuality; then, what kind of analysis this feminism is—in particular, why objectification is specifically male (that's for David Kennedy). I will digress slightly on the subject and object question. Then I will talk about the consequences of setting up a theory this way for questions like falsifiability and uncertainty, and the verb "to be" in feminist discourse.

Gender here is a matter of dominance, not difference. Feminists have noticed that women and men are equally different but not equally powerful. Explaining the subordination of women to men, a political condition, has nothing to do with difference in any fundamental sense. Consequentially, it has a *lot* to do with difference, because the ideology of difference has been so central in its enforcement. Another way to say that is, there would be no such thing as what we know as the sex difference—much less would it be the social issue it is or have the social meaning it has—were it not for male dominance. Sometimes people ask me, "Does that mean you think there's no difference between women and men?" The only way I know how to answer that is: of course there is; the difference is that men have power and women do not. I mean simply that men are not socially supreme and women subordinate by nature; the fact that socially they are, constructs the sex difference as we know it. I mean to suggest that the social meaning of difference—in this I include *différance*—is gender-based.

For those of you who think this is a lot of rhetoric, I want to specify the facts I have in reference. When I speak of male dominance, I mean as its content facts from this culture. The facts have to do with the rate of rape and attempted rape of American women, which is 44 percent. If you ask a random group of women,

"Have you ever been raped or been the victim of an attempted rape?" and do not exclude marital rape, that is the figure.[3] Some 4.5 percent of all women are victims of incest by their fathers, an additional 12 percent by other male family members, rising to a total of 43 percent of all girls before they reach the age of eighteen, if sexual abuse within and outside the family is included. These data, by the way, are predicated on believing women, which Freud had a problem with. You know that the theory of the unconscious was devised to explain how women came to invent experiences of childhood sexual abuse, because Freud did not believe, finally, that they could have happened? If you ask women whether they've been sexually harassed in the last two years, about 15 percent report very serious or physical assaults; about 85 percent of all working women report sexual harassment at some time in their working lives. Between a quarter and a third of all women are battered by men in the family. If you look at homicide data, between 60 percent and 70 percent of murdered women have been killed by a husband, lover, or ex-lover. The same is not true for murdered men. (Men also kill each other in great numbers.) About 12 percent of American women are or have been prostitutes. Prostitution, along with modeling, is the only thing for which women as a group are reputed to be paid—by men—more than men. But then, most prostitutes may never get the money; pimps do. The pornography industry, an exemplary synthesis of the erotization of dominance and submission with capitalism's profit motive, is put at eight billion dollars a year, with three to four times as many outlets as McDonald's restaurants.[4] To conceptualize these data as "the sex difference" acquiesces in and obscures the facts of male power they document and suggest are systematic.

By the way, I mean the word male as an adjective. The analysis of sex is social, not biological. This is not to exempt some men or valorize all women; it is to refer to the standpoint from which these acts I have documented are done, that which makes them invisible, glorious, glamorous, and normal. By male, then, I refer to apologists for these data; I refer to the approach that is integral to these acts, to the standard that has normalized these events so that they define masculinity, to the male sex role, and to the way this approach has submerged its gender to become "the" standard. This is what I mean when I speak of the male perspective or male power. Not all men have equal access to male power, nor can men ever fully occupy women's standpoint. If they do, on occasion, they pay for it; and they can always reclaim male power, which is theirs by default unless consciously disavowed. A woman can also take the male point of view or exercise male power, although she remains always a woman. Our access to male power is not automatic as men's is; we're not born and raised to it. We can aspire to it. Me, for instance, standing up here talking to you—socially this is an exercise of male power. It's hierarchical, it's dominant, it's authoritative. You're listening, I'm talking; I'm active, you're passive. I'm expressing myself; you're taking notes. Women are supposed to be seen and not heard.

Audience: Isn't the relationship between mother and child hierarchical and dominant?

C.M.: In a way, but not exactly in the same sense. It comes to have some hierarchical and dominant aspects under male supremacy, which also unites women and children in powerlessness. In short, I disagree with the Chodorow-Dinnerstein analysis[5] that the mother/child relation is an explanation for male dominance. I think it is only within a context where male power already *exists* that the relation between mother and child can be characterized as one in which the mother is seen as powerful in the sense that the relation becomes one of horror, anxiety, betrayal, cruelty, and—crucially—eroticism. I don't think this relation is *why* male supremacy exists.

Audience: But isn't that the situation we are in— male dominance?

C.M.: It is its reality, yes. But I'm attempting to *explain* that reality. The mother/child relation, described as a relation of dominance, is a consequence of male supremacy, not its causal dynamic. Female mothering does not explain to me why hierarchy is eroticized or even why it is gendered. It doesn't explain why girls don't grow up dominating other women, either. If heirarchy were not eroticized in male-dominant sexuality, I do not think hierarchy would mean what it does, exist where it does, much less be attached to gender, hence to "mother," who

remains a woman. I don't think female mothering is a *why* of male supremacy; I do think women and children are linked in eroticized powerlessness under male supremacy.

Audience: What about female power?

C.M.: Since I think that is a contradiction in terms, socially speaking, I am going to resume what I had planned to say at this point, because I think it will become clear why I think "female power" is a misnomer. Let me know if it doesn't.

Now I want to speak to the question of what sexuality is in this theory. I do not see sexuality as a transcultural container, as essential, as historically unchanging, or as Eros. I define sexuality as whatever a given society eroticizes. That is, sexual is whatever sexual means in a particular society. Sexuality is what sexuality means. This is a political hermeneutical view. Hermeneutics concerns matters of meaning. If sexuality is seen in this way, it is fundamentally social, fundamentally relational, and it is not a thing— which, by the way, does not mean it is not material, in a feminist sense of materiality. Because sexuality arises in relations under male dominance, women are not the principal authors of its meanings. In the society we currently live in, the content I want to claim for sexuality is the gaze that constructs women as objects for male pleasure. I draw on pornography for its form and content, for the gaze that eroticizes the despised, the demeaned, the accessible, the thereto-be-used, the servile, the childlike, the passive, and the animal. *That* is the content of the sexuality that defines gender female in this culture, and visual thingification is its method.

Michelle Barrett asked earlier, how do women come to want that which is not in our interest? (This is a slight reformulation, but I think it is in the spirit of her question.) I think that sexual desire in women, at least in this culture, is socially constructed as that by which we come to want our own self-annihilation. That is, our subordination is eroticized in and as female; in fact, we get off on it to a degree, if nowhere near as much as men do. This is our stake in this system that is not in our interest, our stake in this system that is killing us. I'm saying femininity as we know it is how we come to want male dominance, which most emphatically is not in our interest. Such a critique of complicity—I say this to Gayatri [Spivak]—does not come from an individualistic theory.

The *kind* of analysis that such a feminism is, and, specifically, the standard by which it is accepted as valid, is largely a matter of the criteria one adopts for adequacy in a theory. If feminism is a critique of the objective standpoint as male, then we also disavow standard scientific norms as the adequacy criteria for our theory, because the objective standpoint we criticize is the posture of science. In other words, our critique of the objective standpoint as male is a critique of science as a specifically male approach to knowledge. With it, we reject male criteria for verification. We're not seeking truth in its female counterpart either, since that, too, is constructed by male power. We do not vaunt the subjective. We begin by seeking the truth of and in that which has constructed all this—that is, in gender.

Why is objectivity as a stance specifically male? First of all, familiar to all of you is the social specificity, the particularity, the social situatedness of thought. Social situation is expressed through the concepts people construct to make sense of their situation. Either gender *is* one such social situation, or it is not. If it is, then theories constructed by those with the social experience of men, most particularly by those who are not conscious that gender is a specific social circumstance, will be, at the least, open to being male theories. It would be difficult, it would take a lot of conscious effort, for them not to be. To repeat myself, it is not that I have a biological theory of gender, so that every utterance out of a biologically gendered person's mouth is socially gendered in the same way. I'm saying it is not foreign to us that social conditions shape thought as well as life. Gender either is or is not such a social condition. I'm claiming that it is.

Objectivity is a stance only a subject can take. This is all very interesting on a verbal plane. Gayatri turned this question around; I'll turn it one more time. It is only a subject who gets to take the objective standpoint, the stance which is transparent to its object, the stance that is no stance. A subject is a self. An object is other to that self. Anyone who is the least

bit attentive to gender since reading Simone de Beauvoir knows that it is men socially who are subjects, women socially who are other, objects. Thus the one who has the social access to being that self which takes the stance that is allowed to be objective, that objective person who is a subject, is socially male. When I spoke with David Kennedy about this earlier, he said that the objective subject didn't *have to be* male, so he didn't see how it was gendered. It *could be* any way at all, he said. Well, yes; but my point is that it *isn't* any way at all; it *is* gendered, in fact in the world. If, in order to be gendered, something has to be gendered, those of us in the social change business could pack up and go . . . where? We would give up on changing gender, anyway. Of course it could be any way at all. That it could be and isn't, should be and isn't, is what makes it a political problem.

We notice in language as well as in life that the male occupies both the neutral and the male position. This is another way of saying that the neutrality of objectivity and of maleness are coextensive linguistically, whereas women occupy the marked, the gendered, the different, the forever-female position. Another expression of the sex specificity of objectivity socially is that women have been nature. That is, men have been knowers, mind; women have been "to-be-known," matter, that which is to be controlled and subdued, the acted upon. Of course, this is all a social matter; we live in society, not in the natural world.

Questions of falsifiability look different in this context. One consequence of women's rejection of science in its positivistic form is that we reject the head-counting theory of verification. Structural truths about the meaning of gender may or may not produce big numbers. For example, to say "not only women experience that" in reply to a statement characterizing women's experience, is to suggest that to be properly sex-specific, something must be unique to one sex. Similarly, to say "not all women experience that," as if that contraindicates sex specificity (this point is to Larry Grossberg), is to suggest that to be sex-specific, something must be true of 100 percent of the sex affected. Both of those are implicitly biological criteria for sex: unique and exclusive. Never mind that the biology of sex is not bipolar or exclusive. This is the way the biology of gender is ideologically conceived.

Methodological assumptions have political consequences. One result of this implicitly biological notion of sex specificity is that differences *among* women (notice differences again), such as, crucially, race and class, are seen to undercut the meaningfulness or even the reality of gender. If I say such and so is true of women, and someone responds, but it's not the same for all women, that is supposed to undercut the statement, rather than to point out features that make up the sex specificity of the thing. If gender is a social category, gender is whatever it socially means. All women either will or will not be hit in particular ways by the reality of gender, the totality of which will then comprise the meaning of gender as a social category. In other words, to show that an observation or experience is not the same for all women proves only that it is not biological, not that it is not gendered. Similarly, to say that not only women experience something—for example, to suggest that because some men are raped rape is not an act of male dominance— only suggests that the status of women is not biological. Men can be feminized too, and they know they are when they are raped. The fact that sometimes whites have been slaves does not make Black slavery not racist. That some non-Jews, such as gypsies and gays, were victims of the Holocaust does not mean the Holocaust was not, or was less, anti-Semitic. We know something about the content of Black slavery—that is, of white racism—and about the content of the Holocaust, I trust, that makes it impossible to present isolated if significant counterexamples as if they undercut the specific meaning of the atrocities for the groups who were *defined* by their subjection to them. The fact that lots of white people are poor does not mean that the poverty of Blacks has nothing to do with white racism. It just means that social relations cannot be understood by analogy to machines or bodies or thermodynamics or even quantum mechanics.

It has been suggested that men who experience feelings similar to those women articulate as women may be expressing ways in which being on the bottom of hierarchies can produce similar feelings in people.

The declassed status of student, for example, however temporary, makes a lot of men feel the way most women feel most of the time—except that the men tend to *feel* it, because they've fallen from something. There is nothing like femininity to dignify one's indignity as one's identity. Nor do women and men come to the status of "student" the same. Women have been silenced as women: we have been told we are stupid because we are women, told that our thoughts are trivial because we are women, told that our experiences as women are unspeakable, told that women can't speak the language of significance, had our ideas appropriated by men, only to find those ideas have suddenly become worthy, even creative. Women have been excluded from education as women. This isn't to say we're the only ones who have been excluded from education, but rather that the specific history of that for us *as women* brings us to a structure like that of this conference—in which there's authoritative discourse emanating from the podium and silent receptivity in a mass—in a way that specifically intimidates and has specific exclusionary resonances for us. To those of you who denied this yesterday, I claim the sex specificity of that aspect of this experience.

The next thing I want to address is the methodological question of uncertainty. I want your thoughts on all of this, but in particular on this. I'm coming to think that because men have power over women, women come to epistemological issues situated in a way that sheds a rather distinct light on the indeterminacy/determinacy question as men have agonized over it. Take the problem of "is there a reality and how do I know I'm right about it?" The "is there a there there?" business. How do we deal in the face of Cartesian—updated as existential—doubt? Women know the world is out there. Women know the world is out there because it hits us in the face. Literally. We are raped, battered, pornographed, defined by force, by a world that begins, at least, entirely outside us. No matter what we think about it, how we try to think it out of existence or into a different shape for us to inhabit, the world remains real. Try some time. It exists independent of our will. We can tell that it is there, because no matter what we do, we can't get out of it. Male power is for us—therefore *is*—this kind of fact.

The point of science, as I get it, has been to replace opinion with certainty, to replace religion and faith with the empirical hard stuff. Social science does this by analogy to the physical world: as things move, so society moves. Its laws of motion make society predictable and controllable, or try to. By the way, this analogy, between the social and physical worlds, which underlies the whole "science of society" project, which I'm here calling a specifically male project, has not been very deeply looked into to see whether it applies. Women's situation with respect to that project is that we have *been* "world" for an implicitly male-centered social science. We come to this project as the to-be-known-about, as part of that world to be transformed and controlled. Cartesian doubt—this anxiety about whether the world is really there independent of our will or of our representations, if I can doubt it, maybe it doesn't exist—comes from the luxury of a position of power that entails the possibility of making the world as one thinks or wants it to be. Which is exactly the male standpoint. You can't tell the difference between what you think and the way the world is—or which came first—if your standpoint for thinking and being is one of social power.

Consider the example of faking orgasms, which Gayatri brought up. Men have anxiety that women fake orgasms. Take women's orgasms as an example of something about which one can have Cartesian doubt. "How do I know" she's satisfied, right? Now consider *why* women fake orgasms, rather than how too bad it is that men can't, so that therefore they're unequal to us. I would bet that if we had the power men have, they would *learn*. What I'm saying is, men's power to *make* the world here is their power to make us make the world of their sexual interaction with us the way they want it. They want us to have orgasms; that proves they're virile, potent, effective. We provide them that appearance, whether it's real for us or not. We even get into it. Our reality is, it is far less damaging and dangerous for us to do this, to accept a lifetime of simulated satisfaction, than to hold out for the real thing from them. For them, we

are "world" to their knowledge of world. Their Cartesian doubt is entirely justified: their power to force the world to be their way means that they're forever wondering what's really going on out there.

Heisenberg's uncertainty principle comes close to this awareness. If the way you know the world is this intervention, piercing the veil, making penetrating observations, incisive analyses . . . well, women's social powerlessness gives us the opposite problem. We're forever wondering whether there's anything *other* than the reality of the world men make. Whether there is *any* sphere of the world that responds to our will, our thought. Women are awash in doubt, but ours has never had the credibility of Descartes'. It is our *reality*, even before our knowledge, that is in doubt. Thus I think that the indeterminacy that arises in discourse theory, and in the social text, describes something that, as genders, we are unequally situated in. If you don't determine reality, its indeterminacy— its *un*fixity—is a good deal less apparent to you. Your world is *very determinate*; it is *all too fixed*. It *can't* just be any way at all.

Now I want to say something about the use of the verb "to be" in feminist theory. If the analysis I have given is right, to be realistic about sexuality socially is to see it from the male point of view. To be feminist is to do that with a critical awareness that that is what you are doing. This explains why feminist insights are often criticized for replicating male ideology, why feminists are called "condescending to women," when what we are doing is expressing and exposing how women are condescended to. Because male power has created in reality the world to which feminist insights, when they are accurate, refer, many of our statements will capture that reality, simply exposing it as specifically male for the first time. For example, men say all women are whores. We say men have the power to make this our fundamental condition. So feminism stresses the indistinguishability of prostitution, marriage, and sexual harassment. See: what a woman "is" is what you have *made* women "be." That "is" women, as men make women mean. They have the power to; they *do*—otherwise power means nothing. It's a very empirical "is." Men define women as sexual beings; feminism comprehends that femininity "is" sexual. Men see rape as intercourse; feminists say much intercourse "is" rape. Men say women desire degradation; feminists see female masochism as the ultimate success of male supremacy and marvel at its failures.

If male power makes the world as it "is," theorizing this reality requires capturing it in order to subject it to critique, hence to change. Feminists say women are not individuals. To retort that we "are" will not make it so: it will obscure the need to *make change so that it can be so*. To retort to the feminist charge that women "are" not equal, "Oh, you think women aren't equal to men" is to act as though *saying* we "are" will make it so. What it will do instead, what it has done and is doing, is legitimize the vision that we already "are" equal. That *this* life as we live it now is equality for us. It acts as if the purpose of speech is to say what we want reality to be like, as if it already is that way, as if that will help move reality to that place. This may work in fiction, but it won't work in theory. Rather, if this is reality, nothing needs changing: *this* is freedom; we choose *this*. To me, this answer is about denial and is the opposite of change.

Stanley Aronowitz talked pretty extensively about marxist method. I see two strains in marxist method; it is not monolithic. One is the more objectivist strain, which purports to take the neutral position. The other, which I draw on, is more critical of the necessary situatedness of its own standpoint. This strain purports to capture as thought the flux of history, and it understands itself—more in Lukacs' mode—as reflexive, as participating in an ongoing situation, trapped in it in a way, needing to be self-critical and also having, by virtue of that involvement, some access to the truth of the situation.

Feminism has widely been thought to contain tendencies of liberal feminism, radical feminism, and socialist feminism. Too often, socialist or marxist feminism has applied the objectivist strain in marxism to women and called that marxist feminism. Liberal feminism has applied to women the same objectivism that marxism shares with liberalism, resulting in liberalism applied to women. This, especially on questions of sexuality, is markedly similar to the left view, because of the common maleness of the epistemological posture. What I am calling feminism includes at least some versions of radical feminism, not the biological determinist, but the socially based ones. This feminism is methodologically postmarxist. It is a move to resolve the relationship between marxism and feminism on the level of method. Methodologically, a post-marxist analysis treats women as a social group, not in individualist, naturalist, idealist, moralist, voluntarist, or harmonist terms. (In those terms, we're all really equal, and socially we have a naturally harmonious relation between the genders, which needs, at most, marginal reequilibration). I've noticed that for many people liberal views of sexuality—treating it in terms that are individual, natural, ideal, moral, and voluntarist—seem to coexist remarkably well with otherwise marxist views. In my opinion, no feminism worthy of the name is *not* methodologically post-marxist.

As an example of post-marxist feminism, I want to consider the often-raised question of whether "all women" are oppressed by heterosexuality. The question is posed as if sexual practice were a matter of unconstructed choice. If heterosexuality is the dominant gendered form of sexuality in a society where gender oppresses women through sex, sexuality and heterosexuality are essentially the same thing. This does not erase homosexuality, it merely means that sexuality in that form may be no less gendered. Either heterosexuality is the structure of the oppression of women or it is not. Most people see sexuality as individual and biological and voluntary; that is, they see it in terms of the politically and formally liberal myth structure. If you applied such an analysis to the issue of work—anyone who thinks this is not a valid parallel should target this peculiarly sensitive example— would you agree, as people say about heterosexuality, that a worker chooses to work? Does a worker even meaningfully choose his or her specific line or place of work? If working conditions improve, would you call that worker not oppressed? If you have comparatively good or easy or satisfying or well-paying work, if you even like your work, or have a good day at work, does that mean, from a marxist perspective, your work is not exploited? Those who think that one chooses heterosexuality under conditions that make it compulsory should either explain why it is not compulsory or explain why the word choice can be meaningful here. And I would like you to address a question that I think few here would apply to the workplace, to work, or to workers: whether a good fuck is any compensation for getting fucked. And why everyone knows what that means.

.   .   .

How to make change. Marxism teaches that exploitation and degradation somehow produce resistance and revolution. It's been hard to say why. What I've learned from women's experience with sexuality is that exploitation and degradation produce grateful complicity in exchange for survival. They produce self-loathing to the point of extinction of self, and it is respect for self that makes resistance conceivable. The issue is not why women acquiesce but why we ever do anything but. I would like us to see this as a particular question for explanation and for organizing. My second urgent question has to do with class and with race. I would like to see some consideration of the connections between the theory of sexuality I have outlined and the forms of property possession and ownership *and* the erotization of racial degradation and money. A third urgent issue is the relation between everything I've said and all forms of inequality. Am I describing only one form within a larger system, or is this *the* system, or is this too abstract a question?

I do believe that none of our work can be done the way it has been done if what I am saying is taken seriously. We cannot address aesthetics without considering pornography. We cannot think about sexuality and desire without considering the normalization of rape, and I do not mean rape as surplus repression. We cannot do or criticize science without talking about the masculinity of its premises. We cannot talk about everyday life without understanding its division by gender, or about hegemony without understanding male dominance as a form of it. We cannot talk about production without pointing out that its sex division, as well as sexual harassment and prostitution (and housework), underpins and constitutes the labor market. We cannot talk about the phallus in a way that obscures the penis, and we cannot talk about woman as signifier in a way that loses sight of woman the signified. We need to systematically understand in order to criticize and change, rather than reproduce, the connection between the fact that the few have ruled and used the many in their own interest and for their own pleasure as well as profit and the fact that those few have been men.

NOTES

This talk was delivered at the Conference on Marxism and the Interpretation of Culture, University of Illinois at Champaign-Urbana, July 11, 1983.

1. Catharine A. MacKinnon, "Feminism, Marxism, Method and the State: An Agenda for Theory," 7 *Signs: Journal of Women in Culture and Society* 515 (1982).

2. Catharine A. MacKinnon, "Feminism, Marxism, Method and the State: Toward Feminist Jurisprudence," 8 *Signs: Journal of Women in Culture and Society* 635 (1983).

3. See "Not By Law Alone," note 2. MacKinnon, *Feminism Unmodified.* (Cambridge, Mass: Harvard University Press, 1987).

4. The following notes to "Not By Law Alone" document these data: on incest, note 1; on battery, note 4; on murder, note 5. On pornography, Galloway and Thornton, "Crackdown on Pornography—A No-Win Battle," *U.S. News and World Report*, June 4, 1984, at 84; M. Langelan, "The Political Economy of Pornography," *Aegis: Magazine on Ending Violence against Women* 5–17 (1981); Andrea Dworkin, *Pornography: Men Possessing Women* (1981).

5. Nancy Chodorow, *The Reproduction of Mothering: Psychoanalysis and the Sociology of Gender* (Univ. of CA Press, 1978); Dorothy Dinnerstein, *The Mermaid and the Minotaur: Sexual Arrangements and Human Malaise* (New York: Other Press, 1977).

Study Questions

1. In "Desire and Power" MacKinnon writes that "feminism is a theory of how the erotization of dominance and submission creates gender, creates woman and man in the social form in which we know them." Explain this quotation in your own words.

2. According to MacKinnon, what do rape, sexual harassment, pornography, and battery have to do with the social construction of gender?

Catharine MacKinnon

Sex and Violence: A Perspective

I want to raise some questions about the concept of this panel's title, "Violence against Women," as a concept that may coopt us as we attempt to formulate our own truths. I want to speak specifically about four issues: rape, sexual harassment, pornography, and battery. I think one of the reasons we say that each of these issues is an example of violence against women is to reunify them. To say that aggression against women has this unity is to criticize the divisions that have been imposed on that aggression by the legal system. What I see to be the danger of the analysis, what makes it potentially cooptive, is formulating it—and it *is* formulated this way—these are issues of violence, *not* sex: rape is a crime of violence, not sexuality; sexual harassment is an abuse of power, not sexuality; pornography is violence against women, it is not erotic. Although battering is not categorized so explicitly, it is usually treated as though there is nothing sexual about a man beating up a woman so long as it is with his fist. I'd like to raise some questions about that as well.

I hear in the formulation that these issues are violence against women, not sex, that we are in the shadow of Freud, intimidated at being called repressive Victorians. We're saying we're *op*pressed and they say we're *re*pressed. That is, when we say we're against rape, the immediate response is, "Does that mean you're against sex?" "Are you attempting to impose neo-Victorian prudery on sexual expression?"

This comes up with sexual harassment as well. When we say we're against sexual harassment, the first thing people want to know is, "What's the difference between that and ordinary male-to-female sexual initiation?" That's a good question . . . The same is also true of criticizing pornography. "You can't be against erotica?" It's the latest version of the accusation that feminists are anti-male. To distinguish ourselves from this, and in reaction to it, we call these abuses violence. The attempt is to avoid the critique—we're not against sex—and at the same time retain our criticism of these practices. So we rename as violent those abuses that have been seen to be sexual, without saying that we have a very different perspective on violence and on sexuality and their relationship. I also think a reason we call these experiences violence is to avoid being called lesbians, which for some reason is equated with being against sex. In order to avoid that, yet retain our opposition to sexual violation, we put this neutral, objective, abstract word *violence* on it all.

To me this is an attempt to have our own perspective on these outrages without owning up to having one. To have our point of view but present it as *not* a particular point of view. Our problem has been to label something as rape, as sexual harassment, as pornography in the face of a suspicion that it might be intercourse, it might be ordinary sexual initiation, it might be erotic. To say that these purportedly sexual events violate us, to be against them, we call them not sexual. But the attempt to be objective and neutral avoids owning up to the fact that women do have a specific point of view on these events. It avoids saying that from women's point of view, intercourse, sex roles, and eroticism can be and at times are violent to us as women.

My approach would claim our perspective; we are not attempting to be objective about it, we're attempting to represent the point of view of women. The point of view of men up to this time, called objective, has been to distinguish sharply between rape on the one hand and intercourse on the other; sexual harassment on the one hand and normal, ordinary sexual initiation on the other; pornography or obscenity on the one hand and eroticism on the other. The male point of view defines them by distinction. What women experience does not so clearly distinguish the normal, everyday things from those abuses from which they have been defined by distinction. Not just "Now we're going to take what *you* say is rape and call it violence"; "Now we're going to take what *you* say is sexual harassment and call it violence"; "Now we're going to take what *you* say is pornography and call it violence." We have a deeper critique of what has been done to women's sexuality and who controls access to it. What we are saying is that sexuality in exactly these normal forms often *does* violate us. So long as we say that those things are abuses of violence, not sex, we fail to criticize what has been made of *sex*, what has been done to us *through* sex, because we leave the line between rape and intercourse, sexual harassment and sex roles, pornography and eroticism, right where it is.

I think it is useful to inquire how women and men (I don't use the term *persons*, I guess, because I haven't seen many lately) live through the meaning of their experience with these issues. When we ask whether rape, sexual harassment, and pornography are questions of violence or questions of sexuality, it helps to ask, to whom? What is the perspective of those who are involved, whose experience it is—to rape or to have been raped, to consume pornography or to be consumed through it. As to what these things *mean* socially, it is important whether they are about sexuality to women and men or whether they are

instead about "violence,"—or whether violence and sexuality can be distinguished in that way, as they are lived out.

The crime of rape—this is a legal and observed, not a subjective, individual, or feminist definition—is defined around penetration. That seems to me a very male point of view on what it means to be sexually violated. And it is exactly what heterosexuality as a social institution is fixated around, the penetration of the penis into the vagina. Rape is defined according to what men think violates women, and that is the same as what they think of as the sine qua non of sex. What women experience as degrading and defiling when we are raped includes as much that is distinctive to us as is our experience of sex. Someone once termed penetration a "peculiarly resented aspect" of rape—I don't know whether that meant it was peculiar that it was resented or that it was resented with heightened peculiarity. Women who have been raped often do resent having been penetrated. But that is not all there is to what was intrusive or expropriative of a woman's sexual wholeness.

I do think the crime of rape focuses more centrally on what men define as sexuality than on women's experience of our sexual being, hence its violation. A common experience of rape victims is to be unable to feel good about anything heterosexual thereafter—or anything sexual at all, or men at all. The minute they start to have sexual feelings or feel sexually touched by a man, or even a woman, they start to relive the rape. I had a client who came in with her husband. She was a rape victim, a woman we had represented as a witness. Her husband sat the whole time and sobbed. They couldn't have sex anymore because every time he started to touch her, she would flash to the rape scene and see his face change into the face of the man who had raped her. That, to me, is sexual. When a woman has been raped, and it is sex that she then cannot experience without connecting it to that, it was her sexuality that was violated.

Similarly, men who are in prison for rape think it's the dumbest thing that ever happened . . . It isn't just a miscarriage of justice; they were put in jail for something very little different from what most men do most of the time and call it sex. The only difference is they got caught. That view is nonremorseful and not rehabilitative. It may also be true. It seems to me we have here a convergence between the rapist's view of what he has done and the victim's perspective on what was done to her. That is, for both, their ordinary experiences of heterosexual intercourse and the act of rape have something in common. Now this gets us into intense trouble, because that's exactly how judges and juries see it who refuse to convict men accused of rape. A rape victim has to prove that it was not intercourse. She has to show that there was force and she resisted, because if there was sex, consent is inferred. Finders of fact look for "more force than usual during the preliminaries." Rape is defined by distinction from intercourse—not non-violence, intercourse. They ask, does this event look more like fucking or like rape? But what is their standard for sex, and is this question asked from the *woman's point of view?* The level of force is not adjudicated at her point of violation; it is adjudicated at the standard of the normal level of force. Who sets this standard?

In the criminal law, we can't put everybody in jail who does an ordinary act, right? Crime is supposed to be deviant, not normal. Women continue not to report rape, and a reason is that they believe, and they are right, that the legal system will not see it from their point of view. We get very low conviction rates for rape.[1] We also get many women who believe they have never been raped, although a lot of force was involved. They mean that they were not raped in a way that is legally provable. In other words, in all these situations, there was not *enough* violence against them to take it beyond the category of "sex"; they were not coerced enough. Maybe they were forced-fucked for years and put up with it, maybe they tried to get it over with, maybe they were coerced by something other than battery, something like economics, maybe even something like love.

What I am saying is that unless you make the point that there is much violence in intercourse, as a usual matter, none of that is changed. Also we continue to stigmatize the women who claim rape as having experienced a deviant violation and allow the rest of us to go through life feeling violated but thinking we've never been raped, when there were a great many times when we, too, have had sex and didn't want it. What this critique does that is different from the "violence, not sex" critique is ask a series of questions about normal, heterosexual intercourse and attempt to move the line between heterosexuality on the one hand—intercourse—and rape on the other, rather than allow it to stay where it is.

Having done that so extensively with rape, I can consider sexual harassment more briefly. The way the analysis of sexual harassment is sometimes expressed now (and it bothers me) is that it is an abuse of power, not sexuality. That does not allow us to pursue whether sexuality, as socially constructed in our society through gender roles, is *itself* a power structure. If you look at sexual harassment as power, not sex, what is power supposed to be? Power is employer/employee, not because courts are marxist but because this is a recognized hierarchy. Among men. Power is teacher/student, because courts recognize a hierarchy there. Power is on one side and sexuality on the other. Sexuality is ordinary affection, everyday flirtation. Only when ordinary, everyday affection and flirtation and "I was just trying to be friendly" come into the context of *another* hierarchy is it considered potentially an abuse of power. What is not considered to be a hierarchy is women and men—men on top and women on the bottom. That is not considered to be a question of power or social hierarchy, legally or politically. A feminist perspective suggests that it is.

When we have examples of coequal sexual harassment (within these other hierarchies), worker to worker on the same level, involving women and men, we have a lot of very interesting, difficult questions about sex discrimination, which is supposed to be about gender difference, but does not conceive of gender as a social hierarchy. I think that implicit in race discrimination cases for a brief moment of light was the notion that there is a social hierarchy between Blacks and whites. So that presumptively it's an exercise of power for a white person to do something egregious to a Black person or for a white institution to do something egregious systematically to many

Black people. Situations of coequal power—among coworkers or students or teachers—are difficult to see as examples of sexual harassment unless you have a notion of male power. I think we lie to women when we call it not power when a woman is come onto by a man who is not her employer, not her teacher. What do we labor under, what do we feel, when a man—any man—comes and hits on us? I think we require women to feel fine about turning down male-initiated sex so long as the man doesn't have some *other* form of power over us. Whenever—every and any time—a woman feels conflicted and wonders what's wrong with her that she can't decline although she has no inclination, and she feels open to male accusations, whether they come from women or men, of "why didn't you just tell him to buzz off?" we have sold her out, not named her experience. We are taught that we exist for men. We should be flattered or at least act as if we are—be careful about a man's ego because you never know what he can do to you. To flat out say to him, "You?" or "I don't want to" is not *in* most women's sex-role learning. To say it is, is bravado. And that's because he's a man, not just because you never know what he can do to you because he's your boss (that's two things—he's a man and he's the boss) or your teacher or in some other hierarchy. It seems to me that we haven't talked very much about gender *as* a hierarchy, as a division of power, in the way that's expressed and acted out, primarily I think sexually. And therefore we haven't expanded the definition according to women's experience of sexuality, including our own sexual intimidation, of what things are sexual in this world. So men have also defined what can be called sexual about us. They say, "I was just trying to be affectionate, flirtatious and friendly," and we were just all felt up. We criticize the idea that rape comes down to her word against his—but it really *is* her perspective against his perspective, and the law has been written from *his* perspective. If he didn't mean it to be sexual, it's not sexual. If he didn't see it as forced, it wasn't forced.[2] Which is to say, only male sexual violations, that is, only male ideas of what sexually violates us as women, are illegal. We buy into this when we say our sexual violations are abuses of power, not sex.

Just as rape is supposed to have nothing against intercourse, just as sexual harassment is supposed to have nothing against normal sexual initiation (men initiate, women consent—that's mutual?), the idea that pornography is violence against women, not sex, seems to distinguish artistic creation on the one hand from what is degrading to women on the other. It is candid and true but not enough to say of pornography, as Justice Stewart said, "I know it when I see it."[3] *He* knows what he thinks it is when he sees it—but is that what *I* know? Is that the same "it"? Is he going to know what I know when I see it? I think pretty much not, given what's on the newsstand, given what is not considered hard-core pornography. Sometimes I think what is obscene is what does *not* turn on the Supreme Court—or what revolts them more. Which is uncommon, since revulsion is eroticized. We have to admit that pornography turns men on; it is therefore erotic. It is a lie to say that pornography is not erotic. When we say it is violence, not sex, we are saying, there is this degrading to women, over here, and this erotic, over there, without saying to whom. It is overwhelmingly disproportionately men to whom pornography is erotic. It is women, on the whole, to whom it is violent, among other things. And this is not just a matter of perspective, but a matter of reality.

Pornography turns primarily men on. Certainly they are getting something out of it. They pay incredible amounts of money for it; it's one of the largest industries in the country. If women got as much out of it as men do, we would buy it instead of cosmetics. It's a massive industry, cosmetics. We are poor but we have *some* money; we are some market. We spend our money to set ourselves up as the objects that emulate those images that are sold as erotic to men. What pornography says about us is that we enjoy degradation, that we are sexually turned on by being degraded. For me that obliterates the line, as a line at all, between pornography on one hand and erotica on the other, if what turns men on, what men find beautiful, is what degrades women. It is pervasively present in art, also, and advertising. But it is definitely present in eroticism, if that is what it is. It makes me think that women's sexuality as such is a stigma. We also sometimes have an experience of sexuality authentic somehow in all this. We are not allowed to have it; we are not allowed to talk about it; we are not allowed to speak of it or image it as from our own point of view. And, to the extent we try to assert that we are beings equal with men, we have to be either asexual or virgins.

To worry about cooptation is to realize that lies make bad politics. It is ironic that cooptation often results from an attempt to be "credible," to be strategically smart, to be "effective" on existing terms. Sometimes you become what you're fighting. Thinking about issues of sexual violation as issues of violence not sex could, if pursued legally, lead to opposing sexual harassment and pornography through morals legislation and obscenity laws. It is actually interesting that this theoretical stance has been widely embraced but these legal strategies have not been. Perhaps women realize that these legal approaches would not address the subordination of women to men, specifically and substantively. These approaches are legally as abstract as the "violence not sex" critique is politically abstract. They are both not enough and too much of the wrong thing. They deflect us from criticizing everyday behavior that is pervasive and normal and concrete and fuses sexuality with gender in violation and is not amenable to existing legal approaches. I think we need to think more radically in our legal work here.

Battering is called violence, rather than something sex-specific: this is done to women. I also think it is sexually done to women. Not only in where it is done—over half of the incidents are in the bedroom.[4] Or the surrounding events—precipitating sexual jealousy. But when violence against women is eroticized as it is in this culture, it is very difficult to say that there is a major distinction in the level of sex involved between being assaulted by a penis and being assaulted by a fist, especially when the perpetrator is a man. If women as gender female are defined as sexual beings, and violence is eroticized, then men violating women has a sexual component. I think men rape women because they get off on it in a way that fuses dominance with sexuality. (This is different in emphasis from what Susan Brownmiller says.)[5]

I think that when men sexually harass women it expresses male control over sexual access to us. It doesn't mean they all want to fuck us, they just want to hurt us, dominate us, and control us, and that *is* fucking us. They want to be able to have that and to be able to say when they can have it, to *know* that. That is in itself erotic. The idea that opposing battering is about saving the family is, similarly, abstracted, gender-neutral. There are gender-neutral formulations of all these issues: law and order as opposed to derepression, Victorian morality as opposed to permissiveness, obscenity as opposed to art and freedom of expression. Gender-neutral, objective formulations like these avoid asking *whose* expression, from whose point of view? Whose law and whose order? It's not just a question of who is free to express ourselves; it's not just that there is almost no, if any, self-respecting women's eroticism. The fact is that what we do see, what we are allowed to experience, even in our own suffering, even in what we are allowed to complain about, is overwhelmingly constructed from the male point of view. Laws against sexual violation express what men see and do when they engage in sex with women; laws against obscenity center on the display of women's bodies in ways that men are turned on by viewing. To me, it not only makes us cooptable to define such abuses in gender-neutral terms like violence; when we fail to assert that we are fighting for the affirmative definition and control of our own sexuality, of our own lives as women, and that these experiences violate *that*, we have already been bought.

NOTES

This early synthesis was framed in part to respond to panel members' concerns with cooptation at the National Conference on Women and the Law, Boston, Massachusetts, Apr. 5, 1981.

1. Gerald D. Robin, "Forcible Rape: Institutionalized Sexism in the Criminal Justice System," *Crime and Delinquency* (April 1977) 136–53. "Forcible rape is unique among crimes in the manner in which its victims are dealt with by the criminal justice system. Raped women are subjected to an institutionalized sexism that begins with

the treatment by the police, continues through a male-dominated criminal justice system influenced by pseudo-scientific notions of victim precipitation, and ends with the systematic acquittal of many de facto rapists." Lorenne M. G. Clark and Debra Lewis, *Rape: The Price of Coercive Sexuality* 57 (1977).

2. Examples are particularly clear in England, Canada, and California. Director of Public Prosecutions v. Morgan, 2411 E.R.H.L. 347 (1975); Pappajohn v. The Queen, 11 D.L.R. 3d 1 (1980); People v. Mayberry, 15 Cal. 3d 143, 542 P. 2d 1337 (1975). But cf. People v. Barnes, 228 Cal. Rptr. 228 (Cal. 1986).

3. Jacobellis v. Ohio, 378 U.S. 184, 197 (1964) (Stewart, J., concurring).

4. R. Emerson Dobash and Russell Dobash, *Violence against Wives* (Free Press, 1979) at 14–21.

5. Susan Brownmiller, *Against Our Will: Men, Women and Rape* (Ballantine Books, 1975).

Study Questions

1. In what sense do, "Desire and Power" and "Sex and Violence: A Perspecive," exemplify the dominance approach to sex equality?

Emma Goldman

Woman Suffrage

We boast of the age of advancement, of science, and progress. Is it not strange, then, that we still believe in fetich worship? True, our fetiches have different form and substance, yet in their power over the human mind they are still as disastrous as were those of old.

Our modern fetich is universal suffrage. Those who have not yet achieved that goal fight bloody revolutions to obtain it, and those who have enjoyed its reign bring heavy sacrifice to the altar of this omnipotent diety. Woe to the heretic who dare question that divinity!

Woman, even more than man, is a fetich worshipper, and though her idols may change, she is ever on her knees, ever holding up her hands, ever blind to the fact that her god has feet of clay. Thus woman has been the greatest supporter of all deities from time immemorial. Thus, too, she has had to pay the price that only gods can exact,—her freedom, her heart's blood, her very life.

Nietzsche's memorable maxim, "When you go to woman, take the whip along," is considered very brutal, yet Nietzsche expressed in one sentence the attitude of woman towards her gods.

Religion, especially the Christian religion, has condemned woman to the life of an inferior, a slave. It has thwarted her nature and fettered her soul, yet the Christian religion has no greater supporter, none more devout, than woman. Indeed, it is safe to say that religion would have long ceased to be a factor in the lives of the people, if it were not for the support it receives from woman. The most ardent church-workers, the most tireless missionaries the world over, are women, always sacrificing on the altar of the gods that have chained her spirit and enslaved her body.

The insatiable monster, war, robs woman of all that is dear and precious to her. It exacts her brothers, lovers, sons, and in return gives her a life of loneliness and despair. Yet the greatest supporter and worshiper of war is woman. She it is who instills the love of conquest and power into her children; she it is who whispers the glories of war into the ears of her little ones, and who rocks her baby to sleep with the tunes of trumpets and the noise of guns. It is woman, too, who crowns the victor on his return from the battlefield. Yes, it is woman who pays the highest price to that insatiable monster, war.

From Emma Goldman, *Anarchism and Other Essays*, 1911.

Then there is the home. What a terrible fetich it is! How it saps the very life-energy of woman,—this modern prison with golden bars. Its shining aspect blinds woman to the price she would have to pay as wife, mother, and housekeeper. Yet woman clings tenaciously to the home, to the power that holds her in bondage.

It may be said that because woman recognizes the awful toll she is made to pay to the Church, State, and the home, she wants suffrage to set herself free. That may be true of the few; the majority of suffragists repudiate utterly such blasphemy. On the contrary, they insist always that it is woman suffrage which will make her a better Christian and home keeper, a staunch citizen of the State. Thus suffrage is only a means of strengthening the omnipotence of the very Gods that woman has served from time immemorial.

What wonder, then, that she should be just as devout, just as zealous, just as prostrate before the new idol, woman suffrage. As of old, she endures persecution, imprisonment, torture, and all forms of condemnation, with a smile on her face. As of old, the most enlightened, even, hope for a miracle from the twentieth-century deity,—suffrage. Life, happiness, joy, freedom, independence,—all that, and more, is to spring from suffrage. In her blind devotion woman does not see what people of intellect perceived fifty years ago: that suffrage is an evil, that it has only helped to enslave people, that it has but closed their eyes that they may not see how craftily they were made to submit.

Woman's demand for equal suffrage is based largely on the contention that woman must have the equal right in all affairs of society. No one could, possibly, refute that, if suffrage were a right. Alas, for the ignorance of the human mind, which can see a right in an imposition. Or is it not the most brutal imposition for one set of people to make laws that another set is coerced by force to obey? Yet woman clamors for that "golden opportunity" that has wrought so much misery in the world, and robbed man of his integrity and self-reliance; an imposition which has thoroughly corrupted the people, and made them absolute prey in the hands of unscrupulous politicians.

The poor, stupid, free American citizen! Free to starve, free to tramp the highways of this great country, he enjoys universal suffrage, and, by that right, he has forged chains about his limbs. The reward that he receives is stringent labor laws prohibiting the right of boycott, of picketing, in fact, of everything, except the right to be robbed of the fruits of his labor. Yet all these disastrous results of the twentieth-century fetich have taught woman nothing. But, then, woman will purify politics, we are assured.

Needless to say, I am not opposed to woman suffrage on the conventional ground that she is not equal to it. I see neither physical, psychological, nor mental reasons why woman should not have the equal right to vote with man. But that can not possibly blind me to the absurd notion that woman will accomplish that wherein man has failed. If she would not make things worse, she certainly could not make them better. To assume, therefore, that she would succeed in purifying something which is not susceptible of purification, is to credit her with supernatural powers. Since woman's greatest misfortune has been that she was looked upon as either angel or devil, her true salvation lies in being placed on earth; namely, in being considered human, and therefore subject to all human follies and mistakes. Are we, then, to believe that two errors will make a right? Are we to assume that the poison already inherent in politics will be decreased, if women were to enter the political arena? The most ardent suffragists would hardly maintain such a folly.

As a matter of fact, the most advanced students of universal suffrage have come to realize that all existing systems of political power are absurd, and are completely inadequate to meet the pressing issues of life. This view is also borne out by a statement of one who is herself an ardent believer in woman suffrage, Dr. Helen L. Sumner. In her able work on *Equal Suffrage*, she says: "In Colorado, we find that equal suffrage serves to show in the most striking way the essential rottenness and degrading character of the existing system." Of course, Dr. Sumner has in mind a particular system of voting, but the same applies with equal force to the entire machinery of the representative system. With such a basis, it is difficult to understand how woman, as a political factor, would benefit either herself or the rest of mankind.

But, say our suffrage devotees, look at the countries and States where female suffrage exists. See what woman has accomplished—in Australia, New Zealand, Finland, the Scandinavian countries, and in our own four States, Idaho, Colorado, Wyoming, and Utah. Distance lends enchantment—or, to quote a Polish formula—"it is well where we are not." Thus one would assume that those countries and States are unlike other countries or States, that they have greater freedom, greater social and economic equality, a finer appreciation of human life, deeper understanding of the great social struggle, with all the vital questions it involves for the human race.

The women of Australia and New Zealand can vote, and help make the laws. Are the labor conditions better there than they are in England, where the suffragettes are making such a heroic struggle? Does there exist a greater motherhood, happier and freer children than in England? Is woman there no longer considered a mere sex commodity? Has she emancipated herself from the Puritanical double standard of morality for men and women? Certainly none but the ordinary female stump politician will dare answer these questions in the affirmative. If that be so, it seems ridiculous to point to Australia and New Zealand as the Mecca of equal suffrage accomplishments.

On the other hand, it is a fact to those who know the real political conditions in Australia, that politics have gagged labor by enacting the most stringent labor laws, making strikes without the sanction of an arbitration committee a crime equal to treason.

Not for a moment do I mean to imply that woman suffrage is responsible for this state of affairs. I do mean, however, that there is no reason to point to Australia as a wonder-worker of woman's accomplishment, since her influence has been unable to free labor from the thraldom of political bossism.

Finland has given woman equal suffrage; nay, even the right to sit in Parliament. Has that helped to develop a greater heroism, an intenser zeal than that of the women of Russia? Finland, like Russia, smarts under the terrible whip of the bloody Tsar. Where are the Finnish Perovskaias, Spiridonovas, Figners, Breshkovskaias? Where are the countless numbers of Finnish young girls who cheerfully go to Siberia for

their cause? Finland is sadly in need of heroic liberators. Why has the ballot not created them? The only Finnish avenger of his people was a man, not a woman, and he used a more effective weapon than the ballot.

As to our own States where women vote, and which are constantly being pointed out as examples of marvels, what has been accomplished there through the ballot that women do not to a large extent enjoy in other States; or that they could not achieve through energetic efforts without the ballot?

True, in the suffrage States women are guaranteed equal rights to property; but of what avail is that right to the mass of women without property, the thousands of wage workers, who live from hand to mouth? That equal suffrage did not, and cannot, affect their condition is admitted even by Dr. Sumner, who certainly is in a position to know. As an ardent suffragist, and having been sent to Colorado by the Collegiate Equal Suffrage League of New York State to collect material in favor of suffrage, she would be the last to say anything derogatory; yet we are informed that "equal suffrage has but slightly affected the economic conditions of women. That women do not receive equal pay for equal work, and that, though woman in Colorado has enjoyed school suffrage since 1876, women teachers are paid less than in California." On the other hand, Miss Sumner fails to account for the fact that although women have had school suffrage for thirty-four years, and equal suffrage since 1894, the census in Denver alone a few months ago disclosed the fact of fifteen thousand defective school children. And that, too, with mostly women in the educational department, and also notwithstanding that women in Colorado have passed the "most stringent laws for child and animal protection." The women of Colorado "have taken great interest in the State institutions for the care of dependent, defective, and delinquent children." What a horrible indictment against woman's care and interest, if one city has fifteen thousand defective children. What about the glory of woman suffrage, since it has failed utterly in the most important social issue, the child? And where is the superior sense of justice that woman was to bring into the political field? Where was it in 1903, when the mine owners waged a guerilla war against the Western Miners' Union; when General Bell established a reign of terror, pulling men out of bed at night, kidnapping them across the border line, throwing them into bull pens, declaring "to hell with the Constitution, the club is the Constitution"? Where were the women politicians then, and why did they not exercise the power of their vote? But they did. They helped to defeat the most fair-minded and liberal man, Governor Waite. The latter had to make way for the tool of the mine kings, Governor Peabody, the enemy of labor, the Tsar of Colorado. "Certainly male suffrage could have done nothing worse." Granted. Wherein, then, are the advantages to woman and society from woman suffrage? The oft-repeated assertion that woman will purify politics is also but a myth. It is not borne out by the people who know the political conditions of Idaho, Colorado, Wyoming, and Utah.

Woman, essentially a purist, is naturally bigoted and relentless in her effort to make others as good as she thinks they ought to be. Thus, in Idaho, she has disfranchised her sister of the street, and declared all women of "lewd character" unfit to vote. "Lewd" not being interpreted, of course, as prostitution in marriage. It goes without saying that illegal prostitution and gambling have been prohibited. In this regard the law must needs be of feminine gender: it always prohibits. Therein all laws are wonderful. They go no further, but their very tendencies open all the floodgates of hell. Prostitution and gambling have never done a more flourishing business than since the law has been set against them.

In Colorado, the Puritanism of woman has expressed itself in a more drastic form. "Men of notoriously unclean lives, and men connected with saloons, have been dropped from politics since women have the vote."[1] Could Brother Comstock do more? Could all the Puritan fathers have done more? I wonder how many women realize the gravity of this would-be feat. I wonder if they understand that it is the very thing which, instead of elevating woman, has made her a political spy, a contemptible pry into the private affairs of people, not so much for the good of the cause, but because, as a Colorado woman said, "they

like to get into houses they have never been in, and find out all they can, politically and otherwise."[2] Yes, and into the human soul and its minutest nooks and corners. For nothing satisfies the craving of most women so much as scandal. And when did she ever enjoy such opportunities as are hers, the politician's?

"Notoriously unclean lives, and men connected with the saloons." Certainly, the lady vote gatherers can not be accused of much sense of proportion. Granting even that these busybodies can decide whose lives are clean enough for that eminently clean atmosphere, politics, must it follow that saloon-keepers belong to the same category? Unless it be American hypocrisy and bigotry, so manifest in the principle of Prohibition, which sanctions the spread of drunkenness among men and women of the rich class, yet keeps vigilant watch on the only place left to the poor man. If no other reason, woman's narrow and purist attitude toward life makes her a greater danger to liberty wherever she has political power. Man has long overcome the superstitions that still engulf woman. In the economic competitive field, man has been compelled to exercise efficiency, judgment, ability, competency. He therefore had neither time nor inclination to measure everyone's morality with a Puritanic yardstick. In his political activities, too, he has not gone about blindfolded. He knows that quantity and not quality is the material for the political grinding mill, and, unless he is a sentimental reformer or an old fossil, he knows that politics can never be anything but a swamp.

Women who are at all conversant with the process of politics, know the nature of the beast, but in their self-sufficiency and egotism they make themselves believe that they have but to pet the beast, and he will become as gentle as a lamb, sweet and pure. As if women have not sold their votes, as if women politicians cannot be bought! If her body can be bought in return for material consideration, why not her vote? That it is being done in Colorado and in other States, is not denied even by those in favor of woman suffrage.

As I have said before, woman's narrow view of human affairs is not the only argument against her as a politician superior to man. There are others. Her life-long economic parasitism has utterly blurred her conception of the meaning of equality. She clamors for equal rights with man, yet we learn that "few women care to canvas in undesirable districts."[3] How little equality means to them compared with the Russian women, who face hell itself for their ideal!

Woman demands the same rights as man, yet she is indignant that her presence does not strike him dead: he smokes, keeps his hat on, and does not jump from his seat like a flunkey. These may be trivial things, but they are nevertheless the key to the nature of American suffragists. To be sure, their English sisters have outgrown these silly notions. They have shown themselves equal to the greatest demands on their character and power of endurance. All honor to the heroism and sturdiness of the English suffragettes. Thanks to their energetic, aggressive methods, they have proved an inspiration to some of our own lifeless and spineless ladies. But after all, the suffragettes, too, are still lacking in appreciation of real equality. Else how is one to account for the tremendous, truly gigantic effort set in motion by those valiant fighters for a wretched little bill which will benefit a handful of propertied ladies, with absolutely no provision for the vast mass of working women? True, as politicians they must be opportunists, must take half-measures if they can not get all. But as intelligent and liberal women they ought to realize that if the ballot is a weapon, the disinherited need it more than the economically superior class, and that the latter already enjoy too much power by virtue of their economic superiority.

The brilliant leader of the English suffragettes, Mrs. Emmeline Pankhurst, herself admitted, when on her American lecture tour, that there can be no equality between political superiors and inferiors. If so, how will the workingwomen of England, already inferior economically to the ladies who are benefited by the Shackleton bill,[4] be able to work with their political superiors, should the bill pass? Is it not probable that the class of Annie Keeney, so full of zeal, devotion, and martyrdom, will be compelled to carry on their backs their female political bosses, even as they are carrying their economic masters. They would still have to do it, were universal suffrage for men and women established in England. No matter what the workers do, they are made to pay, always. Still, those

who believe in the power of the vote show little sense of justice when they concern themselves not at all with those whom, as they claim, it might serve most.

The American suffrage movement has been, until very recently, altogether a parlor affair, absolutely detached from the economic needs of the people. Thus Susan B. Anthony, no doubt an exceptional type of woman, was not only indifferent but antagonistic to labor; nor did she hesitate to manifest her antagonism when, in 1869, she advised women to take the places of striking printers in New York.[5] I do not know whether her attitude had changed before her death.

There are, of course, some suffragists who are affiliated with workingwomen—the Women's Trade Union League, for instance; but they are a small minority, and their activities are essentially economic. The rest look upon toil as a just provision of Providence. What would become of the rich, if not for the poor? What would become of these idle, parasitic ladies, who squander more in a week than their victims earn in a year, if not for the eighty million wageworkers? Equality, who ever heard of such a thing?

Few countries have produced such arrogance and snobbishness as America. Particularly is this true of the American woman of the middle class. She not only considers herself the equal of man, but his superior, especially in her purity, goodness, and morality. Small wonder that the American suffragist claims for her vote the most miraculous powers. In her exalted conceit she does not see how truly enslaved she is, not so much by man, as by her own silly notions and traditions. Suffrage can not ameliorate that sad fact; it can only accentuate it, as indeed it does.

One of the great American women leaders claims that woman is entitled not only to equal pay, but that she ought to be legally entitled even to the pay of her husband. Failing to support her, he should be put in convict stripes, and his earnings in prison be collected by his equal wife. Does not another brilliant exponent of the cause claim for woman that her vote will abolish the social evil, which has been fought in vain by the collective efforts of the most illustrious minds the world over? It is indeed to be regretted that the alleged creator of the universe has already presented us with his wonderful scheme of things, else woman suffrage would surely enable woman to outdo him completely.

Nothing is so dangerous as the dissection of a fetich. If we have outlived the time when such heresy was punishable by the stake, we have not outlived the narrow spirit of condemnation of those who dare differ with accepted notions. Therefore I shall probably be put down as an opponent of woman. But that can not deter me from looking the question squarely in the face. I repeat what I have said in the beginning: I do not believe that woman will make politics worse; nor can I believe that she could make it better. If, then, she cannot improve on man's mistakes, why perpetrate the latter?

History may be a compilation of lies; nevertheless, it contains a few truths, and they are the only guide we have for the future. The history of the political activities of men proves that they have given him absolutely nothing that he could not have achieved in a more direct, less costly, and more lasting manner. As a matter of fact, every inch of ground he has gained has been through a constant fight, a ceaseless struggle for self-assertion, and not through suffrage. There is no reason whatever to assume that woman, in her climb to emancipation, has been, or will be, helped by the ballot.

In the darkest of all countries, Russia, with her absolute despotism, woman has become man's equal, not through the ballot, but by her will to be and to do. Not only has she conquered for herself every avenue of learning and vocation, but she has won man's esteem, his respect, his comradeship; aye, even more than that: she has gained the admiration, the respect of the whole world. That, too, not through suffrage, but by her wonderful heroism, her fortitude, her ability, willpower, and her endurance in her struggle for liberty. Where are the women in any suffrage country or State that can lay claim to such a victory? When we consider the accomplishments of woman in America, we find also that something deeper and more powerful than suffrage has helped her in the march to emancipation.

It is just sixty-two years ago since a handful of women at the Seneca Falls Convention set forth a few demands for their right to equal education with men, and access to the various professions, trades, etc. What wonderful accomplishments, what wonderful triumphs! Who but the most ignorant dare speak of woman as a mere domestic drudge? Who dare suggest that this or that profession should not be open to her? For over sixty years she has molded a new atmosphere and a new life for herself. She has become a world-power in every domain of human thought and activity. And all that without suffrage, without the right to make laws, without the "privilege" of becoming a judge, a jailer, or an executioner.

Yes, I may be considered an enemy of woman; but if I can help her see the light, I shall not complain.

The misfortune of woman is not that she is unable to do the work of a man, but that she is wasting her life-force to outdo him, with a tradition of centuries which has left her physically incapable of keeping pace with him. Oh, I know some have succeeded, but at what cost, at what terrific cost! The import is not the kind of work woman does, but rather the quality of the work she furnishes. She can give suffrage or the ballot no new quality, nor can she receive anything from it that will enhance her own quality. Her development, her freedom, her independence, must come from and through herself. First, by asserting herself as a personality, and not as a sex commodity. Second, by refusing the right to anyone over her body; by refusing to bear children, unless she wants them; by refusing to be a servant to God, the State, society, the husband, the family, etc., by making her life simpler, but deeper and richer. That is, by trying to learn the meaning and substance of life in all its complexities, by freeing herself from the fear of public opinion and public condemnation. Only that, and not the ballot, will set woman free, will make her a force hitherto unknown in the world, a force for real love, for peace, for harmony; a force of divine fire, of life-giving; a creator of free men and women.

NOTES

1. *Equal Suffrage*, Dr. Helen Sumner.
2. *Equal Suffrage*.
3. Dr. Helen A. Sumner.

4. Mr. Shackleton was a labor leader. It is therefore self evident that he should introduce a bill excluding his own constituents. The English Parliament is full of such Judases.

5. *Equal Suffrage*, Dr. Helen A. Sumner.

Study Questions

1. Goldman provides at least two arguments against investing energy in getting women the right to vote. What are those arguments? (Hint: One has to do with how women will use the vote, and the other is grounded in her anarchism, i.e., in her skepticism that any form of government could adequately respect the rights of individuals.)

2. In what sense does this article exemplify the dominance approach to sex equality?

Sandra Lee Bartky

Foucault, Femininity, and the Modernization of Patriarchal Power

I

In a striking critique of modern society, Michel Foucault has argued that the rise of parliamentary institutions and of new conceptions of political liberty was accompanied by a darker counter-movement, by the emergence of a new and unprecedented discipline directed against the body. More is required of the body now than mere political allegiance or the appropriation of the products of its labor: The new discipline invades the body and seeks to regulate its very forces and operations, the economy and efficiency of its movements.

The disciplinary practices Foucault describes are tied to peculiarly modern forms of the army, the school, the hospital, the prison, and the manufactory; the aim of these disciplines is to increase the utility of the body, to augment its forces:

> What was then being formed was a policy of coercions that act upon the body, a calculated manipulation of its elements, its gestures, its behaviour. The human body was entering a machinery of power that explores it, breaks it down and rearranges it. A "political anatomy", which was also a "mechanics of power", was being born; it defined how one may have a hold over others' bodies, not only so that they may do what one wishes, but so that they may operate as one wishes, with the techniques, the speed and the efficiency that one determines. Thus, discipline produces subjected and practiced bodies, "docile" bodies.[1]

The production of "docile bodies" requires that an uninterrupted coercion be directed to the very processes of bodily activity, not just their result; this "micro-physics of power" fragments and partitions the body's time, its space, and its movements.[2]

The student, then, is enclosed within a classroom and assigned to a desk he cannot leave; his ranking in the class can be read off the position of his desk in the serially ordered and segmented space of the classroom itself. Foucault tells us that "Jean-Baptiste de la Salle dreamt of a classroom in which the spatial distribution might provide a whole series of distinctions at once, according to the pupil's progress, worth, character, application, cleanliness, and parents' fortune."[3] The student must sit upright, feet upon the floor, head erect; he may not slouch or fidget; his animate body is brought into a fixed correlation with the inanimate desk.

The minute breakdown of gestures and movements required of soldiers at drill is far more relentless:

Bring the weapon forward. In three stages. Raise the rifle with the right hand, bringing it close to the body so as to hold it perpendicular with the right knee, the end of the barrel at eye level, grasping it by striking it with the right hand, the arm held close to the body at waist height. At the second stage, bring the rifle in front of you with the left hand, the barrel in the middle between the two eyes, vertical, the right hand grasping it at the small of the butt, the arm outstretched, the triggerguard resting on the first finger, the left hand at the height of the notch, the thumb lying along the barrel against the moulding. At the third stage. . . .[4]

These "body-object articulations" of the soldier and his weapon, the student and his desk, effect a "coercive link with the apparatus of production." We are far indeed from older forms of control that "demanded of the body only signs or products, forms of expression or the result of labour."[5]

The body's time, in these regimes of power, is as rigidly controlled as its space: The factory whistle and the school bell mark a division of time into discrete and segmented units that regulate the various activities of the day. The following timetable, similar in spirit to the ordering of my grammar school classroom, was suggested for French "écoles mutuelles" of the early nineteenth century:

8:45 entrance of the monitor, 8:52 the monitor's summons, 8:56 entrance of the children and prayer, 9:00 the children go to their benches, 9:04 first slate, 9:08 end of dictation, 9:12 second slate, etc.[6]

Control this rigid and precise cannot be maintained without a minute and relentless surveillance.

Jeremy Bentham's design for the Panopticon, a model prison, captures for Foucault the essence of the disciplinary society. At the periphery of the Panopticon, a circular structure; at the center, a tower with wide windows that opens onto the inner side of the ring. The structure on the periphery is divided into cells, each with two windows, one facing the windows of the tower, the other facing the outside, allowing an effect of backlighting to make any figure visible within the cell. "All that is needed, then, is to place a supervisor in a central tower and to shut up in each cell a madman, a patient, a condemned man, a worker or a schoolboy."[7] Each inmate is alone, shut off from effective communication with his fellows, but constantly visible from the tower. The effect of this is "to induce in the inmate a state of conscious and permanent visibility that assures the automatic functioning of power"; each becomes to himself his own jailer.[8] This "state of conscious and permanent visibility" is a sign that the tight, disciplinary control of the body has gotten a hold on the mind as well. In the perpetual self-surveillance of the inmate lies the genesis of the celebrated "individualism" and heightened self-consciousness which are hallmarks of modern times. For Foucault, the structure and effects of the Panopticon resonate throughout society: Is it surprising that "prisons resemble factories, schools, barracks, hospitals, which all resemble prisons?"[9]

Foucault's account in *Discipline and Punish* of the disciplinary practices that produce the "docile bodies" of modernity is a genuine *tour de force*, incorporating a rich theoretical account of the ways in which instrumental reason takes hold of the body with a mass of historical detail. But Foucault treats the body throughout as if it were one, as if the bodily experiences of men and women did not differ and as if men and women bore the same relationship to the characteristic institutions of modern life. Where is the account of the disciplinary practices that engender the "docile bodies" of women, bodies more docile than the bodies of men? Women, like men, are subject to many of the same disciplinary practices Foucault describes. But he is blind to those disciplines that produce a modality of embodiment that is peculiarly feminine. To overlook the forms of subjection that engender the feminine body is to perpetuate the silence and powerlessness of those upon whom these disciplines have been imposed. Hence, even though a liberatory note is sounded in Foucault's critique of power, his analysis as a whole reproduces that sexism which is endemic throughout Western political theory.

We are born male or female, but not masculine or feminine. Femininity is an artifice, an achievement, "a mode of enacting and reenacting received gender norms which surface as so many styles of the flesh."[10] In what follows, I shall examine those disciplinary practices that produce a body which in gesture and appearance is recognizably feminine. I consider three categories of such practices: those that aim to produce a body of a certain size and general configuration; those that bring forth from this body a specific repertoire of gestures, postures, and movements; and those directed toward the display of this body as an ornamented surface. I shall examine the nature of these disciplines, how they are imposed and by whom. I shall probe the effects of the imposition of such discipline on female identity and subjectivity. In the final section I shall argue that these disciplinary practices must be understood in the light of the modernization of patriarchal domination, a modernization that unfolds historically according to the general pattern described by Foucault.

II

Styles of the female figure vary over time and across cultures: they reflect cultural obsessions and preoccupations in ways that are still poorly understood. Today, massiveness, power, or abundance in a woman's body is met with distaste. The current body of fashion is taut, small-breasted, narrow-hipped, and of a slimness bordering on emaciation; it is a silhouette that seems more appropriate to an adolescent boy or a newly pubescent girl than to an adult woman. Since ordinary women have normally quite different dimensions, they must of course diet.

Mass-circulation women's magazines run articles on dieting in virtually every issue. The *Ladies' Home Journal* of February 1986 carries a "Fat-Burning Exercise Guide," while *Mademoiselle* offers to "Help Stamp Out Cellulite" with "Six Sleek-Down Strategies." After the diet-busting Christmas holidays and later, before summer bikini season, the titles of these features become shriller and more arresting. The reader is now addressed in the imperative mode: Jump into shape for summer! Shed ugly winter fat with the all-new Grapefruit Diet! More women than men visit diet doctors, while women greatly outnumber men in self-help groups such as Weight Watchers and Overeaters Anonymous—in the case of the latter, by well over 90 percent.[11]

Dieting disciplines the body's hungers: Appetite must be monitored at all times and governed by an iron will. Since the innocent need of the organism for food will not be denied, the body becomes one's enemy, an alien being bent on thwarting the disciplinary project. Anorexia nervosa, which has now assumed epidemic proportions, is to women of the late twentieth century what hysteria was to women of an earlier day: the crystallization in a pathological mode of a widespread cultural obsession.[12] A survey taken recently at UCLA is astounding: Of 260 students interviewed, 27.3 percent of the women but only 5.8 percent of men said they were "terrified" of getting fat: 28.7 percent of women and only 7.5 percent of men said they were obsessed or "totally preoccupied" with food. The body images of women and men are strikingly different as well: 35 percent of women but only 12.5 percent of men said they felt fat though other people told them they were thin. Women in the survey wanted to weigh ten pounds less than their average weight; men felt they were within a pound of their ideal weight. A total of 5.9 percent of women and no men met the psychiatric criteria for anorexia or bulimia.[13]

Dieting is one discipline imposed upon a body subject to the "tyranny of slenderness"; exercise is another.[14] Since men as well as women exercise, it is not always easy in the case of women to distinguish what is done for the sake of physical fitness from what is done in obedience to the requirements of femininity. Men as well as women lift weights, do yoga, calisthenics, and aerobics, though "jazzercise" is a largely female pursuit. Men and women alike engage themselves with a variety of machines, each designed to call forth from the body a different exertion: There are Nautilus machines, rowing machines, ordinary and motorized exercycles, portable hip and leg cycles, belt massagers, trampolines; treadmills, arm and leg pulleys. However, given the widespread female obsession with weight, one suspects that many women are working out with these apparatuses in the health club or at the gym with a different aim in mind and in quite a different spirit than the men.

But there are classes of exercises meant for women alone, these designed not to firm or to reduce the body's size overall, but to resculpture its various parts on the current model. M. J. Saffon, "international beauty expert," assures us that his twelve basic facial exercises can erase frown lines, smooth the forehead, raise hollow cheeks, banish crow's feet, and tighten the muscles under the chin.[15] There are exercises to build the breasts and exercises to banish "cellulite," said by "figure consultants" to be a special type of female fat. There is "spot-reducing," an umbrella term that covers dozens of punishing exercises designed to reduce "problem areas" like thick ankles or "saddlebag" thighs. The very idea of "spot-reducing" is both scientifically unsound and cruel, for it raises expectations in women that can never be realized: The pattern in which fat is deposited or removed is known to be genetically determined.

It is not only her natural appetite or unreconstructed contours that pose a danger to women: The very expressions of her face can subvert the disciplinary project of bodily perfection. An expressive face lines and creases more readily than an inexpressive one. Hence, if women are unable to suppress strong emotions, they can at least learn to inhibit the tendency of the face to register them. Sophia Loren recommends a unique solution to this problem: A piece of tape applied to the forehead or between the brows will tug at the skin when one frowns and act as a reminder to relax the face.[16] The tape is to be worn whenever a woman is home alone.

III

There are significant gender differences in gesture, posture, movement, and general bodily comportment: Women are far more restricted than men in their manner of movement and in their lived spatiality. In her classic paper on the subject, Iris Young observes that a space seems to surround women in imagination which they are hesitant to move beyond: This manifests itself both in a reluctance to reach, stretch, and extend the body to meet resistances of matter in motion—as in sport or in the performance of physical tasks—and in a typically constricted posture and general style of movement. Woman's space is not a field

in which her bodily intentionality can be freely realized but an enclosure in which she feels herself positioned and by which she is confined.[17] The "loose woman" violates these norms: Her looseness is manifest not only in her morals, but in her manner of speech, and quite literally in the free and easy way she moves.

In an extraordinary series of over two thousand photographs, many candid shots taken in the street, the German photographer Marianne Wex has documented differences in typical masculine and feminine body posture. Women sit waiting for trains with arms close to the body, hands folded together in their laps, toes pointing straight ahead or turned inward, and legs pressed together.[18] The women in these photographs make themselves small and narrow, harmless; they seem tense; they take up little space. Men, on the other hand, expand into the available space; they sit with legs far apart and arms flung out at some distance from the body. Most common in these sitting male figures is what Wex calls the "proferring position": the men sit with legs thrown wide apart, crotch visible, feet pointing outward, often with an arm and casually dangling hand resting comfortably on an open, spread thigh.

In proportion to total body size, a man's stride is longer than a woman's. The man has more spring and rhythm to his step; he walks with toes pointed outward, holds his arms at a greater distance from his body, and swings them farther; he tends to point the whole hand in the direction he is moving. The woman holds her arms closer to her body, palms against her sides; her walk is circumspect. If she has subjected herself to the additional constraint of high-heeled shoes, her body is thrown forward and off-balance: The struggle to walk under these conditions shortens her stride still more.[19]

But women's movement is subjected to a still finer discipline. Feminine faces, as well as bodies, are trained to the expression of deference. Under male scrutiny, women will avert their eyes or cast them downward; the female gaze is trained to abandon its claim to the sovereign status of seer. The "nice" girl learns to avoid the bold and unfettered staring of the "loose" woman who looks at whatever and whomever she pleases. Women are trained to smile more than men, too. In the economy of smiles, as elsewhere, there is evidence that women are exploited, for they give more than they receive in return; in a smile elicitation study, one researcher found that the rate of smile return by women was 93 percent, by men only 67 percent.[20] In many typical women's jobs, graciousness, deference, and the readiness to serve are part of the work; this requires the worker to fix a smile on her face for a good part of the working day, whatever her inner state.[21] The economy of touching is out of balance, too: men touch women more often and on more parts of the body than women touch men: female secretaries, factory workers, and waitresses report that such liberties are taken routinely with their bodies.[22]

Feminine movement, gesture, and posture must exhibit not only constriction, but grace as well, and a certain eroticism restrained by modesty: all three. Here is field for the operation for a whole new training: A woman must stand with stomach pulled in, shoulders thrown slightly back, and chest out, this to display her bosom to maximum advantage. While she must walk in the confined fashion appropriate to women, her movements must, at the same time, be combined with a subtle but provocative hip-roll. But too much display is taboo: Women in short, low-cut dresses are told to avoid bending over at all, but if they must, great care must be taken to avoid an unseemly display of breast or rump. From time to time, fashion magazines offer quite precise instructions on the proper way of getting in and out of cars. These instructions combine all three imperatives of women's movement: A woman must not allow her arms and legs to flail about in all directions; she must try to manage her movements with the appearance of grace—no small accomplishment when one is climbing out of the back seat of a Fiat—and she is well advised to use the opportunity for a certain display of leg.

All the movements we have described so far are self-movements; they arise from within the woman's own body. But in a way that normally goes unnoticed, males in couples may literally steer a woman everywhere she goes: down the street, around corners, into elevators, through doorways, into her chair

at the dinner table, around the dance-floor. The man's movement "is not necessarily heavy and pushy or physical in an ugly way; it is light and gentle but firm in the way of the most confident equestrians with the best trained horses."[23]

IV

We have examined some of the disciplinary practices a woman must master in pursuit of a body of the right size and shape that also displays the proper styles of feminine motility. But woman's body is an ornamented surface too, and there is much discipline involved in this production as well. Here, especially in the application of make-up and the selection of clothes, art and discipline converge, though, as I shall argue, there is less art involved than one might suppose.

A woman's skin must be soft, supple, hairless, and smooth; ideally, it should betray no sign of wear, experience, age, or deep thought. Hair must be removed not only from the face but from large surfaces of the body as well, from legs and thighs, an operation accomplished by shaving, buffing with fine sandpaper, or foul-smelling depilatories. With the new high-leg bathing suits and leotards, a substantial amount of pubic hair must be removed too.[24] The removal of facial hair can be more specialized. Eyebrows are plucked out by the roots with a tweezer. Hot wax is sometimes poured onto the mustache and cheeks and then ripped away when it cools. The woman who wants a more permanent result may try electrolysis: This involves the killing of a hair root by the passage of an electric current down a needle which has been inserted into its base. The procedure is painful and expensive.

The development of what one "beauty expert" calls "good skin-care habits" requires not only attention to health, the avoidance of strong facial expressions, and the performance of facial exercises, but the regular use of skin-care preparations, many to be applied oftener than once a day: cleansing lotions (ordinary soap and water "upsets the skin's acid and alkaline balance"), wash-off cleansers (milder than cleansing lotions), astringents, toners, make-up removers, night creams, nourishing creams, eye creams, moisturizers, skin balancers, body lotions, hand creams, lip pomades, suntan lotions, sun screens, facial masks. Provision of the proper facial mask is complex: There are sulfur masks for pimples; hot or oil masks for dry areas; also cold masks for dry areas; tightening masks; conditioning masks; peeling masks; cleansing masks made of herbs, cornmeal, or almonds; mud packs. Black women may wish to use "fade creams" to "even skin tone." Skin-care preparations are never just sloshed onto the skin, but applied according to precise rules: Eye cream is dabbed on gently in movements toward, never away from, the nose; cleansing cream is applied in outward directions only, straight across the forehead, the upper lip, and the chin, never up but straight down the nose and up and out on the cheeks.[25]

The normalizing discourse of modern medicine is enlisted by the cosmetics industry to gain credibility for its claims. Dr. Christiaan Barnard lends his enormous prestige to the Glycel line of "cellular treatment activators"; these contain "glycosphingolipids" that can "make older skin behave and look like younger skin." The Clinique computer at any Clinique counter will select a combination of preparations just right for you. Ultima II contains "procollagen" in its anti-aging eye cream that "provides hydration" to "demoralizing lines." "Biotherm" eye cream dramatically improves the "biomechanical properties of the skin."[26] The Park Avenue clinic of Dr. Zizmor, "chief of dermatology at one of New York's leading hospitals," offers not only medical treatment such as dermabrasion and chemical peeling but "total deep skin cleansing" as well.[27]

Really good skin-care habits require the use of a variety of aids and devices: facial steamers; faucet filters to collect impurities in the water; borax to soften it; a humidifier for the bedroom; electric massagers; backbrushes; complexion brushes; loofahs; pumice stones; blackhead removers. I will not detail the implements or techniques involved in the manicure or pedicure.

The ordinary circumstances of life as well as a wide variety of activities cause a crisis in skin-care and require a stepping up of the regimen as well as an additional laying on of preparations. Skin-care discipline requires a specialized knowledge: A woman must know what to do if she has been skiing, taking medication, doing vigorous exercise, boating, or swimming in chlorinated pools; if she has been exposed to pollution, heated rooms, cold, sun, harsh weather, the pressurized cabins on airplanes, saunas or steam rooms, fatigue or stress. Like the schoolchild or prisoner, the woman mastering good skin-care habits is put on a timetable: Georgette Klinger requires that a shorter or longer period of attention be paid to the complexion at least four times a day.[28] Hair-care, like skin-care, requires a similar investment of time, the use of a wide variety of preparations, the mastery of a set of techniques and again, the acquisition of a specialized knowledge.

The crown and pinnacle of good hair care and skin care is, of course, the arrangement of the hair and the application of cosmetics. Here the regimen of hair care, skin care, manicure, and pedicure is recapitulated in another mode. A woman must learn the proper manipulation of a large number of devices—the blow dryer, styling brush, curling iron, hot curlers, wire curlers, eye-liner, lipliner, lipstick brush, eyelash curler, mascara brush—and the correct manner of application of a wide variety of products—foundation, toner, covering stick, mascara, eye shadow, eye gloss, blusher, lipstick, rouge, lip gloss, hair dye, hair rinse, hair lightener, hair "relaxer," etc.

In the language of fashion magazines and cosmetic ads, making up is typically portrayed as an aesthetic activity in which a woman can express her individuality. In reality, while cosmetic styles change every decade or so and while some variation in make-up is permitted depending on the occasion, making up the face is, in fact, a highly stylized activity that gives little rein to self-expression. Painting the face is not like painting a picture; at best, it might be described as painting the same picture over and over again with minor variations. Little latitude is permitted in what is considered appropriate make-up for the office and for most social occasions; indeed, the woman who uses cosmetics in a genuinely novel and imaginative way is liable to be seen not as an artist but as an eccentric. Furthermore, since a properly made-up face is, if not a card of entrée, at least a badge of acceptability in most social and professional contexts, the woman who chooses not to wear cosmetics at all faces sanctions of a sort which will never be applied to someone who chooses not to paint a watercolor.

V

Are we dealing in all this merely with sexual *difference?* Scarcely. The disciplinary practices I have described are part of the process by which the ideal body of femininity—and hence the feminine body-subject—is constructed; in doing this, they produce a "practiced and subjected" body, i.e., a body on which an inferior status has been inscribed. A woman's face must be made up, that is to say, made over, and so must her body: she is ten pounds overweight; her lips must be made more kissable; her complexion dewier; her eyes more mysterious. The "art" of make-up is the art of disguise, but this presupposes that a woman's face, unpainted, is defective. Soap and water, a shave, and routine attention to hygiene may be enough for *him*; for *her* they are not. The strategy of much beauty-related advertising is to suggest to women that their bodies are deficient, but even without such more or less explicit teaching, the media images of perfect female beauty which bombard us daily leave no doubt in the minds of most women that they fail to measure up. The technologies of femininity are taken up and practiced by women against the background of a pervasive sense of bodily deficiency: This accounts for what is often their compulsive or even ritualistic character.

The disciplinary project of femininity is a "set-up": It requires such radical and extensive measures of bodily transformation that virtually every woman who gives herself to it is destined in some degree to fail. Thus, a measure of shame is added to a woman's sense that the body she inhabits is deficient: she ought to take better care of herself; she might after all have jogged that last mile. Many women are without the time or resources to provide themselves with even the

minimum of what such a regimen requires, e.g., a decent diet. Here is an additional source of shame for poor women who must bear what our society regards as the more general shame of poverty. The burdens poor women bear in this regard are not merely psychological, since conformity to the prevailing standards of bodily acceptability is a known factor in economic mobility.

The larger disciplines that construct a "feminine" body out of a female one are by no means race- or class-specific. There is little evidence that women of color or working-class women are in general less committed to the incarnation of an ideal femininity than their more privileged sisters. This is not to deny the many ways in which factors of race, class, locality, ethnicity, or personal taste can be expressed within the kinds of practices I have described. The rising young corporate executive may buy her cosmetics at Bergdorf-Goodman while the counter-server at McDonald's gets hers at the K-Mart; the one may join an expensive "upscale" health club, while the other may have to make do with the $9.49 GFX Body-Flex II Home-Gym advertised in the *National Enquirer*: Both are aiming at the same general result.[29]

In the regime of institutionalized heterosexuality woman must make herself "object and prey" for the man: It is for him that these eyes are limpid pools, this cheek baby-smooth.[30] In contemporary patriarchal culture, a panoptical male connoisseur resides within the consciousness of most women: They stand perpetually before his gaze and under his judgment. Woman lives her body as seen by another, by an anonymous patriarchal Other. We are often told that "women dress for other women." There is some truth in this: Who but someone engaged in a project similar to my own can appreciate the panache with which I bring it off? But women know for whom this game is played: They know that a pretty young woman is likelier to become a flight attendant than a plain one and that a well-preserved older woman has a better chance of holding onto her husband than one who has "let herself go."

Here it might be objected that performance for another in no way signals the inferiority of the performer to the one for whom the performance is intended: The actor, for example, depends on his audience but is in no way inferior to it; he is not demeaned by his dependency. While femininity is surely something enacted, the analogy to theater breaks down in a number of ways. First, as I argued earlier, the self-determination we think of as requisite to an artistic career is lacking here: Femininity as spectacle is something in which virtually every woman is required to participate. Second, the precise nature of the criteria by which women are judged, not only the inescapability of judgment itself, reflects gross imbalances in the social power of the sexes that do not mark the relationship of artists and their audiences. An aesthetic of femininity, for example, that mandates fragility and a lack of muscular strength produces female bodies that can offer little resistance to physical abuse, and the physical abuse of women by men, as we know, is widespread. It is true that the current fitness movement has permitted women to develop more muscular strength and endurance than was heretofore allowed; indeed, images of women have begun to appear in the mass media that seem to eroticize this new muscularity. But a woman may by no means develop more muscular strength than her partner; the bride who would tenderly carry her groom across the threshold is a figure of comedy, not romance.[31]

Under the current "tyranny of slenderness" women are forbidden to become large or massive; they must take up as little space as possible. The very contours a woman's body takes on as she matures— the fuller breasts and rounded hips—have become distasteful. The body by which a woman feels herself judged and which by rigorous discipline she must try to assume is the body of early adolescence, slight and unformed, a body lacking flesh or substance, a body in whose very contours the image of immaturity has been inscribed. The requirement that a woman maintain a smooth and hairless skin carries further the theme of inexperience, for an infantilized face must accompany her infantilized body, a face that never ages or furrows its brow in thought. The face of the ideally feminine woman must never display the marks of character, wisdom, and experience that we so admire in men.

To succeed in the provision of a beautiful or sexy body gains a woman attention and some admiration but little real respect and rarely any social power. A woman's effort to master feminine body discipline will lack importance just because she does it: Her activity partakes of the general depreciation of everything female. In spite of unrelenting pressure to "make the most of what they have," women are ridiculed and dismissed for the triviality of their interest in such "trivial" things as clothes and make-up. Further, the narrow identification of woman with sexuality and the body in a society that has for centuries displayed profound suspicion toward both does little to raise her status. Even the most adored female bodies complain routinely of their situation in ways that reveal an implicit understanding that there is something demeaning in the kind of attention they receive. Marilyn Monroe, Elizabeth Taylor, and Farrah Fawcett have all wanted passionately to become actresses-artists and not just "sex objects."

But it is perhaps in their more restricted motility and comportment that the inferiorization of women's bodies is most evident: Women's typical body language, a language of relative tension and constriction, is understood to be a language of subordination when it is enacted by men in male status hierarchies. In groups of men, those with higher status typically assume looser and more relaxed postures: The boss lounges comfortably behind the desk while the applicant sits tense and rigid on the edge of his seat. Higher-status individuals may touch their subordinates more than they themselves get touched; they initiate more eye contact and are smiled at by their inferiors more than they are observed to smile in return.[32] What is announced in the comportment of superiors is confidence and ease, especially ease of access to the Other. Female constraint in posture and movement is no doubt over-determined: The fact that women tend to sit and stand with legs, feet, and knees close or touching may well be a coded declaration of sexual circumspection in a society that still maintains a double standard, or an effort, albeit unconscious, to guard the genital area. In the latter case, a woman's tight and constricted posture must be seen as the expression of her need to ward off real or symbolic sexual attack. Whatever proportions must be assigned in the final display to fear or deference, one thing is clear: Woman's body language speaks eloquently, though silently, of her subordinate status in a hierarchy of gender.

VI

If what we have described is a genuine discipline—a "system of micro-power that is essentially non-egalitarian and asymmetrical"—who then are the disciplinarians?[33] Who is the top sergeant in the disciplinary regime of femininity? Historically, the law has had some responsibility for enforcement: In times gone by, for example, individuals who appeared in public in the clothes of the other sex could be arrested. While cross-dressers are still liable to some harassment, the kind of discipline we are considering is not the business of the police or the courts. Parents and teachers, of course, have extensive influence, admonishing girls to be demure and ladylike, to "smile pretty," to sit with their legs together. The influence of the media is pervasive, too, constructing as it does an image of the female body as spectacle, nor can we ignore the role played by "beauty experts" or by emblematic public personages such as Jane Fonda and Lynn Redgrave.

But none of these individuals—the skin-care consultant, the parent, the policeman—does in fact wield the kind of authority that is typically invested in those who manage more straightforward disciplinary institutions. The disciplinary power that inscribes femininity in the female body is everywhere and it is nowhere; the disciplinarian is everyone and yet no one in particular. Women regarded as overweight, for example, report that they are regularly admonished to diet, sometimes by people they scarcely know. These intrusions are often softened by reference to the natural prettiness just waiting to emerge: "People have always said that I had a beautiful face and 'if you'd only lose weight you'd be really beautiful.' "[34] Here, "people"—friends and casual acquaintances alike—act to enforce prevailing standards of body size.

Foucault tends to identify the imposition of discipline upon the body with the operation of specific institutions, e.g., the school, the factory, the prison. To do this, however, is to overlook the extent to which discipline can be institutionally *unbound* as well as institutionally bound.[35] The anonymity of disciplinary power and its wide dispersion have consequences which are crucial to a proper understanding of the subordination of women. The absence of a formal institutional structure and of authorities invested with the power to carry out institutional directives creates the impression that the production of femininity is either entirely voluntary or natural. The several senses of "discipline" are instructive here. On the one hand, discipline is something imposed on subjects of an "essentially inegalitarian and asymmetrical" system of authority. Schoolchildren, convicts, and draftees are subject to discipline in this sense. But discipline can be sought voluntarily as well, as, for example, when an individual seeks initiation into the spiritual discipline of Zen Buddhism. Discipline can, of course, be both at once: The volunteer may seek the physical and occupational training offered by the army without the army's ceasing in any way to be the instrument by which he and other members of his class are kept in disciplined subjection. Feminine bodily discipline has this dual character: On the one hand, no one is marched off for electrolysis at the end of a rifle, nor can we fail to appreciate the initiative and ingenuity displayed by countless women in an attempt to master the rituals of beauty. Nevertheless, insofar as the disciplinary practices of femininity produce a "subjected and practiced," an inferiorized, body, they must be understood as aspects of a far larger discipline, an oppressive and inegalitarian system of sexual subordination. This system aims at turning women into the docile and compliant companions of men just as surely as the army aims to turn its raw recruits into soldiers.

Now the transformation of oneself into a properly feminine body may be any or all of the following: a rite of passage into adulthood; the adoption and celebration of a particular aesthetic; a way of announcing one's economic level and social status; a way to triumph over other women in the competition for men or jobs; or an opportunity for massive narcissistic indulgence. The social construction of the feminine body is all these things, but it is at base discipline, too, and discipline of the inegalitarian sort. The absence of formally identifiable disciplinarians and of a public schedule of sanctions serves only to disguise the extent to which the imperative to be "feminine" serves the interest of domination. This is a lie in which all concur: Making up is merely artful play; one's first pair of high-heeled shoes is an innocent part of growing up and not the modern equivalent of foot-binding.

Why aren't all women feminists? In modern industrial societies, women are not kept in line by fear of retaliatory male violence; their victimization is not that of the South African black. Nor will it suffice to say that a false consciousness engendered in women by patriarchal ideology is at the basis of female subordination. This is not to deny the fact that women are often subject to gross male violence or that women and men alike are ideologically mystified by the dominant gender arrangements. What I wish to suggest instead is that an adequate understanding of women's oppression will require an appreciation of the extent to which not only women's lives but their very subjectivities are structured within an ensemble of systematically duplicitous practices. The feminine discipline of the body is a case in point: The practices which construct this body have an overt aim and character far removed, indeed radically distinct, from their covert function. In this regard, the system of gender subordination, like the wage-bargain under capitalism, illustrates in its own way the ancient tension between what is and what appears: The phenomenal forms in which it is manifested are often quite different from the real relations which form its deeper structure.

VII

The lack of formal public sanctions does not mean that a woman who is unable or unwilling to submit herself to the appropriate body discipline will face no sanctions at all. On the contrary, she faces a very severe sanction indeed in a world dominated by men: the refusal of male patronage. For the heterosexual woman, this may mean the loss of a badly needed intimacy; for both heterosexual women and lesbians, it may well mean the refusal of a decent livelihood.

As noted earlier, women punish themselves too for the failure to conform. The growing literature on women's body size is filled with wrenching confessions of shame from the overweight:

> I felt clumsy and huge. I felt that I would knock over furniture, bump into things, tip over chairs, not fit into VW's, especially when people were trying to crowd into the back seat. I felt like I was taking over the whole room. . . . I felt disgusting and like a slob. In the summer I felt hot and sweaty and I knew people saw my sweat as evidence that I was too fat.
>
> I feel so terrible about the way I look that I cut off connection with my body. I operate from the neck up. I do not look in mirrors. I do not want to spend time buying clothes. I do not want to spend time with make-up because its painful for me to look at myself.[36]
>
> I can no longer bear to look at myself. Whenever I have to stand in front of a mirror to comb my hair I tie a large towel around my neck. Even at night I slip my nightgown on before I take off my blouse and pants. But all this has only made it worse and worse. It's been so long since I've really looked at my body.[37]

The depth of these women's shame is a measure of the extent to which all women have internalized patriarchal standards of bodily acceptability. A fuller examination of what is meant here by "internalization" may shed light on a question posed earlier: Why isn't every woman a feminist?

Something is "internalized" when it gets incorporated into the structure of the self. By "structure of the self" I refer to those modes of perception and of self-perception which allow a self to distinguish itself both from other selves and from things which are not selves. I have described elsewhere how a generalized male witness comes to structure woman's consciousness of herself as a bodily being. This, then, is one meaning of "internalization." The sense of oneself as a distinct and valuable individual is tied not only to the sense of how one is perceived, but also to what one knows, especially to what one knows how to do; this is a second sense of "internalization." Whatever its ultimate effect, discipline can provide the individual upon whom it is imposed with a sense of mastery as well as a secure sense of identity. There is a certain contradiction here: While its imposition may promote a larger disempowerment, discipline may bring with it a certain development of a person's powers. Women, then, like other skilled individuals, have a stake in the perpetuation of their skills, whatever it may have cost to acquire them and quite apart from the question whether, as a gender, they would have been better off had they never had to acquire them in the first place. Hence, feminism, especially a genuinely radical feminism that questions the patriarchal construction of the female body, threatens women with a certain de-skilling, something people normally resist: Beyond this, it calls into question that aspect of personal identity which is tied to the development of a sense of competence.

Resistance from this source may be joined by a reluctance to part with the rewards of compliance; further, many women will resist the abandonment of an aesthetic that defines what they take to be beautiful. But there is still another source of resistance, one more subtle perhaps, but tied once again to questions of identity and internalization. To have a body felt to be "feminine"—a body socially constructed through the appropriate practices—is in most cases crucial to a woman's sense of herself as female and, since persons currently can *be* only as male or female, to her sense of herself as an existing individual. To possess such a body may also be essential to her sense of herself as a sexually desiring and desirable subject. Hence, any political project which aims to dismantle the machinery that turns a female body into a feminine one may well be apprehended by a woman as something that threatens her with desexualization, if not outright annihilation.

The categories of masculinity and femininity do more than assist in the construction of personal identities; they are critical elements in our informal social ontology. This may account to some degree for the otherwise puzzling phenomenon of homophobia and

for the revulsion felt by many at the sight of female bodybuilders; neither the homosexual nor the muscular woman can be assimilated easily into the categories that structure everyday life. The radical feminist critique of femininity, then, may pose a threat not only to a woman's sense of her own identity and desirability but to the very structure of her social universe.

Of course, many women *are* feminists, favoring a program of political and economic reform in the struggle to gain equality with men.[38] But many "reform" or liberal feminists, indeed, many orthodox Marxists, are committed to the idea that the preservation of a woman's femininity is quite compatible with her struggle for liberation.[39] These thinkers have rejected a normative femininity based upon the notion of "separate spheres" and the traditional sexual division of labor while accepting at the same time conventional standards of feminine body display. If my analysis is correct, such a feminism is incoherent. Foucault has argued that modern bourgeois democracy is deeply flawed in that it seeks political rights for individuals constituted as unfree by a variety of disciplinary micropowers that lie beyond the realm of what is ordinarily defined as the "political." "The man described for us whom we are invited to free," he says, "is already in himself the effect of a subjection much more profound than himself."[40] If, as I have argued, female subjectivity is constituted in any significant measure in and through the disciplinary practices that construct the feminine body, what Foucault says here of "man" is perhaps even truer of "woman." Marxists have maintained from the first the inadequacy of a purely liberal feminism: We have reached the same conclusion through a different route, casting doubt at the same time on the adequacy of traditional Marxist prescriptions for women's liberation as well. Liberals call for equal rights for women, traditional Marxists for the entry of women into production on an equal footing with men, the socialization of housework and proletarian revolution; neither calls for the deconstruction of the categories of masculinity and femininity.[41] Femininity as a certain "style of the flesh" will have to be surpassed in the direction of something quite different, not masculinity, which is in many ways only its mirror opposite, but a radical and as yet unimagined transformation of the female body.

VIII

Foucault has argued that the transition from traditional to modern societies has been characterized by a profound transformation in the exercise of power, by what he calls "a reversal of the political axis of individualization."[42] In older authoritarian systems, power was embodied in the person of the monarch and exercised upon a largely anonymous body of subjects; violation of the law was seen as an insult to the royal individual. While the methods employed to enforce compliance in the past were often quite brutal, involving gross assaults against the body, power in such a system operated in a haphazard and discontinuous fashion; much in the social totality lay beyond its reach.

By contrast, modern society has seen the emergence of increasingly invasive apparatuses of power: These exercise a far more restrictive social and psychological control than was heretofore possible. In modern societies, effects of power "circulate through progressively finer channels, gaining access to individuals themselves, to their bodies, their gestures and all their daily actions."[43] Power now seeks to transform the minds of those individuals who might be tempted to resist it, not merely to punish or imprison their bodies. This requires two things: a finer control of the body's time and its movements—a control that cannot be achieved without ceaseless surveillance and a better understanding of the specific person, of the genesis and nature of his "case." The power these new apparatuses seek to exercise requires a new knowledge of the individual: Modern psychology and sociology are born. Whether the new modes of control have charge of correction, production, education, or the provision of welfare, they resemble one another; they exercise power in a bureaucratic mode—faceless, centralized, and pervasive. A reversal has occurred: Power has now become anonymous, while the project of control has brought into being a new individuality. In fact, Foucault believes

that the operation of power constitutes the very subjectivity of the subject. Here, the image of the Panopticon returns: Knowing that he may be observed from the tower at any time, the inmate takes over the job of policing himself. The gaze which is inscribed in the very structure of the disciplinary institution is internalized by the inmate: Modern technologies of behavior are thus oriented toward the production of isolated and self-policing subjects.[44]

Women have their own experience of the modernization of power, one which begins later but follows in many respects the course outlined by Foucault. In important ways, a woman's behavior is less regulated now than it was in the past. She has more mobility and is less confined to domestic space. She enjoys what to previous generations would have been an unimaginable sexual liberty. Divorce, access to paid work outside the home, and the increasing secularization of modern life have loosened the hold over her of the traditional family and, in spite of the current fundamentalist revival, of the church. Power in these institutions was wielded by individuals known to her. Husbands and fathers enforced patriarchal authority in the family. As in the ancien régime, a woman's body was subject to sanctions if she disobeyed. Not Foucault's royal individual but the Divine Individual decreed that her desire be always "unto her husband," while the person of the priest made known to her God's more specific intentions concerning her place and duties. In the days when civil and ecclesiastical authority were still conjoined, individuals formally invested with power were charged with the correction of recalcitrant women whom the family had somehow failed to constrain.

By contrast, the disciplinary power that is increasingly charged with the production of a properly embodied femininity is dispersed and anonymous; there are no individuals formally empowered to wield it; it is, as we have seen, invested in everyone and in no one in particular. This disciplinary power is peculiarly modern: It does not rely upon violent or public sanctions, nor does it seek to restrain the freedom of the female body to move from place to place. For all that, its invasion of the body is well-nigh total: The female body enters "a machinery of power that explores it, breaks it down and rearranges it."[45] The disciplinary techniques through which the "docile bodies" of women are constructed aim at a regulation which is perpetual and exhaustive—a regulation of the body's size and contours, its appetite, posture, gestures, and general comportment in space and the appearance of each of its visible parts.

As modern industrial societies change and as women themselves offer resistance to patriarchy, older forms of domination are eroded. But new forms arise, spread, and become consolidated. Women are no longer required to be chaste or modest, to restrict their sphere of activity to the home, or even to realize their properly feminine destiny in maternity: Normative femininity is coming more and more to be centered on woman's body—not its duties and obligations or even its capacity to bear children, but its sexuality, more precisely, its presumed heterosexuality and its appearance. There is, of course, nothing new in women's preoccupation with youth and beauty. What is new is the growing power of the image in a society increasingly oriented toward the visual media. Images of normative femininity, it might be ventured, have replaced the religiously oriented tracts of the past. New too is the spread of this discipline to all classes of women and its deployment throughout the life-cycle. What was formerly the speciality of the aristocrat or courtesan is now the routine obligation of every woman, be she a grandmother or a barely pubescent girl.

To subject oneself to the new disciplinary power is to be up-to-date, to be "with-it"; as I have argued, it is presented to us in ways that are regularly disguised. It is fully compatible with the current need for women's wage labor, the cult of youth and fitness, and the need of advanced capitalism to maintain high levels of consumption. Further, it represents a saving in the economy of enforcement: Since it is women themselves who practice this discipline on and against their own bodies, men get off scot-free.

The woman who checks her make-up half a dozen times a day to see if her foundation has caked or her mascara run, who worries that the wind or rain may spoil her hairdo, who looks frequently to see if her stockings have bagged at the ankle, or who, feeling fat,

monitors everything she eats, has become, just as surely as the inmate of Panopticon, a self-policing subject, a self committed to a relentless self-surveillance. This self-surveillance is a form of obedience to patriarchy. It is also the reflection in woman's consciousness of the fact that *she* is under surveillance in ways that *he* is not, that whatever else she may become, she is importantly a body designed to please or to excite. There has been induced in many women, then, in Foucault's words, "a state of conscious and permanent visibility that assures the automatic functioning of power."[46] Since the standards of female bodily acceptability are impossible fully to realize, requiring as they do a virtual transcendence of nature, a woman may live much of her life with a pervasive feeling of bodily deficiency. Hence, a tighter control of the body has gained a new kind of hold over the mind.

Foucault often writes as if power constitutes the very individuals upon whom it operates:

> The individual is not to be conceived as a sort of elementary nucleus, a primitive atom, a multiple and inert material on which power comes to fasten or against which it happens to strike. . . . In fact, it is already one of the prime effects of power that certain bodies, certain gestures, certain discourses, certain desires, come to be identified and constituted as individuals.[47]

Nevertheless, if individuals were wholly constituted by the power/knowledge regime Foucault describes, it would make no sense to speak of resistance to discipline at all. Foucault seems sometimes on the verge of depriving us of a vocabulary in which to conceptualize the nature and meaning of those periodic refusals of control which, just as much as the imposition of control, mark the course of human history.

Peter Dews accuses Foucault of lacking a theory of the "libidinal body," i.e., the body upon which discipline is imposed and whose bedrock impulse toward spontaneity and pleasure might perhaps become the locus of resistance.[48] Do women's "libidinal" bodies, then, not rebel against the pain, constriction, tedium, semi-starvation, and constant self-surveillance to which they are currently condemned? Certainly they do, but the rebellion is put down every time a woman picks up her eyebrow tweezers or embarks upon a new diet. The harshness of a regimen alone does not guarantee its rejection, for hardships can be endured if they are thought to be necessary or inevitable.

While "nature," in the form of a "libidinal" body, may not be the origin of a revolt against "culture," domination and the discipline it requires are never imposed without some cost. Historically, the forms and occasions of resistance are manifold. Sometimes, instances of resistance appear to spring from the introduction of new and conflicting factors into the lives of the dominated: The juxtaposition of old and new and the resulting incoherence or "contradiction" may make submission to the old ways seem increasingly unnecessary. In the present instance, what may be a major factor in the relentless and escalating objectification of women's bodies—namely, women's growing independence—produces in many women a sense of incoherence that calls into question the meaning and necessity of the current discipline. As women (albeit a small minority of women) begin to realize an unprecedented political, economic, and sexual self-determination, they fall ever more completely under the dominating gaze of patriarchy. It is this paradox, not the "libidinal body," that produces, here and there, pockets of resistance.

In the current political climate, there is no reason to anticipate either widespread resistance to currently fashionable modes of feminine embodiment or joyous experimentation with new "styles of the flesh"; moreover, such novelties would face profound opposition from material and psychological sources identified earlier in this essay. . . . In spite of this, a number of oppositional discourses and practices have appeared in recent years. An increasing number of women are "pumping iron," a few with little concern for the limits of body development imposed by current canons of femininity. Women in radical lesbian communities have also rejected hegemonic images of femininity and are struggling to develop a new female aesthetic. A striking feature of such communities is the extent to which they have overcome the oppressive identification of female beauty and desirability with youth: Here, the physical features of aging—"character" lines and greying hair—not only do not diminish a woman's attractiveness, they may even enhance it. A popular literature of resistance is growing, some of it analytical and reflective, like Kim Chernin's *The Obsession*, some oriented toward practical self-help, like Marcia Hutchinson's recent *Transforming Body Image: Learning to Love the Body You Have*.[49] This literature reflects a mood akin in some ways to that other and earlier mood of quiet desperation to which Betty Friedan gave voice in *The Feminine Mystique*. Nor should we forget that a mass-based women's movement is in place in this country which has begun a critical questioning of the meaning of femininity, if not yet in this, then in other domains of life. We women cannot begin the re-vision of our own bodies until we learn to read the cultural messages we inscribe upon them daily and until we come to see that even when the mastery of the disciplines of femininity produce a triumphant result, we are still only women.

NOTES

1. Michel Foucault, *Discipline and Punish* (New York: Vintage Books, 1979), p. 138.

2. Ibid., p. 28.

3. Ibid., p. 147.

4. Ibid., p. 153. Foucault is citing an eighteenth-century military manual, "Ordonnance du Ier janvier 1766 . . . , titre XI, article 2."

5. Ibid., p. 153.

6. Ibid., p. 150.

7. Ibid., p. 200.

8. Ibid., p. 201.

9. Ibid., p. 228.

10. Judith Butler, "Embodied Identity in De Beauvoir's *The Second Sex*," unpublished manuscript, p. 11, presented to American Philosophical Association, Pacific Division, March 22, 1985. See also Butler's recent monograph *Gender Trouble: Feminism and the Subversion of Identity* (New York: Routledge, 1990).

11. Marcia Millman, *Such a Pretty Face—Being Fat in America* (New York: Norton, 1980), p. 46.

12. Susan Bordo, "Anorexia Nervosa: Psychopathology as the Crystallization of Culture," *Philosophical Forum*, Vol. XVII, No. 2, Winter 1985–86, pp. 73–104. See also Bordo's *Food, Fashion and Power: The Body and The*

Reproduction of Gender (forthcoming, U. of California Press).

13. *USA Today*, May 30, 1985.

14. Phrase taken from the title of Kim Chernin's *The Obsession: Reflections on the Tyranny of Slenderness* (New York: Harper and Row, 1981), an examination from a feminist perspective of women's eating disorders and of the current female preoccupation with body size.

15. M. J. Saffon, *The 15-Minute-A-Day Natural Face Lift* (New York: Warner Books, 1981).

16. Sophia Loren, *Women and Beauty* (New York: William Morrow, 1984), p. 57.

17. Iris Young, "Throwing Like a Girl: A Phenomenology of Feminine Body Comportment, Motility and Spatiality," *Human Studies*, Vol. 3, (1980), pp. 137–156.

18. Marianne Wex, *Let's Take Back Our Space: "Female" and "Male" Body Language as a Result of Patriarchal Structures* (Berlin: Frauenliteraturverlag Hermine Fees, 1979). Wex claims that Japanese women are still taught to position their feet so that the toes point inward, a traditional sign of submissiveness (p. 23).

19. In heels, the "female foot and leg are turned into ornamental objects and the impractical shoe, which offers little protection against dust, rain and snow, induces helplessness and dependence. . . . The extra wiggle in the hips, exaggerating a slight natural tendency, is seen as sexually flirtatious while the smaller steps and tentative, insecure tread suggest daintiness, modesty and refinement. Finally, the overall hobbling effect with its sadomasochistic tinge is suggestive of the restraining leg irons and ankle chains endured by captive animals, prisoners and slaves who were also festooned with decorative symbols of their bondage." Susan Brown-miller, *Femininity* (New York: Simon and Schuster, 1984), p. 184.

20. Nancy Henley, *Body Politics* (Englewood Cliffs, N. J.: Prentice-Hall, 1977), p. 176.

21. For an account of the sometimes devastating effects on workers, like flight attendants, whose conditions of employment require the display of a perpetual friendliness, see Arlie Hochschild, *The Managed Heart: The Commercialization of Human Feeling* (Berkeley, Calif.: University of California Press, 1983).

22. Henley, *Body Politics*, p. 108.

23. Ibid., p. 149.

24. Clairol has just introduced a small electric shaver, the "Bikini," apparently intended for just such use.

25. Georgette Klinger and Barbara Rowes, *Georgette Klinger's Skincare* (New York: William Morrow, 1978), pp. 102, 105, 151, 188, and passim.

26. *Chicago Magazine*, March 1986, pp. 43, 10, 18, and 62.

27. *Essence*, April 1986, p. 25. I am indebted to Laurie Shrage for calling this to my attention and for providing most of these examples.

28. Klinger, *Skincare*, pp. 137–140.

29. In light of this, one is surprised to see a two-ounce jar of "Skin Regeneration Formula," a "Proteolytic Enzyme Cream with Bromelain and Papain," selling for $23.95 in the tabloid *Globe* (April 8, 1986, p. 29) and an unidentified amount of Tova Borgnine's "amazing new formula from Beverly Hills" (otherwise unnamed) going for $41.75 in the *National Enquirer* (April 8, 1986, p. 15).

30. "It is required of woman that in order to realize her femininity she must make herself object and prey, which is to say that she must renounce her claims as sovereign subject." Simone De Beauvoir, *The Second Sex* (New York: Bantam Books, 1968), p. 642.

31. The film *Pumping Iron II* portrays very clearly the tension for female bodybuilders (a tension that enters into formal judging in the sport) between muscular development and a properly feminine appearance.

32. Henley, *Body Politics*, p. 101, 153, and passim.

33. Foucault, *Discipline and Punish*, p. 222.

34. Millman, *Such a Pretty Face*, p. 80. These sorts of remarks are made so commonly to heavy women that sociologist Millman takes the most clichéd as title of her study of the lives of the overweight.

35. I am indebted to Nancy Fraser for the formulation of this point.

36. Millman, *Such a Pretty Face*, pp. 80 and 195.

37. Chernin, *The Obsession*, p. 53.

38. For a claim that the project of liberal or "mainstream" feminism is covertly racist, see Bell Hooks, *Ain't I Woman: Black Women and Feminism* (Boston: South End Press, 1981), Chap. 4. For an authoritative general critique of liberal feminism, see Alison Jaggar, *Feminist Politics and Human Nature* (Totowa, N. J.: Rowman and Allanheld, 1983), Chaps. 3 and 7.

39. See, for example, Mihailo Markovic, "Women's Liberation and Human Emancipation," in *Women and Philosophy*, ed. Carol C. Gould and Marx W. Wartofsky (New York: G. P. Putnam's Sons, 1976), pp. 165–166.

40. Foucault, *Discipline and Punish*, p. 30.

41. Some radical feminists have called for just such a deconstruction. See especially Monique Wittig, *The Lesbian Body* (New York: Avon Books, 1976), and Butler, *Gender Trouble*.

42. Foucault, *Discipline and Punish*, p. 44.

43. Foucault, Colin Gordon, ed., *Power/Knowledge* (Brighton, 1980), p. 151. Quoted in Peter Dews, "Power and Subjectivity in Foucault," *New Left Review*, No. 144, March–April 1984, p. 17.

44. Dews, op. cit., p. 77.

45. Foucault, *Discipline and Punish*, p. 138.

46. Ibid., p. 201.

47. Foucault, *Power/Knowledge*, p. 98. In fact, Foucault is not entirely consistent on this point. For an excellent discussion of contending Foucault interpretations and for the difficulty of deriving a consistent set of claims from Foucault's work generally, see Nancy Fraser, "Michel Foucault: A 'Young Conservative'?" *Ethics*, Vol. 9(?) October 1985, pp. 165–184.

48. Dews, op. cit., p. 92.

49. See Marcia Hutchinson, *Transforming Body Image-Learning to Love the Body You Have* (Trumansburg, N. Y.: Crossing Press, 1985). See also Bordo, "Anorexia Nervosa: Psychopathology as the Crystallization of Culture."

Study Questions

1. According to Foucault, how has the exercise of power changed from premodern to modern times?

2. According to Bartky, how can Foucault's theory be used to shed light on socialization into femininity?

3. According to Bartky, why might women resist throwing off femininity?

4. According to Bartky, how is resistance to the discipline of femininity possible?

5. In what sense does this article exemplify the dominance approach to sex equality?

Audre Lorde

Age, Race, Class, and Sex: Women Redefining Difference

Much of Western European history conditions us to see human differences in simplistic opposition to each other: dominant/subordinate, good/bad, up/down, superior/inferior. In a society where the good is defined in terms of profit rather than in terms of human need, there must always be some group of people who, through systematized oppression, can be made to feel surplus, to occupy the place of the dehumanized inferior. Within this society, that group is made up of Black and Third World people, working-class people, older people, and women.

As a forty-nine-year-old Black lesbian feminist socialist mother of two, including one boy, and a member of an interracial couple, I usually find myself a part of some group defined as other, deviant, inferior, or just plain wrong. Traditionally, in American society, it is the members of oppressed, objectified groups who are expected to stretch out and bridge the gap between the actualities of our lives and the consciousness of our oppressor. For in order to survive, those of us for whom oppression is as american as apple pie have always had to be watchers, to become familiar with the language and manners of the oppressor, even sometimes adopting them for some illusion of protection. Whenever the need for some pretense of communication arises, those who profit from our oppression call upon us to share our knowledge with them. In other words, it is the responsibility of the oppressed to teach the oppressors their mistakes. I am responsible for educating teachers who dismiss my children's culture in school. Black and Third World people are expected to educate white people as to our humanity. Women are expected to educate men. Lesbians and gay men are expected to educate the heterosexual world. The oppressors maintain their position and evade responsibility for their own actions. There is a constant drain of energy which might be better used in redefining ourselves and devising realistic scenarios for altering the present and constructing the future.

Institutionalized rejection of difference is an absolute necessity in a profit economy which needs outsiders as surplus people. As members of such an economy, we have *all* been programmed to respond to the human differences between us with fear and loathing and to handle that difference in one of three ways: ignore it, and if that is not possible, copy it if we think it is dominant, or destroy it if we think it is subordinate. But we have no patterns for relating across our human differences as equals. As a result, those differences have been misnamed and misused in the service of separation and confusion.

Certainly there are very real differences between us of race, age, and sex. But it is not those differences between us that are separating us. It is rather our refusal to recognize those differences, and to examine the distortions which result from our misnaming them and their effects upon human behavior and expectation.

Racism, the belief in the inherent superiority of one race over all others and thereby the right to dominance. Sexism, the belief in the inherent superiority of one sex over the other and thereby the right to dominance. Ageism. Heterosexism. Elitism. Classism.

It is a lifetime pursuit for each one of us to extract these distortions from our living at the same time as we recognize, reclaim, and define those differences upon which they are imposed. For we have all been raised in a society where those distortions were endemic within our living. Too often, we pour the energy needed for recognizing and exploring difference into pretending those differences are insurmountable barriers, or that they do not exist at all. This results in a voluntary isolation, or false and treacherous connections. Either way, we do not develop tools for using human difference as a springboard for creative change within our lives. We speak not of human difference, but of human deviance.

Somewhere, on the edge of consciousness, there is what I call a *mythical norm*, which each one of us

within our hearts knows "that is not me." In america, this norm is usually defined as white, thin, male, young, heterosexual, christian, and financially secure. It is with this mythical norm that the trappings of power reside within this society. Those of us who stand outside that power often identify one way in which we are different, and we assume that to be the primary cause of all oppression, forgetting other distortions around difference, some of which we ourselves may be practising. By and large within the women's movement today, white women focus upon their oppression as women and ignore differences of race, sexual preference, class, and age. There is a pretense to a homogeneity of experience covered by the word *sisterhood* that does not in fact exist.

Unacknowledged class differences rob women of each others' energy and creative insight. Recently a women's magazine collective made the decision for one issue to print only prose, saying poetry was a less "rigorous" or "serious" art form. Yet even the form our creativity takes is often a class issue. Of all the art forms, poetry is the most economical. It is the one which is the most secret, which requires the least physical labor, the least material, and the one which can be done between shifts, in the hospital pantry, on the subway, and on scraps of surplus paper. Over the last few years, writing a novel on tight finances, I came to appreciate the enormous differences in the material demands between poetry and prose. As we reclaim our literature, poetry has been the major voice of poor, working class, and Colored women. A room of one's own may be a necessity for writing prose, but so are reams of paper, a typewriter, and plenty of time. The actual requirements to produce the visual arts also help determine, along class lines, whose art is whose. In this day of inflated prices for material, who are our sculptors, our painters, our photographers? When we speak of a broadly based women's culture, we need to be aware of the effect of class and economic differences on the supplies available for producing art.

As we move toward creating a society within which we can each flourish, ageism is another distortion of relationship which interferes without vision. By ignoring the past, we are encouraged to repeat its mistakes. The "generation gap" is an important social tool for any repressive society. If the younger members of a community view the older members as contemptible or suspect or excess, they will never be able to join hands and examine the living memories of the community, nor ask the all important question, "Why?" This gives rise to a historical amnesia that keeps us working to invent the wheel every time we have to go to the store for bread.

We find ourselves having to repeat and relearn the same old lessons over and over that our mothers did because we do not pass on what we have learned, or because we are unable to listen. For instance, how many times has this all been said before? For another, who would have believed that once again our daughters are allowing their bodies to be hampered and purgatoried by girdles and high heels and hobble skirts?

Ignoring the differences of race between women and the implications of those differences presents the most serious threat to the mobilization of women's joint power.

As white women ignore their built-in privilege of whiteness and define *woman* in terms of their own experience alone, then women of Color become "other," the outsider whose experience and tradition is too "alien" to comprehend. An example of this is the signal absence of the experience of women of Color as a resource for women's studies courses. The literature of women of Color is seldom included in women's literature courses and almost never in other literature courses, nor in women's studies as a whole. All too often, the excuse given is that the literatures of women of Color can only be taught by Colored women, or that they are too difficult to understand, or that classes cannot "get into" them because they come out of experiences that are "too different." I have heard this argument presented by white women of otherwise quite clear intelligence, women who seem to have no trouble at all teaching and reviewing work that comes out of the vastly different experiences of Shakespeare, Molière, Dostoyefsky, and Aristophanes. Surely there must be some other explanation.

This is a very complex question, but I believe one of the reasons white women have such difficulty reading Black women's work is because of their reluctance to see Black women as women and different from themselves. To examine Black women's literature effectively requires that we be seen as whole people in our actual complexities—as individuals, as women, as human—rather than as one of those problematic but familiar stereotypes provided in this society in place of genuine images of Black women. And I believe this holds true for the literatures of other women of Color who are not Black.

The literatures of all women of Color recreate the textures of our lives, and many white women are heavily invested in ignoring the real differences. For as long as any difference between us means one of us must be inferior, then the recognition of any difference must be fraught with guilt. To allow women of Color to step out of stereotypes is too guilt provoking, for it threatens the complacency of those women who view oppression only in terms of sex.

Refusing to recognize difference makes it impossible to see the different problems and pitfalls facing us as women.

Thus, in a patriarchal power system where white-skin privilege is a major prop, the entrapments used to neutralize Black women and white women are not the same. For example, it is easy for Black women to be used by the power structure against Black men, not because they are men, but because they are Black. Therefore, for Black women, it is necessary at all times to separate the needs of the oppressor from our own legitimate conflicts within our communities. This same problem does not exist for white women. Black women and men have shared racist oppression and still share it, although in different ways. Out of that shared oppression we have developed joint defenses and joint vulnerabilities to each other that are not duplicated in the white community, with the exception of the relationship between Jewish women and Jewish men.

On the other hand, white women face the pitfall of being seduced into joining the oppressor under the pretense of sharing power. This possibility does not exist in the same way for women of Color. The tokenism that is sometimes extended to us is not an invitation to join power; our racial "otherness" is a visible reality that makes that quite clear. For white women there is a wider range of pretended choices and rewards for identifying with patriarchal power and its tools.

Today, with the defeat of ERA, the tightening economy, and increased conservatism, it is easier once again for white women to believe the dangerous fantasy that if you are good enough, pretty enough, sweet enough, quiet enough, teach the children to behave, hate the right people, and marry the right men, then you will be allowed to co-exist with patriarchy in relative peace, at least until a man needs your job or the neighborhood rapist happens along. And true, unless one lives and loves in the trenches it is difficult to remember that the war against dehumanization is ceaseless.

But Black women and our children know the fabric of our lives is stitched with violence and with hatred, that there is no rest. We do not deal with it only on the picket lines, or in dark midnight alleys, or in the places where we dare to verbalize our resistance. For us, increasingly, violence weaves through the daily tissues of our living—in the supermarket, in the classroom, in the elevator, in the clinic and the schoolyard, from the plumber, the baker, the saleswoman, the bus driver, the bank teller, the waitress who does not serve us.

Some problems we share as women, some we do not. You fear your children will grow up to join the patriarchy and testify against you, we fear our children will be dragged from a car and shot down in the street, and you will turn your backs upon the reasons they are dying.

The threat of difference has been no less blinding to people of Color. Those of us who are Black must see that the reality of our lives and our struggle does not make us immune to the errors of ignoring and misnaming difference. Within Black communities where racism is a living reality, differences among us often seem dangerous and suspect. The need for unity is often misnamed as a need for homogeneity, and a Black feminist vision mistaken for betrayal of our common interests as a people. Because of the continuous battle against racial erasure that Black women and Black men share, some Black women still refuse to recognize that we are also oppressed as women, and that sexual hostility against Black women is practiced not only by the white racist society, but implemented within our Black communities as well. It is a disease striking the heart of Black nationhood, and silence will not make it disappear. Exacerbated by racism and the pressures of powerlessness, violence against Black women and children often becomes a standard within our communities, one by which manliness can be measured. But these woman-hating acts are rarely discussed as crimes against Black women.

As a group, women of Color are the lowest paid wage earners in america. We are the primary targets of abortion and sterilization abuse, here and abroad. In certain parts of Africa, small girls are still being sewed shut between their legs to keep them docile and for men's pleasure. This is known as female circumcision, and it is not a cultural affair as the late Jomo Kenyatta insisted, it is a crime against Black women.

Black women's literature is full of the pain of frequent assault, not only by a racist patriarchy, but also by Black men. Yet the necessity for and history of shared battle have made us, Black women, particularly vulnerable to the false accusation that anti-sexist is anti-Black. Meanwhile, womanhating as a recourse of the powerless is sapping strength from Black communities, and our very lives. Rape is on the increase, reported and unreported, and rape is not aggressive sexuality, it is sexualized aggression. As Kalamu ya Salaam, a Black male writer points out, "As long as male domination exists, rape will exist. Only women revolting and men made conscious of their responsibility to fight sexism can collectively stop rape."[1]

Differences between ourselves as Black women are also being misnamed and used to separate us from one another. As a Black lesbian feminist comfortable with the many different ingredients of my identity, and a woman committed to racial and sexual freedom from oppression, I find I am constantly being encouraged to pluck out some one aspect of myself and present this as the meaningful whole, eclipsing or denying the other parts of self. But this is a destructive and fragmenting way to live. My fullest concentration of energy is available to me only when I integrate all the parts of who I am, openly, allowing power from particular sources of my living to flow back and forth freely through all my different selves, without the restrictions of externally imposed definition. Only then can I bring myself and my energies as a whole to the service of those struggles which I embrace as part of my living.

A fear of lesbians, or of being accused of being a lesbian, has led many Black women into testifying against themselves. It has led some of us into destructive alliances, and others into despair and isolation. In the white women's communities, heterosexism is sometimes a result of identifying with the white patriarchy, a rejection of that interdependence between women-identified women which allows the self to be, rather than to be used in the service of men. Sometimes it reflects a die-hard belief in the protective coloration of heterosexual relationships, sometimes a self-hate which all women have to fight against, taught us from birth.

Although elements of these attitudes exist for all women, there are particular resonances of heterosexism and homophobia among Black women. Despite the fact that woman-bonding has a long and honorable history in the African and African-American communities, and despite the knowledge and accomplishments of many strong and creative women-identified Black women in the political, social and cultural fields, heterosexual Black women often tend to ignore or discount the existence and work of Black lesbians. Part of this attitude has come from an understandable terror of Black male attack within the close confines of Black society, where the punishment for any female self-assertion is still to be accused of being a lesbian and therefore unworthy of the attention or support of the scarce Black male. But part of this need to misname and ignore Black lesbians comes from a very real fear that openly women-identified Black women who are no longer dependent upon men for their self-definition may well reorder our whole concept of social relationships.

Black women who once insisted that lesbianism was a white woman's problem now insist that Black lesbians are a threat to Black nationhood, are consorting with the enemy, are basically un-Black. These accusations, coming from the very women to whom we look for deep and real understanding, have served to keep many Black lesbians in hiding, caught between the racism of white women and the homophobia of their sisters. Often, their work has been ignored, trivialized, or misnamed, as with the work of Angelina Grimke, Alice Dunbar-Nelson, Lorraine Hansberry. Yet women-bonded women have always been some part of the power of Black communities, from our unmarried aunts to the amazons of Dahomey.

And it is certainly not Black lesbians who are assaulting women and raping children and grandmothers on the streets of our communities.

Across this country, as in Boston during the spring of 1979 following the unsolved murders of twelve Black women, Black lesbians are spearheading movements against violence against Black women.

What are the particular details within each of our lives that can be scrutinized and altered to help bring about change? How do we redefine difference for all women? It is not our differences which separate women, but our reluctance to recognize those differences and to deal effectively with the distortions which have resulted from the ignoring and misnaming of those differences.

As a tool of social control, women have been encouraged to recognize only one area of human difference as legitimate, those differences which exist between women and men. And we have learned to deal across those differences with the urgency of all oppressed subordinates. All of us have had to learn to live or work or coexist with men, from our fathers on. We have recognized and negotiated these differences, even when this recognition only continued the old dominant/subordinate mode of human relationship, where the oppressed must recognize the masters' difference in order to survive.

But our future survival is predicated upon our ability to relate within equality. As women, we must root out internalized patterns of oppression within ourselves if we are to move beyond the most superficial aspects of social change. Now we must recognize differences among women who are our equals, neither inferior nor superior, and devise ways to use each others' difference to enrich our visions and our joint struggles.

The future of our earth may depend upon the ability of all women to identify and develop new definitions of power and new patterns of relating across difference. The old definitions have not served us, nor the earth that supports us. The old patterns, no matter how cleverly rearranged to imitate progress, still condemn us to cosmetically altered repetitions of the same old exchanges, the same old guilt, hatred, recrimination, lamentation, and suspicion.

For we have, built into all of us, old blueprints of expectation and response, old structures of oppression, and these must be altered at the same time as we alter the living conditions which are a result of those structures. For the master's tools will never dismantle the master's house.

As Paulo Freire shows so well in *The Pedagogy of the Oppressed*,[2] the true focus of revolutionary change is never merely the oppressive situations which we seek to escape, but that piece of the oppressor which is planted deep within each of us, and which knows only the oppressors' tactics, the oppressors' relationships.

Change means growth, and growth can be painful. But we sharpen self-definition by exposing the self in work and struggle together with those whom we define as different from ourselves, although sharing the same goals. For Black and white, old and young, lesbian and heterosexual women alike, this can mean new paths to our survival.

> We have chosen each other
> and the edge of each others battles
> the war is the same
> if we lose
> someday women's blood will congeal
> upon a dead planet

> if we win
> there is no telling
> we seek beyond history
> for a new and more possible meeting.[3]

NOTES

Paper delivered at the Copeland Colloquium, Amherst College, April 1980.

1. From "Rape: A Radical Analysis, An African-American Perspective" by Kalamu ya Salaam in *Black Books Bulletin*, vol. 6, no. 4 (1980).

2. Seabury Press, New York, 1970.

3. From "Outlines," unpublished poem.

Study Questions

1. Lorde asserts that "rejection of difference" is essential to a profit economy. What is her argument for this claim? (It is interesting to compare Lorde's argument for this conclusion to Shiva's in "Women's Indigenous Knowledge and Biodiversity Conservation.")

2. Lorde writes, "For as long as any difference between us means one of us must be inferior, then the recognition of any difference is fraught with guilt." What does she mean by this?

3. Lorde exhorts women to "recognize differences among women who are our equals, neither inferior nor superior, and devise ways to use each others' difference to enrich our visions and our joint struggles." What problems does Lorde think will be avoided, and what benefits does she think will be gained, from doing this?

4. In what sense does this article exemplify the dominance approach to sex equality?

John Stoltenberg

Confronting Pornography as a Civil-Rights Issue

In Minneapolis, Minnesota, . . . , a coalition of neighborhood groups . . . were organizing to confront the way the pornography industry was operating in their city. These citizens were angry about the fact that "adult" book and video stores were being located mostly in poor areas and in communities where blacks, Native Americans, and other people of color lived, saturating these neighborhoods with pornography, with a resulting increase in crime and deterioration of the neighborhood. For them pornography was a community issue, a class issue, and a racial issue: They wanted to stop pornography's erosion of the quality of their lives, the land values where they lived, and their physical security. Local citizens groups had tried for over seven years to tackle the problem of pornography in neighborhoods through zoning laws. But these zoning laws had been struck down as unconstitutional, because, as a woman judge on the Minnesota state supreme court opined, they inconvenienced anyone who wanted to buy the stuff; he'd have to travel too far, which would be a nasty incursion on his First Amendment rights. So by the fall of 1983, the Minneapolis City Council was in the process of deliberating on a new zoning law—one that would circumvent this judge's ruling by establishing eight "adult bookstore" zones handily dispersed throughout the city. The issue for neighborhood organizers, however, remained the same: Into *whose* neighborhood would the pornography be zoned?

At the time of these deliberations, Andrea Dworkin and Catharine A. MacKinnon just happened to be in Minneapolis coteaching a course on pornography and law at the University of Minnesota Law School. The two were a formidable team:

• Catharine A. MacKinnon—a feminist lawyer, teacher, writer, and activist—is the constitutional-law scholar who pioneered the legal theory that defined and established sexual harassment as a legal term of art and an actionable form of sex discrimination.[1] Before coming to Minnesota as associate professor teaching sex discrimination and constitutional law, she had taught at Yale, Harvard, and Stanford law schools.

• Andrea Dworkin—at the time a visiting professor in women's studies and law at the University of Minnesota—is a feminist writer, activist, and impassioned public speaker who had addressed scores of Take Back the Night rallies beginning with the first, in San Francisco. She had published extensively about pornography as a women's issue since 1974[2] and had spoken at colleges and demonstrations in the late seventies on "Pornography: The New Terrorism."[3] Pornography plays a role in both causing and justifying all forms of sexual abuse, she believed, and therefore it plays a role in creating and maintaining the civil inferiority of women.[4] "Simply put," according to Dworkin, "if raping women is entertainment, what are women's lives worth?"

John Stoltenberg, "Confronting Pornography as a Civil Rights Issue," from *Refusing to Be a Man*. New York: Routledge, 2000. 120–151. Reprinted by permission of the publisher. Notes have been renumbered.

In October 1983, the Neighborhood Pornography Task Force convinced Dworkin and MacKinnon to appear before the Minneapolis City Council Zoning and Planning Committee to testify about the new zoning ordinance. They testified that they were *opposed* to the zoning approach—because it did absolutely nothing to remedy the real injury that pornography does. Speaking first, Dworkin broached a feminist legal analysis that "[p]ornography is an abuse of the civil rights of women. It is an absolute repudiation of our right to equality under the law and as citizens of this country."[5] Then MacKinnon told the committee, "I suggest that you consider that pornography, as it subordinates women to men, is a form of discrimination on the basis of sex"[6] and proposed that instead of zoning pornography—which indicates, said Dworkin, "that property matters and property values matter but that women don't"[7]—the city could deal with pornography through an amendment to its laws prohibiting sex discrimination. Quite improbably and unexpectedly, the zoning committee unanimously moved to direct the city attorney to pursue this civil-rights approach. Within weeks, the City of Minneapolis hired Dworkin and MacKinnon as consultants—to draft a law recognizing that pornography violates women's civil rights and to organize public hearings that would become a legislative record showing how women's rights are violated by the production and consumption of pornography.

The law they drafted was an amendment to the Minneapolis Civil Rights Ordinance. Essentially it would give the victims of pornography *a chance to fight back*: For the first time in history, this law would allow a woman to try to prove that she had been injured by having pornography forced on her, by being coerced into a pornographic performance, or because pornography was used in some sexual assault on her. It would also allow a woman to sue traffickers in pornography on the basis of the harm pornography does to the civil rights of women as a class. This law, which became widely known as the Dworkin/MacKinnon Civil-Rights Antipornography Ordinance, was "based on the idea—like the principle underlying the Fourteenth Amendment—that

women have *rights* and that those rights are abrogated by systematic sexual subordination."[8]

In December of 1983, there were two days of public hearings on the proposed Ordinance in Minneapolis. Researchers testified; victims testified; people who worked with victims of rape, battery, and child sexual assault testified. It was the first time in history that any legislative body had ever listened to real people's experience of their victimization through pornography.[9] The hearings transcript includes the testimony of Linda Marchiano, who as "Linda Lovelace" was beaten and forced into performing in the film *Deep Throat*. Here is part of her testimony. At the time of the filming, she was married to a man named Chuck Traynor, whom she calls Mr. Traynor.

> During the filming of *Deep Throat*, actually after the first day, I suffered a brutal beating in my room for smiling on the set. It was a hotel room and the whole crew was in one room, there was at least twenty people partying, music going, laughing, and having a good time. Mr. Traynor started to bounce me off the walls. I figured out of twenty people, there might be one human being that would do something to help me and I was screaming for help, I was being beaten, I was being kicked around and again bounced off the walls. And all of a sudden the room next door became very quiet. Nobody, not one person came to help me.
>
> The greatest complaint the next day is the fact that there was bruises on my body. So many people say that in *Deep Throat* I have a smile on my face and I look as though I am really enjoying myself. No one ever asked me how those bruises got on my body.[10]

At another point in her testimony, Linda Marchiano said:

> Mr. Traynor suggested the thought that I do films with a D-O-G and I told him that I wouldn't do it. I suffered a brutal beating, he claims he suffered embarrassment because I wouldn't do it.
>
> We then went to another porno studio, one of the sleaziest ones I have ever seen, and then this guy walked in with his animal and I again started crying. I started crying. I said I am not going to do this and they were all very persistent, the two men involved in making the pornographic film and Mr. Traynor

himself. And I started to leave and go outside of the room where they make these films and when I turned around there was all of a sudden a gun displayed on the desk and having seen the coarseness and the callousness of the people involved in pornography, I knew that I would have been shot and killed.

Needless to say the film was shot and still is one of the hardest ones for me to deal with today.[11]

THE FOUR CAUSES OF ACTION

The Civil-Rights Antipornography Ordinance is a civil law, unlike obscenity laws, which are criminal. Under a criminal law, someone can be tried and sentenced to go to jail if they commit a crime. But under a civil law, someone can be sued and ordered to pay money (which is called damages) or to stop doing something that they're doing (which is called an injunction).

The antipornography ordinance would allow a person access to the local human-rights commission and the civil court if they have a complaint under any of four causes of action. One of these causes of action is called **coercion into pornography**. This cause of action is one that Linda Marchiano could use even though the film *Deep Throat* was made many years ago, because the Ordinance would apply to the last "appearance or sale" of the film made of her coerced performance and *Deep Throat* is still for sale just about everywhere. Linda Marchiano testified in Minneapolis that "every time someone watches that film, they are watching me being raped."[12] The movie is in effect a filmed document of her coerced performances of sex acts.

Today, any movie may be made of any rape and then sold on the market as sexual entertainment. The rape, if the victim is very lucky, could be prosecuted, but the movie is considered "protected speech" under current law. In the last several years, rape-crisis centers have increasingly encountered rapes that have been photographed, and the photographs are being sold. Under current law, nothing can be done to remove the photographs from sale. But the Civil-Rights Antipornography Ordinance is written so that a person whose rape is photographed or who is coerced

into performing for pornography has the right to file a complaint with a human-rights commission or bring a civil suit into court. If they successfully prove their case, they could collect money damages from the whole chain of profit, and that person could also get the pornography made from their coercion off the market in the locality where the Ordinance is in force.

If you know what happens to women victims in rape trials, you have some idea how difficult it is for any woman to prove that she did not consent to an act of forced sex. So imagine the difficulty of proving that you were coerced into performing for pornography when what you were forced to do was to act as if you were thoroughly enjoying what was happening to you. Recognizing that many women trying to use the coercion cause of action would be up against serious pretrial challenges, Dworkin and MacKinnon wrote into the Ordinance a list of "facts or conditions" that cannot in and of themselves be used by the pornographers to get a coercion case dismissed. This list includes "that the person is or has ever been a prostitute," because, among other reasons, it is virtually impossible for a prostitute to get a rape conviction. The list also includes "that the person is connected by blood or marriage to anyone involved in or related to the making of the pornography"; "Linda Lovelace," for example, was married—by force—to the man who was her pimp and torturer. The list also includes "that the person signed a contract . . ."; as Andrea Dworkin has said, "If you can force someone to fuck a dog, you can force them to sign a contract." The complete list includes thirteen items, a virtual catalog of smears used against women's veracity in court:

Proof of one or more of the following facts or conditions shall not, without more, preclude a finding of coercion:

- **a.** that the person is a woman; or
- **b.** that the person is or has been a prostitute; or
- **c.** that the person has attained the age of majority; or
- **d.** that the person is connected by blood or marriage to anyone involved in or related to the making of the pornography; or

e. that the person has previously had, or been thought to have had, sexual relations with anyone, including anyone involved in or related to the making of the pornography; or

f. that the person has previously posed for sexually explicit pictures with or for anyone, including anyone involved in or related to the making of the pornography; or

g. that anyone else, including a spouse or other relative, has given permission on the person's behalf; or

h. that the person actually consented to a use of a performance that is then changed into pornography; or

i. that the person knew that the purpose of the acts or events in question was to make pornography; or

j. that the person showed no resistance or appeared to cooperate actively in the photographic sessions or events that produced the pornography; or

k. that the person signed a contract, or made statements affirming a willingness to cooperate in the production of the pornography; or

l. that no physical force, threats, or weapons were used in the making of the pornography; or

m. that the person was paid or otherwise compensated.[13]

This list was mistakenly interpreted by some opponents of the bill as implying that women cannot ever consent. That's not what this list means at all. In a civil trial for coercion, the burden of proof is on the plaintiff, who must prove that she was actually coerced; and the defendants (the pornographers) can use every means at their disposal to prove that the plaintiff participated willingly. But the legal meaning of this list is that just because a woman is a prostitute or married to the producer or signed a release and so forth, that's not grounds for throwing a case of alleged coercion out of court before it can be tried.

Many people don't realize how pornography actually functions in the lives of its victims. They think of pornography as simply some pictures that some lonely guy masturbates to now and then. But that's not entirely accurate. In fact there are many women on whom pornography is forced, sometimes by husbands, boyfriends, or lovers, and many women who are assaulted in such a way that pornography is directly involved in the assault. For instance, in a random survey of women in San Francisco,[14] 10 percent of the women interviewed said they had been upset by a husband or lover who was pressuring them into doing something that they had seen in pornographic pictures, movies, or books. These are some of the things they said their husbands or boyfriends had asked them to do:

> It was physical slapping and hitting. It wasn't a turn-on; it was more a feeling of being used as an object. What was most upsetting was that he thought it would be a turn-on.

> My husband enjoys pornographic movies. He tries to get me to do things he finds exciting in movies. They include twosomes and threesomes. I always refuse. Also, I was always upset with his ideas about putting objects in my vagina, until I learned this is not as deviant as I used to think. He used to force me or put whatever he wanted into me.

> He forced me to go down on him. He said he'd been going to porno movies. He'd seen this and wanted me to do it. He also wanted to pour champagne on my vagina. I got beat up because I didn't want to do it. He pulled my hair and slapped me around. After that I went ahead and did it, but there was no feeling in it.

> This guy had seen a movie where a woman was being made love to by dogs. He suggested that some of his friends had a dog and we should have a party and set the dog loose on the women. He wanted me to put a muzzle on the dog and put some sort of stuff on my vagina so that the dog would lick there.

> My old man and I went to a show that had lots of tying up and anal intercourse. We came home and proceeded to make love. He went out and got two belts. He tied my feet together with one, and with the other he kind of beat me. I was in the spirit, I really went along with it. But when he tried to penetrate me anally, I couldn't take it, it was too painful. I managed to convey to him verbally to quit it. He did stop, but not soon enough to suit me. Then one time, he

branded me. I still have a scar on my butt. He put a little wax initial thing on a hot plate and then stuck it on my ass when I was unaware.

My boyfriend and I saw a movie in which there was masochism. After that he wanted to gag me and tie me up. He was stoned, I was not. I was really shocked at his behavior. I was nervous and uptight. He literally tried to force me, after gagging me first. He snuck up behind me with a scarf. He was hurting me with it and I started getting upset. Then I realized it wasn't a joke. He grabbed me and shook me by my shoulders and brought out some ropes, and told me to relax, and that I would enjoy it. Then he started putting me down about my feelings about sex, and my inhibitedness. I started crying and struggling with him, got loose, and kicked him in the testicles, which forced him down on the couch. I ran out of the house. Next day he called and apologized, but that was the end of him.[15]

As mounting testimony from pornography victims makes clear, the distinction often made between "fantasy" and real behavior simply doesn't stand up in the world of pornography. If someone forces their fantasy on you, the fantasy is no longer an abstract mental event; and if someone acts out their fantasy of assaulting you, something really happens. Often such "fantasies," modeled after pictorial pornography, are modeled after what really happened to the real woman in the pornography.

In the Civil-Rights Antipornography Ordinance there is a second cause of action called **forcing pornography on a person**. As this cause of action is defined, any person who is forced to watch pornography at home, in a place of work or education, or in public is having their civil rights violated. The person can sue the perpetrator and any institution that lets the abuse occur (just as in cases of sexual harassment). The importance of this cause of action is obvious if you think about battery: There is more and more testimony coming from battered women and from women working in battered-women's shelters about the amount of sexual abuse that is generated in marriages by men who are using pornography. There is also increasing testimony about a growing incidence of pornography-linked sadism in the home, including rape by animals, branding, and maiming.

A third cause of action is called **assault or physical attack due to pornography**. This provision enables anyone who has been raped or injured directly as a result of the use of a specific piece of pornography to sue the perpetrator of the assault for damages. The victim of the assault can also sue anyone who made or sold the specific pornography for money damages and for an injunction against further sale of it in the locality where the law is in force.

A fourth cause of action is called **trafficking in pornography**. A kind of "class action" cause of action, it is based on the notion that pornography is a practice of sex discrimination in and of itself. The trafficking provision basically says that if material meets the definition of pornography in the law, it is sex discrimination by definition; and any woman, acting in behalf of all women, can sue to have it removed from the marketplace because of its impact on the civil status of all women. (But no material may be removed from sale under the trafficking provision without a trial de novo—a full court trial.) There is now a body of proof in the form of clinical evidence, social studies, research studies, and victim testimony that pornography produces hostility, bigotry, and aggression against women, and also attitudes and behaviors of sex discrimination. The words of the preface to the Ordinance summarize these findings:

> Pornography is a systematic practice of exploitation and subordination based on sex that differentially harms and disadvantages women. The harm of pornography includes dehumanization, psychic assault, sexual exploitation, forced sex, forced prostitution, physical injury, and social and sexual terrorism and inferiority presented as entertainment. The bigotry and contempt pornography promotes, with the acts of aggression it fosters, diminish opportunities for equality of rights in employment, education, property, public accommodations, and public services; create public and private harassment, persecution, and denigration; promote injury and degradation such as rape, battery, sexual abuse of children, and prostitution, and inhibit just enforcement of laws against these acts; expose individuals who appear in pornography against their will to contempt, ridicule, hatred, humiliation, and embarrassment and target such women in particular for abuse and physical

aggression; demean the reputations and diminish the occupational opportunities of individuals and groups on the basis of sex; contribute significantly to restricting women in particular from full exercise of citizenship and participation in the life of the community; lower the human dignity, worth, and civil status of women and damage mutual respect between the sexes; and undermine women's equal exercise of rights to speech and action guaranteed to all citizens under the [Constitutions] and [laws] of [place].[16]

Under the trafficking provision of the Ordinance, any woman has a cause of action acting against the subordination of women as a class through the sale and distribution of particular pornography. In addition, any man, child, or transsexual can also sue under this cause of action. They must prove that the pornography has the same impact on their civil status that it has on the civil status of women. This would be easy for children, whose powerlessness in society is closely related to that of women. It would also be theoretically possible for black men and homosexual men, because there exists pornography about them that sexualizes the same kind of hatred and violence that are involved in lynching and gay-bashing.

The following words are from a man named Chuck, who, when he was twenty, after two painful years of marriage, separated from his wife and daughter and felt enormous rage toward women for a year. His words expose the great difference between the world that women live in and the world that men live in— and how pornography and sexual violence keep the civil status of those worlds different and unequal:

> Then one night about a year after I split from my wife, I was out partyin' and drinkin' and smokin' pot. I'd shot up some heroin and done some downers and I went to a porno bookstore, put a quarter in the slot, and saw this porn movie. It was just a guy coming up from behind a girl and attacking her and raping her. That's when I started having rape fantasies.
>
> When I seen that movie, it was like somebody lit a fuse from my childhood on up. When that fuse got to the porn movie, I exploded. I just went for it, went out and raped. It was like a little voice saying, "It's all right, it's all right, go ahead and rape and get your revenge; you'll never get caught. Go out and rip off

some girls. It's all right; they even make movies of it." The movie was just like a big picture stand with words on it saying go out and do it, everybody's doin' it, even the movies.

> So I just went out that night and started lookin'. I went up to this woman and grabbed her breast; then I got scared and ran. I went home and had the shakes real bad, and then I started likin' the feeling of getting even with all women.
>
> The second one was at a college. I tried to talk to this girl and she gave me some off-the-wall story. I chased her into a bathroom and grabbed her and told her that if she screamed, I'd kill her. I had sex with her that lasted about five minutes. When I first attacked her I wasn't even turned on; I wanted to dominate her. When I saw her get scared and hurt, then I got turned on. I wanted her to feel like she'd been drug through mud. I wanted her to feel a lot of pain and not enjoy none of it. The more pain she felt, the higher I felt. . . .
>
> I pulled out of her when I was about to come and I shot in her face and came all over her. It was like I pulled a gun and blew her brains out. That was my fantasy. . . .[17]

THE PENALTIES

The Civil-Rights Antipornography Ordinance has absolutely nothing to do with police action, a morals squad, or a censorship board; it would function entirely in the form of complaints and civil suits brought by individual plaintiffs, not through prosecutions brought by the state. Under the Ordinance, a plaintiff could not get anyone arrested or put in jail, the police could not conduct a raid, and there could not be a criminal prosecution. The justice a plaintiff could get could take these forms, depending on cause of action:

• Under the coercion provision, a person could sue for money damages from the makers and distributors of the pornography—the product of the coercion —and a person could also sue for a court-ordered injunction to get the pornography into which the person was coerced off the market in the place where the Ordinance is law.

• Under the provision about forcing pornography on someone, a person could sue for money damages from the perpetrator and/or the institution under whose authority the forcing occurred, and for a court-ordered injunction to stop any further forcing of the pornography on the plaintiff.

• Under the assault provision, a person could sue the perpetrator of the assault for money damages; in addition, the assault victim could sue the makers and sellers of the pornography that was used in the assault both for money damages and for an injunction against further sale of it where the Ordinance is in effect.

• Similarly, under the trafficking provision, a person could sue for money damages from the makers, sellers, distributors, and exhibitors and for removal of the pornography from sale in the designated city or area because the pornography is sex discrimination. Under the trafficking provision, a person couldn't sue simply on the basis of isolated passages in something, and any injunction could not be enforced without a full court trial.

Coercion, force, assault, and trafficking are self-evidently not "speech"; they are acts, and they must be proven real before anyone can obtain relief under the Ordinance. The Ordinance requires proof of everything—under standard rules of evidence—including whether there was actual coercion, actual force, actual assault, actual trafficking, and whether the material in question actually meets the statutory definition. The only thing the Ordinance does not require proof of is whether these acts constitute sex discrimination. Essentially, the Ordinance says, if as a matter of fact such-and-such happened, then as a matter of law what happened was sex discrimination.

Enforcement of penalties would be by court order, and anyone found not complying with the order could be found in contempt of court through a separate proceeding. Under the Civil-Rights Antipornography Ordinance, there are no penalties for mere possession of any material, even if it meets the definition of pornography in the Ordinance and even if a court orders an injunction against sale of it.

THE STATUTORY DEFINITION OF PORNOGRAPHY

When a case is brought under any of the four causes of action, the plaintiff would have to prove, among other things, that the alleged pornography is in fact pornography as defined in the Ordinance. The statutory definition is a very specific, narrow, and concrete one compared with most definitions in law. It was written based on a thorough study of what is actually made, bought, and sold today; it accurately describes the material actually produced by the ten-billion-dollar-a-year pornography industry. It does not resemble definitions in an obscenity law in any way.

Basically, the Ordinance says, something is pornography if and only if it meets four specific tests. Whether any given material meets the four tests is a matter that must be proved as a finding of fact—by a human-rights commission or a court, in a trial, in an adversarial proceeding; and the burden of proof is on the plaintiff. Rules of evidence would be the same as in any civil proceeding; and depending on how the Ordinance was adopted into local civil-rights law, a judge, a jury, or in some cases the local human-rights commission would decide the factual question. If it cannot be proved that the material meets *all four* tests, then no cause of action involving it can be sustained. The four tests are:

(1) It must be graphic. This means, essentially, that it must be unambiguous—not merely implied or suggested.

And:

(2) It must be sexually explicit. The words "sexually explicit" are not defined within the Ordinance because accumulated case law has given them a meaning—specific genital acts, sadomasochism, and so forth—that courts have already found to be clear. Hence the Ordinance excludes anything that is merely sexually suggestive or anything in which sexual activity is simply implicit, not explicit and graphically shown.

And:

(3) It must be the subordination of women. The word "subordination" is used exactly in its ordinary dictionary meaning: the act of subordinating; the act of placing in a lower order, class, or rank; the act of making subject or subservient, and so forth. (This happens to be a paraphrase of Webster's Third New International, though other dictionaries are pretty similar.) Crucially, the word "subordination" as used in the Ordinance is a noun specifying *an act* (or, as Dworkin and MacKinnon have often called it, a practice). Thus, in order to meet the statutory definition of pornography, something may not merely advocate or express the subordinate status of women; but rather, it must itself actively subordinate women—and there must be proof (in court, in a trial) that it does so.

Because the word "subordination" is unfamiliar in this particular legal context, it has provoked a lot of controversy and confusion; yet the *idea* of subordination has a clear precedent in sex-discrimination law. What is original in the Ordinance is the connection it makes between the harm to a class of people (women) through sex discrimination that takes the particular form of pornography. This unique approach not only defines materials that do harm *on the basis of that harm*; it also defines these materials according to a particular *type* of harm (that is, sex discrimination), and thus it creates a claim under civil-rights law. This legal innovation profoundly distinguishes the civil-rights approach from the history of obscenity litigation in this country, which has never been based on a showing of actual harm to any actual people.

The definition of pornography in the Ordinance is both gender-specific and gender-inclusive. The definition first enumerates what the pornography does according to the ways it uses women, but then a separate clause extends the definition to encompass material that actively subordinates men, children, and transsexuals in the same way that women are subordinated in pornography.

And:

(4) It must include at least one from a list of specific scenarios listed in the Ordinance. The Minneapolis version of the law listed nine scenarios. A later version of the Ordinance was passed in Indianapolis that condensed this list to six and focused on more overtly violent pornography; First: here is the Minneapolis version:

a. women are presented dehumanized as sexual objects, things or commodities; or

b. women are presented as sexual objects who enjoy pain or humiliation; or

c. women are presented as sexual objects who experience sexual pleasure in being raped; or

d. women are presented as sexual objects tied up or cut up or mutilated or bruised or physically hurt; or

e. women are presented in postures of sexual submission; or

f. women's body parts—including but not limited to vaginas, breasts, and buttocks—are exhibited, such that women are reduced to those parts; or

g. women are presented as whores by nature; or

h. women are presented being penetrated by objects or animals; or

i. women are presented in scenarios of degradation, injury, abasement, torture, shown as filthy or inferior, bleeding, bruised, or hurt in a context that makes these conditions sexual.[18]

Here is the Indianapolis list of scenarios:

a. women are presented as sexual objects who enjoy pain or humiliation; or

b. women are presented as sexual objects who experience sexual pleasure in being raped; or

c. women are presented as sexual objects tied up or cut up or mutilated or bruised or physically hurt, or as dismembered or truncated or fragmented or severed into body parts; or

d. women are presented being penetrated by objects or animals; or

e. women are presented in scenarios of degradation, injury, abasement, torture, shown as filthy or inferior, bleeding, bruised, or hurt in a context that makes these conditions sexual; [or]

f. women are presented as sexual objects for domination, conquest, violation, exploitation, possession, or use, or through postures or positions of servility or submission or display.

[Note: Material that meets only this sixth criterion would not be actionable under the Indianapolis trafficking provision—an exception that came to be called "the *Playboy* exemption."][19]

Material has to meet all the parts of the statutory definition or else a lawsuit involving it cannot be brought for any reason—not coercion, not forcing it on someone, not assault, and not trafficking. For example, material that is sexually explicit but premised on equality could never fall under this law. The law does not proscribe graphic nudity by itself, graphic sexual explicitness by itself, any particular graphic connection of similar or different genitals, or any material such as sexist advertising that might arguably subordinate women but that is not sexually explicit, or anything else that is not pornography as defined: "the graphic sexually explicit subordination of women."

THE CIVIL-RIGHTS APPROACH VERSUS OBSCENITY LAW

The statutory definition defines pornography in terms of whom it *harms*—those whom it causes injury to by *putting down*. Obscenity laws do not even mention the word "pornography"; they are criminal laws against *obscenity*, which is often defined in very vague words like "lewd" and "lascivious" (and which case law talks of as "morbid" and "depraved"). The Supreme Court has decided that material is obscene and therefore illegal if it meets the so-called Miller test. One part of this test requires that "the average person, applying contemporary community standards, would find that the work, taken as a whole, appeals to the prurient interest." In effect, this defines obscenity in terms of whom it turns on.

The Civil-Rights Antipornography Ordinance defines pornography that is actionable in terms of injury to victims—either to individual victims or to victims as a class. Obscenity laws, however, are written to outlaw material that offends public morals. A second clause in the Miller test, for instance,

defines material as criminally obscene if "the work depicts or describes, in a patently offensive way, sexual conduct specifically defined by the state law." This refers to the fact that many state obscenity laws specifically prohibit depictions of certain sex acts, including any same-sex sex acts.

A third part of the Miller test permits an obscenity ban if "the work, taken as a whole, lacks serious literary, artistic, political, or scientific value." This part of obscenity laws has allowed pornographers to wrap the exploitation and subordination of women inside high-toned intellectual articles and peddle the product for astronomical profit.

Obscenity laws are inherently subjective and arbitrary in their application because they criminalize a notion of indecency that does no real harm. There's no evidence that obscenity causes any harm. But there's a lot of evidence that pornography—as defined in the civil-rights Ordinance—is harmful.

These two lists summarize the differences between the use of a civil-rights approach to confront pornography and the use of obscenity law.

CIVIL-RIGHTS APPROACH	OBSCENITY LAW
A civil law	A criminal law
Complaint or lawsuit initiated by plaintiff with a cause of action	State prosecution triggered by police officer with a perception of moral offense
Adjudicated by human-rights commission or tried in civil court	Tried in criminal court
Remedies for violated civil rights: money damages and/or injunction	Punishment for violation of statute: imprisonment, fine, censorship
Pornography defined according to harm	Obscenity defined by arousal
Claim based on injury to victim	Crime based on offense to public morals
Class injury: subordination	Community offense: "indecency"

The Civil-Rights Antipornography Ordinance was drafted to address this central harm: the subordination of women. The radical-feminist understanding that women are subordinated, in part, through sex itself is pivotal to the understanding that developed this Ordinance, although it specifically does not address private behavior—it addresses only the subordination of women that is tied to the production, distribution, sale, and consumption of pornography.

Ironically, the emergence of the Civil-Rights Antipornography Ordinance has brought out of the closet unusually widespread support for obscenity laws. Decisions written on it so far by both district- and appeals-court judges have cited obscenity laws reverentially, of course. But even outside the judiciary, everyone from the pornographers to their ACLU front people now seems to think obscenity laws are just dandy. The pornographers routinely budget legal defense as a cost of doing business, a few of their lawyers get hefty fees, not much stuff ever gets prosecuted because the laws don't work very well anymore, even less gets taken off the market, organized crime continues to profit from pornography enormously, and no one who's actually hurt has any rights to recover diddly squat.

In fact the most cogent legal and political critique of obscenity laws today is coming from radical-feminist antipornography activists. Most notably, for instance, Andrea Dworkin has argued vehemently against obscenity laws for five specific reasons:[20]

1. Obscenity laws have become the formula for making pornography. According to present law, so long as the tortured bodies of women are marketed in a socially redeeming wrapper—some literary, artistic, political, or scientific value—it doesn't matter what the pornographers do to women.

2. The prurient-interest test of obscenity is irrelevant to the reality of what is happening to women in pornography. In fact, this test has probably contributed to the production of more and more sadistic pornography, since the more repulsive the material, the less likely a jury would be to believe that an average person would find it sexually arousing. Moreover, the Supreme Court has recently "clarified" the prurient-interest test by taking two synonyms, "lust" and "lasciviousness," and saying that they mean different things, which now means that this criterion is even more meaningless and mind-boggling.

3. The community-standards test is also irrelevant to what pornography does to women. What do community standards mean in a society where violence against women is virtually the norm, where battery is the most commonly committed violent crime, where fewer than one out of every ten women ever makes it through her lifetime unharassed and unassaulted sexually?[21] For that matter, what do community standards mean given the power of pornography to change how much violence and callousness toward women that people will condone, a power that social-science research has demonstrated time and time again? And as Dworkin says, "What would community standards have meant in the segregated South? What would community standards have meant as we approached the atrocity of Nazi Germany? What are community standards in a society where women are persecuted for being women and pornography is a form of political persecution?"[22]

4. Obscenity laws are completely inadequate to the reality of today's technology. They were drafted in an age when obscenity was construed to be essentially writing and drawing, but now there is the mass production and consumption of real photographic documentations of real people being hurt. Meanwhile obscenity laws are constructed on the presumption that it is women's bodies that are dirty, that women's bodies are the filth, which is also a major pornographic theme and which completely misses the point of what happens to real women in and through pornography.

5. Obscenity laws are totally useless for interrupting the bigotry, hostility, aggression, and sexual abuse that pornography creates against women. The only thing obscenity laws have been able to do, at the discretion of police and prosecutors, is occasionally to keep a few items out of the public view. But these laws have had virtually no effect on the availability of pornography to men in private, to individual men, to allmale groups. Pornography is still used in private as part of sexual abuse. The pornography itself is still produced through blackmail, through coercion, through exploitation; and the pornography industry is thriving, making more and more money over more and more women's dead or near-dead bodies. . . .

THE ORDINANCE AND
THE FIRST AMENDMENT

The particular legal and moral issue being raised about pornography today by radical feminists is about how pornography in particular works, what pornography in particular does, and the particular way that in pornography speech and action are meshed.

The issues being raised about pornography by radical feminists are legally and politically original—they are completely different, for instance, from social-purity crusades. The issue of pornography, as raised by radical feminists, turns on whether pornographers should be able to hide behind claimed First Amendment rights in order to promote hostility, bigotry, aggression, and assault against individual women and women as a class.

Casting the issue this way results in social-policy questions such as these:

- How much abuse should the First Amendment shield?
- To what extent does the First Amendment immunize sexual exploitation?
- To what extent is the state's ostensible interest in ending sex discrimination compatible with the pornographer's economic incentive to perpetuate it?
- Does the Fourteenth Amendment's guarantee of equal protection apply to women who are injured in or through pornography?
- If harm is done in part through speech—if there is, for instance, an injury to an individual in the production of the so-called speech, or if something called speech is used to hurt someone thousands and thousands of times over—does the fact that speech is involved mean that the injury may not be redressed?

There are already many existing exceptions to First Amendment protections because certain forms of expression cause harm, especially harm that cannot be redressed or undone by more speech:

- Child pornography, because of a recent Supreme Court decision, is criminally banned. (Both the Media Coalition and the ACLU, incidentally, opposed any law against child pornography, arguing that it must be protected speech.)
- Obscenity, legally, is not even considered speech —even though it exists in words and pictures.
- Libel and group libel are still prohibited, even though there is much confusion about how the laws should be applied and interpreted.
- "Fighting words" are not protected—for instance, a person cannot walk up to you on the street and call you a "fascist," because the presumption is that the insult will provoke violence, and therefore it is not protected.
- Incitement to violence is not protected.
- Blackmail and bribery are crimes done through words that do not have First Amendment protection.

The harm of pornography is not identical to the harm caused by any of these unprotected types of speech, yet there are many similarities in how these exceptions have been argued legally. But because women have been systematically excluded from human-rights considerations, there is not yet a clear-cut precedent for legal arguments for new law that addresses the effects of pornography on women: civil inferiority and sexual abuse. That's why a major part of the effort to pass the Civil-Rights Antipornography Ordinance is to bring into the legal system feminist legal arguments that take the reality of women's lives seriously.

There is a more radical First Amendment issue that the Civil-Rights Antipornography Ordinance brings up as well. The First Amendment protects *those who have already spoken* from state interference. But women and blacks, in particular, have been systematically excluded from public discourse by civil inferiority, economic powerlessness, and violence. Right now, the First Amendment protects those who can buy communication and allows them to use communication as a club against the powerless.

Pornography—the making, the selling, and the use of it—often silences women and makes women afraid to stand up for their rights as equal human beings; meanwhile the rich pornography industry spends millions of dollars on lawyers to protect its right to keep saying to women, in effect: "You are nothing but a whore and men should be able to do anything they want to you."

The First Amendment can be a bulwark of freedom only when it is used and understood and honored in conjunction with rights of equality, in particular the principles underlying the Fourteenth Amendment, which guarantees equal protection under law. One of the main reasons there needs to be this Civil-Rights Antipornography Ordinance is that sexual abuse and civil worthlessness silence women—and in order to have democratic discourse, one must have women's speech.

Strangely, one hears some of the most dire warnings about how this Ordinance could be abused from people in the progressive legal community, those same folks who, under virtually every other circumstance of injustice, look to every possible innovative application of the law for redressing actual harm to actual individuals. But in the case of pornography, they seem to want to make an exception a mile wide. "No," this progressive legal community seems to say, "the harm done by pornography ought not be redressed through any conceivable application of the law." On the issue of pornography, there exists an apparent convergence of legal opinion, from "liberal" to "conservative," to the effect that the law can only "protect" if it is protecting the rights of the exploiters. Even more astonishing is all these lawyers' apparent failure even to imagine that the law might weigh and balance the rights of the exploiters and the rights of the harmed. Their implicit distrust in the law as an instrument of effecting justice here is truly staggering.

WHAT THE CIVIL-RIGHTS APPROACH WOULD ACHIEVE

The Ordinance would definitely hurt the pornography industry. Pornographers could not operate with impunity anymore. They would be hurt economically; they would be at risk legally; and they would be hurt in their social legitimacy, which they very much want. Economically, the Ordinance would, as its drafters

have suggested, "take the profit motive out of rape." The threat of civil liability would be an economic disincentive to actively subordinate women through the production and distribution of materials that do that. Also, through the use of discovery motions in civil trials, information about pornographers' financial dealings and other matters could be obtained. This information could be used, as Dworkin has suggested,[23] to develop prosecutions against organized-crime involvement in the industry.

But just as significantly, the Ordinance would empower victims; it would empower the exploited to fight back against the exploiters.

This would be a feminist law, designed to bring the feminist analysis of women's inequality through sexual exploitation into the center of public policy and constitutional jurisprudence. This is a law that would increase civil liberties—extend the right of speech to many who are now part of a silent, powerless victim class—people who have been hurt and who have no legal way to fight back for justice.

And essentially, this would be an equality law, because it would attack sex inequality and the civil inferiority of women head on: by demanding human rights for women, by demanding human dignity for women, by demanding an end to the buying and selling of women's bodies and sexuality and an end to the profit from sexual abuse that is presented as entertainment.

NOTES

1. See Catharine A. MacKinnon, *Sexual Harassment of Working Women* (New Haven: Yale, 1979).

2. See Andrea Dworkin, *Woman Hating* (New York: Dutton, 1974), pp. 51–90.

3. Reprinted in Andrea Dworkin, *Letters from a War Zone* (London: Secker & Warburg, 1988).

4. See Andrea Dworkin, *Pornography: Men Possessing Women* (New York: Perigee, 1981), and *Right-wing Women* (New York: Perigee, 1983).

5. Andrea Dworkin, unpublished testimony, Zoning and Planning Committee, City of Minneapolis, October 18, 1983 (on file at Organizing Against Pornography, 734 East Lake Street, Minneapolis, Minnesota 55407).

6. Catharine A. MacKinnon, unpublished testimony, Zoning and Planning Committee, City of Minneapolis, October 18, 1983 (on file at Organizing Against Pornography).

7. Dworkin, October 18, 1983, testimony.

8. Undated press release, December 1983 (on file at Organizing Against Pornography).

9. "Minneapolis Asked to Attack Pornography as Rights Issue," *The New York Times*, December 18, 1983; Jeanne Barkey, "Feminists Pioneer Civil Rights Legislation," *Minneapolis Citizens Against Pornography*, Vol. 1, No. 1, Summer 1984 (newsletter on file at Organizing Against Pornography).

10. *Public Hearings on Ordinances to Add Pornography as Discrimination Against Women*, Minneapolis City Council, Government Operations Committee (edition published by Organizing Against Pornography), p. 14.

11. *Public Hearings*, p. 15.

12. *Public Hearings*, p. 16.

13. "Model Antipornography Civil-Rights Ordinance," in *Pornography and Civil Rights: A New Day for Women's Equality*, by Andrea Dworkin and Catharine A. MacKinnon (Minneapolis, Minnesota: Organizing Against Pornography, 1988), pp. 139–140.

14. Research conducted by Diana E. H. Russell, reported in her book *Rape in Marriage* (New York: Macmillan, 1982), pp. 83–84.

15. Excerpts from Diana E. H. Russell's research cited by Dr. Pauline Bart in her testimony before the Minneapolis City Council December 12, 1983, *Public Hearings*, pp. 19–20.

16. "Model Antipornography Civil-Rights Ordinance," in Dworkin and MacKinnon, *Pornography and Civil Rights,* p. 138.

17. From *Men on Rape*, by Timothy Beneke (New York: St. Martin's Press, 1982), pp. 71–74.

18. "An Ordinance of the City of Minneapolis," in Dworkin and MacKinnon, *Pornography and Civil Rights*, p. 101.

19. "Code of Indianapolis and Marion County Indiana," in Dworkin and MacKinnon, *Pornography and Civil Rights*, pp. 113–114.

20. Paraphrased from "Pornography Is a Civil Rights Issue," the testimony of Andrea Dworkin before the Attorney General's Commission on Pornography, January 22, 1986, in Letters From *a War Zone*, by Andrea Dworkin (London: Secker & Warburg, 1988), pp. 285–286.

21. Only 7.8 percent of women never encounter sexual harassment or assault in their lifetime, as calculated by Diana E. H. Russell from her data, cited in Catharine A. MacKinnon, "Pornography, Civil Rights, and Speech," *Harvard Civil Rights-Civil Liberties Review*, Vol. 20, No. 1, winter 1985 (footnote 31).

22. Dworkin, "Pornography Is a Civil-Rights Issue," p. 286.

23. In her testimony before the Attorney General's Commission January 22, 1986.

Study Questions

1. Stoltenberg underscores that the MacKinnon/Dworkin ordinance is a civil rights law rather than an anti-obscenity law. What does he mean by this?

2. According to Stoltenberg, the definition of pornography included in the ordinance "is a very specific, narrow, and concrete one compared with most definitions in law." What *is* the definition, and do you agree with Stoltenberg's assessment of it?

3. The MacKinnon/Dworkin ordinance is criticized for violating the First Amendment right to free speech. Stoltenberg suggests that the ordinance actually protects speech. Explain his point.

4. In what sense does this article exemplify the dominance approach to sex equality?

Lisa Duggan, Nan D. Hunter, and Carole S. Vance

False Promises: Feminist Antipornography Legislation

In the United States, after two decades of increasing community tolerance for dissenting or disturbing sexual or political materials, the 1980s have produced a momentum for retrenchment. In an atmosphere of increased conservatism, support for new repressive legislation of various kinds—from an Oklahoma law forbidding schoolteachers from advocating homosexuality to new antipornography laws passed in Minneapolis and Indianapolis—has emerged as a powerful force.

The antipornography laws have mixed roots of support, however. Though they are popular with the conservative constituencies that traditionally favor legal restrictions on sexual expression of all kinds, they were drafted and are endorsed by antipornography feminists who oppose traditional obscenity and censorship laws. The model law of this type was drawn up in the politically progressive city of Minneapolis by two radical feminists, author Andrea Dworkin and attorney Catharine MacKinnon. It was passed by the city council but vetoed by the mayor. A similar law was enacted in Indianapolis, and then ruled unconstitutional by the Supreme Court in 1986.

Dworkin, MacKinnon and their feminist supporters believe that these proposed antipornography ordinances are not censorship laws. They also claim that the legislative effort behind them is based on feminist support. Both of these claims are dubious at best. Though the new laws are civil laws that allow individuals to sue the makers, sellers, distributors or exhibitors of pornography, and not criminal laws leading to arrest and imprisonment, their censoring impact would be substantially as severe as criminal obscenity laws. Materials could be removed from public availability by court injunction, and publishers and booksellers could be subject to potentially endless legal harassment. Passage of the laws was achieved with the support of right-wing elements who expect the new laws to accomplish what censorship efforts are meant to accomplish. Ironically, many antifeminist conservatives backed these laws, while many feminists opposed them. In Indianapolis, the law was supported by extreme right-wing religious fundamentalists, including members of the Moral Majority, while there was *no* local feminist support. In other cities, traditional pro-censorship forces expressed interest in the new approach to banning sexually explicit materials. Meanwhile, anti-censorship feminists became alarmed at these new developments and are seeking to galvanize feminist opposition to the new antipornography legislative strategy pioneered in Minneapolis.

One is tempted to ask in astonishment; How can this be happening? How can feminists be entrusting the patriarchal state with the task of legally distinguishing between permissible and impermissible sexual images? But in fact this new development is not as surprising as it seems at first. Pornography has come to be seen as a central cause of women's oppression by a significant number of feminists. Andrea Dworkin argues that pornography is the root of virtually all forms of exploitation and discrimination against women. It is a short step from such a belief to the conviction that laws against pornography can end the inequality of the sexes. But this analysis takes feminists very close—indeed far too close—to measures that will ultimately support conservative, antisex, pro-censorship forces in American society, for it is with these forces that women have forged alliances in passing such legislation.

The first feminist-inspired antipornography law was passed in Minneapolis in 1983. Local legislators had been frustrated when their zoning restrictions on porn shops were struck down in the courts. Public hearings were held to discuss a new zoning ordinance. The Neighborhood Pornography Task Force of South and South Central Minneapolis invited Andrea Dworkin and Catharine MacKinnon, who were teaching a course on pornography at the University of Minnesota, to testify. They proposed an alternative that, they claimed, would completely eliminate, rather than merely regulate, pornography. They suggested that pornography be defined as a form of sex discrimination, and that an amendment to the city's civil rights law be passed to proscribe it. City officials hired Dworkin and MacKinnon to develop their new approach and to organize another series of public hearings.

The initial debate over the legislation in Minneapolis was intense, and opinion was divided within nearly every political grouping. By contrast, the public hearings held before the city council were tightly controlled and carefully orchestrated; speakers invited by Dworkin and MacKinnon—sexual abuse victims, counselors, educators and social scientists—testified about the harm pornography does to women. (Dworkin's and MacKinnon's goal was to

compile a legislative record that would help the law stand up to court challenges.) The legislation passed, supported by anti-pornography feminists, neighborhood groups concerned about the effects of porn shops on residential areas, and conservatives opposed to the availability of sexually explicit materials for "moral" reasons.

In Indianapolis, the alignment of forces was different. For the previous two years, conservative antipornography groups had grown in strength and public visibility, but they had been frustrated in their efforts. The police department could not convert its obscenity arrests into convictions; the city's zoning law was also tied up in court challenges. Then Mayor William Hudnut III, a Republican and a Presbyterian minister, learned of the Minneapolis law. Mayor Hudnut thought Minneapolis's approach might be the solution to the Indianapolis problems. Beulah Coughenour, a conservative, Republican Stop ERA activist, was recruited to sponsor the legislation in the City-County Council.

Coughenour engaged MacKinnon as consultant to the city. MacKinnon worked on the legislation with the Indianapolis city prosecutor (a well-known antivice zealot), the city's legal department and Coughenour. The law received the support of neighborhood groups, the Citizens for Decency and the Coalition for a Clean Community. There were no crowds of feminist supporters—in fact, there were no feminist supporters at all. The only feminists to make public statements opposed the legislation, which was nevertheless passed in a council meeting packed with three hundred religious fundamentalists. All twenty-four Republicans voted for its passage; all five Democrats opposed it, to no avail.

Before the Supreme Court ruled it unconstitutional, mutated versions of the Dworkin-MacKinnon bill began to appear. A version of the law introduced in Suffolk County on Long Island in New York emphasized its conservative potential—pornography was said to cause "sodomy" and "disruption" of the family unit, in addition to rape, incest, exploitation and other acts "inimical to the public good." In Suffolk, the law was advanced by a conservative, anti-ERA, male legislator who wished to "restore ladies to what they used to be." The Suffolk County bill clearly illustrates the repressive, antifeminist potential of the new antipornography legislation.

The support of such legislation by antipornography feminists marks a critical moment in the feminist debate over sexual politics. We need to examine carefully these proposals for new laws and expose their underlying assumptions. We need to know why these proposals, for all their apparent feminist rhetoric, actually appeal to conservative antifeminist forces, and why feminists should move in a different direction.

DEFINITIONS: THE CENTRAL FLAW

The antipornography ordinances in Minneapolis and Indianapolis were framed as amendments to municipal civil rights laws. They provide for complaints to be filed against pornography in the same manner that complaints are filed against employment discrimination. If enforced, the laws would make illegal public or private availability (except in libraries) of any materials deemed pornographic.

Such material could be the object of a lawsuit on several grounds. The ordinance would penalize four kinds of behavior associated with pornography: its production, sale, exhibition or distribution ("trafficking"); coercion into pornographic performance; forcing pornography on a person; and assault or physical attack due to pornography.

Under such a law, a woman "acting as a woman against the subordination of women" could file a complaint; men could also file complaints if they could "prove injury in the same way that a woman is injured." The procedural steps in the two ordinances differ, but they generally allow the complainant either to file an administrative complaint with the city's Equal Opportunity Commission (Minneapolis or Indianapolis), or to file a lawsuit directly in court (Minneapolis). If the local commission found the law had been violated, it would file a lawsuit. By either procedure, the court—not "women"—would have the final say on whether the materials fit the definition of pornography, and would have the authority to award monetary damages and issue an injunction (or

court order) preventing further distribution of the material in question.

The Minneapolis ordinance defines pornography as "the sexually explicit subordination of women, graphically depicted, whether in pictures or words." To be actionable, materials would also have to fall within one of a number of categories: nine in the Minneapolis ordinance, six in the Indianapolis version. (The text of the original Minneapolis ordinance, from which the excerpts from the legislation quoted here are taken, is appended to the end of this chapter.)

Although proponents claim that the Minneapolis and Indianapolis ordinances represent a new way to regulate pornography, the strategy is still laden with our culture's old, repressive approach to sexuality. The implementation of such laws hinges on the definition of pornography as interpreted by a court. The definition provided in the Minneapolis legislation is vague, leaving critical phrases such as "the sexually explicit subordination of women," "postures of sexual submission" and "whores by nature" to the interpretation of the citizen who files a complaint and to the judge who hears the case. The legislation does not prohibit only the images of rape and abusive sexual violence that most supporters claim to be its target, but instead drifts toward covering an increasingly wide range of sexually explicit material.

The most problematic feature of this approach is a conceptual flaw embedded in the law itself. Supporters of this type of legislation say that the target of their efforts is misogynist, sexually explicit and violent representation, whether in pictures or words. Indeed, the feminist antipornography movement is fueled by women's anger at the most repugnant examples of pornography. But a close examination of the wording of the model legislative text and examples of purportedly actionable material offered by proponents of the legislation in court briefs suggest that the law is actually aimed at a range of material considerably broader than that which proponents claim is their target. The discrepancies between the law's explicit and implicit aims have been almost invisible to us, because these distortions are very similar to distortions about sexuality in the culture as a whole. The legislation and supporting texts deserve close reading. Hidden beneath illogical transformations, non sequiturs, and highly permeable definitions are familiar sexual scripts drawn from mainstream, sexist culture, that potentially could have very negative consequences for women.

Figure 1

The Venn diagram illustrates the three areas targeted by the law, and represents a scheme that classifies words or images that have any of three characteristics: violence, sexual explicitness or sexism.

Clearly, a text or an image might have only one characteristic. Material can be violent but not sexually explicit or sexist: for example, a war movie in which both men and women suffer injury or death without regard to or because of their gender. Material can be sexist but not sexually explicit or violent. A vast number of materials from mainstream media—television, popular novels, magazines, newspapers—comes to mind, depicting, for example, either distraught housewives or the "happy sexism" of the idealized family, with mom self-sacrificing, other-directed and content. Finally, material can be sexually explicit but not violent or sexist: for example, the freely chosen sexual behavior depicted in some sex education films or women's own explicit writing about sexuality.

As the diagram illustrates, areas can also intersect, reflecting a range of combinations of the three characteristics. Images can be violent and sexually explicit without being sexist—for example, a narrative about a rape in a men's prison, or a documentary about the effect of a rape on a woman. The latter example illustrates the importance of context in evaluating whether material that is sexually explicit and violent is also sexist. The intent of the maker, the context of the film and the perception of the viewer together render a depiction of a rape sympathetic, harrowing, even educational, rather than sensational, victim-blaming and laudatory.

Another possible overlap is between material that is violent and sexist but not sexually explicit. Films or books that describe violence directed against women by men in a way that clearly shows gender antagonism and inequality, and sometimes strong sexual tension, but no sexual explicitness fall into this category—for example, the popular genre of slasher films in which women are stalked, terrified and killed by men, or accounts of mass murder of women, fueled by male rage. Finally, a third point of overlap arises when material is sexually explicit and sexist without being violent—that is, when sex is consensual but still reflects themes of male superiority and female abjectness. Some sex education materials could be included in this category, as well as a great deal of regular pornography.

The remaining domain, the inner core, is one in which the material is simultaneously violent, sexually explicit and sexist—for example, an image of a naked woman being slashed by a knife-wielding rapist. The Minneapolis ordinance, however, does not by any means confine itself to this material.

To be actionable under the law as pornography, material must be judged by the courts to be "the sexually explicit subordination of women, graphically depicted whether in pictures or in words that also includes at least one or more" of nine criteria. Of these, only four involve the intersection of violence, sexual explicitness and sexism, and then only arguably. Even in these cases, many questions remain about whether images with all three characteristics do in fact cause violence against women. And the task of evaluating material that is ostensibly the target of these criteria becomes complicated—indeed, hopeless—because most of the clauses that contain these criteria mix actions or qualities of violence with those that are not particularly associated with violence.

The section that comes closest to the stated purpose of the legislation is clause (iii): "women are presented as sexual objects who experience sexual pleasure in being raped." This clause is intended to cover depictions of rape that are sexually explicit and sexist; the act of rape itself signifies the violence. But other clauses are not so clear-cut, because the list of characteristics often mixes signs or by-products of violence with phenomena that are unrelated or irrelevant to judging violence.

Such a problem occurs with clause (iv): "women are presented as sexual objects tied up or cut up or mutilated or bruised or physically hurt." All these except the first, "tied up," generally occur as a result of violence. "Tied up," if part of consensual sex, is not violent and, for some practitioners, not particularly sexist. Women who are tied up may be participants in nonviolent sex play involving bondage, a theme in both heterosexual and lesbian pornography. (See, for example, *The Joy of Sex* and *Coming to Power*.) Clause (ix) contains another mixed list, in which "injury," "torture," "bleeding," "bruised" and "hurt" are combined with phrases such as "degradation" and "shown as filthy and inferior," neither of which is violent. Depending on the presentation, "filthy" and "inferior" may constitute sexually explicit sexism, although not violence. "Degradation" is a sufficiently inclusive term to cover most acts of which a viewer disapproves.

Several other clauses have little to do with violence at all; they refer to material that is sexually explicit and sexist, thus falling outside the triad of characteristics at which the legislation is supposedly aimed. For example, movies in which "women are presented as dehumanized sexual objects, things, or commodities" may be infuriating and offensive to feminists, but they are not violent.

Finally, some clauses describe material that is neither violent nor necessarily sexist. Clause (v), "women . . . in postures of sexual submission or sexual servility, including by inviting penetration," and clause (viii), "women . . . being penetrated by objects or animals," are sexually explicit, but not violent and not obviously sexist unless one believes that penetration—whether heterosexual, lesbian, or autoerotic masturbation—is indicative of gender inequality and female oppression. Similarly problematic are clauses that invoke representations of "women . . . as whores

by nature" and "women's body parts . . . such that women are reduced to those parts."

Texts cited in support of the Indianapolis law show how broadly it could be applied. In the amicus brief filed on behalf of Linda Marchiano ("Linda Lovelace," the female lead in *Deep Throat*) in Indianapolis, Catharine MacKinnon offered *Deep Throat* as an example of the kind of pornography covered by the law. *Deep Throat* served a complicated function in this brief, because the movie, supporters of the ordinance argue, would be actionable on two counts: coercion into pornographic performance, because Marchiano alleges that she was coerced into making the movie; and trafficking in pornography, because the content of the film falls within one of the categories in the Indianapolis ordinance's definition—that which prohibits presenting women as sexual objects "through postures or positions of servility or submission or display." Proponents of the law have counted on women's repugnance at allegations of coerced sexual acts to spill over and discredit the sexual acts themselves in this movie.

The aspects of *Deep Throat* that MacKinnon considered to be indicative of "sexual subordination" are of particular interest, because any movie that depicted similar acts could be banned under the law. MacKinnon explained in her brief that the film "subordinates women by using women . . . sexually, specifically as eager servicing receptacles for male genitalia and ejaculate. The majority of the film represents 'Linda Lovelace' in, minimally, postures of sexual submission and/or servility." In its brief, the City of Indianapolis concurred: "In the film *Deep Throat* a woman is being shown as being ever eager for oral penetration by a series of men's penises, often on her hands and knees. There are repeated scenes in which her genitalia are graphically displayed and she is shown as enjoying men ejaculating on her face."

These descriptions are very revealing, since they suggest that multiple partners, group sex and oral sex subordinate women and hence are sexist. The notion that the female character is "used" by men suggests that it is improbable that a woman would engage in fellatio of her own accord. *Deep Throat* does draw on several sexist conventions common in advertising and the entire visual culture—the woman as object of the male gaze, and the assumption of heterosexuality, for example. But it is hardly an unending paean to male dominance, since the movie contains many contrary themes. In it, the main female character is shown as both actively seeking her own pleasure and as trying to please men; a secondary female character is shown directing encounters with multiple male partners. The briefs described a movie quite different from the one viewers see.

At its heart, this analysis implies that heterosexual sex itself is sexist; that women do not engage in it of their own volition; and that behavior pleasurable to men is intrinsically repugnant to women. In some contexts, for example, the representation of fellatio and multiple partners can be sexist, but are we willing to concede that they always are? If not, then what is proposed as actionable under the Indianapolis law includes merely sexually explicit representation (the traditional target of obscenity laws), which proponents of the legislation vociferously insist they are not interested in attacking.

Exhibits submitted with the City of Indianapolis brief and also introduced in the public hearing further illustrate this point. Many of the exhibits are depictions of sadomasochism. The court briefs treat S/M material as depicting violence and aggression, not consensual sex, in spite of avowals to the contrary by many S/M practitioners. With this legislation, then, a major question for feminists that has only begun to develop would be closed for discussion. Instead, a simplistic reduction has been advanced as the definitive feminist position. The description of the material in the briefs focused on submissive women and implied male domination, highlighting the similarity proponents would like to find between all S/M narratives and male/female inequality. The actual exhibits, however, illustrated plots and power relations far more diverse than the descriptions provided by MacKinnon and the City of Indianapolis would suggest, including S/M between women and female dominant/male submissive S/M. For example, the Indianapolis brief stated that in the magazine *The Bitch Goddesses*, "women are shown in torture

chambers with their nude body parts being tortured by their 'master' for 'even the slightest offense'. . . . The magazine shows a woman in a scenario of torture." But the brief failed to mention that the dominants in this magazine are all female, with one exception. This kind of discrepancy characterized many examples offered in the briefs.

This is not to say that such representations do not raise questions for feminists. The current lively discussion about lesbian S/M demonstrates that this issue is still unresolved. But in the Indianapolis briefs, all S/M material was assumed to be male dominant/female submissive, thereby squeezing a nonconforming reality into prepackaged, inadequate—and therefore dangerous—categories. This legislation would virtually eliminate all S/M pornography by recasting it as violent, thereby attacking a sexual minority while masquerading as an attempt to end violence against women.

Analysis of clauses in the Minneapolis ordinance and several examples offered in court briefs filed in connection with the Indianapolis ordinance show that the law targets material that is sexually explicit and sexist, but ignores material that is violent and sexist, violent and sexually explicit, only violent, or only sexist.

Certain troubling questions arise here, for if one claims, as some antipornography activists do, that there is a direct relationship between images and behavior, why should images of violence against women or scenarios of sexism in general not be similarly proscribed? Why is sexual explicitness singled out as the cause of women's oppression? For proponents to exempt violent and sexist images, or even sexist images, from regulation is inconsistent, especially since they are so pervasive.

Even more difficulties arise from the vagueness of certain terms crucial in interpreting the ordinances. The term "subordination" is especially important, since pornography is defined as the "sexually explicit subordination of women." The authors of this legislation intend it to modify each of the clauses, and they appear to believe that it provides a definition of sexism that each example must meet. The term is never defined in the legislation, yet the Indianapolis brief, for example, suggests that the average viewer, on the basis of "his or her common understanding of what it means for one person to subordinate another" should be able to decide what is pornographic. But what kind of sexually explicit acts place a woman in an inferior status? To some, *any* graphic sexual act violates women's dignity and therefore subordinates them. To others, consensual heterosexual lovemaking within the boundaries of procreation and marriage is acceptable, but heterosexual acts that do not have reproduction as their aim lower women's status and hence subordinate them. Still others accept a wide range of nonprocreative, perhaps even nonmarital, heterosexuality, but draw the line at lesbian sex, which they view as degrading.

The term "sex object" is also problematic. The city of Indianapolis's brief maintains that "the term sexual object, often shortened to sex object, has enjoyed a wide popularity in mainstream American culture in the past fifteen years, and is used to denote the objectification of a person on the basis of their sex or sex appeal. . . . People know what it means to disregard all aspects of personhood but sex, to reduce a person to a thing used for sex." But, indeed, people do not agree on this point. The definition of "sex object" is far from clear or uniform. For example, some feminist and liberal cultural critics have used the term to mean sex that occurs without strong emotional ties and experience. More conservative critics maintain that any detachment of women's sexuality from procreation, marriage and family objectifies it, removing it from its "natural" web of associations and context. Unredeemed and unprotected by domesticity and family, women—and their sexuality—become things used by men. In both these views, women are never sexually autonomous agents who direct and enjoy their sexuality for their own purposes, but rather are victims. In the same vein, other problematic terms include "inviting penetration," "whores by nature" and "positions of display."

Through close analysis of the proposed legislation one sees how vague the boundaries of the definitions that contain the inner core of the Venn diagram really are. Their dissolution does not happen equally at all points, but only at some: the inner core begins to include sexually explicit and sexist material, and finally expands to include purely sexually explicit

material. Thus "sexually explicit" becomes identified and equated with "violent" with no further definition or explanation.

It is also striking that so many feminists have failed to notice that the proposed laws (as well as examples of actionable material) cover so much diverse work, not just that small and symbolic epicenter where many forms of opposition to women converge. It suggests that for us, as well as for others, sexuality remains a difficult area. We have no clearly developed framework in which to think about sex equivalent to the frameworks that are available for thinking about race, gender and class issues. Consequently, in sex, as in few other areas of human behavior, unexamined and unjustifiable prejudice passes itself off as considered opinion about what is desirable and normal. And finally, sex arouses considerable anxiety, stemming from both the meeting with individual difference and from the prospect—suggested by feminists themselves—that sexual behavior is constructed socially and is not simply natural.

The proposed law takes advantage of everyone's relative ignorance and anxious ambivalence about sex, distorting and oversimplifying what confronts us in building a sexual politic. For example, antipornography feminists draw on several feminist theories about the role of violent, aggressive or sexist representations. The first is relatively straightforward: that these images trigger men into action. The second suggests that violent images act more subtly, to socialize men to act in sexist or violent ways by making this behavior seem commonplace and more acceptable, if not expected. The third assumption is that violent, sexually explicit or even sexist images are offensive to women, assaulting their sensibilities and sense of self. Although we have all used metaphor to exhort women to action or illustrate a point, antipornography proponents have frequently used these conventions of speech as if they were literal statements of fact. But these metaphors have gotten out of hand, as Julie Abraham has noted, for they fail to recognize that the assault committed by a wife-beater is quite different from the visual "assault" of a sexist ad on TV. The nature of that difference is still being clarified in a complex debate within feminism that must continue; this law cuts off speculation, settling on a causal relationship between image and action that is starkly simple, if unpersuasive.

This metaphor also paves the way for reclassifying images that are merely sexist as also violent and aggressive. Thus, it is no accident that the briefs supporting the legislation first invoke violent images and rapidly move to include sexist and sexually explicit images without noting that they are different. The equation is made easier by the constant shifts back to examples of depictions of real violence, almost to draw attention away from the sexually explicit or sexist material that in fact would be affected by the laws.

Most important, what underlies this legislation and the success of its analysis in blurring and exceeding boundaries, is an appeal to a very traditional view of sex: sex is degrading to women. By this logic, any illustrations or descriptions of explicit sexual acts that involve women are in themselves affronts to women's dignity. In its brief, the city of Indianapolis was quite specific about this point: "The harms caused by pornography are by no means limited to acts of physical aggression. The mere existence of pornography in society degrades and demeans all women." Embedded in this view are several other familiar themes: that sex is degrading to women, but not to men; that men are raving beasts; that sex is dangerous for women; that sexuality is male, not female; that women are victims, not sexual actors; that men inflict "it" on women; that penetration is submission; that heterosexual sexuality, rather than the institution of heterosexuality, is sexist.

These assumptions, in part intended, in part unintended, lead us back to the traditional target of obscenity law: sexually explicit material. What initially appeared novel, then, is really the reappearance of a traditional theme. It is ironic that a feminist position on pornography incorporates most of the myths about sexuality that feminism has struggled to displace.

THE DANGERS OF APPLICATION

The Minneapolis and Indianapolis ordinances embody a political view that holds pornography to be a central force in "creating and maintaining" the oppression of women. This view appears in summary form in the legislative findings section at the beginning of the Minneapolis bill, which describes a chain reaction of misogynistic acts generated by pornography. The legislation is based on the interweaving of several themes: that pornography constructs the meaning of sexuality for women and, as well, leads to discrete acts of violence against women; that sexuality is the primary cause of women's oppression; that explicitly sexual images, even if not violent or coerced, have the power to subordinate women; and that women's own accounts of force have been silenced because, as a universal and timeless rule, society credits pornographic constructions rather than women's experiences. Taking the silencing contention a step further, advocates of the ordinance effectively assume that women have been so conditioned by the pornographic world view that if their own experiences of the sexual acts identified in the definition are not subordinating, then they must simply be victims of false consciousness.

The heart of the ordinance is the "trafficking" section, which would allow almost anyone to seek the removal of any materials falling within the law's definition of pornography. Ordinance defenders strenuously protest that the issue is not censorship because the state, as such, is not authorized to initiate criminal prosecutions. But the prospect of having to defend a potentially infinite number of privately filed complaints creates at least as much of a chilling effect against pornographic or sexual speech as does a criminal law. And as long as representatives of the state—in this case, judges—have the ultimate say over the interpretation, the distinction between this ordinance and "real" censorship will not hold.

In addition, three major problems should dissuade feminists from supporting this kind of law: First, the sexual images in question do not cause more harm than other aspects of misogynist culture; second, sexually explicit speech, even in male-dominated society, serves positive social functions for women; and third, the passage and enforcement of antipornography laws such as those supported in Minneapolis and Indianapolis are more likely to impede, rather than advance, feminist goals.

Ordinance proponents contend that pornography does cause violence because it conditions male sexual response to images of violence, and thus provokes violence against women. The strongest research they offer is based on psychology experiments that employ films depicting a rape scene, toward the end of which the woman is shown to be enjoying the attack. The proposed ordinances, by contrast, cover a much broader range of materials than this one specific heterosexual rape scenario. Further, the studies cited by ordinance supporters do not support the theory that pornography causes violence against women.

In addition, the argument that pornography itself plays a major role in the general oppression of women contradicts the evidence of history. It need hardly be said that pornography did not lead to the burning of witches or the English common law treatment of women as chattel property. If anything functioned then as the prime communication medium for woman-hating, it was probably religion. Nor can pornography be blamed for the enactment of laws from at least the eighteenth century that allowed a husband to rape or beat his wife with impunity. In any period, the causes of women's oppression have been many and complex, drawing on the fundamental social and economic structures of society. Ordinance proponents offer little evidence to explain how the mass production of pornography—a relatively recent phenomenon—could have become so potent a causative agent so quickly.

The silencing of women is another example of the harm attributed to pornography. Yet if this argument were correct, one would expect that as the social visibility of pornography has increased the tendency to credit women's accounts of rape would have decreased. In fact, although the treatment of women complainants in rape cases is far from perfect, efforts by the women's movement have resulted in marked improvements. In many places, the corroboration requirement has now been abolished; evidence of a victim's past sexual experiences has been prohibited; and a number of police forces have developed specially trained units and procedures to improve the handling of sexual assault cases. The presence of rape fantasies in pornography may in part reflect a back-lash against these women's movement advances, but to argue that most people routinely disbelieve women who file charges of rape belittles the real improvements made in social consciousness and law.

The third type of harm is a kind of libel: the maliciously false characterization of women as a group of sexual masochists. To claim that all pornography is a lie is a false analogy. If truth is a defense to charges of libel, then surely depictions of consensual sex cannot be thought of as equivalent to a falsehood. For example, some women (and men) do enjoy being tied up or displaying themselves. The declaration by fiat that sadomasochism is a "lie" about sexuality reflects an arrogance and moralism that feminists should combat, not engage in. When mutually desired sexual experiences are depicted, pornography is not "libelous."

Not only does pornography not cause the kind and degree of harm that can justify the restraint of speech, but its existence serves some social functions which benefit women. Pornographic speech has many, often anomalous, characteristics. One is certainly that it magnifies the misogyny present in the culture and exaggerates the fantasy of male power. Another, however, is that the existence of pornography has served to flout conventional sexual mores, to ridicule sexual hypocrisy and to underscore the importance of sexual needs. Pornography carries many messages other than woman-hating; it advocates sexual adventure, sex outside marriage, sex for no reason other than pleasure, casual sex, anonymous sex, group sex, voyeuristic sex, illegal sex, public sex. Some of these ideas appeal to women reading or seeing pornography, who may interpret some images as legitimating their own sense of sexual urgency or desire to be sexually aggressive. Women's experience of pornography is not as universally victimizing as the ordinance would have it.

Antipornography laws, as restrictions on sexual speech, in many ways echo and expand upon the traditional legal analysis of sexually explicit speech under the rubric of obscenity. The Supreme Court has consistently ruled that sexual speech defined as "obscenity" does not belong in the system of public discourse, and is therefore an exception to the First

Amendment and hence not entitled to protection under the free speech guarantee. The definition of obscenity has shifted over the years and remains imprecise. In 1957 the Supreme Court ruled that obscenity could be suppressed regardless of whether it presented an imminent threat of illegal activity. In the opinion of the Supreme Court, graphic sexual images do not communicate "real" ideas. These, it would seem, are found only in the traditionally defined public arena. Sexual themes can qualify as ideas if they use sexuality for argument's sake, but not if they speak in the words and images of "private" life—that is, if they graphically depict sex itself. At least theoretically, and insofar as the law functions as a pronouncement of moral judgment, sex is consigned to remain unexpressed and in the private realm.

The fallacies in this distinction are obvious. Under the U.S. Constitution, for example, it is acceptable to write: "I am a sadomasochist," or even: "Everyone should experiment with sadomasochism in order to increase sexual pleasure." But to write a graphic fantasy about sadomasochism that arouses and excites readers is not protected unless a court finds it to have serious literary, artistic or political value, despite the expressive nature of the content. Indeed, the fantasy depiction may communicate identity in a more compelling way than the "I am" statement. For sexual minorities, sexual acts can be self-identifying and affirming statements in a hostile world. Images of those acts should be protected for that reason, for they do have political content. Just as the personal can be political, so can the specifically and graphically sexual.

Supporters of the antipornography ordinances both endorse the concept that pornographic speech contains no ideas or expressive interest, and at the same time attribute to pornography the capacity to trigger violent acts by the power of its misogyny. The city's brief in defense of the Indianapolis ordinance expanded this point by arguing that all sexually explicit speech is entitled to less constitutional protection than other speech. The antipornography groups have cleverly capitalized on this approach—a product of a totally nonfeminist legal system—to attempt, through the mechanism of the ordinances,

to legitimate a new crusade for protectionism and sexual conservatism.

The consequences of enforcing such a law, however, are much more likely to obstruct than advance feminist political goals. On the level of ideas, further narrowing of the public realm of sexual speech coincides all too well with the privatization of sexual, reproductive and family issues sought by the far right. Practically speaking, the ordinances could result in attempts to eliminate the images associated with homosexuality. Doubtless there are heterosexual women who believe that lesbianism is a "degrading" form of "subordination." Since the ordinances allow for suits against materials in which men appear "in place of women," far-right antipornography crusaders could use these laws to suppress gay male pornography. Imagine a Jerry-Falwell-style conservative filing a complaint against a gay bookstore for selling sexually explicit materials showing men with other men in "degrading" or "submissive" or "objectified" postures—all in the name of protecting women.

And most ironically, while the ordinances would do nothing to improve the material conditions of most women's lives, their high visibility might well divert energy from the drive to enact other, less popular laws that would genuinely empower women—comparable worth legislation, for example, or affirmative action requirements or fairer property and support principles in divorce laws.

Other provisions of the ordinances concern coercive behavior: physical assault which is imitative of pornographic images, coercion into pornographic performance, and forcing pornography on others. On close examination, however, even most of these provisions are problematic.

Existing law already penalizes physical assault, including when it is associated with pornography. Defenders of the proposed legislation often cite the example of models who have been raped or otherwise harmed while in the process of making pornographic images. But victims of this type of attack can already sue or prosecute those responsible. (Linda Marchiano, the actress who appeared in the film *Deep Throat*, has not recovered damages for the physical assaults she describes in her book *Ordeal* because the events happened several years before she decided to try to file a suit. A lawsuit was thus precluded by the statute of limitations.) Indeed, the ordinances do not cover assault or other harm incurred while producing pornography, presumably because other laws already achieve that end.

The ordinances would penalize coercing, intimidating or fraudulently inducing anyone into performing for pornography. Although existing law already provides remedies for fraud or contracts of duress, this section of the proposed ordinance seeks to facilitate recovery of damages by, for example, pornography models who might otherwise encounter substantial prejudice against their claims. Supporters of this section have suggested that it is comparable to the Supreme Court's ban on child pornography. The analogy has been stretched to the point where the City of Indianapolis brief argued that women, like children, need "special protection." "Children are incapable of consenting to engage in pornographic conduct, even absent physical coercion and therefore require special protection," the brief stated. "By the same token, the physical and psychological well-being of women ought to be afforded comparable protection, for the coercive environment in which most pornographic models work vitiates any notion that they consent or 'choose' to perform in pornography."

The reality of women's lives is far more complicated. Women do not become pornography models because society is egalitarian and they exercise a "free choice," but neither do they "choose" this work because they have lost all power for deliberate, volitional behavior. Modeling or acting for pornography, like prostitution, can be a means of survival for those with limited options. For some women, at some points in their lives, it is a rational economic decision. Not every woman regrets having made it, although no woman should have to settle for it. The fight should be to expand the options as well as to insure job safety for women who do become pornography models. By contrast, the impact of the proposed ordinance as a whole would be to drive the pornography industry further underground.

One of the vaguest provisions in the ordinance prohibits "forcing" pornography on a person.

"Forcing" is not defined in the law, and one is left to speculate whether it means forced to respond to pornography, forced to read it or forced to glance at it before turning away. Also unclear is whether the perpetrator must in fact have some superior power over the person being forced—that is, whether there is a meaningful threat that makes the concept of force real.

Again, widely varying situations are muddled, and a consideration of context is absent. "Forcing" pornography on a person "in any public space" is treated identically to using it as a method of sexual harassment in the workplace. The scope of "forcing" could include walking past a newsstand or browsing in a bookstore that had pornography on display. The force involved in such a situation seems mild when compared, for example, to the incessant sexist advertising on television.

The concept behind the "forcing" provision is appropriate, however, in the case of workplace harassment. A worker should not have to endure, especially on pain of losing her job, harassment based on sex, race, religion, nationality or any other factor. This general policy was established by the U.S. courts as part of the guarantees of Title VII of the 1964 Civil Rights Act. Pornography used as a means of harassing women workers is already legally actionable, just as harassment in the workplace by racial slurs is actionable. Any literature endorsing the oppression of women—whether pornography or the Bible—could be employed as an harassment device to impede a woman's access to a job, or to education, public accommodations or other social benefits. It is the usage of pornography in this situation, not the image itself, that is discriminatory. Appropriately, this section of the ordinances provides that only perpetrators of the forcing, not makers and distributors of the images, could be held liable.

Forcing of pornography on a person is also specifically forbidden "in the home." In her testimony before the Indianapolis City Council, Catharine MacKinnon referred to the problem of pornography being "forced on wives in preparation for later sexual scenes." Since only the person who forces the pornography on another can be sued, this provision becomes a kind of protection against domestic harassment. It would allow wives to seek court orders or damages against husbands for some usages of pornography. Although a fascinating attempt to subvert male power in the domestic realm, it nonetheless has problems. "Forcing" is not an easy concept to define in this context. It is hard to know what degree of intrusion would amount to forcing images onto a person who shares the same private space.

More important, the focus on pornography seems a displacement of the more fundamental issues involved in the conflicts that occur between husbands and wives or lovers over sex. Some men may invoke images that reflect their greater power to pressure women into performing the supposedly traditional role of acceding to male desires. Pornography may facilitate or enhance this dynamic of male dominance, but it is hardly the causative agent. Nor would removing the pornography do much to solve the problem. If the man invokes instead his friends' stories about sexual encounters or his experience with other women, is the resulting interaction with his wife substantially different? Focusing on the pornography, rather than on the relationship and its social context, may serve only to channel heterosexual women's recognition of their own intimate oppression toward a movement hailed by the far right as being antiperversion rather than toward a feminist analysis of sexual politics.

The last of the sections that deal with actual coercive conduct is one that attempts to deal with the assault, physical injury or attack of any person in a way that is directly caused by specific pornography. The ordinances would allow a lawsuit against the makers and distributors of pornographic materials that were imitated by an attacker—the only provision of the ordinance that requires proof of causation. Presenting such proof would be extremely difficult. If the viewer's willful decision to imitate the image were found to be an intervening, superseding cause of the harm, the plaintiff would lose.

The policy issues here are no different from those concerning violent media images that are nonsexual: Is showing an image sufficient to cause an act of violence? Even if an image could be found to cause a viewer's behavior, was that behavior reasonably foreseeable? So far, those who have produced violent films have not been found liable under the law when third persons acted out the violence depicted. If this were to change, it would mean, for example, that the producer of the TV movie *The Burning Bed*, which told the true story of a battered wife who set fire to her sleeping husband, could be sued if a woman who saw the film killed her husband in a similar way. The result, of course, would be the end of films depicting real violence in the lives of women.

The ordinances' supporters offer no justification for singling out sexual assault from other kinds of violence. Certainly the experience of sexual assault is not always worse than that of being shot or stabbed or suffering other kinds of nonsexual assault. Nor is sexual assault the only form of violence that is fueled by sexism. If there were evidence that sexual images are more likely to be imitated, there might be some arguable justification for treating them differently. But there is no support for this contention.

Laws which would increase the state's regulation of sexual images present many dangers for women. Although these proposals draw much of their feminist support from women's anger at the market for images of sexual violence, they are aimed not at violence, but at sexual explicitness. Far-right elements recognize the possibility of using the full potential of the ordinances to enforce their sexually conservative worldview, and have supported them for that reason. Feminists should therefore look carefully at the text of these "model" laws in order to understand why many believe them to be a useful tool in *anti*feminist moral crusades.

The proposed ordinances are dangerous because they seek to embody in law an analysis of the role of sexuality and sexual images in the oppression of women with which even all feminists do not agree. Underlying virtually every section of the proposed laws there is an assumption that sexuality is a realm of unremitting, unequaled victimization for women. Pornography appears as the monster that made this so. The ordinances' authors seek to impose their analysis by putting state power behind it. But this analysis is not the only feminist perspective on sexuality. Feminist theorists have also argued that the sexual terrain, however power-laden, is actively contested. Women are agents, and not merely victims, who make decisions and act on them, and who desire, seek out and enjoy sexuality.

APPENDIX: EXCERPTS FROM THE MINNEAPOLIS ORDINANCE

The key provisions of the original Minneapolis ordinance are reprinted below:

1. *Special Findings on Pornography*: The council finds that pornography is central in creating and maintaining the civil inequality of the sexes. Pornography is a systematic practice of exploitation and subordination based on sex which differentially harms women. The bigotry and contempt it promotes, with the acts of aggression it fosters, harm women's opportunities for equality of rights in employment, education, property rights, public accommodations and public services; create pubic harassment and private denigration; promote injury and degradation such as rape, battery and prostitution and inhibit just enforcement of laws against these acts; contribute significantly to restricting women from full exercise of citizenship and participation in public life, including in neighborhoods; damage relations between the sexes; and undermine women's equal exercise of rights to speech and action guaranteed to all citizens under the constitutions and laws of the United States and the State of Minnesota.

gg. *Pornography*. Pornography is a form of discrimination on the basis of sex.

1. Pornography is the sexually explicit subordination of women, graphically depicted, whether in pictures or in words, that also includes one or more of the following:

i. women are presented as dehumanized sexual objects, things or commodities; or
ii. women are presented as sexual objects who enjoy pain or humiliation; or
iii. women are presented as sexual objects who experience sexual pleasure in being raped; or

iv. women are presented as sexual objects tied up or cut up or mutilated or bruised or physically hurt; or
v. women are presented in postures of sexual submission; [or sexual servility, including by inviting penetration;] or
vi. women's body parts—including but not limited to vaginas, breasts, and buttocks—are exhibited, such that women are reduced to those parts; or
vii. women are presented as whores by nature; or
viii. women are presented being penetrated by objects or animals; or
ix. women are presented in scenarios of degradation, injury, abasement, torture, shown as filthy or inferior, bleeding, bruised, or hurt in a context that makes these conditions sexual.

2. The use of men, children, or transsexuals in the place of women . . . is pornography for purposes of . . . this statute.

l. *Discrimination by trafficking in pornography.*
The production, sale, exhibition, or distribution of pornography is discrimination against women by means of trafficking in pornography:

1. City, state, and federally funded public libraries or private and public university and college libraries in which pornography is available for study, including on open shelves, shall not be construed to be trafficking in pornography, but special display presentations of pornography in said places is sex discrimination.
2. The formation of private clubs or associations for purposes of trafficking in pornography is illegal and shall be considered a conspiracy to violate the civil rights of women.
3. Any woman has a cause of action hereunder as a woman acting against the subordination of women. Any man or transsexual who alleges injury by pornography in the way women are injured by it shall also have a cause of action.

m. *Coercion into pornographic performances.* Any person, including a transsexual, who is coerced, intimidated, or fraudulently induced (hereafter, "coerced") into performing for pornography shall have a cause of action against the maker(s), seller(s), exhibitor(s) or distributor(s) of said pornography for damages and for the elimination of the products of the performance(s) from the public view.

1. limitation of action. This claim shall not expire before five years have elapsed from the date of the coerced performance(s) or from the last appearance or sale of any product of the performance(s); whichever date is later;

2. Proof of one or more of the following facts or conditions shall not, without more, negate a finding of coercion:

aa. that the person is a woman; or

bb. that the person is or has been a prostitute; or

cc. that the person has attained the age of majority; or

dd. that the person is connected by blood or marriage to anyone involved in or related to the making of the pornography; or

ee. that the person has previously had, or been thought to have had, sexual relations with anyone including anyone involved in or related to the making of the pornography; or

ff. that the person has previously posed for sexually explicit pictures for or with anyone, including anyone involved in or related to the making of the pornography at issue; or

gg. that anyone else, including a spouse or other relative, has given permission on the person's behalf; or

hh. that the person actually consented to a use of the performance that is changed into pornography; or

ii. that the person knew that the purpose of the acts or events in question was to make pornography; or

jj. that the person showed no resistance or appeared to cooperate actively in the photographic sessions or in the sexual events that produced the pornography; or

kk. that the person signed a contract, or made statements affirming a willingness to cooperate; or

ll. that no physical force, threats, or weapons were used in the making of the pornography; or

mm. that the person was paid or otherwise compensated.

n. *Forcing pornography on a person.* Any woman, man, child, or transsexual who has pornography forced on them in any place of employment, in education, in a home, or in any public place has a cause of action against the perpetrator and/or institution.

o. *Assault or physical attack due to pornography.* Any woman, man, child, or transsexual who is assaulted, physically attacked or injured in a way that is directly caused by specific pornography has a claim for damages against the perpetrator, the maker(s), distributor(s), seller(s), and/or exhibitor(s), and for an injunction against the specific pornography's further exhibition, distribution, or sale. No damages shall be assessed (A) against maker(s) for pornography made, (B) against distributor(s) for pornography distributed, (C) against seller(s) for pornography sold, or (D) against exhibitors for pornography exhibited prior to the effective date of this act.

p. *Defenses.* Where the materials which are the subject matter of a cause of action under subsections (l), (m), (n), or (o) of this section are pornography, it shall not be a defense that the defendant did not know or intend that the materials are pornography or sex discrimination.

Study Questions

1. A central concern about the MacKinnon/Dworkin antipornography legislation raised in this article is that it "vague." Explain this concern.

2. Duggan, Hunter, and Vance write: "Most important, what underlies this legislation and the success of its analysis in blurring and exceeding boundaries, is an appeal to a very traditional view of sex: sex is degrading to women" (second paragraph before the section entitled "The Dangers of Application"). Explain this quotation.

3. Would you support the passage of a MacKinnon/ Dworkin antipornography law in your community? Why or why not?

4. This text includes vocal proponents of and vocal opponents to this type of antipornography legislation under the rubric of dominance approaches to feminism. Does this grouping make sense to you? Why or why not?

Marilyn Frye

Willful Virgin or Do You Have to Be a Lesbian to Be a Feminist?

The connection between lesbianism and feminism has made many women nervous. Many believe that if they associate themselves with feminism they will be associated with lesbianism, and for some that is a frightening, even a disgusting, thought. There is fear of being suspected of approving of lesbians or lesbianism, fear of being identified with lesbians, fear of being suspected of being a lesbian, fear of being lesbian. And there is anger at lesbians for being present, active and assertive as feminists, and for insisting on a connection between lesbianism and feminism.

I will directly provoke and address these fears and this anger here. They are homophobic, more specifically, *gyn*ophobic and lesbian-hating, and they make me impatient. I am going to speak plainly, out of impatience and also out of my own peculiar and slightly perverse optimism.

Every term in my feminism classes, a time comes when heterosexual women students articulate the question: Do you have to be a lesbian to be a feminist? I don't know how much other teachers of Women's Studies hear this question. My classroom is a situation which brings the connection between feminism and lesbianism to one's attention. I am a lesbian, I am "out" to my Women's Studies students, and I expose them to a great deal of strong and empowering feminist thinking by feminists of many cultures and locales who are lesbians. In the classroom, this question signals our arrival at a point where newcomers to feminism are beginning to grasp that sexual acts, sexual desire, and sexual dread and taboo are profoundly political and that feminist politics is as much about the disposition of bodies, the manipulation of desire and arousal, and the bonds of intimacy and loyalty as it is about gender stereotypes, economic opportunity and legal rights. In my classes, this question is a moment of students' coming to terms with the fact that the political is indeed personal, very personal. But what goes on in my class is clearly not the only thing that gives rise to this question. For many students it has already arisen outside this class; they have elsewhere encountered people who apparently believe that if you are a feminist you must be a lesbian. Some students have been just waiting for the chance to pose this question. I usually ask women in my Women's Studies classes if they have ever been called lesbians or dykes or been accused of being lesbian, and always many, often a majority, say they have. One woman was called a lesbian when she rejected the attentions of a man in a bar; another was called "butch" when she opened and held a door for a male friend; another was asked if she was a lesbian when she challenged a man's sexist description of another woman. A woman told her date that she did not want to have sex with him and he called her a dyke. A young woman told her mother that she was going to Washington D.C. for the big pro-choice march; her mother, disapproving and fearing for her daughter's safety, said, "Oh, so now you're going to go off and become a lesbian." A woman who divorced her husband and lives on her own is gossiped about in a way that spreads the suggestion that she is a lesbian. A woman says she is frequently assumed to be a lesbian because of her athletic build and refusal to wear skirts. A woman who does not experience sexual arousal or orgasm with her husband is quizzed about her lesbian tendencies by her doctor and her therapist. A woman reports that her friends refer to her Women's Studies class as her "lesbian class"; several other women say some of their friends do that too.

The message of these exchanges is clearly that a woman who is feminist or does anything or betrays any attitude or desire which expresses her autonomy or deviance from conventional femininity is a lesbian. Hearing this message in these contexts, women are likely to "consider the source"—the message has come from people who are anti-feminist, misogynist or at least unreflective defenders of male privilege or the gender status quo. One might think they are inventing this equation just to intimidate women who are "out of line." But it is more complicated than that. These are not the only people who suggest to newly feminist women that they can't be feminists without being lesbians. Paradoxically, some heterosexual feminists suggest the same thing to them in many ways. Consider what may go on, what often does go on, in the context of Women's Studies in universities and colleges.

In a Women's Studies program somewhere in the U.S. students register with the Women's Studies advisory committee the complaint that their courses are not challenging and radical enough, and a key faculty member surmises that the students who are dissatisfied are lesbian. The dissatisfied students, few of whom are lesbian, pick up on this response, and those who are not lesbian learn that they are out of step because they want their radicalness and rebellion nurtured and they are not lesbian.

Another example: Some students who have been exposed to the thinking and lives of feminist lesbians bring ideas from there into a Women's Studies course

and those ideas are denigrated by that teacher, who identifies them as ideas only a lesbian separatist would consider. Some of those students are not lesbian and yet they have considered those ideas and found them interesting, even compelling, and have found themselves empowered just by thinking about those ideas. They are being told these ideas belong to lesbians, and heterosexual women don't believe those things or even take them seriously.

In many Women's Studies contexts, students are exposed to heterosexual feminist teachers (and sometimes closeted lesbian teachers who are passing as heterosexuals) who model conformity to man-made norms of femininity in appearance, bearing and voice, who argue against any action or politics that would alienate men or non-feminist women, who do not model, approve, or encourage any radical insubordination, any blasphemy against men and their gods, any uncareful enactment of anger. In academic settings it is common that women see these things modeled, hear the violences of men against women unqualifiedly named and condemned, and hear witty mockery of men's arrogances, only by feminists who are lesbian—usually students, more rarely, teachers.

In colleges and universities in the U.S. there is now, after 20 years of hard work, a great deal of feminist knowledge and analysis available to students and there are many students eagerly acquiring a rich understanding of women's subordination in U.S. cultures. Students who are exposed to the well-known data on wife-battering, street rape and acquaintance rape, pornography, child sexual assault, incest and other violences against women, and to any deep and acute feminist analysis of the patriarchal structures of marriage, reproduction and mothering—students who are exposed to feminist analyses of patriarchal religions and of the mythology propagated by popular culture in contemporary societies—students who understand something about women's paid and unpaid work in various modern economies and the practices and institutions which determine the accumulation and distribution of wealth—students who have some idea of the scope and intent of historical conspiracies against women such as the Inquisition, the erasure of women from history, and the post-

World War II propaganda campaign in the U.S. to convert women workers into housewife-consumers—such students catch on that what we are dealing with here is profound, that it goes to the root of this society and what is called "civilization" and is etched into the deepest sources of our own thoughts and passions. They get it that any adequate response to this is going to require radical analysis, radical strategies and radical imagination, and that rebellion will be dangerous and costly. Feminists in the academy have helped students to appreciate the character and magnitude of the problems; students then look to these feminists for resources for responding to the problems—intellectual, spiritual, artistic, emotional, political resources. But when they express this need they often are told, either implicitly or explicitly, that only lesbians crave radical analysis and radical solutions and that only lesbians offer these. They are being told that a strong and angry feminism that will settle for nothing but going to the root of the matter belongs to lesbians. Heterosexual women associated with Women's Studies to a great extent leave the whole task of "being radical" to lesbians, leave the burden, the hopefulness and the excitement of pushing the limits to lesbians. They leave rage and ecstasy to lesbians.

In a variety of contexts, newly feminist women find their assertions and demands met with this implicit or explicit connecting of sexuality and politics. It is a sort of implicit theory of women's sexuality according to which a woman who largely adheres to patriarchal feminine norms in act and attitude and who does not radically challenge or rebel against patriarchal institutions is heterosexual, and a woman who does not comply with feminine norms or who seriously challenges or rebels against patriarchal institutions is a lesbian. The difference between the explicit accusations of lesbianism on the part of non- or anti-feminists and the implicit association of feminist radicalness with lesbianism that occurs in many academic contexts is only a difference in the degree and kind of non-compliance it takes to earn the attributed status of lesbian. Feminists are, by definition, to some degree non-compliant with the patriarchal norms of femininity and rebellious against patriarchal institutions; so

by this theory, feminists are to some degree lesbian. It would follow that those who are *very* feminist, *uncompromisingly* feminist, *extremely* feminist, *radically* feminist, must BE lesbians, flat out.

For the newly feminist woman who is not lesbian, this connecting of feminism (or any sign of female autonomy or rebellion) with lesbianism is very likely to have the effect of making her back off from any radicalness, censor in herself any extremeness of anti-patriarchal thought or action. She has lived all her life in a social climate that makes lesbianism scary and offensive and that makes her believe she herself is not and could never be lesbian. If she is a member of a racialized group, she may also have some sense that to be a lesbian would be disloyal to her home community, or she may have the impression that lesbianism simply does not occur among her people. In such contexts, the equation of feminism and lesbianism is a very effective way to place a very narrow and constraining limit on feminism.

But even though the linking of feminism and lesbianism actually does work—in conjunction with women's homophobia and lesbian-hating—to restrain feminism, and even though our contemporary concept of lesbianism is rooted in theories of sexuality which were invented in a period of fearful and extreme reaction against 19th century feminism, I want to suggest that this notion of a connection between feminism and lesbianism is *not* merely an ad hoc fiction invented by patriarchal loyalists to vilify feminism and intimidate feminists. An intrinsic connection between feminism and lesbianism in a contemporary Euro-American setting is just a historically specific manifestation of an ancient and intrinsic connection between patriarchal/fraternal social order and female heterosexuality.

I believe that all feminist theory and practice eventually conveys one to this proposition; that a central constitutive dynamic and key mechanism of the global phenomenon of male domination, oppression and exploitation of females, is near-universal female heterosexuality. All of the institutions and practices which constitute and materialize this domination (and simultaneously organize males' lives in relation to each other) either presuppose almost-universal female heterosexuality or manufacture, regulate and enforce female heterosexuality, or both.

In saying this, I am using a term, "heterosexuality," which has a particular meaning in contemporary Euro-American cultures and does not translate in any simple way into other cultural contexts. In some cultures the physical intimacy between women which we here think of as central to the concept *lesbian* are not tabooed as they are here—they may not be socially recognized at all, even negatively.[1] But in almost all cultures for at least the last couple of thousand years, to the best of my knowledge, virtually every woman is strenuously required by tradition, law, more and taboo to be in some form of availability, servitude or marriage to a man or men in which she is unconditionally or almost unconditionally sexually accessible to that man or men and in the context of which she carries and bears his or their children. In cultures most shaped by male domination, wives' (females slaves', or servants') compulsory sexual accessibility and service is of a piece with their economic and domestic service and subordination to the man or men to whom they are attached and in some cases to those men's whole fraternity, family or clan.[2] Even though, in many cultures a distinction between two female sexualities, "hetero-" and "lesbian," is not operative, my use of the term "heterosexual" is suitable because I am referring to life-situations and dispositions of female bodies which are defined and determined in terms of female sexual accessibility to males and not in terms of the whole of a female's *own* desire, affectional ties or erotic intimacies, whatever their objects. The point is that virtually all women in patriarchal cultures are rigorously required to be sexual with and for men. When I speak of "the patriarchal institution of female heterosexuality" and suggest that in some sense "it" exists widely across cultures and time, I speak of a nearly global pattern using a term which strictly designates just one of its local manifestations.[3]

For females to be subordinated and subjugated to males on a global scale, and for males to organize themselves and each other as they do, billions of female individuals, virtually all who see life on this planet, must be reduced to a more-or-less willing toleration of subordination and servitude to men. The primary sites of this reduction are the sites of heterosexual relation and encounter—courtship and marriage-arrangement, romance, sexual liaisons, fucking, marriage, prostitution, the normative family, incest and child sexual assault. It is on this terrain of heterosexual connection that girls and women are habituated to abuse, insult, and degradation, that girls are reduced to women—to wives, to whores, to mistresses, to sex slaves, to clerical workers and textile workers, to the mothers of men's children. The secondary sites of the forced female embodiment of subordination are the sites of the ritual preparations of girls and women for heterosexual intercourse, relations, or attachments. I refer to training in proper deportment and attire and decoration, all of which is training in and habituation to bodily restriction and distortion; I refer to diets and exercise and beauty regimens which habituate the individual to deprivation and punishment and to fear and suspicion of her body and its wisdom; I refer to the abduction and seasoning of female sexual slaves; to clitoridectomy and other forms and sorts of physical and spiritual mutilation; all of which have no cultural or economic purpose or function if girls and women do not have to be made ready for husbands and male lovers, pimps, johns, bosses and slavers.

Without (hetero)sexual abuse, (hetero)sexual harassment and the (hetero)sexualization of every aspect of females bodies and behaviors, there would not be patriarchy, and whatever other forms or materializations of oppression might exist, they would not have the shapes, boundaries and dynamics of the racism, nationalism, and so on that we are now familiar with.

The meanings of female heterosexuality are many, and it does not play the same political role in all social and cultural locales. But in most locales it glues each adult woman to one or more men of her caste, class, race, nation, or tribe, making her, willy nilly, a supporter of whatever politic those men adhere to, though she has little or no part in shaping or defining that politic, regardless of whether that politic is liberatory or oppressive, and regardless of whether it is liberatory for women. In the particular cases of races and classes which are politically dominant in their locale, female heterosexuality joins females in racial and/or class solidarity to dominating males and offers for their compliance the bribe of a share of the benefits their men extort from other groups. Female heterosexuality, whether literally *sexual* or not, is profoundly implicated in the racism of white women in our present time and place; the disloyalty to the civilization of white men which Adrienne Rich recommended to white women is not possible without disloyalty to the men with whom one is bonded by the institution of heterosexuality.[4] And in racial or ethnic groups which are oppressed, when a woman is not complying with the norms of female heterosexuality to the satisfaction of some man, he may bully her into line with the argument that her noncompliance or rebellion against the norms of femininity is disloyalty to her race or her community.

Lesbian feminists have noted that if the institution of female heterosexuality is what makes girls into women and is central to the continuous replication of patriarchy, then women's abandonment of that institution recommends itself as one strategy (among others) in the project of dismantling patriarchal structures. And if heterosexual encounters, relations and connections are the sites of the inscription of the patriarchal imperatives on the bodies of women, it makes sense to abandon those sites. And if female heterosexuality is central to the way sexism and racism are knit together in strange paradoxical symbiosis, it makes sense that non-participation in that institution could be part of a strategy for weakening both racism and patriarchy.

Some women speaking in other-than-lesbian feminist voices have responded by saying that withdrawal from participation in the institution of female heterosexuality is only a personal solution and only available to a few; they have said it is not a political, not a systemic strategy. I think, on the contrary, that it can be a systemic strategy, because female heterosexuality is not a given in nature, but is actively and continuously constructed. If women take the construction of ourselves and the institutions and practices which determine and govern us into our own hands, we can construct something else.

Commitment to the naturalness or inevitability of female heterosexuality is commitment to the power relations which are expressed and maintained by the institutions of female heterosexuality in patriarchal cultures around the world. (It is also, by postmodern lights, ahistorical and essentialist.) People who have power maintain that power partly by using that power to make its own historical conditions ahistorical— that is they make the prerequisites of their power into "givens." They naturalize them. A vital part of making generalized male dominance as close to inevitable as a human construction can be is the naturalization of female heterosexuality. Men have been creating ideologies and political practices which naturalize female heterosexuality continuously in every culture since the dawns of the patriarchies. (Both Freud and Lacan are naturalizers of female heterosexuality. They say that female heterosexuality is constructed, but they rescue themselves by going on to say that its construction is determined and made inevitable by the nature of civilization, or the nature of language.)

Female heterosexuality is not a biological drive or an individual woman's erotic attraction or attachment to another human animal which happens to be male. Female heterosexuality is a set of social institutions and practices defined and regulated by patriarchal kinship systems, by both civil and religious law, and by strenuously enforced mores and deeply entrenched values and taboos. Those definitions, regulations, values and taboos are about male fraternity and the oppression and exploitation of women. They are not about love, human warmth, solace, fun, pleasure, or deep knowledge between people. If any of the latter arise within the boundaries of these institutions and practices, it is because fun, solace, pleasure and acknowledgement grow like dandelions and are hard to eradicate, not because heterosexuality is natural or is naturally a site of such benefits.

So, is it possible to be a feminist without being a lesbian? My inclination is to say that feminism, which is thoroughly anti-patriarchal, is not compatible with female heterosexuality, which is thoroughly patriarchal. But I anticipate the following reply:

"You seem to suppose that all relation, connection, or encounter of any passionate or erotic or genital sort or involving any sort of personal commitment between a female and a male must belong to this patriarchal institution called 'female heterosexuality,' that it must be suffocated by this rubric, . . . you seem therefore to suppose that our acts and feelings and meanings are all totally formed by history, social institutions and language. That is a kind of hopeless determinism which is politically fatal and is contradicted by your own presence here as a lesbian."

I agree that I cannot embrace any absolute historical, social determinism. The feminist lesbians' permanent project of defining ourselves and our passions and our communities is a living willful refusal of such determinism. But the free space of creation exists only when it is actively, creatively, aggressively, courageously, persistently occupied. Patriarchal histories and cultures mitigate against such space constantly, by material and conceptual coercion, by bribery, by punishment and by shaping and constraining the imagination. So long as we do not actively, perversely and obstinately create ourselves, lesbians are impossible.

In my essay "To Be And Be Seen," following up on a tip from Sarah Hoagland, I explored at length the proposition that there are no lesbians in the universes of patriarchy. A similar and more generic point is useful here.

The word "virgin" did not originally mean a woman whose vagina was untouched by any penis, but a free woman, one not betrothed, not married, not bound to, not possessed by any man. It meant a female who is sexually and hence socially her own person. In any universe of patriarchy, there are no Virgins in this sense. Even female children are possessed by their male kin and are conceived of as potential wives. Hence Virgins must be unspeakable, thinkable only as negations, their existence impossible. Radically feminist lesbians have claimed positive Virginity and have been inventing ways of living it out, in creative defiance of patriarchal definitions of the real, the meaningful. The question at hand may be conceived this way: *Will* and *can* any women, many women, creatively defy patriarchal definitions of the real and the meaningful to invent and embody modes of living positive Virginity which include women's maintaining erotic, economic, home-making, partnering connections with men? Such Virgins are no more possible *in* patriarchy than are lesbians, and if they impossibly bring themselves into existence, they will be living lives as sexually, socially and politically outlandish and unnatural as the lives undertaken by radically feminist lesbians. What must be imagined here is females who are willing to engage in chosen connections with males, who are wild, undomesticated females, creating themselves here and now.

In a way, it is not my place to imagine these wild females who have occasional and/or committed erotic, reproductive, homemaking, partnered or friendship relations with males. The work and the pleasure of that imagining belong to those who undertake to invent themselves thus. But I do have a vivid, though partial, image of them. It derives both from my own experience as an impossible being and from my intense desire for alliance and sisterhood with women of my acquaintance who engage in relations with men in the patriarchal context but who also seem to me to have a certain aptitude for Virginity. This image expresses that "perverse optimism" which I said at the beginning is one source of this writing/speaking. So I offer for your consideration a sketch of my image of these wild women: (This is not a recipe for political correctness, and I am not legislating: this is a report from my Imagination.)

These Virgins do not attire and decorate themselves in the gear which in their cultures signal female compliance with male-defined femininity and which would form their bodies to such compliance. They do not make themselves "attractive" in the conventional feminine modes of their cultures and so people who can ignore their animal beauty say they are ugly. They maintain as much economic flexibility as they possibly can to ensure that they can revert to independence any time economic partnership is binding them to an alliance less than fully chosen. They would no more have sex when they don't expect to enjoy it than they would run naked in the rain when they don't expect to enjoy it. Their sexual interactions are not sites where people with penises make themselves men and people with vaginas are made women.[5]

These Virgins who connect with men don't try to maintain the fictions that the men they favor are better men than other men. When they are threatened by people who feel threatened by them, they do not point to their connections with men as soothing proof that they really aren't manhaters. They don't avail themselves of male protection. They do not pressure their daughters or their mothers, sisters, friends or students to relate to men in the ways they do so they can feel validated by the other women's choices. They never consider bringing any man with them to any feminist gathering that is not specifically meant to include men, and they help to create and to defend (and they enjoy) women-only spaces.

These Virgins who connect with men are not manipulable by orchestrations of male approval and disapproval, orchestrations of men's and children's needs, real or fake. They are not capable of being reduced to conformity by dread or anxiety about things lesbian, and are unafraid of their own passions for other Virgins, including those who are lesbians. They do not need to be respectable.

These Virgins refuse to enter the institution of marriage, and do not support or witness the weddings of others, including the weddings of their favorite brothers. They are die-hard marriage-resisters. They come under enormous pressure to marry, but they do not give in to it. They do not consider marriage a privilege. Not even the bribe of spousal health insurance benefits lures them into marriage, not even as they and their partners get older and become more anxious about their health and their economic situations.

These Virgins have strong, reliable, creative, enduring, sustaining, ardent friendships with women. Their imagination and their politics are shaped more fundamentally by a desire to empower women and create friendship and solidarity among women than by a commitment to appease, comfort or change men. These Virgins who connect with men do not feel that they could be themselves and be in closets; they are "out" as loose and noncompliant females, a very noticeable phenomenon on the social and political scene. They make themselves visible, audible and tangible to each other, they make community and sisterhood with each other and with lesbian Virgins, and they support each other in their wildness. They frolic and make trouble together. They create ways to have homes and warmth and companionship and intensity with or without a man included. They create value and they create meaning, so when the pressures to conform to patriarchal female heterosexuality are great, they have a context and community of resistance to sustain them and to engage their creative energies in devising new solutions to the problems conformity pretends to solve. They create music, novels, poetry, art, magazines and newspapers, knowledge, skills and tools, political actions and programs. And in their magazines and newspapers, they articulate their imagination, their cultural and political differences, their various values; they berate each other, they support each other, they pay attention to each other.

Are these beings I imagine possible? Can you fuck without losing your virginity? I think everything is against it, but *it's not my call*. I can hopefully image, but the counter-possible creation of such a reality is up to those who want to live it, if anyone does.

Some women have hoped that you *do* have to be a lesbian to be a real, extreme, to-the-root, troublemaking feminist, because then, since they are not lesbians and would never in the world become lesbians, they have an excuse for not thinking or acting radically feminist and not alienating men. Much of what passes for women's fear of lesbianism is really fear of men—fear of what men might do to non-compliant females. But I do not want to provide such an excuse for moderate or safe feminism.

"Do you have to be a lesbian to be a feminist?" is not quite the right question. The question should be "Can a woman be heterosexual and be radically feminist?" My picture is this: you do not have to be a lesbian to uncompromisingly embody and enact a radical feminism, but you also cannot be heterosexual in any standard patriarchal meaning of that word—you cannot be any version of a patriarchal wife. Lesbian or not, to embody and enact a consistent and all-the-way feminism you have to be a heretic, a deviant, an undomesticated female, an impossible being. You have to be a Virgin.

NOTES

This is a slightly revised version of a speech I gave, titled "Do You Have To Be A Lesbian To Be A Feminist?", at the National Women's Studies Association annual conference in June, 1990, in Akron Ohio. I was invited to be one of two speakers in a plenary session which I was told would be on lesbianism, feminism, and homophobia, though when the program came out, there was another title given to the session, a title which did not include the word "lesbian". The original speech was published in *off our backs* in the August/September issue, 1990, and sparked a flood of very critical letters to the editor from women who thought I had answered the title question "yes."

I am happy to acknowledge Carolyn Shafer's help in thinking through and crafting these reflections, and I am indebted also to discussion with Maria Lugones which helped me have the courage to cut through some confusions.

1. In some cultural contexts, this intimacy would not be considered *sexual*. Indeed, in my own time and place, it is difficult for some people to think of intimacy between women as really "sexual." Cf. Frye, "To Be And Be Seen," in *The Politics of Reality: Essays in Feminist Theory* (Freedom, California: The Crossing Press, 1983) 156–158.

2. In the context of European and North American cultures, it may have been a mark of women's increased status (a result of the successes of the 19th Century feminism) that intimate relations among women have come to be taken seriously enough by patriarchal authorities to be seen as an extension of the sexual and to be rigidly forbidden.

3. Thanks to Miriam Johnson for encouraging me to be more mindful, here, of the cultural specificity of the concepts of "lesbian" and "heterosexual". She suggested that the term "wife" more accurately designates what women

are required to be, cross-culturally, than the term "heterosexual". But in the middle-class U.S. culture of which I am a native, at this time the legal and traditional meaning of "wife" is too narrow to designate what I am referring to. Women of my culture are not so strenuously required to marry as they are required to be heterosexual—to be sexually available to a man or men and not to "be sexual with" women.

4. "Disloyal to Civilization: Feminism, Racism, and Gynephobia," *On Lies, Secrets, and Silence* (NY: Norton, 1979) 275–310. See also "White Woman Feminist" in Frye, *Willful Virgin* (Berkeley, CA: The Crossing Press, 1992).

5. These felicitous phrases are due to John Stoltenberg, *Refusing To Be A Man: Essays on Sex and Justice* (Portland, Oregon: Breitenbush Books, Inc.) passim.

Study Questions

1. In paragraph 12, Frye writes that "a central constitutive dynamic and key mechanism of the global phenomenon of male domination, oppression and exploitation of females, is near-universal female heterosexuality." Explain this quotation, paying particular attention to what Frye means by "heterosexuality."

2. What is a "Willful Virgin"?

3. What is your assessment of Frye's "report from my Imagination" near the conclusion of the article? Is Frye's "report" sufficiently attentive to issues of intersectionality?

4. According to Frye, *do* you have to be a lesbian to be a feminist?

5. In what sense does this article exemplify the dominance approach to sex equality?

bell hooks

Seduced by Violence No More

We live in a culture that condones and celebrates rape. Within a phallocentric patriarchal state, the rape of women by men is a ritual that daily perpetuates and maintains sexist oppression and exploitation. We cannot hope to transform "rape culture" without committing ourselves fully to resisting and eradicating patriarchy. In his recent essay "Black America: Multicultural Democracy in the Age of Clarence Thomas and David Duke," Manning Marable writes:

> Rape, spouse abuse, sexual harassment on the job, are all essential to the perpetuation of a sexist society. For the sexist, violence is the necessary and logical part of the unequal, exploitative relationship. To dominate and control, sexism requires violence. Rape and sexual harassment are therefore not accidental to the structure of gender relations within a sexist order.

This is no new revelation. In all our work as thinkers and activists, committed feminist women have consistently made this same point. However, it is important to acknowledge that our movement to transform rape culture can only progress as men come to feminist thinking and actively challenge sexism and male violence against women. And it is even more significant that Marable speaks against a sexist order from his position as an African American social critic.

Black males, utterly disenfranchised in almost every arena of life in the United States, often find that the assertion of sexist domination is their only expressive access to the patriarchal power they are told all men should possess as their gendered birthright. Hence, it should not surprise or shock that many black men support and celebrate "rape culture." That celebration has found its most powerful contemporary voice in misogynist rap music. Significantly, there are powerful alternative voices. Mass media pays little attention to those black men who are opposing phallocentrism, misogyny, and sexism. The "it's-a-dick-thing" version of masculinity that black male pop icons such as Spike Lee and Eddie Murphy promote is a call for "real" black men to be sexist and proud of it, to rape and assault black women and brag about it. Alternative, progressive, black male voices in rap or cinema receive little attention, but they exist. There are even black males who do "rap against rape" (their slogan), but their voices are not celebrated in patriarchal culture.

Overall, cultural celebration of black male phallocentrism takes the form of commodifying these expressions of "cool" in ways that glamorize and seduce. Hence, those heterosexual black males that the culture deems most desirable as mates or erotic partners tend to be pushing a "dick-thing" masculinity. They can talk tough and get rough. They can brag about disciplinin' their women, about making sure the "bitches" respect them. Many black men have a profound investment in the perpetuation and maintenance of rape culture. So much of their sense of value and self-esteem is hooked into the patriarchal macho image; these brothers are not about to surrender their "dick-thing" masculinity. This was most apparent during the Mike Tyson trial. Brothers all over were arguing that the black female plaintiff should not have gone to Tyson's hotel room in the wee hours of the morning if she had no intention of doing the wild thing. As one young brother told me last week, "I mean, if a sister came to my room that late, I would think she got one thing on her mind." When I suggested to him and his partners that maybe a woman could visit the room of a man she likes in the wee hours of the night because she might like to talk, they shook their heads saying, "No way." Theirs is a deeply ingrained sexism, a profoundly serious commitment to rape culture.

Like many black men, they are enraged by any feminist call to rethink masculinity and oppose patriarchy. And the courageous brothers who do, who rethink masculinity, who reject patriarchy and rape culture, often find that they cannot get any play—that the very same women who may critique macho male nonsense contradict themselves by making it clear that they find the "unconscious brothers" more appealing.

On college campuses all over the United States, I talk with these black males and hear their frustrations. They are trying to oppose patriarchy and yet are rejected by black females for not being masculine enough. This makes them feel like losers, that their lives are not enhanced when they make progressive changes, when they affirm feminist movement. Their black female peers confirm that they do indeed hold contradictory desires. They desire men not to be sexist, even as they say, "But I want him to be masculine." When pushed to define "masculine," they fall back on sexist representations. I was surprised by the number of young black women who repudiated the notion of male domination, but who would then go on to insist that they could not desire a brother who could not take charge, take care of business, be in control.

Their responses suggest that one major obstacle preventing us from transforming rape culture is that heterosexual women have not unlearned a heterosexist-based "eroticism" that constructs desire in such a way

that many of us can only respond erotically to male behavior that has already been coded as masculine within the sexist framework. Let me give an example of what I mean. For most of my heterosexual erotic life I have been involved with black males who are into a "dick-thing" masculinity. For more than ten years I was in a nonmonogamous relationship with a black man committed to nonsexist behavior in almost every aspect of daily life—the major exception being the bedroom. I accepted my partner's insistence that his sexual desires be met in any circumstance where I had made sexual overtures (kissing, caressing, and so on). Hence ours was not a relationship in which I felt free to initiate sexual play without going forward and engaging in coitus. Often I felt compelled to engage in sexual intercourse when I did not want to.

In my fantasies, I dreamed of being with a male who would fully respect any body rights, my right to say "no," my freedom not to proceed in any sexual activity that I did not desire even if I initially felt that I wanted to be sexual. When I left this relationship, I was determined to choose male partners who would respect my body rights. For me this meant males who did not think that the most important expression of female love was satisfying male sexual desire. It meant males who could respect a woman's right to say "no," irrespective of the circumstance.

Years passed before I found a partner who respected those rights in a feminist manner, with whom I made a mutual covenant that neither of us would ever engage in any sexual act that we did not desire to participate in. I was elated. With this partner I felt free and safe. I felt that I could choose not to have sex without worrying that this choice would alienate or anger my partner. Though most women were impressed that I had found such a partner, they doubted that this could be a chosen commitment to female freedom on any man's part; they raised suspicious questions. Braggin' about him to girlfriends and acquaintances, I was often told, "Girl, you betta be careful. Dude might be gay." I also began to feel doubts. Nothing about the way this dude behaved was familiar. His was not the usual "dick-thing" masculinity that had aroused feelings of pleasure and danger in me for most of my erotic life. While I liked his alternative behavior, I felt a loss of control—the kind that we experience when we are no longer acting within the socialized framework of both acceptable and familiar heterosexual behavior. I worried that he did not find me really desirable. Then I asked myself whether aggressive emphasis on his desire, on his need for "the pussy" would have reassured me. It seemed to me, then, that I needed to rethink the nature of female heterosexual eroticism, particularly in relation to black culture.

Critically interrogating my responses, I confronted the reality that despite all my years of opposing patriarchy, I had not fully questioned or transformed the structure of my desire. By allowing my erotic desire to still be determined to any extent by conventional sexist constructions, I was acting in complicity with patriarchal thinking. Resisting patriarchy ultimately meant that I had to reconstruct myself as a heterosexual, desiring subject in a manner that would make it possible for me to be fully aroused by male behavior that was not phallocentric. In basic terms, I had to learn how to be sexual with a man in a context where his pleasure and his hard-on is decentered and mutual pleasure is centered instead. That meant learning how to enjoy being with a male partner who could be sexual without viewing coitus as the ultimate expression of desire.

Talking with women of varying ages and ethnicities about this issue, I am more convinced than ever that women who engage in sexual acts with male partners must not only interrogate the nature of the masculinity we desire, we must also actively construct radically new ways to think and feel as desiring subjects. By shaping our eroticism in ways that repudiate phallocentrism, we oppose rape culture.

Whether this alters sexist male behavior is not the point. A woman who wants to engage in erotic acts with a man without reinscribing sexism will be much more likely to avoid or reject situations in which she might be victimized. By refusing to function within the heterosexist framework that condones male erotic domination of women, females would be actively disempowering patriarchy.

Without a doubt, our collective, conscious refusal to act in any way that would make us complicit in the perpetuation of rape culture within the sphere of sexual relations would undermine the structure. Concurrently, when heterosexual women are no longer attracted to macho men, the message sent to men would at least be consistent and clear. That would be a major intervention in the overall effort to transform rape culture.

Study Questions

1. Hooks writes that "one major obstacle preventing us from transforming rape culture is that heterosexual women have not unlearned a heterosexist-based 'eroticism' that constructs desire in such a way that many of us can only respond erotically to male behavior that has already been coded as masculine within the sexist framework" (paragraph 6). Explain this quotation.

2. What, according to hooks, must heterosexual women do in order to resist patriarchy? Compare and contrast hooks's recommendation with Frye's in "Willful Virgin."

3. In what sense does this article exemplify the dominance approach to sex equality?

 Section III

LOCALIZING APPROACHES TO SEX OPPRESSION

Elizabeth Hackett and Sally Haslanger, *"Introduction"*

POSTMODERN FEMINISM

Theoretical Frames

Nancy Fraser and Linda J. Nicholson, *"Social Criticism without Philosophy: An Encounter between Feminism and Postmodernism"*
Judith Butler, from *Gender Trouble*
bell hooks, *"Postmodern Blackness"*

Contextual Studies

Sharon Marcus, *"Fighting Bodies, Fighting Words: A Theory and Politics of Rape Prevention"*
Kate Bornstein, *"Send in the Clowns"*
Susan Bordo, *"Material Girl: The Effacements of Postmodern Culture"*

FEMINIST IDENTITY POLITICS

Theoretical Frames

Barbara Christian, *"The Race for Theory"*
Combahee River Collective, *"A Black Feminist Statement"*
Mari Matsuda, *"On Identity Politics"*

Contextual Studies

Gloria Anzaldúa, *"La Conciencia de la Mestiza: Towards a New Consciousness"*
Angela Davis, *"Mama's Got the Blues: Rivals, Girlfriends, and Advisors"*
Dorothy E. Roberts, *"Punishing Drug Addicts Who Have Babies: Women of Color, Equality, and the Right of Privacy"*

INTRODUCTION

Theories included under the rubric of "General Approaches to Sex Oppression" assume, on the whole, that it is possible to provide a single, universal analysis of what sex oppression consists of; the strategies proposed in that section for addressing sex oppression target the phenomena identified in the analysis as "the problem." The articles in this section question this universality assumption. Instead they propose that sex oppression is not a unified phenomenon that can be given a general analysis, but takes different forms in different contexts, periods, and cultures. The resistance to universalizing accounts of sex oppression has roots in two different, and sometimes seemingly opposed, intellectual and political movements: *postmodernism* and *identity politics*.

Postmodern feminism draws on work in European literary and cultural theory—figures such as Derrida, Lyotard, Foucault, and Lacan—to question the assumptions about language, knowledge, and history that underlie attempts to do social theory on a grand scale. For example, if, as some postmodernists have argued, there is nothing "outside" of social practices themselves to do the work of legitimation, so no possibility of transcendental justification or critique, then feminist theory, like all social theory, must be immanent and local. In other words, feminist theory must consider historically and culturally specific occasions of sex oppression to formulate meaningful critique and to justify alternative social arrangements.

Nancy Fraser and Linda Nicholson provide an introduction to postmodern feminism by considering what postmodernism can offer feminism and vice versa. They argue that although the postmodern rejection of "legitimating metanarratives" provides important lessons about the dangers of theory run amok, feminists should not give up the project of analyzing "societal macrostructures," for social theorists must not "abandon the large theoretical tools needed to address large political problems." Feminist analyses should, however, be "framed by historical narrative and rendered temporally and culturally specific."

The excerpt from Judith Butler's now-classic *Gender Trouble* questions the sources and effects of the categories of sex and gender. Rather than taking them as "given," she exposes them as a product, not a precondition, of social practices. Thus she repositions gender, not as an "external" basis or ground for feminist theory, but as a social formation that feminist theory itself helps constitute. In her essay, "Postmodern Blackness," bell hooks considers whether postmodernism has anything to offer a radical liberation struggle that speaks to the needs of African Americans. Although hesitant, she argues that postmodernism "with its decentered subject can be the space where ties are severed or it can provide the occasion for new and varied forms of bonding. To some extent, ruptures, surfaces, contextuality, and a host of other happenings create gaps that make space for oppositional practices which no longer require intellectuals to be confined by narrow separate spheres with no meaningful connection to the world of the everyday."

The essays by Sharon Marcus, Kate Bornstein, and Susan Bordo draw on postmodern insights to consider how social practices are structured by language and can be changed by altering the scripts (Marcus); the experience of life betwixt and between genders (Bornstein); and the supposed cultural and political plasticity of the gendered and raced body (Bordo).

Identity politics and postmodernism have in common a skepticism toward universalizing social theory. However, where postmodernism's roots are in what might be considered "high theory," the roots of identity politics lie in social activism. The term "identity politics" is used to capture an approach to social justice where the basis for solidarity and organized activism does not lie in shared values or party affiliation, but in shared social "identity," e.g., one's race, gender, sexual orientation, and so on. Those who embrace identity politics argue that members of subordinated groups have a distinctive experience of injustice that is a valuable resource for challenging their marginalization and for establishing greater self-determination. They also point out how the theorizing of economically privileged white feminists often has claimed a false universality. That is, some feminists who embrace identity politics are wary of "grand theory" because historically it has failed to address the experiences of marginalized groups. Feminists engaged in identity politics highlight the significance of racial identity, in particular, when attempting to address issues of sex oppression.

Barbara Christian's essay, "The Race for Theory," highlights some of the tensions between postmodernism and identity politics. Although both approaches have a common theme (i.e., that previously dominant theories have oversimplified the categories of analysis and failed to take into account the complexity of social life), Christian distances herself from postmodernism by highlighting the political significance of theory: Why are we theorizing? About what? And for whom? Writing, speaking, and theorizing are political acts and have distinctive significance for women of color.

The Combahee River Collective's "A Black Feminist Statement" provides a powerful statement of Black feminism's critique of mainstream feminism and the arguments for feminist identity politics. Mari Matsuda defends identity politics from the position of a Japanese American woman and law professor, urging, "Know where you stand, what your privileges are, and who is standing on your toes. And when you holler, 'Get off of my toes!' look around at the others, some most unlike you, who are also stepped on."

Identities are complex, however, and vary over time and across context. Gloria Anzaldúa argues for the value of "a new *mestiza* consciousness . . . a consciousness of the Borderlands." In the tension between binaries, a new consciousness emerges, "and though it is a source of intense pain, its energy comes from continual creative motion that keeps breaking down the unitary aspect of each new paradigm." In considering Black women's blues history, Angela Davis illuminates the tensions between the identities and political strategies of Black middle-class women in the club movement of the early twentieth century, and those of working-class Black women of the same period. Davis's essay not only raises important issues about the internal complexity of groups and the relationship between individuals and groups, but also provides an example of how women—Black working-class women, in particular—have theorized outside of academic institutions. Dorothy Roberts's essay on the legal prosecution of drug-addicted mothers provides clear evidence that centering the experience of a subordinated group can have a profound effect on the theory one produces.[1]

Despite their wide-ranging positions, feminists who embrace identity politics and feminists who embrace postmodernism agree that feminist theory cannot address the problem of sex oppression without attending to the experiences of women of color—and, more generally, women in all their diversity—and without drawing on their insights.

NOTE

1. It is interesting to consider whether the work of Matsuda and Anzaldúa is best grouped under the heading of "Politics of Identity." Is it perhaps better understood as taking a dominance approach, albeit a dominance approach especially attentive to issues of intersectionality?

POSTMODERN FEMINISM

Nancy Fraser and Linda J. Nicholson

Social Criticism without Philosophy:
An Encounter between Feminism and Postmodernism

Feminism and postmodernism have emerged as two of the most important political-cultural currents of the last decade. So far, however, they have kept an uneasy distance from one another. Indeed, so great has been their mutual wariness that there have been remarkably few extended discussions of the relations between them.[1]

Initial reticences aside, there are good reasons for exploring the relations between feminism and postmodernism. Both have offered deep and far-reaching criticisms of the institution of philosophy. Both have elaborated critical perspectives on the relation of philosophy to the larger culture. And, most central to the concerns of this essay, both have sought to develop new paradigms of social criticism which do not rely on traditional philosophical underpinnings. Other differences notwithstanding, one could say that during the last decade feminists and postmodernists have worked independently on a common nexus of problems: They have tried to rethink the relation between philosophy and social criticism so as to develop paradigms of criticism without philosophy.

The two tendencies have proceeded from opposite directions. Postmodernists have focused primarily on the philosophy side of the problem. They have begun by elaborating antifoundational metaphilosophical perspectives and from there have drawn conclusions about the shape and character of social criticism. For feminists, on the other hand, the question of philosophy has always been subordinate to an interest in social criticism. Consequently, they have begun by developing critical political perspectives and from there have drawn conclusions about the status of philosophy. As a result of this difference in emphasis and direction, the two tendencies have ended up with complementary strengths and weaknesses. Postmodernists offer sophisticated and persuasive criticisms of foundationalism and essentialism, but their conceptions of social criticism tend to be anemic. Feminists offer robust conceptions of social criticism, but they tend at times to lapse into foundationalism and essentialism.

Thus, each of the two perspectives suggests some important criticisms of the other. A postmodernist reflection on feminist theory reveals disabling vestiges of essentialism while a feminist reflection on postmodernism reveals androcentrism and political naivete.

It follows that an encounter between feminism and postmodernism will initially be a trading of criticisms. But there is no reason to suppose that this is where matters must end. In fact, each of these tendencies has much to learn from the other; each is in possession of valuable resources which can help remedy the deficiencies of the other. Thus, the ultimate stake of an encounter between feminism and postmodernism is the prospect of a perspective which integrates their respective strengths while eliminating their respective weaknesses. It is the prospect of a postmodernist feminism.

In what follows, we aim to contribute to the development of such a perspective by staging the initial, critical phase of the encounter. In the first section, we examine the ways in which one exemplary postmodernist, Jean-François Lyotard, has sought to derive new paradigms of social criticism from a critique of the institution of philosophy. We argue that the conception of social criticism so derived is too restricted to permit an adequate critical grasp of gender dominance and subordination. We identify some internal tensions in Lyotard's arguments, and we suggest some alternative formulations which could allow for more robust forms of criticism without sacrificing the commitment to antifoundationalism. In the second section, we examine some representative genres of feminist social criticism. We argue that in many cases feminist critics continue tacitly to rely on the sorts of philosophical underpinnings which their own commitments, like those of the postmodernists, ought in principle to rule out. We identify some points at which such underpinnings could be abandoned without any sacrifice of social-critical force. Finally, in a brief conclusion, we consider the prospects for a

postmodernist feminism. We discuss some requirements which constrain the development of such a perspective, and we identify some pertinent conceptual resources and critical strategies.

POSTMODERNISM

Postmodernists seek, inter alia, to develop conceptions of social criticism which do not rely on traditional philosophical underpinnings. The typical starting point for their efforts is a reflection on the condition of philosophy today. Writers like Richard Rorty and Jean-François Lyotard begin by arguing that Philosophy with a capital *P* is no longer a viable or credible enterprise. They go on to claim that philosophy and, by extension, theory in general, can no longer function to *ground* politics and social criticism. With the demise of foundationalism comes the demise of the view that casts philosophy in the role of *founding* discourse vis-à-vis social criticism. That "modern" conception must give way to a new "postmodern" one in which criticism floats free of any universalist theoretical ground. No longer anchored philosophically, the very shape or character of social criticism changes; it becomes more pragmatic, ad hoc, contextual, and local. With this change comes a corresponding change in the social role and political function of intellectuals.

Thus, in the postmodern reflection on the relationship between philosophy and social criticism, the term "philosophy" undergoes an explicit devaluation; it is cut down to size, if not eliminated altogether. Yet, even as this devaluation is argued explicitly, the term "philosophy" retains an implicit structural privilege. It is the changed condition of philosophy which determines the changed character of social criticism and of engaged intellectual practice. In the new postmodern equation, then, philosophy is the independent variable while social criticism and political practice are dependent variables. The view of theory which emerges is not determined by considering the needs of contemporary criticism and engagement. It is determined, rather, by considering the contemporary status of philosophy. This way of proceeding has important consequences, not all of which are positive. Among the results is a certain underestimation and premature foreclosing of possibilities for social criticism and engaged intellectual practice. This limitation of postmodern thought will be apparent when we consider its results in the light of the needs of contemporary feminist theory and practice.

Let us consider as an example the postmodernism of Jean-François Lyotard, since it is genuinely exemplary of the larger tendency. Lyotard is one of the few social thinkers widely considered postmodern who actually uses the term; indeed, it was he himself who introduced it into current discussions of philosophy, politics, society, and social theory. His book *The Postmodern Condition* has become the locus classicus for contemporary debates, and it reflects in an especially acute form the characteristic concerns and tensions of the movement.[2]

For Lyotard, postmodernism designates a general condition of contemporary Western civilization. The postmodern condition is one in which "grand narratives of legitimation" are no longer credible. By grand narratives he means overarching philosophies of history like the Enlightenment story of the gradual but steady progress of reason and freedom, Hegel's dialectic of Spirit coming to know itself, and, most importantly, Marx's drama of the forward march of human productive capacities via class conflict culminating in proletarian revolution. For Lyotard, these metanarratives instantiate a specifically modern approach to the problem of legitimation. Each situates first-order discursive practices of inquiry and politics within a broader totalizing metadiscourse which legitimates them. The metadiscourse narrates a story about the whole of human history which purports to guarantee that the pragmatics of the modern sciences and of modern political processes—the norms and rules which govern these practices, determining what counts as a warranted move within them—are themselves legitimate. The story guarantees that some sciences and some politics have the *right* pragmatics and, so, are the *right* practices.

We should not be misled by Lyotard's focus on narrative philosophies of history. In his conception of legitimating metanarrative, the stress properly belongs on the *meta* and not on the *narrative*. For what most interests him about the Enlightenment, Hegelian, and Marxist stories is what they share with other nonnarrative forms of philosophy. Like ahistorical epistemologies and moral theories, they aim to show that specific first-order discursive practices are well formed and capable of yielding true and just results. *True* and *just* here mean something more than results reached by adhering scrupulously to the constitutive rules of some given scientific and political games. They mean, rather, results which correspond to Truth and Justice as they really are in themselves independently of contingent, historical social practices. Thus, in Lyotard's view, a metanarrative is *meta* in a very strong sense. It purports to be a privileged discourse capable of situating, characterizing, and evaluating all other discourses but not itself to be infected by the historicity and contingency which render first-order discourses potentially distorted and in need of legitimation.

In *The Postmodern Condition*, Lyotard argues that metanarratives, whether philosophies of history or nonnarrative foundational philosophies, are merely modern and dépassé. We can no longer believe, he claims, in the availability of a privileged metadiscourse capable of capturing once and for all the truth of every first-order discourse. The claim to *meta* status does not stand up. A so-called metadiscourse is in fact simply one more discourse among others. It follows for Lyotard that legitimation, both epistemic and political, can no longer reside in philosophical metanarratives. Where, then, he asks, does legitimation reside in the postmodern era?

Much of *The Postmodern Condition* is devoted to sketching an answer to that question. The answer, in brief, is that in the postmodern era legitimation becomes plural, local, and immanent. In this era, there will necessarily be many discourses of legitimation dispersed among the plurality of first-order discursive practices. For example, scientists no longer look to prescriptive philosophies of science to warrant their procedures of inquiry. Rather, they themselves problematize, modify, and warrant the constitutive norms of their own practice even as they engage in it. Instead of hovering above, legitimation descends to the level of practice and becomes immanent in it. There are no special tribunals set apart from the sites where inquiry is practiced. Rather, practitioners assume responsibility for legitimizing their own practice.

Lyotard intimates that something similar is or should be happening with respect to political legitimation. We cannot have and do not need a single, overarching theory of justice. What is required, rather, is a "justice of multiplicities."[3] What Lyotard means by this is not wholly clear. On one level, he can be read as offering a normative vision in which the good society consists in a decentralized plurality of democratic, self-managing groups and institutions whose members problematize the norms of their practice and take responsibility for modifying them as situations require. But paradoxically, on another level, he can be read as ruling out the sort of larger-scale, normative political theorizing which, from a modern perspective at least, would be required to legitimate such a vision. In any case, his justice of multiplicities conception precludes one familiar, and arguably essential, genre of political theory: identification and critique of macrostructures of inequality and injustice which cut across the boundaries separating relatively discrete practices and institutions. There is no place in Lyotard's universe for critique of pervasive axes of stratification, for critique of broad-based relations of dominance and subordination along lines like gender, race, and class.

Lyotard's suspicion of the large extends to historical narrative and social theory as well. Here, his chief target is Marxism, the one metanarrative in France with enough lingering credibility to be worth arguing against. The problem with Marxism, in his view, is twofold. On the one hand, the Marxian story is too big, since it spans virtually the whole of human history. On the other hand, the Marxian story is too theoretical, since it relies on a *theory* of social practice and social relations which claims to *explain* historical change. At one level, Lyotard simply rejects the specifics of this theory. He claims that the Marxian conception of practice as production occludes the diversity and plurality of human practices; and that

the Marxian conception of capitalist society as a totality traversed by one major division and contradiction occludes the diversity and plurality of contemporary societal differences and oppositions. But Lyotard does not conclude that such deficiencies can and should be remedied by a better social theory. Rather, he rejects the project of social theory *tout court*.

Once again, Lyotard's position is ambiguous, since his rejection of social theory depends on a theoretical perspective of sorts of its own. He offers a postmodern conception of sociality and social identity, a conception of what he calls "the social bond." What holds a society together, he claims, is not a common consciousness or institutional substructure. Rather, the social bond is a weave of crisscrossing threads of discursive practices, no single one of which runs continuously throughout the whole. Individuals are the nodes or posts where such practices intersect, and so, they participate in many practices simultaneously. It follows that social identities are complex and heterogeneous. They cannot be mapped onto one another nor onto the social totality. Indeed, strictly speaking, there is no social totality and a fortiori no possibility of a totalizing social theory.

Thus, Lyotard insists that the field of the social is heterogeneous and nontotalizable. As a result, he rules out the sort of critical social theory which employs general categories like gender, race, and class. From his perspective, such categories are too reductive of the complexity of social identities to be useful. There is apparently nothing to be gained, in his view, by situating an account of the fluidity and diversity of discursive practices in the context of a critical analysis of large-scale institutions and social structures.

Thus, Lyotard's postmodern conception of criticism without philosophy rules out several recognizable genres of social criticism. From the premise that criticism cannot be grounded by a foundationalist philosophical metanarrative, he infers the illegitimacy of large historical stories, normative theories of justice, and social-theoretical accounts of macrostructures which institutionalize inequality. What, then, *does* postmodern social criticism look like?

Lyotard tries to fashion some new genres of social criticism from the discursive resources that remain. Chief among these is smallish, localized narrative. He seeks to vindicate such narrative against both modern totalizing metanarrative and the scientism that is hostile to all narrative. One genre of postmodern social criticism, then, consists in relatively discrete, local stories about the emergence, transformation, and disappearance of various discursive practices treated in isolation from one another. Such stories might resemble those told by Michael Foucault, although without the attempts to discern larger synchronic patterns and connections that Foucault sometimes made.[4] Like Michael Walzer, Lyotard evidently assumes that practitioners would narrate such stories when seeking to persuade one another to modify the pragmatics or constitutive norms of their practice.[5]

This genre of social criticism is not the whole postmodern story, however. For it casts critique as strictly local, ad hoc, and ameliorative, thus supposing a political diagnosis according to which there are no large-scale, systemic problems which resist local, ad hoc, ameliorative initiatives. Yet, Lyotard recognizes that postmodern society does contain at least one unfavorable structural tendency which requires a more coordinated response. This is the tendency to universalize instrumental reason, to subject *all* discursive practices indiscriminately to the single criterion of efficiency, or "performativity." In Lyotard's view, this threatens the autonomy and integrity of science and politics, since these practices are not properly subordinated to performative standards. It would pervert and distort them, thereby destroying the diversity of discursive forms.

Thus, even as he argues explicitly against it, Lyotard posits the need for a genre of social criticism which transcends local mininarrative. Despite his strictures against large, totalizing stories, he narrates a fairly tall tale about a large-scale social trend. Moreover, the logic of this story, and of the genre of criticism to which it belongs, calls for judgments which are not strictly practice-immanent. Lyotard's story presupposes the legitimacy and integrity of the scientific and political practices allegedly threatened by performativity. It supposes that one can distin-

guish changes or developments which are *internal* to these practices from externally induced distortions. But this drives Lyotard to make normative judgments about the value and character of the threatened practices. These judgments are not strictly immanent in the practices judged. Rather, they are metapractical.

Thus, Lyotard's view of postmodern social criticism is neither entirely self-consistent nor entirely persuasive. He goes too quickly from the premise that Philosophy cannot ground social criticism to the conclusion that criticism itself must be local, ad hoc, and nontheoretical. As a result, he throws out the baby of large historical narrative with the bathwater of philosophical metanarrative and the baby of social-theoretical analysis of large-scale inequalities with the bathwater of reductive Marxian class theory. Moreover, these allegedly illegitimate babies do not in fact remain excluded. They return like the repressed within the very genres of post-modern social criticism with which Lyotard intends to replace them.

We began this discussion by noting that postmodernists orient their reflections on the character of postmodern social criticism by the falling star of foundationalist philosophy. They posit that, with philosophy no longer able credibly to ground social criticism, criticism itself must be local, ad hoc, and untheoretical. Thus, from the critique of foundationalism, they infer the illegitimacy of several genres of social criticism. For Lyotard, the illegitimate genres include large-scale historical narrative and social-theoretical analyses of pervasive relations of dominance and subordination.[6]

Suppose, however, one were to choose another starting point for reflecting on postfoundational social criticism. Suppose one began, not with the condition of Philosophy, but with the nature of the social object one wished to criticize. Suppose, further, that one defined that object as the subordination of women to and by men. Then, we submit, it would be apparent that many of the genres rejected by postmodernists are necessary for social criticism. For a phenomenon as pervasive and multifaceted as male dominance simply cannot be adequately grasped with the meager critical resources to which they would limit us. On the contrary, effective criticism of this phenomenon requires an array of different methods and genres. It requires at minimum large narratives about changes in social organization and ideology, empirical and social-theoretical analyses of macrostructures and institutions, interactionist analyses of the micropolitics of everyday life, critical-hermeneutical and institutional analyses of cultural production, historically and culturally specific sociologies of gender, and so on. The list could go on.

Clearly, not all of these approaches are local and untheoretical. But all are nonetheless essential to feminist social criticism. Moreover, all can in principle be conceived in ways that do not take us back to foundationalism, even though, as we argue in the next section, many feminists have not wholly succeeded in avoiding that trap.

FEMINISM

Feminists, like postmodernists, have sought to develop new paradigms of social criticism which do not rely on traditional philosophical underpinnings. They have criticized modern foundationalist epistemologies and moral and political theories, exposing the contingent, partial, and historically situated character of what has passed in the mainstream for necessary, universal, and ahistorical truths. They have called into question the dominant philosophical project of seeking objectivity in the guise of a "God's eye view" which transcends any situation or perspective.[7]

However, if postmodernists have been drawn to such views by a concern with the status of philosophy, feminists have been led to them by the demands of political practice. This practical interest has saved feminist theory from many of the mistakes of postmodernism: Women whose theorizing was to serve the struggle against sexism were not about to abandon powerful political tools merely as a result of intramural debates in professional philosophy.

Yet, even as the imperatives of political practice have saved feminist theory from one set of difficulties, they have tended at times to incline it toward another. Practical imperatives have led some feminists to adopt modes of theorizing which resemble the

sorts of philosophical metanarrative rightly criticized by postmodernists. To be sure, the feminist theories we have in mind here are not pure metanarratives; they are not ahistorical normative theories about the transcultural nature of rationality or justice. Rather, they are very large social theories—theories of history, society, culture, and psychology—which claim, for example, to identify causes and constitutive features of sexism that operate cross-culturally. Thus, these social theories purport to be empirical rather than philosophical. But, as we hope to show, they are actually quasi-metanarratives. They tacitly presuppose some commonly held but unwarranted and essentialist assumptions about the nature of human beings and the conditions for social life. In addition, they assume methods and concepts which are uninflected by temporality or historicity and which therefore function de facto as permanent, neutral matrices for inquiry. Such theories then, share some of the essentialist and ahistorical features of metanarratives: They are insufficiently attentive to historical and cultural diversity, and they falsely universalize features of the theorist's own era, society, culture, class, sexual orientation, and ethnic, or racial group.

On the other hand, the practical exigencies inclining feminists to produce quasi-metanarratives have by no means held undisputed sway. Rather, they have had to coexist, often uneasily, with counterexigencies which have worked to opposite effect, for example, political pressures to acknowledge differences among women. In general, then, the recent history of feminist social theory reflects a tug of war between forces which have encouraged and forces which have discouraged metanarrative-like modes of theorizing. We can illustrate this dynamic by looking at a few important turning points in this history.

When in the 1960s, women in the New Left began to extend prior talk about women's rights into the more encompassing discussion of women's liberation, they encountered the fear and hostility of their male comrades and the use of Marxist political theory as a support for these reactions. Many men of the New Left argued that gender issues were secondary because they were subsumable under more basic modes of oppression, namely, class and race.

In response to this practical-political problem, radical feminists such as Shulamith Firestone resorted to an ingenious tactical maneuver: Firestone invoked biological differences between women and men to explain sexism. This enabled her to turn the tables on her Marxist comrades by claiming that gender conflict was the most basic form of human conflict and the source of all other forms, including class conflict.[8] Firestone drew on the pervasive tendency within modern culture to locate the roots of gender differences in biology. Her coup was to use biologism to establish the primacy of the struggle against male domination rather than to justify acquiescence to it.

The trick, of course, is problematic from a postmodernist perspective in that appeals to biology to explain social phenomena are essentialist and monocausal. They are essentialist insofar as they project onto all women and men qualities which develop under historically specific social conditions. They are monocausal insofar as they look to one set of characteristics, such as women's physiology or men's hormones, to explain women's oppression in all cultures. These problems are only compounded when appeals to biology are used in conjunction with the dubious claim that women's oppression is the cause of all other forms of oppression.

Moreover, as Marxists and feminist anthropologists began insisting in the early 1970s, appeals to biology do not allow us to understand the enormous diversity of forms which both gender and sexism assume in different cultures. In fact, it was not long before most feminist social theorists came to appreciate that accounting for the diversity of the forms of sexism was as important as accounting for its depth and autonomy. Gayle Rubin aptly described this dual requirement as the need to formulate theory which could account for the oppression of women in its "endless variety and monotonous similarity."[9] How were feminists to develop a social theory adequate to both demands?

One approach which seemed promising was suggested by Michelle Zimbalist Rosaldo and other contributors in the influential 1974 anthropology collection, *Woman, Culture, and Society*. They argued that common to all known societies was some type of separation between a domestic sphere and a public sphere, the former associated with women and the latter with men. Because in most societies to date, women have spent a good part of their lives bearing and raising children, their lives have been more bound to the domestic sphere. Men, on the other hand, have had both the time and mobility to engage in those out of the home activities which generate political structures. Thus, as Rosaldo argued, while in many societies women possess some or even a great deal of power, women's power is always viewed as illegitimate, disruptive, and without authority.[10]

This approach seemed to allow for both diversity and ubiquity in the manifestations of sexism. A very general identification of women with the domestic and of men with the extra-domestic could accommodate a great deal of cultural variation both in social structures and in gender roles. At the same time, it could make comprehensible the apparent ubiquity of the assumption of women's inferiority above and beyond such variation. This hypothesis was also compatible with the idea that the extent of women's oppression differed in different societies. It could explain such differences by correlating the extent of gender inequality in a society with the extent and rigidity of the separation between its domestic and public spheres. In short, the domestic/public theorists seemed to have generated an explanation capable of satisfying a variety of conflicting demands.

However, this explanation turned out to be problematic in ways reminiscent of Firestone's account. Although the theory focused on differences between men's and women's spheres of activity rather than on differences between men's and women's biology, it was essentialist and monocausal nonetheless. It posited the existence of a domestic sphere in all societies and thereby assumed that women's activities were basically similar in content and significance across cultures. (An analogous assumption about men's activities lay behind the postulation of a universal public sphere.) In effect, the theory falsely generalized to all societies an historically specific conjunction of properties: women's responsibility for early child rearing, women's tendency to spend more time in the geographical space of the home, women's lesser participation in the affairs of the community, a cultural ascription of triviality to domestic work, and a cultural ascription of inferiority to women. The theory thus failed to appreciate that, while each individual property may be true of many societies, the conjunction is not true of most.[11]

One source of difficulty in these early feminist social theories was the presumption of an overly grandiose and totalizing conception of theory. Theory was understood as the search for the one key factor which would explain sexism cross-culturally and illuminate all of social life. In this sense, to theorize was by definition to produce a quasi-metanarrative.

Since the late 1970s, feminist social theorists have largely ceased speaking of biological determinants or a cross-cultural domestic/public separation. Many, moreover, have given up the assumption of monocausality. Nevertheless, some feminist social theorists have continued implicitly to suppose a quasi-metanarrative conception of theory. They have continued to theorize in terms of a putatively unitary, primary, culturally universal type of activity associated with women, generally an activity conceived as domestic and located in the family.

One influential example is the analysis of mothering developed by Nancy Chodorow. Setting herself to explain the internal, psychological dynamics which have led many women willingly to reproduce social divisions associated with female inferiority, Chodorow posited a cross-cultural activity, mothering, as the relevant object of investigation. Her question thus became: How is mothering as a female-associated activity reproduced over time? How does mothering produce a new generation of women with the psychological inclination to mother and a new generation of men not so inclined? The answer she offered was in terms of gender identity: Female mothering produces women whose deep sense of self is relational and men whose deep sense of self is not.[12]

Chodorow's theory has struck many feminists as a persuasive account of some apparently observable psychic differences between men and women. Yet, the theory has clear metanarrative overtones. It posits the existence of a single activity, mothering, which, while differing in specifics in different societies, nevertheless constitutes enough of a natural kind to warrant one label. It stipulates that this basically unitary activity gives rise to two distinct sorts of deep selves, one relatively common across cultures to women, the other relatively common across cultures to men. It claims that the difference thus generated between feminine and masculine gender identity causes a variety of supposedly cross-cultural social phenomena, including the continuation of female mothering, male contempt for women, and problems in heterosexual relationships.

From a postmodern perspective, all of these assumptions are problematic because they are essentialist. But the second one, concerning gender identity, warrants special scrutiny, given its political implications. Consider that Chodorow's use of the notion of gender identity presupposes three major premises. One is the psychoanalytic premise that everyone has a deep sense of self which is constituted in early childhood through one's interactions with one's primary parent and which remains relatively constant thereafter. Another is the premise that this deep self differs significantly for men and for women but is roughly similar among women, on the one hand, and among men, on the other hand, both across cultures and within cultures across lines of class, race, and ethnicity. The third premise is that this deep self colors everything one does; there are no actions, however trivial, which do not bear traces of one's masculine or feminine gender identity.

One can appreciate the political exigencies which made this conjunction of premises attractive. It gave scholarly substance to the idea of the pervasiveness of sexism. If masculinity and femininity constitute our basic and ever present sense of self, then it is not surprising that the manifestations of sexism are systemic. Moreover, many feminists had already sensed that the concept of sex-role socialization, an idea Chodorow explicitly criticized, ignored the depth and intractability of male dominance. By implying that measures such as changing images in school textbooks or allowing boys to play with dolls would be sufficient to bring about equality between the sexes, this concept seemed to trivialize and co-opt the message of feminism. Finally, Chodorow's depth-psychological approach gave a scholarly sanction to the idea of sisterhood. It seemed to legitimate the claim that the ties which bind women are deep and substantively based.

Needless to say, we have no wish to quarrel with the claim of the depth and pervasiveness of sexism nor with the idea of sisterhood. But we do wish to challenge Chodorow's way of legitimating them. The idea of a cross-cultural, deep sense of self, specified differently for women and men, becomes problematic when given any specific content. Chodorow states that women everywhere differ from men in their greater concern with "relational interaction." But what does she mean by this term? Certainly not any and every kind of human interaction, since men have often been more concerned than women with some kinds of interactions, for example, those which have to do with the aggrandizement of power and wealth. Of course, it is true that many women in modern Western societies have been expected to exhibit strong concern with those types of interactions associated with intimacy, friendship, and love, interactions which dominate one meaning of the late twentieth-century concept of relationship. But surely this meaning presupposes a notion of private life specific to modern Western societies of the last two centuries. Is it possible that Chodorow's theory rests on an equivocation on the term *relationship?*[13]

Equally troubling are the aporias this theory generates for political practice. While gender identity gives substance to the idea of sisterhood, it does so at the cost of repressing differences among sisters. Although the theory allows for some differences among women of different classes, races, sexual orientations, and ethnic groups, it construes these as subsidiary to more basic similarities. But it is precisely as a consequence of the request to understand such differences as secondary that many women have denied an allegiance to feminism.

We have dwelt at length on Chodorow because of the great influence her work has enjoyed. But she is not the only recent feminist social theorist who has constructed a quasi-metanarrative around a putatively cross-cultural female-associated activity. On the contrary, theorists like Ann Ferguson and Nancy Folbre,

Nancy Hartsock, and Catharine MacKinnon have built similar theories around notions of sex-affective production, reproduction, and sexuality, respectively.[14] Each claims to have identified a basic kind of human practice found in all societies which has cross-cultural explanatory power. In each case, the practice in question is associated with a biological or quasi-biological need and is construed as functionally necessary to the reproduction of society. It is not the sort of thing, then, whose historical origins need be investigated.

The difficulty here is that categories like sexuality, mothering, reproduction, and sex-affective production group together phenomena which are not necessarily conjoined in all societies while separating off from one another phenomena which are not necessarily separated. As a matter of fact, it is doubtful whether these categories have any determinate cross-cultural content. Thus, for a theorist to use such categories to construct a universalistic social theory is to risk projecting the socially dominant conjunctions and dispersions of her own society onto others, thereby distorting important features of both. Social theorists would do better first to construct genealogies of the *categories* of sexuality, reproduction, and mothering before assuming their universal significance.

Since around 1980, many feminist scholars have come to abandon the project of grand social theory. They have stopped looking for *the* causes of sexism and have turned to more concrete inquiry with more limited aims. One reason for this shift is the growing legitimacy of feminist scholarship. The institutionalization of women's studies in the United States has meant a dramatic increase in the size of the community of feminist inquirers, a much greater division of scholarly labor, and a large and growing fund of concrete information. As a result, feminist scholars have come to regard their enterprise more collectively, more like a puzzle whose various pieces are being filled in by many different people than like a construction to be completed by a single grand theoretical stroke. In short, feminist scholarship has attained its maturity.

Even in this phase, however, traces of youthful quasi-metanarratives remain. Some theorists who have ceased looking for *the* causes of sexism still rely on essentialist categories such as gender identity. This is especially true of those scholars who have sought to develop gynocentric alternatives to mainstream androcentric perspectives but who have not fully abandoned the universalist pretensions of the latter.

Consider, as an example, the work of Carol Gilligan. Unlike most of the theorists we have considered so far, Gilligan has not sought to explain the origins or nature of cross-cultural sexism. Rather, she set herself the more limited task of exposing and redressing androcentric bias in the model of moral development of psychologist Lawrence Kohlberg. Thus, she argued that it is illegitimate to evaluate the moral development of women and girls by reference to a standard drawn exclusively from the experience of men and boys. She proposed to examine women's moral discourse on its own terms in order to uncover its immanent standards of adequacy.[15]

Gilligan's work has been rightly regarded as important and innovative. It challenged mainstream psychology's persistent occlusion of women's lives and experiences and its insistent but false claims to universality. Yet, insofar as Gilligan's challenge involved the construction of an alternative feminine model of moral development, her position was ambiguous. On the one hand, by providing a counterexample to Kohlberg's model, she cast doubt on the possibility of any single, universalist developmental schema. On the other hand, by constructing a female countermodel, she invited the same charge of false generalization she had herself raised against Kohlberg, although now from other perspectives such as class, sexual orientation, race, and ethnicity. Gilligan's disclaimers notwithstanding,[16] to the extent that she described women's moral development in terms of *a* different voice; to the extent that she did not specify which women, under which specific historical circumstances have spoken with the voice in question; and to the extent that she grounded her analysis in the explicitly cross-cultural framework of Nancy Chodorow, her model remained essentialist. It perpetuated in a newer, more localized fashion traces of previous more grandiose quasi-metanarratives.

Thus, vestiges of essentialism have continued to plague feminist scholarship, even despite the decline of grand theorizing. In many cases, including Gilligan's, this represents the continuing subterranean influence of those very mainstream modes of thought and inquiry with which feminists have wished to break.

On the other hand, the practice of feminist politics in the 1980s has generated a new set of pressures which have worked against metanarratives. In recent years, poor and working-class women, women of color, and lesbians have finally won a wider hearing for their objections to feminist theories which fail to illuminate their lives and address their problems. They have exposed the earlier quasi-metanarratives, with their assumptions of universal female dependence and confinement to the domestic sphere, as false extrapolations from the experience of the white, middle-class, heterosexual women who dominated the beginnings of the second wave. For example, writers like Bell Hooks, Gloria Joseph, Audre Lord, Maria Lugones, and Elizabeth Spelman have unmasked the implicit reference to white Anglo women in many classic feminist texts. Likewise, Adrienne Rich and Marilyn Frye have exposed the heterosexist bias of much mainstream feminist theory.[17] Thus, as the class, sexual, racial, and ethnic awareness of the movement has altered, so has the preferred conception of theory. It has become clear that quasi-metanarratives hamper rather than promote sisterhood, since they elide differences among women and among the forms of sexism to which different women are differentially subject. Likewise, it is increasingly apparent that such theories hinder alliances with other progressive movements, since they tend to occlude axes of domination other than gender. In sum, there is growing interest among feminists in modes of theorizing which are attentive to differences and to cultural and historical specificity.

In general, then, feminist scholarship of the 1980s evinces some conflicting tendencies. On the one hand, there is decreasing interest in grand social theories as scholarship has become more localized, issue-oriented, and explicitly fallibilistic. On the other hand, essentialist vestiges persist in the continued use of ahistorical categories like gender identity without reflection as to how, when, and why such categories originated and were modified over time. This tension is symptomatically expressed in the current fascination, on the part of U.S. feminists, with French psychoanalytic feminisms: The latter propositionally decry essentialism even as they performatively enact it.[18] More generally, feminist scholarship has remained insufficiently attentive to the *theoretical* prerequisites of dealing with diversity, despite widespread commitment to accepting it politically.

By criticizing lingering essentialism in contemporary feminist theory, we hope to encourage such theory to become more consistently postmodern. This is not, however, to recommend merely any form of postmodernism. On the contrary, as we have shown, the version developed by Jean-François Lyotard offers a weak and inadequate conception of social criticism without philosophy. It rules out genres of criticism, such as large historical narrative and historically situated social theory, which feminists rightly regard as indispensable. But it does not follow from Lyotard's shortcomings that criticism without philosophy is in principle incompatible with criticism with social force. Rather, as we argue next, a robust postmodern-feminist paradigm of social criticism without philosophy is possible.

TOWARD A POSTMODERN FEMINISM

How can we combine a postmodernist incredulity toward metanarratives with the social-critical power of feminism? How can we conceive a version of criticism without philosophy which is robust enough to handle the tough job of analyzing sexism in all its endless variety and monotonous similarity?

A first step is to recognize, contra Lyotard, that postmodern critique need forswear neither large historical narratives nor analyses of societal macrostructures. This point is important for feminists, since sexism has a long history and is deeply and pervasively embedded in contemporary societies. Thus, postmodern feminists need not abandon the large theoretical tools needed to address large political problems.

There is nothing self-contradictory in the idea of a postmodern theory.

However, if postmodern-feminist critique must remain theoretical, not just any kind of theory will do. Rather, theory here would be explicitly historical, attuned to the cultural specificity of different societies and periods and to that of different groups within societies and periods. Thus, the categories of postmodern-feminist theory would be inflected by temporality, with historically specific institutional categories like the modern, restricted, male-headed, nuclear family taking precedence over ahistorical, functionalist categories like reproduction and mothering. Where categories of the latter sort were not eschewed altogether, they would be genealogized, that is, framed by a historical narrative and rendered temporally and culturally specific.

Moreover, postmodern-feminist theory would be nonuniversalist. When its focus became cross-cultural or transepochal, its mode of attention would be comparativist rather than universalizing, attuned to changes and contrasts instead of to covering laws. Finally, postmodern-feminist theory would dispense with the idea of a subject of history. It would replace unitary notions of woman and feminine gender identity with plural and complexly constructed conceptions of social identity, treating gender as one relevant strand among others, attending also to class, race, ethnicity, age, and sexual orientation.

In general, postmodern-feminist theory would be pragmatic and fallibilistic. It would tailor its methods and categories to the specific task at hand, using multiple categories when appropriate and forswearing the metaphysical comfort of a single feminist method or feminist epistemology. In short, this theory would look more like a tapestry composed of threads of many different hues than one woven in a single color.

The most important advantage of this sort of theory would be its usefulness for contemporary feminist political practice. Such practice is increasingly a matter of alliances rather than one of unity around a universally shared interest or identity. It recognizes that the diversity of women's needs and experiences means that no single solution, on issues like child care, social security, and housing, can be adequate for all.

Thus, the underlying premise of this practice is that, while some women share some common interests and face some common enemies, such commonalities are by no means universal; rather, they are interlaced with differences, even with conflicts. This, then, is a practice made up of a patchwork of overlapping alliances, not one circumscribable by an essential definition. One might best speak of it in the plural as the practice of feminisms. In a sense, this practice is in advance of much contemporary feminist theory. It is already implicitly postmodern. It would find its most appropriate and useful theoretical expression in a postmodern-feminist form of critical inquiry. Such inquiry would be the theoretical counterpart of a broader, richer, more complex, and multilayered feminist solidarity, the sort of solidarity which is essential for overcoming the oppression of women in its "endless variety and monotonous similarity."

NOTES

1. Exceptions are Jane Flax, "Gender as a Social Problem: In and For Feminist Theory," *American Studies/Amerika Studien*, June 1986 [. . .]; Sandra Harding, *The Science Question in Feminism* (Ithaca, NY: Cornell University Press, 1986) and "The Instability of the Analytical Categories of Feminist Theory," *Signs: Journal of Women in Culture and Society*, Vol. 11, No. 4, 1986, pp. 645–664; Donna Haraway, "A Manifesto for Cyborgs: Science, Technology, and Socialist Feminism in the 1980s," *Socialist Review*, No. 80, 1983, pp. 65–107; Alice A. Jardine, *Gynesis: Configurations of Women and Modernity* (Ithaca, NY: Cornell University Press, 1985); Jean-François Lyotard, "Some of the Things at Stake in Women's Struggles," trans. Deborah J. Clarke, Winifred Woodhull, and John Mowitt, *Sub-Stance*, No. 20, 1978; Craig Owens, "The Discourse of Others: Feminists and Postmodernism," *The Anti-Aesthetic: Essays on Postmodern Culture*, ed. Hal Foster (Port Townsend, WA: Bay Press, 1983).

2. Jean-François Lyotard, *The Postmodern Condition: A Report on Knowledge*, trans. G. Bennington and B. Massumi (Minneapolis: University of Minnesota Press, 1984).

3. Ibid. Cf. Jean-François Lyotard and Jean-Loup Thebaud, *Just Gaming* (Minneapolis: University of Minnesota Press, 1987); also Jean-François Lyotard, "The

Differend," *Diacritics*, Fall 1984, trans. Georges Van Den Abbeele, pp. 4–14.

4. See, for example, Michel Foucault, *Discipline and Punish: The Birth of the Prison*, trans. Alan Sheridan (New York: Vintage Books, 1979).

5. Michael Walzer, *Spheres of Justice: A Defense of Pluralism and Equality* (New York: Basic Books, 1983).

6. It should be noted that, for Lyotard, the choice of philosophy as a starting point is itself determined by a metapolitical commitment, namely, to antitotalitarianism. He assumes erroneously, in our view, that totalizing social and political theory necessarily eventuates in totalitarian societies. Thus, the "practical intent" that subtends Lyotard's privileging of philosophy (and which is in turn attenuated by the latter) is anti-Marxism. Whether it should also be characterized as neoliberalism is a question too complicated to be explored here.

7. See, for example, the essays in *Discovering Reality: Feminist Perspectives on Epistemology, Metaphysics, Methodology, and Philosophy of Science*, ed. Sandra Harding and Merrill B. Hintikka (Dordrecht, Holland: D. Reidel, 1983).

8. Shulamith Firestone, *The Dialectic of Sex* (New York: Bantam, 1970).

9. Gayle Rubin, "The Traffic in Women," *Toward an Anthropology of Women*, ed. Rayna R. Reiter, (New York: Monthly Review Press, 1975), p. 160.

10. Michelle Zimbalist Rosaldo, "Woman, Culture, and Society: A Theoretical Overview," *Woman, Culture, and Society*, ed. Michelle Zimbalist Rosaldo and Louise Lamphere (Stanford: Stanford University Press, 1974), pp. 17–42.

11. These and related problems were soon apparent to many of the domestic/public theorists themselves. See Rosaldo's self-criticism, "The Use and Abuse of Anthropology: Reflections on Feminism and Cross-cultural Understanding," *Signs: Journal of Women in Culture and Society*, Vol. 5, No. 3, 1980, pp. 389–417. A more recent discussion, which points out the circularity of the theory, appears in Sylvia J. Yanagisako and Jane F. Collier, "Toward a Unified Analysis of Gender and Kinship," *Gender and Kinship: Essays Toward a Unified Analysis*, ed. Jane Fishburne Collier and Sylvia Junko Yanagisako, (Stanford: Stanford University Press, 1987).

12. Nancy Chodorow, *The Reproduction of Mothering: Psychoanalysis and the Sociology of Gender* (Berkeley: University of California Press, 1978).

13. A similar ambiguity attends Chodorow's discussion of the family. In response to critics who object that

her psychoanalytic emphasis ignores social structures, Chodorow has rightly insisted that the family is itself a social structure, one frequently slighted in social explanations. Yet, she generally does not discuss families as historically specific social institutions whose specific relations with other institutions can be analyzed. Rather, she tends to invoke the family in a very abstract and general sense defined only as the locus of female mothering.

14. Ann Ferguson and Nancy Folbre, "The Unhappy Marriage of Patriarchy and Capitalism," *Women and Revolution*, ed. Lydia Sargent (Boston: South End Press, 1981), pp. 313–338; Nancy Hartsock, *Money, Sex, and Power: Toward a Feminist Historical Materialism* (New York: Longman, 1983); Catharine A. MacKinnon, "Feminism, Marxism, Method, and the State: An Agenda for Theory," *Signs: Journal of Women in Culture and Society*, Vol. 7, No. 3, Spring 1982, pp. 515–544.

15. Carol Gilligan, *In a Different Voice: Psychological Theory and Women's Development* (Cambridge, MA: Harvard University Press, 1983).

16. Cf. Ibid., p. 2.

17. Marilyn Frye, *The Politics of Reality: Essays in Feminist Theory* (Trumansburg, NY: The Crossing Press, 1983); Bell Hooks, *Feminist Theory from Margin to Center* (Boston: South End Press, 1984); Gloria Joseph, "The Incompatible Menage à Trois: Marxism, Feminism and Racism," *Women and Revolution*, ed. Lydia Sargent (Boston: South End Press, 1981), pp. 91–107; Audre Lord, "An Open Letter to Mary Daly," *This Bridge Called My Back: Writings by Radical Women of Color*, ed. Cherríe Moraga and Gloria Anzaldúa (Watertown, MA: Persephone Press, 1981), pp. 94–97; Maria C. Lugones and Elizabeth V. Spelman, "Have We Got a Theory for You! Feminist Theory, Cultural Imperialism and the Demand for the Woman's Voice," *Hypatia, Women's Studies International Forum*, Vol. 6, No. 6, 1983, pp. 578–581; Adrienne Rich, "Compulsory Heterosexuality and Lesbian Existence," *Signs: Journal of Women in Culture and Society*, Vol. 5, No. 4, Summer 1980, pp. 631–660; Elizabeth Spelman, "Theories of Race and Gender: The Erasure of Black Women," *Quest*, Vol. 5, No. 4, 1980/81, pp. 36–62.

18. See, for example, Hélène Cixous, "The Laugh of the Medusa," trans. Keith Cohen and Paula Cohen, *New French Feminisms*, ed. Elaine Marks and Isabelle de Courtivron (New York: Schocken Books, 1981), pp. 245–261; Hélène Cixous and Catherine Clément, *The Newly Born Woman*, trans. Betsy Wing (Minneapolis: University of Minnesota Press, 1986); Luce Irigaray, *Speculum of the Other Woman* (Ithaca, NY: Cornell University Press, 1985) and *This Sex Which Is Not One* (Ithaca, NY: Cornell University Press, 1985); Julia Kristeva, *Desire in Language: A Semiotic Approach to Literature and Art*, ed. Leon S. Roudiez (New York: Columbia University Press, 1980) and "Women's Time," trans. Alice Jardine and Harry Blake, *Signs: Journal of Women in Culture and Society* Vol. 7, No. 1, Autumn 1981, pp. 13–35. See also the critical discussions by Ann Rosalind Jones, "Writing the Body: Toward an Understanding of l'Ecriture Féminine," *The New Feminist Criticism: Essays on Women, Literature and Theory*, ed. Elaine Showalter (New York: Pantheon Books, 1985), and Toril Moi, *Sexual/Textual Politics: Feminist Literary Theory* (London: Methuen, 1985).

Study Questions

1. According to Fraser and Nicholson, postmodernism springs from fairly arcane philosophical concerns. What are those concerns?

2. In its most extreme form, postmodernism seems to preclude "big theory" of any kind. Why would this be of concern to feminists?

3. Fraser and Nicholson write, "A postmodern reflection on feminist theory reveals disabling vestiges of essentialism." What does this mean? Examples of feminist theory cited as displaying such vestiges are the work of Catharine MacKinnon and Carol Gilligan. Do you agree with the authors' assessment of their work?

4. What connection do Fraser and Nicholson draw between the criticisms of mainstream feminist theory made by "poor and working-class women, women of color, and lesbians" and postmodernism?

5. According to Fraser and Nicholson, what characterizes postmodern feminist criticism and why is it desirable?

Judith Butler

From *Gender Trouble*

SUBJECTS OF SEX/GENDER/DESIRE

One is not born a woman, but rather becomes one.
—Simone de Beauvoir

Strictly speaking, "women" cannot be said to exist.
—Julia Kristeva

Woman does not have a sex.
—Luce Irigaray

The deployment of sexuality . . . established this notion of sex.
—Michel Foucault

The category of sex is the political category that founds society as heterosexual.
—Monique Wittig

i. *"Women" as the Subject of Feminism*

For the most part, feminist theory has assumed that there is some existing identity, understood through the category of women, who not only initiates feminist interests and goals within discourse, but constitutes the subject for whom political representation is pursued. But *politics* and *representation* are controversial terms. On the one hand, *representation* serves as the operative term within a political process that seeks to extend visibility and legitimacy to women as political subjects; on the other hand, representation is the normative function of a language which is said either to reveal or to distort what is assumed to be true about the category of women. For feminist theory, the development of a language that fully or adequately represents women has seemed necessary to foster the political visibility of women. This has seemed obviously important considering the pervasive cultural condition in which women's lives were either misrepresented or not represented at all.

Recently, this prevailing conception of the relation between feminist theory and politics has come under challenge from within feminist discourse. The very subject of women is no longer understood in stable or abiding terms. There is a great deal of material that not only questions the viability of "the subject" as the ultimate candidate for representation or, indeed, liberation, but there is very little agreement after all on what it is that constitutes, or ought to constitute, the category of women. The domains of political and linguistic "representation" set out in advance the criterion by which subjects themselves are formed, with the result that representation is extended only to what can be acknowledged as a subject. In other words, the qualifications for being a subject must first be met before representation can be extended.

Foucault points out that juridical systems of power *produce* the subjects they subsequently come to represent.[1] Juridical notions of power appear to regulate

From *Gender Trouble* (New York: Routledge/Taylor & Francis Books, Inc., 1990). Reprinted with permission. Notes have been renumbered and edited.

political life in purely negative terms—that is, through the limitation, prohibition, regulation, control and even "protection" of individuals related to that political structure through the contingent and retractable operation of choice. But the subjects regulated by such structures are, by virtue of being subjected to them, formed, defined, and reproduced in accordance with the requirements of those structures. If this analysis is right, then the juridical formation of language and politics that represents women as "the subject" of feminism is itself a discursive formation and effect of a given version of representational politics. And the feminist subject turns out to be discursively constituted by the very political system that is supposed to facilitate its emancipation. This becomes politically problematic if that system can be shown to produce gendered subjects along a differential axis of domination or to produce subjects who are presumed to be masculine. In such cases, an uncritical appeal to such a system for the emancipation of "women" will be clearly self-defeating.

The question of "the subject" is crucial for politics, and for feminist politics in particular, because juridical subjects are invariably produced through certain exclusionary practices that do not "show" once the juridical structure of politics has been established. In other words, the political construction of the subject proceeds with certain legitimating and exclusionary aims, and these political operations are effectively concealed and naturalized by a political analysis that takes juridical structures as their foundation. Juridical power inevitably "produces" what it claims merely to represent; hence, politics must be concerned with this dual function of power: the juridical and the productive. In effect, the law produces and then conceals the notion of "a subject before the law"[2] in order to invoke that discursive formation as a naturalized foundational premise that subsequently legitimates that law's own regulatory hegemony. It is not enough to inquire into how women might become more fully represented in language and politics. Feminist critique ought also to understand how the category of "women," the subject of feminism, is produced and restrained by the very structures of power through which emancipation is sought.

Indeed, the question of women as the subject of feminism raises the possibility that there may not be a subject who stands "before" the law, awaiting representation in or by the law. Perhaps the subject, as well as the invocation of a temporal "before," is constituted by the law as the fictive foundation of its own claim to legitimacy. The prevailing assumption of the ontological integrity of the subject before the law might be understood as the contemporary trace of the state of nature hypothesis, that foundationalist fable constitutive of the juridical structures of classical liberalism. The performative invocation of a nonhistorical "before" becomes the foundational premise that guarantees a presocial ontology of persons who freely consent to be governed and, thereby, constitute the legitimacy of the social contract.

Apart from the foundationalist fictions that support the notion of the subject, however, there is the political problem that feminism encounters in the assumption that the term *women* denotes a common identity. Rather than a stable signifier that commands the assent of those whom it purports to describe and represent, *women*, even in the plural, has become a troublesome term, a site of contest, a cause for anxiety. As Denise Riley's title suggests, *Am I That Name?* is a question produced by the very possibility of the name's multiple significations.[3] If one "is" a woman, that is surely not all one is; the term fails to be exhaustive, not because a pregendered "person" transcends the specific paraphernalia of its gender, but because gender is not always constituted coherently or consistently in different historical contexts, and because gender intersects with racial, class, ethnic, sexual, and regional modalities of discursively constituted identities. As a result, it becomes impossible to separate out "gender" from the political and cultural intersections in which it is invariably produced and maintained.

The political assumption that there must be a universal basis for feminism, one which must be found in an identity assumed to exist cross-culturally, often accompanies the notion that the oppression of women has some singular form discernible in the universal or hegemonic structure of patriarchy or masculine domination. The notion of a universal patriarchy has been widely criticized in recent years for its failure to account for the workings of gender oppression in the concrete cultural contexts in which it exists. Where those various contexts have been consulted within such theories, it has been to find "examples" or "illustrations" of a universal principle that is assumed from the start. That form of feminist theorizing has come under criticism for its efforts to colonize and appropriate non-Western cultures to support highly Western notions of oppression, but because they tend as well to construct a "Third World" or even an "Orient" in which gender oppression is subtly explained as symptomatic of an essential, non-Western barbarism. The urgency of feminism to establish a universal status for patriarchy in order to strengthen the appearance of feminism's own claims to be representative has occasionally motivated the shortcut to a categorial or fictive universality of the structure of domination, held to produce women's common subjugated experience.

Although the claim of universal patriarchy no longer enjoys the kind of credibility it once did, the notion of a generally shared conception of "women," the corollary to that framework, has been much more difficult to displace. Certainly, there have been plenty of debates: Is there some commonality among "women" that preexists their oppression, or do "women" have a bond by virtue of their oppression alone? Is there a specificity to women's cultures that is independent of their subordination by hegemonic, masculinist cultures? Are the specificity and integrity of women's cultural or linguistic practices always specified against and, hence, within the terms of some more dominant cultural formation? If there is a region of the "specifically feminine," one that is both differentiated from the masculine as such and recognizable in its difference by an unmarked and, hence, presumed universality of "women"? The masculine/feminine binary constitutes not only the exclusive framework in which that specificity can be recognized, but in every other way the "specificity" of the feminine is once again fully decontextualized and separated off analytically and politically from the constitution of class, race, ethnicity, and other axes of power relations that both constitute "identity" and make the singular notion of identity a misnomer.[4]

My suggestion is that the presumed universality and unity of the subject of feminism is effectively undermined by the constraints of the representational discourse in which it functions. Indeed, the premature insistence on a stable subject of feminism, understood as a seamless category of women, inevitably generates multiple refusals to accept the category. These domains of exclusion reveal the coercive and regulatory consequences of that construction, even when the construction has been elaborated for emancipatory purposes. Indeed, the fragmentation within feminism and the paradoxical opposition to feminism from "women" whom feminism claims to represent suggest the necessary limits of identity politics. The suggestion that feminism can seek wider representation for a subject that it itself constructs has the ironic consequence that feminist goals risk failure by refusing to take account of the constitutive powers of their own representational claims. This problem is not ameliorated through an appeal to the category of women for merely "strategic" purposes, for strategies always have meanings that exceed the purposes for which they are intended. In this case, exclusion itself might qualify as such an unintended yet consequential meaning. By conforming to a requirement of representational politics that feminism articulate a stable subject, feminism thus opens itself to charges of gross misrepresentation.

Obviously, the political task is not to refuse representational politics—as if we could. The juridical structures of language and politics constitute the contemporary field of power; hence, there is no position outside this field, but only a critical genealogy of its own legitimating practices. As such, the critical point of departure is *the historical present*, as Marx put it. And the task is to formulate within this constituted frame a critique of the categories of identity that contemporary juridical structures engender, naturalize, and immobilize.

Perhaps there is an opportunity at this juncture of cultural politics, a period that some would call "postfeminist," to reflect from within a feminist perspective on the injunction to construct a subject of feminism. Within feminist political practice, a radical rethinking of the ontological constructions of identity appears to be necessary in order to formulate a representational politics that might revive feminism on other grounds. On the other hand, it may be time to entertain a radical critique that seeks to free feminist theory from the necessity of having to construct a single or abiding ground which is invariably contested by those identity positions or anti–identity positions that it invariably excludes. Do the exclusionary practices that ground feminist theory in a notion of "women" as subject paradoxically undercut feminist goals to extend its claims to "representation"?[5]

Perhaps the problem is even more serious. Is the construction of the category of women as a coherent and stable subject an unwitting regulation and reification of gender relations? And is not such a reification precisely contrary to feminist aims? To what extent does the category of women achieve stability and coherence only in the context of the heterosexual matrix?[6] If a stable notion of gender no longer proves to be the foundational premise of feminist politics, perhaps a new sort of feminist politics is now desirable to contest the very reifications of gender and identity, one that will take the variable construction of identity as both a methodological and normative prerequisite, if not a political goal.

To trace the political operations that produce and conceal what qualifies as the juridical subject of feminism is precisely the task of *a feminist genealogy* of the category of women. In the course of this effort to question "women" as the subject of feminism, the unproblematic invocation of that category may prove to *preclude* the possibility of feminism as a representational politics. What sense does it make to extend representation to subjects who are constructed through the exclusion of those who fail to conform to unspoken normative requirements of the subject? What relations of domination and exclusion are inadvertently sustained when representation becomes the sole focus of politics? The identity of the feminist subject ought not to be the foundation of feminist politics, if the formation of the subject takes place within a field of power regularly buried through the assertion of that foundation. Perhaps, paradoxically, "representation" will be shown to make sense for feminism only when the subject of "women" is nowhere presumed.

ii. The Compulsory Order of Sex/Gender/Desire

Although the unproblematic unity of "women" is often invoked to construct a solidarity of identity, a split is introduced in the feminist subject by the distinction between sex and gender. Originally intended to dispute the biology-is-destiny formulation, the distinction between sex and gender serves the argument that whatever biological intractability sex appears to have, gender is culturally constructed: hence, gender is neither the causal result of sex nor as seemingly fixed as sex. The unity of the subject is thus already potentially contested by the distinction that permits of gender as a multiple interpretation of sex.

If gender is the cultural meanings that the sexed body assumes, then a gender cannot be said to follow from a sex in any one way. Taken to its logical limit, the sex/gender distinction suggests a radical discontinuity between sexed bodies and culturally constructed genders. Assuming for the moment the stability of binary sex, it does not follow that the construction of "men" will accrue exclusively to the bodies of males or that "women" will interpret only female bodies. Further, even if the sexes appear to be unproblematically binary in their morphology and constitution (which will become a question), there is no reason to assume that genders ought also to remain as two.[7] The presumption of a binary gender system implicitly retains the belief in a mimetic relation of gender to sex whereby gender mirrors sex or is otherwise restricted by it. When the constructed status of gender is theorized as radically independent of sex, gender itself becomes a free-floating artifice, with the consequence that *man* and *masculine* might just as easily signify a female body as a male one, and *woman* and *feminine* a male body as easily as a female one.

This radical splitting of the gendered subject poses yet another set of problems. Can we refer to a "given" sex or a "given" gender without first inquiring into how sex and/or gender is given, through what means? And what is "sex" anyway? Is it natural, anatomical, chromosomal, or hormonal, and how is a feminist critic to assess the scientific discourses which purport to establish such "facts" for us?[8] Does sex have a history?[9] Does each sex have a different history, or histories? Is there a history of how the duality of sex was established, a genealogy that might expose the binary options as a variable construction? Are the ostensibly natural facts of sex discursively produced by various scientific discourses in the service of other political and social interests? If the immutable character of sex is contested, perhaps this construct called "sex" is as culturally constructed as gender; indeed, perhaps it was always already gender, with the consequence that the distinction between sex and gender turns out to be no distinction at all.[10]

It would make no sense, then, to define gender as the cultural interpretation of sex, if sex itself is a gendered category. Gender ought not to be conceived merely as the cultural inscription of meaning on a pregiven sex (a juridical conception); gender must also designate the very apparatus of production whereby the sexes themselves are established. As a result, gender is not to culture as sex is to nature; gender is also the discursive/cultural means by which "sexed nature" or "a natural sex" is produced and established as "prediscursive," prior to culture, a politically neutral surface *on which* culture acts. . . . At this juncture it is already clear that one way the internal stability and binary frame for sex is effectively secured is by casting the duality of sex in a prediscursive domain. This production of sex *as* the prediscursive ought to be understood as the effect of the apparatus of cultural construction designated by *gender*. How, then, does gender need to be reformulated to encompass the power relations that produce the effect of a prediscursive sex and so conceal that very operation of discursive production? . . .

CONCLUSION: FROM PARODY TO POLITICS

I began with the speculative question of whether feminist politics could do without a "subject" in the category of women. At stake is not whether it still makes sense, strategically or transitionally, to refer to women in order to make representational claims in

their behalf. The feminist "we" is always and only a phantasmatic construction, one that has its purposes, but which denies the internal complexity and indeterminacy of the term and constitutes itself only through the exclusion of some part of the constituency that it simultaneously seeks to represent. The tenuous or phantasmatic status of the "we," however, is not cause for despair or, at least, it is not *only* cause for despair. The radical instability of the category sets into question the *foundational* restrictions on feminist political theorizing and opens up other configurations, not only of genders and bodies, but of politics itself.

The foundationalist reasoning of identity politics tends to assume that an identity must first be in place in order for political interests to be elaborated and, subsequently, political action to be taken. My argument is that there need not be a "doer behind the deed," but that the "doer" is variably constructed in and through the deed. This is not a return to an existential theory of the self as constituted through its acts, for the existential theory maintains a prediscursive structure for both the self and its acts. It is precisely the discursively variable construction of each in and through the other that has interested me here.

The question of locating "agency" is usually associated with the viability of the "subject," where the "subject" is understood to have some stable existence prior to the cultural field that it negotiates. Or, if the subject is culturally constructed, it is nevertheless vested with an agency, usually figured as the capacity for reflexive mediation, that remains intact regardless of its cultural embeddedness. On such a model, "culture" and "discourse" *mire* the subject, but do not constitute that subject. This move to qualify and enmire the preexisting subject has appeared necessary to establish a point of agency that is not fully *determined* by that culture and discourse. And yet, this kind of reasoning falsely presumes (a) agency can only be established through recourse to a prediscursive "I," even if that "I" is found in the midst of a discursive convergence, and (b) that to be *constituted* by discourse is to be *determined* by discourse, where determination forecloses the possibility of agency.

Even within the theories that maintain a highly qualified or situated subject, the subject still encounters its discursively constituted environment in an opposi-tional epistemological frame. The culturally enmired subject negotiates its constructions, even when those constructions are the very predicates of its own identity. In Beauvoir, for example, there is an "I" that does its gender, that becomes its gender, but that "I," invariably associated with its gender, is nevertheless a point of agency never fully identifiable with its gender. That *cogito* is never fully *of* the cultural world that it negotiates, no matter the narrowness of the ontological distance that separates that subject from its cultural predicates. The theories of feminist identity that elaborate predicates of color, sexuality, ethnicity, class, and able-bodiedness invariably close with an embarrassed "etc." at the end of the list. Through this horizontal trajectory of adjectives, these positions strive to encompass a situated subject, but invariably fail to be complete. This failure, however, is instructive: what political impetus is to be derived from the exasperated "etc." that so often occurs at the end of such lines? This is a sign of exhaustion as well as of the illimitable process of signification itself. It is the *supplément*, the excess that necessarily accompanies any effort to posit identity once and for all. This illimitable et cetera, however, offers itself as a new departure for feminist political theorizing.

If identity is asserted through a process of signification, if identity is always already signified, and yet continues to signify as it circulates within various interlocking discourses, then the question of agency is not to be answered through recourse to an "I" that preexists signification. In other words, the enabling conditions for an assertion of "I" are pro-vided by the structure of signification, the rules that regulate the legitimate and illegitimate invocation of that pronoun, the practices that establish the terms of intelligibility by which that pronoun can circulate. Language is not an *exterior medium or instrument* into which I pour a self and from which I glean a reflection of that self. The Hegelian model of self-recognition that has been appropriated by Marx, Lukacs, and a variety of contemporary liberatory dis-courses presupposes a potential adequation between the "I" that confronts its world, including its language,

as an object, and the "I" that finds itself as an object in that world. But the subject/object dichotomy, which here belongs to the tradition of Western epistem-ology, conditions the very problematic of identity that it seeks to solve.

What discursive tradition establishes the "I" and its "Other" in an epistemological confrontation that subsequently decides where and how questions of knowability and agency are to be determined? What kinds of agency are foreclosed through the positing of an epistemological subject precisely because the rules and practices that govern the invocation of that subject and regulate its agency in advance are ruled out as sites of analysis and critical intervention? That the epistemological point of departure is in no sense inevitable is naively and pervasively confirmed by the mundane operations of ordinary language—widely documented within anthropology—that regard the subject/object dichotomy as a strange and contingent, if not violent, philosophical imposition. The language of appropriation, instrumentality, and distanciation germane to the epistemological mode also belong to a strategy of domination that pits the "I" against an "Other" and, once that separation is effected, creates an artificial set of questions about the knowability and recoverability of that Other.

As part of the epistemological inheritance of con-temporary political discourses of identity, this binary opposition is a strategic move within a given set of signifying practices, one that establishes the "I" in and through this opposition and which reifies that opposition as a necessity, concealing the discursive apparatus by which the binary itself is constituted. The shift from an *epistemological* account of identity to one which locates the problematic within practices of *signification* permits an analysis that takes the epistemological mode itself as one possible and contingent signifying practice. Further, the question of *agency* is reformulated as a question of how signification and resignification work. In other words, what is signified as an identity is not signified at a given point in time after which it is simply there as an inert piece of entitative language. Clearly, identities *can* appear as so many inert substantives; indeed, epistemological models tend to take this appearance as their point of theoretical departure. However, the substantive "I" only appears as such through a signifying practice that seeks to conceal its own workings and to naturalize its effects. Further, to qualify as a substantive identity is an arduous task, for such appearances are rule-generated identities, ones which rely on the consistent and repeated invocation of rules that condition and restrict culturally intelligible practices of identity. Indeed, to understand identity as a *practice*, and as a signifying practice, is to understand culturally intelligible subjects as the resulting effects of a rule-bound discourse that inserts itself in the pervasive and mundane signifying acts of linguistic life. Abstractly considered, language refers to an open system of signs by which intelligibility is insistently created and contested. As historically specific organizations of language, discourses present themselves in the plural, coexisting within temporal frames, and instituting unpredictable and inadvertent convergences from which specific modalities of discursive possibilities are engendered.

As a process, signification harbors within itself what the epistemological discourse refers to as "agency." The rules that govern intelligible identity, i.e., that enable and restrict the intelligible assertion of an "I," rules that are partially structured along matrices of gender hierarchy and compulsory heterosexuality, operate through *repetition*. Indeed, when the subject is said to be constituted, that means simply that the subject is a consequence of certain rule-governed discourses that govern the intelligible invocation of identity. The subject is not *determined* by the rules through which it is generated because signification is *not a founding act, but rather a regulated process of repetition* that both conceals itself and enforces its rules precisely through the production of substantializing effects. In a sense, all signification takes place within the orbit of the compulsion to repeat; "agency," then, is to be located within the possibility of a variation on that repetition. If the rules governing signification not only restrict, but enable the assertion of alternative domains of cultural intelligibility, i.e., new possibilities for gender that contest the rigid codes of hierarchical binarisms, then it is only *within* the practices of repetitive signifying that a subversion of identity becomes possible. The injunction *to be* a given gender produces necessary failures, a variety of incoherent configurations that in their multiplicity exceed and defy the injunction by which they are generated. Further, the very injunction to be a given gender takes place through discursive routes: to be a good mother, to be a heterosexually desirable object, to be a fit worker, in sum, to signify a multiplicity of guarantees in response to a variety of different demands all at once. The coexistence or convergence of such discursive injunctions produces the possibility of a complex reconfiguration and redeployment; it is not a transcendental subject who enables action in the midst of such a convergence. There is no self that is prior to the convergence or who maintains "integrity" prior to its entrance into this conflicted cultural field. There is only a taking up of the tools where they lie, where the very "taking up" is enabled by the tool lying there.

What constitutes a subversive repetition within signifying practices of gender? I have argued ("I" deploy the grammar that governs the genre of the philosophical conclusion, but note that it is the grammar itself that deploys and enables this "I," even as the "I" that insists itself here repeats, redeploys, and—as the critics will determine—contests the philosophical grammar by which it is both enabled and restricted) that, for instance, within the sex/gender distinction, sex poses as "the real" and the "factic," the material or corporeal ground upon which gender operates as an act of cultural *inscription*. And yet gender is not written on the body as the torturing instrument of writing in Kafka's "In the Penal Colony" inscribes itself unintelligibly on the flesh of the accused. The question is not: what meaning does that inscription carry within it, but what cultural apparatus arranges this meeting between instrument and body, what interventions into this ritualistic repetition are possible? The "real" and the "sexually factic" are phantasmatic constructions—illusions of substance—that bodies are compelled to approximate, but never can. What, then, enables the exposure of the rift between the phantasmatic and the real whereby the real admits itself as phantasmatic? Does this offer the possibility for a repetition that is not fully constrained by the injunction to reconsolidate naturalized identities? Just as bodily surfaces are enacted *as* the natural, so these surfaces can become the site of a dissonant and denaturalized performance that reveals the performative status of the natural itself.

Practices of parody can serve to reengage and reconsolidate the very distinction between a privileged and naturalized gender configuration and one that appears as derived, phantasmatic, and mimetic— a failed copy, as it were. And surely parody has been used to further a politics of despair, one which affirms a seemingly inevitable exclusion of marginal genders from the territory of the natural and the real. And yet this failure to become "real" and to embody "the natural" is, I would argue, a constitutive failure of all gender enactments for the very reason that these ontological locales are fundamentally uninhabitable. Hence, there is a subversive laughter in the pastiche-effect of parodic practices in which the original, the authentic, and the real are themselves constituted as effects. The loss of gender norms would have the effect of proliferating gender configurations, destabilizing substantive identity, and depriving the naturalizing narratives of compulsory heterosexuality of their central protagonists: "man" and "woman." The parodic repetition of gender exposes as well the illusion of gender identity as an intractable depth and inner substance. As the effects of a subtle and politically enforced performativity, gender is an "act," as it were, that is open to splittings, self-parody, self-criticism, and those hyperbolic exhibitions of "the natural" that, in their very exaggeration, reveal its fundamentally phantasmatic status.

I have tried to suggest that the identity categories often presumed to be foundational to feminist politics, that is, deemed necessary in order to mobilize feminism as an identity politics, simultaneously work to limit and constrain in advance the very cultural possibilities that feminism is supposed to open up. The tacit constraints that produce culturally intelligible "sex" ought to be understood as generative political structures rather than naturalized foundations.

Paradoxically, the reconceptualization of identity as an *effect*, that is, as *produced* or *generated*, opens up possibilities of "agency" that are insidiously foreclosed by positions that take identity categories as foundational and fixed. For an identity to be an effect means that it is neither fatally determined nor fully artificial and arbitrary. That the *constituted* status of identity is misconstrued along these two conflicting lines suggests the ways in which the feminist discourse on cultural construction remains trapped within the unnecessary binarism of free will and determinism. Construction is not opposed to agency; it is the necessary scene of agency, the very terms in which agency is articulated and becomes culturally intelligible. The critical task for feminism is not to establish a point of view outside of constructed identities; that conceit is the construction of an epistemological model that would disavow its own cultural location and, hence, promote itself as a global subject, a position that deploys precisely the imperialist strategies that feminism ought to criticize. The critical task is, rather, to locate strategies of subversive repetition enabled by those constructions, to affirm the local possibilities of intervention through participating in precisely those practices of repetition that constitute identity and, therefore, present the immanent possibility of contesting them.

This theoretical inquiry has attempted to locate the political in the very signifying practices that establish, regulate, and deregulate identity. This effort, however, can only be accomplished through the introduction of a set of questions that extend the very notion of the political. How to disrupt the foundations that cover over alternative cultural configurations of gender? How to destabilize and render in their phantasmatic dimension the "premises" of identity politics?

This task has required a critical genealogy of the naturalization of sex and of bodies in general. It has also demanded a reconsideration of the figure of the body as mute, prior to culture, awaiting signification, a figure that cross-checks with the figure of the feminine, awaiting the inscription-as-incision of the masculine signifier for entrance into language and culture. From a political analysis of compulsory heterosexuality, it has been necessary to question the construction of sex as binary, as a hierarchical binary. From the point of view of gender as enacted, questions have emerged over the fixity of gender identity as an interior depth that is said to be externalized in various forms of "expression." The implicit construction of the primary heterosexual construction of desire is shown to persist even as it appears in the mode of primary bisexuality. Strategies of exclusion and hierarchy are also shown to persist in the formulation of the sex/gender distinction and its recourse to "sex" as the prediscursive as well as the priority of sexuality to culture and, in particular, the cultural construction of sexuality as the prediscursive. Finally, the epistemological paradigm that presumes the priority of the doer to the deed establishes a global and globalizing subject who disavows its own locality as well as the conditions for local intervention.

If taken as the grounds of feminist theory or politics, these "effects" of gender hierarchy and compulsory heterosexuality are not only misdescribed as foundations, but the signifying practices that enable this metaleptic misdescription remain outside the purview of a feminist critique of gender relations. To enter into the repetitive practices of this terrain of signification is not a choice, for the "I" that might enter is always already inside: there is no possibility of agency or reality outside of the discursive practices that give those terms the intelligibility that they have. The task is not whether to repeat, but how to repeat or, indeed, to repeat and, through a radical proliferation of gender, *to displace* the very gender norms that enable the repetition itself. There is no ontology of gender on which we might construct a politics, for gender ontologies always operate within established political contexts as normative injunctions, determining what qualifies as intelligible sex, invoking and consolidating the reproductive constraints on sexuality, setting the prescriptive requirements whereby sexed or gendered bodies come into cultural intelligibility. Ontology is, thus, not a foundation, but a normative injunction that operates insidiously by installing itself into political discourse as its necessary ground.

The deconstruction of identity is not the deconstruction of politics; rather, it establishes as political the very terms through which identity is articulated.

This kind of critique brings into question the foundationalist frame in which feminism as an identity politics has been articulated. The internal paradox of this foundationalism is that it presumes, fixes, and constrains the very "subjects" that it hopes to represent and liberate. The task here is not to celebrate each and every new possibility qua possibility, but to redescribe those possibilities that *already* exist, but which exist within cultural domains designated as culturally unintelligible and impossible. If identities were no longer fixed as the premises of a political syllogism, and politics no longer understood as a set of practices derived from the alleged interests that belong to a set of ready-made subjects, a new configuration of politics would surely emerge from the ruins of the old. Cultural configurations of sex and gender might then proliferate or, rather, their present proliferation might then become articulable within the discourses that establish intelligible cultural life, confounding the very binarism of sex, and exposing its fundamental unnaturalness. What other local strategies for engaging the "unnatural" might lead to the denaturalization of gender as such?

NOTES

1. See Michel Foucault, "Right of Death and Power over Life," in *The History of Sexuality, Volume 1, An Introduction*, trans. Robert Hurley (New York: Vintage, 1980), originally published as *Histoire de la sexualité 1: La volonté de savoir* (Paris: Gallimard, 1978). In that final chapter, Foucault discusses the relation between the juridical and productive law. His notion of the productivity of the law is clearly derived from Nietzsche, although not identical with Nietzsche's will-to-power. The use of Foucault's notion of productive power is not meant as a simpleminded "application" of Foucault to gender issues. . . .

2. References throughout this work to a subject before the law are extrapolations of Derrida's reading of Kafka's parable "Before the Law," in *Kafka and the Contemporary Critical Performance: Centenary Readings*, ed. Alan Udoff (Bloomington: Indiana University Press, 1987).

3. See Denise Riley, *Am I That Name?: Feminism and the Category of "Women" in History* (New York: Macmillan, 1988).

4. See Sandra Harding, "The Instability of the Analytical Categories of Feminist Theory," in *Sex and Scientific Inquiry*, eds. Sandra Harding and Jean F. O'Barr (Chicago: University of Chicago Press, 1987), pp. 283–302.

5. I am reminded of the ambiguity inherent in Nancy Cott's title, *The Grounding of Modern Feminism* (New Haven: Yale University Press, 1987). She argues that the early twentieth-century U.S. feminist movement sought to "ground" itself in a program that eventually "grounded" that movement. Her historical thesis implicitly raises the question of whether uncritically accepted foundations operate like the "return of the repressed"; based on exclusionary practices, the stable political identities that found political movements may invariably become threatened by the very instability that the foundationalist move creates.

6. I use the term *heterosexual matrix* . . . to designate that grid of cultural intelligibility through which bodies, genders, and desires are naturalized. I am drawing from Monique Wittig's notion of the "heterosexual contract" and, to a lesser extent, on Adrienne Rich's notion of "compulsory heterosexuality" to characterize a hegemonic discursive/epistemic model of gender intelligibility that assumes that for bodies to cohere and make sense there must be a stable sex expressed through a stable gender (masculine expresses male, feminine expresses female) that is oppositionally and hierarchically defined through the compulsory practice of heterosexuality.

7. For an interesting study of the *berdache* and multiple-gender arrangements in Native American cultures, see Walter L. Williams, *The Spirit and the Flesh: Sexual Diversity in American Indian Culture* (Boston: Beacon Press, 1988). See also, Sherry B. Ortner and Harriet Whitehead, eds., *Sexual Meanings: The Cultural Construction of Sexuality*, (New York: Cambridge University Press, 1981). For a politically sensitive and provocative analysis of the *berdache*, transsexuals, and the contingency of gender dichotomies, see Suzanne J. Kessler and Wendy McKenna, *Gender: An Ethnomethodological Approach* (Chicago: University of Chicago Press, 1978).

8. A great deal of feminist research has been conducted within the fields of biology and the history of science that assess the political interests inherent in the various discriminatory procedures that establish the scientific basis for sex. See Ruth Hubbard and Marian Lowe, eds., *Genes and Gender*, vols. 1 and 2, (New York: Gordian Press, 1978, 1979); the two issues on feminism and science of *Hypatia: A Journal of Feminist Philosophy*, vol. 2, No. 3, Fall 1987, and vol. 3, No. 1, Spring 1988, and especially The Biology and Gender Study Group, "The Importance of Feminist Critique for Contemporary Cell Biology" in this last issue (Spring 1988); Sandra Harding, *The Science Question in Feminism*, (Ithaca: Cornell University Press, 1986); Evelyn Fox-Keller, *Reflections on Gender and Science*, (New Haven: Yale University Press, 1984); Donna Haraway, "In the Beginning was the Word: The Genesis of Biological Theory," *Signs: Journal of Women in Culture and Society*, Vol. 6, No. 3, 1981; Donna Haraway, *Primate Visions* (New York: Routledge, 1989); Sandra Harding and Jean F. O'Barr, *Sex and Scientific Inquiry*, (Chicago: University of Chicago Press, 1987); Anne Fausto-Sterling, *Myths of Gender: Biological Theories About Women and Men* (New York: Norton, 1979).

9. Clearly Foucault's *History of Sexuality* offers one way to rethink the history of "sex" within a given modern Eurocentric context. For a more detailed consideration, see Thomas Lacquer and Catherine Gallagher, eds., *The Making of the Modern Body: Sexuality and Society in the 19th Century*, (Berkeley: University of California Press, 1987), originally published as an issue of *Representations*, No. 14, Spring 1986.

10. See my "Variations on Sex and Gender: Beauvoir, Wittig, Foucault," in *Feminism as Critique* eds. Seyla Benhabib and Drucilla Cornell (Basil Blackwell, dist. by University of Minnesota Press, 1987).

Study Questions

1. Drawing on Foucault, Butler says that "juridical systems of power *produce* the subjects they subsequently come to represent" (section i, paragraph 3). What systems are at issue here? In what sense are subjects *produced* by these systems?

2. Butler continues, "[T]he feminist subject turns out to be discursively constituted by the very political system that is supposed to facilitate its emancipation." What does she mean by this? Is this a problem? Why or why not?

3. According to Butler, supposing that *women* are the subjects on whose behalf feminism strives poses several further problems. Briefly explain two of them.

4. Butler criticizes the sex/gender distinction in section ii. What is her argument? And what is her conclusion, i.e., should we collapse the notions of sex and gender?

5. In the section entitled "Conclusion: From Parody to Politics," Butler is concerned not only with the cultural embeddedness of the subject, but also with the possibility of *agency* for embedded subjects. If there is no "I" outside of culture who freely expresses itself through the use of language and culture; but instead the "I" is constituted/produced in and by signifying practices, then is the "I" culturally determined? Is free agency impossible? What is Butler's answer to this question? How do *repetition* and *parody* play a role in her answer?

bell hooks

Postmodern Blackness

Postmodernist discourses are often exclusionary even as they call attention to, appropriate even, the experience of "difference" and "Otherness" to provide oppositional political meaning, legitimacy, and immediacy when they are accused of lacking concrete relevance. Very few African-American intellectuals have talked or written about postmodernism. At a dinner party I talked about trying to grapple with the significance of postmodernism for contemporary black experience. It was one of those social gatherings where only one other black person was present. The setting quickly became a field of contestation. I was told by the other black person that I was wasting my time, that "this stuff does not relate in any way to what's happening with black people." Speaking in the presence of a group of white onlookers, staring at us as though this encounter were staged for their benefit, we engaged in a passionate discussion about black experience. Apparently, no one sympathized with my insistence that racism is perpetuated when blackness is associated solely with concrete gut level experience conceived as either opposing or having no connection to abstract thinking and the production of critical theory. The idea that there is no meaningful connection between black experience and critical thinking about aesthetics or culture must be continually interrogated.

My defense of postmodernism and its relevance to black folks sounded good, but I worried that I lacked conviction, largely because I approach the subject cautiously and with suspicion.

Disturbed not so much by the "sense" of postmodernism but by the conventional language used when it is written or talked about and by those who speak it, I find myself on the outside of the discourse looking in. As a discursive practice it is dominated primarily by the voices of white male intellectuals and/or academic elites who speak to and about one another with coded familiarity. Reading and studying their writing to understand postmodernism in its multiple manifestations, I appreciate it but feel little inclination to ally myself with the academic hierarchy and exclusivity pervasive in the movement today.

Critical of most writing on postmodernism, I perhaps am more conscious of the way in which the focus on "Otherness and difference" that is often alluded to in these works seems to have little concrete impact as an analysis or standpoint that might change the nature and direction of postmodernist theory. Since much of this theory has been constructed in reaction to and against high modernism, there is seldom any mention of black experience or writings by black people in this work, specifically black women (though in more recent work one may see a reference to Cornel West, the black male scholar who has most engaged postmodernist discourse). Even if an aspect of black culture is the subject of postmodern critical writing, the works cited will usually be those of black men. A work that comes immediately to mind is Andrew Ross's chapter "Hip, and the Long Front of Color" in *No Respect: Intellectuals and Popular Culture*; while it is an interesting reading, it constructs black culture as though black women have had no role in black cultural production. At the end of Meaghan Morris' discussion of postmodernism in her collection of essays *The Pirate's Fiance: Feminism and Postmodernism*, she provides a bibliography of works by women, identifying them as important contributions to a discourse on postmodernism that offer new insight as well as challenging male theoretical hegemony. Even though many of the works do not directly address postmodernism, they address similar concerns. There are no references to works by black women.

The failure to recognize a critical black presence in the culture and in most scholarship and writing on postmodernism compels a black reader, particularly a black female reader, to interrogate her interest in a subject where those who discuss and write about it seem not to know black women exist or even to consider the possibility that we might be somewhere writing or saying something that should be listened to, or producing art that should be seen, heard, approached with intellectual seriousness. This is especially the case with works that go on and on about the way in which postmodernist discourse has opened up a theoretical terrain where "difference and Otherness" can be considered legitimate issues in the academy. Confronting both the absence of recognition of black female presence that much postmodernist theory re-inscribes and the resistance on the part of most black folks to hearing about real connection between postmodernism and black experience, I enter a discourse, a practice, where there may be no ready audience for my words, no clear listener, uncertain then, that my voice can or will be heard.

During the sixties, black power movement was influenced by perspectives that could easily be labeled modernist. Certainly many of the ways black folks addressed issues of identity conformed to a modernist universalizing agenda. There was little cri-

tique of patriarchy as a master narrative among black militants. Despite the fact that black power ideology reflected a modernist sensibility, these elements were soon rendered irrelevant as militant protest was stifled by a powerful, repressive postmodern state. The period directly after the black power movement was a time when major news magazines carried articles with cocky headlines like "Whatever Happened to Black America?" This response was an ironic reply to the aggressive, unmet demand by decentered, marginalized black subjects who had at least momentarily successfully demanded a hearing, who had made it possible for black liberation to be on the national political agenda. In the wake of the black power movement, after so many rebels were slaughtered and lost, many of these voices were silenced by a repressive state; others became inarticulate. It has become necessary to find new avenues to transmit the messages of black liberation struggle, new ways to talk about racism and other politics of domination. Radical postmodernist practice, most powerfully conceptualized as a "politics of difference," should incorporate the voices of displaced, marginalized, exploited, and oppressed black people. It is sadly ironic that the contemporary discourse which talks the most about heterogeneity, the decentered subject, declaring breakthroughs that allow recognition of Otherness, still directs its critical voice primarily to a specialized audience that shares a common language rooted in the very master narratives it claims to challenge. If radical postmodernist thinking is to have a transformative impact, then a critical break with the notion of "authority" as "mastery over" must not simply be a rhetorical device. It must be reflected in habits of being, including styles of writing as well as chosen subject matter. Third world nationals, elites, and white critics who passively absorb white supremacist thinking, and therefore never notice or look at black people on the streets or at their jobs, who render us invisible with their gaze in all areas of daily life, are not likely to produce liberatory theory that will challenge racist domination, or promote a breakdown in traditional ways of seeing and thinking about reality, ways of constructing aesthetic theory and practice. From a different standpoint, Robert Storr makes a similar critique in the global issue of *Art in America* when he asserts:

> To be sure, much postmodernist critical inquiry has centered precisely on the issues of "difference" and "Otherness." On the purely theoretical plane the exploration of these concepts has produced some important results, but in the absence of any sustained research into what artists of color and others outside the mainstream might be up to, such discussions become rootless instead of radical. Endless second guessing about the latent imperialism of intruding upon other cultures only compounded matters, preventing or excusing these theorists from investigating what black, Hispanic, Asian and Native American artists were actually doing.

Without adequate concrete knowledge of and contact with the non-white "Other," white theorists may move in discursive theoretical directions that are threatening and potentially disruptive of that critical practice which would support radical liberation struggle.

The postmodern critique of "identity," though relevant for renewed black liberation struggle, is often posed in ways that are problematic. Given a pervasive politic of white supremacy which seeks to prevent the formation of radical black subjectivity, we cannot cavalierly dismiss a concern with identity politics. Any critic exploring the radical potential of postmodernism as it relates to racial difference and racial domination would need to consider the implications of a critique of identity for oppressed groups. Many of us are struggling to find new strategies of resistance. We must engage decolonization as a critical practice if we are to have meaningful chances of survival even as we must simultaneously cope with the loss of political grounding which made radical activism more possible. I am thinking here about the postmodernist critique of essentialism as it pertains to the construction of "identity" as one example.

Postmodern theory that is not seeking to simply appropriate the experience of "Otherness" to enhance the discourse or to be radically chic should not separate the "politics of difference" from the politics of racism. To take racism seriously one must consider the plight of underclass people of color, a vast majority of whom are black. For African-Americans our collective condition prior to the advent of postmodernism and perhaps more tragically expressed under current postmodern conditions has been and is characterized by continued displacement, profound alienation, and despair. Writing about blacks and postmodernism, Cornel West describes our collective plight:

> There is increasing class division and differentiation, creating on the one hand a significant black middle-class, highly anxiety-ridden, insecure, willing to be co-opted and incorporated into the powers that be, concerned with racism to the degree that it poses contraints on upward social mobility; and, on the other, a vast and growing black underclass, an underclass that embodies a kind of walking nihilism of pervasive drug addiction, pervasive alcoholism, pervasive homicide, and an exponential rise in suicide. Now because of the deindustrialization, we also have a devastated black industrial working class. We are talking here about tremendous hopelessness.

This hopelessness creates longing for insight and strategies for change that can renew spirits and reconstruct grounds for collective black liberation struggle. The overall impact of postmodernism is that many other groups now share with black folks a sense of deep alienation, despair, uncertainty, loss of a sense of grounding even if it is not informed by shared circumstance. Radical postmodernism calls attention to those shared sensibilities which cross the boundaries of class, gender, race, etc., that could be fertile ground for the construction of empathy—ties that would promote recognition of common commitments, and serve as a base for solidarity and coalition.

Yearning is the word that best describes a common psychological state shared by many of us, cutting across boundaries of race, class, gender, and sexual practice. Specifically, in relation to the post-modernist deconstruction of "master" narratives, the yearning that wells in the hearts and minds of those whom such narratives have silenced is the longing for critical voice. It is no accident that "rap" has usurped the primary position of rhythm and blues music among young black folks as the most desired sound or that it began as a form of "testimony" for the underclass. It has enabled underclass black youth to develop a critical voice, as a group of young black men told me, a "common literacy." Rap projects a critical voice, explaining, demanding, urging. Working with this insight in his essay "Putting the Pop Back into Postmodernism," Lawrence Grossberg comments:

> The postmodern sensibility appropriates practices as boasts that announce their own—and consequently our own—existence, like a rap song boasting of the imaginary (or real—it makes no difference) accomplishments of the rapper. They offer forms of empowerment not only in the face of nihilism but precisely through the forms of nihilism itself: an empowering nihilism, a moment of positivity through the production and structuring of affective relations.

Considering that it is as subject one comes to voice, then the postmodernist focus on the critique of identity appears at first glance to threaten and close down the possibility that this discourse and practice will allow those who have suffered the crippling effects of colonization and domination to gain or regain a hearing. Even if this sense of threat and the fear it evokes are based on a misunderstanding of the postmodernist political project, they nevertheless shape responses. It never surprises me when black folks respond to the critique of essentialism, especially when it denies the validity of identity politics by saying, "Yeah, it's easy to give up identity, when you got one." Should we not be suspicious of postmodern critiques of the "subject" when they surface at a historical moment when many subjugated people feel themselves coming to voice for the first time? Though an apt and oftentimes appropriate comeback, it does not really intervene in the discourse in a way that alters and transforms.

Criticisms of directions in postmodern thinking should not obscure insights it may offer that open up our understanding of African-American experience. The critique of essentialism encouraged by postmodernist thought is useful for African-Americans concerned with reformulating outmoded notions of identity. We have too long had imposed upon us from both the outside and the inside a narrow, constricting notion of blackness. Postmodern critiques of essentialism which challenge notions of universality and static overdetermined identity within mass culture and mass consciousness can open up new possibilities for the construction of self and the assertion of agency.

Employing a critique of essentialism allows African-Americans to acknowledge the way in which class mobility has altered collective black experience so that racism does not necessarily have the same impact on our lives. Such a critique allows us to affirm multiple black identities, varied black experience. It also challenges colonial imperialist paradigms of black identity which represent blackness one-dimensionally in ways that reinforce and sustain white supremacy. This discourse created the idea of the "primitive" and promoted the notion of an "authentic" experience, seeing as "natural" those expressions of black life which conformed to a preexisting pattern or stereotype. Abandoning essentialist notions would be a serious challenge to racism. Contemporary African-American resistance struggle must be rooted in a process of decolonization that continually opposes re-inscribing notions of "authentic" black identity. This critique should not be made synonymous with a dismissal of the struggle of oppressed and exploited peoples to make ourselves subjects. Nor should it deny that in certain circumstances this experience affords us a privileged critical location from which to speak. This is not a reinscription of modernist master narratives of authority which privilege some voices by denying voice to others. Part of our struggle for radical black subjectivity is the quest to find ways to construct self and identity that are oppositional and liberatory. The unwillingness to critique essentialism on the part of many African-Americans is rooted in the fear that it will cause folks to lose sight of the specific history and experience of African-Americans and the unique sensibilities and culture that arise from that experience. An adequate response to this concern is to critique essentialism while emphasizing the significance of "the authority of experience." There is a radical difference between a repudiation of the idea that there is a black "essence" and recognition of the way black identity has been specifically constituted in the experience of exile and struggle.

When black folks critique essentialism, we are empowered to recognize multiple experiences of black identity that are the lived conditions which make diverse cultural productions possible. When this diversity is ignored, it is easy to see black folks as falling into two categories: nationalist or assimilationist, black-identified or white-identified. Coming to terms with the impact of postmodernism for black experience, particularly as it changes our sense of identity, means that we must and can rearticulate the basis for collective bonding. Given the various crises facing African-Americans (economic, spiritual, escalating racial violence, etc.), we are compelled by circumstance to reassess our relationship to popular culture and resistance struggle. Many of us are as reluctant to face this task as many non-black postmodern thinkers who focus theoretically on the issue of "difference" are to confront the issue of race and racism.

Music is the cultural product created by African-Americans that has most attracted postmodern theorists. It is rarely acknowledged that there is far greater censorship and restriction of other forms of cultural production by black folks—literary, critical writing, etc. Attempts on the part of editors and publishing houses to control and manipulate the representation of black culture, as well as the desire to promote the creation of products that will attract the widest audience, limit in a crippling and stifling way the kind of work many black folks feel we can do and still receive recognition. Using myself as an example, that creative writing I do which I consider to be most reflective of a postmodern oppositional sensibility, work that is abstract, fragmented, non-linear narrative, is constantly rejected by editors and publishers. It does not conform to the type of writing they think black women should be doing or the type of writing they believe will sell. Certainly I do not think I am the only black person engaged in forms of cultural production, especially experimental ones, who is constrained by the lack of an audience for certain kinds of work. It is important for postmodern thinkers and theorists to constitute themselves as an audience for such work. To do this they must assert power and privilege within the space of critical writing to open up the field so that it will be more inclusive. To change the exclusionary practice of postmodern critical discourse is to enact a postmodernism of resistance. Part of this intervention entails black intellectual participation in the discourse.

In his essay "Postmodernism and Black America," Cornel West suggests that black intellectuals "are marginal—usually languishing at the interface of Black and white cultures or thoroughly ensconced in Euro-American settings." He cannot see this group as potential producers of radical postmodernist thought. While I generally agree with this assessment, black intellectuals must proceed with the understanding that we are not condemned to the margins. The way we work and what we do can determine whether or not what we produce will be meaningful to a wider audience, one that includes all classes of black people. West suggests that black intellectuals lack "any organic link with most of Black life" and that this "diminishes their value to Black resistance." This statement bears traces of essentialism. Perhaps we need to focus more on those black intellectuals, however rare our presence, who do not feel this lack and whose work is primarily directed towards the enhancement of black critical consciousness and the strengthening of our collective capacity to engage in meaningful resistance struggle. Theoretical ideas and critical thinking need not be transmitted solely in written work or solely in the academy. While I work in a predominantly white institution, I remain intimately and passionately engaged with black community. It's not like I'm going to talk about writing and thinking about postmodernism with other academics and/or intellectuals and not discuss these ideas with underclass non-academic black folks who are family, friends, and comrades. Since I have not broken the ties that bind me to underclass poor black community, I have seen that knowledge, especially that which enhances daily life and strengthens our capacity to survive, can be shared. It means that critics, writers, and academics have to give the same critical attention to nurturing and cultivating our ties to black community that we give to writing articles, teaching, and lecturing. Here again I am really talking about cultivating habits of being that reinforce awareness that knowledge can be disseminated and shared on a number of fronts. The extent to which knowledge is made available, accessible, etc. depends on the nature of one's political commitments.

Postmodern culture with its decentered subject can be the space where ties are severed or it can provide the occasion for new and varied forms of bonding. To some extent, ruptures, surfaces, contextuality, and a host of other happenings create gaps that make space for oppositional practices which no longer require intellectuals to be confined by narrow separate spheres with no meaningful connection to the world of the everyday. Much postmodern engagement with culture emerges from the yearning to do intellectual work that connects with habits of being, forms of artistic expression, and aesthetics that inform the daily life of writers and scholars as well as a mass population. On the terrain of culture, one can participate in critical dialogue with the uneducated poor, the black underclass who are thinking about aesthetics. One can talk about what we are seeing, thinking, or listening to; a space is there for critical exchange. It's exciting to think, write, talk about, and create art that reflects passionate engagement with popular culture, because this may very well be "the" central future location of resistance struggle, a meeting place where new and radical happenings can occur.

Study Questions

1. At the beginning of this article, hooks challenges the idea that postmodernism has no "relevance to black folks," positing that such a suggestion perpetuates racism. What is her argument for this claim?

2. Hooks goes on to acknowledge reservations about postmodernism, but then asserts: "If radical postmodernist thinking is to have a transformative impact, then a critical break with the notion of 'authority' as 'mastery over' must not simply be a rhetorical device. It must be reflected in habits of being, including styles of writing as well as chosen subject matter" (paragraph 6). Explain this quotation.

3. Hooks also identifies as "problematic" the ways in which the postmodern critique of identity is often posed. What is her concern about how this critique is often posed? Hooks suggests that the postmodern critique of identity nonetheless can be of use to oppressed groups, and to African Americans in particular. Explain both hooks's reservations about this critique and what she sees as its potential usefulness to African Americans.

4. Ultimately, does hooks embrace or eschew postmodern thinking? Explain your answer.

Sharon Marcus

Fighting Bodies, Fighting Words: A Theory and Politics of Rape Prevention

Some recent arguments about the incompatibility of poststructuralist theory and feminist politics designate rape and the raped woman's body as symbols of the real. Mary E. Hawkesworth, in an article entitled "Knowers, Knowing, Known: Feminist Theory and Claims of Truth," defines two tendencies of what she calls "postmodern" thought—a conflation of reality and textuality, and an emphasis on the impossibility of ascertaining the meaning of texts. Toward the end of her essay she states:

> The undesirable consequences of the slide into relativism that results from too facile a conflation of world and text is particularly evident when feminist concerns are taken as a starting point. Rape, domestic violence, and sexual harassment . . . are not fictions or figurations that admit of the free play of signification. The victim's account of these experiences is not simply an arbitrary imposition of a purely fictive meaning on an otherwise meaningless reality. A victim's knowledge of the event may not be exhaustive; . . . But it would be premature to conclude from the incompleteness of the victim's account that all other accounts (the assailant's, defense attorney's, character witnesses' for the defendant) are equally valid or that there are no objective grounds on which to distinguish between truth and falsity in divergent interpretations.[1]

Hawkesworth makes three claims: that rape is real; that to be real means to be fixed, determinate, and transparent to understanding; and that feminist politics must understand rape as one of the real, clear facts of women's lives. As her argument unfolds it contradicts each of these claims. The subject of the second quoted sentence is "rape"; the subject of the third quoted sentence is "the victim's account of these experiences." This substitution of account for event implies the very inseparability of text and world which Hawkesworth had previously criticized in postmodern thought, and indeed leads her to reverse her characterization of postmodernism: where earlier in the piece postmodernism conflated the fictive and the real, here it problematically separates them because it considers a woman's account of rape "an arbitrary imposition of a purely fictive meaning on an otherwise meaningless reality." The subject of the paragraph shifts again in the fourth quoted sentence, this time to the rape trial, which Hawkesworth insists will adjudicate among competing accounts of the rape; she ends the paragraph with a barrage of legalistic terms—"the standards of evidence, criteria of relevance, paradigms of explanation and norms of truth" which, she holds, one can and must use to determine the truth value of rape accounts. Such a conclusion in

fact jettisons feminism's selective political focus on the raped woman, since "standards of evidence" and "norms of truth" derive their prestige from their claims to apply equally to all men and women, all points of view, and all situations. Hawkesworth's argument that the reality of rape must be the "starting point" of feminist politics thus leads her to espouse a supposedly apolitical system of objective judgment. Her climactic assertion that "there are some things that can be known" could be the summing-up of a rapist's defense as easily as that of his prosecution.

Hawkesworth intends to distinguish this empiricist, epistemological view of rape from the textual, postmodern view. Where she insists on rape's reality, she sees postmodernism insisting on rape's indeterminacy as an event, and hence on the impossibility of ascribing blame to a rapist and innocence to a victim.[2] Where she turns to the legal determination of blame, Michel Foucault, a theorist whom she associates with postmodernism, cautions against repressive measures which might stigmatize male sexuality and advocates instead making economic reparation to raped women.[3] Yet ultimately Hawkesworth adopts the same *perspective* on rape that her postmodern opponents do: in the eyes of all these thinkers, rape has always already occurred and women are always either already raped or already rapable. Hawkesworth believes that women can derive power from proving that they have been made powerless and from identifying the perpetrators of this victimization. Postmodernists take issue with the notions of law, action, knowledge, and identity which would enable a woman to label a man her rapist. But for both parties, when they think about rape, they inevitably see a raped woman.

Hawkesworth does not address this fundamental fit between her view of rape and the postmodern one; nor does she rebut the specific content of postmodern analyses of rape. Rather, she asserts the incompatibility of postmodern theories of language and reality with feminist political action against rape. This assertion actually contradicts one of feminism's most powerful contentions about rape—that rape is a question of language, interpretation, and subjectivity. Feminist thinkers have asked: Whose words count in a rape and a rape trial? Whose "no" can never mean "no"? How do rape trials condone men's misinterpretations of women's words? How do rape trials consolidate men's subjective accounts into objective "norms of truth" and deprive women's subjective accounts of cognitive value?[4] Feminists have also insisted on the importance of *naming* rape as violence and of collectively narrating stories of rape.[5] Though some of these theorists might explicitly assert that rape is real, their emphasis on *recounting* rape suggests that in their view actions and experiences cannot be said to exist in politically real and useful ways until they are perceptible and representable. A feminist politics which would fight rape cannot exist without developing a language about rape, nor, I will argue, without understanding rape to be a language. What founds these languages are neither real nor objective criteria, but political decisions to exclude certain interpretations and perspectives and to privilege others.

In this essay I propose that we understand rape as a language and use this insight to imagine women as neither already raped nor inherently rapable. I will argue against the political efficacy of seeing rape as the fixed reality of women's lives, against an identity politics which defines women by our violability, and for a shift of scene from rape and its aftermath to rape situations themselves and to rape *prevention*. Many current theories of rape present rape as an inevitable material fact of life and assume that a rapist's ability to physically overcome his target is the foundation of rape. Susan Brownmiller represents this view when she states in her influential 1975 book, *Against Our Will: Men, Women, and Rape*, that "in terms of human anatomy the possibility of forcible intercourse incontrovertibly exists. This single factor may have been sufficient to have caused the creation of a male ideology of rape. When men discovered that they could rape, they proceeded to do it."[6] Such a view takes violence as a self-explanatory first cause and endows it with an invulnerable and terrifying facticity which stymies our ability to challenge and demystify rape. To treat rape simply as one of what Hawkesworth calls "the realities that circumscribe women's lives" can mean to consider rape as terrifyingly unnameable and unrepresentable, a reality that lies beyond our grasp and which we can only experience as grasping and encircling us.[7] In its efforts to convey the horror and iniquity of rape, such a view often concurs with masculinist culture in its designation of rape as a fate worse than, or tantamount to, death; the apocalyptic tone which it adopts and the metaphysical status which it assigns to rape implies that rape can only be feared or legally repaired, not fought.

Feminist antirape literature, activism, and policy development on rape in the United States during the last two decades have increasingly concentrated on police procedures and legal definitions of rape. This focus can produce a sense of futility: rape itself seems to be taken for granted as an occurrence and only postrape events offer possible occasions for intervention. Although feminist drives to change the legal definition of rape, to increase the penalties for rape and to render the terms of a rape trial less prejudicial to the raped woman have publicized rape's seriousness as a crime, an almost exclusive insistence on equitable reparation and vindication in the courts has limited effectiveness for a politics of rape prevention. Quite literally, the rape has already occurred by the time a case comes to court; a verdict of guilty can in no way avert the rape itself, and no one has proven a direct link between increased penalties and convictions for a crime and a decreased incidence of that crime. The notorious racism and sexism of the United States police and legal systems often compromise the feminist goals of a rape trial. Interracial rape cases constitute a minority of rapes committed and rapes brought to trial, but when the rapist is white, exhibit significantly lower rates of conviction than intraracial rape cases, and much higher rates of conviction when the rapist is Afro-American. In both intra- and interracial rape trials, raped Afra-Americans often do not obtain convictions even in the face of overwhelming evidence of brutalization; raped white women have great difficulty in obtaining convictions against white rapists. In the relatively smaller percentage of cases where they have been raped by Afro-Americans, white women often obtain legal victories at the cost of juries' giving currency to racist prejudices and to patronizing ideologies of female protection. These biases fabricate and scapegoat a rapist of color and implicitly condone the exploitation and rape of women of color.[8] Finally, courtroom trials assert first and foremost their own legitimacy and power to judge events, and only grant power to the vindicated party on the condition that the court's power be acknowledged.

Attempts to stop rape through legal deterrence fundamentally choose to *persuade men* not to rape. They thus assume that men simply have the power to rape and concede this primary power to them, implying that at best men can secondarily be dissuaded from using this power by means of threatened punishment from a masculinized state or legal system. They do not envision strategies which will enable women to sabotage men's power to rape, which will empower women to take the ability to rape completely out of men's hands.

We can avoid these self-defeating pitfalls by regarding rape not as a fact to be accepted or opposed, tried or avenged, but as a process to be analyzed and undermined as it occurs. One way to achieve this is to focus on what actually happens during rape attempts and on differentiating as much as possible among various rape situations in order to develop the fullest range of rape prevention strategies.[9] Another way to refuse to recognize rape as the real fact of our lives is to treat it as a *linguistic* fact: to ask how the violence of rape is enabled by narratives, complexes and institutions which derive their strength not from outright, immutable, unbeatable force but rather from their power to structure our lives as imposing cultural scripts. To understand rape in this way is to understand it as subject to change.

The definition of rape as a linguistic fact can be taken several ways. One common conjunction of rape and language refers to the many images of rape which our culture churns out, representations which often transmit the ideological assumptions and contradictions of rape—women are rapable, women deserve rape/women provoke rape, women want rape, women are ashamed of being raped/women publicly lie about being raped. While these cultural productions can collude in and perpetuate rape in definite and complicated ways, the statement that rape is a linguistic fact should not be taken to mean that such linguistic forms actually rape women.

Another crucial, literal way to understand rape as a linguistic fact is to highlight the presence of speech in rape. Contrary to received wisdom, which imagines rape as a wordless, absolutely impersonal attack, most rapists take verbal initiatives with their targets in addition to deploying physical aggression. Many rapists initially engage their targets in friendly or threatening conversation; many speak a great deal during the rape and demand that the women whom they rape either talk to them or recite particular phrases. Internalized strictures on what can be spoken and on what is unspeakable—which restrict men and women differently—structure rape situations as much as physical inequalities do, particularly when a woman knows a rapist—the most prevalent rape situation.[10] Women's noncombative responses to rapists often derive as much from the self-defeating rules which govern polite, empathetic feminine conversation as they do from explicit physical fear.[11] To prevent rape, women must resist self-defeating notions of polite feminine speech as well as develop physical self-defense tactics.

A "continuum" theory of sexual violence links language and rape in a way that can be taken to mean that representations of rape, obscene remarks, threats and other forms of harassment should be considered equivalent to rape. Such a definition substitutes the remarks and threats which gesture toward a rape for the rape itself, and thus contradicts the very meaning of "continuum," which requires a temporal and logical distinction between the various stages of a rape attempt. In a "continuum" theory which makes one type of action, a verbal threat, immediately substitutable for another type of action, sexual assault, the time and space between these two actions collapse and once again, rape has always already occurred. Such verbal acts should be countered and censured for what they are—initiatives to set up a rape situation. To make them metaphors for rape itself, however, occludes the gap between the threat and the rape—the gap in which women can try to intervene, overpower and deflect the threatened action.[12]

Yet another way to analyze rape as a linguistic fact argues that rape is structured like a language, a language which shapes both the verbal *and* physical interactions of a woman and her would-be assailant. To say that rape is structured like a language can account both for rape's prevalence and its potential prevention. Language is a social structure of meanings which enables people to experience themselves as speaking, acting, and embodied subjects.[13] We can outline the language of rape in the United States along raced and gendered axes. The language of rape seeks to induce in white women an exclusive and erroneous fear of nonwhite men as potential rapists and legitimizes white men's sexual violence against all women as well as their retributive violence against nonwhite men in the name of protecting or avenging white women. At various historical moments this language has intensively designated Afra-Americans as targets of rape attempts—so much so that generations of Afro-Americans have developed definite languages of resistance to rape. Simultaneously or at other times, the language of rape may also address women of color as generic "women." The language of rape solicits women to position ourselves as endangered, violable, and fearful and invites men to position themselves as legitimately violent and entitled to women's sexual services. This language structures physical actions and responses as well as words, and forms, for example, the would-be rapist's feelings of powerfulness and our commonplace sense of paralysis when threatened with rape.

As intractably real as these physical sensations may appear to us, however, they appear so because the language of rape speaks through us, freezing our own sense of force and affecting the would-be rapist's perceptions of our lack of strength. Rapists do not prevail simply because as men they are really, biologically, and unavoidably stronger than women. A rapist follows a social script and enacts conventional, gendered structures of feeling and action which seek to draw the rape target into a dialogue which is skewed against her. A rapist's ability to accost a woman verbally, to demand her attention, and even to attack her physically depends more on how he positions himself relative to her socially than

it does on his allegedly superior physical strength. His *belief* that he has more strength than a woman and that he can use it to rape her merits more analysis than the putative fact of that strength, because that belief often produces as an effect the male power that appears to be rape's cause.

I am defining rape as a scripted interaction which takes place in language and can be understood in terms of conventional masculinity and femininity as well as other gender inequalities inscribed before an individual instance of rape. The word "script" should be taken as a metaphor conveying several meanings. To speak of a rape script implies a *narrative* of rape, a series of steps and signals whose typical initial moments we can learn to recognize and whose final outcome we can learn to stave off. The concept of a narrative avoids the problems of the collapsed continuum described earlier, in which rape becomes the inevitable beginning, middle, and end of any interaction. The narrative element of a script leaves room and makes time for revision.[14]

We are used to thinking of language as a tool which we preexist and can manipulate, but both feminist and poststructuralist theories have persuasively contended that we only come to exist through our emergence into a preexistent language, into a social set of meanings which scripts us but does not exhaustively determine our selves. In this sense the term "rape script" also suggests that social structures *inscribe* on men's and women's embodied selves and psyches the misogynist inequalities which enable rape to occur. These generalized inequalities are not simply prescribed by a totalized oppressive language, nor fully inscribed before the rape occurs—rape itself is one of the specific techniques which continually scripts these inequalities anew. Patriarchy does not exist as a monolithic entity separate from human actors and actresses, impervious to any attempts to change it, secure in its role as an immovable first cause of misogynist phenomena such as rape; rather, patriarchy acquires its consistency as an overarching descriptive concept through the aggregation of microstrategies of oppression such as rape. Masculine power and feminine powerlessness neither simply precede nor cause rape; rather, rape is one of culture's many modes of feminizing women. A rapist chooses his target because he recognizes her to be a woman, but a rapist also strives to imprint the gender identity of "feminine victim" on his target. A rape act thus imposes as well as presupposes misogynist inequalities; rape is not only scripted—it also scripts.[15]

To take male violence or female vulnerability as the first and last instances in any explanation of rape is to make the identities of rapist and raped preexist the rape itself. If we eschew this view and consider rape as a scripted interaction in which one person auditions for the role of rapist and strives to maneuver another person into the role of victim, we can see rape as a *process* of sexist gendering which we can attempt to disrupt. Contrary to the principles of criminology and victimology, all rapists do not share fixed characteristics, nor do they attack people who are clearly marked as rape victims. Rape does not happen to preconstituted victims; it momentarily makes victims. The rapist does not simply *have* the power to rape; the social script and the extent to which that script succeeds in soliciting its target's participation help to create the rapist's power. The rape script preexists instances of rape but neither the script nor the rape act results from or creates immutable identities of rapist and raped.

The script should be understood as a framework, a grid of comprehensibility which we might feel impelled to use as a way of organizing and interpreting events and actions. We may be swayed by it even against our own interests—few women can resist utterly all the current modes of feminization—but its legitimacy is never complete, never assured. Each act can perform the rape script's legitimacy or explode it. By defining rape as a scripted performance, we enable a gap between script and actress which can allow us to rewrite the script, perhaps by refusing to take it seriously and treating it as a farce, perhaps by resisting the physical passivity which it directs us to adopt. Ultimately, we must eradicate this social script. In the meantime, we can locally interfere with it by realizing that men elaborate masculine power in relation to imagined feminine powerlessness; since we are solicited to help create this power, we can act to destroy it. This is not to say that women must

demonstrate resistance to provide *legal* proof that sexual overtures were undesired. A resistance criterion for defining rape has often been used to absolve rapists by expecting women trained in passivity to be able to display the same levels of aggressivity as men.[16] But clearly it is preferable to have stopped a rape attempt ourselves than to have our raped selves vindicated in court. We should not be required to resist to prove our innocence at some later judicial date, but we should do so to serve our own immediate interests.

Before we can combat the creation of our powerlessness and of the rapist's power, we need a more detailed understanding of the underpinnings of the rape script. The rape script takes its form from what I will call a *gendered grammar of violence*, where grammar means the rules and structure which assign people to positions within a script. Between men of different races, this grammar predicates white men as legitimate subjects of violence between all men and as subjects of legitimate sexual violence against all women; it portrays men of color as ever-threatening subjects of illegitimate violence against white men and illegitimate sexual violence against white women. In an intraracial context, this grammar generically predicates men as legitimate perpetrators of sexual violence against women. I will address the difference between violence between men and sexual violence in greater detail below, but within the category of general violence we should distinguish among "legitimate violence between," "illegitimate violence against," and "legitimate violence against." Legitimate violence *between* men signifies a competitive pact between potential equals which permits venues for violence; in the United States today, this suggests an intraracial configuration of sparring partners. Illegitimate violence *against* implies that the violence is an unjustifiable and unthinkable attack which challenges social inequalities and can thus legitimately be responded to in unthinkable ways such as lynching; dominant U.S. culture tends to label most initiatives by men of color against whites as "illegitimate violence against." Intraracial male violence against women does not challenge social inequalities and hence is commonly thought to be legitimate; women's resistance to this violence is considered unthinkable and often condemned when it occurs. The dominant grammar of rape subsumes intraracial sexual violence under the rubric of gender; it does not activate race as a meaningful factor when a man rapes a woman of the same race. Nor does the dominant grammar of rape actively acknowledge paragrammars of gender which do not foster marking women as objects of violence, just as the dominant grammar of language does not acknowledge paralanguages to be anything more than opaque and ungrammatical "dialects."

The gendered grammar of violence predicates men as the objects of violence and the operators of its tools, and predicates women as the objects of violence and the subjects of fear. This grammar induces men who follow the rules set out for them to recognize their gendered selves in images and narratives of aggression in which they are agents of violence who either initiate violence or respond violently when threatened. A grammatically correct mirror of gender reflects back to men heroic images in which they risk death, brave pain and never suffer violence to be done to them without attempting to pay it back in kind. This mirror reflects back to women images which conflate female victimization and female value; this grammar encourages women to become subjects by imagining ourselves as objects.

Feminist theory has widely acknowledged that when women follow social conventions we recognize and enact our gendered selves as objects of violence. It is by now a feminist truism—but nonetheless still an important feminist truth—that the criteria of feminine beauty and worthy feminine behavior, if enacted without any modification, create a trammeled, passive person. Our culture's various techniques of feminization tend to buttress the rape script, since the femininity they induce "makes a feminine woman the perfect victim of sexual aggression."[17] Studies of rape scenarios enable us to differentiate at least two grammatical positions appointed to and adopted by some women in a rape script, both of which go against women's interest in preventing rape. An interpretive stance of *empathy*, a quality deemed feminine even when detached from female practitioners, prods some women to identify with rapists rather than to defend themselves from rapists' desire to destroy their targets. One author, Frederick Storaska, even advocates empathy as a mode of self-defense, reasoning that men rape to compensate for a lack of self-esteem and love; he thus claims that when women respond lovingly to potential rapists, they no longer feel compelled to rape.[18] Even if we accept this dubious premise for heuristic purposes, we still observe that it places all human agency on the male side: to avert rape, a woman must make a man feel like a full human being, rather than force him to recognize *her* will and humanity. A second, communicative stance of *responsiveness* encourages women not to take the offensive in a dialogue with a would-be rapist but to stay within the limits he sets—she can consent or not consent, acquiesce to his demands or dissuade him from them, but she does not actively interrupt him to shift the terms of discussion.[19]

Though feminist theorists of rape have thoroughly analyzed how women serve as objects of violence, they have focused less consistently on how women become *subjects of fear* and what effect this subjection has on our enactment of rape scripts. (By subjection, I mean a process which does not simply oppress, dominate and destroy women but one which incites us to become subjects by subjecting us to fear.) Various theories have recognized that rape causes fear, but have ignored the other half of the vicious circle —that often rapes succeed as a result of women's fears. In *The Female Fear*, Margaret T. Gordon and Stephanie Riger have argued that the distribution of fear corresponds to the other unequal distributions of privilege in U.S. society.[20] Even though women in fact are neither the sole objects of sexual violence nor the most likely targets of violent crimes, women constitute the majority of fearful subjects; even in situations where men are empirically more likely to suffer from violent crimes, they express less fear than women do, and tend to displace this fear onto a concern for their mothers, sisters, wives, and daughters which usually takes the form of restricting their mobility by means of warning these women not to go out alone or at night.[21]

The grammar of violence assigns women a disadvantageous position in the rape script because it identifies us as objects of violence and because it offers the insidious inducement of a subject position which assigns us an active role vis-à-vis *fear*—a role which is all the more insidious for its apparent agency. Whereas masculine fear triggers the notorious "fight-or-flight" response, feminine fear inspires the familiar sensations of "freezing"—involuntary immobility and silence. Women learn to recognize ourselves as subjects of this fear and thus to identify with a state which does not elaborate our subjectivity but dissolves it. This fear may differ from one rape situation to another. Acquaintance and marital rapes distort the contract of male protection of women and shatter the community of care established between lovers; they may produce an uncanny, dreadful estrangement from familiar expectations. A sudden attack by a stranger may produce shocked, stunned terror. At the broadest level, however, the grammar of violence dictates that feminine fear concentrate the self on the anticipation of pain, the inefficacy of action, and the conviction that the self will be destroyed. Feminine fear precipitates all violence and agency outside of its subject; it thus disables its subject from risking possible pain or death in order to defend herself, since that risk can seem viable only if the subject perceives herself as possessing some violent capacity on which she can draw to try to survive pain or elude injury. Feminine fear also seems to entail a complete identification of a vulnerable, sexualized body with the self; we thus come to equate rape with death, the obliteration of the self, but see no way we can draw on our selves to save that self and stave off rape.

In terms of rape prevention, this grammar of violence and fear also structures what can be called an *instrumental* theory of rape and determines ideas about feminine self-defense. The instrumental theory of rape, propounded by Susan Brownmiller in *Against Our Will*, argues that men rape because their penises possess the objective capacity to be weapons, tools, and instruments of torture.[22] Traditional self-defense advice given to women assumes this quasi-invincibility of the male body and advocates passive avoidance techniques. This counsel cautions against the use of any type of weapon unless the woman can be sure to use it effectively; the implication is that unless one is

absolutely certain that one's actions will be effective, one should not attempt to defend one's self at all. When police manuals do mention that one can wield impromptu weapons, they tend to cite flimsy and obsolete accessories such as hatpins, rather than suggest that women carry more serviceable objects. These same manuals often neglect to mention male genitalia when they designate the vulnerable points of a potential rapist's body, thus perpetuating the myth of the unassailably powerful penis. These views enact, in effect, a gendered polarization of the grammar of violence in which the male body can wield weapons, can make itself into a weapon, and benefits from an enforced ignorance concerning its own vulnerability; the female body is predicated by this grammar as universally vulnerable, lacking force, and incompetent to supplement its deficiencies with tools which could vanquish the penis's power by dissimulating it. In a culture which relentlessly urges women to make up for our lacks by accessorizing, we are told that we cannot manage bodily accessories if we manipulate them for purposes of self-defense, and that we will be best served by consenting to be accessories to our own violation. We are taught the following fallacy—that we can best avoid getting hurt by letting someone hurt us. We absorb the following paradox—that rape is death, but that in a rape the only way to avoid death is to accept it. Consenting to the death of rape forms our only possibility of fighting for our lives, but these lives will have been destroyed by the rape. Fear forges the link between these contradictory statements: rape is so terrifying because it is like death, and this totalizing fear disables us from combating the rape.

We can begin to develop a feminist discourse on rape by displacing the emphasis on what the rape script promotes—male violence against women—and putting into place what the rape script stultifies and excludes—women's will, agency, and capacity for violence. One of the few books on rape prevention, Pauline Bart's and Patricia H. O'Brien's remarkable *Stopping Rape: Successful Survival Strategies*, has persuasively disproved the widespread belief that resistance to rape will lead only to injury because it will anger the would-be rapist. The authors deftly point out that "advising women to either comply or risk injury assumes that rape itself does not result in injury." They also show that in their sample, there "was no relationship between the women's use of physical resistance and the rapists' use of additional force over and above the rape attempt," and that passive responses often led to increased violence on the rapist's part.[23] Their surveys of women who prevented rape attempts consistently show that resistance does work, and that often minimal signs of it—an assertive remark, a push, a loud scream, flight—can suffice to block a man from continuing a rape attempt. Many women were able to prevent rape even when the rapist threatened them with a gun or knife. We can translate this finding into the terms of our grammatical framework by saying that the grammar of violence defines rape as an act committed against a subject of fear and not against a subject of violence—not, that is, against someone whom the would-be rapist assumes would attempt to fight back.[24] This assumption forms such an integral part of the rape script that we can say that simply by fighting back, we cease to be grammatically correct feminine subjects and thus become much less legible as rape targets.

In order to understand the difference which fighting back can make, we must distinguish sexualized violence from subject-subject violence. Sexualized violence anticipates and seeks its target's subjection as a subject of fear, defenselessness, and acquiescence to injury. In subject-subject violence, each interlocutor expects and incites violence in the other, whereas in sexualized violence women are excluded from this community of violence.[25] Subject-subject violence underlies intraracial masculine homosocial competition, in which men fight one another with the understanding that they are following the same rules and that one man can expect to receive from another any violence which he metes out to him. Although on one level the men are opponents, on another level they cooperate in their agreement to play the same game.

This gentleman's agreement does not obtain in a rape situation. Bart and O'Brien's analysis shows that unassertive, accommodating strategies which assume a contract situation of "mutual self-interest and good-will" fall to persuade a rapist who in no way identifies with the interests or subjectivity of his target.[26] Flight can work more effectively than rational negotiations since it simply breaks away from a script of polite, empathetic response to a potential aggressor. Verbal self-defense can successfully disrupt the rape script by refusing to concede the rapist's power. Treating the threat as a joke; chiding the rapist; bargaining to move to a different place, to perform only certain acts, or to have the rapist put any weapons he might have aside, are all examples of verbal methods which have in some cases thwarted rape attempts because they assert a woman's agency, not her violability, and a woman's power, rather than her fearful powerlessness. A rapist confronted with a wisecracking, scolding, and bossy woman may lose his grip on his power to rape; a rapist responded to with fear may feel his power consolidated. While we cannot underestimate the power of talking back and talking at the rapist, physical retaliation goes even further to disrupt the grammer of rape. Directed physical action is as significant a criterion of humanity in our culture as words are, and we must develop our capacities for violence in order to disrupt the rape script. Most women feel more able to use verbal strategies than physical ones—but it is precisely this feeling which indicates that the rape script has colonized our minds and bodies, positioning us as vulnerable to rape. Physical action poses the greatest challenge to most women as we think about preventing rape—and because it is our greatest point of resistance, it is the grammatical dictum we could flout to our greatest advantage.[27] The use of physical retaliation undermines the powerlessness which the scenario of violence and fear scripts for us. By talking back and fighting back we place ourselves as subjects who can engage in dialogic violence and respond to aggression in kind; in addition to offering us an opportunity to elude or even overpower an assailant, self-defense undermines a would-be rapist by catapulting him out of his role of omnipotent attacker and surprising him into having to fight someone whom he had marked out as a purely acquiescent victim.

Legislation backs up the objectifying violence of the rape script by not defining rape as an assault, which would fall under the rubric of subject-subject violence against persons, but as a sexual offense. This definition separates sexual parts from the person and views them as objects which have been violated. I have been arguing that to prevent rape, we must resist a would-be rapist's attempt to place us in a sexualized, gendered position of passivity and that instead we fend off the rape by positioning ourselves as if we were in a fight. For definitional purposes, however, rape is clearly neither sex nor simple assault. Rape could best be defined as a sexualized and gendered attack which imposes sexual difference along the lines of violence. Rape engenders a sexualized female body defined as a wound, a body excluded from subject-subject violence, from the ability to engage in a fair fight. Rapists do not beat women at the game of violence, but aim to exclude us from playing it altogether.

We have seen that subject-subject violence presumes a contractual relation between its participants, who engage with one another as equals who agree to disagree. This subject of contractual relations also underwrites the subject of property ownership. In capitalist culture one owns property by virtue of being free to contract with equals to exchange it. Alienability and the power to contract for the transfer of alienable goods form the basis of property in things, in others, and in one's self. A masculine capacity to alienate the self in a risky encounter which involves a contractual exchange of aggression positions men as the subjects of property in themselves. This capacity, combined with a sense of entitlement to women-as-property, positions men as potential rapists in the rape script. Violation entails the invasion and destruction of property; it is the obverse of alienation which demarcates the boundaries of a property and maintains its integrity in the face of circulation. Since women are considered to be property and thus not to own it, it is not possible to enter into contracts with us and thus implausible that we would resist attempts to appropriate us.[28] If what one owns expresses what one is worth and hence what one merits, women seem to own only our violation—hence we are often said to "deserve" rape.

Many feminist theorists have focused on how the infliction of violence against putative female objects is related to the view that women are also considered objects of property. Lorenne Clark and Debra Lewis, in *Rape: The Price of Coercive Sexuality*, have offered a thoughtful analysis of the relationships among rape culture, rape laws, and property laws. They show that the adherents of rape culture see female sexuality as a property which only men can truly own, which women often hoard, which can thus justifiably be wrested from us, and which women themselves merely hold in trust for a lawful owner. Rape thus becomes the theft or violation of one man's property rights by another. Clark and Lewis advocate transforming rape from a crime against a valuable object to a crime which violates a female person's right to contract to exchange her own sexual property. They thus seek to reinforce women's property in themselves and to guarantee women's "right to the exclusive ownership and control of their own bodies."[29]

This move criticizes male property in women but sustains a definition of female sexuality as violable property. The call for female ownership of this property does not displace this injurious definition; it merely erects legal impediments to carrying out naturalized violations. While I have argued that we can prevent rape by positioning ourselves as subjects of violence and objects of fear, to assume property-in-ourselves and that our selves are property will only extend, not challenge, the hold which rape scripts have over women. The rape script strives to put women in the place of objects; property metaphors of rape similarly see female sexuality as a circumscribable thing.[30] The theft metaphor makes rape mirror a simplified model of castration: a single sexual organ identifies the self, that organ is conceived of as an object that can be taken or lost, and such a loss dissolves the self. These castration and theft metaphors reify rape as an irrevocable appropriation of female sexuality.

The rape script describes female bodies as vulnerable, violable, penetrable, and wounded; metaphors of rape as trespass and invasion retain this definition intact. The psychological corollary of this property metaphor characterizes female sexuality as inner space, rape as the invasion of this inner space, and antirape politics as a means to safeguard this inner space from contact with anything external to it. The entire female body comes to be symbolized by the vagina, itself conceived of as a delicate, perhaps inevitably damaged and pained inner space.

Antirape activists have often criticized the false demarcation between an inside and outside of rape in terms of geographical space: rape culture spawns spatial contradictions by warning women not to go outside because of possible rape, but most rapes occur inside women's homes. Denaturalizing this myth unveils the boundary between inside and outside and indicates the irrelevance of this inside/outside distinction for fighting rape: if rape can occur inside, then "inside" is no longer what it is meant to be—sheltering, separate and distinct from an unsafe, external realm. Yet antirape theorists often continue to map external and internal spatial divisions onto the female body by using invasion as a metaphor for rape. This metaphor coheres with the gendered grammar of violence outlined earlier, since positions vis-à-vis violence coincide with spatial coordinates: a subject of violence acts on an object of violence to define her as the boundary between exterior and interior, which he crosses, and as the immobilized space through which he moves.[31] Precisely because the invasion metaphor coheres so strongly with the grammar of sexualized violence, we should question its efficacy in helping women fight rape. The need to define rape and to assert its existence can distract us from plotting its vanishing point. To combat rape, we do not need to insist on the reality of an inside/outside distinction between the female body and the world; this distinction may be one of the rape script's effects, but if so, it is this distinction we must dissolve in order to undo rape.

Neither all women nor all rape survivors represent rape as an invasion of female sexual property. Bart and O'Brien's work has shown that many women represent rape as the extraction of a service and define it "as something done with a penis, not something done to a vagina."[32] My previous claim that rape scripts gender suggests that we view rape not as the invasion of female inner space, but as the forced creation of female sexuality as a violated inner space.

The horror of rape is not that it steals something from us but that it makes us into things to be taken. Thus, to demand rights to ourselves as property and to request protection for our vulnerable inner space is not enough. We do not need to defend our "real" bodies from invasion but to rework this elaboration of our bodies altogether. The most deep-rooted upheaval of rape culture would revise the idea of female sexuality as an object, as property, and as an inner space.

Such a revision can and should take multiple directions. One possible alternative to figuring female sexuality as a fixed spatial unit is to imagine sexuality in terms of time and change. The use of past sexual history in rape trials to determine the probability of consent and to invoke claims of right based on past consent (used to defend the rape rights of boyfriends and husbands), demonstrate that rape culture consistently denies female sexuality the ability to change over time. Rather than secure the right to alienate and own a spatialized sexuality, antirape politics can claim women's right to a self that could differ from itself over time without then having to surrender its effective existence as a self. The title of a book on acquaintance rape, "I Never Called It Rape," provides an emblem of this conception of female sexuality. This title expresses a nonunified consciousness for which the act of naming the active desire not to have intercourse does not coincide with the nonconsensual sexual act; it insists that this split self can come to power and knowledge over time. The title conceives of female sexuality not as a discrete object whose violation will always be painfully and instantly apparent, but as an intelligible process whose individual instances can be reinterpreted and renamed over time.

I have argued against understanding rape as the forced entry of a real inner space and for considering it as a form of invagination in which rape scripts the female body as a wounded inner space. We can elude the limits of an empiricist approach by developing a politics of fantasy and representation. Rape exists because our experience and deployment of our bodies is the effect of interpretations, representations, and fantasies which often position us in ways amenable to the realization of the rape script: as paralyzed, as incapable of physical violence, as fearful. New cultural productions and reinscriptions of our bodies and our geographies can help us begin to revise the grammar of violence and to represent ourselves in militant new ways. In the place of a tremulous female body or the female self as an immobilized cavity, we can begin to imagine the female body as subject to change, as a potential object of fear and agent of violence. Conversely, we do not have to imagine the penis as an indestructible weapon which cannot help but rape; we can take the temporality of male sexuality into consideration and bear in mind the fragility of erections and the vulnerability of male genitalia. *Stopping Rape* reports the words of one woman who had been threatened with death unless she cooperated with her rapist: " 'If he's going to kill me he'll just have to kill me. I will not let this happen to me. And I grabbed him by his penis, I was trying to break it, and he was beating me all over the head with his fists, I mean, just as hard as he could. I couldn't let go. I was just determined I was going to yank it out of the socket. And then he lost his erection . . . pushed me away and grabbed his coat and ran.' "[33]

I have tried to show that such self-defense is not merely an immediately effective and practical strategy; as female violence and as the refusal to accept the rapist's body as powerfully real and really powerful, this self-defense strikes at the heart of rape culture. Self-defense of course offers no final solution: it will not always be sufficient to ward off rape and it should certainly not be necessary. While the ethical burden to prevent rape does not lie with us but with rapists and a society which upholds them, we will be waiting a very long time if we wait for men to decide not to rape. To construct a society in which we would know no fear, we may first have to frighten rape culture to death.

NOTES

I would like to thank Sylvia Brownrigg, Judith Butler, Jennifer Callahan, Susan Maslan, Mary Poovey, and Joan Scott for their critical readings of earlier drafts of this essay. My thanks also go to all the women and men who have talked about rape with me as well as to the participants in the National Graduate Women's Studies Conference in February 1990 where I presented these ideas.

1. Mary E. Hawkesworth, "Knowers, Knowing, Known: Feminist Theory and Claims of Truth," *Signs: Journal of Women in Culture and Society*, 14, 3 (1989), p. 555.

2. Hawkesworth does not cite specific poststructuralist discussions of rape. For more detailed discussions of the relationship between textural criticism and sexual violence, see Teresa de Lauretis, "The Violence of Rhetoric: Considerations on Representation and Gender," in *Technologies of Gender: Essays on Theory, Film, and Fiction* (Bloomington: Indiana University Press, 1987), pp. 31–50; Frances Ferguson, "Rape and the Rise of the Novel," *Representations*, 20 (Fall 1987), pp. 88–112; and Ellen Rooney, "Criticism and the Subject of Sexual Violence," *Modern Language Notes*, 98, 5 (December 1983).

3. See Monique Plaza, "Our Damages and Their Compensation: Rape: The Will Not to Know of Michel Foucault," *Feminist Issues* (Summer 1981), pp. 25–35. She cites Foucault's statements in *La folie encerciée* (Paris: Seghers/Laffont, 1977).

4. See, for example, Anna Clark, *Women's Silence, Men's Violence: Sexual Assault in England, 1770–1845* (London: Pandora Press, 1987); Lorenne Clark and Debra Lewis, *Rape: The Price of Coercive Sexuality* (Toronto: The Women's Press, 1977); Angela Davis, *Women, Race and Class* (New York: Vintage Books, 1981), esp. "Rape, Racism and the Myth of the Black Rapist," pp. 172–201; Delia Dumaresq, "Rape—Sexuality in the Law," *mlf*, 5 & 6 (1981), pp. 41–59; Sylvia Walby, Alex Hay, and Keith Soothill, "The Social Construction of Rape," *Theory Culture and Society*, 2, 1 (1983), pp. 86–98; Susan Estrich, *Real Rape* (Cambridge: Harvard University Press, 1987); Frances Ferguson, "Rape and the Rise of the Novel"; Susan Griffin, *Rape: The Politics of Consciousness*, Rev. 3rd ed. (San Francisco: Harper and Row, 1986); Liz Kelly, *Surviving Sexual Violence* (Minneapolis: University of Minnesota Press, 1988); Andren Medea and Kathleen Thompson, *Against Rape* (New York: Farrar, Straus and Giroux, 1974); Ken Plummer, "The Social Uses of Sexuality: Symbolic Interaction, Power and Rape" in *Perspectives on Rape and Sexual Assault*, June Hopkins, ed. (London: Harper & Row, 1984), pp. 37–55; Elizabeth A. Stanko, *Intimate Intrusions: Women's Experience of Male Violence* (London: Routledge & Kegan Paul, 1985).

5. See *I Never Called It Rape: The Ms. Report on Recognizing, Fighting, and Surviving Date and Acquaintance Rape* (New York: Harper and Row, 1988).

6. Susan Brownmiller, *Against Our Will: Men, Women and Rape* (New York: Simon and Schuster, 1975), p. 14.

7. Mary E. Hawkesworth, "Knowers, Knowing, Known," p. 555.

8. Members of other groups such as Hispanics and Native Americans have and still do experience similar inequities: our culture's alacrity to blend sexual and racial oppression means that any other group in the process of becoming racially stigmatized could find itself enmeshed in these webs of injustice. However, Afro-Americans have historically borne the brunt of symbolizing rapist and raped to the white imagination, and it is for this reason that I refer specifically to Afro- and Afra-Americans as well as to the more generic group "men and women of color." For further discussion of rape and antiblack racism, see Hazel Carby, " 'On the Threshold of Woman's Era': Lynching, Empire, and Sexuality in Black Feminist Theory," in *Critical Inquiry*, 12 (Autumn 1985), pp. 262–277; Angela Davis, *Women, Race and Class*; Jacqueline Dowd Hall, " 'The Mind That Burns In Each Body': Women, Rape, and Racial Violence," in *Powers of Desire*, edited by Ann Snltow, Christine Stansell, and Sharon Thompson (New York: Monthly Review Press, 1983), pp. 328–49; Rennie Simson, "The Afro-American Female: The Historical Context of the Construction of Sexual Identity," in *Powers of Desire*, pp. 229–35; Deborah Gray White, *Ar'n't I a Woman: Female Slaves in the Plantation South* (New York: W. W. Norton & Co., 1985).

9. See, for example, Pauline Bart and Patricia O'Brien, *Stopping Rape: Successful Survival Strategies* (New York: Pergamon Press, 1985), especially chapter 3, "The Rape Situation," pp. 23–31.

10. See Andrea Medea and Kathleen Thompson, *Against Rape*, p. 25.

11. See Nancy Henley, *Body Politics: Power, Sex, and Nonverbal Communication* (New Jersey: Prentice-Hall, 1977); Robin Lakoff, *Language and Woman's Place* (New York: Octagon Books, 1976), and Sally McConnell-Ginet, Ruth Borker, Nelly Furman, eds., *Women and Language in Literature and Society* (New York: Praeger, 1980).

12. The way in which the continuum theory equates all signs of intended, projected violence with realized, completed violence curiously mirrors myths that women provoke rape (and thus cannot be said to be raped at all). These "provocation" theories interpret all perceptions of female sociability—a smile, a nod, or even saying nothing at all —as signifying sexual consent and as thus obviating the need for further negotiation. Here too, the time and space between acts vanishes and women become always already

raped, "seduced," or "seductive." For a demonstration that efforts to keep seduction and rape logically distinct continually fall because seduction and rape alike define female sexuality as passive, see Ellen Rooney, "Criticism and the Subject."

13. For discussions of the relevance of this definition of language to feminist analyses, see Teresa de Lauretis, "Violence of Rhetoric," especially pp. 41–42, and Joan W. Scott, "Deconstructing Equality-Versus-Difference: Or, The Uses of Poststructuralist Theory for Feminism," *Feminist Studies*, 14, 1 (Spring 1988), p. 34.

14. My definition of a script differs from the sociological one posed, for example, by Judith Long Laws and Pepper Schwartz in *Sexual Scripts: The Social Construction of Female Sexuality* (Hinsdale: The Dryden Press, 1977). They write: "By sexual scripts we mean a repertoire of acts and statuses that are recognized by a social group, together with the rules, expectations, and sanctions governing these acts and statuses" (2). This definition focuses on scripts as prefabricated interactions between bearers of fixed roles, rather than as a process which in every instance must strive to reproduce itself and its performers. Although the authors note that the institutionalization of one script entails that "alternative scripts are denigrated or denied," they conceptualize each individual script as secure from implosion and internal contestation (6). I argue that these scripts are self-contradictory and can be challenged from within. One crucial contradiction of the rape script is that it casts women as weak victims yet posits massive amounts of force and violence as necessary to rape us. We can thus draw from the rape script itself the implication that we may possess more force than the script leads us to think we do.

15. Angela Davis makes a similar point when she argues that rape by slave owners and overseers was the one act which differentiated between slave men and slave women. Rape from without inaugurates sexual difference within a group of men and women otherwise equal, hence otherwise indistinguishable. *Women, Race and Class*, pp. 23–4.

16. See Susan Estrich, *Real Rape*.

17. Susan Griffin, *Rape: The Power of Consciousness*, p. 16.

18. Frederick Storaska, *How to Say No to a Rapist and Survive*, cited in Pauline Bart and Patricia O'Brien, *Stopping Rape*, passim.

19. See Ellen Rooney, "*Criticism and the Subject*," for a critique of "consent" as a criterion of rape and the ways in which it precludes the theorization of female sexuality.

20. Margaret T. Gordon and Stephanle Riger, *The Female Fear* (New York: Free Press, 1989), p. 118.

21. Ibid., p. 54.

22. See Susan Brownmiller, *Against Our Will*, p. 14.

23. Pauline Bart and Patricia H. O'Brien, *Stopping Rape*, pp. 40–41.

24. See, for example, the Queen's Bench Foundation report on interviews with rapists: when asked why they chose a target, 82.2% said because she was "available" and 71.2% because she was "defenseless"—terms which amount to the same meaning, since "available" here means "available to be raped." *Rape: Prevention and Resistance* (Queen's Bench Foundation: San Francisco, 1976).

25. Teresa de Lauretis follows Rene Girard in calling this type of subject-subject violence " 'violent reciprocity' . . . which is socially held in check [and promoted] by the institution of kinship, ritual, and other forms of mimetic violence (war and sport come immediately to mind)." "Violence of Rhetoric" p. 43.

26. Pauline Bart and Patricia H. O'Brien, *Stopping Rape*, pp. 109–10.

27. Jeffner Allen underlines this point when she criticizes "non-violence as a patriarchal construct" and as a "heterosexual virtue [which] charges women to be 'moral,' virtuously non-violent in the face of the 'political,' the violent male-defined world. The ideology of heterosexual virtue entitles men to terrorize—possess, humiliate, violate, objectify—women and forecloses the possibility of women's active response to men's sexual terrorization." *Lesbian Philosophy: Explorations* (Palo Alto: Institute of Lesbian Studies, 1986), pp. 29, 35.

28. See Maria Mies, *Patriarchy and Accumulation on a World Scale: Women in the International Division of Labor* (London: Zed Books, 1986), p. 169.

29. Lorenne Clark and Debra Lewis, *Rape: The Price of Coercive Sexuality*, p. 166.

30. Clark and Lewis are not the only authors to use the rape metaphor; Pauline Bart and Patricia H. O'Brien compare rape laws to trespassing laws, *Stopping Rape*, p. 21; the *Ms.* report on acquaintance rape compares definitions of rape with those of theft, p. 22, and Susan Estrich makes several analogies between theft and rape, *Real Rape*, pp. 14, 40–41.

31. See Teresa de Lauretis, "Violence of Rhetoric," pp. 43–44.

32. Pauline Bart and Patricia H. O'Brien, *Stopping Rape*, p. 20.

33. Ibid., p. 38.

Study Questions

1. Marcus considers the view that "[m]any current theories of rape present rape as an inevitable material fact of life and assume that a rapist's ability to physically overcome his target is the foundation of rape" (paragraph 5). What reasons does she give for rejecting this view?

2. Explain three possible meanings of the claim that we should understand "rape as a *linguistic* fact" (paragraph 8). Does this view have the result that women can be raped by words?

3. What does Marcus mean by a "rape script" (paragraph 14)? What is valuable (in Marcus's view) in viewing rape as a "scripted interaction"? Do you agree? Give an example of another gender-related "scripted interaction."

4. What is the difference between "legitimate violence between" and "illegitimate violence against" and "legitimate violence against" (paragraph 18)? Give examples.

5. Marcus offers several proposals for what we might do to "develop a feminist discourse on rape" that seeks to undermine the rape script. Summarize *one* of her proposals and critically evaluate it. Do you agree that the proposal would help undermine the rape script? Do you think it is a good idea? Why or why not?

6. Do you have other suggestions about how we might work to undermine the rape script? Please explain.

7. In what sense does this article take a postmodern feminist approach?

Kate Bornstein

Send in the Clowns

A few weeks after I told my mother that I was going to become her daughter, she called me with a question. "Are you sure," she asked, "this change of yours isn't just another role? You've always been an actor, is this just another part, maybe your most challenging one?" At the time, I was offended. How dare she, I asked myself, compare my life's struggle with some part! But, looking back, it really was a good question. Thanks, mom.

Real gender freedom begins with fun. Here, you get what might be called The Gender Blender, a sort of whirling confusion of leather and rhinestones. These creatures do not spring full-born from the forehead of the culture; gender blenders earn their feather boa wings step by step, feather by feather.

> The easiest way to spot a newly transgendered person is that he or she moves just a bit slower than most people; he or she is unlearning old ways of moving, and picking up new ways of moving. So one of the first things you try to do is to move at a normal pace, because you don't want to be laughed at. You don't want the high school kids pointing and yelling. You don't want to see the looks of disgust on people's faces. So you learn how to blend in. It's called "passing."

> [The standup comic] seems to know no fear of humiliation and thus appears to be dangerously outside the boundaries of social control.
>
> —David Marc, *Comic Visions: Television Comedy and American Culture*, 1989

Humiliation is a whip of the defenders of gender. Humiliation is sanctioned at virtually every level of the culture: people can laugh at a transgendered person; but when there's no fear of being humiliated for one's portrayal of gender, there's less opportunity for the culture to exert control.

> I was on my way to a surgeon's office on the upper East Side. It was rush hour, and the train station was packed. There was a large crowd of people avoiding an old man who was standing in the middle of the passageway. I heard his voice up ahead, above the noise of the crowd.
>
> "Sir, twenty-five cents, please."
>
> Or he'd say, "Lady, got a quarter?"
>
> I was reaching into my bag for some change, just as the motion of the crowd brought me almost face to face with him.
>
> He was so grimy.
>
> He stank of urine and wine.
>
> He looked right at me.
>
> "Lady?" he said.
>
> "Mister?" he said.
>
> "Say, what the fuck are you?" he said. And he began to laugh.
>
> He laughed. And he laughed. He just laughed. And the crowd carried me further down the passageway, and I could still hear him laughing.

We're taught to pay attention to the humiliation, because it can be enforced by violence, the other whip of the system. Violence against transgendered people makes freedom from the fear of humiliation tricky to say the least. So you have some choices: you can get real good at hiding, or you can get beat up. You can commit suicide—or you learn how to laugh. There are actually quite a few opportunities to laugh, but fear keeps us from looking at those opportunities.

Cross-culturally, the individuals who have freed themselves from the fear of humiliation are clowns, fools, jesters, and tricksters. This can be Coyote, Uncle Tolpa, Br'er Rabbit, Raccoon Dog, or any number of documented practitioners of what Scoop Nisker calls *crazy wisdom* in cultures around the world.

> The great fool, like Einstein, wonders about the obvious and stands in awe of the ordinary, which makes him capable of revolutionary discoveries about space and time. The great fool lives outside the blinding circle of routine, remaining open to the surprise of each moment. We are the foolish ones, complacent in our understanding. We take for granted the miraculous dance of creation, but the great fool continuously sees it for the first time. The revelations of the great fool often show us where we are going, or—more often—where we are.
> —Scoop Nisker, *Crazy Wisdom*, 1990

What do fools have in common? Well, they don't play by the rules, they laugh at most rules, and they encourage us to laugh at ourselves. Their pranks of substituting one thing for another create instability and uncertainty, making visible the lies imbedded in a culture. Fools demonstrate the wisdom of simplicity and innocence. These are valuable crafts, these are skills we could use in our problem-laden world.

> The market value of comedy ascends in the face of a plausible end to history.
> —David Marc, *Comic Visions: Television Comedy and American Culture*, 1989

Any healthy civilization would certainly have people performing these fool skills at every level of the culture. In *our* civilization, the only people doing these things are considered trouble-makers, whatever their line of work.

> The only true art is art that raises questions and implicates people.
> —Holly Hughes, *Sphinxes Without Secrets*, 1990

There's room in our Eurocentric culture for a class of clowns, jesters, tricksters, and fools. In fact, there are a lot of positions open. Since very few people are volunteering, since people laugh at us anyway, and since we have such wit, charm, and impeccable fashion sense, I think transgendered people should move right into these roles.

> I mentioned this once in writing, and it raised the question of how does someone who's not an actor or writer, and who (sensibly) doesn't want to **be** an actor or a writer, get along in this role. I think it's just a matter of incorporating a sense of humor into our daily lives. I think it has a lot to do with taking the tendency people have for laughing at us, and laughing **first**, so as to highlight and defuse that mechanism. That doesn't take talent; it takes living life at one's right size. It takes an admission of one's outsider status, and a wish to help others expand their points of view. It takes compassion.

WHO ARE THE FOOLS?

The fool's role can be taken on at the secretary's desk as easily as on the stage. The clown can perform in a circus or on a bus. The jester can take the ear of a king, or the ear of a neighbor. The trickster can fool the Congress of the United States, or the folks down at the general store.

Today's more widely-known fools are the solo performers, monologists, standups, anyone who addresses or performs before any audience, like the odd instructor or professor. These folks are the twentieth century's answer to the roving minstrel or countryside jester. Some of the many gender blenders of our times are fools like these:

• **Sandy Stone**, singled out for attack by Janice Raymond in her book, *The Transsexual Empire*, in 1979. After a dozen years of recovery and research, Stone is once more back on the scene with her rib-tickling, devilish essay, "The Empire Strikes Back: A Posttranssexual Manifesto."

• **Elvis Herselvis**, a San Francisco–based lesbian writer and Elvis impersonator; and **Glamoretta Rampage**, (AKA San Francisco–based writer and performer, Justin Bond), the charming wife of Elvis Herselvis.

• **Shelley Mars**, performance artist and Drag King *extraordinaire* from New York City.

• Writer, director **Ingrid Wilhite**, whose two films *Fun With a Sausage*, and *The Mister Sisters*, stretch the limits of lesbian identity, and nicely blur the lines of gender identity and sexual orientation.

• **The Sisters of Perpetual Indulgence, Inc.**, is, per their own literature ". . . a controversial order of gay, bisexual, and transgender 'nuns' of various religious backgrounds founded in Iowa in the mid-1970s." The Sisters hold various fund-raising events to benefit various AIDS-related groups.

SISTER SAM WANTS YOU!
JOIN QUEER ARMY TODAY!
NO WARS—FABULOUS PARADES!
—from a recruitment flier by The Sisters of
Perpetual Indulgence, 1992

• The late **Doris Fish**, Australia and San Francisco; the late **"Tippi,"** San Francisco; the late **Ethyl Eichelberger**, New York: three transgendered performance artists with AIDS who died within a year of each other.

There are perhaps better-known kings and queens of drag. Milton Berle, Nipsey Russell, and Lucille Ball come to mind immediately. But I think that using drag on stage as a gimmick, a *shtick*, is an appropriation; it's different than living a transgendered life and then using that life for material on stage or screen. The contrast between transgender as gimmick and transgender as life marks one major difference between mainstream theater and what might be called queer theater.

There's a strength in knowing we have our own comics, our own jokers. But here it gets tricky. The pressure and temptation is to create art or politics for a particular group, which is in turn based on some inflexible identity: special interest groups, identity politics, whatever you want to call it. The group becomes loyal audience, supporters, and followers, if for no other reason than the fool is speaking their language, performing their lives.

But this is so important: the fool became a fool by flexing the rules, the boundaries of the group, and this is antithetical to the survival dynamic of most groups. A group remains a group by being inflexible: once it stretches its borders, it's no longer the same group. A fool, in order to survive, must not identify long with any rigidly-structured group. When more and more of the fool's work is done for a particular identity-based group, then the fool becomes *identified* with the group. The fool is indeed foolish who serves a special interest, and will quickly cease being a fool.

So where do all these transgender fools go, if not to lead or participate in some grand and glorious transgender revolution? They climb yet another step on the ladder of transgender evolution: they move toward some spiritual awareness and practice.

We must never forget that art is not a form of propaganda, it is a form of truth.
—John Fitzgerald Kennedy

Study Questions

1. Compare and contrast Bornstein's suggestion that transgendered people are well suited to play the role of "fool" to Butler's remarks in the excerpt from *Gender Trouble* about repetition and parody.

2. In the last line of the penultimate paragraph Bornstein writes, "The fool is indeed foolish who serves a special interest, and will quickly cease being a fool." Explain this quotation.

3. In what sense does this article take a postmodern feminist approach?

Susan Bordo

Material Girl

The Effacements of Postmodern Culture

PLASTICITY AS POSTMODERN PARADIGM

In a culture in which organ transplants, life-extension machinery, microsurgery, and artificial organs have entered everyday medicine, we seem on the verge of practical realization of the seventeenth-century imagination of body as machine. But if we have technically and technologically realized that conception, it can also be argued that metaphysically we have deconstructed it. In the early modern era, machine imagery helped to articulate a totally determined human body whose basic functionings the human being was helpless to alter. The then-dominant metaphors for this body —clocks, watches, collections of springs—imagined a system that is set, wound up, whether by nature or by God the watchmaker, ticking away in predictable, orderly manner, regulated by laws over which the human being has no control. Understanding the system, we can help it to perform efficiently, and we can intervene when it malfunctions. But we cannot radically alter its configuration.

Pursuing this modern, determinist fantasy to its limits, fed by the currents of consumer capitalism, modern ideologies of the self, and their crystallization in the dominance of United States mass culture, Western science and technology have now arrived, paradoxically but predictably (for it was an element, though submerged and illicit, in the mechanist con-

ception all along), at a new, postmodern imagination of human freedom from bodily determination. Gradually and surely, a technology that was first aimed at the replacement of malfunctioning parts has generated an industry and an ideology fueled by fantasies of rearranging, transforming, and correcting, an ideology of limitless improvement and change, defying the historicity, the mortality, and, indeed, the very materiality of the body. In place of that materiality, we now have what I will call cultural plastic. In place of God the watchmaker, we now have ourselves, the master sculptors of that plastic. This disdain for material limits and the concomitant intoxication with freedom, change, and self-determination are enacted not only on the level of the contemporary technology of the body but in a wide range of contexts, including much of contemporary discourse on the body, both popular and academic. In this essay, looking at a variety of these discursive contexts, I attempt to describe key elements of this paradigm of plasticity and expose some of its effacements— the material and social realities it denies or renders invisible.

PLASTIC BODIES

"Create a masterpiece, sculpt your body into a work of art," urges *Fit* magazine. "You visualize what you want to look like, and then you create that form." "The challenge presents itself: to rearrange things."[1] The precision technology of body-sculpting, once the secret of the Arnold Schwarzeneggers and Rachel McLishes of the professional body-building world, has now become available to anyone who can afford the price of membership in a gym (Figure 2). "I now look at bodies," says John Travolta, after training for the movie *Staying Alive*, "almost like pieces of clay that can be molded."[2] On the medical front, plastic surgery, whose repeated and purely cosmetic employment has been legitimated by Michael Jackson, Cher, and others, has become a fabulously expanding industry, extending its domain from nose jobs, face lifts, tummy tucks, and breast augmentations to collagen-plumped lips and liposuction-shaped ankles, calves, and buttocks (Figure 3). In 1989, 681,000 procedures were done, up 80 percent over 1981; over half of these were performed on patients between the ages of eighteen and thirty-five.[3] The trendy *Details* magazine describes "surgical

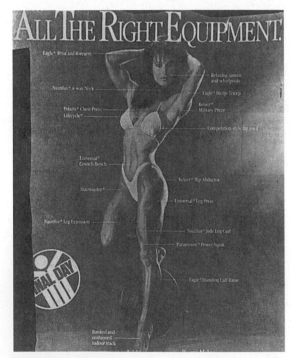

Figure 2

stretching, tucking and sucking" as "another fabulous [fashion] accessory" and invites readers to share their cosmetic-surgery experiences in their monthly column "Knife-styles of the Rich and Famous." In that column, the transportation of fat from one part of the body to another is described as breezily as changing hats might be:

> Dr. Brown is an artist. He doesn't just pull and tuck and forget about you. . . . He did liposuction on my neck, did the nose job and tightened up my forehead to give it a better line. Then he took some fat from the side of my waist and injected it into my hands. It goes in as a lump, and then he smooths it out with his hands to where it looks good. I'll tell you something, the nose and neck made a big change, but nothing in comparison to how fabulous my hands look. The fat just smoothed out all the lines, the veins don't stick up anymore, the skin actually looks soft and great. [But] you have to be careful not to bang your hands.[4]

Popular culture does not apply any brakes to these fantasies of rearrangement and self-transformation. Rather, we are constantly told that we can "choose" our own bodies (Figures 4 and 5). "The proper diet, the right amount of exercise and you can have, pretty much, any body you desire," claims Evian. Of course, the rhetoric of choice and self-determination and the breezy analogies comparing cosmetic surgery to fashion accessorizing are deeply mystifying. They efface, not only the inequalities of privilege, money, and time that prohibit most people from indulging in these practices, but the desperation that characterizes the lives of those who do. "I will do anything, *anything*, to make myself look and feel better," says Tina Lizardi (whose "Knife-styles" experience I quoted from above). Medical science has now designated a new category of "polysurgical addicts" (or, in more casual references, "scalpel slaves") who return for operation after operation, in perpetual quest of the elusive yet ruthlessly normalizing goal, the "perfect" body.[5] The dark underside of the practices of body transformation and rearrangement reveals botched and sometimes fatal operations, exercise addictions, eating disorders. And of course, despite the claims of the Evian ad, one cannot have *any* body that one

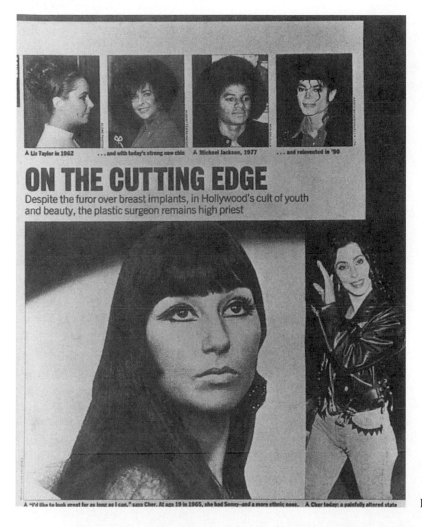

A Liz Taylor in 1962 ...and with today's strong new chin A Michael Jackson, 1977 ...and rejuvenated in '90

ON THE CUTTING EDGE
Despite the furor over breast implants, in Hollywood's cult of youth and beauty, the plastic surgeon remains high priest

A "I'd like to look great for as long as I can," says Cher. At age 19 in 1965, she had Sonny—and a more ethnic nose.   A Cher today: a painfully altered state

Figure 3

wants—for not every body will *do*. The very advertisements whose copy speaks of choice and self-determination visually legislate the effacement of individual and cultural difference and circumscribe our choices (Figure 6).

That we are surrounded by homogenizing and normalizing images—images whose content is far from arbitrary, but is instead suffused with the dominance of gendered, racial, class, and other cultural iconography—seems so obvious as to be almost embarrassing to be arguing here. Yet contemporary understandings of the behaviors I have been describing not only con-

struct the situation very differently but do so in terms that preempt precisely such a critique of cultural imagery. Moreover, they reproduce, on the level of discourse and interpretation, the same conditions that postmodern bodies enact on the level of cultural practice: a construction of life as plastic possibility and weightless choice, undetermined by history, social location, or even individual biography. A 1988 "Donahue" show offers my first illustration.

The show's focus was a series of television commercials for DuraSoft colored contact lenses. In these commercials as they were originally aired, a woman

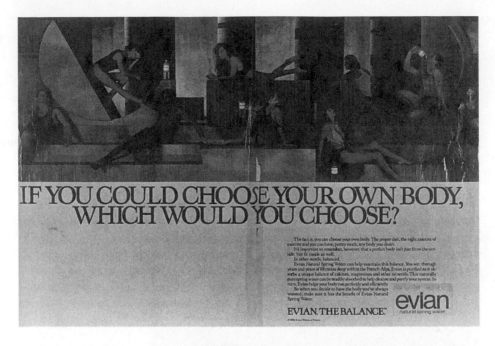

IF YOU COULD CHOOSE YOUR OWN BODY,
WHICH WOULD YOU CHOOSE?

Figures 4 and 5

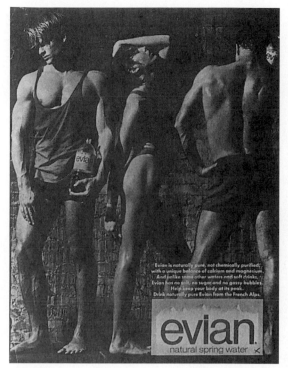

Figure 6

"wrong" with any inclinations to "make it a political question." Here are some comments taken from the transcript of the show:

"Why does it have to be a political question? I mean, people perm their hair. It's just because they like the way it looks. It's not something sociological. Maybe black women like the way they look with green contacts. It's to be more attractive. It's not something that makes them—I mean, why do punk rockers have purple hair? Because they feel it makes them feel better." [white woman]

"What's the fuss? When I put on my blue lenses, it makes me feel good. It makes me feel sexy, different, the other woman, so to speak, which is like fun." [black woman]

"I perm my hair, you're wearing make-up, what's the difference?" [white woman]

"I want to be versatile . . . having different looks, being able to change from one look to the other." [black female model]

"We all do the same thing, when we're feeling good we wear new makeup, hairstyles, we buy new clothes. So now it's contact lenses. What difference does it make?" [white woman]

"It goes both ways . . . Bo Derek puts her hair in cornstalks, or corn . . . or whatever that thing is called. White women try to get tan." [white woman]

"She's not trying to be white, she's trying to be different." [about a black woman with blue contact lenses]

"It's fashion, women are never happy with themselves."

"I put them in as toys, just for fun, change. Nothing too serious, and I really enjoy them." [black woman][6]

was shown in a dreamlike, romantic fantasy—for example, parachuting slowly and gracefully from the heavens. The male voiceover then described the woman in soft, lush terms: "If I believed in angels, I'd say that's what she was—an angel, dropped from the sky like an answer to a prayer, with eyes as brown as bark." [Significant pause] "No . . . I *don't think so*." [At this point, the tape would be rewound to return us to:] "With eyes as violet as the colors of a child's imagination." The commercial concludes: "DuraSoft colored contact lenses. Get brown eyes a second look" (cf. Figure 7).

The question posed by Phil Donahue: Is this ad racist? Donahue clearly thought there was controversy to be stirred up here, for he stocked his audience full of women of color and white women to discuss the implications of the ad. But Donahue was apparently living in a different decade from most of his audience, who repeatedly declared that there was nothing "wrong" with the ad, and everything

Some points to note here: first, putting on makeup, styling hair, and so forth are conceived of only as free *play*, fun, a matter of creative expression. This they surely are. But they are also experienced by many women as necessary before they will show themselves to the world, even on a quick trip to the corner mailbox. The one comment that hints at women's (by now depressingly well documented) dissatisfaction with their appearance trivializes that dissatisfaction and puts it beyond the pale of cultural critique: "It's fashion." What she means is, "It's *only* fashion,"

Figure 7

whose whimsical and politically neutral vicissitudes supply endless amusement for women's eternally superficial values. ("Women are never happy with themselves.") If we are never happy with ourselves, it is implied, that is due to our female nature, not to be taken too seriously or made into a political question.

Second, the content of fashion, the specific ideals that women are drawn to embody (ideals that vary historically, racially, and along class and other lines) are seen as arbitrary, without meaning; interpretation is neither required nor even appropriate. Rather, all motivation and value come from the interest and allure—the "sexiness"—of change and difference itself. Blue contact lenses for a black woman, it is admitted, make her "other" ("the other woman"). But that "other" is not a racial or cultural "other"; she is sexy because of the piquancy, the novelty, the erotics of putting on a different self. *Any* different self would do, it is implied.

Closely connected to this is the construction of *all* cosmetic changes as the same: perms for the white women, corn rows on Bo Derek, tanning, makeup, changing hairstyles, blue contacts for black women —all are seen as having equal political valance (which is to say, *no* political valance) and the same cultural meaning (which is to say, *no* cultural meaning) in the heterogeneous yet undifferentiated context of the things "all" women do "to be more attractive." The one woman in the audience who offered a different construction of this behavior, who insisted that the styles we aspire to do not simply reflect the free play of fashion or female nature—who went so far, indeed, as to claim that we "are brainwashed to think blond hair and blue eyes is the most beautiful of all," was regarded with hostile silence. Then, a few moments later, someone challenged: "Is there anything *wrong* with blue eyes and blond hair?" The audience enthusiastically applauded this defender of democratic values.

This "conversation"—a paradigmatically postmodern conversation, as I will argue shortly—effaces the same general elements as the rhetoric of body transformation discussed earlier. First, it effaces the inequalities of social position and the historical origins which, for example, render Bo Derck's corn rows and black women's hair-straightening utterly noncommensurate. On the one hand, we have Bo Derek's privilege, not only as so unimpeachably white as to permit an exotic touch of "otherness" with no danger of racial contamination, but her trend-setting position as a famous movie star. Contrasting to this, and mediating a black woman's "choice" to straighten her hair, is a cultural history of racist body-discriminations such as the nineteenth-century comb-test, which allowed admission to churches and clubs only to those blacks who could pass through their hair without snagging a fine-tooth comb hanging outside the door. (A variety of comparable tests— the pine-slab test, the brown bag test—determined whether one's skin was adequately light to pass muster.)[7]

Second, and following from these historical practices, there is a disciplinary reality that is effaced in the construction of all self-transformation as equally arbitrary, all variants of the same trivial game, without differing cultural valance. I use the term *disciplinary* here in the Foucauldian sense, as pointing to practices that do not merely transform but *normalize* the subject. That is, to repeat a point made earlier, not every body will do. A 1989 poll of *Essence* magazine readers revealed that 68 percent of those who responded wear their hair straightened chemically or by hot comb.[8] "Just for fun"? For the kick of being "different"? When we look at the pursuit of beauty as a normalizing discipline, it becomes clear that not all body transformations are the same. The general tyranny of fashion—perpetual, elusive, and instructing the female body in a pedagogy of personal inadequacy and lack—is a powerful discipline for the normalization of *all* women in this culture. But even as we are all normalized to the requirements of appropriate feminine insecurity and preoccupation with appearance, more specific requirements emerge in different cultural and historical contexts, and for different groups. When Bo Derek put her hair in corn rows, she was engaging in normalizing feminine practice. But when Oprah Winfrey admitted on her show that all her life she has desperately longed to have "hair that swings from side to side" when she shakes her head (Figure 8), she revealed the power of racial as well as gender normalization, normalization not only to "femininity," but to the Caucasian standards of beauty that still dominate on television, in movies, in popular magazines. (When I was a child, I felt the same way about my thick, then curly, "Jewish" hair as Oprah did about hers.) Neither Oprah nor the *Essence* readers nor the many Jewish women (myself included) who ironed their hair in the 1960s have creatively or playfully invented themselves here.

Figure 8

Figure 9

DuraSoft knows this, even if Donahue's audience does not. Since the campaign first began, the company has replaced the original, upfront magazine advertisement with a more euphemistic variant, from which the word *brown* has been tastefully effaced. (In case it has become too subtle for the average reader, the model now is black—although it should be noted that DuraSoft's failure to appreciate brown eyes also renders the eyes of most of the world not worth "a second look" [Figure 9].) In the television commercial, a comparable "brownwash" was effected; here "eyes as brown as . . ." was retained, but the derogatory nouns—"brown as boots," "brown as bark"—were eliminated. The announcer simply was left speechless: "eyes as brown as . . . brown as . . . ," and then, presumably having been unable to come up with an enticing simile, shifted to "violet." As in the

expurgated magazine ad, the television commercial ended: "Get *your* eyes a second look."

When I showed my students these ads, many of them were as dismissive as the "Donahue" audience, convinced that I was once again turning innocent images and practices into political issues. I persisted: if racial standards of beauty are not at work here, then why no brown contacts for blue-eyed people? A month later, two of my students triumphantly produced a DuraSoft ad for brown contacts (Figure 10), appearing in *Essence* magazine, and with an advertising campaign directed solely at *already* brown-eyed consumers, offering the promise *not* of "getting blue eyes a second look" by becoming excitingly darker, but of "subtly enhancing" dark eyes, by making them *lighter* brown. The creators of the DuraSoft campaign

Figure 10

clearly know that not all differences are the same in our culture, and they continue, albeit in ever more mystified form, to exploit and perpetuate that fact.[9]

PLASTIC DISCOURSE

The "Donahue" DuraSoft show (indeed, any talk show) provides a perfect example of what we might call a postmodern conversation. All sense of history and all ability (or inclination) to sustain cultural criticism, to make the distinctions and discriminations that would permit such criticism, have disappeared. Rather, in this conversation, "anything goes"—and any positioned social critique (for example, the woman who, speaking clearly from consciousness of racial oppression, insisted that the attraction of blond hair and blue eyes has a cultural meaning significantly different from that of purple hair) is immediately destabilized. Instead of distinctions, endless *differences* reign—an undifferentiated pastiche of differences, a grab bag in which no items are assigned any more importance or centrality than any others. Television is, of course, the great teacher here, our prime modeler of plastic pluralism: if one "Donahue" show features a feminist talking about battered wives, the next show will feature mistreated husbands. Women who love too much, the sex habits of priests, disturbed children of psychiatrists, daughters who have no manners, male strippers, relatives who haven't spoken in ten years all have their day alongside incest, rape, and U.S. foreign policy. All are given equal weight by the great leveler—the frame of the television screen.

This spectacle of difference defeats the ability to sustain coherent political critique. Everything is the same in its unvalanced difference. ("I perm my hair, you're wearing makeup, what's the difference?") Particulars reign, and generality—which collects, organizes, and prioritizes, suspending attention to particularity in the interests of connection, emphasis, and criticism—is suspect. So, whenever some critically charged generalization was suggested on Donahue's DuraSoft show, someone else would invariably offer a counterexample—I have blue eyes, and I'm a black woman; Bo Derek wears corn rows—to fragment the critique. What is remarkable is that people accept these examples as *refutations* of social critique. They almost invariably back down, utterly confused as to how to maintain their critical generalization in the face of the destabilizing example. Sometimes they qualify, claiming they meant some people, not all. But of course they meant neither all nor some. They meant *most*—that is, they were trying to make a claim about social or cultural *patterns*—and that is a stance that is increasingly difficult to sustain in a postmodern context, where we are surrounded by endlessly displaced images and are given no orienting context in which to make discriminations.

Those who insist on an orienting context (and who therefore do not permit particulars to reign in all their absolute "difference") are seen as "totalizing," that is, as constructing a falsely coherent and morally coercive universe that marginalizes and effaces the experiences and values of others. ("Is there anything *wrong* with blue eyes and blond hair?") As someone who is frequently interviewed by local television and newspaper reporters, I have often found my feminist arguments framed in this way, as they were in an article on breast-augmentation surgery. After several pages of "expert" recommendations from plastic surgeons, my cautions about the politics of female body transformation (none of them critical of individuals contemplating plastic surgery, all of them of a cultural nature) were briefly quoted by the reporter, who then went on to end the piece with a comment on *my* critique—from the director of communications for the American Society of Plastic and Reconstructive Surgery:

> Those not considering plastic surgery shouldn't be too critical of those who do. It's the hardest thing for people to understand. What's important is if it's a problem to that person. We're all different, but we all want to look better. We're just different in what extent we'll go to. But none of us can say we don't want to look the best we can.[10]

With this tolerant, egalitarian stroke, the media liaison of the most powerful plastic surgery lobby in the country presents herself as the protector of "difference" against the homogenizing and stifling regime of the feminist dictator.

Academics do not usually like to think of themselves as embodying the values and preoccupations of popular culture on the plane of high theory or intellectual discourse. We prefer to see ourselves as the demystifyers of popular discourse, bringers-to-consciousness-and-clarity rather than unconscious reproducers of culture. Despite what we would *like* to believe of ourselves, however, we are always within the society that we criticize, and never so strikingly as at the present postmodern moment. All the elements of what I have here called postmodern conversation—intoxication with individual choice and creative *jouissance*, delight with the piquancy of particularity

and mistrust of pattern and seeming coherence, celebration of "difference" along with an absence of critical perspective differentiating and weighing "differences," suspicion of the totalitarian nature of generalization along with a rush to protect difference from its homogenizing abuses—have become recognizable and familiar in much of contemporary intellectual discourse. Within this theoretically self-conscious universe, moreover, these elements are not merely embodied (as in the "Donahue" show's DuraSoft conversation) but explicitly thematized and *celebrated*, as inaugurating new constructions of the self, no longer caught in the mythology of the unified subject, embracing of multiplicity, challenging the dreary and moralizing generalizations about gender, race, and so forth that have so preoccupied liberal and left humanism.

For this celebratory, academic postmodernism, it has become highly unfashionable—and "totalizing" —to talk about the grip of culture on the body. Such a perspective, it is argued, casts active and creative subjects as passive dupes of ideology; it gives too much to dominant ideology, imagining it as seamless and univocal, overlooking both the gaps which are continually allowing for the eruption of "difference" and the polysemous, unstable, open nature of all cultural texts. To talk about the grip of culture on the body (as, for example, in "old" feminist discourse about the objectification and sexualization of the female body) is to fail to acknowledge, as one theorist put it, "the cultural work by which nomadic, fragmented, active subjects confound dominant discourse."[11]

So, for example, contemporary culture critic John Fiske is harshly critical of what he describes as the view of television as a "dominating monster" with "homogenizing power" over the perceptions of viewers. Such a view, he argues, imagines the audience as "powerless and undiscriminating" and overlooks the fact that:

> Pleasure results from a particular relationship between meanings and power. . . . There is no pleasure in being a "cultural dope." . . . Pleasure results from the production of meanings of the world and of self that are felt to serve the interests of the reader rather than those of the dominant. The subordinate

may be disempowered, but they are not powerless. There is a power in resisting power, there is a power in maintaining one's social identity in opposition to that proposed by the dominant ideology, there is a power in asserting one's own subcultural values against the dominant ones. There is, in short, a power in being different.[12]

Fiske then goes on to produce numerous examples of how *Dallas, Hart to Hart*, and so forth have been read (or so he argues) by various subcultures to make their own "socially pertinent" and empowering meanings out of "the semiotic resources provided by television."

Note, in Fiske's insistent, repetitive invocation of the category of power, a characteristically postmodern flattening of the terrain of power relations, a lack of differentiation between, for example, the power involved in creative *reading* in the isolation of one's own home and the power held by those who control the material production of television shows, or the power involved in public protest and action against the conditions of that production and the power of the dominant meanings—for instance, racist and sexist images and messages—therein produced. For Fiske, of course, there *are* no such dominant meanings, that is, no element whose ability to grip the imagination of the viewer is greater than the viewer's ability to "just say no" through resistant reading of the text. That ethnic and subcultural meaning *may* be wrested from *Dallas* and *Hart to Hart* becomes for Fiske proof that dominating images and messages are only in the minds of those totalitarian critics who would condescendingly "rescue" the disempowered from those forces that are in fact the very medium of their creative freedom and resistance ("the semiotic resources of television").

Fiske's conception of power—a terrain without hills and valleys, where all forces have become "resources"—reflects a very common postmodern misappropriation of Foucault. Fiske conceives of power as in the *possession* of individuals or groups, something they "have"—a conception Foucault takes great pains to criticize—rather than (as in Foucault's reconstruction) a dynamic of noncentralized forces, its dominant historical forms attaining their hegemony, not from magisterial design or decree, but through

multiple "processes, of different origin and scattered location," regulating and normalizing the most intimate and minute elements of the construction of time, space, desire, embodiment.[13] This conception of power does *not* entail that there are no dominant positions, social structures, or ideologies emerging from the play of forces; the fact that power is not held by any *one* does not mean that it is equally held by *all*. It is in fact not "held" at all; rather, people and groups are positioned differentially within it. This model is particularly useful for the analysis of male dominance and female subordination, so much of which is reproduced "voluntarily," through our self-normalization to everyday habits of masculinity and femininity. Within such a model, one can acknowledge that women may indeed contribute to the perpetuation of female subordination (for example, by embracing, taking pleasure in, and even feeling empowered by the cultural objectification and sexualization of the female body) without this entailing that they have power in the production and reproduction of sexist culture.

Foucault does insist on the *instability* of modern power relations—that is, he emphasizes that resistance is perpetual and unpredictable, and hegemony precarious. This notion is transformed by Fiske (perhaps under the influence of a more deconstructionist brand of postmodernism) into a notion of resistance as *jouissance*, a creative and pleasurable eruption of cultural "difference" through the "seams" of the text. What this celebration of creative reading as resistance effaces is the arduous and frequently frustrated historical struggle that is required for the subordinated to articulate and assert the value of their "difference" in the face of dominant meanings—meanings which often offer a pedagogy directed at the reinforcement of feelings of inferiority, marginality, ugliness. During the early fifties, when *Brown v. the Board of Education* was wending its way through the courts, as a demonstration of the destructive psychological effects of segregation black children were asked to look at two baby dolls, identical in all respects except color. The children were asked a series of questions: which is the nice doll? which is the bad doll? which doll would you like to play with? The majority of black children, Kenneth Clark reports, attributed the positive characteristics to the white doll, the negative characteristics to the black. When Clark asked one final question, "Which doll is like you?" they looked at him, he says, "as though he were the devil himself" for putting them in that predicament, for forcing them to face the inexorable and hideous logical implications of their situation. Northern children often ran out of the room; southern children tended to answer the question in shamed embarrassment. Clark recalls one little boy who laughed, "Who am I like? That doll! It's a nigger and I'm a nigger!"[14]

Failing to acknowledge the psychological and cultural potency of normalizing imagery can be just as effective in effacing people's experiences of racial oppression as lack of attentiveness to cultural and ethnic differences—a fact postmodern critics sometimes seem to forget. This is not to deny what Fiske calls "the power of being different"; it is, rather, to insist that it is won through ongoing political *struggle* rather than through an act of creative interpretation. Here, once again, although many postmodern academics may claim Foucault as their guiding light, they differ from him in significant and revealing ways. For Foucault, the metaphorical terrain of resistance is explicitly that of the "battle"; the "points of confrontation" may be "innumerable" and "instable," but they involve a serious, often deadly struggle of embodied (that is, historically situated and shaped) forces.[15] Barbara Kruger exemplifies this conception of resistance in a poster that represents the contemporary contest over reproductive control through the metaphor of the body as battleground (Figure 11). Some progressive developers of children's toys have self-consciously entered into struggle with racial and other forms of normalization. The Kenya Doll (Figure 12) comes in three different skin tones ("so your girl is bound to feel pretty and proud") and attempts to create a future in which hair-straightening *will* be merely one decorative option among others. Such products, to my mind, are potentially effective "sites of resistance" precisely because they recognize that the body is a battleground whose self-determination has to be fought for.

The metaphor of the body as battleground, rather than postmodern playground, captures, as well, the

Figure 11

practical difficulties involved in the political struggle to empower "difference." *Essence* magazine has consciously and strenuously tried to promote diverse images of black strength, beauty, and self-acceptance. Beauty features celebrate the glory of black skin and lush lips; other departments feature interviews with accomplished black women writers, activists, teachers, many of whom display styles of body and dress that challenge the hegemony of white Anglo-Saxon standards. The magazine's advertisers, however, continually play upon and perpetuate consumers' feelings of inadequacy and insecurity over the racial characteristics of their bodies. They insist that, in order to be beautiful, hair must be straightened and eyes lightened; they almost always employ models with fair skin, Anglo-Saxon features, and "hair that moves," insuring association of their products with

Figure 12

fantasies of becoming what the white culture most prizes and rewards.

This ongoing battle over the black woman's body and the power of its "differences" ("differences" which actual black women embody to widely varying degrees, of course) is made manifest in the twentieth-anniversary issue, where a feature celebrating "The Beauty of Black" faced an advertisement visually legislating virtually the opposite (and offering, significantly, "escape") (Figures 13 and 14). This invitation to cognitive dissonance reveals what *Essence* must grapple with, in every issue, as it tries to keep its message of African American self-acceptance clear and dominant, while submitting to economic necessities on which its survival depends. Let me make it clear here that such self-acceptance, not the reverse tyranny that constructs light-skinned and Anglo-featured African Americans as "not black enough," is the message *Essence* is trying to convey, against a culture that *denies* "the Beauty of Black" at every

turn. This terrain, clearly, is not a playground but a minefield that constantly threatens to deconstruct "difference" *literally* and not merely literarily.

"MATERIAL GIRL": MADONNA AS POSTMODERN HEROINE

John Fiske's conception of "difference," in the section quoted above, at least imagines resistance as challenging specifiable historical forms of dominance. Women, he argues, connect with subversive "feminine" values leaking through the patriarchal plot of soap operas; blacks laugh to themselves at the glossy, materialist-cowboy culture of *Dallas*. Such examples suggest a resistance directed against *particular* historical forms of power and subjectivity. For some postmodern theorists, however, resistance is imagined as the refusal to embody *any* positioned subjectivity at all; what is celebrated is continual creative escape from location, containment, and definition. So, as Susan Rubin Suleiman advises, we must move beyond the valorization of historically suppressed values (for example, those values that have been culturally constructed as belonging to an inferior, female domain and generally expunged from Western science, philosophy, and religion) and toward "endless complication" and a "dizzying accumulation of narratives."[16] She appreciatively (and perhaps misleadingly) invokes Derrida's metaphor of "incalculable choreographies"[17] to capture the dancing, elusive, continually changing subjectivity that she envisions, a subjectivity without gender, without history, without location. From this perspective, the truly resistant female body is, not the body that wages war on feminine sexualization and objectification, but the body that, as Cathy Schwichtenberg has put it, "uses simulation strategically in ways that challenge the stable notion of gender as the edifice of sexual difference . . . [in] an erotic politics in which the female body can be refashioned in the flux of identities that speak in plural styles."[18] For this erotic politics, the new postmodern heroine is Madonna.

This celebration of Madonna as postmodern heroine does not mark the first time Madonna has been

Figure 13

portrayed as a subversive culture-figure. Until the early 1990s, however, Madonna's resistance has been interpreted along "body as battleground" lines, as deriving from her refusal to allow herself to be constructed as a passive object of patriarchal desire. John Fiske, for example, argues that this was a large part of Madonna's original appeal to her "wanna-bes"—those hordes of middle-class pre-teeners who mimicked Madonna's moves and costumes. For the "wanna-bes," Madonna demonstrated the possibility of a female heterosexuality that was independent of patriarchal control, a sexuality that defied rather than rejected the male gaze, teasing it with her own gaze, deliberately trashy and vulgar, challenging anyone to

Figure 14

call her a whore, and ultimately not giving a damn how she might be judged. Madonna's rebellious sexuality, in this reading, offered itself, not as coming into being through the look of the "other," but as self-defining and in love with, happy with itself—an attitude that is rather difficult for women to achieve in this culture and that helps to explain, as Fiske argues, her enormous appeal for pre-teen girls.[19] "I like the way she handles herself, sort of take it or leave it; she's sexy but she doesn't need men . . . she's kind of there all by herself," says one. "She gives us ideas. It's really women's lib, not being afraid of what guys think," says another.[20]

Madonna herself, significantly and unlike most sex symbols, has never advertised herself as disdainful of feminism or constructed feminists as man-haters. Rather, in a 1985 *Time* interview, she suggests that her lack of inhibition in "being herself" and her "luxuriant" expression of "strong" sexuality constitute her brand of feminist celebration.[21] Some feminist theorists would agree. Molly Hite, for example, argues that "asserting female desire in a culture in which female sexuality is viewed as so inextricably conjoined with passivity" is "transgressive":

> Implied in this strategy is the old paradox of the speaking statue, the created thing that magically begins to create, for when a woman writes—self-consciously from her muted position as a woman and not as an honorary man—about female desire, female sexuality, female sensuous experience generally, her performance has the effect of giving voice to pure corporeality, of turning a product of the dominant meaning-system into a producer of meanings. A woman, conventionally identified with her body, writes about that identification, and as a consequence, femininity—silent and inert by definition—erupts into patriarchy as an impossible discourse.[22]

Not all feminists would agree with this, of course. For the sake of the contrast I want to draw here, however, let us grant it, and note, as well, that an argument similar to Fiske's can be made concerning Madonna's refusal to be obedient to dominant and normalizing standards of female *beauty*. I am now talking, of course, about Madonna in her more fleshy days. In those days, Madonna saw herself as willfully out of step with the times. "Back in the fifties," she says in the *Time* interview, "women weren't ashamed of their bodies." (The fact that she is dead wrong is not relevant here.) Identifying herself with her construction of that time and what she calls its lack of "suppression" of femininity, she looks down her nose at the "androgynous" clothes of our own time and speaks warmly of her own stomach, "not really flat" but "round and the skin is smooth and I like it." Contrasting herself to anorectics, whom she sees as self-denying and self-hating, completely in the thrall of externally imposed standards of worthiness, Madonna (as she saw herself) stood for self-definition through the assertion of her own (traditionally "female" and now anachronistic) body-type (Figure 15).

Of course, this is no longer Madonna's body type. Shortly after her 1987 marriage to Sean Penn she began a strenuous reducing and exercise program,

Figure 15

now runs several miles a day, lifts weights, and has developed, in obedience to dominant contemporary norms, a tight, slender, muscular body (Figure 16). Why did she decide to shape up? "I didn't have a flat stomach anymore," she has said. "I had become well-rounded." Please note the sharp about-face here, from pride to embarrassment. My goal here, however, is not to suggest that Madonna's formerly voluptuous body was a nonalienated, freely expressive body, a "natural" body. While the slender body is the current cultural ideal, the voluptuous female body is a cultural form, too (as are all bodies), and was a coercive ideal in the fifties. My point is that in terms of Madonna's own former lexicon of meanings—in which feminine voluptuousness and the choice to be round in a culture of the lean were clearly connected to spontaneity, self-definition, and defiance of the cultural gaze—the terms set by that gaze have now triumphed. Madonna has been normalized; more

precisely, she has self-normalized. Her "wanna-bes" are following suit. Studies suggest that as many as 80 percent of nine-year-old suburban girls (the majority of whom are far from overweight) are making rigorous dieting and exercise the organizing discipline of their lives.[23] They do not require Madonna's example, of course, to believe that they must be thin to be acceptable. But Madonna clearly no longer provides a model of resistance or "difference" for them.

None of this "materiality"—that is, the obsessive body-praxis that regulates and disciplines Madonna's life and the lives of the young (and not so young) women who emulate her—makes its way into the representation of Madonna as postmodern heroine. In the terms of this representation (in both its popular and scholarly instantiations) Madonna is "in control of her image, not trapped by it"; the proof lies in her ironic and chameleon-like approach to the construction of her identity, her ability to "slip in and out of character at will," to defy definition, to keep them guessing.[24] In this coding of things, as in the fantasies of the polysurgical addict (and, as I argue elsewhere in this volume, the eating-disordered woman), *control* and *power*, words that are invoked over and over in discussions of Madonna, have become equivalent to *self-creating*. Madonna's new body has no material history; it conceals its continual struggle to maintain itself, it does not reveal its pain. (Significantly, Madonna's "self-exposé," the documentary *Truth or Dare*, does not include any scenes of Madonna's daily workouts.) It is merely another creative transformation of an ever-elusive subjectivity. "More Dazzling and Determined Not to Stop Changing," as *Cosmopolitan* describes Madonna: ". . . whether in looks or career, this multitalented dazzler will never be trapped in *any* mold!"[25] The plasticity of Madonna's subjectivity is emphasized again and again in the popular press, particularly by Madonna herself. It is how she tells the story of her "power" in the industry: "In pop music, generally, people have one image. You get pigeonholed. I'm lucky enough to be able to change and still be accepted . . . play a part, change characters, looks, attitudes."[26]

Madonna claims that her creative work, too, is meant to escape definition. "Everything I do is meant

madonna: broadway bound

Living proof that exercise does pay off. Madonna shows her shape in revealing clothes that hug every curve. The blazer redefined, opposite page. In navy linen (Moreau), it falls sensuously into a deep décolletage. With delicate white organza cuffs (Hurel). By Christian Lacroix Haute Couture. When you bare a lot of skin, it must be firm and smooth. Crème Cou at Décolleté by Stendhal moisturizes neck and breast area instantly. Daring silhouette, right. The stretch cotton halter with built-in bra in shades of bronze, ends in a peplum skirt, about $1,910. Mauve bicycle pants in stretch cotton with lace trim, about $377. Both by Jean Paul Gaultier. See Fashion Guide for details and stores, next to last page.

141

Figure 16

to have several meanings, to be ambiguous," she says. She resists, however (in true postmodern fashion), the attribution of serious artistic intent; rather (as she told *Cosmo*), she favors irony and ambiguity, "to entertain myself" and (as she told *Vanity Fair*) out of "rebelliousness and a desire to fuck with people."[27] It is the postmodern nature of her music and videos that has most entranced academic critics, whose accolades reproduce in highly theoretical language the notions emphasized in the popular press. Susan McClary writes:

Madonna's art itself repeatedly deconstructs the traditional notion of the unified subject with finite ego boundaries. Her pieces explore . . . various ways of constituting identities that refuse stability, that remain fluid, that resist definition. This tendency in her work has become increasingly pronounced; for instance, in her recent controversial video "Express Yourself" . . . she slips in and out of every subject position offered within the video's narrative context . . . refusing more than ever to deliver the security of a clear, unambiguous message or an "authentic" self.[28]

Later in the same piece, McClary describes "Open Your Heart to Me," which features Madonna as a porn star in a peep show, as creating "an image of open-ended *jouissance*—an erotic energy that continually escapes containment."[29] Now, many feminist viewers may find this particular video quite disturbing, for a number of reasons. First, unlike many of Madonna's older videos, "Open Your Heart to Me" does not visually emphasize Madonna's subjectivity or desire—as "Lucky Star," for example, did through frequent shots of Madonna's face and eyes, flirting with and controlling the reactions of the viewer. Rather, "Open Your Heart to Me" places the viewer in the position of the voyeur by presenting Madonna's body as object, now perfectly taut and tightly managed for display. To be sure, we do not identify with the slimy men, drooling over Madonna's performance, who are depicted in the video; but, as E. Ann Kaplan has pointed out, the way men view women *in* the filmic world is only one species of objectifying gaze. There is also the viewer's gaze, which may be encouraged by the director to be either more or less objectifying.[30] In "Open Your Heart to Me," as in virtually all rock videos, the female body is offered to the viewer purely as a spectacle, an object of sight, a visual commodity to be consumed. Madonna's weight loss and dazzling shaping-up job make the spectacle of her body all the more compelling; we are riveted to her body, fascinated by it. Many men and women may experience the primary reality of the video as the elicitation of desire *for* that perfect body; women, however, may also be gripped by the desire (very likely impossible to achieve) to *become* that perfect body.

These elements can be effaced, of course, by a deliberate abstraction of the video from the cultural context in which it is historically embedded—the continuing containment, sexualization, and objectification of the female body—and in which the viewer is implicated as well and instead treating the video as a purely formal text. Taken as such, "Open Your Heart to Me" presents itself as what E. Ann Kaplan calls a "postmodern video": it refuses to "take a clear position vis-à-vis its images" and similarly refuses a "clear position for the spectator within the filmic world . . . leaving him/her decentered, confused."[31]

McClary's reading of "Open Your Heart to Me" emphasizes precisely these postmodern elements, insisting on the ambiguous and unstable nature of the relationships depicted in the narrative of the video, and the frequent elements of parody and play. "The usual power relationship between the voyeuristic male gaze and object" is "destabilized," she claims, by the portrayal of the male patrons of the porno house as leering and pathetic. At the same time, the portrayal of Madonna as porno queen–object is deconstructed, McClary argues, by the end of the video, which has Madonna changing her clothes to those of a little boy and tripping off playfully, leaving the manager of the house sputtering behind her. McClary reads this as "escape to androgyny," which "refuses essentialist gender categories and turns sexual identity into a kind of play." As for the gaze of the viewer, she admits that it is "risky" to "invoke the image of porn queen in order to perform its deconstruction," but concludes that the deconstruction is successful: "In this video, Madonna confronts the most pernicious of her stereotypes and attempts to channel it into a very different realm: a realm where the feminine object need not be the object of the patriarchal gaze, where its energy can motivate play and nonsexual pleasure."[32]

I would argue, however, that despite the video's evasions of clear or fixed meaning there *is* a dominant position in this video: it is that of the objectifying gaze. One is not *really* decentered and confused by this video, despite the "ambiguities" it formally contains. Indeed, the video's postmodern conceits, I would suggest, facilitate rather than deconstruct the presentation of Madonna's body as an object on display. For in the absence of a coherent critical position telling us how to read the images, the individual images themselves become preeminent, hypnotic, fixating. Indeed, I would say that ultimately this video is entirely about Madonna's body, the narrative context virtually irrelevant, an excuse to showcase the physical achievements of the star, a video centerfold. On this level, any parodic or destabilizing element appears as cynically, mechanically tacked on, in bad faith, a way of claiming trendy status for what is really just cheesecake—or, perhaps, soft-core pornography.

Indeed, it may be worse than that. If the playful "tag" ending of "Open Your Heart to Me" is successful in deconstructing the notion that the objectification, the sexualization of women's bodies is a serious business, then Madonna's *jouissance* may be "fucking with" her youthful viewer's perceptions in a dangerous way. Judging from the proliferation of rock and rap lyrics celebrating the rape, abuse, and humiliation of women, the message—not Madonna's responsibility alone, of course, but hers among others, surely—is getting through. The artists who perform these misogynist songs also claim to be speaking playfully, tongue-in-cheek, and to be daring and resistant transgressors of cultural structures that contain and define. Ice T, whose rap lyrics gleefully describe the gang rape of a woman—with a flashlight, to "make her tits light up"—claims that he is only "telling it like it is" among black street youth (he compares himself to Richard Wright), and he scoffs at feminist humorlessness, implying, as well, that it is racist and repressive for white feminists to try to deny him his indigenous "style." The fact that Richard Wright embedded his depiction of Bigger Thomas within a critique of the racist culture that shaped him, and that *Native Son* is meant to be a *tragedy*, was not, apparently, noticed in Ice T's postmodern reading of the book, whose critical point of view he utterly ignores. Nor does he seem concerned about what appears to be a growing fad—not only among street gangs, but in fraternity houses as well—for gang rape, often with an unconscious woman, and surrounded by male spectators. (Some of the terms popularly used to describe these rapes include "beaching"—the woman being likened to a "beached whale"—and "spectoring," to emphasize how integral a role the onlookers play.)

My argument here is a plea, not for censorship, but for recognition of the social contexts and consequences of images from popular culture, consequences that are frequently effaced in postmodern and other celebrations of "resistant" elements in these images. To turn back to Madonna and the liberating postmodern subjectivity that McClary and others claim she is offering: the notion that one can play a porno house by night and regain one's androgynous innocence by day does not seem to me to be a refusal of essentialist categories about gender, but rather a new inscription of mind/body dualism. What the body does is immaterial, so long as the imagination is free. This abstract, unsituated, disembodied freedom, I have argued in this essay, glorifies itself only through the effacement of the material praxis of people's lives, the normalizing power of cultural images, and the continuing social realities of dominance and subordination.

NOTES

Earlier versions of this essay were delivered at the 1988 meetings of the Society for Phenomenology and Existentialist Philosophy, Duke University, Syracuse University, the 1990 meetings of the Popular Culture Association, the State University of New York at Binghamton's 1990 Conference on Feminism and Cultural Studies: Theory, History, Experience, and Sienna College. I thank all those who offered comments on those occasions, and Cynthia Willett and Cathy Schwichtenberg for reading an earlier written draft and making suggestions on it . . .

1. Quoted in Trix Rosen, *Strong and Sexy* (New York: Putnam, 1983), pp. 72, 61.

2. "Travolta: 'Your Really Can Make Yourself Over,'" *Syracuse Herald-American*, Jan. 13, 1985.

3. "Popular Plastic Surgery," *Cosmopolitan* (May 1990): 96.

4. Tina Lizardi and Martha Frankel, "Hand Job," *Details* (Feb. 1990): 38.

5. Jennet Conant, Jeanne Gordon, and Jennifer Donovan, "Scalpel Slaves Just Can't Quit," *Newsweek* (Jan. 11, 1988): 58–59.

6. "Donahue" transcript 05257, n.d., Multimedia Entertainment, Cincinnati, Ohio.

7. Dahleen Glanton, "Racism Within a Race," *Syracuse Herald-American*, Sept. 19, 1989.

8. *Essence* reader opinion poll (June 1989): 71.

9. Since this essay first appeared, DuraSoft has altered its campaign once more, renaming the lenses "Complements" and emphasizing how "natural" and subtle they are. "No one will know you're wearing them," they assure. One ad for "Complements" features identical black twins, one with brown eyes and one wearing blue lenses, as if to show that DuraSoft finds nothing "wrong" with brown eyes. The issue, rather, is self-determination: "Choosing your very own eye color is now the most natural thing in the world."

10. Linda Bien, "Building a Better Bust," *Syracuse Herald-American*, March 4, 1990.

11. This was said by Janice Radway in an oral presentation of her work, Duke University, Spring, 1989.

12. John Fiske, *Television Culture* (New York: Methuen, 1987), p. 19.

13. Michel Foucault, *Discipline and Punish* (New York: Vintage, 1979), p. 138.

14. Related in Bill Moyers, "A Walk Through the Twentieth Century: The Second American Revolution," PBS Boston.

15. Foucault, *Discipline and Punish*, pp. 26–27.

16. Susan Rubin Suleiman, "(Re)Writing the Body: The Politics and Poetics of Female Eroticism," in Susan Rubin Suleiman, ed., *The Female Body in Western Culture* (Cambridge: Harvard University Press, 1986), p. 24.

17. Jacques Derrida and Christie V. McDonald, "Choreographies," *Diacritics* 12, no. 2 (1982): 76.

18. Cathy Schwichtenberg, "Postmodern Feminism and Madonna: Toward an Erotic Politics of the Female Body," paper presented at the University of Utah Humanities Center, National Conference on Rewriting the (Post)Modern: (Post)Colonialism/Feminism/Late Capitalism, March 30–31, 1990.

19. John Fiske, "British Cultural Studies and Television," in Robert C. Allen, ed., *Channels of Discourse* (Chapel Hill: University of North Carolina Press, 1987), pp. 254–90.

20. Quoted in John Skow, "Madonna Rocks the Land," *Time* (May 27, 1985): 77.

21. Skow, "Madonna Rocks the Land," p. 81.

22. Molly Hite, "Writing—and Reading—the Body: Female Sexuality and Recent Feminist Fiction," in *Feminist Studies* 14, no. 1 (Spring 1988): 121–22.

23. "Fat or Not, 4th Grade Girls Diet Lest They Be Teased or Unloved," *Wall Street Journal*, Feb. 11, 1986.

24. Catherine Texier, "Have Women Surrendered in MTV's Battle of the Sexes?" *New York Times*, April 22, 1990, p. 31.

25. *Cosmopolitan* (July 1987): cover.

26. David Ansen, "Magnificent Maverick," *Cosmopolitan* (May 1990): 311.

27. Ansen, "Magnificent Maverick," p. 311; Kevin Sessums, "White Heat," *Vanity Fair* (April 1990): 208.

28. Susan McClary, "Living to Tell: Madonna's Resurrection of the Fleshy," *Genders*, no. 7 (Spring 1990): 2.

29. McClary, "Living to Tell," p. 12.

30. E. Ann Kaplan, "Is the Gaze Male?" in Ann Snitow, Christine Stansell, and Sharon Thompson, eds., *Powers of Desire: The Politics of Sexuality* (New York: Monthly Review Press, 1983), pp. 309–27.

31. E. Ann Kaplan, *Rocking Around the Clock: Music Television, Postmodernism and Consumer Culture* (New York: Methuen, 1987), p. 63.

32. McClary, "Living to Tell," p. 13.

Study Questions

1. What does Bordo mean by "postmodern" (e.g., she speaks of the "postmodern" imagination, of "postmodern" conversations, and "postmodern" bodies)?

2. Explain two of the ways that, according to Bordo, a postmodern approach to the body "effaces" our social, historical, and/or individual situations. Compare Bordo's concern here with Wendell's worries about postmodernism in "The Social Construction of Disability."

3. In the second paragraph of the section entitled "Plastic Discourse," Bordo argues that the postmodern "spectacle of difference defeats the ability to sustain coherent political critique." Explain her argument.

4. Does Bordo think that it is possible to resist the dominant cultural meanings of the body? How?

Barbara Christian

The Race for Theory

I have seized this occasion to break the silence among those of us, critics, as we are now called, who have been intimidated, devalued by what I call the race for theory. I have become convinced that there has been a takeover in the literary world by Western philosophers from the old literary elite, the neutral humanists. Philosophers have been able to effect such a takeover because so much of the literature of the West has become pallid, laden with despair, self-indulgent, and disconnected. The New Philosophers, eager to understand a world that is today fast escaping their political control, have redefined literature so that the distinctions implied by that term, that is, the distinctions between everything written and those things written to evoke feeling as well as to express thought, have been blurred. They have changed literary critical language to suit their own purposes as philosophers, and they have reinvented the meaning of theory.

My first response to this realization was to ignore it. Perhaps, in spite of the egocentrism of this trend, some good might come of it. I had, I felt, more pressing and interesting things to do, such as reading and studying the history and literature of black women, a history that had been totally ignored, a contemporary literature bursting with originality, passion, insight, and beauty. But, unfortunately, it is difficult to ignore this new takeover, because theory has become a commodity that helps determine whether we are hired or promoted in academic institutions—worse, whether we are heard at all. Due to this new orientation, works (a word that evokes labor) have become texts. Critics are no longer concerned with literature but with other critics' texts, for the critic yearning for attention has displaced the writer and has conceived of herself or himself as the center. Interestingly, in the first part of this century, at least in England and America, the critic was usually also a writer of poetry, plays, or novels. But today, as a new generation of professionals develops, she or he is increasingly an academic. Activities such as teaching or writing one's response to specific works of literature have, among this group, become subordinated to one primary thrust—that moment when one creates a theory, thus fixing a constellation of ideas for a time at least, a fixing which no doubt will be replaced in another month or so by somebody else's competing theory as the race accelerates. Perhaps because those who have effected the takeover have the power (although they deny it) first of all to be published, and thereby to determine the ideas that are deemed valuable, some of our most daring and potentially radical critics (and by *our* I mean black, women, Third World) have been influenced, even co-opted, into speaking a language and defining their discussion in terms alien to and opposed to our needs and orientation. At least so far, the creative writers I study have resisted this language.

For people of color have always theorized—but in forms quite different from the Western form of abstract logic. And I am inclined to say that our theorizing (and I intentionally use the verb rather than the noun) is often in narrative forms, in the stories we create, in riddles and proverbs, in the play with language, because dynamic rather than fixed ideas seem more to our liking. How else have we managed to survive with such spiritedness the assault on our bodies, social institutions, countries, our very humanity? And women, at least the women I grew up around, continuously speculated about the nature of life through pithy language that unmasked the power relations of their world. It is this language, and the grace and pleasure with which they played with it, that I find celebrated, refined, critiqued in the works of writers like Toni Morrison and Alice Walker. My folk, in other words, have always been a race for theory—though more in the form of the hieroglyph, a written figure that is both sensual and abstract, both beautiful and communicative. In my own work I try to illuminate and explain these hieroglyphs, which is, I think, an activity quite different from the creating of the hieroglyphs themselves. As the Buddhists would say, the finger pointing at the moon is not the moon.

In this discussion, however, I am more concerned with the issue raised by my first use of the term, *the race for theory*, in relation to its academic hegemony, and possibly of its inappropriateness to the energetic emerging literatures in the world today. The pervasiveness of this academic hegemony is an issue continually spoken about—but usually in hidden groups, lest we, who are disturbed by it, appear ignorant to the reigning academic elite. Among the folk who speak in muted tones are people of color, feminists, radical critics, creative writers, who have struggled for much longer than a decade to make their voices, their various voices, heard, and for whom literature is not an occasion for discourse among critics but is necessary nourishment for their people and one way by which they come to understand their lives better. Clichéd though this may be, it bears, I think, repeating here.

The race for theory—with its linguistic jargon; its emphasis on quoting its prophets; its tendency toward "biblical" exegesis; its refusal even to mention specific works of creative writers, far less contemporary ones; its preoccupations with mechanical analyses of language, graphs, algebraic equations; its gross generalizations about culture—has silenced many of us to the extent that some of us feel we can no longer discuss our own literature, and others have developed intense writing blocks and are puzzled by the incomprehensibility of the language set adrift in literary circles. There have been, in the last year, any number of occasions on which I had to convince literary critics who have pioneered entire new areas of critical inquiry that they did have something to say. Some of us are continually harassed to invent wholesale theories regardless of the complexity of the literature we study. I, for one, am tired of being asked to produce a black feminist literary theory as if I were a mechanical man. For I believe such theory is prescriptive—it ought to have some relationship to practice. Because I can count on one hand the number of people attempting to be black feminist literary critics in the world today, I consider it presumptuous of me to invent a theory of how we *ought* to read. Instead, I think we need to read the works of our writers in our various ways and remain open to the intricacies of the intersection of language, class, race, and gender in the literature. And it would help if we share our process, that is, our practice, as much as possible because, finally, our work *is* a collective endeavor.

The insidious quality of this race for theory is symbolized for me by a term like "minority discourse," a label that is borrowed from the reigning theory of the day but which is untrue to the literatures being produced by our writers, for many of our literatures (certainly Afro-American literature) are central, not minor. I have used the passive voice in my last sentence construction, contrary to the rules of black English, which like all languages has a particular value system, because I have not placed reponsibility on any particular person or group. But that is precisely because this new ideology has become so prevalent among us that it behaves like so many of the other ideologies with which we have had to contend. It appears to have neither head nor center. At the least, though, we can say that the terms "minority" and "discourse" are located firmly in a Western dualistic or "binary" frame which sees the rest of the world as minor and tries to convince the rest of the world that it *is* major, usually through force and then through language, even as it claims many of the ideas that we, its "historical" other, have known and spoken about for so long. For many of us have never conceived of ourselves only as somebody's *other*.

Let me not give the impression that by objecting to the race for theory I ally myself with or agree with the neutral humanists who see literature as pure expression and will not admit to the obvious control of its production, value, and distribution by those who have power, who deny, in other words, that literature is, of necessity, political. I am studying an entire body of literature that has been denigrated for centuries by such terms as *political*. For an entire century Afro-American writers, from Charles Chestnutt in the nineteenth century through Richard Wright in the 1930s, Imamu Baraka in the 1960s, Alice Walker in the 1970s, have protested the literary hierarchy of dominance which declares when literature is literature, when literature is great, depending on what it thinks is to its advantage. The black arts movement of the 1960s, out of which black studies, the feminist literary movement of the 1970s, and women's studies grew, articulated precisely those issues, which came *not* from the declarations of the New Western Philosophers but from these groups' reflections on their own lives. That Western scholars have long believed their ideas to be universal has been strongly opposed by many such groups. Some of my colleagues do not see black critical writers of previous decades as eloquent enough. Clearly they have not read Richard Wright's "Blueprint for Negro Writing," Ralph Ellison's *Shadow and Act*, Charles Chesnutt's resignation from being a writer, or Alice Walker's "Search for Zora Neale Hurston." There are two reasons for this general ignorance of what our writer-critics have said. One is that black writing has been generally ignored in this country. Because we, as Toni Morrison has put it, are seen as a discredited people, it is no surprise, then, that our creations are also discredited. But this is also due to the fact that, until recently, dominant critics in the Western world have also been

creative writers who have had access to the upper-middle-class institutions of education, and, until recently, our writers have decidedly been excluded from these institutions and in fact have often been opposed to them. Because of the academic world's general ignorance about the literature of black people, and of women, whose work too has been discredited, it is not surprising that so many of our critics think that the position arguing that literature is political begins with these New Philosophers. Unfortunately, many of our young critics do not investigate the reasons *why* that statement—literature is political—is now acceptable when before it was not; nor do we look to our own antecedents for the sophisticated arguments upon which we can build in order to change the tendency of any established Western idea to become hegemonic.

For I feel that the new emphasis on literary critical theory is as hegemonic as the world it attacks. I see the language it creates as one that mystifies rather than clarifies our condition, making it possible for a few people who know that particular language to control the critical scene. That language surfaced, interestingly enough, just when the literature of peoples of color, black women, Latin Americans, and Africans began to move to "the center." Such words as *center* and *periphery* are themselves instructive. *Discourse*, *canon*, *texts*, words as Latinate as the tradition from which they come, are quite familiar to me. Because I went to a Catholic mission school in the West Indies I must confess that I cannot hear the word "canon" without smelling incense, that the word "text" immediately brings back agonizing memories of biblical exegesis, that "discourse" reeks for me of metaphysics forced down my throat in those courses that traced *world* philosophy from Aristotle through Aquinas to Heidegger. "Periphery" too is a word I heard throughout my childhood, for if anything was seen as being at the periphery, it was those small Caribbean islands that had neither land mass nor military power. Still I noted how intensely important this periphery was, for U.S. troups were continually invading one island or another if any change in political control ever seemed to be occurring. As I lived among folk for whom language was an absolutely necessary way of validating our existence, I was told that the minds of the world lived only in the small continent of Europe. The metaphysical language of the New Philosophy, then, I must admit, is repulsive to me and is one reason why I raced from philosophy to literature, because the latter seemed to me to have the possibilities of rendering the world as large and as complicated as I experienced it, as sensual as I knew it was. In literature I sensed the possibility of the integration of feeling/knowledge, rather than the split between the abstract and the emotional in which Western philosophy inevitably indulged.

Now I am being told that philosophers are the ones who write literature; that authors are dead, irrelevant, mere vessels through which their narratives ooze; that they do not work nor have they the faintest idea what they are doing—rather, they produce texts as disembodied as the angels. I am frankly astonished that scholars who call themselves Marxists or post-Marxists could seriously use such metaphysical language even as they attempt to deconstruct the philosophical tradition from which their language comes. And as a student of literature, I am appalled by the sheer ugliness of the language, its lack of clarity, its unnecessarily complicated sentence constructions, its lack of pleasurableness, its alienating quality. It is the kind of writing for which composition teachers would give a first-year student a resounding F.

Because I am a curious person, however, I postponed readings of black women writers I was working on and read some of the prophets of this new literary orientation. These writers did announce their dissatisfaction with some of the cornerstone ideas of their own tradition, a dissatisfaction with which I was born. But in their attempt to change the orientation of Western scholarship, they, as usual, concentrated on themselves and were not in the slightest interested in the worlds they had ignored or controlled. Again I was supposed to know *them*, while they were not at all interested in knowing *me*. Instead, they sought to "deconstruct" the tradition to which they belonged even as they used the same forms, style, and language of that tradition, forms that necessarily embody its values. And increasingly as I read them and saw their substitution of their philosophical writings for literary ones, I began to have the uneasy feeling that their folk were not producing any literature worth mentioning. For they always harkened back to the masterpieces of the past, again reifying the very texts they said they were deconstructing. Increasingly, as *their* way, *their* terms, *their* approaches remained central and became the means by which one defined literary critics, many of my own peers who had previously been concentrating on dealing with the other side of the equation—the reclamation and discussion of past and *present* Third World literatures—were diverted into continually discussing the new literary theory.

From my point of view as a critic of contemporary Afro-American women's writing, this orientation is extremely problematic. In attempting to find the deep structures in the literary tradition, a major preoccupation of the new New Criticism, many of us have become obsessed with the nature of reading itself to the extent that we have stopped writing about literature being written today. Since I am slightly paranoid, it has begun to occur to me that the literature being produced *is* precisely one of the reasons why this new philosophical-literary-critical theory of relativity is so prominent. In other words, the literature of blacks, women of South America and Africa, and so forth, as overtly "political" literature was being preempted by a new Western concept which proclaimed that reality does not exist, that everything is relative, and that every text is silent about something—which indeed it must necessarily be.

There is, of course, much to be learned from exploring how we know what we know, how we read what we read, an exploration which, of necessity, can have no end. But there also has to be a "what," and that "what," when it is even mentioned by the New Philosophers, are texts of the past, primarily Western male texts, whose norms are again being transferred onto Third World and female texts as theories of reading proliferate. Inevitably a hierarchy has now developed between what is called theoretical criticism and practical criticism, as mind is deemed superior to matter. I have no quarrel with those who wish to philosophize about how we know what we know. But I do resent the fact that this particular orientation is so privileged, and has diverted so many of us from doing the first readings of the literature being written today as well as of past works about which nothing has been written. I note, for example, that there is little work done on Gloria Naylor, that most of Alice Walker's works have not been commented on—despite the rage around *The Color Purple*—that there has yet to be an in-depth study of Frances Harper, the nineteenth-century abolitionist poet and novelist. If our emphasis on theoretical criticism continues, critics of the future may have to reclaim the writers we are now ignoring, that is, if they are even aware these artists exist.

I am particularly perturbed by the movement to exalt theory, as well, because of my own adult history. I was an active member of the black arts movement of the sixties and know how dangerous theory can become. Many today may not be aware of this, but the black arts movement tried to create black literary theory and in doing so became prescriptive. My fear is that when theory is not rooted in practice, it becomes prescriptive, exclusive, elitish.

An example of this prescriptiveness is the approach the black arts movement took toward language. For it, blackness resided in the use of black talk which they defined as hip urban language. So that when Nikki Giovanni reviewed Paule Marshall's *Chosen Place, Timeless People*, she criticized the novel on the grounds that it was not black, for the language was too elegant, too white. Blacks, she said, did not speak that way. Having come from the West Indies where we do, some of the time, speak that way, I was amazed by the narrowness of her vision. The emphasis on *one way* to be black resulted in the works of Southern writers being seen as nonblack because the black talk of Georgia does not sound like the black talk of Philadelphia. Because the ideologues, like Baraka, came from the urban centers, they tended to privilege their way of speaking, thinking, writing, and to condemn other kinds of writing as not being black enough. Whole areas of the canon were assessed according to the dictum of the black arts nationalist point of view, as in Addison Gayle's *The Way of the New World*, and other works were ignored because they did not fit the scheme of cultural nationalism. Older writers like Ralph Ellison and James Baldwin

were condemned because they saw that the intersection of Western and African influences resulted in a new Afro-American culture, a position with which many of the black nationalist idealogues disagreed. Writers were told that writing love poems was not being black. Further examples abound.

It is true that the black arts movement resulted in a necessary and important critique both of previous Afro-American literature and of the white-established literary world. But in attempting to take over power, it, as Ishmael Reed satirizes so well in *Mumbo Jumbo*, became much like its opponent, monolithic and downright repressive.

It is this tendency toward the monolithic, monotheistic, and so on, that worries me about the race for theory. Constructs like the *center* and the *periphery* reveal that tendency to want to make the world less complex by organizing it according to one principle, to fix it through an idea which is really an ideal. Many of us are particularly sensitive to monolithism because one major element of ideologies of dominance, such as sexism and racism, is to dehumanize people by stereotyping them, by denying them their variousness and complexity. Inevitably, monolithism becomes a metasystem, in which there is a controlling ideal, especially in relation to pleasure. Language as one form of pleasure is immediately restricted and becomes heavy, abstract, prescriptive, monotonous.

Variety, multiplicity, eroticism are difficult to control. And it may very well be that these are the reasons why writers are often seen as *persona non grata* by political states, whatever form they take, because writers/artists have a tendency to refuse to give up their way of seeing the world and of playing with possibilities; in fact, their very expression relies on that insistence. Perhaps that is why creative literature, even when written by politically reactionary people, can be so freeing, for in having to embody ideas and recreate the world, writers cannot merely produce "one way."

The characteristics of the black arts movement are, I am afraid, being repeated again today, certainly in the other area to which I am especially tuned. In the race for theory, feminists, eager to enter the halls of power, have attempted their own prescriptions. So often I have read books on feminist literary theory that restrict the definition of what *feminist* means and overgeneralize about so much of the world that most women as well as men are excluded. And seldom do feminist theorists take into account the complexity of life—that women are of many races and ethnic backgrounds with different histories and cultures and that as a rule women belong to different classes that have different concerns. Seldom do they note these distinctions, because if they did they could not articulate a theory. Often as a way of clearing themselves they do acknowledge that women of color, for example, do exist, then go on to do what they were going to do anyway, which is to invent a theory that has little relevance for us.

That tendency toward monolithism is precisely how I see the French feminist theorists. They concentrate on the female body as the means to creating a female language, because language, they say, is male and necessarily conceives of woman as other. Clearly many of them have been irritated by the theories of Lacan for whom language is phallic. But suppose there are peoples in the world whose language was invented primarily in relation to women, who after all are the ones who relate to children and teach language. Some native American languages, for example, use female pronouns when speaking about non-gender-specific activity. Who knows who, according to gender, created languages. Further, by positing the body as the source of everything, French feminists return to the old myth that biology determines everything and ignore the fact that gender is a social rather than a biological construct.

I could go on critiquing the positions of French feminists who are themselves more various in their points of view than the label used to describe them, but that is not my point. What I am concerned about is the authority this school now has in feminist scholarship—the way it has become *authoritative discourse*, monologic, which occurs precisely because it does have access to the means of promulgating its ideas. The black arts movement was able to do this for a time because of the political movements of the 1960s—so too with the French feminists who could not be inventing "theory" if a space had not been created by the women's movement. In both cases, both groups posited a theory that excluded many of the people who made that space possible. Hence, one of the reasons for the surge of Afro-American women's writing during the 1970s and its emphasis on sexism in the black community is precisely that when the ideologues of the 1960s said *black*, they meant *black male*.

I and many of my sisters do not see the world as being so simple. And perhaps that is why we have not rushed to create abstract theories. For we know there are countless women of color, both in America and in the rest of the world, to whom our singular ideas would be applied. There is, therefore, a caution we feel about pronouncing black feminist theory that might be seen as a decisive statement about Third World women. This is not to say we are not theorizing. Certainly our literature is an indication of the ways in which our theorizing, of necessity, is based on our multiplicity of experiences.

There is at least one other lesson I learned from the black arts movement. One reason for its monolithic approach had to do with its desire to destroy the power that controlled black people, but it was a power that many of its ideologues wished to achieve. The nature of our context today is such that an approach which desires power single-mindedly must of necessity become like that which it wishes to destroy. Rather than wanting to change the whole model, many of us want to be at the center. It is this point of view that writers like June Jordan and Audre Lorde continually critique even as they call for empowerment, as they emphasize the fear of difference among us and our need for leaders rather than a reliance on ourselves.

For one must distinguish the desire for power from the need to become empowered—that is, seeing oneself as capable of and having the right to determine one's life. Such empowerment is partially derived from a knowledge of history. The black arts movement did result in the creation of Afro-American studies as a concept, thus giving it a place in the university where one might engage in the reclamation of Afro-American history and culture and pass it on to others. I am particularly concerned that institutions such as black studies and women's studies, fought for with such vigor and at some sacrifice, are not often seen as important by many of our black or women scholars precisely because the old hierarchy of traditional departments is seen as superior to these "marginal" groups. Yet, it is in this context that many others of us are discovering the extent of our complexity, the interrelationships of different areas of knowledge in relation to a distinctly Afro-American or female experience. Rather than having to view our world as subordinate to others, or rather than having to work as if we were hybrids, we can pursue ourselves as subjects.

My major objection to the race for theory, as some readers have probably guessed by now, really hinges on the question, "For whom are we doing what we are doing when we do literary criticism?" It is, I think, the central question today, especially for the few of us who have infiltrated the academy enough to be wooed by it. The answer to that question determines what orientation we take in our work, the language we use, the purposes for which it is intended.

I can only speak for myself. But what I write and how I write is done in order to save my own life. And I mean that literally. For me, literature is a way of knowing that I am not hallucinating, that whatever I feel/know *is*. It is an affirmation that sensuality is intelligence, that sensual language is language that makes sense. My response, then, is directed to those who write what I read and to those who read what I read—put concretely—to Toni Morrison and to people who read Toni Morrison (among whom I would count few academics). That number is increasing, as is the readership of Alice Walker and Paule Marshall. But in no way is the literature Morrison, Marshall, or Walker create supported by the academic world. And, given the political context of our society, I do not expect that to change soon. For there is no reason, given who controls these institutions, for them to be anything other than threatened by these writers.

My readings do presuppose a need, a desire among folk who, like me, also want to save their own lives. My concern, then, is a passionate one, for the literature of people who are not in power has always been in danger of extinction or of co-optation, not

because we do not theorize but because what we can even imagine, far less who we can reach, is constantly limited by societal structures. For me, literary criticism is promotion as well as understanding, a response to the writer to whom there is often no response, to folk who need the writing as much as they need anything. I know, from literary history, that writing disappears unless there is a response to it. Because I write about writers who are now writing, I hope to help ensure that their tradition has continuity and survives.

So my "method," to use a new "lit. crit." word, is not fixed but relates to what I read and to the historical context of the writers I read *and* to the many critical activities in which I am engaged, which may or may not involve writing. It is a learning from the language of creative writers, which is one of surprise, so that I might discover what language I might use. For my language is very much based on what I read and how it affects me, that is, on the surprise that comes from reading something that compels you to read differently, as I believe literature does. I, therefore, have no set method, another prerequisite of the new theory, since for me every work suggests a new approach. As risky as that might seem, it is, I believe, what intelligence means—a tuned sensitivity to that which is alive and therefore cannot be known until it is known. Audre Lorde puts it in a far more succinct and sensual way in her essay, "Poetry Is Not a Luxury."

> As they become known to and accepted by us, our feelings and the honest exploration of them become sanctuaries and spawning grounds for the most radical and daring of ideas. They become a safe-house for that difference so necessary to change and the conceptualization of any meaningful action. Right now, I could name at least ten ideas I would have found intolerable or incomprehensible and frightening, except as they came after dreams and poems. This is not idle fantasy, but a disciplined attention to the true meaning of "it feels right to me." We can train ourselves to respect our feelings and to transpose them into a language so they can be shared. And where that language does not yet exist, it is our poetry which helps to fashion it. Poetry is not only dream and vision; it is the skeleton architecture of our lives. It lays the foundations for a future of

change, a bridge across our fears of what has never been before.[1]

NOTE

1. Audre Lorde, "Poetry Is Not a Luxury," in Audre Lorde, *Sister Outsider* (Trumansburg, N.Y.: Crossing Press, 1984), 37.

Study Questions

1. According to Chrstian, how have the "New Philosophers" redefined literature (what is the old definition, what is the new one)?

2. Christian describes a "new orientation" toward theory. Describe three features of this form of theorizing as she understands it. Can you identify any of these features in other works in this book?

3. Christian says, "The insidious quality of this race for theory is symbolized for me by a term like 'minority discourse.' " (paragraph 6). Explain her criticism of this term. Christian argues that the new form of theory is politically problematic. Explain three of her reasons for thinking this.

4. What does Christian propose as an alternative approach to literature?

Combahee River Collective

A Black Feminist Statement

We are a collective of Black feminists who have been meeting together since 1974.[1] During that time we have been involved in the process of defining and clarifying our politics, while at the same time doing political work within our own group and in coalition with other progressive organizations and movements. The most general statement of our politics at the present time would be that we are actively committed to struggling against racial, sexual, heterosexual, and class oppression and see as our particular task the development of integrated analysis and practice based upon the fact that the major systems of oppression are interlocking. The synthesis of these oppressions creates the conditions of our lives. As Black women we see Black feminism as the logical political movement to combat the manifold and simultaneous oppressions that all women of color face.

We will discuss four major topics in the paper that follows: (1) the genesis of contemporary Black feminism; (2) what we believe, i.e., the specific province of our politics; (3) the problems in organizing Black feminists, including a brief herstory of our collective; and (4) Black feminist issues and practice.

1. THE GENESIS OF CONTEMPORARY BLACK FEMINISM

Before looking at the recent development of Black feminism we would like to affirm that we find our origins in the historical reality of Afro-American women's continuous life-and-death struggle for survival and liberation. Black women's extremely negative relationship to the American political system (a system of white male rule) has always been determined by our membership in two oppressed racial and sexual castes. As Angela Davis points out in "Reflections on the Black Woman's Role in the

Community of Slaves," Black women have always embodied, if only in their physical manifestation, an adversary stance to white male rule and have actively resisted its inroads upon them and their communities in both dramatic and subtle ways. There have always been Black women activists—some known, like Sojourner Truth, Harriet Tubman, Frances E. W. Harper, Ida B. Wells Barnett, and Mary Church Terrell, and thousands upon thousands unknown—who had a shared awareness of how their sexual identity combined with their racial identity to make their whole life situation and the focus of their political struggles unique. Contemporary Black feminism is the outgrowth of countless generations of personal sacrifice, militancy, and work by our mothers and sisters.

A Black feminist presence has evolved most obviously in connection with the second wave of the American women's movement beginning in the late 1960s. Black, other Third World, and working women have been involved in the feminist movement from its start, but both outside reactionary forces and racism and elitism within the movement itself have served to obscure our participation. In 1973 Black feminists, primarily located in New York, felt the necessity of forming a separate Black feminist group. This became the National Black Feminist Organization (NBFO).

Black feminist politics also have an obvious connection to movements for Black liberation, particularly those of the 1960s and 1970s. Many of us were active in those movements (civil rights, Black nationalism, the Black Panthers), and all of our lives were greatly affected and changed by their ideology, their goals, and the tactics used to achieve their goals. It was our experience and disillusionment within these liberation movements, as well as experience on the periphery of the white male left, that led to the need to develop a politics that was antiracist, unlike those of white women, and antisexist, unlike those of Black and white men.

There is also undeniably a personal genesis for Black feminism, that is, the political realization that comes from the seemingly personal experiences of individual Black women's lives. Black feminists and many more Black women who do not define themselves as feminists have all experienced sexual oppression as a constant factor in our day-to-day existence. As children we realized that we were different from boys and that we were treated differently. For example, we were told in the same breath to be quiet both for the sake of being "ladylike" and to make us less objectionable in the eyes of white people. As we grew older we became aware of the threat of physical and sexual abuse by men. However, we had no way of conceptualizing what was so apparent to us, what we *knew* was really happening.

Black feminists often talk about their feelings of craziness before becoming conscious of the concepts of sexual politics, patriarchal rule, and most importantly, feminism, the political analysis and practice that we women use to struggle against our oppression. The fact that racial politics and indeed racism are pervasive factors in our lives did not allow us, and still does not allow most Black women, to look more deeply into our own experiences and, from that sharing and growing consciousness, to build a politics that will change our lives and inevitably end our oppression. Our development must also be tied to the contemporary economic and political position of Black people. The post World War II generation of Black youth was the first to be able to minimally partake of certain educational and employment options, previously closed completely to Black people. Although our economic position is still at the very bottom of the American capitalistic economy, a handful of us have been able to gain certain tools as a result of tokenism in education and employment which potentially enable us to more effectively fight our oppression.

A combined antiracist and antisexist position drew us together initially, and as we developed politically we addressed ourselves to heterosexism and economic oppression under capitalism.

2. WHAT WE BELIEVE

Above all else, our politics initially sprang from the shared belief that Black women are inherently valuable, that our liberation is a necessity not as an adjunct to somebody else's but because of our need as human persons for autonomy. This may seem so obvious as to sound simplistic, but it is apparent that no other ostensibly progressive movement has ever considered our specific oppression as a priority or worked seriously for the ending of that oppression. Merely naming the pejorative stereotypes attributed to Black women (e.g. mammy, matriarch, Sapphire, whore, bulldagger), let alone cataloguing the cruel, often murderous, treatment we receive, indicates how little value has been placed upon our lives during four centuries of bondage in the Western hemisphere. We realize that the only people who care enough about us to work consistently for our liberation is us. Our politics evolve from a healthy love for ourselves, our sisters and our community which allows us to continue our struggle and work.

This focusing upon our own oppression is embodied in the concept of identity politics. We believe that the most profound and potentially the most radical politics come directly out of our own identity, as opposed to working to end somebody else's oppression. In the case of Black women this is a particularly repugnant, dangerous, threatening, and therefore revolutionary concept because it is obvious from looking at all the political movements that have preceded us that anyone is more worthy of liberation than ourselves. We reject pedestals, queenhood, and walking ten paces behind. To be recognized as human, levelly human, is enough.

We believe that sexual politics under patriarchy is as pervasive in Black women's lives as are the politics of class and race. We also often find it difficult to separate race from class from sex oppression because in our lives they are most often experienced simultaneously. We know that there is such a thing as racial-sexual oppression which is neither solely racial nor solely sexual, e.g., the history of rape of Black women by white men as a weapon of political repression.

Although we are feminists and lesbians, we feel solidarity with progressive Black men and do not advocate the fractionalization that white women who are separatists demand. Our situation as Black people necessitates that we have solidarity around the fact of race, which white women of course do not need to have with white men, unless it is their negative solidarity as racial oppressors. We struggle together with Black men against racism, while we also struggle with Black men about sexism.

We realize that the liberation of all oppressed peoples necessitates the destruction of the political-economic systems of capitalism and imperialism as well as patriarchy. We are socialists because we believe the work must be organized for the collective benefit of those who do the work and create the products, and not for the profit of the bosses. Material resources must be equally distributed among those who create these resources. We are not convinced, however, that a socialist revolution that is not also a feminist and antiracist revolution will guarantee our liberation. We have arrived at the necessity for developing an understanding of class relationships that takes into account the specific class position of Black women who are generally marginal in the labor force, while at this particular time some of us are temporarily viewed as doubly desirable tokens at white-collar and professional levels. We need to articulate the real class situation of persons who are not merely race-less, sexless workers, but for whom racial and sexual oppression are significant determinants in their working/economic lives. Although we are in essential agreement with Marx's theory as it applied to the very specific economic relationships he analyzed, we know that his analysis must be extended further in order for us to understand our specific economic situation as Black women.

A political contribution which we feel we have already made is the expansion of the feminist principle that the personal is political. In our consciousness-raising sessions, for example, we have in many ways gone beyond white women's revelations because we are dealing with the implications of race and class as well as sex. Even our Black women's style of talking/testifying in Black language about what we have experienced has a resonance that is both cultural and political. We have spent a great deal of energy delving into the cultural and experiential nature of our oppression out of necessity because none of these matters has ever been looked at before. No one before has ever examined the multilayered texture of Black women's lives. An example of this kind of revelation/ conceptualization occurred at a meeting as we discussed the ways in which our early intellectual interests had been attacked by our peers, particularly Black males. We discovered that all of us, because we were "smart" had also been considered "ugly," i.e., "smart-ugly." "Smart-ugly" crystallized the way in which most of us had been forced to develop our intellects at great cost to our "social" lives. The sanctions in the Black and white communities against Black women thinkers is comparatively much higher than for white women, particularly ones from the educated middle and upper classes.

As we have already stated, we reject the stance of lesbian separatism because it is not a viable political analysis or strategy for us. It leaves out far too much and far too many people, particularly Black men, women, and children. We have a great deal of criticism and loathing for what men have been socialized to be in this society: what they support, how they act, and how they oppress. But we do not have the misguided notion that it is their maleness, per se— i.e., their biological maleness—that makes them what they are. As Black women we find any type of biological determinism a particularly dangerous and reactionary basis upon which to build a politic. We must also question whether lesbian separatism is an adequate and progressive political analysis and strategy, even for those who practice it, since it so completely denies any but the sexual sources of women's oppression, negating the facts of class and race.

3. PROBLEMS IN ORGANIZING BLACK FEMINISTS

During our years together as a Black feminist collective we have experienced success and defeat, joy and pain, victory and failure. We have found that it is very difficult to organize around Black feminist issues, difficult even to announce in certain contexts that we *are* Black feminists. We have tried to think about the reasons for our difficulties, particularly since the white women's movement continues to be strong and to grow in many directions. In this section we will discuss some of the general reasons for the organizing problems we face and also talk specifically about the stages in organizing our own collective.

The major source of difficulty in our political work is that we are not just trying to fight oppression on one front or even two, but instead to address a whole range of oppressions. We do not have racial, sexual, heterosexual, or class privilege to rely upon, nor do we have even the minimal access to resources and power that groups who possess any one of these types of privilege have.

The psychological toll of being a Black woman and the difficulties this presents in reaching political consciousness and doing political work can never be underestimated. There is a very low value placed upon Black women's psyches in this society, which is both racist and sexist. As an early group member once said, "We are all damaged people merely by virtue of being Black women." We are dispossessed psychologically and on every other level, and yet we feel the necessity to struggle to change the condition of all Black women. In "A Black Feminist's Search for Sisterhood," Michele Wallace arrives at this conclusion:

> "We exist as women who are Black who are feminists, each stranded for the moment, working independently because there is not yet an environment in this society remotely congenial to our struggle— because, being on the bottom, we would have to do what no one else has done: we would have to fight the world."[2]

Wallace is pessimistic but realistic in her assessment of Black feminists' position, particularly in her allusion to the nearly classic isolation most of us face. We might use our position at the bottom, however, to make a clear leap into revolutionary action. If Black women were free, it would mean that everyone else would have to be free since our freedom would necessitate the destruction of all the systems of oppression.

Feminism is, nevertheless, very threatening to the majority of Black people because it calls into question some of the most basic assumptions about our existence, i.e., that sex should be a determinant of power relationships. Here is the way male and female voices were defined in a Black nationalist pamphlet from the early 1970s.

> "We understand that it is and has been traditional that the man is the head of the house. He is the leader of the house/nation because his knowledge of the world is broader, his awareness is greater, his understanding is fuller and his application of this information is wiser . . . After all, it is only reasonable that the man be the head of the house because he is able to defend and protect the development of his home . . . Women cannot do the same things as men—they are made by nature to function differently. Equality of men and women is something that cannot happen even in the abstract world. Men are not equal to other men, i.e. ability, experience or even understanding. The value of men and women can be seen as in the value of gold and silver—they are not equal but both have great value. We must realize that men and women are a complement to each other because there is no house/family without a man and his wife. Both are essential to the development of any life."[3]

The material conditions of most Black women would hardly lead them to upset both economic and sexual arrangements that seem to represent some stability in their lives. Many Black women have a good understanding of both sexism and racism, but because of the everyday constrictions of their lives cannot risk struggling against them both.

The reaction of Black men to feminism has been notoriously negative. They are, of course, even more threatened than Black women by the possibility that Black feminists might organize around our own needs. They realize that they might not only lose valuable and hard-working allies in their struggles but that they might also be forced to change their habitually sexist ways of interacting with and oppressing Black women. Accusations that Black feminism divides the Black struggle are powerful deterrents to the growth of an autonomous Black women's movement.

Still, hundreds of women have been active at different times during the three-year existence of our group. And every Black woman who came, came out of a strongly-felt need for some level of possibility that did not previously exist in her life.

When we first started meeting early in 1974 after the NBFO first eastern regional conference, we did not have a strategy for organizing, or even a focus. We just wanted to see what we had. After a period of months of not meeting, we began to meet again late in the year and started doing an intense variety of consciousness-raising. The overwhelming feeling that we had is that after years and years we had finally found each other. Although we were not doing political work as a group, individuals continued their involvement in Lesbian politics, sterilization abuse and abortion rights work, Third World Women's International Women's Day activities, and support activity for the trials of Dr. Kenneth Edelin, Joan Little, and Inéz García. During our first summer, when membership had dropped off considerably, those of us remaining devoted serious discussion to the possibility of opening a refuge for battered women in a Black community. (There was no refuge in Boston at that time.) We also decided around that time to become an independent collective since we had serious disagreements with NBFO's bourgeois-feminist stance and their lack of a clear political focus.

We also were contacted at that time by socialist feminists, with whom we had worked on abortion rights activities, who wanted to encourage us to attend the National Socialist Feminist Conference in Yellow Springs. One of our members did attend and despite the narrowness of the ideology that was promoted at that particular conference, we became more aware of the need for us to understand our own economic situation and to make our own economic analysis.

In the fall, when some members returned, we experienced several months of comparative inactivity and internal disagreements which were first conceptualized as a Lesbian-straight split but which were also the result of class and political differences. During the summer those of us who were still meeting had determined the need to do political work and to move beyond consciousness-raising and serving exclusively as an emotional support group. At the beginning of 1976, when some of the women who had not wanted to do political work and who also had voiced disagreements stopped attending of their own accord, we again looked for a focus. We decided at that time, with the addition of new members, to become a study group. We had always shared our reading with each other, and some of us had written papers on Black feminism for group discussion a few months before this decision was made. We began functioning as a study group and also began discussing the possibility of starting a Black feminist publication. We had a retreat in the late spring which provided a time for both political discussion and working out interpersonal issues. Currently we are planning to gather together a collection of Black feminist writing. We feel that it is absolutely essential to demonstrate the reality of our politics to other Black women and believe that we can do this through writing and distributing our work. The fact that individual Black feminists are living in isolation all over the country, that our own numbers are small, and that we have some skills in writing, printing, and publishing makes us want to carry out these kinds of projects as a means of organizing Black feminists as we continue to do political work in coalition with other groups.

4. BLACK FEMINIST ISSUES AND PROJECTS

During our time together we have identified and worked on many issues of particular relevance to Black women. The inclusiveness of our politics makes us concerned with any situation that impinges upon the lives of women, Third World and working people. We are of course particularly committed to working on those struggles in which race, sex and class are simultaneous factors in oppression. We might, for example, become involved in workplace organizing at a factory that employs Third World women or picket a hospital that is cutting back on already inadequate health care to a Third World community, or set up a rape crisis center in a Black neighborhood. Organizing around welfare and daycare concerns might also be a focus. The work to be done and the countless issues that this work represents merely reflect the pervasiveness of our oppression.

Issues and projects that collective members have already worked on are sterilization abuse, abortion rights, battered women, rape and health care. We have also done many workshops and educationals on Black feminism on college campuses, at women's conferences, and most recently for high school women.

One issue that is of major concern to us and that we have begun to publicly address is racism in the white women's movement. As Black feminists we are made constantly and painfully aware of how little effort white women have made to understand and combat their racism, which requires among other things that they have a more than superficial comprehension of race, color, and Black history and culture. Eliminating racism in the white women's movement is by definition work for white women to do, but we will continue to speak to and demand accountability on this issue.

In the practice of our politics we do not believe that the end always justifies the means. Many reactionary and destructive acts have been done in the name of achieving "correct" political goals. As feminists we do not want to mess over people in the name of politics. We believe in collective process and a nonhierarchical distribution of power within our own group and in our vision of a revolutionary society. We are committed to a continual examination of our politics as they develop through criticism and self-criticism as an essential aspect of our practice. In her introduction to *Sisterhood is Poweful* Robin Morgan writes:

> "I haven't the faintest notion what possible revolutionary role white heterosexual men could fulfill, since they are the very embodiment of reactionary-vested-interest-power."

As Black feminists and Lesbians we know that we have a very definite revolutionary task to perform and we are ready for the lifetime of work and struggle before us.

NOTES

The Combahee River Collective is a Black feminist group in Boston whose name comes from the guerrilla action conceptualized and led by Harriet Tubman on June 2, 1863, in the Port Royal region of South Carolina. This action freed more than 750 slaves and is the only military campaign in American history planned and led by a woman.

1. This statement is dated April 1977.
2. Michele Wallace, "A Black Feminist's Search for Sisterhood," The Village Voice, 28 July 1975, pp. 6–7.
3. Mumininas of Committee for Unified Newark, Mwanamke Mwananchi (The Nationalist Woman), Newark, N.J., © 1971, pp. 4–5.

Study Questions

1. What does the Collective mean by "identity politics"?

2. Why does the Collective oppose lesbian separatism?

3. What is the Collective's political agenda, and how does a commitment to identity politics influence that agenda?

4. Does it make sense to group the Collective's statement under the heading "Politics of Identity"? (Is it perhaps equally legitimately characterized as making a dominance feminist argument?)

Mari Matsuda

On Identity Politics

This chapter was a keynote address to the Minority Section of the American Association of Law Schools, delivered at a 1995 luncheon[1] honoring Professor Richard Delgado for his contributions to scholarship. Professor Delgado was one of the first legal scholars to write explicitly from the perspective of a person of color. His work, and the work of many of the professors gathered at the luncheon, represents the intellectual strengths of identity politics.

Why write as a Japanese-American woman? Why not just as a law professor?

When I started teaching, well-meaning colleagues urged me to mask identity. "Don't get ghettoized in women's issues. Don't write about race, you'll become known as partisan rather than scholarly." Unfortunately, the same advice is handed out to aspiring teachers today. "Don't let your politics show on your resumé." Just this year a professor on an appointments committee asked whether I knew of any women or people of color who were not doing race and gender "stuff." All the names I sent to him

were of people writing in those areas, and, he suggested, "We have enough of that." To anyone who longs for recognition as just a law professor, I wish you well. You should keep coming to minority section activities anyway. I promise you that you will need us someday. To those of you who are claiming your identity in your work, I would like to share my responses to the anti-identity crowd.

First, let me summarize the naysayers. In addition to the well-meaning colleagues who bring career advice about staying out of the ghetto, various pundits, academics, politicians, and theorists from all over the political map are attacking the new scholarship of identity. PC bashing is old news, and the only news is how doggedly attached the media are to old news—the same story, again and again, about how the multicultural thought police are taking over the academy.[2] If we had a dollar for every time this claim pops up in the press, we could save the NAACP.[3]

In addition to this PC bashing, there is a seemingly sophisticated claim that theoretical, scholarly use of identity is a dead end. In polite terms, this theoretical turn decries nationalism, narrowness, polemics, essentialism, vulgarization, parochialism, balkanization, and sidetracking from the main theoretical issues. "All this talk about race is masking class difference" is one such line. In less polite terms, the anti-identity theorists talk about guilt tripping, mau-mauing, or, as one critic said of my work, "self-aggrandizing slop." To talk about who we are as relevant to what we believe, in this view, is self-absorbed, narcissistic, and boring as well as a bullying move to silence others.

You may have noticed an inversion in many of these claims. The old school—masked identities, dominant narratives passing for universal—is portrayed as open and ecumenical. Challenges to this hegemony are seen as bullying and balkanizing. "We all got along until they discovered their identity." The cluster of African-American or Asian or Latino students huddling in the corner of the cafeteria is seen as excluding the roomful of Anglos, not vice versa.

Because these kinds of inverting attacks are so obviously a result of someone's inability to share power, it seems a waste of time to respond. The path-breaking work in critical race theory, feminist theory, and gay and lesbian studies is the best refutation. "We can't turn our whole life into a response," a critical race theorist once said to me.

We have not. We have spent most of our time doing work in the communities we care about, doing the scholarship that is inspiring to us. Nonetheless, the critical chorus grows more insistent, confuses students, affects hiring decisions, and remains the darling of the media monopoly. In addition, there is a legitimate debate in progressive circles about the utility of identity as an organizing device and in forming political theory. A brief response is in order.

Why racial identity—why now? Because it is still a radical act to stand in my shoes and speak when someone who looks like me is not supposed to do what I do. This is resistance. None of us were supposed to become law professors, write books, teach elites, or speak with authority about the words and systems that were designed to keep our kin under control. Most of us are here because someone in our family decided we could do more with our lives than what our teachers, what the dominant culture, said we could do. We were not mentored by our law professors. We were not the assumed, the chosen. Our students are still unsure of our capabilities. I see it as a form of resistance to stand in the front of the room on the first day of class and introduce myself as a Japanese-American, a feminist, and your law professor.

I was raised in a culture of modesty. The Japanese say, do not be the *deru kugi*, the nail that sticks out, or you will get hit on the head. How do I reconcile this with talking about myself and my identity on the first day of class? First of all, passing is impossible. This may be news to some of our colleagues, but most of us know this is true. More important, who I am colors how I see the world, how I understand questions of law and justice. By claiming, exploring, and questioning my own identity in an explicit way, I seek truth, and I seek to encourage my students to do the same.

I can take on the cloak of the detached universal, but it is an uncomfortable garment. It is not me, and I do not do my best work wearing it. I seek self-liberation when I write from my particular stance. The most brilliant and moving work coming from our community represents the liberated voice. I hear amidst the click of your keyboards the amazing sound of people doing something they never thought they would be able to do: speaking with their own voices in their professional lives. I hear Español climbing out of the footnotes up into the text. I see references to sexual identity becoming part of the analysis, not just the anecdote. I feel rhythm sneaking out of the subtitles to shape the flow of paragraphs. We are so much the richer for this work. People are actually reading law review articles for a change, passing photocopies along to friends. Practicing lawyers, miles away from the academy, are reading critical race theory because it reads well. "There was nothing like this," they say, "when I was in law school."

The fact that much of the new scholarship reads so well invites the charge that it is lightweight, the academic equivalent of a Kwanzaa cookbook. This would be true if nationalist gestures were served up in place of hard, theoretical work. The writing speaks for itself. It is no accident that the works of critical race theory are among the most cited throughout the academy by judges, scholars, and textbook writers. The ideas have value, and they are new and provocative precisely because they come from identities previously kept in the closet. The tradition of self-criticism, much a part of the political and cultural practices many of us are familiar with, adds to the rigor of this work.

But enough said about the value of speaking in one's own voice. I would like to address the politics of it. "What about Eastern Europe?" someone is bound to ask when I say I do not think identity politics is a bad thing. I think this view misunderstands and, again, inverts history. It assumes that racial identity is the cause of racial division rather than a product of it.

Our culture, our identity, is not entirely of our own making. We participate in and act upon what we are handed by history. I am the granddaughter of immigrant toilers. I choose to remember this and to celebrate the survival, resilience, and culture of my people. The Japanese American Citizens League takes positions on immigrant rights and against internments and relocations—of the Navajo, the Haitians, and antiwar protesters in the 1970s—because of a deliberate choice to remember what was done to us and to forge a political identity around it. This is a choice not every Japanese-American makes. There is agency involved in the way one uses identity, but it is not completely autonomous from what history hands us.

So what about Eastern Europe? I am no area expert, but I do know this: it was the Cold War that armed this region to the teeth, and it is the ideology of

militarism and patriarchy that teaches that might makes right. It is the lust for wealth, power, spatial conquest, and raw materials that has driven wars for as long as the record of history, and ethnic identity is used in this deadly game. It is not inevitable that cultural differences lead to political division. Too often "clan fighting" or "ethnic hatred" is an easy explanation for conflicts actually generated by colonialism, cold war militarism, or economic exploitation.

There is a political agenda to the balkanization line. If ethnic identity is the cause of ethnic strife, the solution is for everyone to stop claiming ethnic identity and be "just like me." This is an obvious move away from recognizing the effects of systems of domination like racism or class exploitation.

This is not to say that mau-mauing is a good thing. A regressive use of identity politics is one that seeks merely to reverse conditions of domination and put one's own group on top. What a useless exercise. Nowhere in the critical race theory literature will you find anyone doing this. It is interesting that the critique of vulgar nationalism is made anyway, without citation.

This, again, is an inversion. For some people, any attempt to discuss the particularities of experience must be for the purposes of creating a new domination. Us and Them, someone has to be the alpha dog. If you are talking about your people, it must be because you want to exclude my people. This is a massive projection, the kind of projection made by hangers-on of the old order. It is like the white South Africans who fantasized that the end of apartheid would mean a bloodbath of revenge, massive relocation of people from their homes, and brutalizing punishments for the old regime. The gentleness of what in fact is going on in South Africa today shows whose mind was really on brutality, whose heart held secrets of self-loathing.

No one is saying that all people of color think alike. Neither are we saying that our color is irrelevant to our intellectual development. It is not an either-or situation. Let me say it again plainly because there is such a will to disbelieve: it is not either-or. We live in a complex, dynamic world. For many of us the heritage and experience of being part of one or more oppressed groups in twentieth-century America is a rich part of our lives. From the food on our table, to the music we listen to as we drive, to the protests we march in, to the theory we struggle with, something resonates from the place we call home. This is not all we are, and not everyone who looks like us hears the same call. But it is there, it is real, and, as the young people say, get used to it.

I do not know of any other politics of social change that works other than the one that asks people to explore deeply their own location on the axes of power. Know where you stand, what your privileges are, and who is standing on your toes. And when you holler, "Get off of my toes!" look around at the others, some most unlike you, who are also stepped on. The vibrancy of gay/lesbian political activism, in these dark days for progressives in the United States, shows how this formula still works, however imperfectly, to get folks in their marching shoes.

In summary, vulgar nationalism—that is not what we do. Progressive identity politics—there is no other way. Am I guilt tripping colleagues? I can only succeed if they have something to feel guilty about. Who we are is no longer a secret. We gather as the minority section out of a sense of affinity and politics that is good for our souls, our digestion, and our work. The result, of late, is distinguished scholarship, seeking human liberation, and reaching a readership wider than any law professor ever dreamed possible.[4]

There resides, in our particularities, a new and profound universality. I believe that is where our work is headed, and I rejoice at such good company as we move toward that home.

NOTES

1. American Association of Law Schools Minority Section Luncheon Address, New Orleans, January 1995, Professor Robin Barnes, Organizer.

2. See, e.g., Lynne V. Cheney, *Why Our Culture and Our Country Have Stopped Making Sense—and What We Can Do about It* (New York: Simon & Schuster, 1995).

3. The NAACP faced a serious fiscal crisis at the time of this speech.

4. For examples of critical race theory writing, see K. Crenshaw; N. Gotanda, G. Pellet, and K. Thomas, *Critical Race Theory* (New York. The New Press, 1995).

Study Questions

1. Matsuda makes a case for "speaking in one's own voice." What is that case, and how do her remarks compare with Alcoff's thoughts on speaking only for oneself?

2. What does Matsuda mean by "progressive identity politics," and what reasons does she provide for embracing it?

3. Compare and contrast Matsuda's understanding of identity politics with that of the Combahee River Collective.

4. Compare and contrast Matsuda's remarks in paragraph 16 with Audre Lorde's discussion of difference in "Age, Race, Class, and Sex."

5. Does it make sense to group Matsuda's article under the heading "Politics of Identity"? (Is she perhaps equally legitimately characterized as making a dominance feminist argument?)

Gloria Anzaldúa

La conciencia de la mestiza

Towards a New Consciousness

Por la mujer de mi raza
hablará el espíritu.[1]

Jose Vascocelos, Mexican philosopher, envisaged *una raza mestiza, una mezcla de razas afines, una raza de color—la primera raza síntesis del globo.* He called it a cosmic race, *la raza cósmica*, a fifth race embracing the four major races of the world.[2] Opposite to the theory of the pure Aryan, and to the policy of racial purity that white America practices, his theory is one of inclusivity. At the confluence of two or more genetic streams, with chromosomes constantly "crossing over," this mixture of races, rather than resulting in an inferior being, provides hybrid progeny, a mutable, more malleable species with a rich gene pool. From this racial, ideological, cultural and biological cross-pollinization, an "alien" consciousness is presently in the making—a new *mestiza* consciousness, *una conciencia de mujer*. It is a consciousness of the Borderlands.

UNA LUCHA DE FRONTERAS / A STRUGGLE OF BORDERS

Because I, a *mestiza*,
continually walk out of one culture

and into another,
because I am in all cultures at the same time,
alma entre dos mundos, tres, cuatro,
me zumba la cabeza con lo contradictorio.
Estoy norteada por todas las voces que me hablan
simultáneamente.

The ambivalence from the clash of voices results in mental and emotional states of perplexity. Internal strife results in insecurity and indecisiveness. The mestiza's dual or multiple personality is plagued by psychic restlessness.

In a constant state of mental nepantilism, an Aztec word meaning torn between ways, *la mestiza* is a product of the transfer of the cultural and spiritual values of one group to another. Being tricultural, monolingual, bilingual, or multilingual, speaking a patois, and in a state of perpetual transition, the *mestiza* faces the dilemma of the mixed breed: which collectivity does the daughter of a darkskinned mother listen to?

El choque de un alma atrapado entre el mundo del espíritu y el mundo de la técnica a veces la deja entullada. Cradled in one culture, sandwiched between two cultures, straddling all three cultures and their value systems, *la mestiza* undergoes a struggle of flesh, a struggle of borders, an inner war. Like all people, we perceive the version of reality that our culture communicates. Like others having or living in more than one culture, we get multiple, often opposing messages. The coming together of two self-consistent but habitually incompatible frames of reference[3] causes *un choque*, a cultural collision.

Within us and within *la cultura chicana*, commonly held beliefs of the white culture attack commonly held beliefs of the Mexican culture, and both attack commonly held beliefs of the indigenous culture. Subconsciously, we see an attack on ourselves and our beliefs as a threat and we attempt to block with a counterstance.

But it is not enough to stand on the opposite river bank, shouting questions, challenging patriarchal, white conventions. A counterstance locks one into a duel of oppressor and oppressed; locked in mortal combat, like the cop and the criminal, both are reduced to a common denominator of violence. The counterstance refutes the dominant culture's views and beliefs, and, for this, it is proudly defiant. All reaction is limited by, and dependent on, what it is reacting against. Because the counterstance stems from a problem with authority—outer as well as inner—it's a step towards liberation from cultural domination. But it is not a way of life. At some point, on our way to a new consciousness, we will have to leave the opposite bank, the split between the two mortal combatants somehow healed so that we are on both shores at once and, at once, see through serpent and eagle eyes. Or perhaps we will decide to disengage from the dominant culture, write it off altogether as a lost cause, and cross the border into a wholly new and separate territory. Or we might go another route. The possibilities are numerous once we decide to act and not react.

A TOLERANCE FOR AMBIGUITY

These numerous possibilities leave *la mestiza* floundering in uncharted seas. In perceiving conflicting information and points of view, she is subjected to a swamping of her psychological borders. She has discovered that she can't hold concepts or ideas in rigid boundaries. The borders and walls that are supposed to keep the undesirable ideas out are entrenched habits and patterns of behavior; these habits and patterns are the enemy within. Rigidity means death. Only by remaining flexible is she able to stretch the psyche horizontally and vertically. *La mestiza* constantly has to shift out of habitual formations; from convergent thinking, analytical reasoning that tends to use rationality to move toward a single goal (a Western mode), to divergent thinking,[4] characterized by movement away from set patterns and goals and toward a more whole perspective, one that includes rather than excludes.

The new *mestiza* copes by developing a tolerance for contradictions, a tolerance for ambiguity. She learns to be an Indian in Mexican culture, to be Mexican from an Anglo point of view. She learns to juggle cultures. She has a plural personality, she operates in a pluralistic mode—nothing is thrust out, the good the bad and the ugly, nothing rejected, nothing abandoned. Not only does she sustain contradictions, she turns the ambivalence into something else.

She can be jarred out of ambivalence by an intense, and often painful, emotional event which inverts or resolves the ambivalence. I'm not sure exactly how. The work takes place underground—subconsciously. It is work that the soul performs. That focal point or fulcrum, that juncture where the mestiza stands, is where phenomena tend to collide. It is where the possibility of uniting all that is separate occurs. This assembly is not one where severed or separated pieces merely come together. Nor is it a balancing of opposing powers. In attempting to work out a synthesis, the self has added a third element which is greater than the sum of its severed parts. That third element is a new consciousness—a mestiza consciousness—and though it is a source of intense pain, its energy comes from continual creative motion that keeps breaking down the unitary aspect of each new paradigm.

En unas pocas centurias, the future will belong to the mestiza. Because the future depends on the breaking down of paradigms, it depends on the straddling of two or more cultures. By creating a new mythos—that is, a change in the way we perceive reality, the way we see ourselves, and the ways we behave—*la mestiza* creates a new consciousness.

The work of *mestiza* consciousness is to break down the subject-object duality that keeps her a prisoner and to show in the flesh and through the images in her work how duality is transcended. The answer to the problem between the white race and the colored, between males and females, lies in healing the split that originates in the very foundation of our lives, our culture, our languages, our thoughts. A massive uprooting of dualistic thinking in the individual and collective consciousness is the beginning of a long struggle, but one that could, in our best hopes, bring us to the end of rape, of violence, of war.

LA ENCRUCIJADA / THE CROSSROADS

A chicken is being sacrificed
    at a crossroads, a simple mound of earth
a mud shrine for *Eshu*,
    Yoruba god of indeterminacy,
who blesses her choice of path.
    She begins her journey.

Su cuerpo es una bocacalle. La mestiza has gone from being the sacrificial goat to becoming the officiating priestess at the crossroads.

As a *mestiza* I have no country, my homeland cast me out; yet all countries are mine because I am every woman's sister or potential lover. (As a lesbian I have no race, my own people disclaim me; but I am all races because there is the queer of me in all races.) I am cultureless because, as a feminist, I challenge the collective cultural/religious male-derived beliefs of Indo-Hispanics and Anglos; yet I am cultured because I am participating in the creation of yet another culture, a new story to explain the world and our participation in it, a new value system with images and symbols that connect us to each other and to the planet. *Soy un amasamiento*, I am an act of kneading, of uniting and joining that not only has produced both a creature of darkness and a creature of light, but also a creature that questions the definitions of light and dark and gives them new meanings.

We are the people who leap in the dark, we are the people on the knees of the gods. In our very flesh, (r)evolution works out the clash of cultures. It makes us crazy constantly, but if the center holds, we've made some kind of evolutionary step forward. *Nuestra alma el trabajo*, the opus, the great alchemical work; spiritual *mestizaje*, a "morphogenesis,"[5] an inevitable unfolding. We have become the quickening serpent movement.

Indigenous like corn, like corn, the *mestiza* is a product of crossbreeding, designed for preservation under a variety of conditions. Like an ear of corn—a female seed-bearing organ—the *mestiza* is tenacious, tightly wrapped in the husks of her culture. Like kernels she clings to the cob; with thick stalks and strong brace roots, she holds tight to the earth—she will survive the crossroads.

Lavando y remojando el maíz en agua de cal, despojando el pellejo. Moliendo, mixteando, amasando, haciendo tortillas de masa.[6] She steeps the corn in lime, it swells, softens. With stone roller on *metate*, she grinds the corn, then grinds again. She kneads and moulds the dough, pats the round balls into *tortillas*.

We are the porous rock in the stone *metate*
squatting on the ground.
We are the rolling pin, *el maíz y agua*,
la masa harina. Somos el amasijo.
Somos lo molido en el metate.
We are the *comal* sizzling hot,
the hot *tortilla*, the hungry mouth.
We are the coarse rock.
We are the grinding motion,
the mixed potion, *somos el molcajete.*
We are the pestle, the *comino, ajo, pimienta*,
We are the *chile colorado*,
the green shoot that cracks the rock.
We will abide.

EL CAMINO DE LA MESTIZA /
THE MESTIZA WAY

Caught between the sudden contraction, the breath sucked in and the endless space, the brown woman stands still, looks at the sky. She decides to go down, digging her way along the roots of trees. Sifting through the bones, she shakes them to see if there is any marrow in them. Then, touching the dirt to her forehead, to her tongue, she takes a few bones, leaves the rest in their burial place.

She goes through her backpack, keeps her journal and address book, throws away the muni-bart metromaps. The coins are heavy and they go next, then the greenbacks flutter through the air. She keeps her knife, can opener and eyebrow pencil. She puts bones, pieces of bark, *hierbas*, eagle feather, snakeskin, tape recorder, the rattle and drum in her pack and she sets out to become the complete *tolteca*.[7]

Her first step is to take inventory. *Despojando, desgranando, quitando paja.* Just what did she inherit from her ancestors? This weight on her back—which is the baggage from the Indian mother, which the baggage from the Spanish father, which the baggage from the Anglo?

Pero es difícil differentiating between *lo heredado, lo adquirido, lo impuesto.* She puts history through a sieve, winnows out the lies, looks at the forces that we as a race, as women, have been a part of. *Luego bota lo que no vale, los desmientos, los desencuentos, el embrutecimiento. Aguarda el juicio, hondo y enraízado, de la gente antigua.* This step is a conscious rupture with all oppressive traditions of all cultures and religions. She communicates that rupture, documents the struggle. She reinterprets history and, using new symbols, she shapes new myths. She adopts new perspectives toward the darkskinned, women and queers. She strengthens her tolerance (and intolerance) for ambiguity. She is willing to share, to make herself vulnerable to foreign ways of seeing and thinking. She surrenders all notions of safety, of the familiar. Deconstruct, construct. She becomes a *nahual*, able to transform herself into a tree, a coyote, into another person. She learns to transform the small "I" into the total Self. *Se hace moldeadora de su alma. Según la concepción que tiene de sí misma, así será.*

QUE NO SE NOS OLVIDE
LOS HOMBRES

"Tú no sirves pa' nada—
you're good for nothing.
Eres pura vieja."

"You're nothing but a woman" means you are defective. Its opposite is to be *un macho*. The modern meaning of the word "machismo," as well as the concept, is actually an Anglo invention. For men like my father, being "macho" meant being strong enough to protect and support my mother and us, yet being able to show love. Today's macho has doubts about his ability to feed and protect his family. His "machismo" is an adaptation to oppression and poverty and low self-esteem. It is the result of hierarchical male dominance. The Anglo, feeling inadequate and inferior and powerless, displaces or transfers these feelings to the Chicano by shaming him. In the Gringo world, the Chicano suffers from excessive humility and self-effacement, shame of self and self-deprecation. Around Latinos he suffers from a sense of language inadequacy and its accompanying discomfort; with Native Americans he suffers from a racial amnesia which ignores our common blood, and from guilt because the Spanish part of him took their land and oppressed them. He has an excessive compensatory hubris when around Mexicans from the other side. It overlays a deep sense of racial shame.

The loss of a sense of dignity and respect in the macho breeds a false machismo which leads him to put down women and even to brutalize them. Coexisting with his sexist behavior is a love for the mother which takes precedence over that of all others. Devoted son, macho pig. To wash down the shame of his acts, of his very being, and to handle the brute in the mirror, he takes to the bottle, the snort, the needle, and the fist.

Though we "understand" the root causes of male hatred and fear, and the subsequent wounding of women, we do not excuse, we do not condone, and we will no longer put up with it. From the men of our race, we demand the admission/acknowledgment/disclosure/testimony that they wound us, violate us, are afraid of us and of our power. We need them to say they will begin to eliminate their hurtful put-down ways. But more than the words, we demand acts. We say to them: We will develop equal power with you and those who have shamed us.

It is imperative that mestizas support each other in changing the sexist elements in the Mexican-Indian culture. As long as woman is put down, the Indian and the Black in all of us is put down. The struggle of the mestiza is above all a feminist one. As long as *los hombres* think they have to *chingar mujeres* and each other to be men, as long as men are taught that they are superior and therefore culturally favored over *la mujer*, as long as to be a *vieja* is a thing of derision, there can be no real healing of our psyches. We're halfway there—we have such love of the Mother, the good mother. The first step is to unlearn the *puta/virgen* dichotomy and to see *Coatlapopeuh-Coatlicue* in the Mother, *Guadalupe*.

Tenderness, a sign of vulnerability, is so feared that it is showered on women with verbal abuse and blows. Men, even more than women, are fettered to gender roles. Women at least have had the guts to break out of bondage. Only gay men have had the courage to expose themselves to the woman inside them and to challenge the current masculinity. I've encountered a few scattered and isolated gentle straight men, the beginnings of a new breed, but they are confused, and entangled with sexist behaviors that they have not been able to eradicate. We need a new masculinity and the new man needs a movement.

Lumping the males who deviate from the general norm with man, the oppressor, is a gross injustice. *Asombra pensar que nos hemos quedado en ese pozo oscuro donde el mundo encierra a las lesbianas. Asombra pensar que hemos, como femenistas y lesbianas, cerrado nuestros corazónes a los hombres, a nuestros hermanos los jotos, desheredados y marginales como nosotros.* Being the supreme crossers of cultures, homosexuals have strong bonds with the queer white, Black, Asian, Native American, Latino, and with the queer in Italy, Australia and the rest of the planet. We come from all colors, all classes, all races, all time periods. Our role is to link people with each other—the Blacks with Jews with Indians with Asians with whites with extraterrestrials. It is to transfer ideas and information from one culture to another. Colored homosexuals have more knowledge of other cultures; have always been at the forefront (although sometimes in the closet) of all liberation struggles in this country; have suffered more injustices and have survived them despite all odds. Chicanos need to acknowledge the political and artistic contributions of their queer. People, listen to what your *jotería* is saying.

The mestizo and the queer exist at this time and point on the evolutionary continuum for a purpose. We are a blending that proves that all blood is intricately woven together, and that we are spawned out of similar souls.

SOMOS UNA GENTE

*Hay tantísimas fronteras
que dividen a la gente,
pero por cada frontera
existe también un puente.*

—Gina Valdés

Divided Loyalties

Many women and men of color do not want to have any dealings with white people. It takes too much time and energy to explain to the downwardly mobile, white middle-class women that it's okay for us to want to own "possessions," never having had any nice furniture on our dirt floors or "luxuries" like washing machines. Many feel that whites should help their own people rid themselves of race hatred and fear first. I, for one, choose to use some of my energy to serve as mediator. I think we need to allow whites to be our allies. Through our literature, art, *corridos*, and folktales we must share our history with them so when they set up committees to help Big Mountain Navajos or the Chicano farmworkers or *los Nicaragüenses* they won't turn people away because of their racial fears and ignorances. They will come to see that they are not helping us but following our lead.

Individually, but also as a racial entity, we need to voice our needs. We need to say to white society: We need you to accept the fact that Chicanos are different, to acknowledge your rejection and negation of us. We need you to own the fact that you looked upon us as less than human, that you stole our lands, our personhood, our self-respect. We need you to make public restitution: to say that, to compensate for your own sense of defectiveness, you strive for power over us, you erase our history and our experience because it makes you feel guilty—you'd rather forget your brutish acts. To say you've split yourself from minority groups, that you disown us, that your dual consciousness splits off parts of yourself, transferring the "negative" parts onto us. (Where there is persecution of minorities, there is shadow projection. Where there is violence and war, there is repression of shadow.) To say that you are afraid of us, that to put distance between us, you wear the mask of contempt. Admit that Mexico is your double, that she exists in the shadow of this country, that we are irrevocably tied to her. Gringo, accept the doppelganger in your psyche. By taking back your collective shadow the intracultural split will heal. And finally, tell us what you need from us.

BY YOUR TRUE FACES WE WILL KNOW YOU

I am visible—see this Indian face—yet I am invisible. I both blind them with my beak nose and am their blind spot. But I exist, we exist. They'd like to think I have melted in the pot. But I haven't, we haven't.

The dominant white culture is killing us slowly with its ignorance. By taking away our self-determination, it has made us weak and empty. As a people we have resisted and we have taken expedient positions, but we have never been allowed to develop unencumbered —we have never been allowed to be fully ourselves. The whites in power want us people of color to barricade ourselves behind our separate tribal walls so they can pick us off one at a time with their hidden weapons; so they can whitewash and distort history. Ignorance splits people, creates prejudices. A misinformed people is a subjugated people.

Before the Chicano and the undocumented worker and the Mexican from the other side can come together, before the Chicano can have unity with Native Americans and other groups, we need to know the history of their struggle and they need to know ours. Our mothers, our sisters and brothers, the guys who hang out on street corners, the children in the playgrounds, each of us must know our Indian lineage, our afro-*mestisaje*, our history of resistance.

To the immigrant *mexicano* and the recent arrivals we must teach our history. The 80 million *mexicanos* and the Latinos from Central and South America must know of our struggles. Each one of us must know basic facts about Nicaragua, Chile and the rest of Latin America. The Latinoist movement (Chicanos, Puerto Ricans, Cubans and other Spanish-speaking people working together to combat racial discrimination in the market place) is good but it is not enough. Other than a common culture we will have nothing to hold us together. We need to meet on a broader communal ground.

The struggle is inner: Chicano, *indio*, American Indian, *mojado*, *mexicano*, immigrant Latino, Anglo in power, working class Anglo, Black, Asian—our psyches resemble the border-towns and are populated by the same people. The struggle has always been inner, and is played out in the outer terrains. Awareness of our situation must come before inner changes, which in turn come before changes in society. Nothing happens in the "real" world unless it first happens in the images in our heads.

EL DÍA DE LA CHICANA

I will not be shamed again
Nor will I shame myself.

I am possessed by a vision: that we Chicanas and Chicanos have taken back or uncovered our true faces, our dignity and self-respect. It's a validation vision.

Seeing the Chicana anew in light of her history. I seek an exoneration, a seeing through the fictions of white supremacy, a seeing of ourselves in our true guises and not as the false racial personality that has been given to us and that we have given to ourselves. I seek our woman's face, our true features, the positive and the negative seen clearly, free of the tainted biases of male dominance. I seek new images of identity, new beliefs about ourselves, our humanity and worth no longer in question.

Estamos viviendo en la noche de la Raza, un tiempo cuando el trabajo se hace a lo quieto, en el oscuro. El día cuando aceptamos tal y como somos y para en donde vamos y porque—ese día será el día de la Raza. Yo tengo el conpromiso de expresar mi visión, mi sensibilidad, mi percepción de la revalidación de la gente mexicana, su mérito, estimación, honra, aprecio, y validez.

On December 2nd when my sun goes into my first house, I celebrate *el día de la Chicana y el Chicano.* On that day I clean my altars, light my *Coatlalopeuh* candle, burn sage and copal, take *el baño para espantar basura,* sweep my house. On that day I bare my soul, make myself vulnerable to friends and family by expressing my feelings. On that day I affirm who we are.

On that day I look inside our conflicts and our basic introverted racial temperament. I identify our needs, voice them. I acknowledge that the self and the race have been wounded. I recognize the need to take care of our personhood, of our racial self. On that day I gather the splintered and disowned parts of *la gente mexicana* and hold them in my arms. *Todas las partes de nosotros valen.*

On that day I say, "Yes, all you people wound us when you reject us. Rejection strips us of self-worth; our vulnerability exposes us to shame. It is our innate identity you find wanting. We are ashamed that we need your good opinion, that we need your acceptance. We can no longer camouflage our needs, can no longer let defenses and fences sprout around us. We can no longer withdraw. To rage and look upon you with contempt is to rage and be contemptuous of ourselves. We can no longer blame you, nor disown the white parts, the male parts, the pathological parts, the queer parts, the vulnerable parts. Here we are weaponless with open arms, with only our magic. Let's try it our way, the mestiza way, the Chicana way, the woman way.

On that day, I search for our essential dignity as a people, a people with a sense of purpose—to belong and contribute to something greater than our *pueblo.* On that day I seek to recover and reshape my spiritual identity. *¡Anímate! Raza, a celebrar el día de la Chicana.*

EL RETORNO

All movements are accomplished in six stages, and the seventh brings return.

—I Ching[8]

Tanto tiempo sin verte casa mía, mi cuna,
mi hondo nido de la huerta.

—"Soledad"[9]

I stand at the river, watch the curving, twisting serpent, a serpent nailed to the fence where the mouth of the Rio Grande empties into the Gulf.

I have come back. *Tanto dolor me costó el alejamiento.* I shade my eyes and look up. The bone beak of a hawk slowly circling over me, checking me out as potential carrion. In its wake a little bird flickering its wings, swimming sporadically like a fish. In the distance the expressway and the slough of traffic like an irritated sow. The sudden pull in my gut, *la tierra, los aguaceros.* My land, *el viento soplando la arena, el lagartijo debajo de un nopalito. Me acuerdo como era antes. Una región desértica de vasta llanuras, costeras de baja altura, de escasa lluvia, de chaparrales formados por mesquites y huizaches.* If I look real hard I can almost see the Spanish fathers who were called "the cavalry of Christ" enter this valley riding their burros, see the clash of cultures commence.

Tierra natal. This is home, the small towns in the Valley, *los pueblitos* with chicken pens and goats picketed to mesquite shrubs. *En las colonias* on the other side of the tracks, junk cars line the front yards of hot pink and lavender-trimmed houses—Chicano architecture we call it, self-consciously. I have missed the TV shows where hosts speak in half and half, and where awards are given in the category of Tex-Mex music. I have missed the Mexican cemeteries blooming with artificial flowers, the fields of aloe vera and red pepper, rows of sugar cane, of corn hanging on the stalks, the cloud of *polvareda* in the dirt roads behind a speeding pickup truck, *el sabor de tamales de rez y venado.* I have missed *la yegua colorada* gnawing the wooden gate of her stall, the smell of horse flesh from Carito's corrals. *He hecho menos las noches calientes sin aire, noches de linternas y lechuzas* making holes in the night.

I still feel the old despair when I look at the unpainted, dilapidated, scrap lumber houses consisting mostly of corrugated aluminum. Some of the poorest people in the U.S. live in the Lower Rio Grande Valley, an arid and semi-arid land of irrigated farming, intense sunlight and heat, citrus groves next to chaparral and cactus. I walk through the elementary school I attended so long ago, that remained segregated until recently. I remember how the white teachers used to punish us for being Mexican.

How I love this tragic valley of South Texas, as Ricardo Sánchez calls it; this borderland between the Nueces and the Rio Grande. This land has survived possession and ill-use by five countries: Spain, Mexico, the Republic of Texas, the U.S., the Confederacy, and the U.S. again. It has survived Anglo-Mexican blood feuds, lynchings, burnings, rapes, pillage.

Today I see the Valley still struggling to survive. Whether it does or not, it will never be as I remember it. The borderlands depression that was set off by the 1982 peso devaluation in Mexico resulted in the closure of hundreds of Valley businesses. Many people lost their homes, cars, land. Prior to 1982, U.S. store owners thrived on retail sales to Mexicans who came across the border for groceries and clothes and appliances. While goods on the U.S. side have become 10, 100, 1000 times more expensive for Mexican buyers, goods on the Mexican side have become 10, 100, 1000 times cheaper for Americans. Because the Valley is heavily dependent on agriculture and Mexican retail trade, it has the highest unemployment rates along the entire border region; it is the Valley that has been hardest hit.[10]

"It's been a bad year for corn," my brother, Nune, says. As he talks, I remember my father scanning the sky for a rain that would end the drought, looking up into the sky, day after day, while the corn withered on its stalk. My father has been dead for 29 years, having worked himself to death. The life span of a Mexican farm laborer is 56—he lived to be 38. It shocks me that I am older than he. I, too, search the sky for rain. Like the ancients, I worship the rain god and the maize goddess, but unlike my father I have recovered their names. Now for rain (irrigation) one offers not a sacrifice of blood, but of money.

"Farming is in a bad way," my brother says. "Two to three thousand small and big farmers went bankrupt in this country last year. Six years ago the price of corn was $8.00 per hundred pounds," he goes on. "This year it is $3.90 per hundred pounds." And, I think to myself, after taking inflation into account, not planting anything puts you ahead.

I walk out to the back yard, stare at *los rosales de mamá.* She wants me to help her prune the rose bushes, dig out the carpet grass that is choking them. *Mamagrande Ramona también tenía rosales.* Here every Mexican grows flowers. If they don't have a piece of dirt, they use car tires, jars, cans, shoe boxes. Roses are the Mexican's favorite flower. I think, how symbolic—thorns and all.

Yes, the Chicano and Chicana have always taken care of growing things and the land. Again I see the four of us kids getting off the school bus, changing into our work clothes, walking into the field with Papí and Mamí, all six of us bending to the ground. Below our feet, under the earth lie the watermelon seeds. We cover them with paper plates, putting *terremotes* on top of the plates to keep them from being blown away by the wind. The paper plates keep the freeze away. Next day or the next, we remove the plates, bare the tiny green shoots to the elements. They survive and grow, give fruit hundreds of times the size of the seed. We water them and hoe them. We harvest them. The vines dry, rot, are plowed under. Growth, death, decay, birth. The soil prepared again and again, impregnated, worked on. A constant changing of forms, *renacimientos de la tierra madre*.

> This land was Mexican once
>   was Indian always
>   and is.
>   And will be again.

NOTES

1. This is my own "take off" on Jose Vasconcelos' idea. Jose Vasconcelos, *La Raza Cósmica: Misión de la Raza Ibero-Americana* (México: Aguilar S.A. de Ediciones, 1961).

2. Vasconcelos.

3. Arthur Koestler termed this "bisociation." Albert Rothenberg, *The Creative Process in Art, Science, and Other Fields* (Chicago, IL: University of Chicago Press, 1979), 12.

4. In part, I derive my definitions for "convergent" and "divergent" thinking from Rothenberg, 12–13.

5. To borrow chemist Ilya Prigogine's theory of "dissipative structures." Prigogine discovered that substances interact not in predictable ways as it was taught in science, but in different and fluctuating ways to produce new and more complex structures, a kind of birth he called "morphogenesis," which created unpredictable innovations. Harold Gilliam, "Searching for a New World View," *This World* (January, 1981), 23.

6. *Tortillas de masa harina*: corn tortillas are of two types, the smooth uniform ones made in a tortilla press and usually bought at a tortilla factory or supermarket, and *gorditas*, made by mixing *masa* with lard or shortening or butter (my mother sometimes puts in bits of bacon or *chicharrones*).

7. Gina Valdés, *Puentes y Fronteras: Coplas Chicanas* (Los Angeles, CA: Castle Lithograph, 1982), 2.

8. Richard Wilhelm, *The I Ching or Book of Changes*, trans. Cary F. Baynes (Princeton, NJ: Princeton University Press, 1950), 98.

9. *"Soledad"* is sung by the group, Haciendo Punto en Otro Son.

10. Out of the twenty-two border counties in the four border states, Hidalgo County (named for Father Hidalgo who was shot in 1810 after instigating Mexico's revolt against Spanish rule under the banner of *la Virgen de Guadalupe*) is the most poverty-stricken county in the nation as well as the largest home base (along with Imperial in California) for migrant farmworkers. It was here that I was born and raised. I am amazed that both it and I have survived.

Study Questions

1. According to Anzaldúa, why is a "new consciousness" needed, and why are mestizas particularly well positioned to forge one?

2. In Anzaldúa's account, what ought to characterize this new consciousness?

3. Anzaldúa writes, "The struggle of the mestiza is above all a feminist one" (paragraph 6 of *"El camino de la mestiza*/The Mestiza Way"). What are her reasons for believing this?

4. In the paragraphs immediately following, what connection does Anzaldúa posit between "the queer" and the new consciousness?

5. What do you take to be the significance, if any, of Anzaldúa's style of writing (e.g., it is multilingual, nonlinear, genre-blending, makes use of metaphor)?

6. Does it make sense to group this excerpt from Anzaldúa under the heading "Politics of Identity"? (Is she perhaps equally legitimately characterized as making a dominance feminist argument?)

Angela Davis

Mama's Got the Blues

Rivals, Girlfriends, and Advisors

Trust no man, trust no man, no further than your eyes can see
I said, trust no man, no further than your eyes can see
He'll tell you that he loves you and swear it is true
The very next minute he'll turn his back on you
Ah, trust no man, no further than your eyes can see.
—"Trust No Man"[1]

Classic blues comprised an important elaboration of black working-class social consciousness. Gertrude Rainey's and Bessie Smith's songs constituted historical preparation for social protest. They also foreshadowed a brand of protest that refused to privilege racism over sexism, or the conventional public realm over the private as the preeminent domain of power. Because women's blues were not ideologically structured by the assumptions that defined the prominent black women's organizations of the era as middle-class, they could issue more direct and audacious challenges to male dominance. It is important, I think, to understand women's blues as a working-class form that anticipates the politicalization of the "personal" through the dynamic of "consciousness-raising," a phenomenon associated with the women's movement of the last three decades.

Studies of feminist dimensions in African-American women's historical activism tend to focus on individuals and organizations solidly anchored in the developing black middle class. Paula Giddings points out that while the mission of the black women's club movement was fundamentally antiracist, it shared certain class assumptions with the white women's movement it criticized:

> The Black women's club movement did have a number of things in common with the White club movement. . . . [T]he membership of both organizations consisted mostly of middle-class educated women who were steeped in the Protestant ethic. Neither group questioned the superiority of middle-class values or way of life, or had any romantic notions of the inherent nobility of the poor, uneducated masses; education and material progress were values that Black and White women shared. Both also believed in the importance of the home and the woman's moral influence within it. Black and White women saw the family as a microcosm and cornerstone of society.[2]

When the National Association of Colored Women was founded in 1896, it chose for its motto "Lifting as We Climb." This motto called upon the most educated, most moral, and most affluent African-American women to recognize the extent to which the dominant culture's racist perceptions linked them with the least educated, most immoral, and most impoverished black women. Mary Church Terrell described this cross-class relationship as a determination "to come into the closest possible touch with the masses of our women, through whom the womanhood of our people is always judged." More explicitly, "[s]elf-preservation demands that [educated black women] go among the lowly, illiterate and even the vicious, to whom they are bound by ties of race and sex . . . to reclaim them."[3] While this posture was certainly admirable and helped to produce a distinguished tradition of progressive activism among black middle-class women from the NACW to the National Council of Negro Women and similar organizations today, what was and remains problematic is the premise that middle-class women embody a standard their poorer sisters should be encouraged to emulate.

The black women's club movement was especially concerned with the notion of "defending our name" against pervasive charges of immorality and sexual promiscuity.[4] Given the extent to which representations of black inferiority emanating from the dominant culture were bound up with notions of racial hypersexualization—the deployment of the myth of the black rapist to justify lynching is the most obvious example—it is hard to imagine that women like Fannie Barrier Williams, Ida B. Wells, and Mary Church Terrell could have been as effective as they were without defending the sexual purity of their sisters. Yet, in the process of defending black women's moral integrity and sexual purity, they almost entirely denied sexual agency. . . . [S]exuality was one of the few realms in which masses of African-American women could exercise autonomy—and thus tangibly distinguish their contemporary status from the history of enslavement. Denial of sexual agency was in an important respect the denial of freedom for working-class black women.

The women about whom Gertrude Rainey and Bessie Smith sing are precisely those who were perceived by the club women as in need of salvation. Yet, middle-class women were not the only black women who engaged in community-building. I want to suggest that women's blues provided a cultural space for community-building among working-class black women, and that it was a space in which the coercions of bourgeois notions of sexual purity and "true womanhood" were absent.

During the period following World War I, large numbers of black people left the South or moved from rural areas into southern cities and thus into new job markets. At the same time, a distinctly post-slavery music culture was widely disseminated, thus accelerating and complicating the development of a postslavery working-class consciousness. Yet, blues scholars working within the discipline of musicology are rarely concerned with the ideological implications of the blues, and historians studying the African-American past rarely turn to blues history. In the few works that attempt to probe blues history for insights about the development of black cultural consciousness, masculinist bias almost inevitably leads to a failure to take seriously the efforts of women blues musicians and the female reception of their work. As a consequence, the central part played by women both in the blues and in the history of African-American cultural consciousness is often ignored.

Perhaps women's blues history has been so readily marginalized because the most frequently recurring themes of women's blues music revolve around male lovers and the plethora of problems posed by heterosexual relationships complicated by expressions of autonomous female sexuality. As I have attempted to point out, these love themes have complex social implications. Moreover, it is usually left unremarked that these songs provide a rich and complex backdrop for working-class women's lives, reflecting how they dealt with and experienced each other. Blues lyrics often construct these intragender relationships as antagonistic, as negotiations of encounters between competitors and rivals. At the same time, there are songs that highlight friendship, sisterhood, love, and solidarity between women. These range from Gertrude Rainey's "Prove It on Me Blues"[5]—and other songs recorded by women of that era celebrating sexual love between women—to songs such as Bessie Smith's "A Good Man Is Hard to Find," presenting advice to women on how to conduct themselves within their heterosexual relationships.[6]

. . . [T]he abundance of themes revolving around love and sexuality in women's blues indicate the extent to which, for African Americans during the decades following emancipation, sexual love was experienced as physical and spiritual evidence—and the blues as aesthetic evidence—of freedom. From this historical vantage point, competition and rivalry in love may be seen as evidence of the historical construction of black working-class individuality. Although sexual rivalries no doubt existed among the emergent black middle class, ideological prohibitions required women either to be silent or to engage in a "proper" way of speaking about such matters.

As slave music suggests, the conditions for physical and spiritual survival during slavery (as well as the survival of transmuted African ancestral cultures) defined the value of the individual as subordinate to the community. The abolition of slavery, while it did not bring economic and political freedom, created a backdrop for new kinds of relationships between black individuals and thus for a different valuation of the individual in general. The new African Americans—women and men alike—came to perceive their individual selves not only as welded together within the community, but as different from and in opposition to one another as well. For working-class women and men, the blues both allowed and furnished cultural representations of this new individuality.

Blues portraits of women in competition with each other for sexual partners—as "vicious" as they may have appeared to women like Mary Church Terrell—revealed working-class women as capable of exercising some measure of agency in choosing their partners. This is not to deny the problematic aspects of blues constructions of female jealously and rivalry, sometimes to the point of violence. On the contrary,

while representations of female sexual agency no doubt played a progressive role by encouraging assertiveness and independence among black women, these representations simultaneously legitimized a tradition of real and often murderous violence between women. As African-American women forged a continuum of independent womanhood—in contradiction to the prevailing ideology of women's place—they also affirmed, in frequently exaggerated forms, sexist models of women's conduct. While this contradictory character of the emergence of black female working-class individuality is far from inconsequential—and I will later identify some of the ways these contradictions are manifested in blues performances—I want to emphasize, for the moment, the importance of women's blues as a site for the independent elaboration and affirmation of subjectivity and community for women of the black working class. Through the blues, black women were able to autonomously work out—as audiences and performers—a working-class model of womanhood. This model of womanhood was based in part on a collective historical memory of what had been previously required of women to cope with slavery. But more important, it revealed that black women and men, the blues audience, could respond to the vastly different circumstances of the postslavery era with notions of gender and sexuality that were, to a certain extent, ideologically independent of the middle-class cult of "true womanhood." In this sense, as Hazel Carby has pointed out, the blues was a privileged site in which women were free to assert themselves publicly as sexual beings.

Beginning with W. E. B. Du Bois's essay in *Darkwater*, many studies have emphasized the extent to which black working-class women's relative economic independence summoned various modes of female consciousness that emphasized strength, resilience, and autonomy.[7] However, such arguments often assume a strictly causal relationship between the economic conditions of slavery—which inflicted responsibilities for production on women that were equal to those placed on men—and the gendered consciousness among working-class black women that privileged independence.[8] I want to emphasize women's blues as an important cultural mediator for this gendered consciousness that transformed collective memories of slavery as it worked with a new social construction of love and sexuality. The blues provided a space where women could express themselves in new ways, a space in which they sometimes affirmed the dominant middle-class ideology but also could deviate from it.

I begin with the most complicated expressions of women's independence and assertiveness, in which an independent sense of women's strength was interwoven with themes of female rivalry over a male lover. "Rough and Tumble Blues," composed and recorded by Gertrude "Ma" Rainey, presents a powerful, fighting, rough-and-tumble woman, who boasts about her assertiveness and power. Her boasts, however, are directed at the women—Mama Tree Top Tall and Miss Shorty Toad—who have their eyes on her man. Her power is established partly by virtue of her ability to support the man financially— evidenced by the fact that she has bought him a "struttin' suit." The final verse of this song proclaims:

> I got rough and killed three women 'fore the police
>   got the news
> I got rough and killed three women 'fore police got
>   the news
> 'Cause mama's on the warpath with those rough and
>   tumble blues.[9]

A similar song, "Wringing and Twisting Blues," composed by Paul Carter and also recorded by Rainey, announces the protagonist's desire to poison the woman for whom her lover left her:

> But if I know that woman that caused my heart to
>   moan
> I'd cook a special dinner, invite her to my home
> . . . . . .
> If she eats what's on my table, she will be graveyard
>   bound
> I'll be right there to tell her, when they put her in the
>   ground
> "You're the cause of me having those wringin' and
>   a-twistin' blues."[10]

There are comparable images of female violence directed against other women in Bessie Smith's songs:

> But if I find that gal
> That tried to steal my pal
> I'll get her told, just you wait and see.[11]

Or, in more aggressive terms:

> St. Louis gal, I'm gonna handle you, I said man-
>   handle you
> . . . . . .
> Your life won't be worth a dime
> You stole my pal, St. Louis gal
>
> I'm goin' a-huntin', root-dooti-doot
> You know just what I'm gonna shoot
> You stole my pal, St. Louis gal.[12]

Such representations of jealousy and violence need not be taken literally. However, we should keep in mind the current discourse on racialized violence that merges real violence and representations of violence. Critiques of gangsta rap, for example, argue for a rather simple and mechanical relation between cultural images and material reality. Of course, the murders of rappers Tupac Shakur and Biggie Smalls within six months of one another in late 1996 and early 1997 tended to affirm this. But, with respect to the role of violence in Rainey's and Smith's work, I am arguing that these performed lyrics provide a glimpse of a kind of working-class women's community-building that, rather than advocating violence, proclaims women's complexity by refusing to deny or downplay female antagonism. The jealousy and competitiveness that was so openly expressed in the blues surely also characterized middle-class women's relations with each other. Remaining unnamed and unacknowledged, these antagonisms must have had vast political consequences about which we could not even begin to speculate today.

Jealousy and rivalry, as they defined female blues subjects' attitudes toward other women, do not always erupt into actual or imagined violence as in the songs cited above. Often, there is simply suspicion, as in Bessie Smith's "Empty Bed Blues":

> Lord, he's got that sweet somethin', and I told my
>   gal friend Lou

He's got that sweet somethin', and I told my gal
    friend Lou
From the way she's ravin', she must have gone and
    tried it too.

"Empty Bed Blues, Part II" concludes with a word of
advice offered to other women:

When you get good lovin', never go and spread the
    news
Yeah, it will double cross you and leave you with
    them empty bed blues.[13]

In a similar vein, "He's Got Me Goin'"—a song
replete with erotic imagery—reveals a subject so
utterly captivated by her lover that she fears other
women may hear about him and try to attract his
attentions:

'Fraid to advertise my man, simply scared to death
These gals'll hear about him and try him for they
    self.[14]

Unmitigated jealousy, however, is not always the
posture assumed by jealous blues subjects. The blues
never remain fixed on one perspective, but rather
different songs—sometimes the same song—explore
experiences from various vantage points. This feature
of the blues, the aesthetic incorporation of several
perspectives and dimensions, may be interpreted
as reflective of West African philosophical outlooks
and representational strategies. Beneath the apparent
simplicity and straightforwardness of the blues, complex visions—reflecting the complexity with which
reality is perceived—can always be uncovered. This
is another way in which the blues are located on an
African cultural continuum.[15]

Some songs describe the woman succumbing to
feelings of jealousy. In other songs, jealousy is named
and acknowledged—even celebrated as an important
subject and a powerful blues theme. Still other songs
reveal a critical attitude toward jealousy, pointing
to its potential destructiveness. Within the body of
Gertrude Rainey's work, all three of these attitudes
are evident. In "Sleep Talking Blues," the protagonist
warns her man of the disastrous consequences of
calling another woman's name in his sleep:

When you talk in your sleep, be sure your mama's
    not awake
When you talk in your sleep, be sure your mama's
    not awake
You call another woman's name, you'll think you
    wake up in a earthquake.[16]

In "Jealous Hearted Blues"—one of Lovie Austin's
compositions—jealousy is repeatedly named, as the
jealous woman acknowledges the extent to which she
has been overcome by this emotion. The following
chorus is repeated four times:

Yes I'm jealous, jealous, jealous hearted me
Lord, I'm just jealous, jealous as I can be.

Indeed, the protagonist is so utterly driven by her
jealousy that she announces this measure:

Gonna buy me a bulldog to watch him while I sleep
To keep my man from making his midnight creep.[17]

Finally, in "Jealousy Blues," an analytical and
implicitly critical posture is assumed. This song
focuses on the catastrophic potential of jealousy
for relationships and for one's psychological well-
being, as well as on its violence and its material
consequences:

If all the world is evil, all the world is evil, oh jeal-
    ousy is the worst of all
It'll make you mad and lonely, your sweet love will
    feel so pale
It'll steal your loving daddy, have many folks in
    jail.[18]

The most complicated evocation of jealousy can
be found in "My Man Blues," a song written by
Bessie Smith and performed as a duet with Clara
Smith, who was known during the period as the
Empress's most serious musical rival. The piece is
about competition for the attentions of a man who
each woman insists belongs to her. There are powerful resonances in this song: the actual competitive
relationship between the two Smiths as entertainers;
the rivalry in general between women; and a troubled
but unmistakable reconciliation:

Bessie: Clara, who was that man I saw you with the other day?

Clara: Bessie, that was my smooth black daddy that we call Charlie Gray.

Bessie: Don't you know that's my man? Yes, that's a fact.

Clara: I ain't seen your name printed up and down his back.

Bessie: You better let him be.

Clara: What, old gal? Because you ain't talkin' to me.

Bessie: That's my man, I want him for my own.

Clara: [Spoken] No! No! [Sung] He's my sweet daddy. You'd better leave that man alone.

Bessie: See that suit he got on? I bought it last week.

Clara: I been buyin' his clothes for five years, for that is my black sheik.

[*CHARLIE WHISTLES*]

[*SPOKEN*]

Bessie: Is that you, honey?

Charlie: 'Tain't nobody but—who's back there?

Clara: It sounds like Charlie.

Bessie: It 'tis my man, sweet papa Charlie Gray.

Clara: Your man? How do you git that way?

Bessie: Now, look here, honey. I been had that man for sumpteen years.

Clara: Child, don't you know I'll turn your damper down?

Bessie: Yes, Clara, and I'll cut you every way but loose!

Clara: Well, you might as well be get it fixed.

Bessie: Well, then.

[*SUNG*]

Bessie: I guess we got to have him on cooperation plan.
         I guess we got to have him on cooperation plan.

[*SPOKEN*]

Clara: Bessie!

Bessie: Clara!

[*SUNG*]

Both: Ain't nothin' different 'bout all those other two-time men.

[*SPOKEN*]

Bessie: How 'bout it?

Clara: Suits me.

Bessie: Suits me too.

Clara: Well, then.[19]

Edward Brooks has called this humorous song "a fascinating document . . . which completely dispels the doubts of some commentators about Bessie Smith's supremacy over her nearest rival."[20] With respect to the content of the song, the women apparently are equal competitors for the love of the same man. That this rivalry is presented in broadly comic terms encourages in the audience a critical attitude toward such conduct on the part of women. What is most striking about this song is its resolution: the two women agree to share the man over whom they have been engaging in a verbal duel. Bessie proposes to Clara, "I guess we got to have him on cooperation plan." Her suggestion seems to imply how futile it is for them to be so consumed by jealousy that they constantly are at loggerheads with one another. At this point in the song, their focus on the male lover is displaced by their mutual acknowledgment of each other: each calls the other's name. And, in the final moments of the song, they sing together for the first time, agreeing that, since most other men would be as unfaithful as the one over whom they have been battling, they may as well act on Bessie's suggestion. The reconciliation with which the piece concludes, as comically as it may be formulated, alludes to a possibility of sisterhood and solidarity that is forged in and through struggles around sexuality.

The concluding posture of "My Man Blues" is especially interesting for the way it provides an imagined alternative to the notions of women's community-building on which middle-class black club women relied. From their vantage point, women could only come together in defense of sexual purity. In other words, sexuality could only play a role in community-building as an object of ideological protest and cleansing. Of course, the kind of political work the club women set out to do would have been impossible had they not denied the sexually motivated antagonisms so central in blues discourse. In light of the emergence of sexuality in recent decades as an important arena of political struggle, it is important, nevertheless, to understand the blues as a form that did allow explicit articulations and explorations of sexual politics.

There are far more songs of advice among women's blues recordings than there are songs of female competition. One of the principal modes of community-building in women's blues is that of sharing experiences for the purpose of instructing women how to conduct their lives. Many of the songs that describe the difficulties of romantic partnerships are pedagogical in character. In some instances, the instruction warns women to beware of the powers of seduction some men possess, as in the following stanza from Bessie Smith's "Lookin' for My Man Blues":

He's a red hot papa, melt hearts as cold as ice
He's a red hot papa, melt hearts as cold as ice
Girls, if he ever love you once, you bound to love
    him twice.[21]

Or, as in Ma Rainey's "Trust No Man," women are instructed to "[t]rust no man, no further than your eyes can see."[22]

There are also songs that advise women how to avoid triangular entanglements—and how to keep other women from eyeing their men. In Bessie Smith's "Keep It to Yourself," there is an underlying perception of other women as competitors and rivals. However, the instruction seeks to avoid active rivalry over men:

If your man is nice and sweet, servin' you lots of
    young pigmeat
Oh, yeah, keep it to yourself
. . . . . .
If your man is full of action, givin' you a lots of
    satisfaction
Oh, yeah, keep it to yourself
. . . . . .
If he tries to treat you right, give you lovin' every
    night
Oh, yeah, keep it to yourself

He don't fall for no one, he don't call for no one
He don't give nobody his L-O-V-E, 'cause it's yours
With your man you've got the best go, don't broad-
    cast it on nobody's radio
Oh, yeah, keep it to yourself.[23]

There is an interesting dialectic here between the individual woman and the larger female community. While women are clearly perceived as antagonists —as potential intruders into others' relationships— they are also viewed as possessing common fears and common interests. They are located both outside and inside a community of women. This aesthetic community of women emerges in its most developed form when blues women share stories about abusive partners or advise their sisters how to conduct themselves in relation to such men. Daphne Duval Harrison points out in her pioneering study of the classic blues singers that "[a]dvice to other women is a staple among women's blues themes, especially on how to handle your men."[24] Much of this advice seems to accept male supremacy without overtly challenging it, but it also displays unmistakable oppositional attitudes in its rejection of sexual passivity as a defining characteristic of womanhood.

A process similar to the consciousness-raising strategies associated with the 1960s women's liberation movement unfolds in these songs, which are conversations among women about male behavior in which the traditional call-and-response structure of West African–based music takes on a new feminist meaning. Consciousness-raising groups affirmed the most dramatic insight of the early women's liberation movement: the personal is political. Individual women shared personal experiences with the aim of rendering explicit the underlying politics shaping women's lives. Because of the complicated racial politics of the 1960s, which defined the women's movement as white, and because of its emphasis on personal micropolitics (often seen as a retreat from the macropolitics of race), black women generally found it difficult to identify with the strategy of consciousness-raising. In retrospect, however, it is possible to detect ways in which the sharing of personal relationships in blues culture prefigured consciousness-raising and its insights about the social construction of individual experience. Seen in this light, the blues women can be understood as being responsible for the dissemination of attitudes toward male supremacy that had decidedly feminist implications.

That the blues is a highly "personal" aesthetic form in no way diminishes its important social and political dimensions. Lawrence Levine has pointed out that

[t]he blues was the most highly personalized, indeed, the first almost completely personalized

music that Afro-Americans developed. It was the first important form of Afro-American music in the United States to lack the kind of antiphony that had marked other black musical forms. The call and response form remained, but in blues it was the singer who responded to himself or herself either verbally or on an accompanying instrument. In all these respects blues was the most typically American music Afro-Americans had yet created and represented a major degree of acculturation to the individualized ethos of the larger society. . . .[25]

Levine is certainly accurate in his emphasis on the personal and personalizing dimensions of the blues, but he fails to recognize a more complicated persistence of the call-and-response form. The blues in performance creates space for spontaneous audience response in a manner that is similar to religious testifying. Just as the sermon lacks vitality when no response is forthcoming from the congregation, so the blues performance falls flat without the anticipated affirmations of the audience. It was this invitation to respond that rendered women's blues such a powerful site for the construction of working-class consciousness and one of the only arenas in which working-class black women could become aware of the deeply social character of their personal experiences.

The contemporary blues woman Koko Taylor has pointed out that the songs she writes and performs do not always reflect her own individual experiences. Yet, as she insists, she knows that among the women in her audiences, some will certainly identify with the situation she constructs:

> Now when I write a song, I'm thinking about people in general, everyday living. Just look around, you know. Say, for instance, like when I wrote this tune "Baby Please Don't Dog Me." You know what I'm saying. I'm thinking about, O.K., here is some woman begging and she's pleading, Baby please don't dog me, when you know that you're doing wrong yourself. . . . Now that shoe might not fit my feet. That shoe might not fit your feet. But that shoe do fit somebody's feet. It's some woman out there is really thinking, she really feels the way that I'm singing about, what I'm talking about in this song. It's some woman somewhere really feels this way. These are the words she would like to say.[26]

Call-and-response persists in women's blues through the construction of fictional subjects who assert their sexuality in a variety of ways. Such subjects permit a vast array of individual women to locate themselves within a blues community without having to abstract themselves from their personal lives. Rainey and Smith sang songs about women who had numerous male lovers, women angry about male sexual behavior, and women who loved women. Moreover, individual women were able to respond to and comment on the problems of other women without having to reveal the autobiographical sources of their authority and wisdom.

"The widespread use of the call-and-response discourse mode among African-Americans," black feminist sociologist Patricia Hill Collins points out,

> illustrates the importance placed on dialogue. Composed of spontaneous verbal and nonverbal interaction between speaker and listener in which all of the speaker's statements, or "calls," are punctuated by expressions, or "responses," from the listener, this Black discourse mode pervades African American culture. The fundamental requirement of this interactive network is active participation of all individuals. For ideas to be tested and validated, everyone in the group must participate.[27]

Collins defines call-and-response disourse as an essential dimension of the "Afrocentric feminist epistemology" she proposes. While she invokes black women musicians like Billie Holiday and Aretha Franklin in her discussion of yet another dimension of this alternative epistemology, the ethic of caring, she does not discuss the musical roots of call-and-response discourse. Such a discussion—particularly in relation to blues women like Bessie Smith—would render her compelling argument even more powerful. Collins is concerned with the possibility of knowledge production that suppresses neither the individual at the expense of the general welfare, nor feelings at the expense of rational thought. The participatory character of the blues affirms women's community without negating individual feelings.

Without the assumption of such an imagined community, the advice song in women's blues simply could not work. Gertrude Rainey's "Trust No Man," composed by Lillian Hardaway Henderson, is one of the finest examples of the advice song:

I want all you women to listen to me
Don't trust your man no further than your eyes can
    see
I trusted mine with my best friend
But that was the bad part in the end

Trust no man, trust no man, no further than your eyes
    can see
I said trust no man, no further than your eyes can see
He'll tell you that he loves you and swear it is true
The very next minute he'll turn his back on you
Ah, trust no man, no further than your eyes can see.[28]

Singing "I want all you women to listen to me" in the first verse of the song, Rainey constructs an audience, an imagined community of women. It is clear on the recording that Rainey is inviting response—even to this mechanical reproduction of her live performance. Her advice is framed and delivered in such a way that any woman listening can discover a way to identify with her admonition. The appeal is so powerful that it is easy to imagine the responses that came forth during her live performances. As if to preclude any doubt as to the invitation to respond, Rainey included spoken words in the second chorus: "Say! Take Ma Rainey's advice! Don't trust *no* man. I mean, not even your own man!" She concludes this spoken session with the words: "Just don't trust nobody! You see where it got me, don't you? He sure will leave you."

Bessie Smith's "Safety Mama" is a song of advice that counsels women to take strong stands with the men with whom they are involved, and to take measures to guarantee their own economic independence:

Let me tell you how and what one no-good man done
    to me
He caught me pretty, young, and wild, after that he
    let me be

He'd taken advantage of my youth, and that you
    understand
So wait awhile, I'll show you, child, just how to treat
    a no-good man

Make him stay at home, wash and iron
Tell all the neighbors he done lost his mind

Give your house rent shake on Saturday night
Monday morning you'll hold collectors good and
    tight.[29]

. . . What is also striking about "Safety Mama" is that it emphatically counsels women to find ways of supporting themselves financially. Certainly, black women were compelled to work for a living, but for many decades following the abolition of slavery, the jobs that were available to them were limited to domestic work. "Safety Mama" suggests that rather than rely on their men—and perhaps also to avoid the perpetual servitude to which so many working black women were condemned—they organize rent parties in order to acquire funds to meet their landlords' demands. By the 1920s these "house rent shakes" had developed into a community institution in the urban North, aiding men and women alike to raise the money necessary to "hold collectors good and tight." The imagined women's community in this song is one that refuses to place women in sexual and economic subordination to men. It affirms working-class women's independence. Again, it is possible to envision the enthusiastic responses that came from Smith's female audiences.

Another advice song recorded by Bessie Smith . . . is "Pinchback Blues." It proposes to arm women with the power to resist men who attempt to use sexual attractiveness to exploit women. As in "Safety Mama" and Rainey's "Trust No Man," "Pinchback" opens with an evocation of a female community. "Girls," Smith states in the spoken introduction, "I wanna tell you about these sweet men. These men goin' 'round here tryin' to play cute. I'm hard on you, boys, yes sir." She then proceeds to narrate an experience of having been lured into a relationship that led to marriage with a "sweet man" who then refused to get a job to support either his female partner or himself:

I fell in love with a sweet man once, he said he loved
    me too
He said if I'd run away with him what nice things he
    would do

I'd travel around from town to town, how happy
    I would feel
But don't you know, he would not work . . .

Universalizing the lesson drawn from these experiences, Smith offers direct advice to her female audience:

> . . . girls, take this tip from me
> Get a workin' man when you marry, and let all these
>   sweet men be
> . . . . . .
> There's one thing about this married life that these
>   young girls have got to know
> If a sweet man enter your front gate, turn out your
>   lights and lock your door.[30]

The admonition "get a working man" is even more than a sound bit of advice to a woman who wishes to acquire a measure of material security. It suggests an identification with workers—and by extension, the values and perhaps also the collective consciousness associated with the working class. Women are urged to seek out solid working men and to learn how to resist the temptations of parasitic men who try to dazzle with their good looks and smooth talk.

It is interesting that Bessie Smith's appearance in the 1929 motion picture *St. Louis Blues*[31]—the only extant recording of her image on film—was in the role of a woman who did not take the advice offered in "Pinchback Blues." In this film, which incorporates an overabundance of racist and sexist stereotypes, the character she plays is abused and exploited by a handsome, light-skinned, disloyal, crapshooting man who has obviously attached himself to her for the sole purpose of taking her money. "Bessie," the character she plays in the film, has bought clothes for "Jimmy" (played by Jimmy Mordecai), allowed him to live in the hotel room she is renting, and provided him with money. He, in turn, is involved with a thin, light-skinned woman (played by Isabel Washington) who fits a Eurocentric definition of feminine beauty.

The plot of this film, superficially constructed around Bessie Smith's performance of W. C. Handy's "St. Louis Blues," is based on Jimmy's taunting abandonment of Bessie, who is so utterly mesmerized by him that she pleads with him to stay even as she lies on the floor after being battered by him. When the scoundrel returns—the setting for this scene is a luxurious Harlem nightclub—she experiences a momentary exhilaration. However, she is soon overcome with despair once more because, as it turns out, Jimmy's romantic invitation to dance is simply a ploy to steal the money she has hidden in her garter. The film concludes with the pinchback, Jimmy, in a posture of triumph, and the victimized woman, Bessie, in a state of paralyzing depression.

The choice of Bessie Smith for the part in the film has been attributed to W. C. Handy, who, as a collaborator on the film, suggested to the director, Dudley Murphy, that she be cast in the leading role. "She had made the definitive version of the title tune," Chris Albertson has pointed out, and her powerful voice was one of the few that could be heard over the projected accompaniment of a forty-two-voice mixed choir, jazz band, and strings.[32] It is not difficult to understand Smith's decision to make this film. During the late twenties, the popularity of blues had begun to wane and many leading blues singers—Alberta Hunter and Ethel Waters included—increasingly began to sing Tin Pan Alley products and to seek roles in musicals. Smith had starred in a Broadway production that had flopped, and she, like other black women entertainers, was eager to break into the revolutionary medium of talking pictures. But black singers who had been able to exercise a certain measure of autonomy and control over their music found that the new medium used and abused their talents at the whims of producers and directors.

St. Louis Blues deserves criticism not only for its exploitation of racist stereotypes but for its violation of the spirit of the blues. Its direct translation of blues images into a visual and linear narrative violates blues discourse, which is always complicated, contextualized, and informed by that which is unspoken as well as by that which is named. *St. Louis Blues*, the film, flagrantly disregards the spirit of women's blues by leaving the victimized woman with no recourse. In the film, the response is amputated from the call. Although the advice song "Pinchback Blues" evokes a male figure who bears a striking resemblance to the character of Jimmy in the film, "Pinchback" warns women to stay away from such con men. In other women's blues that allude to these men, even when the criticism is not open and direct, the female subjects are never left in a state of absolute despair. Such a posture violates the spirit of women's blues. It is precisely the presence of an imagined community of supportive women that rescues them from the existential agony that Smith portrays at the end of *St. Louis Blues*.

There are also a number of advice songs that suggest how women should conduct themselves in relationships with men who are worthy partners. A cover Bessie Smith recorded of Alberta Hunter's "A Good Man Is Hard to Find" is a typical woman-to-woman advice blues of this kind. It eventually became a standard. This song is unique in that it does not evoke an individual's experiences but rather is directed, in its entirety, to the female audience, articulating their collective experiences with their sexual partners. The persisting problems women encounter in their relationships are named: the unfaithful male lover whose actions provoke tumultuous feelings of jealousy in his female partner, as well as fantasies (if not realities) of violent assault. The main advice in this song is that if a woman does find a man who is loyal, respectful, and sensitive, she should know how to reciprocate:

> Lord, a good man is hard to find, you always get
>   another kind
> Yes, and when you think that he's your pal
> You look and find him fooling 'round some old gal
> Then you rave, you are crazed, you want to see him
>   down in his grave
>
> So if your man is nice, take my advice
> Hug him in the morning, kiss him at night
> Give him plenty lovin', treat your good man right
> 'Cause a good man nowadays sho' is hard to find.[33]

There is a series of songs among the recordings of Gertrude Rainey and Bessie Smith in which the woman who is experiencing difficulties in love shares her problems and her feelings with other women. These songs implicitly emphasize the dialectical relation between the female subject and the community of women within which this individuality is imagined. In an aesthetic realm, these songs construct a women's community in which individual women

are able to locate themselves on a jagged continuum of group experiences. They encourage intimacy and familiarity between women. They contextualize particular events in the personal histories of the songs' subjects—often actions by their male partners that have wrought havoc in their lives—as stories they are sharing with their girlfriends. These girlfriends console them by implicitly confirming similar events in their own histories, thus providing emotional support and enabling women to confront such disruptive moments with attitudes that move from victimization to agency. Ma Rainey, for example, begins "Jelly Bean Blues" by asking, "Did you ever wake up with your good man on your mind?"[34] The song then proceeds to describe the subject's state of mind in the aftermath of her lover's desertion. The initial question establishes a relationship of intimacy and familiarity with her female audience.

Bessie Smith's version of Rainey's composition "Moonshine Blues" makes a few minor but significant changes, including the substitution in one stanza of "girls" for "lord." Smith thus explicitly conjures up a supportive female community. In Rainey's rendition:

> I feel like screamin', I feel like cryin'
> Lord, I been mistreated, folks, and don't mind
>   dyin'.[35]

In Smith's version:

> Girls, I feel like screamin', I feel like cryin'
> I been mistreated, and I don't mind dyin'.[36]

Of course, Rainey, following the traditional patterns of blues discourse, is announcing her plight, publicizing her private woes, and thus, in this stanza, invokes her entire community—the folks—while directing her feelings of despair to the Lord. Smith, on the other hand, seeks solace not in the Lord but rather from the girls.

In "You Don't Understand," recorded by Bessie Smith in 1929, a collective female presence is invoked in the first line. The subject realizes that it is futile to try to persuade the man she loves to return to her: "Here I am, girls of mine, pleading but it's all in vain."[37] The entire text, with the exception of the opening phrase, is directed to the unresponsive man. Ma Rainey's "Titanic Man Blues" begins with a similar invocation: "Everybody fall in line, going to tell you 'bout that man of mine." From the story that follows, it is obvious that she is addressing herself to women. After this opening phrase, the female figure in the song proceeds to direct her comments to a lover she plans to leave, ending each verse with this statement: "It's the last time, Titanic, fare thee well."[38] It is as if she invites a community of women to be present at a ritualistic shunning. Invoking the presence of sympathetic women summons up the courage the woman needs in order to eject this man from her life.

Bessie Smith's "I Used to Be Your Sweet Mama" is one of the most stunning examples of sharing among women for the purpose of summoning up the emotional strength necessary to challenge male supremacy in personal relationships:

> All you women understand
> What it is to be in love with a two-time man
> The next time he calls me sweet mama in his lovin'
>   way
> This is what I'm going to say
>
> "I used to be your sweet mama, sweet papa
> But now I'm just as sour as can be."

Again, this song anticipates the 1960s strategy of consciousness-raising. Affirming that the women in her listening audience have a common understanding of disloyal lovers, the protagonist creates, on the basis of that collective experience, a rehearsal space. One easily can imagine the testifying that punctuated Bessie Smith's performances of this song. She must have received enthusiastic shouts of encouragement from the women in her audiences as she sang, "This is what I'm going to say," and certainly as she informed her audience what she would tell "sweet papa":

> "So don't come stallin' around my way expectin'
>   any love from me
> You had your chance and proved unfaithful
> So now I'm gonna be real mean and hateful
> I used to be your sweet mama, sweet papa
> But now I'm just as sour as can be."

> I ain't gonna let no man worry me sick
> Or turn this hair of mine gray
> Soon as I catch him at his two-time tricks
> I'm gonna tell him to be on his way
> To the world I scream, "No man can treat me mean
> And expect my love all the time."
> When he roams away, he'd better stay
> If he comes back he'll find
>
> "You've had your chance and proved unfaithful
> So now I'm gonna be real mean and hateful
> I used to be your sweet mama, sweet papa
> But now I'm just as sour as can be."[39]

Such songs as this and Rainey's "Trust No Man," in part because they evoked enthusiastic, testifying responses from their female audiences, would have been considered distasteful by middle-class club women. Formally educated women assumed that such cultural expressions tended to confirm the dominant culture's association of black women with sexual license and immorality. As the club women went about their work of "defending our name," they disassociated themselves from working-class women's blues culture, and assumed the missionary role of introducing "true womanhood" to their less fortunate sisters. In fact, they were defending the name of the female contingent of the black bourgeoisie. It did not occur to them then—and may not be obvious to us today—that this women's blues community was in fact defending the name of its own members. And while the club women achieved great victories in the historical struggles they undertook against racism, and forcefully affirmed black women's equality in the process, the ideological terrain on which they operated was infused with assumptions about the inherent inferiority of poor—and especially sexually assertive—women. In hindsight, the production, performance, and reception of women's blues during the decade of the twenties reveal that black women's names could be defended by working-class as well as middle-class women. Women's blues also demonstrate that working-class women's names could be defended not only in the face of the dominant white culture but in the face of male assertions of dominance in black communities as well.

NOTES

1. Gertrude "Ma" Rainey, "Trust No Man," Paramount 12395, Aug. 1926. Reissued on *Ma Rainey*, Milestone M-47021, 1974.

2. Paula Giddings, *When and Where I Enter: The Impact of Black Women on Race and Sex in America* (New York: Morrow, 1984), p. 95.

3. Mary Church Terrell, "What Role Is the Educated Negro Woman to Play in the Uplifting of Her Race?" quoted in Giddings, p. 98.

4. This theme of the Black women's club movement was first formulated by Fannie Barrier Williams in an address she gave at a worldwide gathering of women during the 1983 World Columbian Exposition:

I regret the necessity of speaking to the question of the moral progress of our women because the morality of our home life has been commented on so despairingly and meanly that we are placed in the unfortunate position of being defenders of our name. . . . While I duly appreciate the offensiveness of all references to American slavery, it is unavoidable to charge to that system every moral imperfection that mars the character of the colored American. The whole life and power of slavery depended upon an enforced degradation of everything human in the slaves. The slave code recognized only animal distinctions between the sexes and ruthlessly ignored those ordinary separations of the sexes that belong to the social state. It is a great wonder that two centuries of such demoralization did not work a complete extinction of all the moral instincts.

The Present Status and Intellectual Progress of Colored Women (Chicago, 1893), quoted in Eleanor Flexner, *Century of Struggle: The Woman's Rights Movement in the United States* (New York: Atheneum, 1974), pp. 187–88.

5. Gertrude "Ma" Rainey. "Prove It on Me Blues," Paramount 12668, June 1928. Reissued on *Ma Rainey*, Milestone M-47021, 1974.

6. Bessie Smith, "A Good Man Is Hard to Find," Columbia 14250-D, Sept. 27, 1927. Reissued on *The Empress*, Columbia CG 30818, 1972.

7. W. E. B. Du Bois, *Darkwater: Voices from Within the Veil* (New York: Harcourt, Brace & Howe, 1920). See Patricia Hill Collins's account of the epistemological implications of this discourse in *Black Feminist Thought* (Boston: Unwin Hyman, 1990).

8. See Angela Y. Davis, *Women, Race, and Class* (New York: Random House, 1981), chap. 1.

9. Gertrude "Ma" Rainey, "Rough and Tumble Blues," Paramount 112311, 1926. Reissued on *The Immortal Ma Rainey*, Milestone MLP-2001, 1966.

10. Gertrude "Ma" Rainey, "Wringing and Twisting Blues," Paramount 12338, Dec. 1925. Reissued on *The Immortal Ma Rainey*, Milestone MLP-2001, 1966. In another verse, the means of poisoning the rival are detailed:

I had some green cucumbers, some half done tripe and greens
Some buttermilk and codfish, some sour kidney beans.

These images from black culinary culture reflect a number of myths—as well as realities—regarding dangerous foods: unripe cucumbers, uncooked pork, milk and fish (considered a deadly combination), and beans gone bad.

11. Bessie Smith, "Any Woman's Blues," Columbia 13001-D, Oct. 16, 1923. Reissued on *Any Woman's Blues*, Columbia G 30126, 1972.

12. Bessie Smith, "St. Louis Gal," Columbia 13005-D, Sept. 24, 1923. Reissued on *Any Woman's Blues*, Columbia G 30126,1972.

13. Bessie Smith, "Empty Bed Blues," Columbia 14312-D, Mar. 20, 1928. Reissued on *Empty Bed Blues*, Columbia CG 30450,1972.

14. Bessie Smith, "He's Got Me Goin'," Columbia 14464-D, Aug. 20, 1929. Reissued on *Any Woman's Blues*, Columbia G 30126, 1972.

15. As an aside, this makes for an interesting contribution to the debate on modernism and African-American culture, especially considering the similarities between the techniques associated with Cubism in the visual arts and the blues perspective. See Houston Baker's *Modernism and the Harlem Renaissance* (Chicago and London: University of Chicago Press, 1987).

16. Gertrude "Ma" Rainey, "Sleep Talking Blues," Paramount 12760, Sept. 1928. Reissued on *Ma Rainey*, Milestone M-47021, 1974.

17. Gertrude "Ma" Rainey, "Jealous Hearted Blues," Paramount 12252, Dec. 1925. Reissued on *Ma Rainey*, Milestone M-47021, 1974.

18. Gertrude "Ma" Rainey, "Jealousy Blues," Paramount 12364, March 1926. Reissued on *Oh My Babe Blues*, Biograph BLP-12011, n.d.

19. Bessie Smith, "My Man Blues," Columbia 14098-D, Sept. 1925. Reissued on *Nobody's Blues but Mine*, Columbia CG 31093, 1972.

20. Edward Brooks, *The Bessie Smith Companion* (New York: Da Capo, 1982), p. 95.

21. Bessie Smith, "Lookin' for My Man Blues," Columbia 14569-D, Sept. 28, 1927. Reissued on *The Empress*, Columbia CG 30818, 1972.

22. Gertrude "Ma" Rainey, "Trust No Man," Paramount 12395, Aug. 1926. Reissued on *Ma Rainey*, Milestone M-47021, 1974.

23. Bessie Smith. "Keep It to Yourself," Columbia 14516-D, Mar. 27, 1930. Reissued on *Any Woman's Blues*, Columbia G 30126, 1972.

24. Daphne Duval Harrison, *Black Pearls: Blues Queens of the 1920s* (New Brunswick: Rutgers Univ. Press, 1988), p. 110.

25. Lawrence Levine, *Black Culture and Black Consciousness* (New York: Oxford Univ. Press, 1975), p. 221.

26. Koko Taylor in *Wild Women Don't Have the Blues*, dir. Christine Dall, Calliope Film Resources, 1989, videocassette.

27. Collins, p. 213.

28. Rainey, "Trust No Man."

29. Bessie Smith, "Safety Mama," Columbia 14634-D, Nov. 20, 1931. Reissued on *The World's Greatest Blues Singer*, Columbia CG 33, 1972.

30. Bessie Smith, "Pinchback Blues," Columbia 14025-D, Apr. 5, 1924. Reissued on *Empty Bed Blues*, Columbia CG 30450, 1972.

31. *St. Louis Blues*, dir. Dudley Murphy, Gramercy Studio of RCA Photophone, presented by Radio Pictures, 1929. W. C. Handy coauthored the script for this film, the release of which occasioned a protest by the NAACP.

32. Chris Albertson, *Bessie* (New York: Stein & Day, 1972), p. 159.

33. Bessie Smith, "A Good Man Is Hard to Find."

34. Gertrude "Ma" Rainey, "Jelly Bean Blues," Paramount 12238, Feb. 1927. Reissued on *Ma Rainey*, Milestone M-47021, 1974.

35. Gertrude "Ma" Rainey, "Moonshine Blues," Paramount 12603, Dec. 1927. Reissued on *Ma Rainey*, Milestone M-47021, 1974.

36. Bessie Smith, "Moonshine Blues," Columbia 14018-D, Apr. 19, 1924. Reissued on *Empty Bed Blues*, Columbia CG 30450, 1972.

37. Bessie Smith, "You Don't Understand," Columbia 14487-D, Oct. 11, 1929. Reissued on *Any Woman's Blues*, Columbia G 30126, 1972.

38. Gertrude "Ma" Rainey, "Titanic Man Blues," Paramount 12374, Jan. 1926. Reissued on *Blues the World Forgot*, Biograph BLP-12001, n.d.

39. Bessie Smith, "I Used to Be Your Sweet Mama," Columbia 1492-D, Feb. 9, 1928. Reissued on *Empty Bed Blues*, Columbia CG 30450, 1972.

Study Questions

1. Davis asserts that the blues reveal an attitude toward sexuality that is at odds with that promoted by the black women's club movement. Describe these two attitudes and what Davis says accounts for each.

2. Davis argues that the blues were an important site of community-building for working-class black women. According to Davis, how do the themes, in blues songs, of jealousy and the difficulties of romantic partnerships contribute to this community building?

3. According to Davis, the blues "prefigure" many aspects of feminism typically traced to the 1970s and after, such as the refusal to privilege racism over sexism, the practice of consciousness-raising, and the recognition of sexuality as "an important arena of political struggle." What does Davis mean by this?

4. Does it make sense to characterize Davis as drawing on a politics of identity in this excerpt?

5. Does the fact that Davis is not a member of the groups about which she is writing raise problems for her work?

Dorothy E. Roberts

Punishing Drug Addicts Who Have Babies:
Women of Color, Equality, and the Right of Privacy

PROLOGUE

A former slave named Lizzie Williams recounted the beating of pregnant slave women on a Mississippi cotton plantation: "I[']s seen nigger women dat was fixin' to be confined do somethin' de white folks didn't like. Dey [the white folks] would dig a hole in de ground just big 'nuff fo' her stomach, make her lie face down an whip her on de back to keep from hurtin' de child."

In July 1989, Jennifer Clarise Johnson, a twenty-three-year-old crack addict, became the first woman in the United States to be criminally convicted for exposing her baby to drugs while pregnant. Florida law enforcement officials charged Johnson with two counts of delivering a controlled substance to a minor after her two children tested positive for cocaine at birth. Because the relevant Florida drug law did not apply to fetuses, the prosecution invented a novel interpretation of the statute. The prosecution obtained Johnson's conviction for passing a cocaine metabolite from her body to her newborn infants during the sixty-second period after birth and before the umbilical cord was cut.

I. INTRODUCTION

A growing number of women across the country have been charged with criminal offenses after giving birth to babies who test positive for drugs. The majority of these women, like Jennifer Johnson, are poor and black. Most are addicted to crack cocaine. The prosecution of drug-addicted mothers is part of an alarming trend toward greater state intervention into the lives of pregnant women under the rationale of protecting the fetuses from harm. This intervention has included compulsory medical treatment, greater restrictions on abortion, and increased supervision of pregnant women's conduct.

Such government intrusion is particularly harsh for poor women of color. They are the least likely to obtain adequate prenatal care, the most vulnerable to government monitoring, and the least able to conform to the white, middle-class standard of motherhood. They are therefore the primary targets of government control.

The prosecution of drug-addicted mothers involves two fundamental tensions. First, punishing a woman for using drugs during pregnancy pits the state's interest in protecting the future health of a child against the mother's interest in autonomy over her reproductive life—interests that until recently had not been thought to be in conflict. Second, such prosecutions represent one of two possible responses to the problem of drug-exposed babies. The government may choose either to help women have healthy pregnancies or to punish women for their prenatal conduct. Although it might seem that the state could pursue both of these avenues at once, the two responses are ultimately irreconcilable. Far from deterring injurious drug use, prosecution of drug-addicted mothers in fact deters pregnant women from using available health and counseling services, because it causes women to fear that, if they seek help, they could be reported to government authorities and charged with a crime. Moreover, prosecution blinds the public to the possibility of nonpunitive solutions and to the inadequacy of the nonpunitive solutions that are currently available.

The debate between those who favor protecting the rights of the fetus and those who favor protecting the rights of the mother has been extensively waged in the literature. This article does not repeat the theoretical arguments for and against state intervention. Rather, it suggests that both sides of the debate have largely overlooked a critical aspect of government prosecution of drug-addicted mothers. Can we determine the legality of the prosecutions simply by weighing the state's abstract interest in the fetus against the mother's abstract interest in autonomy? Can we determine whether the prosecutions are fair simply by deciding the duties a pregnant woman owes to her fetus and then assessing whether the defendant has met them? Can we determine the constitutionality of the government's actions without considering the race of the women being singled out for prosecution?

Before deciding whether the state's interest in preventing harm to the fetus justifies criminal sanctions against the mother, we must first understand the mother's competing perspective and the reasons for the state's choice of a punitive response. This article seeks to illuminate the current debate by examining the experiences of the class of women who are primarily affected—poor black women.

Providing the perspective of poor black women offers two advantages. First, examining legal issues from the viewpoint of those whom they affect most helps to uncover the real reasons for state action and to explain the real harms that it causes. It exposes the way in which the prosecutions deny poor black women a facet of their humanity by punishing their reproductive choices. The government's choice of a punitive response perpetuates the historical devaluation of black women as mothers. Viewing the legal issues from the experiential standpoint of the defendants enhances our understanding of the constitutional dimensions of the state's conduct.

Second, examining the constraints on poor black women's reproductive choices expands our understanding of reproductive freedom in particular and of the right of privacy in general. Much of the literature discussing reproductive freedom has adopted a white middle-class perspective, which focuses narrowly on abortion rights. The feminist critique of privacy doctrine has also neglected many of the concerns of poor women of color.

My analysis presumes that black women experience various forms of oppression simultaneously, as a complex interaction of race, gender, and class that is more than the sum of its parts. It is impossible to isolate any one of the components of this oppression or to separate the experiences that are attributable to one component from experiences attributable to the others. The prosecution of drug-addicted mothers cannot be explained as simply an issue of gender inequality. Poor black women have been selected for punishment as a result of an inseparable combination of their gender, race, and economic status. Their devaluation as mothers, which underlies the prosecutions, has its roots in the unique experience of slavery and has been perpetuated by complex social forces. . . .

This article advances an account of the constitutionality of prosecutions of drug-addicted mothers which explicitly considers the experiences of poor black women. The constitutional arguments are based on theories both of racial equality and of the right of privacy. I argue that punishing drug addicts who choose to carry their pregnancies to term unconstitutionally burdens the right to autonomy over reproductive decisions. Violation of poor black women's reproductive rights helps to perpetuate a racist hierarchy in our society. The prosecutions thus impose a standard of motherhood that is offensive to principles of both equality and privacy. This article provides insight into the particular and urgent struggle of women of color for reproductive freedom. Further, I intend my constitutional critique of the prosecutions to demonstrate the advantages of a discourse that combines elements of racial equality and privacy theories in advocating the reproductive rights of women of color. . . .

II. BACKGROUND: THE STATE'S PUNITIVE RESPONSE TO DRUG-ADDICTED MOTHERS

A. The Crack Epidemic and the State's Response

Crack cocaine appeared in America in the early eighties, and its abuse has grown to epidemic proportions. Crack is especially popular among inner-city women. Indeed, evidence shows that, in several urban areas in the United States, more women than men now smoke crack. Most crack-addicted women are of childbearing age, and many are pregnant. This phenomenon has contributed to an explosion in the number of newborns affected by maternal drug use; some experts estimate that as many as 375,000 drug-exposed infants are born every year. In many urban hospitals, the number of these newborns has quadrupled in the last five years. A widely cited 1988 study conducted by the National Association for Perinatal Addiction Research and Education (NAPARE) found that 11 percent of newborns in thirty-six hospitals surveyed were affected by their mothers' illegal drug use during pregnancy. In several hospitals, the proportion of drug-exposed infants was as high as 15 and 25 percent.

Babies born to drug-addicted mothers may suffer a variety of medical, developmental, and behavioral problems, depending on the nature of their mother's substance abuse. Immediate effects of cocaine ex-

posure can include premature birth, low birth weight, and withdrawal symptoms. Cocaine-exposed children have also exhibited neurobehavioral problems, such as mood dysfunction, organizational deficits, poor attention, and impaired human interaction, although it has not been determined whether these conditions are permanent. Congenital disorders and deformities have also been associated with cocaine use during pregnancy. According to NAPARE, babies exposed to cocaine have a tenfold greater risk of suffering Sudden Infant Death Syndrome (SIDS).

Data on the extent and potential severity of the adverse effects of maternal cocaine use are controversial. The interpretation of studies of cocaine-exposed infants is often clouded by the presence of other fetal risk factors, such as the mother's use of additional drugs, cigarettes, or alcohol, and her socio-economic status. For example, the health prospects of an infant are significantly threatened because pregnant addicts often receive little or no prenatal care and may be malnourished. Moreover, because the medical community has given more attention to studies showing adverse effects of cocaine exposure than to those that deny these effects, the public has a distorted perception of the risks of maternal cocaine use. Researchers have not yet authoritatively determined the percentage of infants exposed to cocaine who actually experience adverse consequences.

The response of state prosecutors, legislators, and judges to the problem of drug-exposed babies has been punitive. They have punished women who use drugs during pregnancy by depriving these mothers of custody of their children, by jailing them during their pregnancy, and by prosecuting them after their babies are born.

The most common penalty for a mother's prenatal drug use is the permanent or temporary removal of her baby. Hospitals in a number of states now screen newborns for evidence of drugs in their urine and report positive results to child welfare authorities. Some child protection agencies institute neglect proceedings to obtain custody of babies with positive toxicologies based solely on these tests. More and more government authorities are also removing drug-exposed newborns from their mothers immediately after birth pending an investigation of parental fitness. In these investigations, positive neonatal toxicologies often raise a strong presumption of parental unfitness, circumventing the inquiry into the mother's ability to care for her child, which is customarily necessary to deprive a parent of custody.

A second form of punishment is the "protective" incarceration of pregnant drug addicts charged with unrelated crimes. In 1988, a Washington, D.C., judge sentenced to jail for the duration of her pregnancy a thirty-year-old woman named Brenda Vaughn, who pleaded guilty to forging $700 worth of checks. The judge stated at sentencing that he wanted to ensure that the baby would be born in jail to protect it from its mother's drug abuse. Although the Vaughn case has received the most attention, anecdotal evidence suggests that defendants' drug use during pregnancy often affects judges' sentencing decisions.

Finally, women have been prosecuted after the birth of their children for having exposed the fetuses to drugs or alcohol. Creative statutory interpretations that once seemed little more than the outlandish concoctions of conservative scholars are now used to punish women. Mothers of children affected by prenatal substance abuse have been charged with crimes such as distributing drugs to a minor, child abuse and neglect, manslaughter, and assault with a deadly weapon.

This article considers the constitutional implications of criminal prosecution of drug-addicted mothers because, as Part IV explains, this penalty most directly punishes poor black women for having babies. When the government prosecutes, its intervention is not designed to protect babies from the irresponsible actions of their mothers (as is arguably the case when the state takes custody of a pregnant addict or her child); rather, the government criminalizes the mother as a consequence of her decision to bear a child.

B. The Disproportionate Impact on Poor Black Women

Poor black women bear the brunt of prosecutors' punitive approach. These women are the primary targets of prosecutors, not because they are more likely to be guilty of fetal abuse, but because they are black and poor. Poor women, who are disproportionately black, are in closer contact with government agencies, and their drug use is therefore more likely to be detected. Black women are also more likely to be reported to government authorities, in part because of the racist attitudes of health care professionals. Finally, their failure to meet society's image of the ideal mother makes their prosecution more acceptable.

To charge drug-addicted mothers with crimes, the state must be able to identify those who use drugs during pregnancy. Because poor women are generally under greater government supervision—through their associations with public hospitals, welfare agencies, and probation officers—their drug use is more likely to be detected and reported. Hospital screening practices result in disproportionate reporting of poor black women. The government's main source of information about prenatal drug use is hospitals' reporting of positive infant toxicologies to child welfare authorities. This testing is implemented almost exclusively by hospitals serving poor minority communities. Private physicians who serve more affluent women perform less of this screening for two reasons: they have a financial stake both in retaining their patients' business and securing referrals from them, and they are socially more like their patients.

Hospitals administer drug tests in a manner that further discriminates against poor black women. One common criterion triggering an infant toxicology screen is the mother's failure to obtain prenatal care, a factor that correlates strongly with race and income. Worse still, many hospitals have no formal screening procedures, relying solely on the suspicions of health care professionals. This discretion allows doctors and hospital staff to perform tests based on their stereotyped assumptions about drug addicts.

Health care professionals are much more likely to report black women's drug use to government authorities than they are similar drug use by their wealthy white patients. A study recently reported in the *New England Journal of Medicine* demonstrated this racial bias in the reporting of maternal drug use.

Researchers studied the results of toxicologic tests of pregnant women who received prenatal care in public health clinics and in private obstetrical offices in Pinellas County, Florida. Substance abuse by pregnant women did not correlate substantively with racial or economic categories, nor was there any significant difference between public clinics and private offices. Despite similar rates of substance abuse, however, black women were ten times more likely than whites to be reported to public health authorities for substance abuse during pregnancy. Although several possible explanations can account for this disparate reporting, both public health facilities and private doctors are more inclined to turn in pregnant black women who use drugs than pregnant white women who use drugs.

It is also significant that, out of the universe of material conduct that can injure a fetus, prosecutors have focused on crack use. The selection of crack addiction for punishment can be justified neither by the number of addicts nor the extent of the harm to the fetuses. Excessive alcohol consumption during pregnancy, for example, can cause severe fetal injury, and marijuana use may also adversely affect the unborn. The incidence of both these types of substance abuse is high as well. In addition, prosecutors do not always base their claims on actual harm to the child; rather, they base it on the mere delivery of crack by the mother. Although different forms of substance abuse prevail among pregnant women of various socio-economic levels and racial and ethnic backgrounds, inner-city black communities have the highest concentrations of crack addicts. Therefore, selecting crack abuse as the primary fetal harm to be punished has a discriminatory impact that cannot be medically justified.

Focusing on black crack addicts rather than on other perpetrators of fetal harms serves two broader social purposes. First, prosecution of these pregnant women serves to degrade women whom society views as undeserving to be mothers and to discourage them from having children. If prosecutors had instead chosen to prosecute affluent women addicted to alcohol or prescription medication, the policy of criminalizing prenatal conduct very likely would have

suffered a hasty demise. Society is much more willing to condone the punishment of poor women of color who fail to meet the middle-class ideal of motherhood.

In addition to legitimizing fetal rights enforcement, the prosecution of crack-addicted mothers diverts public attention from social ills such as poverty, racism, and a misguided national health policy— implying instead that shamefully high black infant death rates are caused by the bad acts of individual mothers. Poor black mothers thus become the scapegoats for the black community's ill health. Punishing them assuages any guilt the nation might feel at the plight of an underclass with infant mortality at rates higher than those in some less developed countries. Making criminals of black mothers apparently helps to relieve the nation of the burden of creating a health care system that ensures healthy babies for all its citizens.

For a variety of reasons, then, an informed appraisal of the competing interests involved in the prosecutions must take account of the race of the women affected. Part III examines a significant aspect of black women's experience that underlies the punishment of crack-addicted mothers.

III. THE DEVALUATION OF BLACK MOTHERHOOD

The systematic, institutionalized denial of reproductive freedom has uniquely marked black women's history in America. An important part of this denial has been the devaluation of black women as mothers. A popular mythology that degrades black women and portrays them as less deserving of motherhood reinforces this subordination. This mythology is one aspect of a complex set of images that deny black humanity in order to rationalize the oppression of blacks.

In this part, I will discuss three manifestations of the devaluation of black motherhood: the original exploitation of black women during slavery; the more contemporary, disproportionate removal of black children from their mothers' custody; and sterilization abuse. Throughout this part, I will also show how several popular images denigrating black mothers—the licentious Jezebel; the careless, incompetent mother; the domineering matriarch; and the lazy welfare mother—have reinforced and legitimated their devaluation.

A. *The Slavery Experience*

The essence of black women's experience during slavery was the brutal denial of autonomy over reproduction. Female slaves were commercially valuable to their masters not only for their labor but also for their capacity to produce more slaves. Henry Louis Gates, Jr., writing about the autobiography of a slave named Harriet A. Jacobs, observes that it "charts in vivid detail precisely how the shape of her life and the choices she makes are defined by her reduction to a sexual object, an object to be raped, bred or abused." Black women's childbearing during slavery was thus largely a product of oppression rather than an expression of self-definition and personhood.

The method of whipping pregnant slaves that was used throughout the South vividly illustrates the slaveowners' dual interest in black women as workers and childbearers. Slaveowners forced women to lie face down in a depression in the ground while they were whipped, thus allowing the masters to protect the fetus while abusing the mother. It serves as a powerful metaphor for the evils of a fetal protection policy that denies the humanity of the mother. It is also a forceful symbol of the convergent oppressions inflicted on slave women: they were subjugated at once both as blacks and as females.

From slavery on, black women have fallen outside the scope of the American ideal of womanhood. Slaveowners forced slave women to perform strenuous labor, which contravened the Victorian female roles prevalent in the dominant white society. Angela Davis has observed: "Judged by the evolving nineteenth-century ideology of femininity, which emphasized women's roles as nurturing mothers and gentle companions and housekeepers for their husbands, Black women were practically anomalies." Black women's historical deviation from traditional female roles has engendered a mythology that denies their womanhood.

One of the most prevalent images of slave women was the character of Jezebel, a woman governed by her sexual desires. As early as 1736, the *South Carolina Gazette* described "African Ladies" as women "of 'strong robust constitution' who were 'not easily jaded out' but able to serve their lovers 'by Night as well as Day.'" This ideological construct of the licentious Jezebel legitimated white men's sexual abuse of black women. The stereotype of black women as sexually promiscuous helped to perpetuate their devaluation as mothers.

The myth of the "bad" black woman was deliberately and systematically perpetuated after slavery ended. For example, historian Philip A. Bruce's book *The Plantation Negro as a Freeman*, published in 1889, strengthened popular views of black degeneracy, male and female. Bruce traced the alleged propensity of the black man to rape white women to the "wantonness of the women of his own race" and "the sexual laxness of plantation women as a class." This image of the sexually loose, impure black woman, which originated in slavery, persists in modern American culture.

Under slavery, black women were also systematically denied the rights of motherhood. Slave mothers had no legal claim to their children; slave masters owned not only black women but also their children. They alienated slave women from their children by selling them to other slaveowners and by controlling childrearing. In 1851, Sojourner Truth reminded the audience at a women's rights convention that society denied black women even the limited dignity of Victorian womanhood accorded white women of the time, including the right of mothering:

> Dat man ober dar say dat women needs to be helped into carriages, and lifted ober ditches, and to have de best place every whar. Nobody eber heap me into carriages, or ober mud puddles, or gives me any best place . . . and ar'n't I a woman? Look at me! Look at my arm! . . . I have plowed, and planted, and gathered into barns, and no man could head me—and ar'n't I a woman? I could work as much and eat as much as a man (when I could get it), and bear de lash as well—and ar'n't I a woman? I have borne thirteen children and seen em mos' all sold off into slavery,

and when I cried out with a mother's grief, none but Jesus heard—and ar'n't I a woman?

Black women struggled in many ways to resist the efforts of slave masters to control their reproductive lives. They used contraceptives and abortifacients, escaped from plantations, feigned illness, endured severe punishment, and fought back rather than submit to slave masters' sexual domination. Free black women with the means to do so purchased freedom for their daughters and sisters. Black women, along with black men, succeeded remarkably often in maintaining the integrity of their family life despite slavery's disrupting effects.

B. The Disproportionate Removal of Black Children

The disproportionate number of black mothers who lose custody of their children through the child welfare system is a contemporary manifestation of the devaluation of black motherhood. This disparate impact of state intervention results in part from black families' higher rate of reliance on government welfare. Because welfare families are subject to supervision by social workers, instances of perceived neglect are more likely to be reported to governmental authorities than neglect on the part of more affluent parents. Black children are also removed from their homes in part because of the child welfare system's cultural bias and application of the nuclear family pattern to black families. Black childrearing patterns that diverge from the norm of the nuclear family have been misinterpreted by government bureaucrats as child neglect. For example, child welfare workers have often failed to respect the longstanding cultural tradition in the black community of shared parenting responsibility among blood-related and nonblood kin. The state has thus been more willing to intrude upon the autonomy of poor black families, and in particular of black mothers, while protecting the integrity of white, middle-class homes.

This devaluation of black motherhood has been reinforced by stereotypes that blame black mothers for the problems of the black family. This scapegoating dates back to slavery, when black mothers were

blamed for the devastating effects on their children of both poverty and the abuse of black women. When a one-month-old slave girl named Harriet died in the Abbeville District of South Carolina on December 9, 1849, the census marshal reported the cause of death as "[s]mothered by carelessness of [her] mother." This report was typical of the U.S. census mortality schedules for the southern states in its attribution of a black infant death to accidental suffocation by the mother. Census marshal Charles M. Pelot explained: "I wish it to be distinctly understood that nearly all the accidents occur in the negro population, which goes clearly to prove their great carelessness and total inability to take care of themselves." It now appears that the true cause of these suffocation deaths was Sudden Infant Death Syndrome. Black children died at a dramatically higher rate because of the hard physical work, poor nutrition, and abuse that their slave mothers endured during pregnancy.

The scapegoating of black mothers has manifested itself more recently in the myth of the black matriarch, the domineering female head of the black family. White sociologists have held black matriarchs responsible for the disintegration of the black family and the consequent failure of black people to achieve success in America. Daniel Patrick Moynihan popularized this theory in his 1965 report, *The Negro Family: The Case for National Action*. According to Moynihan: "At the heart of the deterioration of the fabric of the Negro society is the deterioration of the Negro family. It is the fundamental cause of the weakness of the Negro community. . . . In essence, the Negro community has been forced into a matriarchal structure which, because it is so out of line with the rest of the American society, seriously retards the progress of the group as a whole." Thus, Moynihan attributed the cause of black people's inability to overcome the effects of racism largely to the dominance of black mothers.

C. The Sterilization of Women of Color

Coerced sterilization is one of the most extreme forms of control over a woman's reproductive life. By permanently denying her the right to bear children, sterilization enforces society's determination that a woman does not deserve to be a mother. Unlike white women, poor women of color have been subjected to sterilization abuse for decades. The disproportionate sterilization of black women is yet another manifestation of the dominant society's devaluation of black women as mothers.

Sterilization abuse has taken the form both of blatant coercion and trickery and of subtle influences on women's decisions to be sterilized. In the seventies, some doctors conditioned delivering babies and performing abortions on black women's consent to sterilization. In a 1974 case brought by poor teenage black women in Alabama, a federal district court found that an estimated 100,000 to 150,000 poor women were sterilized annually under federally funded programs. Some of these women were coerced into agreeing to sterilization under the threat that their welfare benefits would be withdrawn unless they submitted to the operation. Despite federal and state regulations intended to prevent involuntary sterilization, physicians and other health care providers continue to urge women of color to consent to sterilization because they view these women's family sizes as excessive and believe these women are incapable of effectively using other methods of birth control.

Current government funding policy perpetuates the encouragement of sterilization of poor, and thus of mainly black, women. The federal government pays for sterilization services under the Medicaid program, while it often does not provide or encourage information about or access to other contraceptive techniques and abortion. In effect, sterilization is the only publicly funded birth control method readily available to poor women of color.

Popular images of the undeserving black mother serve to legitimate government policy as well as the practices of health care providers. The myth of the black Jezebel has been supplemented by the contemporary image of the lazy welfare mother who breeds children at the expense of taxpayers in order to increase the amount of her welfare check. This view of black motherhood provides the rationale for society's restrictions on black female fertility. It is this image of the undeserving black mother that

ultimately underlies the government's choice to punish crack-addicted women.

IV. PROSECUTING DRUG ADDICTS AS PUNISHMENT FOR HAVING BABIES

Informed by the historical and present devaluation of black motherhood, we can better understand prosecutors' reasons for punishing drug-addicted mothers. This article views such prosecutions as punishing these women, in essence, for having babies; judges such as the one who convicted Jennifer Johnson are pronouncing not so much "I care about your baby" as "You don't deserve to be a mother."

It is important to recognize at the outset that the prosecutions are based in part on a woman's pregnancy and not on her illegal drug use alone. Prosecutors charge these defendants not with drug use but with child abuse or drug distribution—crimes that relate to their pregnancy. Moreover, pregnant women receive harsher sentences than do drug-addicted men or women who are not pregnant.

The unlawful nature of drug use must not be allowed to confuse the basis of the crimes at issue. The legal rationale underlying the prosecutions does not depend on the illegality of drug use. Harm to the fetus is the crux of the government's legal theory. Criminal charges have been brought against women for conduct that is legal but is alleged to have harmed the fetus.

When a drug-addicted woman becomes pregnant, she has only one realistic avenue to escape criminal charges—abortion. Thus, she is penalized for choosing to have the baby rather than choosing to have an abortion. In this way, the state's punitive action may coerce women to have abortions rather than risk being charged with a crime. Thus, it is the choice of carrying a pregnancy to term that is being penalized.

There is also good reason to question the government's justification for the prosecutions—the concern for the welfare of potential children. I have already discussed the selectivity of the prosecutions with respect to poor black women. This focus on the conduct of one group of women weakens the state's rationale for the prosecutions.

The history of overwhelming state neglect of black children casts further doubt on its professed concern for the welfare of the fetus. When a society has always closed its eyes to the inadequacy of prenatal care available to poor black women, its current expression of interest in the health of unborn black children must be viewed with suspicion. The most telling evidence of the state's disregard of black children is the high rate of infant death in the black community. In 1987, the mortality rate for black infants in the United States was 17.9 deaths per thousand births—more than twice the figure of 8.6 for white infants. In New York City, while infant mortality rates in upper- and middle-income areas were generally less than 9 per thousand in 1986, the rates exceeded 19 in the poor black communities of the South Bronx and Bedford-Stuyvesant and reached 27.6 in Central Harlem.

The main reason for these high mortality rates is inadequate prenatal care. Most poor black women face financial and other barriers to receiving proper care during pregnancy. In 1986, only half of all pregnant black women in the United States received adequate prenatal care. It appears that in the eighties, black women's access to prenatal care has actually declined. The government has chosen to punish poor black women rather than to provide the means for them to have healthy children.

The cruelty of this punitive response is heightened by the lack of available drug treatment services for pregnant drug addicts. Protecting the welfare of drug addicts' children requires, among other things, adequate facilities for the mother's drug treatment. Yet a drug addict's pregnancy serves as an obstacle to obtaining this treatment. Treatment centers either refuse to treat pregnant women or are effectively closed to them, because the centers are ill-equipped to meet the needs of pregnant addicts. Most hospitals and programs that treat addiction exclude pregnant women because their babies are more likely to be born with health problems requiring expensive care. Program directors also feel that treating pregnant addicts is worth neither the increased cost nor the risk of tort liability.

Moreover, there are several barriers to pregnant women who seek to use centers that will accept them. Drug treatment programs are generally based on male-oriented models that are not geared to the needs of women. The lack of accommodations for children is perhaps the most significant obstacle to treatment. Most outpatient clinics do not provide child care, and many residential treatment programs do not admit children. Furthermore, treatment programs have traditionally failed to provide the comprehensive services that women need, including prenatal and gynecological care, contraceptive counseling, appropriate job training, and counseling for sexual and physical abuse. Predominantly male staffs and clients are often hostile to female clients and employ a confrontational style of therapy that makes many women uncomfortable. Moreover, long waiting lists make treatment useless for women who need help during the limited duration of their pregnancies.

Finally, and perhaps most important, ample evidence reveals that prosecuting addicted mothers may not achieve the government's asserted goal of healthier pregnancies; indeed, such prosecutions will probably lead to the opposite result. Pregnant addicts who seek help from public hospitals and clinics are the ones most often reported to government authorities. The threat of prosecution based on this reporting forces women to remain anonymous and thus has the reverse effect of deterring pregnant drug addicts from seeking treatment. For this reason, the government's decision to punish drug-addicted mothers is irreconcilable with the goal of helping them.

Pregnancy may be a time when women are most motivated to seek treatment for drug addiction and to make positive lifestyle changes. The government should capitalize on this opportunity by encouraging drug-addicted women to seek help and by providing them with comprehensive treatment. Punishing pregnant women who use drugs only exacerbates the causes of addiction—poverty, lack of self-esteem, and hopelessness. Perversely, this makes it more likely that poor black women's children—the asserted beneficiaries of the prosecutions—will suffer from the same hardships. . . .

D. Unconstitutional Government Standards for Procreation: The Intersection of Privacy and Equality

The equal protection clause and the right of privacy provide the basis for two separate constitutional challenges to the prosecution of drug-addicted mothers. The singling out of black mothers for punishment combines in a single government action several wrongs prohibited by both constitutional doctrines. Black mothers are denied autonomy over procreative decisions because of their race. The government's denial of black women's fundamental right to choose to bear children serves to perpetuate the legacy of racial discrimination embodied in the devaluation of black motherhood. The full scope of the government's violation can better be understood, then, by a constitutional theory that acknowledges the complementary and overlapping qualities of the Constitution's guarantees of equality and privacy. Viewing the prosecutions as imposing a racist government standard for procreation uses this approach.

Poor crack addicts are punished for having babies because they fail to measure up to the state's ideal of motherhood. Prosecutors have brought charges against women who use drugs during pregnancy without demonstrating any harm to the fetus. Moreover, a government policy that has the effect of punishing primarily poor black women for having babies evokes the specter of racial eugenics, especially in light of the history of sterilization abuse of women of color. These factors make clear that these women are not punished simply because they may harm their unborn children; rather, they are punished because the combination of their poverty, race, and drug addiction is seen as making them unworthy of procreating.

This aspect of the prosecutions implicates both equality and privacy interests. The right to bear children goes to the heart of what it means to be human. The value we place on individuals determines whether we see them as entitled to perpetuate themselves in their children. Denying a woman the right to bear children—or punishing her for exercising that right—deprives her of a basic part of her humanity. When this denial is based on race, it also functions to preserve a racial hierarchy that essentially disregards black humanity.

The abuse of sterilization laws designed to effect eugenic policy demonstrates the potential danger of governmental standards for procreation. During the first half of the twentieth century, the eugenics movement embraced the theory that intelligence and other personality traits are genetically determined and therefore inherited. This hereditarian belief, coupled with the reform approach of the Progressive Era, fueled a campaign to remedy America's social problems by stemming biological degeneracy. Eugenicists advocated compulsory sterilization to prevent reproduction by people who were likely to produce allegedly defective offspring. Eugenic sterilization was thought to improve society by eliminating its "socially inadequate" members. Around the turn of the century, many states enacted involuntary sterilization laws directed at those deemed burdens on society, including the mentally retarded, mentally ill, epileptics, and criminals.

In a 1927 decision, *Buck v. Bell*, the Supreme Court upheld the constitutionality of a Virginia involuntary sterilization law. The plaintiff, Carrie Buck, was described in the opinion as "a feeble minded white woman" committed to a state mental institution who was "the daughter of a feeble minded mother in the same institution, and the mother of an illegitimate feeble minded child." The court approved an order of the mental institution that Buck undergo sterilization. Justice Holmes, himself an ardent eugenicist, gave eugenic theory the imprimatur of constitutional law in his infamous declaration: "Three generations of imbeciles are enough."

The salient feature of the eugenic sterilization laws is their brutal imposition of society's restrictive norms of motherhood. Governmental control of reproduction in the name of science masks racist and classist judgments about who deserves to bear children. It is grounded on the premise that people who depart from social norms do not deserve to procreate. Carrie Buck, for example, was punished by sterilization not because of any mental disability, but because of her deviance from society's social and sexual norms.

Explanations of the eugenic rationale reveal this underlying moral standard for procreation. One eugenicist, for example, justified his extreme approach of putting the socially inadequate to death as " 'the surest; the simplest, the kindest, and most humane means for preventing reproduction among those *whom we deem unworthy of the high privilege.*' " Dr. Albert Priddy, the superintendent of the Virginia Colony, similarly explained the necessity of eugenic sterilization in one of his annual reports: the " 'sexual immorality,' of 'anti-social' 'morons' rendered them 'wholly unfit for exercising the *right of motherhood.*' "

Fourteen years after *Buck v. Bell*, the Supreme Court acknowledged the danger of the eugenic rationale. Justice William Douglas recognized both the fundamental quality of the right to procreate and its connection to equality in a later sterilization decision, *Skinner v. Oklahoma*. *Skinner* considered the constitutionality of the Oklahoma Habitual Criminal Sterilization Act authorizing the sterilization of persons convicted two or more times for "felonies involving moral turpitude." An Oklahoma court had ordered Skinner to undergo a vasectomy after he was convicted once of stealing chickens and twice of robbery with firearms. The statute, the court found, treated unequally criminals who had committed intrinsically the same quality of offense. For example, men who had committed grand larceny three times were sterilized, but embezzlers were not. The court struck down the statute as a violation of the equal protection clause. Declaring the right to bear children to be "one of the basic civil rights of man," the court applied strict scrutiny to the classification and held that the government failed to demonstrate that the statute's classifications were justified by eugenics or the inheritability of criminal traits.

Skinner rested on grounds that linked equal protection doctrine and the right to procreate. Justice Douglas framed the legal question as "a sensitive and important area of human rights." The reason for the court's elevation of the right to procreate was the court's recognition of the significant risk of discriminatory selection inherent in state intervention in reproduction. The court also understood the genocidal implications of a government standard for

procreation: "In evil or reckless hands [the government's power to sterilize] can cause races or types which are inimical to the dominant group to wither and disappear." The critical role of procreation to human survival and the invidious potential for government discrimination against disfavored groups makes heightened protection crucial. The court understood the use of the power to sterilize in the government's discrimination against certain types of criminals to be as invidious "as if it had selected a particular race or nationality for oppressive treatment."

Although the reasons advanced for the sterilization of chicken thieves and the prosecution of drug-addicted mothers are different, both practices are dangerous for similar reasons. Both effectuate ethnocentric judgments by the government that certain members of society do not deserve to have children. As the court recognized in *Skinner*, the enforcement of a government standard for childbearing denies the disfavored group a critical aspect of human dignity.

The history of compulsory sterilization demonstrates that society deems women who deviate from its norms of motherhood—in 1941, teenaged delinquent girls like Carrie Buck who bore illegitimate children; today, poor black crack addicts who use drugs during pregnancy—"unworthy of the high privilege" of procreation. The government therefore refuses to affirm their human dignity by helping them to overcome obstacles to good mothering. Rather, it punishes them by sterilization or criminal prosecution and thereby denies them a basic part of their humanity. When this denial is based on race, the violation is especially serious. Governmental policies that perpetuate racial subordination through the denial of procreative rights, which threaten at once racial equality and privacy, should be subject to the highest scrutiny. . . .

VIII. CONCLUSION

Our understanding of the prosecutions of drug-addicted mothers must include the perspective of the women whom they most directly affect. The prosecutions arise in a particular historical and political context that has constrained reproductive choice for poor women of color. The state's decision to punish drug-addicted mothers rather than to help them stems from the poverty and race of the defendants and from society's denial of their full dignity as human beings. Viewing the issue from their vantage point reveals that the prosecutions punish for having babies women whose motherhood has historically been devalued.

A policy that attempts to protect fetuses by denying the humanity of their mothers will inevitably fail. We must question such a policy's true concern for the dignity of the fetus, just as we question the motives of the slave owner who protected the unborn slave child while whipping his pregnant mother. Although the master attempted to separate the mother and fetus for his commercial ends, their fates were inextricably intertwined. The tragedy of crack babies is initially a tragedy of crack-addicted mothers: both are part of a larger tragedy of a community that is suffering a host of indignities, including, significantly, the denial of equal respect for its women's reproductive decisions.

It is only by affirming the personhood and equality of poor women of color that the survival of their future generations will be ensured. The first principle of the government's response to the crisis of drug-exposed babies should be the recognition of their mothers' worth and entitlement to autonomy over their reproductive lives. A commitment to guaranteeing these fundamental rights of poor women of color, rather than punishing them, is the true solution to the problem of unhealthy babies.

Study Questions

1. Roberts suggests that the prosecution of drug-addicted mothers "involves two fundamental tensions" (section I, paragraph 3). What are these two tensions?

2. In Roberts's view, the ongoing debate over state intervention has "overlooked a critical aspect of government prosecution of drug-addicted mothers" (section I, paragraph 4). What is this critical aspect, and what method does she recommend as a way to illuminate it?

3. Why, according to Roberts, do poor black women "bear the brunt of prosecutors' punitive approach" to fetal exposure to drugs (section II b, paragraph 1)?

4. Describe one of the "myths" of black motherhood and explain how, according to Roberts, it has reinforced the devaluation of Black mothers.

5. Roberts maintains that poor crack addicts are not punished simply because of the harm they may cause the fetus, but "because the combination of their poverty, race, and drug addiction is seen as making them unworthy of procreating" (section VII d, paragraph 2). What is her argument for this? Supposing it is true, what are the implications?

6. Does it make sense to characterize Roberts as drawing on a politics of identity in this excerpt?

7. Does the fact that Roberts is not a member of the group about which she is writing raise problems for her work?

Section IV
FEMINIST ALLIES?

INTRODUCTION

It is relatively uncontroversial to describe the material included in this text up to this point as "feminist." A great deal of recent scholarship exists, however, in which gender and sex figure prominently, but to which the label "feminist" is not so straightforwardly applied. The following section briefly introduces three contemporary liberatory projects that have produced such scholarship—i.e., postcolonial theory, neo-materialist theory, and queer theory—and raises questions about the projects' relationships to feminism. These are chosen as prominent examples of politically engaged research that takes up gender issues. Many others could have been equally good choices.

The question arises: what is the relationship between such gender-sensitive research and feminist theory? Considering, more specifically, postcolonial theory, neo-materialist theory, and queer theory, does feminist theory complement these projects, compete with them, even conflict with them? Plausibly the projects center on the emancipation of a group, or the elimination of a form of subordination, different from that centered by feminism; nevertheless can each benefit from the insights of the other? Or are the projects, on the contrary, inconsistent with feminism because they are insufficiently attentive to, for example, women or sexism? A third possibility is that postcolonial theory, neo-materialist theory, and/or queer theory are successor projects to feminism, effectively absorbing feminism into a more inclusive, overarching liberatory agenda. Or perhaps it is feminism that provides the more inclusive rubric, thus positioning one or more of these projects as aspects of feminism. And there are, of course, other possible relationships.

Obviously one's assessment of the relationship between feminism and these projects will hinge on one's understanding of feminism, as well as on one's understanding of the three projects under discussion. The readings included up to this point are designed to help readers clarify their thoughts about the scope and nature of feminism. Needless to say, the small selection of entries that follows cannot provide a comparable overview of the three projects represented. The entries do, however, introduce the three projects themselves, as well as suggest some of the alliances and turf struggles between them and feminism.

The section begins with Nancy Fraser's article, "Multiculturalism, Antiessentialism, and Radical Democracy," which situates feminism within a broader quest for radical democracy. In Fraser's view, feminist debates over equality, difference, identity, and fragmentation have left us with a false dichotomy between a politics of recognition and a politics of redistribution. Fraser proposes that to address the issues raised by "multiple intersecting differences," we must "theorize our relation to the other political struggles surrounding us" and forge "democratic mediations." The piece thus motivates an inquiry into libratory projects other than feminism.

Two articles on *postcolonial theory* follow. Leela Gandhi argues that, while much works against what she regards as "the potential unity between postcolonialism and feminism," much is to be gained from their alliance. In particular, she calls for an "offensive against the aggressive myth of both imperial and nationalist masculinity." Ann Stoler's "Carnal Knowledge and Imperial Power" can be read as an example of the kind of work for which Gandhi is calling; Stoler analyzes how sexual control was "foundational" to the colonization of Asia.

The section following offers two essays that consider the relationship between feminism and *neo-materialist theory*. We begin with a now-classic essay by Iris Young, "Socialist Feminism and the Limits of Dual Systems Theory." Young argues that we cannot adequately understand women's subordination by regarding patriarchy and capitalism as two relatively autonomous systems impacting women's lives. Instead, she calls for a unified feminist historical materialism that is sensitive to the interaction between the cultural and the material sources of injustice. Gwyn Kirk's essay takes up this challenge by arguing for "an ecological feminism that focuses on the social and material reasons for women's environmental concerns, has an integrated view of spiritual politics, and can integrate class, race, and gender in theory and practice."

Last but far from least are the articles about *queer theory*. Leslie Feinberg's "Walking Our Talk" addresses the appropriate scope of trans liberation, arguing that nothing less than a fully inclusive agenda will do. In "Thinking Sex," an article often cited as germinal to lesbian and gay studies, Gayle Rubin identifies feminism as an inadequate venue for a radical theory of sexuality. Judith Butler takes issue with Rubin's claim, as well as with other theorists' claims about the relationship between lesbian and gay studies and feminism, in the excerpt from "Against Proper Objects" included here. Finally, in "Black (W)holes and the Geometry of Black Female Sexuality," Evelynn Hammonds ponders whether queer theory may—at long last—provide a venue in which black feminist critics can "make visible black women's self-defined sexualities."

Nancy Fraser

Multiculturalism, Antiessentialism, and Radical Democracy

A Genealogy of the Current Impasse in Feminist Theory

"Democracy" is today an intensely contested word that means different things to different people, even as everyone claims to be for it. Should we take it to mean free-market capitalism plus multiparty elections, as many former Cold Warriors now insist? Or should we understand democracy in the stronger sense of self-rule? And if so, does that mean that every distinct nationality should have its own sovereign state in an "ethnically cleansed" territory? Or does it rather mean a process of communication across differences, where citizens participate together in discussion and decision making to determine collectively the conditions of their lives? And in that case, finally, what is required to ensure that *all* can participate *as peers*? Does democracy require social equality? The recognition of difference? The absence of systemic dominance and subordination?[1]

"Radical democracy" must be distinguished from rival conceptions of democracy by a distinctive set of answers to these questions. What, then, might its distinctive answers be? I assume that to be a radical democrat today is to appreciate—and to seek to eliminate—two different kinds of impediments to democratic participation. One such impediment is social inequality; the other is the misrecognition of difference. Radical democracy, on this interpretation, is the view that democracy today requires both economic redistribution and multicultural recognition.

This, however, is only the outline of an answer. To try to flesh it out is to become immediately embroiled in difficult questions about the relation between equality and difference. These questions are variously debated today with respect to gender, sexuality, nationality, ethnicity, and "race." What are the differences that make a difference for democracy? Which differences merit public recognition and/or political representation? Which differences, in contrast, should be considered irrelevant to political life and treated instead as private matters? Which kinds of differences, finally, should a democratic society seek to promote? And which, on the contrary, should it aim to abolish?

Radical democrats, like everyone else, cannot avoid confronting these questions. But to answer them is no simple matter. Current U.S. discussions are at an impasse, I think, impeded by some unfortunate tendencies. One is the tendency to focus one-sidedly on cultural politics to the neglect of political economy. This is the thrust of current arguments over identity politics, which rage across the whole spectrum of "new social movements." These arguments pit antiessentialists, committed to deconstructing group identities, against multiculturalists, eager to recognize and revalue group differences. The issue at bottom is the politics of recognition: *Which* politics of recognition best serves the victims of misrecognition? Revaluation of difference or deconstruction of identity?

The argument in this form is unresolvable. It remains on the terrain of identity politics, where the misrecognition of difference is constructed as a "cultural" problem and dissociated from political economy. In fact, injustices of recognition are thoroughly imbricated with injustices of distribution. They cannot be adequately addressed in isolation from the latter. Radical democrats will never succeed in untying the gordian knots of identity and difference until we leave the terrain of identity politics. This means resituating cultural politics in relation to social politics and linking demands for recognition with demands for redistribution.

This, at any rate, is the thesis I shall argue in this chapter. I shall approach it somewhat indirectly, however. I shall reconstruct the history of recent U.S. feminist debates about difference in order to show how and where our present difficulties arise. Where possible, I shall also suggest ways of getting around them.

This approach requires a clarification. Despite the explicit focus on feminist debates, my interest here is not confined to feminism per se. Rather, I aim to use a reconstruction of feminist debates to illustrate a more general trajectory. Analogous lines of argument could be developed from other starting points, such as the debates concerning "race." They, too, I believe, would reveal a progressive tendency to divorce the cultural politics of recognition from the social politics of redistribution—to the detriment of efforts to develop a credible vision of radical democracy.

"GENDER DIFFERENCE": EQUALITY OR DIFFERENCE?

Academic feminist theory in the United States is at an impasse today, perfectly mirroring the larger radical-democratic impasse. We are currently spinning our wheels arguing over identity politics, having succumbed to two unfortunate temptations. One is the tendency to adopt an undiscriminating form of antiessentialism, which treats all identities and differences as repressive fictions. The other is the mirror-opposite tendency to adopt an undiscriminating version of multiculturalism, which celebrates all identities and differences as worthy of recognition. In fact, both of these tendencies share a common root: they fail to connect the cultural politics of identity and difference to the social politics of justice and equality. Dissociating the politics of recognition from the politics of redistribution, both tendencies impede feminist efforts to develop a credible vision of radical democracy.

To see this, we need only reconstruct the history of debates about difference in second-wave U.S. feminism. These debates divide roughly into three phases. In the first phase, which lasted from the late 1960s through about the mid-1980s, the main focus was "gender difference." In the second phase, which ran roughly from the mid-1980s to the early 1990s, the main focus shifted to "differences among women." A third phase, which is currently under way, is focused on "multiple intersecting differences." Of course, to plot the trajectory of debate in this way is necessarily to simplify and abstract. But it also makes possible the sort of bird's-eye view that can reveal an otherwise hidden inner logic.

In the first phase, the principal antagonists were "equality feminists" and "difference feminists." And the main questions that divided them were, first, the nature and causes of gender injustice, and second, its appropriate remedy, hence, the meaning of gender equity. Let me describe the two sides schematically, ignoring many nuances and subtleties.

Equality feminists saw gender difference as an instrument and artifact of male dominance. What passes for such difference in a sexist society, they claimed, are either misogynist lies told to rationalize women's subordination (for example, we are said to be irrational and sentimental, *therefore* unfit for intellectual work but well suited to domesticity) or the socially constructed results of inequality (we have

actually *become* anxious about math or fearful of success *because* we have been differently treated). In either case, to stress gender difference is to harm women. It is to reinforce our confinement to an inferior domestic role, hence to marginalize or exclude us from all those activities that promote true human self-realization, such as politics, employment, art, the life of the mind, and the exercise of legitimate authority. It is also to deprive us of our fair share of essential social goods, such as income, jobs, property, health, education, autonomy, respect, sexual pleasure, bodily integrity, and physical safety.

From the equality perspective, then, gender difference appeared to be inextricable from sexism. The political task was thus clear: the goal of feminism was to throw off the shackles of "difference" and establish equality, bringing women and men under a common measure. To be sure, liberal feminists, radical feminists, and socialist feminists might dispute how best to achieve this goal, but they nevertheless shared a common vision of gender equity, which involved minimizing gender difference.

This equality perspective dominated the U.S. women's movement for nearly a decade from the late 1960s. In the late 1970s, however, it was sharply challenged by the rise of a new, "difference" feminism, which has also been called "cultural feminism." Difference feminists rejected the equality view as androcentric and assimilationist. From their perspective, getting women included in traditionally male pursuits was an insufficiently radical goal because it uncritically adopted the biased masculinist view that only men's activities were truly human, thereby depreciating women's. Far from challenging sexism, then, equality feminism actually reproduced it—by devaluing femininity. What was needed instead was another sort of feminism, one that opposed the undervaluation of women's worth by recognizing gender difference and revaluing femininity.

Difference feminists accordingly proposed a new, positive, interpretation of gender difference. Women really did differ from men, they claimed, but such difference did not mean inferiority. Some insisted, on the contrary, that nurturing, peace-loving women were morally superior to competitive, militaristic men. Others preferred to drop all talk of inferiority and superiority, to recognize two different "voices" of equivalent value, and to demand a respectful hearing for woman's voice. In either case, they agreed that gender difference was real and deep, the most fundamental human difference. All women shared a common "gender identity" *as women*. All suffered a common harm when that identity was depreciated. All, therefore, were sisters under the skin. Feminists need only articulate the positive content of femininity in order to mobilize this latent solidarity. The way to do justice to women, in sum, was to *recognize*, not minimize, gender difference.

Here, then, were the stakes in the first difference debate within second-wave U.S. feminism. The movement stood poised between two conflicting views of gender difference, two alternative accounts of gender injustice, and two opposing visions of gender equity. The proponents of equality saw gender difference as the handmaiden of male domination. For them, the central injustices of sexism were women's marginalization and the maldistribution of social goods. And the key meaning of gender equity was equal participation and redistribution. Difference feminists, in contrast, saw gender difference as the cornerstone of women's identity. For them, accordingly, androcentrism was sexism's chief harm. And the centerpiece of gender equity was the recognition and revaluation of femininity.

This debate raged for several years on both the cultural and the political planes, but it was never definitively settled. Part of the difficulty was that each side had convincing criticisms of the other. The proponents of difference successfully showed that the egalitarians presupposed "the male as norm," a standard that disadvantaged women. The egalitarians argued just as cogently, however, that the difference side relied on stereotypical notions of femininity, which reinforced existing gender hierarchies. Neither side, therefore, had a fully defensible position. Yet each had an important insight. The egalitarian insight was that no adequate account of sexism could overlook women's social marginalization and unequal share of resources; hence, no persuasive vision of gender equity could omit the goals of equal participation and

fair distribution. The difference insight was that no adequate account of sexism could overlook the problem of androcentrism in the construction of cultural standards of value; hence, no persuasive vision of gender equity could omit the need to overcome such androcentrism.

What, then, was the moral to be drawn? Henceforth, feminists would have to find a way to accommodate both of these insights. We would need to develop a perspective that opposed social inequality and cultural androcentrism simultaneously. Such a perspective would effectively combine a politics of redistribution with a politics of recognition, but not as two separate matters. Rather, it would have to integrate social demands with cultural demands, seeking to change culture and political economy in tandem.

"DIFFERENCES AMONG WOMEN"

As it turned out, U.S. feminists did not resolve the equality/difference impasse by developing such a new perspective. Rather, by the mid-1980s, the entire framework of the debate had been altered so radically that the problem could no longer be posed in those terms. In the interim, leading feminist currents had come to reject the view that gender difference could be fruitfully discussed in isolation from other axes of difference, especially "race," ethnicity, sexuality, and class. And so the equality/difference debate was displaced. The focus on "gender difference" gave way to a focus on "differences among women," inaugurating a new phase of feminist debate.

This shift in focus was largely the work of lesbians and feminists of color. For many years they had protested forms of feminism that failed to illuminate their lives and address their problems. African-American women, for example, had invoked their history of slavery and resistance, waged work, and community activism to contest assumptions of universal female dependence on men and confinement to domesticity. Meanwhile, Latina, Jewish, Native-American, and Asian-American feminists had protested the implicit reference to white Anglo women in many mainstream feminist texts. Lesbians, finally, had unmasked assumptions of normative heterosexuality in the classic feminist accounts of mothering, sexuality, gender identity, and reproduction.

Mainstream U.S. feminism, all these voices insisted, was *not* a feminism for all women. It privileged the standpoint of the white Anglo heterosexual middle-class women who had so far dominated the movement. It falsely extrapolated from their experiences and conditions of life in ways that were inappropriate, even harmful, to other women. Thus, the very movement that claimed to liberate women ended up reproducing within its own ranks the racism and the heterosexism, the class hierarchies and the ethnic biases, that were endemic in U.S. society.

For many years, such voices had been largely confined to the margins of U.S. feminism. By the mid to late 1980s, however, they had moved, in the prophetic words of bell hooks, "from [the] margins to [the] center" of discussion.[2] Many erstwhile doubters were now willing to concede the point: the movement had been so exclusively preoccupied with gender difference that it had neglected the differences among women.

"Difference feminism" was the most obvious culprit. Its purportedly universal accounts of feminine gender identity and women's different voice could now be seen for what they actually were: culturally specific stereotypical idealizations of middle-class, heterosexual, white-European femininity, idealizations that had as much to do with hierarchies of class, "race," ethnicity, and sexuality as with hierarchies of gender. And yet, equality feminism was culpable, too. Assuming that all women were subordinated to all men in the same way and to the same degree, it had falsely universalized the specific situation of white, middle-class heterosexual women and concealed their implication in hierarchies of class, "race," ethnicity, and sexuality. Thus, neither side of the old equality/difference debate could withstand the critique. Although one side had stressed male/female similarity and the other side male/female difference, the end result was effectively the same: both had obscured important differences among women. In both cases, consequently, the attempt to build sisterhood backfired. False universalizations of *some* women's situation

and *some* women's identity ideals had not promoted feminist solidarity. They led, on the contrary, to anger and schism, to hurt and mistrust.

But the difficulty went deeper still. In repressing differences among women, the mainstream movement had also repressed axes of subordination other than gender—once again, class, "race," ethnicity, nationality, and sexuality.[3] It therefore repressed what Deborah King has called "multiple jeopardy," the multiple forms of subordination faced by lesbians, women of color, and/or poor and working-class women.[4] Consequently, the mainstream movement failed to grasp the multiple affiliations of such women, their loyalty to more than one social movement. For example, many women of color and/or lesbians remain committed to fighting *alongside* men of color and/or gays in antiracist and/or gay-liberation movements, while simultaneously fighting *against* the sexism of their male comrades. But a feminism focused only on gender difference failed fully to grasp this situation. By suppressing axes of subordination other than gender, it also suppressed differences *among men*. And that created a double bind for women who are subject to multiple jeopardy: it effectively pressured them to choose between loyalty to their gender and loyalty to their "race," class, and/or sexuality. The either/or imperative denied their reality of multiple jeopardy, multiple affiliation, and multiple identity.

The exclusive focus on "gender difference" proved increasingly counterproductive as "identity politics" proliferated in the 1980s. Now the political scene was crowded with "new social movements," each politicizing a different "difference." Gays and lesbians were mobilized around sexual difference in order to fight against heterosexism; movements of African Americans, Native Americans, and other peoples of color had politicized "racial" difference in order to contest racial subordination; and a wide range of ethnically and religiously identified groups were struggling for recognition of cultural differences within an increasingly multiethnic nation.[5] Thus, feminists found themselves sharing political space with all these movements, but not in the sense of a parallel, side-by-side coexistence. Rather, all the various movements cut across one another. And each was going through an analogous process of discovering the other differences within itself.

In this context, the need for a reorientation was clear. Only if feminists were willing to abandon an exclusive focus on gender difference could we cease interpreting other difference claims as threats to the unity of women. Only if we were willing to grapple with axes of subordination other than gender could we theorize our relation to the other political struggles surrounding us. Only by abandoning the view of ourselves as a self-contained social movement, finally, could we fully grasp the true situation: that gender struggles were occurring on the broader terrain of civil society, where multiple axes of difference were being contested simultaneously and where multiple social movements were intersecting.

"MULTIPLE INTERSECTING DIFFERENCES": ANTIESSENTIALISM OR MULTICULTURALISM?

By around 1990, therefore, the decisive U.S. feminist debate was poised to shift from "differences among women" to "multiple intersecting differences." The result should have been an enormous gain. What had appeared at first to be a turning inward (instead of focusing on our relation to men, we would focus on the relations among ourselves) seemed instead to invite a turning outward (instead of focusing on gender alone, we would focus on its relation to other crosscutting axes of difference and subordination). In this way, the whole range of politicized differences would become grist for the feminist mill. Not only gender but also "race," ethnicity, nationality, sexuality, and class would now require feminist theorization.[6] And all struggles against subordination would now need somehow to be linked up with feminism.

To make such a shift should not in principle have required scuttling the project of combining a politics of redistribution with a politics of recognition. Indeed, the discussions of "differences among women" never explicitly challenged that project. Nor did anything in the logic of attending to such differences entail the need to abandon efforts to integrate a cultural politics

of identity and difference with a social politics of justice and equality. But to make such a shift did complicate that project. Henceforth, it would be necessary to resituate the task of integrating redistribution and recognition in a new, more complex political field. Cultural demands would have to interimbricate with social demands across the entire spectrum of crosscutting axes of domination.

Once again, however, U.S. feminists have not (yet) developed such an approach. On the contrary, as we enter the third and current phase of debate about difference, the politics of recognition is becoming increasingly dissociated from the politics of redistribution, and the former is increasingly eclipsing the latter. The result is a truncated problematic, which is impeding efforts to develop a credible vision of radical democracy.

In the current phase, the feminist discussion joins the more general discussion of radical democracy. Today, "radical democracy" is being proposed as a rubric for mediating various struggles over "multiple intersecting differences," hence for linking various social movements.[7] As such, it appeals on at least two planes. On the one hand, it seems to correct the balkanizing tendencies of identity politics and to promote broader political alliances. On the other hand, and at the same time, it seems to offer a "postsocialist" vision of the good society and to contest hegemonic conservative understandings of democracy. It is no wonder, then, that feminists seeking to develop a viable theoretical and political outlook oriented to "multiple intersecting differences" are increasingly turning to radical democracy.[8]

Yet the meaning of "radical democracy" remains underdeveloped. Functioning chiefly as a counterweight to identity politics, it remains largely confined to the cultural-political plane. Thus, current discussion tends to bracket political economy. It is so far unclear, therefore, how precisely the project of a radical democracy can connect a cultural politics of recognition to a social politics of redistribution. Unless it manages to connect them, however, "radical democracy" will not be genuinely democratic. It will not succeed in forging democratic mediations among "multiple intersecting differences."

The difficulties become clear when we examine the current debates that form the context for discussions of radical democracy. These debates focus chiefly on group identity and cultural difference, and they divide into two related streams. One of the streams can be designated "antiessentialism"; it cultivates a skeptical attitude toward identity and difference, which it reconceptualizes as discursive constructions. A second stream can be designated "multiculturalism"; it cultivates a positive view of group differences and group identities, which it seeks to revalue and promote. Although both streams of discussion are in some respects insightful, neither is entirely satisfactory. Meanwhile, the conjoining of the two in current debates about radical democracy results in a one-sided, truncated, "culturalist" problematic.

One problem is that both discussions rely on one-sided views of identity and difference. The antiessentialist view is skeptical and negative; it sees all identities as inherently repressive and all differences as inherently exclusionary. The multiculturalist view, in contrast, is celebratory and positive; it sees all identities as deserving of recognition and all differences as meriting affirmation. Thus, neither approach is sufficiently differentiated. Neither provides a basis for distinguishing democratic from antidemocratic identity claims, just from unjust differences. Neither, as a result, can sustain a viable politics or a credible vision of radical democracy.

A second problem, which undergirds the first, is that both current approaches have lost the dual focus on redistribution and recognition. Both antiessentialism and multiculturalism are concerned virtually exclusively with injustices of cultural misrecognition. Both neglect injustices of political-economic maldistribution. Neither, therefore, provides an adequate political framework.

Let me briefly sketch the main contours of each approach, focusing on its understanding of difference. I shall try to show that the weaknesses in both cases can be traced to a common source, namely, a failure to appreciate that cultural differences can be freely elaborated and democratically mediated only on the basis of social equality.

I begin with antiessentialism—as it is debated within feminist circles. Proponents of antiessentialism propose to avoid the errors of difference feminism by radically reconceiving identity and difference. They begin from the assumption that the differences among women go "all the way down"; hence, there is no way of being a woman that is not already "raced," sexed, and classed; therefore, gender has no invariant essence or core. Yet they also reject approaches that would divide women (and men) into ever smaller subgroups, each with its own distinct identity and its own claim for recognition.[9] In contrast to such approaches, antiessentialists appreciate that neither differences nor identities are simply given as a matter of fact in virtue of a group's "objective" character or social position. Rather, they are discursively constructed. Differences and identities are performatively created through cultural processes of being claimed and elaborated; they do not preexist such processes. They could always in principle be otherwise. Thus, existing differences and identities can be performatively undone or altered by being dis-claimed or differently elaborated.[10]

What follows politically from this view? Clearly, antiessentialism rejects any politics—feminist or otherwise—that essentializes identity and difference. But some of its exponents go further still. Stressing that all collective identities are "fictional" because constructed, they regard all with a skeptical eye. From this perspective, politicized identity terms such as *women* must always necessarily be exclusionary; they can be constructed only through the repression of difference. Any collective identification, therefore, will be subject to critique from the standpoint of what it excludes. Feminist identity is no exception. Thus, the black-feminist critique of white bias in feminism is not only a protest against racism; it also protests a logical necessity. Any attempt to claim a black feminist identity, therefore, could only repeat the exclusionary gesture.

I shall henceforth call this "the deconstructive version of antiessentialism." In this version, the only "innocent" political practice is negative and deconstructive. It involves unmasking the repressive and exclusionary operation that enables every construction of identity. Thus, it is not the job of feminism, in this view, to construct a feminine identity or a collective feminist subject; it is, rather, our task to deconstruct every construction of "women." Rather than take for granted the existence of gender difference and hence of "women," we should expose the processes by which gender binarism and, therefore, "women" are constructed. The political aim of feminism, then, is to destabilize gender difference and the gender identities that accompany it. A privileged strategy is dissidence and parody.[11] But beyond this, we should ally with other social movements with analogous deconstructive aims, for example, with critical "race" theorists committed to deconstructing black/white difference and with queer theorists working to deconstruct the homo/hetero difference but not, in contrast, with Afrocentrists seeking to consolidate black identity, nor with proponents of gay and lesbian identity.

What should we make of this discussion? In my view the outcome is mixed. On the one hand, antiessentialism makes a major advance by conceptualizing identities and differences as discursively constructed instead of as objectively given. But the politics of the deconstructive version are simplistic. By this, I do not mean only the obvious difficulty that sexism cannot be dismantled by an exclusively negative, deconstructive practice. I mean also the further difficulties that arise when deconstructive antiessentialists try the theoretical equivalent of pulling a rabbit out of a hat, when they try, that is, to deduce a normative politics of culture from an ontological conception of identity and difference. And I mean, finally, limitations linked to the failure to pursue the question of how to integrate an antiessentialist politics of recognition with an egalitarian politics of redistribution.

The difficulty can be put like this: Deconstructive antiessentialists appraise identity claims on ontological grounds alone. They do not ask, in contrast, how a given identity or difference is related to social structures of domination and to social relations of inequality. Nor do they ask what sort of political economy would be required to sustain nonexclusionary identi-

ties and antiessentialist understandings of difference. They risk succumbing, as a result, to a night in which all cows are gray: all identities threaten to become equally fictional, equally repressive, and equally exclusionary. But this is tantamount to surrendering any possibility of distinguishing emancipatory and oppressive identity claims, benign and pernicious differences. Thus, deconstructive antiessentialists evade the crucial political questions of the day: Which identity claims are rooted in the defense of social relations of inequality and domination? And which are rooted in a challenge to such relations? Which identity claims carry the potential to expand actually existing democracy? And which, in contrast, work against democratization? Which differences, finally, should a democratic society seek to foster, and which, on the contrary, should it aim to abolish?

Yet antiessentialism has no monopoly on these problems. They are shared, I contend, by the other major stream of U.S. discussion, the stream focused on "multiculturalism." Multiculturalism has become the rallying cry for a potential alliance of new social movements, all of whom seem to be struggling for the recognition of difference. This alliance potentially unites feminists, gays and lesbians, members of racialized groups and of disadvantaged ethnic groups in opposition to a common enemy: namely, a culturally imperialist form of public life that treats the straight, white-Anglo, middle-class male as the human norm, in relation to which everyone else appears deviant. The goal of the struggle is to create multicultural public forms, which recognize a plurality of different, equally valuable ways of being human. In such a society, today's dominant understanding of difference as deviance would give way to a positive appreciation of human diversity. All citizens would enjoy the same formal legal rights in virtue of their common humanity. But they would also be recognized for what differentiates them from one another, their cultural particularity.

This, at least, is the most common U.S. understanding of multiculturalism. It has dominated intense debates over education in the mainstream public sphere. Conservatives have attacked proponents of

Women's Studies, African-American Studies, Gay-and-Lesbian Studies, and Ethnic Studies, charging that we have inappropriately politicized the curriculum by replacing Great Works selected for their enduring universal value with inferior texts chosen on ideological, affirmative-action grounds. Thus, the argument turns on the interpretation of "difference." Whereas defenders of traditional education persist in viewing difference negatively, as deviance from a single universal norm, multiculturalists view difference positively, as cultural variation and diversity, and demand its representation in educational curricula, as well as elsewhere in public life.

Feminists and radical democrats are understandably committed to defending some version of multiculturalism against the conservative attacks. But we should nevertheless reject the version I have just sketched, which I will henceforth call "the pluralist version."[12] The pluralist version of multiculturalism is premised on a one-sided understanding of difference: difference is viewed as intrinsically positive and inherently cultural. This perspective accordingly celebrates difference uncritically while failing to interrogate its relation to inequality. Like the American pluralist tradition from which it descends, it proceeds—contrary to fact—as if U.S. society contained no class divisions or other deep-seated structural injustices, as if its political economy were basically just, as if its various constituent groups were socially equal. Thus, it treats difference as pertaining exclusively to culture.[13] The result is to divorce questions of difference from material inequality, power differentials among groups, and systemic relations of dominance and subordination.

All this should ring warning bells for feminists who would be radical democrats. We should recognize this view as a cousin of the old "difference feminism." The latter's core elements are recycled here in a more general form and extended to differences other than gender. Where difference feminism made cultural androcentrism the central injustice and revaluation of femininity the chief remedy, pluralist multiculturalism substitutes the more general injustice of cultural imperialism and the more general remedy of revaluing all disrespected identities. But the structure of the thinking is the same. And so are the structural weaknesses.

Like difference feminism, pluralist multiculturalism tends to substantialize identities, treating them as given positivities instead of as constructed relations. It tends, consequently, to balkanize culture, setting groups apart from one another, ignoring the ways they cut across one another, and inhibiting cross-group interaction and identification. Losing sight of the fact that differences intersect, it regresses to a simple additive model of difference.

Like difference feminism, moreover, pluralist multiculturalism valorizes existing group identities. It assumes that such identities are fine as they are, only some need additional respect. But some existing group identities may be importantly tied to existing social relations of domination, and they might not survive the transformation of those relations. Moreover, some group identities—or strands thereof—are incompatible with others. For example, one cannot consistently affirm a white-supremacist identity and an antiracist identity simultaneously; affirming some identities—or some strands of some identities—requires transforming others. Thus, there is no avoiding political judgments about better and worse identities and differences. These, however, pluralist multiculturalism cannot make.

Pluralist multiculturalism, finally, is the mirror image of deconstructive antiessentialism. Whereas that approach threatened to delegitimate all identities and differences, this one seems to celebrate them all indiscriminately. Thus, its politics are equally one-sided. It, too, maintains an exclusive and one-sided focus on the cultural politics of recognition, while neglecting the social politics of redistribution. Consequently, it too evades the crucial political questions of the day: Which identity claims are rooted in the defense of social relations of inequality and domination? And which are rooted in a challenge to such relations? Which identity claims carry the potential to expand actually existing democracy? And which, in contrast, work against democratization? Which differences, finally, should a democratic society seek to foster, and which, on the contrary, should it aim to abolish?

CONCLUDING THESES: TOWARD A CREDIBLE VISION OF RADICAL DEMOCRACY

It is no accident that both deconstructive antiessentialism and pluralist multiculturalism fail in the same way, for the weaknesses of both share a common root: both fail to connect a cultural politics of identity and difference to a social politics of justice and equality. Both fail, that is, to link struggles for recognition to struggles for redistribution. Neither appreciates the crux of the connection: *cultural differences can be freely elaborated and democratically mediated only on the basis of social equality.*

In this sense, both approaches are victims of an unmastered history. With the wisdom of hindsight, we can now see that both are haunted by echoes of the old equality/difference debate. The failure to resolve that debate left both current discussions with a truncated problematic. Both antiessentialism and multiculturalism have sought to correct the deficiencies of difference feminism, but they remain on the latter's own terms. Both approaches restrict themselves to the plane of culture, which they treat in abstraction from social relations and social structures, including political economy. And so both try to elaborate a cultural politics of difference in abstraction from a social politics of equality. Put differently, both approaches repress the insights of equality feminism concerning the need for equal participation and fair distribution. As a result, both are left without the resources needed to make crucial political distinctions. Thus, neither can sustain a viable politics in a period of multiple, intersecting difference claims. And neither can model a credible vision of radical democracy.

What, finally, can we learn from this story? How can we use its lessons to develop a credible vision of radical democracy? And where should we go from here?

Let me conclude by proposing three theses.

First, there is no going back to the old equality/difference debate in the sense of an exclusive focus

on any single axis of difference. The shift from "gender difference" to "differences among women" to "multiple intersecting differences" remains an unsurpassable gain, but this does not mean that we should simply forget the old debate. Rather, we now need to construct a new equality/difference debate, one oriented to multiple intersecting differences. We need, in other words, to reconnect the problematic of cultural difference with the problematic of social equality.

Second, there is no going back to essentialized understandings of identity and difference. The antiessentialist view of identities and differences as relationally constructed represents an unsurpassable gain, but this does not mean that we should pursue an exclusively deconstructive politics. Rather, we should develop an alternative version of antiessentialism, one that permits us to link an antiessentialist cultural politics of recognition with an egalitarian social politics of redistribution.

Third, there is no going back to the monocultural view that there is only one valuable way of being human. The multicultural view of a multiplicity of cultural forms represents an unsurpassable gain, but this does not mean that we should subscribe to the pluralist version of multiculturalism. Rather, we should develop an alternative version that permits us to make normative judgments about the value of different differences by interrogating their relation to inequality.

In sum, we must find a way to combine the struggle for an antiessentialist multiculturalism with the struggle for social equality. Only then will we be able to develop a credible model of radical democracy and a politics that is adequate to our time. A promising rallying cry for this project is "No recognition without redistribution."[14]

NOTES

1. Research for this essay was supported by the Institut für die Wissenschaften vom Menschen, Vienna, and the Dean of the Graduate Faculty of the New School for Social Research. I am grateful for helpful comments from Cornelia Klinger and Eli Zaretsky.

2. bell hooks, *Feminist Theory: From Margin to Center* (Boston: South End Press, 1984).

3. An important exception was the socialist-feminist current of the late 1960s and the 1970s. Socialist-feminists had always insisted on relating gender divisions to class divisions and, to a lesser degree, to racial divisions, but with the decline of the New Left, their influence waned.

4. Deborah King, "Multiple Jeopardy, Multiple Consciousness," *Signs* 14, no. 1 (autumn 1988): 42–72.

5. The relative absence of nationalist struggles—the exceptions being some Native-American and Puerto-Rican currents—distinguishes U.S. identity politics from that in many other areas of the world.

6. The reverse is also true: gender must now be theorized from the perspective of these other differences.

7. See, for example, Ernesto Laclau and Chantal Mouffe, *Hegemony and Socialist Strategy* (London: Verso, 1985), and David Trend, ed., *Radical Democracy* (New York: Routledge, 1995).

8. See, for example, Judith Butler, *Bodies That Matter* (New York: Routledge, 1993), and the various contributors to Trend, *Radical Democracy*.

9. This seems to be the logic of many multicultural approaches to difference. It mars the otherwise very thoughtful discussion in Elizabeth V. Spelman, *Inessential Woman: Problems of Exclusion in Feminist Thought* (Boston: Beacon Press, 1988).

10. For an argument to this effect, see Judith Butler, *Gender Trouble: Feminism and the Subversion of Identity* (New York: Routledge, Chapman & Hall, 1990), which elaborates a performative theory of gender.

11. Ibid.

12. Not all versions of multiculturalism are "pluralist" in the sense I describe here. The pluralist version is an ideal typical reconstruction of what I take to be the majority understanding of multiculturalism. It is also mainstream in the sense of being the version that is usually debated in mainstream public spheres. Other versions are discussed in Linda Nicholson, "To Be or Not to Be: Charles Taylor on The Politics of Recognition," *Constellations* 3, no. 1 (1996): 1–16, and in Michael Warner et al., "Critical Multiculturalism," *Critical Inquiry* 18, no. 3 (spring 1992): 530–56.

13. In so doing, pluralist multiculturalism construes difference on the standard U.S. model of ethnicity, in which an immigrant group preserves some identification with its "old country" cultural heritage, while integrating into U.S. society; since the ethnic group is thought not to occupy any distinctive structural position in the political economy, its difference is wholly cultural. Pluralist multiculturalism generalizes this ethnicity model to gender, sexuality, and "race," which the model does not in fact fit. For a critique of the ethnicity model, see Nicholson, "To Be or Not to Be."

14. For a first attempt to work out some of the implications of this project, see Fraser, "From Redistribution to Recognition?" Chapter 1 in Fraser, *Justice Interruptus: Critical Reflections on the "Postsocialist" Condition* (Routledge, 1997).

Study Questions

1. What does Fraser mean (in outline) by "radical democracy"? What does she mean by "identity politics"?

2. Fraser maintains that in order to achieve social justice, we must understand the connection between "the cultural politics of identity and difference" and "the social politics of justice and equality." Explain how, according to Fraser, "second-wave U.S. feminism" (from the 1960s through the mid-1980s) failed to establish the needed connection. What steps did U.S. academic feminism of the 1980s and 1990s take toward bridging the two sets of issues?

3. Explain Fraser's critique of "the deconstructive version of antiessentialism."

4. Explain Fraser's critique of "the pluralist version of multiculturalism."

5. Explain the connection Fraser wants to make between issues of cultural difference and issues of social justice. What are the advantages of her view over deconstructive antiessentialism and pluralist multiculturalism?

POSTCOLONIAL THEORY

Leela Gandhi
Postcolonialism and Feminism

In *Culture and Imperialism*, Said concedes that *Orientalism* fails to theorise adequately the resistance of the non-European world to the material and discursive onslaught of colonialism. This recent book announces its departure from Said's earlier and disablingly one-sided account of the colonial encounter: "Never was it the case that the imperial encounter pitted an active Western intruder against a supine or inert non-Western native; there was *always* some form of active resistance and, in the overwhelming majority of cases, the resistance finally won out" (Said 1993, p. xii). However, despite this apparent recantation, Said stubbornly refuses to elevate anti-colonial *resistance* to the status of anti-colonial *critique*. The culture of resistance, he argues, finds its theoretical and political limit in the chauvinist and authoritarian boundaries of the postcolonial nation-State—itself a conformity-producing prison-house which reverses, and so merely replicates, the old colonial divisions of racial consciousness. Moreover, in its exclusively anti-Western focus, anti-colonial nationalism deflects attention away from internal orthodoxies and injustices —"the nation can become a panacea for *not* dealing with economic disparities, social injustice, and the capture of the newly independent state by a nationalist elite" (1993, p. 262). Thus, Said insists, a comprehensive dismantling of colonial hierarchies and structures needs to be matched by a reformed and imaginative reconception of colonised society and culture. It

requires an enlightened intellectual consensus which "refuses the short term blandishments of separatist and triumphalist slogans in favour of the larger, more generous human realities of community *among* cultures, peoples, and societies" (1993, p. 262). In other words, the intellectual stirrings of anti-colonialism can only be properly realised when nationalism becomes more "critical of itself"—when it proves itself capable of directing attention "to the abused rights of all oppressed classes" (1993, p. 264).

Said's intervention urges postcolonialism to reconsider the significance of all those other liberationist activities in the colonised world—such as those of the women's movement—which forcefully interrupt the triumphant and complacent rhetoric of the anti-colonial nation-State. "Students of postcolonial politics", he laments, "have not . . . looked enough at ideas that minimise orthodoxy and authoritarian or patriarchal thought, that take a severe view of the coercive nature of identity politics" (1993, p. 264). And yet, despite the force of Said's appeal, it is difficult for postcolonialism to entirely withdraw its loyalties from anti-colonial nationalism. Accordingly, it has always been troubled by the conflicting claims of nationalism and feminism. In this chapter we will focus on the discordance of race and gender within colonised cultures with a view to elucidating some of the issues surrounding the contiguities and oppositions between feminist and postcolonial theory.

IMPERIALIST FEMINISMS:
WOMAN (IN)DIFFERENCE

Until recently, feminist and postcolonial theory have followed what Bill Ashcroft et al. call "a path of convergent evolution" (Ashcroft et al., 1995, p. 249). Both bodies of thought have concerned themselves with the study and defence of marginalised "Others" within repressive structures of domination and, in so doing, both have followed a remarkably similar theoretical trajectory. Feminist and postcolonial theory alike began with an attempt to simply invert prevailing hierarchies of gender/culture/race, and they have each progressively welcomed the poststructuralist invitation to refuse the binary oppositions upon which patriarchal/colonial authority constructs itself. It is only in the last decade or so, however, that these two parallel projects have finally come together in what is, at best, a very volatile and tenuous partnership. In a sense, the alliance between these disciplinary siblings is informed by a mutual suspicion, wherein each discourse constantly confronts its limits and exclusions in the other. In the main, there are three areas of controversy which fracture the potential unity between postcolonialism and feminism: the debate surrounding the figure of the "third-world woman"; the problematic history of the "feminist-as-imperialist"; and finally, the colonialist deployment of "feminist criteria" to bolster the appeal of the "civilising mission".

The most significant collision and collusion of postcolonial and feminist theory occurs around the contentious figure of the "third-world woman". Some feminist postcolonial theorists have cogently argued that a blinkered focus on racial politics inevitably elides the "double colonisation" of women under imperial conditions. Such theory postulates the "third-world woman" as victim par excellence—the forgotten casualty of both imperial ideology, and native and foreign patriarchies. While it is now impossible to ignore the feminist challenge to the gender blindness of anti-colonial nationalism, critics such as Sara Suleri are instructive in their disavowal of the much too eager "coalition between postcolonial and feminist theories, in which each term serves to reify the potential pietism of the other" (Suleri 1992, p. 274).

The imbrication of race and gender, as Suleri goes on to argue, invests the "third-world woman" with an iconicity which is almost "too good to be true" (1992, p. 273).

Suleri's irascible objections to the postcolonial–feminist merger require some clarification. They need to be read as a refusal to, as it were, surrender the "third-world woman" to the sentimental and often opportunistic enamourment with "marginality", which . . . has come to characterise the metropolitan cult of "oppositional criticism". As Spivak writes, "If there is a buzzword in cultural critique now, it is 'marginality'" (Spivak 1993, p. 55). We now take it on trust that the consistent invocation of the marginal/subjugated has helped reform the aggressive canonicity of high Western culture. And yet, even as the margins thicken with political significance, there are two problems which must give pause. First, as Spivak insists, the prescription of non-Western alterity as a tonic for the ill health of Western culture heralds the perpetration of a "new Orientalism". Second, the metropolitan *demand* for marginality is also troublingly a *command* which consolidates and names the non-West as interminably marginal. By way of example, we might reconsider Deleuze and Guattari's celebration of "minor" or "deterritorialised" discourses in their influential study, *Kafka: Toward a Minor Literature* (Deleuze & Guattari 1986). These discourses or literatures, the authors inform us, inhere in "points of nonculture or underdevelopment, linguistic Third World zones by which a language can escape, an animal enter into things, an assemblage come into play" (1986, p. 27). In Deleuze and Guattari's revolutionary manifesto, the third world becomes a stable metaphor for the "minor" zone of nonculture and underdevelopment. Moreover, its value inheres only in its capacity to politicise or—predictably— "subvert" major, that is to say, more developed, cultural formations. Once again, then, as Gayatri Spivak suggests, the margin is at the service of the centre: "When a cultural identity is thrust upon one because the centre wants an identifiable margin, claims for marginality assure validation from the centre" (Spivak 1993, p. 55). The "third-world woman" is arguably housed in an "identifiable margin". And as critics like

Suleri and Spivak insist, this accommodation is ultimately unsatisfactory.

In an impressionistic and quasi-poetic book *Woman, Native, Other*, Trinh T. Minh-ha firmly attributes the rise of the "third-world woman" to the ideological tourism of Western/liberal feminism. Trinh's book elaborates its critique through a fictionalised—and yet all too familiar—account of the paternalistic and self-congratulatory tokenism which sustains "Special Third World Women's" readings, workshops, meetings and seminars. In every such event, Trinh argues, the veneer of cross-cultural, sisterly colloquium disguises an unpleasant ideology of separatism. Wherever she goes, the "native woman" is required to exhibit her ineluctable "difference" from the primary referent of Western feminism: "It is as if everywhere we go, we become Someone's private zoo" (Trinh 1989, p. 82). This voyeuristic craving for the colourful alterity of native women seriously compromises the seemingly egalitarian politics of liberal feminism. The consciousness of difference, identified by Trinh, sets up an implicit culturalist hierarchy wherein almost inevitably the "native woman" suffers in contrast with her Western sibling. By claiming the dubious privilege of "preparing the way for one's more 'unfortunate' sisters", the Western feminist creates an insuperable division between "I-who-have-made-it and You-who-cannot-make-it" (1989, p. 86). Thus, Trinh concludes, the circulation of the "Special Third World Women's Issue", only serves to advertise the specialness of the mediating first(?) world woman.

In her influential article "Under Western eyes: feminist scholarship and colonial discourses", Chandra Talpade Mohanty similarly discerns the play of a discursive colonialism in the "production of the 'Third World Woman' as a singular monolithic subject in some recent (Western) feminist texts" (Talpade Mohanty 1994, p. 196). Talpade Mohanty uses the term "colonialism" very loosely to imply any relation of structural domination which relies upon a self-serving suppression of "the heterogeneity of the subject(s) in question" (1994, p. 196). The analytic category "third-world woman" is, thus, colonialist for two reasons— first, because its ethnocentric myopia disregards the enormous material and historical differences between "real" third-world women; and second, because the composite "Othering" of the "third-world woman" becomes a self-consolidating project for Western feminism. Talpade Mohanty shows how feminists working within the social sciences invoke the narrative of "double colonisation" principally to contrast the political immaturity of third-world women with the progressive ethos of Western feminism. Thus, the representation of the average third-world woman as "ignorant, poor, uneducated, tradition-bound, domesticated, family-oriented, victimised", facilitates and privileges the self-representation of Western women "as educated, modern, as having control over their own bodies and 'sexualities', and the 'freedom' to make their own decisions" (1994, p. 200). In other words, the implied cultural lack of the "third-world woman" fortifies the redemptive ideological/political plenitude of Western feminism. To a large extent, Trinh's and Talpade Mohanty's critiques of liberal-feminist imperialism draw upon Said's understanding of colonial discourse as the cultural privilege of representing the subjugated Other. Both Said's Orientalist offenders and Talpade Mohanty's feminist opportunists, seem to speak the third world through a shared vocabulary which insists: they cannot represent themselves; they must be represented. The "third-world woman" can thus be seen as yet another object of Western knowledges, simultaneously knowable and unknowing. And as Talpade Mohanty laments, the residual traces of colonialist epistemology are all too visible in the:

> appropriation and codification of "scholarship" and "knowledge" about women in the third world by particular analytic categories employed in writings on the subject which take as their primary point of reference feminist interests which have been articulated in the US and western Europe (1994, p. 196).

Gayatri Spivak deserves mention here for her relentless challenge to all those specious knowledge systems which seek to regulate the articulation of what she calls the "gendered subaltern". Although most of Spivak's scattered oeuvre touches upon the touchy politics of knowing the Other, her early essay "French feminism in an international frame" (1987) is exemplary in its attention to the narcissism of the liberal-feminist investigator. In this essay, Spivak details the problematic elisions which run through Julia Kristeva's *About Chinese Women*—a text which emerged out of the sporadic French academic interest in China during the 1970s. Spivak's essay pursues Kristeva's itinerant gaze to the sun-soaked expanse of Huxian Square, where a crowd of un-speaking women picturesquely awaits the theorist's peroration. In her characteristic style, Spivak starts to interrupt Kristeva's musings and, in so doing, fore-grounds the discrepancy between the visible silence of the observed Chinese women and the discursive cacophony of the observing French feminist. Spivak's exercise makes a simple point: we never *hear* the object(s) of Kristeva's investigation represent them-selves. Yet, in the face of her mute native material, Kristeva abandons all scholarly decorum to hypothe-sise and generalise about China in terms of millennia, and always, as Spivak wryly observes, "with no encroachment of archival evidence" (Spivak 1987, p. 137). Eventually, as Kristeva's prose starts to slip away from any reference to the verity of the onlook-ing gathering at Huxian Square, her fluency becomes an end in itself; a solipsistic confirmation of the investigator's discursive privilege. Indeed, as Spivak points out, the material and historical scene before Kristeva is only ever an occasion for self-elaboration:

> Her question, in the face of those silent women, is about her *own* identity rather than theirs . . . This too might be characteristic of the group of thinkers to whom I have, most generally, attached her. In spite of their occasional interest in touching the *other* of the West, of metaphysics, of capitalism, their repeated question is obsessively self-centred: if we are not what official history and philosophy say we are, who then are we (not), how are we (not)? (Spivak 1987, p. 137).

Spivak's incisive reading catches the authoritative knower in the act of "epistemic violence"—or author-itarian knowing. *About Chinese Women* is really a book about Kristeva: a text which deploys, once again, the difference of the "third-world woman" as grist to the mill of Western theory. Trinh's concluding remarks on the generic third-world women's seminar

are relevant here: "We did not come to hear a Third World member speak about the First(?) World, We came to listen to that voice of difference likely to bring us *what we can't have* and to divert us from the monotony of sameness" (Trinh 1989, p. 88).

The critics we have been reviewing raise significant and trenchant objections to the Western feminist investment in postcolonial matters. And yet their own critique suffers from serious limitations. Trinh, Talpade Mohanty and Spivak each idealise and essentialise the epistemological opacity of the "real" third-world woman. By making her the bearer of meanings/experiences which are always in excess of Western analytic categories, these critics para-doxically re-invest the "third-world woman" with the very iconicity they set out to contest. This newly reclaimed figure is now postulated as the triumphant site of anti-colonial resistance. Trinh's rampant prose valorises the racial, gendered body itself as a rev-olutionary archive, while Spivak, somewhat feebly, urges the academic feminist to *speak to* the subaltern woman, to learn from her repository of lived experi-ence. If these proposals for change are somewhat suspect, it is also worth noting that each of the critics under consideration is guilty of the sort of reversed ethnocentrism which haunts Said's totalising critique of Orientalism. In refuting the composite and mono-lithic construction of "native women", Spivak et al. unself-consciously homogenise the intentions of all Western feminists/feminisms. As it happens, there are always other stories tell—on both sides of the fence which separates postcolonialism from feminism.

GENDERED SUBALTERNS: THE (OTHER) WOMAN IN THE ATTIC

In its more irritable moments, then, postcolonial theory tends to regard liberal feminism as a type of neo-Orientalism. Said, we may recall, diagnoses Orientalism as a discourse which invents or orien-talises the Orient for the purposes of imperial con-sumption: "The Orient that appears in Orientalism, then, is a system of representations framed by a whole set of forces that brought the Orient into Western learning, Western consciousness, and later, Western empire" (Said 1991 [1978], pp. 202–3). Liberal feminism, it is argued, similarly throws in its lot with colonial knowledge systems whenever it postulates— or "worlds"—the "third-world woman" as a composite and monolithic category for analysis.

As Talpade Mohanty argues:

> Without the overdetermined discourse that creates the "*third* world", there would be no (singular and privileged) first world. Without the "third-world woman", the particular self-presentation of western women . . . would be problematical . . . the definition of "the third-world woman" as a monolith might well tie into the larger economic and ideological praxis of "disinterested" scientific inquiry and pluralism which are the surface manifestations of a latent economic and cultural colonization of the "non-western" world (Talpade Mohanty 1994, pp. 215–16)

Thus, the axioms of imperialism are said to repeat themselves in every feminist endeavour to essentialise or prescriptively name the alterity/difference of native female Others.

The domestic quarrel between postcolonialism and feminism does not end here. If Western feminism stands convicted for its theoretical articulation of the "third-world woman", it is also blamed for the way in which it simultaneously occludes the historical claims of this figure. To a large extent, both "faults" inhere in the privilege of "representation" claimed by hegemonic feminist discourses. They are two sides of the same coin. Thus, liberal academic feminism is said to silence the "native woman" in its pious attempts to represent or speak for her. Kristeva's *About Chinese Women*, as we have seen, is a case in point. In her essay "Can the subaltern speak?", Spivak famously elaborates some other contexts wherein contesting representational systems violently displace/silence the figure of the "gendered subaltern". As she writes:

> Between patriarchy and imperialism, subject-constitution and object-formation, the figure of the woman disappears, not into a pristine nothingness, but a violent shuttling which is the displaced figuration of the "third-world woman" caught between tradition and modernisation (Spivak 1988 [1985], p. 306).

This essay argues that the "gendered subaltern" disappears because we never hear her speak about herself. She is simply the medium through which competing discourses represent their claims; a palimpsest written over with the text of other desires, other meanings.

Spivak's earlier essay, "Three women's texts and a critique of imperialism" (1985), offers another take on the "disappearance" of the "gendered subaltern" within liberal feminist discourses. Her arguments here open up a crucial area of disagreement between postcolonialism and feminism. Rather than chronicle the liberal feminist appropriation of the "gendered subaltern", this essay queries the conspicuous absence of the "third-world woman" within the literature which celebrates the emerging "female subject in Europe and Anglo-America" (Spivak 1985, p. 243). Spivak argues that the high feminist norm has always been blinkered in its "isolationist admiration" for individual female achievement. A rereading of women's history shows that the "historical moment of feminism in the West" was itself defined "in terms of female access to individualism" (1985, p. 246). Yet nowhere does feminist scholarship stop to consider where the battle for female individualism was played out. Nor does it concern itself with the numerous exclusions and sacrifices which might attend the triumphant achievements of a few female individuals. Spivak's essay is posed as an attempt to uncover the repressed or forgotten history of Euro-American feminism. Once again the margins reveal the mute figure of gendered subalterneity: "As the female individualist, not quite/ not male, articulates herself in shifting relationship to what is at stake, the 'native female' as such (*within* discourse, *as* a signifier) is excluded from a share in this emerging norm" (1985, pp. 244–5).

Spivak furnishes her theoretical hypothesis with a sensitive and well-known critique of *Jane Eyre*. While feminist critics have conventionally read this novel as an allegorical account of female self-determination, Spivak in contrast argues that Jane Eyre's personal progress through Brontë's novel is predicated upon the violent effacement of the half-caste Bertha Mason. Bertha's function in the novel, we are told, "is to render indeterminate the boundary between human and animal and thereby weaken her entitlement under the spirit if not the letter of the Law" (1985, p. 249). Jane gradually claims the entitlements lost by her dark double. Her rise to the licit centre of the novel, Spivak insists, requires Bertha's displacement to the fuzzy margins of narrative consciousness—it is fuelled, in this sense, by the Creole woman's literal and symbolic self-immolation.

Spivak's polemical reading of *Jane Eyre* firmly situates this cult text of Western feminism in the great age of European imperialism. The cultural and literary production of nineteenth-century Europe, she argues, is inextricable from the history and success of the imperialist project. Thus, and insofar as feminism seeks its inspirational origins in this period, it must also reconsider its historical complicity with imperialist discourses. The terms of Spivak's general challenge to feminism are elaborated in Jenny Sharpe's recent book, *Allegories of Empire* (1993). Sharpe further complicates the negotiations between feminism and postcolonialism by exhuming the difficult figure of the female imperialist, thereby exposing women's role in not only the politics but also the practice of empire. How might feminism respond to the individual achievements of this figure? Recent critics and historians have argued that the feminist battle for individual rights was considerably more successful in the colonies than "at home". While European civil society remained undecided as to whether women possessed the attributes and capacities of individuals, its colonial counterpart—in places like India—was considerably more amenable to the good offices of the white female subject. The imperial "memsahib", as Rosemary Marangoly George argues, "was a British citizen long before England's laws caught up with her" (Marangoly George 1993, p. 128). And yet she was only anchored as a full individual through her racial privileges.

The figure of the "feminist imperialist"—much like that of the "third-world woman"—fractures the potential unity between postcolonial and feminist scholarship. By way of example we might briefly turn to Pat Barr's early book, *The Memsahibs*. This nostalgic and eulogistic study betrays the faultlines of a narrowly "feminist" approach to the ideologically fraught figure of the female imperialist. Barr is fierce and persuasive in her desire to reclaim the "memsahib" from the satirical pen of male writers like Kipling and also from the apparent neglect of the masculinist archive: "What they did and how they responded to their alien environment were seldom thought worthy of record, either by themselves or by contemporary chroniclers of the male-dominated imperial scenario" (Barr 1976, p. 1). So also and correctly Barr teaches us to read the memsahib's life in hot and dusty India as a *career*. Her favourite "memsahib", Honoria Lawrence, makes a vocation out of good humour: "Irritable she sometimes was, but never frivolous, nor procrastinating when it came to the duty of cheering her absent husband . . ." (1976, p. 71). Honoria's letters and diaries—enthusiastically cited by Barr—consistently professionalise the activities of wife- and mother-in-exile, housekeeper and hostess. She writes, in this vein, of the hiatus prior to her marriage and departure for India as an enervating period of unemployment: "the unemployed energies, the unsatisfied desire for usefulness would eat me up" (1976, p. 35). Empire transforms such a life of indolence into work. The "wives of the Lawrences and their followers", as Barr records, "were vowed to God just as definitely as their husbands, were as closely knit in a community of work and religion" (1976, p. 103).

Barr's analysis confirms the soundness of her feminist credentials. She is ideologically pristine in the way in which she encourages her readers to appreciate the domestic labour of her heroines. And yet how might postcolonialism even begin to condone this feminist investment in imperial career opportunities. As it happens, the "contribution" of the "memsahib" can only be judged within the racial parameters of the imperial project. This, then, is Barr's conclusive defence of her protagonists: "For the most part, the women loyally and stoically accepted their share of the white people's burden and lightened the weight of it with their quiet humour, their grace, and often their youth" (1976, p. 103). Not content to stop here, Barr goes on to valorise the grassroots feminism of her protagonists. The "angel" in the colonial home, we are told, joins the ranks of colonial missionaries to universalise the gospel of bourgeois domesticity. In the fulfilment of this endeavour she regularly turns her evangelical eye upon the glaring problem of the backward "Indian female". The indefatigable Annette Ackroyd braves the collective wrath of Indian patriarchy to instruct "pupils in practical housework and to the formation of orderly and industrious habits" (Barr 1976, p. 166), while her compatriot, Flora Annie Steele, promises the Punjabi Education Board a "primer on Hygiene for the Girls' Middle School examination to take the place of the perfectly useless Euclid" (Barr 1976, p. 160). However, whereas Barr sees only a history of self-empowerment in the figures of the well-meaning memsahibs Steele and Ackroyd, the postcolonial critic is prevented from such unreserved celebration by the recognition that these women's constitution as fully fledged "individual subjects" is, in the end, inextricable from the hierarchies which inform the imperial project. Once again, their achievements/privileges are predicated upon the relative incivility of the untutored "Indian female". Meanwhile, in the wings, Spivak's "gendered subaltern" silently awaits further instruction.

CONFLICTING LOYALTIES: BROTHERS V. SISTERS

In the course of its quarrel with liberal feminism, postcolonialism—as we have been arguing—fails conclusively to resolve the conflicting claims of "feminist emancipation" and "cultural emancipation". It is unable to decide, as Kirsten Holst Petersen puts it, "which is the more important, which comes first, the fight for female equality or the fight against Western cultural imperialism?" (Holst Peterson in Ashcroft et al. 1995, p. 252). These are not, of course, new questions. For if contemporary liberal feminism derives its ancestry in part from the imperialist "memsahib", postcolonialism, no less, recuperates stubborn nationalist anxieties about the "woman question" which typically dichotomise the claims of "feminism" and "anticolonialism". Frantz Fanon's apology for Algerian women in his book, *A Dying Colonialism* is a case in point. Fanon postulates the "veiled Algerian woman" as a site for the playing out of colonial and anticolonial rivalries. Accordingly, the colonial critique of Algerian patriarchy is read as a strategic attempt to fragment the unity of national revolution. The coloniser, Fanon tells us, destructures Algerian society through its women: "If we want to destroy the structure of Algerian society, its capacity for resistance, we must first of all conquer the women; we must go and find them behind the veil where they hide themselves and in the houses where the men keep them out of sight" (Fanon 1965, pp. 57–8). Fanon's rhetoric self-consciously politicises the veil or the *haik*, thereby reconstituting colonialism as the project of "unveiling Algeria". Against this, nationalism appropriates the feminine *haik* as a metaphor for political elusiveness. The Algerian woman becomes a fellow revolutionary simply through her principled "no" to the coloniser's "reformist" invitation. She learns also to revolutionise her feminine habit: "she goes out into the street with three grenades in her handbag or the activity report of an area in her bodice" (1965, p. 50). Fanon's appeal to the loyalties of Algerian women elaborates a characteristic nationalist anxiety which Spivak brilliantly summarises in the sentence: "White men are saving brown women from brown men" (Spivak 1988 [1985], p. 296). Thus, in Fanon's understanding, the claims of brown compatriotism must necessarily exceed the disruptive petition of white (feminist) interlopers. The veiled Algerian woman, he confidently announces, "in imposing such a restriction on herself, in choosing a form of existence limited in scope, was deepening her consciousness of struggle and preparing for combat" (1965, p. 66). Despite the force of Fanon's argument, interloping feminist readers may very well question his authoritative representation of Algerian womanhood and find themselves in agreement with Partha Chatterjee's recent book, *The Nation and Its Fragments*, which argues that nationalist discourse is finally "a discourse *about* women; women do not speak here" (Chatterjee 1993, p. 133). Seen in these terms, postcolonial theory betrays its own uneasy complicity with nationalist discourses whenever it announces itself as the only legitimate mouthpiece for native women.

In another context, the publication of the American author Katherine Mayo's accusatory book, *Mother India*, in 1927 (republished in 1986) distils some further controversies surrounding the Western feminist intervention into the "native woman question". This sensationalist book reads, as Gandhi observed, like a drain inspector's report. Under the guise of "disinterested inquiry", Mayo embarks on a furious invective against the unhappy condition of Indian women. In page after page she inventories the brutishness of Indian men, the horrors of child-marriage, the abjection of widowhood and, of course, the atavistic slavishness, illiteracy and unsanitary habits of Indian wives. Mayo's book, understandably, caused an uproar. Most prominent male Indian nationalists penned furious rejoinders to her allegations, and a spate of books appeared under titles like *Father India: A Reply to Mother India, A Son of Mother India Answers* and *Unhappy India*. In the face of Mayo's assessment of Indians as unfit for self-rule—on account of their heinous attitudes toward women—sane critics like Gandhi and Tagore, calmly dismissed the book as another tired apology for the colonial civilising mission. Other more traumatised critics, in their anti-feminist vitriol, betrayed troubling aspects of the nationalist possessiveness about "native women".

The anonymous but indisputably male author of the hysterical *Sister India*, for example, insists that Mayo's feminist criterion are simply foreign to India. He invokes the rhetoric of cultural authenticity to argue that the emancipation of Indian women must be couched in an indigenous idiom. Mayo's recommendations are flawed primarily because they invite Indian women to become poor copies of their Western counterparts:

> It would be an evil day for India if Indian women indiscriminately copy and imitate Western women. Our women will progress in their own way . . . We are by no means prepared to think that the Western woman of today is a model to be copied. What has often been termed in the West as the emancipation

of women is only a glorified name for the disintegration of the family ("World Citizen" 1927, p. 163).

Not only does *Sister India* demonise Western feminism, it also reveals the extent to which the nation authenticates its distinct cultural identity through its women. Partha Chatterjee's work on Indian anticolonial nationalism is instructive here—drawing attention to the subtle nuances of the nationalist compromise with the invasive hegemony of colonial/Western values. Indian nationalists, he argues, dealt with the compulsive claims of Western civilisation by dividing the domain of culture into two discrete spheres—the material and the spiritual. It was hard to contest the superiority and domination of the West in the *material* sphere. But on the other hand, as texts like Gandhi's *Hind Swaraj* proclaimed, no cultural rival could possibly match the superiority of India's *spiritual* essence. Thus, as Chatterjee writes, while it was deemed necessary to cultivate and imitate the material accomplishments of Western civilisation, it was compulsory to simultaneously preserve and police the spiritual properties of national culture. And in the catalogue of the nation's spiritual effects, the home and its keeper acquired a troublesome pre-eminence. In Chatterjee's words: "The home in its essence must remain unaffected by the profane activities of the material world—and woman is its representation" (Chatterjee 1993, p. 120).

This, then, is the context for the nationalist trepidation about the "Westernisation" of Indian women. The irate author of *Sister India* takes his cue from nationalist discourse in his anxiety that Mayo's book might urge the custodians of national (spiritual) domesticity to bring Europe imitatively into the foundational home. Chatterjee's sources reveal that the nationalist investment in "authentic" Indian womanhood resulted in the nomination of a new enemy—the hapless "memsahib". As he writes:

> To ridicule the idea of a Bengali woman trying to imitate the ways of a *memsaheb* . . . was a sure recipe calculated to evoke raucous laughter and moral condemnation in both male and female audiences . . . What made the ridicule stronger was the

constant suggestion that the Westernised woman was fond of useless luxury and cared little for the well-being of the home (1993, p. 122).

Thus, in order to establish the necessary *difference* between Indian and Western women, (male) nationalism systematically demonised the "memsahib"—as a particularly ugly passage about Katherine Mayo from *Sister India* exemplifies: "She is an old maid of 49, and has all along, been absorbed in the attempt to understand the mystery of sex. If she were a married lady, she would have easily understood what the mystery was . . . As soon as she gets married, she will be an improved girl, and an improved woman" ("World Citizen" 1927, pp. 103–4).

In this account of nationalist anxieties about Western "feminism" we can discern the historical origins of the postcolonial animosity toward liberal feminism. Equally, it is important to note that the traumatic nationalist negotiation of the "woman question" establishes a direct and problematic enmity between "brown men" and "white women". No one has understood or articulated this historical hostility more eloquently than E. M. Forster in his *A Passage To India*. The native men of Forster's Chandrapore despise the memsahibs. "Granted the exceptions", as Forster's Aziz agrees, "all Englishwomen are haughty and venal" (Forster 1979, p. 33). This disdain is, of course, amply reciprocated, and as Mrs Callendar, the wife of the local civil surgeon, observes: "the best thing one can do to a native is to let him die" (1979, p. 44). Forster's fictional counterpart, Fielding, accurately diagnoses the implacable hostility between "memsahibs" and "native men": "He had discovered that it is possible to keep in with Indians and Englishmen, but that he who would also keep in with Englishwomen must drop the Indians. The two wouldn't combine" (1979, p. 74). These tensions, announced from the very beginning of the novel, famously explode in the Marabar Caves incident. From this point onward, the superior race clusters around the inferior sex, while the inferior race announces its allegiance to the superior sex. Between the female victim, Adela Quested, and the colonised underdog, Dr Aziz, the choices are, indeed, very stark. The choices between the obnoxious Katherine Mayo and the awful author of *Sister India* are starker still. Yet this is, surely, a very old quarrel and it is possible for postcolonialism and feminism to exceed the limits of their respective histories.

BETWEEN MEN: RETHINKING THE COLONIAL ENCOUNTER

A productive area of collaboration between postcolonialism and feminism presents itself in the possibility of a combined offensive against the aggressive myth of both imperial and nationalist masculinity. In the last few years, a small but significant group of critics has attempted to reread the colonial encounter in these terms as a struggle between competing masculinities. We have already seen how colonial and colonised women are postulated as the symbolic mediators of this (male) contestation. If anti-colonial nationalism authenticated itself through female custodians of spiritual domesticity, the male imperial ethic similarly distilled its "mission" through the figure of the angel in the colonial home. Anne McClintock's recent book, *Imperial Leather*, points to some aspects of the empire's investment in its women. As she writes: "Controlling women's sexuality, exalting maternity and breeding a virile race of empire-builders was widely perceived as the paramount means for controlling the health and wealth of the male imperial body" (McClintock 1995, p. 47). Other writers have also drawn attention to ways in which the colonial civilising mission represented itself through the self-sacrificing, virtuous and domesticated figure of the "white" housewife. The figure of woman, Jenny Sharpe argues, was "instrumental in shifting a colonial system of meaning from self-interest and moral superiority to self-sacrifice and racial superiority" (1993, p. 7).

In this context, McClintock usefully foregrounds the hidden aspect of sexual rivalry which accompanied the restitution and reinvention of imperial/anti-colonial "manliness" and patriarchy. She argues that the masculinity of empire was articulated, in the first instance, through the symbolic feminisation of conquered geographies, and in the erotic economy of colonial "discovery" narratives. Vespucci's mythic disclosure of the virginal American landscape is a case in point: "Invested with the male prerogative of naming, Vespucci renders America's identity a dependent extension of his, and stakes male Europe's territorial rights to her body and, by extension, the fruits of her land" (1995, p. 26). In another context, Fanon shows how this threat of territorial/sexual dispossession produces, in the colonised male, a reciprocal fantasy of sexual/territorial repossession: "I marry white culture, white beauty, white whiteness. When my restless hands caress those white breasts, they grasp white civilisation and dignity and make them mine" (Fanon 1967, p. 63). Needless to say, these competing desires find utterance in competing anxieties. Sharpe's work suggests that the discourse of rape surrounding English women in colonial India positions Englishmen as their avengers, thereby permitting violent "strategies of counterinsurgency to be recorded as the restoration of moral order" (Sharpe 1993, p. 6). Correspondingly, Fanon insists that the "aura" of rape surrounding the veiled Algerian woman provokes the "native's bristling resistance" (Fanon 1967, p. 47).

Fanon's exploration, in *Black Skin, White Masks*, of the sexual economy underpinning the colonial encounter in Algeria leads him to conclude that the colonised black man is the "real" Other for the colonising white man. Several critics and historians have extended this analysis to the Indian context to argue that colonial masculinity defined itself with reference to the alleged effeminacy of Indian men. The infamous Thomas Macaulay, among others, gives full expression to this British disdain for the Indian apology for maleness:

> The physical organisation of the Bengali is feeble even to effeminacy. He live[s] in a constant vapour bath. His pursuits are sedentary, his limbs delicate, his movements languid. During many ages he has been trampled upon by men of bolder and hardy deeds. Courage, independence, veracity, are qualities to which his constitution and his situation are equally unfavourable (cited in Rosselli 1980, p. 122).

In other words, India is colonisable because it lacks real men. Macaulay's description fully illustrates what Ashis Nandy describes as the colonial homology between sexual and political dominance. By insisting upon the racial effeminacy of the Bengali (not quite) male, Macaulay reformulates the colonial relationship in terms of the "natural" ascendancy of men over women. Accordingly, he renders as hypermasculine the unquestioned dominance of European men at home and abroad. As Nandy writes:

> Colonialism, too, was congruent with the existing Western sexual stereotypes and the philosophy of life which they represented. It produced a cultural consensus in which political and socio-economic dominance symbolised the dominance of men and masculinity over women and femininity (Nandy 1983, p. 4).

The discourse of colonial masculinity was thoroughly internalised by wide sections of the nationalist movement. Some nationalists responded by lamenting their own emasculation, others by protesting it. Historians have drawn attention, in this regard, to the reactive resurgence of physical and, relatedly, militaristic culture within the Indian national movement.

Ashis Nandy elides the story of Indian nationalism's derivative masculinity to tell an altogether different—and considerably more interesting—story about dissident androgyny. *The Intimate Enemy* (1983) theorises the emergence of a protest against the colonial cult of masculinity, both within the Indian national movement and also on the fringes of nineteenth-century British society. Nandy's analysis reclaims diverse figures like Gandhi and Oscar Wilde. Gandhi, as Nandy shows us, repudiated the nationalist appeal to maleness on two fronts—first, through his systematic critique of male sexuality; and second, through his self-conscious aspiration for bisexuality or the desire, as he put it, to become "God's eunuch" (see Mehta 1977, p. 194). Gandhi's radical self-fashioning gives "femaleness" an equal share in the making of anti-colonial subjectivity. So also, by refusing to partake in the disabling logic of colonial sexual binaries, he successfully complicates the authoritative signature of colonial masculinity. From the other side, Wilde similarly protests the dubious worth of manly British robustness. As with Gandhi, his critique of conventional sexual identities and sexual norms threatens what Nandy describes as "a basic postulate of the colonial attitude in Britain" (Nandy 1983, p. 44). There are countless other examples—Edward Carpenter, Lytton Strachey and Virginia Woolf are all, as Nandy writes, "living protests against the world view associated with colonialism" (1983, p. 43). Postcolonialism and feminism own a potential meeting ground in these figures—in Carpenter's thesis about the "intermediate sex" and in Woolf's contentious delineation of androgyny. And perhaps there is some hope of a cross-cultural and inter-theoretical accord in Woolf's passionate and feminist critique of bellicose colonial masculinity in *Three Guineas*:

> We can still shake out eggs from newspapers; still smell a peculiar and unmistakable odour in the region of Whitehall and Westminister. And abroad the monster has come more openly to the surface. There is no mistaking him there. He has widened his scope. He is interfering now with your liberty; he is dictating how you shall live; he is making distinctions not merely between sexes, but between the races. You are feeling in your own persons what your mothers felt when they were shut out, when they were shut up, because you are Jews, because you are democrats, because of race, because of religion (Woolf [1938] reprinted 1992, p. 304).

Much like Wilde and Gandhi, Woolf's denunciation of aggressive masculinity supplies the basis of a shared critique of chauvinist national and colonial culture. While some critics have fruitfully explored the terms of such a critique, its full potential awaits theoretical elaboration.

REFERENCES

Ashcroft, et al. (eds) 1995, *The Postcolonial Studies Reader*, Routledge, London.

Barr, P. 1976, *The Memsahibs: The Women of Victorian India*, Secker & Warburg, London.

Chatterjee, P. 1993, *The Nation and Its Fragments*, Princeton University Press, Princeton, New Jersey.

Deleuze, G. & Guattari, F. 1986, *Kafka: Toward a Minor Literature*, trans. Dana Polan, University of Minnesota Press, Minneapolis.

Fanon, F. 1965, *A Dying Colonialism*, trans. Haakon Chevalier, Grove Press, New York.

——— 1967, *Black Skin, White Masks*, trans. Charles Lam Markmann, Grove Press, New York.

Forster, E. M. 1979, *A Passage to India*, ed. Oliver Stallybrass, Penguin, Harmondsworth.

Marangoly George, R. 1993, "Homes in the Empire, empires in the home," *Cultural Critique*, vol. 26, pp. 95–128.

Mayo, K. 1986, *Mother India*, Indian edn, Anmol Publications, Delhi.

McClintock, A. 1995, *Imperial Leather: Race, Gender and Sexuality in the Colonial Contest*, Routledge, London.

Mehta, V. 1977 *Mahatma Gandhi and his Apostles*, Andre Deutsch, London.

Nandy, A. 1983, *The Intimate Enemy*, Oxford University Press, Delhi.

Rosselli, J. 1980, "The self-image of effeteness: physical education and nationalism in nineteenth century Bengal," *Past and Present*, vol. 86, pp. 121–48.

Said, E. 1991 [1978], *Orientalism*. 3rd ed. Penguin, Harmondsworth.

——— 1993, *Culture and Imperialism*, Chatto & Windus, London.

Sharpe, J. 1993, *Allegories of Empire*, University of Minnesota Press, Minneapolis.

Spivak, G. 1985, "Three women's texts and a critique of imperialism," *Critical Inquiry*, vol. 12, pp. 242–61.

——— 1987, "French feminism in an international frame," in *In Other Worlds: Essays in Cultural Politics*, Methuen, New York, pp. 134–53.

——— 1988, "Can the subaltern speak?" reprinted in *Marxist Interpretations of Culture*, eds Cary Nelson & Lawrence Grossberg, MacMillan Education, Basingstoke, pp. 271–313.

——— 1993, *Outside in the Teaching Machine*, Routledge, New York.

Suleri, S. 1992, *The Rhetoric of English India*, University of Chicago Press, Chicago.

Talpade Mohanty, C. 1994, "Under Western eyes," reprinted in *Colonial Discourse and Postcolonial Theory: A Reader*, eds. Patrick Williams & Laura Chrisman, Columbia University Press, New York, pp. 196–220.

Trinh, T. Minh-ha 1989, *Woman, Native, Other*, Indiana University Press, Bloomington.

Woolf, V. 1992, *A Room of One's Own & Three Guineas*, ed. Morag Shiach, Oxford University Press, Oxford.

"World Citizen" 1927, *Sister India*.

Study Questions

Gandhi posits "three areas of controversy which fracture the potential unity between postcolonialism and feminism: the debate surrounding the figure of the 'third-world woman'; the problematic history of the 'feminist-as-imperialist'; and finally, the colonialist deployment of 'feminist criteria' to bolster the appeal of the 'civilising mission'" (paragraph 3).

1. Explain what Gandhi means by the "area of controversy" having to do with "the figure of the 'third-world woman.'"

2. Explain what Gandhi means by the "area of controversy" having to do with "the 'feminist-as-imperialist.'"

3. Explain what Gandhi means by the "area of controversy" having to do with "the colonialist deployment of 'feminist criteria.'"

4. In Gandhi's view, what is the appropriate response to such deployments of "feminist criteria"? And according to Gandhi, what inappropriate response have some Indian nationalists embraced?

5. In her conclusion Gandhi notes: "A productive area of collaboration between postcolonialism and feminism presents itself in the possibility of a combined offensive against the aggressive myth of both imperial and nationalist masculinity." Explain this quotation.

Ann Laura Stoler

Carnal Knowledge and Imperial Power

Gender, Race, and Morality in Colonial Asia

Over the last fifteen years the anthropology of women has fundamentally altered our understanding of colonial expansion and its consequences for the colonized. More recent attention to the structures of colonial authority has placed new emphasis on the quotidian assertion of European dominance in the colonies, on imperial interventions in domestic life, and thus on the cultural prescriptions by which European women and men lived. Having focused on how colonizers have viewed the indigenous Other, we are beginning to sort out how Europeans in the colonies imagined themselves and constructed communities built on asymmetries of race, class, and gender—entities significantly at odds with the European models on which they were drawn.

Feminist attempts to engage the gender politics of Dutch, French, and British imperial cultures converge on some strikingly similar observations; namely, that European women in these colonies experienced the cleavages of racial dominance and internal social distinctions very differently than men precisely because of their ambiguous positions as both subordinates in colonial hierarchies and as active agents of imperial culture in their own right. Concomitantly, the majority of European women who left for the colonies in the late nineteenth and early twentieth centuries confronted profoundly rigid restrictions on their domestic, economic, and political options, more limiting than those of metropolitan Europe at the time and sharply contrasting with the opportunities open to colonial men.

In one form or another, these studies raise a basic question: In what ways were gender inequalities essential to the structure of colonial racism and imperial authority? Was the strident misogyny of imperial

Ann Stoler, "Carnal Knowledge and Imperial Power: Gender, Race, and Morality in Colonial Asia," from *The Gender/Sexuality Reader* edited by Michaela Di Leonardo. Reproduced by permission of Routledge/Taylor & Francis Books, Inc. Notes have been deleted.

thinkers and colonial agents a byproduct of received metropolitan values ("they just brought it with them"), a reaction to contemporary feminist demands in Europe ("women need to be put back in their breeding place"), or a novel and pragmatic response to the conditions of conquest? Was the assertion of European supremacy in terms of patriotic manhood and racial virility an expression of imperial domination or a defining feature of it?

Focusing on French Indochina and the Dutch East Indies in the early twentieth century but drawing on other contexts, I suggest that the very categories of "colonizer" and "colonized" were secured through forms of sexual control that defined the domestic arrangements of Europeans and the cultural investments by which they identified themselves. In treating the sexual and conjugal tensions of colonial life as more than a political trope for the tensions of empire writ small, but as a part of the latter in socially profound and strategic ways, I examine how gender-specific sexual sanctions and prohibitions not only demarcated positions of power but prescribed the personal and public boundaries of race.

Colonial authority was constructed on two powerful but false premises. The first was the notion that Europeans in the colonies made up an easily identifiable and discrete biological and social entity; a "natural" community of common class interests, racial attributes, political affinities, and superior culture. The second was the related notion that the boundaries separating colonizer from colonized were thus self-evident and easily drawn. Neither premise reflected colonial realities. Tensions between bureaucrats and planters, settlers and transients, missionaries and metropolitan policy makers, *petits blancs* (lower-class whites), and monied entrepreneurs have always made Euro-colonial communities more socially fractious and politically fragile than many of their members professed. Internal divisions developed out of competing economic and political agendas— conflicts over access to indigenous resources, frictions over appropriate methods for safeguarding European privilege and power, competing criteria for reproducing a colonial elite and for restricting its membership.

The markers of European identity and the criteria for community membership were never fixed. Rather, they defined fluid, permeable, and historically disputed terrain. The colonial politics of exclusion was contingent on constructing categories. Colonial control was predicated on identifying who was "white," who was "native," and which children could become citizens rather than subjects, designating who were legitimate progeny and who were not.

What mattered was not only one's physical properties but also who counted as "European" and by what measure. Skin shade was too ambiguous; bank accounts were mercurial; religious beliefs and education were crucial but never completely sufficient. Social and legal standing derived from the cultural prism through which color was viewed, from the silences, acknowledgments, and denials of the social circumstances in which one's parents had sex. Sexual unions based on concubinage, prostitution, or church marriage derived from the hierarchies of rule; but in turn, they were negotiated relations, contested classifications, which altered individual fates and the very structure of colonial society. Ultimately inclusion or exclusion required regulating the sexual, conjugal, and domestic life of *both* Europeans in the colonies and their colonized subjects.

POLITICAL MESSAGES AND SEXUAL METAPHORS

Colonial observers and participants in the imperial enterprise expressed unwavering interest in the sexual interface of the colonial encounter. Probably no subject is discussed more than sex in colonial literature and no subject more frequently invoked to foster the racist stereotypes of European society. With the sustained presence of Europeans in the colonies, sexual prescriptions by class, race, and gender became increasingly central to the politics of empire and subject to new forms of scrutiny by colonial states.

The salience of sexual symbols as graphic representations of colonial dominance is relatively unambiguous and well-established. Edward Said, for example, has argued that the sexual submission and possession of Oriental women by European men "fairly *stands for* the pattern of relative strength between East and West, and the discourse about the Orient that it enabled." He describes Orientalism as a "male perception of the world," "a male power-fantasy," "an exclusively male province," in which the Orient is penetrated, silenced, and possessed. Sexuality, then, serves as a loaded metaphor for domination, but Said's critique is not (nor does it claim to be) about those relations between women and men. Sexual images illustrate the iconography of rule, not its pragmatics. Sexual asymmetries and visions convey what is "really" going on elsewhere, at another political epicenter. They are tropes to depict other centers of power.

Sexual domination has been carefully considered as a discursive symbol, instrumental in the conveyance of other meanings, but has been less often treated as the substance of imperial policy. Was sexual dominance, then, merely a graphic substantiation of who was, so to speak, on the bottom and who was on the top? Was the medium the message, or did sexual relations always "mean" something else, stand in for other relations, evoke the sense of *other* (pecuniary, political, or some possibly more subliminal) desires? This analytic slippage between the sexual symbols of power and the politics of sex runs throughout the colonial record—as well as through contemporary commentaries on it. Some of this may be due to the polyvalent quality of sexuality; symbolically rich and socially salient at the same time. But sexual control was more than a convenient metaphor for colonial domination; it was, as I argue here, a fundamental class and racial marker implicated in a wider set of relations of power.

In the sections that follow I look at the relationship between the domestic arrangements of colonial communities and their wider political structures. Part I draws on colonization debates over a broad period (sixteenth-twentieth c.) in an effort to identify the long-term intervention of colonial authorities in issues of "racial mixing," settlement schemes, and sexual control. In examining debates over European family formation, over the relationship between subversion and sex, I look at how evaluations of concubinage, and of morality more generally, changed with new forms of racism and new gender-specific expressions of them. . . .

PART I: SEX AND OTHER CATEGORIES OF COLONIAL CONTROL

Who bedded and wedded with whom in the colonies of France, England, Holland, and Iberia was never left to chance. Unions between Annamite women and French men, between Portuguese women and Dutch men, between Spanish men and Inca women produced offspring with claims to privilege, whose rights and status had to be determined and prescribed. From the early 1600s through the twentieth century the sexual sanctions and conjugal prohibitions of colonial agents were rigorously debated and carefully codified. It is in these debates over matrimony and morality that trading and plantation company officials, missionaries, investment bankers, military high commands, and agents of the colonial state confronted one another's visions of empire and the settlement patterns on which rule would rest.

In 1622, the Dutch East Indies Company (VOC) arranged for the transport of six poor but marriageable young Dutch women to Java, providing them with clothing, a dowry upon marriage, and a contract binding them to five years in the Indies. Aside from this and one other short-lived experiment, immigration of European women to the East was consciously restricted for the next two hundred years. VOC shareholders argued against female emigration on several counts: the high cost of transporting married women and daughters; the possibility that Dutch women (with stronger ties than men to the Netherlands?) might hinder permanent settlement by goading their burgher husbands to quickly lucrative but nefarious trade, and then repatriate to display their newfound wealth; the fear that Dutch women would enrich themselves through private trade and encroach on the company's monopoly; and the prediction that their children would be sickly and force families to repatriate, ultimately depleting the colony of permanent and loyal settlers.

The Dutch East Indies Company enforced the sanction against female migration by selecting bachelors as their European recruits and by promoting both extramarital relations and legal unions between low-ranking employees and imported slave women. Although there were Euro-Asian marriages, government regulations made concubinage a more attractive option by prohibiting European men with native wives and children from returning to Holland. The VOC saw households based on Euro-Asian unions, by contrast, as having distinct advantages; individual employees would bear the costs of dependents; children of mixed unions were considered stronger and healthier; and Asian women made fewer (economic and emotional) demands. Finally, it was thought that men would be more likely to settle permanently by establishing families with local roots.

Concubinage served colonial interests in other ways. It permitted permanent settlement and rapid growth by a cheaper means than the importation of European women. Salaries of European recruits to the colonial armies, bureaucracies, plantation companies, and trading enterprises were kept artificially low. This was possible not only because the transport of European women and family support was thereby eliminated, as was often argued, but also because local women provided domestic services for which new European recruits would otherwise have had to pay. In the mid-nineteenth century, such arrangements were de rigueur for young civil servants intent on setting up households on their own. Despite some clerical opposition by the nineteenth century concubinage was the most prevalent living arrangement for European men. Nearly half of the Indies' European male population in the 1880s was unmarried and living with Asian women. It was only in the early twentieth century that concubinage was politically condemned.

In Asia and Africa, corporate and government decision-makers invoked the social services that local women supplied as "useful guides to the language and other mysteries of the local societies." The medical and cultural know-how of local women was credited with keeping many European men alive in their initial confrontation with tropical life.

Handbooks for incoming plantation employees bound for Tonkin, Sumatra, and Malaya urged men to find a bed-servant as a prerequisite to quick acclimatization. In Malaysia, commercial companies encouraged the procurement of local "companions for psychological and physical well-being"; to protect European staff from the ill-health that sexual abstention, isolation, and boredom were thought to bring. Even in the British empire, where the colonial office formally banned concubinage in 1910, it was tacitly condoned and practiced long after. In the Indies, a simultaneous sanction against concubinage among civil servants was only selectively enforced; it had little effect on domestic arrangements outside of Java and no perceptible impact on the European households in Sumatra's newly opened plantation belt where Japanese and Japanese *huishoudsters* (as Asian mistresses were sometimes called) remained the rule rather than the exception.

While the term concubinage commonly referred to the cohabitation outside of marriage between European men and Asian women, in fact, it glossed a wide range of arrangements that included sexual access to a non-European woman as well as demands on her labor and legal rights to the children she bore. Thus, to define it as cohabitation perhaps suggests more social privileges than most women who were involved in such relations enjoyed. Many colonized women combined sexual and domestic service within the abjectly subordinate contexts of slave or "coolie" and lived in separate quarters. On the plantations in East Sumatra, for example, where such arrangements were structured into company policies of labor control, Javanese women picked from the coolie ranks often retained their original labor contracts for the duration of their sexual and domestic service.

To say that concubinage reinforced the hierarchies on which colonial societies were based is not to say that it did not make those distinctions more problematic at the same time. In such regions as North Sumatra, grossly uneven sex ratios often made for intense competition among male workers and their European supervisors for indigenous women. *Vrouwen perkara* (disputes over women) resulted in assaults on whites, new labor tensions, and dangerous incursions into the standards deemed essential for white prestige. Metropolitan critics were particularly disdainful of these liaisons on moral grounds—all the more so when these unions *were* sustained and affectively significant relationships, thereby contradicting the racial premise of concubinage as an emotionally unfettered convenience. But perhaps most important, the tension between concubinage as a confirmation and compromise of racial hierarchy was realized in the progeny that it produced, "mixed bloods," poor "Indos," and abandoned *métis* children who straddled the divisions of ruler and ruled and threatened to blur the colonial divide. These *voorkinderen* (literally, "children from a previous marriage/union," but in this colonial context usually marking illegitimate children from a previous union with a non-European woman) were economically disadvantaged by their ambiguous social status and often grew up to join the ranks of the impoverished whites.

Concubinage was a domestic arrangement based on sexual service and gender inequalities that "worked" as long as European identity and supremacy were clear. When either was thought to be vulnerable, in jeopardy, or less than convincing, at the turn of the century and increasingly through the 1920s, colonial elites responded by clarifying the cultural criteria of privilege and the moral premises of their unity. Structured sex in the politically safe context of prostitution, and where possible in the more desirable context of marriage between "full-blooded" Europeans, replaced concubinage.

Restrictions on European Women in the Colonies

Colonial governments and private business not only tolerated concubinage but actively encouraged it—principally by restricting the emigration of European women to the colonies and by refusing employment to married male European recruits. Although most accounts of colonial conquest and settlement suggest that European women chose to avoid early pioneering ventures, the choice was rarely their own. In the Indies, a government ordinance of 1872 made it impossible for any soldier below the rank of sergeant major to be married; and even above that rank, conditions were very restrictive. In the Indies army, marriage was a privilege of the officer corps, whereas barrack-concubinage was instituted and regulated for the rank and file. Through the 1920s and 1930s, formal and informal prohibitions set by banks, estates, and government services operating in Africa, South Asia, and Southeast Asia restricted marriage during the first three to five years of service while some simply prohibited it altogether.

Many historians assume that these bans on employee marriage and on the emigration of European women lifted when specific colonies were politically stable, medically upgraded, and economically secure. In fact marriage restrictions lasted well into the twentieth century, long after rough living and a scarcity of amenities had become conditions of the past. In India as late as 1929, British employees in the political service were still recruited at the age of twenty-six and then prohibited from marriage during their first three probationary years. On the Ivory Coast, employment contracts in the 1920s also denied marriage with European women before the third tour, which meant a minimum of five years' service, so that many men remained unmarried past the age of thirty.

European demographics in the colonies were shaped by these economic and political exigencies and thus were enormously skewed by sex. Among the laboring immigrant and native populations as well as among Europeans in the late nineteenth and early twentieth centuries, the number of men was, at the very least, double that of women, and sometimes exceeded the latter by twenty-five times. Although in the Netherlands Indies, the overall ratio of European women to men rose from 47:100 to 88:100 between 1900 and 1930, representing an absolute increase from 4,000 to 26,000 Dutch women, in outlying areas such as on Sumatra's plantation belt in 1920 there were still only 61 European women per 100 men. On Africa's Ivory Coast, European sex ratios through 1921 were still 1:25. In controlling the availability of European women and the sorts of sexual access allowed, colonial state and corporate authorities avoided salary increases as well as the proliferation of a lower-class European settler population. Such policies in no way muted the internal class distinctions within the European communities; they simply shaped the social geography of the colonies by fixing the conditions under which European privileges could be attained and reproduced.

Sex, Subversion, and White Prestige

The marriage prohibition revealed how deeply the conduct of private life and the sexual proclivities individuals expressed were tied to corporate profits and the security of the colonial state. Nowhere was the connection between sex and subversion more openly contested than in North Sumatra in the early 1900s. Irregular domestic arrangements were thought to encourage subversion as strongly as acceptable unions could avert it. Family stability and sexual "normalcy" were thus linked to political agitation or quiescence in very concrete ways.

Since the late nineteenth century, the major North Sumatran tobacco and rubber companies had neither accepted married applicants nor allowed them to take wives while in service. Company authorities argued that new employees with families in tow would be a financial burden, risking the emergence of a "European proletariat" and thus a major threat to white prestige. Low-ranking plantation employees protested against these company marriage restrictions, an issue that mobilized their ranks behind a broad set of demands. Under employee pressure, the prohibition was relaxed to a marriage ban for the first five years of service.

Domestic arrangements thus varied as government officials and private businesses weighed the economic versus political costs of one arrangement over another, but such calculations were invariably meshed. Europeans in high office saw white prestige and profits inextricably linked, and attitudes toward concubinage reflected that concern. Thus in Malaya through the 1920s, concubinage was tolerated precisely because "poor whites" were not. Government and plantation administrators argued that white prestige would be imperiled if European men became impoverished in attempting to maintain middle-class life styles and European wives. Colonial morality and the place of concubinage in it was relative, given the

"particular anathema with which the British regarded 'poor whites.'" In late nineteenth century Java, in contrast, concubinage itself was considered to be a major source of white pauperism and vigorously condemned at precisely the same time that a new colonial morality passively condoned illegal brothels.

What constituted morality vacillated, as did the very definition of white prestige—and what its defense should entail. A discursive obsession with white prestige was a basic feature of colonial mentality. White prestige and its protection loom as the primary cause of a long list of otherwise inexplicable colonial postures, prejudices, fears, and violences. What upheld that prestige was not a constant; concubinage was socially lauded at one time and seen as a political menace at another. White prestige was a gloss for different intensities of racist practice, gender specific and culturally coded. Although many accounts contend that white women brought an end to concubinage, its decline came with a much wider shift in colonial relations along more racially segregated lines—in which the definitions of prestige shifted and in which Asian, Creole, and European-born women were to play new roles.

PART II: EUROPEAN WOMEN AND RACIAL BOUNDARIES

Perhaps nothing is as striking in the sociological accounts of European colonial communities as the extraordinary changes that are said to accompany the entry of white women. These adjustments shifted in one direction: toward European life styles accentuating the refinements of privilege and new etiquettes of racial difference. Housing structures in the Indies were partitioned, residential compounds in the Solomon Islands enclosed, servant relations in Hawaii formalized, dress codes in Java altered, food and social taboos in Rhodesia and the Ivory Coast codified. Taken together, these changes encouraged new kinds of consumption and new social services catering to these new demands.

The arrival of large numbers of European women thus coincided with an embourgeoisment of colonial communities and with a significant sharpening of racial categories. European women supposedly required more metropolitan amenities than men and more spacious surroundings to allow it; they had more delicate sensibilities and therefore needed suitable quarters—discrete and enclosed. Women's psychological and physical constitutions were considered more fragile, demanding more servants for the chores they should be spared. In short, white women needed to be maintained at elevated standards of living, in insulated social spaces cushioned with the cultural artifacts of "being European." Segregationist standards were what women "deserved," and more importantly what white male prestige required that they maintain.

Racist but Moral Women, Innocent but Immoral Men

Colonial rhetoric on white women was full of contradictions. At the same time that new female immigrants were chided for not respecting the racial distance of local convention, an equal number of colonial observers accused these women of being more avid racists in their own right. Allegedly insecure and jealous of the sexual liaisons of European men with native women, bound to their provincial visions and cultural norms, European women, it was and is argued, constructed the major cleavages on which colonial stratification rested. Thus Percival Spear, in commenting on the social life of the English in eighteenth-century India, asserted that women "widened the racial gulf" by holding to "their insular whims and prejudices". Writing about French women in Algeria two hundred years later, the French historian Pierre Nora claimed that these "parasites of the colonial relationship in which they do not participate directly, are generally more racist than men and contribute strongly to prohibiting contact between the two societies." For the Indies, "it was jealousy of the dusky sirens . . . but more likely some say . . . it was . . . plain feminine scandalization at free and easy sex relations" that caused a decline in miscegenation.

Such bald examples are easy to find in colonial histories of several decades ago. Recent scholarship is more subtle but not substantially different. In the European community on the French Ivory Coast, ethnographer Alain Tirefort contends that "the presence of the white woman separated husbands from indigenous life by creating around them a zone of European intimacy." Gann and Duignan state simply that it was "the cheap steamship ticket for women that put an end to racial integration in British Africa." In such narratives, European women are positioned both as marginal players on the colonial stage and as principal actors. They are charged with dramatically reshaping the face of colonial society, imposing racial distance in African and Asian contexts where "relatively unrestrained social intermingling . . . had been prevalent in earlier year." European women are not only the true bearers of racist beliefs but also hard-line operatives who put racism into practice, encouraging class distinctions among whites while fostering new racial antagonisms, formerly muted by sexual access.

Are we to believe that sexual intimacy with European men yielded social mobility and political rights for colonized women? Or even less likely, that because British civil servants bedded with Indian women, somehow Indian men had more "in common" with British men and enjoyed more parity? Colonized women could sometimes parlay their positions into personal profit and small rewards, but these were *individual* negotiations with no social, legal, or cumulative claims. European male sexual access to native women was not a leveling mechanism for asymmetries in race, class, or gender.

Male colonizers positioned European women as the bearers of a redefined colonial morality. But to suggest that women fashioned this racism out of whole cloth is to miss the political chronology in which new intensities of racist practice arose. In the African and Asian contexts already mentioned, the arrival of large numbers of European wives, and particularly the fear for their protection, followed from new terms and tensions in the colonial contract. The presence and protection of European women was repeatedly invoked to clarify racial lines. It coincided with perceived threats to European prestige, increased racial conflict, covert challenges to the colonial order, outright expressions of nationalist resistance, and internal dissension among whites themselves.

If white women were the primary force behind the decline of concubinage, as is often claimed, they did so as participants in a much broader shift in racial politics and colonial plan. This is not to suggest that European women were passive in this process, as the dominant themes in many of their novels attest. Many European women did oppose concubinage— not because they were categorically jealous of, and threatened by, Asian women as often claimed, but, more likely, because of the double standard it condoned for European women. The voices of European women had little resonance until their objections coincided with a realignment in racial and class politics in which they were strategic to both.

Race and the Politics of Sexual Peril

The gender-specific requirements for colonial living were constructed on heavily racist evaluations, which pivoted on images of the heightened sexuality of colonized men. In this frame, European women needed protection because men of color had "primitive" sexual urges and uncontrollable lust, aroused by the sight of white women. In some colonies, that sexual threat remained an unlabeled potential; in others it was given a specific name. The "Black Peril" referred throughout Africa and much of the British Empire to the professed dangers of sexual assault on white women by black men.

In Southern Rhodesia and Kenya in the 1920s and 1930s, preoccupations with the "Black Peril" gave rise to the creation of citizens' militias, ladies' riflery clubs, and investigations as to whether African female domestic servants would not be safer to employ than men. In New Guinea, alleged attempted assaults on European women by Papuan men prompted the passage of the White Women's Protection Ordinance of 1926, which provided "the death penalty for any person convicted for the crime of rape or attempted rape upon a European woman or girl." And in the Solomon Islands authorities introduced public flogging in 1934 as punishment for "criminal assaults on [white] females."

What do these cases have in common? First, the rhetoric of sexual assault and the measures used to prevent it had virtually no correlation with actual incidences of rape of European women by men of color. Just the contrary: there was often no ex post facto evidence, nor any at the time, that rapes were committed or that rape attempts were made. Moreover, the rape laws were race specific; sexual abuse of black women was not classified as rape and therefore was not legally actionable, nor did rapes committed by white men lead to prosecution. If these accusations of sexual threat were not prompted by the fact of rape, what did they signal and to what were they tied?

Allusions to political and sexual subversion of the colonial system went hand in hand. The term "Black Peril" referred to sexual threats, but it also connoted the fear of insurgence, of some perceived nonacquiescence to colonial control more generally. Concern over protection of white women intensified during real and perceived crises of control—provoked by threats to the internal cohesion of the European communities or by infringements on its borders. Thus colonial accounts of the Mutiny in India in 1857 are full of descriptions of the sexual mutilation of British women by Indian men despite the fact that no rapes were recorded. In New Guinea, the White Women's Protection Ordinance followed a large influx of acculturated Papuans into Port Moresby in the 1920s. Resistant to the constraints imposed on their dress, movement, and education, whites perceived them as arrogant, "cheeky," and without respect. In post– World War I Algeria, the political unease of *pieds noirs* (local French settlers) in the face of "a whole new series of [Muslim] demands" manifested itself in a popular culture newly infused with strong images of sexually aggressive Algerian men.

Second, rape charges against colonized men were often based on perceived transgressions of social space. "Attempted rapes" turned out to be "incidents" of a Papuan man "discovered" in the vicinity of a white residence, a Fijian man who entered a European patient's room, a male servant poised at the bedroom of a European woman asleep or in half-dress. With such a broad definition of danger in a culture of fear, all colonized men of color were threatening as sexual and political aggressors.

Third, accusations of sexual assault frequently followed upon heightened tensions within European communities—and renewed efforts to find consensus within them. Rape accusations in South Africa, for example, coincided with a rash of strikes between 1890 and 1914 by both African and white miners. As in Rhodesia after a strike by white railway employees in 1929, the threat of native rebellion brought together conflicting members of the European community in common cause where "solidarity found sustenance in the threat of racial destruction."

During the late 1920s, when labor protests by Indonesia workers and European employees were most intense, Sumatra's corporate elite expanded their vigilante organizations, intelligence networks, and demands for police protection to ensure their women were safe and their workers "in hand."

In Sumatra's plantation belt, subsidized sponsorship of married couples replaced the recruitment of single Indonesian workers and European staff, with new incentives provided for family housing and *gezinvorming* ("family formation") in both groups. This recomposed labor force of family men in "stable households" explicitly weeded out politically "undesirable elements" and the socially malcontent. With the marriage restriction finally lifted for European staff in the 1920s, young men sought wives among Dutch-born women while on leave in Holland or through marriage brokers by mail. Higher salaries, upgraded housing, elevated bonuses, and a more mediated chain of command between colonized fieldworker and colonial staff served to clarify both national and racial affinities and to differentiate the further political interests of European from Asian workers.

The remedies searched for to alleviate sexual danger were sought in new prescriptions for securing white control; increased surveillance of native men, new laws stipulating severe corporeal punishment for the transgression of sexual and social boundaries, and the creation of areas made racially off-limits. These went with a moral rearmament of the European community and reassertions of its cultural identity. Charged with guarding cultural norms, European women were instrumental in promoting white solidarity. It was partly at their own expense, as they were to be nearly as closely policed as colonized men.

Policing European Women and Concessions to Chivalry

Although native men were the ones legally punished for alleged sexual assaults, European women were frequently blamed for provoking those desires. New arrivals from Europe were accused of being too familiar with their servants, lax in their commands, indecorous in their speech and in their dress. In Papua New Guinea, "everyone" in the Australian community agreed that rape assaults were caused by a "younger generation of white women" unschooled in the proper treatment of servants. In Rhodesia as in Uganda, sexual anxieties persisted in the absence of any incidents and restricted women to activities within the European enclaves. The immorality act of 1916 "made it an offense for a white woman to make an indecent suggestion to a male native." As in the American South, "the etiquette of chivalry controlled white women's behavior even as [it] guarded caste lines." A defense of community, morality, and white male power was achieved by increasing control over and consensus among Europeans, by reaffirming the vulnerability of white women and the sexual threat posed by native men, and by creating new sanctions to limit the liberties of both.

European colonial communities in the early twentieth century assiduously controlled the movements of European women, and, where possible, imposed on them restricted and protected roles. This is not to say that European women did not work; some openly questioned the sexist policies of their male superiors. However, by and large their tasks buttressed rather than contested the established racial order.

Particularly in the colonies with small European communities as opposed to those of large-scale settlement, there were few opportunities for women to be economically independent or to act politically on their own. The "revolt against chivalry"—the protest of American Southern white women to lynchings of black men for alleged rape attempts—had no counterpart among European women in Asia and Africa. Firmly rejecting expansion based on the "poor white" (petit blanc) Algerian model, French officials in Indochina dissuaded *colons* with insufficient capital from entry and promptly repatriated those who tried to remain. Single women were seen as the quintessential petits blancs; with limited resources and shopkeeper aspirations, they presented the dangerous possibility that straitened circumstances would lead them to prostitution, thereby degrading European prestige at large.

Professional competence did not leave single European women immune from marginalization. Single professional women were held in contempt as were European prostitutes, with surprisingly similar objections. White prostitutes threatened prestige, while professional women needed protection; both fell outside the social space to which European colonial women were assigned—namely, as custodians of family welfare and respectability, and as dedicated and willing subordinates to, and supporters of, colonial men. . . .

CONCLUSION

I have focused here on the multiple levels at which sexual control figured in the substance, as well as the iconography, of racial policy and imperial rule. But colonial politics was not just about sex; nor did sexual relations reduce to colonial politics. On the contrary, sex in the colonies was about sexual access and reproduction, class distinctions and racial demarcations, nationalism and European identity—in different measure and not at all at the same time. These major shifts in the positioning of women were not, as we might expect, signaled by the penetration of capitalism per se but by more subtle changes in class politics, imperial morality, and as responses to the vulnerabilities of colonial control. European culture and class politics resonated in colonial settings; class and gender discriminations were transposed into racial distinctions and reverberated in the metropole as they were fortified on colonial ground. Sexual control was both an instrumental image for the body politic, a salient part standing for the whole, and itself fundamental to how racial politics were secured and how colonial projects were carried out.

Study Questions

1. In this excerpt from her intersectional analysis of sexual control in colonial Asia, Stoler argues that sexual control was "foundational to how racial politics were secured and how colonial projects were carried out." What does she mean by this?

2. In your opinion, is this article an example of feminist theory? Postcolonial theory? Both? What ought the relationship be between these types of theorizing?

NEO-MATERIALIST THEORY

Iris M. Young

Socialist Feminism and the Limits of Dual Systems Theory

Socialist feminist theory is perhaps the most vital and profound development in contemporary Marxist theory and is also central to advances in feminist social theory.[1] This growing body of theoretical and analytical literature locates itself in the tradition of Marxism, but agrees with the radical feminist claim

Iris M. Young, "Socialist Feminism and the Limits of Dual Systems Theory," The Socialist Review 50.51 (1980): 169–188. Copyright 1980 by *The Socialist Review*. Reproduced with permission of *The Socialist Review* in the format Textbook via Copyright Clearance Center. Notes have been renumbered and edited.

that traditional Marxian theory cannot adequately comprehend the bases, structure, dynamic, and detail of women's oppression. It thus seeks to supplement the Marxian theory of class society with at least elements of the radical feminist analysis of sexist society.

The predominant manner of accomplishing this synthesis of Marxism and radical feminism has been through what I call the "dual systems theory." Stated briefly, for I will define it at more length in what follows, the dual systems theory says that women's oppression arises from two distinct and relatively autonomous systems. The system of male domination, most often called "patriarchy," produces the specific gender oppression of women; the system of the mode of production and class relations produces the class oppression and work alienation of most women. Patriarchy "interacts" with the system of the mode of production—in our case, capitalism—to produce the concrete phenomena of women's oppression in society.

As one committed to the project of incorporating many radical feminist insights into a theory of women's situation within the tradition of Marxism, I used to accept the dual systems theory. Recently, however, it has begun to seem inadequate. In this paper I express some of my discomfort with the dual systems theory by raising some theoretical and practical questions about it.

My primary motive in raising these critical questions is political: I wish to see the political principles of socialist feminism furthered. By socialist feminist politics I mean the following: a socialist movement must pay attention to women's issues and support the autonomous organization of women in order to succeed, and all socialist organizing should be conducted with a feminist consciousness; and feminist struggle and organizing should be anticapitalist in its thrust and should make explicit connections between the oppression of women and other forms of oppression. The dual systems theory is a better basis for these principles than any other existing theory of women's situation under capitalism, but I have begun to think that it does not serve well enough and that it even fosters analyses and practices contrary to those principles.

THE ORIGINS OF DUAL SYSTEMS THEORY

The feminist break with the new left and the resulting contemporary women's movement stand as perhaps the most revolutionary and lasting effect of the movements of the 1960s. Quickly these new-wave feminists, who called themselves radical feminists, began developing questions, categories, and analyses that broke wholly new ground and irrevocably altered the perceptions of most progressive people. For the first time we had systematic accounts of such unspeakable phenomena as rape and heterosexism. Those identifying themselves as radical feminists continue to develop their analyses with extraordinary insight.

Like the feminist politics and movement that began by distinguishing itself from the radical left, many of the early theoretical works of radical feminism, such as Firestone's *Dialectic of Sex* and Millett's *Sexual Politics*, began from a confrontation with Marxism. We do not need to summarize the details of the arguments they developed. They concluded that Marxism failed as a theory of history and a theory of oppression because it did not account for the origins, structure, and dynamic of male domination and failed to recognize sex oppression as the most fundamental oppression. Radical feminism thus rejected Marxian theory as a basis for understanding women's oppression and rejected the socialist movement as a viable means of organizing to alter the social structure.

Some feminist women, however, acknowledged the radical feminist criticisms of the socialist movement but did not wish to separate from that movement entirely. Believing that eliminating capitalist economic institutions would not itself liberate women, these emerging socialist feminists nevertheless found this a necessary condition for that liberation. The socialist feminists agreed with the radical feminist claim that traditional Marxian theory cannot articulate the origins and structure of sex oppression in a way that accounts for the presence of this oppression as a pervasive and fundamental element of most societies. But they did not wish thereby to reject entirely the Marxist theory of history or critique of capitalism.

Accepting and rejecting elements of both radical feminism and Marxist socialism, the socialist feminists found themselves with a political and a theoretical problem. The political problem was how to participate in a movement for socialism without sacrificing feminist autonomy and without forfeiting feminist criticism of socialists. Socialist feminist politics has also had to grapple with how to orient feminist organizing and self-help projects in such a way that they recognize the particular oppressions of race and poverty, and promote critique of capitalist institutions.

The theoretical problem socialist feminists face is how to synthesize Marxian theory and radical feminist theory into a viable theory of social reality in general and of women's oppression in particular. The solution to this problem emerged as the dual systems theory. One of the earliest statements of the dual systems theory is Linda Phelps's "Patriarchy and Capitalism." In discussing women's situation in contemporary society, she claims that we must talk of two distinct systems of social relations: patriarchy and capitalism.

> If sexism is a social relationship in which males have authority over females, *patriarchy* is a term which describes the whole system of interaction which arises from that basic relationship, just as capitalism is a system built on the relationship between capitalist and worker. Patriarchal and capitalist social relationships are two markedly different ways that human beings have interacted with each other and have built social, political and economic institutions.[2]

According to Phelps, patriarchy and capitalism constitute distinct systems of oppression because the principles of authority differ and because they have distinct histories. Capitalism and patriarchy, moreover, contradict as well as reinforce each other as they interact in contemporary society.

More recently, Zillah Eisenstein has attempted to articulate in a more complex fashion this relation between the dual systems of capitalism and patriarchy. In her formulation, a mode of production (e.g., capitalism) and patriarchy are distinct systems in their structures but nevertheless support each other.

> This statement of the mutual dependence of patriarchy and capitalism not only assumes the malleability of patriarchy to the needs of capital, but assumes the malleability of capital to the needs of patriarchy. When one states that capitalism needs patriarchy in order to operate efficiently one is really noting that male supremacy, as a system of sexual hierarchy, supplies capitalism (and systems previous to it) with the necessary order and control. . . . To the extent that the concern with profit and the concern with societal control are inextricably connected (but cannot be reduced to each other), patriarchy and capitalism become an integral process; specific elements of each system are necessitated by the other.[3]

Other dual systems theorists claim a less harmonious relationship between capitalism and patriarchy. Heidi Hartmann, for example, claims that at times during the history of modern society the interests of the system of patriarchy have struggled against the interests of the system of capitalism and that the patriarchal interests have won out.[4]

I have been referring to "the" dual systems theory not in order to designate one unified body of theory, but to refer to a general *type* of theoretical approach. Those who subscribe to a dual systems approach to understanding women's oppression differ significantly in the categories they use and in their particular formulations of the dual systems account. The two systems are not always called "patriarchy" and "capitalism." The terms "mode of production" and "mode of reproduction" frequently designate the two types of system.[5] Gayle Rubin criticizes both "patriarchy" and "reproduction" as terms to designate the system of male domination. She prefers the term "sex/gender system" as a neutral category that can stand as the analogue in the realm of sex power to the system of production in the realm of class power.[6] Among the other categories that have been proposed to designate the system underlying male domination, as distinct from the mode of production, are "sex/affective production"[7] and the "relations of procreation."[8]

Development of the dual systems approach has fostered major theoretical, analytical, and practical advances over traditional Marxist treatments of "the women question" and has contributed to a revitalization of Marxist method. Socialist feminist analyses springing from the dual systems approach have examined in detail the relationship of women's specific oppression to capitalist institutions in a way that otherwise might not have occurred. The dual systems theory has directed the attention of socialists to phenomena in capitalist society that lie beyond the production process, but nevertheless are central for understanding the contemporary economy and ideology—such as family relations, advertising and sexual objectification, consumer culture, and so on.

As the first attempt to synthesize Marxism and radical feminisn, the dual systems theory has been a crucial theoretical development, and I do not wish to belittle its contribution. I suspect, however, that it may now be holding socialist feminists back from developing further theoretical insights and practical strategies. In what follows I shall argue that the dual systems theory has not succeeded in confronting and revising traditional Marxist theory enough, because it allows Marxism to retain in basically unchanged form its theory of economic and social relations, on to which it merely grafts a theory of gender relations.

IDEOLOGICAL AND PSYCHOLOGICAL APPROACHES

There are numerous variations in dual-systems accounts. Some develop more important insights than others. In this essay I do not wish to review the work of all the major dual systems theorists. In criticizing the dual systems approach I will be reconstructing what I see as the basic form of those accounts. Where I refer to specific works, I am using them as examples of a general approach.

All dual systems accounts begin from the premise that the system of male domination is structurally independent of the relations of production described by Marxian theory. Given this assumption, the dual systems theorists must specify the independent origins and structure of the system(s) of gender relations and articulate their relation to the system(s) of production relations. In my reading I have seen two general approaches to articulating the nature of the

system of gender relations. The first understands the system of patriarchy as an ideological and psychological structure independent of specific social, economic, and historical relations. This version of the dual systems theory then attempts to give an account of the interaction of the ideological and psychological structures of patriarchy with the social and economic structures of class society. The second version of the dual systems theory considers patriarchy itself to be a particular system of social relations of production (or "reproduction") relatively independent of the relations of production that Marxists traditionally analyze. Some dual systems theorists, such as Rubin, combine both versions of the dual systems theory, but most writers tend toward one or the other.

Juliet Mitchell's approach in *Psychoanalysis and Feminism* is an example of the first, ideological-psychological version, as indeed are most theories that rely on Freudian theory as the basis of a theory of male domination.[9] Mitchell clearly states the autonomy of the systems of patriarchy and capitalism, one being ideological and the other material.

> Though, of course, ideology and the given mode of production are interdependent, one cannot be reduced to the other nor can the same laws be found to govern the other. To put the matter schematically, in analyzing contemporary Western society we are (as elsewhere) dealing with two autonomous areas: the economic mode of capitalism and the ideological mode of patriarchy.[10]

Mitchell understands patriarchy as a universal and formal structure of kinship patterning and psychic development that interacts with the particular structure of a mode of production.

> Men enter into the class-dominated structures of history while women (as women, whatever their work in actual production) remain defined by the kinship pattern of organization. Differences of class, historical epoch, specific social situation alter the expression of femininity; but in relation to the law of the father, women's position across the board is a comparable one.[11]

In this account, the patriarchal structures that Freudian theory articulates exist as a pre- or nonhistorical ideological backdrop to transformations in social and economic relations of the mode of production. This ideological and psychological structure lying outside economic relations persists in the same form throughout them. Mitchell does not wish to deny, of course, that the concrete situation of women differs in varying social circumstances. She accounts for this variation in women's situation by the way in which particular structures of a given mode of production intersect with the universal structures of patriarchy.

This version of the dual systems theory inappropriately dehistoricizes and universalizes women's oppression. It may be true that in all male-dominated societies there are common elements to the situation of women and the social relations in which they stand. Relations having to do with children are not least of these. Such elements, however, by no means exhaust the distinctiveness of women's situation. It is absurd to suggest, as does Mitchell, that women as women stand outside history. Women participate in the social relations of production, as well as most other social relations, in *gender-specific* ways that vary enormously in form and content from one society or epoch to another. Describing such differences in the specific characteristics of sexist oppression as merely "expressions" of one and the same universal system of male domination trivializes the depth and complexity of women's oppression.

There are certain practical dangers, moreover, in representing male domination as universal in form. On the one hand, it tends to create a false optimism regarding the possibility of a common consciousness among women. This can lead to serious cultural, ethnic, racial, and class biases in the account of the allegedly common structures of patriarchy.[12] On the other hand, the notion of a single system of patriarchy that persists in basically unchanged form through different epochs paralyzes feminist action because it represents the beast we are struggling against as so ancient and monolithic.

The main problem with this version of the dual systems theory, however, is that it does not in fact succeed in giving the alleged system of patriarchy equal weight with and independence from the system of production. It conceives of all concrete social relations as belonging to the economic system of production. Thus it gives no material weight to the system of patriarchy, which it defines in its basic structure as independent of the mode and relations of production, the social relations that proceed from them, and the processes of historical change. Thus this version of the dual systems theory ends by ceding to the traditional theory of production relations the primary role in giving an account of women's concrete situation. The theory of patriarchy supplies the *form* of women's oppression, but traditional Marxist theory supplies its content, specificity, and motors of change. Thus this version of the dual systems theory fails to challenge traditional Marxism because it cedes to that Marxism theoretical hegemony over historically material social relations.[13]

This version of the dual systems theory tends to identify gender differentiation with male domination. Gender is a culturally produced psychological structure that also expresses itself in images, symbols, and ideologies. Thus far the feminist appropriation of psychoanalysis in the work of such thinkers as Mitchell, Rubin, Chodorow, and Dinnerstein[14] represents the best theory of the origins and structure of gender that we have. Without doubt any account of the situation and oppression of women must contain such a gender theory as an element. But gender theory in itself cannot explain how men in a particular society occupy an *institutionalized* position of superiority and privilege. For men can occupy and maintain such an institutionalized position of superiority only if the organization of social and economic relations gives them a level of control over and access to resources that women do not have. However important an ideological-psychological account of gender identity and symbolization may be for a theory of women's oppression, it is not sufficient. A feminist theory must account for male domination as structured in a set of specific, though variable, social and economic relations, with specific material effects on the relations of men and women.[15] Feminism cannot allow gender-blind traditional Marxism to have the last word on the structure and movement of social relations of labor and other social relations.

PATRIARCHY AS
A SOCIAL STRUCTURE

A number of dual systems theorists have recognized these weaknesses in the first version of the dual systems theory and thus have sought to develop an account of patriarchy as a system distinct from capitalism, yet based in a set of specific social relations. Heidi Hartmann, for example, maintains that patriarchy is a set of social relations with a material base that lies in men's control over women's labor and in women's exclusion from access to essential productive resources.[16] She clearly subscribes to the dual systems approach: patriarchy should be understood as a system of domination distinct from capitalism, with its own "laws of motion." It is not clear, however, how one can maintain both these positions. In order to succeed in separating capitalism and patriarchy, this social-structural version of the dual systems theory requires articulating a structure by which we can isolate the social relations of production belonging to patriarchy from those belonging to capitalism. Hartmann's account does not develop such a structure of social relations, however, and she even admits that it is difficult to isolate structures specific to patriarchy.[17]

Dual systems theorists commonly tackle this problem of isolating the material relations specific to patriarchy by positing what Rosalind Petchesky has called the "model of separate spheres."[18] In this model women and men historically have had their primary places in separate spheres of production, from which arise distinct relations of production. Almost invariably this model poses the family as the locus of the women's productive sphere and social relations outside the family as the locus of men's. The model of separate spheres seems to provide us with the distinct structures and histories that the dual systems theory requires. The history of patriarchy will be constituted in the history of relations in the "domestic" sphere, while the history of class society will be constituted in the "public" sphere, on which traditional Marxism focuses.

Ann Ferguson, for example, argues that women are the exploited workers in the distinct sphere of production that she calls sex/affective production, a type of production distinct from the production of material goods. This type of production, like the production of material goods, goes through different historical states, or modes of production. In contemporary society the mode of sex/affective production is the nuclear family. Inside the family women produce sex/affective goods that their husbands appropriate, and hence women in contemporary society constitute an exploited class in the strict Marxian sense.[19] Those socialist feminists who regard the family under capitalism as a vestige of the feudal mode of production also hold that women's situation is structured by the interaction of two modes of production,[20] as do those who wish to distinguish a "mode of reproduction" from mode of production.[21]

The model of separate spheres appears to hypostasize a separation peculiar to capitalism—that between family and work—into a universal form. In all precapitalist societies, the family is the primary unit of production, and kinship relations are a powerful determinant of economic relations. Separation of productive activity from the household and kinship relations, and the creation of two spheres of social life, is one of the defining characteristics of capitalist society itself, as a number of writers have pointed out.[22] Projecting this separation onto the structure of all societies—or at least all male-dominated class societies—cannot but obscure crucial differences between precapitalist and capitalist societies with respect to the situation of women.

Precisely because the separation of domestic from economic life is peculiar to capitalism, use of that separation as the basis for the analysis of women's situation in contemporary society may be playing right into the hands of bourgeois ideology. Bourgeois ideology itself promoted and continues to promote the identification of women with the home, domesticity, affective relations, and "nonproductive" activity, and defines these as structurally distinct from the "public" world of "real" economic life. For this reason socialist feminists should be suspicious of this identification of women's situation with a distinct sphere of private domestic relations, and above all should be wary of utilizing such an identification as a basis of their own analytic framework.

We should also ask whether the separation itself does not obscure a more basic integration. A number of analyses have emphasized the degree to which the alleged separation of the domestic and affective sphere from the economic sphere is ultimately illusory. Weinbaum and Bridges, for example, argue quite persuasively that contemporary capitalism not only has rationalized and socialized production operations in accordance with its domination and profit needs, but has rationalized and socialized the allegedly private work of consumption as well.[23] Other theorists, such as Marcuse, suggest that contemporary capitalism has actually entered into and rationalized sexual and affective relations for its own ends.[24]

The main problem with the model of separate spheres, however, is that because it assumes the family as the primary sphere of patriarchal relations, it fails to bring into focus the character of women's specific oppression as women outside the family. For example, it is difficult to view the use of women as sexual symbols to promote consumption as a function of some separate sphere distinct from the economic requirements of monopoly capitalism. When more than half of women over sixteen are working outside as well as inside the home, the model of separate spheres, and the focus on domestic life that it encourages, may divert attention from a capitalism that increasingly exploits women in gender-specific paid work.

The character of women's oppression in the contemporary workplace has specifically sexist forms that cannot be encompassed by traditional accounts of relations of production. For example, sexual harassment is a routine way that superiors discipline women workers. More broadly, in contemporary society not only images of "sexy" women foster capitalist accumulation, but also real live women are employed for their "sexual" labor—for being sexy on their jobs, suggesting sexiness to customers, and performing many jobs whose main function is being sexy in one way or another. The dual systems theory does not seem to have the theoretical equipment to comprehend these diverse kinds of sexist oppression outside the family and personal sphere.

The only means the dual systems theory has for doing so is to view gender-structured phenomena of the capitalist economy and workplace as modeled on or effects of relations in the family, and this in fact is the strategy for explanation adopted by many dual systems theorists. Admitting and trying to explain the pervasiveness of gender structuration in all spheres of contemporary society, however, seriously weakens the model of separate spheres on which the explanation of that gender structuration is based in the dual systems theory. It would be much more direct to construct a theory of capitalist patriarchy as a unified system entailing specific forms of gender structuring in its production relations and ideology.

Viewing gender phenomena of the contemporary capitalist workplace as modeled on or effects of family relations, moreover, still tends to play down the specific oppression of women outside family life and to give inordinate emphasis to the family. It also misses the specific character of the sexist oppression of the workplace and other realms outside the family. Patriarchal oppression outside family life in contemporary society depends on impersonal, routinized, and generalized behavior as opposed to the personal relations of oppression that characterize the patriarchal family.

My criticisms of the dual systems approach to socialist feminist theorizing ultimately issue in the claim that dual systems theory does not go far enough. The dual systems approach accepts the traditional Marxian theory of production relations, historical change, and analysis of the structure of capitalism in basically unchanged form. It rightly criticizes that theory for being essentially gender-blind, and hence seeks to supplement Marxist theory of capitalism with feminist theory of a system of male domination. Taking this route, however, tacitly endorses the traditional Marxian position that "the woman question" is auxiliary to the central questions of a Marxian theory of society.

The dual systems theory, that is, declines from confronting Marxism *directly* in its failure to take account of the situation and oppression of women. Our nascent historical research coupled with our feminist intuition tells us that the labor of women occupies a central place in any system of production, that gender division is a basic axis of social structuration in all hitherto existing social formations, and that gender hierarchy serves as a pivotal element in most systems of social domination. If traditional Marxism has no theoretical place for such hypotheses, it is not merely an inadequate theory of women's oppression, but also an inadequate theory of social relations, relations of production, and domination. *We need not merely a synthesis of feminism with traditional Marxism, but also a thoroughly feminist historical materialism, which regards the social relations of a particular historical social formation as one system in which gender differentiation is a core attribute.*

DUAL SYSTEMS THEORY AND POLITICS

Socialist feminists insist that no political program or political activity is truly socialist unless it attends to the unique situation and oppression of women. Likewise, socialist feminists insist that feminist analyses and political activity should always look for ways of exposing the class- and race-differentiated character of patriarchal oppression, as well as its internal connection with the dynamic of profit. For example, in the sphere of reproductive rights, socialist feminists have emphasized the racist character of sterilization abuse and recent attacks on abortion rights. They have also taken pains to expose the interests of the medical establishment and drug companies in keeping women ignorant of our bodies and dependent on expensive and often dangerous means of birth control, birthing, and "curing" menopause.

Precisely what distinguishes the politics of socialist feminism is this commitment to the practical unity of the struggle against capitalism and the struggle for women's liberation. The dual systems theory, however, can tend to sever this practical unity, which socialist feminism has been trying to achieve since its inception. Thus the politics of socialist feminism would be better served by a theory of capitalist society that explicitly incorporated gender differentiation

into its structural analysis, and hence took the oppression of women as a core aspect of the system.

Some socialist feminists might fear that such a "one system" theory would undermine arguments for the necessity of an autonomous women's movement, for a cornerstone of socialist feminist politics has been its conviction that women should be organized autonomously in groups in which they alone have decision-making power. Women must have the space to develop positive relations with each other, apart from men, and we can best learn to develop our own organizing, decision-making, speaking, and writing skills in an environment free of male dominance or paternalism. Only by being separately organized can feminist women confront the sexism of socialist men. And only in an autonomous women's movement can socialist women unify with women who see the need for struggle against male domination but do not see that struggle as integrated with an anticapitalist struggle.

The dual systems theory arose at least in part from this socialist feminist recognition of the strategic necessity of a women's movement allied with but autonomous from the mixed socialist movement. If capitalism and patriarchy are each distinct systems, mutually influencing but nevertheless ultimately separate and irreducible, it follows most plausibly that the struggle against patriarchy should be organizationally distinct from the struggle against capitalism.

I am convinced of the necessity of separately organizing women around issues relating to our own situation. Without such an autonomous women's movement the socialist movement itself cannot survive and grow. One can argue for the strategic necessity of such an autonomous women's movement, however, without postulating male domination and capitalist domination as distinct social systems. One only need appeal to the indisputable practical realities that capitalist patriarchal society structures the lives of women in special ways and that these capitalist patriarchal structures give to most men relative privilege and power. From this analysis it does not follow that there are two distinct systems of social relations. The dual systems theory can have the damaging effect of justifying a segregation of feminist concerns to the women's movement. This segregation means that socialists outside the women's movement need not take feminism seriously, and those who work in that movement must justify how their political work relates to socialism.

Because it does not confront traditional Marxian theory directly enough as a theory of social relations and oppression, the dual systems theory allows many socialists not to take feminism as seriously as they should. It can tend to justify the dismissal of feminist organizing by socialists not persuaded of the centrality of women's oppression to contemporary capitalism, and it can tend to justify their not bringing issues of women's oppression to the fore in their own practice. To be sure, the failure of many socialists to take feminist concerns seriously as socialist concerns reflects a political tension that no theory will alone heal. Nevertheless, confinement of feminist concerns to the periphery of socialist organizing would be more difficult for nonfeminist socialists to justify if socialist feminists confronted them with a theory of capitalist society that showed that society to be patriarchal in its essence and internal structure.

The necessity for all socialist work to have a feminist dimension and for socialists in the mixed left to take seriously issues surrounding women's oppression becomes most pressing under contemporary conditions. The new right does not appear to separate capitalism and patriarchy into distinct systems. Those attacking women's and gay rights ally unambiguously with those attacking unions or those promoting increased armaments. The new right has a total platform, the main plank of which is defense of the sanctity of the monogamous heterosexual many-children family. With a theory of capitalist patriarchy that showed its relations of labor and hierarchy as one gender-structured system in which the oppression of women is a core element, socialist feminists would be in a better position to argue and enact this practical necessity.

Because the mixed left does not take feminism as seriously as it should, many socialists who choose to concentrate all their energy on women's issues feel called upon, and often enough are called upon, implicitly or explicitly, to justify the socialist character of their work. On the other hand, not all socialists

with strong feminist commitments wish to devote their political energies to specifically women's issues, nor should they. They then often are called upon to demonstrate the feminist meaning of their work. As a result of these tensions, many socialist feminists feel as though they ought to do twice as much work— socialist work on the one hand, and feminist work on the other. As long as we define patriarchy as a system ultimately distinct from capitalism, this practical tension appears necessary.

This "double shift" syndrome, of course, cannot be overcome by theory alone. Socialist women who choose to devote all their energies to separately organizing women around women's issues, however, should have the full active support and recognition of a socialist movement that perceives such work as in itself vital political work. Within the mixed left, moreover, feminist consciousness should be so incorporated that one could justifiably understand oneself as engaging in feminist work on issues not immediately concerning women's situation. We are a long way from that situation today. A major reason for this, I claim, is lack of a theory of capitalist society that would foster analyses revealing the patriarchal meaning of nearly every aspect of society.

I have been concentrating most of my argument here on the claim that all socialist political work should be feminist in its thrust and that socialists should recognize feminist concerns as internal to their own. Likewise, socialist feminists take as a basic principle that feminist work should be anticapitalist in its thrust and should link women's situation with the phenomena of racism and imperialism. Once again, this political principle would best be served by a social theory that regards these phenomena as aspects of a single system of social relations. With such a theory we would be in a better position to argue to other feminists that they must attend to issues of class and race in their analysis and organizing.

TOWARD A UNIFIED THEORY

I am not prepared here to offer even the outlines of such a theory. In concluding I will merely offer some of the general elements I believe such a theory should contain and some of the basic issues it should address.

A feminist historical materialism must be a total social theory, not merely a theory of the situation and oppression of women. That theory will take gender differentiation as its basic starting point, in the sense that it will seek always to keep the fact of gender difference in the center of its accounts and will reject any account that obscures gender-differentiated phenomena. It will take gender statuses, gender hierarchy and domination, changes in gender relations, gender ideologies, etc., as central aspects of any social formation. These must be analyzed in any account of a social formation, and other aspects of the social formation must be linked to them.

Following the lead of the early radical feminists, a feminist historical materialism must explore the hypothesis that class domination arises from and/or is intimately tied to patriarchal domination. We cannot simply assume that sex domination causes class society, as most radical feminists have done. But we must take seriously the question of whether there is a causal relation here, to what extent there is, and precisely how the causal relations operate if and when they exist.

A feminist historical materialism must be a truly *materialist* theory. This does not mean that it must "reduce" all social phenomena to economic phenomena, narrowly understood as processes of the production and distribution of material goods. Following Delphy and Williams, among others, I understand a materialist account as one that considers phenomena of "consciousness"—e.g., intellectual production, broad social attitudes and beliefs, cultural myths, symbols, images, etc.—as rooted in real social relationships.[25] This should not imply "reducing" such phenomena of consciousness to social structures and social relationships, nor does it even mean that the phenomena of consciousness cannot be treated as having a logic of their own. Nor should it mean that phenomena like attitudes and cultural definitions cannot enter as elements into the explanation of a particular structure of social relationships, though I would claim they can never be the sole explanation. This requirement mainly calls for a methodological priority to concrete social institutions and practices, along with the material conditions in which they take place.

The concrete social relations of gender and the relations in which these stand to other types of interaction and domination must appear at the core of the theory. In another paper I have suggested that a feminist historical materialism might utilize gender division of labor as a central category. This category would refer to all structured gender differentiation of laboring activity in a particular society, where "labor" includes any task or activity that the society defines as necessary.[26] Whether or not this is the correct approach, a feminist historical materialism should remain Marxist in the sense that it takes the structure of laboring activity and the relations arising from laboring activity, broadly defined, as a crucial determinant of social phenomena. Accepting that Marxist premise, it must also find a way of analyzing social relations arising from laboring activity in gender-differentiated terms.

Finally, a feminist historical materialism must be thoroughly *historical*. It must eschew any explanations that claim to apply to societies across epochs. In practice this means that a feminist historical materialism must be suspicious of any claims to universality regarding any aspect of women's situation. If there exist any circumstances common to the situation of all women, these must be discovered empirically, not presupposed. We must develop a theory that can articulate and appreciate the vast differences in the situation, structure, and experience of gender relations in different times and places. At the same time, however, we want a single theory that can be utilized to analyze vastly different social structures. This means we need a set of basic categories that can be applied to differing social circumstances in such a way that their specificity remains and yet comparison is possible. In addition to such a set of categories we need a theoretical method that will guide us in our explanation of the particular phenomena in a particular society.

The remarks in this section have been very abstract. I intend only to outline some general directions for moving toward a feminist social theory in which the basic insights of Marxism can be absorbed and developed. Whether the above criteria for a socialist-feminist theory are correct can be decided only by embarking on the theoretical task in light of our practical needs.

NOTES

I am grateful to Heidi Hartmann, Nancy Hartsock, Ruth Milkman, Sandra Bartky, and Alison Jaggar for their comments and criticisms on earlier versions of this paper.

1. I say feminist social theory, not all feminist theory, for I think that current works of radical feminism, like Daly's *Gyn/Ecology* (Boston: Beacon Press, 1978), make profound and in some cases unparalleled contributions to theory and analysis of cultural symbols and patriarchal mythology.

2. Linda Phelps, "Patriarchy and Capitalism," *Quest*, vol. 2 no. 2 (Fall 1975), p. 39.

3. Zillah Eisenstein, "Developing a Theory of Capitalist Patriarchy," in Eisenstein, ed., *Capitalist Patriarchy and the Case for Socialist Feminisn* (New York: Monthly Review Press, 1979), p. 27.

4. See Heidi Hartmann, "The Unhappy Marriage of Marxism and Feminism: Toward a More Progressive Union," in Lydia Sargent, ed., *Women and Revolution* (Boston: South End Press, 1980); this paper, which was originally coauthored with Amy Bridges, has received wide distribution among socialist feminists. . . . On similar points see also Hartmann's paper "Capitalism, Patriarchy, and Job Segregation by Sex," in Eisenstein, ed., *Capitalist Patriarchy*.

5. See, for example, Jane Flax, "Do Feminists Need Marxism?", *Quest*, vol. 3, no. 1 (Summer 1976), p. 55.

6. Gayle Rubin, "The Traffic in Women: Notes on the Political Economy of Sex," in Rayna Reiter, ed., *Toward an Anthropology of Women* (New York: Monthly Review Press, 1976), p. 167.

7. Ann Ferguson, "Women as a New Revolutionary Class," in Pat Walker, ed., *Between Labor and Capital* (Boston: South End Press, 1979), pp. 279–312.

8. Alison Jaggar develops this term in *Feminist Politics and Human Nature* (Totowa, N.J.: Rowman and Allenheld, 1983).

9. Compare Flax's approach in her "Do Feminists Need Marxism?"

10. Juliet Mitchell, *Psychoanalysis and Feminism* (New York: Vintage Books, 1974), p. 409.

11. Mitchell, p. 409.

12. See Mina Davis Caulfield, "Universal Sex Oppression?—A Critique from Marxist Anthropology," *Catalyst*, nos. 10–11 (Summer 1977), pp. 60–77. She points to some consequences of cultural bias that result from the assumption of a universal and common sex oppression, specifically with respect to the way we regard Third World women. I have articulated in another place some contrary attributes of sexism as experienced by black women and white women in America; see "Proposals for Socialist Feminist Theory," in *Women Organizing*, publication of the Socialist Feminist Commission of the New American Movement, no. 2 (June 1978). Eisenstein, in "Developing a Theory," does a good job of laying out the variables that differently structure the lives of different groups of women in such a way that it is not possible to speak of a common situation.

13. Compare McDonough and Harrison's criticism of Mitchell in "Patriarchy and Relations of Production," in Kuhn and Wolpe, eds., *Feminism and Materialism* (London: Routledge and Kegan Paul, 1978), pp. 12–25.

14. In addition to Mitchell and Rubin, already cited, see Nancy Chodorow, *The Reproduction of Mothering* (Berkeley: University of California Press, 1978), and Dorothy Dinnerstein, *The Mermaid and the Minotaur* (New York: Harper and Row, 1976).

15. This is similar to a point that Christine Delphy makes in her paper "For a Feminist Materialism," in *Close to Home: A Materialist Analysis of Women's Oppression* (Amherst: University of Massachusetts Press, 1984), pp. 211–19. She takes a strong stand against all psychological reductionism that would explain social structures and social relations in psychological terms.

16. Hartmann, "Unhappy Marriage."

17. Hartmann, 1978 manuscript, pp. 38–39.

18. Rosalind Petchesky, "Dissolving the Hyphen: A Report on Marxist-Feminist Groups 1–5," in Eisenstein, *Capitalist Patriarchy*, pp. 373–90.

19. Ferguson, pp. 279–312.

20. This is basically Mitchell's position in *Women's Estate* (New York: Vintage Books, 1973); see also Sheila Rowbotham, *Women's Consciousness, Man's World* (Middlesex: Penguin Books, 1973), pp. 61–63.

21. Flax, "Do Feminists Need Marxism?"

22. See Eli Zaretsky, *Capitalism, the Family, and Personal Life* (New York: Harper and Row, 1976); Ann Oakley, *Woman's Work: The Housewife, Past and Present* (New York: Vintage Books, 1974); and Roberta Hamilton, *The Liberation of Women: A Study of Patriarchy and Capitalism* (London: George Allen and Unwin, 1978).

23. Batya Weinbaum and Amy Bridges, "The Other Side of the Paycheck: Monopoly Capital and the Structure of Consumption," in Eisenstein, ed., *Capitalist Patriarchy*, pp. 190–205.

24. See Herbert Marcuse, *One Dimensional Man* (Boston: Beacon Press, 1964), chapter 3.

25. Delphy, "For a Feminist Materialism"; Raymond William, *Marxism and Literature* (New York: Oxford University Press, 1977), part 2.

26. Iris Young, "Beyond the Unhappy Marriage: A Critique of the Dual Systems Theory," in Sargent, ed., *Women and Revolution*.

Study Questions

1. What is "dual systems theory"? What are the two "systems" involved? How are the systems allegedly related? (Give an example of one dual system theory's answer to this question.)

2. Explain two advantages of a dual systems approach over a single system approach.

3. Explain two disadvantages of a dual systems approach.

4. Young recommends a "*thoroughly feminist historical materialism*" (emphasis in original) as an improvement over a dual systems approach. What does she mean by a "thoroughly feminist historical materialism," and how is it an improvement? In particular,

   • what does she mean when she says that the theory must be *materialist*?
   • what does she mean when she says that the theory must be *historical*?
   • what does she mean when she says that the theory must be *thoroughly feminist*?

Gwyn Kirk

Standing on Solid Ground

A Materialist Ecological Feminism

• A billion people in the world lack safe drinking water, and some 80 percent of all disease in poor countries is caused by contaminated water (Seager and Olson 1986). An estimated 40,000–50,000 children die each day worldwide, mainly in Africa and Asia, from malnutrition and a lack of clean water.

• Millions of industrial and agricultural workers are employed in hazardous conditions. Oil companies, chemical companies, and textile and electronics producers are responsible for severe environmental devastation through their regular manufacturing processes as well as industrial "accidents," but operate without meaningful environmental constraints (Chavez 1993; Noble 1993).

• In India, Africa, and Latin America, vast acres once used for subsistence crops have been diverted into cash crop production to earn hard currency to pay the interest on overseas loans. In some places new dams make water available for large-scale irrigation of cash crops, but many poor women have to carry water and firewood increasing distances for home use (Shiva 1988).

• A significant number of babies without brains have been born to women on both sides of the Rio Grande, polluted by U.S.-controlled *maquiladora* industries on the Mexican side of the river, and to Pacific Island women who were exposed to radiation during atomic tests or subsequently through irradiated land and water (de Ishtar 1994; Dibblin 1989; Women Working for a Nuclear Free and Independent Pacific 1987).

- In the U.S., children's health is compromised by environmental factors such as lead in paints and gasoline, air pollution, traffic hazards, and violence that often involves the use of handguns, with significant differences between those living in inner cities and suburban neighborhoods (Hamilton 1993; Phoenix 1993).

- Under pressure of poverty, some Native American reservations in the U.S., as well as African and Pacific Island nations, import toxic wastes from industrialized countries and regions as one of the few ways they can earn income, particularly foreign exchange, by providing landfill sites (Center for Investigative Reporting 1990; Center for Third World Organizing 1991; Third World Network 1988).

- In the U.S., breast cancer, which is increasingly linked to environmental causes, affects one woman in nine—many more in some areas—and has killed more women than the AIDS epidemic (Arditti and Schreiber 1992). Native American women whose land and water are heavily polluted have initiated research into the likelihood that their breast milk is toxic (Cook 1985, 1993).

- In the past few years several patents have been taken out on genetically engineered parts of plants and animals, including the cell lines of a U.S. man and an indigenous man from Papua New Guinea, and many more patents are pending (Juma 1989).

The purpose of this chapter is to show how gender, race, class, imperialism, and the global capitalist economy are connected to ecological destruction, and how effective analysis and activism need to be informed by a broad, integrative materialist framework. Given the vast scope and critically serious nature of environmental devastation, I am dismayed that relatively few feminists in the U.S. appear to be

concerned with this issue. I see the theoretical frameworks that dominate U.S. feminist discourse and activism—liberalism, radical feminism, and postmodernism—as the least useful approaches for understanding ecological issues, and the pre-eminence of these perspectives is a serious limitation to feminist work in this area.

Women are the backbone of grassroots organizing around ecological issues worldwide. Well-known examples come from the Chipko (tree-hugging) movement in India (Anand 1983; Shiva 1988), the Kenyan women's green belt movement (Maathai 1988), Micronesian women working in communities devastated by atomic testing (de Ishtar 1994; Women Working for a Nuclear Free and Independent Pacific 1987), U.S. women organizing against toxic dumps and incinerators (Zeff 1989), Native American women's research on toxicity in breast milk (Cook 1985, 1993), and many projects in Asia, Africa, and Latin America that promote sustainable agriculture (Durning 1989b). Much environmental activism in the U.S. is currently undertaken by women of color and poor white women, arising from their daily experiences of poverty and degraded physical environments and often drawing on analyses of race and class rather than gender. While women's engagement with environmental issues comes out of a variety of situations and experiences, I argue that an understanding of their close material connection to the nonhuman environment puts such women on the cutting edge of resistance to ecological destruction, and that such analysis should also be a crucial part of any feminist oppositional project.

Ecological feminists and women environmental activists need to understand and challenge the source of environmental devastation: the unsustainable priorities, values, and living standards of industrialized countries based on highly militarized, capitalist economies. A materialist framework identifies economic and political institutions as the perpetrators of ecologically unsound investment; it offers a basis for understanding how the seemingly random instances listed above are connected and suggests appropriate public action—locally, nationally, and internationally. It allows one to see global connections across lines of race, class, and nation, and to build alliances across these lines of difference. While emphasizing women's activism here, I do not consider women to be solely responsible for planetary caretaking.

FEMINISM AND ECOLOGY: SEEING THE WOOD FOR THE TREES

There are several ways to make theoretical links between feminism and ecology, with varied roots in feminist theories (Daly 1979; Griffin 1978; Warren 1991), feminist spirituality (Sjöö and Mor 1987; Spretnak 1982; Starhawk 1987), social ecology (Bookchin 1990; King 1990), and socialism (Mellor 1992). While some ecofeminists embrace this eclecticism (Spretnak 1990), many proponents and detractors find it confusing and incoherent. Some reject ecofeminism as essentialist; others see it as synonymous with goddess worship and earth-centered spiritualities (Biehl 1991) or animal rights (Adams 1990; Gaard 1993). Women of color critics argue that, as with much western feminism, ecofeminism privileges gender over race and class (Agarwal 1992). English-language ecofeminist anthologies have been dominated by a concern with ethics, personal transformation, and earth-centered spirituality drawn from prehistoric Europe-idealist rather than materialist concerns (Adams 1993; Caldecott 1983*; Diamond and Orenstein 1990*; Plant 1989*), and the contributions and perspectives of women of color are marginal in these collections, which tend to assume a unitary theoretical framework. Joni Seager uses the term "ecological feminism" in an attempt to sidestep the confusion surrounding ecofeminism (Seager 1991). I consider this theoretical quagmire briefly in order to define a solid place to stand.

AN ESSENTIAL, CARING WOMEN'S NATURE?

The fact that women are disproportionately involved in campaigning around environmental issues and against militarism at a grassroots level worldwide is a phenomenon for explanation. Some ecofeminist writers assume an essential, caring woman's nature (Gray 1979); many critique this as a facile essentialism that necessarily limits women's activities and perspectives within the constraints of traditional roles as wives, mothers, domestic workers, and caretakers (paid and unpaid). For the past decade academic discussions of ecofeminism in the U.S. have been bogged down by arguments about essentialism and the related claim that women are closer to nature—a complex concept—than men. This claim implies a separation between people and the nonhuman world that is highly problematic. Nature is not something "out there" somewhere. Rather, people are intimately connected to the nonhuman world in the most profound yet mundane way, through the air we breathe, the food we eat, the water we drink, and so on. But this long drawn out argument about essentialism is also unnecessary and can be avoided by focusing on women's socialization as caretakers across many cultures, with overwhelming responsibility for caring for children, the sick, the elderly, and the well-being of their communities, as family members, friends, and neighbors, or professionally as nurses, teachers, and social workers. I see women's caring work—and this includes environmental knowledge and activism, especially in rural areas where women are farmers and herbalists who understand the visceral interconnections between people and the nonhuman world—as part of this gendered division of labor. Women and men are socialized very differently in many cultures. While it may be fascinating to hypothesize about why this gendered socialization and division of labor first arose, one does not need to speculate about "essentials" to see a clear experiential connection between these aspects of women's lives and their environmental activism.

CONNECTING SPIRITUALITY AND POLITICS

As many scholars have noted, the European "Enlightenment" tradition—from which such liberatory political philosophies as liberalism, Marxism, and socialism have been developed—is fundamentally dualistic and constructs hierarchical relationships between polarized concepts such as mind and body, matter and spirit, and reason and spirituality, which are also basic oppositional categories of contemporary western thought (Merchant 1981; Plumwood 1993). This routine construction of hierarchy and the justification of difference in terms of inequality has had profound consequences. Pre-Enlightenment philosophies such as European paganism and the worldviews of indigenous peoples in the Americas, India, Australia, New Zealand, and the Pacific do not make these separations (Booth 1990; LaDuke 1993; Sanchez 1993; Shiva 1988; Starhawk 1987). On these views, spirituality and politics, for example, are not dissociated categories but interrelated approaches to life. A spiritual belief in the interconnectedness of all life forms is then the springboard for environmental activism against governments and corporations that repudiate such connections by destroying or contaminating the earth, air, and water as well as a multitude of life forms.

This question of a legitimate connection between politics and spirituality—also a complex term—seriously divides U.S. environmentalists, ecosocialists, and ecofeminists. For some, ecofeminism is held to be synonymous with goddess worship and embraced or rejected on that basis. Distinctions should be made here between goddess religions, earth-centered spiritualities in their many cultural forms and contexts, rituals and the cultural underpinnings of specific rituals, organized male-dominated religions, and the origins of people's passionate but seemingly secular beliefs which lead them into political action. This issue needs exploring in more depth, but I note that many Native American, African American, and Chicano environmentalists in the U.S. do not polarize spirituality and politics as some U.S. Greens and ecofeminists do, though even the most secular activists derive their passion for social and economic justice from a fundamental belief, for example in people's equality or intrinsic value. Indeed, the perspective I put forward here may also run into this problem. In an attempt to avoid charges of essentialism and goddess-worship I emphasize the material basis for women's environmental activism, because

western thought has no conception of a blended spiritual politics. This is very different from individualist spiritualities that focus on personal growth, betterment, and salvation without also incorporating an oppositional political practice. Particularly egregious in this respect are those "New Age" spiritualities that appropriate Native American rituals and concepts, often turning them into commodities for sale without taking on a wider concern for and resistance to the continuing oppression of Native Americans. Scientists who have proposed that the earth is a self-regulating system, personified as Gaia, the ancient Greek goddess of the earth (Lovelock 1988; Margulis and Lovelock 1974), have attracted "New Age" environmentalists as well as hard-core polluters to the idea that Gaia can look after herself. But to throw out all spiritual beliefs as superstitious mumbo-jumbo, as Bookchin and Beihl do, is to continue to uphold a disconnected view of life, which ecological feminism should seek to transcend (King 1990).

INTEGRATIVE FRAMEWORKS: CLASS, RACE, GENDER, AND NATION

A key insight of ecofeminism put forward in the germinal works of Susan Griffin and Carolyn Merchant, for example, is the connection between the domination of women and the domination of nature, often feminized and sexualized as in "virgin forest," "rape of the earth," "penetrating the wilderness," and so on. Sources—whether forests, seeds, or women's bodies—are turned into resources to be objectified, controlled, used, and only valued when placed in a system that produces profits (Mies and Shiva 1993; Shiva 1988). But this is not just a matter of women and nature. In the service of capital accumulation, white-dominated, capitalist patriarchy also creates "otherness" and oppresses people of color and poor people worldwide. This continual process of objectification is the central mechanism underlying systems of oppression based on class, race, gender, and nation (Plumwood 1993). Thus the oppression of women, racism, and ecological destruction are directly linked to economic exploitation.

In practice there is an enormous gap between much U.S. ecofeminist writing and the perspectives of grassroots activists involved in the environmental justice movement—predominantly women, many of whom see their activism not only in terms of gender, but also and often more importantly in terms of race and/or class arising from their daily experiences and understandings of the world as women of color or white working-class women. As I outline briefly below, the global capitalist economy is intrinsically antiecological. If ecological feminism is to inform a vital ecological politics in the U.S. we need to emphasize the interconnections among oppressions, activists, and movements; to frame issues broadly to mobilize wide-ranging involvement and support, rather than emphasizing points of disagreement; and to show how the process of capital accumulation is reinforced by the ideological articulation of difference based on gender, ethnicity, and culture. While I agree with those who argue that much U.S. ecofeminism is overly concerned with sexism at the expense of class and race, what is often missing from environmental justice activism is an explicit recognition of sexism as a crucial mechanism of oppression. This is very different from acknowledging that most grassroots environmental activists are women, and it means embracing theoretical perspectives that see women's liberation as fundamental to ecological soundness and a sustainable world.

In summary, I argue for an ecological feminism that focuses on the social and material reasons for women's environmental concerns, has an integrated view of spiritual politics, and can integrate class, race, and gender in theory and practice. Fundamental to this approach is an understanding of the profoundly antiecological nature of the global capitalist economy.

THE ANTIECOLOGICAL GLOBAL ECONOMY

The widespread nature of environmental destruction is an integral part of capitalist as well as state-planned economies (O'Connor 1994). This discussion focuses on capitalist economics now dominant worldwide, which, while not identical, share a logic of capital accumulation. Key principles of capitalist economies include the following:

- They are based on production for profit, not needs—admittedly a tricky concept that varies from context to context—and inevitably result in considerable inequalities of wealth, material comfort, safety, social standing, and opportunities for work, education, and self-expression among people in the same nation and between nations.
- They are inherently expansionist, always seeking new markets, new commodities, and generating new "needs."
- They are intrinsically wasteful, routinely producing trash, derelict land and buildings, and polluted environments as businesses establish themselves, operate until they have exhausted the opportunities for profit-making, and either close down or move on.
- Growth = Progress. There is an inbuilt assumption that economic growth is the same as progress—a more complex concept with economic, intellectual, social, and moral dimensions. Wealth is seen only in terms of material wealth.
- Capital must be able to move at will and without loyalty or commitment to the people of a particular area, so that businesses can always maximize their operating costs, pitting workers in one region or country against those in another.
- Immediate costs and short-run considerations dominate corporate and government decision-making. The role of governments is to maintain political and economic conditions favorable to profit-making through laws, regulations, tax breaks, and other incentives.

Current inequalities between countries are often based on older inequalities resulting from colonization. While the details differed from place to place and from one colonial power to another, colonialism invariably involved the distortion of local economies with dependence on a few agricultural products or "raw materials"—people, timber, minerals, and cash crops. Throughout the second half of the twentieth century, virtually all former colonies have gained political independence but have remained linked to their colonizers politically through organizations like the British Commonwealth and economically through the activities of established firms and transnational corporations and loans from governments and banks based in northern countries. There are also ties of culture and language, as many members of the new political and business elites were educated at prestigious universities in colonial capitals. Whether the hand-over of political power was relatively smooth or accompanied by extreme turmoil and bloodshed, newly independent governments have been under pressure to improve living conditions for their populations and have borrowed capital to finance economic development. This combination of circumstances has led many commentators to characterize the continuing economic inequalities between rich and poor countries as "neocolonialism" (George 1988; Payer 1991).

EXTERNAL DEBT AND STRUCTURAL ADJUSTMENT

This is the contemporary context for international trade. Currently many countries pay more for imports than they earn in exports, leading to external debt or a balance of payments deficit. In 1991, for example, the U.S. budget deficit dropped to $66.2 billion, the first time it had fallen below $100 billion since 1983. Over $1.3 trillion is jointly owed by governments of Latin America, Asia, Africa, and the Caribbean to northern governments and commercial banks. The sixteen major borrowers in Latin America owe a total of $420 billion; between 1982 and 1990, $160 billion was transferred from Latin America to the developed world in debt repayments (O'Reilly 1991). Partly because countries of western Europe and North America have such serious balance of payments problems themselves—increasingly a focus of political debate and domestic policy-making—they have put a great deal of pressure on other debtor countries to repay loans. Indeed, since the mid-1980s, African

governments have transferred $2 billion more to the International Monetary Fund in interest payments than they have received in new loans (Beresford 1994). Loans have to be repaid in "hard" currency— U.S. dollars, Japanese yen, British pounds, French francs, Swiss francs, and German marks—which can be exchanged on world currency markets. Thus debtor nations have to sell goods and services that richer countries want to buy, or that can earn hard currency from poorer countries, with clear implications for the physical environment. Such products include raw materials (hardwoods, oil, copper, gold, diamonds); cash crops (sugar, tobacco, coffee, tea, tropical fruits and flowers); drug-producing crops (coca, marijuana, opium poppies), processed illicit drugs, and weapons. Debtor countries may also export labor (construction workers, maids, and mail-order brides); lease land for military bases or trash dumps; or develop their tourist assets—sunny beaches, beautiful landscapes, and "exotic" young women and children involved in sex tourism.

As well as selling goods and services to offset their external debt, the World Bank and the International Monetary Fund have pressured all debtor nations to make stringent changes in their economies to qualify for new loans, with the aim of increasing the profitablity of the economy and making it more export-focused (Barnet and Cavanagh 1994; Danaher 1994; Reed 1992; Sparr 1994; Vickers 1990). Measures relevant to environmental concerns include

—cuts in government subsidies and the abolition of price controls, particularly on food, fuel, and public transportation;
—selling nationalized industries or at least a majority shareholding to private corporations often from outside the country;
—improving profitability for corporations through wage controls, tax breaks, loans, and credit, or provision of infrastructure such as better roads or rail transport; and
—increasing the output of cash crops by increasing yields and/or increasing the amount of land in cash crop production.

In parts of Latin America, governments have been willing to allow international environmental organizations and foreign banks exclusive control of specific parcels of land to be left undeveloped—"debt-for-nature swaps"—as a way of dealing with a small proportion of their debt (Madrid 1990*; O'Cleireacain 1990*). Many activist groups in southern countries oppose the repayment of external debts and challenge the structural/social adjustment policies that are making many people's lives much harder. They argue that many foreign loans were used by their countries' elites for inappropriate, prestige development in urban centers that have not benefited the majority of the population, or that the country has already lost enormous wealth to northern countries due to centuries of colonization.

THE POLITICS OF SURVIVAL

This global economic context—characterized by complex inequalities based on class, race, gender, and nation—frames ecological issues and politics. I now look at several examples which illustrate how such inequalities impact ecological concerns and grassroots environmental projects, particularly focusing on development and health. These examples come from the U.S. and southern countries, from very different contexts and life situations; not all of them concern women exclusively. Thus my discussion has an inevitable unevenness and requires the reader to shift between varied contexts while at the same time keeping in mind the overarching framework, so that these are not seen as random cases.

AGRICULTURAL DEVELOPMENT: FEEDING THE WORLD

Women's role as primary agricultural producers in many parts of Africa, Latin America, and Asia gives them direct experience and detailed knowledge of ecological issues. Women make up 80 percent of the subsistence farmers in sub-Saharan Africa, for example. They are the main users of water in agriculture and forestry, as well as domestic life, and they carry it each day, sometimes several miles. Women are also responsible for finding fuel—wood, crop residues, and manure—another time-consuming and arduous

daily task. While some women are involved in cash crop production, a gendered division of labor and the gender bias of many economic development projects means that men produce most cash crops and receive the income from them. Increasingly, cash crops compete with subsistence agriculture for available land, labor, and water. To provide food for their families, women farm more marginal land and walk further for water and fuel (Agarwal 1992; Dankelman and Davidson 1988). They may well understand ecologically sound agricultural practices but are pressured into farming steep hillsides or cutting trees for fuelwood, for example, thus worsening soil erosion and flooding during heavy rains. Such women work sixteen-hour days, seven days a week, juggling farming with cooking, cleaning, laundry, and child care —though according to national income accounting none of this counts as productive work because it is not done for wages (Waring 1988).

The world of agricultural development agencies, transnational corporations, and government policymakers is dominated by capitalist and neo-colonial notions of economic development and material progress, where large-scale, chemically dependent, capital-intensive mechanized agriculture, usually producing cash crops for export, is the model promoted and funded by international financial institutions. An extensive literature on women and development offers trenchant critiques of such maldevelopment for its emphasis on cash crops at the expense of viable subsistence agriculture; its exclusion of women from much development policy-making; and its promotion of ecologically unsound agricultural practices (Braidotti and others 1994; Dankelman and Davidson 1988; ISIS Women's International Information and Communications Service 1984; Rodda 1990; Sen and Grown 1987; Shiva 1988). The so-called Green Revolution with hybrid "high-yield" seeds that require massive inputs of chemical fertilizers, pesticides, and regular irrigation, has not improved food security for poor people in the "two-thirds world,"[1] but has been an ecological disaster that has turned plants and farmers into consumers of chemicals (Shiva 1991). New hybrid varieties are more susceptible to drought, disease, and pests, and—the biggest contradiction of all—are not fertile, so farmers cannot recycle their own seed for the next year's planting but must buy more each season from chemical companies—an example of a new commodity creating new "needs" as part of the expansionist process of capital accumulation.

SCIENCE REDESIGNS NATURE: BIOTECHNOLOGY AND GENETIC ENGINEERING

Going beyond this plant-breeding technology is genetic engineering, a remarkable new form of biotechnology capable of changing the very nature of life itself (Juma 1989; Spallone 1992). It involves the manipulation of genetic material—DNA—so that it is possible to implant human genes in animals, for example, and animal genes in people, creating combinations that could never be achieved through selective breeding as traditionally practiced. Other examples include research on human embryos intended to identify genes responsible for various genetic "defects" that can be corrected in the womb, making genetically engineered designer babies a real possibility. A cancerous mouse, created and patented by Harvard University and DuPont, is already available for sale to cancer researchers. The use of genetically engineered bovine growth hormone, introduced in the U.S. in 1994, will increase milk production. Genetically engineered bio-pesticides and seeds will have far-reaching effects on agriculture and are considered the most lucrative products of this technology—seeds being the crucial first link in the food chain (Mather 1995; Raeburn 1995). Enormous profits are to be made, as is clear from even a casual glance at the business pages.

Genetic engineering is being vigorously promoted as the answer to many problems: curing disease, eliminating mental illness and physical disabilities, reducing crime, curing infertility, as well as increasing genetic diversity and ridding the world of hunger, claims which need to be looked at very critically. While researchers, promoters, and investors argue that everyone stands to benefit from this new technology,

it is important to note that it is controlled by a small number of transnational corporations and research facilities in northern countries, in contrast to traditional plant and animal breeding practices developed in specific settings, known to many farmers and passed on from generation to generation. Clearly this will reinforce the power of elites and further marginalize the poor. World hunger, for example, is not caused by deficiencies in crop varieties but by the consumption habits of rich countries and the unequal distribution of wealth and political power in the world (Moore Lappé and Collins 1986). Pineapples from the Philippines, strawberries from Mexico, and carnations from Colombia are all imported into the U.S. and are grown on land that could otherwise produce food for local needs, as is also the case with sugar cane, tea, and coffee. As well as increasing milk production, bovine growth hormone makes cows more vulnerable to disease, for which they are given powerful antibiotics and other drugs on a regular basis, which in turn affects the quality of their milk. The percentage of human diseases whose cause can be traced to genetic defects is very small. Most disabilities are caused by accidents and environmental or occupational exposure. By focusing on a tiny proportion of diseases, genetic engineering gives them enormous attention, while the study of most illnesses is ignored and poorly funded. Social causes are also ignored. Rather than genetic factors, poor prenatal care, directly traceable to socioeconomic class, is the primary cause of birth defects, with environmental or drug-related effects close behind.

Besides engineering genetic material, people's thinking is also being engineered to accept it (Shiva 1993). Genetic engineering suggests fantastic or terrifying possibilities and assumes that there are technical solutions to problems with economic and social causes. Thus, discussions that should be taking place in the political arena have been transferred to biological experts who present their work to their funders and professional colleagues in obscure, scientific language. Research and activist groups like the Research Foundation for Science, Technology and Natural Resource Policy in India,[2] the Pure Food Campaign in the U.S.,[3] and the Feminist Network of Resistance to Reproductive and Genetic Engineering[4] (with groups in sixteen countries) are piecing together available information and challenging the underlying assumptions and practices of genetic engineering as it affects agriculture and human reproduction, though there is little public debate in the U.S. on this issue, which has such far-reaching effects—many of which, like the release of genetically engineered organisms into the environment, are simply not known. Beyond the political and economic details, what is at stake here are opposing systems of knowledge and value.

WHO OWNS LIFE?
ETHNOSCIENTIFIC KNOWLEDGE,
INTELLECTUAL PROPERTY

Despite the incursions of profit-driven agriculture in Africa, Asia, Latin America, and the Caribbean, there are thousands of small-scale, ecologically sound development projects, many of them organized by women, described by Alan Durning as the "best hope for global prosperity and ecology" (Durning 1989a). Many rural farmers struggle to continue to use ecological practices and appropriate technology, and to draw on long-standing ethnoscientific knowledge— for instance, the National Council of Women of Kenya's Green Belt Movement, which has spread to many other African countries. Started in 1977 by biologist Wangari Maathai, this program was initiated and promoted by women as a solution to diminishing supplies of fuelwood and desertification in rural Kenya. By the mid-1980s Kenyan women had planted more than 2 million trees (Maathai 1988; Maathai 1991). Other projects rely on the introduction of appropriate technology to reduce the long hours women spend working for subsistence (Charlton 1984; Dankelman and Davidson 1988; Leonard 1989).

Ecologically sound development projects also have their counterparts in the U.S., including women's economic projects in rural and urban areas and on Native American reservations; organic farms; seed banks that safeguard genetic diversity and promote the use of old, established seed varieties that can withstand drought and pests; and community gardening in inner cities (Bagby 1990). The 4-H Urban Gardening project in Detroit,[5] for example, coordinates well over 100 small gardens citywide and relies on the expertise of local people, mostly elderly African American women, who raise vegetables for individual use and to supplement food prepared at senior centers, as well as producing crops for sale: loofah sponges, fresh herbs, honey, and worm boxes for fishing. Many of these women were brought up in rural areas in the southern United States, where they learned about gardening before coming to Detroit for work in the 1930s and '40s. By drawing on local people's knowledge and interests, providing fresh produce at little financial cost, and using the land in an ecologically sound and productive way, these gardening projects combine aspects of economic, ecological, and cultural survival. Besides growing vegetables and flowers, they contribute to the revitalization of inner-city communities and a sense of empowerment that comes from self-reliance. When people are outdoors working they also make neighborhoods safer by their presence, watchfulness, and care. An additional goal is to teach young people about gardening, strengthening connections between the generations and helping young people become more self-supporting. A rural example from the U.S. is Ganados del Valle/Tierra Wools in northern New Mexico, a worker cooperative of twenty people—most of them women— which owns some 3,000 head of Churro sheep and produces high-quality, handwoven rugs and clothing and organic lamb.[6] Its objectives include economic development, environmental protection, cultural revival and conservation, workplace democracy, and social justice (Jackson 1991; Pulido 1993).

Sociologist and activist Devón Peña notes that, as ethnobotanists, Chicanas in northern New Mexico know the backcountry in great detail because they go there at different seasons to gather herbs for medicinal purposes (Peña 1992). This detailed knowledge has been passed on by older people, as is also the case with some Native Americans and others who live in rural areas. Though many who have been raised in cities have not had the opportunity to learn such things, feminists involved in women's health in the past twenty years have encouraged women to become more knowledgeable and self-reliant with regard to health, and have published herbal guides as part of this work (Gladstar 1993; Potts 1988). On other continents, indigenous people—often women—also have a detailed knowledge of local plants—their medicinal properties and usefulness for many domestic tasks—learned from their mothers and grandmothers and gradually developed over many generations. Increasingly, the pharmaceutical industry is interested in developing medicines from plant material from tropical regions, which are the richest and most diverse sources of plant life. Seventy-five percent of plants that "provide active ingredients for prescription drugs originally came to the attention of researchers because of their uses in traditional medicine" (Kloppenburg 1991). Western agribusiness insists that plant and animal resources from the two-thirds world are public property, part of a common human heritage, but when they are developed by pharmaceutical companies they become private property for sale, graphically described by Vandana Shiva as "biopiracy." As well as medicines, many staple food crops now produced in northern countries, such as corn and potatoes, have been adapted from tropical crops. According to Jack Kloppenburg, "Indigenous people have in effect been engaged in a massive program of foreign aid to the urban populations of the industrialized north" (Kloppenburg 1991). This commodification of knowledge in a capitalist context raises complex questions about who owns knowledge of life forms and whether indigenous peoples should have intellectual property rights and be compensated for their knowledge, a debate that feminists in industrial countries should participate in. Genetic engineers who seek protection for modified life forms by taking out patents on their "inventions" pose a similar challenge.

WORKING FOR WELLNESS: ENVIRONMENTAL HEALTH

Capitalist production processes—whether in the agricultural, industrial, service, or information sectors—are a crucial aspect of health for workers and those who live and work near toxic workplaces. The explosion of the Union Carbide chemical plant near Bhopal, India, in 1984, which killed and maimed thousands of people, is a graphic example of lax safety standards routinely adopted as a way to cut production costs (Kurzman 1987; Shrivastava 1987). While many labor organizers oppose unsafe working conditions, companies often frame the issue in either/or terms and pit jobs against a better working environment. Firing particular individuals or threatening to relocate the plant elsewhere are common management strategies in this struggle for improved working conditions (Moses 1993; Noble 1993).

In the U.S., hazardous working conditions and toxic wastes disproportionately affect lower-income neighborhoods, particularly those housing people of color, in a correspondence so striking it merits the term "environmental racism" (Bullard 1990; Bullard 1993; Hofrichter 1993; Lee 1987; Schwab 1994; Szasz 1994). Many women are involved in campaigning against toxic pollution in the workplace and the community in an environmental justice movement significant for its racial diversity (Kraus 1993; Zeff et al. 1989). Typically they get involved because they become ill themselves or through caring for a sick relative, often a child. Activists piece together information to find the source of the illness, publicize their findings, and take on agricultural or industrial corporations and city agencies responsible for contamination. The Citizens' Clearinghouse for Hazardous Wastes,[7] founded by Lois Gibbs in the early 1980s, provides resource materials to local groups and publishes news of local campaigns (Gibbs 1995). Other organizations actively pursuing these issues at regional and national levels include the National Women's Health Network[8] (Nelson et al. 1990), the Southwest Organizing Project,[9] the Center for Third World Organizing,[10] and the United Farm Workers of America (U.F.W.),[11] which opposes the extensive use of pesticides in commercial fruit and vegetable production. For some years the U.F.W. has called for a boycott of California table grapes to protest the fact that farm workers and their families, particularly women and children, suffer severe health effects due to pesticide exposure, and as leverage in negotiating better conditions in work contracts. Such produce is not good for consumers either. Middle-class parents were very effective in getting the pesticide Alar banned in the late 1980s because it damaged children's health (Mott and Snyder 1987; Witte Garland 1989), with no apparent awareness or concern for farm workers exposed to it in the course of their work. In many parts of the U.S. mainly white, middle-class consumers avoid contaminated produce by buying organic, which does nothing to improve conditions for most farm workers or to reduce the effects of chemical pesticides and fertilizers on land and water. Much more needs to be done to build alliances between farm workers—many of whom are Mexican Americans and Central Americans—and consumer groups. This will include increased education and public awareness of the dangers of pesticides and the low nutritional value of much mass-produced food, as well as support for farmer's markets, producer/consumer cooperatives, and other alternative agricultural projects.

WOMEN'S HEALTH, FETAL HEALTH

For U.S. women, cancer is the second leading cause of death, and breast cancer currently affects one in nine women, though the figures are much higher in some areas. Rita Arditti and Tatiana Schrieber argue that cancers have environmental causes, evidenced by dramatic differences in cancer rates between geographical locations and the identification of specific substances including asbestos, chemicals, and ionizing radiation, which are linked to cancer (Arditti and Schreiber 1992). They conclude that cancer is not only largely environmental in origin but also largely preventable, a view that underlies the work of groups like the Women's Community Cancer Project.[12]

Women and children are "ecological markers" with regard to toxics and often show signs of disease earlier than men do, either due to low body weight in the case of children, or because their bodies are said by health professionals to be "unhealthy environments" for their babies (Chavkin 1984; Nelson 1990). In some cases women in the U.S. have been barred from jobs involving routine exposure to toxic

chemicals so that they cannot sue their employers should they give birth to a disabled child—a form of fetal protection where women are seen in terms of their reproductive potential rather than as people in their own right. A Supreme Court decision in April 1991, for example, barred Johnson Controls, an auto battery manufacturer in Milwaukee, from keeping fertile women out of high-paying jobs involving exposure to lead (Daniels 1993). While some feminists hailed this as a victory for equal rights, others saw it as the right to be treated equally badly. The decision does not address the more fundamental issue of hazardous workplaces, regardless of gender. Men's reproductive systems are also affected by toxics—as has at last been officially accepted in some extreme cases, such as exposure to the defoliant Agent Orange during the Vietnam War, and exposure to radioactivity in nuclear plants and through nuclear weapons tests (Gibbs 1995). A Native American women's initiative concerning connections between the health of a mother and the health of her baby is the Akwasasne Mother's Milk project, started in the early 1980s by midwife Kasti Cook (Cook 1985, 1993). Akwasasne, "the land where the partridge drums," home of the Mohawk Nation (near Rooseveltown, NY), is affected by severe chemical pollution flowing through the Great Lakes system as well as from nearby industries. Akwasasne women became concerned that by eating local vegetables, fish, and other wildlife they might be exposing their babies to toxic pollution through their breast milk and questioned whether they should continue breast feeding. Despite the economic costs and against their tradition of supporting themselves from the land, they decided to stop eating locally produced food—garden produce, fish, and small game animals—and to monitor their situation carefully. More recent analysis of breast milk samples is not as bad as originally feared but still gives no cause for complacency. Another egregious example involves women from Micronesia in the western Pacific who have been campaigning for years about the catastrophic effects of atmospheric atomic tests conducted by the British, French, and U.S. governments in the 1950s and early 1960s (de Ishtar 1994; Women Working for a Nuclear Free and Independent Pacific

1987). Whole islands have been irradiated and soil and drinking water contaminated. Some women have given birth to "jelly fish babies" without skeletons who live only a few hours. Other children survive despite severe illnesses and disabilities caused by radiation.

The general relationship between environmental hazards and health needs much more detailed research and public debate (Gibbs 1995; Nelson 1990), including research on environmental causes of illnesses like cancer, chemical sensitivities to pollution, and allergies, and support for holistic medical practices that do not rely on drugs and surgery.

POPULATION: TOO MANY PEOPLE FOR WHAT?

The issue of population is another key one for ecological feminism. The discourse about fertility and population is also a discourse about race. With white populations falling in comparison to people of color in the U.S., it is white women who are offered so-called fertility treatments and whose right to safe, accessible abortion is being eroded. The question of why so many young people in this country are apparently infertile, for example, is salient here. In the U.S. infertility is looked upon as a personal failing to be remedied by treatment, another example of a new product meeting a new "need," even though infertility treatments have a spectacularly low success rate so far and are very expensive. They are aimed at middle-class women as a way of widening individual choice, but the relationship between infertility and environmental hazards is rarely examined, and feminist critiques of reproductive technologies have tended to focus on their invasiveness and the lack of power and knowledge consumers have compared to medical experts (Arditti et al. 1984; Corea 1985, 1987; Stamworth 1988). Sterilization without women's full knowledge or under duress has been a common practice in the U.S. among poor women, especially Latinas, African Americans, and Native Americans. In the 1950s and '60s Puerto Rican women were used in trials of contraceptive pills later

made available in the U.S. in much lower dosages. Currently poor African American women and Latinas are much more likely than white women to be encouraged to use the long-acting contraceptive Norplant, implanted under the skin, on the assumption that their pregnancies are not desirable and that these women would be unreliable if they used other contraceptive methods.

There is also a similar, distinctly racist dimension to the environmental debate about population globally. Simply looking at numbers of people and rates of population growth, prominent environmentalists in northern countries argue that many nations, particularly in Africa and Asia, must cut their high rates of population increase. They talk in terms of the limited carrying capacity of the planet to support human life and pose the "problem of overpopulation" as a central (sometimes *the* central) environmental concern. Anne and Paul Ehrlich, for example, emphasize the inevitable, destructive potential of this "population bomb," implying that two-thirds world women, more than anyone else, threaten the survival of the planet (Ehrlich and Ehrlich 1990). Deep ecologists have gone much further, calling for drastic reductions in population. An *Earth First!* contributor who wrote under the pseudonym Miss Ann Thropy made the outrageous claim that if AIDS did not exist it would have had to be invented, or that starving people in Africa should be left to die so that the human population can be brought back into balance with the carrying capacity of the land (Miss Ann Thropy 1991). Framing the issue this way is ideologically loaded and racist and obscures several central questions: the varied cultural and economic reasons poor people have children; the inverse relationship between women's status and family size; why men are not required to take responsibility for their sexuality and fertility; the political reasons for starvation and hunger; the skewed distribution of wealth on an international level, where industrialized countries consume most of the world's resources and generate most of the waste, especially the chemicals and gases that deplete the ozone layer. The U.S., for example, which has 6 percent of the world's population, uses some 40 percent of the world's resources. "A family of eight in Rwanda or Nicaragua neither depletes nor pollutes the Earth anywhere near the amount that does a family of four in Great Britain or the United States" (Hynes 1991). Feminist researchers like Betsy Hartmann, director of the Population and Development Program,[13] emphasize this relationship between population and consumption, positing a "problem of overconsumption" on the part of the North (Bandarage 1994; Hartmann 1991; Hartmann 1995; Moore Lappé and Schurman 1988). Many southern countries are working to reduce their population growth and recognize only too well the difficulties they face in terms of food security. It is important to see this in the context of external debt outlined above. One reason it is difficult to feed fast-growing populations in southern countries is that an increasing acreage once used for subsistence crops now produces cash crops for export as a way of earning hard currency and making repayments on foreign loans.

MILITARY SACRIFICE AREAS: OUTPOSTS OF EMPIRE

A final example to illustrate my general argument concerns military activities, which cause the most severe, long-term environmental destruction worldwide (Seager 1993). This includes weapons production, storage, and testing, as well as outright war. In many wars farmland, deserts, and forests are routinely mined, making them extremely dangerous and unusable for years to come. In the Vietnam War, chemical defoliants were used to destroy the forests. During the Gulf War, U.S. bombers did untold environmental damage, including an unprecedented attack on oil wells that continued to burn for many months after the war was officially over, giving off a thick, noxious smoke that completely blotted out the light. The production of nuclear weapons is another case in point. The mining of uranium, the development of weapons-grade plutonium, and the assembly and testing of warheads have contaminated indigenous peoples' lands in North America, southern Africa, Australia, and the Pacific, and have affected the health of countless people through contaminated air and water (Birks and Ehrlich 1989; Christensen 1988). The half-life of weapons-grade plutonium is 24,000 years, so this is a long-term problem of overwhelming dimensions, currently with no solution. Many community organizations in the U.S. have been campaigning for years against nuclear processing plants and dump sites, which leak radioactive particles into the air and ground water, ironically in the name of national security.[14] Not only do these processes treat the land as disposable, they treat people the same way. Many Native Americans see uranium mining on reservations as racist and genocidal, though it often provides the only well-paid work available. People from the Pacific view the decision to test atomic weapons in their islands, which France continued in French Polynesia until January 1996, as imperialist and racist in the extreme. During agreements to end the UN Trusteeship of Micronesia in 1969, then U.S. Secretary of State Henry Kissinger said, "There's only 90,000 people out there, who gives a damn?" (Women Working for a Nuclear Free and Independent Pacific 1987). He did not say people of color, but the implication is clear.

As the world economy becomes more integrated and more reliant on automation, there are fewer chances of employment for many people. At the same time military budgets have risen in virtually every country to a staggering total, with arms sales a major export for many industrialized countries (Collinson 1989; Leger-Sivard 1991). Poorer countries also trade arms, a key source of hard currency. For many young men, whether in U.S. inner cities or war-torn countries like Afghanistan and Sri Lanka, guns are far easier to get than jobs, while many women worldwide campaign against militarism and military values. Women in Sri Lanka have come together across lines of ethnicity and culture to try to stop civil war. Jewish and Palestinian women are working together to oppose the military violence of the Israeli state. Women in the Pacific Island of Belau have been crucial in the campaign to retain their country's nuclear-free constitution—incidentally the only one in the world—against great political and economic pressure from the U.S. to use Belau as a navy base.

Women's antimilitarist campaigning in northern countries, especially in the 1980s, included many demonstrations, vigils, and peace encampments outside military bases, factories making weapons components, bomb assembly plants, and military tracking stations. The Women's Pentagon Action (1983) protested military priorities and the vast resources allocated to them, and the widespread, everyday culture of violence manifested in war toys, films, and video games, an important factor in the construction of militarized masculinity (Enloe 1990). Greenham Common Women's Peace Camp in England, which started in 1981 as a protest against the siting of U.S. nuclear cruise missiles, linked violence against women and children, military violence, and ecological destruction. Greenham inspired dozens of other peace camps in North America, western Europe, Australia, and New Zealand, and many thousands of women there participated in campaigns of nonviolent direct action—protests that were imaginative, colorful, and assertive, with powerful artistic and ritual elements (Cook and Kirk 1983; Harford and Hopkins 1984). Greenham women also campaigned for the demilitarization of what used to be common land, making connections with others whose land has been annexed in the interests of military domination, including indigenous people of North America, Australia, Aoteroa (New Zealand), and the Pacific Islands. This antimilitarist activism was the source of much ecofeminist theorizing and practice, though it was criticized by women of color for being overly concerned with gender at the expense of race and class (Amos and Parmer 1984; Omolade 1989*). This tendency, together with the inevitable ebb and flow of any voluntary campaign, made for a limited theoretical understanding, and this feminist peace movement has not sustained itself into the 1990s.

PRINCIPLES OF A MATERIALIST ECOLOGICAL FEMINISM

With these examples I have outlined a broad basis for a materialist ecological feminism, which will have many cultural variants depending on specific circumstances. Based on this discussion I suggest the following general principles for a materialist ecological feminist theory and practice. It should

- include the experiences and perspectives of women dealing with ecological issues as a matter of survival;
- recognize the linear expansionism of capitalist economies as fundamental to ecological devastation;
- link the domination of women by men, people of color by white people, nonhuman nature by human beings—understanding that the connection between ecological sustainability and social justice is structural and not just a campaigning strategy based on coalitions of different groups;
- challenge existing industrial and agricultural production processes that involve the routine use of toxins, excessive packaging and waste, the pollution of the workplace and surrounding environment, and the oil-intensive transport of goods over great distances;
- challenge the overconsumption and materialism of rich countries and elites in poor countries, opposing prevalent ideas about modernization, growth, and progress;
- call for a reduction in production such that the goals of the economy are reoriented to the production and reproduction of life;
- frame issues in ways that include women and men of different backgrounds and experience, to enable diverse groups to work together across race, class, and national lines;
- move from a framework of oppression to a framework of resistance;
- oppose personal and military violence;
- promote sustainable, life-affirming projects that link economic and cultural survival.

AGENDAS FOR ACTION

These principles give rise to extensive agendas for action. I see two fundamental questions for feminists in industrialized countries who are concerned about ecological issues. What is involved in creating sustainable economies worldwide? How can we work toward this change?

Ecological feminism needs to be involved with sustainable agriculture, restoration ecology, and health in the broad sense of well-being. It must oppose the structural/social economic adjustment policies of northern governments, as well as militarism and the culture of violence it generates and requires. This means opening up a public debate that challenges and opposes the values and practices of this economic system—its hazardous production processes as well as its consumerist ideology—rather, framing progress in terms of sustainability, connectiveness, and true security. It involves promoting vibrant local economic projects so that people are not dependent on the whims of corporate investors and developers, building up communities where young people are needed, where they can develop skills and gain respect for themselves and each other through meaningful work and participation in community projects and decision-making (Boggs 1994; Kirk 1996). It involves expanding and strengthening many existing, small-scale projects including community gardens; farmers' markets; cooperative organic farming; backyard gardening and composting; the design and building of eco-housing; repairing, reusing, and recycling discarded materials, vacant land, and derelict buildings, especially in blighted postindustrial cities; promoting technologies that rely on renewable resources. There need to be many more such projects, though the next challenge is to scale them up without destroying them.

This agenda also means questioning what constitutes valid knowledge and who can claim authority and expertise. It assumes that people may need to be made aware of these issues—a task for formal schooling and informal community-based education—and that they should be active participants in decision-making with control over their means of livelihood. It means challenging the assumptions and practice of genetic engineering as it applies to the production of seeds, plants, and animals, as well as human reproduction; challenging institutionalized science as a

major contributor to ecological destruction—indeed, as Carolyn Merchant puts it, the death of nature—but promoting what Lin Nelson calls the "kitchen table science" of women piecing together information about polluters, and the ethnoscience of women farmers in the Himalaya or Native American and Chicana herbalists. It requires research which is of interest and value to activists and policy-makers, rather than an abstract academic feminism increasingly coopted by patriarchal notions of scholarship. It needs organizations and contexts where working relationships between activists, researchers, and policy-makers can develop, and where students can learn this approach in practice. It will require extensive democratization of political processes and institutions locally, nationally, and internationally.

Clearly, what I am outlining here is both a long-term agenda and something already happening in small ways through many projects. Such a broad perspective may seem utterly daunting given the basic contradiction between exploitative economic systems and a world without environmental destruction or violence, but many women and men are grappling with these issues and making changes. Local, regional, national, and international networks of feminists and environmental justice activists, admittedly small and rather fragile, currently link organizers, researchers, and policy-makers around many of the issues I raise here. Examples include Development Alternatives for Women in a New Era (DAWN) active in Asia, Africa, Latin America, and the Caribbean; Women Working for a Nuclear Free and Independent Pacific, with groups in Britain, Australia, and the Pacific; and Women's Environment and Development Organization in New York. Fifteen hundred women from all continents gathered in Miami in November 1991 to develop a women's agenda to take to the UN Conference on Environment and Development in Brazil in June 1992. This World Women's Congress for a Healthy Planet[15] included women who work for UN agencies, elected politicians, teachers, scholars, journalists, students, and activists—women who are working inside formal governmental structures, in lobbying and educational work, and through grassroots organizing. It was the first major international women's gathering to discuss ecological issues and showed the growing strength of women's analysis and organizing.

Environmental issues have enormous potential for bringing people together across lines of gender, race, class, and nation in projects and movements that radically challenge white-dominated, patriarchal capitalism and include transformative agendas and strategies for sustainable living. At root this is about taking on the whole economic system and the systems of power—personal and institutional—that sustain it, working to transform relationships of exploitation and oppression. This means that northern countries must consume far fewer of the world's resources. Feminists and environmentalists need to challenge the fundamentals of materialism and consumerism, creating a definition of wealth that includes health, physical energy and strength, safety and security, time, skills, talents, wisdom, creativity, love, community support, a connection to one's history and cultural heritage, and a sense of belonging. This is not a philosophy of denial nor a romanticization of poverty, though it does involve a fundamental paradigm shift in a country—indeed a world—so dominated by the process of capital accumulation and the allure of material wealth. There is a need for greater dialogue between those from rich and poor countries, and between middle-class and poorer people in rich countries like the U.S., but this needs to move from a politics of solidarity—implying support for others in struggle—to a politics of engagement, where we are in struggle together.

This is a pivotal time in human history. The point is not to pursue the liberal ideal of equal opportunity for material development in a world that is heading toward even greater ecological destruction; to intellectually deconstruct the complexities of reality without apparent interest in practical reconstruction; or to buy "Green" products—where the emphasis is still on consumption (Hynes 1991; Mies 1993), but to transform relationships among people and between people and the nonhuman world so there is the possibility that our children's children will inherit a healthier planet and will be able to live in more truly human ways.

NOTES

1. I follow Charlotte Bunch in using this term to emphasize the fact that the majority of the world's people live in the so-called Third World, while recognizing that such shorthand terms are all problematic: "First World/Third World" assumes the superiority of North America and Western Europe. Economic development terms, which rank countries as "developed," "undeveloped," "underdeveloped," or "developing" assumes a unitary view of development and progress following the industrial capitalism of western Europe and North America. Hemispheres of political influence—West and East—is also a simplification; as is the distinction between countries of the North and South. Comparing countries also masks serious inequalities within them.

2. Research Foundation for Science, Technology and Natural Resource Policy, A60 Hauz Khas, New Delhi, 110 016, India. Journal: *Bija—the Seed: A Quarterly Monitor on Biodiversity, Biotechnology and Intellectual Property Rights.*

3. The Pure Food Campaign, 1130 17th Street NW, #300, Washington, DC 20036.

4. Feminist Network of Resistance to Reproductive and Genetic Engineering (FINRRAGE). The U.S. contact is Janice Raymond, Women's Studies Department, University of Massachusetts, Amherst, MA 01003.

5. 4-H Urban Gardens is a project of Michigan State University, Department of Agriculture, Wayne County Cooperative Extension Service, 640 Temple Street, sixth floor, Detroit, MI 48201.

6. Tierra Wools, P.O. Box 118, Los Ojos, NM 87551.

7. Citizens' Clearinghouse for Hazardous Wastes, P.O. Box 6806, Falls Church, VA 22040. Newsletter: *Everyone's Backyard.*

8. National Women's Health Network, 1325 G Street N.W., Washington, DC 20005.

9. Southwest Organizing Project, 211 Tenth Street S.W., Albuquerque, NM 87102.

10. Center for Third World Organizing, 1218 East 21 Street, Oakland, CA 94606. Bimonthly journal: *Third Force.*

11. United Farm Workers of America, P.O. Box 62–La Paz, Keene, CA 93531. Film; *The Wrath of Grapes.*

12. Women's Community Cancer Project, c/o The Women's Center, 46 Pleasant Street, Cambridge, MA 02139.

13. Population and Development Program, Hampshire College, Amherst, MA 01002.

14. Radioactive Waste Campaign, 625 Lafayette Street, New York, NY 10003; the Military Toxics Project, Tides Foundation, P.O. Box 845, Sabattus, ME 04280.

15. Women's World Congress for a Healthy Planet, 845 Third Avenue, 15th floor, New York, NY 10022.

* Indicates full bibliographic information not supplied in original.

REFERENCES

Adams, Carol J. 1990. *The Sexual Politics of Meat: A Feminist-Vegetarian Critical Theory*. New York: Continuum Books.

Agarwal, Bina. 1992. "The Gender and Environment Debate: Lessons from India." *Feminist Review* 18 (1): 119–157.

Amos, Valerie and Pratisha Parmer. 1984. "Challenging Imperial Feminism." *Feminist Review* 17: 3–19.

Anand, Anita. 1983. Saving Trees, Saving Lives: Third World Women and the Issue of Survival. In *Reclaim the Earth: Women Speak Out for Life on Earth*, edited by Leonie Caldecott and Stephanie Leland. 182–88. London: Women's Press.

Arditti, Rita, Renate Duelli Klein, and Shelley Minden, ed. 1984. *Test-Tube Women: What Future for Motherhood?* Boston: Pandora Press.

Arditti, Rita and Tatiana Schreiber. 1992. Breast Cancer: The Environmental Connection. *Resist* (246).

Bagby, Rachel. 1990. Daughters of Growing Things. In *Reweaving the World: The Emergence of Ecofeminism*, eds. Irene Diamond and Gloria Orenstein. 231–248. San Francisco: Sierra Club Books.

Bandarage, Asoka. 1994. Population and Development: Toward a Social Justice Agenda. *Monthly Review* 46 (4): 40–50.

Barnet, Richard and Michael Cavanagh. 1994. *Global Dreams: Imperial Corporations and the New World Order*. New York: Simon and Schuster.

Beresford, David. 1994. *The Guardian* (London), July 20, 11.

Biehl, Janet. 1991. *Rethinking Ecofeminist Politics*. Boston: South End Press.

Birks, John and Anne Ehrlich, eds. 1989. *Hidden Dangers: The Environmental Consequences of Preparing for War*. San Francisco: Sierra Club Books.

Boggs, Grace Lee. 1994. "Beyond Corporate Bondage." *The Witness* (May): 18–20.

Bookchin, Murray. 1990. *The Ecology of Freedom: The Emergence and Dissolution of Hierarchy*. Toronto: Black Rose Books.

Booth, Annie L. and Jacobs, Harvey M. 1990. Ties that Bind: Native American Beliefs as a Foundation for Environmental Consciousness. *Environmental Ethics* 12 (Spring): 27–43. Braidotti, Rita, Ewa Charkiewicz, Sabine Hausler, and Saskia Wieringa. 1994. *Women, the Environment and Sustainable Development: Towards a Theoretical Synthesis*. London and NJ: Zed Books/INSTRAW, 1994.

Braidotti, Rosi, et al. 1994. *Women, the Environment and Sustainable Development*. London: Zed Books and INSTRAW.

Bullard, Robert D. 1990. *Dumping in Dixie: Race, Class, and Environmental Quality*. Boulder: Westview Press.

Bullard, Robert D., ed. 1993. *Confronting Environmental Racism: Voices from the Grassroots*. Boston: South End Press.

Center for Investigative Reporting. 1990. *Global Dumping Ground: The International Traffic in Hazardous Waste*. Washington: Seven Locks Press.

Center for Third World Organizing, ed. 1991. *The Minority Trendsletter*. Vol. 4. special issue on Toxics and Communities of Color. Oakland: Center for Third World Organizing.

Charlton, Sue Ellen. 1984. *Women in Third World Development*. Boulder and London: Westview.

Chavez, Cesar. 1993. "Farm Workers at Risk." In *Toxic Struggles: The Theory and Practice of Environmental Justice*, ed. Richard Hofrichter. 163–170. Philadelphia and Gabriola Island, BC: New Society Publishers.

Chavkin, Wendy, ed. 1984. *Double Exposure: Women's Health Hazards on the Job and at Home*. New York: Monthly Review Press.

Christensen, John. 1988. *Deadly Defense: Military Radioactive Landfills*. New York: Radioactive Waste Campaign.

Collinson, Helen. 1989. *Death on Delivery: The Impact of the Arms Trade on the Third World*. London: Campaign Against the Arms Trade.

Cook, Alice and Gwyn Kirk. 1983. *Greenham Women Everywhere*. Boston: South End Press.

Cook, Katsi. 1985. A Community Health Project: Breastfeeding and Toxic Contaminants. *Indian Studies* (Spring): 14–16.

Cook, Katsi. 1993. Update: First Environment Project. *Indigenous Woman* 1 (3): 39–41.

Corea, Gena. 1985. *The Mother Machine: From Artificial Insemination to Artificial Wombs*. San Francisco: Harper and Row.

Corea, Gena et al. 1987. *Man-made Women: How New Reproductive Technologies Affect Women*. Bloomington: Indiana University Press.

Daly, Mary. 1979. *Gyn/Ecology: The Metaethics of Radical Feminism*. Boston: Beacon Press.

Danaher, Kevin, ed. 1994. *Fifty Years is Enough: The case against the World Bank and the I.M.F*. Boston: South End Press.

Daniels, Cynthia R. 1993. *At Women's Expense: State Power and the Politics of Fetal Rights*. Cambridge, MA: Harvard University Press.

Dankelman, Irene and Joan Davidson, eds. 1988. *Women and the Environment in the Third World: Alliance for the Future*. London: Earthscan.

de Ishtar, Zohl. 1994. *Daughters of the Pacific*. Melbourne: Spinifex Press.

Dibblin, Jane. 1989. *Day of Two Suns: U.S. Nuclear Testing and the Pacific Islanders*. New York: New Amsterdam Books.

Durning, Alan. 1989a. Grass-roots Groups are our Best Hope for Global Prosperity and Ecology. *Utne Reader* (July/August): 40–49.

Durning, Alan. 1989b. Groundswell at the Grassroots. *World Watch* (Nov/Dec): 16–23.

Ehrlich, Paul and Anne Ehrlich. 1990. *The Population Explosion*. New York: Simon and Schuster.

Enloe, Cynthia. 1990. *Bananas, Beaches and Bases: Making Feminist Sense of International Politics*. Berkeley: University of California Press.

Gaard, Greta. 1993. *Ecofeminism: Women, Animals, Nature*. Philadelphia: Temple University Press.

George, Susan. 1988. *A Fate Worse than Debt*. London: Penguin Books.

Gibbs, Lois. 1995. *Dying from Dioxin: A Citizens' Guide to Reclaiming Our Health and Rebuilding Democracy*. Boston: South End Press.

Gladstar, Rosemary. 1993. *Herbal Healing for Women: Simple Home Remedies for Women of All Ages*. New York: Simon and Schuster.

Gray, Elizabeth Dodson. 1979. *Green Paradise Lost*. Wellesley, MA: Roundtable Press.

Griffin, Susan. 1978. *Woman and Nature: The Roaring Inside Her*. San Francisco: Harper Colophon.

Hamilton, Cynthia. 1993. Coping with Industrial Exploitation. In *Confronting Environmental Racism: Voices from the Grassroots*, ed. Robert D. Bullard. 63–76. Boston: South End Press.

Harford, Barbara and Sarah Hopkins. 1984. *Women at the Wire*. London: Women's Press.

Hartmann, Betsy. 1991. The Ecology Movement: Targeting Women for Population Control. *Ms. Magazine* (May/June): 83.

Hartmann, Betsy. 1995. *Reproductive Rights and Wrongs: The Global Politics of Population Control*. Revised ed., Boston: South End Press.

Hofrichter, Richard, ed. 1993. *Toxic Struggles: The Theory and Practice of Environmental Justice*. Philadelphia: New Society Publishers.

Hynes, Patricia H. 1991. The Race to Save the Planet: Will Women Lose? *Women's Studies International Forum* 14 (5): 473–78.

ISIS Women's International Information and Communications Service. 1984. *Women in Development: A Resource Guide for Organization and Action*. Philadelphia: New Society Publishers.

Jackson, Donald Dale. 1991. Around Los Ojos, Sheep and Land are Fighting Words. *Smithsonian* (April): 37–47.

Juma, Calestous. 1989. *The Gene Hunters: Biotechnology and the Scramble for Seeds*. Princeton, NJ: Princeton University Press.

King, Ynestra. 1990. Healing the Wounds: Feminism, Ecology, and the Nature/Culture Dualism. In *Reweaving the World: The Emergence of Ecofeminism*, eds. Irene Diamond and Gloria Orenstein. 106–121. San Francisco: Sierra Club Books.

Kirk, Gwyn. 1996 (forthcoming). Rebuilding, Recreating, Respiriting the City from the Ground Up": A Movement in the Making. *Capital, Nature, Socialism*.

Kloppenburg, Jack. 1991. No Hunting! Biodiversity, Indigenous Rights, and Scientific Poaching. *Cultural Survival Quarterly* 15 (3): 14–18.

Krauss, Celene. 1993. Blue-Collar Women and Toxic Wastes Protests: The Process of Politicization. In *Toxic Struggles: The Theory and Practice of Environmental Justice*, ed. Richard Hofrichter. 107–117. Philadelphia and Gabriola Island, BC: New Society Publishers.

Kurzman, Dan. 1987. *A Killing Wind: Inside Union Carbide and the Bhopal Catastrophe*. New York: McGraw-Hill.

LaDuke, Winona. 1993. A Society Based on Conquest Cannot Be Sustained: Native Peoples and the Environmental Crisis. In *Toxic Struggles: The Theory and Practice of Environmental Justice*, ed. Richard Hofrichter. 98–106. Philadelphia and Gabriola Island, BC: New Society Publishers.

Lee, Charles. 1987. *Toxic Wastes and Race in the United States*. New York: Commission for Racial Justice, United Church of Christ.

Leger-Sivard, Ruth. 1991. *World Militaries and Social Expenditures 1990*. Washington DC: World Priorities Inc.

Leonard, Ann, ed. 1989. *Seeds: Supporting Women's Work in the Third World*. New York: The Feminist Press.

Lovelock, James. 1988. *The Ages of Gaia: A Biography of Our Living Earth*. New York: Bantam Books.

Maathai, Wangari. 1988. *The Green Belt Movement: Sharing the Approach and the Experience*. Nairobi: Environmental Liaison Center International.

Maathai, Wangari. 1991. Foresters without Diplomas. *Ms. Magazine* (March/April): 74–5.

Margulis, L. and J. E. Lovelock. 1974. Biological Modulation of the Earth's Atmoshpere. *Icarus* 21: 471–89.

Mather, Robin. 1995. *A Garden of Unearthly Delights: Bioengineering and the Future of Food*. New York: Dutton.

Mellor, Mary. 1992. *Breaking the Boundaries: Towards a Feminist Green Socialism*. London: Virago Press.

Merchant, Carolyn. 1981. *The Death of Nature: Ecology and the Scientific Revolution*. San Francisco: Harper and Row.

Mies, Maria. 1993. The Need for a New Vision: the Subsistence Perspective. In *Ecofeminism*, eds. Maria Mies and Vandana Shiva. London and NJ: Zed Books. 297–324.

Maria Mies and Vandana Shiva. 1993. *Ecofeminism*. London and NJ: Zed Books.

Miss Ann Thropy. 1991. Overpopulation and Industrialism. In *Earth First! Reader*, ed. John Davis. Salt Lake City: Peregrine Smith Books. 137–143.

Moore Lappé, Frances and Joseph Collins. 1986. *World Hunger: Twelve Myths*. New York: Grove Press.

Moore Lappé, Frances and Rachel Schurman. 1988. *Taking Population Seriously*. San Francisco: Institute for Food and Development Policy.

Moses, Marian. 1993. Farmworkers and Pesticides. In *Confronting Environmental Racism: Voices from the Grassroots*, ed. Robert D. Bullard. Boston: South End Press. 161–178.

Mott, Lawrie and Karen Snyder. 1987. *Pesticide Alert: A Guide to Pesticides in Fruit and Vegetables*. San Francisco: Sierra Club Books.

Nelson, Lin. 1990. "The Place of Women in Polluted Places." In *Reweaving the World: The Emergence of Ecofeminism,* eds. Irene Diamond and Gloria Orenstein. San Francisco: Sierra Club Books. 172–187.

Nelson, Lin, Regina Kenen, and Susan Klitzman. 1990. *Turning Things Around: A Women's Occupational and Environmental Health Resource Guide*. Washington DC: National Women's Health Network.

Noble, Charles. 1993. Work: The Most Dangerous Environment. In *Toxic Struggles: The Theory and Practice of Environmental Justice*, ed. Richard Hofrichter. Philadelphia and Gabriola Island, BC: New Society Publishers. 171–78.

O'Connor, Martin, ed. 1994. *Is Capitalism Sustainable? Political Economy and the Politics of Ecology*. New York: Guildford Press.

O'Reilly, Brian. 1991. Cooling Down the World Debt Bomb. *Fortune*, 20 May, 123.

Payer, Cheryl. 1991. *Lent and Lost: Foreign Credit and Third World Development*. London and NJ: Zed Books.

Peña, Devón. 1992. The "Brown" and the "Green": Chicanos and Environmental Politics in the Upper Rio Grande. *Capitalism, Nature, Socialism: A Journal of Socialist Ecology* 3 (1): 79–103.

Phoenix, Janet. 1993. Getting the Lead Out of the Community. In *Confronting Environmental Racism: Voices from the Grassroots*, ed. Robert D. Bullard. Boston: South End Press. 77–92.

Plumwood, Val. 1993. *Feminism and the Mastery of Nature*. New York: Routledge.

Potts, Billie. 1988. *Witches Heal: Lesbian Herbal Self-Sufficiency*. 2nd. ed., Ann Arbor, MI: DuReve Publications.

Pulido, Laura. 1993. Sustainable Development at Ganados del Valle. In *Confronting Environmental Racism: Voices from the Grassroots*, ed. Robert D. Bullard. Boston: South End Press. 123–140.

Raeburn, Paul. 1995. *The Last Harvest: The Genetic Gamble that Threatens to Destroy American Agriculture*. New York: Simon and Schuster.

Reed, David, ed. 1992. *Structural Adjustment and the Environment*. London: Earthscan.

Rodda, Annabel. 1990. *Women and the Environment*. London and NJ: Zed Books.

Sanchez, Carole Lee. 1993. Animal, Vegetable, and Mineral: The Sacred Connection. In *Ecofeminism and the Sacred*, ed. Carol J. Adams. New York: Continuum Books.

Schwab, Jim. 1994. *Deeper Shades of Green: The Rise of Blue-Collar and Minority Environmentalism in America*. San Francisco: Sierra Club Books.

Seager, Joni. 1991. Making Feminist Sense of Environmental Issues. *Sojourner* (Feb).

Seager, Joni. 1993. *Earth Follies: Coming to Feminist Terms with the Global Environmental Crisis*. New York: Routledge.

Seager, Joni and Ann Olson, ed. 1986. *Women in the World: An International Atlas*. New York: Pan Books.

Sen, Gita and Caren Grown. 1987. *Development, Crises, and Alternative Visions: Third World Women's Perspectives*. New York: Monthly Review Press.

Shiva, Vandana. 1988. *Staying Alive: Women, Ecology and Development*. London and NJ: Zed Books.

Shiva, Vandana. 1991. *The Violence of the Green Revolution: Ecological Degradation and Political Conflict*. London and NJ: Zed Books.

Shiva, Vandana. 1993. *Monocultures of the Mind: Perspectives on Biodiversity and Biotechnology*. London and N.J.: Zed Books.

Shrivastava, Paul. 1987. *Bhopal: Anatomy of a Crisis*. Cambridge, MA: Ballinger Publishers.

Sjöö, Monica and Barbara Mor. 1987. *The Great Cosmic Mother: Rediscovering the Religion of the Earth*. San Francisco: Harper and Row.

Spallone, Pat. 1992. *Generation Games: Genetic Engineering and the Future of Our Lives*. London: Women's Press.

Sparr, Pamela. 1994. *Mortgaging Women's Lives: Feminist Critiques of Structural Adjustment*. London and NJ: Zed Books.

Spretnak, Charlene, ed. 1982. *The Politics of Women's Spirituality*. New York: Anchor Books.

Spretnak, Charlene. 1990. Ecofeminism: Our Roots and Flowering. In *Reweaving the World: The Emergence of Ecofeminism*, eds. Irene Diamond and Gloria Orenstein. San Francisco: Sierra Club Books. 3–14.

Stamworth, Michelle. 1988. *Reproductive Technologies: Gender, Motherhood, and Medicine*. Minneapolis: University of Minnesota Press.

Starhawk. 1987. *Truth or Dare: Encounters with Power, Authority, and Mystery*. San Francisco: Harper and Row.

Szasz, Andrew. 1994. *Ecopopulism: Toxic Waste and the Movement for Environmental Justice*. Minneapolis: University of Minnesota Press.

Third World Network. 1988. *Toxic Terror: Dumping of Hazardous Wastes in the Third World*. Penang: Third World Network.

Vickers, Jeanne. 1990. *Women and the World Economic Crisis*. London and NJ: Zed Books.

Waring, Marilyn. 1988. *If Women Counted: A New Feminist Economics*. San Francisco: Harper and Row.

Warren, Karen, ed. 1991. *Hypatia*. Vol. 6. Special issue on Ecological Feminism.

Witte Garland, Anne. 1989. *For Our Kids' Sake: How to Protect Your Child Against Pesticides in Food*. New York: Natural Resources Defense Council.

Women Working for a Nuclear Free and Independent Pacific. 1987. *Pacific Women Speak: Why Haven't You Known?* Oxford: Green Line.

Zeff, Robin Lee, Marsha Love, and Karen Stults, eds. 1989. *Empowering Ourselves: Women and Toxics Organizing*. Falls Church, VA: Citizens Clearinghouse for Hazardous Wastes.

Study Questions

1. According to Kirk, what explains women's disproportionate involvement in environmental and peace activism?

2. What reasons does Kirk offer for thinking that an adequate ecological feminism must take (all of) race, class, gender, and nation into account?

3. Pick one of Kirk's case studies and consider (a) how capitalism, racism, sexism, and/or colonialism (etc.) helps determine current circumstances, (b) what (presumably more just) alternatives are possible, and (c) what trade-offs would be required to move from the existing system to one of the alternatives.

4. What does Kirk recommend we do to bring about social change that will satisfy the principles of ecological feminism?

Leslie Feinberg

Walking Our Talk

I am home, working at my computer. I can hear Minnie Bruce's keyboard clicking and clacking nearby as she puts the finishing touches on an epic poem.

As I reach the conclusion of this book, I am facing another springtime of travel. It is 1998. But the majority of my life is not spent at a podium, invited by people who respect my work. Instead, when I'm out in public, I spend far too much of my precious time and energy trying to find a safe public toilet, or negotiating my way past groups of hostile people who block my path. I spend a lot of time at the gym trying to work off the tension of being stared at—glared at—wherever I go. But I am considered an unwelcome intruder in either the women's or the men's dressing room in the health club.

Most days I feel very isolated—marginalized most places I go. Really, the only places in the world where I fit are the spaces that have been liberated by political struggles. That's what makes it possible for me to speak to students and faculty at universities and colleges, youth groups, community organizations, rallies, and demonstrations. A big chunk of my life is spent editing a weekly socialist newspaper, attending meetings, organizing Deaf and disabled accessibility for rallies, doing group childcare so that parent activists can attend protests, sealing envelopes, faxing press releases, and leafleting at subway stops.

I spend much of my life doing volunteer grassroots organizing because I believe this is the way to win fundamental and lasting change for everyone, including myself, whose life is constricted or injured or disrespected by the system we live under.

Change. Most of us yearn for it. What kind of change do you want? What kind of change is trans liberation fighting for?

What are the goals of the trans movement?

It depends on who you ask. When a movement first begins to surge, many people from all walks of life who share that oppression rise up together and want to put forward one strong demand. But as the movement develops, many divergent ideas are voiced.

How could it be otherwise? I've sat in sleazy diners in the middle of the night listening to homeless teenage drag queens rage against the cops who beat them mercilessly and then demand sex, and against the system that won't cut them a single break. I've sat in conferences with cross-dressers who own banks and railroads, hold high-level government offices, and run television studios. What demands can all these trans people agree on? What definition of liberation? At what points will their political paths diverge?

Some of our issues are so sharply defined and clear we'd be hard pressed to debate them. For example, no matter how you identify yourself, I'm sure you and I agree the devaluation of trans lives must end. No one should be chased down the street or beaten bloody because of what they're wearing or how they define or present themselves. No one should be out of work, paid lower wages, or arbitrarily fired because of their identity. No one who is ill or injured should be turned away from medical care.

Should we stop there? I know I can't.

I feel the necessity to fight for the rights of transsexual men and women to respectful and affordable medical care, and to defend the right of intersexual people to make their own informed decisions about their own bodies. I stand up for every individual's right to their expression of gender, free from criticism or condemnation.

Trans people—everyone in fact—have a right to safe, sanitary, single-occupancy toilets. All trans people deserve identification papers that reflect our lives respectfully. Trans youths have a right to a home and an education; trans elders deserve sensitive care; trans prisoners need defense against prison officials who allow and encourage others to gang rape them.

If you do not identify as a trans person, you can make a significant contribution to our movement. I know many people who do not experience the oppression directly feel diminished and degraded by how trans people are treated. Thousands of people have told me, in conversations, e-mail, letters, and telephone calls, about the pain they felt in the pit of their stomach when a drag queen or transsexual or butch female was verbally harassed in public.

"I didn't know what to do," is what I hear most often. "I didn't want to embarrass the person or call more attention to them. What should I do the next time?" This is frequently the response of a caring, good-hearted person who was caught in a situation that they were never socially prepared for. Each of these people left the situation feeling shaken, emotionally raw, and powerless.

The answer is: There is no formula. There is only this guideline: What would you want a sympathetic stranger to do if you were in a similar situation? It's not easy to deflect the lightning bolts of hate and ridicule directed at one person toward yourself. It's not easy for anyone to stand up to a bully or bullies. You may stand completely alone with that trans person. Or that trans person, caught in the snare of public humiliation, may not even acknowledge your support.

But you may surprise yourself, too. You may tap into that seam of rocky courage that made you the honest, sensitive person you are today. You may inspire other strangers, temporarily silenced by fear, to speak up.

There are other fronts to this fight. Someone on the job might spark a confrontation, for example, because a transsexual coworker, who is transitioning from male-to-female, is using the women's bathroom. If you were in that situation, what you would want a coworker to do for you? You can offer to escort her to the bathroom, so everyone sees you are not buying into the fear being whipped up. You can dispel anxiety that transsexual women pose any danger to another woman. You can face down the loudest bigots, knowing that if trans-phobia goes unchallenged, sexism and anti-lesbian, gay, and bi prejudices will intensify, too.

Each friend and coworker and neighbor and family member you tell about your actions will be more prepared for the moment they defend a trans person. And you may discover that some of them had—or have—trans friends and lovers, but didn't know that you were an open enough person to be confided in. Our loved ones need every iota of support and solidarity that we as trans people do.

You may still leave these confrontations feeling rattled and raw. I know I do. But one thing is sure: You won't feel powerless. You will grow as a person who has come to grips with the fact that the way you are a woman or a man is one way to be, not the only way to be. You will have learned to spot bigotry in another cloaked form. Your pride and confidence in yourself will grow. And you will be a treasured ally.

So, what are the goals of trans liberation? There is not one single answer. If you ask me, the aim should not fall a yard short of genuine social and economic liberation for everyone. How to build a movement capable of achieving that objective, however, is the crux of the matter at hand.

Confronting all forms of gender-phobia and transphobia are very important to me. But I have worked hard all my life and have almost nothing to show for it. In large part because I am a visibly-identified trans person, I've had low-paying jobs that offer no pension and pay a pittance into Social Security. How will I survive as a blue-collar trans elder? I have to literally scrape together hundreds of dollars every month on health insurance. The urgent need for *affordable* health care is just as real for me as the need to tear down the brick walls of bigotry that block my access. Rent devours a bigger chunk of my income every year.

And I face many other struggles. For example, my partner and I have very few rights as a same-sex couple. I am female in a woman-hating society. And I am regularly confronted with anti-Semitism. The oppressions I battle are layered, and all weigh heavily on me.

We're still in the beginning stages of the trans movement. And so the question of what will be the consciousness of this movement is still up for grabs. How this question is settled will have long-term ramifications. Are we simply attempting to win legislative victories? As important as these reforms are, they do not address the root causes of trans oppression.

The majority of trans people suffer from police harassment, assault, racism, sexism, high unemployment, low wages, job insecurity, homelessness, lack of health care, and high rents. The problem for trans people isn't just backward attitudes, it's the system. It's an economic system that is profit-driven—valuing only the bottom line—so people's needs always come last. This Robin-Hood-in-reverse system robs the poor to enrich a tiny fraction of the population. Yet that small wealthy class has learned in a highly refined way that the success to maintaining its rule is to split up the majority, make us point our fingers at one another, focus our anger at each other.

Our trans movement is getting stronger because we're fighting. But the progress that we've made is fragile. History teaches us that when an economic crisis hits, the process of scapegoating becomes more intense and more violent. African-American, Latino, Asian, and Arab peoples, lesbians, gay men, and bisexuals, feminists, trans people—and others who have been in the forefront of progress—will increasingly find themselves in the crosshairs. And the gains we made will all be under siege, as well.

To safeguard what we've won and to move forward requires securing, solidifying, and making more permanent alliances with others who are hurt by the same system. Consciousness plays an important role in cementing this coalition. Shared consciousness becomes a material force because what you're fighting for and what you are determined to win together has a big impact on how your foes react to you.

For example, if in the course of the Vietnam war the U.S. anti-war movement had only demanded negotiations, that would have been defined as the outer limit of the debate in this country.

But the consciousness of all the Vietnamese who were fighting the seemingly overwhelming Pentagon forces was that they weren't going to give up. They were going to fight to the death for their freedom. This determination of the Vietnamese had a profound impact on the consciousness of people in the United States. The growing consciousness here became: We don't want one more person to die!

The resolve of the Vietnamese and its effect on anti-war consciousness in the United States had a deep and pervasive impact on those who had the most to gain and the least to lose by refusing to fight—U.S. soldiers. By 1971, one out of four of all U.S. military soldiers worldwide—not just those in Vietnam—had either gone AWOL or deserted. And many other soldiers—individually and as groups—actively resisted the war in Vietnam, refused to put down rebellions in inner cities in the United States, held sit-down actions, fragged abusive officers, and participated in other acts of rebellion. The might of their combined consciousness made it very hard for the brass to conduct a war.

Or look at the consciousness of impoverished working-class people in the United States during the

1930s. People were so poor during the Depression that they were literally starving to death in the streets. They joined the ranks of massive protests and made it clear they were going to keep fighting until they got some justice. And that social upheaval resulted in the reform package known as the New Deal.

The Social Security Act wasn't passed because people lobbied politicians. It was passed because in cities across the country tens of thousands of unemployed people marched and rallied and waged militant strikes. When the landlords evicted tenants, organizing committees moved them back in; when the electric companies shut off people's lights and gas, progressive organizers came in and turned them back on. There was a growing radicalization—a rising tide of struggle.

And when people started to fight together in the mid-1930s on issues of economic and social security and the right to unionize, it brought Black/white unity to the fore. People needed each other in order to win their demands. As a result, the number of lynchings in this country plunged precipitously.

The Klan and lynchings were developed as barbarous weapons of counter-revolutionary terror to dismantle the tremendous social victories of African Americans during Black Reconstruction, and later to maintain an apartheid-like police state in the southern half of this country. Between 1866 and 1933 there were some 5,000 recorded lynchings in the United States. The rate reached a horrendous height around the beginning of the economic Depression in 1929.

The sharpest and most significant decrease in lynchings in this country, however, was around 1933 and 1934, during a period of acute capitalist economic crisis. Those years coincided with the rise of a mass workers' movement that organized African-American and white workers together into the CIO—the Congress of Industrial Organizations. It coincided with the rise of the 1934 general strikes of workers in San Francisco and Toledo and Minneapolis and military factory occupations—known as sit-down strikes—that swept from auto workers, to electric storage battery makers, to hosiery workers.

This ascending workers' movement did not put an end once and for all to lynchings. But it pushed back this and other forms of terror. And the degree to which right-wing violence has surged or been suppressed since then has depended on the relative strength of the working class in its struggle against the wealthy owning class. When the majority of working people awaken to their own class interests and act together to take collective action, the social equation is dramatically changed in a period of such rising struggle.

Many movements have come before the trans liberation movement: the movement to abolish slavery, women's suffrage, workers' rights, civil rights, gay liberation, anti-Vietnam war, women's liberation, Deaf and disabled liberation. These social movements have had a profound social impact on U.S. life.

Does our trans movement have to start from scratch or can we build on what we've learned from the last 150 years? What lessons can we glean from struggles that preceded ours? What are the best tactics and strategy to win our demands? How can we not only protect our victories, but gain new ground?

And where is the mass movement in the streets that trans liberation can ally itself with? Where is the struggle today that can turn the tide of reaction? Where are the hundreds of thousands in the streets, marching and demanding justice, like the protests of the 1930s that won the right to unionize, to Social Security, to welfare and unemployment insurance, to public housing? Today, Corporate America and its politicians are taking the reforms of the New Deal off the table. Where is the massive, angry response?

Is a mass upsurge possible today? If so, can we make the demands of the trans communities a strong voice within that tide of resistance? Who can we look toward to build such a movement?

All our lives we have been taught that those of us who do the work of the world are not the agents of historical change. Instead, we are told that the only way we can have any impact on the direction of the economy, or society as a whole, is to vote once every four years for one of two parties that are funded by and beholden to big business.

Since the 1930s, the Republican and Democratic Party have played hard cop, soft cop when it comes to domestic economic policy. The Democratic Party has taken credit for legislative reforms like the New Deal. But do the Democrats really deserve that credit? This is an important question, especially since some in the lesbian, gay, bi, and trans communities look to the Democratic Party as a vehicle of progressive reform. So how the New Deal was won, for example, has meaning for our movement.

Franklin Roosevelt, a Democrat, took office three years after the cataclysmic 1929 capitalist economic crash. His administration presided during a powerful mass upsurge of the working class that threatened to erupt into a general working-class rebellion. The Roosevelt administration was in charge of trying to quell this pre-revolutionary surge. His job was to save capitalism. And the New Deal was meant to do just that. And so the New Deal was a great legislative victory wrested through struggle. Workers won it.

Democrat Lyndon Johnson was similarly forced to make concessions as a result of the great struggles of the 1960s. His administration created new social programs like the "War on Poverty" in order to buy social peace at home, while waging war in Vietnam. These policies, plus the strong war economy, helped isolate young middle-class activists and keep rebellion from sweeping the entire working class.

The Democratic Party cannot lead us forward to trans liberation. They've led us into war and economic austerity: Woodrow Wilson led the United States into World War I; Franklin Roosevelt led the country into World War II. Truman started the Korean War. John Kennedy and Lyndon Johnson began and widened the Vietnam War.

The reactionary drive to slash social services began during the late 1970s, when Democrat Jimmy Carter started draining social services to fuel a $2 trillion military buildup. And he was the mastermind of the union-busting plan to attack the air traffic controllers—implemented by Reagan in 1981—that was the opening gun of the current anti-labor offensive.

The process of transferring wealth from working people to the wealthy continued after Reagan. The rate actually accelerated during the first four years of the Clinton Democratic administration.

Whether a Democrat or a Republican presides, both parties administer the same system on behalf of big business. As the trans struggle unfolds, it will become critical to develop an independent movement that can free itself from the grip of "lesser-of-two-evils" politics of waiting to get another Democrat in office.

The truth is, you and I are the stuff that great leaders are made of. We don't have to wait for a distinguished white man on a horse or a politician wealthy enough to win office in a multimillion dollar campaign to usher in justice and equality. The ranks of rebellions and revolutions that have shaped human history have been made up of people like you and me. That history lesson has been purposefully kept from us.

Where is the great social movement in the streets that will help support and strengthen our demand for trans liberation? Will we see it in our lifetimes? No crystal ball exists to predict mass awakening. But laws of motion and development do exist: Repression breeds resistance. That's the lesson of Stonewall.

And remember what Sylvia Rivera said about that rebellion? "I always believed that we would have a fight back. I just didn't know it would be that night."

When I was growing up in the 1950s, the right-wing repression was ferocious. Working-class families like my own went about our lives, going to work, going to school, paying the bills, feeding the cat. We couldn't see the momentous struggles of the 1960s on the horizon. We didn't realize that the repression was making it impossible not to struggle, not to fight back.

Of all the periods of human history, I am excited to live in this particular epoch. In just five decades, I have witnessed technology outstrip anything I saw as a child in a Buck Rogers movie, or anything I read by Jules Vernes—Mars probes, Pentium chips, laser microsurgery. Yet sweatshop conditions today—in this country and around the world—are reminiscent of the nineteenth century exploitation of labor that I read about as a child in Charles Dickens's novels. It is this contradiction that creates the material basis for the inevitable rise of an independent, anti-capitalist movement by the working class.

Will trans people be in the front ranks of these battles? Of course we will be. Wherever oppression has existed, we have been at the forefront of struggles.

History has recorded the names of many trans warriors. We all grew up hearing about Joan of Arc, for example. Few of us, though, were taught that she was a masculine, cross-dressing female. Joan of Arc was an illiterate, peasant teenager. She became a brilliant leader of a peasant army because she was able to rise to the demands of the historical moment in which she lived.

So did the cross-dressed leaders of urban rebellions like "Captain" Alice Clark, a cross-dressed female who led a crowd of women and cross-dressed males in England in 1629 in an uprising over the high cost of grain. So did Rebecca and her Daughters—peasant guerrilla armies that shaped Welsh history by fighting British occupation in the nineteenth century. So did Louisa Capetillo, the Puerto Rican cross-dresser and socialist feminist who led tobacco workers in battles against their bosses in the early twentieth century. So did Magnus Hirschfeld, a Jewish, gay, feminine, socialist leader at the turn of the twentieth century who led a movement for the rights of trans people and same-sex love in Germany. So did Marsha Johnson and Sylvia Rivera, impoverished drag queens who fought the cops at the Stonewall Rebellion in 1969.

The irony is that many of those trans leaders did not fight only for civil rights for transgender, transsexual, intersexual, lesbian, gay, and bisexual people. They fought colonization, unjust wars, hunger, privatization of land, gouging taxation, repression by the police and military, homelessness, and economic exploitation. They fought for the rights of everyone who was tyrannized and downtrodden.

We remember their names for the same reason we remember Nat Turner's and Sojourner Truth's and John Brown's—because they fought back, even when the economic and social system that oppressed them seemed invincible. Imagine how during the nineteenth century in the United States it must have seemed as though slavery could last forever. There was no mass movement. They didn't have millions of followers. But Nat Turner, Sojourner Truth, and John Brown fought back anyway. In doing so, they became *catalysts* to the movement to abolish slavery.

The people who make a difference in history are those who fight for freedom—not because they're guaranteed to succeed—but because it's the right thing to do. And that's the kind of fighters that history demands today. Not those who worship the accomplished fact. Not those who can only believe in what is visible today. But instead, people of conscience who dedicate their lives to what needs to be won, and what can be won.

I am confident that you and I will find each other, shoulder-to-shoulder, in that historic struggle.

Study Questions

1. According to Feinberg, what political strategy will bring about "lasting and fundamental change for everyone"? What is Feinberg's argument for adopting this strategy?

2. According to Feinberg, what ought to be the goals of trans liberation? Explain.

3. This article focuses a great deal on economics. In Feinberg's view, what does economics have to do with trans liberation?

Gayle S. Rubin

Thinking Sex: Notes for a Radical Theory of the Politics of Sexuality

II SEXUAL THOUGHTS

"You see, Tim," Phillip said suddenly, "your argument isn't reasonable. Suppose I granted your first point that homosexuality is justifiable in certain instances and under certain controls. Then there is the catch: where does justification end and degeneracy begin? Society must condemn to protect. Permit even the intellectual homosexual a place of respect and the first bar is down. Then comes the next and the next until the sadist, the flagellist, the criminally insane demand their places, and society ceases to exist. So I ask again: where is the line drawn? Where does degeneracy begin if not at the beginning of individual freedom in such matters?"

(Fragment from a discussion between two gay men trying to decide if they may love each other, from a novel published in 1950.)

A radical theory of sex must identify, describe, explain, and denounce erotic injustice and sexual oppression. Such a theory needs refined conceptual tools which can grasp the subject and hold it in view. It must build rich descriptions of sexuality as it exists in society and history. It requires a convincing critical language that can convey the barbarity of sexual persecution.

Several persistent features of thought about sex inhibit the development of such a theory. These assumptions are so pervasive in Western culture that they are rarely questioned. Thus, they tend to reappear in different political contexts, acquiring new rhetorical expressions but reproducing fundamental axioms.

One such axiom is sexual essentialism—the idea that sex is a natural force that exists prior to social life and shapes institutions. Sexual essentialism is embedded in the folk wisdoms of Western societies, which consider sex to be eternally unchanging, asocial, and transhistorical. Dominated for over a century by medicine, psychiatry, and psychology, the academic study of sex has reproduced essentialism. These fields classify sex as a property of individuals. It may reside in their hormones or their psyches. It may be construed as physiological or psychological. But within these ethnoscientific categories, sexuality has no history and no significant social determinants.

During the last five years, a sophisticated historical and theoretical scholarship has challenged sexual essentialism both explicitly and implicitly. Gay history, particularly the work of Jeffrey Weeks, has led this assault by showing that homosexuality as we know it is a relatively modern institutional complex. Many historians have come to see the contemporary institutional forms of heterosexuality as an even more recent development. An important contributor to the new scholarship is Judith Walkowitz, whose research

Gayle Rubin, "Thinking Sex," from *Pleasure and Danger: Exploring Female Sexuality*, edited by Carole S. Vance, Pandora Press, London, 1989. Notes have been edited and renumbered.

has demonstrated the extent to which prostitution was transformed around the turn of the century. She provides meticulous descriptions of how the interplay of social forces such as ideology, fear, political agitation, legal reform, and medical practice can change the structure of sexual behavior and alter its consequences.

Michel Foucault's *The History of Sexuality* has been the most influential and emblematic text of the new scholarship on sex. Foucault criticizes the traditional understanding of sexuality as a natural libido yearning to break free of social constraint. He argues that desires are not preexisting biological entities, but rather, that they are constituted in the course of historically specific social practices. He emphasizes the generative aspects of the social organization of sex rather than its repressive elements by pointing out that new sexualities are constantly produced. And he points to a major discontinuity between kinship-based systems of sexuality and more modern forms.

The new scholarship on sexual behavior has given sex a history and created a constructivist alternative to sexual essentialism. Underlying this body of work is an assumption that sexuality is constituted in society and history, not biologically ordained. This does not mean the biological capacities are not prerequisites for human sexuality. It does mean that human sexuality is not comprehensible in purely biological terms. Human organisms with human brains are necessary for human cultures, but no examination of the body or its parts can explain the nature and variety of human social systems. The belly's hunger gives no clues as to the complexities of cuisine. The body, the brain, the genitalia, and the capacity for language are all necessary for human sexuality. But they do not determine its content, its experiences, or its institutional forms. Moreover, we never encounter the body unmediated by the meanings that cultures give to it. To paraphrase Lévi-Strauss, my position on the relationship between biology and sexuality is a "Kantianism without a transcendental libido."

It is impossible to think with any clarity about the politics of race or gender as long as these are thought of as biological entities rather than as social constructs. Similarly, sexuality is impervious to political

analysis as long as it is primarily conceived as a biological phenomenon or an aspect of individual psychology. Sexuality is as much a human product as are diets, methods of transportation, systems of etiquette, forms of labor, types of entertainment, processes of production, and modes of oppression. Once sex is understood in terms of social analysis and historical understanding, a more realistic politics of sex becomes possible. One may then think of sexual politics in terms of such phenomena as populations, neighborhoods, settlement patterns, migration, urban conflict, epidemiology, and police technology. These are more fruitful categories of thought than the more traditional ones of sin, disease, neurosis, pathology, decadence, pollution, or the decline and fall of empires.

By detailing the relationships between stigmatized erotic populations and the social forces which regulate them, work such as that of Allan Bérubé, John D'Emilio, Jeffrey Weeks, and Judith Walkowitz contains implicit categories of political analysis and criticism. Nevertheless, the constructivist perspective has displayed some political weaknesses. This has been most evident in misconstructions of Foucault's position.

Because of his emphasis on the ways that sexuality is produced, Foucault has been vulnerable to interpretations that deny or minimize the reality of sexual repression in the more political sense. Foucault makes it abundantly clear that he is not denying the existence of sexual repression so much as inscribing it within a large dynamic. Sexuality in Western societies has been structured within an extremely punitive social framework, and has been subjected to very real formal and informal controls. It is necessary to recognize repressive phenomena without resorting to the essentialist assumptions of the language of libido. It is important to hold repressive sexual practices in focus, even while situating them within a different totality and a more refined terminology.

Most radical thought about sex has been embedded within a model of the instincts and their restraints. Concepts of sexual oppression have been lodged within that more biological understanding of sexuality. It is often easier to fall back on the notion of a natural

libido subjected to inhumane repression than to refor-
mulate concepts of sexual injustice within a more
constructivist framework. But it is essential that we
do so. We need a radical critique of sexual arrangements that has the conceptual elegance of Foucault
and the evocative passion of Reich.

The new scholarship on sex has brought a welcome insistence that sexual terms be restricted to
their proper historical and social contexts, and a cau-
tionary scepticism towards sweeping generalizations.
But it is important to be able to indicate groupings
of erotic behavior and general trends within erotic
discourse. In addition to sexual essentialism, there
are at least five other ideological formations whose
grip on sexual thought is so strong that to fail to discuss them is to remain enmeshed within them. These
are sex negativity, the fallacy of misplaced scale, the
hierarchical valuation of sex acts, the domino theory
of sexual peril, and the lack of a concept of benign
sexual variation.

Of these five, the most important is sex negativity.
Western cultures generally consider sex to be a dangerous, destructive, negative force. Most Christian
tradition, following Paul, holds that sex is inherently
sinful. It may be redeemed if performed within marriage for procreative purposes and if the pleasurable
aspects are not enjoyed too much. In turn, this idea
rests on the assumption that the genitalia are an
intrinsically inferior part of the body, much lower and
less holy than the mind, the "soul," the "heart," or
even the upper part of the digestive system (the status
of the excretory organs is close to that of the genitalia). Such notions have by now acquired a life of
their own and no longer depend solely on religion for
their perseverance.

This culture always treats sex with suspicion. It
construes and judges almost any sexual practice in
terms of its worst possible expression. Sex is presumed
guilty until proven innocent. Virtually all erotic
behavior is considered bad unless a specific reason to
exempt it has been established. The most acceptable
excuses are marriage, reproduction, and love. Sometimes scientific curiosity, aesthetic experience, or a
long-term intimate relationship may serve. But the
exercise of erotic capacity, intelligence, curiosity, or

creativity all require pretexts that are unnecessary for
other pleasures, such as the enjoyment of food, fiction, or astronomy.

What I call the fallacy of misplaced scale is a
corollary of sex negativity. Susan Sontag once commented that since Christianity focused "on sexual
behavior as the root of virtue, everything pertaining
to sex has been a 'special case' in our culture." Sex
law has incorporated the religious attitude that hereti-
cal sex is an especially heinous sin that deserves the
harshest punishments. Throughout much of European
and American history, a single act of consensual anal
penetration was grounds for execution. In some states,
sodomy still carries twenty-year prison sentences.
Outside the law, sex is also a marked category. Small
differences in value or behavior are often experienced
as cosmic threats. Although people can be intolerant,
silly, or pushy about what constitutes proper diet, differences in menu rarely provoke the kinds of rage,
anxiety, and sheer terror that routinely accompany
differences in erotic taste. Sexual acts are burdened
with an excess of significance.

Modern Western societies appraise sex acts according to a hierarchical system of sexual value. Marital,
reproductive heterosexuals are alone at the top of the
erotic pyramid. Clamoring below are unmarried
monogamous heterosexuals in couples, followed by
most other heterosexuals. Solitary sex floats ambigu-
ously. The powerful nineteenth-century stigma on
masturbation lingers in less potent, modified forms,
such as the idea that masturbation is an inferior
substitute for partnered encounters. Stable, long-term
lesbian and gay male couples are verging on respectability, but bar dykes and promiscuous gay men are
hovering just above the groups at the very bottom of
the pyramid. The most despised sexual castes currently include transsexuals, transvestites, fetishists,
sadomasochists, sex workers such as prostitutes and
porn models, and the lowliest of all, those whose
eroticism transgresses generational boundaries.

Individuals whose behavior stands high in this
hierarchy are rewarded with certified mental health,
respectability, legality, social and physical mobility,
institutional support, and material benefits. As sexual
behaviors or occupations fall lower on the scale, the

individuals who practice them are subjected to a presumption of mental illness, disreputability, criminality, restricted social and physical mobility, loss of institutional support, and economic sanctions.

Extreme and punitive stigma maintains some sexual behaviors as low status and is an effective sanction against those who engage in them. The intensity of this stigma is rooted in Western religious traditions. But most of its contemporary content derives from medical and psychiatric opprobrium.

The old religious taboos were primarily based on kinship forms of social organization. They were meant to deter inappropriate unions and to provide proper kin. Sex laws derived from Biblical pronouncements were aimed at preventing the acquisition of the wrong kinds of affinal partners: consanguineous kin (incest), the same gender (homosexuality), or the wrong species (bestiality). When medicine and psychiatry acquired extensive powers over sexuality, they were less concerned with unsuitable mates than with unfit forms of desire. If taboos against incest best characterized kinship systems of sexual organization, then the shift to an emphasis on taboos against masturbation was more apposite to the newer systems organized around qualities of erotic experience.

Medicine and psychiatry multiplied the categories of sexual misconduct. The section on psychosexual disorders in the *Diagnostic and Statistical Manual of Mental and Physical Disorders (DSM)* of the American Psychiatric Association (APA) is a fairly reliable map of the current moral hierarchy of sexual activities. The APA list is much more elaborate than the traditional condemnations of whoring, sodomy, and adultery. The most recent edition, *DSM-III*, removed homosexuality from the roster of mental disorders after a long political struggle. But fetishism, sadism, masochism, transsexuality, transvestism, exhibitionism, voyeurism, and pedophilia are quite firmly entrenched as psychological malfunctions. Books are still being written about the genesis, etiology, treatment, and cure of these assorted "pathologies."

Psychiatric condemnation of sexual behaviors invokes concepts of mental and emotional inferiority rather than categories of sexual sin. Low-status sex practices are vilified as mental diseases or symptoms of defective personality integration. In addition, psychological terms conflate difficulties of psychodynamic functioning with modes of erotic conduct. They equate sexual masochism with self-destructive personality patterns, sexual sadism with emotional aggression, and homoeroticism with immaturity. These terminological muddles have become powerful stereotypes that are indiscriminately applied to individuals on the basis of their sexual orientations.

Popular culture is permeated with ideas that erotic variety is dangerous, unhealthy, depraved, and a menace to everything from small children to national security. Popular sexual ideology is a noxious stew made up of ideas of sexual sin, concepts of psychological inferiority, anti-communism, mob hysteria, accusations of witchcraft, and xenophobia. The mass media nourish these attitudes with relentless propaganda. I would call this system of erotic stigma the last socially respectable form of prejudice if the old forms did not show such obstinate vitality, and new ones did not continually become apparent.

All these hierarchies of sexual value—religious, psychiatric, and popular—function in much the same ways as do ideological systems of racism, ethnocentrism, and religious chauvinism. They rationalize the well-being of the sexually privileged and the adversity of the sexual rabble.

Figure 1 diagrams a general version of the sexual value system. According to this system, sexuality that is "good," "normal," and "natural" should ideally be heterosexual, marital, monogamous, reproductive, and non-commercial. It should be coupled, relational, within the same generation, and occur at home. It should not involve pornography, fetish objects, sex toys of any sort, or roles other than male and female. Any sex that violates these rules is "bad," "abnormal," or "unnatural." Bad sex may be homosexual, unmarried, promiscuous, non-procreative, or commercial. It may be masturbatory or take place at orgies, may be casual, may cross generational lines, and may take place in "public," or at least in the bushes or the baths. It may involve the use of pornography, fetish objects, sex toys, or unusual roles (see Figure 1).

The charmed circle:
Good, Normal, Natural, Blessed Sexuality

Heterosexual
Married
Monogamous
Procreative
Non-commercial
In pairs
In a relationship
Same generation
In private
No pornography
Bodies only
Vanilla

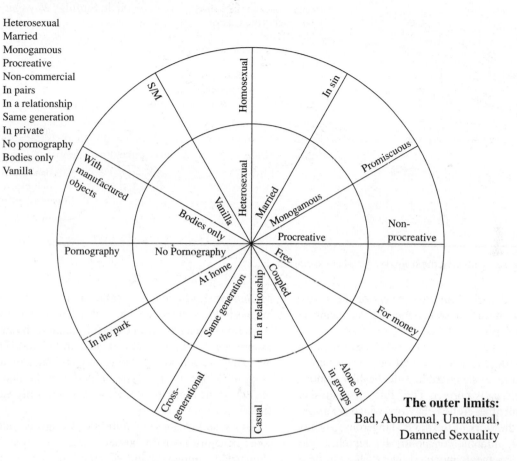

The outer limits:
Bad, Abnormal, Unnatural,
Damned Sexuality

Homosexual
Unmarried
Promiscuous
Non-procreative
Commercial
Alone or in groups
Casual
Cross-generational
In public
Pornography
With manufactured objects
Sadomasochistic

Figure 1 The sex hierarchy: the charmed circle vs. the outer limits

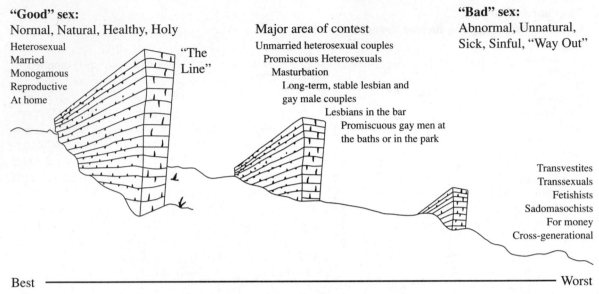

"Good" sex:
Normal, Natural, Healthy, Holy

Heterosexual
Married
Monogamous
Reproductive
At home

"The Line"

Major area of contest

Unmarried heterosexual couples
Promiscuous Heterosexuals
Masturbation
Long-term, stable lesbian and
gay male couples
Lesbians in the bar
Promiscuous gay men at
the baths or in the park

"Bad" sex:
Abnormal, Unnatural,
Sick, Sinful, "Way Out"

Transvestites
Transsexuals
Fetishists
Sadomasochists
For money
Cross-generational

Best ——————————————————————————————————————— Worst

Figure 2 The sex hierarchy: the struggle over where to draw the line

Figure 2 diagrams another aspect of the sexual hierarchy: the need to draw and maintain an imaginary line between good and bad sex. Most of the discourses on sex, be they religious, psychiatric, popular, or political, delimit a very small portion of human sexual capacity as sanctifiable, safe, healthy, mature, legal, or politically correct. The "line" distinguishes these from all other erotic behaviors, which are understood to be the work of the devil, dangerous, psychopathological, infantile, or politically reprehensible. Arguments are then conducted over "where to draw the line," and to determine what other activities, if any, may be permitted to cross over into acceptability.[1]

All these models assume a domino theory of sexual peril. The line appears to stand between sexual order and chaos. It expresses the fear that if anything is permitted to cross this erotic DMZ, the barrier against scary sex will crumble and something unspeakable will skitter across.

Most systems of sexual judgment—religious, psychological, feminist, or socialist—attempt to determine on which side of the line a particular act falls. Only sex acts on the good side of the line are accorded moral complexity. For instance, heterosexual encounters may be sublime or disgusting, free or forced,

healing or destructive, romantic or mercenary. As long as it does not violate other rules, heterosexuality is acknowledged to exhibit the full range of human experience. In contrast, all sex acts on the bad side of the line are considered utterly repulsive and devoid of all emotional nuance. The further from the line a sex act is, the more it is depicted as a uniformly bad experience.

As a result of the sex conflicts of the last decade, some behavior near the border is inching across it. Unmarried couples living together, masturbation, and some forms of homosexuality are moving in the direction of respectability (see Figure 2). Most homosexuality is still on the bad side of the line. But if it is coupled and monogamous, the society is beginning to recognize that it includes the full range of human interaction. Promiscuous homosexuality, sadomasochism, fetishism, transsexuality, and cross-generational encounters are still viewed as unmodulated horrors incapable of involving affection, love, free choice, kindness, or transcendence.

This kind of sexual morality has more in common with ideologies of racism than with true ethics. It grants virtue to the dominant groups, and relegates vice to the underprivileged. A democratic morality should judge sexual acts by the way partners treat one another, the level of mutual consideration, the presence or absence of coercion, and the quantity and quality of the pleasures they provide. Whether sex acts are gay or straight, coupled or in groups, naked or in underwear, commercial or free, with or without video, should not be ethical concerns.

It is difficult to develop a pluralistic sexual ethics without a concept of benign sexual variation. Variation is a fundamental property of all life, from the simplest biological organisms to the most complex human social formations. Yet sexuality is supposed to conform to a single standard. One of the most tenacious ideas about sex is that there is one best way to do it, and that everyone should do it that way.

Most people find it difficult to grasp that whatever they like to do sexually will be thoroughly repulsive to someone else, and that whatever repels them sexually will be the most treasured delight of someone, somewhere. One need not like or perform a particular sex act in order to recognize that someone else will, and that this difference does not indicate a lack of good taste, mental health, or intelligence in either party. Most people mistake their sexual preferences for a universal system that will or should work for everyone.

This notion of a single ideal sexuality characterizes most systems of thought about sex. For religion, the ideal is procreative marriage. For psychology, it is mature heterosexuality. Although its content varies, the format of a single sexual standard is continually reconstituted within other rhetorical frameworks, including feminism and socialism. It is just as objectionable to insist that everyone should be lesbian, non-monogamous, or kinky, as to believe that everyone should be heterosexual, married, or vanilla—though the latter set of opinions are backed by considerably more coercive power than the former.

Progressives who would be ashamed to display cultural chauvinism in other areas routinely exhibit it towards sexual differences. We have learned to cherish different cultures as unique expressions of human inventiveness rather than as the inferior or disgusting habits of savages. We need a similarly anthropological understanding of different sexual cultures.

Empirical sex research is the one field that does incorporate a positive concept of sexual variation. Alfred Kinsey approached the study of sex with the same uninhibited curiosity he had previously applied to examining a species of wasp. His scientific detachment gave his work a refreshing neutrality that enraged moralists and caused immense controversy. Among Kinsey's successors, John Gagnon and William Simon have pioneered the application of sociological understandings to erotic variety. Even some of the older sexology is useful. Although his work is imbued with unappetizing eugenic beliefs, Havelock Ellis was an acute and sympathetic observer. His monumental *Studies in the Psychology of Sex* is resplendent with detail.

Much political writing on sexuality reveals complete ignorance of both classical sexology and modern sex research. Perhaps this is because so few colleges and universities bother to teach human sexuality, and because so much stigma adheres even to scholarly investigation of sex. Neither sexology nor sex research has been immune to the prevailing sexual value system. Both contain assumptions and information which should not be accepted uncritically. But sexology and sex research provide abundant detail, a welcome posture of calm, and a well-developed ability to treat sexual variety as something that exists rather than as something to be exterminated. These fields can provide an empirical grounding for a radical theory of sexuality more useful than the combination of psychoanalysis and feminist first principles to which so many texts resort. . . .

VI THE LIMITS OF FEMINISM

We know that in an overwhelmingly large number of cases, sex crime is associated with pornography. We know that sex criminals read it, are clearly influenced by it. I believe that, if we can eliminate the distribution of such items among impressionable children, we shall greatly reduce our frightening sex-crime rate.

(J. Edgar Hoover)

In the absence of a more articulated radical theory of sex, most progressives have turned to feminism for guidance. But the relationship between feminism and sex is complex. Because sexuality is a nexus of the relationships between genders, much of the oppression of women is borne by, mediated through, and constituted within, sexuality. Feminism has always been vitally interested in sex. But there have been two strains of feminist thought on the subject. One tendency has criticized the restrictions on women's sexual behavior and denounced the high costs imposed on women for being sexually active. This tradition of feminist sexual thought has called for a sexual liberation that would work for women as well as for men. The second tendency has considered sexual liberalization to be inherently a mere extension of male privilege. This tradition resonates with conservative, anti-sexual discourse. With the advent of the anti-pornography movement, it achieved temporary hegemony over feminist analysis.

The anti-pornography movement and its texts have been the most extensive expression of this discourse. In addition, proponents of this viewpoint have condemned virtually every variant of sexual expression as anti-feminist. Within this framework, monogamous lesbianism that occurs within long-term, intimate relationships and which does not involve playing with polarized roles, has replaced married, procreative heterosexuality at the top of the value hierarchy. Heterosexuality has been demoted to somewhere in the middle. Apart from this change, everything else looks more or less familiar. The lower depths are occupied by the usual groups and behaviors: prostitution, transsexuality, sadomasochism, and cross-generational activities. Most gay male conduct, all casual sex, promiscuity, and lesbian behavior that does involve roles or kink or non-monogamy are also censured. Even sexual fantasy during masturbation is denounced as a phallo-centric holdover.

This discourse on sexuality is less a sexology than a demonology. It presents most sexual behavior in the worst possible light. Its descriptions of erotic conduct always use the worst available example as if it were representative. It presents the most disgusting pornography, the most exploited forms of prostitution, and the least palatable or most shocking manifestations of sexual variation. This rhetorical tactic consistently misrepresents human sexuality in all its forms. The picture of human sexuality that emerges from this literature is unremittingly ugly.

In addition, this anti-porn rhetoric is a massive exercise in scapegoating. It criticizes non-routine acts of love rather than routine acts of oppression, exploitation, or violence. This demon sexology directs legitimate anger at women's lack of personal safety against innocent individuals, practices, and communities. Anti-porn propaganda often implies that sexism originates within the commercial sex industry and subsequently infects the rest of society. This is sociologically nonsensical. The sex industry is hardly a feminist utopia. It reflects the sexism that exists in the society as a whole. We need to analyze and oppose the manifestations of gender inequality specific to the sex industry. But this is not the same as attempting to wipe out commercial sex.

Similarly, erotic minorities such as sadomasochists and transsexuals are as likely to exhibit sexist attitudes or behavior as any other politically random social grouping. But to claim that they are inherently anti-feminist is sheer fantasy. A good deal of current feminist literature attributes the oppression of women to graphic representations of sex, prostitution, sex education, sadomasochism, male homosexuality, and transsexualism. Whatever happened to the family, religion, education, child-rearing practices, the media, the state, psychiatry, job discrimination, and unequal pay?

Finally, this so-called feminist discourse recreates a very conservative sexual morality. For over a century, battles have been waged over just how much shame, distress, and punishment should be incurred by sexual activity. The conservative tradition has promoted opposition to pornography, prostitution, homosexuality, all erotic variation, sex education, sex research, abortion, and contraception. The opposing, pro-sex tradition has included individuals like Havelock Ellis, Magnus Hirschfeld, Alfred Kinsey, and Victoria Woodhull, as well as the sex education movement, organizations of militant prostitutes and homosexuals, the reproductive rights movement, and organizations such as the Sexual Reform League of the 1960s. This motley collection of sex reformers, sex educators, and sexual militants has mixed records on both sexual and feminist issues. But surely they are closer to the spirit of modern feminism than are moral crusaders, the social purity movement, and anti-vice organizations. Nevertheless, the current feminist sexual demonology generally elevates the anti-vice crusaders to positions of ancestral honor, while condemning the more liberatory tradition as anti-feminist. In an essay that exemplifies some of these trends, Sheila Jeffreys blames Havelock Ellis, Edward Carpenter, Alexandra Kollantai, "believers in the joy of sex of every possible political persuasion," and the 1929 congress of the World League for Sex Reform for making "a great contribution to the defeat of militant feminism."

The anti-pornography movement and its avatars have claimed to speak for all feminism. Fortunately, they do not. Sexual liberation has been and continues to be a feminist goal. The women's movement may have produced some of the most retrogressive sexual thinking this side of the Vatican. But it has also produced an exciting, innovative, and articulate defense of sexual pleasure and erotic justice. This "pro-sex" feminism has been spearheaded by lesbians whose sexuality does not conform to movement standards of purity (primarily lesbian sadomasochists and butch/femme dykes), by unapologetic heterosexuals, and by women who adhere to classic radical feminism rather than to the revisionist celebrations of femininity which have become so common. Although the anti-porn forces have attempted to weed anyone who disagrees with them out of the movement, the fact remains that feminist thought about sex is profoundly polarized.

Whenever there is polarization, there is an unhappy tendency to think the truth lies somewhere in between. Ellen Willis has commented sarcastically that "the feminist bias is that women are equal to men and the male chauvinist bias is that women are inferior. The unbiased view is that the truth lies somewhere in between." The most recent development in the feminist sex wars is the emergence of a "middle" that seeks to evade the dangers of anti-porn fascism, on the one hand, and a supposed "anything goes" libertarianism, on the other. Although it is hard to criticize a position that is not yet fully formed, I want to draw attention to some incipient problems.

The emergent middle is based on a false characterization of the poles of the debate, construing both sides as equally extremist. According to B. Ruby Rich, "the desire for a language of sexuality has led feminists into locations (pornography, sadomasochism) too narrow or overdetermined for a fruitful discussion. Debate has collapsed into a rumble." True, the fights between Women Against Pornography (WAP) and lesbian sadomasochists have resembled gang warfare. But the responsibility for this lies primarily with the anti-porn movement, and its refusal to engage in principled discussion. S/M lesbians have been forced into a struggle to maintain their membership in the movement, and to defend themselves against slander. No major spokeswoman for lesbian S/M has argued for any kind of S/M supremacy, or advocated that everyone should be a sadomasochist. In addition to self-defense, S/M lesbians have called for appreciation for erotic diversity and more open discussion of sexuality. Trying to find a middle course between WAP and Samois is a bit like saying that the truth about homosexuality lies somewhere between the positions of the Moral Majority and those of the gay movement.

In political life, it is all too easy to marginalize radicals, and to attempt to buy acceptance for a moderate position by portraying others as extremists. Liberals have done this for years to communists. Sexual radicals have opened up the sex debates. It is shameful to deny their contribution, misrepresent their positions, and further their stigmatization.

In contrast to cultural feminists, who simply want to purge sexual dissidents, the sexual moderates are willing to defend the rights of erotic non-conformists to political participation. Yet this defense of political rights is linked to an implicit system of ideological condescension. The argument has two major parts. The first is an accusation that sexual dissidents have not paid close enough attention to the meaning, sources, or historical construction of their sexuality. This emphasis on meaning appears to function in much the same way that the question of etiology has functioned in discussions of homosexuality. That is, homosexuality, sadomasochism, prostitution, or boy-love are taken to be mysterious and problematic in some way that more respectable sexualities are not. The search for a cause is a search for something that could change so that these "problematic" eroticisms would simply not occur. Sexual militants have replied to such exercises that although the question of etiology or cause is of intellectual interest, it is not high on the political agenda and that, moreover, the privileging of such questions is itself a regressive political choice.

The second part of the "moderate" position focuses on questions of consent. Sexual radicals of all varieties have demanded the legal and social legitimation of consenting sexual behavior. Feminists have criticized them for ostensibly finessing questions about "the limits of consent" and "structural constraints" on consent. Although there are deep problems with the political discourse of consent, and although there are certainly structural constraints on sexual choice, this criticism has been consistently misapplied in the sex debates. It does not take into account the very specific semantic content that consent has in sex law and sex practice.

As I mentioned earlier, a great deal of sex law does not distinguish between consensual and coercive behavior. Only rape law contains such a distinction. Rape law is based on the assumption, correct in my view, that heterosexual activity may be freely chosen or forcibly coerced. One has the legal right to engage in heterosexual behavior as long as it does not fall under the purview of other statutes and as long as it is agreeable to both parties.

This is not the case for most other sexual acts. Sodomy laws, as I mentioned above, are based on the assumption that the forbidden acts are an "abominable and detestable crime against nature." Criminality is intrinsic to the acts themselves, no matter what the desires of the participants. "Unlike rape, sodomy or an unnatural or perverted sexual act may be committed between two persons both of whom consent, and, regardless of which is the aggressor, both may be prosecuted." Before the consenting adults statute was passed in California in 1976, lesbian lovers could have been prosecuted for committing oral copulation. If both participants were capable of consent, both were equally guilty.

Adult incest statutes operate in a similar fashion. Contrary to popular mythology, the incest statutes have little to do with protecting children from rape by close relatives. The incest statutes themselves prohibit marriage or sexual intercourse between adults who are closely related. Prosecutions are rare, but two were reported recently. In 1979, a 19-year-old Marine met his 42-year-old mother, from whom he had been separated at birth. The two fell in love and got married. They were charged and found guilty of incest, which under Virginia law carries a maximum ten-year sentence. During their trial, the Marine testified, "I love her very much. I feel that two people who love each other should be able to live together." In another case, a brother and sister who had been raised separately met and decided to get married. They were arrested and pleaded guilty to felony incest in return for probation. A condition of probation was that they not live together as husband and wife. Had they not accepted, they would have faced twenty years in prison.

In a famous S/M case, a man was convicted of aggravated assault for a whipping administered in an S/M scene. There was no complaining victim. The session had been filmed and he was prosecuted on the basis of the film. The man appealed his conviction by arguing that he had been involved in a consensual sexual encounter and had assaulted no one. In rejecting his appeal, the court ruled that one may not consent to an assault or battery "except in a situation involving ordinary physical contact or blows incident to sports such as football, boxing, or wrestling." The court went on to note that the "consent of a person without legal capacity to give consent, such as a child or insane person, is ineffective," and that "It is a matter of common knowledge that a normal person in full possession of his mental faculties does not freely consent to the use, upon himself, of force likely to produce great bodily injury." Therefore, anyone who would consent to a whipping would be presumed non compos mentis and legally incapable of consenting. S/M sex generally involves a much lower level of force than the average football game, and results in far fewer injuries than most sports. But the court ruled that football players are sane, whereas masochists are not.

Sodomy laws, adult incest laws, and legal interpretations such as the one above clearly interfere with consensual behavior and impose criminal penalties on it. Within the law, consent is a privilege enjoyed only by those who engage in the highest-status sexual behavior. Those who enjoy low-status sexual behavior do not have the legal right to engage in it. In addition, economic sanctions, family pressures, erotic stigma, social discrimination, negative ideology, and the paucity of information about erotic behavior, all serve to make it difficult for people to make unconventional sexual choices. There certainly are structural constraints that impede free sexual choice, but they hardly operate to coerce anyone into being a pervert. On the contrary, they operate to coerce everyone toward normality.

The "brainwash theory" explains erotic diversity by assuming that some sexual acts are so disgusting that no one would willingly perform them. Therefore, the reasoning goes, anyone who does so must have been forced or fooled. Even constructivist sexual theory has been pressed into the service of explaining away why otherwise rational individuals might engage in variant sexual behavior. Another position that is not yet fully formed uses the ideas of Foucault and Weeks to imply that the "perversions" are an especially unsavory or problematic aspect of the construction of modern sexuality. This is yet another version of the notion that sexual dissidents are victims of the subtle machinations of the social system. Weeks and Foucault would not accept such an interpretation, since they consider all sexuality to be constructed, the conventional no less than the deviant.

Psychology is the last resort of those who refuse to acknowledge that sexual dissidents are as conscious and free as any other group of sexual actors. If deviants are not responding to the manipulations of the social system, then perhaps the source of their incomprehensible choices can be found in a bad childhood, unsuccessful socialization, or inadequate identity formation. In her essay on erotic domination, Jessica Benjamin draws upon psychoanalysis and philosophy to explain why what she calls "sadomasochism" is alienated, distorted, unsatisfactory, numb, purposeless, and an attempt to "relieve an original effort at differentiation that failed." This essay substitutes a psycho-philosophical inferiority for the more usual means of devaluing dissident eroticism. One reviewer has already construed Benjamin's argument as showing that sadomasochism is merely an "obsessive replay of the infant power struggle."

The position which defends the political rights of perverts but which seeks to understand their "alienated" sexuality is certainly preferable to the WAP-style bloodbaths. But for the most part, the sexual moderates have not confronted their discomfort with erotic choices that differ from their own. Erotic chauvinism cannot be redeemed by tarting it up in Marxist drag, sophisticated constructivist theory, or retro-psychobabble.

Whichever feminist position on sexuality—right, left, or center—eventually attains dominance, the existence of such a rich discussion is evidence that the feminist movement will always be a source of interesting thought about sex. Nevertheless, I want to challenge the assumption that feminism is or should be the privileged site of a theory of sexuality. Feminism is the theory of gender oppression. To assume automatically that this makes it the theory of sexual oppression is to fail to distinguish between gender, on the one hand, and erotic desire, on the other.

In the English language, the word "sex" has two very different meanings. It means gender and gender identity, as in "the female sex" or "the male sex." But sex also refers to sexual activity, lust, intercourse, and arousal, as in "to have sex." This semantic merging reflects a cultural assumption that sexuality is reducible to sexual intercourse and that it is a function of the relations between women and men. The cultural fusion of gender with sexuality has given rise to the idea that a theory of sexuality may be derived directly out of a theory of gender.

In an earlier essay, "The Traffic in Women," I used the concept of a sex/gender system, defined as a "set of arrangements by which a society transforms biological sexuality into products of human activity." I went on to argue that "Sex as we know it—gender identity, sexual desire and fantasy, concepts of childhood—is itself a social product." In that essay, I did not distinguish between lust and gender, treating both as modalities of the same underlying social process.

"The Traffic in Women" was inspired by the literature on kin-based systems of social organization. It appeared to me at the time that gender and desire were systemically intertwined in such social formations. This may or may not be an accurate assessment of the relationship between sex and gender in tribal organizations. But it is surely not an adequate formulation for sexuality in Western industrial societies. As Foucault has pointed out, a system of sexuality has emerged out of earlier kinship forms and has acquired significant autonomy.

> Particularly from the eighteenth century onward, Western societies created and deployed a new apparatus which was superimposed on the previous one, and which, without completely supplanting the latter, helped to reduce its importance. I am speaking of the deployment of *sexuality*. . . . For the first [kinship], what is pertinent is the link between partners and definite statutes; the second [sexuality] is concerned with the sensations of the body, the quality of pleasures, and the nature of impressions.

The development of this sexual system has taken place in the context of gender relations. Part of the modern ideology of sex is that lust is the province of men, purity that of women. It is no accident that pornography and the perversions have been considered part of the male domain. In the sex industry, women have been excluded from most production and consumption, and allowed to participate primarily as workers. In order to participate in the "perversions," women have had to overcome serious limitations on their social mobility, their economic resources, and their sexual freedoms. Gender affects the operation of the sexual system, and the sexual system has had gender-specific manifestations. But although sex and gender are related, they are not the same thing, and they form the basis of two distinct arenas of social practice.

In contrast to my perspective in "The Traffic in Women," I am now arguing that it is essential to separate gender and sexuality analytically to reflect more accurately their separate social existence. This goes against the grain of much contemporary feminist

thought, which treats sexuality as a derivation of gender. For instance, lesbian feminist ideology has mostly analyzed the oppression of lesbians in terms of the oppression of women. However, lesbians are also oppressed as queers and perverts, by the operation of sexual, not gender, stratification. Although it pains many lesbians to think about it, the fact is that lesbians have shared many of the sociological features and suffered from many of the same social penalties as have gay men, sadomasochists, transvestites, and prostitutes.

Catharine MacKinnon has made the most explicit theoretical attempt to subsume sexuality under feminist thought. According to MacKinnon, "Sexuality is to feminism what work is to marxism . . . the molding, direction, and expression of sexuality organizes society into two sexes, women and men." This analytic strategy in turn rests on a decision to "use sex and gender relatively interchangeably." It is this definitional fusion that I want to challenge.

There is an instructive analogy in the history of the differentiation of contemporary feminist thought from Marxism. Marxism is probably the most supple and powerful conceptual system extant for analyzing social inequality. But attempts to make Marxism the sole explanatory system for all social inequalities have been dismal exercises. Marxism is most successful in the areas of social life for which it was originally developed—class relations under capitalism.

In the early days of the contemporary women's movement, a theoretical conflict took place over the applicability of Marxism to gender stratification. Since Marxist theory is relatively powerful, it does in fact detect important and interesting aspects of gender oppression. It works best for those issues of gender most closely related to issues of class and the organization of labor. The issues more specific to the social structure of gender were not amenable to Marxist analysis.

The relationship between feminism and a radical theory of sexual oppression is similar. Feminist conceptual tools were developed to detect and analyze gender-based hierarchies. To the extent that these overlap with erotic stratifications, feminist theory has some explanatory power. But as issues become less those of gender and more those of sexuality, feminist analysis becomes misleading and often irrelevant. Feminist thought simply lacks angles of vision which can fully encompass the social organization of sexuality. The criteria of relevance in feminist thought do not allow it to see or assess critical power relations in the area of sexuality.

In the long run, feminism's critique of gender hierarchy must be incorporated into a radical theory of sex, and the critique of sexual oppression should enrich feminism. But an autonomous theory and politics specific to sexuality must be developed.

It is a mistake to substitute feminism for Marxism as the last word in social theory. Feminism is no more capable than Marxism of being the ultimate and complete account of all social inequality. Nor is feminism the residual theory which can take care of everything to which Marx did not attend. These critical tools were fashioned to handle very specific areas of social activity. Other areas of social life, their forms of power, and their characteristic modes of oppression, need their own conceptual implements. In this essay, I have argued for theoretical as well as sexual pluralism.

VII CONCLUSION

. . . these pleasures which we lightly call physical . . .

(Colette)

Like gender, sexuality is political. It is organized into systems of power, which reward and encourage some individuals and activities, while punishing and suppressing others. Like the capitalist organization of labor and its distribution of rewards and powers, the modern sexual system has been the object of political struggle since it emerged and as it has evolved. But if the disputes between labor and capital are mystified, sexual conflicts are completely camouflaged.

The legislative restructuring that took place at the end of the nineteenth century and in the early decades of the twentieth was a refracted response to the emergence of the modern erotic system. During that period, new erotic communities formed. It became possible to be a male homosexual or a lesbian in a way it had

not been previously. Mass-produced erotica became available, and the possibilities for sexual commerce expanded. The first homosexual rights organizations were formed, and the first analyses of sexual oppression were articulated.

The repression of the 1950s was in part a backlash to the expansion of sexual communities and possibilities which took place during World War II. During the 1950s, gay rights organizations were established, the Kinsey reports were published, and lesbian literature flourished. The 1950s were a formative as well as a repressive era.

The current right-wing sexual counter-offensive is in part a reaction to the sexual liberalization of the 1960s and early 1970s. Moreover, it has brought about a unified and self-conscious coalition of sexual radicals. In one sense, what is now occurring is the emergence of a new sexual movement, aware of new issues and seeking a new theoretical basis. The sex wars out on the streets have been partly responsible for provoking a new intellectual focus on sexuality. The sexual system is shifting once again, and we are seeing many symptoms of its change.

In Western culture, sex is taken all too seriously. A person is not considered immoral, is not sent to prison, and is not expelled from her or his family, for enjoying spicy cuisine. But an individual may go through all this and more for enjoying shoe leather. Ultimately, of what possible social significance is it if a person likes to masturbate over a shoe? It may even be non-consensual, but since we do not ask permission of our shoes to wear them, it hardly seems necessary to obtain dispensation to come on them.

If sex is taken too seriously, sexual persecution is not taken seriously enough. There is systematic mistreatment of individuals and communities on the basis of erotic taste or behavior. There are serious penalties for belonging to the various sexual occupational castes. The sexuality of the young is denied, adult sexuality is often treated like a variety of nuclear waste, and the graphic representation of sex takes place in a mire of legal and social circumlocution. Specific populations bear the brunt of the current system of erotic power, but their persecution upholds a system that affects everyone.

The 1980s have already been a time of great sexual suffering. They have also been a time of ferment and new possibility. It is up to all of us to try to prevent more barbarism and to encourage erotic creativity. Those who consider themselves progressive need to examine their preconceptions, update their sexual educations, and acquaint themselves with the existence and operation of sexual hierarchy. It is time to recognize the political dimensions of erotic life.

NOTE

1. Throughout this essay I treated transgender behavior and individuals in terms of the sex system rather than the gender system, although transvestites and transsexuals are clearly transgressing gender boundaries. I did so because transgendered people are stigmatized, harassed, persecuted, and generally treated like sex "deviants" and perverts. But clearly this is an instance of the ways in which my classificatory system does not quite encompass the existing complexities. The schematic renderings of sexual hierarchies in Figures 1 and 2 were oversimplified to make a point. Although the point remains valid, the actual power relationships of sexual variation are considerably more complicated.

Study Questions

1. Rubin argues that society feels compelled to "draw and maintain an imaginary line between good and bad sex." What kind of sex falls on each side of Rubin's line? According to Rubin, why is such line-drawing inappropriate?

2. What alternative means for determining the morality of sex acts does Rubin propose? Does her alternative strike you as an improvement? As sufficiently attentive to feminist concerns?

3. What is Rubin's argument for the conclusion that feminism is an inadequate venue for a radical theory of sexuality? Do you agree with Rubin on this point?

Judith Butler

Against Proper Objects[1]

A set of paradoxes has emerged within recent debates in feminist and queer theory that complicates any effort to stage a simple stand off between the two domains. Within queer studies generally, a methodological distinction has been offered which would distinguish theories of sexuality from theories of gender and, further, allocate the theoretical investigation of sexuality to queer studies, and the analysis of gender to feminism. Consider the introduction to *The Lesbian and Gay Studies Reader* in which an "analogy" (xv) with women's studies is offered as a way of understanding the range of issues pertaining to lesbian and gay studies. Citing a 1975 essay written by feminist historian Joan Kelly-Gadol, the editors write that "women's history is not meant to be additive . . . rather, women's history seeks to establish the centrality of *gender* as a fundamental category of historical analysis and understanding—a category central, in other words, to each of those previously existing subdepartments of history" (xv). Applauding the feminist effort to make gender into "a central category of analysis." the editors seek to make the same kind of claim for the objects of research proper to lesbian and gay studies: "Lesbian/gay studies does for *sex* and *sexuality* approximately what women's studies does for gender" (xv).

AGAINST METHODOLOGY

In laying out the "proper" domain for feminist analysis, the editors of *The Lesbian and Gay Studies Reader* formulate the methodological domain of women's studies as that which "includes any research that treats gender (whether female or male) as a central category of analysis." The parenthetical reference to "female or male" suggests that these terms are interchangeable with the notion of gender, although conventional formulations of the sex/gender distinction associated "sex" with female or male—or with the problematic of a continuum between them—and "gender" with the social categories of men and women. This brief and parenthetical suggestion that gender might be understood as equivalent to "female or male" thus appears to rest on a conflation of sex with gender.

Significantly, though "female or male" appear in this formulation of feminism, the term "sex" does not; gender appears to be reduced to sex in this sentence at the same time that the term "sex" remains merely implied. One might think this is a small point. Note, however, that the term "sex" does become explicit in the next sentence, but only as one of the two proper objects of lesbian and gay studies: "sex and sexuality." In this second context, "sex" appears to mean "sexual desire and practice," but also the Foucaultian sense of "sex" as a regime of identity or a fictional ideal by which sex as anatomy, sensation, acts, and practice are arbitrarily unified.[2] If, as appears likely, the Foucaultian meaning of "sex" is implied by its mention in this context, then "sex" would include the matter of "female or male" mentioned above. Thus, the editors lead us through analogy from a feminism in which gender and sex are conflated to a notion of lesbian and gay studies in which "sex" encompasses and exceeds the purview of feminism: "sex" in this second instance would include not only questions of identity and attribute (female or male), but discourses of sensation, acts, and sexual practice as well.

To the extent that the analogy "works" through reference to a term—"sex"—which commonly concerns both feminism and lesbian/gay studies, that commonality must be denied—through elision or through the semantic splitting and redistribution of its constitutive parts. Whereas "sex" in the elided sense attributed to feminism will mean only identity and attribute, "sex" in the explicit and lesbian/gay sense will include and supersede the feminist sense: identity, attribute, sensation, pleasures, acts, and practices. Thus "sex" in the sense deployed by lesbian and gay studies is understood to include the putative feminist binary (female or male), but also to imply the second proper object of lesbian and gay studies: "sexuality."

I belabor the structure of this analogy because the terms that the analogy seeks to compare are not as separate as they may at first appear. And if the terms are separated in arbitrary or illegible ways (as in the case of "gender [female or male]") it is because such a separation, however falsifying or arbitrary, assists in making the methodological claim that is supposed to ground lesbian and gay studies as an "autonomous" enterprise.

As the analogy is now set up, feminism is figured as concerned not only with one aspect of "sex"—putative anatomical identity—but with no aspects of sexuality. Is this a description of feminist practice, one which follows feminism's own self-restriction of its own methodological concerns to that of "gender" (reduced to "sex" in its biological formulations)? Where would the feminist traditions in favor of enhancing sexual freedom fit in such a scheme, much less those that analyze the interrelation of gender and sexuality? Or is it that, whenever feminism engages in such claims it can now be said no longer to be feminism, but rather to belong to the methodology of lesbian and gay studies? Perhaps the restriction of feminism to gender, construed as biological binary, is nothing other than a prescribed restriction of feminist practice to terms illegible to feminist criticism performed in the service of augmenting claims made by lesbian and gay studies for methodological autonomy?

Even if we accept Foucault's proposal to consider "sex" as a fictional unity, a speculative ideal, which compounds the semantic senses of sex as identity, sensation, and practice, to name a few, are we to accept Foucault's presumption that "sex" is as monolithic and unified a category as it seems? Does "sex" not gain that appearance of a monolithic unity, a speculative ideal, to the extent that it covers over "sexual difference" or, rather, assimilates sexual difference to the category of "sex"? In so far as lesbian and gay studies relies on *this* notion of sex, then it appears to take as one of its grounds, its founding methodological claims, a refusal of sexual difference in the theoretical constitution of "sex" as a proper object of study.

The terms of the analogy suggest as much once we consider that the theoretical distinction between feminist and lesbian/gay studies effects a refusal of the first term, "gender," through an assimilation of its elided sense, "sex," to the second set of terms: "sex and sexuality." Indeed, only by reducing feminism to "gender," then implicitly conflating gender with sex, i.e. "female or male," and then explicitly declaring "sex" to be one of its two proper objects, can lesbian and gay studies establish itself as the proper successor to feminism. This place, however, is established in part through assimilating sexual difference to sex in such a way that sexual difference itself is refused through the trajectory of the sublation. Sexual difference, irreducible to "gender" or to the putative biological disjunction of "female or male," is rhetorically refused through the substitution by which a unitary "sex" is installed as the proper object of inquiry.

The appropriation of this view by lesbian and gay studies suggests that the analogy which opens the discussion of proper objects is hardly benign, and that the "ground" is established through a refusal, perhaps a repudiation, of the significance of sexual difference. The distinction between the two domains works in at least two ways. The second term (gay and lesbian studies) is distinguished from the first (feminist studies) through a separation of the *kinds* of objects they pursue. To the extent, however, that the second pursues a kind of object ("sex") that both refuses and includes the object of the first ("female or male"), that distinction becomes the rhetorical means by which a repudiation is performed. The repudiation begins with the reduction of gender to sex—a caricature of

feminist theoretical work of the last twenty years—which then stages the possibility of an assimilation of that caricatured version of feminism to the putatively more expansive terrain of lesbian and gay studies. That assimilation takes place through elision, but also as a chiasmic effect. Considered as analogy, the terms are discrete: considered as an historical account encoded in the terms of analogy, lesbian and gay studies improves upon the terms of feminism; considered as chiasm, the analogy breaks down, and the terms which appear to be parallel (gender and sex/sexuality) or the same ("sex" in the elided sense and "sex" in the explicit sense) are neither, and the narrative of supersession loses its plausibility.

If the "sex" which feminism is said to study constitutes one dimension of the multi-dimensional "sex" that lesbian and gay research is said to study, then the implicit argument is that lesbian and gay studies does precisely what feminism is said to do, but does it in a more expansive and complex way. This distinction between "sex" as anatomical identity and "sex" as regime or practice will become quite crucial to the formulation of lesbian/gay studies as the analysis of sex and sexuality, for the ambiguity of sex as act and identity will be split into univocal dimensions in order to make the claim that the kind of sex that one *is* and the kind of sex that one *does* belong to two separate kinds of analysis: feminist and lesbian/gay, respectively.

And yet, "sex" carries different valences in each context for which the above framework cannot give an adequate account. The terms of the analogy are falsifying to the extent that the object of feminism cannot be reduced to "gender (female or male)," and the "sex" where of lesbian and gay studies speaks—*to the extent that it defines itself against feminism*—is constituted through a repudiation of sexual difference, a move which many lesbian and gay scholars would surely refuse, including no doubt the editors of the volume in question. Indeed, what is at issue is clearly *not* a question of what the editors of the volume intend, given that all three have made strong contributions to feminist scholarship, but rather with a set of political and historical implications of the analogy between feminism and lesbian/gay studies which have been difficult to discern for many of us who work within and between these domains of study.[3]

The problem here is not just the fairly obvious one that there is little, if any, feminist research that would make use of the oxymoron, "gender (male or female)" as a methodological point of departure. Even Joan Kelly-Gadol's cited article construes the notion of "sex" as a fully social category and, though published in 1975, a year after the publication of Gayle Rubin's "The Traffic in Women," it does not pursue the implications of the sex/gender distinction as is done in the subsequent work of Sherry Ortner, Harriet Whitehead, Moira Gaetens, Evelyn Fox Keller, and Joan W. Scott.[4] Perhaps more salient here is that "gender" has denoted not a set of attributes or identities, but a framework of differential analysis and "a primary way of signifying relationships of power" (Scott, *Gender* 44). Feminist efforts to refuse the reduction of gender to a disjunctive and biological binarism have been quite central to several disciplines for several decades: a) the work on the biological sciences of Ruth Hubbard, Anne Fausto-Sterling, Monique Wittig, Donna Haraway, Helen Longino to name but a few; b) the massive literature within feminism that not only explores the links among gender, race, and sexuality, but shows how "gender" is produced through these overlapping articulations of power. This scholarship in the fields of Third World and postcolonial feminism has called into question in different ways not only the exclusive focus of feminism on gender, but the centrality of racial and class formations in the constitution of gender itself. Feminists posing these kinds of questions include Norma Alarcón, Cherríe Moraga, Chandra Mohanty, Valerie Smith, Hortense Spillers, Gayatri Chakravorty Spivak, among scores of others.

Although the problems associated with the sex/gender distinction are many, it seems clear that the more general question of the relation of the biological and the cultural—which includes scholarly reflection on the production of the very distinction between the two categories—has commanded feminist intellectual attention from the beginning of the Second Wave. That there are competing feminist views on how that tension ought to be formulated is clear, but few, if any, feminist texts proceed with a simple parenthetical conflation of the two. In fact, what is incisive and valuable in feminist work is precisely the kind of thinking that calls into question the settled grounds of analysis. And even the recourse to sexual difference within feminist theory is at its most productive when it is taken not as a ground, foundation, or methodology, but as a *question* posed but not resolved.

What separates the putative object of feminism—gender, construed as sex—from the putative object of lesbian and gay studies—sex, construed as sexuality—is a chiasmic confusion in which the constitutive ambiguity of "sex" is denied in order to make arbitrary territorial claims. And though the language of the editorial introduction to the volume appears to appreciate the feminist precedent, this is an idealization which is perhaps not without its aggression. Indeed, lesbian and gay studies in this form cannot articulate its own "proper object" outside the terms of this analogy with feminism, an analogy that relegates feminism to an analysis of "gender" reduced to a biological frame and evacuated of all sexuality. In this sense, the very formulation of lesbian and gay studies depends upon the evacuation of a sexual discourse from feminism. And what passes as a benign, even respectful, analogy with feminism is the means by which the fields are separated, where that separation requires the desexualization of the feminist project and the appropriation of sexuality as the "proper" object of lesbian/gay studies.

The institution of the "proper object" takes place, as usual, through a mundane sort of violence. Indeed, we might read moments of methodological founding as pervasively anti-historical acts, beginnings which fabricate their legitimating histories through a retroactive narrative, burying complicity and division in and through the funereal figure of the "ground."

The use of the analogy between feminist and lesbian/gay also presumes that the problem of precedent might be adequately addressed through recourse to a binary frame. Lesbian and gay studies will be derived from feminism, and yet, the editors argue, there will continue to be important communication between the two domains.[5] But what constitutes these domains as sequential and distinct, framed by analogy and its binary presumption? How is it that this framing of lesbian/gay in relation to feminism forecloses the field of social differences from which both projects emerge? In particular, terms such as "race" and "class" are ruled out from having a constitutive history in determining the parameters of either field. Whether the position is for or against the centrality of gender to sexuality, it is gender and sexuality alone that remain the common objects of contention. The presumption is that they can be compared and contrasted, but that the binary frame presumed and instituted through the analogy is itself self-evidently "proper."

AGAINST THE ANTI-PORNOGRAPHY PARADIGM

The anti-pornography movement through the 80s and, more recently, the assimilation of feminist politics to the discourse on victimization, have succeeded in rendering popular a view of feminism in which positions of gender are strictly correlated with positions of domination or subordination within sexuality. Feminist positions such as Catharine MacKinnon's offer an analysis of sexual relations as structured by relations of coerced subordination, and argue that acts of sexual domination constitute the social meaning of being a "man," as the condition of coerced subordination constitutes the social meaning of being a "woman." Such a rigid determinism assimilates any account of sexuality to rigid and determining positions of domination and subordination, and assimilates those positions to the social gender of man and woman. But that deterministic account has come under continuous criticism from feminists not only for an untenable account of female sexuality as coerced subordination, but for the totalizing view of heterosexuality as well— one in which all power relations are reduced to relations of domination—and for the failure to distinguish the presence of coerced domination in sexuality from pleasurable and wanted dynamics of power. The Barnard Conference in 1983 entitled "The Scholar and the Feminist IX" publically staged the debate between feminists who would elevate their readings of pornographic "victimization" to the model for all

gender relations, and those who drew on strong feminist traditions of promoting sexual freedom for women to counter the pornography paradigm for thinking sexuality. These latter feminists consistently refused the assimilation of all sexuality to coercive models of domination, and refused as well the assimilation of models of domination to socially fixed positions of gender within a totalizing map of patriarchal domination.

The feminist tradition in favor of sexual freedom,[6] with strong ties to radical sexual theory and activism, has been clearly voiced by numerous scholars, some of whom, such as Ellen Dubois and Judith Walkowitz, have explicitly argued for the historical links between a progressive sexual politics and feminist aims.[7] This tradition has continued in the writings of Dorothy Allison, bell hooks, Cherríe Moraga, Joan Nestle, Esther Newton, Sarah Schulman, and others. Central to Carole Vance's reformulation of this position is a consideration of both the pleasure and the danger of women's sexual freedom, where danger carries both the anti-erotic threat of coerced sexuality, as in rape, battery, and the mundane masculinist rituals of intimidation, and the highly erotic promise of transgressing traditional restrictions on women's sexuality. This purposefully ambiguous agenda thus offered and continues to offer an important alternative to the anti-pornography framework in which every instance of the sexual ambiguity of power is quickly resolved into univocal positions of coercive domination.

Significantly, this very feminist tradition in which both pleasure and danger govern the discourse on sexuality is elided in the articulation of lesbian/gay from feminist in the founding methodology of queer studies. Those radical sexual positions within feminism offered an alternative to the MacKinnon framework and made it possible for many women to remain feminists in spite of the rising popularity of the feminist framework of female victimization. To restrict the proper object of feminism to gender, and to appropriate sexuality as the proper object of lesbian/gay studies, is either to deny this important feminist contribution to the very sexual discourse in which lesbian and gay studies emerged or to argue, implicitly, that the feminist contributions to thinking sexuality culminate in the supersession of feminism by lesbian and gay studies.

The appropriation of Gayle Rubin's influential essay, "Thinking Sex" (1983), as a founding piece in gay and lesbian studies is especially important in understanding the way in which this act of methodological founding depends upon—and enacts—a restriction of the scope of feminist scholarship and activism. Important to underscore is the above-mentioned feminist context in which Rubin's essay was published, and the criticisms of some feminist paradigms she offered. Rubin clearly argued that feminism ought not to be the only or the primary theoretical model for understanding sexuality, but her call was not for a lesbian/gay theoretical frame, but for an analysis that might account for the regulation of a wide range of sexual minorities.[8]

Whereas the editors of *The Lesbian and Gay Studies Reader* are right to claim in the introduction to their reprinting of "Thinking Sex" that "[feminism] does not and cannot provide by itself a full explanation for the oppression of sexual minorities," they do not supply any grounds for the claim that lesbian and gay studies can provide by itself a more appropriate framework for the analysis of sexual minorities. A close reading of Rubin's essay suggests indeed that it would be as much a mistake to hand over the thinking of sexuality to feminism—as its proper object—as it would be to hand it over to lesbian and gay studies—as its proper object.

In the final two pages of the essay, Rubin effects a number of controversial moves which have set the stage for conceptualizing gender and sexuality as two separable domains of analysis. She opposes reductive monocausal accounts in which either all of sexuality is attributable to gender or all of gender is construed as the causal effect of regimes of sexuality. If sexual relations cannot be reduced to gender positions, which seems true enough, it does not follow that an analysis of sexual relations apart from an analysis of gender relations is possible. Their interrelation may have a necessity that is neither causal nor fixed for all time. Indeed, in the place of a methodological separation of lesbian/gay and feminist studies, it may be that non-reductive and non-causal accounts of the relation

of gender and sexuality are in order. The separation of the two domains by Rubin is meant to contest those feminist efforts "which treat sexuality as a derivation of gender" (308). Understood this way, the separation of the two domains is to be contextualized within the effort to dispute those feminist frameworks which seek to establish sexuality, and sexual domination in particular, as the scene by which gender positions are installed and consolidated along an axis of domination and submission.

Rubin's critique of the causal reduction of sexuality to gender in "Thinking Sex" signalled an important departure from her earlier work. Whereas in "The Traffic in Women: Towards a 'Political Economy' of Sex," gender was construed as the instrument and effect of sexual regimes, in "Thinking Sex" Rubin refers to sexuality as an "autonomous" (309) domain. This separation of gender and sexuality suggests that feminism, considered as an analysis of gender, is not necessarily the most appropriate discourse for considering the kinds of power relations within which sexuality is formed and regulated. Rubin refers to the fusion of two different meanings of "sex" whereby to be a sex implies having sex in a given way, that is, that "sexuality is reducible to sexual intercourse and that it is a function of the relations between women and men" (307). Where and when a feminist analysis accepts this cultural presumption, feminism actively recapitulates heterosexist hegemony. For example, MacKinnon's view of feminism is one which makes free use of the copula in which causal relations are elliptically asserted through the postulation of equivalences, i.e. within the structures of male dominance, conceived exclusively as heterosexual, sex is gender is sexual positionality. Although MacKinnon seeks to explain this hegemony, the terms by which the explanation proceeds tend to freeze the relations described, thus recapitulating the very cultural presumption of a heterosexually framed scene of sexual domination. *But when and where feminism refuses to derive gender from sex or from sexuality, feminism appears to be part of the very critical practice that contests the heterosexual matrix, pursuing the specific social organization of each of these relations as well as their capacity for social transformation.*

Significantly, Rubin situates her own position historically. She begins the argument by claiming quite clearly that a "rich discussion [on sexuality] is evidence that the feminist movement will always be a source of interesting thought about sex," and then proceeds to question whether "feminism is or ought to be the privileged site of a theory of sexuality." This sentence is then followed by another in which feminism is given definition: "Feminism is the theory of gender oppression," and then, "it does not follow that a theory of gender oppression, that is, an analysis of oppression on the basis of gender, will offer up an adequate theory of sexual oppression, oppression on the basis of sexual practice" (307).

Toward the end of this short theoretical conclusion of the "Thinking Sex" essay, Rubin returns to feminism in a gestural way, suggesting that "in the long run, feminism's critique of gender hierarchy must be incorporated into a radical theory of sex, and the critique of sexual oppression should enrich feminism. But an autonomous theory and politics specific to sexuality must be developed" (309). Hence, for Rubin, a separate account of sexual oppression, one which accounts for sexual minorities, including queers, sadomasochists, transvestites, inter-generational partners, and prostitutes is an historical necessity in 1983. The contemporary appropriation of this position for founding lesbian and gay studies thus reduces the expansive category of sexual minorities to the representation of one group of members on the list.

According to the logic of Rubin's argument, it would be as wrong to claim that gender can only or best be understood in the context of class (as some Marxists have argued) as it would be to claim that sexuality can only or best be understood in the context of gender (as some feminists have argued). By extension, it would be equally fallacious to claim that sexuality is only or best understood in the context of lesbian and gay studies. Indeed, according to Rubin's logic, sexuality is no more likely to receive a thorough analysis under the rubric of lesbian and gay studies than it is under that of feminist studies. Not only do central notions like the racialization of sexuality get dropped or domesticated as "instances" of either feminism or lesbian and gay studies, but the notion of sexual minorities, which include sex workers, transsexuals, and cross-generational partners, cannot be adequately approached through a framework of lesbian and gay studies. One need only consider the absurdity of the claim that the history and politics of prostitution is best served within the framework of lesbian and gay studies. Similarly, the important dissonance between transsexuality and homosexuality is lost when and if the claim is made that the analysis of transsexuality is best served within the frame of lesbian and gay studies. Indeed, to the extent that lesbian and gay studies refuses the domain of gender, it disqualifies itself from the analysis of transgendered sexuality altogether. And though it is clear that lesbian and gay studies may have some interesting perspectives to contribute to the analysis of heterosexuality, it would be quite a leap to claim that heterosexuality ought now to become the exclusive or proper object of lesbian and gay studies. Yet, all of these improbable claims are invited by the methodological announcement that "sex and sexuality" constitute the proper object of inquiry for lesbian and gay studies and, by implication, *not* the proper object for other kinds of inquiry.

Rubin's essay called for political attention to be paid to "sexual minorities" who are not always women, and who constitute a class of sexual actors whose behavior is categorized and regulated by the state in invasive and pathologizing ways. The expansive and coalitional sense of "sexual minorities" cannot be rendered interchangeable with "lesbian and gay," and it remains an open question whether "queer" can achieve these same goals of inclusiveness.

HAS "THE LONG RUN" ARRIVED?

It is important to appreciate the way in which Rubin's revision of the early essay is simultaneous with her effort to separate a theory and politics of sexuality from one of feminism. In some ways, it is the figure of MacKinnon against whom Rubin's own position is articulated. It is, after all, MacKinnon who in Rubin's terms "attempt[s] to subsume sexuality under feminist thought." She does this by arguing that genders are the direct consequence of the social constitution of sexuality. In MacKinnon's terms, "the molding, direction, and expression of sexuality organizes society into two sexes, women and men" ("Traffic" 182).

As important as it is to oppose the theory and politics of MacKinnon's version of gender oppression, Rubin's tactic of separating sexuality from the sphere of feminist critique has taken on implications that could not have been foreseen when the essay was written. With the recent media success of anti-pornography feminists, and the veritable identification of feminism with a MacKinnon-style agenda, feminism has become identified with state-allied regulatory power over sexuality. This shift in public discourse has backgrounded those *feminist* positions strongly opposed to MacKinnon's theory and politics, including Rubin's own.[9] As a result, those feminist positions which have insisted on strong alliances with sexual minorities and which are skeptical of the consolidation of the regulatory power of the state have become barely legible as "feminist." A further expropriation of the tradition of sexual freedom from the domain of feminism has taken place, then, through the odd twist by which feminism is said no longer to have "sexuality" as one of its objects of inquiry.

Rubin's own essay, however, works along slightly different lines. In "Thinking Sex," Rubin seeks recourse to Foucault to put into question the very relation between kinship relations and gender that had been at the center of "The Traffic in Women." She writes,

> It appeared to me at that time that gender and desire were systematically intertwined in such social formations. This may or may not be an accurate assessment of the relationship between sex and gender in tribal organizations. But it is surely not an adequate formulation for sexuality in Western industrial societies. As Foucault has pointed out, a system of sexuality has emerged out of earlier kinship forms and has acquired significant autonomy. (307)

In *The History of Sexuality* Foucault claims that from the 18th century onward, there is a new apparatus superimposed on the system of kinship, the emergence of and deployment of "sexuality."[10] He then proceeds to make a distinction which seems to have central importance for Rubin in "Thinking Sex": with respect to kinship, he argues, "what is pertinent is the link between partners and definite statutes," and in sexuality, what is pertinent is "the sensations of the body, the quality of pleasures, and the nature of impressions" (106). Whereas kinship appears to be regulated by juridical strictures pertaining to persons and their appropriate social functions, sexuality takes impressions and sensations as the field to be regulated.

Rubin's own essay in which this citation appears is primarily concerned with juridical efforts in the early 1980s to restrict sexual acts and practices, to narrow the notion of juridical consent, and to banish sexual activity from public spaces. In support of the claim that sexuality constitutes a new domain of regulation, and that sexual oppression is distinct from gender oppression, she offers an historical argument that sexuality is no longer formed or constrained by kinship. The presumption here is that gender oppression can be understood through the regulation of kinship, and that kinship no longer operates as it once did to install and perpetuate gender relations through the regulation of sexuality within specific constraints of kinship, that is, through the workings of sanction and prohibition. Kinship formed the focus of Rubin's "Traffic" essay, and the effect of the historical distinction that she makes here between kinship and sexuality is to claim that the latter essay supersedes the former.

But is this supersession possible? Is the historical and analytic distinction between kinship and sexuality finally tenable? Rubin's focus in "Traffic" on kinship as a way of regulating sexuality implied that in the absence of explicit rules and institutions, kinship survives psychically as the force of prohibition and guilt in sexual life. Hence, the feminist justification for the turn to psychoanalysis was grounded precisely in this requirement to read the traces of kinship in psychic life. The putatively historical shift from kinship to sexuality, associated with the methodological shift from gender to sexuality, necessitates a turn from psychoanalysis to Foucault. But can the latter term (of any of these pairs) be fully or meaningfully separated from the former?[11]

The argument in "Thinking Sex" that posits the anachronism of kinship is supported by a Foucaultian historiography in which state-sponsored efforts at population control and the heightened medicalization of sexuality are figured as replacing kinship as the organizing structure of sexuality. This new deployment, argues Foucault, proceeds through diagnosis and normalization rather than through taboos and sanctions. And yet, the limiting presumption of a European history constrains the plausibility of the narration of such a "shift." How do the geopolitical constraints of that history restrict the generalizability of the argument in whose service it is invoked? And even if certain forms of kinship within certain European contexts lose the power to organize sexuality unilaterally, and public discourses on sexuality become more central, are there reconfigured forms of kinship that result from this very shift and which exert an organizational force on sexuality?

In following Foucault's scheme, Rubin severs the newer deployment of sexuality from the older regime of kinship, dropping the psychoanalytic analysis offered in "Traffic" and offering in its place a regime-theory of sexuality, which would include psychoanalysis itself as one of its regulatory modes. The credibility of this argument rests on the proposition that the modern, medicalized regime by which sensation and pleasure are normalized is not in the service of "family values" or a given normative view of kinship relations. That it is sometimes in precisely that service suggests that whereas it would be a mistake to argue that kinship relations uniformly govern the regulation of sexuality, it would be equally mistaken to claim their radical separability. In fact, the analysis of sexual minorities, offered as a separate class, requires to be thought in relation to an analysis of normative kinship. Consider the various juridical efforts to control inter-generational sexuality in which the figure of the sexually endangered child is almost always positioned outside the home, thus veiling the sexual abuse of children within the home in the service of an idealized view of the family as a desexualized safe haven for children. Consider as well the prohibitions on public sex which redraw the public/private distinction, and reprivatize sexual relations, where notions

of "privacy" apply almost exclusively to the state-sanctioned forms of heterosexual conjugality (cf. Bowers v. Hardwick). Consider as well the sequestration of HIV positive prostitutes and gay men, and the construction of both venues for sexuality as causally—rather than conditionally—linked to the disease; the moralizing against those at risk for AIDS by virtue of their sexual practices directly supports the ideological fiction of marriage and the family as the normalized and privileged domain of sexuality.

We might read the desire for a sexuality beyond kinship as a sign of a certain utopian strain in sexual thinking which is bound to fail, and which requires that our conceptions of kinship remain frozen in their most highly normative and oppressive modes. Those who imagine themselves to be "beyond" kinship will nevertheless find terms to describe those supporting social arrangements which constitute kinship. Kinship in this sense is not to be identified with any of its positive forms, but rather as a site of redefinition which can move beyond patrilineality, compulsory heterosexuality, and the symbolic overdetermination of biology. Examples of the convergence of queer and kinship concerns include the "buddy" system set up by Gay Men's Health Crisis and other AIDS service organizations to fulfill the social and medical support needs of its patients; laws legitimating lesbian and gay parenting and adoption; legal claims of guardianship; the rights to make medical decisions for incapacitated lovers; the right to receive and dispose of the body of a deceased lover, to receive property, to execute the will. And in lesbian and gay human rights work, it is common to find that lesbian and gay rights are not recognized as "human" rights precisely because lesbians and gay men, along with other sexual minorities, are not perceived as sufficiently "human" given their estrangement or opposition to the normative kinship configurations by which the "human" becomes recognizable.

The effort to think sexuality outside of its relation to kinship is, thus, not the same as thinking sexuality apart from reproduction, for reproductive relations constitute only one dimension of kinship relations. To claim that the two domains ought to be thought in relation to one another is not to claim that sexuality ought to remain restricted within the terms of kinship; on the contrary, it is only to claim that the attempt to contain sexuality within the domain of legitimate kinship is supported by moralizing and pathologizing discourses and institutions. It is that complicity—and the risks of breaking with that complicity—that requires us to understand the two domains in relation to each other.

Apart from these explicit demands and difficulties of kinship, and their clear relation to the regulation of sexual life, there is perhaps a less tangible desire to be discerned in the theoretical effort to separate the analysis of sexuality from the study of kinship, namely, the desire to desire beyond the psyche, beyond the traces of kinship that psyches bear. These include the formative and consequential markings of culturally specific familial organizations, powerful and shaping experiences of sexual prohibition, degradation, excitation, and betrayal.

Politically, the costs are too great to choose between feminism, on the one hand, and radical sexual theory, on the other. Indeed, it may be precisely the time to take part in what Rubin in 1984 foresaw as the necessity, "in the long run," for feminism to offer a critique of gender hierarchy that might be incorporated into a radical theory of sex, and for radical sexual theory to challenge and enrich feminism. Both sets of movements might also strengthen the feminist effort to displace MacKinnon's structurally static account of gender, its pro-censorship position, and its falsifying cultural generalizations about the eternally victimized position of women.[12]

THE TROUBLE WITH GENDER

A characterization of feminism as an exclusive focus on gender thus misrepresents the recent history of feminism in several significant ways: 1) the history of radical feminist sexual politics is erased from the proper characterization of feminism; 2) the various anti-racist positions developed within feminist frameworks for which gender is no more central than race, or for which gender is no more central than colonial positionality or class—the domains of socialist femin-ism, postcolonial feminism, Third World feminism—are no longer part of the central or proper focus of feminism; 3) the MacKinnon account of gender and sexuality is taken as paradigmatic of feminism, and the strong feminist opposition to her work is excluded from the parameters of feminism; 4) gender is reduced to sex (and sometimes to sex-assignment), rendered fixed or "given," and the contested history of the sex/gender distinction is displaced from view; 5) the normative operation of gender in the regulation of sexuality is denied. The result is that the sexual contestation of gender norms is no longer an "object" of analysis within either frame, as it crosses the very domains of analysis that this methodological claim for lesbian and gay studies strains to keep apart. [. . .]

NOTES

1. Throughout this essay I draw upon Biddy Martin's conceptualization of the problematic relation between gender and sexuality in contemporary feminist and queer studies. Not only in conversation, but in her written work as well, she has insisted on theory as a "moving between" what have become, for some, polarized or separate positions. She deftly argues in "Sexuality without Genders and Other Queer Utopias" against certain trends within contemporary theory on the construction of social identities. Bodies, she writes, ought not to be described as simple effects of discourse or as the malleable surface of social inscription, but considered in a more complex and intimate relation with psychic reality. She claims as well that there are problems with theories that tend to foreground gender at the expense of sexuality and race, sexuality at the expense of gender and race, and race at the expense of sexuality and gender. Her analysis offers a set of trenchant critiques which show that certain political agendas are served through the foregrounding of one determinant of the body over others, but also that those very theories are weakened by their failure to broach the complex interrelations of these terms.

2. Foucault himself argues against the use of sex as "fictitious unity . . . [and] causal principle": "[T]he notion of 'sex' made it possible to group together, in an artificial unity, anatomical elements, biological functions, conducts, sensations, and pleasures, and it enabled one to make use of this fictitious unity as a causal principle, an omnipresent

meaning: sex was thus able to function as a unique signifier and as a universal signified" (*History* 154).

3. My argument here is with the implicit reasoning whereby a grounding of lesbian and gay studies takes place, a form of argumentation which has been reiterated in a variety of contexts, and which the editors of the volume cite implicitly from those sources. In fact, I would argue that much of the scholarship of Abelove, Barale, and Halperin has important feminist dimensions, and that they have marked several essays in the volume they edited as contributing to a dialogue between feminism and queer studies. Indeed, I think it would be a mistake, finally uninteresting and unproductive, to hold any of these authors—or any others—responsible for the analogy in question. The analogy is much more important as a theoretical development with cultural currency that exceeds the particular articulations it receives in the works of specific authors.

4. The editors cite both the late Joan Kelly-Gadol and Joan W. Scott as examples of feminists who have made gender into a central focus for women's history. Yet both of these writers have insisted that the turn to gender opens up the question of how a monolithic history might be retold in which the presumption of symmetry between men and women is contested. Interestingly, the framework for lesbian and gay studies that is founded through this analogy with their work assumes a symmetry that their work contests.

5. The editors write "Lesbian/gay studies does for *sex* and *sexuality* approximately what women's studies does for gender. That does not mean that sexuality and gender must be strictly partitioned. On the contrary, the problem of how to understand the connections between sexuality and gender continues to furnish an illuminating topic of discussion in both women's studies and lesbian/gay studies; hence, the degree of overlap or of distinctness between the fields of lesbian/gay studies and women's studies is a matter of lively debate and ongoing negotiation" (xv–xvi).

6. The feminist tradition of sexual freedom appears most recently to be identified with a strong defense of civil liberties and, on occasion, an affiliation with civil libertarianism. But nineteenth century socialist traditions of sexual freedom were centrally concerned with a critique of the family and with state institutions. A contemporary articulation of a feminist theory of freedom needs to be developed in relation to a critique of individualism, of centralized state power in its regulatory dimensions, and the interrelation between the two.

7. The volumes *Pleasure and Danger* edited by Carole S. Vance and *Powers of Desire: The Politics of Sexuality* edited by Ann Snitow, Christine Stansell, and Sharon

Thompson were centrally important in waging this critique of the anti-pornography paradigm.

8. In *Epistemology of the Closet*, Eve Kosofsky Sedgwick makes use of Rubin's distinction between gender and sexuality to argue that sexuality has a kind of ambiguity that gender does not. Sedgwick claims that "virtually all people are publically and unalterably assigned to one or the other gender, and from birth. . . ." On the other hand, "sexual orientation, with its far greater potential for rearrangement, ambiguity, and representational doubleness . . . offer(s) the apter deconstructive object" (34). Sedgwick thus identifies the question of gender with the question of sex-assignment, and then appears to make the presumption that the assignment of sex "works"—a presumption that psychoanalytic theory, which retains an emphasis on unconscious fantasy, would call into question. Even if one were to accept the reduction of gender with its complex social variability to the notion of sex-assignment (a pre-feminist construal of "gender"), it seems that "assignment" might be reconsidered in terms of the complex dynamic of social interpellation, whereby being called "a girl" is simply not enough to make it so. The problem of assuming an assignment can be understood only through a consideration of psychic resistance and ambivalence proper to a theory of identification, processes which collectively call into question the efficacy of "assignment" both as a social performative and as the basis for a theory of gender.

For an extended analysis of Sedgwick's account of gender, see Biddy Martin's excellent essay, "Sexualities Without Genders and Other Queer Utopias." Martin considers those passages in which Sedgwick understands feminism to be exclusively concerned with "the question of who is to have control of women's (biologically) distinctive reproductive capability" (*Epistemology* 28). Such a restriction of feminist work to this particular question miscontrues the range of feminist engagements with questions of reproduction, but also with non-reproductive sexuality. If we consider those feminist questions not as who controls women's reproductive capacities, but rather, as whether women may lay claim to sexual freedom outside the domain of reproduction, then the question of *sexuality* proves as central to the feminist project as the question of *gender*.

By separating sexuality from gender in this way, Sedgwick also restricts the scope of Rubin's coalitional understanding of "sexual minorities." Whereas Rubin saw the turn to sexuality as a way to provide a framework which would include and link queers, transgendered people, cross-generational partners, prostitutes, Sedgwick understands sexuality as the proper domain of lesbian and gay studies or, rather, of "an antihomophobic inquiry" (15). By separating the notion of gender from sexuality, Sedgwick narrows the notion of sexual minorities offered by Rubin, distancing queer studies from the consideration of trans-gendered persons, transgendered sexualities, transsexuality, transvestism, cross-dressing, and cross-gendered identifica-tion. Although Sedgwick appears to defend this method-ological separation, her own readings often make rich and brilliant use of the problematic of cross-gendered identifi-cation and cross-sexual identification. See, for instance, "White Glasses" in *Tendencies*.

Finally, it seems that we might accept the irreducibility of sexuality to gender or gender to sexuality, but still insist on the necessity of their interrelationship. If gender is more than a "stigmata," a "tag" that one wears, but is, rather, a normative institution which seeks to regulate those expres-sions of sexuality that contest the normative boundaries of gender, then gender is one of the normative means by which the regulation of sexuality takes place. The threat of homosexuality thus takes the form of a threat to established masculinity or established femininity, although we know that those threats can reverse their direction, enabling precisely the occasions for the proliferation of what is to be prohibited.

9. See the work of Wendy Brown, Carol Clover, Drucilla Cornell, Lisa Duggan, bell hooks, Nan Hunter, Molly Ladd-Taylor, Anne McClintock, Mandy Merck, Carole Vance, and Linda Williams, to name a few.

10. For a fuller elaboration, see my "Sexual Inversions."

11. Teresa de Lauretis's recent *The Practice of Love* crosses feminist with gay and lesbian studies in such a way that sexuality is not reducible to gender and neither is Foucault fully incompatible with psychoanalysis.

12. See Chandra Mohanty's "Under Western Eyes" not for a critique of MacKinnon per se, but for the colonialist consequences of the universalization of women's subordi-nation implied by western versions of feminism which dis-associate gender oppression from racial, cultural, and geopolitical specificities.

WORKS CITED

Abelove, Henry, Michèle Aina Barale, and David M. Halperin, eds. *The Lesbian and Gay Studies Reader*. New York: Routledge, 1993.

de Lauretis, Teresa. *The Practice of Love: Lesbian Sexuality and Perverse Desire*. Bloomington: Indiana UP, 1994.

Foucault, Michel. *The History of Sexuality: An Introduction*. Trans. Robert Hurley. New York: Pantheon, 1978. Vol. 1 of *The History of Sexuality*. 3 vols. 1978–86.

Martin, Biddy. "Sexualities Without Genders and Other Queer Utopias." *Diacritics* [Special issue on "Critical Crossings."] Ed. Judith Butler and Biddy Martin. 24.2–3 (1994): 104–21.

Rubin, Gayle. "Thinking Sex: Notes for a Radical Theory of the Politics of Sexuality." Vance, 267–319. Rpt. in Abelove, Barale, and Halperin 3–44.

———. "The Traffic in Women: Notes on the 'Political Economy' of Sex." *Toward an Anthropology of Women*. Ed. Rayna R. Reiter. New York: Monthly Review, 1975. 157–210.

Scott, Joan W. "Gender as a Useful Category of Analysis." *Gender and The Politics of History*. New York: Columbia UP, 1988. 28–52.

Sedgwick, Eve Kosofsky. *Epistemology of the Closet*. Berkeley: U of California P, 1991.

———. *Tendencies*. Durham: Duke UP, 1993.

Vance, Carole S., ed. *Pleasure and Danger: Exploring Female Sexuality*. London: Routledge, 1984.

Study Questions

1. Discussing the analogy between women's studies and lesbian/gay studies drawn by the editors of *The Lesbian and Gay Studies Reader*, Butler writes, "What separates the putative object of feminism—gender, construed as sex—from the putative object of lesbian and gay studies—sex construed as sexuality—is a chiasmic confusion in which the constitutive ambiguity of 'sex' is denied in order to make arbitrary territorial claims" (paragraph 14). Explain this quotation.

2. Among the undesirable consequences Butler identifies as stemming from the characterization of feminism as focusing exclusively on gender is the expulsion of "radical feminist sexual politics" and "socialist feminism, postcolonial feminism, [and] Third World feminism" from the proper domain of feminism (last paragraph). Explain her argument for this claim.

3. Butler concludes, "Politically, the costs are too great to choose between feminism, on the one hand, and radical sexual theory, on the other." Compare this position to Rubin's in "Thinking Sex." With which author are you in greater agree-ment? Why?

Evelynn Hammonds

Black (W)holes and the Geometry of Black Female Sexuality

> The female body in the West is not a unitary sign. Rather, like a coin, it has an obverse and a reverse: on the one side, it is white; on the other, not-white or, prototypically, black. The two bodies cannot be separated, nor can one body be understood in isolation from the other in the West's metaphoric construction of "woman." White is what woman is; not-white (and the stereotypes not-white gathers in) is what she had better not be. Even in an allegedly postmodern era, the not-white woman as well as the not-white man are symbolically and even theoretically excluded from sexual difference. Their function continues to be to cast the difference of white men and white women into sharper relief.
>
> (O'Grady 14)

When asked to write for the second special issue of *differences* on queer theory I must admit I was at first hesitant even to entertain the idea. Though much of what is now called queer theory I find engaging and intellectually stimulating, I still found the idea of writing about it disturbing. When I am asked if I am queer I usually answer yes even though the ways in which *I* am queer have never been articulated in the *body* of work that is now called queer theory. Where should I begin, I asked myself? Do I have to start by adding another adjective to my already long list of self-chosen identities? I used to be a black lesbian, feminist, writer, scientist, historian of science, and activist. Now would I be a black, queer, feminist, writer, scientist, historian of science, and activist? Given the rapidity with which new appellations are created I wondered if my new list would still be up to date by the time the article came out. More importantly, does this change

or any change I might make to my list convey to anyone the ways in which I am queer?

Even a cursory reading of the first issue of *differences* on queer theory or a close reading of *The Lesbian and Gay Studies Reader* (Abelove, Barale, and Halperin)—by now biblical in status—would lead me to answer no. So what would be the point of my writing for a second issue on queer theory? Well, I could perform that by now familiar act taken by black feminists and offer a critique of every white feminist for her failure to articulate a conception of a racialized sexuality. I could argue that while it has been acknowledged that race is not simply additive to, or derivative of sexual difference, few white feminists have attempted to move beyond simply stating this point to describe the powerful effect that race has on the construction and representation of gender and sexuality. I could go further and note that even when race is mentioned it is a limited notion devoid of complexities. Sometimes it is reduced to biology and other times referred to as a social construction. Rarely is it *used* as a "global sign," a "metalanguage," as the "ultimate trope of difference, arbitrarily contrived to produce and maintain relations of power and subordination" (Higginbotham 255).

If I were to make this argument, I wonder under what subheading such an article would appear in *The Lesbian and Gay Studies Reader*? Assuming, of course, that they would want to include it in the second edition. How about "Politics and Sex"? Well, it would certainly be political but what would anybody learn about sex from it? As I look at my choices I see that I would want my article to appear in the section, "Subjectivity, Discipline, Resistance." But where would I situate myself in the group of essays that discuss "lesbian experience," "lesbian identity," "gender insubordination," and "Butch-Femme Aesthetic"? Perhaps they wouldn't want a reprint after all and I'd be off the hook. Maybe I've just hit one of those "constructed silences" that Teresa de Lauretis wrote about as one of the problems in lesbian and gay studies ("Queer" viii).

When *The Lesbian and Gay Studies Reader* was published, I followed my usual practice and searched for the articles on black women's sexuality. This reading practice has become such a commonplace in my life I have forgotten how and when I began it. I never open a book about lesbians or gays with the expectation that I will find some essay that will address the concerns of my life. Given that on the average most collections don't include writers of color, just the appearance of essays by African-Americans, Latinos, and Native Americans in this volume was welcome. The work of Barbara Smith, Stuart Hall, Phillip Brian Harper, Gloria Hull, Deborah McDowell, and, of course, Audre Lorde has deeply influenced my intellectual and political work for many years as has the work of many of the other writers in this volume.

Yet, despite the presence of these writers, this text displays the consistently exclusionary practices of lesbian and gay studies in general. In my reading, the canonical terms and categories of the field: "lesbian,"

"gay," "butch," "femme," "sexuality," and "subjectivity" are stripped of context in the works of those theorizing about these very categories, identities, and subject positions. Each of these terms is defined with white as the normative state of existence. This is an obvious criticism which many have expressed since the appearance of this volume. More interesting is the question of whether the essays engaging with the canonical terms have been in any way informed by the work of the writers of color that do appear in the volume. The essays by Hull and McDowell both address the point I am trying to make. Hull describes the life of Angelina Weld Grimké, a poet of the Harlem Renaissance whose poetry expressed desire for women. This desire is circumscribed, underwritten, and unspoken in her poetry. McDowell's critical reading of Nella Larsen's *Passing* also points to the submersion of sexuality and same-sex desire among black women. In addition, Harper's essay on the death of Max Robinson, one of the most visible African-Americans of his generation, foregrounds the silence in black communities on the issue of sexuality and AIDS. "Silence" is emphasized as well in the essay by Ana Maria Alonso and Maria Teresa Koreck on the AIDS crisis in "Hispanic" communities. But the issue of silence about so-called deviant sexuality in public discourse and its submersion in private spaces for people of color is never addressed in theorizing about the canonical categories of lesbian and gay studies in the reader. More important, public discourse on the sexuality of particular racial and ethnic groups is shaped by processes that pathologize those groups, which in turn produce the submersion of sexuality and the attendant silence(s). Lesbian and gay theory fails to acknowledge that these very processes are connected to the construction of the sexualities of whites, historically and contemporaneously.

QUEER WORDS AND QUEER PRACTICES

I am not by nature an optimist, although I do believe that change is possible and necessary. Does a shift from lesbian to queer relieve my sense of anxiety over whether the exclusionary practices of lesbian and gay studies can be resolved? If queer theory is, as de Lauretis notes in her introduction to the first special issue of *differences*, the place where "we [would] be willing to examine, make explicit, compare, or confront the respective histories, assumptions, and conceptual frameworks that have characterized the self-representations of North American lesbians and gay men, of color and white," and if it is "from there, [that] we could then go on to recast or reinvent the terms of our sexualities, to construct another discursive horizon, another way of thinking the sexual," then *maybe* I had found a place to explore the ways in which queer, black, and female subjectivities are produced (iv–v). Of course, I first had to gather more evidence about this shift before I jumped into the fray.

In her genealogy of queer theory, de Lauretis argues that the term was arrived at in the effort to avoid all the distinctions in the discursive protocols that emerged from the standard usage of the terms *lesbian* and *gay*. The kind of distinctions she notes include the need to add qualifiers of race or national affiliation to the labels, "lesbian" and "gay." De Lauretis goes on to address my central concern. She writes:

> The fact of the matter is, most of us, lesbians and gay men, do not know much about one another's sexual history, experiences, fantasies, desire, or modes of theorizing. And we do not know enough about ourselves, as well, when it comes to differences between and within lesbians, and between and within gay men, in relation to race and its attendant differences of class or ethnic culture, generational, geographical, and socio-political location. We do not know enough to theorize those differences. (viii; emphasis added)

She continues:

> Thus an equally troubling question in the burgeoning field of "gay and lesbian studies" concerns the discursive constructions and constructed silences around the relations of race to identity and subjectivity in the practices of homosexualities and the representations of same sex desire. (viii)

In my reading of her essay, de Lauretis then goes on to attribute the problem of the lack of knowledge of the experiences of gays and lesbians of color to gays and lesbians of color. While noting the problems of their restricted access to publishing venues or academic positions, she concludes that "perhaps, to a gay writer and critic of color, defining himself gay is not of the utmost importance; he may have other more pressing priorities in his work and life" (ix). This is a woefully inadequate characterization of the problem of the visibility of gays and lesbians of color. Certainly institutional racism, homophobia, and the general structural inequalities in American society have a great deal more to do with this invisibility than personal choices. I have reported de Lauretis's words at length because her work is symptomatic of the disjuncture I see between the stated goals of the volume she edited and what it actually enacts.

Despite the presence of writers of color, the authors of the essays in the *differences* volume avoid interrogating their own practices with respect to the issue of difference. That is to say to differences of race, ethnicity, and representation in analyzing subjectivity, desire, and the use of the psychoanalytic in gay and lesbian theory. Only Ekua Omosupe explicitly addresses the issue of black female subjectivity, and her essay foregrounds the very issue that queer theory ostensibly is committed to addressing. Omosupe still sees the need to announce her skepticism at the use of the term *lesbian* without the qualifier, "black," and addresses the lack of attention to race in gay and lesbian studies in her analysis of Adrienne Rich's work (108). For her, the term "lesbian" without the racial qualifier is simply to be read as "white" lesbian. Despite her criticism, however, she too avoids confronting difference within the category of black lesbian, speaking of "the" black lesbian without attention to or acknowledgment of a multiplicity of identities or subject positions for black women. She notes that the title of Audre Lorde's collected essays is *Sister Outsider*, which she argues is "an apt metaphor for the Black lesbian's position in relation to the white dominant political cultures and to her own Black community as well" (106). But metaphors reveal as much as they conceal and Omosupe cannot tell us what kind of outsider Lorde is, that is to say what sexual practices, discourses, and subject positions within her black community she was rebelling against. As with the Hull and McDowell essays, Omosupe's article acknowledges silence, erasure, and invisibility as crucial issues in the dominant discourses about black female sexuality, while the essay and the volume as a whole continue to enact this silence.

Thus, queer theory as reflected in this volume has so far failed to theorize the very questions de Lauretis announces that the term "queer" will address. I disagree with her assertion that we do not know enough about one another's differences to theorize differences between and within gays and lesbians in relation to race. This kind of theorizing of difference, after all, isn't simply a matter of empirical examples. And we do know enough to delineate what queer theorists *should* want to know. For me it is a question of knowing specifically about the production of black female queer sexualities: if the sexualities of black women have been shaped by silence, erasure, and invisibility in dominant discourses, then are black lesbian sexualities doubly silenced? What methodologies are available to read and understand this perceived void and gauge its direct and indirect effects on that which is visible? Conversely, how does the structure of what is visible, namely white female sexualities, shape those not-absent-though-not-present black female sexualities which, as O'Grady argues, cannot be separated or understood in isolation from one another? And, finally, how do these racialized sexualities shaped by silence, erasure, and invisibility coexist with other sexualities, the closeted sexualities of white queers, for example? It seems to me that there are two projects here that need to be worked out. White feminists must re-figure (white) female sexualities so that they are not theoretically dependent upon an absent yet-ever-present pathologized black female sexuality. I am not arguing that this figuration of (white) female sexuality must try to encompass completely the experiences of black women, but that it must include a conception of the power relations between white and black women as expressed in the representations of sexuality (Higginbotham 252).[1] This model of power, as Judith Butler has argued, must avoid setting up "racism and homophobia and misogyny as parallel or analogical relations," while recognizing that "what

has to be thought through, is the ways in which these vectors of power require and deploy each other for the purpose of their own articulation" (18). Black feminist theorists must reclaim sexuality through the creation of a counternarrative that can reconstitute a present black female subjectivity and that includes an analysis of power relations between white and black women and among different groups of black women. In both cases I am arguing for the development of a complex, relational but not necessarily analogous, conception of racialized sexualities (JanMohamed 94). In order to describe more fully what I see as the project for black feminist theorists, I want to turn now to a review of some of the current discussions of black women's sexuality.

THE PROBLEMATIC OF SILENCE

To name ourselves rather than be
named we must first see ourselves. For
some of us this will not be easy. So
long unmirrored, we may have
forgotten how we look. Nevertheless,
we can't theorize in a void; we must
have evidence.

(O'Grady 14)

Black feminist theorists have almost universally described black women's sexuality, when viewed from the vantage of the dominant discourses, as an absence. In one of the earliest and most compelling discussions of black women's sexuality, the literary critic Hortense Spillers wrote: "black women are the beached whales of the sexual universe, unvoiced, misseen, not doing, awaiting *their* verb" ("Interstices" 74). For writer Toni Morrison, black women's sexuality is one of the "unspeakable things unspoken," of the African-American experience. Black women's sexuality is often described in metaphors of speech-lessness, space, or vision, as a "void" or empty space that is simultaneously ever visible (exposed) and invisible and where black women's bodies are always already colonized. In addition, this always already colonized black female body has so much sexual potential that it has none at all ("Interstices" 85). Historically, black women have reacted to this repressive force of the hegemonic discourses on race and sex with silence, secrecy, and a partially self-chosen invisibility.

Black feminist theorists, historians, literary critics, sociologists, lawyers, and cultural critics have drawn upon a specific historical narrative which purportedly describes the factors that have produced and maintained perceptions of black women's sexuality (including their own). Three themes emerge in this history: first, the construction of the black female as the embodiment of sex and the attendant invisibility of black women as the unvoiced, unseen everything that is not white; second, the resistance of black women both to negative stereotypes of their sexuality and to the material effects of those stereotypes on their lives; and, finally, the evolution of a "culture of dissemblance" and a "politics of silence" by black women on the issue of their sexuality. The historical narrative begins with the production of the image of a pathologized black female "other" in the eighteenth century by European colonial elites and the new biological scientists. By the nineteenth century, with the increasing exploitation and abuse of black women during and after slavery, U.S. black women reformers began to develop strategies to counter negative stereotypes of their sexuality and their use as a justification for the rape, lynching, and other abuses of black women by whites. Although some of the strategies used by black women reformers might have initially been characterized as resistance to dominant and increasingly hegemonic constructions of their sexuality, by the early twentieth century black women reformers promoted a public silence about sexuality which, it could be argued, continues to the present.[2] This "politics of silence," as described by historian Evelyn Brooks Higginbotham, emerged as a political strategy by black women reformers who hoped by their silence and by the promotion of proper Victorian morality to demonstrate the lie of the image of the sexually immoral black woman (262). Historian Darlene Clark Hine argues that the "culture of dissemblance" that this politics engendered was seen as a way for black women to "protect the sanctity of inner aspects of their lives" (915). She defines this culture as "the behavior and attitudes of Black women that created the appearance of openness and disclosure but actually shielded the truth of their inner lives and selves from their oppressors" (915). "Only with secrecy," Hinc argues, "thus achieving a self-imposed invisibility, could ordinary Black women accrue the psychic space and harness the resources needed to hold their own" (915). And by the projection of the image of a "super-moral" black woman, they hoped to garner greater respect, justice, and opportunity for all black Americans (915). Of course, as Higginbotham notes, there were problems with this strategy. First, it did not achieve its goal of ending the negative stereotyping of black women. And second, some middle-class black women engaged in policing the behavior of poor and working-class women and any who deviated from a Victorian norm in the name of protecting the "race."[3] My interpretation of the conservatizing and policing aspect of the "politics of silence" is that black women reformers were responding to the ways in which any black woman could find herself "exposed" and characterized in racist sexual terms no matter what the truth of her individual life, and that they saw this so-called deviant individual behavior as a threat to the race as a whole. Finally, one of the most enduring and problematic aspects of the "politics of silence" is that in choosing silence black women also lost the ability to articulate any conception of their sexuality.

Without more detailed historical studies we will not know the extent of this "culture of dissemblance," and many questions will remain to be answered.[4] Was it expressed differently in rural and in urban areas; in the north, west, or south? How was it maintained? Where and how was it resisted? How was it shaped by class? And, furthermore, how did it change over time? How did something that was initially adopted as a political strategy in a specific historical period become so ingrained in black life as to be recognizable as a culture? Or did it? What emerges from the very incomplete history we have is a situation in which black women's sexuality is ideologically located in a nexus between race and gender, where the black female subject is not seen and has no voice.

Methodologically, black feminists have found it difficult even to fully characterize this juncture, this point of erasure where African-American women are located. As legal scholar Kimberlé Crenshaw puts it, "Existing within the overlapping margins of race and gender discourse and the empty spaces between, it is a location whose very nature resists telling" (403). And this silence about sexuality is enacted individually and collectively by black women and by black feminist theorists writing about black women.

It should not surprise us that black women are silent about sexuality. The imposed production of silence and the removal of any alternatives to the production of silence reflect the deployment of power against racialized subjects, "wherein those who could speak did not want to and those who did want to speak were prevented from doing so" (JanMohamed 105). It is this deployment of power at the level of the social and the individual which has to be historicized. It seems clear that we need a methodology that allows us to contest rather than reproduce the ideological system that has up to now defined the terrain of black women's sexuality. Spillers made this point over a decade ago when she wrote: "Because black American women do not participate, as a category of social and cultural agents, in the legacies of symbolic power, they maintain no allegiances to a strategic formation of texts, or ways of talking about sexual experience, that even remotely resemble the paradigm of symbolic domination, except that such a paradigm has been their concrete disaster" ("Interstices" 80). To date, through the work of black feminist literary critics, we know more about the elision of sexuality by black women than we do about the possible varieties of expression of sexual desire.[5] Thus what we have is a very narrow view of black women's sexuality. Certainly it is true, as Crenshaw notes, that "in feminist contexts, sexuality represents a central site of the oppression of women; rape and the rape trial are its dominant narrative trope. In antiracist discourse, sexuality is also a central site upon which the repression of blacks has been premised; the lynching narrative is embodied as its trope" (405). Sexuality is also, as Carol Vance defines it, "simultaneously a domain of restriction, repression, and danger as well as a

domain of exploration, pleasure, and agency" (1). The restrictive, repressive, and dangerous aspects of black female sexuality have been emphasized by black feminist writers while pleasure, exploration, and agency have gone under-analyzed.

I want to suggest that black feminist theorists have not taken up this project in part because of their own status in the academy. Reclaiming the body as well as subjectivity is a process that black feminist theorists in the academy must go through themselves while they are doing the work of producing theory. Black feminist theorists are themselves engaged in a process of fighting to reclaim the body—the maimed immoral black female body—which can be and still is used by others to discredit them as producers of knowledge and as speaking subjects. Legal scholar Patricia Williams illuminates my point: "no matter what degree of professional I am, people will greet and dismiss my black femaleness as unreliable, untrustworthy, hostile, angry, powerless, irrational, and probably destitute . . ." (95). When reading student evaluations, she finds comments about her teaching and her body: "I marvel, in a moment of genuine bitterness, that anonymous student evaluations speculating on dimensions of my anatomy are nevertheless counted into the statistical measurement of my teaching proficiency" (95). The hypervisibility of black women academics and the contemporary fascination with what bell hooks calls the "commodification of Otherness" (21) means that black women today find themselves precariously perched in the academy. Ann duCille notes:

> Mass culture, as hooks argues, produces, promotes, and perpetuates the commodification of Otherness through the exploitation of the black female body. In the 1990s, however, the principal sites of exploitation are not simply the cabaret, the speakeasy, the music video, the glamour magazine; they are also the academy, the publishing industry, the intellectual community. (592)

In tandem with the notion of silence, black women writers have repeatedly drawn on the notion of the "invisible" to describe aspects of black women's lives in general and sexuality in particular. Lorde

writes that "within this country where racial difference creates a constant, if unspoken distortion of
vision, Black women have on the one hand always
been highly visible, and on the other hand, have been
rendered invisible through the depersonalization of
racism" (91). The hypervisibility of black women
academics means that visibility too can be used to
control the intellectual issues that black women can
and cannot speak about. Already threatened with being
sexualized and rendered inauthentic as knowledge
producers in the academy by students and colleagues
alike, this avoidance of theorizing about sexuality
can be read as one contemporary manifestation of
their structured silence. I want to stress here that the
silence about sexuality on the part of black women
academics is no more a "choice" than was the silence
practiced by early twentieth-century black women.
This production of *silence* instead of *speech* is an
effect of the institutions such as the academy which
are engaged in the commodification of Otherness.
While hypervisibility can be used to silence black
women academics it can also serve them. Lorde has
argued that the "visibility which makes us most
vulnerable," that of being black, "is that which is the
source of our greatest strength." Patricia Hill Collins's
interpretation of Lorde's comment is that "paradoxically, being treated as an invisible Other gives black
women a peculiar angle of vision, the outsider-within
stance that has served so many African-American
women intellectuals as a source of tremendous
strength" (94).

Yet, while invisibility may be somewhat useful
for academicians, the practice of a politics of silence
belies the power of such a stance for social change.
Most important, the outsider-within stance does not
allow space for addressing the question of other
outsiders, namely black lesbians. Black feminist
theorizing about black female sexuality, with a few
exceptions—Cheryl Clarke, Jewelle Gomez, Barbara
Smith, and Audre Lorde—has been relentlessly
focused on heterosexuality. The historical narrative
that dominates discussion of black female sexuality
does not address even the possibility of a black lesbian sexuality, or of a lesbian or queer subject.
Spillers confirms this point when she notes that "the

sexual realities of black American women across the
spectrum of sexual preference and widened sexual
styles tend to be a missing dialectical feature of the
entire discussion" ("Interstices" 91).

At this juncture, then, I cannot cast blame for a
lack of attention to black lesbian sexuality solely on
white feminist theorists. De Lauretis argues that
female homosexualities may be conceptualized as
social and cultural forms in their own right, which are
undercoded or discursively dependent upon more
established forms. They (and male homosexualities)
therefore act as "an agency of social process whose
mode of functioning is both interactive and yet resistant, both participatory and yet distinct, claiming at
once equality and difference, and demanding political and historical representation while insisting on its
material and historical specificity" ("Queer" iii). If
this is true, then theorizing about black lesbian sexuality is crucially dependent upon the existence of a
conception of black women's sexuality in general.
I am not arguing that black lesbian sexualities are
derivative of black female heterosexualities, but only
that we cannot understand the latter without understanding it in relation to the former. In particular,
since discussions of black female sexuality often turn
to the issue of the devastating effects of rape, incest,
and sexual abuse, I want to argue that black queer
female sexualities should be seen as one of the sites
where black female desire is expressed.

Discussions of black lesbian sexuality have most
often focused on differences from or equivalencies
with white lesbian sexualities, with "black" added to
delimit the fact that black lesbians share a history
with other black women. However, this addition
tends to obfuscate rather than illuminate the subject
position of black lesbians. One obvious example of
distortion is that black lesbians do not experience
homophobia in the same way as do white lesbians.
Here, as with other oppressions, the homophobia
experienced by black women is always shaped by
racism. What has to be explored and historicized is
the specificity of black lesbian experience. I want
to understand in what way black lesbians are "outsiders" within black communities. This, I think,
would force us to examine the construction of the

"closet" by black lesbians. Although this is the topic for another essay, I want to argue here that if we accept the existence of the "politics of silence" as an historical legacy shared by all black women, then certain expressions of black female sexuality will be rendered as dangerous, for individuals and for the collectivity. From this it follows then that the culture of dissemblance makes it acceptable for some heterosexual black women to cast black lesbians as proverbial traitors to the race.[6] And this in turn explains why black lesbians who would announce or act out desire for women—whose deviant sexuality exists within an already pre-existing deviant sexuality—have been wary of embracing the status of "traitor" and the attendant loss of community such an embrace engenders.[7] Of course, while some black lesbians have hidden the truth of their lives, there have been many forms of resistance to the conception of lesbian as traitor within black communities. Audre Lorde is one obvious example. Lorde's claiming of her black and lesbian difference "forced both her white and Black lesbian friends to contend with her historical agency in the face of [this] larger racial/sexual history that would reinvent her as dead" (Karla Scott, qtd. in de Lauretis, *Practice* 36). I would also argue that Lorde's writing, with its focus on the erotic, on passion and desire, suggests that black lesbian sexualities can be read as one expression of the reclamation of the despised black female body. Therefore, the works of Lorde and other black lesbian writers, because they foreground the very aspects of black female sexuality which are submerged—that is, female desire and agency—are critical to our theorizing of black female sexualities. Since silence about sexuality is being produced by black women and black feminist theorists, that silence itself suggests that black women do have some degree of agency. A focus on black lesbian sexualities, I suggest, implies that another discourse—other than silence—can be produced.

I also suggest that the project of theorizing black female sexualities must confront psychoanalysis. Given that the Freudian paradigm is the dominant discourse which defines how sexuality is understood in this postmodern time, black feminist theorists have to answer the question posed by Michele Wallace: "is

the Freudian drama transformed by race in a way that would render it altered but usable?" (*Invisibility* 231) While some black feminists have called the psychoanalytic approach racist, others such as Spillers, Mae Henderson, and Valerie Smith have shown its usefulness in analyzing the texts of black women writers. As I am not a student of psychoanalytic theory, my suggested responses to Wallace's question can only be tentative at best. Though I do not accept all aspects of the Freudian paradigm, I do see the need for exploring its strengths and limitations in developing a theory of black female sexualities.

It can readily be acknowledged that the collective history of black women has in some ways put them in a different relationship to the canonical categories of the Freudian paradigm, that is, to the father, the maternal body, to the female-sexed body (Spillers, "Mama's"). On the level of the symbolic, however, black women have created whole worlds of sexual signs and signifiers, some of which align with those of whites and some of which do not. Nonetheless, they are worlds which always have to contend with the power that the white world has to invade, pathologize, and disrupt those worlds. In many ways the Freudian paradigm implicitly depends on the presence of the black female other. One of its more problematic aspects is that in doing so it relegates black women's sexuality to the irreducibly abnormal category in which there are no distinctions between homosexual and heterosexual women. By virtue of this lack of distinction, there is a need for black women, both lesbian and heterosexual, to, as de Lauretis describes it, "reconstitute a female-sexed body as a body for the subject and for her desire" (*Practice* 200). This is a need that is perhaps expressed differently by black women than by white women, whose sexualities have not been subjected to the *same* forces of repression and domination. And this seems to me to be a critical place where the work of articulating black female sexualities must begin. Disavowing the designation of black female sexualities as inherently abnormal, while acknowledging the material and symbolic effects of the appellation, we could begin the project of understanding how differently located black women engage in reclaiming the body and expressing desire.

What I want to propose requires me to don one of my other hats, that of a student of physics. As I struggled with the ideas I cover in this essay, over and over again I found myself wrestling with the juxtaposed images of "white" (read normal) and "black" (read not white and abnormal) sexuality. In her essay, "Variations on Negation," Michele Wallace invokes the idea of the black hole as a trope that can be used to describe the invisibility of black creativity in general and black female creativity specifically (*Invisibility* 218). As a former physics student, I was immediately drawn to this image. Yet it also troubled me.[8] As Wallace rightfully notes, the observer outside of the hole sees it as a void, an empty place in space. However, it is not empty; it is a dense and full place in space. There seemed to me to be two problems: one, the astrophysics of black holes, i.e. how do you deduce the presence of a black hole? And second, what is it like inside of a black hole? I don't want to stretch this analogy too far so here are my responses. To the first question, I suggest that we can detect the presence of a black hole by its effects on the region of space where it is located. One way that physicists do this is by observing binary star systems. A binary star system is one that contains two bodies which orbit around each other under mutual gravitational attraction. Typically, in these systems one finds a visible apparently "normal" star in close orbit with another body such as a black hole, which is not seen optically. The existence of the black hole is inferred from the fact that the visible star is in orbit and its shape is distorted in some way or it is detected by the energy emanating from the region in space around the visible star that could not be produced by the visible star alone.[9] Therefore, the identification of a black hole requires the use of sensitive detectors of energy and distortion. In the case of black female sexualities, this implies that we need to develop reading strategies that allow us to make visible the distorting and productive effects these sexualities produce in relation to more visible sexualities. To the second question— what is it like inside of a black hole?—the answer is that we must think in terms of a different geometry. Rather than assuming that black female sexualities are structured along an axis of normal and perverse

paralleling that of white women, we might find that for black women a different geometry operates. For example, acknowledging this difference I could read the relationship between Shug and Celie in Alice Walker's *The Color Purple* as one which depicts desire between women and desire between women and men simultaneously, in dynamic relationship rather than in opposition. This mapping of the geometry of black female sexualities will perhaps require black feminist theorists to engage the Freudian paradigm more rigorously, or it may cause us to disrupt it.

CAN I GET HOME FROM HERE?

I see my lesbian poetics as a way of entering into a dialogue—from the margins—with Black feminist critics, theorists and writers. My work has been to imagine an historical Black woman-to-woman eroticism and living —overt, discrete, coded, or latent as it might be. To imagine Black women's sexuality as a polymorphous erotic that does not exclude desire for men but also does not privilege it. To imagine, without apology, voluptuous Black women's sexualities.

(Clarke 224)

So where has my search taken me? And why does the journey matter? I want to give a partial answer to the question I posed at the beginning of this essay. At this juncture queer theory has allowed me to break open the category of gay and lesbian and begin to question how sexualities and sexual subjects are produced by dominant discourses and then to interrogate the reactions and resistances to those discourses. However, interrogating sites of resistance and reaction did not take me beyond what is generally done in gay and lesbian studies. The turn to queer should allow me to explore, in Clarke's words, the "overt, discrete, coded, or latent" and "polymorphous" eroticism of differently located black women. It is still not clear to me, however, that other queer theorists will resist the urge to engage in a re-ranking, erasure, or appropriation of sexual subjects who are at the margins of dominant discourses.

Why does my search for black women's sexuality matter? Wallace once wrote that she feared being called elitist when she acted as though cultural criticism was as crucial to the condition of black women as health, the law, politics, economics, and the family. "But," she continued, "I am convinced that the major battle for the 'other' of the 'other' [Black women] will be to find voice, transforming the construction of dominant discourse in the process" (*Invisibility* 236). It is my belief that what is desperately needed is more rigorous cultural criticism detailing how power is deployed through issues like sexuality and the alternative forms that even an oppressed subject's power can take. Since 1987, a major part of my intellectual work as an historian of U.S. science and medicine has addressed the AIDS crisis in African-American communities. The AIDS epidemic is being used, as Simon Watney has said, to "inflect, condense and rearticulate the ideological meanings of race, sexuality, gender, childhood, privacy, morality and nationalism" (ix). The position of black women in this epidemic was dire from the beginning and worsens with each passing day. Silence, erasure, and the use of images of immoral sexuality abound in narratives about the experiences of black women with AIDS. Their voices are not heard in discussions of AIDS, while intimate details of their lives are exposed to justify their victimization. In the "war of representation" that is being waged through this epidemic, black women are victims that are once again the "other" of the "other," the deviants of the deviants, regardless of their sexual identities or practices. While white gay male activists are using the ideological space framed by this epidemic to contest the notion that homosexuality is "abnormal" and to preserve the right to live out their homosexual desires, black women are rendered silent. The gains made by queer activists will do nothing for black women if the stigma continues to be attached to their sexuality. The work of black feminist critics is to find ways to contest the historical construction of black female sexualities by illuminating how the dominant view was established and maintained and how it can be disrupted. This work might very well save some black women's lives. I want this epidemic to be used to foment the sexual revolution that black Americans never had (Giddings 462). I want it to be used to make visible black women's self-defined sexualities.

Visibility in and of itself, however, is not my only goal. Several writers, including bell hooks, have argued that one answer to the silence now being produced on the issue of black female sexuality is for black women to see themselves, to mirror themselves (61). The appeal to the visual and the visible is deployed as an answer to the legacy of silence and repression. As theorists, we have to ask what we assume such reflections would show. Would the mirror black women hold up to themselves and to each other provide access to the alternative sexual universe within the metaphorical black hole? Mirroring as a way of negating a legacy of silence needs to be explored in much greater depth than it has been to date by black feminists theorists. An appeal to the visual is not uncomplicated or innocent. As theorists we have to ask how vision is structured, and, following that, we have to explore how difference is established, how it operates, how and in what ways it constitutes subjects who *see* and *speak* in the world (Haraway, "Promises" 313). This we must apply to the ways in which black women are seen and not seen by the dominant society and to how they see themselves in a different landscape. But in overturning the "politics of silence" the goal cannot be merely to be seen: visibility in and of itself does not erase a history of silence nor does it challenge the structure of power and domination, symbolic and material, that determines what can and cannot be seen. The goal should be to develop a "politics of articulation." This politics would build on the interrogation of what makes it possible for black women to speak and act.

Finally, my search for black women's sexuality through queer theory has taught me that I need not simply add the label queer to my list as another naturalized identity. As I have argued, there is no need to re-produce black women's sexualities as a silent void. Nor are black queer female sexualities simply identities.

Rather, they represent discursive and material terrains where there exists the possibility for the active production of speech, desire, and agency.

NOTES

My thanks to Joan Scott, Mary Poovey, Donna Penn, and Geeta Patel for their support and for their thoughtful and incisive critiques of the ideas in this essay.

1. Here I am referring to the work of Stuart Hall and especially Hazel Carby: "We need to recognize that we live in a society in which dominance and subordination are structured through processes of racialization that continuously interact with other forces of socialization. . . . But processes of racialization, when they are mentioned at all in multicultural debates are discussed as if they were the sole concern of those particular groups perceived to be racialized subjects. Because the politics of difference work with concepts of individual identity, rather than structures of inequality and exploitation, processes of racialization are marginalized and given symbolic meaning only when subjects are black" ("Multicultural" 193).

2. See Higginbotham, Hine, Giddings, Carby (*Reconstructing*), and Brown ("What").

3. See Carby, "Policing." Elsa Barkley Brown argues that the desexualization of black women was not just a middle-class phenomenon imposed on working-class women. Though many working-class women resisted Victorian notions of womanhood and developed their own notions of sexuality and respectability, some also, from their own experiences, embraced a desexualized image ("Negotiating" 144).

4. The historical narrative discussed here is very incomplete. To date there are no detailed historical studies of black women's sexuality.

5. See analyses of novels by Nella Larsen and Jessie Fauset in Carby (*Reconstructing*), McDowell, and others.

6. I participated in a group discussion of two novels written by black women, Jill Nelson's *Volunteer Slavery* and Audre Lorde's *Zami*, where one black woman remarked that while she thought Lorde's book was better written than Nelson's, she was disturbed that Lorde spoke so much about sex and "aired all of her dirty linen in public." She held to this even after it was pointed out to her that Nelson's book also included descriptions of her sexual encounters.

7. I am reminded of my mother's response when I "came out" to her. She asked me why, given that I was already black and that I had a non-traditional profession for a woman, I would want to take on one more thing that would make my life difficult. My mother's point, which is echoed by many black women, is that in announcing my homosexuality I was choosing to alienate myself from the black community.

8. I was disturbed by the fact that the use of the image of a black hole could also evoke a negative image of black female sexuality reduced to the lowest possible denominator, i.e. just a "hole."

9. The existence of the second body in a binary system is inferred from the periodic Doppler shift of the spectral lines of the visible star, which shows that it is in orbit, and by the production of X-ray radiation. My points are taken from the discussion of the astrophysics of black holes in Wald, chapters 8 and 9.

WORKS CITED

Abelove, Henry, Michèle Barale, and David Halperin, eds. *The Lesbian and Gay Studies Reader*. New York: Routledge, 1993.

Alonso, Ana Maria, and Maria Teresa Koreck. "Silences, 'Hispanics,' AIDS, and Sexual Practices." Abelove, Barale, and Halperin 110–126.

Brown, Elsa Barkley. "Negotiating and Transforming the Public Sphere: African American Political Life in the Transition From Slavery to Freedom." *Public Culture* 7.1 (1994): 107–46.

———. "'What Has Happened Here': The Politics of Difference in Women's History and Feminist Politics." *Feminist Studies* 18.2 (1992): 295–312.

Busia, Abena, and Stanlie James. *Theorizing Black Feminisms: The Visionary Pragmatism of Black Women*. New York: Routledge, 1993.

Butler, Judith. *Bodies That Matter: On the Discursive Limits of "Sex."* New York: Routledge, 1993.

Carby, Hazel. "The Multicultural Wars." Wallace and Dent 187–99.

———. "Policing the Black Woman's Body in the Urban Context." *Critical Inquiry* 18 (1992): 738–55.

———. *Reconstructing Womanhood: The Emergence of the Afro-American Woman Novelist*. New York: Oxford, 1987.

Clarke, Cheryl. "Living the Texts Out: Lesbians and the Uses of Black Women's Traditions." Busia and James 214–27.

Collins, Patricia Hill. *Black Feminist Thought, Knowledge, Consciousness, and the Politics of Empowerment.* Cambridge: Unwin Hyman, 1990.

Crenshaw, Kimberlé. "Whose Story Is It Anyway?: Feminist and Antiracist Appropriations of Anita Hill." Morrison 402–40.

de Lauretis, Teresa. *The Practice of Love: Lesbian Sexuality and Perverse Desire.* Bloomington: Indiana UP, 1994.

———. "Queer Theory: Lesbian and Gay Sexualities: An Introduction." *differences: A Journal of Feminist Cultural Studies* 3.2 (1991): iii–xviii.

duCille, Ann. "The Occult of True Black Womanhood: Critical Demeanor and Black Feminist Studies." *Signs* 19.3 (1994): 591–629.

Giddings, Paula. "The Last Taboo." Morrison 441–65.

Gomez, Jewelle. "A Cultural Legacy Denied and Discovered: Black Lesbians in Fiction by Women." Smith 110–123.

Haraway, Donna. "The Promises of Monsters: A Regenerative Politics for Inappropriate/d Others." *Cultural Studies.* Ed. Laurence Grossberg, Cary Nelson, and Paula Treichler. New York: Routledge, 1992. 295–337.

———. "Situated Knowledges: The Science Question in Feminism and the Privilege of Partial Perspective." *Simians, Cyborgs, and Women: The Reinvention of Nature.* New York: Routledge, 1991.

Henderson, Mae Gwendolyn. "Speaking in Tongues: Dialogics, Dialectics, and the Black Woman Writer's Literary Tradition." Wall 16–37.

Higginbotham, Evelyn Brooks. "African-American Women's History and the Metalanguage of Race." *Signs* 17.2 (1992): 251–74.

Hine, Darlene Clark. "Rape and the Inner Lives of Black Women in the Middle West: Preliminary Thoughts on the Culture of Dissemblance." *Signs* 14.4 (1989): 915–20.

hooks, bell. "Selling Hot Pussy: Representations of Black Female Sexuality in the Cultural Marketplace." *Black Looks: Race and Representation.* Boston: South End, 1992. 61–76.

Hull, Gloria T. " 'Lines She Did Not Dare': Angela Weld Grimké, Harlem Renaissance Poet." Abelove, Barale, and Halperin 453–66.

JanMohamed, Abdul. "Sexuality On/Of the Racial Border: Foucault, Wright, and the Articulation of 'Racialized Sexuality.' " *Discourses of Sexuality: From Artistotle to AIDS.* Ed. Domna Stanton. Ann Arbor: U of Michigan P, 1992. 94–116.

Lorde, Audre. *Sister Outsider, Essays and Speeches.* Trumansburg, NY: Crossing, 1984.

———. *Zami: A New Spelling of My Name.* Trumansburg, NY: Crossing, 1982.

McDowell, Deborah E. " 'It's Not Safe. Not Safe at All': Sexuality in Nella Larsen's *Passing.*" Abelove, Barale, and Halperin 616–625.

Morrison, Toni, ed. *Race-ing Justice, En-gendering Power: Essays on Anita Hill, Clarence Thomas and the Construction of Social Reality.* New York: Pantheon, 1992.

Nelson, Jill. *Volunteer Slavery: My Authentic Negro Experience.* Chicago: Noble, 1993.

O'Grady, Lorraine. "Olympia's Maid: Reclaiming Black Female Subjectivity." *Afterimage* (1992): 14–23.

Omosupe, Ekua. "Black/Lesbian/Bulldagger." *differences: A Journal of Feminist Cultural Studies* 3.2 (1991): 101–11.

Smith, Barbara. "Towards a Black Feminist Criticism." *Conditions* 2 (1977): 25–44.

———, ed. *Home Girls: A Black Feminist Anthology.* New York: Kitchen Table, 1983.

Smith, Valerie. "Black Feminist Theory and the Representation of the 'Other.' " Wall 38–57.

Spillers, Hortense. "Interstices: A Small Drama of Words." Vance 73–100.

———. "Mama's Baby, Papa's Maybe: An American Grammar Book." *Diacritics* Summer 17.2 (1987): 65–81.

Vance, Carole, ed. *Pleasure and Danger: Exploring Female Sexuality.* London: Pandora, 1989.

———. "Pleasure and Danger: Toward a Politics of Sexuality." Vance 1–24.

Wald, Robert. *Space, Time, and Gravity: The Theory of the Big Bang and Black Holes.* 2nd edition. Chicago: U of Chicago P, 1992.

Wall, Cheryl, ed. *Changing Our Own Words: Essays on Criticism, Theory, and Writing by Black Women.* New Brunswick: Rutgers UP, 1989.

Wallace, Michele. *Invisibility Blues: From Pop to Theory.* New York: Verso, 1990.

Wallace, Michele and Gina Dent, eds. *Black Popular Culture.* Seattle: Bay, 1992.

Walker, Alice. *The Color Purple.* New York: Harcourt, 1982.

Watney, Simon. *Policing Desire: Pornography, AIDS and the Media.* Minneapolis: U of Minnesota P, 1989.

Williams, Patricia J. *The Alchemy of Race and Rights: Diary of a Law Professor.* Cambridge: Harvard UP, 1991.

Study Questions

1. According to Hammonds, in what ways have lesbian/gay studies and queer studies failed to address the issue of diversity among lesbians and gays?

2. What three factors have theorists pointed to in explaining the perceptions of Black women's sexuality over time? Give an example of each.

3. According to Hammonds, what is the "politics of silence"? What are the advantages and disadvantages, in her account, of such a politics?

4. Hammonds draws an analogy between "black holes" in physics and Black female creativity. Explain the analogy. How does the analogy contribute to Hammonds's discussion of Freudian psychology?

5. What does Hammonds mean by a "politics of articulation," and how does it go beyond a politics of "visibility"?